You've Been Framed

You've Been Framed

How to Reframe Your Wealth Management Business and Renew Client Relationships

Ray Sclafani

WILEY

To my beloved wife, life-learning partner, best friend, and soul mate. Sally, I love you with all of my heart! Your unending love and support has provided me the confidence to dream big for us. It's corny, it's true: You complete me. Cent'anni, BAV! Love, Harry!

To our boys, Jonathan and Nicholas. You both inspire me, each day, to become the most I can be. You are God's greatest blessings that Mom and I could ever have hoped for. May you both soar to heights far above what we could have ever dreamed. I only hope this work is an example of possibility for you. Remember to laugh and play along the way!

To my mom, who showed me the way—who has been and I know will always be there for me. I love you.

To Nana, who sent me that $25 in college and helped feed me when I had nothing. I love you. Happy 93 years young!

To my clients, current and past, who have trusted in me, partnered, and been willing to give me a chance. Thank you, from the bottom of my heart, for believing in our work together.

To every great financial advisor across the globe. Your work inspires me. May you continue to positively impact the lives of your clients and change the world for the better in the noble work you do each and every day. Thank you for your unending commitment to excellence.

Contents

Foreword

When I first met Ray Sclafani in the early part of this century, he was leading the wholesaling team for Alliance Bernstein's mutual funds. He struck me as an earnest, caring, driven executive who was confident in his abilities but not naïve enough to think he had all the tools necessary to be truly great. In other words, he was a perfect student.

Since then, I have had hundreds of interactions with Ray both personally and in combination with the clients he has served. I was there in the beginning as he started to frame out his business structure for his new business, ClientWise. Since then, he has helped hundreds of financial professionals transform the way they organize their practices and consciously execute a plan.

I was struck by his willingness to hear feedback with an open attitude and his commitment to making decisions based on these ideas. I found him to be one of the hardest-working people in this business, who never settled for mediocrity and who never tolerated being average. Interestingly, this is the basic tenet of his book, *You've Been Framed*.

Ray is able to draw on his many years in business development, management, and ownership to craft a compelling narrative for entrepreneurs seeking to get to a new level of fulfillment with their firms. I found his modular approach to helping advisors evaluate, address, and resolve challenges to be especially thoughtful. It allows readers to contemplate a question, then refer back to the relevant sections of the book to process the optimal outcome.

The financial services profession is going through a profound change. What has worked in the past will not work in the future. Today's economics, demographics, and regulatory environment introduce a whole new set of challenges for the business. In my experience, I find the profession divided into two camps: those who live in the past and complain about the present and those who see the present as a catalyst for the future.

What Ray has done with this book is give structure to those who wish to transform their business from a vehicle for generating income to one that makes an impact on the lives of others. It is an important addition to your business book library.

Mark C. Tibergien

Acknowledgments

It was in the spring of 2003, as I recall, that Dan Sullivan of Strategic Coach suggested to me that I consider building my own firm. Soon thereafter, he challenged me to write a book. Well, years later, I decided for myself that it was time. Thanks, Dan . . . for the freedom, the fun, and the challenge to think creatively, follow my unique ability, and make every day a positive focus. You helped me make this work possible.

There are many friends, colleagues, and neighbors who helped shape me as a human and as a professional.

Joan Weltz, may God rest her soul, taught me in the fourth and fifth grade at P.S. 79 in Whitestone, Queens, that it was okay to try new things and that even if I wasn't great at something, I could learn and take risks. She gave me the confidence to know, even at a young age, that it was the adventures in life that brought great surprises—and that a move to Texas was BIG!

It was Mr. Bennett of J. J. Pearce High School who had such vision and figured out how to mobilize so many high school kids to show up at 0-dark-thirty—to shoe-polish marks on the parking lot to teach us how to march our way right onto that football field every Friday night and believe. He was also the guy who told me I couldn't be the leader of the band. Whew! That was important.

Also to be remembered are the many professors at Baylor University who took such great care to make sure I made it, who supported me, who taught me lots of life lessons, and who helped make me into who I am today.

Then there was the one trip, and the only trip, where I would learn from my Uncle Len how to commute, at 17, from Bayside by bus, the Q16, to Flushing for the 7 train to Grand Central, where I would change to the 4 or 5 downtown to Wall Street, before walking up Broadway to 140. During that trip, it was Uncle Len who taught me how to fold (back in those days) a *Wall Street Journal*, which one must read each and every morning. Thanks for the tokens, Uncle Len! And yes, I did mix the tokens up a bit!

I gratefully acknowledge, too, my former colleagues at Alliance Capital, who just seemed to know exactly where to place me so that I could achieve great results, each and every time: Alan Halfenger, who took a young 17-year-old, gave him a job, and told him just what to do to succeed, and Willie Mae, who ran that mailroom and taught me the importance of locking the safe. It was Jim Yockey who took a chance on me and taught me about the advisor, about learning what was important to helping each advisor build a business, about building the database, and about running a business. But there are so many others who came after Jim, especially Bob Errico, to whom I owe a career. Although Bob may never know how much that visit to Texas meant, while having that lunch at The Palm, it was a full life lesson that would provide career guidance for the many years to come. John, Rick, Mike, Dave, and all of the others! What a ride! Thanks for the memories, the lessons, and the lifetime of friendship. And for all of those great runs through the Park and around the city! Every morning was an individual lesson in what matters.

I send a huge thank you to Bob Powers, who rests in peace; whose wisdom, stories, and catchphrases are priceless, each and every morning, then and now; and who kept me going and thinking and becoming. So, "send in the clowns . . ."

Dr. Marvin Sadovsky, who taught me about communication, partnering, and the belief systems in neurolinguistics, helped me to create this work. That outcome frame is all I ever needed. Thanks for that!

Mr. Carrol Meredith, who also rests in peace, and who spent hours teaching me about this business, was always there for me. His commitment to Merrill Lynch, to his advisors, and to his clients was awe inspiring. Carrol represented all that there was in the phrase, "Do right by others."

My favorite running partner and Jewish father, Harold Rubin, who has been so willing to share his wisdom about life, about work, and about this business, has helped me shape my thinking about the future of financial services.

Thank you to our total team at ClientWise, which has provided such a powerful platform of possibility, for future growth, for our clients, and for ourselves to partner and achieve the unimaginable.

Sophia Harbas, our director of coaching services at ClientWise, has been with me every single professional step of the way, a best friend for Beth and me, and a thinking partner who always knows how to think out of the box. Thanks for being you . . . for leading and for inspiring me to press forward and do our best for others. Your unselfish acts of kindness and partnership are an example for us all. Thanks for the journey. The best is indeed yet to come!

Thank you to Lisa Hanna, our chief of staff, who more than nine years ago signed up for more than I think we both could think of at the time. I'm still amazed at how she keeps the trains running on schedule and fits it all in!

Thank you, Beth Holly. Your attention to detail and project management has truly made this work come together. Thank you very much, Christina. Or is it Kristina?

Last but not least, thank you to Mark Tibergien, for whose knowledge about this industry and vision for where we should come together to think about the future we all owe a great deal. His contributions and dedication that have helped so many others, his intellect and passion, mean more to me than those of any other professional I have ever met. Thank you, Mark!

Introduction

This book is built on the following premise: *Financial advising is a noble profession.* As a financial industry veteran of more than 25 years, I have been witness to the amazing work that advisors do every day to help other people live satisfying, fulfilling, and successful lives.

Financial professionals do meaningful work. They help their clients to design the lives they want to lead and then help them live to the fullest, whether by guiding clients through the challenges of transitioning toward retirement, preparing for and selling a family-owned business when there is no next generation to take it over, making adjustments to original plans because of a divorce, or sending a child to the college of his or her choice. Financial professionals provide support to clients taking care of unexpected health care costs with aging parents and are there as clients work through the financial and maybe even emotional implications of a spouse's death. The most effective financial advisors also speak to their clients about philanthropic giving, endowment work, and setting up trusts, helping to create a positive influence that radiates out into society.

I call it impact work. Why? Because when advisors do their jobs well, not only does their work impact this generation, but it also carries forward through multiple generations. If a financial advisor does a great job with his or her client, that client's children and grandchildren will be better off because of that partnership, as will the charities and endowments to which the client contributes. Society will be better off, too, as advisors have helped clients maximize both their wealth and their ability to pay that wealth forward.

Advisors themselves have an opportunity to create change by the way in which they conduct their practices. As Dan Sullivan puts it, financial advisors of the future will have the opportunity to "innovate more and more fundamental solutions to economic, political, and

KEY CONCEPT

Financial advising done at its best is impact work that allows the advisor to make a positive difference in the life of the client, in the lives of the client's heirs, and in all of the diverse parts of society that that client's life touches.

social issues."[1] I am reminded of one advisor client of my firm who has found a way to start schools in Africa for girls and another who is involved in an annual bicycle giveaway to underprivileged children. Sullivan points to the example of an advisor who created a divorce mediation program that could be used not only in financial services but also in legal and counseling services. Whether on a small, medium, or big scale, that's true impact. It's what our profession looks like at its best and what it can be more and more as we move into the future.

GOOD VERSUS EVIL IN THE FINANCIAL INDUSTRY

The idea of the financial profession being noble sounds a lot like heresy if we rely only on what we see in the media. There, we don't hear about the positive side of the financial industry; we hear instead about financial traders under criminal investigation, brokerage firms facing fines, scammers using Ponzi schemes to cheat investors, and decent Americans having their homes foreclosed on due to a mortgage industry gone awry. We see the rawest side of the financial industry depicted in films that showcase sex, drugs, and corruption (*The Wolf of Wall Street* comes to mind); we may witness our neighbors shaking their heads at the mention of the latest financial scandal among the big banks on the evening news or their social-media feed; and we may hear our friends and family complaining about the greed associated with the industry.

In reality, these portrayals represent only a small segment of the financial profession, and they certainly don't represent the typical financial advisor. If you are a financial advisor, you know as I do that the majority of individuals in our industry are principled, hardworking, and committed to serving others. They are taking client calls the night before a holiday because they want to make sure their clients get the service they deserve. They are reading up on the tax code on weekends to make sure they have the latest information for their clients long before April 15 rolls around. They update their knowledge of the capital markets frequently. They are curious about people, and they are excellent listeners. They are dedicated to their clients' financial health and prosperity, and they are not counting their paychecks as the media sometimes suggests.

While it's true that being a financial advisor and being the founder of a financial advisory firm have monetary benefits, the majority of the financial professionals with whom I have had the honor of serving and partnering are empathic, notable for their deep integrity, and committed to serving others. Throughout this book, you will read many of their stories, which reveal the approach they are taking to help accelerate their own success and how they partner with clients. I have the unique good fortune of occupying a front-row seat to observe the work of the best in the business, and I will share what I've learned with you.

 KEY CONCEPT

Despite media coverage of negative and scandalous financial industry stories, financial advisors are, by a wide margin, hardworking, principled, knowledgeable, and generous individuals who are a credit to the industry and to their clients.

WHO THIS BOOK IS FOR

As you decide whether to purchase this book or whether to read deeper, you may be wondering whether this book is for you, given that there are so many different types of financial professionals out there. In fact, this book is for financial advisors of any type—wirehouse, independent broker-dealer, and registered investment advisors—who are interested in enriching and/or expanding their teams, strengthening their client relationships, and growing their practices.

In particular, if you are an advisor who knows you have something valuable to offer your clients but you are asking yourself whether you and your firm are doing an effective job of communicating that value, this book is for you. If you are a financial advisor who has found yourself thinking about your professional brand lately and wondering if it is developed enough to attract your ideal client, this book is also for you. Maybe you have yet to define your own brand or specific value proposition, but you do know that you'd like to grow your practice, and you recognize that there is room for you to do a better job of marketing your services. Or perhaps you've been pigeonholed by some of your clients: They don't understand the full breadth of services you offer, and you're ready to break out of that narrow mold and create a brand that is as big as you now are. If so, this book is for you.

This book is also for those advisors who want to be able to sell their firm someday and who are seriously thinking about an exit strategy. This book will help these advisors clarify their value proposition to clients and learn to document that value, so others on the team can replicate the unique capabilities and approach of their firm and scale them over time for greater profit.

Last, this book is for those advisors who believe in the potential of this profession to help people live better lives and who are interested in having a positive impact on others and leaving a legacy.

 Come Together: Calling Advisors from Every Channel

We have all heard the debates regarding which channel serves clients the best. We have witnessed regulations being created to designate which advisors can claim that they have a fiduciary relationship with their clients. And we have seen the rivalry that can occur between professionals in competing channels. We will not engage in that debate here. In fact, we will proceed under the premise that every channel has its value and that we all have something to learn from one another.

Regardless of the channel in which an advisor chooses to operate—wirehouse, independent broker-dealer, hybrid, insurance, or registered investment advisor, to name a few—almost all financial advisors are working diligently to provide the very best they can for their clients. These advisors are committed to doing well by their clients, regardless of any public suspicion that it's all about making money for themselves.

There are debates about whether the wirehouse folks have allegiance to their clients versus their corporations, for example, but I invite you to set those debates aside for now and focus instead on the reality that all financial advisors, regardless of channel, are in this together.

Even with the differences among us, we are all part of the same industry, and it is up to us to set the tone of engagement for the future. Go competitive and go negative and we only feed the public's perception that advisors are focused on profits rather than people. Choose instead to see value in different approaches and to opt for collaboration, and we not only help create a positive face for the public but we also increase the chances of elevating our own industry. If we remain client focused and "client-wise," we can all benefit. In a rising tide, all boats will rise together.

THE GOODS: WHAT THIS BOOK CONTAINS

This book provides all the tools you need to consider how you may wish to reframe yourself, your team, and your firm, as well as to engage in the actual reframe. While the reframe itself ultimately will be unique to your firm and your clients, the process to get there is consistent across firms, as I and my team have tested, refined, and perfected it over the years with thousands of financial advisors. We share it here with you. In fact, I have included in this book everything I believe you will need to successfully reframe your practice. This includes key concepts to help you understand the philosophy behind reframing, assessment tools to help you identify important patterns, coaching questions that enable you to reflect, a step-by-step formula for engaging in the reframe, hands-on exercises to move forward, and industry insight from top financial leaders that will make your reframe even more effective. You will also be given access to online resources and an online community of other financial professionals with whom you can engage, chat, brainstorm, ask questions, and share insight to make sure you don't have to go it alone.

This book is divided into three sections. "Part I: You Gotta Believe" covers the thinking and philosophy behind why the reframe is

Are You Ready?

To successfully engage in the reframing process, you must be willing to hear feedback from others with an attitude of openness, invest the effort to reflect on that feedback, and make a series of important decisions about what you want to really stand for, now and in the future. You must also be ready to do the necessary work in a consistent way if you're going to succeed. This book can serve as a useful tool in the development of your frame and the frames of your firm and your team of professionals. If you are open and engaged in the process, it will work for you.

important. This part will help you create new thinking patterns that can inspire and motivate you to engage in the hard work of reframing your practice. You have to be open to the possibility of some shifts in your thinking and beliefs before you can engage in the reframing process. You may also find out while reading this first part of the book that you're on the right track and/or that how you're currently framed is exactly how you wish to be framed. That can help increase the confidence of all members of your team, including you as the leader, while keeping you all motivated and energized to continue on your path of success and development.

Then, "Part II: Five Steps to Reframing Your Business" gives you a step-by-step plan for how to effectively reframe your practice. This section is full of support tools—coaching questions, checklists, exercises, online resources, and more—to help you create a powerful new frame that will help you meet your goals for your practice. In particular, Part II will help you

- determine how your clients are currently framing you,
- explore what you'd really like to be seen as representing and match this up with your clients' actual needs,
- create a marketing story to communicate your new frame to others,
- reengage your clients with your new story so they can fully partake in your firm's services and tell others about your story, and

■ build a network of trustworthy professionals who will help you deliver on your promise to your clients and spread the word about what you do.

Part II will help you create an authentic marketing approach that builds a bridge between what you want to provide and what your clients need, so you can grow your business in a conscious and purposeful way that meets both criteria. It's the ultimate setup for long-term success, whether that's defined as selling your business someday for the greatest return or watching your firm continue into the next generation.

In "Part III: Now What?" you will learn how to assess whether you have effectively reframed your practice by looking for 10 specific signals. This can be as rewarding as hearing your client tell someone else about your services and nailing them spot on or as simple as discovering that you like to go to work once again. Part III will also review key concepts, talk about the future of advising, and highlight some of the additional free resources awaiting you online as you engage in reframing your business. These resources include helpful checklists, articles, and opportunities to converse with other financial leaders.

JOINING TOGETHER TO CREATE A NOBLE PROFESSION

I sincerely believe that the financial profession is a noble one and that advisors have the potential to make a huge impact on their clients and the world. This book is meant to help advisors reach their full potential so they can not only achieve their own goals as business owners but also benefit their clients, transform the industry, and change the world. Are you ready to join me?

I'm invested in the journey and here's why.

My dedication to the financial industry is rooted in my long history with the profession. I first joined the industry at 17 years of age, when I was fortunate enough to get a job working at 140 Broadway in downtown Manhattan as a summer intern for Alliance Capital, which was really beginning to grow as a mutual fund company. Although I was born in New York, I had moved to Texas at age 11; six years later, I came back to New York to learn the ropes in financial services. I ended up earning enough summer money at Alliance Capital to put myself through my first year of college at Baylor University.

At Baylor, I learned a lot about myself, a lot about values, and a lot about integrity. I owe a great deal to the university and to the many professors there who invested in helping to shape who I am today. I was taught at Baylor that we get to grow up to be whatever we wish to be, to be curious and learn from others, and to be a journey learner. I remember, too, one of my professors reminding me upon graduation that the journey for learning had only just begun.

For 20 years, I chose to work in the asset management space for Alliance Capital, which became Alliance Bernstein, in multiple capacities. I started in operations when I was 17, where I learned the business from the inside out; next, I moved into an inside sales role and then a field sales professional role, meeting with financial advisors, which I did for more than a decade. Then I was recruited to be part of the leadership team, where I was responsible for leading the bank channel, the independent financial planning channel, the registered investment advisor channel, and the insurance channel. It was a long, prosperous, and wonderful career that gave me an opportunity to understand the financial industry in a way that an outsider cannot.

I had always felt called to make a difference in the lives of others, so I decided to engage in that calling more fully: I left Alliance Bernstein and trained to become a professional certified coach. By January 2006, I had launched ClientWise, dedicated to coaching the financial professionals with whom I'd worked for so long. In this work, I have the pleasure of leading a team of coaches who help many top professional advisors discover how their clients view them and discern how they would like their clients to view them in the future. These coaches also work with advisors as they rebuild their frames and grow their referral networks to create businesses with greater value, purpose, and longevity.

In addition to leading a team of more than 25 coaches and growing ClientWise, I have the pleasure of traveling the United States and internationally to speak to, train, and coach top-tier financial professionals. I continue to discover that as highly capable as advisors are, there are still discrepancies—sometimes big, sometimes small—between how they see themselves and how others see them, clients and team members included. That is why I have written this book. It excites me to be an advocate for financial advisors and for the great work many of them do for others. I think that if advisors listen to clients, connect to their own passions, and match the two, their work can truly change the world.

I bring a unique background to my current work as an executive coach and CEO of a coaching company dedicated to financial professionals. While other coaches in this space may have covered the financial industry as journalists or have come out of a more general business background, I have worked directly in the financial industry for more than two decades, rising through the ranks and learning how the business operates, from rainmaking and relationship development to team building and practice management.

I also have a personal familiarity with the process of reframing, having done it many times over the years: as a Texan working in New York City, a New Yorker working in Texas, a salesman who became a leader, a field sales guy who moved to the home office, a wholesaler that grew to be a national sales director, and a financial services leader who became an executive coach to financial leaders.

Ultimately, my intention in writing this book is to make a positive difference in the lives of others, from the financial professionals who read this book to the clients they serve, who will be affected for the better. But it's a journey that we have to take together. If we are going to evolve the industry and pull so many clients up with us, we must agree to listen to our clients, try new pathways, work hard, and go back again to our clients to listen to their feedback until we get things right. In the process, we can fall back in love with the profession and spend our time doing more of what we love.

Are you out, or are you in?

Harold Rubin, a good friend of mine who is also a mentor, will often remind me that my job is to grow into the most that I can be each and every day. "Yesterday is over," Harold will say. "What do you plan to do today to become the most that you can be?" I would like to challenge you to ask yourself this same question. By engaging in the reframe process, you will have the capability to ask and answer, "How can we be the best we can be today and in the future for our clients and ourselves?"

HOW TO READ THIS BOOK

While this book can be read from start to finish, you don't have to read the chapters in a particular order or even read the book cover to cover. Feel free to focus on those chapters that most excite you and resonate with you or to view a snapshot of each chapter by reading the key concepts, coaching questions, and industry-insight examples in each. Be sure not to miss the alerts, too, for the complimentary online tools that are available to you on the ClientWise eXchange™ (youvebeenframed.clientwise.com). These unique tools and resources can help you and your team to reframe yourselves, achieve the goals you have set, and ultimately make the kind of difference in the lives of others you hope to make. Icons are used throughout the book to signal each of these different elements.

🔑 Key Concept

⚙ Coaching Corner

💡 Industry Insight

❌ The eXchange™

The eXchange™ is a first-of-its-kind platform that provides financial advisors with access to proprietary content developed by my company, ClientWise, since 2006 while working with top performers in the industry. As a reader, you will have access to a special book-related set of tools on the eXchange™, as well as to other financial professionals who have read this book.[2] The eXchange™ also provides access to a network of high-performing financial professionals across the nation and the ability to engage with the world's highest-credentialed executive coaches. The membership on the eXchange™ continues to grow; I invite you to take advantage of this opportunity to join.

CONCLUSION

In an industry marked by constant change, the ability to reframe oneself, one's team, and one's practice is essential. Fiduciary standards will continue to evolve, compensation will continue to change, and new technology will continue to emerge, regularly disrupting both the way we do business and the type of service that clients expect and the government demands. Today, it is the robo-advisor; tomorrow, it will be something else, and we can only predict so much.

The ability to reframe your practice will give you the agility you require to stay relevant in tomorrow's world. It will provide you with the tools you need to articulate your value to the client when competing technologies emerge, downward pressure on compensation continues, and the unforeseen changes of tomorrow take place. The ability to reframe will ensure you are ready for that change and that you will be able to evolve again and again over time as the marketplace shifts into its next iteration. Reframing ensures relevance!

NOTES

1. Dan Sullivan, "The Twelve Predictions: Excerpted from *Creative Destruction*, Module 1" (Toronto, Canada: The Strategic Coach, 2007), 3, www.strategiccoach.com/downloads/prb_12Predictions.pdf.
2. The eXchange™ can be found at youvebeenframed.clientwise.com.

PART I

You Gotta Believe

CHAPTER **1**

You've Been Framed!

I am willing to bet that as a financial services professional, you show up every day and work hard for your clients. You make phone calls, have in-person meetings, and do quarterly and annual reviews. You crunch numbers when required; you get in your car or on the plane when you need to be somewhere important for your clients; and you do your homework, reading the financial papers, the tax code, and new industry regulations. You tell your team, if you have one, what to do and how to operate to ensure success for the client and the firm. You're working hard and doing everything right. Or are you?

That is the question. As much as work and life are busy, and as easy as it would be to give a quick nod of a yes, if you are really and truly honest with yourself as a financial services professional, the answer has to be "maybe," because you can't really know how you are doing until you take the time to assess.

Have you asked yourself lately how you are doing with your financial services business? Not just in terms of top-line and bottom-line numbers, but in terms of everything that leads to a truly successful career, business, and client community? Here are some questions to consider as you contemplate how successful you really are today.

- Do you have a clear understanding of your firm's unique value, and have you documented that value for yourself and your clients, so that the business not only thrives but also can be replicated, scaled, and sold if desired?

- Are you providing your clients with the comprehensive wealth management services they deserve, or do you just focus on those products and services that you can and care to offer? If you don't offer them, are you willing and able to connect your clients to other respected professionals?

- Have you learned to truly partner with your clients, or are you stuck in the old model of just selling to your clients or telling them what they should do, rather than inviting them to co-create in the process?

- Do you have a team of capable folks who work well together and whom your clients trust, rely on, and value?

- How clear are you about how you charge for your services and the true value that the client finds in what you provide?

- Are you and every member of your team clear about what differentiates you from other financial advisors and the many choices your clients have today?

- How are you working to be relevant in the lives of the heirs of your clients' wealth?

- Do you have the ability to step away from your business to take an extended vacation or a break or, if need be, to deal with a personal or family illness?

- Do you have the desired amount of work–life balance on a day-to-day basis, allowing you to eat right, exercise, spend time with family and friends, and enjoy life however you like to do best?

- Do you have a rock-solid succession plan in place for how your business will continue after you choose to move on to something new or to retire? When put to the test, will that succession plan really work?

These are just some of the questions to explore if you are ready to assess how successful your financial services practice is today—questions that will be explored directly and implicitly in this book.

In the process of asking these questions, you may discover that you are right on track with your business and find greater peace of mind, motivation, and energy in that. Or you may discover it's time for a major reframe. Alternately, you may discover that you simply want to recalibrate your business and your approach to bring greater satisfaction to the work that you do and to your client's satisfaction in the support you provide them.

Whether you simply want to get your numbers up, you have some doubts about where your business is going right now, or you are a lifelong learner, this book has something for you. It will take you on a journey of assessing the state of your financial services practice today, and it will provide you with all the tools you need to reframe for the future if you discover that this is necessary for greater success or more satisfaction.

Like it or not, we've all been framed—whether we've framed ourselves or allowed others to frame us. You are about to become conscious of the way you are framed today—by your team, your clients, the public, and the media—so you can make intentional decisions to ensure that the frame others see you within is the one you meant for them to use. By learning to frame yourself intentionally, you will tap into the fullest degree of your and your firm's potential. Let's look deeper at what it means to be framed.

WHAT'S A FRAME?

The perspective through which people view advisors is the *frame*: the set of beliefs through which others see and define you, your team, and your business. The frame is constructed of those words the client, the media, your team, or anyone else uses to describe what it is that you do and the way in which you do it. The frame may be accurate or it may be false. It may be positive or it may be negative. Do you have a clue how others are framing you?

Wealth management advisor Charles Prothro, CFP, CLU, ChFC, and AEP of Charles Prothro Financial, describes the frame as follows:

"When somebody frames me, they put a wall around me. They put me inside something and they don't necessarily let me out of it—just like a picture frame."[1] Prothro knows all about what it means to be framed, as he was in the life insurance business for 22 years before expanding his business to offer other financial services. "Everyone knew me as a life insurance man. They knew what that meant. They understood that. I would walk into [. . . a client's] life and I was a life insurance policy walking into the room."[2]

Then one day, Prothro gave an insurance check to one of his clients whose husband had just passed away, and a look in her eyes told him that she had no idea what to do with all that money—where to put it or how to invest it. He didn't have a Series 7 license and wasn't in a position to be providing financial advice. Prothro explains, "That's when I walked in the office and told myself, 'I'm never going to have that happen again.'"[3]

Prothro decided then and there to reframe his business to be about more than insurance. He hired an experienced credentialed investment planner and Certified Financial Planner, and he augmented his own credentials to include those of Certified Financial Planner and Chartered Financial Consultant. Prothro also changed his company name from that of his flagship insurance company to Charles Prothro Financial to help him convey the reframe to his clients. Just as important, he made time to educate his clients on the new services he and his team could offer.

Clients responded well to the reframe, with comments like, "Charlie, I'm so glad to know this. I always wanted you to get in this type of business . . . it just adds to the things you're doing for us."[4] Another grateful and appreciative client noted, "Charlie, you treated me the same when I was sending you $50.00 a month for a life insurance policy as you do now with all of our investment dollars."[5] For Prothro, it's all about serving the client fully—and stretching, growing, and reframing to make that happen effectively.

 KEY CONCEPT

People tend to view financial advisors through a particular perspective or *frame*. The frame is made up of the set of beliefs through which a person sees, defines, and understands the advisor.

Sometimes the frame gets created by what people see and hear in the media. In the first two decades of the twenty-first century, the media brought to the public news of some nasty events in the financial industry, including the collapse of large banks such as Lehman Brothers, Washington Mutual, and IndyMac; massive illegal-trading discoveries such as the estimated $6.2 billion lost by JPMorgan Chase's "London Whale";[6] and violations of securities laws by supposedly trustworthy banks. Bernie Madoff's Ponzi scheme certainly did damage and left a mark.

After August 2008, hundreds of thousands of Americans watched their investment portfolios and retirement accounts take a nosedive during the Great Recession, while homeowners who were given ill-advised loans struggled to handle mortgage payments. All of these unfortunate issues contributed to a series of potential negative frames that the public sometimes placed on the financial professional.

Not all frames are negative, but this is a helpful place to start because we can see how damaging they can be. Here are some examples of the more negative frames that people may consciously or unconsciously assign to those in the financial services profession:

- Financial advisors are self-serving, greedy, and unprincipled.
- Financial advisors don't really help people; they just sell investments to make themselves richer.
- Most advisors at brokerage houses are just sales automatons peddling the company line.
- My father's financial advisor is old fashioned and I never want to work with him/her.
- My advisor can't do anything for me besides build my retirement portfolio.

Then there are the frames that get placed on advisors due to the way they began their careers. Advisors often admit to me that if they started as insurance sales professionals, they are usually framed as that. If they started as stockbrokers, they are only known as investment advisors. If they started as financial planners selling limited partnerships, they are still viewed by many clients as salespeople. Even after these advisors have expanded, their clients still frame them in old ways that do not acknowledge any growth.

Not every advisor is framed in these ways, nor with every client or prospective client, but certainly these are real frames being used to view some in our industry. Do you want to risk being framed in limiting ways?

INDUSTRY INSIGHT: REFRAMING FOR THE WIN

Erin Botsford, CEO and founder of Botsford Financial Group, understood the value of reframing early in her career. When she first got into the business in the early 1990s, she quickly discovered that clients coming into her office had a "preconceived notion" of her as either a stockbroker or an insurance agent, when in fact she was a certified financial planner.[7]

In addition to being framed with the wrong job description, Botsford also discovered that clients framed her whole profession of financial services as being quite low on the totem pole of professionals and advisors with whom they worked. In Botsford's view, her clients framed their attorneys at the highest level; beneath that, clients put their CPAs and then "probably their Mercedes dealer," she said; financial advisors were situated "way underneath."

Through a blend of mentorship, hard work, recognition of her unique value, and outright brains for the job, Botsford began to reframe herself. She went from being framed as a stockbroker on the bottom rung of the ladder of her clients' trusted advisors to being a savvy and cherished financial advisor who understood estate planning top to bottom. Both clients and other professionals in the field began to turn to her when they needed support in this area. Today, Botsford's firm serves clients in more than 30 states.

Botsford began her early reframe by taking the advice of her mentor, Amy Leavitt, Certified Financial Planner (now of Leavitt Associates), to learn everything she could about estate planning. With Leavitt's support, Botsford identified one of the best estate planning attorneys in the Dallas area and partnered with her to mutually refer clients. But first, Botsford spent a year learning from her new partner how to read and understand estate planning documents, scouring them and learning to point out what was good and bad about them.

Within a year, Botsford became über-skilled at assessing estate planning documents, which allowed her to have brilliant conversations with her clients on the topic—and which won their trust, their business, and their introductions to new future clients. Suddenly, Botsford had a big advantage over her competitors, and high-net-worth clients began seeking out her unique services.

Although there are other important facets to Botsford's growth from solo advisor to CEO of a 15-plus-employee firm, her early reframing efforts had a major positive influence on her success as an advisor and businessperson. Over the years, Botsford has been named one of *Barron's* Top 100 Independent Financial Advisors and Top 100 Women Financial Advisors, one of *D Magazine*'s Best Financial Planners, and a *Texas Monthly* Dallas/Fort Worth Five Star Wealth Manager.

Using this book, you can help ensure that your clients see you according to your desired frame, not the frame that they've constructed based on

- negative images from the media,
- their experience working with former advisors, or
- your own ineffective storytelling about your brand!

I know some amazing financial leaders who understand the importance of having a clear brand and who have put generous time and money into the effort, but even the best of the best are sometimes surprised when they explore how their clients perceive them and discover that perceptions don't match up in all areas with their intended brand or frame. This book will give advisors the guidance they need to make a purposeful and effective reframe rather than allowing a de facto, limiting frame to stand unchallenged.

Paul Pagnato, founder and managing director of Pagnato Karp, is very purposeful in how he frames his company. There are three distinct ways in which he works with his team to frame Pagnato Karp: First, they aim to be "recognized as true fiduciaries in the marketplace—[as] a business, a firm and advisors that provide 100 percent pure, objective, transparent advice. That's number one, and very, very important to us." Second, Pagnato works to frame his company as working with the ultra-high-net-worth family and, third, as a family office solution. To implement the frame, Pagnato and team are careful to take a holistic rather than a single-area approach. He believes the latter only leads to frustration and recommends that advisors consider how everything they are doing to frame themselves ties together, whether it's their marketing materials, how their presentation looks, their website, or their print, radio, television, and social media output. Pagnato states, "I believe what has worked for us is looking holistically at all aspects of the marketing, the public relations, the media and branding. It's a comprehensive solution [executed] in a comprehensive way."[8]

KEY CONCEPT

Being aware of your frame is the first step in taking charge of it, by making sure you are defined by your values and work rather than by negative impressions created by scandalous news stories, clients' past experiences with other advisors, or an inaccurate message you are inadvertently sending.

Gabe is an example of an advisor who is stuck in an outmoded frame. He started out 15 years ago selling life insurance and was thought of at the time as a reliable and excellent insurance agent. Fifteen years later, he still has many of the same clients. How do they frame Gabe all these years later? As a reliable and excellent insurance agent. Reliable and excellent are good; unfortunately, the insurance part is flawed because Gabe and his now 10-person firm do more than sell insurance. They also build estate plans, offer beneficiary-designation review, and do tax advising. But most of Gabe's long-term clients don't know about these new services. Gabe never took the time to reframe what he does for his clients, so they have no clue that he provides these other services; he is losing potential business as a result.

Now let's look at a frame that is working effectively for a financial firm. Building Futures Inc. is a firm that offers small to midsize developers and builders lending support, fee analysis, asset protection, and more. Led by their marketing-minded CEO, Miriam, not only has the firm taken the time to get clear on who their audience is and the value Building Futures brings to that audience, but it also regularly communicates its services and value to clients through monthly correspondence and during client check-ins. This firm has taken the steps necessary to create alignment between the value it delivers to clients and what clients perceive it to do. The frame their clients see them through is the one they've carefully and clearly communicated to clients through both service and language. As a result, their clients naturally use that frame to think about and describe the firm, so their firm benefits.

On the one hand, framing is another way to talk about branding and marketing your company—distilling its value and communicating that value with your target market. On the other hand, I would argue that framing, as compared to branding and marketing, more clearly acknowledges the most important element of your success as an advisor: the client! When we talk about branding and marketing, it's easy to fall into the one-sided approach of blaring through a megaphone to the public what services you provide without ever having a dialogue with your target client or stopping to ask, "What does the client, whom my firm is built to serve, actually want and need from my business and our team?"

The process of framing outlined in this book holds the client at the center of the relationship. When you reframe your firm or your team, you will begin and conclude the process by engaging in a series of larger conversations with the client. Provide your clients what they need and your business will grow.

KEY CONCEPT

Reframing begins and ends with the client: what the client needs, what the client believes about you and what you have to offer, and what the client gains in his or her relationship with you as a financial advisor.

THE FIVE LEVELS OF FRAMING

Have you ever met somebody who remembers you from a career 20 years ago and who isn't aware of your career path or how far you've come? And then you reconnect with the person and he or she realizes, "Wow, you've had a lot of different work experiences." It's like the young kid working in an office mailroom who grows up and becomes the CEO of the company but whom people still think of as the young kid in the mailroom. That's framing, and it happens every day.

Framing can happen on multiple levels: at personal, firm, and team levels; among advocates; and within the industry (as shown in Figure 1.1). Personal framing relates to how people view you as an individual person: mailroom clerk versus CEO, nice guy or grouchy

Figure 1.1 The Five Levels of Framing

woman, ambitious employee versus unmotivated worker, reliable individual versus unreliable person, well organized versus disorganized, and so on. Each of these ideas represents a different possible personal frame that you may or may not be pleased with. Soliciting feedback from others is a way to learn more about how they frame you on a personal level.

The firm frame refers to how clients view your practice: its "personality" and values, the kind of clients it works with, the services it provides, and the value it offers to clients. For example, is your firm seen as a team of wealth management partners for the client or as a bunch of sales guys and gals waiting to tell the client about the latest investment opportunity? Do your clients think you only do financial planning, or do they know that you offer other wealth management services as well? The firm frame gets even more complex if you are affiliated with a broker-dealer. Now you have to consider the way your clients may automatically view you based on your association with a given broker-dealer as well as the way you would like them to frame you based on your firm's unique personality, values, and enterprise value.

The team frame refers to how the people on your team view you as a leader. Do they see you as fair or unfair? Stable or erratic? Collaborative or dictatorial? Dedicated or distant? Do they see you as taking company profits without being engaged in the practice, or do they see you as a driver of the practice's success? Although their frames vary, team members see every leader through one kind of frame or another. How does your team frame you?

Advocates frame you, too. Advocates are others who serve as ambassadors for you, your firm, or your team. They believe in you and are willing to promote and refer your services to others. It's important to educate advocates on what your intended frame is so they can help you spread the word and attract the right clients for your business.

The last frame relates to how the public views the entire financial industry. This frame is formed in large part by the media, whether through TV commercials that poke fun at the advisor, scandalous headlines in the newspaper, or unbecoming film productions. Although advisors can't do much to control the industry frame, they can control how they are viewed by their clients, their team, and their advocates by having a well-defined frame that they communicate consistently with clients, potential clients, advocates, and the public.

KEY CONCEPT

Reframing happens at the personal, firm, team, advocate, and industry levels. Being aware of these frames is the first step in taking control of them.

COACHING CORNER

How do you think others are framing you, your team, and your firm? The best way to find out is to ask others, but begin with your own hunch. What answers come to mind?

Reframing: What's the Payoff?

It will take effort for advisors to make a reframe—time and resources to interview clients, to brainstorm the new frame, to incorporate the client services the advisors can provide and the clients desire, to create new marketing collateral, and to communicate the new frame to clients—but there is an attractive payoff:

- Informed clients who actively seek your services
- Increased enterprise value
- More client introductions
- A bigger, healthier practice
- Increased personal wealth through your thriving practice
- Freedom to do what you love within and outside of the firm
- Increased job satisfaction
- More work–life balance
- Chance to leave a legacy
- Opportunity to sell the firm if and when desired
- Opportunity to make a greater impact in clients' lives and the world at large

The reframing process is one of discovery. It involves gathering valuable information from current clients and then going within the team to identify and refine what the firm does well and would like to be doing in the future. The end result is a conscious reframe that allows advisors to build satisfying and saleable practices that have a positive impact and can sustain themselves over time. Success is just a reframe away . . .

CONCLUSION

The truth is that as a financial advisor, you've been framed, like it or not. Perhaps you have framed yourself; perhaps you have allowed others to frame you. Many of the frames will be good; some will be not so good. This book is going to help identify the ways you are currently framed by clients, prospective clients, and other trusted advisors and centers of influence. This book will also help you take a purposeful

KEY CONCEPT

By taking charge of how you are framed, you will be able to provide your best services to the clients whose needs match your skills, maximizing your performance and the clients' outcomes.

---

approach to reframing the way these others see you so that it matches the firm and professional you are today and plan to be tomorrow.

Why leave the framing to chance when you have the power to build your brand in an intentional way? Only by taking the time to discern your value, match it to the needs of your ideal clients, and learn to tell a story about that value through your marketing communication efforts and client and advocate conversations can you be sure that you are creating the team and practice that you truly want to be. That's what we will do together in this book, which is filled with unique takeaways that can significantly alter your financial practice for the better, tomorrow and well into the future.

We will begin by looking at five of the common reframes that advisors can make if they are ready to operate as the best in the business do.

NOTES

1. Charles Prothro, personal interview, March 23, 2015, transcript, p. 1.
2. Ibid.
3. Ibid. p. 2.
4. Ibid. p. 5.
5. Ibid.
6. Patricia Hurtado, "The London Whale," *Bloomberg QuickTake*, last modified April 23, 2015, accessed May 29, 2015, www.bloombergview.com/quicktake/the-london-whale.
7. Erin Botsford, personal interview, March 10, 2015, transcript, pp. 1–2.
8. Paul Pagnato, personal interview, March 23, 2015, transcript, p. 4.

CHAPTER **2**

What the Best in the Business Don't Want You to Know

The Five Wealth Management Reframes

What is it that separates the highest-performing financial advisors from everyone else? Is it the ability to sell big? Is it awesome technical expertise? Is it uncanny insight into markets, or is it super-savvy people skills? All of these traits help the best performers rise to the top, but at the core of these advisors' success is . . .

the ability to innovate.

Top-performing advisors—or those whom I call the "best in the business"—can change on the fly and know how to adjust. They shift, modify, and improve as circumstances and contexts change, and they are improving all the time. These advisors are not afraid to reframe when needed; in fact, they know that they will fall behind, maybe even fail, if they don't.

What the top-performing advisors don't want other advisors to know is that they are successful in the business because they are really good at adjusting. Right? No one wins the game because they insist on sticking with the game plan regardless of what they see happening on the playing field. The only way to win is to adjust, and the best in the business *don't* want you to know that they are masters at adapting to changing circumstances. What's more, they are also really good at empowering those around them—on their teams and in their firms—to adjust, too.

Another way to think of it is as a willingness to reframe. Reframing is really about getting a read on where your clients are today and making adjustments to give them the value they desire and deserve. It's about assessing the characteristics of today's world and refining your business to serve clients in this emerging context.

This business is about change. We've seen more change in the past few years than we've seen in the decade prior. Those who survive and thrive embrace the changes and make the appropriate shifts, adjustments, and reframes required to succeed. Those who produce weaker results keep doing the same things over and over while expecting better results. But as Albert Einstein once said, that kind of behavior is the definition of insanity.

 KEY CONCEPT

Circumstances, contexts, the world, your and your clients' situations: They are always changing. To be a successful financial advisor, you need to be able to adjust your plans—or *reframe*—on the fly.

At ClientWise, my executive coaching company for financial leaders, we observe practice management and study leadership every day. We have coached thousands of financial advisors, including those ranked in *Barron's* Top 1,000, and we have studied many financial services firms, small and large. I have spoken to advisors all over the country and the world, including Australia, Canada, Hong Kong, and the United Kingdom, and delivered talks to meetings and conferences at Merrill Lynch, Royal Bank of Canada, Northwestern Mutual, Morgan Stanley,

MetLife, Ameriprise Financial, TIAA-CREF, JPMorgan Chase, Raymond James, Nationwide Financial, the Money Management Institute, and *Barron's*. In collaborating with advisors from these different groups, I have learned about where they have succeeded (versus failed) and why.

In our observations and analyses at ClientWise of the top-performing advisors, we have discovered that those who are most successful have *reframed* themselves for wealth management in the twenty-first century. They have discovered that the old game plan no longer works and have engaged in the following five key reframes. These reframes have given them a distinct competitive advantage over others in the industry, allowing them to grow their practices into the most successful entities that they can be. Table 2.1 presents the five reframes—outlining the shifts from the old frames to the new frames—for effective wealth management practices in the twenty-first century.

In each of these five reframes, there is a pattern of partnership. Advisors can only provide comprehensive wealth management by partnering with others, internally and externally, to augment their own specialties and expertise (Reframe #1). Advisors also interact with clients using a partnering relationship rather than a sales-to-customer relationship (Reframe #2). In addition, advisors partner with team members to ensure the best service and outcomes are provided to clients (Reframe #3). What's more, advisors no longer tell clients what

Table 2.1 Wealth Management Practice Reframes for the Twenty-First Century

	Old Frame		New Frame
Reframe #1	I provide my clients with one particular financial service.	→	I provide my clients with comprehensive wealth management that begins with outcomes-based financial planning.
Reframe #2	I sell to my clients.	→	I partner with my clients.
Reframe #3	I am the best at serving my clients.	→	My team is the best at serving our clients.
Reframe #4	I know what is of value to my clients.	→	My clients and my team work together to define what value our clients need and what value my team can provide.
Reframe #5	I allow clients to rent my services until I choose to stop practicing.	→	I build a legacy business that serves multiple generations to come.

they should value; rather, advisors partner with clients to discover what clients need and value and then improve their own practices to provide that (Reframe #4). Last, advisors build a business that outlasts them by partnering with younger financial advisors whom they mentor and to whom they pass their wisdom (Reframe #5).

Today's high-performing advisors have recognized the cultural shift from hierarchy to equality and from authority to partnership. Whether it's the way the Internet has allowed consumer access to information—leveling the playing field between consumers and the professionals who serve them—or the emergence of the sharing economy where people can bypass traditional corporations and turn directly or near directly to others for a car ride, room stay, or grocery delivery, the world is now flatter than ever.

Translate this phenomenon to the world of financial advising and we start to see a shift from a vertical relationship to a more horizontal one. How does this look in practice? It's the advisor moving from behind the desk to sit beside clients. It's not an approach of, "I have all of the information and you need me." Instead, it's an approach of, "All of the information is in the public domain, and my job is to help you make sense of it and to remove the complexity associated with wealth management."

High-performing advisors have recognized this shift from a hierarchical to a collaborative relationship, and they have made the reframes necessary to build their practices on this premise of partnership: advisor to client, but also advisor to internal and external teams as well.

 KEY CONCEPT

The most successful financial advisors have embraced five key reframes of the client–advisor relationship: Successful advisors provide *comprehensive* wealth management services (rather than a single service), they *partner* with clients (rather than sell to them), they provide the services of a *team* (rather than being the sole advisor), they listen to their clients to determine their *individual values* (rather than assuming that this client's goals are the same as other clients' goals), and they build a business that serves and will be around for *future generations* (rather than existing just for the duration of the advisor's working life).

What Makes You the Best in the Business?

Let's talk about what it means to be "best in the business." At Client-Wise, we define the best in the business as those who

- are clear on their enterprise value
- have pristine client relationships
- track record of stellar regulatory compliance
- operate as part of a team
- have strategic hiring strategies to attract, develop, and retain superior human capital
- have sustainable businesses that can outlive their founder
- have next-generation client coverage
- have high retention scores when clients pass away

Assets under management is one way to judge success, but there are so many other factors by which to gauge success as well, from quality of client relationships and ethical track record to business sustainability.

REFRAME #1: I PROVIDE MY CLIENTS WITH COMPREHENSIVE WEALTH MANAGEMENT THAT BEGINS WITH OUTCOMES-BASED FINANCIAL PLANNING

The first secret of the most successful advisory firms is this: Financial advising is no longer just about offering one particular service such as investment advising, insurance, or financial planning. It's about providing support across all the areas of wealth management that are essential to clients: investing, financial planning, financial management, financial reporting, risk management, family continuity, trusteeship, and/or philanthropy (as illustrated in Figure 2.1).

Admittedly, since 2010 there has been a trend for advisors to move from calling themselves "financial advisors" and "financial consultants" to "wealth management advisors." Yet many have made the switch without actually adjusting or reframing the services they offer. These folks call themselves wealth management advisors, but they still focus solely or mainly on investments or whatever individual service they have traditionally offered.

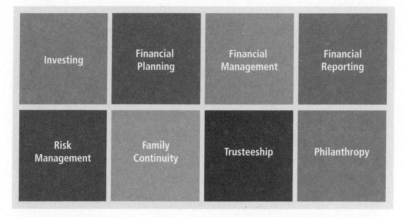

Figure 2.1 Areas of Wealth Management

In contrast, the best in the business understand that this evolution in title goes far beyond semantics. It offers an opportunity for the advisor to go wider and deeper than finances—beyond dollar signs in the bank account and stocks and bonds in the retirement fund—to serve the diverse areas that relate to a client's wealth. Think opportunity! The end result is that these particular firms are able to attract new clients interested in comprehensive support, to capture additional business from existing clients who need and want more, and to increase overall client retention as clients remain satisfied and find value in these firms' offerings.

THE eXchange™
Online Tool 2.1: Your Wealth Management Checklist

How do you define wealth management, and what pieces of wealth management are you best suited to offer? Where do the gaps remain? Building relationships with other select professionals will allow you to do what you love and still support your clients across their wealth management needs. Visit the eXchange™ and complete Your Wealth Management Checklist to focus on which wealth management services your firm would like to offer directly, versus those you can connect your clients to through other professionals on your external team.

At the core of this particular reframe is outcomes-based financial planning to deliver the comprehensive approach of wealth management. We must put financial planning at the core! The financial plan ensures that the advisor and client take everything wealth related into account. For example, there will be no grossly overweighting one stock because you don't realize the client already has investments there, and you won't sell the client life insurance when he or she already has it.

As David B. Armstrong, CFA, president and cofounder of Monument Wealth Management, notes, the financial plan answers the big question of *what is the money for?*[1] As important of a question as that is, plenty of advisors and clients may not have taken the time to answer it. Yet understanding what the money one is making, saving, growing, and managing is for ensures that advisors and clients know how to build the right type of wealth management plan. It also enables them to assess if they are achieving their goals and, if not, to make adjustments along the way.

 COACHING CORNER

The pie of opportunity to service and support clients is big. Which areas of wealth management are you serving? Which ones would you like to serve? Do you have trusted partners and professionals to whom you can refer clients for those areas you don't serve? Reframing your practice will allow you to work through these questions to an end result that helps you grow your business and increase client satisfaction. The hands-on reframing work can be done later in the book, but now is a good time to begin contemplating what kind of wealth management services you currently offer and which ones you may want to expand into in the future.

Where the advisor or firm does not have a skill set, partnerships with other respected professionals can be built. The best of the best do this skillfully. They learn about trusted professionals by going directly to clients to invite them to share their networks, and then they go about building a team of professional advocates that can be used again and again to offer clients a web of support. The advisor stays in the lead, making his or her advice and network indispensable to the client so that others in the network remain partners rather than competitors. A new way of running the wealth management business takes shape, and everyone benefits in the process.

KEY CONCEPT

Moving from calling oneself a financial advisor to embracing the new term *wealth management advisor* should be more than a change in job title. True wealth management involves providing a range of services to help clients achieve their financial goals. If you do not have the specific skill set your client needs, partner with respected professionals who do. Everyone—you, your clients, and your partners—will benefit from the teamwork.

 The Benefits of Reframing to Offer Comprehensive Wealth Management

- Clients get their wealth management needs met, meet their financial-related goals, and maximize their wealth and impact on family and community.
- Advisors increase client retention and grow their client base while also creating a strong pipeline of future business through fruitful partnerships with others in the wealth management community.
- Firms have the potential to develop a unique value proposition that renders them ready for a liquidity event down the road.
- Advisors enjoy more meaningful work as they deliver services matched with their own interests while meeting the real needs of their target clients.
- Society benefits as individuals' wealth is maximized and opportunities for philanthropic giving increased.

REFRAME #2: I PARTNER WITH MY CLIENTS

The second reframe of top advisory firms is that they have stopped *selling* to their clients and started *partnering* with their clients. In a sales relationship, the advisor has a series of financial products and/or services that he or she suggests to the client for purchase or investment. In a partnering relationship, instead of suggesting what to buy, the advisor works with the client to formulate wealth goals and to co-create a plan for achieving those goals. Investments may well be made in support of those goals, but it comes out of a partnering rather than a sales relationship.

In a wealth management partnership, it's not about the advisor's agenda, but the client's agenda. As a result, the advisor uses his or her expertise to support the client and the client's goals at the same time that the client is brought more intimately into the relationship to be an active participant in meeting goals and creating financial success.

In the view of Geri Eisenman Pell, CEO of Pell Wealth Partners, it's not that the sales piece is "bad" or has to be removed entirely from the equation, but there is a big difference between being a "product pusher" and someone who offers financial products to clients in service of a well-thought-out financial plan.[2] As Pell puts it, "If you lead with financial planning and if you're always filling a need that a person has and never filling your need to sell a product, then . . . there's no negative connotation to it." Pell understands that the client comes first and has always taken the latter approach. As a result, she explains, "I've never had anybody say to me, 'You're just selling this because it's a product you want to offload.' Never."

The best advisors recognize that the value of the profession is no longer to simply sell to—or even advise or consult with—the client, but instead to create this partnership. They know how to enter into an equal relationship with the client rather than defaulting to the more traditional one-way relationship that has characterized the profession for so long, in which the advisor is the authority and the client is merely the recipient of advice and technical expertise.

The change in the industry from an approach of "sales driven by the advisor" to "partnership driven in service of the client" follows the natural evolution seen in other industries. There we see the relationship between expert and consumer has shifted from a vertical one to a horizontal one as the Internet has given people access to everything, from information to products to services, and has empowered them to step into the role of equal in many areas. In health care, patients now have easy access to online medical advice and their medical records, empowering them to ask doctors more questions and self-report more information to improve their care. In the financial industry, clients can now manage their own portfolios through online accounts, and they have access to the latest financial news, allowing them to be more educated in conversations with their advisors and to make more informed requests.

As clients have become empowered by access to information, they also have developed an expectation that they will be treated as partners in all of their important relationships. They expect their relationship with their financial advisor to be no different. The best in the business recognize this and actively work to create healthy partnerships with clients.

As CEO Pell points out, all too often firms fall into the trap of thinking that investing for their clients and reporting back to them on those investments is enough. In fact, clients need an in-tune, agile advisor who can detect clients' unique financial concerns and respond to them in a satisfactory way. That's partnership.

Pell recounts a telling story on the subject, in which she met an ultra-high-net-worth woman at a charity event who confessed that the brokerage firm that served her and her husband was missing the mark at truly hearing and responding to their concerns.[3]

The husband had some serious financial concerns that were keeping him up at night. Although "the blue shirts" of the firm, as the woman called them, agreed to meet with the couple, the conversation centered around technical jargon that did nothing to put the couple at ease. As a result, the husband continued to suffer from insomnia due to his ineffectively allayed financial concerns. A firm skilled in partnership would have caught their true concerns through active listening and worked through them in dialogue and follow-up action with the clients.

 KEY CONCEPT

Rather than selling to the client, your goal should be to partner with the client so that you understand this particular client's needs, which you can then work to meet. Clients are more informed than ever before, thanks to the Internet, so they often already have an idea of where they want to go but need help getting there. Clear communication with your client leads to a stronger relationship, which increases the likelihood of a long-term partnership and successful attainment of financial goals.

Five Steps to an Effective Advisor–Client Partnership

At ClientWise, we encourage advisors to use the following structure to create a healthy partnership. This approach involves more than just an attitude of equality. There are specific actions the advisor engages in to create a successful collaboration.

1. The advisor invites the client to enter into a joint *partnership agreement* that outlines the expectations for the relationship on both sides.

2. The advisor works to *build an effective relationship with the client by fostering trust* and treating the client with respect.

3. The advisor *asks powerful questions* of the client and *actively listens* for answers.

4. The advisor works with the client to *set goals, make plans, and design actions.*

5. The advisor *manages the progress of the client* toward meeting those goals and *provides accountability* for the client regarding follow-through on plans and proposed actions.

It's no mistake that the steps just outlined for creating a healthy wealth management partnership mimic several of the core competencies of the coaching profession.[4] As a coaching firm, ClientWise has intentionally leveraged many of the valuable principles of coaching when training financial leaders on how to create more effective partnerships. It's our goal to share the secrets of coaching with financial advisors, giving them the power to create superb partnerships with their clients. This allows these advisors to move beyond just an attitude of equality to having real tools for building effective partnerships. It also helps them advance beyond their competitors' ability to deliver. In the end, creating a healthy partnership comes from being able to set the foundation for an effective partnership, create a trustworthy relationship, communicate effectively, and facilitate learning and results.

In addition to being what clients *want* today, partnership is also what clients *need* today, and the best advisors are recognizing this. Clients are busier than ever; they are flooded daily with data and communications to process and manage, and the varying elements of their wealth picture have become more complex. Today's client welcomes the support of a wealth management partner who is attentive to the whole wealth picture *and* willing to engage with the client as a collaborator. The best in the business see these opportunities and engage.

REFRAME #3: MY TEAM IS THE BEST AT SERVING OUR CLIENTS

What the best in the business also don't want you to know is that they are not doing it all anymore. They are engaged in the firm but in a different way, using all of their knowledge, wisdom, and experience to *lead a team*, so they are able to truly enjoy the work they do for clients without feeling stretched thin, and so they can deliver on their promise to always be there for the client.

Instead of carrying the mind-set of "I am the best at serving my clients," the best in the business have reframed to "My team is the best at serving our clients." These advisors have broken away from the notion that they have to do it all or that they all have to do it. They are enabling their teams to be the best at serving clients so they don't have to handle the sizable endeavor alone.

The truth is that it's a tough business to work in alone: managing the portfolios, working solo with clients, running the numbers, working to win new clients, and so on. The best in the business, however, get to enjoy using their wisdom to lead a group of people working interdependently to support the client. There is true satisfaction in that. These leaders aren't about doing everything themselves; they are about engaging in a different way that draws on their wisdom and lets them stay involved while retaining the freedom to grow well beyond the early days of their practice, when they were occupied doing everything.

In the old days, many advisors could successfully go it alone. It was hard work, but it was doable. As the financial advising profession has grown more sophisticated, however, the need for a team has increased. Not only has the profession moved from the more narrow financial advising and consulting approach to the more comprehensive wealth management approach with all its growth ramifications, but the work that advisors do within any area of wealth management now has several important pieces to it: technical expertise, client service, client relationship, marketing/acquisitions, and practice management

Figure 2.2 Areas of the Wealth Management Practice

(as illustrated in Figure 2.2). This is in addition to the effort that must now be expended to grow the team of the firm, such as hiring human capital, building company culture and values, managing the team daily, and leading the firm with a long-term strategy in mind.

To expect a single advisor to handle all of these responsibilities is both unrealistic and absurd. The firm suffers, the client suffers, the advisor suffers, or most likely all three do. Building a team takes time, effort, and patience, yes. But the reward in return is freedom for the

 KEY CONCEPT

As the number of services wealth management advisors are expected to provide has increased, so too has the need for a team of advisors. A one-person financial advising shop used to be realistic, but now, to provide the diverse range of services, keep up with all of the tasks involved in running and growing a business, and provide the best advising experience for clients, such a setup is not ideal. Share the work and multiply your success!

firm's leader, who now has the space to focus on the parts of the firm that he or she enjoys; in the process, the client gets better service and support.

At ClientWise, we define a *true team* as a group of people who are fully committed to mutually defined and extraordinary success of the group as a unit and who hold themselves mutually accountable for the achievement of that success, as well as the methods by which that success is achieved. Let's break that down a bit. Team is

- a group of people
- committed as a unit to mutually defined success and
- engaged in holding each other accountable.

The best in the business recognize that it's about more than just adding people to the roster or bringing people together; it's about getting the right people onto the bus—people who are engaged in defining success and committed to achieving it. The best in the business also understand the meaning and value of accountability and know how to create a culture in which the team holds one another responsible for taking the steps toward success.

 COACHING CORNER

How does the notion of team fit into your financial services practice today? How might it fit into your practice tomorrow? Where is team already strong in your practice, and where do you feel motivated to make improvements?

REFRAME #4: MY CLIENTS AND MY TEAM WORK TOGETHER TO DEFINE WHAT VALUE OUR CLIENTS NEED AND WHAT VALUE MY TEAM CAN PROVIDE

In the old way of operating, advisors worked under the assumption that they knew best what clients needed. They sought value and tried to deliver it to their clients. Today, the best advisors have reframed this idea. It's no longer a case of the advisor pushing so-called value onto the client, but rather a case of advisors inviting clients into a discussion to define what value they seek. The advisor and the advisor's team can then work together to refine and provide that value, both directly and by making the right professional connections for the client.

Most firms are already providing clients value—value that is desirable, useful, and of interest for the future. Yet clients often don't know what that value really is. How often have you heard a client say, "I didn't know you could help me with life insurance"? Or, "I didn't know you could help me with a mortgage." An advisor may offer 10 services, but the client often only knows of two.

In another example of missed value, the client may realize that she meets with her advisor on a yearly basis without understanding that this meeting is more than a sales opportunity for the advisor to get in front of the client: It is actually an important opportunity to check in on the status of action plans and to recalibrate goals. Advisors provide value to clients, but if the client is too busy or not sufficiently informed to recognize the value, frankly, much of its power gets lost. The best of the best advisors recognize the importance of not only becoming intentional about the kind of wealth management services they offer, but they also realize that they have to continually educate the client on what these services are and how they provide value to the client.

 KEY CONCEPT

Clients cannot take advantage of services you offer that they do not know about or don't realize that they need. Make sure both you and your client understand what value your client needs and what value your team can provide.

At ClientWise, we provide advisors with a specific process for partnering with clients to explore their understanding of a firm's current value proposition. During this process, advisors also engage with clients to gather insight into the value that these clients seek, work with their team to refine the firm's value proposition, and then return to the client to share what the refined offerings now are. This process is at the heart of reframing one's wealth management practice and will be explored in full in Part II of the book.

Five Steps to Reframing

1. Collect: Advisors speak to clients to identify where they see value in the firm and where they would like to see more value (we call it the *ClientWise Conversation*™).

2. Define: Advisors clearly and intentionally rebrand/reframe themselves by defining their unique profile of wealth management services in response to the client conversation and advisors' own wishes and interests.

3. Design: Advisors create the marketing materials to communicate that brand/frame to clients, professional advocates, and the public.

4. Inform: Advisors go back to clients and educate them on what wealth management services are offered and the accompanying value of each.

5. Renew: Advisors regularly check in with clients to jointly explore what they have achieved together (since they last met, over the course of the year, and over their life's work together). Over time, the clients should be able to describe this value themselves, and advisors should continue to solicit new feedback.

The insight clients can provide during the partnering process can be an invaluable part of your reframing campaign. After all, what use is a reframe if you're offering services that clients aren't interested in? You can offer the most brilliant products in the world and communicate your new frame to your clients brilliantly, but your efforts will be useless if what you are offering isn't what clients want. Once you've taken your client feedback to the drawing board and revised the value your firm can provide on the basis of what clients are looking for, then you are ready to present your reframed services to your clients.

The reframing process enables the advisor to evoke what it is that clients value most while concurrently reminding clients about all the valuable work the firm has done and continues to do for them. During this process, advisors actively educate clients on the value they bring to clients while putting energy into seeking clients' feedback on value and responding to it.

Top-performing advisors know that they can never take for granted that the client appreciates their value—or even understands what they really do. As a result, these advisors invest time and energy in helping to frame and reframe the very value they provide for clients. This enables clients to understand the full benefits of the wealth management partnership and to increase motivation to stay with a firm over the long term. Clients will be more prepared and inclined to make effective referrals to the firm, too, with the potential to bring in new business and help the firm grow. Not only will clients then understand the firm's value—and thus have the capacity to appreciate it—but they will also have the words to tell others about the firm's value. It's a powerful mix that deepens the potential for a firm's success and longevity.

 COACHING CORNER

What value does your firm currently offer to clients? What do you think your clients would say if asked to describe your firm's value? What areas would be known versus unknown? You will have an opportunity to get more insight into these questions in Part II of the book, using the ClientWise Conversation™, but now is a great time to start considering your firm's value and the way your clients perceive it.

REFRAME #5: I BUILD A LEGACY BUSINESS THAT SERVES MULTIPLE GENERATIONS TO COME

For some advisors, it's natural to operate on the premise that your business will run as long as you do, and then, when you choose to walk away, it will be time to close the doors. The alternative—creating a succession plan, hiring the right advisors to follow in your footsteps, and taking the time to develop and mentor these advisors—is not necessarily attractive to the advisor who gets a thrill from winning business or running the numbers but not necessarily from mentoring the next generation. What's more, it's resource intensive to build your business to outlast you. Yet, the best in the business are finding a way to do just that.

The reasons are twofold. First, the best in the business recognize that to win the most clients, they need to have advisors who can work with all kinds of people, across every adult age group, rather than serving as the one and only advisor for each and every client. Today, an advisor's potential clients span four generations: the greatest generation, the boomers, the Gen Xers, and the millennials. Advisors who are the best in the business realize that younger clients have their own way of operating that may best be catered to by advisors of a younger generation, too. Some of these younger clients don't want to work with "Daddy's broker." The best in the business are making sure that these folks don't have to.

Second, the best in the business see the unique value of their experience and expertise and don't want to let them slip away when they choose to retire or step away from the business. There's no replacement for the body of knowledge that an advisor has developed over the decades as the industry has grown and changed: the ability to recognize trends and patterns, given that history repeats itself; the capacity to construct an investment portfolio rather than follow model portfolios; an understanding of the bond market; or the emotional intelligence of how to communicate with people.

The industry needs that wisdom to be passed on, as there is a scarcity of younger advisors joining the industry. According to Accenture, only 5 percent of U.S. financial advisors are younger than 30 years old.[5] In part, this is because there has been a trend, post-2008, for firms to hire experienced advisors from existing firms rather than recruiting and training younger individuals out of college. In addition, there is some speculation that grads are less interested in applying for these positions.[6]

Don't we owe it to our industry, to the public, and to ourselves to mentor the next generation of advisors and to pass our knowledge on to them, so they can continue to serve and support and we can enjoy the peace of mind that comes with passing on a legacy? Financial well-being enables the accomplishment of so much else: from being able to take care of one's family and send children to college to being able to invest in philanthropy. That's part of what makes advising a noble profession. If we hold our role to be invaluable in people's lives, then we need to treat our profession with the respect it deserves, helping it to live on in the next generation of well-prepared advisors. The best in the business—who are defined by more than just assets under management—understand this.

KEY CONCEPT

It may be most comfortable to work with peers as clients and not worry about what happens once you leave the advising business, but clients need and deserve to be more than your current paycheck. To truly elevate the wealth management profession, serve your clients, and leave a positive legacy, look to the future and mentor the next generation of advisors for your clients' sake as well as the future of wealth advising.

 Top 10 Secrets of the Best in the Business

While we're busy learning from the best in the business, let's go beyond the five reframes of the top advisors. Here is my top 10 list of what the best in the business are doing right now, including the five reframes but going further. I can tell you from coaching and training thousands of advisors since 2006 that the following practices are true of most of them.

The best in the business . . .

1. are intensely focused on growth and are willing to engage in a reframe.

2. understand that they cannot go it alone in today's world and that building a strong team is essential.

3. have already expanded their definition of wealth management to include a more comprehensive approach that has planning at its foundation.

4. are willing to take the time to get clear on how they uniquely define wealth management services offered by their firm.

5. are clear about their unique value proposition rather than just having a canned elevator speech.

6. have conditioned clients to understand the real value of their advisory firm, getting them invested in what the firm has to offer and turning them into loyal advocates.

7. know how important it is to attract human capital and are willing to invest in the process of finding the right individuals for the team.

(Continued)

(Continued)

8. have stopped selling to clients and are truly partnering.
9. believe in the importance of leadership development for themselves and their teams, moving folks on a trajectory from sales to technical expertise to leadership.
10. are comfortable partnering with other professionals to support clients across the full wealth management spectrum.

CONCLUSION

The best in the business know that continual improvement is essential to success. They are open to reframing themselves today and tomorrow, as needed, to meet the demands of their clients, the marketplace, and the industry. Remember only this, and you will be well on your way to operating at top capacity. Whether it's in the realm of how they manage client relationships, what kind of financial instruments and services they offer, or the way in which they develop their teams to be more robust and innovative, the top advisors place a value on growth and improvement that ensures they are attractive to existing and new clients alike. It reminds me of the story of the lion and gazelle.

As the story goes, every morning in Africa, a gazelle wakes up and it knows it has to run faster than the slowest lion or it will be eaten. Every day in Africa, a lion wakes up, and it knows it has to run faster than the slowest gazelle or it will starve. The point of the story is this: It doesn't matter if you are a lion or a gazelle—every day you've got to wake up and be running. How does this relate to the advisor? Regardless of your channel, the environment in which you operate is in constant flux—your clients, your profession, and your industry. So if you don't plan on changing, well . . . plan to be outrun.

I know, that sounds terrible, doesn't it? But there's truth to it. Our industry is constantly moving and evolving, with new regulations being added, the demographics of our clients changing (younger, female, ethnically diverse), and clients expecting more and new things from their advisors. To meet the consequent demands, advisors have got to get up and start moving.

Top advisors are in search of continual growth and have their ears to the ground on trends. They have open minds, can see possibility, and enjoy a capacity for creative thinking as well as change. All of these things allow top advisors and advisory firms to recognize the trends of today and respond to them. Lifelong learning, paired with insight into the trends of today, is what keeps the best the best.

You can create your own success by learning from others who lead the way, because there is truly a slice of the pie available to every advisor who is willing to adapt and reframe for tomorrow's world. With a realization of how expansive wealth management really is and an interest in connecting with clients' vast needs, there is fascinating, meaningful, and impactful work available for every interested financial advisor.

If you want to increase the number of clients that you serve, if you want to increase your revenue, if you want to increase profits, and if you want to build a business that truly has enterprise value and is really sustainable, then you have to change and improve. You have to really care about how you are being framed, and you have to be able to make a reframe when necessary. The Japanese call this process of continual improvement *kaizen*.[7] If you have a bigger future in mind, then you have to care about what people think about your brand. This is what the best in the business know and are acting on every single day.

The five reframes of the best in the business provide a roadmap for how you can best focus on growing and improving. The chapters that follow will take a deeper look at each of these reframes.

NOTES

1. David B. Armstrong, CFA, personal interview, March 6, 2015, transcript, p. 3.
2. Geri Eisenman Pell, personal interview, March 10, 2015, transcript, pp. 5–6.
3. Ibid., p. 8.
4. International Coaching Federation, "Core Competencies," accessed February 23, 2015, www.coachfederation.org/credential/landing.cfm?ItemNumber=2206&navItemNumber=576.
5. Accenture, *Advisor Succession Planning: Managing the Retirement of Baby Boomer Advisors*, 2013, accessed February 27, 2015, www.accenture.com/SiteCollectionDocuments/PDF/Accenture-CM-AWAMS-POV-Advisor-Succession-Planning-Final-Mar2013-web.pdf, p. 5.
6. Rachel Abrams, "A Hunt to Find the Next Generation of Financial Advisors." *DealBook* (blog), *New York Times*, June 24, 2014, http://dealbook.nytimes.com/2014/06/24/a-hunt-to-find-the-next-generation-of-financial-planners/?_r=0.
7. Kaizen Institute, "What is Kaizen?," accessed February 27, 2015, www.kaizen.com/about-us/definition-of-kaizen.html.

CHAPTER 3

Death of a Salesman/ Saleswoman and Rise of the Wealth Advisor

One of the most significant problems financial advisors face is that the public does not know what they actually do. A person gets handed a business card from an advisor affiliated with a broker-dealer and assumes the advisor sells investments. A person receives a phone call from an advisor affiliated with an insurance agency and believes it precedes an insurance sale. But often, these frames and perceptions are outdated or inaccurate.

The current perceptual frame of the vast majority of the public is that most financial advisors are simply salespeople or that they only handle financial transactions. The thinking tends to be that the type of product, sale, or other financial transaction is limited to the business that the parent organization has historically done. The public doesn't realize that the wirehouse advisor might offer financial planning, providing a goals-based approach to designing a wealth strategy, or that the agent affiliated with an insurance company offers other services beyond insurance that include a financial planning approach. They don't distinguish between wealth management and investment management, or know that their current advisor can probably do far more for them than he or she is already doing. To be frank, when it comes to understanding what advisors do, the public is fairly uninformed.

The blame for this lack of understanding lies squarely with those of us in the financial services profession. Is it realistic to expect the public to have followed the evolution of our industry from a selling profession to an advising profession to a partnering profession? Is the public responsible for understanding the practical ramifications of new federal regulations and legislation on the way we do business, what we call ourselves, and how we are able to serve them? The answer to both questions is a clear no. In an industry as technical, complex, and ever-changing as financial services, it is up to advisors and financial services organizations to educate the public and clients on the function and value of wealth management advisors.

This reality gets at the heart of the challenge for advisors today: They are framed all the time by the very people they want to serve. More often than not, the client or potential client's frame is a mis-frame that leads to lost opportunity and lost business because clients are turned off by salespeople, they don't realize the full value they can attain by working with advisors, or both.

The best in the business have discovered that the sales frame is an important area to reframe. They've moved from the old frame of "I sell to my clients" to the new frame of "I partner with my clients." This chapter will explore that reframe in depth.

THE MIS-FRAME

Yes, it is true: Advisors have been framed as part of one of the least trusted groups in America—salespeople. It's not my intent to give financial advisors or salespeople a bad rap. However, all we have to do is think of the unlikable Willy Loman character in Arthur Miller's play *Death of a Salesman*, or the stereotype of the aggressive, self-serving used-car salesman to be reminded of the negative images that get associated with sales.

Because the public tends to think of the work of financial advisors as revolving around selling investments, life insurance, financial plans, and so on, every negative image associated with sales is, on a regular basis, automatically assigned to the advisor: pushy, self-interested, inauthentic, untrustworthy, obnoxious—you name it. As a result and without even opening one's mouth, the advisor who hangs a business shingle, affiliates with a brokerage firm, or hands out a business card has been framed.

What's more, when the financial services industry takes a misstep that shows up in the news headlines, the "greedy salesperson" frame is merely reinforced. Also reinforced is the idea that the industry (and therefore most financial advisors) is only interested in how much money can be made off of people.

In addition to the potential negative connotation of selling, the selling approach no longer accurately captures what advisors do. Today, wealth management advisors are doing financial planning, estate planning, tax minimization, and many other wealth-related activities, but the public often assumes that these individuals are simply selling investments because that is what many in the industry used to do. It's unfortunate because advisors lose an opportunity to provide more to their clients, and clients miss out on an opportunity to be served more comprehensively.

 KEY CONCEPT

Most people do not realize that financial advisors no longer merely sell products; rather, advisors partner with clients to help them manage wealth and meet financial goals. It is up to financial advisors to clear up this misperception.

THE ROOTS OF THE INDUSTRY

The public has come by the negative salesperson frame honestly. In the early days of the profession (around the 1920s), the advisor was called "the customer's man" or the "customer's broker." The job of the customer's man was to place and take orders and to buy bonds and stocks. The customer's man sold investments to clients. Along the same lines, an insurance agent in this time period was called a "special agent." What a special agent did was sell life insurance products to customers.

Over time, the customer's man became "the stockbroker." The stockbroker also took orders from the client, managed the account, and bought and sold securities. As time went on, this financial professional became known as "the account executive." Whether the advisor was a customer's broker, a stockbroker, or an account executive, he or she was still an agent in the business of sales. The advisor in these times made money by buying and selling stocks, bonds, insurance, and other financial instruments to clients and by earning a commission or fee on the sale itself. The incentive was for the agent to buy and sell, all while making money for his or her client to retain the right to keep trading the client's account. The idea of financial planning as a whole or comprehensive wealth management had not yet come into play for the industry.

At the time, there was also a series of "county roads." If you got started in the business by joining an insurance firm, you sold life insurance. If you got started in a "boiler room" selling stocks and bonds, you were a broker. If you got started with the old IDS (Investors Diversified Services, Inc.), for example, you sold financial plans. Each of these individual firms primarily sold one product. Each product was its own individual county road.

The Glass-Steagall Act of 1933 changed things forever when it allowed a merger of professions, so that bankers could sell investment products, investment professionals could sell life insurance, and life insurance people could do financial planning. Suddenly, the service roads of the industry merged together onto a superhighway. Insurance agents began selling investment plans, investment managers began selling banking products, and bankers were all of a sudden selling investment products. Even the independent planners who might have been investment managers were helping clients minimize taxes by working with their clients' estate planners and writing insurance policies. The individual-product sale was over. The role of the wealth advisor was born.

KEY CONCEPT

The 1933 Glass-Steagall Act laid the groundwork for the profession of wealth advising by allowing bankers, life insurance agents, investment managers, and other professionals to sell multiple kinds of financial products.

After World War II, financial planning was born to meet the growing needs of Americans.[1] Suddenly, financial professionals were doing more than selling: They were helping clients create a financial roadmap for the future.

During the next few decades, the work of financial professionals continued to gain credibility as the industry organized to provide technical training and designations. Suddenly, multiple designations appeared in the industry. Members of the profession obtained CFPs, CHFCs, and CLUs; they earned CIMA Chartered Professional Wealth Advisor certifications. All of these designations helped to build some level of efficacy for an industry that was starving for a clearer identity and for credibility. The industry was also slowly but surely moving away from sales.

A further critical development occurred in 1969 when 13 individuals met in Chicago (predecessors to the Certified Financial Planner Board of Standards) and developed the notion that the public could gain value from a "profession that integrated knowledge and practices from the many, often-fragmented areas of the financial services industry."[2] The role of the advisor as a supportive expert who helped the client understand varying pieces of the financial industry—beyond investments—emerged. The move toward wealth management was underway, albeit without the name yet.

The trajectory of evolution faced by professionals in the industry is captured in Figure 3.1.

SALES, NO MORE

There was a time when the financial professional as salesperson was enough. In fact, as late as the 1980s, the stockbroker was a symbol of American success. The baby boomers working with them wanted the

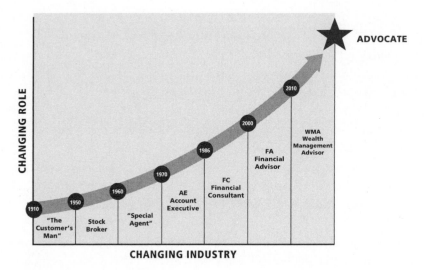

Figure 3.1 Evolving Role of the Financial Advisor

best of everything, including the best advice about which stocks to choose for their portfolios. Stockbrokers were held in high regard by the boomers, who were outearning their parents and transforming the economy in the process.

Then, during the 1990s, the boomers discovered the Internet, and many started doing their own trades online. What's more, after 30 years of brute-force traditional sales marketing from advisors, consisting of millions of cold calls a day, the public had become burned out on the sales approach that financial people had often provided to them. In addition, the public was smart enough to recognize that they could save the broker's commission by buying and selling on their own.

Suddenly, brokers-as-salespeople were needed less and less, and so these professionals transformed themselves into financial advisors, offering a more consultative and needs-based approach. However, many newly minted "advisors" were still essentially operating as salespeople, identifying their clients' needs to position products for sale. They were trying to do the same work disguised under a new name, even though the demands of the marketplace had changed. The sales approach was often endemic to the whole organization, a sign of the organizational strategy at large and an indicator of the culture of the industry.

Being a broker or a consultative seller is no longer enough. Today, the boomers are approaching retirement in large numbers and are leading increasingly complex lives. They need someone who can help them achieve not only their financial goals but also their life goals. They expect better service with lower fees. They've been through the ups and downs of the market and are skeptical of sales pitches. In response to the boomers' higher expectations, a new type of investment professional is being born.

The need for a new kind of advisor is not just due to boomers, though. Today's clientele—boomers, Gen Xers, and millennials alike—is sophisticated and different. In a flattening world where vertical hierarchies are transforming into horizontal relationships, the client expects to be brought into the planning process, not to be told to simply trust and accept the advisor's stock picks and financial recommendations. What's more, clients want to work with a financial professional who knows how to match goals with planning and investing.

In the old days, when investing was still out of reach and clouded in mystery for the mainstream person, clients needed their brokers and advisors to guide them on investments and to effect transactions for them. I can still remember giving a seminar in the late 1990s in Wichita, Kansas, regarding a privatization fund my firm was selling. Heavy snow was falling as I pulled into the parking lot and I remember thinking that no one would show up in such bad weather. Instead, 250 people made up my audience, and I developed laryngitis because I had to talk loudly enough for everyone to hear me. Similar bad weather at a seminar in Oklahoma City did not deter folks from attending that time, either. Neither did other such circumstances all over the country. People were coming to these seminars because they had to come; it was the only way to get information at the time.

Today, people don't have to come to these presentations or seek out advisors to get information on investing: They can get it on the Internet. There they can research, buy, and sell investments, managing their own portfolios with ease.

For the youngest generations, who are tech-savvy digital natives, online money management comes naturally. When one of my sons was in high school, for example, he surprised me one day by letting me know he had started managing his own investment portfolio online. While we had had some conversations along the way to set the stage for his interest in finances, the initiative was all his own and he had no trouble getting set up online. The world is different now. The reality is that 20, 30, 40, and 50 years ago, financial advisors were needed to effect transactions, make trades, and sell stuff; today, those services are no longer necessary.

KEY CONCEPT

Today's clients are sophisticated consumers with experience in managing their money and investments online. An experienced advisor can offer this new breed of client help in planning out what steps he or she needs to take to meet his or her financial goals.

WELCOME TO THE WORLD OF WEALTH ADVISING

With the "death of the salesman" in financial services, we are seeing the "birth of the wealth advisor." Christopher P. Jordan, founder and CEO of LEXCO Wealth Management, has seen this transformation take place in his own career.

Prior to founding LEXCO, Jordan worked as a partner in an advisory firm that placed a heavy emphasis on sales quotas and selling loaded mutual funds and other commission-based products. Interested in taking a more holistic approach to wealth management, he started his own firm that focused on service rather than sales. "With high-net-worth clients, you've got to offer something more than just a product," says Jordan. By taking a comprehensive approach to meeting his clients' needs, Jordan has created a highly successful practice. LEXCO Wealth Management has been ranked the number seven branch in the nation with National Planning Corporation,[3] and Jordan's now 17-person firm has been ranked "three years running as one of the top 10 offices in the nation at his Broker/Dealer."[4]

For Jordan, being a wealth advisor means bringing together a team of people to help his clients achieve their goals. He communicates regularly with a broad network of estate planners, insurance specialists, CPAs, attorneys, mortgage experts, and other professionals who can help his clients create an integrated financial plan. "In today's marketplace, you've got be different," says Jordan. "Our team-based approach is one way in which we differentiate our firm while helping our clients simplify their financial lives."[5]

Because Jordan makes it easier for his clients to reach their goals, his clients see him as a trusted advisor rather than simply a salesman. He has shifted from the old frame of "I provide my clients with one particular financial service" to "I provide my clients with comprehensive wealth management that begins with outcomes-based financial planning."

KEY CONCEPT

Finding a way to differentiate yourself and/or your firm from others in the field is a key to success.

Having started LEXCO in 1999, Jordan has been an early leader in the movement to evolve the financial services industry away from sales and into holistic wealth management. Unlike some professionals in the industry who have caught on to the title change from financial advisor to wealth management advisor without actually deepening their practices, Jordan has built a firm that can deliver on its promise to help clients manage the full breadth of their wealth.

COACHING CORNER

Take a moment to reflect on the philosophy and approach behind how you serve your clients. Where are you possibly still stuck in a sales approach? Where are you succeeding at providing comprehensive wealth management?

 How Should Advisors Charge Today?

It's a dirty little secret, but I believe that what is really holding us back as an industry is the way that many financial advisors are compensated. Many

(Continued)

> **(Continued)**
>
> financial advisors receive the largest percentage of their compensation on the basis of managing a client's portfolio. Right there, advisors are incentivized to focus on investments rather than goal setting, planning, or any of the other diverse areas of a client's wealth picture.
>
> The industry can rise up to meet this new opportunity to manage wealth when it becomes clearer about charging clients a fee not just on the assets that are being managed but rather on the time and delivery of the wealth plan and strategy. Inclusive in that wealth plan and strategy is the design, implementation, and delivery of all things related to wealth management. Advisors need to be able to charge a higher fee when they provide more services.
>
> As we evolve from a transactional industry where we sold lots of products to an industry where we are advising rather than selling, we need to move beyond the old compensation structure of charging a fee for the assets under management to what some advisors are already doing—charging clients fees for helping them with all things related to their wealth.

A New Way to Benchmark

At the core of wealth management is a financial plan that is paired with the client's goals and vision for the future. When I worked at Alliance Bernstein, we called it "benchmarking the beach house." If the client's goal was to buy a vacation home, we created a financial plan that took into consideration the amount of money that would be needed to eventually make the purchase, and we designed a plan that included the monthly savings and time frame required to reach this goal. If a client was saving for a child's college education and tuition was expected to cost a quarter million dollars, we would determine how much money the client needed to save each month to get there x number of years from now.

Another way to think of this is benchmarking to a family index or a personal index—to those goals that are important to the client and the client's family. Instead of just putting a lot of money in a portfolio and looking to get the most performance out of it (benchmarking to the S&P or other index), the wealth advisor helps the client create a plan that supports specific client goals—a plan that pegs to the family index, the personal index, or that list of things that represent the client's vision of success. In a big-picture sense, a wealth advisor provides guidance around the design of the client's future and how personal wealth will help the client achieve what it is he or she wants to achieve. The wealth advisor serves as a guide, certainly possessing all of the technical competencies needed to support the client but also having the relational ability to help the client through the process of discovering how he or she wants the future to look and how the advisor can actively participate in managing wealth to get there.

This is where the coaching aspect of wealth management comes in. I'm not referring to coaching in the athletic sense, where the coach tells the player on the field which plays to run and which goals to achieve, but the kind of coaching we see in business, where executive coaches partner with leaders to help them set their own agenda and then achieve it through planning, support, and accountability. Today's wealth advisor allows the client to take more of a leadership role in the partnership than has ever occurred in the past. Together, they are coauthors and cocreators in the design of a wealth strategy that supports the client's goals and vision for the future. The client brings the dreams, personal insight, and motivation to engage; the advisor brings the technical expertise, professional insight, and relational capacity to guide the client through the discovery and execution of the plan.

KEY CONCEPT

Today's wealth advisors function as coaches, helping clients achieve their dreams and goals by offering professional expertise, insight, and support.

THE eXchange™

Online Tool 3.1: Ten Reasons Your Clients Will Love You for Offering True Wealth Management

Visit the eXchange™ to discover 10 reasons your clients will love you for offering true wealth management. Feel free to adapt this list to your brand and to include it in

(*Continued*)

(Continued)

your firm's marketing literature so you can share it with clients and teach them more about why comprehensive wealth management sets you apart from other firms.

INDUSTRY INSIGHT: USING THE FINANCIAL PLAN TO GAUGE SUCCESS

David B. Armstrong, CFA, president and cofounder of Monument Wealth Management, can still remember the day a disgruntled potential client called him and asked if he could come in for an appointment with Monument because he wasn't happy with his current financial advisor.[6] When Armstrong inquired about why the man on the line—let's call him Mike—was unhappy with his advisor, his answer was simple: "I don't think they are making me enough money."

Armstrong replied by asking, "What kind of return do you need in order to feel like you are making a lot of money?" and Mike explained that actually, he didn't know, it was just how he felt about the situation. Mike took another moment to think and then clarified things further. He explained how the S&P 500 had been up 30 percent the previous year, while Mike's portfolio had only gone up by 14 percent. He did not feel good about that and blamed his advisors.

Armstrong did not disagree, and here's why. As it turns out, Mike's firm had not worked with him to create a financial plan. Armstrong shared that if Mike had had a plan, he would know exactly how to gauge whether his firm was helping him achieve success. So Armstrong asked Mike, "What if your plan only called for your portfolio to be up 7 percent and you were up 14 percent? Would you feel good about that?" Within that context, the client's answer was yes.

The moral of this story, according to Armstrong, is to begin with a financial plan and then use that plan—rather than the S&P 500—to benchmark success. The financial plan is so valuable because it serves as a reminder to people on a quarterly basis what their long-term goal is and how they're going to get there. It allows the advisor and client to assess whether true success is being achieved and signals when the wealth management strategy needs to be adjusted.

As the financial services industry moves away from being sales based, there is a huge opportunity for wealth advisors to start having what I call *larger conversations* with clients. Larger conversations include discussing things like

- How would you like your life to look in five years? Ten years? Twenty years?
- What wealth strategy and financial plan can we create together to help you get there?
- What are all of the pieces of the wealth picture that we need to consider to make sure we maximize success?
- What parts of the plan are you most comfortable with? Are you willing to commit to and engage with the plan? Is the plan realistic? If not, how do we need to adjust the plan?

Advisors are used to the idea of financial planning. It's the discovery piece related to helping the client verbalize the vision behind the plan that's the newer piece for most advisors. This is where advisors can bring new value to clients—by using coaching and relational skills to elicit what the Kinder Institute refers to as "the human side of financial planning."[7]

The Kinder Institute refers to the process as *life planning*:

> In Life Planning we discover a client's deepest and most profound goals through a [. . .] process of structured and non-judgmental inquiry. Then, using a mix of professional and advanced relationship skills, we inspire clients to pursue their aspirations, discuss and resolve obstacles, create a concrete financial plan, and provide ongoing guidance as clients accomplish their objectives.[8]

In the past, advisors were technical experts helping clients buy, sell, and trade to make more money; today, advisors are more than technical experts, and their goal is more than sales. Advisors are partnering with their clients to increase their wealth in ways that match their unique goals. Coaching skills are a powerful way to unlock a client's goals, motivation, engagement, and commitment.

New approaches to advising bring new challenges, but the good news is that advisors don't have to start from scratch in developing the discovery process. Instead, they can borrow tricks and tools of the trade right from the executive coaching profession, which for years has been helping leaders identify goals, create action plans, and achieve them through support and accountability. It's the same coaching process that ClientWise explores with our financial professional clients every day; this book will provide these coaching techniques to help advisors engage in a successful discovery process with clients.

The time has come for advisors to start having much larger, more impactful conversations with clients, and to consistently do so. No longer is advising just about managing people's money or selling them a financial plan or convincing them to buy a life insurance policy. It's all about *partnering* with clients to help them identify their unique goals for the future, collaborating to create a goal-based financial plan that the client is able to commit to, and checking in over time to ensure the plan is on track and working.

 COACHING CORNER

What does it mean to you to truly partner with your clients? Think of or write down five ways in which you enjoy partnering with clients and/or you would like to partner with clients in the future.

 Three Reasons to Make the Shift from Sales or Consultant to Wealth Advisor

From the customer's man, stockbroker, and account executive to the financial consultant, financial advisor, and now wealth advisor, those in the financial services profession have a huge opportunity to make a fundamental difference in people's lives while growing their practices in the process. Here are three reasons to make the shift.

1. By partnering with clients rather than selling to them or even directing them, advisors unlock the collaborative power of a team. By pairing the advisor's expertise with the client's interests and motivations, the chances of maximizing wealth grow exponentially.

2. By engaging clients in a discovery process focused on setting goals, the advisor ensures that the financial plan gets constructed

in a way that matches the unique needs of the client. Again, this increases client motivation to participate; just as important, it ensures client satisfaction when the right goals are ultimately reached.

3. By shifting to an approach of comprehensive wealth management rather than remaining focused on just one piece of the client's financial picture, advisors create huge value for the client who operates in a busy world and hardly has the time or expertise to manage on his or her own the many elements of his or her wealth.

As a bonus, because the client has co-created the plan with the advisor, advisors don't have to spend time getting the client to commit to the plan, as the client is already on board.

CONCLUSION

It is time for the death of the salesman and the rise of the wealth advisor. It is time for advisors to move away from a transactional sales approach, and even the consulting approach, and toward forming deeper relationships with clients. It is time for advisors to serve clients by stepping into the lead role of coordinating the many professionals that are needed to deliver true wealth management. It is time, too, to change the way advisors charge for their services while redefining the value they provide. And it is time to develop an intimate understanding of each client's unique needs as clients move toward a future just their own. While sales will always remain a part of our job as advisors, being wealth advisors means spending less time selling products and more time marketing ourselves as trusted advisors and then delivering on that promise.

Although many advisors have moved along a trajectory from sales to financial advising and now to overall wealth management, many clients are still stuck framing advisors as salespeople. That mind-set affects clients' willingness to engage with the advisor; it affects their ability to seek the services advisors provide. Finally, it limits clients' ability to tell others about the advisor's value. It is up to advisors to educate clients, their other trusted advisors, and the public on the vast new ways that they can support clients. The reward will be more business, more introductions from the other professionals, and, ultimately, more loyal client advocates who are willing to help their advisors find additional clients. The reward will be an industry that is elevated as the public begins to understand the significant service that advisors provide to the community at large.

The lesson for advisors may be just as much about learning to see and frame themselves differently—not as transactional agents, but as partners with the client and as custodians of the client's whole wealth picture. For some, this very well might reveal the opportunity to add that more human element to the picture through stronger relational work; for others, it might be the opportunity to provide more technical expertise for clients. The end result will be more satisfied clients and more satisfied advisors, too, who are engaged in meaningful work that yields results and has an impact.

As advisors and as an industry, it is time to rise up and give more to our clients. We need to shift from selling to supporting, from telling to discovery, from hierarchy to partnership, and from one piece of the wealth pie to the whole wealth picture. Today, the value proposition for the client is in that partnership. Those advisors who are able to evoke from the client insights and desires about what they want their wealth to do for them will have the competitive advantage.

In this new phase of the profession, managing money, selling life insurance policies, writing financial plans, rebalancing portfolios, minimizing taxes, and providing banking services all become the technical back-end piece of advising. The front-end piece—the piece that is most powerful—is forward-facing partnering and communicating with the client.

The truth is that being a salesperson is not noble. But helping individuals discover, pursue, and achieve their goals is. As clients achieve their goals, they have the ability to pay it forward, and everyone benefits.

NOTES

1. "About CFP Board." CFP Board website (n.d.), CFP Board's Early Days section, accessed May 29, 2015, www.cfp.net/about-cfp-board/about-cfp-board/history.

2. Ibid.

3. Financial Advisor Profile: Christopher Paul Jordan, President & CEO." LEXCO Wealth Management website (n.d.), accessed May 29, 2015, http://lexcowealth.com/advisors/christopher-p-jordan.

4. Ibid.

5. This information is being cited from an article written by Ray Sclafani that is titled "From Broker to Facilitator," which can be found at: www.clientwise.com/leadership/articles/evolution-of-the-facilitator.

6. David B. Armstrong, CFA, personal interview, March 6, 2015, transcript, pp. 5, 12.

7. The Kinder Institute of Life Planning website (n.d.), "What Is Life Planning?" section, accessed May 29, 2015, www.kinderinstitute.com/professional.html.

8. Ibid.

CHAPTER 4

The Big, Fat Lie

S ome frames, like the advisor-as-salesperson frame, are problematic because they limit clients' ideas about what the advisor can do for them, reducing profits in the process. Other frames may be right on track—well placed and with good intentions—yet if the advisor fails to live up to them, client trust gets broken, damaging the advisor's reputation. We'll look at one such frame—that of "we'll always be there for you"—in this chapter.

It's a strange irony: Advisors regularly frame themselves as planners for their clients, but paradoxically, many advisors fail to plan—not for their clients but for themselves and their businesses when it comes to continuity, succession, and longevity. As asset management and distribution analytics firm Cerulli Associates has indicated, only 29 percent of advisors have a succession plan at all.[1] A full 59 percent of advisors within five years of retirement do not have a succession plan.[2] Those advisors who do have a succession plan may just be fooling themselves into thinking it's adequate. The plan may look good on paper, but when put to the reality test, it can easily fall apart, as will become clear later in this chapter.

KEY CONCEPT

The best advisors have plans in place not only for their clients but also for themselves and their businesses, ensuring that if the advisor ever has to step away from work, the clients will smoothly transition to their new advisor or team.

WE'LL ALWAYS BE THERE FOR YOU . . . UNTIL WE AREN'T

Picture the following television commercial to gain insight into the "we'll always be there for you" frame. The screen shows a young married couple bringing their first child home from the hospital. It flashes to the baby's fifth birthday party, with the happy mom and dad giving their child a new bike. Next thing on the screen is the child's college graduation, followed by footage of the adult child having her own child, with the loving grandparents nearby. The commercial closes with all three generations sitting on a bench outside an assisted living facility. The tagline of a financial services company appears at the bottom of the screen as a voiceover promises, "We'll be there."

This commercial, representative of those we've seen from financial services companies over the years, conveys the promise that every advisor makes to his or her clients, whether overtly or implicitly: the promise to be there for the client through all of life's transitions, at each and every turn where financial support is needed. Whether it's through TV, print, or online advertising; marketing materials; or the conversations advisors have with clients, most advisors and financial services firms court and reassure clients on the basis of this premise that they can be relied on no matter how much time passes or how uncertain life becomes. The reality is, however, that many advisors do not have an effective plan to ensure that the client will truly be taken care of over the years. I call this failure *the big, fat lie.*

Clients would be shocked to know that their financial advisor might not actually have a plan in place if he or she were to become ill or disabled or pass away, leaving both the clients and the advisor's family unattended. A client who has signed on with an advisor who's middle aged may be horrified 15 years down the road when that advisor dies during the client's retirement years with no satisfactory replacement in place. Clients who have been told for years by their advisor that another firm is ready to take over in the case of illness or absence may be disappointed to learn when this contingency comes true that they don't like working with the replacement or that the replacement has changed plans and does not want to work with them.

I'm reminded of a busy, successful advisor who lost sight in one eye and then the other. Although he had a partner, his partner decided that he no longer wanted to work with the advisor, and the advisor could not serve his clients on his own with his new disability. His clients were suddenly without an advisor, left to fend for themselves. The noble promise of the advisor is to be there for the client through all of life's transitions—loyal and steadfast, like a rock-solid partner, rather than an opportunist who is merely renting the relationship. It's the way that advisors frame themselves for clients, directly or indirectly. Unfortunately, even the most well-meaning advisors sometimes fail to fulfill this pledge and thus fall prey to telling a big, fat lie that they will always be there for clients, when at some point, in reality, they simply can't or won't.

KEY CONCEPT

If you are framing yourself as an advisor who can help clients prepare for a lifetime of financial challenges, it is incumbent upon you to prepare for a time when you cannot or will not be working with your clients directly anymore. If you do not make adequate succession plans, you are lying to your clients.

Sunbathing in Florida at the Clients' Expense

The example of Mick will give more clarity on how advisors are challenged to follow through on their promises to clients and how they sometimes render that promise a big, fat lie. Mick is a financial advisor who runs his own firm. He has been in the industry for 35 years and has had his own business for 25. Mick has a group of more than 100 clients whom he has served for many years. He has more than

$150 million in assets under management and a sales assistant that knows the clients, perhaps better than Mick does. Mick has long enjoyed running his own operation because it allows him to work personally with his clients, as he feels will best benefit them, without being beholden to a larger corporate strategy that may or may not jive with his clients' needs and lives.

Because Mick has always put his clients' needs first, even going beyond his commitment to them by making house calls and working during holidays, they absolutely love him. He is authentic, reliable, and personable. Mick's clients feel they can trust him now and into the future. He has always told them that he will be with them through all of life's stages, and he certainly has been there to provide support as his clients have bought homes, put their children through college, and dealt with the illnesses of spouses and aging parents.

But at age 62, as Mick is starting to wind down professionally, the question is, What will happen to his clients in the process? Mick has told his clients he will be there for them through all of life's big moments, but Mick is starting to disengage. The cold, hard facts are that Mick really wants to spend more time in Boca Raton and enjoy the sun while continuing to get paid as if he were working full time. How honest does he need to be with himself and his clients about his ability to serve them? Should Mick just keep taking his percentage while spending less and less time at the office, or should he make some changes to ensure that his clients are receiving all that they deserve, now and after Mick's gone?

It's a question that every advisor will eventually have to ask him- or herself as well, to ensure the best possible client outcomes and, frankly, to avoid engaging in any malfeasance. It's time for advisors to invest in the human capital needed to truly deliver for the client, or to be honest with clients about the degree to which they can serve.

How Good Is Your Succession Plan?

With the average age of financial advisors in America being 50.9 years old, Mick has lots of company.[3] Advisors across the land are graying, looking toward retirement, scaling back on clients, and figuring out how to transition out of their firms. The latest data from

Cerulli Associates reveals that 5 percent of wirehouse advisors are expected to retire in the next five years and 35 percent will retire in the next 10 years, while 25 percent of independent broker-dealers and 30 percent of registered investment advisors indicate that they will leave their practices or retire in the next 10 years. Across all channels, one in four advisors is expected to leave the industry in the next 10 years. Financial services clients across the land are going to be affected as their advisors disengage or drop out of the industry.

For advisors who do have a succession plan in place, the effectiveness of that plan can easily be called into question. Let's take a look at Mick's situation to understand how. Traditionally, advisors like Mick who run a small operation have put plans into place to transition out of their firms by creating a buy/sell agreement with another advisor who will take over in case of sickness, retirement, or death. While this is certainly a good alternative to having no agreement, noble advisors have got to ask themselves whether such an agreement is really enough.

COACHING CORNER

What does your succession plan look like today? How would you rate it on a scale of 1 to 5 (5 being best)? Be honest. Then pick three things you'd like to do to improve your succession plan in the coming year and mark time on your calendar to start making them happen.

THE eXchange™
Online Tool 4.1: Succession Planning Checklist

Visit the eXchange™ to download a Succession Planning Checklist for use or adaptation by your firm.

Take a moment to imagine how this all might play out not nearly as well as desired. Five years from now, Mick decides he is ready to retire. He triggers his buy/sell agreement with a younger advisor, Joe, and sends a letter to all of his clients, along with making a personal phone call to each, letting them know about his retirement and providing Joe's contact information to ensure continuity of support. This sounds fair, and it certainly meets a minimum standard of ethics. Yet how are Mick's clients going to feel when they learn that after years of working with Mick, they are now expected to switch to a completely different advisor at a different firm whose style is different than Mick's—right in the middle of their own important life changes? Are they going to feel a sense of comfort and connection with Joe, or are they going to feel like they've been dropped in the lap of a random new advisor that they may—or may not—like?

Further complicating the issue, Joe may discover that right now, he only has room to take on 10 new clients rather than Mick's 100. Or he may only want to work with those of Mick's clients who need financial planning and investment strategies support but not retirement advice or estate planning, as Mick was apt to provide. It's not unrealistic to think that Joe's firm has evolved since he and Mick first created their agreement or that Joe simply did not accurately predict what kind of new clients he'd like to take on when the time came, yet this will leave many of Mick's clients out in the cold. Mick—a dedicated, reliable, and caring advisor—is no longer able to deliver on the promise that his firm will be there for his clients through all of their life stages. As Mick's succession plan disintegrates under pressure, it becomes clear that well-intentioned Mick has peddled his clients a big, fat lie without ever meaning to.

 KEY CONCEPT

Once you have a succession plan in place, revisit it regularly to make sure your arrangements are still realistic, and make any necessary adjustments.

I don't know a single advisor who would tell me that he or she is not focused on helping clients achieve their goals in the event of his or her absence. I've said it before and I'll say it again: The majority of advisors are principled, dedicated, and client-focused professionals.

They want the absolute best for their clients! Yet many of them are telling their clients a big, fat lie—that they will always be there for them, when in fact they have no succession plan or the one they do have in place isn't particularly strong. To operate with integrity and to fulfill the promise of the "we'll always be there for you" frame that most advisors convey to clients, advisors will need to take a look at their succession planning to assess how effective it really is. Ultimately, they will need to make a shift from the old frame of "I allow clients to rent my services until I choose to stop practicing" to "I build a legacy business that serves multiple generations to come."

 ## Will You Rust or Will You Rise?

Admittedly, there's a counterperspective to the headlines and statistics that proclaim that financial advisors are about to retire in droves. After traveling around the country and working with thousands of advisors, I have started to modify this theory to state that financial advisors are about to *semiretire* in droves. Instead of retiring, aging advisors are tending to hold on to the "good life" by maintaining their client roster and retaining the associated income stream while spending fewer hours engaged on the job. Voila! Semiretirement, here come the advisors. Who wants to stop working when you can make 1 percent on assets under management while spending mornings on the back nine and afternoons poolside? Sounds enticing.

A Loss of Legacy. Think of it this way. Not only are advisors doing a disservice to their clients if they disengage—clients get less of the advisor's time and attention and really will be lost when the advisor stops working completely—but they are also allowing their own businesses to decay instead of leaving behind a legacy. Is this the vision that most advisors have for their businesses—that the business will thrive while they are in the heart of their working years and then, as they age, the business will simply rust away? Some advisors will say they have support staff who will be there to fulfill the promises. However, in most instances, the support staff has not been developed to a point of being able to keep offering the same degree of service. What's more, the client often does not have a relationship with the staff,

(Continued)

(Continued)

is uninterested in being served by them, and will just choose to go elsewhere. This is the hard truth.

A Loss of Wisdom. One of my biggest fears, as a financial services veteran who cares about the industry, is that aging advisors will disengage more and more from their work without letting clients know that they've gone on indefinite hiatus and that there's no good backup waiting in the wings. For clients, it's the worst of all worlds, as their advisors become less hands-on in their approach without providing the client suitable supplementation to what they now can offer from the place of semiretirement. For the industry, mass semiretirement of advisors until they simply rust away would be a tragedy, too. Why? As older advisors drop out of the industry, their expertise and wisdom will be lost rather than passed on to the next generation. What a shame it would be—and a disservice to the industry and clients—to let so much technical, service, and relational savvy disappear.

The answer for aging and semiretiring advisors is to build out a team. Sounds like hard work at first, but once the team is in place, the seasoned advisor gains the freedom to work less and enjoy life more, while running a firm that can be bought down the road, internally or externally. That makes for a much better ending to the story for mature advisors than simply rusting away.

Rent-an-Advisor

It's not that advisors want to leave clients so they are hung out to dry. This approach of serving the client until the advisor can't serve the client anymore has often just been the way of things.

Right now, most advisors are set up so that they allow clients to rent the relationship with them. The client pays the advisor for his or her services until the advisor no longer can or will provide them, then the client is required to rent a new advisor.

However, there is an alternative to this approach—and the best in the business are already using it. It's about building a *team of professionals* to support the client and creating a firm culture that transcends the single advisor. Suddenly, the client is no longer renting one advisor but has access to an entire team for the long term, a team that won't expire when a single "lease" is up.

The advisors on that team have common values and work within a common culture, so if the need to switch advisors arises, the transition is far smoother than in the case of Mick's clients being sent cold turkey to Joe. Throughout the years, the client knows that there will be support regardless of whether his or her lead advisor has to step away due to illness or other circumstances.

Your clients depend on you for guidance now and into the future. They also hope that the money they've worked so hard to save will be managed well when their children inherit it, and they would love to see their kids go on to work with Mom and Dad's trusted advisor. What are you doing to make that happen?

 KEY CONCEPT

One succession strategy is to have a team of professionals in place for the duration of the advisor–client relationship. This way, when the lead advisor steps out, the rest of the team is positioned to carry out the original promise of a lifetime of service.

 COACHING CORNER

Imagine that you were forced to step away from your advising work for a long period. How would your clients be taken care of? What kind of plan do you have in place? What areas of your plan are strong? What areas of the plan could you stand to improve?

 INDUSTRY INSIGHT: A PROMISE TO OFFER TRUE WEALTH MANAGEMENT

Another version of the big, fat lie is the promise by advisors to offer clients wealth management services when, in fact, they are delivering only partial wealth

(Continued)

(Continued)

management that focuses on one area of wealth alone, such as investments. In the past five years, the use of the term *wealth management* to describe the work that advisors do has become more and more commonplace. Yet it is often a case of rebranding without reframing, as firms have caught on to the desired industry lingo without making actual changes in the way they do business. For Rob Nelson, president of NorthRock Partners, the reframe for his work from more traditional financial advising to comprehensive wealth management was authentic.

For years, Nelson worked as a financial advisor for one of the largest financial services companies in the United States, where he learned the ins and outs of the business and grew from being a newbie advisor to a seasoned one. Nelson enjoyed the work and respected his firm but, over time, realized it was time for him to reframe himself so he could deliver on the inherent promise he felt he made to his clients to truly take care of them. He wanted to offer more comprehensive support than he could at his traditional advisory firm: tax planning and preparation, banking, bill payment, legal issues, and estate planning.

Nelson wanted to be able to support his clients in all aspects of their financial lives and with less confinement, so he took the leap and became a registered investment advisor. The good news was that Nelson now had the freedom to partner with any custodian in the financial services industry who he felt was right for his clients; the bad news was that he could work with any custodian in the financial services industry, which would be no small feat: Nelson and his new firm would now have to do everything on their own. The new challenges were worth it, however. "It ended up being one of the best decisions I've ever made," said Nelson.[4]

To successfully make the transition, Nelson spoke openly with his existing clients of 10 and 20 years and shared with them the direction his new firm would be going in and why. In becoming a registered investment advisor, Nelson explained, he would be gaining more flexibility to serve clients based on what they truly needed, not what Nelson's former organization happened to offer. The client response to Nelson's transition was overwhelmingly supportive. As it turned out, they never felt that they had a relationship with Nelson's former employer; rather, they felt that they had a relationship with him. His employer held their assets, but Nelson was their trusted advisor, and they felt confident that he could continue to be after he moved on to being an RIA. As Nelson explains, "It was actually a little less of an event for my clients than it was for me. They still needed to have a faith moment when it came down to moving their assets to another custodian and starting to work with us in a different way, but it went really well."[5]

Separating from his former firm made it easier for Nelson to frame himself accurately online. When clients shared his name with others, they would often Google him as a first point of contact. In the past, his former employer's website would naturally pop up, which had branding that was different from that of Nelson's personal style of advising. After the switch to being his own firm, a Google search would bring up NorthRock Partners, which immediately reflected Nelson's style of advising and offering true wealth management. He was able to create the desired client experience from the start.

With his new firm launched, Nelson was able to offer his clients a deeper relationship in banking, give true advice, gain clearer control of assets, help them with their legal and estate planning in a deeper way, and even do some of that trust work on site. His intention to deliver true wealth management had become a reality and was more than lip service. He knew it was a success by the way clients invited him into their lives. Nelson finds that when he's working with a professional athlete who's thinking about changing teams, the athlete wants his family there so they can participate in the discussion about what such a change would mean. If one of Nelson's corporate executive clients is considering changing to a new employer, he or she invites Nelson's team to be there. If a client has a divorce on the horizon, a lot of times it's the spouse and Nelson's team who know about it. It's the ultimate sign of trust, resulting from the "deep-rooted relationships"[6] that Nelson has developed with his clients. Nelson has been there for many challenging as well as feel-good moments during which his clients would say he has made a real difference in their lives. Goodbye, big, fat lie.

THE NEXT GENERATION OF ADVISORS

As noted earlier, there is currently a scarcity of young financial advisors in the industry, with only 5 percent of the 315,000 advisors working in the United States younger than 30.[7] This scarcity is believed to exist for a number of reasons. After the economic crisis of 2008–2009, many big firms stopped recruiting new grads and started hiring experienced advisors from other firms.[8]

Further, young people themselves appear to have little interest in joining the world of traditional financial advising. As Scott Smith, a Cerulli Associates director, puts it, "You're asking a 26-year-old to take his parents' phone book and convince all their friends to hand over substantial sums of money. Young people have a greater interest in being more holistic planners, and less transactional."[9] Enter opportunity, however. As the industry shifts more toward comprehensive wealth advising and away from a transactions-based approach, it may be a lure for the younger generation.

Younger advisors are certainly needed. As boomers get more and more ready to transfer their wealth to their Gen X and millennial children and as the millennials grow up into bona fide adults, the need for the next generation of advisors increases. The cold, hard truth is that most young people don't want to work with Daddy's broker. They need someone who understands the way they think, play, communicate, live, and work. What an opportunity this presents to savvy financial services firms who are willing to build a team of advisors that spans the generations. Doing so increases opportunities for business today as well as the opportunity to sell the firm down the line to an internal player.

Paul Pagnato, founder and managing director of Pagnato Karp, explains it like this: "Individuals like to work with and hire an advisor that they're similar to in age. There are a lot of studies done, and someone who is 28 or 30 years old typically wants to work with someone that's 30 years old. They don't want to work with someone who is 60 years old. I believe that is an issue and that's going to be a challenge in the marketplace."[10]

Pagnato believes this situation brings opportunity, too. With their ease in using and embracing technology, he sees Gen X and millennial advisors with plenty to offer clients as technology plays a greater role in how money is managed. He is optimistic, too, that "as the financial system is healed [post-2008], you'll see more advisors coming into the marketplace that are younger" as hiring trends increase.[11]

When asked what advice he would give to advisors in their 20s and 30s, Pagnato suggests that these young advisors train and enter the business as a fiduciary rather than associating with a broker-dealer. "I believe that is where the puck is going, that is clearly where all the regulators are going, [and] it is clearly where the assets are going," notes Pagnato. "You can look at all the data, and the money is flowing to the independents that are more embracive of the fiduciary standards [while] . . . society as a whole is becoming much more socially responsible . . . People want to work with companies that are doing the right thing, and that's what the fiduciary standard is all about. It's about doing the right thing."[12]

KEY CONCEPT

A tremendous opportunity exists for younger advisors: Not only do younger clients want to work with advisors who understand them, but having younger advisors on a financial services team helps put to rest older clients' and employers' succession fears.

CONCLUSION

For years, advisors have been framing themselves as able to serve clients through all of life's transitions and stages. Yet sadly, many of them are sole practitioners, and their businesses, which they worked so hard to build, will dry up and eventually fade away. This will leave clients scrambling in search of a new advisor to "rent" from a place of weakness and surprise rather than strength. These advisors are principled practitioners who value integrity, but they end up failing to fulfill their promise to always be there for clients.

The solution, as it turns out, is quite simple: Build a team of advisors that allows the advisor to create a robust business that survives— and thrives—even when the lead advisor steps away.

Once again, it's a call for all of us in the industry to be noble. If we really want to think about the financial services profession in a bigger way and if we are truly grateful for the great profession that we've had the pleasure to be part of, then it's incumbent upon us to really think about the successful service of the client. That means thinking about transitioning our roles now, with all the wisdom we've accumulated over the years, to other advisors on the team.

As advisors build a team and their clients grow comfortable with wanting to work with the team, advisors can work less, let the team do more, and increase the enterprise value of their business. That's something to celebrate!

NOTES

1. Accenture, *Advisor Succession Planning: Managing the Retirement of Baby Boomer Advisors,* 2013, accessed March 17, 2015, www.accenture.com/SiteCollectionDocuments/PDF/Accenture-CM-AWAMS-POV-Advisor-Succession-Planning-Final-Mar2013-web.pdf, p. 4, paras. 1–2.

2. Matthew Heimer, "Will Your Advisor Retire Before You Do?," *MarketWatch Encore* (blog), July 19, 2013, http://blogs.marketwatch.com/encore/2013/07/19/will-your-adviser-retire-before-you-do/.

3. *FA* Staff, "43% of Advisors Nearing Retirement, Says Cerulli," *Financial Advisor Online,* January 17, 2014, www.fa-mag.com/news/43--of-all-advisors-are-approaching-retirement--says-cerulli-16661.html.

4. Rob Nelson, personal interview, April 28, 2015, transcript, p. 2.

5. Rob Nelson, personal interview, April 28, 2015, transcript, p. 3.

6. Rob Nelson, personal interview, April 28, 2015, transcript, p. 8.

7. Rachel Abrams, "A Hunt to Find the Next Generation of Financial Advisors," *DealBook* (blog), *New York Times,* June 24, 2014, http://dealbook.nytimes.com/2014/06/24/a-hunt-to-find-the-next-generation-of-financial-planners/?_r=1.

8. Mark Miller, "Wanted: Financial Advisors Who Aren't about to Hang It Up," *Reuters*, February 20, 2014, www.reuters.com/article/2014/02/20/us-column-miller-finan-cialadvisers-idUSBREA1J1N920140220.

9. Ibid.

10. Paul Pagnato, personal interview, March 23, 2015, transcript, p. 5.

11. Ibid.

12. Ibid.

CHAPTER **5**

Lone Ranger
to Leader™

A s the advising profession has moved from a focus on sales to technical expertise to wealth management partnership, the kind of firms that the most successful advisors build is changing, too. Today, it's no longer about running a one-person operation; now it's all about team. In fact, according to Fidelity Investments, 84 percent of high-performing advisors work in a team configuration versus only 48 percent of other advisors.[1]

Why the need for team? As the advising profession moves from offering a single product or service to providing whole wealth management, advisors can't go it alone anymore. There are now too many pieces of wealth management for one person to have the time or expertise to manage them all: financial planning, investing, banking, taxes, life insurance, estate planning, and more. Then, layer onto that a more sophisticated advising profession than ever before, involving the need for rainmaking, relational skills, technical skills, service skills, marketing skills, and so on . . . and you need a team to thrive.

In addition, if the client, the client's family, and the heirs to the client's wealth are going to be able to depend on an advisor, then advisors are going to have to build something that's truly going to outlast them, and that begins with a team. Having a strong team in place helps advisors operate out of integrity and avoid telling the big, fat lie that they will always be there for the client when they can't actually deliver.

Unfortunately, some advisors are still operating as sole practitioners, whether in practice or in principle. Some have stubbornly remained sole advisor in their firms, avoiding the hassle of taking on new advisors. Others who do have a team often keep the team members in the background when it comes to client relations, creating a bottle-neck that puts too much pressure on the advisor and compromises the organization. It's another case of advisors framing themselves in an outdated way that is detrimental to their business: the old frame of "I am the best at serving my clients" versus the new frame used by the best in the business, "My team is the best at serving our clients." At ClientWise, we refer to this as framing oneself as a lone ranger (old frame) versus as a leader (new frame).

What's a lone ranger? Lone rangers do much of the work them-selves. Lone rangers have chosen not to build team or, if they have a group of people working for them, the team may not operate as effec-tively as it could. Lone rangers believe they are the only one who can advise the client.

Working as a lone ranger can be exciting and rewarding. Yet it can be difficult and exhausting, too, especially when trying to sustain production and grow the business to higher levels. Yes, you can work harder and longer, but you're still likely to hit a limit with how far you can grow the business alone or without a true team.

If you believe, as emphasized earlier in this book, that the way of the future really is comprehensive wealth management—and if you believe that the client deserves more, today and in the future—then you've got to get other team members on board. This reframe is of value to you, the advisor, too. It frees you to focus on the work you love doing the most, it ensures that you can step away from the business when needed, and it gives you an advantage over competitors. The team reframe creates a win–win situation for advisor and client alike.

KEY CONCEPT

Going it alone is a tempting path, given its straightforward nature, but becoming a team leader expands your business opportunities: in the array of services you can offer your clients, in the number of clients you can take on, and in the length of time you can truthfully promise to serve your clients.

Where are you on the journey from lone ranger to leader? This chapter will help you explore this question and give you tools to improve your leadership skills and team performance, wherever you are on the lone-ranger-to-leader spectrum.

THE eXchange™
Online Tool 5.1: Leader's Journey Assessment

Take stock of where you are on the leadership journey by completing the brief, 15-item Leader's Journey Assessment on the eXchange™. This will help you identify your current areas of strength as a team leader versus opportunities for growth.

SURRENDER INDEPENDENCE TO INTERDEPENDENCE

The evolution from lone ranger to leader involves a major reframe. You must shift from framing yourself as the one and only—or the primary operator—of your business to framing yourself as the skilled leader of a competent team.

Advisors using the sales approach may tend to frame themselves as a lone ranger, as they are usually most comfortable in the trenches, where they can be sure of making the sale. But even those advisors who operate from a technical or wealth management approach can easily fall into the lone ranger mentality. In working with a client, they may take the "trust me" approach and make the relationship all about them, not about their team or even the client's participation and partnership.

In making themselves the primary person who interacts with, manages, and influences the client, these advisors are setting up potential disappointments in the future: disappointment if the advisor is unable to deliver everything promised due to lack of time and availability, if the advisor has blind spots on particular areas of wealth management that compromise chances of successfully meeting client goals, and/or if and when the advisor has to withdraw from the lead role of managing the client's wealth due to retirement, illness, or something else.

 KEY CONCEPT

Being a lone ranger means being vulnerable to external circumstances (e.g., illness, accident, having too many demands on your time) as well as internal ones (specialties you have not been trained in, areas in which you are unaware of your weaknesses). Creating a team of professionals circles the wagons, bulking up your coverage and thereby protecting both you and your clients.

The truth is that you have to let go to grow. For example, you may need to let go of the beliefs that

- the client service model has to be delivered by only you;
- you are the only one who can do a client review; or
- you possess all of the technical knowledge associated with delivering wealth management and that you can be the relationship manager, technician, rainmaker, operations person, and administrative manager.

These are some of the universal beliefs that lone rangers may need to let go of to become a leader.

Then there are those pieces that lone rangers will need to let go of that are unique to their particular firm, due to varying skill sets, strengths, client needs, and so forth. Regardless of the unique profile of a given firm and situation, the advisor undoubtedly will need to be willing to hand certain functions and responsibilities over to others on the team so the firm can offer true wealth management.

Another way to describe this is as surrendering independence to interdependence: letting go of the idea that you need to do everything yourself and replacing it with the notion that your job is to lead others in working as a team to get everything done for the client and the business. It's a reframe from rainmaker to CEO, from lone ranger to leader. When you're a salesperson working by yourself, you're "eating what you kill," so to speak. When you're a leader or a CEO, you've got to find the ability to let go and trust that in building this team, the profits will not only come but increase because you will be able to better serve the client.

COACHING CORNER

Regardless of whether you have a team, in what ways do you think you may still be operating as a lone ranger? Take some time to think about the way you spend your time each day. What kinds of lone ranger activities are you involved in? What kinds of leadership activities are you engaged in? Where would you feel comfortable making adjustments to help make the reframe from lone ranger to leader?

Surrendering independence for interdependence is not easy. One of my high-performing lone ranger clients, Bill, was certainly resistant at first. Bill was bringing in $18 million a year in income because he had done such an effective job of figuring out how to manage people's investments. He had been doing such a good job, in fact, that people had been telling him his whole adult life of how great a job he was doing and that he should keep up the good work. He was a phenom and everyone wanted more of him, so he just kept doing more.

When I introduced the concept of building a true team around him, Bill was shocked. All of the feedback he had received for years said that he should keep working his professional magic and manage more and more investment portfolios. Now I was encouraging him to learn how to step back and give some control to a team of professionals that he would have to build around himself?

Bill expressed concern that the high performance he had been generating for years might drop if he was no longer doing the investing himself. His statement on the topic was along the lines of, "Why would I ever want to risk having mediocre performance for my clients? They're paying me to run their portfolios; I'm going to run their portfolios."

Interestingly, when pressed further on the point, Bill shared that he already had a team—after all, he had hired a bunch of people to process all of the work he generated. I explained to him that what he had was a work group, not a team, and that he could tell the difference between the two by asking what would happen if he was removed from the work equation. "So," I asked him, "what would happen if you ever got injured or sick?"

The whole tent of his operation would fold—and Bill knew it. So we worked together to build a true team around him: better utilizing current team members, hiring new ones, building a network of other professional advocates in the wider wealth management business, and fostering an effective team culture. Over time, clients began to be able to rely on other people rather than just Bill, and they got more services than Bill alone could provide.

It turned out that Bill's clients, while they valued his investment expertise and capability, also needed more from him. They needed a true partner to design wealth strategies that could help them live the lives they truly wished to live. Now Bill and his team can meet those needs, and, should anything happen to him, Bill's tent won't fold.

In the old days, when you sold one instrument, you could go it alone. In today's wealth management business, you've got to include other people. You may play the role of lead wealth management advisor, but the team will also have a service leader, a technical person, and more—not just the CPA and the attorney, but other technicians like the relocation specialist, the private equity firm, the business valuation person, the primary banker, or the tax return preparer. Then you will have your traditional team as well, to cover areas like marketing, business, development, technology, and compliance. Some of these folks will be on your internal team; others may be on your virtual team, depending on the kind of firm you would like to run and whatever is needed to serve the client. One thing is certain: A team is needed to deliver true wealth management.

 The Three Kinds of Advisors to Add to Your Team

The most effective teams have three advisor roles in common. Several additional roles can be filled by team members or consultants dedicated to providing support in other areas, but these three advisor roles are central to delivering on the promises you make to your clients.

Senior Lead Advisor: The senior lead advisor is dedicated primarily to rainmaking activities, consistently filling the pipeline by taking meetings with new potential clients and centers of influence and bringing them on board. The secondary role of the senior lead advisor is as a strategic relationship manager, who only gets involved with clients when they need a more senior partner to help make a crucial decision. If a client is especially important to your team's success or a situation necessitates a higher level of care, the senior lead advisor might be brought in to partner with these clients in achieving their financial goals.

Lead Advisor: The lead advisor's primary role is relationship manager. Focused on complete client care, the lead advisor ensures that no accounts are leaving and that the team is delivering on the promises made to the client. The lead advisor also has a secondary set of four crucial responsibilities: (1) uncovering new assets from existing clientele, (2) finding new revenue opportunities to service existing clients more effectively, (3) connecting to the heirs of your clients' wealth and knowing when and where that wealth is ready to transition, and (4) building Loyal Client Advocates™ by engaging client relationships on a deeper level to uncover the potential clients within their networks.

Service Advisor: The service advisor takes care of all follow-through and follow-up. He or she is essentially responsible for completing the work promised to the client, so sometimes the service advisor is front and center with clients and other times he or she is behind the scenes, making sure all client information and paperwork is complete and in order. In addition, these service advisors will move into lead advisor and senior lead advisor roles according to your succession plan needs. You want your clients to be as comfortable with them as possible, and the longevity of their involvement will help with this.

The benefit of a team is that it allows you to home in on core competencies and the unique value you bring to the team with increased focus and efficiency. This won't be possible if you or any of your team members are wearing "all the hats," or trying to play the roles of senior lead advisor and lead advisor simultaneously. While you may work together to accomplish some of these responsibilities, only one team member is the driver of each.

TEAM DEFINED

For those advisors who do have teams today but who find that their teams are not operating at top capacity, the root of the problem may be found by looking at the way the team originally formed. In the beginning, when an advisor got started in the business, in any channel, the advisor was responsible for doing it all. The more successful the advisor became, the more he or she needed extra people to support the work. The result? The advisor hired staff members and created a "team."

Over time, the advisor became even more successful and therefore needed to hire more staff members, further growing the "team." The cycle continued until the advisor woke up one day to realize he or she had become a manager with a lot of mouths to feed on the so-called team.

Managing the team took lots of time and was not particularly enjoyable. What's more, the advisor never empowered the team members to create strong relationships with the client, so the client still depended on the advisor in spite of there being a team. More and more of the advisor's time got eaten up by the team instead of being freed up by it.

What happened in these situations? Instead of building an interdependent team that was able to make the advisor's life easier, the advisor built a work group that took lots of care and feeding. It's a common mistake that ends with the same results: The work group and the client remain dependent on the advisor because he or she did not follow the steps necessary to create an interdependent team empowered to build relationships with the client, and the advisor becomes overtaxed and overburdened as responsibilities grow rather than diminish. No wonder some advisors shudder at the idea of creating a team, while others run "teams" that are not nearly as productive and helpful to the advisor as they could be.

At ClientWise, we define *team* in the following way:

A true team is a group of people who are fully committed to mutually defined and extraordinary success of the group as a unit and who hold themselves accountable for the achievement of that success as well as the methods by which that success is achieved.

A team is a group of people who are committed to joint success, a success that is extraordinary. How does one define *extraordinary*? The team gets to decide. For a true team to exist, all of the members need to have an opportunity to help define success. That's a little uncomfortable for the high-performing lone ranger used to calling the shots and trusting his or her own judgment. It calls the lone ranger to stretch out of his or her comfort zone. But remember, too, that the lone ranger is becoming a leader, and leaders have the privileged position of helping the group set the vision; the leader has an essential role in defining what success looks like for the team.

KEY CONCEPT

A team is not simply a group of people working on a project. The members of a true team are committed to achieving a shared goal. Everyone on the team agrees on what the goal entails, and everyone on the team contributes their skills and dedication while holding their fellow team members accountable for their contributions, leading to extraordinary success.

Team Accountability

A team is responsible for holding its members *accountable for the achievement* of their extraordinary, mutually defined success. The team members also hold each other *accountable for the methods* they use to achieve that success. So, as the journey toward success is undertaken, team members tune in to how the rest of the team is executing to get to that success. They hold one another accountable to getting stuff done and doing it in the best way. In addition, it's not a case of success at any cost but rather coming by success honestly and with integrity.

Let's look at that word *accountability*. In a financial sense, accountability is responsibility for the way that money is used and managed. In a governance sense, accountability refers to the liability or blameworthiness of a nonprofit or corporate entity in a given situation or general fashion. In a team sense, accountability involves holding others responsible, but the blame component is removed altogether.

The kind of accountability I am referring to here, with a true team, is a more expansive and collaborative experience. We're not talking oversight boards or authoritarian rule. We're talking team meetings, goal setting, and regular check-ins. It is about the magic that comes from being present, engaged, and aware of what each team member has agreed to contribute and work toward and staying in conversation to support the execution of the plan. On a true team, there is a grass-roots culture of positive accountability. Supportive questions like "Hey, how's it going with Project X?" and "Is there anything you want to talk through on Y?" bubble up authentically and organically.

KEY CONCEPT

Accountability does not mean blame. On true teams, accountability is collaborative: Team members check with each other to make sure everyone is present, engaged, aware, supported, and on the path to executing the group's plan.

 Five Ways to Win Your Clients Over to the Team Reframe

At first, some clients may not feel comfortable letting their lone ranger advisors reframe themselves into leaders. Clients may trust the single advisor but may not yet have faith in the rest of the team—whether the team was formerly kept in the background or is altogether new. If this is the reality, the advisor may have to make a case to clients for why the transformation from lone ranger to leader is in the clients' best interest. Here are five ways to win clients over to the team idea. Remember: The most important part of this process is engaging the client and helping make him or her part of the lone-ranger-to-leader transformation.

1. Set up a meeting (ideally in person) with the client to let him or her know personally that you are cultivating your existing team or a new team to better serve the client.

2. Share the ways in which you are hopeful that the team will be able to better serve the client (e.g., be able to offer new

services across the wealth management spectrum, ensure that someone is always there for the client if you ever get sick or need to step away; provide a more robust team up and down the advisory chain to ensure quality of service; free you up to be there for the client during the big, strategic decisions; serve the client's heirs with advisors of varying ages and a succession plan in place; etc.).

3. Give the client a brief overview of the roles of each existing and new team member and share two or three strengths of that team member.

4. Ask the client what concerns he or she may have regarding the transition to a team approach; listen to the responses and validate the client's perspective ("I appreciate your concerns and look forward to working through them together. As our client, you always come first, and if you are not happy with the team, we want to know about it so we can continue to develop the team in a way that best supports you").

5. Ask for permission from the client to check in regularly to gather feedback on how the team is doing to make improvements and continue to develop them—and follow through.

It may be a process of education to help clients understand the value of the advisor shifting from the lone ranger approach to the team approach. Taking the time to speak personally with the client, outlining the benefits of the team approach, listening to client concerns, and circling back for team feedback can all make for a smoother and more successful transition.

The Old Team Structure versus the New Team Structure

The team reframe is not just about moving from being a lone ranger to leader of a team: It is also about moving from the old style to the new style of teaming. Teams of the past were built on a structure that put the advisor at the center of the group dynamic as a sort of gate-keeper between staff members and clients (as reflected in Figure 5.1). This put the advisor in a position of power, but it also created many

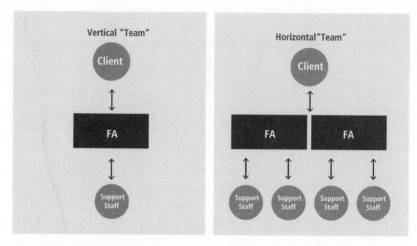

Figure 5.1 Old Team Structures

opportunities for the advisor to become a bottleneck as the bulk of what the client needed passed directly through the advisor; similarly, the bulk of the staff's work was also passed through the advisor on its way to the client.

As it turns out, the old form of a team wasn't really a team at all. If you removed the advisor, the team would implode because the client had the relationship with the advisor, not anyone else on the team. The advisor was "the man" or "the woman" to deal with on all issues. Sure, the client might be served by the staff in some ways, but the client did not view them as professional advisors. To create true interdependence, you've got to get other professionals working with the client.

Enter the new team structure, which places the client at the center of the group dynamic. As shown in Figure 5.2, the work flow travels directly from each team member to the client as well as through the team itself.

The new team structure removes the challenge of advisor bottle-necks, builds trust between the client and all team members, and encourages collaboration among team members. Information and work flow easily and efficiently from those with expertise and ownership in a given area to the client or through the team first when team input is needed.

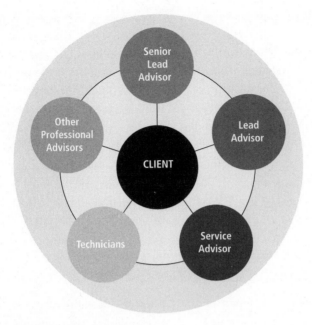

Figure 5.2 New Team Structure

KEY CONCEPT

Traditionally, the client interacted solely with the advisor, who intentionally acted as a gatekeeper but inadvertently ended up being a bottleneck. To best serve clients, top teams now encourage interaction between the client and all of the members of the team, building trust between the client and the team and making all of the team's knowledge and skill available to the client.

THE eXchange™

Online Tool 5.2: A Guide to Defining Your High-Performing Team

Visit the eXchange™ for a 12-question guide to defining your unique high-performing team.

DO YOU HAVE A TEAM OR DO YOU HAVE A WORK GROUP?

Whenever I speak to advisors across the country about the need to have a team in place to deliver true wealth management, the responses vary. Some admit they have no team in place, others describe their team with confidence, and still others wonder if they are on the right track with their current team. I like to ask advisors in the last two situations to consider whether they have a true team or, instead, a work group.

A work group is made up of staff members and/or contractors to whom the advisor hands off work. Each member of the work group has individual goals that the advisor has set, but the group has not come together as a whole to mutually define success. Work group members may or may not happen to interact with each other, and they are not charged with keeping each other accountable.

You know you have a work group if

- you've hired a bunch of "staff" to work on individual projects, tasks, or roles, but you have not brought these individuals together to coalesce as a group with a common vision for success;
- you have defined what success means for the group without taking their input;
- you have resisted adding smart, intelligent technicians and relationship managers to the group in lieu of "worker bees"; and
- you hand off service work to the team but not relational work.

You know you have a work group when you eliminate the founder and the entire business implodes because the client is not accustomed to dealing with anyone but the founder. The founder is not so unlike a pole in a circus tent. Pull the pole down and what happens to the tent? It collapses.

KEY CONCEPT

If the members of your "team" work completely independently, do not share goals, do not interact, and do not help hold each other accountable, you have a work group, not a team. Consider implementing a true team structure to boost your team's performance and results.

In contrast, you know you have a true team when the client believes he or she is being served by the whole group rather than just the leader. If asked, the client would express that the team brings him or her more value than if the client worked with the lead advisor alone. In addition, you know you have a team when

- you observe members at a meeting and see every individual having a voice, speaking up, and taking a leadership role;
- day-to-day, you see team members acting as owners of their share of the business;
- you see team members working together, treating each other with respect, and supporting each other; and
- you sense a culture of inclusivity, collaboration, and camaraderie.

Last, if you have a true team, the members will believe the work that they are doing is contributing to team success for the benefit of the client. They will find their work joyful and will feel they are operating at their best.

 ## COACHING CORNER

Take some time to think about the group of people that are supporting you and your business. Is it a team or a work group? How do you know?

 Ten Tips for Fostering Team Behavior and Creating Sustainability and Success

1. Encourage storytelling, reminiscing, and anecdote sharing at team meetings. This can be focused on personal experiences related to key team goals and projects as well as personal experiences unrelated to work.

2. Find opportunities to talk with team members on an impromptu face-to-face basis to connect and share.

3. Create regular team social events and, on occasion, include family.

(Continued)

(Continued)

4. Create opportunities to share individual team members' feelings about the team's common intent and purpose, team goals, and ambience.

5. Create powerful team meetings that will be opportunities for the entire team to do real work together.

6. Consider the habit of "working together frequently" as a discussion topic for a team meeting. There will be more ownership if everyone is involved in the discussion and has agreed to actions.

7. Reinforce and talk about the team's shared goals whenever possible.

8. Actively identify where collective thinking or collective work should be used and would be more powerful than individual thinking and work (e.g., planning for the future, solving problems, and creating new approaches).

9. If team members are in the same office, minimize use of e-mail; drop in to see people face-to-face. If team members are not in the same office, encourage more use of the telephone, conference calls, and Skype versus e-mail.

10. Give feedback regularly. Be specific, be timely, and offer praise publicly.

CONCLUSION

Like it or not, as a professional in the financial services industry, you've been framed. Because you (or your predecessors) originally entered this business by selling a financial product, clients tend to view you as a salesperson. Most of them don't know that you've moved on from advising on a single product to offering more options. Although clients would love to work with a partner, many of them don't realize that you can be that to them—or already are—because, quite frankly, you may not have taken the time to educate them on your evolved role as a financial or wealth management advisor. Your job title may reflect the change, but busy clients may still be clueless.

I hope you are now a believer. If you agree that you are no longer a salesperson, you're a partner; if you're no longer interested in telling people you will always be there for them when in fact you don't have a succession plan in place; and if you are ready to trade the lone ranger mentality for the leader mentality, it's time to turn to Part II of this book, where you can begin to do the real work of reframing yourself, your team, and your business.

First, you get to have a conversation with your clients to gather input and learn about how they are framing you; then, you will have a chance to spend time with your team identifying how you would actually like to be framed. In the process, you will get to answer questions like, What kind of executive do you want to be? What kind of team do you want to build? And what do you want that team to be known for?

These are exciting times. No longer are you limited to advising on a single product. You don't have to sell; you can partner. What's more, you get to be the designer of your business, making conscious choices about what kind of clients you'd like to work with and the kind of services you are inspired to provide to these clients.

You no longer have to do it all, either, nor should you. You can build or develop your team to play key roles in serving the client so you are freed up to focus on the parts of the business you love, however you define them. There are a range of professionals out there for you to bring on, too, as part of your team, to support the client where you may not do so internally.

It's an opportunity for you to lead not just your team and your business but the industry, too. By reaching out to other financial professionals and taking them on as team members rather than mere referral sources, you set a new standard of collegiality in the industry and create a model of true wealth management for the client—one where the client is taken care of in all regards. That's noble!

NOTE

1. Fidelity Investments, *Plan, Diversify, and Differentiate: Three Strategies of High-Performing Advisors*, 2014, accessed May 31, 2015, https://nationalfinancial.fidelity.com/app/literature/view?itemCode=9587275&renditionType=pdf.

PART II

Five Steps to Reframing Your Business

CHAPTER **6**

Discovering Your Current Frame

The ClientWise Conversation™

So here we are in the twenty-first-century world of the financial services profession. As explored in Part I, no longer is the advisor's role to sell to the client; now it is to partner with the client. In a marketplace where a team is needed, no longer is it effective to operate with the mentality of a lone ranger rather than a leader. What's more, a transformation is well underway, with advisors moving from providing a single product or service to offering a total wealth management solution for clients.

Whether advisors choose to deliver all of the products and services related to their particular brand of wealth management or not, being relevant in the life of the ideal client, knowing who they serve, and designing a total solution to meet the needs of that client are paramount. Even if the advisor outsources the other products and services, designing a total solution for the client is part of what the future advisory relationship will be about; it's what will make the advisor and advisory team or firm relevant.

It is also time in the twenty-first century for advisors to review with their clients what kind of value they provide and how they do it. In today's consumer-friendly marketplace, where the client has ample access to information, opportunities galore to do it him- or herself, and plenty of choices of whom to use as a provider of financial services, the advisor no longer has the liberty of simply deciding what he or she wants to provide the client. The wise advisor invites clients into the process of defining what is of value to them.

Not that it's all drudgery and obligation—along the way, the advisor has the freedom to refine the value the client needs so it matches the advisor's passions and strengths. In some cases, the advisor may seek out a new, better-matched target-client base if the gap between what the client wants and the advisor can deliver is large, or the advisor may build out a team to address gaps. In any case, the conversation must always begin with the client; from there, the advisor can shape this newly gained understanding to create a firm that can serve the right people in the right way.

Last, today's successful advisors take the long view. Not only do they promise their clients that they will always be there for them and their families, but they also build practices that can deliver on that promise. They work with their clients to involve their heirs in the wealth management process; they build diverse teams that can appeal to clients of different age groups. They develop trust between their clients and their teams, so everyone knows what to do if the lead advisor has to step away for a time due to illness, need for respite, or something else. These advisors have a real, live succession plan in place, evidenced by the way they are developing their team and strengthening clients' relationships with the team over time. These are, in essence, the five big reframes that successful advisors of today are engaging in (see Part I for more information).

 KEY CONCEPT

The conversation about your role as a financial advisor, how you are framed, and the services you do and should offer must always—always!—begin with the client.

Figure 6.1 The Five Steps to Reframing Your Wealth Management Business

Any one of these reframes—as well as the unique reframes that a given advisor would like to make in terms of what clientele the advisor serves and how—involves a process. Reframing does not happen overnight, and it does not happen without engaging in specific action. Five specific steps to reframing (shown in Figure 6.1) will help you get the results you desire.

Step 1: Collect data. Before you can reframe your wealth management practice, you first need to understand how you are being framed. To do so, you'll be going right to your clients to find out how they frame you today. That's step 1, collecting information about your current frame. This is the step that we'll explore in this chapter.

Step 2: Define frame. Next, it's time to "go within" your firm and/or your team and engage in the process of envisioning what your new frame will be. That's step 2 of the reframing process: defining the new frame. Here you will be asking and answering, "How do you want your clients to frame you in the future?"

This process will involve looking at the kind of value you'd like to provide versus the kind of value that your clients are seeking. If there is a gap, this process will involve resolving the discrepancy, whether to tweak the kind of services you offer to meet the needs of your current client list, to build out a team to meet those needs, or to outline a new ideal client list to match your own strengths and interests as an advisor.

Step 3: Build frame. After you define what new frame you want to be seen through, you will be ready to build the new frame. This will involve a new frame for your team as well as a new frame for you as a leader. It will also entail creating new marketing assets that consistently portray your new frame. That's step 3: building the new frame.

Step 4: Renew relationships. Once the new frame is in place, it's time to go back to your clients and communicate the new frame by renewing relationships. Here, you will educate your clients on your new frame, including the new kind of wealth management you are set to deliver, its value to clients, and the way your team will be integral to its delivery. That's step 4: renewing relationships.

Step 5: Create advocates. Last, to help the new frame "stick" and to encourage the growth of your firm, you will spend time creating advocates for your firm. Some will be clients, some will be other professionals, but all will understand the new frame and be able to communicate it consistently to others. That's step 5: creating advocates who are willing to accurately frame you while making introductions between you and potential new clients.

When followed with integrity, these five steps will help you reframe your practice so that it becomes the most effective version of itself, one with clear value that clients desire and that you and your team enjoy providing.

 KEY CONCEPT

Reframing your wealth management business involves five important steps: collecting information on your current frame, defining your new frame, building your new frame, renewing relationships, and creating advocates.

Now that we've taken a high-level look at the five-step process for reframing your wealth management business, we will spend the rest of the chapter drilling down into step 1 so you can master it.

Who Are You Reframing For?

Like it or not, you've been framed! The truth is that everybody frames you, so everybody eventually needs to learn about your reframe. Sometimes it is your client who is framing you, but sometimes it is your own team. Similarly, the professionals who refer you work and to whom you refer work probably have a frame for you as well.

All of these audiences not only would benefit from experiencing your reframe, but they also must learn about your new reframe for it to be truly effective. The reframe can only work if you are consistent with the message you deliver across audiences.

Because you are constantly learning and the industry is ever changing, your firm will (or should) always evolve, too. Therefore, by extension, parts of your frame likely will always be changing. After all, to thrive in financial services, you will always need to be innovating, creating capacity, adding new capabilities and human capital, creating new processes, adding and changing new services . . . whew! This list seems endless. I'm sure you get the point.

It's important to recognize that you will always need to be thinking about how you're being framed, how you and your firm want to be framed, and what you consistently need to be doing to make sure there is a clear alignment with how you're being framed and how you want to be framed as a leader, a team, and a firm! Isn't nice to know that you now have a process for how to do this, now and in the future?

You'll likely revisit this process for many years to come. I invite you to edit it, adjust it, and make it your own. Let me know how it's working for you. Join our community to get help from others who are also leading a reframing process, hear their stories, and share your own. After all, that's what our ClientWise™ community is all about.

No matter which audience you'd like to reframe yourself for, the reframing process outlined in this part of the book will work. For example, although this chapter focuses on using step 1 of the reframing process with clients, you can just as easily use this step with other professionals to whom you send and from whom you receive work. Simply substitute the word *professional* for *client* as you read through the passage and you will have the guidance you need to interview other professionals. (Note: We recommend that you interview the professionals you work most closely with.)

THE CLIENTWISE CONVERSATION™

The first step of the reframing process is to have a conversation with your clients, as well as with professionals with whom you work, to better understand how they frame you: how they perceive you, your services, your team, and your firm (see Figure 6.2).

I suggest using a very clear script and set of talking points for how this conversation should run, which my firm developed in 2006 and has been road-testing ever since, with more than 50,000 advisors having completed this process (and you may be one of them).

The ultimate goal with this conversation, which we call the Client-Wise Conversation™, is to collect data from the marketplace today so you can look for patterns and get a clear picture of how you are being framed . . . or mis-framed, as the case may actually be.

For example, do your clients see you as selling insurance without realizing that you also provide guidance on building an investment portfolio? Do your clients perceive you as old school, even though you now have advisors on staff who are from the millennial generation? Do your clients think you operate solo when, in fact, you have a team? Chances are that as you discover how clients frame you, you will also discover that to some degree they mis-frame you, meaning that there is a gap between the value they understand you to provide and the kind of value you actually provide.

You need to know why your clients mis-frame you so that you know where a reeducation process may need to take place during the reframe process. For example, your clients may need to be informed that you do more than sell insurance, that you have advisors with whom their heirs may be more comfortable speaking, and that you have a team in place should you ever need to step away due to family illness or any other eventuality.

Figure 6.2 Reframe Step 1: Collect Data from the Marketplace

Getting a read on the client's frame for you will also provide you with feedback on how well you are currently doing with framing your business. It gives you a baseline of your current "frame job." It will let you know if the conversations you've been having with clients have been effective, if your marketing material is clear and accurate, and if those who send you new business have been framing you the right way.

It's altogether possible that you will discover that you have been doing a great job framing yourself, in which case you can simply plan to build from here during steps 2 and 3 of the reframing process—define and build. Alternatively, you might discover small discrepancies, or you might be surprised to discover big gaps between the ways you'd like to be seen by clients and the ways they appear to actually see you. Regardless of the outcome, you will have more clarity on how accurately your clients frame you today so that you have the data you need to move forward with the reframe process.

KEY CONCEPT

Because your clients are perhaps the most important asset your firm holds today, the first step of the reframing process is to have a conversation with your clients, as well as with professionals with whom you work, to better understand how they frame you—that is, how they perceive you, your services, your team, and your firm.

INDUSTRY INSIGHT: WISE CLIENTS, WISE ADVISOR

As Tom Weilert of Weilert Wunderlick Armstrong in Dallas would admit, he didn't believe he had the time to conduct the ClientWise Conversation™ with clients—yet as soon as he had completed the first five interviews, he realized that he needed to make time. Tom has now interviewed nearly every one of his clients because he realizes how much he can learn from them, and his business has benefited greatly.

For the first 30 years of Weilert's career, he was accurately framed as an insurance specialist. When he and his partners decided that they were going to expand their firm to offer holistic retirement-income distribution planning that incorporated multigenerational estate planning, they knew that the massive change would require additional team members and, perhaps more important, a reframe. Enter the Client-Wise Conversation™.

Weilert started his ClientWise Conversations™ close to home. His first interviews were with in-house staff and close professional associates. What he found in the process was that although he already had the trust of his staff and network of professionals, the descriptions they gave of the services his business provided were completely inconsistent. He needed to take charge of his frame.

As the transitions to the business came and the conversations with clients began and continued, the benefits of this open communication shone through. "What the ClientWise Conversation™ did was help us frame our own firm up in our own mind," says Weilert. Knowing how clients saw them helped to direct the efforts of Weilert and his partners. "What the ClientWise Conversation™ forced us to do was to find ourselves. Once we had a definition of who we were, then we could begin to educate the client."[1]

The transition from insurance to retirement-income distribution planning took time and many, many conversations. With each new round of feedback came new ideas for the firm and new promises to make and keep. Some clients weren't able to re-frame the firm in their minds, sticking with the old frame of insurance specialist, but others were thrilled with the new services, and additional clients came aboard.

Today, Weilert Wunderlick Armstrong has a clear vision of itself, a wide client base, a strong value statement, a four-characteristic definition of an ideal client, 16 diverse areas taken into consideration while planning distributions, and a partner structure that ensures the firm will be around to follow through on their promise of multigenerational wealth and risk management. And to think, this all started with a (ClientWise) conversation.

It's time to have a conversation with your clients to discover how they are framing you. At ClientWise, we have developed a set of five specific questions that together form the ClientWise Conversation™; these questions will help you collect the feedback you need to move forward with the framing process. In fact, we strongly urge you to use these exact questions, in this exact order. We have tested them with well over 50,000 advisors and have made adjustments along the way so that you don't have to. The five questions are as follows:

1. What is the one thing you value most about how my firm and I serve you?

2. What is the one thing you would most like me to change or improve about my firm and how I serve you?

3. If you were to describe the services that my firm and I offer you, to clients like yourself, what would you say?

4. If you were to describe what we've achieved together for as long as we've worked together, what would you say?

5. Among your other professional advisors in your life, who do you trust the most and why?

Each and every one of these questions is included for a reason, which we will explore in the remainder of the chapter. But let's start with some guidance on how best to set up the meeting.

 The ClientWise Conversation™: Who, When, and Where?

Who? You may be wondering who should be interviewing clients and professionals and gathering information. In general, I like to recommend that the advisor conduct these conversations because it is an opportunity for you to continue to build trust directly with the client and to demonstrate your very real commitment to the framing process. There is also a personal touch that only you can give as the advisor.

That being said, there may be times where the situation calls for someone else to conduct the interviews. Perhaps you feel that someone on your team has the right people skills to do the most effective job, such as your HR director, your chief marketing officer, or a registered assistant who has interacted with the client a great deal.

Alternatively, you may have a relationship with a consulting or coaching firm that you trust and feel would do an excellent job interfacing with clients on your behalf. This can be helpful in cases where you feel the clients would be able to be more open and honest with their input if they are able to speak to someone with a bit of distance from you.

When? As for when to conduct the ClientWise Conversation™, I strongly recommend that you schedule it as its own conversation rather

(Continued)

(Continued)

than trying to tag it onto the end of normal client review. Many advisors will try to maximize their time by dumping this interview at the back end of a client review. That's totally understandable, and yet it isn't really ideal for getting the most out of the conversation.

If, in the end, you feel that you must conduct the ClientWise Conversation™ at the end of a client review, there is a way to do it that will serve you best. When you set the appointment for the client review, ask the client for permission to add the ClientWise Conversation™ to the agenda. Then, at the start of the meeting, check in again to request permission and make sure the client is still okay with this piece of the agenda.

When the client review is complete and the client expresses satisfaction with it, ask permission to move into the ClientWise Conversation™. If the client agrees, take a break to reset the room: Open the door, get a cup of coffee, head to the bathroom. When the client returns to the room, he or she will bring greater openness than would have occurred without the break.

Where? At ClientWise, our research and the experiences shared with us by our coaching clients indicate that this model is most powerful when used in a face-to-face conversation. These have a much more personal touch and people tend to linger in them longer, so you have more time with a client and can gather far more information than is generally possible by phone. Therefore, we strongly recommend this approach whenever possible.

THE eXchange™

Online Tool 6.1: Checklist for Conducting the ClientWise Conversation™ after a Client Review

For a how-to checklist on conducting the ClientWise Conversation™ successfully at the end of a client review, if a separate meeting is not possible, visit the eXchange™.

KEY CONCEPT

There are three different entities that can conduct the ClientWise Conversation™: You as the advisor may conduct it yourself, you may choose to have someone on your team conduct the conversation with the client, or you may hire a consultant to facilitate the conversation.

THE MEETING SETUP

Before you get into the logistics of setting up the ClientWise Conversation™, ask yourself, are you willing to do this work? The best and the brightest in the business, those who are really ambitious and courageous and want to grow and deliver top-drawer services for their clients, find the time to have these conversations. If you want to move to that proverbial next level, then you have to want to do this work, too. You're going to need to carve out time in your schedule to invite others to the meeting and, most important, to conduct the actual conversation.

As you think about the time commitment, plan on interviewing 20 to 25 clients for a period of 20 to 30 minutes each. Not five to 10, but 20 to 25. There's a good reason for this: It helps to have time to practice and warm up. With the first five people you speak to, you may find yourself struggling to remember the questions. The next five, you may get the questions right but may not capture the answers in the most helpful way. By the next five, you are likely to get into a groove and then be able—with the next five to 10—to really start to hear specific patterns of feedback.

As you prepare to engage in the ClientWise Conversation™, another question to ask yourself is whether you are open to having conversations with clients that will allow you to improve your own sense of self-awareness. Feedback is only meaningful if you are able to hear it from an open and nondefensive perspective. Take some time to think about whether you are ready to be open-minded in this process and genuinely interested in hearing your clients' responses. If fear or disinterest comes up, consider talking to a coach certified by the International Coach Federation who can help you sort through those responses and clear your mind to be open to the results.

When you are feeling motivated and open to feedback, it's time to start teeing up meetings with your clients. Plan to start with whomever you would consider to be the five easiest clients for you to have this kind of conversation with. They should also be clients whose opinions you respect and who can provide you with honest input.

Before you pick up the phone to invite clients to set up a date and time to have the in-person ClientWise Conversation™, be sure to prepare for even this introductory call. Think about the client and the relationship you have built with him or her. Think about the kinds of conversations you've had with this client over the years when he or she has provided you with feedback. Bring a sense of understanding of the client and a sincere appreciation for what you have built together into the call. The client will sense it in your voice, and you will be prepared to connect with the client on issues relevant to the client's wealth, life goals, career goals, friends, and family as you've regrounded yourself in your past work together.

So let's talk about the setup. First, schedule an appointment for the in-person meeting. When you make the phone call to each client, explain that you want to ask for an appointment to get some input about how you are serving them.

In particular, explain

- that you are looking for ways to improve your practice
- because your business is growing and
- that you're calling a select few clients
- whose opinions you respect a great deal, like theirs,
- and would it be possible for them to meet with you in person within a reasonable time frame, such as the next week or two, for 20 to 25 minutes,
- so you can get some feedback on what's working, what's not working, and what could be done to improve their experience with your firm.

With a lead-in like that, how can your client say anything but yes?

Once your client has agreed to meet with you and you both have the conversation on the calendar, you'll need to prepare for the appointment. Begin by identifying what you genuinely appreciate about the client: not one thing you appreciate, but three things you appreciate, as you're going to share these at the in-person meeting.

Next, see if you can answer the five questions on the client's behalf before even having the meeting. What do you think he or she will say to each of the questions? Then, be prepared for the possibility that the client may share much more (or less) than you might have thought.

Perhaps there are other questions that are important to you, too, such as how important the client believes it is to be connecting to the heirs of his or her wealth; how comfortable he or she is with the other members of the team; how the client would describe wealth management; how confident, on a scale of 1 to 5, 5 being the best, the client is in the plan to achieve the goals and outcomes for his or her wealth; and so on. If so, add them to the end of your script for the conversation, to be posed after the five questions have been asked.

Also, think about the types of "other trusted advisors" your client might be working with (e.g., accountant, banker, realtor, etc.), as you'll be inquiring about this piece, too, and it helps to have some thoughts about what you want to know in case the client needs some clarification or prompting. In addition, rehearse your calls with someone. In fact, the first call to make when rehearsing could just start, "Hi, Mom . . ." You never know! Keep it light, friendly, and relaxed.

 COACHING CORNER

With whom would you like to conduct the ClientWise Conversation™? Think about both clients and professionals whom you serve and know. When you are ready, make a list of 20 to 25 clients you'd like to speak with, and another list of the same number of professionals you'd like to speak with. The first five people you interview in either group should be those who are easiest for you to speak to and connect with. Schedule the more challenging interviews after that.

KEY CONCEPT

Be sure to prepare for the ClientWise Conversation™. Do this by opening your mind to hear and accept whatever feedback you may receive, calling clients to schedule an appointment for the conversation, blocking out your time for these conversations, figuring out what you appreciate about your clients, and rehearsing how the conversation will go.

 Five Steps to a Successful ClientWise Conversation™

1. Meet with the client in person rather than over the phone; it's more personal and gives the client time and space to provide more in-depth answers.

2. Make the meeting one on one, rather than showing up with three team members and risking intimidating the client.

3. Come from a position of strength, not weakness. Explain to the client that as your business continues to grow, you are always looking for ways to improve and better serve your clients.

4. Avoid becoming defensive; instead, let the client know that his or her insight is important to you, listen, and take notes to show you are taking the client seriously.

5. Use the five most important words early and often: "Tell me more about that."

Launching the Conversation: Questions 1 and 2

You've set up the meeting and now it is time to speak with your client, preferably in person and at a meeting that is separate from a client review. Before you dive into the questions, you can launch the meeting with some helpful techniques. At ClientWise, we ask all of our clients to begin the meeting by again stating its purpose. For example:

"Joe, I wanted to meet with you and ask you to help me think about the way I am running my practice. I value your opinion, and I would like to ask you for some honest feedback."

It's helpful to ground the client in the purpose of the meeting as this will be a new kind of conversation, probably unlike those you've had before. There will be no discussion of investments, financial planning, or the capital markets as you are meeting with the client to invite him or her to provide you with feedback about you and your practice. This opening comment will also build trust and rapport with your client as you express that you appreciate his or her feedback.

Remember, too, as you launch the conversation that you are coming from a position of strength. Your attitude is one of excitement and openness because your practice is doing well and you would like to do even better at serving clients in the ways they need. It's all part of a philosophy of continual improvement or lifelong learning.

The next step we ask all of our clients to take is to tell the person three things that you like or admire about him or her. For example:

"I have always appreciated how knowledgeable you are about what I do, and how thorough you are about doing your homework before we meet."

"I really appreciate how you always confirm our appointments and make sure it is convenient for me. That kind of sensitivity is unusual."

"I value the trust you put in me, especially the way you follow my advice when I make recommendations."

By telling the other person three things you like or admire about him or her, you are setting a positive tone for the meeting and further building trust. (Of course, these observations need to be authentic to be effective.) Recent research by a Japanese team has shown that not only do compliments serve as social rewards that have a positive effect on recipients not unlike that of money, but they also motivate people to perform better after receiving them.[2] You want your clients' help, and this is a great method to start paving the way to get it!

There are no right or wrong words to acknowledge your clients; simply offer them some evidence that you understand them and value specific things about them. In fact, having a perfect script is probably a mistake. Your acknowledgment should be tailored to the client you are talking to and personal to them. Authenticity and sincerity are the most important elements to this step.

 KEY CONCEPT

Start your meeting on a positive note by giving your client three authentic compliments. When you build trust by showing you appreciate someone on an individual level, that person is inclined to return the favor, which will pave the way to a productive conversation.

With the meeting launched, you can begin asking the five Client-Wise Conversation™ questions, beginning with Question 1 and then moving on to Question 2. To be effective, the questions need to be asked in the order they are given. The reason for this lies in value. Often, it's easier for the clients to identify first what is working for them, what they value, and how they enjoy working with you today.

Most interviewers assume that the current setup is working well and thus want to skip that part of the interview in favor of getting to the question of what can be done better. If you take that approach, you'll likely hear from clients that the relationship is fine, they are happy, and they wouldn't change much. "Keep doing what you're doing," you'll be likely to hear.

This is not the feedback you are looking for! Instead, give clients the space to start thinking and talking about their experiences with you over the years, and this will warm them up to giving you the constructive feedback you are asking for.

Do not, under any circumstances, think that you can mail these questions out in some sort of written or typed survey. It's best if you do not even send them to the client in advance. I had one Morgan Stanley advisor in Chicago call me to specifically tell me the ClientWise Conversation™ didn't work. When I responded with some questions of my own to figure out why, I discovered that he had mass mailed the five questions to all 400 of his clients and got (surprise surprise!) very little response. You need the questions answered, and you need them answered truthfully, with your clients' authentic responses. These answers are best acquired in person.

Also important to note, the conversation will be richer than just the five questions with authentic answers by your clients. As your clients answer the five questions I have provided here, you will learn information that may raise additional questions for you. Plan to ask any follow-up questions that spring to mind and to be in the flow of the conversation. Remember, however, that in the first meeting, you must cover all five of the questions. Start with Question 1:

What is the one thing you value most about how my firm and I serve you?

This question allows you to begin the inquiry by gathering positive information, which is likely to put both you and the client at ease. Most people don't particularly enjoy giving negative or constructive feedback, whereas they are far more willing and/or comfortable saying something positive. So this is an icebreaker question. Of course, it's more than an icebreaker. At its heart, it is a means of determining how exactly the client perceives your value as a professional. You are gathering data to let you know how your clients are currently framing your business. What value do they think you provide them?

As with all of these questions, it's important to word them as they are shown here. The wording has been chosen expressly and tested across thousands of situations. In the case of Question 1, notice that the question doesn't ask, "What is the most important way that you feel my firm and I serve you?" It asks, "What is the one thing . . . ?" Neurolinguistics research shows that people tend to freeze up or struggle to answer a question about "the most important" something, whereas they answer "one thing" questions with greater ease and creativity.

The request to pull the superlative, tip-top, number one "most important thing" answer out of the air raises the blood pressure of the person trying to come up with a brilliant, insightful, unassailable response; in fact, psychology professor Barry Schwartz has called the quest to make the perfect choice "a recipe for misery."[3] Spare your clients the torture and stick with "one thing"! After all, they are likely to give you more than one thing anyway!

The Five Most Important Words

Regardless of how the client responds to your questions, the five most important words you will use during the ClientWise Conversation™ are these: "Tell me more about that." These are powerful words that will encourage your client to expand, to offer you even more data, and to share more deeply. This will give you an even clearer sense of how you are being framed. In addition, by showing a sense of interest and curiosity in your client's comments, you will also have a chance to build greater rapport with the client.

It's all about active listening, focusing your attention on the client through the words you use and the posture you hold. Active listening involves responding to a client's words with statements that encourage him or her to say more, such as "Expand upon that, please" or "What did you mean when you said ____?" With active listening, you will also take time to make sure you truly understand what it is that the client is trying to communicate to you. For example, you may repeat back to the client what you think you heard, and then ask, "Did I get that right?" inviting the client to confirm, clarify, or correct the meaning.

In addition, it will help you to be mindful of the different levels of communication that are really taking place during the conversation. At level 1 exist the words that the clients give you. Your job is to hear their words. This is about what the clients have to say, not what your thoughts and opinions are.

At level 2 is the meaning of the clients' words. What they are saying may mean something different to them than it does to you. Last, consider level 3 of the communication, that is, reading between the lines. What can you intuit by what your clients are saying to you? Try to listen at a really deep level, and check in with your clients to ensure that your intuition is correct. Don't be afraid to say, "I think I'm hearing you say something else" or "Let me see if I'm really understanding you" and then stating the message you think you are receiving. It is better to check in and be corrected than to not check in and proceed with making changes in your firm on the basis of a misunderstanding of client feedback.

After you have asked your client what is the one thing that he or she values most about your firm and you've taken time to listen and document the answer, it's time to ask Question 2:

What is the one thing you would most like me to change or improve about my firm and how I serve you?

With this question, you are moving on to gather information about how you can be a more effective partner to your clients. If the answer resonates and/or you discover a pattern across multiple clients, you can build this change into the reframe. Wow, is this question powerful! Who has better insight into how you can best serve the client than the client him- or herself? Your client is a treasure trove of useful information on how you can effectively reframe your business. As long as you are able to build trust during the conversation and maintain an open attitude rather than being defensive, you have the potential to learn some very useful information with this question.

In fact, one of my clients, an advisor from the Midwest, affiliated with one of the big brokerage houses, informed me that this question saved him from losing his biggest client. I picked up the phone one day to hear him share, "I just want you to know that you saved my career." I will admit that I was stunned. Truth be told, I had never met the man—let's call him Paul—but he had gone through one of our coaching programs and had learned the ClientWise Conversation™ from his ClientWise coach.

Paul explained the following: "My number one client, who is a chief executive of a major company, was about to leave me—until I asked him, 'What is the one thing I could change or improve?' His answer was, 'Stop calling my home number and leaving messages for me to call you back. Send me an e-mail, it would be preferred, and, oh, by the way, go set up an appointment and meet my wife. She really has no clue about the finances, and you need to educate her.'"

Why did Paul's client make these requests? Here's what was really happening. This client was the chief executive of an international company and found himself traveling all over the world. Paul would call the client for his periodic check-in because this client was an ultra-high-net-worth individual, and he had a very large investment portfolio. A trainer or consultant somewhere along the way had told Paul that this was the right thing to do, the "best practice."

But here's the thing: The client never asked for Paul to call him monthly and certainly not at his home number. Instead of this being a good thing for the client, it was causing him all sorts of headaches, because each time Paul would leave a voice mail on the home machine, the client's wife would think that something had gone wrong with the couple's investment portfolio, so she would call the husband in the middle of the night, say, Tokyo time, waking him up to ask, "Hey, by the way, the advisor just called and left this message. Is everything okay?"

The truth of the matter was that nothing was wrong at all, but Paul's "best practice" home number check-in caused all sorts of stress, disruption, and headaches for the client. The client was ready to dump his "annoying" advisor who just wouldn't let up with the monthly calls to his home phone—until his advisor took the time to gather feedback from him. Question 2 saved this advisor from losing his biggest client.

It saved him his career, too, because this client had referred over 50 clients to him who were all high-net-worth individuals and employees of the international firm that the client led. If the client had left the advisor, the rest of these clients would have departed, too.

Instead, this story has a fantastic ending. Instead of losing his client, Paul actually reframed his business and gained new clients by developing a whole education series to better educate the spouses of his clients. The ClientWise Conversation™ helped him realize that he was not connecting with half of his clients—the spouses—and he made a meaningful change in his value proposition as a result. In fact, it has become the centerpiece to his value proposition, as he primarily works with C-suite executives, many of whom are married and appreciate this piece of support.

This story makes you wonder what you will discover when you ask your clients about the one thing that they would most like you to change or improve about your firm and how it serves them, doesn't it?

 KEY CONCEPT

Asking clients what they value about your firm and what they would change about your services can result in new insights and new ideas for you, and more personalized services for your clients. Be sure to follow up client comments often with the request, "Tell me more about that."

Document, Document, Document

Another key aspect of the ClientWise Conversation™ is to document everything you are hearing the client share. Ask the client for permission to do so, with words like, "The insight and the words and phrases that you are sharing with me are really important. Do you mind if I take notes?"

Then, as you take notes, try to capture the client's words and phrases rather than simply paraphrasing. The reason is that words and phrases mean different things to different people. For example, when facilitating workshops, I often write the word TENDER up on the board and hear back from the group that it means so many different things to different people: chicken, steak, soft, small boat, Elvis ("Love Me Tender"). This is just one example of how words mean different things to different people. Try that out, by the way, at your next team meeting. Ask everyone at the same time what the word on the board means to them. It's always a laugh, but it makes the point that checking in about what words and phrases mean to different people really matters.

So, to ensure you are capturing your client's intended meaning, write down his or her words, not your own interpretation of them. As part of this process, also make absolutely sure that you understand what those words and phrases mean. Understanding precisely what the client means will ensure you gather useful data to consider later when constructing your new frame.

In the end, documenting the client's responses will help you later be able to look for patterns in the data that you collect because the patterns will give you all the insight that you need to have. Plan to put these notes in an Excel spreadsheet or other template that works for you so you can analyze it later.

 THE eXchange™

Online Tool 6.2: ClientWise Conversation™ Data Collector

Visit the eXchange™ for a note-taking template that you can use during the Client-Wise Conversation™ to capture your client's answers.

Question 3

When my firm first designed the questions in the ClientWise Conversation™ back in 2006, we made a mistake. There were only four questions at the time, not five, and that's because we didn't know that Question 3—the next one that you will use when conducting the ClientWise Conversation™—would not provide us with the kind of feedback we anticipated. Whoops! The question read as follows:

If you were to describe the services that my firm and I offer you, to clients like yourself, what would you say?

In Question 3, we were trying to get at the heart of what kind of services clients believed their advisors provided to them. That's fair enough, I think, with a question like this one. Yet, the answer that thousands of clients provided when asked this question was altogether different than the one we expected. Instead of saying things like, "You offer reasonably priced life insurance" or "You help clients build strong retirement portfolios," they said things like, "I trust you," "You take care of my family," "You've always been there for me," and "I can count on you."

The clients' answers had everything to do with building a trustful relationship. It had very little to do with answering the actual question, which invited people to describe the advisor's services—unless, of course, building a trusting relationship was the one most important thing that the advisor was providing to the client as a service.

Jonathan Beukelman, Managing Director of Wealth Management at the Beukelman Group,[4] discovered a similar reality early in his career and ultimately used it to help him frame himself for clients in a way that would be truly helpful to them. As a natural listener, Beukelman asked questions of his prospects and clients early on. In response, they told him the interesting truth that they didn't get particularly excited to hear about all the great investments his firm had told him to talk about to them.

What they really wanted was his support with the big questions, like how to pass their money down to their kids in the best way, how to educate their children about money, and how to make sure that they didn't ruin the next generation by not transitioning their wealth properly. This information helped Beukelman understand early on the value of the support relationship he could supply his clients. Most people need more than a mutual fund manager, Beukelman discovered— they need a financial advisor. What clients needed was not one piece, but the whole picture.

Over the years, when Beukelman has asked his clients what they need from him, they will often express concerns regarding their adult children. Beukelman doesn't shy away from talking directly to his clients' children, often when the kids are in their early twenties. Instead, he says lightheartedly, "Let me at them."

Over the course of his conversations with them, Beukelman has discovered that some of these kids "just need . . . patient conversation."[5] Instead of focusing on money management per se, Beukelman focuses on listening to these individuals and helping to keep a "fire in their gut" so they have the motivation to manage their money well, to "just go on and attack it."[6] Beukelman, whose firm specializes in managing family wealth, understands that the value of the advisor to the client is in the trusting relationship he and his team can provide, not in their ability to sell services to them.

We discovered the same reality as Beukelman when road-testing Question 3 of the ClientWise Conversation™: From the clients' view, the greatest value they receive from their advisor is to have a trusting relationship. In fact, this was the number one answer that was given when we asked clients, "If you were to describe the services that my firm and I offer you, to clients like yourself, what would you say?" We had learned something very important by asking Question 3. Clearly, though, we needed to add a different question to elicit the client's view on what kind of services the advisor offered. That's where Question 4 came in.

Yet, we did not remove Question 3 as we felt it was incredibly important to retain for two reasons. First, we believed that advisors needed to hear out loud from their clients how important the trusting relationship was to clients. Second, we knew that enabling the clients to enunciate for themselves that the trusting relationship was important to them would have a powerful impact on the clients. Both advisors and clients would gain a firsthand understanding, in the moment, of how much value the trusting relationship brings to clients, a value that could not be easily replicated by switching to another firm.

KEY CONCEPT

Asking clients to describe the services you provide usually reveals the most important asset in your relationship with the client: the trusting relationship itself.

 Avoid the Dance of Being Defensive

No matter what answers you get during the ClientWise Conversation™, you never want to fall into defending yourself or your firm. Instead of responding to the clients right on the spot with counter-comments to their points, focus instead on listening clearly, encouraging additional comments, and taking notes. Plan to remain singularly focused on gathering the data. Because you are not yet at the point where you know how you will want to reframe your business, stay in listening mode rather than speaking mode. You will have a chance to speak to the clients in a future conversation to address their concerns (step 4: renewing relationships). That conversation will take place when you are crystal clear on how you want to reframe yourself, your team, and/or your firm.

Question 4

Question 4 centers around achievement. It's a powerful question because it gets the clients to say in their own words what it is you have achieved together. It gets them to describe the value of your services out loud.

> If you were to describe what we've achieved together for as long as we've worked together, what would you say?

When the clients believe they have achieved something and they are able to articulate that something—when they own and know for themselves what they have achieved in partnership with you, the advisor— there is magic. The client makes a real connection in his or her mind between what you do as an advisor and why it is valuable to him or her.

Now if you as the advisor tell the client, "This is of value to you," the client won't believe it; it won't sink in or feel real or authentic. But if clients say out loud what is of value to them, it becomes real. Therein lies the genius of Question 4.

KEY CONCEPT

Asking the client about what the two of you have achieved together illuminates for you what is of value to the client, and illuminates for the client the value that you provide to him or her.

 ### Asking "What Have We Achieved Together?" During Client Reviews

I would argue that every single advisor needs to ask a client Question 4 on every single client review, not just during the ClientWise Conversation™. What's more, advisors need to get really smart about documenting what the client believes he or she has achieved in working with the advisor. There needs to be a memorialization of this value discussion after every client review. Send an e-mail; send a letter. "Really great that we were able to connect today to review the outcomes and goals that you have for your wealth and your life as it relates to your family. By the way, it was great to hear you say that we achieved X since we last met."

At the end of the year when there is an annual review, ask Question 4 and recap the things that the client believes were achieved over the course of a year; for example, "We've rebalanced investment portfolios, we've retitled life insurance policies, we've updated an estate plan, we've together made a decision about who would take care of the kids if something were to happen to Mom and Dad. We helped a child find the right college to go to, and we funded that second home. We provided a line of credit to buy that second business or to expand the business." These are all really powerful achievements.

Question 5

The last question that needs to be asked during the ClientWise Conversation™ is Question 5:

> Among your other professional advisors in your life, who do you trust the most and why?

There are two reasons that an advisor wants to ask Question 5. First, you want to know who the other trusted advisors are in the client's life. From a competitive perspective and a client-influence perspective, you have to identify and understand who else has your client's ear and business so you know where you stand relative to them.

Second, when we study the best in the business—those who are most successful—what we notice is that they have a network of professionals with whom they partner so that they can provide comprehensive wealth management. The answer to Question 5 will provide you with essential data for building your network of professionals with whom you partner.

Note that I am not talking about the old, trite centers of influence or professional alliances for the benefit of getting referrals. Referrals are not even what you want. What you really want are introductions, and you only get formal introductions if you have professional partnerships with people.

By asking Question 5 of your clients, you will be able to gather key information that will help you in the reframe to develop those professional partnerships and to provide complete wealth management. The reality is that if you are going to deliver wealth management, you will likely specialize in only one piece of wealth management and need to build out a team for the rest.

For example, if you are a financial planner, you may still need on your team a primary banker, a primary insurance agent, a primary business valuation specialist, a health care consultant, a person to handle the concentrated stock position, and more. As your client goes through one or more life transitions, you are likely to have a need to connect him or her to one of these other professionals on your team. If you are proactive about building this team, all roads can lead back to you as the financial planner or wealth advisor.

The best way to build this network is to ask your existing clients, "Hey, by the way, among your other trusted advisors, who do you trust the most and why? Because from time to time, my clients need to connect with these other types of professionals, and the way we have built our network is by asking our clients who they trust the most and why, to determine whether or not we want to add them to our professional network for the benefit of our clients, because we are building a

community—a community of clients and a community of professionals that together can help our clients achieve their goals and dreams
and hopes and desires."

As you are building your network, you are also creating goodwill
with the clients and deepening their potential to trust in you—to understand that you will truly be able to take care of them because you
have a robust team, not just of partners, but of partners that your
clients trust.

KEY CONCEPT

Finding out which other professionals are advising your clients lets you know where
you stand with your clients and provides the potential opportunity to expand your
professional network.

COACHING CORNER

Imagine that during the ClientWise Conversation™, a client tells you several areas
where he has been disappointed with your firm, and in the process he expresses that
he has even considered leaving your firm. How would you respond to such a client
during the conversation? Let this scenario play out in your mind, or even better,
role-play it with a colleague so you can practice responding out loud.

The Meeting Wrap-Up

As the meeting comes to a close, you will want to let the client know
that his or her input was really valuable and helpful. Do not forget to
thank your client for his or her time, ideas, and candor. Plan, too, to
ask permission of the client to be able to have a follow-up conversation in the future with a question like one of the following. (That being said, there are some clients you will not go back to because they
weren't really helpful. If you feel this is the case for a particular client,
you can skip this step.)

"Would it be okay if we circle back to you in a couple of months and share with you our key findings?"

"Would it be okay if we came back to you and demonstrated some of the items we are improving, perhaps [from a technology perspective or from a processing perspective or from a messaging perspective]?"

"Would it be all right if I come back and share with you regarding the value that we really want to bring to our clients?"

"Would you mind my sharing those key insights and what changes and improvements we have decided to make?"

"I have some work to do. Thanks for your input. I want to come back to you after I've done some thinking and learning because we want to reshape, we're improving, and we want to include you in the improving part of the process so you're aware of what we've done; is that OK?"

By closing in this way, you will demonstrate that you are taking the client and his or her opinion seriously and that this is not simply a matter of you looking to get referrals from the client. It conveys that you are engaging in an authentically driven process around identifying how you are being framed today.

In addition to going back to your client in the future with the results of your reframe, plan to make it a habit as a team, every 18 to 20 months, to have this kind of conversation with your client. This will allow you to get a fresh read on how you are being framed at that stage in time and to identify whether steps you've taken to reframe your business are working.

 ## From ClientWise Conversation™ to Analysis

You made the calls, you scheduled the visits, you kept the appointments, you had the conversations. You've got a pile of notes and ringing ears, and the question that arises is, "Now what?" Gathering data was only step 1; now you need to make sense of it all. That is, you need to analyze your data.

Start by reviewing what you wrote. Think back to what your clients said and how they said it. With everything refreshed in your mind, begin to do the following:

- Look for patterns in client responses.
- Ask the team for input on the client responses.
- Ask yourself, what words and phrases did you hear?
- Identify the gaps between how the client frames you and how you want to be framed.
- Determine how you and the team can use what you have discovered in your daily work, beginning right now.
- Start documenting what you achieve each and every quarter with the client.

Mentally processing all of the information and using it to make changes to your practice (during future steps of the reframing process) will not be an overnight operation, so be patient with yourself. In some cases, at some point in the future, circumstances may trigger a memory of a client comment, and you may have an "aha!" moment when the significance or application of the client's observation suddenly makes sense. Think of this analyzing process as a marathon, not a sprint. Use what you can, when you can, and accept that if something does not make sense now, it may in the future.

CONCLUSION

In reality, your clients may not understand exactly what it is that you do. They may not realize the unique nature of your value proposition, or they may find it difficult to articulate what it is you do that is different from the thousands of other financial advisors in the marketplace. The only way to find out whether this is the case is by taking the time to talk with them. That's what step 1 of the reframing process is all about.

It's a powerful opportunity to be in conversation with your best clients in a new and different way. There's no discussion of investments, financial planning, or the capital markets; you are meeting with the clients to invite them to provide you feedback about you and your practice.

In the process, you will gather data that allows you to create a baseline of how you are being framed. You will have a rich pool of information that you can analyze and identify patterns in how your clients view your services, what they value most about you, and the things they would like to see you change. In step 2, you will spend time defining what you would like your new frame to be. With the baseline for how others are framing you at the ready and your new vision for how you want to be framed, you'll be set to close the gap. No longer will you have to guess at how to frame yourself for clients; you'll have the information needed to create your desired reframe.

NOTES

1. Tom Weilert, personal interview, March 13, 2015, transcript, pp. 10–11.
2. Janice Wood, "Compliments Can Improve Performance," *PsychCentral*, November 11, 2011, accessed March 25, 2015, http://psychcentral.com/news/2012/11/11/compliments-can-improve-performance/47462.html.
3. As quoted in Alina Tugend, "Too Many Choices: A Problem That Can Paralyze," *New York Times*, February 26, 2010, www.nytimes.com/2010/02/27/your-money/27shortcuts.html?_r=1.
4. Jonathan Beukelman, personal interview, March 13, 2015, transcript, p. 3.
5. Ibid., p. 4.
6. Ibid.

CHAPTER **7**

Defining Your New Frame by Discovering Your Value

I f you've completed step 1 of the reframing process, you've done the meaningful work of collecting and analyzing a large amount of information from your clients and the professionals with whom you work and interact. You've looked for significant patterns and taken note of important gaps. You know what it is that clients value about your services, and you know the areas where they would seek you to make changes. In all, you now have a tremendous pool of information that you can use to inform you as you *define your new frame*. That's step 2 of the reframing process (see Figure 7.1).

The information in step 1 of the reframing process has come from the outside, so to speak—from your clients and the other professionals you have interviewed. Now it's time to look within yourself, your team, and the organization for wisdom and guidance on what you believe a good reframe will be for the firm. The data you have gathered from

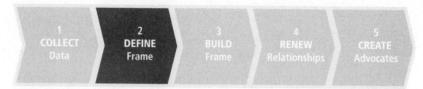

Figure 7.1 Reframe Step 2: Define Your New Frame

clients and professionals, coupled with the insights and ideas you generate by brainstorming internally with your team, will provide you with the valuable information you need to define an effective frame that supports your clients in a way that works for them and, at the same time, is reflective of a purpose you and your team are excited to fulfill.

How will you ultimately decide to define your new frame? Maybe you have a passion for helping entrepreneurs and decide to reframe yourself as an advisory firm dedicated to serving small to midsize organizations with an entrepreneurial bent by offering cash management, liability management, asset transfer, and other services this group needs. Maybe you will choose to reframe as a firm that provides support to professional athletes on signing bonuses, budgeting, retirement planning, and more. You might instead choose to cater to family-owned businesses or to ultra-high-net-worth millennials, providing services customized just for them. The frame you define will be as unique as you and your team, your strengths, your interests, and your clients.

Erin Botsford, CEO and founder of Botsford Financial Group, has framed her firm on the basis of some of her significant experiences growing up. When Botsford was 11 years old, her father died and left her mother with six kids and a $10,000 life insurance policy.[1] Botsford and her family went from middle-class status to poverty in an instant. When Botsford was 16 years old, she was in a car accident in which she collided with a man on a motorcycle; the motorcyclist died in the crash. Her mother had to put a second mortgage on their home to pay for the fees to defend Botsford, who was eventually found innocent.

On the basis of these and other early life experiences, Botsford developed an outlook that risk management was the core of the financial advisory work she did with clients. In her words, her firm's "entire focus is helping people protect their money, their assets, and their life's work."[2] Not surprisingly, the tagline after her company name on her website reads, "the keepers and protectors of our clients' lifestyles, as they define them.™" Last, the company bio explains, "The Botsford Group is a comprehensive wealth management firm, specializing in Asset Protection and Risk Management strategies for business owners and senior executives of Fortune 500 companies."[3] How's that for a clear frame, designed to take the best care of Botsford's clients, in a way that Botsford can authentically stand behind?

Like Botsford, you can specialize in working with your ideal clients in a way that is supportive to them while also being grounded in the authentic purpose of your team. You get there by defining and building the right frame. Having interviewed your clients in step 1 of the reframe using the ClientWise Conversation™, you're off to a great start. This chapter will provide you with six questions you can use to interview yourself and your own team to define your new frame in a customized way that works for both you and your clients.

The ultimate goal of defining the right frame for your firm and your clients is to be able to provide true value to your clients. By taking the time to define your new frame (and, later, to build it), you will be able to regularly generate value that is unique to your firm and that provides your ideal clients with just what they need to be successful.

Note, too, that this process of defining a new frame for your firm is durable and can be used again and again. The best in the business are always looking for ways to adjust and improve, and one of the effective ways to do that is to tweak and redefine one's frame. Therefore, think of the frame-defining step not as a one-time event but rather as a process that can be used over and over again to refine and improve the

 KEY CONCEPT

Before you can build a new frame, you need to figure out what you have to offer and what the clients you want to serve need. This information will come from internal and external sources. Look at the information you have already gathered with an open mind, let it guide you and your thinking as you prepare to reframe, and remember that your goal in the reframe is to provide true value to your clients.

frame. If you're committed to building enterprise value, teach those at your firm to consistently listen, grow, and improve. Now, that's sustainable!

You know how your clients frame your firm because you've interviewed them with the ClientWise Conversation™. With that valuable information at the forefront of your mind, you are ready to look inward and ask yourself and your team the following six questions to continue the exploration process and determine how best to define your new frame (see Figure 7.2).

First, *what is your noble purpose?* What are you trying to meaningfully accomplish by running your organization, beyond making a good living for yourself and your team? Why does your firm exist? Knowing your noble purpose will give you a foundation you can return to time and again as you ask yourself the remainder of the questions needed to define your new frame.

Second, *who do you want your business to be built to serve?* Who are you passionate about supporting? Another way of asking this question is, who is your ideal client? You can determine your ideal client by identifying your specific target group, your niche within that target group, and then your ideal clients within that niche. Once you know who your firm is going to be built to serve, you are ever closer to defining your new frame.

Once you've identified the group you would like to build your business to serve, ask *what are this group's main concern(s)?* With this question, the goal is to identify the needs of your ideal client types.

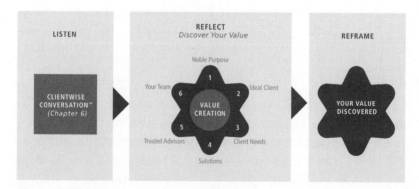

Figure 7.2 The Wealth Management Reframe Process

Here's another way to ask the question: What do you know that your ideal clients need that they don't even know they need, because you're an expert in working with them? You can start with your ideal clients' main concern/s and, from there, break that down into their various needs—both known and unknown.

With this valuable information in hand, you will be ready to ask yourself, *What solutions or solutions will you provide to your ideal clients?* It's brainstorming time. Recognize a client need? Find a solution. But, first, let's be clear here. Solutions are not just the *products* that you are compensated for delivering, they're also the *services* you are or are not compensated for delivering. What custom services do you provide? What intellectual capital do you offer? Value occurs not only in the products you offer but also in the services you provide through your firm's signature approach.

Next, to deliver the desired solutions to your ideal clients with your signature approach, it's likely you will want and need to invite other trusted advisors into the process. Unless you are ready to grow into a mega-organization, chances are you will want or need to build out a strong professional network to be able to truly serve your clients' full spectrum of needs. That's where the next question comes in as you are defining your new frame: *What other trusted advisors work with your ideal clients?* Part of your value to the client is to serve as a facilitator: The root of this word is *facile,* which means "easy." How much easier can you make your clients' lives by identifying the other advisors with whom they need to work and by developing a relationship with these advisors so that you can make them even more available to your clients and at just the right times?

Asking Questions 2, 3, 4, and 5 as you define your new frame can generate some fascinating and useful results. A number of years ago, I conducted a series of workshops with several groups of more than 50 advisors each over the course of several months in Princeton, New Jersey, that used this process to help them define their new frames. The room was abuzz with conversation, creativity, and innovation. All in all, the groups generated more than 25 pages of ideas, focused on more than 35 different target client groups. Take a look at some of the unique results that these advisors generated toward possible future reframes (see Table 7.1).

Table 7.1 Sample Work of Advisors Brainstorming About the Needs and Solutions of Their Ideal Clients and About Their Trusted Advisors

Target Market	Needs	Solutions	Trusted Advisors
Real estate developers	Known: ■ Estate planning ■ Diversification ■ Confidentiality ■ Multiple existing advisor relationships ■ Sophistication ■ Tax sensitivity Unknown: ■ Leverage ■ Life insurance ■ Tax strategies ■ Consolidation of financial picture	Known: ■ International trust ■ Offshore products ■ Wealth management tools ■ Multicurrency ■ Airplane financing ■ Mortgage of multiple residences Unknown (intangible): ■ Referral to international corporate finance group ■ Doing business in native language ■ Expertise in doing cross-border transactions ■ Personal representations	■ Real estate agent ■ Materials/construction owners ■ Government agencies ■ Existing clients in sector ■ Bankers ■ Chamber of Commerce ■ Professional associations
Lawyers	Known: ■ High taxable income ■ Time management ■ Irregular cash flow ■ Disability insurance ■ Stock options/stock concentration Unknown: ■ 401(k) (but no pension stream) ■ Board of directors exposure ■ Estate planning, tax treatment of life insurance	■ High taxable income review, fixed income strategy, max retirement contribution ■ Irregular cash flow & estimated tax issue—managed cash reserve ■ Stock concentration—prepaid forward, exchange funds, charitable swing ■ 401(k)/pension-structure retirement income ■ Board of directors exposure, Sarbanes–Oxley ■ Estate planning & life insurance, ILIT	■ Real estate broker ■ Insurance broker ■ Employment lawyer

Target Market	Needs	Solutions	Trusted Advisors
People with philanthropic interests	Known: ■ Current and planned giving ■ Make a difference ■ Leave a legacy ■ Tax sensitivity Unknown: ■ How charitable gifts affect their overall financial and estate plan ■ How to maximize your charitable gifts	■ Proactive approach to maximize charitable giving ■ Ongoing relationships, not transactional ■ Identify center for philanthropy ■ Specific vehicles	■ Estate attorney ■ CPA ■ Professional fundraiser ■ Directors of planned giving ■ Family foundations

Table 7.1 captures sample answers to the Questions 2–5 in the frame-defining process:

1. What is your noble purpose?
2. Who do you want your business to be built to serve (ideal clients)?
3. What are this group's main concern/s (and related needs)?
4. What solution or solutions will you provide to your ideal clients?
5. What other trusted advisors work with your ideal clients?

Once advisors and firms have gotten clear on their noble purpose, ideal clients, needs, solutions, and professional networks, advisors can ask the last question of the frame-defining process:

6. What team would you like to build to fulfill your noble purpose?

With Question 6, you will identify what kind of a team you will need to build to fulfill your noble purpose and deliver the promised value to your ideal client. Once all six of these questions are answered, you will be well positioned to authentically describe who you serve and what you stand for, which conveys the new frame in a nutshell and will be used to inform all of the marketing material that gets built during the next part of the reframing process.

THE eXchange™

Online Tool 7.1: Example Needs, Target Market, Solutions, and Centers of Influence

There's no replacement for what can be created by great minds working together in a single room. The information generated in Table 7.1 on the different target groups advisors can work with, along with their associated needs, solutions, and centers of influence, is evidence of that. Download this amazing free content from the eXchange™ (youvebeenframed.clientwise.com) to help get your own creative juices flowing as you define your new frame.

KEY CONCEPT

Once you have defined your noble purpose, identified your ideal clients, understood their needs, brainstormed solutions to their problems, built a strong professional network to support you and your clients, created a team to deliver your value, and can authentically describe what you do and who you do it for, what you need to do to reframe will be clear.

QUESTION 1: WHAT IS YOUR NOBLE PURPOSE?

By now, you know that my view is that the work that financial advisors do, when done well, is truly noble work. I say this because I've been a witness to greatness by many financial professionals who have genuinely helped clients build and implement successful financial plans that have helped those clients get a clear vision about what they wanted to achieve and take those necessary steps to attain the results they had hoped for. When an advisory team does their work well, they impact hundreds, perhaps even thousands, of families: They can change communities. In fact, when they do their work really well, they create sustainable firms using effective succession planning and employ those next-generation advisors who can connect to the heirs of their clients' wealth and impact generations to come.

When defining your new frame, start with the purpose of your firm. It's the purpose that keeps the team focused on the prize, serving others. It's the purpose that keeps the other trusted advisors with whom the advisory team has chosen to partner for the benefit of the clients trustful of that professional partnership for the benefit of others. It's the purpose that allows for successful client acquisition strategies to work with ease.

The purpose should be an ambition that is significant in size, aspirational in scope, and possible to achieve that will serve your clients, yourself, and your organization. For example, a firm's purpose might be to help as many individuals as possible, including ourselves, to develop sufficient financial freedom to be able to engage in work or play driven only by their passion, rather than settled for because of need, by the time they are sixty years old. You get the picture. Significant in size. Aspirational in scope. Possible to achieve.

There is a sense of nobility in the purposeful work of financial advisors that I often observe but isn't well articulated by the advisor or advisory team. Yet it's my view that the team's purpose ought to be central to the frame. As we coach in our Lone Ranger to Leader™ programs at ClientWise, the common purpose and intent make up the larger, more inspiring ideas and aims that will drive your team's definition of wealth management, who the ideal client is, what products and services your team chooses to offer, the intellectual property and signature approach that your team will design and implement, and what the team's client service model is. The purpose is what will guide how you build the team that will serve your clients as well.

 COACHING CORNER

What is your firm's noble purpose? Take time on your own with pen and paper to reflect on this question and to sketch it out; bring your team together to explore this question and discuss. The next chapter of this book also provides details on how to work with your team to identify a common purpose. Begin this process now, as it will provide you with the foundation for defining the rest of your frame.

KEY CONCEPT

Your firm's noble purpose can be the central, inspirational point around which you and your team revolve. That purpose should be significant in size, aspirational in scope, and possible to achieve to the benefit of your clients, yourself, and your organization.

QUESTION 2: WHO'S YOUR IDEAL CLIENT?

Now that you know what your noble purpose is, you are ready to answer the question, whom do you want your firm built to serve? In simpler terms, who, exactly, is your client? There's a very good reason why redefining begins with getting clear on who your target client is—because your job as a firm is to provide value to your clients, and the only way to do that is to understand whom you are working with. Only when you understand this can you determine their needs and thus know what solutions to provide. The value is in the solutions!

Having a specific client you are serving will affect your entire approach to your business. So, it's time to brainstorm on your target market and, from there, create your ideal client profile. Within a target market, there are niches, and within those niches, there are ideal clients. For example, say you have identified dentists as the target market. Yet within the category of dentists are a variety of specialists, such as general dentists, oral pathologists, periodontists, orthodontists, endodontists, pedodontists, oral and maxillofacial surgeons, and so on. Within those niches, there is an ideal client type for your firm; this is the kind of person you'd like to work with in terms of their characteristics, attitude, outlook, demographics, and more. For example, you may choose to serve periodontists who (ideal client type) live in the Northeast, have families, want to retire by 50 years of age, and enjoy investing their money but want a partner to ensure they make smart decisions.

Plan to do this ideal client brainstorming activity with your team—led by you, someone on your team, or even a coaching or consulting firm. Start by taking a look at the top 50 clients of your firm. Look for patterns of how you met them, what you like about them, what you may dislike about them, how much energy and time they require, who excites you, who you enjoy speaking with, and who your team despises when their name comes up on the caller ID. There will be groups of individuals that you enjoy serving most, and then there will be those that you may find difficult to serve. This is a very good exercise for a person to consider when identifying the ideal client type.

Some things you may want to consider when going through this client analysis are the following:

- Do you enjoy haggling over fees?
- When you explain your fee structure, which clients ask tough questions but value your services?
- Who understands the rising expenses associated with running a financial advisory firm?
- Who couldn't care less and doesn't want you to meet with their children, grandchildren, or heirs?
- Who finds it easy to introduce you to their friends and colleagues?
- Who wants no part in thinking about helping your firm grow and doesn't understand the benefits when your firm does grow?
- If you could work with any individual client, who would it be and why?
- Think of one of your favorite clients and write down a list of characteristics that make this client unique. Repeat as desired.
- What are the characteristics and demographics of your ideal client (e.g., age, gender, career field, education level, geographic location)?

The results of engaging in this exercise may surprise you or they may seem excitingly right on track. Either way, they will provide you with a clear starting point for identifying your ideal clients and defining your new frame.

KEY CONCEPT

Identify your target niche market as well as the characteristics that define your ideal client. The diamonds will be found in the details.

Here's a look at some of the unique and varied target market niches that were generated by the same group of advisors who created the materials shown in Table 7.1: Asian business owners, special needs associations, aircraft owners, women in transition (widows, divorcees, new-job hunters), trucking company owners, oil executives, farmers/ranchers/landowners, NFL and PGA athletes, lobbyists, and tribal governments. As you can see, no target client was off limits when these advisors gave themselves time and space to brainstorm about the possibilities. Table 7.2 shows additional example target markets and niches, along with example ideal client types.

I'm often asked, can my firm serve only one type of ideal client? The answer is, of course. It's your firm. You get to choose. But in doing so, consider how you will scale and build a firm that is profitable, sustainable, and long lasting while serving a single type of ideal client. Think about what types of services and service models will allow you to render something more complex and of high value to your ideal client. Alternatively, you may find that team members can play a number of technical roles that serve a variety of ideal client types. For example, managing investment portfolios is a professional service that can be centralized, while the advisors in the firm can deliver customized services for each ideal client type, such as the financial planning and relationship management.

Table 7.2 Examples of Target Markets, Niches, and Ideal Client Types

Target Market	Niche	Ideal Client
C-suite execs	IT industry	West Coast based, workaholic seeking more work–life balance, within five years of retirement
Women	Working mothers who are 40+ years old	Full-time employed, worried about saving for college, appreciates the value of advice
Professional athletes	Football players	Been injured, so appreciates the finite aspect of their career; humble; good sense of humor; effective communicator
Nonprofit leaders	Leads a health-related agency	U.S. based with international travel, master's degree or above, excellent business sense

Who will your ideal client be? By setting aside time on your and the team's calendars to ask and answer this question, you will gain essential information needed to define your new frame.

COACHING CORNER

What group of individuals would you like to serve as your clients and why? Start with your ideal target market and, from there, narrow down to your ideal target niche or niches. Next, think about your ideal clients' age, interests, demographics, characteristics, and any other descriptors that make them unique and of interest to you as clients. As you work through this exercise, feel free to write down as many answers as come to mind. Later, review them and circle those that most excite you, then rank order them. Which ideal clients are you starting to focus on?

QUESTION 3: WHAT ARE YOUR CLIENTS' NEEDS?

Once you have determined who your ideal client is, you are ready to move on to exploring with your team what your clients' needs are. This step is essential. If you don't know what your clients' needs are, then you may well end up providing services and solutions that are of no use or interest to them.

It's like standing on a street corner in northern Alaska selling beach equipment straight from a Florida beachside stand. You may be very proud of offering the best suntan lotion, sunglasses, towels, beach chairs, and beach umbrellas, but your clients, who don't value these things, will be scratching their heads and saying to you, "But we don't do the beach here." Your clients, in this situation, need parkas and winter hats with flappy ears, not picnic coolers and popsicles. It's a case of misaligned services and client needs and no one—neither the advisor nor the client—wants that. While this is an extreme example, you get the point.

Looking at Figure 7.3, you can see how offering the wrong kind of services to your particular clients will lead to a miss in terms of client satisfaction. You can provide the most excellent version of your services, but if the client doesn't need them, who cares? Certainly not the client.

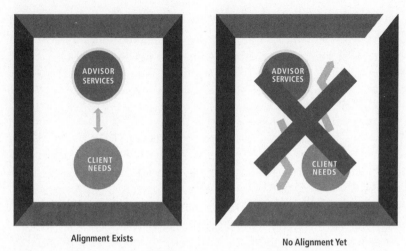

Alignment Exists   No Alignment Yet

Figure 7.3 Aligned versus Unaligned Advisor Services and Client Needs

The reality is that if you provide services that your clients don't need or value, you will struggle to retain clients or gain new ones. On the flip side, if you provide services that your clients want, need, and value, they will be willing to pay you today and tomorrow. That's a win–win situation for everyone.

Here are some questions you can ask yourself and the team to identify your clients needs:

- What kind of support does your client need to successfully manage his or her wealth?
- What would make your client sleep better at night or jump for joy in the morning when it comes to finance-related matters?
- What services can you provide to ensure your client avoids future pitfalls and challenges? Any others that you can think of to add?
- What needs does your client have without even realizing it?

Identifying your clients' needs sets you up to provide solutions to them. Who doesn't want to have their needs met? Solutions and support equal satisfied clients who remain loyal to the organization.

KEY CONCEPT

After you've identified your ideal target clients, put in the work to figure out the specific client needs within your chosen niche. Taking the time to understand your client is the first step in serving that client.

Here are some example client needs (see Table 7.3) generated by the group of advisors who brainstormed the data revealed in Table 7.1.

Table 7.3 Examples of Client Needs

Target Market	Needs
Business owners	Known: ■ Taxes ■ Profitability ■ Liquidity ■ Cash management ■ Retirement benefits ■ Making payroll Unknown: ■ Costs of cash management ■ Succession plan ■ Exit strategy ■ Liquidity strategy—family ■ Estate planning/asset protection ■ Organizing personal life ■ Holistic vs. atomistic ■ Lending capabilities
Asian business owners	Known: ■ Retirement planning ■ Estate tax issue ■ Currency ■ Risk of political issues ■ Language barrier Unknown: ■ Liability ■ Insurance ■ Estate presentation ■ Currency hedge ■ Offshore strategy

(Continued)

Table 7.3 (*Continued*)

Target Market	Needs
Aircraft owners	Known: ■ Financing needs ■ Refurbishing ■ System upgrades Unknown: ■ Upgrade ■ Types of financing
Blue-collar retirees with large 401(k)s	Known: ■ Structuring income ■ Estate planning ■ Largest source of liquid assets Unknown: ■ Multiple cash flow solutions ■ Minimize adverse tax consequences

As you explore your clients' needs, don't stop at the surface or the obvious. Dig deeper, investigating the unknown needs of your clients, too. That is where the magic is. The clients don't know what they don't know, but if you're an expert at serving those clients, you likely have insights into the things your clients need that they don't even know they need.

These unknown needs are where an advisor can provide real value. Let's go back to our dentist example. Perhaps your firm is built to serve small- to medium-sized dentistry practices. The dentists at a particular practice have done a good job setting up a retirement plan for themselves and their staff. But what they don't know is the importance of insurance-related services, or what their succession strategy is, or what continuity planning is about, or what their exit strategy is, or how to value the business, or how to set up an ownership structure that would allow the sale of the business internally or externally with ease.

But with your research, experience, and expertise, your firm has built a network of business valuation specialists, attorneys, and insurance professionals who specialize, like you, in serving this target market. Because of your approach, you've worked out an arrangement with this group of professionals. All of you have agreed who your ideal client really is, and together you believe you can serve this group more effectively than any other wealth management group out there. You see, the unknown needs are where the value is.

Supporting your clients' unknown needs is a huge part of the value you will be providing once you deliver on your new frame! You can set yourself up for success in the future by uncovering your clients' known and unknown needs now.

Last, don't forget about all that valuable data you gathered during the ClientWise Conversation™. Take a look back at the results from those conversations and pull out the varying needs that your clients evidenced there. There is no more reliable data on your clients than that they've given you themselves. So where the needs are relevant to your ideal client profile, plan to pull those into your new frame.

INDUSTRY INSIGHT: DEFINING YOUR BRAND ON THE BASIS OF YOUR BELIEFS

When asked for his thoughts on how advisors can go about successfully framing themselves, Gregory Mech, managing director at The CAPROCK Group, naturally drifted to the notion that the process has to begin with one's values. Mech explained, "It becomes really important as we enter an exercise like reframing that we understand our own values, our own beliefs, and . . . what our higher purpose is because that's going to be the foundation from which all of our behaviors radiate."[4] In contrast, Mech believes that many times the process of rebranding or reframing "becomes an exercise in advertising or spin."[5] Such an approach is, in his view, misplaced.

For Mech, it's about authenticity. "The thing that comes to mind for me, as I think about rebranding and reframing," Mech described, "is just because you say you are doesn't mean you are."[6] He referenced the example of Tesla Motors versus Fisker Automotive: two automobile companies that each promised the public that they would provide a luxury automobile that was environmentally sound. Tesla followed through and sold more than 2,250 Roadsters in 31 countries between 2008 and March 2012;[7] Fisker crashed and burned after a two-year delay, a release in 2011, and then a production stop in 2012 due to a lack of financial resources.[8]

Mech believes that many financial services firms fall into the same trap as Fisker: framing themselves a certain way without then delivering on that frame. In Mech's view, it's a recipe for disaster. He has taken a different approach and it has worked for him.

(Continued)

(Continued)

Mech frames his work today in a way that meshes with his values and beliefs—and then he delivers. He noted, "I help families discover and understand what matters most to them, and then I help them fulfill whatever that goal or destiny might be. That fits with me because I . . . believe I'm here to help steward clients who don't necessarily have the financial intelligence to get to where they want to go, to help them make good decisions, to act as their advocate." According to Mech, his clients will confirm that he does just that. As he explained, "That's an important distinction . . . because unless people have that mutual understanding or agreement that, in fact, that is your brand and that is what is delivered by the brand . . . it's not meaningful."[9]

QUESTION 4: WHAT SOLUTIONS DO YOU PROVIDE?

With your clients' needs identified, you are ready to move on to what *solutions* you are going to provide your clients. These are the things your clients are going to pay you for. Now it's all about your creating value for your client.

No longer are you subjected to a guessing game on what kind of solutions to provide for your clients, because the work you've done in defining their needs has set you up for success. All you need to do is take the time with your team to consider the solutions to which these needs logically point.

KEY CONCEPT

Knowing the needs of your client means you're halfway to serving that client. Commit to finding and providing the solutions to their problems.

Let's say your ideal clients are women in transition (women who have been widowed, have divorced, lost a job, are changing jobs, and others) and one of their *needs* is to manage their money so it lasts. The question becomes, what kind of *solutions* can you provide to help these clients ensure that their money indeed lasts over the long haul? This question could be answered a number of ways, depending on the firm, its strengths, and its vision. Here is what the test group of 50 advisors came up with:

- Spending plan
- Retirement income service
- Women's education
- Quarterly seminars
- Long-term care
- Annuities
- Portfolio management
- Estate plan
- Trusted IRA
- Tax issue guidance
- Social connection/emotional empathy

What services would you come up with? However you answer this question will help you further clarify what your frame has the potential to look like in the future.

Another way to look at this piece of the framing process is as defining what wealth management looks like for your firm. You know that wealth management is more than investment management or sales; you know that true wealth management is meant to be comprehensive. What needs to be clarified now is how you want to define wealth management for your firm. Here are some questions to help you and your team engage in this part of the process:

- Look at each of the needs of your clients. What one or more solutions do you believe could address each need?
- If the client were your son, daughter, niece, nephew, dear friend, or anyone that you cared about deeply, what kind of solutions would you want to make sure they had access to?
- Imagine you had unlimited time, human capital, and money at your disposal. What kind of solutions would you be excited about developing, providing, and/or connecting your client to?
- Imagine you are at a conference dedicated to your ideal client type, and you display a poster with all of the solutions you can provide for this group. List 10 items that you'd be sure to put on this list.

As you work through this piece of the process, give yourself the freedom to imagine anything and everything. Brainstorm in a team setting and/or in solitude with a blank sheet of paper and a pen, with a plan to take it into the team setting at a later time. Think about how you brainstorm best and get others on your team involved, too. Bottom line: The sky's the limit during this idea stage, so plan to set all constraints, concerns, and reality checks aside.

What to Do When Your Current Clients Don't Need Your Services

At the core of defining a new frame for your team and your firm is the process of aligning the kind of services your clients need and the kind of services you are willing, interested, and able to provide. As you engage in the process of defining your new frame, it will become clear to you whether the services you currently provide match up with your ideal client profile. If not, that's a sign that something's gotta give. There are only two ways out of the dilemma: Change your clients or change your services! The answer is up to you, but if a gap is discovered, this issue must be addressed.

While considering what solutions you will be providing to your ideal clients, think, too, about the development of your own intellectual property. For example, you may have developed a specific approach to wealth management that you've named and that you can trademark if you haven't already. You may have a step-by-step planning process, designed to help a business owner exit his or her business, that you can document and formalize. Or you may have knowledge that you can convert into checklists, questionnaires, and assessments that you can give to your clients to help them make decisions about how best to manage their wealth.

INDUSTRY INSIGHT: TURNING INTELLECTUAL CAPITAL INTO INTELLECTUAL PROPERTY

Michael Tannery, cofounder and CEO of Tannery & Company Wealth Management, has done a fantastic job of turning his company's ideas and processes into intellectual property that his firm can use to win new business and also share with existing clients so they can better manage their wealth.

One of the novel ideas that turned into a product Tannery and his firm created is a workbook titled *I Was Married, I Got a Divorce, I'm a Success.* The father of three children, Tannery went through his own divorce 17 years ago, during which he experienced the emotional and financial issues associated with being a divorced parent. Tannery used this experience to create a workbook that his firm now gives to its clients who are undergoing a divorce.

The book has 12 exercises focused on not just the financial aspects of divorce but the emotional aspects, too. Tannery explained that after his divorce, "what I understood wasn't just the financial side . . . I understood the emotional timeline that occurs."[10] Tannery took that knowledge and created a book that helps his clients.

This workbook also helps Tannery open the door to lasting partnerships with other professionals. When he and his team call on family lawyers, they give them this book. The lawyers quickly realize that this is a differentiating factor for Tannery's firm versus other financial services firms they typically encounter.

Tannery is also sure to share success stories of the way he has been able to help his divorcing clients. One of his favorites is how he was able to help two clients swap houses: a client in the middle of a divorce who needed to downsize and another client who was ready to upsize. In the process, Tannery saved both clients a total of $60,000 in real estate commissions.

Another favorite success story is the time one of his clients, a divorced woman, asked for suggestions on how to collect an outstanding business bill from a client. After taking Tannery's advice and successfully obtaining the check (in the thousands of dollars), the woman called Tannery to thank him and said before hanging up, "You are the best husband I never had. I love you."[11] She called right back, at which point Tannery said, "It's okay, I love you too," and they laughed. Tannery describes this kind of relationship with the client as not being "a romantic love, but it's just an incredible connection and trust because they know that we're here for them no matter what's going on." Tannery gets that the value of his firm to his clients is first and foremost the trusting relationship.

In sharing these client-centered success stories, along with his divorce workbook, with the professionals he is courting to become part of his network, Tannery frames his firm as a true advocate for the client. Not surprisingly, he finds that these professionals are interested in learning more about partnering with him.

COACHING CORNER

Pick your favorite questions in the previous two sections on identifying client needs and generating solutions. Grab a blank sheet of paper or open up your computer and write the answers. Alternatively, find a colleague to do this exercise with and talk through it out loud.

QUESTION 5: WHAT OTHER TRUSTED ADVISORS WORK WITH YOUR TARGET GROUP?

After all of that productive brainstorming, you may have a substantial list of possible solutions you can provide to your target client. Before fears can possibly take over and stop you in your tracks with questions like, "How am I going to deliver all of these services?" or "Is my team really up to the challenge?" you can work on answering with your team the next question involved in defining your new frame: Which other trusted advisors work with your target group?

These trusted advisors are an important piece of your new frame. Once you get them on board, you can turn that wish list of client solutions into true wealth management that you, your firm, and your professional network can deliver. Check out the following list of trusted professionals that my test group of 50 advisors generated for their target clients of women executives.

CPAs	Recruiters/ headhunters	Contractors
Attorneys		Architects
Divorce attorneys	Insurance specialists	Salon/day spa employees
Psychologists	Human resources	
Physicians	Bankers	Teachers, camp counselors
Spiritual counselors	IT specialists	
Advertising/PR firms	Commercial realtors	American Business Women's Association
Women's organizations	Interior designers	

National Association of Women Business Owners	Affinity groups within corporations	Churches
Chamber of Commerce	Business journals and industries	Book clubs
	Women's magazines and periodicals	Meetup.com
		Volunteer/ community services
		Alumnae

How's that for being thorough? Your list does not need to be as long as this one, but it does show how expansive one's thinking can be when engaging in this exercise.

There is nothing fancy or complex about generating a list of trusted professionals for your target market. It's a matter of taking the time to think this piece through. Here are a few questions to help you and your team work through this step with ease.

- Look at each solution you've written down for your target clients. What kind of professional/s would be in a good position to offer that solution?
- Think about the other professionals you currently have a relationship with or have always meant to reach out to. Which of these professionals would be well suited to offer additional support to your target client?
- Pull out the data collected as you were engaging in the Client-Wise Conversation™. What trusted advisors did your clients share then who also would be suited to supporting your newly identified target client?

Because their wealth management needs are diverse, clients most likely need support from more than you and your firm, yet they probably don't want to have to look elsewhere. If you can take the guesswork out of whom else they should be talking to and introduce them to other trusted professionals who can support them, your clients' trust and appreciation of you will grow. And in the future, when they need another service or introduction, who will they naturally go to? You. That puts you in a position to provide them with additional services, make other introductions, build more goodwill, and allow the cycle of loyalty to continue.

KEY CONCEPT

It may be impossible for your firm to provide every single service that your clients need. Building a network of professionals to whom you can refer clients for the services you don't cover still leaves you in the position of being the answer to your clients' questions. This is a good position from which to build trust, goodwill, rapport, satisfaction, and loyalty.

QUESTION 6: WHAT TEAM WOULD YOU LIKE TO BUILD TO FULFILL YOUR NOBLE PURPOSE?

You know what your noble purpose is, who your ideal client is, what their known and unknown needs are, what solutions you'd like to provide them to meet their needs, and who the trusted advisors are that can help in effectively providing these solutions to your clients. You are ready to determine what team you will need and want to build to fulfill your noble purpose and support the needs of your ideal clients. The following chapter will guide you on how to fully address Question 6. But for now, start to think about what kind of team you will need to form. You've already started to consider what trusted advisors to add to your network or external team, so begin to think about who will need to be on your internal team. What kind of professionals will you want to hire; what roles will need to be filled; and what traits, values, and characteristics do you want to add to your team?

KEY CONCEPT

The previous steps of redefining your frame have identified your noble purpose, who your ideal client is, what your clients need, what you can provide, and what other services your professional network enables. The final step of defining your new frame is to figure out who you need on your firm's internal team to meet the needs of your clients.

CAPTURING YOUR VALUE

When it comes to defining your new frame, the sum of the whole is greater than any individual part. When you bring together your noble purpose, your ideal client, the solutions you provide to meet the needs of your ideal clients, and the teams—internal and external—that you put together to deliver those solutions, you have created a frame for your firm that will allow you to deliver your value!

Wouldn't it be great if you could explain your value to clients in a clear way? That's when your marketing materials will come in handy. Your marketing materials will describe your purpose, who you do serve, and how you deliver value.

THE eXchange™
Online Tool 7.2: Brainstorming the New Frame

Noble purpose, target market, needs, solutions, centers of influence, and value-delivering team, what a comprehensive list! For access to a step-by-step guide for defining your new frame, including additional brainstorming ideas for your team to tackle, go to the eXchange™ at youvebeenframed.clientwise.com.

 Just Say No to the Elevator Speech

Advisors often have an insatiable appetite for coming up with the perfect statement to provide when asked, "What do you do?" It's the proverbial elevator speech: how to pitch your company in a single sentence before the lift hits the tenth floor. "Hello, my name is Ray. I am a wealth advisor at Newco Wealth Management and we provide peace of mind." Ridiculous! The elevator speech worked in an era of sales, when advisors were pitching. Today, in the era of partnership, it usually falls flat.

While there are certainly times that you will need to be able to pitch your company quickly, I encourage you to think about how to best describe your noble purpose and the types of clients your firm is built

(Continued)

(Continued)

to serve. Yes, it's okay to be specific and authentic. You might even be surprised at the reaction you get from others, who are used to hearing the typical elevator pitch.

The elevator speech was, in many ways, based on capturing a client's attention (self-serving). Your authentic description of your company, grounded in your noble purpose and confident in your depiction of your ideal client, is more focused in how you are able to help the client (other directed). It is less about having a handy marketing statement and more about taking a genuine approach that is in alignment with your firm's values and capabilities. Focus on articulating your client's real needs and being client centered and client wise.

What's more, the elevator speech often stays right there in the elevator, whereas being authentic about who you serve and how you serve them will guide all that your company does. It will show up in your annual client reviews, team meetings, conversations with other professionals, hiring practices, and more. It will also show up throughout your marketing material, which will become clear when you engage in the next step of the reframing process: building your new frame.

CONCLUSION

Whether you answer the six questions related to defining your new frame in a daylong meeting with your team or flesh them out over a series of team meetings, this process will take some time and dedication, but it's worth it. If you engage in this process authentically, giving it the time and mental "open space" it deserves, the end result, honestly, will be magnificent.

You will have the words to convey to your clients the power of what you can do for them. You will be able to deliver services customized to their very needs, and, in return, your clients will develop a love for what you can do for them. They will trust you, appreciate you, and remain loyal to you. They will want to tell others about you, and they might even do a happy dance in your honor when they wake up in the morning.

NOTES

1. Erin Botsford, personal interview, March 10, 2015, transcript, p. 5.

2. The Botsford Group, "Botsford Financial Group—Founder's Message," video, 3:18, posted March 5, 2015, www.botsfordfinancial.com/index.php.

3. The Botsford Group, "About Us: Our Firm," accessed April 9, 2015, www.botsfordfinancial.com/our_firm.php.

4. Gregory Mech, personal interview, March 16, 2015, transcript, p. 2.

5. Ibid.

6. Ibid.

7. Rishiraj Ranawat, "Tesla Roadster: The Car of the Future?," Ozytive, February 28, 2013, www.ozytive.com/2013/02/28/tesla-roadster-the-car-of-the-future/.

8. Bradley Berman, "Henrik Fisker Resigns from Fisker Automotive," *Wheels* (blog), *New York Times*, March 13, 2013, http://wheels.blogs.nytimes.com/2013/03/13/henrik-fisker-resigns-from-fisker-automotive/?_r=0.

9. Gregory Mech, personal interview, March 16, 2015, transcript, p. 3.

10. Ibid., p. 6.

11. Ibid., p. 8.

CHAPTER **8**

Building Your New Frame

N ow that you know what your new frame is going to be—that is, you've defined your ideal clients, client needs, corporate solutions, professional network, and value statement in step 2 of the reframe process—you are ready to go about step 3: building your new frame (see Figure 8.1).

Building the new frame includes three key elements:

1. Reframing your team
2. Reframing yourself as a leader
3. Reframing your marketing assets

Every successful and sustainable reframe includes each of these parts.

First, you want to know how to best design your team. It's time to develop, build, adjust, tweak, and/or augment your team so you can deliver the wealth management services outlined in your new frame from step 2 of the reframing process.

The human capital is what is going to make your newly framed business "go." Remember, you may think you're in the wealth management business, but really, you're in the human capital business that

Figure 8.1 Reframe Step 3: Build Your Frame

delivers wealth management. Your team is integral to the delivery of your value proposition.

You start with building your team first because your team has the potential to provide valuable contributions to the new marketing materials you'll soon be creating, whether from a content, a design, or an administrative capacity. Your team is also likely to be featured in your marketing materials, so it's best to figure out what your team looks like now.

Advisors often believe they have their team in place. But start to think about the sustainability of growth. Is the team you have today the team you will need to deliver your newly framed wealth management services? How confident are you that you have built a strategic hiring plan that will get you where you are planning to go? Have you considered all of the capacity that you'll need to expand or adjust for, the new capabilities that you'll likely want to add and grow into, and the creativity that you believe is necessary to create the interdependency that you desire for the team to soar? It bears repeating that you need to consider each of these three parts: capacity considerations, capability and technical skills, and creativity in those others you'll need to make your firm grow exponentially.

Once your updated team has been put together, you will continue to build your new frame by assessing and reframing your own leadership skills to make them maximally effective. There are several behaviors, many of which will be covered in this chapter, that you can adopt to help you bring your team together to successfully deliver your reframed wealth management services.

With a strong team supporting your reframed organization, you and the team will be ready to co-create your marketing communications plan and strategy. Included in that marketing plan is the task of developing communications that can be delivered across five modes of communication—phone, mail, electronic media, in person, and third party. Here the focus will be on putting your new frame into evidence at each of the different points of contact through which your client sees you, your potential client meets you, and the professionals with whom you interact encounter you.

Remember, at this point, many advisors might just *tell* the team what they are building rather than involving them and encouraging them to share their best thinking and input. It will not be so if you are truly engaging in a team and leadership reframe. These reframes will have you valuing every team member's contribution and inviting them into the process of collaboration to meet common goals that advance your organization and the clients' goals, including the creation of your valuable marketing assets.

Together you can work to convey information on your new frame consistently across all media and points of interaction with others. Consistency, consistency, consistency! It is only through the consistent message you communicate to others that your reframe can occur effectively. That consistency needs to occur with you as a leader, with your team, and with all of your other trusted advisors—those professional advocates you are including as part of your extended wealth management team.

 KEY CONCEPT

An essential part of the reframing process is your team. Not only do they deliver your firm's services to your clients, but they also are a source of information, insight, and (consistent!) messaging during the reframing process.

LONE RANGER TO LEADER™

The following may be the most important part of any chapter in this entire book. No matter what the stage of your business, whether you are a sole practitioner (*solopreneur*), you have built a successful team structure, or you are a partner in a larger firm, the journey toward developing powerful leadership skills is exactly that: a journey. For our industry to evolve and mature, we must together focus on building our own leadership skills as well as those of the leaders of tomorrow. It will take time and effort; it will involve adjustments, new behaviors, and new ways of thinking. But no longer will it be acceptable to go it alone; no longer will it be acceptable to move as a lone ranger.

The industry is in fact moving in the right direction. At ClientWise, we recently conducted a survey of more than 600 wealth management professionals to gauge whether they are on teams, and, if so, what these teams look like. In fact, 80 percent of those who responded indicated they were working in a team setting! Figure 8.2 shows some of the interesting results we learned from those respondents who were working on a team.

If we are going to be honest and authentic in our approach with clients when we are telling them that we'll be there through life transitions with them, then we need to lead effective teams that can deliver to our clients now and in the future. No one advisor can be there always and forever, whereas the team has depth and reliability that can be trusted to truly and consistently deliver.

So the journey of building your team is in large part the journey of transforming from lone ranger to leader. Many advisors get stuck playing the part of the lone ranger because for a long time, they were

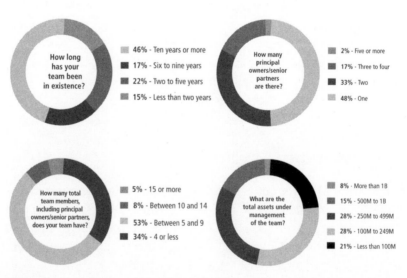

Figure 8.2 Team Makeup of More Than 300 Advisors (Answered by 323 Respondents)

the primary and sole practitioner who acquired the client, met with the client to build a plan, went back to the office, input all the data into the software, built the plan, went back to the client and represented the plan, and then went back to the office to put all the information to work and to manage the portfolio. Even those who years ago decided to build a team or even partner with other advisors to build a firm often find themselves working now in silos, alone, as lone rangers. For our industry to sustain itself and grow in providing true value for the client, we must evolve from lone rangers to leaders.

It's true that behind the scenes, these lone rangers may have had a support person doing a lot of the support-person kind of work, and yet in many cases the client really never saw any other professional other than that sole practitioner. Even in some financial advisory firms where there are already teams of professionals in place, there may still be a lead advisor operating with a lone ranger mind-set by hanging on to being the individual who's the primary contact for each client. This approach cannot sustain itself—in this model, the real loser is the client.

Unfortunately, a lone ranger can only manage a finite number of clients. What's more, true wealth management is too diverse to be handled by one professional. Trying to funnel all of the necessary wealth management tasks through one lone ranger–style lead advisor is likely doing a disservice to the client as the advisor struggles to meet the full breadth of important client demands.

 INDUSTRY INSIGHT: BUILDING A TEAM FROM SCRATCH

Jonathan Beukelman, Managing Director of Wealth Management at the Beukelman Group, remembers when he first built a real team for his firm. The first big transition came when he moved from having a part-time virtual assistant that he shared with other firms to hiring his own in-house assistant. It meant investing extra money to hire someone to have in house, all the more so because Beukelman recruited a financial advisor, rather than an admin person, to do the job. The advisor had to take a leap of faith, as it was technically a step down on his career ladder, but Beukelman promised him that he was on a mission to grow the company and he would carry this advisor with him.[1]

(Continued)

(Continued)

Looking back, Beukelman has no regrets about the decision to hire his own assistant. It seemed to kick-start the beginning of something new, different, bigger, and better for his company. As Beukelman noted, "Once you get your own assistant, you feel internally that you actually have something."[2] With the support of an assistant, he found that he could communicate his value proposition better. Together, they could go deeper with clients and get more things done.

Today, Beukelman's firm has seven employees, and his initial employee—the advisor assistant—has grown with the firm. He has trained each new employee who has come on board, getting them up to speed, and he has run the business side of the firm for a long time, freeing up Beukelman to focus on other areas of the business.

To help clients get comfortable with the idea of working with a team, Beukelman and his firm are careful to share the team frame early on with prospects and new clients. They let clients know that there are multiple people on the team who will be working with the client in their particular areas of expertise. "For me, being able to communicate to clients, each individual person on the team and what their skill set is and how it comes together for the client, works pretty well," Beukelman explained.[3]

Beukelman takes pride in the fact that he does not have a team where each advisor simply works with his or her own set of clients in isolation; instead, his team tends to touch each client from the vantage point of their own expertise. Although the process is "not without challenges,"[4] Beukelman finds that as clients get to know the team, they typically learn who to reach out to in order to receive the specific support they require at a given time. According to him, the whole process runs pretty seamlessly.

The interesting thing is that even if every hiring decision that was made in putting together the team wasn't perfect, it all worked out in the end. Even if people did not land in the right spots when they first came on board the Beukelman Group, they were eventually moved to the area that best suited them.

Perhaps this is because Beukelman was smart enough to hire folks that had the right characteristics to fit into the vision he had for his firm's culture. He noted, "I had people that were extremely upbeat, that could work with clients on a consistent basis, and that would be there and committed to them."[5] As Beukelman interviewed people for his team, he looked for people who owned the things they were involved in. He wanted people who would take the business and the caretaking of clients' money as seriously as he did, and he found them.

At ClientWise, we have developed an extensive, four-part, 16-hour executive training program to help advisors grow from lone rangers to leaders and to help their teams evolve from lone ranger teams to true teams, not just work groups. (A *work group* is made up of staff members and/or contractors to whom the advisor hands off work; each member of the work group has individual goals that the advisor has set, but the group has not come together as a whole to mutually define success.) While all of material from the executive training program cannot be covered in this single chapter and will likely be the topic of a different book, I outline here fundamental aspects of that journey to help you build the new team frame in terms of who is on your team and how you can lead them most effectively.

 KEY CONCEPT

It's tempting to stick with a lone ranger approach to wealth management, but it's not necessarily in the clients' best interest for you to do so. Allowing a true team with diverse talents to handle the many tasks involved with effectively handling your clients' needs does not mean giving up control. Rather, sharing the work with your team's talented members will free you up to focus on your strengths and to build a stronger business.

Building Your Team

While defining your new frame in step 2, you took time to identify the professionals who would be on your *external team*; now it's time to get clear on what your *internal team* will look like.

If you are a solopreneur, you will be assessing whether you want or need to have an internal team and, if so, what it will look like. If you already stand at the head of a team in your organization, you can use this step to assess what changes, if any, need to be made to your team roster to be able to successfully and sustainably deliver on your new frame for your clients, now and in the future.

Here are some questions to consider as you engage in the brainstorming process of who you want and need on your new team:

- Are you prepared and committed to building an internal team to successfully deliver your newly framed wealth management services, or will your external team be sufficient? How comfortable are you leading the team, or do you want to bring in someone else to be CEO, given your particular interests, strengths, and skill set?

■ Are you willing to take the time and energy to truly lead an internal team, not just run a work group? How open are you to learning and improving new leadership skills so you can be the most effective leader you can be?

■ What will you have to let go of to become the most effective leader for your team and your clients? How committed are you to developing the human capital on your team, codesigning professional development plans, and giving feedback and advice from a collaborative perspective? Are you ready and willing to do so? If not, what do you need to work through before you can move forward? While you may have imagined your work as a technician or as a financial advisor, how have you imagined yourself leading your wealth management firm?

■ On a scale of 1 to 10 (1 being lowest functioning and 10 being highest functioning), how effective do you believe your current team is at achieving its goals? If less than 10, where could changes be made to improve team functioning? Personnel? Job roles? Leadership? Team culture?

By beginning to answer these questions, you will set the stage for understanding what kind of internal team makes the most sense for your firm. You will get clearer on your own willingness to lead a team and discover obstacles that may be standing in your way.

 Building a Team with the Right Capabilities

Although your team will have some unique requirements given your particular brand of wealth management, there are some foundational capabilities that every financial services team should have:

■ Rainmaking
■ Relationship management

- Technical capability
- Operational and administrative structure

At ClientWise, we recommend having the following three different kinds of advisors to help cover these capabilities. First, there is the *senior lead advisor,* who is dedicated primarily to rainmaking activities. This advisor's secondary role is as a strategic relationship manager, who only gets involved when a more senior partner is needed to help make a crucial decision.

Next, there is a *lead advisor,* whose primary role is to be a relationship advisor. Focused on complete client care, the lead advisor ensures that no accounts are leaving and that the team is delivering on the promises made to the client.

Last, there is a *service advisor,* who takes care of all follow-through and follow-up. He or she is essentially responsible for completing the work promised to the client. Sometimes the service advisor is front and center with clients, and other times he or she is behind the scenes, making sure all client information and paperwork is complete and in order.

It bears saying that as you undergo this process of building a team, not everyone has the same desire to step into the leadership role. If you happen to find yourself feeling uncertain about taking on that mantle, be honest with yourself. Talk to a coach credentialed by the International Coach Federation who specializes in working in the financial services industry or perhaps a mentor or respected other. Then give yourself time to determine whether it's a matter of moving past fear and potential obstacles or if you would simply prefer to spend your time engaging in the core of the financial services technical work rather than leading others who do so. You may also need to seriously consider how you are developing the future company and developing tomorrow's leaders, today. After all, if you are truly doing legacy work, leadership requires you to plan ahead for tomorrow. You deserve it. Your clients deserve it. And the firm you're building will have greater enterprise value.

Most of us have told the clients that we'll be there with them through their life transitions, so let's do that. It's simply not enough having a buy–sell agreement with another advisor down the block, with whom the client hasn't built a long-lasting relationship. It's not enough if you work in a large brokerage firm and you're counting on the office manager to distribute your client roster to other advisors in the office should something happen to you or you retire. You must plan, and you must plan ahead. Again, you deserve it. It's your life's work, after all. And, more important, your clients deserve it!

If in doubt regarding whether to build an internal team, explore what your goals for your company are and make some decisions about what is most important to you: doing work you love in the way you love to do it versus growing the company and its potential reach. Realistically, remaining a solopreneur (even with an external team to support you) may limit the number of clients you have and the depth of services you can offer. Yet this is your life and your business, and you get to make the call on how you want to shape and run both. Be conscious, get clear, and move forward in the way that is right for you. However you choose to structure your business, though, always keep in mind the promises you've made to clients and make sure you can follow through on them.

When you are ready to engage in building your internal team, check out the Coaching Corner exercise that follows.

 COACHING CORNER

Take some time to contemplate who you would like to have on your internal team. What skill sets, characteristics, and values are essential to each person's unique role and the overall team's success? In what ways may you need to restructure your current team members' job descriptions to be able to deliver your reframed wealth management services? What personnel changes, if any, do you anticipate needing to make to create your new team? Keep in mind that any well-balanced team will be able to win new clients, manage ongoing client relationships, engage in the technical aspects of the business, and operate and run the business.

THE eXchange™

Online Tool 8.1: A Guide to Defining Your High-Performing Team

Visit the eXchange™ for a 12-question guide to defining your unique high-performing team. Also visit the eXchange™ for a strategic hiring guide, sample job descriptions, and competency-based interview questions.

Leading Your Team

The design of your new team is just the first step in getting your team ready to deliver the new frame. It's also important to assess your own behaviors and make shifts where needed so that you are the most effective leader that you can be.

Make the Transition

At ClientWise, we invite advisors to enter into 10 transitions to grow into sophisticated leaders of highly effective teams. We have found that even those advisors already serving in leadership roles find that they grow when they put in the effort to move through these transitions. Here are the first three transitions. You will either believe these or you won't. If you don't believe these, you must reassess how prepared you are to truly build a strong team. You must believe:

- I am *part of a team* instead of a lone ranger.
- I see *team success* as more important than individual success.
- I am CEO or leader of the team, which means I must consistently engage in leadership activities.

It is interesting that the word *team* shows up three times in these statements, whereas *leadership* only appears once. It is not by accident that more emphasis is put on the group than the individual here. It is only by shifting from an individual perspective to the group or team perspective that an advisor may become a true leader.

In the old days, the leader had the mind-set of "boss." The top advisor, who was usually the biggest producer, drove the agenda and goals and told the "team" what to do and how to do it. In fact, this kind of structure isn't a team at all, it's a work group. That kind of work group doesn't fly in today's business landscape. Today the leader has to be capable of having the same mentality that he or she will ask of direct reports—a mentality that he or she is part of a team and that team success is more important than individual success.

It's all part of Total Team Leadership™, a term we've coined at ClientWise that is defined as follows:

> a leader and team who engage in the exchange of leadership among themselves in a manner that evokes meaningful contribution from every team member, showcases the strengths of each team member, and advances consistent and effective group decision making.

There is a true sense of inclusiveness in this new kind of financial services leader. Gone is the old structure of leader dictating down to direct reports; instead, we see the new structure in which the leader steps into the role of equal team member and then moves fluidly from this place into the leadership role of holding the vision, facilitating, and managing as needed, while empowering every member of the team to step up and lead. The leader needs to be able to move easily between his or her role as team member and team leader, and team members must be able to easily perceive that movement. It's the magic of team in the twenty-first century. This is especially true if you plan on bringing younger talent, the millennial, into the business. In the Total Team Leadership™ model, everyone has a voice and is expected to contribute to team goals.

 KEY CONCEPT

Effective teams are no longer work groups that unthinkingly follow the orders of a hierarchically superior "boss." Rather, team members are empowered contributors who have a voice in decision making and an investment in the group's success.

How does the advisor move through these three leadership transitions? Table 8.1 shows the different behaviors that the advisor can engage in to move through these transitions successfully.

Table 8.1 Ten Behaviors for Transitioning into a Total Team Leader

Transition	Behavior
I am part of a team instead of a lone ranger.	1. Regularly act as a member of the team instead of a leader. 2. Invite the members of the team to teach you so that shared learning occurs rather than simply top-down learning. 3. Share leadership with other members of the team. 4. Model attending to team goals and not just individual goals.
I see team success as more important than individual success.	5. Move easily and often from personally oriented activity to team productivity. 6. Align and merge your individual goals into team goals and encourage your team members to do the same. 7. Celebrate and reward team behavior and success.
I am CEO or leader of the team, which means I must consistently engage in leadership activities.	8. Model team behavior. 9. Encourage team participation. 10. Feel and evidence pleasure from helping to shape team achievement.

Allowing the importance of team to permeate all that you do will create an environment that helps your team coalesce, get inspired, and move forward to achieve the common goals of the team and the organization. The way to get from here to there is to commit to making the leadership *transitions* by diving into the associated *behaviors*.

THE eXchange™

Online Tool 8.2: Ten Steps to Leading a Highly Effective Team

Visit the eXchange™ for a printable checklist of the 10 leadership behaviors you can engage in to become the most effective leader for your team.

COACHING CORNER

Look at the 10 leadership behaviors featured in Table 8.1. Where are you currently doing well? Where do you see potential for your growth? Pick three behaviors you'd like to work on and add reminders to your calendar to work on each one for a month during the next three months. Rinse and repeat.

(Continued)

(Continued)

Also, in the eXchange™, you'll find a leadership self-assessment and an assessment for team members of their leader(s). The learning comes from the gaps, where the leader evaluates him- or herself and the team members evaluate his or her leadership ability.

Finding Common Purpose

As you are practicing and implementing Total Team Leadership™, you can set your team up for success by working with them to create a common intent, or common purpose, that will bind, motivate, and guide the group toward the desired future. At ClientWise, we define common intent and purpose as follows:

> an ambition that is significant in size, aspirational in scope, and possible to achieve that will serve your clients, yourselves, and your organization.

Common intent and purpose gets at the more inspiring ideas and aims that will drive your team's definition of wealth management, who the ideal client is, what solutions you offer, and what value you bring to the client. The most valuable common intents and purposes have an aim that is broader than the team itself and that includes an emotional component. Compare the following.

> To increase assets under management by *X* percent
>
> versus
>
> To help as many individuals as possible, including ourselves, to develop sufficient financial freedom to be able to engage in work or play driven only by their passion by the time they are 60

At ClientWise, we define our common intent and purpose as the following:

> Transforming the industry, one advisor at a time. For we believe that financial advising is noble work and when we make a positive impact in the life of one advisor, we make an impact positively on the lives of hundreds, for generations to come. When we impact 10,000 or more advisors and their firms, we've helped to transform

an industry for the better, creating a more mature and everlasting industry of noble workers.

Your team's common intent and purpose will get at why you do what you do. Another way of thinking of it is, what is the real purpose of your company besides making money? Simon Sinek, in his book *Start with Why*,[6] has created a terrific model for uncovering common purpose. Sinek argues that people don't buy what you do; they buy why you do it, which is an important point to have clear in the minds of everyone on your team. If your core values—if your driving passions—do not match up with those of your potential clients, you will have a much harder time bringing those clients into your fold.

In his TED talk, Sinek used the example of Dr. Martin Luther King Jr., who inspired people to follow him not because he told people what to do but because he told them what he believed. Sinek noted that 250,000 people showed up to listen to Dr. King's "I Have a Dream" speech, not his "I Have a Plan" speech. Further, they made the often lengthy trip to hear him speak not for Dr. King, but for themselves.[7]

You can foster the creation of a common intent and purpose by doing the following:

1. Start, encourage, and continue the conversation to set common intent and purpose.
2. Ensure that the common intent and purpose are large enough and aspirational enough to both bond and motivate the team at a deep level.
3. Engage team members to continue to connect with and commit to the team's common intent and purpose.
4. Model connecting to and acting in response to the team's common intent and purpose.

Common intent and purpose reflect why teams are actually created. Teams come together to do work that is larger than an individual, where collective energy and capacity combine to achieve something that an individual could or would never do alone. Common intent and purpose also make it easy for team members individually and collectively to move in the same direction, support one another, and serve clients at the highest level.

Common intent and purpose not only work to motivate your team and help them stay clear on the team's reason for being, they can also serve as great filters when you are hiring new team members to make sure they are a good fit. They also act as useful filters for determining what kind of clients you will work with because your ideal clients will value what you do and why, as encapsulated in your common intent and purpose.

 KEY CONCEPT

Common intent and purpose will pull your current team together and help you attract and retain clients and new team members who share your vision and values.

REFRAMING YOUR MARKETING COLLATERAL

You've reframed your team and your own leadership style to help you lead your reframed team as effectively as possible. With these areas reframed, you are ready to create the marketing materials needed to effectively and consistently communicate your new frame to the world: to current clients, potential clients, other professionals, and more. These materials will be based on the frame you have defined previously in step 2: your ideal client, client needs, client solutions, professional network, and value statement.

Think Marketing Assets

The thing about a reframe is that to make it stick, you need to educate people about it while consistently communicating it. So as exciting as it may be that you have developed a new frame that caters to your clients' needs and your own interests and skill sets, it will be relatively meaningless if you don't put it into evidence across your marketing materials.

You have a new story to tell; your marketing materials need to reflect the new story so others can learn and understand it. You also need the assets that you can share with your loyal client advocates and the professional advocates who will tell your story. You must arm them with the tools and resources to make their jobs easier in supporting you and your team.

Think of your marketing materials as assets. It's a term advisors are familiar with, and I use it to help remind us of how valuable our marketing materials are to our businesses' growth, success, and sustainability. Consider some of the ways in which the term *asset* is defined, then consider these within the context of your marketing materials:

- "A resource with economic value that an individual, corporation or country owns or controls with the expectation that it will provide future benefit."[8]

- "Something valuable that an entity owns, benefits from, or has use of, in generating income."[9]

- "A useful or valuable quality, skill, or person."[10]

That last definition gets to the heart of the competitive advantage that your marketing assets can create for you. Most advisors are not marketers or branders; if you rally your own team and/or bring in marketing experts to help you brand your firm, you will not only stand out among your competitors but also increase your ability to win clients.

In sum, your marketing materials are nothing short of valuable assets for your organization. You need to invest in them—through time, brainpower, and money—and then, if you execute well, you can expect a return on that investment.

Will your marketing assets have value per se? As you can guess, my answer to that question is yes. In the near term, your marketing assets are an integral mode of acquiring new clients, keeping current clients satisfied, and providing your professional network with the communication tools for making introductions to you from new clients. If your marketing materials help you win engagements with your ideal clients and retain current clients, they are providing you with economic value in the form of dollars those new clients bring in.

 KEY CONCEPT

Your marketing materials are assets that need to describe your organization's reframe consistently. Invest time, talent, and resources into these essential tools for informing your potential clients and partners about who you are, what you do, and what you stand for.

In the longer term, your up-to-date, well-framed marketing assets can help you to sell your company successfully at the appropriate time, should you choose to do so, because they are your brand in evidence. They are an essential tool to continually attract your ideal client so you can continue to provide your firm's unique definition of wealth management services.

How many resources (time, money, and effort) are you willing to spend on your marketing assets if you know that they will bring you a high multiple in returns?

The Five Modes of a Marketing Communications Plan

It's a shift for some advisors to imagine putting a lot of energy into branding or marketing their firm. They may prefer to be out in the field meeting clients, back in the office doing the research, putting together the financial plan, or creating the client presentation. They may not have ever realized how powerful their marketing assets can be, or they may know how important they are and have just not found the time to keep them up to date.

Either way, to successfully engage in the reframe, advisors need to make it a priority to give their marketing materials an update or an overhaul. Even those advisors who already have excellent marketing assets will likely need to look into redoing and updating their materials to reflect their new frame. Designing new marketing materials is a key step in the reframing process.

Marketing assets exist across five media, as described in Table 8.2.

As you can see, there are a lot of ways to reach your ideal clients and attract them to your new brand of wealth management services. Instead of jumping into a big marketing campaign across all of these media (can you say "overwhelming"?), I encourage you to create instead a presentation that includes the key elements of your new frame. This can serve as a central resource for guiding the development of any future marketing campaigns as well as an internal training tool for your newly framed team. We call this the *capability deck.*

Creating Your Capability Deck

If you are or ever were in financial services in a corporate or large organizational setting, chances are that you have made hundreds of pitch

Table 8.2 Five Major Modes of Marketing Assets

Asset Type	Definition	Examples
Electronic	Any material that gets posted or distributed digitally to convey your frame and attract your ideal clients	Website Social media Blog Videos E-mails E-newsletter
Old-fashioned "snail mail" (print)	Any print material that gets sent to individuals via traditional mail to convey your frame and attract your ideal clients	Newsletter Annual report Financial plans Client statements Invoices Holiday greetings Special offers & announcements
Phone	Any devices used to ensure that the conversations you have with individuals over the phone convey your frame and attract ideal clients; these often come in the form of scripts that you and your team follow when engaging in phone conversations	Phone talking points and scripts for ■ speaking with potential clients ■ onboarding new clients ■ conducting phone check-ins with clients
In person	Any materials you can use or give when meeting with potential or current clients in person to convey your frame and attract and retain your ideal clients	Talking points and scripts for ■ new client meeting ■ client review Company brochure Business cards Financial plan Investment reports
Third party	Any materials you provide to your advocates, both clients and professionals, to make it easy for them to accurately frame you for potential clients and attract them to your business	Advocate brochure Referral postcards Company fact sheet Conversation scripts (phone and in person)

books in your career, maybe even thousands. It's the PowerPoint presentation with your firm's logo stamped all over it, a matching color scheme, lists of bulleted facts and figures, attention-getting quotations, colorful graphs and charts, a company vision statement, service descriptions, client promises, and clip art images that whiz onto the screen. It's a sales tool. Pitch books are old fashioned.

Instead, create a capability deck that is fully client oriented. Make it useful. Create it in a way that it will convey your new frame. Make it the most powerful presentation that you ever create, with well-constructed and highly meaningful information for helping you communicate to clients and other professionals why you do what you do, who you do it for, and how you do what you do that is unique and distinguishing. The reframe capability deck is your opportunity to pull together all of the market research and analysis that you conducted during the ClientWise Conversation™ (step 1 of the reframe) and while defining your new frame (step 2). It's your storyboard, so to speak: a springboard for communicating your new frame to clients (step 4) and your network of advocates (step 5).

Your capability deck should cover the following topics:

- Why you do what you do
- Who your firm is built to serve
- Known needs of your clients
- Unknown needs of your clients
- Solutions you provide to your clients
- Your unique, client-outcome-oriented wealth management process
- Your team of trusted professionals (internal and external)
- What the client could expect if he or she was to work with your firm, the process for becoming a client, and how the client will be served after signing on

If you have more than one ideal client type, separate these out, so each deck reflects one type's own unique needs, solutions, wealth management process, and trusted advisors. Consider whether your wealth management process has to be adjusted on the basis of the ideal client type. For example, your wealth management process would look different for professional athletes who earn income early in their careers that may need to last a lifetime compared to corporate executives who plan on working until age 55. You'll want your presentation to reflect those differences. Although the core of your presentation will likely remain consistent across client types, you may need to customize certain parts of it, such as your client engagement model.

As you build your capability deck, look back at the frame you created in step 2 of the reframing process, including any work you may have generated when completing Online Tool 7.2: Brainstorming the New Frame. Refine it and revise it as needed, including it in the capability deck to accurately convey your new frame. Once it is complete, you can use the capability deck internally to guide how you build all of your new marketing assets and as a tool to educate and frame yourself and your firm in front of clients, prospective clients, and other trusted advisors. It will also be an outstanding training tool for every member of your team.

 KEY CONCEPT

A *capability deck* is a client-oriented marketing tool that conveys not only what you can do for the client but why you do what you do, who you do it for, and how what you do is like what no one else does. It is an excellent tool for communicating your reframe.

Organizing Your Marketing Campaign

With your capability deck created, you will have a central resource to guide your new marketing campaign, which should be executed across the five marketing modes in Table 8.2: electronic, mail, phone, in person, and third party. To keep your marketing campaign manageable and ensure a professional product, consider hiring a marketing firm or outside expert to help you create and implement it. Some financial services firms are well positioned to take care of the marketing themselves—if so, you probably already know who you are. If in doubt, interview other marketing professionals who can help you. At a minimum, you will learn something in the process; at a maximum, you will find support for your firm if you ultimately decide that you need or desire it.

THE eXchange™

Online Tool 8.3: Marketing Firms to Help You Build Your Brand

We've created a resource group of marketing firms that specialize in the financial services industry. Go to the eXchange™ for a list of firms that you might find useful.

As you begin to put your marketing strategy and plan together, consider the order in which you should create your new assets. Which are essentials that must be created before you can launch the new frame, and which assets can be added later on or as you go? For example, a good website and business cards are a must at the start of the new frame, whereas referral postcards for your advocates and holiday greetings can be created down the line. You may find yourself creating talking points or scripts for phone and in-person conversations on an as-needed basis—before the next scheduled client review or your next lunch date with one of your advocates, for example.

When you have decided which campaigns you want to tackle first, give each one a name and list the following details for each:

- Expected payoff/ROI
- Target market, niche, and ideal client profile
- Possible offer(s)
- Relevant messages
- Delivery options
- Who on the team is involved
- Start and end dates of the campaign

Table 8.3 shows a sample campaign.

Table 8.3 represents just one of the infinite possibilities for how a firm may choose to construct their marketing strategy and plan. In fact, this is an example of just one particular campaign among what could be multiple campaigns to help target different types of ideal clients. For example, the financial services firm represented in Table 8.3 might also include pediatric physician assistants and pediatric nurse practitioners on their ideal client list, which might require two additional customized marketing campaigns.

Table 8.3 Marketing Campaign Example

Campaign	Expected Payoff/ ROI	Target Market	Ideal Client Profile	Possible Offer(s)	Relevant Messages	Delivery Options
Pediatrician outreach	75–100 client leads generated	Physicians	Pediatricians w/ practices ≤ 5 years old	■ One free session of wealth management counseling ■ Complimentary financial plans for physician's family ■ Link to a downloadable checklist: *Wealth Management Issues for the Pediatrician Who Owns an Independent Practice*	■ We have been successfully working with physicians for over 15 years to mitigate risk and build sustainable wealth management strategies. ■ We have spoken to more than 250 pediatricians' offices nationwide to understand their needs, and we have developed targeted solutions to address them.	■ Quarterly e-newsletter to existing database of 2,500 physicians ■ Postcard mailer to 2,000 pediatricians' offices ■ Sponsor a lunch at national pediatricians' conference in May

What will your marketing strategy and plan look like? Which campaigns will it involve and how can these campaigns be executed? As you contemplate the execution of your marketing strategy, plan to prioritize campaigns and phase them in over time to ensure you and your team can successfully manage them and get the most out of them. Brainstorm with abandon; plan with reality in mind; execute with consistency; and enjoy watching the very real results as your new ideal clients come in the door over time.

THE eXchange™
Online Tool 8.4: Marketing Campaign Organizer™

It's time to create your marketing campaign. Visit the eXchange™ to download and print a Marketing Campaign Organizer™ that will allow you to outline your next marketing campaign, including target market, ideal client profile, possible offers, relevant messages, delivery options, who is involved, start and end dates, and expected ROI.

CONCLUSION

The creation of marketing assets is admittedly a big task and will take time. Have a plan and engage others to help you create milestones for all of the assets your firm would like to build to reflect your new frame or enhance your previous frame, based on what you've now co-created as a team. For those tempted to succumb to the mental block of "I can't do it!" I offer the following advice.

First, you've got a team now; enlist them in working toward your common intent and purpose.

Second, although compliance is a very real consideration when it comes to how you can legally present your firm in your marketing materials, move ahead by investigating the rules of what you can and can't do and consult an expert when needed. Instead of leading with "I can't," start with what it is that you really do and stand for, then partner with those in the compliance area to help your message come alive in a way that clearly and authentically frames what you do.

Last, engage the professional advice and guidance of a marketing consultant or hire an expert to work in house to help you do the custom writing, designing, and publishing that will be required. Your message to your firm's ideal client, distributed across multiple media, must not get stale.

While this may currently be problematic for advisors affiliated with any of the large brokerage firms today, this will need to change in time. The new rules for marketing today, called *inbound marketing* or *content marketing*, mean that if you want to be known as an expert, you must consistently publish your content so you are viewed as relevant.

For those of you who are able to do this now, get more serious about how you can put yourself forward as an expert in your field and among those your firm is truly built to serve. Build a terrific marketing organization that communicates all that you do, so you can get to serving many others for generations to come.

When excellent marketing is not just window dressing but opens the door to excellent client support, our whole industry moves forward. Invest in creating authentic marketing assets, take the time to build the right team for your particular kind of wealth management, and find the courage and patience to push your own leadership skills ever higher, into the realm of "we are a team." In doing so, the frame that you and your team have so consciously created and constructed for your clients will become a living reality that inspires others in the industry—and even beyond—to do the same.

NOTES

1. Jonathan Beukelman, personal interview, March 13, 2015, transcript, p. 6.
2. Ibid.
3. Ibid.
4. Ibid.
5. Ibid., p. 7.
6. Simon Sinek, *Start with Why: How Great Leaders Inspire Everyone to Take Action* (New York: Portfolio, 2011).
7. "Start with Why—How Great Leaders Inspire Action," YouTube video, 18:01, from a TEDxPugetSound talk, posted by TEDx Talks, September 28, 2009, www.youtube .com/watch?v=u4ZoJKF_VuA.
8. *Investopedia: Dictionary,* s.v. "Asset," accessed April 2, 2015, www.investopedia.com/ terms/a/asset.asp.
9. *BusinessDictionary.com,* s.v. "Asset," accessed April 2, 2015, www.businessdictionary .com/definition/asset.html.
10. *Cambridge Dictionaries Online,* s.v. "Asset," retrieved April 2, 2015, http://dictionary. cambridge.org/dictionary/british/asset.

PART III

Now What?

CHAPTER **9**

Teaching Others How to Frame You

Renewing Relationships

The preparation for your reframe is complete. You've collected data from your clients and professional network; you've used it, along with your team brainstorm, to inform how you want to define your new frame; and you've built your new frame by revamping your team and creating your new marketing assets. Your new frame is now ready to share with your clients. This is step 4 of the reframing process (see Figure 9.1). At ClientWise, we refer to it as *renewing relationships* because you are not just telling your client about your new frame, you are focusing on strengthening your relationship with the client more than ever as you make it clear that the reframe is based on all you've learned from your clients and is there to help you serve the client better.

You may be thinking, "But I've just tweaked our brand—why do I need to make a production of the rollout?" First, give yourself and your team the credit everyone deserves. After all, it took a great deal

Figure 9.1 Reframe Step 4: Renew Relationships

of effort to commit to and follow through on this very important work, and you all deserve recognition for that work. Second, you may have a good handle on what you do and what you've always done, but remember that your clients may not have always seen you in the frame you think you have for yourself. If nothing else, reaching out now gives you a reason to renew your relationship with your clients while ensuring that you and your clients are currently on the same page, looking at the same frame.

As with each of the previous steps of the reframe, step 4 involves a process imbued with intent. This step's focus is on educating the client on your new frame within the context of renewing your relationship with the client. You will be teaching your client about your new frame, but doing so in a way that is grounded in the client relationship and your partnership together.

It is not a top-down approach of "Hey, client, this is our new brand!" but instead a partnering approach that began when you asked for client feedback during the ClientWise Conversation™ (step 1) and is now logically progressing as you return to the client with an update on what you've built after collecting client feedback. In Figure 9.2, compare and contrast these two approaches to delivering the new frame.

In step 4, as throughout the reframing process, the client will always be at the center of what you do. This process began with clients when you collected data from them, and it continued with clients when you analyzed their feedback and used it to inform how you wanted to define your new frame. You also spent a great deal of time envisioning who your ideal clients would be, and now you are returning to your clients to reinvigorate your relationships with a check-in and the positive news on all you have been building to better serve them.

It's all about authentically renewing your relationship with the client—sharing with the client what you've learned from client

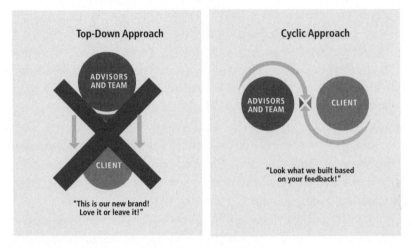

Figure 9.2 Sharing the New Frame with Your Clients

feedback, informing him or her why you are designing the firm the way you now are, and inviting the client to engage with you as you grow into a new and even better version of your organization.

KEY CONCEPT

When presenting the new frame, plan to renew your relationship with your client, whose feedback shaped your current frame and whose future feedback will influence changes yet to come.

There are three major aspects to renewing the client relationship: presenting the new frame to your existing clients at an in-person meeting, actively transitioning your existing clients to working with your new and improved team, and acquiring new clients for your new company. It all begins with the Client Renewal Conversation.

DELIVERING THE FRAME, DELIVERING THE FIRM

You've rebuilt your marketing assets, and you now have a capability deck that showcases with whom you work, what you provide your clients in terms of solutions and value, and why. Now you're ready to set up meetings with your existing clients to share your new frame with them. You are going to have a Client Renewal Conversation in which you reframe yourself with clients who have known you a certain way for so long.

How long have your clients known you, and how were you framed when they first met you, perhaps long ago? How much has your firm evolved since then, and how much has your own role changed? You will be having the Client Renewal Conversation with existing clients who already know you as a firm—and perhaps have known you a particular way for some time now. This conversation is about getting these individuals comfortable with and even excited about your reframed firm and the potential value it can bring to them.

If you recall how to get the most out of the ClientWise Conversation™, you will likely see some similarities between the best ways to approach the ClientWise Conversation™ and to have the Client Renewal Conversation. Here are the important elements of the Client Renewal Conversation:

- *Start by inviting your clients to meet in person for the Client Renewal Conversation.* It's easier to make a connection when face-to-face than over the phone, and this typically provides you more space and time to connect with the client.

- *Come from a position of strength* when you invite your clients to meet and when you speak to them at the meeting itself. Explain how you are a learning organization and always working to improve your service to clients. You're excited to share with them some ways you plan to better serve your clients and get their continued feedback.

- *Plan to meet with each of your clients to introduce your new frame to them.* Think about which clients you need to meet with personally versus which clients your team members may be best positioned to meet with. For example, if you have expanded your team to include a lead advisor who will be handling certain relationships as the primary advisor, it may make sense for that advisor to meet with those clients. Consider issues like how comfortable you expect your client to be in meeting with you versus other team members, and decide on the basis of your expectations for success.

- *Bring key members of your team to the meeting.* Whereas you attended the ClientWise Conversation™ solo, so as not to overwhelm or "team up" on the client, the Client Renewal Conversation is a good time to introduce your clients to any new members of your team. But get your clients' permission to bring additional people; if they would prefer to meet only with you, respect that and plan to transition them over to your new team in the future. As you bring team members to the meeting, you may not be taking as much of a lead as you had in the past. You're allowing others to share leadership and take ownership of the meeting.

- *Showcase your new frame* by walking the clients through your capability presentation. I call this process "delivering the firm." Share with the clients who your new and improved firm is built to serve, how you serve them, and why you serve them. Answer for them the following questions: What are your solutions and how will these meet the needs of your clients? What is your unique wealth management process? What value do you bring to the client? Who is on your team to make all of this possible?

- *Be consistent and clear as you deliver your message.* If you want people to think differently about your firm, you have to explain your new frame in a way that is understandable and consistent throughout. Make sure that your words and visual aids at the meeting all match up with one another and the new frame.

- *Highlight your new team and your own role in the new frame.* If your role has changed in the new frame, let your clients know what new responsibilities you will be carrying versus delegating and why. Introduce your new team members and let the clients know that these changes will allow you to deliver the full value you've promised for the benefit of the clients. Ask the clients for permission to bring team members onto their account.

- *Listen to your clients' reactions and feedback.* Take the time to observe your clients' reactions to the new frame; ask for questions, feedback, and input. Your relationship with each client is a partnership, so clients' voices really matter.

KEY CONCEPT

The Client Renewal Conversation consists of scheduling in-person meetings with your clients to showcase your new frame. Plan on opening from a position of strength, being clear and consistent in your message, highlighting the new team and new roles in the frame, and listening to client feedback and reactions.

As much as you are talking during the Client Renewal Conversation, you are also coming from a place of curiosity and listening. This is an opportunity to show clients that you listened to them during the ClientWise Conversation™ and that your new frame incorporates what you learned. It's also an important time to gauge your client's reaction to your new frame and respond to it.

As during the ClientWise Conversation™, it's important to be open to feedback rather than defensive. Respond to client concerns with curiosity and interest and be prepared to listen for what the client is really saying (e.g., "Tell me more." "Can you say more about that?" "I'm really glad you took the time to share your thoughts on this.").

It can be helpful, too, to redirect the client to the benefits of your new frame, underscoring or reviewing the ways in which you anticipate your new frame can bring the client greater wealth, offer the client greater support, save the client time, and so on. I've often found that as long as the reframe will benefit clients (i.e., you can answer what I call the WIIFM question, or "What's in it for me?"), they are fine with the new and improved firm. After all, clients do want to see that you are growing, improving, and learning: Expansion on your part benefits them.

By being intentional in your communications with clients and even explaining how your reframe is grounded in integrity—reflective of your firm's strengths and passions—you will help to build trust with clients and, with trust, loyalty.

As you engage in the Client Renewal Conversation, plan as well to clarify the answer to the question, How will you be able to deliver on the promise made to clients that you will be here for them through life transitions? You can't live forever, which means you may not actually be there for your clients through all of life's transitions; your team, however, can.

During the Client Renewal Conversation, you can highlight for clients the growth that you have planned for your team to ensure your firm's sustainability. Another way of saying this is that you've made strategic hiring decisions and you've got a solid succession plan in place. That should be reassuring news to your client.

KEY CONCEPT

Remember that there are two sides to the Client Renewal Conversation: It is just as much about listening as about talking. Keep an open mind to your clients' reactions and feedback.

Renewing relationships, on a larger scale, should really be an ongoing process. It's a ritual that you'll want to build into your interactions with clients, being sure to check in with them in this way every 18 months more formally, delivering the firm with every client interaction and every client review. Consistency! Consistency! In this way, as your organization continues to evolve, you can keep your clients up to date on the ways in which you can better serve them, not just today but tomorrow, too.

In fact, I encourage you to approach your clients from a perspective of discovery each and every time you interact with them. How have their lives changed? Things happen all the time in people's lives. Clients buy new pieces of real estate. They sell one company and buy another. They inherit some money they didn't know they were going to inherit. They take vacations, their children go off to college, or they check their parents into nursing homes. Really know their families, their children, and their heirs.

While you are discovering things about your clients, you should also be revealing the changes happening in your firm. As an organization, you are always changing. Maybe you have hired a certified financial planner or added some new technology. Maybe you've launched some new services or tweaked your processes. The client needs to know about these things; keep him or her informed. And, of course, do so in a way that is consistent with your new frame. As things at your firm change, explain how and why these changes support the value that you continually strive to deliver to clients. Through this consistent messaging, you will reinforce your clients' ability to think of your firm in the new and improved way.

Things change in your clients' lives, and things change at your company. By approaching your clients with curiosity about what is going on in their lives, you will also pave the way for you to share what has changed lately at your organization. Stay sharp by regularly renewing the relationship with your clients.

KEY CONCEPT

The Client Renewal Conversation is not a one-time event. Change is ever occurring with your clients and with you. Check in regularly so you can keep up with your clients' needs and they can stay aware of the services you offer.

COACHING CORNER

With which clients do you need to set up meetings to have the Client Renewal Conversation? Plan to go back to all of the clients whom you value. If any of these individuals no longer meet your ideal client profile, prepare for the difficult conversation in which you and they work together to determine whether your firm continues to be the right one for them and, if not, what firm might be a better fit. Otherwise, enjoy the journey of delivering your firm to your valued clients.

INDUSTRY INSIGHT: PREPARING TO WORK WITH THE HEIRS OF YOUR CLIENTS

In 2009, Diane Doolin, senior vice president of the Doolin Group at Morgan Stanley and a *Barron's* "Top 100 Women" financial advisor, knew she wanted to differentiate herself from other financial advisors. She was interested in how she could serve not just her clients but their whole families. Doolin decided to attend a presentation on the topic of passing on values as well as money, designed for business founders and their heirs as well as professional advisors. When she arrived, she was surprised to find that the room was filled with business owners and wealthy families but no advisors aside from herself and her business partner.

What surprised Doolin even more, however, was the moment when one of the speakers, Roy Williams, president and founder of the Williams Group, shared that 70 percent of all wealth transfers fail. It was an "aha!" moment for Doolin, who suddenly realized that advisors knew how to manage money well, execute estate planning documents well, and transfer money in a tax-efficient way. The money got to the heirs. It was within families that problems occurred because of lack of trust and communication, heirs not being prepared, and family values not being shared in conversations.

Doolin thought, "As financial planners, we have the perfect plan in place, [and] the returns are terrific. But all that being said, what if after the money is passed on, everything falls apart? What are we really doing of value here [. . .] if it ends with this generation?" Doolin was inspired to do better by her clients.

She met with Roy Williams and his partner, Vic Preisser, an executive coach and mentor to heirs with the Williams Group, who shared the highlights of what they had learned over the years in serving high-net-worth families. At first, Doolin was excited at the prospect of using the information she was gaining to better serve her clients and their families and, in turn, her business. Before long, however, she realized that what she was discovering was "way too big" to keep it from the industry.

The result is the Institute for Preparing Heirs®, a training company (of which Doolin is a founding director) that serves financial advisors who work with high-net-worth multigenerational families. The Institute offers advisors a variety of tools and resources to help advisors better serve their high-net-worth families, including white papers, family conversation-starter checklists, family meeting resources, marketing resources, webinars, and training videos. As the Institute has coalesced and grown, Doolin has been in the thick of it, testing new tools and resources as they are developed.

When asked how her financial advisory practice has benefited from the time she has given to the Institute, Doolin explained how it helps her in every conversation she has with clients. It deepens her relationship with clients and opens up the door for her to work with their children, parents, and other family members. In describing the "inheritance conversation" that she has with clients, Doolin noted, "This conversation is, with the highest intention, a relationship builder. It can impact your business in a positive, relationship-oriented way. You attract really nice people when you have good intentions for their family; it's a whole different way of doing things."

Doolin has seen quantitative benefits as well. After running her annual Client University, with topics such as "How, What, and When Do I Tell the Kids?" "Your Estate Plan Is Set, But Is Your Family Prepared?" and, for women, "Assuming the Mantle of Family Financial Leadership," Doolin received a phone call from a woman who wanted her to set up a family foundation for her. She was interested in working with Doolin because of her focus on involving the family. Today, this particular client relationship is at $40 million, and Doolin anticipates that it could go much higher.

(Continued)

(*Continued*)

Doolin suggests that advisors think of the opportunity to assist clients in transferring their wealth to families as a chance to keep up with the times by reinventing themselves. She recalled how in the past advisors had to reframe themselves from being transactional brokers who bought and sold stocks to "advice givers" or professional advisors regarding asset allocation. Over time, advisors became "trusted advisors"; today, she believes that the new shift for those in the industry is to become "the trusted family advisor." It's time, Doolin said, for the advisor to look not just at Mr. and Mrs. Jones, but at their whole family as the client.

TRANSITIONING CURRENT CLIENTS TO THE TEAM FRAME

During the Client Renewal Conversation, you will introduce your new team to the client, whether in person or through your capability deck. The team reframe, like so much of the reframe process, will need to be ongoing. You've got to do some additional transition work to help the client get comfortable working with your new or revamped team.

The next time you interact with the client, plan to continue the discussion you began during the Client Renewal Conversation in which you let the client know you've built out or revamped your team and why, grounding your answers in how the team can benefit the client. Continue to communicate to get the client's permission to bring other team members into your work with the client, and then start getting your team members involved so they are sharing responsibility for the client.

 KEY CONCEPT

Remember that the Client Renewal Conversation is also about your team. It provides the opportunity to talk about the talents and services the team members have to offer and to introduce them in person as conversation participants.

On a practical level, as you move forward, you should never be on a client review alone again. Bring other team members to the calls, and slowly but surely you will find that your client will develop trust for the rest of your team, not just you. Share leadership, allowing others on the team to provide advice and guidance.

Here's where the three types of advisors described in Chapters 4 and 8—senior, lead, and service advisors—come in. Make sure that other members of the team are participating in a way that the client can see; over time, as your team achieves successes, the client will have greater faith in it. In sum, have a plan, be consistent, and never be the only one conducting the client review again.

When it comes to reframing your new team that delivers wealth management for your firm, you will likely have three kinds of clients:

1. *Those who trust you inherently and are excited about the new and improved firm.* They are enthusiastic about the new capabilities, the new capacity, and better client service you'll be offering. Heck, many of these types of clients would do anything you suggested, so if you're on board, they're on board.

2. *Those who will need some time to embrace these changes and improvements.* You'll need to calibrate how long you're willing to wait for them to transition with you.

3. *Those who, no matter what, will only work with you.* There are two types of these clients: those who you will likely continue to work with, and those who will likely not make the journey to the new and improved firm.

As you engage in the transition process, it will become clear who is who. Be grateful for those who trust you inherently and are excited about the process; take your time with those who seem open to the team idea but are not as fast to trust and transition. As for those clients who have framed you as the only one they should be dealing with, you will have to decide how to reconcile this with your new frame. Are you willing to stay tied to your old role with this client for their business, or is it time to let the client go? You get to make the choice.

INDUSTRY INSIGHT: GETTING CLIENTS COMFORTABLE WORKING WITH THE TEAM

Kelly Campbell, founder and CEO of Campbell Wealth Management, shared the story of how he successfully transitioned his clients to working with his team many years

(Continued)

(Continued)

ago. In particular, he recounted what it was like to remove himself from review meetings with clients.

At first, Campbell admits, he wasn't as intentional as he could have been when transitioning himself out of meetings. Instead, he casually suggested to a couple of his employees that perhaps they could attend the review meetings for two clients that week. He was sure to join the meetings for a time, but then he departed.

This worked all right, but, over time, Campbell became much more intentional about laying the groundwork for the process and would explain to clients early on that they would be meeting with his service team for review meetings. He would let them know that he had built this team expressly to deliver reviews to the clients, to give them the best service possible, and so they would always have someone to talk to, given that he is typically in meetings all day.

Today, occasionally, a client will ask Campbell if he can pop into the meeting, and he does. But he finds that all he needs to do now is say hello or answer a couple of questions and then he can depart.

This has all been part of a larger team reframe that Campbell undertook early on. As he brought in new clients, he introduced all of his team members, then explained his role in business development, certain team members' roles in service, and other team members' roles in managing client portfolios. With this clear communication up front, Campbell finds that clients are comfortable working with the team, and the firm is set up for success to deliver the best service possible to its clients.

Campbell suggested that advisors undertaking the team reframe learn to trust the way they've designed their team and carry that confidence forward when informing clients about the team. "You've got to trust the system," Campbell stated, "and you've got to tell that to clients. 'This is the way our program works.'"[1]

When asked how he handles it when a client is unwilling to work with others on the team besides him, Campbell explained that his firm won't take that person as a client. He noted that this is rarely the case—and often, when it is, other issues are going on as well—but he is clear that his clients have to be comfortable working with his team.

Campbell believes that his clients undoubtedly benefit from the team approach. He noted, "They get a dedicated service team . . . they get their questions answered thoroughly and much more quickly."[2] In addition, they get a financial plan conducted for them once a year, something that Campbell couldn't offer if he worked as a lone ranger. Campbell believes firmly in the importance of the financial plan and its ability to help the firm and the client make sure they are on track and headed in the right direction. It's just one of the many areas of value that he can offer to his clients because of his team frame.

ACQUIRING NEW CLIENTS FOR YOUR NEW FRAME

With the time you've spent helping your existing clients understand your new frame and the energy you've invested in renewing those relationships, you are well on your way to making the transition to your new and improved company. From here, you have the freedom and opportunity to acquire new clients—those ideal individuals whom you so consciously identified earlier in the reframing process.

If you've already had the Client Renewal Conversation with your existing clients, chances are that you'll find it relatively easy to frame your firm for prospective and new clients. These are the easiest individuals of all for whom to frame your company, as this is the very first time they are meeting you.

Simply use all of the materials you've created to communicate your new frame—capability deck, updated website, introductory video, documented engagement models, and the like—to share with your prospects and new clients what your firm does, who you do it for, why you do it, and what your team looks like.

With such a clear and conscious process in place, you are likely to discover that the right clients start being attracted to your firm, almost as if by magic. Of course, with you and your team having invested hours of effort in this process so far, it's not magic at all. It is, however, the growth of the seeds of change you have planted.

At ClientWise, we teach advisors a process to guide them from attracting clients to acquiring clients to integrating them into their firm. It's called the 3 Stages of the Client Acquisition Process™: Stage 1, Campaign Management; Stage 2, Opportunity Management; and Stage 3, New Client Integration. Figure 9.3 provides a snapshot of this process.

In Stage 1, you focus on generating, managing, and converting leads. As you move through this stage, be clear about the most effective ways that you, your team, and your designated rainmakers can generate new leads for the business. Your marketing team should be clear about the most effective way to nurture those leads to determine whether those potential clients are the right fit for your business. Your relationship managers should be clear about the timeline the potential client wishes to engage in and what value that potential client sees in the wealth management services your firm offers. Your relationship

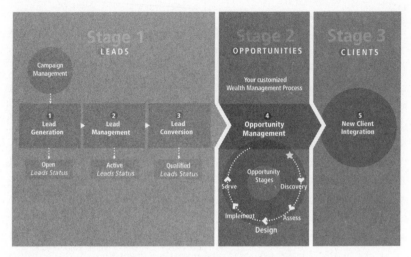

Figure 9.3 The Three Stages of the Client Acquisition Process™

managers should also set expectations before your team partners with the client so that clear outcomes are outlined and an appropriate timeline—one that works for both client and firm—to achieve those outcomes is established.

I find it important at this point to make the following recommendations. Often the teams' timeline is faster than that of the potential client. Therefore, let the client know that to deliver on the promises you're making, you'll need to marshal the resources to get it right. You'll need to know what his or her timeline looks like, so you can best move at the pace at which he or she wishes to move. This demonstrates your sincere desire to honor their timeline while also allowing you and your team to deliver.

Also, it's important at this stage to be absolutely certain that you get a commitment from the prospective client that, no matter what, lines of communication will remain open. No one ever likes a prospect that goes dark. By setting the stage and agreement up front that this won't be the case, if and when it does, you'll have a terrific way to go back to the client and remind the client of your agreement or you'll decide that this prospective client and his or her communication style are just not the right fit for your business.

Once you determine that a lead is either interested in working with your firm or qualified to work with your firm, you move into Stage 2,

Opportunity Management. Your lead is now an opportunity because he or she has shown interest or shown evidence of being qualified to work with you, increasing the chances that he or she will ultimately convert to being your client.

In Stage 2, it is time to go deeper in helping prospective clients understand your frame by allowing them to take your firm for a "test drive." Introduce them to your team, take time to explain your customized wealth management processes, and perhaps even offer them, in vivo, a sampling of what you do so they can get a feel for its value firsthand. This may entail sharing some of your unique materials, such as checklists, white papers, or self-assessments, or it might involve going so far as to create a financial plan together. During Stage 2, you will use your customized wealth management process to engage the prospective client and provide an opportunity for him or her to sample the value of your firm's signature approach.

Ultimately, you will design Stage 2 in a way that works best for your firm, but the following five steps can offer you a generic starting point:

1. *Discover* everything you can learn about the prospective client.
2. *Assess* the prospective client's current situation.
3. *Design* a wealth plan in complete partnership with the prospective client.
4. *Introduce* the wealth plan and begin the process of delivering value.
5. *Invite* the prospective client to sign on as a client with your firm so that you may implement the wealth plan and start serving the client in a complete wealth management way.

These five steps represent a generic approach to Stage 2, and we recognize that many advisors will want to customize it to meet their business and client needs. If you have not already, we encourage you to customize your process, both for your comfort and to individualize your approach to the specific clients you are working with. These five steps can provide a starting point.

By learning more about the prospective client and allowing him or her to learn more about your firm, you can use Stage 2 to determine whether the prospective client is both interested *and* qualified to work with your firm. If the client emerges as being both, ask him or her to become a client. Enter Stage 3: New Client Integration.

Stage 3 begins once a prospective client has agreed to work with your firm. It's time for onboarding. Regardless of how effective your firm was at conducting Stages 1 and 2, this next stage of onboarding is equally essential to the process to ensure the longevity of the client relationship. Successful onboarding can be achieved by delivering to the client the value that was promised to him or her during Stages 1 and 2.

During Stage 3, you will welcome your new client and deepen the relationship; you will get the appropriate paperwork completed and begin all of the technical work required to set up a new client within the firm. You may share guidelines for what is expected for how you work with clients and how they are invited to partner with the firm. Every firm has its own unique onboarding process; you can go to the ClientWise eXchange™ to get other ideas and tools to help you design your own process. First impressions last a lifetime, so plan to get it right up front!

KEY CONCEPT

The next step of your focused growth and change as a firm is acquiring new clients. This often happens quite naturally, as your deliberate crafting of services and clear vision of what you do attracts people who share your outlook and need your specific talents.

THE eXchange™
Online Tool 9.1: Ninety-Nine Discovery Questions

Much has been written about the discovery phase of wealth management, but if you would like additional support, feel free to visit the eXchange™ to access 99 discovery questions you can use in this first stage of the wealth management process.

At ClientWise, we've been tracking those advisors who have had extraordinary success for multiple years in a row, bringing in new clients, acquiring new relationships, and uncovering new client assets and opportunities to serve. Advisors are often asking me, because we coach so many top professionals, what's the secret to client acquisition? What are the best in the business doing to grow their client base? The answer is pretty simple, but very few execute on this. First, the best in the business are clear about how they want to be framed and intentional about being consistent. They are selective. They don't take every client. They turn away from opportunities where they wouldn't be at their best and help those they turn away find the appropriate financial professional. In other words, they know who they serve and they're focused! Second, they have built a process. Oftentimes, they follow our proven process for Building Loyal Client Advocates™ and are intentional about building their Professional Advocate Network™. Yes, it's true. They look for introductions, not referrals. Loyal client advocates and professional advocates accont for more than 70 percent of net new relationships among those who are having extraordinary success bringing on new relationships.

THE eXchange™

Online Tool 9.2: Improve Your Client Acquisition Process

For a printable copy of the Three Stages of the Client Acquisition Process™, along with an associated exercise to help you improve your current process and set goals, visit the eXchange™.

CONCLUSION

At its core, step 4, renewing relationships, is about engaging in a conversation with clients who have known you all these years so you can reframe yourself and your firm for them. Knowingly or unknowingly, you've trained your clients over time to see you in a certain way; now it's time to retrain them to understand the new and improved value you provide for the fee that you are charging them.

Of course, this is much more than an opportunity to teach clients about your new frame and your new and improved value to them as a firm. It's an essential moment to deepen your relationship with the clients—both their trust in you and their belief that you are the right firm for them.

206 ▶ NOW WHAT?

You go into the Client Renewal Conversation with a client-centered attitude that the client can detect and appreciate. You inform the client of the ways in which you heard what was said in that earlier ClientWise Conversation™, along with the feedback of other clients, and demonstrate how you have decided to incorporate that feedback into your new frame.

Learning can become wisdom when you understand it consciously and can share it with someone else. Renewing relationships is an opportunity to turn the learning you've experienced during earlier stages of the reframe into just such wisdom.

With your existing client relationships renewed and your frame well defined and designed, you are ready to carry the frame into the future. This will involve teaching new clients about your frame as you acquire and integrate them into your practice. It also should involve generating ongoing content that allows you to continue educating your clients to understand and value your new frame: blog posts, white papers, e-newsletters, freebie checklists, assessments, and whatever other materials you have cited as candidates for your marketing campaign.

Remember: Whether you are courting prospective clients at an in-person meeting, generating ongoing marketing content, or meeting with an existing client for a review, it is ever so important to communicate your new frame in a consistent way. If you want people to think of you differently, you have to remain faithful to the message that you want to deliver each and every time you encounter them. It takes time for the message to settle in—and it's a good message that you've worked hard to craft. Capitalize on it!

NOTES

1. Kelly Campbell, personal interview, March 12, 2015, transcript, p. 4.
2. Ibid., p. 5.

CHAPTER **10**

Sharing the Frame
It's All About Advocacy

Your new frame would not be complete without a strong network of trusted professionals and clients to help you spread the word about the rich kind of wealth management you now deliver. At ClientWise, we call this network the *loyal advocate network* and consider it an essential part of any financial advisor's success. It is step 5 of the reframing process (see Figure 10.1). Here's why.

In ClientWise's research of more than 500 top financial advisors, advisors indicated that 71 percent of the business that they were currently winning was a direct result of new client relationships that had originated from introductions and personal connections through their network of advocates. In addition, our research showed that the most successful financial advisors spent 41 percent or more of their

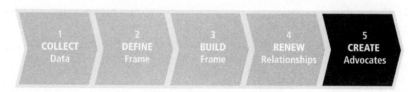

Figure 10.1 Reframe Step 5: Create a Loyal Advocate Network

time in client outreach and acquisition, and that the method for client acquisition with the most effective results, in terms of assets collected, was an advocate approach.

At ClientWise, we feel that a robust advocate network is essential to the health and success of your business, which is why it is included as the fifth and last step of the reframing process. According to a study by the IBM Institute of Business Value,[1] other benefits of having a strong network of advocates include (1) advocates are 60 percent less likely to be sensitive to fees, and (2) advocates are twice as likely to consolidate 80 percent of their assets with one wealth management firm. At ClientWise, we have witnessed that advocates not only know the value of their advisors but are also glad to communicate it to others. Advocates are more than clients or professionals with whom you will engage; they are partners who will work with you toward a successful future.

 KEY CONCEPT

In a study of 500 financial advisors, nearly three-quarters of new business was found to have resulted from introductions and personal connections through an advocate network.

WHAT IS A LOYAL ADVOCATE?

Among the many words used to describe *advocate* are *backer, campaigner, champion, expounder, promoter, proponent, supporter,* and *upholder.*[2] According to Merriam-Webster,[3] an advocate is someone who "works for a cause or a group" or "a person who argues for or supports a cause or policy." In the context of growing your business, *advocate* has an even more particular meaning. At ClientWise, we don't just refer to advocates but to loyal advocates, and we define the term as follows.

A *loyal advocate* is someone who appreciates and understands what you do, thoroughly understands the benefits to themselves and others of being in a relationship with you, can clearly articulate both what you do and the benefits of it to others, and is actively engaged in introducing you to prospective clients for the benefit of you and the prospective client.

At the core of it, loyal advocates are *partners* with you, and you are partners with them. Worthy partners are those who believe and understand the value of the excellence and commitment that they bring to clients. Partners communicate, support one another, and are willing to help one another, oftentimes when there is no remuneration, because partners are playing the long game and they believe in the nobility of the work they are doing.

There are two kinds of loyal advocates:

- client advocates
- professional advocates.

The first group, Loyal Client Advocates™ (LCAs), consists of your clients who are willing to advocate for you. Many LCAs have such strong relationships with their financial advisors that they think and behave more like a partner than a client. Think about how powerful that is—to have your clients as partners. These are the clients who want to see you succeed; who will go out of their way to help you connect with those they believe will benefit from all that you offer; and who know that their friends, family, colleagues, and network are best served when they are working with you.

The second group consists of the professionals (e.g., business valuation specialists, business brokers, estate attorneys, CPAs, bankers, realtors, executive coaches, and physicians, just to name a few) who are willing to advocate for you and who seek to serve any mutual clients at a deeper level by being in a relationship with you. In truth, any professional who is on your external team should be a loyal advocate. If they are not, reconsider whether they should really be part of the team. Why would you send business to one of these other professionals on your wealth management team unless you could feel confident that they would advocate for you to their clients as well?

Both client and professional advocates meet a list of *seven specific criteria*. Loyal advocates

1. appreciate and understand what you do.
2. thoroughly understand the benefits of being in relationship with you.
3. are able to articulate well what you do and the benefits to others in a manner that is consistent with how you wish to be framed.
4. want to be actively engaged in partnering with you to make the necessary introductions to prospective clients for your benefit.
5. are natural connectors.
6. have influence with others when they make an introduction.
7. have a strong network of individuals to whom they can make useful introductions.

Let's look at each of those criteria more closely. It's a must that individuals be able to appreciate and understand you if they are to be loyal advocates. They also need to be able to articulate well what it is that you do. If they don't, they will just keep framing you to others using your old frame or will otherwise mis-frame you.

 KEY CONCEPT

Loyal advocates meet seven criteria: They understand what you do, understand the benefits of partnering with you, can communicate the benefits of partnering with you, can make introductions to prospective clients, are natural connectors, influence others, and have a strong network of individuals to introduce you to.

Beyond having the appreciation and ability to tell others accurately about what you do, individuals who are going to be your advocates need to be *connectors* and *influencers*: those who find it easy to connect you to others and enjoy making introductions (connectors) and who are also able to impact the decisions that these people make because they are held in high esteem by them (influencers).

Connectors and influencers are more than people who have a network; they are people who are able to effectively use their network or "Rolodex." Knowing how to take that Rolodex and introduce others to your network is what connecting is all about. After those introductions are made, influence is the invaluable quality of having the standing that allows a person to influence people. Also important, loyal advocates can make qualified connections—that is, introduce you to people that matter to you and your business.

I know lots of people who have a network but don't know how to make an introduction, and, when they do, it doesn't come with ease. I also know lots of folks who both have a network and are able, with ease, to make a connection, but they have no influence, so when they make an introduction, it generally falls flat because the person who is being introduced is bothered by the introduction. "Oh goodness, why again did you say Joe wants us to meet? He's always doing this and wasting my time!" Well, that won't go well. Get my point? You've got to build advocate relationships with those who meet all of these seven criteria, as each is an important part of enabling a valuable partnership.

Last, for individuals to become part of your loyal advocate network, they must have a willingness and capability to play the role of advocate for you. Ultimately, individuals can appreciate you and understand what you do, articulate well what you do, be a great connector, have influence, and know the right people, but if they don't want to be actively engaged in advocating for you, then they're not going to be able to help you gain the potential benefits of a loyal advocate network. They have to be motivated and willing to engage in the process.

 KEY CONCEPT

The best loyal advocates are connectors, who have many contacts, and influencers, whose advice carries weight with the members of their network.

It's a lot to expect of people to be advocates. Is this realistic? Attainable? Results from an IBM Institute of Business study point in the direction of *yes*. Of 1,311 U.S. wealth management clients who had been with their firm for an average of 10+ years and who had investable assets over $500,000, 43 percent of these individuals identified themselves with characteristics of an advocate as defined in that study.[4] That is, they were likely to refer new business, consolidate more of their portfolios with their primary firm, and resist competitive offers.

Clearly, not every client will have the characteristics of an LCA as defined here in this chapter. In fact, most clients will not have all of the characteristics to be called an LCA. Given that reality, the top financial advisors focus on that small population of clients (5 percent or less) who want to be engaged with the financial advisor and who are most likely to provide new client introductions consistently and proactively. Not everyone has a network, nor the influence. Some are more comfortable than others in making an introduction. And others may not have the time to make an introduction. This is about quality over quantity.

If you are wondering how many advocates it is realistic to expect to attain, consider the following. It is reasonable to expect that each advisor on the team can attain five LCAs on his or her own. Generally, the leader or partners in the financial advisory firm or team take the role of developing professional advocates and strategic alliances. That being said, since these professional advocates are instrumental to delivering the promises made regarding wealth management, often it's the other advisors on the team that serve as the hands-on collaborators with the professionals for the benefit of the client.

Take a moment now to consider your loyal advocates. Who are they, and how do you know that they are able to advocate for you? Chances are that you've got some folks who are in the ballpark of being your advocates, but if they don't meet all seven criteria, they don't represent a loyal advocate—at least, not yet.

Unfortunately, most advisors think they have a lot of people who are advocating for them, when the truth of the matter is that they have a lot of people who may like them without being able to serve as real advocates. At ClientWise, we suggest using a formal process for building your network of advocates so you can be sure that you have true loyal advocates on your side. We call this process the *advocate approach*.

Creating LCAs is more than a key strategy to building your firm's client base—it's essential. At ClientWise, we believe in the power of LCAs to such a degree that we have developed a series of training programs on the subject, along with 45 pages of supporting material. While the present chapter does not provide enough space to cover the subject of LCAs to its fullest depth, it will give an overview of the process of building LCAs to provide greater insight to get you started.

Although I realize that not every reader will be interested in working with a coaching or consulting firm to help them build their LCA network, I would be doing advisors a disservice if I did not encourage them to consider doing so. In reality, there are many mistakes that advisors tend to make when building the LCA network and many pitfalls to the process; thus, it is truly helpful to have support to ensure that things go well. Because building the LCA network, with its seven criteria, is a unique process that ClientWise has designed, we have lots of useful insight into the specific ways to avoid these mistakes and pitfalls. We've built a series of programs to help advisors build their LCA network, whether they've got a week or 12 weeks and whether they are building LCAs on their own or embarking on a journey with their team. When you are ready to build your LCA network, I encourage you to consider availing yourself of a resource such as one of these programs.

 COACHING CORNER

Take some time to answer the following questions. Write them down or discuss them with another person on your team.

1. Are there any concepts about developing a team of loyal advocates that you are uncomfortable with or any beliefs you have that might limit your ability to develop your advocate network? If so, what are they and how will you move past them?

2. Why do you refer people to other professionals, and what can you learn from that process that will help you create your strategies for developing your loyal advocate network?

3. What would you like to shift or change in your thinking or actions to be more powerful in developing your loyal advocate network?

THE eXchange™

Online Tool 10.1: The Advocate Approach Self-Assessment™

ClientWise has created a tool to help you determine how engaged in the advocate approach you already are. The Advocate Approach Self-Assessment™ was developed to help you assess the depth and strength of your advocate approach in an easy and effective way. You can take the assessment by visiting the eXchange.™

 ## The Difference between a Referral and Advocacy

When most advisors hear the word *advocacy,* they think of referrals, but there is a difference. A referral is a simple act that occurs when someone gives your name and contact info to someone else and suggests they contact you to learn more about your services. Another version is when someone gives you a person's contact information and tells you to call them. You might hear, "Call my buddy Rick. He could really benefit from what you do." Or, "Call my kids and get to know them better." Then when you ask if the client wants to be involved in the process, he or she says no.

Advocacy, in contrast, occurs when a person is able to tell others about your services and is willing to take the time to make an introduction between you and the person. Whereas a referral involves just giving your contact info to someone else and leaving it to the person to possibly follow up, an introduction involves a person getting actively involved in connecting you with the prospective client. This could entail the advocate

- sending a joint e-mail to you and the person to get you connected,
- getting you both on the phone line together,
- or even arranging an in-person meeting with everyone present.

An advocate engages in a formal handoff between you and the client and then stays in touch to hear how things are going between the two of you. In fact, as you build your loyal advocates, both clients and professionals, you'll learn that the true advocate is eager to partner with you to determine together how a proper handoff should occur.

If you can't find yourself advocates, then a referral is better than nothing at all. And yet why not go deeper than a referral? An advocate offers so much more. First, people tend to be more inclined to follow up with you if you have been introduced to them by someone they know and respect, if only out of courtesy for their contact. Second, people tend to be more comfortable initiating a working relationship with those that are known by someone they know. A study by Nielsen gives some insight here: Ninety-two percent of global consumers report that they trust "earned media," such as word-of-mouth or recommendations from friends and family, above all other forms of advertising.[5]

Third, advocates—true loyal advocates who meet the seven criteria—can be relied upon to generate new business for you more effectively than referrals. They are not only willing to be actively involved in helping you grow your business, but they also have the contacts, influence, and understanding of your business and its benefits to be able to do so.

It's always better for someone else to tell your story. Touting your own virtues can come across as sales-y; the listener knows at minimum that you are biased and have a vested interest in influencing them. In contrast, if a respected outside party is communicating your virtues to someone, the listener typically perceives more objectivity and credibility behind the positive words. Thus, the value of advocacy over referrals!

BUILDING CLIENT ADVOCATES

Most advisors know people who are willing to tell others about them and who are already doing so to the best of their ability. Yet, most people with the opportunity to advocate have difficulty transferring the trusting relationship they have with their advisor into a form of communication that really excites the potential new client.

The communication sometimes goes like this: "You have to meet my advisor. I have the best relationship with [him/her]." Or "She's a great money manager." Or "He's really good at helping you choose the right insurance plan." Unfortunately, the family member, friend, or colleague hearing these words does not necessarily discover the value for him- or herself in generic statements like these. The advocate approach can be used to enable advisors to help others describe what these advisors do in a way that's unique, differentiating, and compelling to potential clients.

Benefits of the Advocate Approach

The advocate approach was developed in response to research that ClientWise conducted with over 500 of the most successful financial advisors in the business who have vibrant, highly profitable practices. This approach was then field-tested. For those financial advisors who followed the steps of the advocate approach and did the necessary work, the approach created highly successful results with significant growth in client numbers, amount of assets managed, and significant increases in revenue for the financial advisor. To see the potential that engaging in this process holds for you, conduct the exercise in Figure 10.2.

Enter your best estimates in the fields of Figure 10.2 and do the calculations to get a clearer idea of what the payoff could be in building an LCA network for your firm.

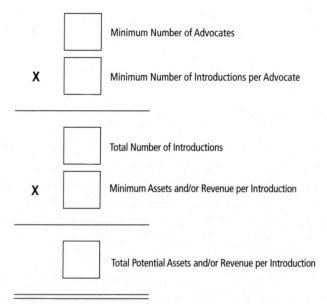

Figure 10.2 Total Potential Value of the LCA Network

This exercise allows you to put into real numbers the benefits of using the advocate approach. For example, if a financial advisor cultivated only a small contingent of three to five client advocates who, in turn, introduced three to five of their close associates, friends, and family throughout the course of the year, that would lead to 10 to 25 new client relationships annually for your business. In turn, if the same numbers applied when building professional advocates, that number would double, leading to a total of 20 to 50 new client relationships each year. That's more than power in numbers—it's power in relationships. Over the last decade in coaching advisors and teams building these processes, I've learned firsthand that the advocate is the gift that keeps on giving. Once you establish the advocate partnership and nurture the relationship by building a custom service model for them, they not only will continue to share their relationships and network with you, they will also accelerate the sharing. You'll find you have more and more in common over the many years you'll work intentionally together. One key hint here: You must build a custom service model for them and continue to spend time together. This is step 5 of the process, and you'll hear more about this later in this chapter.

KEY CONCEPT

Using the advocate approach can grow your business exponentially. Do not underestimate its importance.

The advocacy approach has five steps, as shown in Figure 10.3. It's an elegant process, one that should be learned and mastered by all of the members of your team, especially your lead advisors.

Discover

The advocate approach begins with something you already know well: having the ClientWise Conversation™ with a client. The goal here

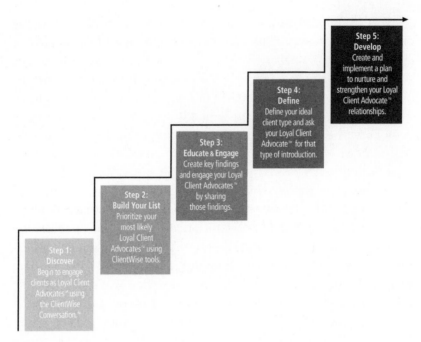

Figure 10.3 Five Steps to Building Loyal Client Advocates™

is to get a sense of whether the client appreciates and understands what you do, understands the benefits received by being in a relationship with you, and can articulate them. Here, you are *discovering*, or assessing, whether this particular client is well suited to be an advocate for you. In addition, you are gathering information on any other professionals that you may want to bring into your advocate network.

It's now time to pick up the phone and ask your most promising potential advocates for a face-to-face meeting. Your side of the conversation doesn't have to follow this script exactly, but the gist will be this: "As my business continues to grow, I'm always looking for ways to improve what it is that we do as a firm to serve clients just like you. I'm meeting with a very select group; I value your opinion and would welcome your feedback on a few items. Would you be willing to meet with me for twenty to thirty minutes over a cup of coffee or lunch?"

When you meet with your client, begin the ClientWise Conversation™. Let's review the five questions that make up the ClientWise Conversation™:

1. What is the one thing you value most about how my firm and I serve you?

2. What is the one thing you would most like me to change or improve about my firm and how I serve you?

3. If you were to describe the services that my firm and I offer you, to clients like yourself, what would you say?

4. If you were to describe what we've achieved together for as long as we've worked together, what would you say?

5. Among your other professional advisors in your life, who do you trust the most and why?

By the time clients are done answering these questions, you will have a clearer sense of how well they understand and appreciate what you do, as well as how effective they are at articulating your frame. You also will receive a review of their trusted advisors, or even possibly get the names of some new ones for you to reach out to.

You will need to think about how and when to reintroduce the ClientWise Conversation.™ You've already conducted it once, but this will be your chance to do so again, since your client has been informed about your new frame.

As for when, let some time pass between when you conducted your last conversation with the client (which will be the Client Renewal Conversation) and when you conduct the next ClientWise Conversation™ to be respectful of the client's time. This will also give the client the opportunity to experience receiving your services and support within your new frame, before you jump back in to learn more about how well they understand and appreciate what you do and how well they can articulate what you offer. Leave this up to the client, but there will be some that you go back to and some you won't. For the ones you do return to, you shouldn't wait more than six to eight weeks at the most.

Some advisors worry about bothering the client with another conversation. That is why we are careful to allow sufficient time to pass between the Client Renewal Conversation and the next ClientWise Conversation™. In addition, the ClientWise Conversation™, with its very specific steps and recommendations around how to conduct it, will ensure that you remain respectful of the client when speaking to him or her (see Chapter 6 for details). Remember, too, that it is recommended that you conduct the ClientWise Conversation™ on a periodic basis with every client to gauge from time to time how effectively you are framing your firm. You are not conducting this conversation for self-serving reasons but because you truly want to serve the clients better by understanding from their answers how you are doing in their eyes.

KEY CONCEPT

The first step of the advocate approach is discovery, which is accomplished through a face-to-face meeting and ClientWise Conversation™ with the client. Discuss what and how your firm is doing and assess whether the client can articulate your new frame accurately to potential new clients.

As you proceed through the ClientWise Conversation™ with your clients, we recommend that you begin to segment your clients into those who are already LCAs, those who have the potential to be LCAs, and those who are not likely to be loyal advocates.

THE eXchange™

Online Tool 10.2: Potential Client Advocate Checklist

Visit the eXchange™ for a checklist that will help you categorize clients as loyal advocates versus potential loyal advocates.

Build Your List

After you conduct the ClientWise Conversation™, it's time to build your list of potential client advocates (professional advocates come later in the process). To make that determination, you will have to consider which clients are currently actively engaged in partnering with you to make the necessary introductions to prospective clients for your benefit and the benefit of the prospective client. Evaluate who is sending you new clients, at what level are they sending you new clients, how valuable those introductions are, and whether the number of introductions from each client is increasing or decreasing. From there, you will be able to determine and build a list of which of your clients will be your best LCAs.

It bears repeating that not all clients will become (or have the potential to become) client advocates. In truth, you will have more clients who are not client advocates than those who are. As a result, you will want to invest your time in developing advocacy with those clients who either are already or are likely to become an integral part of your advocate network.

 KEY CONCEPT

After discovering your clients' potential as advocates through ClientWise Conversations™, consider how many new clients your current clients have already sent your way. With this information in hand, build a list of clients who show the most promise of being LCAs.

As you determine who your current LCAs are, consider the following points as well. Those clients with the potential to be loyal advocates generally provide multiple introductions, and established advocates almost always generate multiple introductions. In addition, advocates enjoy sending good, valuable introductions to you, not just individuals who have little potential to serve your practice. Indeed, some advocates refer clients who generate fees that are worth as much, if not more, than the original referring source. Plan to track where your introductions to new clients are coming from so you can be sure to get clear on who your strongest LCAs are.

THE eXchange™
Online Tool 10.3: New Client Introduction Tracking Sheet

Visit the eXchange™ to download a New Client Introduction Tracking Sheet that you can use while assessing your introductions over the past 24 months. You can also use this tracking sheet going forward to keep a record of every new introduction.

COACHING CORNER

Take time to sit down and look at your introductions for the last 24 months by clients. List which clients have sent you new clients and their level of assets.

Educate and Engage

After you have interviewed your clients with the ClientWise Conversation™ and built your list of current and potential LCAs, you are ready to assess the findings of the recent ClientWise Conversation™ and share those findings with the clients.

THE eXchange™
Online Tool 10.4: Loyal Client Advocate Approach™ Key Findings Worksheet

Go to the eXchange™ and download the Loyal Client Advocate Approach™ Key Findings Worksheet for help summarizing key data you gathered during the Client-Wise Conversation™.

Once you have a handle on the findings of the ClientWise Conversation™, approach your current and potential client advocates on the phone to educate and engage them. Take this time to share the ClientWise Conversation™ findings with these clients and ask to set up a meeting to discuss the clients' advocacy or possible advocacy.

As a review of the steps just discussed and to expand on them, the process should go as follows:

- Request a meeting by phone.
- State the purpose of the meeting (to share what you've learned from the ClientWise Conversation™ and get the client's take on whether he or she thinks you've gotten it right, or not).
- Share the key findings from your worksheet.
- Acknowledge the client's continued help and insights, and mention two or three things that have been useful from the conversation. It is important that you offer things that have been authentically useful or illuminating for you.
- Ask the client for permission to have a third, larger conversation.

Note that you will not have this educate-and-engage conversation with all of the clients who you initially interviewed at the beginning of the advocacy approach. You will use the results from the Loyal Client Advocate Approach™ Key Findings Worksheet—and your intuition and discretion—to determine how many clients you intend to educate and engage and who those clients are. Plan to start with those clients who already appear to be advocates and then move to those who appear to be potential advocates. Prioritize who you speak with first on the basis of where you see the best potential for return on your time and effort and the best potential to build deeper, more engaged relationships.

Note that there will be some clients that you will determine, based on their feedback, that you're not likely to return to. However, those that were eager to connect with you and were willing to share their input, you will likely want to go back to. These are the folks that will be eager to learn what you've discovered and who want to know about the changes and improvements you plan on making to your business and team.

When you request another meeting, be sure to protect the relationship by giving the client permission to say no if the client appears hesitant. At this point, the client will have either said an unqualified yes, maybe, or no. Don't push for a yes if the client is reluctant. You will have a chance to ask again if you think that it will not injure the relationship. If the client says no, accept it gracefully and thank the client again for his or her time and opinions to date. For those clients who are willing to have the next meeting, thank them and tell them you will call in the next week or so to schedule another conversation. That conversation will be step 4, define, in the Loyal Client Advocate Approach™.

Finally, watch your time. This conversation should last no more than an hour unless the client seems to be so engaged that he or she doesn't want to stop. It is critically important that in that hour, you complete the entire conversation.

 KEY CONCEPT

The next step of building LCAs is educating and engaging the clients you have identified as potential advocates. Via phone call, share what you've learned in past conversations, acknowledge their past help and insights, and ask for a third in-person conversation to explore their future advocacy. If your client seems reluctant to step into the advocate role, do not push.

Define

You have now laid the foundation for conversation. You have done the research, identified your highest potential LCAs, and asked them for a larger conversation about working more closely with you. You have a list of clients who have indicated that they are willing and want to have this larger conversation with you. You are now ready for the conversation that actually moves into your most important request of your LCAs: the request for introductions.

What you will be engaging in is not the typical referral conversation; this part of the conversation will help you create a working relationship with your client. It will teach you how to ask for the right kind of introduction so that your client can connect you to exactly the kind of prospective clients you are looking for: the ideal client that you defined when creating your new frame.

The conversation will be as follows:

- Request a meeting by phone.
- State the purpose of the meeting at its beginning.

- Protect the relationship by providing an out if the client is not willing to become engaged on a deeper level with you and your practice.
- Protect the relationship by reinforcing confidentiality.
- Ask directly for the client to work closer with you to develop new clients.
- Share your ideal client type.
- Be specific in asking the client to make an introduction.
- Thank the LCA for the conversation and any introductions that have been given, and ask whether you can be of service in any way to the LCA.

For those who are potential advocates, you will aim to educate and engage them around advocacy; for those who are already your advocates, you can focus on deepening their connection to their role as an advocate.

KEY CONCEPT

The next step of the advocate approach is to meet again with your potential advocate in person. Ask the client to work closely with you to develop new clients for your firm, but be aware of any hesitance on your client's part; protect your relationship and reinforce confidentiality with your client before all other considerations. Identify your ideal client type, specifically ask for introductions, sincerely thank your LCA, and ask how you can be of service to the LCA.

 A Conversation Script: Inviting Clients to Be Loyal Advocates

1. Request a meeting by phone.

Hello, Karen. In our last meeting, I mentioned I would like to have a larger conversation with you and you were generously willing to do that. I am looking forward to that conversation

(Continued)

(*Continued*)

and wanted to get it on the calendar. Would you be available to meet with me in the next few days or next week?

2. **State the purpose of the meeting at its beginning.**

   When we last met, I said that I wanted to have a larger conversation about working closer with you in growing my business selectively. I want to share my vision around that, get your input, and ask for your help.

3. **Protect the relationship by providing an out if the client is not willing to become engaged on a deeper level with you and your practice.**

   As I stated last time, I want you to know that our friendship comes first. Whatever else may happen, it is critically important to me that we protect our relationship. So, please feel free to let me know if at any time I have asked something that doesn't feel right for you.

4. **Protect the relationship by reinforcing confidentiality.**

   It goes without saying, but I'd like to say it anyway. Confidentiality is key. I view all of my conversations with all of my clients with the highest degree of confidentiality. You can be assured that I will never betray that sense of trust and privacy.

5. **Ask directly for the client to work closer with you to develop new clients**.

   Karen, would you be willing to be in a working relationship with me to help me find individuals like you who need and would benefit from the wealth management services that I provide?

6. **Share your ideal client type**.

   Karen, I really appreciate your partnership. As you think about those who might benefit from my services, I want you to know that experience has shown me that I am most effective serving the following types of clients. [You would then go on to explain your ideal client type or types, leaving room for your potential LCA to ask questions, make suggestions, or put forth the name of a potential client.]

7. **Be specific in asking the client to make an introduction.**

   Once you have explained your ideal client type, ask your LCA for introductions of that type. In addition, if you know the name of someone the LCA could introduce you to, ask for an introduction to that person, specifically using language similar to the language below.

   Karen, in the past you've spoken about Hal Holcrumb. As you mentioned, I focus on working with executives at manufacturing firms. I'd like to ask you a question. Knowing what you know about me and how I like to serve and work with clients like you, do you think that Mr. Holcrumb is the sort of person who I'd like to work with?

8. **Thank the LCA for the conversation, any introductions that have been made, and ask whether you can be of service in any way to the LCA.**

   Because you are building a deeper relationship with the LCA, it is critical that every conversation end with a personal acknowledgment of and thanks to the LCA. In addition, since the LCA is supporting you at a significant level, it is important that you seek to support the LCA in the same manner. I discuss that more fully in the next section.

Develop

You now have active LCAs. You have done the work to start the relationships and are on your way to finding these relationships rewarding both personally and professionally. Indeed, most financial advisors who develop LCAs regard them as some of the most meaningful and significant relationships in their lives.

Those financial advisors have not only undertaken the actions that create the relationships, they have also continued to *nurture and deepen* their LCA relationships. They do this not only because it makes sense from a business standpoint but also because the relationships create a foundational community of good, successful people who support one another.

Your work moving forward will be to design how you will develop, nurture, and sustain your LCA community. You must start by recognizing that the LCA relationship is different from your relationships with other clients. The client advocate relationship, at its best, is a tremendously intimate relationship because LCAs regularly put their reputations at risk by recommending you. They have that much faith in who you are and that much faith in your ability to serve those who are important to them.

You must recognize the scope of the LCA's very personal investment in a working relationship with you in your business and engage with him or her with equal personal investment. To nurture and sustain these relationships, you must do three things:

1. Develop rules and a structure for handling introductions with each LCA into which the LCA has real input.
2. Develop a special service model for LCAs that reflects the depth of your relationship with your LCAs.
3. Stay in touch with your LCAs regularly and at a significant level.

None of these actions are particularly difficult to achieve, but they all take intention, partnership with your LCAs, and a personal touch on your part. Much has been written about the best, most effective ways to generate referrals, but note that this method is not about generating an endless stream of referrals. Rather, it is about partnering with a select group of clients who meet all of the criteria to be considered advocates.

KEY CONCEPT

Now that you have LCAs, take care of them. Take every opportunity to nurture and deepen your partnering relationship. They are putting their reputations on the line by recommending you and your services. Stay in touch and truly listen to what they have to say.

BUILDING PROFESSIONAL ADVOCATES

In addition to client advocates, professional advocates represent the other side of the advocacy coin that is so important to developing a successful wealth management practice, and the last important piece of the reframing process. Professional advocates are important in part because they will provide you with introductions to new clients, but also because you will need them to support your clients and wealth management business; thus, you will want to introduce your clients to these professionals as well. At ClientWise, what we've learned is that the best in the business are building these networks of other professionals, not only for business development opportunities, but more so because to fulfill the promises made to clients, they will need a team of other professionals to round out their own wealth management business. The quality introductions from these other professionals should only be considered a strategic by-product of building the network correctly.

For example, most advisors will not be involved in doing a client's taxes, preparing their estate documents, valuing their business for sale, providing a client's life insurance solutions, and so forth. As a result, working closely with other professionals who can provide these services becomes paramount. Advisors need other professionals in their network both to win new business and to support their clients in the best way possible.

The process of building professional advocates is similar to (although not the same as) the process of building client advocates. While the remainder of this chapter will not delve in depth into the how-to's of building professional advocates, Figure 10.4 provides an overview of the process that you can review to gain greater insight.

To build a professional advocate program with the greatest growth potential possible, we recommend that you seek the help of a coach or mentor for each step. To help you implement the tools in this program rapidly and in a fully customized way, you may wish to seek the help of a professional coach who has a complete coaching skill set as well as experience in the industry. ClientWise also offers in-depth training on this topic, which goes beyond what could realistically be included in this chapter.

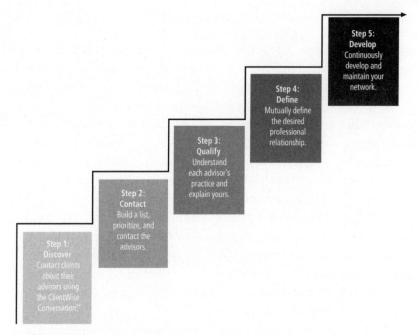

Figure 10.4 Five Steps to Building Professional Advocates

Steps 1 and 2: Discover and Contact

You have already conducted the first step of this process when building your LCAs, so you will not need to repeat that step now, but it is included here to show the full process from start to finish.

The second step is to build your list of potential professional advocates, to categorize and prioritize them according to current versus potential advocates, and then to contact these professionals. When deciding who goes on this list, don't just include the professionals that your clients recommended—also consider all of the professionals you already know and/or work with. Aim for a list of 50 to 75 professionals and centers of influence.

There are many centers of influence to consider as your advocates. For some on this list, the introduction process will be a two-way street; for others, it is just a one-way boulevard in your direction.

- Valuation consultant or business broker
- Realtor

- Certified public accountant
- Personal coach or advisor
- Attorney
- Chamber of Commerce leader
- Business owner
- Community or political leader
- Other financial advisors
- Doctor
- Church or synagogue leader
- Professor, teacher, principal, other school officials

This list of possible centers of influence can help you brainstorm who you'd like to include on your customized list of potential professional advocates.

After collecting the names and phone numbers of other professional advisors and centers of influence from your clients, it is time to list and prioritize them. To ensure that you are investing your resources where they are most likely to pay off, it is helpful to focus first on those professional advisors who will help you best serve your ideal client type, as defined by you during the earlier step 2 of the reframing process (see Figure 10.5).

Once your list of professionals is built, it's time to contact your target professionals. One of the hardest things for some financial professionals is to make the first contact with another advisor. Even though it may be uncomfortable, your goal should be to meet with every one of the high-potential professionals mentioned to you during your client meetings.

Priority Categories

Figure 10.5 Priority Categories for Potential Professional Advocates

Will everyone respond positively to your request and be willing to meet with you? No. But a surprising percentage of professionals will, and many of the most successful centers of influence in your community will be happy to, as well. The most successful financial advisors have learned that their success is directly related to their degree of connectedness to others in the community. On the basis of our research and experience at ClientWise, I can confidently predict that at least half of the people you call will meet with you.

KEY CONCEPT

Another source of advocates is your and your clients' professional networks. Follow similar steps (discover, contact, qualify, define, develop) to engage professional advocates as you do for client advocates, but look to people you work with, people your clients work with, and other centers of influence when considering who to recruit for your network.

COACHING CORNER

Take some time to think about centers of influence you know who could potentially be good advocates for you and your business.

Step 3: Qualify

The third step of building professional advocates is to understand each professional's practice and explain your practice as well to these advocates—to deliver your frame. We recommend that you do this in two separate meetings, using the first meeting to learn about what the professional does in his or her practice and then, if you are still interested in working with this professional, using the second meeting to educate the professional on your own frame.

At the first meeting, plan to

1. set the agenda (i.e., purpose of the meeting, what you want to cover, the amount of time allocated, and "check-in for acceptance");

2. ask specific questions to better understand the professional advisor and his or her practice, and take notes;

3. begin to discern whether you want to work with this professional advisor; and

4. schedule the next appointment, if you see the potential for a mutually beneficial relationship.

Some sample questions to consider asking are

- How did you get started in your profession?
- What is it about your profession that appeals most to you?
- What distinguishes you from others in your field?
- In your opinion, what is the most challenging factor people in your profession face today?
- How do you promote your services?
- With the exception of anything that might be considered confidential, what are some of the things you and our mutual client have accomplished?

After the interview is complete, take time to discern whether you want to work with this professional advisor. Follow the guidance of author Janet G. Elsea in her book *First Impression Best Impression* and consider what the professional looked like during the interview, what he or she sounded like, what he or she said, and how well he or she listened. What are your initial instincts, thoughts, and/or feelings regarding whether you would be able to have a productive relationship with this professional?

 THE eXchange™

Online Tool 10.5: Interview Questions for Potential Professional Advocates

For a list of additional possible questions to ask potential professional advocates, visit the eXchange™.

At the second meeting with the professional with whom you'd like to collaborate, it's time to take out your capability deck and use it to communicate all that you now do. That's step 4 of the following recommended process:

1. Set the agenda (i.e., purpose of the meeting, what you want to cover, the amount of time allocated, and "check-in for acceptance").

2. Recap what you learned from the first meeting to confirm your understanding and convey that you listened carefully to what the professional advisor had to say. Look for an acknowledgment from the professional advisor that you got it right. Now you may move forward.

3. Once you've received that acknowledgment, ask for permission to discuss your practice.

4. Run the professional through your capability presentation to educate them on your frame.

5. Ask the professional advisor how he or she would describe you and your practice.

6. Schedule the next appointment to manage expectations and mutually define the desired introduction relationship, which is to be based on mutual advocacy.

▼ Advocates as a Sounding Board but Not an Advisory Council

As you are making decisions about how to change and improve your firm and how to grow your business, your advocates can be your sounding board to get direct feedback on your services, your offerings, and the decisions you need to make. This approach is not to be confused with creating an advisory council or an advisory board. While I've seen those work remarkably successfully, one of the things I would caution advisors against is creating an advisory board with a formal structure, because that often comes with unintended consequences.

The two most significant potential unintended consequences are as follows. First, some of your advocates may not get along with each other and may not want to serve on a board more formally together. Second, boards have term limits, and you want your advocates to be evergreen rather than having a term limit attached. Because of these unintended consequences, I'm not a fan of formalizing an advisory board. From time to time, though, it makes sense to pull advocates together as a sounding board.

Step 4: Define

Once the proper groundwork has been laid (as described in the previous three steps), it is time to talk business from a mutual advocacy perspective. The third meeting is when you mutually define the desired professional relationship. Start, as always, with you setting the agenda. Next, acknowledge what you value most about the other professional advisor's practice and then seek an acknowledgment about what he or she values most about your practice. You might also discuss the synergies in the way each of you serves your clients.

You can then proceed to ask the professional advisor to describe his or her most desired client types so you understand what type of introduction the advisor would most like you to make for him or her, followed by you describing your most desired client type.

Last, plan to discuss your expectations for the relationship with the other professional. Keep focused on the possibilities of working together and discuss what that might look like. Authenticity and openness are fundamental to establishing and maintaining productive relationships.

Once you and another professional advisor understand each other's most desired client types, it is important to promptly manage each other's expectations about how you might collaborate and work together for the benefit of others. Nothing strains a new advocacy relationship faster than one party thinking (often erroneously) that the other is not holding up their end of the bargain. It may be helpful to summarize your working relationship in a document or e-mail, so you both can use it for reference.

Step 5: Develop

The last step in the process of building your professional advocate network is to continuously develop and maintain the network you've worked so hard to initiate. Plan to speak and meet with your professional advocates on a regular basis, as often as monthly, if possible. Over time, if your relationship with a particular network member proves to be unproductive for you despite your best efforts, drop it and invest your resources where they are likely to produce a better return.

Remember, it's not quantity that counts here, but quality. You don't need to have a list of 50 professional advocates. No one has the time or resources to maintain that many relationships. A handful of professional advisors who are committed to working closely with you for mutually beneficial reasons is all you need.

CONCLUSION

Why advocacy? When it comes to informing potential clients about your services, it's always better to have somebody else tell your story than for you to. This applies as much to family members and heirs as it does to any other type of new client.

Isn't it better to have your clients advocate to their family for the work that you have done together than for you to just singlehandedly try to build relationships with their kids and grandkids and inheritors of the clients' wealth? Credibility is so much stronger this way. As a result, the most important work you can do as an advisor is to proactively, intentionally build relationships with others who will serve as your advocates and be able to tell your story, in some ways perhaps even more elegantly and authentically than you can.

Note that even if your current clients are already advocating for you to others—friends, colleagues, families, and so on—you've still got to check back in continually with clients to keep them up to date on your services because your firm is evolving and growing, too. So you've always got to be educating your advocates—always updating and inviting them to learn more about the changes and improvements that you're making and informing them how you're proactively building out your team and your firm to meet the ever-changing needs of the financial services environment because it's a moving target. You will know your advocacy approach is working well when you start to witness that you're getting new clients from your loyal advocates and when you observe that your loyal advocates see great value in the work that you do by the words they use to describe your services.

Sustainable growth gets easier over time when others are advocating for your services. There's a bonus, too: It always feels good when others go out of their way to help you succeed. It's humbling that your advocates believe in the greater good of what you, your team, and your firm are all about.

Transfer of trust is easier when an advocate makes that handoff.

NOTES

1. Brian Lincoln and Bob Heffernan, *Building Client Advocacy: New Opportunities for Wealth Management Firms*. IBM Institute for Business Value, 2008, www.ibm.com/services/us/gbs/bus/pdf/gbw03021-usen-02-advocacy-wm.pdf.

2. *Roget's New Millennium Thesaurus*, 1st ed. (version 1.2.1), s.v. "advocate."

3. *Merriam-Webster OnLine*, s.v. "advocate," accessed May 6, 2015, www.merriam-webster.com/dictionary/advocate.

4. Lincoln and Heffernan, *Building Client Advocacy*.

5. "Global Trust in Advertising and Brand Messages," Nielsen Company, last modified April 10, 2012, accessed May 6, 2015, www.nielsen.com/us/en/insights/reports/2012/global-trust-in-advertising-and-brand-messages.html.

Conclusion

Ten Signals of a Successful Reframe

You've made it to the end of this book and, if you've been working the program as you go, very possibly the end of the reframing process for yourself and your firm. The question now is, how will you know if your reframe has been successful?

Like smoke signals that are used to communicate from a long distance, there are also signals that will appear after you've engaged in the reframe process that will provide you with insight that you are making progress on your reframing journey. These are universal signals for which you can be on the lookout, regardless of your particular reframe.

Then, there will be those signals that are unique to your firm and its particular reframe. This chapter provides guidance on both types of signals, describing what the common signals of success are as well as how to develop a list of customized signals to help you know that your unique reframe is going well.

But first, let's talk about this notion of an end to the reframing process. While it is true that there are five clear steps to reframing your wealth management firm, the truth is that reframing is an ongoing journey. *It's about dialogue as much as it is about destination.* The process of reframing is really one big feedback loop between your firm and your clients that should continue over months and years. This dialogue between you and your clients (as well as between you and your network of advocates) will enable your firm to continue to evolve to meet the shifting needs of your clients as well as the changing demands of the financial landscape. A willingness to treat the reframing process as a continuing journey will enable you to not only grow with the times but also expand your career and practice in a way that satisfies you personally and professionally. In other words, what you've now learned is a sustainable process.

The reality is that there is no "shazam!" moment within the reframe process in which your business will be tidily wrapped up with a bow and done evolving. Your vision for your practice will change; you will receive input from clients and professionals that will help shape that change. There might be a need to introduce new services. Your logo might change. The tax code will get updated and you'll have to adjust to it. Your knowledge will grow and affect the way you run your practice. As a result, the reframe process will, by necessity, need to be continual rather than finite. As you continue to attract new talent to your business, their input will be valuable to co-creating your future firm.

And yet, as you work through any given reframe, you will arrive at clear vistas where you will be able to appreciate the growth you've engaged in and enjoy its benefits. From these vistas—solid plateaus to which you will ascend during your journey of reframing—you will discover that all of your strategizing, effort, and teamwork have culminated in something real and powerful. You will be able to assess your success on the basis of the unique milestones you have set for yourself, as well as the list in this chapter of 10 universal signals of success that occur with effective reframing. By becoming familiar with the universal and unique signals of success, you will have the information you need to recognize when your reframe process is going well and when it needs some adjusting.

KEY CONCEPT

Reframing is an ongoing journey, but there are milestones, both universal and unique, to look for to ascertain whether you have successfully reframed along the way.

YOU KNOW YOUR REFRAME IS WORKING IF . . .

By now, it is clear that the journey of reframing takes time, patience, and work. There may be times that you and your team will be slogging through the "foggy woods," unsure of the progress you've made and unclear just how close or far your destination really is. Keep the following in mind for just such a moment: *Do not quit,* because you might be closer than you think. Instead, keep your antennae up; look for clues that your reframe is working; and, when you discover them, notice, appreciate, and celebrate them.

After the reframe has begun, you will start to see things change; you will see flutters of progress, inertia that is transforming into movement. Be attuned to these initial signs of change because it is in these areas that you will discover the "juice" of motivation to keep you going; these initial signs also will give you the confidence to continue moving ahead with the reframe. Don't forget to take the time to look up, either—you may just see a smoke signal in the distance letting you know you are close.

Universal Signals That Your Reframe Is Working

The signals that your reframe is working track well to many of the aspects of the reframe that you've worked through, so they will likely sound familiar.

You will know that your reframe is working when:

- Your *team* works excitedly together to enact the frame you've mutually designed and you can see that team members feel they're partners in the delivery of the new frame.

- Your *clients* exhibit confidence in working with members of your team because they trust their technical capability, relational capability, decisional capability, problem-solving capability, and so on.

- You ask clients to describe what it is you have achieved in the number of years you've worked together and they have a powerful and valuable answer, one that reflects the very frame you intended to build.

- Each client review is more powerful than the last.

- Your business profits are rising and doubling every three to five years.

- Another professional invites you to join in serving one of his or her clients and that professional frames you in a way that's exactly as you want to be framed.

- You find that it has gotten easier to run your business because your team, your advocates, and your clients want you to succeed.

- You are attracting new young talent to your team each year with ease.

- You see loyalty and longevity in your existing employees, who are excited about the strategic plan for growth because they're equal partners in having created that plan.

- You've got an operating agreement and a mechanism in place for the other talented members of your firm to find their "path to partner" and potentially (or have already) become owners in a sustainable and growing business.

The universal signals of success are many, then, and these represent some of the top ones. There will be unique signals of success, too. Read on to learn more about detecting them.

 KEY CONCEPT

Among the universal signals of a successful reframe are a loyal and engaged team; clients happy with your partnership and the results you achieve for them; rising profits; and goodwill and accurate framing from clients, partners, and employees.

THE eXchange™

Online Tool C.1: A Checklist: Signals of Reframing Success

Visit the eXchange™ for a downloadable checklist of these and other universal signals that your reframe has been a success.

Unique Signals That Your Reframe Is Working

In addition to the universal signals of success, you can gauge your progress against a list of signals that you've laid out for yourself in advance that are indicators of your success. Here are some tips on how to do so:

- Collaborate with your team members to develop a list of items that signal you are meeting with success. Be as specific as possible.
- Include project milestones on your list that will show you have accomplished a meaningful task or an initiative related to your reframe.
- Share this list with your advocates and invite their ideas, comments, and feedback.
- Update your list of unique signals on the basis of what you have learned from your advocates.
- Gather input from your loyal advocates and determine whether they also see a shift in the frame of your firm.

Once your list of unique signals has been completed, you can go about gathering information to help you see which signals are actually occurring.

KEY CONCEPT

Unique signals for gauging the success of your reframe can be whatever you feel represents what you want to achieve. Work with your team to figure out a list of milestones, share the list of milestones with advocates for feedback, update your list as necessary, and check back with your advocates to see if the milestones are being met and your frame is shifting per your plan.

It's critical that you do the following three things (which are the most effective) to gather this information: (1) make your own observations, (2) assess business results, and (3) invite feedback from clients and professionals. As for observations, watch your team in action, ask questions of your clients and listen to their answers, and check in with your advocates to get a sense of how things are going from an outside perspective.

Analyze business results by paying attention to important data such as how your client base is increasing, how many introductions you are receiving, for what percentage of clients you are serving additional family members, etc. Create metrics for analyzing your business that link to your strategic goals so you can truly assess how your business is growing.

Most important, return to your clients consistently and repeatedly to gain insight into how they think you are doing. What do they feel you have accomplished together? What do they value most about your services and support? Once you've gathered everyone's feedback and added it to your observations and the business results, you will be in a position to evaluate where you are as a firm and what, if anything, you still need to do to achieve a successful reframe.

KEY CONCEPT

Being aware of your firm's current situation is key for the evaluation process to be successful. Gather data and make observations, analyze your business results, and listen to client feedback to gauge your reframing success.

COACHING CORNER

Set aside 30 to 60 minutes to work with your team to identify what will constitute your unique signals of success. Plan to revisit that list with your team in a few months to assess which signals you have met so far; which you still hope to meet; which new signals you'd like to add; and which signals, if any, you feel missed the mark and should be removed from the list.

Ten Signals That Your Reframe *Isn't* Working

In spite of best efforts or good intentions, sometimes the reframe doesn't occur as effectively as we'd like. Here are some signs that it isn't working yet:

1. You're not getting introductions to prospective clients.
2. You feel alone in running the business.
3. You have a work group that reports individually to you, rather than a team invested in supporting one another through mutual accountability.
4. Clients and/or partners continue to frame you in the old way.
5. You aren't winning new clients.
6. Your assets aren't growing; your revenues aren't growing.
7. You feel like the business isn't fun anymore.
8. You are feeling burnt out.
9. There's turnover on your team.
10. Team members seem disengaged from the work and/or are unwilling to go the extra mile.

If you discover a preponderance of these signals or you otherwise have reason to believe that your reframe isn't working yet, set some time aside to investigate why. Have you worked all five steps of the reframing process? Have you put in sufficient time, teamwork, and resources when engaging in these steps? Are the services you offer out of alignment with what your ideal clients truly need? Have you failed to communicate your frame effectively?

An answer of yes to any of these questions could point you in the right direction for making adjustments. Use this book as a resource and/or consider working with a coach to further identify areas for improvement so you can get back on track and enjoy the many benefits of reframing yourself, your team, and your organization.

GO TO THE CLIENTWISE eXchange™

Along the journey of your reframe, you're going to test things out. You're going to make some new moves and you're going to try some new things, like a different message, different people, a different logo, or a different service model or approach. If you'd really like to be successful, you've got to get feedback from others; you have to test out whether your message is hitting the mark. We invite you to become a part of our community of reframers along the journey toward future success. We invite you to share your own reframes with us and with our community of advisors and leaders who are thinking about their own reframes and success.

When you find yourself in the midst of a reframe in the future, consider going to the eXchange™ to share your story just as advisors in this book have shared theirs. I believe that your own successes and challenges can offer useful lessons for others and, at ClientWise, we'd welcome hearing about it all on the eXchange™, which offers a platform for users to communicate with each other. You will find a specific group called "You've Been Framed," which you'll be able to join and participate in. We welcome you to learn more about the community and take advantage of what's been built here for you to learn alongside others who are also committed to growth and reframing as leaders. As you move through the reframe process, your team will learn and grow; your clients will share new ideas; you will deepen your own leadership skills. Those of us at ClientWise and in the ClientWise community would enjoy hearing about it and are willing to help you.

You never have to go it alone, then—not just because of the eXchange™ but because there are coaching and consulting companies like ClientWise that specialize in working with financial advisors and can partner with you to achieve any of the essential steps to reframing, from gathering client feedback and identifying ideal client type(s) to building the marketing assets needed to launch your new frame. What's more, you can bring coaching into your organization by training to earn the ClientWise Certified Financial Services Coach Designation, the only International Coach Federation (ICF)–approved course designed specifically to assist financial professionals in obtaining the vital skills needed to become an ICF-accredited coach. The options for support and community are waiting for you when you are ready.

KEY CONCEPT

You can find support for your reframe and help others by sharing what you've learned from your reframe by participating on the eXchange™.

CONCLUSION

No matter where you are in your business—no matter what your level of success—the most important thing is to consistently have an eye toward the future focused on how you, your team, and your firm want to be framed. Be willing to evolve, change, and grow as a journey learner.

Be curious about others, too. How can you help them achieve success? What do they find valuable in your existing partnership—both technical and relational aspects—and what would they love to have more of and less of from you and your firm in the future? Be curious about how others view you, your team, and your firm.

If we are to treat advising as a noble profession, then we must take the servant-leadership approach. This means becoming deeply connected to clients' needs as well as leading others on your team to connect deeply with clients. When we do our work well, we can truly shape the lives of others—those in our communities and in the world.

That being said, our industry is not without its challenges. We need to continue to raise the bar on fiduciary standards; we need to bring new talent into the industry; we need to find a way to not just help the ultra-affluent or the mass-affluent but also help every neighbor so that we can positively impact everyone's life. That may mean that your firm donates time to help those others.

We can feel good about the work that we do if we focus on the needs of our clients and also find a way to share the benefits of our work with everyone. It's time the public really understood the value of advice and the value you bring to helping shape a better world. Get out there and frame yourselves, renew client relationships, and expand your reach, and you will help many others reach their goals and live the lives they wish to lead. We can—and, I'm confident, will—build a sustainable approach to the financial advising business.

Together, we can make this happen.

Additional Resources

Your purchase of *You've Been Framed* provides you with not only a comprehensive text but also access to online tools, available free on the ClientWise eXchange™ (youvebeenframed.clientwise.com), to assist you in your reframing journey. Each book-related tool on the eXchange™ is listed below for your convenience; more detailed descriptions of these tools can be found in each book chapter.

The truth is that I couldn't imagine writing this book without sharing these tools with you. Why? *You've Been Framed* is meant to be a starting point for your work and for a conversation that we in the industry can have with one another; the eXchange™ is a forum through which that work and conversation can continue. What's more, as the financial services profession and industry continue to evolve, the tools on the eXchange™ will be updated to keep things relevant, useful, and fresh.

The ClientWise eXchange™ is thus the container that allows this book to continue to evolve. No matter when you purchase the book or where you pick it up, so long as you're willing to take advantage of the many resources that exist online, they're yours. I invite you to join other financial leaders and your peers on the eXchange™ at youvebeenframed.clientwise.com so we can continue the conversation together!

Chapter 2
Online Tool 2.1: Your Wealth Management Checklist
   A list highlighting key elements of each area of wealth management.

Chapter 3
Online Tool 3.1: Ten Reasons Your Clients Will Love You for Offering True Wealth Management
   A list of 10 reasons your clients will love you for offering true wealth management that can be customized to your practice.

Chapter 4
Online Tool 4.1: Succession Planning Checklist
   A checklist to use or adapt while planning your firm's leadership succession.

Chapter 5

Online Tool 5.1: Leader's Journey Assessment
    A 15-item assessment that will help you identify your current areas of
        strength as a team leader versus opportunities for growth.
Online Tool 5.2: A Guide to Defining Your High-Performing Team
    A 12-question guide to defining your unique high-performing team.

Chapter 6

Online Tool 6.1: Checklist for Conducting the ClientWise Conversation™
    after a Client Review
    A how-to checklist on conducting the ClientWise Conversation™
        successfully at the end of a client review, if a separate meeting
        is not possible.
Online Tool 6.2: ClientWise Conversation™ Data Collector
    A note-taking template to use during the ClientWise conversation to
        capture the client data.

Chapter 7

Online Tool 7.1: Example Needs, Target Market, Solutions, and Centers
    of Influence
    A template to help you define your new frame by thinking about the
        different target groups advisors can work with, along with their
        associated needs, solutions, and centers of influence.
Online Tool 7.2: Brainstorming the New Frame
    A step-by-step guide for defining your new frame, including a list of
        more than 70 power words and a variety of power phrases.

Chapter 8

Online Tool 8.1: A Guide to Defining Your High-Performing Team
    A 12-question guide to defining your unique high-performing team.
Online Tool 8.2: Ten Steps to Leading a Highly Effective Team
    A printable checklist of the 10 leadership behaviors you can engage
        in to become the most effective leader for your team.
Online Tool 8.3: Marketing Firms to Help You Build Your Brand
    A list of marketing firms that specialize in the financial services
        industry.
Online Tool 8.4: Marketing Campaign Organizer™
    An organizer that will help you outline your next marketing campaign,
        prompting thought about your target market, ideal client profile,
        possible offers, relevant messages, delivery options, who is
        involved, start and end dates, and expected ROI.

Chapter 9

Online Tool 9.1: Ninety-Nine Discovery Questions
    Ninety-nine discovery questions you can use to learn about the client.

Online Tool 9.2: Improve Your Client Acquisition Process
> A printable copy of the Three Stages of the Client Acquisition Process™ and an associated exercise to help you improve your current process and set goals.

Chapter 10

Online Tool 10.1: The Advocate Approach Self-Assessment™
> A tool to help you determine how engaged in the advocate approach you already are.

Online Tool 10.2: Potential Client Advocate Checklist
> A checklist that will help you categorize clients into loyal advocates versus potential loyal advocates.

Online Tool 10.3: New Client Introduction Tracking Sheet
> A tracking sheet that can be used to assess your introductions over the past 24 months and to record every new introduction.

Online Tool 10.4: Loyal Client Advocate Approach™ Key Findings Worksheet
> A worksheet to help summarize key data you gathered during the ClientWise Conversation™.

Online Tool 10.5: Interview Questions for Potential Professional Advocates
> A list of additional possible questions to ask potential professional advocates.

Conclusion

Online Tool C.1: A Checklist: Signals of Reframing Success
> A downloadable checklist of signals that your reframe has been a success.

About the Author

Ray Sclafani is founder and CEO of ClientWise, the premier coaching and training company serving the financial services industry. Through ClientWise, Ray has provided coaching or created and presented workshops for, among others, Merrill Lynch, Morgan Stanley Wealth Management, UBS, LPL, Ameriprise Financial, Raymond James, MetLife, and Northwestern Mutual. In addition, he has spoken on request to major industry conferences and company events for firms such as Raymond James and FSC Securities, as well as the FPA National Conference, the John Hancock Funds Wholesaler Conference, the Nationwide Financial Summit Sales Conference, the MetLife Presidents' Conference, the Northwestern Mutual Forum, Northwestern Mutual's annual meeting, *Barron's* Winner's Circle Summit, and *Barron's* Top Advisory Teams Summit.

Prior to his leadership role at ClientWise, Ray served in the financial industry, where he worked at Alliance Bernstein for 20 years in several key roles, including founder and managing director of the Advisor Institute at Alliance Bernstein, where he developed and directed an extensive series of programs directed at creating sustainable motivation, increased sales, and deepened client relationships.

Through significant coaching education and practice, Ray earned the Professional Certified Coach (PCC) designation from the International Coach Federation, the leading independent professional association for coaches. He also holds a Master's Certification in Neuro-Linguistics from the International Association for Neuro-Linguistic Programming and has participated in The Strategic® Coach Program for 17 years. Ray holds a BA from Baylor University and lives in Bedford, New York, with his wife and true life partner, Beth, and their two sons, who continually inspire his work and his passion for excellence.

Index

Note: Page references in *italics* refer to figures.

[NOT] 478

[AND] 478

[OR] 478

[NAND] 478

[NOR] 478

[XOR] 478

DISCRETE MATHEMATICS

DISCRETE MATHEMATICS

Kenneth A. Ross | Charles R. B. Wright

Department of Mathematics | University of Oregon

PRENTICE-HALL, INC. | Englewood Cliffs, N.J. 07632

Library of Congress Cataloging in Publication Data

Ross, Kenneth A.
  Discrete mathematics.

  Includes indexes.
  1. Electronic data processing—Mathematics.
I. Wright, Charles R. B.   II. Title.
QA76.9.M35R67   1985   511   84-15978
ISBN 0-13-215286-X

Editorial/production supervision: *Nicholas C. Romanelli*
Manufacturing buyer: *John Hall*
Cover design: *Lundgren Graphics, Ltd.*
Cover art: *Photo by Michael de Camp, from The Image Bank*

Printed in the United States of America

10 9 8 7 6 5 4 3 2

ISBN 0-13-215286-X

Prentice-Hall International, Inc., *London*
Prentice-Hall of Australia Pty. Limited, *Sydney*
Editora Prentice-Hall do Brasil, Ltda., *Rio de Janeiro*
Prentice-Hall Canada Inc., *Toronto*
Prentice-Hall Hispanoamericana, S.A., *Mexico*
Prentice-Hall of India Private Limited, *New Delhi*
Prentice-Hall of Japan, Inc., *Tokyo*
Prentice-Hall of Southeast Asia Pte. Ltd., *Singapore*
Whitehall Books Limited, *Wellington, New Zealand*

To Emily and Laurel Ross
and Karen Wright

CONTENTS

x   *Contents*

PREFACE

||||||||||||||||||||||||||||||||||||||||||||||||||||||||||||||||||||||||||||||||||||||||||||||||||||||||||||||||||||||||||||||||||||||||||||||||||||||||||||||||||||||||||||||||||||||||||||||||||

The term "discrete mathematics" is used broadly to describe the kind of mathematics in which properties such as nearness and smoothness—the key ideas of calculus—are not at issue. In this book the term means the basic noncalculus mathematics a computer science student needs. Some of the material is algebra, some is logic, some is combinatorics or graph theory. Some of the sets we deal with are finite and others are infinite.

Although we do draw on computer science for motivation, we assume no previous experience in the subject. When it is necessary to discuss an application such as logical circuit design in some detail, we provide the needed background, but otherwise we have avoided including topics which are more properly taught in courses in computer science. Of course the choice of topics is a matter of judgment. We have left out a discussion of automata, because the power of mathematics is not very clear in an elementary treatment of the subject. Coding theory is exciting mathematics, but to say anything useful requires more algebra than we develop here. Our treatments of algorithm verification and of time and space complexity are woven into the accounts of other subjects—for instance the division algorithm—rather than set off separately. Algorithm verification is one of the main applications of logic, induction and recursion. We have provided the tools for it, and we have also provided a number of algorithms which come up naturally in the study of relations and graphs. Some of them are written in English and some in a self-explanatory pseudo-code, with the choice of format made for maximum clarity.

We have included more abstract algebra than is absolutely necessary for the undergraduate computer science curriculum today. All of the evidence indicates that in the years to come, computer science will require a higher level of mathematical sophistication, involving more and more advanced mathematics. To give students some of the tools they will need in the future, we have developed enough of the theory of groups to treat nontrivial applications involving symmetry. The discussion of groups also serves as a model for other algebraic systems and for the general algebraic approach which we have taken in much of the book.

One of our main goals is the development of mathematical maturity. We and our colleagues have used this material successfully for several years with average students at the level of beginning calculus, and we find that by the end of two terms they are ready for upperclass work. The presentation begins with an intuitive approach which becomes more and more rigorous as the students' appreciation for proofs and skill at building them increase. Our account is careful but informal. As we go along we illustrate the way mathematicians attack problems, and show the power of an abstract approach. We have aimed to make the account simple enough so the students can learn it and complete enough so they won't have to learn it again.

Chapter 0 gives an introduction to graphs and algorithms and suggests some of the kinds of problems we will consider later. It can be covered quickly, but should not be skipped. Chapters 1, 2, 3, 4 and 7 contain the core material on sets, logic, functions, relations and algebra. The remaining chapters are independent of each other, except that some of the material on digraphs in Sections 8.1 and 8.2 is required in Sections 10.5, 11.2, 11.5 and 11.6.

We have broken the discussion of logic into two parts: Chapter 2 contains the propositional calculus and an introduction to induction, and Chapter 6 presents the predicate calculus, recursion and generalized induction. We have found that the material goes down better in two bites, and that revisiting logic helps reinforce Chapter 2.

Various choices of topics are possible for a one-semester course. One program which ties together relations, graphs and algorithms consists of Chapters 0, 1, 2, 3, 7, Sections 4.1, 4.2, 4.3 on matrices, algebra and relations, and Sections 8.1, 8.4 and 8.7 on graphs, with Sections 8.2, 8.8 and 8.9 as time permits. A two-semester course can cover the whole book. We strongly recommend coordinating the choice and sequence of topics covered with the computer science courses which the students are taking concurrently. The interactive potential is enormous.

It is a pleasure to acknowledge the helpful comments and suggestions given by our students and colleagues. In particular, we thank our colleagues Frank Anderson, Micheal Dyer, James Harper, David Harrison, William Kantor, Richard Koch, Ivan Niven, Margaret Owens, Andrzej Proskurowski, Stephen Prothero, Mark Reeder and Jerry Wolfe. From among our students, the most helpful comments came from Joyce Eaton, Kenneth Peale and Cathy Phillips.

It is a pleasure also to thank our editor, Bob Sickles, and the members of the staff at Prentice-Hall. In particular, the professional wisdom and experience of Nicholas C. Romanelli are largely responsible for the successful transformation from manuscript to book.

TO THE STUDENT ESPECIALLY

We know that words like "obviously" and "clearly" can be very annoying; they have sometimes bothered us too. When you see them occasionally in this book they are intended as hints. If you don't find the passage obvious or clear, you are probably making the situation too complicated or reading something unintended into the text. Take a break; then back up and read the material again. Similarly, the examples are meant to be helpful. If you are pretty sure you know the ideas involved, but an example seems much too hard, skip over it on first reading and then come back later. If you aren't very sure of the ideas, though, take a more careful look at the example.

Exercises are an important part of the book. They give you a chance to check your understanding and to practice thinking and writing clearly and mathematically. As the book goes on, more and more exercises ask you for proofs. We use the words "show" and "prove" interchangeably, though "show" is more common when a calculation is enough of an answer and "prove" suggests some reasoning is called for. "Prove" means "give a convincing argument or discussion to show why the assertion is true." What you write should be convincing to an instructor, to a fellow student, and to yourself the next day. Proofs should include words and sentences, not just computations, so that the reader can follow your thought processes. Use the proofs in the book as models, especially at first. The discussion of logical proofs in Chapter 2 will also help. Perfecting the ability to write a "good" proof is like perfecting the ability to write a "good" essay or give a "good" oral presentation. They all take practice. Don't be discouraged when one of your proofs fails to convince an expert (say a teacher or a grader). Instead, try to see what failed to be convincing.

Each chapter ends with a list of the main points it covers and with some suggestions for how to use the list to review. One of the best ways to learn material which you plan to use again is to tie each new idea to as many familiar concepts and situations as you can, and to visualize settings in which the new fact would be helpful to you. We have included lots of examples in the text to make this process easier. The review lists can be used to go over the material in the same way by yourself or with fellow students.

Answers or hints to most odd-numbered exercises are given in the back of the book. Wise students will look at the answers only after trying seriously to do the problems. When a proof is called for we usually give a hint or an outline of a proof, which you should first understand and then expand upon. A symbols index appears on the inside of the front cover and the Greek alphabet on the inside of the back cover. At the back of the book there is an index of topics. Starting on page 556 there is a brief dictionary of terms that we use in the text without explanation, but which some readers may have forgotten or never encountered. Look at these items right now to see where they are and what they contain, and then join us for Chapter 0.

K.A. Ross / C.R.B. Wright

0

INTRODUCTION TO GRAPHS

AND TREES

The purpose of this text is to present an introduction to several topics in discrete mathematics that are used in or are related to topics in computer science. The presentation will stress precise and mathematical thought, an ingredient essential to both disciplines and in fact to all sciences. However, in practice, such precision is preceded by intuition, which is often obtained by an analysis of examples.

In this chapter we give an informal introduction to graphs and trees. These are topics that are easily grasped, and for which the concepts are easily illustrated with pictures. Our discussion is often intuitive, but it is not careless. In later chapters we will fill in the mathematical formality which is left out for now. While reading and studying our small easy examples, you should try to imagine large complex ones. Ask yourself whether the thought processes remain valid. We understand complex situations by first understanding simple ones.

§ *0.1 Graphs*

You are already undoubtedly familiar with the idea of a graph as a picture of a function. The word "graph" is also used to describe a different kind of structure which arises in a variety of natural settings and which is the subject of this section. In a loose sense these new graphs are diagrams which, properly interpreted, contain information. The graphs we are concerned with are like road maps, circuit diagrams or flowcharts in the sense that they depict connections or relationships between various parts of the diagram.

The diagrams in Figure 1 are from a variety of settings. Figure 1(a) shows a simple flowchart. Figure 1(b) might represent five warehouses of a trucking firm and truck routes between them, labeled with their distances.

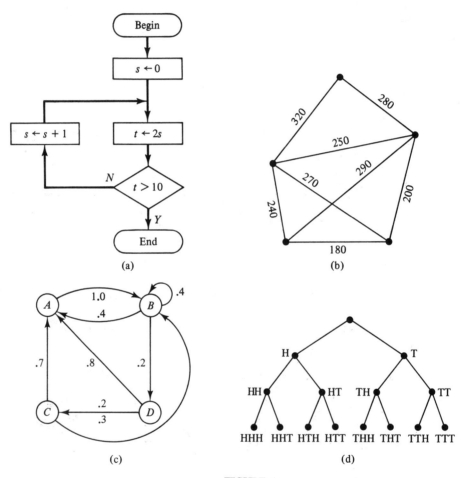

FIGURE 1

Figure 1(c) could be telling us about the probability that a rat located in one of four cages will move to one of the other three or stay in its own cage. Figure 1(d) might depict possible outcomes of a repeated experiment such as coin tossing [Heads or Tails]. What do all these diagrams have in common? Each consists of a collection of objects—boxes, circles or dots—and some lines between the objects. Sometimes the lines are directed; that is, they are arrows. Sometimes the objects are labeled, and sometimes the lines are. Later we will worry about arrows and labels, but for now we just concentrate on the objects and lines.

The essential features of a **graph** are its objects and connecting lines; see Figure 2. The objects, drawn here as dots, are called **vertices** [plural of **vertex**] and the connecting lines are called **edges**. The graphs in Figures 2(a) and 2(b)

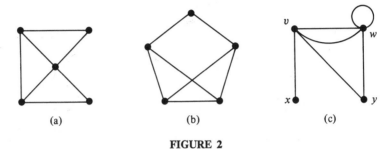

(a)   (b)   (c)

FIGURE 2

have 5 vertices and 7 edges. The crossing of the two lines in Figure 2(b) is irrelevant and is just a peculiarity of our drawing. The graph in Figure 2(c) has 4 vertices and 6 edges. Two of its edges connect vertex v to vertex w; they are called **multiple edges** or **parallel edges**. One of its edges connects the vertex w to itself; such an edge is called a **loop**.

In graph theory we are interested in sequences of edges that link up with each other to form a **path**. To illustrate the idea, we redraw Figure 2(c) in Figure 3(a) and label the edges as well as the vertices. Examples of paths are $d\,b\,f\,e$ [Figure 3(b)] and $c\,f\,e\,b\,a$ [Figure 3(c)]. Note that the drawing alone

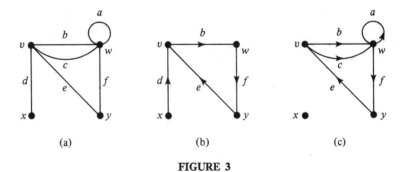

(a)   (b)   (c)

FIGURE 3

does not tell us what path we have in mind: Figure 3(c) is also a picture of the paths $b\,a\,f\,e\,c$ and $c\,a\,f\,e\,b$. Paths can repeat edges: $b\,a\,b\,e\,f\,a\,a\,b$ is a path. The **length** of a path is the number of edges in the path. Thus $b\,a\,b\,e\,f\,a\,a\,b$ has length 8.

Adjacent edges in a path must have a vertex in common. So a path determines a sequence of vertices. The vertex sequences for the paths discussed above are as follows:

The path	Its vertex sequence
$d\,b\,f\,e$	$x\,v\,w\,y\,v$
$c\,f\,e\,b\,a$	$v\,w\,y\,v\,w\,w$
$b\,a\,f\,e\,c$	$v\,w\,w\,y\,v\,w$
$c\,a\,f\,e\,b$	$v\,w\,w\,y\,v\,w$
$b\,a\,b\,e\,f\,a\,a\,b$	$v\,w\,w\,v\,y\,w\,w\,w\,v$

Note several items. The number of vertices in a vertex sequence is one larger than the number of edges in the path. When a loop appears in a path, its vertex is repeated in the vertex sequence. Vertex sequences treat parallel edges the same and so different paths, such as $b\,a\,f\,e\,c$ and $c\,a\,f\,e\,b$, can have the same vertex sequence. If a graph has no parallel edges or multiple loops, then vertex sequences do uniquely determine paths. In this case the edges can be described by just listing the two vertices which they connect and we may describe a path by its vertex sequence.

A path is a **closed path** if the first and last vertices of its vertex sequence are the same. Some closed paths in Figure 3(a) are $b\,a\,b\,e\,f\,a\,a\,b$, $d\,c\,f\,e\,d$ with vertex sequence $x\,v\,w\,y\,v\,x$, and $f\,e\,b$ with vertex sequence $w\,y\,v\,w$. A **cycle** is a closed path that is efficient in the sense that it repeats no edges and the vertices of its vertex sequence are all distinct except for the first and last ones. Thus $f\,e\,b$ is a cycle. The closed path $d\,c\,f\,e\,d$ repeats the edge d and its vertex sequence $x\,v\,w\,y\,v\,x$ repeats the vertex v. The closed path $c\,a\,f\,e$ is not a cycle; it doesn't repeat any edges but its vertex sequence $v\,w\,w\,y\,v$ repeats the vertex w.

A graph is **acyclic** if it contains no cycles. A path is **acyclic** if the subgraph consisting of the vertices and edges of the path is acyclic. The graph in Figure 4 is not acyclic, since $v\,u\,y\,x\,w\,v$ is a cycle. The path $s\,t\,v\,w\,x\,y\,z$ *is* acyclic.

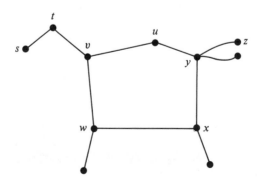

FIGURE 4

So is the path $u\,v\,t\,v\,w$; the side trip $v\,t\,v$ is not a cycle. The path $u\,v\,t\,v\,w\,x$ $y\,z\,y\,u$ is not acyclic, since the subgraph it determines contains the cycle $u\,v\,w\,x\,y\,u$.

One of the oldest problems involving graphs is the Königsberg bridge problem, which asks whether it is possible to take a walk in the town shown in Figure 5(a) crossing each bridge exactly once and returning home. The

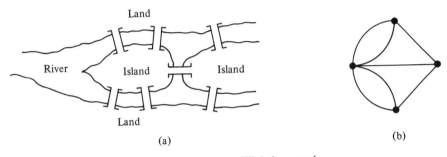

(a)

(b)

Königsberg graph

FIGURE 5

Swiss mathematician Leonhard Euler [pronounced OIL-er] solved this problem in 1736. He constructed the graph shown in Figure 5(b), replacing the land areas by vertices and the bridges joining them by edges. The question then became: Is there a closed path in this graph which uses each edge exactly once? We call such a path an **Euler circuit**. Euler showed that no such path exists for the graph in Figure 5(b). To see why, we need one more concept. The **degree** of a vertex in a graph is the number of edges connected to that vertex. In Figure 6 we have written the degrees beside the vertices. Note that a loop contributes 2, not 1, to the degree of a vertex. Euler showed that a graph which has an Euler circuit must have all vertices of even degree. So the

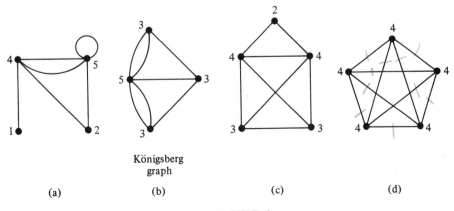

(a)

Königsberg
graph

(b)

(c)

(d)

FIGURE 6

only graph in Figure 6 that could possibly have an Euler circuit is (d). Does it?

Let's see why an Euler circuit forces all vertices to have even degree. Start at some vertex on the circuit and follow the circuit from vertex to vertex, erasing each edge as you go along it. When you go through a vertex you erase one edge going in and one going out, or else you erase a loop. Either way, the erasure reduces the degree of the vertex by 2. Eventually every edge gets erased and all vertices have degree 0. So all vertices must have had even degree to begin with.

Euler also proved that his result almost goes the other way. That is, if every vertex has even degree, this is almost enough to assure us that the graph has an Euler circuit. Almost? Look at Figure 7. This is a picture of a graph

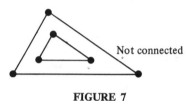

FIGURE 7

since it consists of vertices and edges, even though it's not connected like our earlier examples. [A graph is **connected** if given any two vertices there is a path connecting them.] Every vertex in Figure 7 has even degree, but obviously[1] this graph has no Euler circuit because the graph is not connected. Here is what Euler showed.

Euler's Theorem[2] If all the vertices of a connected graph have even degree, then the graph has an Euler circuit.

To really understand this theorem we should be able to find a proof, or develop an algorithm or procedure that would always produce an Euler circuit. Indeed, these two approaches are intimately connected. A full understanding of a proof often leads to an algorithm, and behind every algorithm there's a proof. Here's a simple explanation of Euler's theorem, which we illustrate using Figure 8. Start with any vertex, say w, and any edge connected to it, say a. The other vertex, x in this case, has even degree and has been used an odd number of times [once] and so there is an unused edge leaving x. Pick one, say b. Continue in this way. The process won't stop until the starting vertex w is reached since, whenever any other vertex is reached, only an odd number of its edges have been used. In our example, this algorithm might

---

[1]See the preface for a discussion concerning this very annoying word.
[2]Some terms, like "theorem," are explained briefly in the dictionary which starts on page 556. Most technical terms can be found by way of the index.

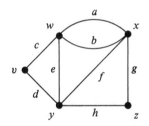

FIGURE 8

start out with edges *a b e* and vertices *w x w y*. At *y* we can choose any of three edges: *d, f,* or *h*. If we select *f*, the rest of the process is determined. We end up with the Euler circuit *a b e f g h d c* with vertex sequence *w x w y x z y v w*.

Simple, wasn't it? Well, it is too simple. What would have happened if, when we first reached vertex *y*, we had chosen edge *d*? After choosing edge *c*, we'd be trapped at vertex *w* and our path *a b e d c* would have missed edges *f, g* and *h*. Our explanation and our algorithm must be too simple. In our example it is clear that edge *d* should have been avoided when we first reached vertex *y*, but why? What general principle should have warned us to avoid this choice? Think about it. We will continue this discussion in the next section.

EXERCISES 0.1

1. Which of the following vertex sequences describe paths in the graph drawn in Figure 9(a)?
   (a) *s t u v w x y z*   (b) *t v w z y x*
   (c) *s t u s*   (d) *t u s s*
   (e) *v w v w v w v*   (f) *w v u s t v w*

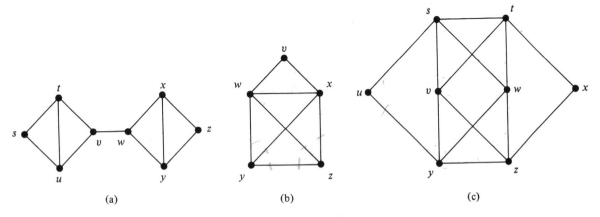

FIGURE 9

2. Which paths in Exercise 1 are closed paths?

3. Which paths in Exercise 1 are cycles?

4. For the graph in Figure 9(a), give the vertex sequence of a shortest path connecting the following pairs of vertices and give its length.
   (a) s and v (b) s and z
   (c) u and y (d) v and w

5. For each pair of vertices in Exercise 4, give the vertex sequence of a longest path connecting them that repeats no edges. Is there a longest path connecting them?

6. Which graphs in Figure 9 have Euler circuits? For those that don't, give an explanation. For those that do, give an Euler circuit.

7. True or False. "True" means "true in all circumstances under consideration." Consider a graph.
   (a) If there is an edge from a vertex u to a vertex v, then there is an edge from v to u.
   (b) If there is an edge from a vertex u to a vertex v and an edge from v to a vertex w, then there is an edge from u to w.

8. Repeat Exercise 7 with the word "edge" replaced by "path" everywhere.

9. Repeat Exercise 7 with the word "edge" replaced by "path of even length" everywhere.

10. Repeat Exercise 7 with the word "edge" replaced by "path of odd length" everywhere.

11. Give an example of a graph with vertices x, y and z with the following three properties:
    (i)   there is a cycle using vertices x and y;
    (ii) there is a cycle using vertices y and z;
    (iii) no cycle uses vertices x and z.

12. (a) For each graph in Figure 6 calculate
        (i) the sum of the degrees of all of the vertices;
        (ii) the number of edges.
    (b) Compare your answers to part (a) and make a conjecture.
    (c) Use the "erasing edge" idea to justify your conjecture in part (b).
    (d) Can a graph have an odd number of vertices of odd degree?

13. Suppose that a cycle contains a loop. What is its length? Can a cycle contain two loops?

§0.2   Special Paths and Trees

We continue our discussion of Euler's theorem and the example in Figure 8 of §0.1, which we reproduce in Figure 1(a). As we select edges let's remove them from the graph and consider the subgraphs so obtained. Our path started out with edges $a\ b\ e$; Figure 1(b) shows the graph with these edges removed. In our successful search for an Euler circuit we next selected f, and we noted that if we had selected d we were doomed. Figure 1(c) shows the graph if f is also removed while Figure 1(d) shows the graph if instead d is removed.

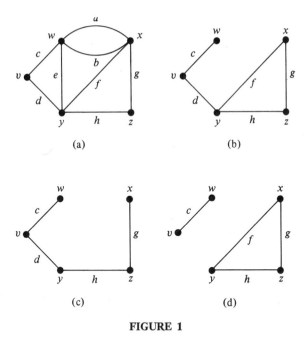

FIGURE 1

There is a difference: removal of d disconnected the graph while removal of f did not. This is the clue for an algorithm that works. At each vertex, FLEURY'S algorithm instructs us to select, if possible, an edge whose removal will not disconnect the graph. If this is not possible, there is exactly one edge available. We select it; then remove it and the vertex from the graph.

The original choice of edges $a\,b\,e\,f\,g\,h\,d\,c$ satisfied the restrictions of FLEURY'S algorithm. Let's illustrate the procedure again, starting at vertex z; see Figure 2(a). Select edges h and f so that we are at vertex x; Figure 2(b) shows these edges removed. Selection of edge g would disconnect the graph; vertex z would be isolated from the rest of the graph. So we select edge a so that we are at vertex w [Figure 2(c)]. Now choosing b would disconnect the graph, so we select c or e, say c. The rest of the procedure is forced. When we remove d, we remove the isolated vertex v. Then we remove e and the isolated vertex y. Etc. See Figures 2(d)–2(f). The Euler circuit obtained is $h\,f\,a\,c\,d\,e\,b\,g$ with vertex sequence $z\,y\,x\,w\,v\,y\,w\,x\,z$.

Euler's theorem tells us which graphs have closed paths using each edge exactly once, and FLEURY'S algorithm gives a way to construct the paths when they exist. In contrast, much less is known about graphs with paths which go through each vertex exactly once. The Scottish mathematician Sir William Hamilton was one of the first to study such graphs, and at one time even marketed a puzzle based on the problem. A closed path is called a **Hamilton circuit** if it uses every vertex of the graph exactly once, except for the last vertex, which duplicates the first vertex. The difference between finding

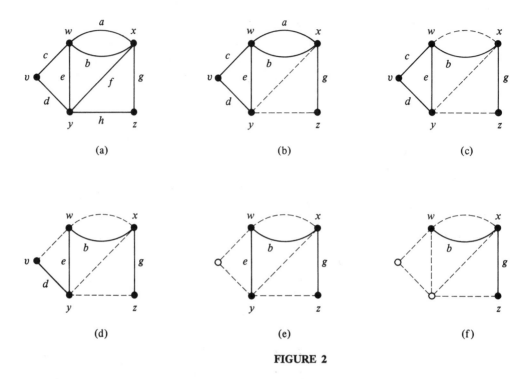

FIGURE 2

an Euler circuit and a Hamilton circuit is the difference between inspecting streets and inspecting street lights at corners.

Consider the graphs in Figure 3. The graph in Figure 3(a) certainly has a Hamilton circuit which will be an Euler circuit too. The graph in Figure 3(b) has no Hamilton circuit: any path that used every vertex would have to use the central vertex more than once. It does have an Euler circuit. Why? The 8-vertex graph in Figure 3(c) has many Hamilton circuits; the arrows indicate how one of them goes. This graph has no Euler circuit. Why? The 7-vertex graph in Figure 3(d) has no Hamilton circuit. To see this, note that each edge connects an upper vertex to a lower vertex. If there were a Hamilton

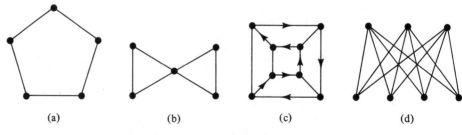

FIGURE 3

circuit, its vertex sequence would alternate between upper and lower vertices and would consist of exactly 8 vertices. The first and eighth vertices would have to be different [one would be upper and one would be lower] and yet they would have to be the same to complete the circuit. We conclude that no such circuit exists.

With Euler's theorem, the theory of Euler circuits is very nice and complete. What can be proved about Hamilton circuits? Under certain conditions, graphs will have so many edges compared to the number of vertices that they must have Hamilton circuits. But the graph in Figure 3(a) has very few edges and yet it has a Hamilton circuit. And the graph in Figure 3(d) has lots of edges but no Hamilton circuit. It turns out that there is no known simple characterization of those connected graphs possessing Hamilton circuits. The concept of Hamilton circuit seems very close to that of Euler circuit, and yet the theory of Hamilton circuits is vastly more complicated. In particular, no efficient algorithm is known for finding Hamilton circuits. The problem is a special case of the Traveling Salesperson Problem. Here one begins with a graph whose edges are assigned **weights** that may represent mileage, cost, computer time or some other quantity that we wish to minimize. In Figure 4 the weights might represent mileage between cities on a traveling salesperson's route. The goal is to find the shortest round trip that visits each city exactly

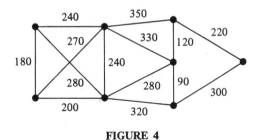

FIGURE 4

once. That is, the goal is to find a Hamilton circuit minimizing the sum of the weights of the edges. A nice algorithm solving this problem would also be able to find Hamilton circuits in an unweighted graph, since we could always assign weight 1 to each edge.

We next consider a different problem that resembles the Hamilton circuit problem but which is much easier to solve. Given a connected weighted graph, the goal is to find a connected subgraph using all vertices and having minimal total weight. [The **total weight** of a subgraph is the sum of the weights of its edges.] For example, suppose Figure 4 represents distances between cities and that the goal is to connect all cities by pipelines using the minimum possible number of miles of pipeline. It turns out that minimal connected subgraphs are always acyclic, since removal of an edge from a cycle will not disconnect a graph. Acyclic connected graphs are so important that they get a special name: they are called **trees**. We'll devote a whole chapter to them, including applications to such computer science topics as data structures and reverse Polish notation.

Figure 5 contains some examples of trees. Incidentally, we regard the trees in Figures 5(a) and 5(b) as essentially the same. Their pictures are differ-

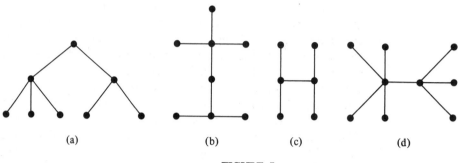

(a)   (b)   (c)   (d)

FIGURE 5

ent but the essential structure [vertices and edges] is the same. They share all graph-theoretic properties such as the numbers of vertices and edges, the number of vertices of each degree, etc. To make this clear, we have redrawn them in Figures 6(a) and 6(b) and labeled corresponding vertices. The trees in Figures 6(c) and 6(d) are also essentially the same.

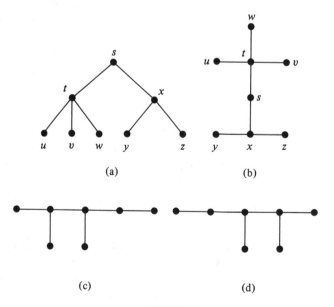

(a)   (b)

(c)   (d)

FIGURE 6

Now back to the problem of minimal connected subgraphs that use all vertices. As we remarked, such a subgraph must be a tree. It is called a **minimal spanning tree**. A connected graph always has at least one minimal spanning tree; let's look at a simple algorithm for finding one. To use the algorithm we first list the edges of the graph in order of their weights. Let's use subscripts and list the edges as $e_1, e_2, e_3, \ldots$ where e_1 is the edge of lowest weight, e_2 is the edge of next lowest weight, etc. If two edges have the same weight, it doesn't matter which comes first. Using this convention we redraw the "pipeline" Figure 4 in Figure 7. Note that the labels on edges e_6 and e_7

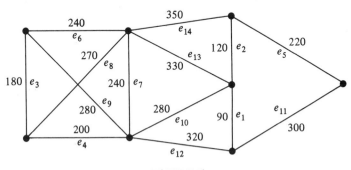

FIGURE 7

could be interchanged. So could the ones on edges e_9 and e_{10}. Our algorithm begins with no edges at all and selects the edges $e_1, e_2, \ldots$ in order, except that at each step we don't use an edge if its selection would create a cycle. Figure 8(a) shows the subgraph obtained after selecting edges e_1, e_2, e_3, e_4, e_5 and e_6. The algorithm rejects edges e_7, e_8 and e_9 because the addition of any of these to the graph in Figure 8(a) would create a cycle. The algorithm next accepts edge e_{10} and rejects the remaining edges. At the end, the algorithm provides the spanning tree in Figure 8(b). The total weight of this minimal spanning tree is

$$90 + 120 + 180 + 200 + 220 + 240 + 280 = 1330;$$

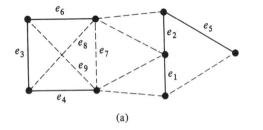

(a)

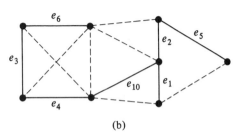

(b)

FIGURE 8

1330 miles of pipeline would be needed to connect all the cities in Figure 4. This algorithm is often called a **greedy algorithm**. Can you see a reason for the name?

Suppose we want a spanning tree for a connected graph whose edges aren't weighted. No problem. We assign all edges the same weight, say 1, order the edges in any way we like and apply the algorithm described in the last paragraph. Different orderings may provide different spanning trees. If we want *all* spanning trees, then the problem gets more complicated. Of course, we could apply our algorithm to each ordering, but note, for example, that there are[3]

$$14! = 14 \cdot 13 \cdot 12 \cdot 11 \cdot 10 \cdot 9 \cdot 8 \cdot 7 \cdot 6 \cdot 5 \cdot 4 \cdot 3 \cdot 2 \cdot 1$$

$$\approx 8.72 \cdot 10^{10}$$

possible orderings of the edges for the graph in Figure 7. Even computers don't like to face this many computations. To find all spanning trees one would be advised to look for a better approach, but we will not pursue this matter.

The symbol 14! just used is read "14 factorial." In general, $n!$ is read "n factorial" and is shorthand for

$$n(n-1)(n-2) \cdots 3 \cdot 2 \cdot 1 = 1 \cdot 2 \cdot 3 \cdots (n-2)(n-1)n.$$

Procedures or algorithms that lead to approximately $n!$ steps when one has n vertices or edges are regarded as ineffective because $n!$ grows incredibly rapidly as n gets large. Procedures that lead to something like n^2 steps [or n^3 or $n\sqrt{n}$, say, depending on the circumstances] are regarded as reasonably effective. It is in roughly this sense that we regard FLEURY'S algorithm for finding Euler circuits as acceptable. There are no known effective algorithms for finding Hamilton circuits or even for deciding whether one exists in a particular graph.

EXERCISES 0.2

1. Which of the graphs in Figure 9 have Euler circuits? Hamilton circuits? Give the vertex sequence of a Hamilton or Euler circuit in each case in which one exists.

2. Use FLEURY'S algorithm to find an Euler circuit in the graph of Figure 9(b).

3. Apply FLEURY'S algorithm to the graph of Figure 9(a) until it breaks down. Start at vertex w.

---

[3]The notation $\approx$ means "approximately equals."

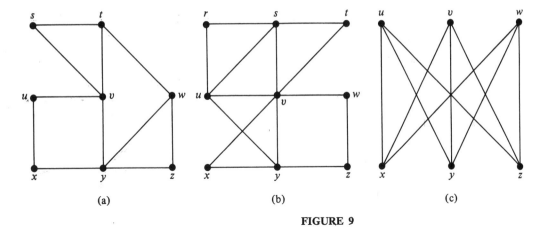

FIGURE 9

4. Repeat Exercise 3 for the graph in Figure 9(c).

5. Which of the graphs in Figure 2 of § 0.1 have Hamilton circuits?

6. Count the number of spanning trees in the graphs of Figure 10.

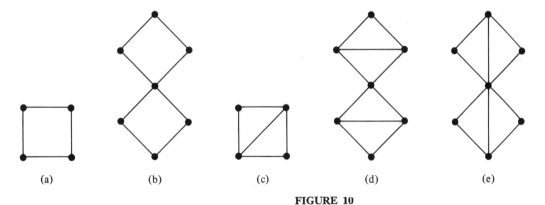

FIGURE 10

7. In the pipeline problem of Figure 7, the labels on edges e_6 and e_7 could have been interchanged. Interchange them and apply the algorithm for minimal spanning trees to the new sequence of edges. What is the total weight of your new spanning tree?

8. Reverse the order of the edges in Figure 7, i.e., switch the names on e_1 and e_{14}, on e_2 and e_{13}, etc. Redraw the figure and apply the algorithm for minimal spanning trees to this sequence of edges. The tree you get will be a "maximal spanning tree" with respect to the weights in Figure 7. What is its total weight?

9. (a) For each tree in Figure 5, count the number of vertices and the number of edges, and compare the answers.

(b) On the basis of your work in part (a), make a general conjecture concerning a tree with n vertices.

(c) Why must a connected graph with n vertices have at least $n - 1$ edges? *Hint:* It has at least one spanning tree.

10. Vertices of a tree having degree 1 are called **leaves**.
   (a) Count the leaves on the trees in Figure 5.
   (b) Every tree [with more than one vertex] has at least two leaves. Think about this and see if you can give an explanation.
   (c) Draw three trees each of which has exactly two leaves.

11. Consider the tree in Figure 11(a).
   (a) Select several pairs of vertices and, for each pair, give all paths connecting them which repeat no edges.
   (b) Based on your work in part (a), make a general conjecture about trees.

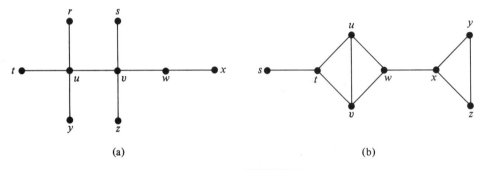

(a)   (b)

FIGURE 11

12. (a) Consider the graph in Figure 11(b). Here is the vertex sequence for a path from u to z: $u\,t\,s\,t\,v\,w\,u\,v\,w\,x\,z\,y\,z$. Cut out parts of this path to get an acyclic path from u to z which repeats no edges. *Hint:* Why visit a vertex twice?
   (b) Describe a general algorithm which, given a path from a vertex u to a vertex v, produces an acyclic path from u to v.

13. Consider the graph in Figure 11(b).
   (a) Which edges are parts of cycles? For example, edge $t\,u$ is part of the cycle $t\,u\,w\,v\,t$.
   (b) Which edges have the property that their removal from the graph would disconnect the graph?
   (c) Can you make a general conjecture based on this example?

14. Consider a tree with n vertices. It has exactly $n - 1$ edges [Exercise 9] and so the sum of the degrees of its vertices is $2n - 2$ [Exercise 13 of § 0.1].
   (a) A certain tree has two vertices of degree 4, one vertex of degree 3 and one vertex of degree 2. If the other vertices have degree 1, how many vertices are there in the graph? *Hint:* If the tree has n vertices, $n - 4$ of them will have to have degree 1.
   (b) Draw a tree as described in part (a).

15. Repeat Exercise 14 for a tree with two vertices of degree 5, three of degree 3, two of degree 2 and the rest of degree 1.

§ *0.3* *Matrices for Graphs*

Informally, a graph consists of dots and lines, i.e., vertices and edges. How can we, or a computer, describe such a structure in an unambiguous manner? We might list all vertices and all edges and specify for each edge which vertices it connects. This is how we will finally define a graph after we have introduced sets and functions. Another way to completely describe a graph would be to consider all pairs of vertices and to associate with each pair the number of edges connecting them. Since there might be loops in the graph, we allow ourselves to consider pairs where the two vertices are actually the same vertex. By arranging these numbers of edges in a suitable rectangular format we get what's called the matrix of a graph. [The plural of "matrix" is "matrices."]

As an illustration, we find the matrix of the graph in Figures 2(c) and 3(a) of § 0.1, which we have redrawn in Figure 1(a). We will want to list the vertices in order, so we have renamed them v_1, v_2, v_3, v_4, using subscripts to indicate the order. The matrix **M** of the graph is given in Figure 1(b).

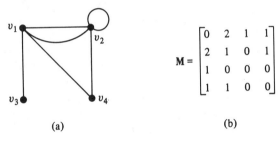

$$\mathbf{M} = \begin{bmatrix} 0 & 2 & 1 & 1 \\ 2 & 1 & 0 & 1 \\ 1 & 0 & 0 & 0 \\ 1 & 1 & 0 & 0 \end{bmatrix}$$

(a)   (b)

FIGURE 1

The entries in **M** tell how many edges there are between one vertex and another. For example, the entry 1 in the fourth horizontal row and second vertical column of **M**, designated M[4, 2], is the number of edges from the fourth vertex v_4 to the second vertex v_2. There is just one such edge, so the entry is 1. [See Figure 2(a).] Similarly, M[1, 2] = 2 because there are two edges connecting v_1 to v_2 [Figure 2(b)], and M[3, 4] = 0 since there are no edges from v_3 to v_4. More generally, the entry M[i, j] in row i and column j is the number of edges from vertex v_i to vertex v_j. When we describe the location of an entry in a matrix we always tell first which row it's in and then which column.

Note that the matrix **M** contains all the information about the connections in the graph, so we can recover the graph from its matrix alone, without the picture. And we can read some information right off the matrix. For example, there are parallel edges if and only if some matrix entry is larger than 1. The loops are all indicated on the main diagonal; see Figure 2(c).

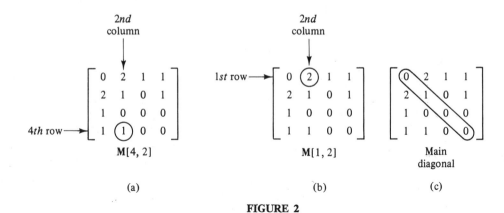

FIGURE 2

The entry $M[2, 2] = 1$ shows that there is a loop at v_2. The other diagonal matrix entries are 0 and so there are no other loops. If a vertex v_i has no loops, its degree is simply the sum of the entries of the ith row [or column]. For example, v_1 has degree 4 since the entries in row 1 add to 4. Finally, observe that the matrix of a graph will be symmetric about the main diagonal, since $M[i, j] = M[j, i]$ for all choices of i and j. Some properties of graphs are not easy to read from their matrices [e.g., the existence of Hamilton circuits], but sometimes we will be able to manipulate the matrices to learn about the graphs.

In § 0.2 we made somewhat vague references to graphs that are "essentially the same." We will not make the notion really precise [the magic word will be "isomorphism"] until after we have a precise set-theoretic definition of graph. But here is an observation that might help give you a sense of what we are looking for. Two graphs are essentially the same [i.e., are "isomorphic"] if their vertices can be ordered so that the matrices of the two graphs are identical. Figure 3 shows all possible trees with 6 vertices. Any tree with 6 vertices

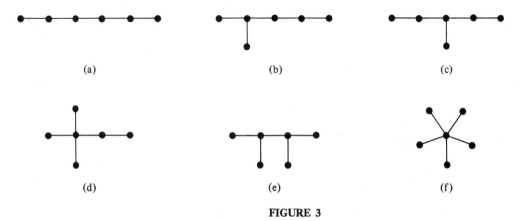

FIGURE 3

must be isomorphic with exactly one of the given trees, and no two trees in the figure are isomorphic with each other.

Isomorphic graphs must share graph-theoretic properties; they must have the same numbers of edges, vertices, loops, cycles of length 4, vertices of even degree, etc. One might hope that there would be a reasonably short list of properties such that any two graphs that shared the properties on the list would have to be isomorphic. No such luck. In general, there are no easy ways to check whether two graphs are isomorphic. Of course, if you can find some graph-theoretic property that they do *not* share, you are done and the graphs *aren't* isomorphic.

As an illustration, with suitable choices for their orderings the graphs in Figures 3(b) and 3(c) have matrices

$$\begin{bmatrix} 0 & 1 & 0 & 0 & 0 & 0 \\ 1 & 0 & 1 & 0 & 0 & 1 \\ 0 & 1 & 0 & 1 & 0 & 0 \\ 0 & 0 & 1 & 0 & 1 & 0 \\ 0 & 0 & 0 & 1 & 0 & 0 \\ 0 & 1 & 0 & 0 & 0 & 0 \end{bmatrix} \text{ and } \begin{bmatrix} 0 & 1 & 0 & 0 & 0 & 0 \\ 1 & 0 & 1 & 0 & 0 & 0 \\ 0 & 1 & 0 & 1 & 0 & 1 \\ 0 & 0 & 1 & 0 & 1 & 0 \\ 0 & 0 & 0 & 1 & 0 & 0 \\ 0 & 0 & 1 & 0 & 0 & 0 \end{bmatrix}.$$

We can see that these two graphs are put together differently, so are not isomorphic, since one graph has two leaves [i.e., vertices of degree 1] connected to its vertex of degree 3 while the other graph has only one. This information is contained in the matrices, but we have to be looking for it to find it. At first glance the matrices look different, but not a *lot* different, so we might think we could just rearrange rows and columns to turn one into the other. One way to check this out would be to try all 6! possible orderings of the graph of Figure 3(b) and see if any of the matrices we get are identical with our matrix for Figure 3(c). That factorial sign tells us that in general such a method of checking isomorphism is impractical for large graphs. No method is known which is substantially better than this for arbitrary graphs, though much more effective algorithms are available for graphs of special types, such as trees.

Given a graph, it would be nice to be able to recognize which vertices can be reached from other vertices. Also, it would be useful to know how long the paths between them have to be. Let's tackle a simpler problem. Which vertices can be reached using paths of length 2? While we are at it, we'll keep track of how many such paths there are. We illustrate the ideas using the graph of Figure 1(a), reproduced in Figure 4(a) with the edges labeled. In Figure 4(b) we have created a new graph by connecting pairs of vertices by one edge for each path of length 2 between them in Figure 4(a). There are 6 loops at vertex v_1 because $b\,b$, $b\,c$, $c\,b$, $c\,c$, $d\,d$ and $e\,e$ are paths of length 2 from v_1 to v_1. The 3 edges from v_2 to v_4 represent the paths $b\,e$, $c\,e$ and $a\,f$

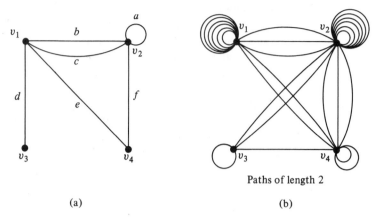

Paths of length 2

(a)   (b)

FIGURE 4

from v_2 to v_4. No edge in Figure 4(b) connects v_1 and v_3 since there are no paths of length 2 connecting these vertices.

The tedious analysis of the last paragraph for creating Figure 4(b) can be avoided by using the matrix **M** for the original graph. Let's count again the paths of length 2 from v_1 to v_2. Such a path passes through v_1, v_2, v_3 or v_4 on the way, so we can count the number of paths from v_1 to v_2 through v_1, the number through v_2, through v_3 and through v_4 and add these numbers to get the total. Now to get the number of paths with vertex sequence v_1 v_2 v_2, for example, we count the edges from v_1 to v_2 and the edges from v_2 to v_2 and multiply these numbers to get $2 \cdot 1 = 2$. The corresponding paths are $b\, a$ and $c\, a$. The numbers we multiply, **M**[1, 2] and **M**[2, 2], are given in the matrix **M**. The general situation for paths from v_1 to v_2 is illustrated in Table 1. The total number of paths of length 2 from v_1 to v_2 is thus

$$\mathbf{M}[1, 1] \cdot \mathbf{M}[1, 2] + \mathbf{M}[1, 2] \cdot \mathbf{M}[2, 2] + \mathbf{M}[1, 3] \cdot \mathbf{M}[3, 2] + \mathbf{M}[1, 4] \cdot \mathbf{M}[4, 2]$$
$$= 3.$$

TABLE 1

Vertex v_i	Number of edges from v_1 to v_i	Number of edges from v_i to v_2	Number of paths with vertex sequence v_1 v_i v_2
v_1	$\mathbf{M}[1, 1] = 0$	$\mathbf{M}[1, 2] = 2$	$\mathbf{M}[1, 1] \cdot \mathbf{M}[1, 2] = 0 \cdot 2 = 0$
v_2	$\mathbf{M}[1, 2] = 2$	$\mathbf{M}[2, 2] = 1$	$\mathbf{M}[1, 2] \cdot \mathbf{M}[2, 2] = 2 \cdot 1 = 2$
v_3	$\mathbf{M}[1, 3] = 1$	$\mathbf{M}[3, 2] = 0$	$\mathbf{M}[1, 3] \cdot \mathbf{M}[3, 2] = 1 \cdot 0 = 0$
v_4	$\mathbf{M}[1, 4] = 1$	$\mathbf{M}[4, 2] = 1$	$\mathbf{M}[1, 4] \cdot \mathbf{M}[4, 2] = 1 \cdot 1 = 1$

This turns out to be the entry in the first row and second column of a matrix called the "product matrix" $\mathbf{MM} = \mathbf{M}^2$. It is the sum of products of entries from the first row of **M** and the second column of **M**. We won't pursue this further now, but only want to observe that forming product matrices is a purely mechanical process that computers and many people can perform quickly, and the entries in M^2 tell us the number of paths of length 2 connecting vertices. In other words, M^2 is the matrix for the graph in Figure 4(b). Similarly, the entries in the product $M^2M = M^3$ tell us the number of paths of length 3 connecting vertices. Etc.

There is another matrix of interest related to a graph. It is the **reachability matrix R**. An entry $R[i, j]$ is 1 if there is some path from vertex v_i to v_j and it is 0 otherwise. Thus **R** can be determined once all of the powers $M^2, M^3, M^4, \ldots$ are. This looks like an infinite task, but fortunately a theorem tells us the following: If a graph has n vertices and there is a path from v_i to v_j, then there is a path from v_i to v_j having length $\leq n$. Hence **R** can be determined once the powers $M^2, M^3, \ldots, M^n$ are known. Our example has 4 vertices, so it suffices to examine M, M^2, M^3 and M^4. As with any connected graph, the reachability matrix **R** for our example will consist of all 1's. We can tell that our little graph is connected just by looking at its picture, but the matrix procedures would be useful for testing the connectedness of a very large graph or one which was known to us only by its matrix.

We end this section by indicating why the famous Four-Color Theorem is a theorem in graph theory. The theorem asserts that every map in the plane consisting of connected regions without holes can be colored with four colors without coloring two adjacent regions the same color. The theorem was not proved until 1976, after decades of work. The proof finally given used mathematical ingenuity to reduce the problem to a question which could be settled by a computer search. It was one of the first proofs of a significant mathematical result using a computer as a tool.

Given a map, we can construct a graph by viewing regions as vertices and putting an edge between vertices if and only if their corresponding regions are adjacent. We illustrate this in Figure 5. The map coloring problem turns into a vertex coloring problem; vertices connected by an edge must be given different colors. Note that we do not regard Arizona and Colorado [nor Utah and New Mexico] as adjacent.

We said at the beginning that this chapter is meant to be an informal introduction to some of the mathematical topics which are important in computer science and which are the focus of the rest of the book. Our goal has been to provide interesting and concrete examples of problems and methods, so an informal approach was suitable. When we try to generalize from the examples, however, we will need to be careful. It is easy to be fooled into believing that facts about special examples we know and love are true in general. To be sure we can trust our conclusions, we need to start from precisely stated definitions and proceed logically.

In Chapter 1 we lay the foundation and establish some working notation. Chapter 2 begins our study of logic. The material will get harder to read—

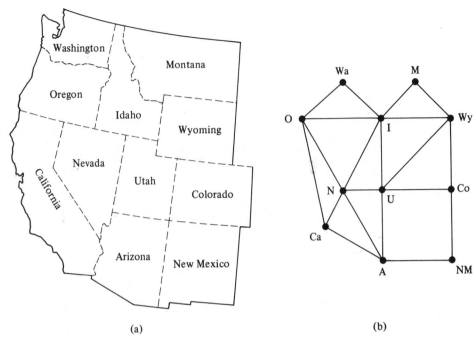

(a)   (b)

FIGURE 5

less like a novel—but the payoff is the knowledge that our conclusions are true, and not just plausible assertions. One reason you are reading this book is to learn some facts. Another reason, perhaps even more important, is to get practice working with logical arguments. That practice is about to start.

EXERCISES 0.3

1. Give the matrices for the trees in Figure 3.
2. Write matrices for the graphs in Figure 6.

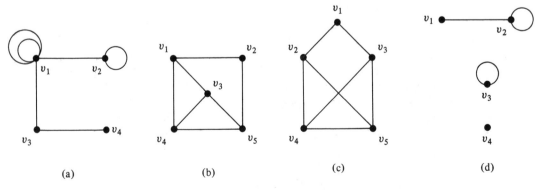

(a)   (b)   (c)   (d)

FIGURE 6

3. Are the graphs in Figures 6(b) and 6(c) isomorphic? Explain.

4. The trees in Figure 7 all have 6 vertices. Indicate which tree in Figure 3 each is isomorphic with.

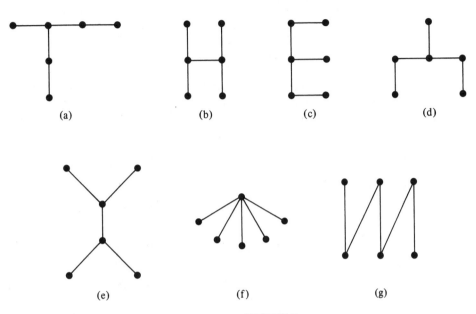

FIGURE 7

5. Draw pictures of all connected graphs with 4 edges and 4 vertices. Don't forget loops and parallel edges.

6. For each matrix in Figure 8, draw a graph having the matrix.

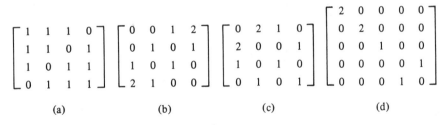

FIGURE 8

7. Show that two of the graphs with matrices in Figure 8 are isomorphic.

8. Make a table similar to Table 1 to count the paths of length 2 from v_1 to itself in Figure 4(a).

9. Consider the graph in Figure 6(d).
   (a) Draw the graph that shows all paths of length 2, as we did in Figure 4(b).
   (b) Is the graph in part (a) connected?
   (c) Give the matrix for the graph in part (a).
   (d) Give the reachability matrix **R**.

10. Repeat Exercise 9 for the graph in Figure 3(a); see Exercise 1.

11. Repeat Exercise 9 for the graph in Figure 3(c); see Exercise 1.

12. Use Figure 5 to show that some maps require 4 different colors. *Hint:* Color Nevada and all its neighbors.

13. Let **M** be the matrix for a graph. Give a formula for the degree of a vertex v_i in terms of **M** that works even if there are loops at v_i. *Suggestion:* Look at the matrices for the graphs in Figures 1, 6(a) or 6(d).

14. Consider the matrix of some graph.
   (a) Suppose all the numbers in some row are 0. What does this tell us about the corresponding vertex?
   (b) Suppose all the numbers in some row are nonzero. What does this tell us about the vertex?
   (c) What can you conclude about connectedness of the graph in the situations described in parts (a) and (b)?

CHAPTER HIGHLIGHTS

To check your understanding of the material in this chapter, we recommend that you consider each item listed below and:

   (a) Satisfy yourself that you can define each concept and describe each method.
   (b) Give at least one reason why the item was included in the chapter.
   (c) Think of at least one example of each concept and at least one situation in which the fact or method would be useful.

This chapter is intended to be informal. More precise definitions and justifications of some of the material appear in later chapters.

Concepts

graph
   vertex, edge, degree
   path
      length, vertex sequence
      cycle
      Euler circuit
      Hamilton circuit
   connected
   tree
   weighted graph
      minimal spanning tree
   matrix description of graph
      reachability matrix
   graph isomorphism

Facts

A graph has an Euler circuit if and only if it is connected and all its vertices
have even degree.

The simpleminded approach to constructing Euler circuits can fail.

Hamilton circuits are in general hard to construct.

Graph isomorphism can be hard to detect.

Map coloring can be converted to a question about graphs.

Methods

FLEURY'S algorithm to construct Euler circuits.

Greedy algorithm to construct minimal spanning trees.

Preview of matrix methods for finding number of paths and reachability.
[More on this later.]

1

SETS

In this chapter we introduce the notation and terminology of set theory that is basic for the remainder of the book.

§1.1 Some Special Sets

In the past few decades it has become traditional to use set theory as the underlying basis for mathematics. That is, the concepts of "set" and "membership" are taken as basic undefined terms and the rest of mathematics is defined or described in these terms. A set is a collection of objects; the definition of a set must be unambiguous in the sense that it must be possible to decide whether particular objects belong to the set. We will usually denote sets by capital letters such as A, B, S or X. Objects are usually denoted by lowercase letters such as a, b, s or x. An object a which belongs to a set S is called a **member** of S or **element** of S. If a is an object and A is a set we write $a \in A$ to mean that a is a member of A and $a \notin A$ to mean that a is not a member of A. The symbol $\in$ can be read as a verb phrase "is an element of," "belongs to" or "is in" or as the preposition "in," depending on context.

Specific sets can be written in a variety of ways. A few especially common and important sets will be given their own names, i.e., their own symbols. We will reserve the symbol $\mathbb{N}$ for the set of **natural numbers**:

$$\mathbb{N} = \{0, 1, 2, 3, 4, 5, 6, \ldots\}.$$

Note that we include 0 among the natural numbers.

We write $\mathbb{P}$ for the set of **positive integers**:

$$\mathbb{P} = \{1, 2, 3, 4, 5, 6, 7, \ldots\}.$$

Many mathematics texts write this set as $\mathbb{N}$ instead. The set of all **integers**, positive, zero or negative, will be denoted by $\mathbb{Z}$ [for the German word "Zahl"]. Numbers of the form m/n where $m \in \mathbb{Z}$, $n \in \mathbb{Z}$ and $n \neq 0$ are called **rational numbers** [since they are ratios of integers]. The set of all rational numbers is denoted by $\mathbb{Q}$. The set of all **real numbers**, rational or not, is denoted by $\mathbb{R}$. Thus $\mathbb{R}$ contains all the numbers in $\mathbb{Q}$ and $\mathbb{R}$ also contains $\sqrt{2}, \sqrt{3}, \sqrt[3]{2}, -\pi, e$ and many many other numbers.

Small finite sets can be listed using braces { } and commas. For example, $\{2, 4, 6, 8, 10\}$ is the set consisting of the five positive even integers less than 12 and $\{2, 3, 5, 7, 11, 13, 17, 19\}$ consists of the eight primes less than 20. Readers who need to be reminded what "even" or "prime" mean may consult the dictionary inside the back cover. Two sets are **equal** if they contain the same elements. Thus

$$\{2, 4, 6, 8, 10\} = \{10, 8, 6, 4, 2\} = \{2, 8, 2, 6, 2, 10, 4, 2\};$$

the order of the listing is irrelevant and there is no advantage [or harm] in listing elements more than once.

Large finite sets and even infinite sets can be listed with the aid of the mathematician's etcetera, namely three dots . . . , provided the meaning of the three dots is clear. Thus $\{1, 2, 3, \ldots, 1000\}$ represents the set of positive integers less than or equal to 1000 and $\{3, 6, 9, 12, \ldots\}$ presumably represents the infinite set of positive integers that are divisible by 3. On the other hand, the meaning of $\{1, 2, 3, 5, 8, \ldots\}$ may be less than perfectly clear. The somewhat vague use of three dots is not always satisfactory, especially in computer science, and we will develop techniques for unambiguously describing such sets without using dots.

Sets are often described by properties of their elements via the notation

$$\{ \quad : \quad \}.$$

Before the colon a variable [n or x, for instance] is indicated and after the colon the properties are given. For example,

$$\{n : n \in \mathbb{N} \quad \text{and} \quad n \text{ is even}\}$$

represents the set of nonnegative even integers, i.e., the set $\{0, 2, 4, 6, 8, 10, \ldots\}$. The colon is always read "such that" and so the above is read "the set of all n such that n is in $\mathbb{N}$ and n is even." Similarly,

$$\{x : x \in \mathbb{R} \quad \text{and} \quad 1 \leqq x < 3\}$$

represents the set of all real numbers that are greater than or equal to 1 and less than 3. The number 1 belongs to the set, but 3 does not. Just to streamline notation, the last two sets can be written as

$$\{n \in \mathbb{N} : n \text{ is even}\} \quad \text{and} \quad \{x \in \mathbb{R} : 1 \leq x < 3\}.$$

The first set is then read "the set of all n in $\mathbb{N}$ such that n is even."

Another way to list a set is to specify a rule for obtaining its elements using some other set of elements. For example, $\{n^2 : n \in \mathbb{N}\}$ represents the set of all integers that are the squares of integers in $\mathbb{N}$, i.e.,

$$\{n^2 : n \in \mathbb{N}\} = \{m \in \mathbb{N} : m = n^2 \text{ for some } n \in \mathbb{N}\}$$
$$= \{0, 1, 4, 9, 16, 25, 36, \ldots\}.$$

Note that this set equals $\{n^2 : n \in \mathbb{Z}\}$. Similarly, $\{(-1)^n : n \in \mathbb{N}\}$ represents the set obtained by evaluating $(-1)^n$ for all $n \in \mathbb{N}$, so that

$$\{(-1)^n : n \in \mathbb{N}\} = \{-1, 1\}.$$

This set has only two elements.

Now consider two sets S and T. We say that T is a **subset** of S provided every element of T belongs to S. If T is a subset of S, we write $T \subseteq S$. The symbol $\subseteq$ can be read as "is a subset of." Two sets S and T are **equal** if they contain the same elements. Thus $S = T$ if and only if $T \subseteq S$ and $S \subseteq T$.

EXAMPLE 1   (a) We have $\mathbb{P} \subseteq \mathbb{N}$, $\mathbb{N} \subseteq \mathbb{Z}$, $\mathbb{Z} \subseteq \mathbb{Q}$, $\mathbb{Q} \subseteq \mathbb{R}$. As with the familiar inequality $\leq$, we can run these assertions together:

$$\mathbb{P} \subseteq \mathbb{N} \subseteq \mathbb{Z} \subseteq \mathbb{Q} \subseteq \mathbb{R}.$$

(b) Since 2 is the only even prime, we have

$$\{n \in \mathbb{P} : n \text{ is prime and } n \geq 3\} \subseteq \{n \in \mathbb{P} : n \text{ is odd}\}.$$

(c) Consider again any set S. Obviously $x \in S$ implies $x \in S$ and so $S \subseteq S$. That is, we regard a set as a subset of itself. This is why we use the notation $\subseteq$ rather than $\subset$. This usage is analogous to our usage of $\leq$ for real numbers. The inequality $x \leq 5$ is valid for many numbers, like 3, 1 and -73. It is also valid for $x = 5$, i.e., $5 \leq 5$. This last inequality looks a bit peculiar because we actually know more, namely $5 = 5$. But $5 \leq 5$ says that "5 is less than 5 or else 5 is equal to 5," and this is a true statement. Similarly, $S \subseteq S$ is true even though we know more, namely $S = S$. Statements like "$5 = 5$," "$5 \leq 5$," "$S = S$" or "$S \subseteq S$" do no harm and are often useful to call attention to the fact that a particular case of a more general statement is valid. $\square$[1]

Occasionally we will write $T \subset S$ to mean that $T \subseteq S$ and $T \neq S$, i.e., T is a subset of S different from S. This usage of $\subset$ is analogous to our usage of $<$ for real numbers. If $T \subset S$ we say that T is a **proper subset** of S.

---

[1]We will use $\square$ to signify the end of an example or proof.

We next introduce notation for some special subsets of $\mathbb{R}$, called **intervals**. For $a, b \in \mathbb{R}$ with $a < b$, we define

$$[a, b] = \{x \in \mathbb{R} : a \leq x \leq b\}; \quad (a, b) = \{x \in \mathbb{R} : a < x < b\};$$
$$[a, b) = \{x \in \mathbb{R} : a \leq x < b\}; \quad (a, b] = \{x \in \mathbb{R} : a < x \leq b\}.$$

The general rule is that brackets [,] signify that the endpoints are to be included and parentheses (,) signify that they are to be excluded. Intervals of the form $[a, b]$ are called **closed**; ones of the form (a, b) are **open**. It is also convenient to use the term "interval" for some unbounded sets which we describe using the symbols ∞ and $-\infty$; they do not represent real numbers but are simply part of the notation for the sets. Thus

$$[a, \infty) = \{x \in \mathbb{R} : a \leq x\}; \quad (a, \infty) = \{x \in \mathbb{R} : a < x\};$$
$$(-\infty, b] = \{x \in \mathbb{R} : x \leq b\}; \quad (-\infty, b) = \{x \in \mathbb{R} : x < b\}.$$

Set notation must be dealt with carefully. For example, [0, 1], (0, 1) and $\{0, 1\}$ all denote different sets. In fact, the intervals [0, 1] and (0, 1) are infinite sets while $\{0, 1\}$ has only two elements.

Consider the following sets:

$$\{n \in \mathbb{N} : 2 < n < 3\}, \quad \{x \in \mathbb{R} : x^2 < 0\},$$
$$\{r \in \mathbb{Q} : r^2 = 2\}, \quad \{x \in \mathbb{R} : x^2 + 1 = 0\}.$$

These sets have one property in common: they contain no elements. From a strictly logical point of view, they contain the same elements and so they are equal in spite of the different descriptions. This unique set having no elements at all is called the **empty set**. We will use two notations for it, the suggestive { } and the standard $\varnothing$. The symbol $\varnothing$ is not a Greek phi ϕ; it is borrowed from the Norwegian alphabet and non-Norwegians should read it as "empty set." We regard $\varnothing$ as a subset of every set S because we regard the statement "$x \in \varnothing$ implies $x \in S$" as logically true in a vacuous sense. You should probably take this explanation on faith until you study § 2.4.

Sets are themselves objects and so can be members of other sets. The set $\{\{1, 2\}, \{1, 3\}, \{2\}, \{3\}\}$ has four members, namely $\{1, 2\}, \{1, 3\}, \{2\}$ and $\{3\}$. If we had a box containing two sacks full of marbles we would consider it to be a box of sacks, rather than a box of marbles, so it would contain two members. Likewise, if A is a set, then $\{A\}$ is a set with one member, namely A, no matter how many members A itself has. A box containing an empty sack contains something, namely a sack, so it is not an empty box. In the same way, $\{\varnothing\}$ is a set with one member, whereas $\varnothing$ is a set with no members, so $\{\varnothing\}$ and $\varnothing$ are different sets. We have $\varnothing \in \{\varnothing\}$ and even $\varnothing \subseteq \{\varnothing\}$, but $\varnothing \notin \varnothing$.

The set of all subsets of a set S is called the **power set** of S and will be denoted $\mathcal{P}(S)$. Clearly the empty set $\varnothing$ and the set S itself are elements of $\mathcal{P}(S)$, i.e., $\varnothing \in \mathcal{P}(S)$ and $S \in \mathcal{P}(S)$.

EXAMPLE 2   (a) We have $\mathcal{P}(\varnothing) = \{\varnothing\}$ since $\varnothing$ is the only subset of $\varnothing$.

(b) Consider a typical one-element set, say $S = \{a\}$. Then $\mathcal{P}(S) = \{\varnothing, \{a\}\}$ has two elements.

(c) If $S = \{a, b\}$ and $a \neq b$, then $\mathcal{P}(S) = \{\varnothing, \{a\}, \{b\}, \{a, b\}\}$ has four elements.

(d) If $S = \{a, b, c\}$ has three elements, then

$$\mathcal{P}(S) = \{\varnothing, \{a\}, \{b\}, \{c\}, \{a, b\}, \{a, c\}, \{b, c\}, \{a, b, c\}\}$$

has eight elements.

(e) Let S be a finite set. Note that if S has n elements and if $n \leq 3$, then $\mathcal{P}(S)$ has 2^n elements, as shown in parts (a)–(d) above. This is not an accident, as we show in Example 6 of § 2.5.

(f) If S is infinite, then $\mathcal{P}(S)$ is also infinite, of course. □

We introduce one more special kind of set, denoted by Σ^*. Sets like this, which may be unfamiliar to many readers, will recur throughout this book. The idea is to allow a rather general, but precise, mathematical treatment of languages. First we need an alphabet. An **alphabet** is a finite nonempty set Σ [Greek capital sigma] whose members are symbols, often called **letters** of Σ, and which is subject to some minor restrictions which we will discuss at the end of this section. Given an alphabet Σ, a **word** is any finite string of letters from Σ. We denote the set of all words using letters from Σ by Σ^* [sigma-star]. Any subset of Σ^* is called a **language** over Σ.

EXAMPLE 3   (a) Let $\Sigma = \{a, b, c, d, \ldots, z\}$ consist of the twenty-six letters of the "English" alphabet. *Any* string of letters from Σ belongs to Σ^*. Thus Σ^* contains *math, is, fun, aint, lieblich, amour, zzyzzoomph, etcetera*, etc. Since Σ^* contains *a, aa, aaa, aaaa, aaaaa*, etc., Σ^* is clearly an infinite set. To be definite, we could define the **American language** L to be the subset of Σ^* consisting of words in the latest edition of *Webster's New World Dictionary of the American Language*. Thus

$$L = \{a, aachen, aardvark, aardwolf, \ldots, zymurgy\},$$

a large but finite set.

(b) To get simple examples and yet illustrate the ideas, we will frequently take Σ to be a 2-element set $\{a, b\}$. In this case Σ^* contains *a, b, ab, ba, bab, babbabb*, etc.; again Σ^* is infinite.

(c) If $\Sigma = \{0, 1\}$, then the set B of words in Σ^* that begin with 1 is exactly the set of binary notations for positive integers. That is,

$$B = \{1, 10, 11, 100, 101, 110, 111, 1000, 1001, \ldots\}. \quad \square$$

There is a special word in Σ* somewhat analogous to the empty set, called the **empty word** or **null word**; it is the string with no letters at all and is denoted by ϵ [Greek lowercase epsilon].

EXAMPLE 4   (a) If Σ = {a, b}, then

Σ* = {ε, a, b, aa, ab, ba, bb, aaa, aab, aba, abb, baa, bab, bba, . . .}.

(b) If Σ = {0, 1, 2}, then

Σ* = {ε, 0, 1, 2, 00, 01, 02, 10, 11, 12, 20, 21, 22, 000, 001, 002, . . .}.

(c) If Σ = {a}, then

Σ* = {ε, a, aa, aaa, aaaa, aaaaa, aaaaaa, . . .}.

This example doesn't contain very useful languages, but it will serve to illustrate various concepts.

(d) Various computer languages fit our definition of language. For example, the alphabet Σ for one version of ALGOL has 113 elements. Σ includes letters, the digits 0, 1, 2, . . . , 9 and a variety of operators, including sequential operators like "go to" and "if." As usual, Σ* contains all possible finite strings of letters from Σ, without regard to meaning. The subset of Σ* consisting of those strings accepted for execution by an ALGOL compiler on a given computer is a well-defined and useful subset of Σ*; we could call it the ALGOL language determined by the compiler. ☐

As promised, we now discuss the restrictions needed for Σ. Suppose that Σ contains not only the symbols a and b but also the symbol ab. Is the string aab a string of three letters a, a and b in Σ or a string of two letters a and ab? There is no way to tell. So if a, b and ab have some particular significance in an application, the ambiguity here may make it impossible to attach a meaning to the word aab. As another example, we would not want Σ to contain ab, aba and bab; if it did, the letters in the word

$$ababab = (ab)(ab)(ab) = (aba)(bab)$$

would be ambiguous. To avoid these problems, we do not allow Σ to contain letters which are themselves strings beginning with other letters of Σ. Thus Σ = {a, b, c}, Σ = {a, b, ca} and Σ = {a, b, Ab} are allowed, but Σ = {a, b, c, ca} is not. With this agreement, we can unambiguously define **length**(w) for a word w in Σ* to be the number of letters from Σ in w, counting each appearance of a letter. For example, if Σ = {a, b}, then length(aab) = length(bab) = 3. We also define length(ε) = 0. A more precise definition is given in § 3.5.

One final word: We will use w, w_1, etc. as variable names for words. This should cause no confusion even though w also happens to be a letter of the English alphabet.

EXAMPLE 5   If $\Sigma = \{a, b\}$ and $A = \{w \in \Sigma^* : \text{length}(w) = 2\}$, then $A = \{aa, ab, ba, bb\}$. If

$$B = \{w \in \Sigma^* : \text{length}(w) \text{ is even}\},$$

then B is the infinite set $\{\epsilon, aa, ab, ba, bb, aaaa, aaab, aaba, aabb, \ldots\}$. Note that A is a subset of B.   ☐

EXERCISES 1.1

Terms such as "divisible," "prime" and "even" are defined in the dictionary at the back of the book.

1. List five elements in each of the following sets.
 (a) $\{n \in \mathbb{N} : n \text{ is divisible by } 5\}$ (b) $\{2n + 1 : n \in \mathbb{P}\}$
 (c) $\mathcal{P}(\{1, 2, 3, 4, 5\})$ (d) $\{2^n : n \in \mathbb{N}\}$
 (e) $\{1/n : n \in \mathbb{P}\}$ (f) $\{r \in \mathbb{Q} : 0 < r < 1\}$
 (g) $\{n \in \mathbb{N} : n + 1 \text{ is prime}\}$

2. List the elements in the following sets.
 (a) $\{1/n : n = 1, 2, 3, 4\}$
 (b) $\{n^2 - n : n = 0, 1, 2, 3, 4\}$
 (c) $\{1/n^2 : n \in \mathbb{P}, n \text{ is even}\quad \text{and}\quad n < 11\}$
 (d) $\{2 + (-1)^n : n \in \mathbb{N}\}$

3. List five elements in each of the following sets.
 (a) Σ^* where $\Sigma = \{a, b, c\}$
 (b) $\{w \in \Sigma^* : \text{length}(w) \leq 2\}$ where $\Sigma = \{a, b\}$
 (c) $\{w \in \Sigma^* : \text{length}(w) = 4\}$ where $\Sigma = \{a, b\}$
 Which sets above contain the empty word ϵ?

4. Determine the following sets, i.e., list their elements if they are nonempty and write $\varnothing$ if they are empty.
 (a) $\{n \in \mathbb{N} : n^2 = 9\}$ (b) $\{n \in \mathbb{Z} : n^2 = 9\}$
 (c) $\{x \in \mathbb{R} : x^2 = 9\}$ (d) $\{n \in \mathbb{N} : 3 < n < 7\}$
 (e) $\{n \in \mathbb{Z} : 3 < |n| < 7\}$ (f) $\{x \in \mathbb{R} : x^2 < 0\}$
 (g) $\{n \in \mathbb{N} : n^2 = 3\}$ (h) $\{x \in \mathbb{Q} : x^2 = 3\}$
 (i) $\{x \in \mathbb{R} : x < 1\quad \text{and}\quad x \geq 2\}$ (j) $\{3n + 1 : n \in \mathbb{N}\quad \text{and}\quad n \leq 6\}$
 (k) $\{n \in \mathbb{P} : n \text{ is prime}\quad \text{and}\quad n \leq 15\}$ [Recall that 1 isn't prime.]

5. How many elements are there in the following sets? Write ∞ if the set is infinite.
 (a) $\{n \in \mathbb{N} : n^2 = 2\}$ (b) $\{n \in \mathbb{Z} : 0 \leq n \leq 73\}$
 (c) $\{n \in \mathbb{Z} : 5 \leq |n| \leq 73\}$ (d) $\{n \in \mathbb{Z} : 5 < n < 73\}$
 (e) $\{n \in \mathbb{Z} : n \text{ is even}\quad \text{and}\quad |n| \leq 73\}$
 (f) $\{x \in \mathbb{Q} : 0 \leq x \leq 73\}$ (g) $\{x \in \mathbb{Q} : x^2 = 2\}$
 (h) $\{x \in \mathbb{R} : x^2 = 2\}$ (i) $\{x \in \mathbb{R} : .99 < x < 1.00\}$
 (j) $\mathcal{P}(\{0, 1, 2, 3\})$ (k) $\mathcal{P}(\mathbb{N})$
 (l) $\{n \in \mathbb{N} : n \text{ is even}\}$ (m) $\{n \in \mathbb{N} : n \text{ is prime}\}$
 (n) $\{n \in \mathbb{N} : n \text{ is even and prime}\}$ (o) $\{n \in \mathbb{N} : n \text{ is even or prime}\}$

6. How many elements are there in the following sets? Write ∞ if the set is infinite.
 (a) $\{-1, 1\}$ (b) $[-1, 1]$
 (c) $(-1, 1)$ (d) $\{n \in \mathbb{Z} : -1 \leq n \leq 1\}$

(e) Σ^* where $\Sigma = \{a, b, c\}$

(f) $\{w \in \Sigma^* : \text{length}(w) \leq 4\}$ where $\Sigma = \{a, b, c\}$

7. Consider the sets

$$A = \{n \in \mathbb{P} : n \text{ is odd}\}, \qquad B = \{n \in \mathbb{P} : n \text{ is prime}\},$$
$$C = \{4n + 3 : n \in \mathbb{P}\}, \qquad D = \{x \in \mathbb{R} : x^2 - 8x + 15 = 0\}.$$

Which of these sets are subsets of which? Consider all sixteen possibilities.

8. Consider the sets $\{0, 1\}$, $(0, 1)$ and $[0, 1]$. True or False.

(a) $\{0, 1\} \subseteq (0, 1)$

(b) $\{0, 1\} \subseteq [0, 1]$

(c) $(0, 1) \subseteq [0, 1]$

(d) $\{0, 1\} \subseteq \mathbb{Z}$

(e) $[0, 1] \subseteq \mathbb{Z}$

(f) $[0, 1] \subseteq \mathbb{Q}$

(g) $1/2$ and $\pi/4$ are in $\{0, 1\}$

(h) $1/2$ and $\pi/4$ are in $(0, 1)$

(i) $1/2$ and $\pi/4$ are in $[0, 1]$

9. Consider the following three alphabets: $\Sigma_1 = \{a, b, c\}$, $\Sigma_2 = \{a, b, ca\}$ and $\Sigma_3 = \{a, b, Ab\}$. Determine to which of Σ_1^*, Σ_2^* and Σ_3^* each word below belongs, and give its length as a member of each set to which it belongs.

(a) *aba*

(b) *bAb*

(c) *cba*

(d) *cab*

(e) *caab*

(f) *baAb*

10. Here is a question to think about. Let $\Sigma = \{a, b\}$ and imagine, if you can, a dictionary for all the nonempty words of Σ^* with the words arranged in the usual alphabetical order. All the words *a*, *aa*, *aaa*, *aaaa*, etc. must appear before the word *ba*. How far into the dictionary will you have to dig to find the word *ba*? How would the answer change if the dictionary contained only those words in Σ^* of length 20 or less?

11. Suppose that w is a nonempty word in Σ^*.

(a) If the first [i.e., leftmost] letter of w is deleted, is the resulting string in Σ^*?

(b) How about deleting letters from both ends of w? Are the resulting strings still in Σ^*?

(c) If you had a device which could recognize letters in Σ and could delete letters from strings, how could you use it to determine if an arbitrary string of symbols is in Σ^*?

§ *1.2*   *Set Operations*

In this section we introduce operations that allow us to create new sets from old sets. We define the **union** $A \cup B$ and **intersection** $A \cap B$ of sets A and B as follows:

$$A \cup B = \{x : x \in A \text{ or } x \in B \text{ or both}\};$$

$$A \cap B = \{x : x \in A \text{ and } x \in B\}.$$

We added "or both" to the definition of $A \cup B$ for emphasis and clarity. In ordinary English, the word "or" has two interpretations. Sometimes it is the **inclusive or** and means one or the other or both. This is the interpretation when a college catalog asserts: A student's program must include 2 years of science or 2 years of mathematics. At other times, "or" is the **exclusive or** and means one or the other but not both. This is the interpretation when a menu offers soup or salad. In mathematics we always interpret **or** as the "inclusive or" unless explicitly specified to the contrary. Sets A and B are said to be **disjoint** if they have no elements in common, i.e., if $A \cap B = \varnothing$.

For sets A and B, the **relative complement** $A\backslash B$ is the set of objects that are in A and not in B:

$$A\backslash B = \{x : x \in A \quad \text{and} \quad x \notin B\} = \{x \in A : x \notin B\}.$$

It is the set obtained by removing from A all the elements of B that happen to be in A.

The **symmetric difference** $A \oplus B$ of the sets A and B is the set

$$A \oplus B = \{x : x \in A \quad \text{or} \quad x \in B \quad \text{but not both}\}.$$

Note the use of the "exclusive or" here. It follows from the definition that

$$A \oplus B = (A \cup B)\backslash(A \cap B) = (A\backslash B) \cup (B\backslash A).$$

It is sometimes convenient to illustrate relations between sets with pictures called **Venn diagrams**, in which sets correspond to subsets of the plane. See Figure 1, where the indicated sets have been shaded in.

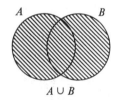

$A \cup B$

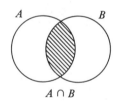

$A \cap B$

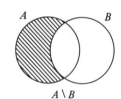

$A \backslash B$

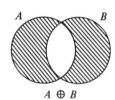

$A \oplus B$

FIGURE 1

EXAMPLE 1   (a) Let $A = \{n \in \mathbb{N} : n \leq 11\}$, $B = \{n \in \mathbb{N} : n$ is even and $n \leq 20\}$ and $E = \{n \in \mathbb{N} : n$ is even$\}$. Then we have

$$A \cup B = \{0, 1, 2, 3, 4, 5, 6, 7, 8, 9, 10, 11, 12, 14, 16, 18, 20\},$$

$$A \cap B = \{0, 2, 4, 6, 8, 10\},$$

$$A \backslash B = \{1, 3, 5, 7, 9, 11\},$$

$$B \backslash A = \{12, 14, 16, 18, 20\},$$

$$A \oplus B = \{1, 3, 5, 7, 9, 11, 12, 14, 16, 18, 20\}.$$

We also have $E \cap B = B$, $B \backslash E = \{\ \}$,

$$E \backslash B = \{n \in \mathbb{N} : n \text{ is even} \quad \text{and} \quad n \geq 22\} = \{22, 24, 26, 28, \ldots\},$$

$$\mathbb{N} \backslash E = \{n \in \mathbb{N} : n \text{ is odd}\} = \{1, 3, 5, 7, 9, 11, \ldots\},$$

$$A \oplus E = \{1, 3, 5, 7, 9, 11\} \cup \{n \in \mathbb{N} : n \text{ is even} \quad \text{and} \quad n \geq 12\}$$

$$= \{1, 3, 5, 7, 9, 11, 12, 14, 16, 18, 20, 22, \ldots\}.$$

(b) Consider the intervals $[0, 2]$ and $(0, 1]$. Then $(0, 1] \subseteq [0, 2]$ and so

$$(0, 1] \cup [0, 2] = [0, 2] \quad \text{and} \quad (0, 1] \cap [0, 2] = (0, 1].$$

Moreover, we have

$$(0, 1] \setminus [0, 2] = \{ \ \},$$

$$[0, 2] \setminus (0, 1] = \{0\} \cup (1, 2] \quad \text{and} \quad [0, 2] \setminus (0, 2) = \{0, 2\}.$$

(c) Let $\Sigma = \{a, b\}$, $A = \{\epsilon, a, aa, aaa\}$, $B = \{\epsilon, b, bb, bbb\}$ and $C = \{w \in \Sigma^* : \text{length}(w) \leqq 2\}$. Then we have

$$A \cup B = \{\epsilon, a, b, aa, bb, aaa, bbb\}, \qquad A \cap B = \{\epsilon\},$$

$$A \setminus B = \{a, aa, aaa\}, \qquad\qquad B \setminus A = \{b, bb, bbb\},$$

$$A \cap C = \{\epsilon, a, aa\}, \qquad\qquad B \setminus C = \{bbb\},$$

$$C \setminus A = \{b, ab, ba, bb\}, \qquad\qquad A \setminus \Sigma = \{\epsilon, aa, aaa\}. \quad \square$$

It is often convenient to work within some fixed set such as $\mathbb{N}$, $\mathbb{R}$ or Σ^*. That is, it is convenient to fix some set U, which we call the **universe** or **universal set**, and to consider only elements in U and subsets of U. For $A \subseteq U$ the relative complement $U \setminus A$ is called the **absolute complement** or simply the **complement** of A and is denoted by A^c. Note that the relative complement $A \setminus B$ can be written in terms of the absolute complement: $A \setminus B = A \cap B^c$. In the Venn diagrams in Figure 2 we have drawn the universe U as a rectangle and shaded in the indicated sets.

EXAMPLE 2 (a) If the universe is $\mathbb{N}$, and A and E are as in Example 1(a), then

$$A^c = \{n \in \mathbb{N} : n \geqq 12\} \quad \text{and} \quad E^c = \{n \in \mathbb{N} : n \text{ is odd}\}.$$

(b) If the universe is $\mathbb{R}$, then $[0, 1]^c = (-\infty, 0) \cup (1, \infty)$, $(0, 1)^c = (-\infty, 0] \cup [1, \infty)$ and $\{0, 1\}^c = (-\infty, 0) \cup (0, 1) \cup (1, \infty)$. For any $a \in \mathbb{R}$, $[a, \infty)^c = (-\infty, a)$ and $(a, \infty)^c = (-\infty, a]$. $\square$

Note that the last two Venn diagrams in Figure 2 show that $A^c \cap B^c = (A \cup B)^c$. This set identity and many others are true in general. Table 1 lists some basic identities for sets and set operations. Don't be overwhelmed by them; look at them one at a time. As some of the names of the laws suggest, many of them are analogues of laws from algebra. The idempotent laws are new [certainly $a + a = a$ fails for most numbers], and there is only one distributive law for numbers. Of course, the laws involving complementation are new. All sets in Table 1 are presumed to be subsets of some universal set U.

Because of the associative laws, we can write the sets $A \cup B \cup C$ and $A \cap B \cap C$ without any parentheses and cause no confusion.

The identities in Table 1 can be verified in one of two ways. One can shade in the corresponding sets of a Venn diagram and observe that they are

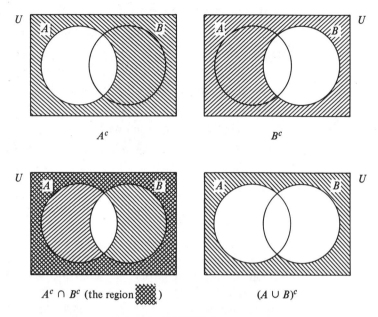

A^c

B^c

$A^c \cap B^c$ (the region ▦)

$(A \cup B)^c$

FIGURE 2

TABLE 1. *Laws of Algebra of Sets*

1a. $A \cup B = B \cup A$ b. $A \cap B = B \cap A$	commutative laws
2a. $(A \cup B) \cup C = A \cup (B \cup C)$ b. $(A \cap B) \cap C = A \cap (B \cap C)$	associative laws
3a. $A \cup (B \cap C) = (A \cup B) \cap (A \cup C)$ b. $A \cap (B \cup C) = (A \cap B) \cup (A \cap C)$	distributive laws
4a. $A \cup A = A$ b. $A \cap A = A$	idempotent laws

5a. $A \cup \varnothing = A$
  b. $A \cup U = U$
  c. $A \cap \varnothing = \varnothing$
  d. $A \cap U = A$
	identity laws

6. $(A^c)^c = A$	double complementation
7a. $A \cup A^c = U$ b. $A \cap A^c = \varnothing$	
8a. $U^c = \varnothing$ b. $\varnothing^c = U$	
9a. $(A \cup B)^c = A^c \cap B^c$ b. $(A \cap B)^c = A^c \cup B^c$	DeMorgan laws

equal. Alternatively, one can show that sets S and T are equal by showing that $S \subseteq T$ and $T \subseteq S$; these inclusions can be verified by showing that $x \in S$ implies $x \in T$ and by showing that $x \in T$ implies $x \in S$. We give examples of both sorts of arguments, leaving most of the verifications to the interested reader.

EXAMPLE 3   The DeMorgan law 9a is illustrated by Venn diagrams in Figure 2. Here is a proof in which we first show $(A \cup B)^c \subseteq A^c \cap B^c$ and then we show $A^c \cap B^c \subseteq (A \cup B)^c$.

To show $(A \cup B)^c \subseteq A^c \cap B^c$, we consider an element x in $(A \cup B)^c$. Then $x \notin A \cup B$. In particular, $x \notin A$ and so we must have $x \in A^c$. Similarly, $x \notin B$ and so $x \in B^c$. Therefore $x \in A^c \cap B^c$. We have shown that $x \in (A \cup B)^c$ implies $x \in A^c \cap B^c$; hence $(A \cup B)^c \subseteq A^c \cap B^c$.

To show the reverse inclusion $A^c \cap B^c \subseteq (A \cup B)^c$, we consider x in $A^c \cap B^c$. Then $x \in A^c$ and so $x \notin A$. Also $x \in B^c$ and so $x \notin B$. Since $x \notin A$ and $x \notin B$, we conclude that $x \notin A \cup B$, i.e., $x \in (A \cup B)^c$. Hence $A^c \cap B^c \subseteq (A \cup B)^c$. ☐

EXAMPLE 4   The distributive law 3b is demonstrated in Figure 3. The picture of the set $A \cap (B \cup C)$ is double-hatched ▓.

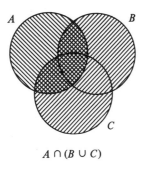 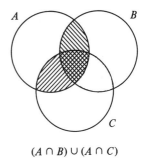

$A \cap (B \cup C)$ $(A \cap B) \cup (A \cap C)$

FIGURE 3

Here is a proof where we show that the sets are subsets of each other. First consider $x \in A \cap (B \cup C)$. Then x is in A for sure. Also x is in $B \cup C$. So either $x \in B$, in which case $x \in A \cap B$, or else $x \in C$, in which case $x \in A \cap C$. In either case, we have $x \in (A \cap B) \cup (A \cap C)$. This shows that $A \cap (B \cup C) \subseteq (A \cap B) \cup (A \cap C)$.

Now consider $y \in (A \cap B) \cup (A \cap C)$. Either $y \in A \cap B$ or $y \in A \cap C$; we consider the two cases separately. If $y \in A \cap B$, then $y \in A$ and $y \in B$, so $y \in B \cup C$ and hence $y \in A \cap (B \cup C)$. Similarly, if $y \in A \cap C$

then $y \in A$ and $y \in C$, so $y \in B \cup C$ and thus $y \in A \cap (B \cup C)$. Since $y \in A \cap (B \cup C)$ in both cases, we've shown that $(A \cap B) \cup (A \cap C) \subseteq A \cap (B \cup C)$. We already proved the opposite inclusion and so the two sets are equal.   ☐

The proofs using Venn diagrams seem much easier than the proofs where we analyze inclusions elementwise. Proofs by picture make many people nervous; on the other hand, the Venn diagram for A, B, C has eight regions [see Figure 4] and these comprise all the logical possibilities, so that proofs

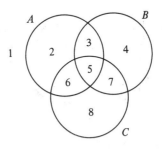

FIGURE 4

using Venn diagrams are in fact valid. A much more serious objection to proofs via Venn diagrams is that they hide the thought process, i.e., the logic used to shade the diagrams is not specified. If we had written out the reasoning behind the diagrams in Figure 3, the proof would have been as long as the elementwise proof in Example 4. The latter proof relies only on logic and would be easier to communicate to a computer or to intelligent life in some far-off galaxy. Another reason for avoiding Venn diagrams is that they are hard to draw whenever there are more than three sets. Still, nearly everyone who works with mathematics uses pictures, including Venn diagrams, to help understand mathematical situations.

Table 1 gives a few of the basic relationships in set theory. Many other relationships exist. They can be verified using one of three methods: (1) Venn diagrams; (2) elementwise arguments as in Examples 3 and 4; (3) applying the laws in Table 1. Sometimes proofs will combine methods (2) and (3).

EXAMPLE 5   We give three proofs for the relationship

$$(A \cup B) \cap A^c \subseteq B.$$

Proof 1.   See Figure 5. The picture for $(A \cup B) \cap A^c$ is double-hatched and is clearly a subset of B.

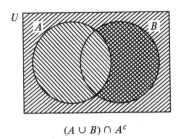 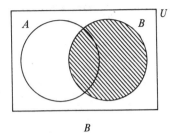

$(A \cup B) \cap A^c$ B

FIGURE 5

Proof 2. We show that $x \in (A \cup B) \cap A^c$ implies $x \in B$. Consider x in $(A \cup B) \cap A^c$. Then $x \in A^c$ and so $x \notin A$. Since x is also in $A \cup B$, it is in A or in B, so it follows that x must be in B.

Proof 3. Using the laws of algebra in Table 1 we obtain

$$(A \cup B) \cap A^c = A^c \cap (A \cup B) \qquad \text{commutativity 1b}$$
$$= (A^c \cap A) \cup (A^c \cap B) \qquad \text{distributivity 3b}$$
$$= (A \cap A^c) \cup (A^c \cap B) \qquad \text{commutativity 1b}$$
$$= \varnothing \cup (A^c \cap B) \qquad \text{7b}$$
$$= (A^c \cap B) \cup \varnothing \qquad \text{commutativity 1a}$$
$$= A^c \cap B. \qquad \text{identity law 5a}$$

This identity agrees, of course, with the picture on the left in Figure 5. Now it is clear that $A^c \cap B \subseteq B$, since if $x \in A^c \cap B$ then x must be in B. □

EXAMPLE 6 The symmetric difference $\oplus$ is also an associative operation:

$$(A \oplus B) \oplus C = A \oplus (B \oplus C).$$

We can see this by looking at the Venn diagrams in Figure 6. On the left we have hatched $A \oplus B$ one way and C the other. Then $(A \oplus B) \oplus C$ is the

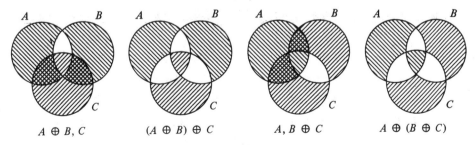

$A \oplus B, C$ $(A \oplus B) \oplus C$ $A, B \oplus C$ $A \oplus (B \oplus C)$

FIGURE 6

set hatched one way or the other but not both. Doing the same sort of thing with A and $B \oplus C$ gives us the same set, so the sets $(A \oplus B) \oplus C$ and $A \oplus (B \oplus C)$ are equal.

Of course it is also possible to prove this fact without appealing to the pictures. You may want to construct such a proof yourself. Be warned, though, that a detailed argument will be fairly complicated. $\square$

Since $\oplus$ is associative, the expression $A \oplus B \oplus C$ is unambiguous. Note that an element belongs to this set provided it belongs to exactly one or to all three of the sets A, B and C.

EXERCISES 1.2

1. Let $U = \{1, 2, 3, 4, 5, \ldots, 12\}$, $A = \{1, 3, 5, 7, 9, 11\}$, $B = \{2, 3, 5, 7, 11\}$, $C = \{2, 3, 6, 12\}$ and $D = \{2, 4, 8\}$. Determine the sets
   (a) $A \cup B$ (b) $A \cap C$
   (c) $(A \cup B) \cap C^c$ (d) $A \setminus B$
   (e) $C \setminus D$ (f) $B \oplus D$
   (g) How many subsets are there of C?

2. Let $A = \{1, 2, 3\}$, $B = \{n \in \mathbb{P} : n \text{ is even}\}$ and $C = \{n \in \mathbb{P} : n \text{ is odd}\}$.
   (a) Determine $A \cap B$, $B \cap C$, $B \cup C$ and $B \oplus C$.
   (b) List all subsets of A.
   (c) Which of the following sets are infinite? $A \oplus B$, $A \oplus C$, $A \setminus C$, $C \setminus A$.

3. In this exercise the universe is $\mathbb{R}$. Determine the following sets.
   (a) $[0, 3] \cap [2, 6]$ (b) $[0, 3] \cup [2, 6]$
   (c) $[0, 3] \setminus [2, 6]$ (d) $[0, 3] \oplus [2, 6]$
   (e) $[0, 3]^c$ (f) $[0, 3] \cap \varnothing$

4. Let $\Sigma = \{a, b\}$, $A = \{a, b, aa, bb, aaa, bbb\}$, $B = \{w \in \Sigma^* : \text{length}(w) \geq 2\}$ and $C = \{w \in \Sigma^* : \text{length}(w) \leq 2\}$.
   (a) Determine $A \cap C$, $A \setminus C$, $C \setminus A$ and $A \oplus C$.
   (b) Determine $A \cap B$, $B \cap C$, $B \cup C$ and $B \setminus A$.
   (c) Determine $\Sigma^* \setminus B$, $\Sigma \setminus B$ and $\Sigma \setminus C$.
   (d) List all subsets of Σ.
   (e) How many sets are there in $\mathcal{P}(\Sigma)$?

5. In this exercise the universe is Σ^* where $\Sigma = \{a, b\}$. Let A, B and C be as in Exercise 4. Determine the following sets.
   (a) $B^c \cap C^c$ (b) $(B \cap C)^c$
   (c) $(B \cup C)^c$ (d) $B^c \cup C^c$
   (e) $A^c \cap C$ (f) $A^c \cap B^c$
   (g) Which of these sets are equal? Why?

6. The following statements involve subsets of some nonempty universal set U. Tell whether each is true or false. For each false one, give an example for which the statement is false.

(a) $A \cap (B \cup C) = (A \cap B) \cup C$ for all A, B, C.

(b) $A \cup B \subseteq A \cap B$ implies $A = B$.

(c) $(A \cap \varnothing) \cup B = B$ for all A, B.

(d) $A \cap (\varnothing \cup B) = A$ whenever $A \subseteq B$.

(e) $A \cap B = A^c \cup B^c$ for all A, B.

7. For any set A, what is $A \oplus A$? $A \oplus \varnothing$?

8. Use Venn diagrams to prove the following.

(a) $A \cap (B \oplus C) = (A \cap B) \oplus (A \cap C)$

(b) $A \oplus B \subseteq (A \oplus C) \cup (B \oplus C)$

9. Prove the generalized DeMorgan law $(A \cap B \cap C)^c = A^c \cup B^c \cup C^c$. *Hint:* First apply the DeMorgan law 9b to the sets A and $B \cap C$. The elementwise method can be avoided.

10. Prove the following without using Venn diagrams.

(a) $A \cap B \subseteq A$ and $A \subseteq A \cup B$ for all sets A and B.

(b) If $A \subseteq B$ and $A \subseteq C$, then $A \subseteq B \cap C$.

(c) If $A \subseteq C$ and $B \subseteq C$, then $A \cup B \subseteq C$.

(d) $A \subseteq B$ if and only if $B^c \subseteq A^c$.

Note. In the remaining exercises, you may use any method of proof.

11. Prove the distributive law 3a.

12. Prove that $(A^c) \oplus (B^c) = A \oplus B$ for any subsets A and B of some universal set U.

13. Prove the following absorption laws.

(a) $A \cup (A \cap B) = A$ (b) $A \cap (A \cup B) = A$

14. (a) Prove that $A \subseteq B$ if and only if $A \cup B = B$. This is really two assertions: "$A \subseteq B$ implies $A \cup B = B$" and "$A \cup B = B$ implies $A \subseteq B$."

(b) Prove that $A \subseteq B$ if and only if $A \cap B = A$.

15. Prove or disprove. [A proof needs to be a general argument, but a single counterexample is sufficient for a disproof.]

(a) $A \cap B = A \cap C$ implies $B = C$.

(b) $A \cup B = A \cup C$ implies $B = C$.

(c) $A \cap B = A \cap C$ and $A \cup B = A \cup C$ imply $B = C$.

(d) $A \cup B \subseteq A \cap B$ implies $A = B$.

(e) $A \oplus B = A \oplus C$ implies $B = C$.

16. (a) Show that relative complementation is not commutative; that is, $A \setminus B = B \setminus A$ can fail.

(b) Show that relative complementation is not associative: $(A \setminus B) \setminus C = A \setminus (B \setminus C)$ can fail.

(c) Show, however, that $(A \setminus B) \setminus C \subseteq A \setminus (B \setminus C)$ for all A, B and C.

17. Draw a Venn diagram for four sets A, B, C and D. Be sure to have a region for all sixteen possible sets such as $A \cap B^c \cap C^c \cap D$.

18. Show that $A \setminus B \subseteq C$ if and only if $A \setminus C \subseteq B$.

§ *1.3   Subscripts and Indexing*

Subscript notation comes in handy when we are dealing with a large collection of objects, especially if they are similar; here large often means "more than 3 or 4." For example, letters x, y and z are adequate when dealing with equations involving three or fewer unknowns. But if there are ten unknowns or if we wish to discuss the general situation of n unknowns [n some unspecified integer in $\mathbb{P}$], then $x_1, x_2, \ldots, x_n$ would be a good choice for the names of the unknowns. Here the unknowns are distinguished by the little numbers 1, 2, $\ldots, n$ which are called **subscripts**. As another example, a general nonzero polynomial has the form

$$a_n x^n + a_{n-1} x^{n-1} + \cdots + a_2 x^2 + a_1 x + a_0,$$

where $a_n \neq 0$. Here n is the degree of the polynomial and the $n + 1$ possible coefficients are labeled $a_0, a_1, \ldots, a_n$ using subscripts. For example, the polynomial $x^3 + 4x^2 - 73$ fits this general scheme; to see this, let $n = 3$, $a_3 = 1$, $a_2 = 4$, $a_1 = 0$ and $a_0 = -73$.

A similar situation arises in set theory. A simple way to handle n sets is to name them $A_1, A_2, \ldots, A_n$. An infinite sequence of sets is also possible: $A_1, A_2, \ldots$ or $\{A_k : k \in \mathbb{P}\}$. Of course the subscripts could begin with 0 or some other integer. We sometimes think of the subscripts as indexing [or labeling] the collection of sets. In this case, we may say the collection of sets is **indexed** by the set of subscripts. For example, $\{A_k : k \in \mathbb{P}\}$ is a family of sets indexed by $\mathbb{P}$ while $B_0, B_1, B_2, \ldots$ represents a family of sets indexed by $\mathbb{N}$.

EXAMPLE 1   (a) For each n in $\mathbb{P}$ let

$$D_n = \{k \in \mathbb{Z} : k \text{ is divisible by } n\}.$$

Recall that 0 is divisible by all integers. Some of the sets D_n defined above are

$D_1 = \mathbb{Z}$,

$D_2 = \{k \in \mathbb{Z} : k \text{ is divisible by } 2\} = \{k \in \mathbb{Z} : k \text{ is even}\}$
   $= \{\ldots, -10, -8, -6, -4, -2, 0, 2, 4, 6, 8, 10, \ldots\}$,

$D_5 = \{\ldots, -30, -25, -20, -15, -10, -5, 0, 5, 10, 15, 20, 25, 30, \ldots\}$.

By a slight abuse of notation, we might also write

$$D_n = \{0, \pm n, \pm 2n, \pm 3n, \ldots\}.$$

The family of sets $\{D_n : n \in \mathbb{P}\}$ is indexed by $\mathbb{P}$.

(b) For $n \in \mathbb{P}$ we define the following intervals in $\mathbb{R}$:

$$A_n = [-n, n] \quad \text{and} \quad B_n = [n, 2n].$$

Thus $A_3 = [-3, 3]$ and $B_3 = [3, 6]$, for instance. Both collections $\{A_n : n \in \mathbb{P}\}$ and $\{B_n : n \in \mathbb{P}\}$ are indexed by $\mathbb{P}$.

(c) Let Σ be an alphabet. For each $k \in \mathbb{N}$, Σ^k is defined to be the set of all words in Σ^* having length k. In symbols,

$$\Sigma^k = \{w \in \Sigma^* : \text{length}(w) = k\}.$$

This "power notation" will seem quite appropriate in the context of § 4.4. Note that the sets Σ^k are disjoint, that $\Sigma^0 = \{\epsilon\}$, and that $\Sigma^1 = \Sigma$. The family of sets $\{\Sigma^k : k \in \mathbb{N}\}$ is indexed by $\mathbb{N}$.

In the case that $\Sigma = \{a, b\}$, we have $\Sigma^0 = \{\epsilon\}$, $\Sigma^1 = \Sigma = \{a, b\}$, $\Sigma^2 = \{aa, ab, ba, bb\}$, etc.

(d) We allow the possibility that two sets with different indices are the same. For instance, consider the set M of memory locations in a given computer and for $n \in \mathbb{N}$ let

$$M_n = \{x \in M : x \text{ contains } n\}.$$

Then $M_0, M_1, M_2, \ldots$ is a family of sets indexed by $\mathbb{N}$ and $M_n = \varnothing$ for all large enough values of n. It could also happen that $M_n = \varnothing$ for certain small values of n, too.

If we let $L_n = \{x \in M : x \text{ contains a number less than } n\}$, then $L_0, L_1, L_2, \ldots$ is indexed by $\mathbb{N}$, $L_0 \subseteq L_1 \subseteq L_2 \subseteq \cdots$ and $L_n = L_{n+1}$ is possible. $\quad\square$

We have used the symbol Σ as a name for an alphabet. In mathematics the big Greek sigma $\sum$ has a standard use as a general summation sign. The terms following it are to be summed according to how $\sum$ is decorated. For example, consider the expression

$$\sum_{k=1}^{10} k^2.$$

The decorations "$k = 1$" and "10" tell us to sum the numbers k^2 obtained by successively setting $k = 1$, then $k = 2$, then $k = 3$, etc. on up to $k = 10$. That is,

$$\sum_{k=1}^{10} k^2 = 1 + 4 + 9 + 16 + 25 + 36 + 49 + 64 + 81 + 100 = 385.$$

The letter k is a variable [it varies from 1 to 10] and it could be replaced by any other variable. Thus

$$\sum_{k=1}^{10} k^2 = \sum_{j=1}^{10} j^2 = \sum_{r=1}^{10} r^2.$$

We can also consider more general sums like

$$\sum_{k=1}^{n} k^2$$

in which the stopping point n can take on different values. Each value of n

gives a particular value of the sum; for each choice of n the variable k takes on the values from 1 to n. Here are some of the sums represented by $\sum_{k=1}^{n} k^2$.

Value of n	The sum
$n = 1$	$1^2 = 1$
$n = 2$	$1^2 + 2^2 = 1 + 4 = 5$
$n = 3$	$1^2 + 2^2 + 3^2 = 14$
$n = 4$	$1^2 + 2^2 + 3^2 + 4^2 = 30$
$n = 10$	$1^2 + 2^2 + 3^2 + 4^2 + 5^2 + 6^2 + 7^2 + 8^2 + 9^2 + 10^2$
	$= 385$
$n = 73$	$1^2 + 2^2 + 3^2 + 4^2 + \cdots + 73^2 = 132{,}349$

We can also discuss even more general sums like

$$\sum_{k=1}^{n} x_k \quad \text{and} \quad \sum_{j=m}^{n} a_j.$$

Here it is understood that $\{x_k : 1 \leq k \leq n\}$ represents some collection of numbers indexed by $\{k \in \mathbb{N} : 1 \leq k \leq n\}$ and that $\{a_j : m \leq j \leq n\}$ represents a collection of numbers indexed by $\{j \in \mathbb{N} : m \leq j \leq n\}$. Presumably $m \leq n$ since otherwise there would be nothing to sum.

In analogy with $\sum$, the big Greek pi $\prod$ is a general product sign. As explained in § 0.2, for $n \in \mathbb{P}$ the product of the first n integers is called n **factorial** and written $n!$ Thus

$$n! = 1 \cdot 2 \cdot 3 \cdots n = \prod_{k=1}^{n} k.$$

The expression $1 \cdot 2 \cdot 3 \cdots n$ is somewhat confusing for small values of n like 1 and 2; it really means "multiply consecutive integers until you reach n." The expression $\prod_{k=1}^{n} k$ is less ambiguous. Here are the first few values of $n!$

$1! = 1$	$5! = 1 \cdot 2 \cdot 3 \cdot 4 \cdot 5 = 120$
$2! = 1 \cdot 2 = 2$	$6! = 720$
$3! = 1 \cdot 2 \cdot 3 = 6$	$7! = 5040$
$4! = 1 \cdot 2 \cdot 3 \cdot 4 = 24$	$8! = 40{,}320$

For technical reasons $n!$ is also defined for $n = 0$; $0!$ is defined to be 1. The definition of $n!$ will be reexamined in § 3.4.

Next consider a family of sets A_k indexed by some nonempty set I of integers; I may be finite or infinite. The **union** $\bigcup_{k \in I} A_k$ is defined to be the set of elements that belong to at least one of the sets A_k. That is,

$$\bigcup_{k \in I} A_k = \{x : x \in A_k \text{ for at least one value of } k \in I\}.$$

Likewise, the **intersection** $\bigcap_{k \in I} A_k$ is defined by

$$\bigcap_{k \in I} A_k = \{x : x \in A_k \quad \text{for all} \quad k \in I\}.$$

If I has the form $\{k \in \mathbb{Z} : m \leq k \leq n\}$, we write these sets as $\bigcup_{k=m}^{n} A_k$ and $\bigcap_{k=m}^{n} A_k$. For example,

$$\bigcup_{k=0}^{20} A_k = \{x : x \in A_k \quad \text{for some} \quad k \in \mathbb{N} \quad \text{such that} \quad 0 \leq k \leq 20\}$$
$$= A_0 \cup A_1 \cup A_2 \cup A_3 \cup \cdots \cup A_{19} \cup A_{20}.$$

If I is infinite and has the form $\{k \in \mathbb{Z} : k \geq m\}$ we write

$$\bigcup_{k=m}^{\infty} A_k \quad \text{for} \quad \bigcup_{k \in I} A_k \quad \text{and} \quad \bigcap_{k=m}^{\infty} A_k \quad \text{for} \quad \bigcap_{k \in I} A_k.$$

Note that the symbol ∞ here is convenient, but does not represent one of the values of the subscripts.

EXAMPLE 2   (a) For $n \in \mathbb{P}$, let

$$D_n = \{k \in \mathbb{Z} : k \text{ is divisible by } n\}.$$

Then we have

$$D_3 \cap D_5 = \{k \in \mathbb{Z} : k \text{ is divisible by both 3 and 5}\}$$
$$= \{k \in \mathbb{Z} : k \text{ is divisible by 15}\} = D_{15}$$
$$= \{0, \pm15, \pm30, \pm45, \ldots\},$$

and

$$D_3 \cup D_5 = \{k \in \mathbb{Z} : k \text{ is divisible by 3 or 5}\}$$
$$= \{0, \pm3, \pm5, \pm6, \pm9, \pm10, \pm12, \pm15, \pm18, \pm20, \ldots\}.$$

Note that

$$\bigcap_{n \in \mathbb{P}} D_n = \bigcap_{n=1}^{\infty} D_n = \{0\}.$$

In fact, if I is any infinite subset of $\mathbb{P}$, then

$$\bigcap_{n \in I} D_n = \{k \in \mathbb{Z} : k \text{ is divisible by all } n \text{ in } I\} = \{0\}.$$

(b) Let $A_n = [-n, n]$ and $B_n = [n, 2n]$ for $n \in \mathbb{P}$. For example, $A_5 = [-5, 5]$ and $B_7 = [7, 14]$. Observe that

$$\bigcap_{n=4}^{73} A_n = [-4, 4], \quad \bigcup_{n=4}^{73} A_n = [-73, 73] \quad \text{and} \quad \bigcup_{n=1}^{\infty} A_n = \mathbb{R}.$$

Note that the sets B_n "slide along $\mathbb{R}$" as n increases:

So clearly $B_2 \cap B_6 = \{\ \}$ and $\bigcap_{n=1}^{\infty} B_n = \{\ \}$. But not all pairs of sets B_n, B_m are disjoint. For example,

$$B_5 \cap B_8 = [8, 10] \quad \text{and} \quad \bigcap_{n=4}^{8} B_n = \{8\}.$$

(c) If Σ is an alphabet, then

$$\bigcup_{k=0}^{\infty} \Sigma^k = \bigcup_{k \in \mathbb{N}} \Sigma^k = \Sigma^*. \quad \square$$

EXAMPLE 3   The DeMorgan laws in § 1.2 extend as follows. Let $\{A_k : k \in I\}$ be a collection of subsets of some universe U that is indexed by I. Then

$$\left(\bigcup_{k \in I} A_k\right)^c = \bigcap_{k \in I} A_k^c \quad \text{and} \quad \left(\bigcap_{k \in I} A_k\right)^c = \bigcup_{k \in I} A_k^c.$$

We verify the first equality. Suppose that $x \in (\bigcup_{k \in I} A_k)^c$. Then $x \notin \bigcup_{k \in I} A_k$ and so $x \notin A_k$ for all $k \in I$. Hence we have $x \in A_k^c$ for all $k \in I$ and so $x \in \bigcap_{k \in I} A_k^c$. Thus we have $(\bigcup_{k \in I} A_k)^c \subseteq \bigcap_{k \in I} A_k^c$. For the reverse inclusion, consider $x \in \bigcap_{k \in I} A_k^c$. Then $x \in A_k^c$ for all $k \in I$. So $x \notin A_k$ for all $k \in I$. Consequently $x \notin \bigcup_{k \in I} A_k$, i.e., $x \in (\bigcup_{k \in I} A_k)^c$. This shows that $\bigcap_{k \in I} A_k^c \subseteq (\bigcup_{k \in I} A_k)^c$ and so the sets must be equal. $\square$

So far we have only considered indexed families of sets, but we can use indexing to provide labels for the objects in any collection.

EXAMPLE 4   In § 0.2 we considered a graph with 14 edges, and named the edges e_1, e_2, ..., e_{14}. We could say that we indexed the set E of edges using the set $\{1, 2, \ldots, 14\}$. That is,

$$E = \{e_i : i \in \{1, 2, \ldots, 14\}\}. \quad \square$$

In § 2.5 we will be concerned with families of propositions that are indexed by the set $\mathbb{P}$. By a **proposition** we mean an unambiguous sentence that is either true or false, but not both.

EXAMPLE 5   (a) Here are some propositions: "New York is the capital of the United States." "Every graph has an even number of edges." "73 is a prime number." "$3 + 3 = 5$." "More examples are presented in § 2.1."

(b) Here are some nonpropositions: "Do not walk on the grass!" "Give to the mathematics department of your choice." "Mathematics courses are easier than computer science courses." "$4x - 1 = 2x$." The third example is ambiguous since its truth value [True or False] varies from person to person. The fourth example is ambiguous since x isn't specified, but it becomes a proposition if we write "$4x - 1 = 2x$ for all $x \in \mathbb{R}$" or "$4x - 1 = 2x$ for some $x \in \mathbb{R}$." More examples of nonpropositions appear in Examples 3 and 4 of § 2.1. ☐

EXAMPLE 6 For each choice of n in $\mathbb{P}$ the equation "$n^2 = 2^n$" is a proposition. For $n = 2$ and 4 it is true; for other values of n it is false. If we let $A(n)$ be the proposition "$n^2 = 2^n$" then the set $\{A(1), A(2), \ldots\}$ is a set of propositions indexed by $\mathbb{P}$. Similarly, if we let $B(n)$ be "$n^3 + 1$ is divisible by 3," $C(n)$ be "$1 + 2 + \cdots + n = 1 \cdot 2 \cdots n$," and $D(n)$ be "$n^3 - 4n + 6$ is divisible by 3," then the sets of propositions $\{B(1), B(2), \ldots\}$, $\{C(1), C(2), \ldots\}$ and $\{D(1), D(2), \ldots\}$ are indexed by $\mathbb{P}$. The propositions $B(n)$ are true for some values of n [for example, $n = 2, 5$ and 11] but not for others. Note that the propositions $C(n)$ could have been written "$\sum_{k=1}^{n} k = n!$" The first few $C(n)$'s are

Value of n	Proposition $C(n)$
$n = 1$	$1 = 1$
$n = 2$	$1 + 2 = 1 \cdot 2$
$n = 3$	$1 + 2 + 3 = 1 \cdot 2 \cdot 3$
$n = 4$	$1 + 2 + 3 + 4 = 1 \cdot 2 \cdot 3 \cdot 4$
$n = 5$	$1 + 2 + 3 + 4 + 5 = 1 \cdot 2 \cdot 3 \cdot 4 \cdot 5$

For $n = 1$ or 3, $C(n)$ is true, but otherwise $C(n)$ is false. The first few $D(n)$'s are

Value of n	Proposition $D(n)$
$n = 1$	$1^3 - 4 \cdot 1 + 6 = 3$ is divisible by 3
$n = 2$	$2^3 - 4 \cdot 2 + 6 = 6$ is divisible by 3
$n = 3$	$3^3 - 4 \cdot 3 + 6 = 21$ is divisible by 3
$n = 4$	$4^3 - 4 \cdot 4 + 6 = 54$ is divisible by 3
$n = 5$	$5^3 - 4 \cdot 5 + 6 = 111$ is divisible by 3

Note that the first five values of n yield true propositions. Is this accidental or a pattern? It turns out that the proposition $D(n)$ is true for every value of n. With enough determination and/or hardware, one could check this for thousands of values of n. But this would not be a proof; conceivably the result fails for some gigantic n. In § 2.5 we will see how to settle this sort of question once and for all; this particular example is dealt with in Exercise 8 of that section. ☐

Frequently propositions indexed by $\mathbb{P}$ will be written as $p(n)$. Thus $p(1)$ is the first proposition, $p(2)$ is the second proposition, $\ldots$, $p(n)$ is the nth proposition.

EXAMPLE 7 Consider the propositions

$$p(n) = \text{“}11^n - 4^n \text{ is divisible by } 7.\text{”}$$

Then $p(1)$ is the proposition "$11 - 4$ is divisible by 7," $p(4)$ is the proposition "$11^4 - 4^4$ is divisible by 7," etc. ☐

EXERCISES 1.3

1. Calculate

(a) $\dfrac{7!}{5!}$

(b) $\dfrac{10!}{6!\,4!}$

(c) $\dfrac{9!}{0!\,9!}$

(d) $\dfrac{8!}{4!}$

(e) $\displaystyle\sum_{k=0}^{5} k!$

(f) $\displaystyle\prod_{j=3}^{6} j$

2. Simplify

(a) $\dfrac{n!}{(n-1)!}$

(b) $\dfrac{(n!)^2}{(n+1)!\,(n-1)!}$

3. Calculate

(a) $\displaystyle\sum_{k=1}^{n} 3^k$ for $n = 1, 2, 3$ and 4,

(b) $\displaystyle\sum_{k=3}^{n} k^3$ for $n = 3, 4$ and 5,

(c) $\displaystyle\sum_{j=n}^{2n} j$ for $n = 1, 2$ and 5.

4. Calculate

(a) $\displaystyle\sum_{i=1}^{10} (-1)^i$

(b) $\displaystyle\sum_{k=0}^{3} (k^2 + 1)$

(c) $\left(\displaystyle\sum_{k=0}^{3} k^2 \right) + 1$

(d) $\displaystyle\prod_{n=1}^{5} (2n + 1)$

(e) $\displaystyle\prod_{j=4}^{8} (j - 1)$

5. (a) Calculate $\displaystyle\prod_{r=1}^{n} (r - 3)$ for $n = 1, 2, 3, 4$ and 73.

(b) Calculate $\displaystyle\prod_{k=1}^{m} \dfrac{k+1}{k}$ for $m = 1, 2$ and 3. Give a formula for this product for all $m \in \mathbb{P}$.

6. (a) Calculate $\displaystyle\sum_{k=0}^{n} 2^k$ for $n = 1, 2, 3, 4$ and 5.

(b) Use your answers to part (a) to guess a general formula for this sum.

7. For $n \in \mathbb{P}$, let $D_n = \{k \in \mathbb{Z} : k \text{ is divisible by } n\}$. Determine

(a) $D_2 \cap D_5$

(b) $D_2 \cap D_3 \cap D_5$

(c) $D_2 \cap D_4$

(d) $D_4 \cap D_6$

(e) $D_4 \oplus D_6$

(f) D_2^c

8. In this exercise the universe is $\mathbb{R}$. Let

$$A = \bigcup_{n=0}^{\infty} [2n, 2n+1] \quad \text{and} \quad B = \bigcup_{n=1}^{\infty} [2n-1, 2n].$$

(a) Determine the sets $A \cup B$ and $A \cap B$. *Suggestion:* Draw pictures of A and B as subsets of $\mathbb{R}$.

(b) Give four positive numbers in A^c.

(c) Give four positive numbers in B^c.

(d) Determine $A^c \cap B^c$.

9. In this exercise the universe is $\mathbb{N}$. For each $n \in \mathbb{P}$, let $A_n = \{n, n+1, n+2, \ldots\}$ $= \{k \in \mathbb{N} : k \geq n\}$ and $B_n = \{0, 1, 2, \ldots, 2n\} = \{k \in \mathbb{N} : k \leq 2n\}$.

(a) Write down A_n and B_n for $n = 2$ and $n = 4$.

(b) Write down A_1^c, A_2^c and A_4^c.

(c) Determine $A_n \cap B_n$ and A_n^c for $n = 1, 2, 3$ and 7.

(d) Determine $\bigcup\limits_{n=3}^{6} A_n$, $\bigcup\limits_{n=3}^{6} B_n$, $\bigcap\limits_{n=3}^{6} B_n$, $\bigcap\limits_{n=3}^{6} A_n$.

(e) Determine $\bigcup\limits_{n=3}^{\infty} A_n$, $\bigcup\limits_{n=3}^{\infty} B_n$, $\bigcap\limits_{n=3}^{\infty} B_n$, $\bigcap\limits_{n=3}^{\infty} A_n$.

(f) Determine $\bigcup\limits_{n=1}^{5} A_n^c$ and $\bigcup\limits_{n=1}^{\infty} (A_n \cup B_n)^c$.

10. Let $A_0 = \{n \in \mathbb{Z} : n \text{ is divisible by } 5\}$ and for $k \in \mathbb{P}$ let $A_k = \{n + k : n \in A_0\}$.

(a) List several elements in each of the sets A_1, A_2, A_3, A_4, A_5 and A_6.

(b) What is the relationship between A_5 and A_0? A_6 and A_1? A_{30} and A_0?

(c) Generalize your answers to part (b).

(d) What is $\bigcup\limits_{k=0}^{4} A_k$? $\bigcup\limits_{k=1}^{5} A_k$?

11. Let Σ be an alphabet and, for $k \in \mathbb{N}$, let $\Sigma^k = \{w \in \Sigma^* : \text{length}(w) = k\}$.

(a) What is $\bigcup\limits_{k=0}^{n} \Sigma^k$ for each $n \in \mathbb{N}$?

(b) Describe the set $\bigcup\limits_{k \in \mathbb{N}} \Sigma^{2k}$.

12. Let $\Sigma = \{a, b\}$ and for $n \in \mathbb{N}$ let

$$A_n = \{w \in \Sigma^* : \text{the letter } a \text{ occurs in } w \text{ exactly } n \text{ times}\}.$$

(a) Describe the members of A_0.

(b) List five elements in A_1 and five elements in A_4.

(c) What is $\bigcup\limits_{n \in \mathbb{N}} A_n$?

(d) Explain briefly why the inclusion $A_n \subseteq \bigcup\limits_{k=n}^{\infty} \Sigma^k$ is valid for all n.

(e) For $m \in \mathbb{N}$, let B_m be the set of all words w in Σ^* in which the letter b occurs exactly m times. Explain why $A_n \cap B_m \subseteq \Sigma^{n+m}$ for all m and n.

13. Prove the second generalized DeMorgan law stated in Example 3.

14. For $n \in \mathbb{P}$, let $A(n)$ be the proposition "$\sum\limits_{k=1}^{n} k = \frac{1}{2}n(n+1)$." Verify that $A(n)$ is true for $n \leq 5$.

15. For $n \in \mathbb{P}$, let $p(n)$ be the proposition "$11^n - 4^n$ is divisible by 7." Verify that $p(n)$ is true for $n = 1, 2, 3$.

16. For $n \in \mathbb{P}$, let $p(n)$ be the proposition "$n^3 - n$ is divisible by 6." Check whether this is true for each $n \leq 5$. Do you have a conjecture for $n \geq 6$?

17. For $n \in \mathbb{P}$, let $p(n)$ be the proposition "$n! > n^2$." Which of the propositions $p(1), p(2), p(3), p(4), p(5), p(6)$ are true? Do you have a conjecture for $n \geq 7$?

18. For $n \in \mathbb{P}$, let $p(n)$ be the proposition "$2n^2 - 2n + 7$ is prime." Determine whether this is true for each $n \leq 5$. Do you have a conjecture for $n \geq 6$?

§1.4   Ordered Pairs, Matrix Notation

Consider two sets S and T. For each element s in S and each element t in T, we form an **ordered pair** $\langle s, t \rangle$. Here s is the first element of the ordered pair, t is the second element and the order is important. Thus $\langle s_1, t_1 \rangle = \langle s_2, t_2 \rangle$ if and only if $s_1 = s_2$ and $t_1 = t_2$. The set of all ordered pairs $\langle s, t \rangle$ is called the **product of S and T** and written $S \times T$:

$$S \times T = \{\langle s, t \rangle : s \in S \text{ and } t \in T\}.$$

If $S = T$ we sometimes write S^2 for $S \times S$.

EXAMPLE 1   (a) Let $S = \{1, 2, 3, 4\}$ and $T = \{a, b, c\}$. Then $S \times T$ consists of the twelve ordered pairs listed on the left in Figure 1. We could also depict these

$\langle 1, c \rangle$	$\langle 2, c \rangle$	$\langle 3, c \rangle$	$\langle 4, c \rangle$		c	o	o	o	o
$\langle 1, b \rangle$	$\langle 2, b \rangle$	$\langle 3, b \rangle$	$\langle 4, b \rangle$		b	o	o	o	o
$\langle 1, a \rangle$	$\langle 2, a \rangle$	$\langle 3, a \rangle$	$\langle 4, a \rangle$		a	o	o	o	o
						1	2	3	4

List of $\{1, 2, 3, 4\} \times \{a, b, c\}$ Picture of $\{1, 2, 3, 4\} \times \{a, b, c\}$

FIGURE 1

pairs as corresponding points in labeled rows and columns, in the manner shown on the right in the figure. The reader should list or draw $T \times S$ and note that $T \times S \neq S \times T$.

(b) If $S = \{1, 2, 3, 4\}$, then $S^2 = S \times S$ has sixteen ordered pairs; see Figure 2. Note that $\langle 2, 4 \rangle \neq \langle 4, 2 \rangle$; these ordered pairs involve the same two numbers, but in different orders. In contrast, the *sets* $\{2, 4\}$ and $\{4, 2\}$

$\langle 1, 4 \rangle$	$\langle 2, 4 \rangle$	$\langle 3, 4 \rangle$	$\langle 4, 4 \rangle$		4	o	o	o	o
$\langle 1, 3 \rangle$	$\langle 2, 3 \rangle$	$\langle 3, 3 \rangle$	$\langle 4, 3 \rangle$		3	o	o	o	o
$\langle 1, 2 \rangle$	$\langle 2, 2 \rangle$	$\langle 3, 2 \rangle$	$\langle 4, 2 \rangle$		2	o	o	o	o
$\langle 1, 1 \rangle$	$\langle 2, 1 \rangle$	$\langle 3, 1 \rangle$	$\langle 4, 1 \rangle$		1	o	o	o	o
						1	2	3	4

List of $\{1, 2, 3, 4\}^2$ Picture of $\{1, 2, 3, 4\}^2$

FIGURE 2

are the same. Also note that $\langle 2, 2 \rangle$ is a perfectly good ordered pair in which the first element happens to equal the second element. On the other hand, the set $\{2, 2\}$ is just the set $\{2\}$ in which 2 happens to be written twice. If you are used to seeing ordered pairs written (a, b), you may wonder why we do it differently. We do so because we don't want to confuse ordered pairs with open intervals. For us $(2, 4)$ is the set $\{x \in \mathbb{R} : 2 < x < 4\}$.

(c) The set $\mathbb{N}^2 = \mathbb{N} \times \mathbb{N}$ is infinite but we can draw part of it; see Figure 3. The solid points represent $\langle 3, 0 \rangle$, $\langle 1, 5 \rangle$ and $\langle 4, 2 \rangle$. Note that $\mathbb{N}^2 = \{\langle m, n \rangle : m, n \in \mathbb{N}\}$.

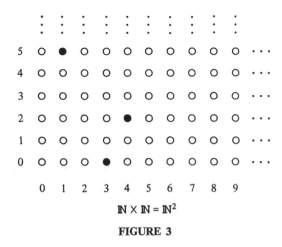

$$\mathbb{N} \times \mathbb{N} = \mathbb{N}^2$$

FIGURE 3

(d) Part of the set $\mathbb{R}^2 = \mathbb{R} \times \mathbb{R} = \{\langle x, y \rangle : x, y \in \mathbb{R}\}$ is sketched in Figure 4. The solid dots represent the points $\langle 3, 0 \rangle$, $\langle \frac{1}{2}, 1 \rangle$ and $\langle -2, 2 \rangle$. The set $\mathbb{R}^2$ gives a coordinate system for the plane, since every point in the

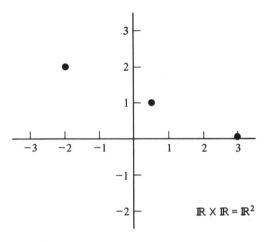

$$\mathbb{R} \times \mathbb{R} = \mathbb{R}^2$$

FIGURE 4

plane corresponds to exactly one ordered pair of real numbers, i.e., to an element of $\mathbb{R}^2$. ⬛

We are often interested in subsets of product sets.

EXAMPLE 2   (a) Let $S = \{1, 2, 3\}$ and $T = \{0, 1, 2, 3\}$. The pictures of the following subsets of $S \times T$ are indicated in Figure 5:

$$A = \{\langle m, n \rangle \in S \times T : m + n \leq 3\},$$
$$B = \{\langle m, n \rangle \in S \times T : m - n = 2\},$$
$$C = \{\langle m, n \rangle \in S \times T : \max \{m, n\} = 3\},$$
$$D = \{\langle m, n \rangle \in S \times T : m = 1\}.$$

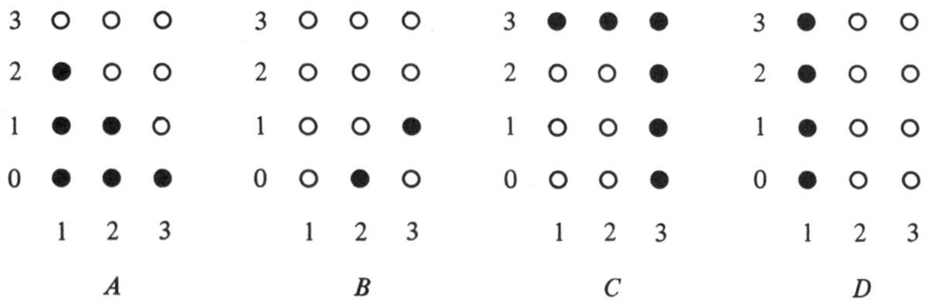

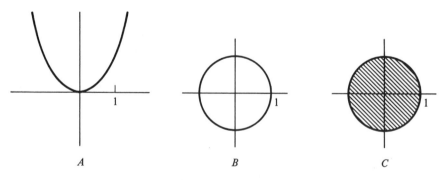

FIGURE 5

(b) The pictures of the following subsets of $\mathbb{R}^2$ are sketched in Figure 6:

$$A = \{\langle x, y \rangle \in \mathbb{R}^2 : y = x^2\}, \qquad B = \{\langle x, y \rangle \in \mathbb{R}^2 : x^2 + y^2 = 1\},$$
$$C = \{\langle x, y \rangle \in \mathbb{R}^2 : x^2 + y^2 \leq 1\}. \quad ⬛$$

FIGURE 6

We next define the product of any finite number of sets. Thus, consider n sets $S_1, S_2, \ldots, S_n$. The **product set** $S_1 \times S_2 \times \cdots \times S_n$ consists of all **ordered n-tuples** $\langle s_1, s_2, \ldots, s_n \rangle$ where $s_1 \in S_1, s_2 \in S_2$, etc. That is,

$$S_1 \times S_2 \cdots \times S_n = \{\langle s_1, s_2, \ldots, s_n \rangle : s_k \in S_k \text{ for } k = 1, 2, \ldots, n\}.$$

Just as with ordered pairs, two ordered n-tuples $\langle s_1, s_2, \ldots, s_n \rangle$ and $\langle t_1, t_2, \ldots, t_n \rangle$ are regarded as equal if all the corresponding entries are equal: $s_k = t_k$ for $k = 1, 2, \ldots, n$. If the sets $S_1, S_2, \ldots, S_n$ are all equal, to S say, we may write S^n for the product $S_1 \times S_2 \times \cdots \times S_n$.

EXAMPLE 3 Just as $\mathbb{R}^2$ gives a coordinate system for the plane, $\mathbb{R}^3$ gives a coordinate system for the usual 3-dimensional space in which we think we live. The set

$$\{\langle x, y, z \rangle \in \mathbb{R}^3 : x^2 + y^2 + z^2 \leqq 1\}$$

corresponds to the solid ball with center $\langle 0, 0, 0 \rangle$ and radius 1. ☐

The set $\mathbb{R}^n$ is called n-**dimensional real space**, and many geometrical notions can be extended to $\mathbb{R}^n$ for $n \geqq 4$ even though it is difficult to visualize and draw suitable pictures. Our interest in $\mathbb{R}^n$ will be more algebraic, though we will rely on our intuition from $\mathbb{R}^3$ to give us some rough feeling for geometry in $\mathbb{R}^n$. For example, $\mathbb{R}^n$ is the suitable universal set when considering equations with n unknowns. For instance, the solution set S for the system

$$x^2 + 2xy - y^2 - z - w = 0$$
$$x + 2xz - z^2 - 2yw = 0$$
$$x^2 + 2xw - y^2 - 3z^2 + w^3 = 0$$

is some [horrible] subset of $\mathbb{R}^4$. It is clear that S contains $\langle 0, 0, 0, 0 \rangle$ and $\langle 1, 1, 1, 1 \rangle$, but not much else is clear about S.

Systems of equations with several unknowns are much easier to handle if all the equations are **linear**; this means that each equation has the form

$$a_1 x_1 + a_2 x_2 + \cdots + a_n x_n = b$$

where the coefficients $a_1, a_2, \ldots, a_n, b$ are constants. Here $x_1, x_2, \ldots, x_n$ represent the n unknown real values; equivalently, the unknown is an element $\langle x_1, x_2, \ldots, x_n \rangle$ of $\mathbb{R}^n$. The equation is called "linear" from the fact that if $n = 2$ its graph is a straight line. Systems of linear equations can be solved and understood best with the aid of matrices. We will not solve any systems of linear equations here since this skill is covered in texts on matrix theory and linear algebra. Our goal here is simply to observe the link between systems of linear equations and matrices.

EXAMPLE 4 The system

$$2x - 3y + z = 4$$
$$x + y - 5z = 7$$

is completely described by the coefficients 2, −3, 1, 4, 1, 1, −5 and 7, provided we know which coefficient goes where. We can take care of that by presenting them in their proper location,

$$\begin{bmatrix} 2 & -3 & 1 \\ 1 & 1 & -5 \end{bmatrix}$$

for the left-hand side and $\begin{bmatrix} 4 \\ 7 \end{bmatrix}$ for the right-hand side.   □

More generally, if we have m linear equations in n unknowns, it is convenient to index the coefficients by double subscripts as follows:

$$a_{11}x_1 + a_{12}x_2 + \cdots + a_{1n}x_n = b_1$$
$$a_{21}x_1 + a_{22}x_2 + \cdots + a_{2n}x_n = b_2$$
$$a_{31}x_1 + a_{32}x_2 + \cdots + a_{3n}x_n = b_3$$
$$\vdots$$
$$a_{m1}x_1 + a_{m2}x_2 + \cdots + a_{mn}x_n = b_m.$$

The rectangular array of coefficients

$$\mathbf{A} = \begin{bmatrix} a_{11} & a_{12} & \cdots & a_{1n} \\ a_{21} & a_{22} & \cdots & a_{2n} \\ a_{31} & a_{32} & \cdots & a_{3n} \\ \vdots & \vdots & & \vdots \\ a_{m1} & a_{m2} & \cdots & a_{mn} \end{bmatrix}$$

is called the **coefficient matrix** for the system. In general, a **matrix** is a rectangular array. Many computer languages allow the definition of n-dimensional arrays for $n = 2, 3, 4, \ldots$, and with such languages one can describe matrices as 2-dimensional arrays. In many instances special algorithms are also available for performing operations with matrices which would not be appropriate for higher-dimensional arrays. The matrix $\mathbf{A}$ above has m horizontal rows and n vertical columns and is called an $m \times n$ **matrix**. It is traditional to use capital letters, such as $\mathbf{A}$, for matrices. The entry in the ith row and jth column is denoted by a_{ij} and we sometimes write $\mathbf{A}$ as $[a_{ij}]$. Whenever double indexes are used in matrix theory, rows precede columns! Sometimes, as in § 0.3, we denote the entry in the ith row and jth column by $\mathbf{A}[i, j]$; this notation is preferable in computer science since it avoids subscripts. In this text a **matrix** has real entries unless otherwise specified. Note that an $m \times n$ matrix can be viewed as a collection of real numbers indexed by the product set $\{1, 2, \ldots, m\} \times \{1, 2, \ldots, n\}$.

EXAMPLE 5   (a) The matrix

$$A = \begin{bmatrix} 2 & -1 & 0 & 3 & 2 \\ 1 & -2 & 1 & -1 & 3 \\ 3 & 0 & 1 & 2 & -3 \end{bmatrix}$$

is a 3×5 matrix. If we write $A = [a_{ij}]$, then $a_{11} = 2$, $a_{31} = 3$, $a_{13} = 0$, $a_{35} = -3$, etc. If we use the notation $A[i, j]$, then $A[1, 2] = -1$, $A[2, 1] = 1$, $A[2, 2] = -2$, etc.

(b) If B is the 3×4 matrix defined by $B[i, j] = i - j$, then $B[1, 1] = 1 - 1 = 0$, $B[1, 2] = 1 - 2 = -1$, etc. and so

$$B = \begin{bmatrix} 0 & -1 & -2 & -3 \\ 1 & 0 & -1 & -2 \\ 2 & 1 & 0 & -1 \end{bmatrix}.$$ □

There are at least five reasons why matrices are important in the mathematical sciences.

1. They arise in solving systems of linear equations, as we hinted at in the previous paragraph. We will briefly discuss this point of view again in § 4.1. However, entire texts and courses are devoted to the study of matrices and systems of equations, and we will not duplicate their efforts.

2. Matrices are a convenient device for storing information that is naturally indexed by two variables. This is especially true in business, economics and computer science.

3. Many physical phenomena are linear or very nearly linear in nature and so matrices arise in the mathematical descriptions of these phenomena.

4. As hinted at in § 0.3, matrices are a valuable tool in graph theory, which we will study in Chapter 8.

5. The set of $n \times n$ matrices has a very rich algebraic structure, which is of interest in itself and is also a source of inspiration in the study of more abstract algebraic structures. We will introduce addition of matrices later in this section and we will introduce other algebraic operations on matrices in Chapter 4. More general algebraic systems will be studied in Chapter 11.

For positive integers m and n, we write $\mathfrak{M}_{m,n}$ for the set of all $m \times n$ matrices. Two matrices A and B in $\mathfrak{M}_{m,n}$ are **equal** provided all their corresponding entries are equal, i.e., $A = B$ provided $a_{ij} = b_{ij}$ for all i and j where $1 \leq i \leq m$ and $1 \leq j \leq n$. Matrices that have the same number of rows as columns are called **square matrices**. Thus A is a square matrix if A

belongs to $\mathfrak{M}_{n,n}$ for some $n \in \mathbb{P}$. The **transpose** $\mathbf{A}^T$ of a matrix $\mathbf{A} = [a_{ij}]$ in $\mathfrak{M}_{m,n}$ is the matrix in $\mathfrak{M}_{n,m}$ whose entry in the ith row and jth column is a_{ji}. That is, $\mathbf{A}^T[i, j] = \mathbf{A}[j, i]$. For example, if

$$\mathbf{A} = \begin{bmatrix} 2 & -1 & 0 & 4 \\ 3 & 2 & -1 & 2 \\ 4 & 0 & 1 & 3 \end{bmatrix}, \quad \text{then} \quad \mathbf{A}^T = \begin{bmatrix} 2 & 3 & 4 \\ -1 & 2 & 0 \\ 0 & -1 & 1 \\ 4 & 2 & 3 \end{bmatrix}.$$

The first row in $\mathbf{A}$ becomes the first column in $\mathbf{A}^T$, etc.

Matrices that have only one row, i.e., $1 \times n$ matrices, are often called **row vectors**, while matrices that have only one column, i.e., $m \times 1$ matrices, are called **column vectors**. The transpose of a row vector is a column vector and the transpose of a column vector is a row vector. Thus $[2 \quad 4 \quad -3 \quad -1]$ is a row vector and its transpose

$$\begin{bmatrix} 2 \\ 4 \\ -3 \\ -1 \end{bmatrix}$$

is a column vector. We sometimes view an $m \times n$ matrix as composed of m row vectors or of n column vectors.

Two matrices $\mathbf{A}$ and $\mathbf{B}$ can be added if they are the same size, that is, if they belong to the same set $\mathfrak{M}_{m,n}$. In this case, the **sum** is obtained by adding corresponding entries. More explicitly, if $\mathbf{A} = [a_{ij}]$ and $\mathbf{B} = [b_{ij}]$ are in $\mathfrak{M}_{m,n}$, then $\mathbf{A} + \mathbf{B}$ is the matrix $\mathbf{C} = [c_{ij}]$ in $\mathfrak{M}_{m,n}$ defined by

$$c_{ij} = a_{ij} + b_{ij} \quad \text{for} \quad 1 \leq i \leq m \quad \text{and} \quad 1 \leq j \leq n.$$

Equivalently, we define

$$(\mathbf{A} + \mathbf{B})[i, j] = \mathbf{A}[i, j] + \mathbf{B}[i, j] \quad \text{for} \quad 1 \leq i \leq m \quad \text{and} \quad 1 \leq j \leq n.$$

Since m or n can be 1, this definition applies in particular to row vectors and to column vectors.

EXAMPLE 6   (a) Consider

$$\mathbf{A} = \begin{bmatrix} 2 & 4 & 0 \\ -1 & 3 & 2 \\ -3 & 1 & 2 \end{bmatrix}, \quad \mathbf{B} = \begin{bmatrix} 1 & 0 & 5 & 3 \\ 2 & 3 & -2 & 1 \\ 4 & -2 & 0 & 2 \end{bmatrix}, \quad \mathbf{C} = \begin{bmatrix} 3 & 1 & -2 \\ -5 & 0 & 2 \\ -2 & 4 & 1 \end{bmatrix}.$$

Then we have

$$\mathbf{A} + \mathbf{C} = \begin{bmatrix} 5 & 5 & -2 \\ -6 & 3 & 4 \\ -5 & 5 & 3 \end{bmatrix},$$

but $\mathbf{A} + \mathbf{B}$ and $\mathbf{B} + \mathbf{C}$ are not defined. Of course the sums $\mathbf{A} + \mathbf{A}$, $\mathbf{B} + \mathbf{B}$ and $\mathbf{C} + \mathbf{C}$ are also defined; for example,

$$\mathbf{B} + \mathbf{B} = \begin{bmatrix} 2 & 0 & 10 & 6 \\ 4 & 6 & -4 & 2 \\ 8 & -4 & 0 & 4 \end{bmatrix}.$$

(b) Consider the row vectors

$$\mathbf{v}_1 = [-2 \quad 1 \quad 2 \quad 3], \qquad \mathbf{v}_2 = [4 \quad 0 \quad 3 \quad -2], \qquad \mathbf{v}_3 = [1 \quad 3 \quad 5]$$

and the column vectors

$$\mathbf{v}_4 = \begin{bmatrix} 1 \\ 2 \\ -3 \\ 2 \end{bmatrix}, \qquad \mathbf{v}_5 = \begin{bmatrix} 0 \\ 3 \\ -2 \end{bmatrix} \quad \text{and} \quad \mathbf{v}_6 = \begin{bmatrix} 4 \\ 1 \\ 5 \end{bmatrix}.$$

The only sums of distinct vectors here that are defined are

$$\mathbf{v}_1 + \mathbf{v}_2 = [2 \quad 1 \quad 5 \quad 1] \quad \text{and} \quad \mathbf{v}_5 + \mathbf{v}_6 = \begin{bmatrix} 4 \\ 4 \\ 3 \end{bmatrix}. \quad \square$$

Elements in $\mathbb{R}^n$ are also often called **vectors**. We add them just as if they were row vectors:

$$\langle x_1, x_2, \ldots, x_n \rangle + \langle y_1, y_2, \ldots, y_n \rangle = \langle x_1 + y_1, x_2 + y_2, \ldots, x_n + y_n \rangle.$$

EXERCISES 1.4

1. Let $A = \{a, b, c\}$ and $B = \{a, b, d\}$.
   (a) List or draw the ordered pairs in $A \times A$.
   (b) List or draw the ordered pairs in $A \times B$.
   (c) List or draw the set $\{\langle x, y \rangle \in A \times B : x = y\}$.
2. Let $S = \{0, 1, 2, 3, 4\}$ and $T = \{0, 2, 4\}$.
   (a) How many ordered pairs are in $S \times T$? $T \times S$?
   (b) List or draw the elements in $\{\langle m, n \rangle \in S \times T : m < n\}$.
   (c) List or draw the elements in $\{\langle m, n \rangle \in T \times S : m < n\}$.
   (d) List or draw the elements in $\{\langle m, n \rangle \in S \times T : m + n \geq 3\}$.
   (e) List or draw the elements in $\{\langle m, n \rangle \in T \times S : mn \geq 4\}$.
   (f) List or draw the elements in $\{\langle m, n \rangle \in S \times S : m + n = 10\}$.
3. For each of the following sets, list all elements if the set has fewer than seven elements. Otherwise, list exactly seven elements of the set.
   (a) $\{\langle m, n \rangle \in \mathbb{N}^2 : m = n\}$
   (b) $\{\langle m, n \rangle \in \mathbb{N}^2 : m + n \text{ is prime}\}$
   (c) $\{\langle m, n \rangle \in \mathbb{P}^2 : m = 6\}$

(d) $\{\langle m, n \rangle \in \mathbb{P}^2 : \min \{m, n\} = 3\}$
(e) $\{\langle m, n \rangle \in \mathbb{P}^2 : \max \{m, n\} = 3\}$
(f) $\{\langle m, n \rangle \in \mathbb{N}^2 : m^2 = n\}$

4. List five elements in each of the following sets.
   (a) $\{\langle m, n, p \rangle \in \mathbb{N}^3 : m + n = p\}$
   (b) $\{\langle m, n, p \rangle \in \mathbb{N}^3 : m = p = 1\}$
   (c) $\{\langle m, n, p, q \rangle \in \mathbb{N}^4 : mnpq = 0\}$

5. Sketch the following sets.
   (a) $\{\langle m, n \rangle \in \mathbb{N}^2 : -1 \leq m - n \leq 1\}$
   (b) $\{\langle m, n \rangle \in \mathbb{N}^2 : m - n \leq 2\}$

6. Sketch the following subsets of $\mathbb{R}^2$.
   (a) $A = \{\langle x, y \rangle \in \mathbb{R}^2 : x = y^2\}$
   (b) $B = \{\langle x, y \rangle \in \mathbb{R}^2 : x \leq y^2\}$
   (c) $C = \{\langle x, y \rangle \in \mathbb{R}^2 : x \geq 0, y \geq 0, x + y = 1\}$
   (d) $D = \{\langle x, y \rangle \in \mathbb{R}^2 : x \geq 0, y \geq 0, x + y \leq 1\}$

7. Consider $A = \{\langle x, y \rangle \in \mathbb{R}^2 : 2x - y = 4\}$, $B = \{\langle x, y \rangle \in \mathbb{R}^2 : x + 3y = 9\}$
   and $C = \{\langle x, y \rangle \in \mathbb{R}^2 : y = 2x\}$. Find
   (a) $A \cap B$ (b) $A \cap C$
   (c) $B \cap C$ (d) $A^c \cup C^c$

8. Solve $\langle 2x - y, x + 2y \rangle = \langle 3, 4 \rangle$ for x and y.

9. Let $\Sigma = \{a, b, c, d\}$.
   (a) List seven elements of the set

   $$\{\langle w_1, w_2 \rangle \in \Sigma^* \times \Sigma^* : \text{length}(w_1) = \text{length}(w_2)\}.$$

   (b) List all the elements in the set

   $$\{\langle x, y, z \rangle \in \Sigma^3 : xyz \text{ is a word in the English language}\}.$$

   For example, the ordered triple $\langle b, a, d \rangle$ belongs to this set.

10. Consider the matrix

$$\mathbf{B} = \begin{bmatrix} 1 & 2 & -2 & 1 \\ 3 & 0 & 1 & 2 \\ 2 & -1 & 4 & 1 \\ 0 & -3 & 1 & 3 \end{bmatrix}.$$

   Evaluate

   (a) b_{12} (b) b_{21} (c) b_{23} (d) $\sum_{i=1}^{4} b_{ii}$

11. Consider the matrices

$$\mathbf{A} = \begin{bmatrix} -1 & 0 & 2 \\ 1 & 3 & -2 \\ 4 & 2 & 3 \end{bmatrix}, \quad \mathbf{B} = \begin{bmatrix} 6 & 8 & 5 \\ 4 & -2 & 7 \\ 3 & 1 & 2 \end{bmatrix}, \quad \mathbf{C} = \begin{bmatrix} 1 & 3 \\ 2 & -4 \\ 5 & -2 \end{bmatrix}.$$

   Calculate the following when they exist.
   (a) $\mathbf{A}^T$ (b) $\mathbf{C}^T$ (c) $\mathbf{A} + \mathbf{B}$

  (d) $\mathbf{A} + \mathbf{C}$ (e) $(\mathbf{A} + \mathbf{B})^T$ (f) $\mathbf{A}^T + \mathbf{B}^T$

  (g) $\mathbf{B} + \mathbf{B}^T$ (h) $\mathbf{C} + \mathbf{C}^T$ (i) $(\mathbf{A} + \mathbf{A}) + \mathbf{B}$

12. Consider the following elements in $\mathbb{R}^3$:

$$\mathbf{v}_1 = \langle 1, 0, 0 \rangle, \qquad \mathbf{v}_2 = \langle 0, -1, 1 \rangle, \qquad \mathbf{v}_3 = \langle 1, 0, -1 \rangle.$$

Find

  (a) $\mathbf{v}_1 + \mathbf{v}_2$ (b) $\mathbf{v}_1 + \mathbf{v}_3$

  (c) $\mathbf{v}_3 + \mathbf{v}_2$ (d) $(\mathbf{v}_1 + \mathbf{v}_2) + \mathbf{v}_1$

13. Let $\mathbf{A} = [a_{ij}]$ and $\mathbf{B} = [b_{ij}]$ be matrices in $\mathfrak{M}_{4,3}$ defined by $a_{ij} = (-1)^{i+j}$ and $b_{ij} = i + j$. Find the following matrices when they exist.

  (a) $\mathbf{A}^T$ (b) $\mathbf{A} + \mathbf{B}$ (c) $\mathbf{A}^T + \mathbf{B}$

  (d) $\mathbf{A}^T + \mathbf{B}^T$ (e) $(\mathbf{A} + \mathbf{B})^T$ (f) $\mathbf{A} + \mathbf{A}$

14. Let $\mathbf{A}$ and $\mathbf{B}$ be matrices in $\mathfrak{M}_{3,3}$ defined by $\mathbf{A}[i, j] = ij$ and $\mathbf{B}[i, j] = i + j^2$.

  (a) Find $\mathbf{A} + \mathbf{B}$.

  (b) Calculate $\sum_{i=1}^{3} \mathbf{A}[i, i]$.

  (c) Calculate $\sum_{i=1}^{3} \left(\sum_{j=1}^{3} \mathbf{B}[i, j] \right)$ and $\sum_{j=1}^{3} \left(\sum_{i=1}^{3} \mathbf{B}[i, j] \right)$.

  (d) Does $\mathbf{A}$ equal its transpose $\mathbf{A}^T$?

  (e) Does $\mathbf{B}$ equal its transpose $\mathbf{B}^T$?

15. (a) List the six 3×3 matrices whose rows are row vectors $[1 \quad 0 \quad 0]$, $[0 \quad 1 \quad 0]$ and $[0 \quad 0 \quad 1]$.

  (b) Which matrices in part (a) are equal to their transposes?

16. In this exercise, $\mathbf{A}$ and $\mathbf{B}$ represent matrices. True or False.

  (a) $(\mathbf{A}^T)^T = \mathbf{A}$ for all $\mathbf{A}$.

  (b) If $\mathbf{A}^T = \mathbf{B}^T$, then $\mathbf{A} = \mathbf{B}$.

  (c) If $\mathbf{A} = \mathbf{A}^T$, then $\mathbf{A}$ is a square matrix.

  (d) If $\mathbf{A}$ and $\mathbf{B}$ are the same size, then $(\mathbf{A} + \mathbf{B})^T = \mathbf{A}^T + \mathbf{B}^T$.

17. For each $n \in \mathbb{N}$, let

$$\mathbf{A}_n = \begin{bmatrix} 1 & n \\ 0 & 1 \end{bmatrix} \quad \text{and} \quad \mathbf{B}_n = \begin{bmatrix} 1 & (-1)^n \\ -1 & 1 \end{bmatrix}.$$

  (a) Give $\mathbf{A}_n^T$ for all $n \in \mathbb{N}$.

  (b) Find $\{n \in \mathbb{N} : \mathbf{A}_n^T = \mathbf{A}_n\}$.

  (c) Find $\{n \in \mathbb{N} : \mathbf{B}_n^T = \mathbf{B}_n\}$.

  (d) Find $\{n \in \mathbb{N} : \mathbf{B}_n = \mathbf{B}_0\}$.

18. For sets S, T and V, prove

  (a) $(S \cap T) \times V = (S \times V) \cap (T \times V)$

  (b) $(S \cup T) \times V = (S \times V) \cup (T \times V)$

19. In § 1.1 we mentioned that all of mathematics can be defined or described in terms of "set" and "membership." For example, the **ordered pair** $\langle s, t \rangle$ with first entry s and second entry t can be defined as the set $\{\{s\}, \{s, t\}\}$, in which s and t obviously play different roles. Show that this definition satisfies the basic property of ordered pairs:

$$\langle s_1, t_1 \rangle = \langle s_2, t_2 \rangle \quad \text{if and only if} \quad s_1 = s_2 \quad \text{and} \quad t_1 = t_2.$$

CHAPTER HIGHLIGHTS

To check your understanding of the material in this chapter, we recommend that you consider each item listed below and:

(a) Satisfy yourself that you can define each concept and each notation.

(b) Give at least one reason why the item was included in the chapter.

Concepts

set [undefined]
    member = element, subset
    equal, disjoint
    set operations
    universe, complement
    Venn diagram
indexed collection
ordered pair, product of sets
vector, matrix, matrix sum
coefficient matrix of a system of linear equations
alphabet, language, word, length of word

Examples and Notation

$\mathbb{N}$, $\mathbb{P}$, $\mathbb{Z}$, $\mathbb{Q}$, $\mathbb{R}$, $\mathfrak{M}_{m,n}$

$\in$, $\notin$, $\{\ \}$, $\{\ :\ \}$, $\subseteq$, $\subset$

$\varnothing = \{\ \} = $ empty set

$\mathcal{P}(S)$, $\cup$, $\cap$, $A \setminus B$, $A \oplus B$

$\bigcup\limits_{k \in I} A_k$, $\bigcap\limits_{k \in I} A_k$

$\sum$ [summation notation], $\prod$ [product notation]

$n!$

$\langle s, t \rangle$, $\langle s_1, \ldots, s_n \rangle$, $S \times T$, $S_1 \times \cdots \times S_n$

S^n, $\mathbb{R}^n$

Σ^*

Facts

Laws of set algebra [Table 1 of § 1.2].
Additional laws proved from them [e.g., Examples 5 and 6 of § 1.2].

Methods

Use of Venn diagrams.
Reasoning from definitions and previously established facts.

2

ELEMENTARY LOGIC

AND INDUCTION

In this chapter and in Chapter 6 we give an informal introduction to logic. Mathematicians, computer scientists, and in fact all scientists need to be able to recognize valid and invalid arguments, and should be aware of some techniques of logic. Thus our emphasis will be on logic as a working tool, though we will give some hints as to what is involved in a careful formal treatment of the subject. The last section of the chapter introduces mathematical induction.

§ 2.1 *Propositional Calculus*

Propositional calculus is the study of the logical relationships between objects called propositions, which are usually interpretable as meaningful assertions in real-life contexts. For us, a **proposition** will be any sentence that is either true or false, but not both. That is, it is a sentence that can be assigned the truth value **true** or the truth value **false**, and not both. We do not need to know what its truth value is in order to consider a proposition.

EXAMPLE 1   The following are propositions:

(a) Julius Caesar was president of the United States.
(b) The world is flat.
(c) The Soviet Union is the world's largest country in area.
(d) $2 + 2 = 4$.

(e) $2 + 3 = 7$.

(f) $2^{89301} + 1$ is a prime number.

(g) The number 4 is positive and the number 3 is negative.

(h) If a tree has n vertices, then it has exactly $n - 1$ edges.

(i) $2^n + n$ is a prime number for infinitely many n.

(j) Every even integer greater than 4 is the sum of two prime numbers.

Note that propositions (d) and (e) are mathematical sentences, where "$=$" serves as the verb "equals" or "is equal to." Clearly proposition (f) is true or false, even though we have no idea which. Proposition (g) is false, since 3 is not negative. If this is not clear now, it will become clear soon, since (g) is the compound proposition: "4 is positive *and* 3 is negative." We have no idea whether proposition (i) is true or false, though some mathematicians may know the answer. On the other hand, as of the writing of this book *no one knows* whether proposition (j) is true; its truth is known as "Goldbach's conjecture." □

EXAMPLE 2   Here are some more propositions:

(a) Every connected graph has an Euler circuit.

(b) $x + y = y + x$ for all $x, y \in \mathbb{R}$.

(c) $\mathbf{A} = \mathbf{A}^T$ for all 2×2 matrices $\mathbf{A}$.

(d) $2^n = n^2$ for some $n \in \mathbb{N}$.

(e) It is not true that 3 is an even integer or 7 is a prime.

(f) If the world is flat, then $2 + 2 = 4$.

Propositions (a), (b) and (c) are really infinite sets of propositions covered by the phrase "Every" or "for all." And proposition (d) is a special sort of proposition because of the phrase "for some." Propositions of these types will be studied systematically in §§ 6.1 and 6.2. Proposition (e) is a somewhat confusing compound proposition whose truth value will be easy to analyze after the study of this chapter. Our propositional calculus will allow us to construct propositions like that in (f), even when they may appear silly or even paradoxical. □

EXAMPLE 3   The following sentences are not propositions:

(a) Your place or mine?

(b) Why is induction important?

(c) Go directly to jail.

(d) Help me, please.

(e) $x - y = y - x$.

The reason that sentence (e) is not a proposition is that the symbols are not specified. If the intention is

(e′) $x - y = y - x$ for all $x, y \in \mathbb{R}$,

then this is a false proposition. If the intention is

(e″) $x - y = y - x$ for some $x, y \in \mathbb{R}$,

or

(e‴) $x - y = y - x$ for all x, y in $\{0\}$,

then this is a true proposition. The problem of unspecified symbols will be dealt with in § 6.1. □

EXAMPLE 4   Of course, in the real world there are ambiguous propositions:

(a) Teachers are overpaid.
(b) Doctors are rich.
(c) It was cold in Minneapolis in January 1924.
(d) Math is fun.
(e) Trees are more interesting than matrices.
(f) $A^2 = 0$ implies $A = 0$ for all A.

The difficulty with sentence (f) is that the set of allowable A's is not specified. Proposition (f) is true for all $A \in \mathbb{R}$. It turns out that (f) is meaningful, but false, for the set of all 2×2 matrices A. Ambiguous propositions should either be made unambiguous or abandoned. We will not concern ourselves with this process, but assume that our propositions are unambiguous. □

In the propositional calculus, we will generally use lower case letters such as $p, q, r, \ldots$ to stand for propositions and we will combine propositions to obtain compound propositions using standard connective symbols:

$\neg$ for "not" or negation;
$\wedge$ for "and";
$\vee$ for "or" [inclusive];
$\rightarrow$ for "implies" or the conditional implication;
$\leftrightarrow$ for "if and only if" or the biconditional.

Other connectives, such as $\oplus$, appear in the exercises.

After we illustrate in Example 5 how some of the propositions in Examples 1 and 2 can be viewed as compound propositions, we will carefully discuss each of the connective symbols and explain how they affect the truth values of compound propositions.

EXAMPLE 5   (a) Recall proposition (g) in Example 1: "The number 4 is positive and the number 3 is negative." This can be viewed as the compound proposition $p \wedge q$ where $p = $ "4 is positive" and $q = $ "3 is negative."
        (b) Proposition (f) in Example 2, "If the world is flat, then $2 + 2 = 4$," can be viewed as the compound proposition $r \rightarrow s$ where $r = $ "the world is flat" and $s = $ "$2 + 2 = 4$."

(c) Proposition (e) in Example 2 says "It is not true that 3 is an even integer or 7 is a prime." This is $\neg(p \vee q)$ where $p = $ "3 is even" and $q = $ "7 is a prime." Actually, proposition (e) is poorly written and can also be interpreted to mean $(\neg p) \vee q$.

(d) Let's look again at Example 2(d): "$2^n = n^2$ for some $n \in \mathbb{N}$." This proposition turns out to be decomposable as

$$"p(0) \vee p(1) \vee p(2) \vee p(3) \vee \cdots"$$

or

$$"p(n) \quad \text{for some} \quad n \in \mathbb{N}"$$

where $p(n)$ is the simple proposition "$2^n = n^2$." However, these two constructions are not allowed in the propositional calculus. Hence the propositional calculus will be inadequate for our needs and we will study the more general predicate calculus in Chapter 6. We begin with the propositional calculus in order to deal with the basic connectives and concepts first. □

The fundamental assumption in the propositional calculus is that the truth values of a proposition built up from other propositions by using logical connectives are completely determined by the truth values of the original propositions and the way the proposition is built up from them. Thus, given propositions p and q, the truth values of the compound propositions $\neg p$, $p \wedge q$, $p \vee q$, $p \rightarrow q$ and $p \leftrightarrow q$ will be determined by the truth values of p and q. Since there are only four different combinations of truth values for p and q, we can simply give tables to describe the truth values of the compound propositions for all combinations.

The proposition $\neg p$ should be true exactly when p is false. Most mathematicians and many computer scientists symbolize truth values as T or F [for True or False], while others symbolize them as 1 or 0 [for True or False]. The truth tables for $\neg p$ are:

p	$\neg p$
F	T
T	F

p	$\neg p$
0	1
1	0

Henceforth we will use 0's and 1's to signify False and True. The truth table for $p \wedge q$ is

p	q	$p \wedge q$
0	0	0
0	1	0
1	0	0
1	1	1

The table is read horizontally. For example, the third line tells us that if p is true and q is false, then the compound proposition $p \wedge q$ is to have truth value false. Note that $p \wedge q$ has truth value true exactly when both p *and* q are true.

As we explained in § 1.2, the use of "or" in the English language is somewhat ambiguous, but our use of $\vee$ will not be ambiguous. We define $\vee$ as follows:

p	q	$p \vee q$
0	0	0
0	1	1
1	0	1
1	1	1

Most people would agree with the truth value assignments for the first three lines. The fourth line states that we regard $p \vee q$ to be true if both p and q are true. This is the "inclusive or," sometimes written "and/or." Thus $p \vee q$ is true if p is true or q is true *or both*. The "exclusive or," symbolized $\oplus$, means that one or the other is true but not both; see Exercise 15.

The **conditional implication** $p \to q$ means that the truth of p implies the truth of q. In other words, if p is true, then q must be true. The only way that this can fail is if p is true while q is false.

p	q	$p \to q$
0	0	1
0	1	1
1	0	0
1	1	1

The following are English language equivalents to $p \to q$: "p implies q," "if p, then q," "p only if q," "p is a sufficient condition for q," and "q is a necessary condition for p." The first two are straightforward and we will usually avoid the other three; but see Exercises 17 and 18.

The first two lines of the truth table for $p \to q$ may bother some people because it looks as if false propositions imply anything. In fact, we are simply defining the *compound proposition $p \to q$* to be true if p is false. This usage of implication appears in ordinary English. Suppose that a politician promises "If I am elected, then taxes will be lower next year." If the politician is not elected, we would surely not regard him or her as a liar, no matter how the tax rates changed.

We will discuss the biconditional $p \leftrightarrow q$ after we introduce general truth tables.

A **truth table** for a compound proposition built up from propositions $p, q, r, \ldots$ is a table giving the truth values of the compound proposition in terms of the truth values of $p, q, r, \ldots$. We call $p, q, r, \ldots$ the **variables** of the table and of the compound proposition. One can determine the truth values of the compound proposition by determining the truth values of subpropositions working from the inside out, as we now illustrate.

EXAMPLE 6 Here is a truth table for the compound proposition $(p \wedge q) \vee \neg(p \to q)$. Note that there are still only four rows, because there are still only four distinct combinations of truth values for p and q.

column 1 2	3	4	5	6
p q	$p \wedge q$	$p \to q$	$\neg(p \to q)$	$(p \wedge q) \vee \neg(p \to q)$
0 0	0	1	0	0
0 1	0	1	0	0
1 0	0	0	1	1
1 1	1	1	0	1

The values in columns 3 and 4 are determined by the values in columns 1 and 2. The values in column 5 are determined by the values in column 4. The values in column 6 are determined by the values in columns 3 and 5. The sixth column gives the truth values of the complete compound proposition.

One can use a simpler truth table, with the same thought processes, by writing the truth values under the connectives, as follows:

p q	$(p \wedge q)$	$\vee$	$\neg(p \to q)$	
0 0	0	0	0	1
0 1	0	0	0	1
1 0	0	1	1	0
1 1	1	1	0	1
step 1 1	2	4	3 2	

The values at each step are determined by the values at earlier steps. For example, the values at the third step were determined by the values in the last column. The values at the fourth step were determined by the values in the third and fifth columns. The column created at the last step gives the truth values of the compound proposition. ∎

The simpler truth tables become more advantageous as the compound propositions get more complicated.

EXAMPLE 7 Here is the truth table for

$$(p \rightarrow q) \wedge [(q \wedge \neg r) \rightarrow (p \vee r)].$$

p q r	$(p \rightarrow q)$	$\wedge$	$[(q \wedge \neg r) \rightarrow (p \vee r)]$			
0 0 0	1	1	0	1	1	0
0 0 1	1	1	0	0	1	1
0 1 0	1	0	1	1	0	0
0 1 1	1	1	0	0	1	1
1 0 0	0	0	0	1	1	1
1 0 1	0	0	0	0	1	1
1 1 0	1	1	1	1	1	1
1 1 1	1	1	0	0	1	1
step 1 1 1	2	5	3	2	4	2

Notice that the rows of a truth table could be given in any order; we've chosen a systematic order for the truth combinations of p, q, r partly to be sure we have listed them all. □

The **biconditional** $p \leftrightarrow q$ is defined by the truth table for $(p \rightarrow q) \wedge (q \rightarrow p)$:

p q	$(p \rightarrow q)$	$\wedge$	$(q \rightarrow p)$
0 0	1	1	1
0 1	1	0	0
1 0	0	0	1
1 1	1	1	1
step 1 1	2	3	2

That is,

p q	$p \leftrightarrow q$
0 0	1
0 1	0
1 0	0
1 1	1

Thus $p \leftrightarrow q$ is true if both p and q are true or if both p and q are false. The following are English language equivalents to $p \leftrightarrow q$: "p if and only if q," "p is a necessary and sufficient condition for q" and "p precisely if q."

It is worth emphasizing that the compound propositions $p \rightarrow q$ and $q \rightarrow p$ are quite different; they have different truth tables. The proposition $q \rightarrow p$ is called the **converse** of the proposition $p \rightarrow q$.

EXERCISES 2.1

1. Let p, q, r be the following propositions:

$$p = \text{"It is raining."}$$

$$q = \text{"The sun is shining."}$$

$$r = \text{"There are clouds in the sky."}$$

Translate the following into logical notation, using p, q, r and logical connectives.
   (a) It is raining and the sun is shining.
   (b) If it is raining, then there are clouds in the sky.
   (c) If it is not raining, then the sun is not shining and there are clouds in the sky.
   (d) The sun is shining if and only if it is not raining.
   (e) If there are no clouds in the sky, then the sun is shining.

2. Let p, q, r be as in Exercise 1. Translate the following into English sentences.
   (a) $(p \wedge q) \rightarrow r$
   (b) $(p \rightarrow r) \rightarrow q$
   (c) $\neg p \leftrightarrow (q \vee r)$
   (d) $\neg(p \leftrightarrow (q \vee r))$
   (e) $\neg(p \vee q) \wedge r$

3. (a) Give the truth values of the propositions in parts (a)–(e) of Example 1.
   (b) Do the same for all parts of Example 2. In Example 2(e), indicate which interpretation you are using; see Example 5(c).

4. Which of the following are propositions? Give the truth values of the propositions.
   (a) $x^2 = x$ for all $x \in \mathbb{R}$.
   (b) $x^2 = x$ for some $x \in \mathbb{R}$.
   (c) $x^2 = x$.
   (d) $x^2 = x$ for exactly one $x \in \mathbb{R}$.
   (e) $xy = xz$ implies $y = z$.
   (f) $xy = xz$ implies $y = z$ for all $x, y, z \in \mathbb{R}$.
   (g) $w_1 w_2 = w_1 w_3$ implies $w_2 = w_3$ for all words $w_1, w_2, w_3 \in \Sigma^*$.

5. Consider the ambiguous sentence "$x^2 = y^2$ implies $x = y$ for all x, y."
   (a) Make the sentence into an unambiguous proposition whose truth value is true.
   (b) Make the sentence into an unambiguous proposition whose truth value is false.

6. Determine the truth values of the following compound propositions.
   (a) If $2 + 2 = 4$, then $2 + 4 = 8$.
   (b) If $2 + 2 = 5$, then $2 + 4 = 8$.
   (c) If $2 + 2 = 4$, then $2 + 4 = 6$.
   (d) If $2 + 2 = 5$, then $2 + 4 = 6$.
   (e) If the earth is flat, then Julius Caesar was the first president of the United States.
   (f) If the earth is flat, then George Washington was the first president of the United States.

(g) If George Washington was the first president of the United States, then the earth is flat.

(h) If George Washington was the first president of the United States, then $2 + 2 = 4$.

7. Suppose that $p \rightarrow q$ is known to be false. Give the truth values for
    (a) $p \wedge q$ (b) $p \vee q$ (c) $q \rightarrow p$

8. Construct truth tables for
    (a) $p \wedge \neg p$ (b) $p \vee \neg p$
    (c) $p \leftrightarrow \neg p$ (d) $\neg \neg p$

9. Construct truth tables for
    (a) $\neg(p \wedge q)$ (b) $\neg(p \vee q)$
    (c) $\neg p \wedge \neg q$ (d) $\neg p \vee \neg q$

10. Construct the truth table for $(p \rightarrow q) \rightarrow [(p \vee \neg q) \rightarrow (p \wedge q)]$.

11. Construct the truth table for $[(p \vee q) \wedge r] \rightarrow (p \wedge \neg q)$.

12. Construct the truth table for $[(p \leftrightarrow q) \vee (p \rightarrow r)] \rightarrow (\neg q \wedge p)$.

13. Construct truth tables for
    (a) $\neg(p \vee q) \rightarrow r$ (b) $\neg((p \vee q) \rightarrow r)$
This exercise shows that one must be careful with parentheses. We will discuss this matter further in Example 6 of § 3.5.

14. (a) Write a compound proposition that is true when exactly one of the three propositions p, q and r is true.
    (b) Write a compound proposition that is true when exactly two of the three propositions p, q and r are true.

15. The "exclusive or" connective $\oplus$ is defined by the truth table

p	q	$p \oplus q$
0	0	0
0	1	1
1	0	1
1	1	0

    (a) Show that $p \oplus q$ has the same truth table as $\neg(p \leftrightarrow q)$.
    (b) Construct a truth table for $p \oplus p$.
    (c) Construct a truth table for $(p \oplus q) \oplus r$.
    (d) Construct a truth table for $(p \oplus p) \oplus p$.

16. Give the converses of the following propositions.
    (a) $q \rightarrow r$.
    (b) If it is raining, then there are clouds in the sky.
    (c) If $x^2 = x$, then $x = 0$ or $x = 1$.
    (d) If $2 + 2 = 4$, then $2 + 4 = 8$.

17. Even though we will normally use "implies" and "if . . . , then" to describe implication, other word orders and phrases often arise in practice, as in the examples below. Let p, q and r be the propositions:

$$p = \text{"the flag is set,"}$$

$$q = \text{"}I = 0\text{,"}$$

$$r = \text{"subroutine } S \text{ is completed."}$$

Translate each of the following propositions into symbols, using the letters p, q, r and the logical connectives.

(a) If the flag is set, then $I = 0$.

(b) Subroutine S is completed if the flag is set.

(c) The flag is set if subroutine S is not completed.

(d) Whenever $I = 0$ the flag is set.

(e) Subroutine S is completed only if $I = 0$.

(f) Subroutine S is completed only if $I = 0$ or the flag is set.

   Note the ambiguity in part (f); there are two different answers, each with its own claim to validity. Would punctuation help?

18. Consider the following propositions:

$$r = \text{"ODD}(N) = T\text{,"}$$

$$m = \text{"the output goes to the monitor,"}$$

$$p = \text{"the output goes to the printer."}$$

Translate the following, as in Exercise 17.

(a) The output goes to the monitor if $\text{ODD}(N) = T$.

(b) The output goes to the printer whenever $\text{ODD}(N) = T$ is not true.

(c) $\text{ODD}(N) = T$ only if the output goes to the monitor.

(d) The output goes to the monitor if the output goes to the printer.

(e) $\text{ODD}(N) = T$ or the output goes to the monitor if the output goes to the printer.

19. Is the following a proposition? "This sentence is false." If so, what is its truth value?

§ 2.2   *Tautologies*

An important class of compound propositions consists of those that are always true no matter what the truth values of the variables p, q, etc. are. Such a compound proposition is called a **tautology**. Why would we ever be interested in a proposition that is always true, and hence is pretty boring? The answer is that we are going to be dealing with some rather complicated-looking propositions which we hope to show are true, and the way that we will show their truth will be by using other propositions that are known to be true always. We begin with a very simple tautology.

EXAMPLE 1   (a) The classical tautology is the compound proposition $p \rightarrow p$:

p	$p \rightarrow p$
0	1
1	1

(b) The compound proposition $[p \wedge (p \rightarrow q)] \rightarrow q$ is a tautology:

p q	$[p \wedge (p \rightarrow q)]$	$\rightarrow$	q
0 0	0 1	1
0 1	0 1	1
1 0	0 0	1
1 1	1 1	1
step 1 1	3 2	4

(c) $\neg(p \vee q) \leftrightarrow (\neg p \wedge \neg q)$ is a tautology:

p q	$\neg(p \vee q)$	$\leftrightarrow$	$(\neg p \wedge \neg q)$
0 0	1 0	1	1 1 1
0 1	0 1	1	1 0 0
1 0	0 1	1	0 0 1
1 1	0 1	1	0 0 0
step 1 1	3 2	4	2 3 2

A compound proposition that is always false is called a **contradiction.** Clearly a compound proposition P is a contradiction if and only if $\neg P$ is a tautology.

EXAMPLE 2   The classical contradiction is the compound proposition $p \wedge \neg p$:

p	p	$\wedge$	$\neg p$
0	0	0	1
1	1	0	0

Two compound propositions P and Q are regarded as **logically equivalent** if they have the same truth values for all choices of truth values of the variables p, q, etc. In other words, the final columns of their truth tables must be the same. When this occurs, we write $P \Leftrightarrow Q$. Since $P \leftrightarrow Q$ has truth values true precisely when the truth values of P and Q agree, we see that:

$$P \Leftrightarrow Q \quad \textit{if and only if} \quad P \leftrightarrow Q \quad \textit{is a tautology.}$$

The observation that $P \Leftrightarrow Q$ will be especially useful in cases where P and Q look quite different from each other. See, for instance, the formulas in Table 1.

EXAMPLE 3   (a) In view of Example 1(c), the compound propositions $\neg(p \vee q)$ and $\neg p \wedge \neg q$ are logically equivalent. That is, $\neg(p \vee q) \Leftrightarrow (\neg p \wedge \neg q)$.
      (b) The very nature of the connectives $\vee$ and $\wedge$ suggests that $p \vee q \Leftrightarrow q \vee p$ and $p \wedge q \Leftrightarrow q \wedge p$. Of course, one can verify these assertions by showing that $(p \vee q) \leftrightarrow (q \vee p)$ and $(p \wedge q) \leftrightarrow (q \wedge p)$ are tautologies.

It is worth stressing the difference between $\Leftrightarrow$ and $\leftrightarrow$. The expression "$P \Leftrightarrow Q$" is an assertion, namely that P and Q are logically equivalent, i.e., $P \leftrightarrow Q$ is a tautology. The expression "$P \leftrightarrow Q$" simply represents some compound proposition that might or might not be a tautology.

In Table 1 we list a number of logical equivalences selected for their usefulness. To obtain a table of tautologies, replace each $\Leftrightarrow$ by $\leftrightarrow$. These tautologies can all be verified by truth tables. However, most of them should be intuitively reasonable. Many of the entries in Table 1 have names, which we have given, but there is no need to memorize them all. In the table, t represents any tautology and c represents any contradiction.

TABLE 1. Logical Equivalences

1. $\neg\,\neg p \Leftrightarrow p$	double negation
2a. $(p \lor q) \Leftrightarrow (q \lor p)$ b. $(p \land q) \Leftrightarrow (q \land p)$ c. $(p \leftrightarrow q) \Leftrightarrow (q \leftrightarrow p)$	commutative laws
3a. $[(p \lor q) \lor r] \Leftrightarrow [p \lor (q \lor r)]$ b. $[(p \land q) \land r] \Leftrightarrow [p \land (q \land r)]$	associative laws
4a. $[p \lor (q \land r)] \Leftrightarrow [(p \lor q) \land (p \lor r)]$ b. $[p \land (q \lor r)] \Leftrightarrow [(p \land q) \lor (p \land r)]$	distributive laws
5a. $(p \lor p) \Leftrightarrow p$ b. $(p \land p) \Leftrightarrow p$	idempotent laws
6a. $(p \lor c) \Leftrightarrow p$ b. $(p \lor t) \Leftrightarrow t$ c. $(p \land c) \Leftrightarrow c$ d. $(p \land t) \Leftrightarrow p$	identity laws
7a. $(p \lor \neg p) \Leftrightarrow t$ b. $(p \land \neg p) \Leftrightarrow c$	
8a. $\neg(p \lor q) \Leftrightarrow (\neg p \land \neg q)$ b. $\neg(p \land q) \Leftrightarrow (\neg p \lor \neg q)$ c. $(p \lor q) \Leftrightarrow \neg(\neg p \land \neg q)$ d. $(p \land q) \Leftrightarrow \neg(\neg p \lor \neg q)$	DeMorgan laws
9. $(p \to q) \Leftrightarrow (\neg q \to \neg p)$	contrapositive
10a. $(p \to q) \Leftrightarrow (\neg p \lor q)$ b. $(p \to q) \Leftrightarrow \neg(p \land \neg q)$	implication
11a. $(p \lor q) \Leftrightarrow (\neg p \to q)$ b. $(p \land q) \Leftrightarrow \neg(p \to \neg q)$	
12a. $[(p \to r) \land (q \to r)] \Leftrightarrow [(p \lor q) \to r]$ b. $[(p \to q) \land (p \to r)] \Leftrightarrow [p \to (q \land r)]$	
13. $(p \leftrightarrow q) \Leftrightarrow [(p \to q) \land (q \to p)]$	equivalence
14. $[(p \land q) \to r] \Leftrightarrow [p \to (q \to r)]$	exportation law
15. $(p \to q) \Leftrightarrow [(p \land \neg q) \to c]$	reductio ad absurdum

The logical equivalences 2, 3, 4, 8 and 9 should be recognized by name, especially 9, the **contrapositive** rule.

Given two compound propositions P and Q, we say that P **logically implies** Q provided Q has truth value true whenever P has truth value true. We write $P \Rightarrow Q$ when this occurs. Note that *$P \Rightarrow Q$ if and only if the compound proposition $P \to Q$ is a tautology*, i.e., $P \to Q$ is never false. Equivalently, P and Q never simultaneously have the truth values 1 and 0, respectively, so when P is true, Q is true and when Q is false, P is false.

EXAMPLE 4   We have $[p \wedge (p \to q)] \Rightarrow q$ since $[p \wedge (p \to q)] \to q$ is a tautology by Example 1(b).   ☐

In Table 2 we list some useful logical implications. Each entry becomes a tautology if $\Rightarrow$ is replaced by $\to$. As with Table 1, many of the implications have names that need not be memorized.

TABLE 2. *Logical Implications*

16.	$p \Rightarrow (p \vee q)$	addition
17.	$(p \wedge q) \Rightarrow p$	simplification
18.	$(p \to c) \Rightarrow \neg p$	absurdity
19.	$[p \wedge (p \to q)] \Rightarrow q$	modus ponens
20.	$[(p \to q) \wedge \neg q] \Rightarrow \neg p$	modus tollens
21.	$[(p \vee q) \wedge \neg p] \Rightarrow q$	disjunctive syllogism
22.	$p \Rightarrow [q \to (p \wedge q)]$	
23.	$[(p \leftrightarrow q) \wedge (q \leftrightarrow r)] \Rightarrow (p \leftrightarrow r)$	transitivity of $\leftrightarrow$
24.	$[(p \to q) \wedge (q \to r)] \Rightarrow (p \to r)$	transitivity of $\to$ *or* hypothetical syllogism
25a.	$(p \to q) \Rightarrow [(p \vee r) \to (q \vee r)]$	
b.	$(p \to q) \Rightarrow [(p \wedge r) \to (q \wedge r)]$	
c.	$(p \to q) \Rightarrow [(q \to r) \to (p \to r)]$	
26a.	$[(p \to q) \wedge (r \to s)] \Rightarrow [(p \vee r) \to (q \vee s)]$	constructive dilemmas
b.	$[(p \to q) \wedge (r \to s)] \Rightarrow [(p \wedge r) \to (q \wedge s)]$	
27a.	$[(p \to q) \wedge (r \to s)] \Rightarrow [(\neg q \vee \neg s) \to (\neg p \vee \neg r)]$	destructive dilemmas
b.	$[(p \to q) \wedge (r \to s)] \Rightarrow [(\neg q \wedge \neg s) \to (\neg p \wedge \neg r)]$	

In checking logical implications $P \Rightarrow Q$ it is only necessary to analyze the rows of the truth table where P is true or where Q is false.

EXAMPLE 5   (a) We verify the implication $(p \wedge q) \Rightarrow p$. We need only consider the case where $p \wedge q$ is true, i.e., both p and q are true. Thus we consider the truncated table:

p q	(p ∧ q)	→	p
1 1	1	1	

(b) We verify the implication 26a. The full truth table would require 16 rows. However, we need only consider the cases where the implication $(p \lor r) \to (q \lor s)$ might be false. Thus it is enough to look at the cases for which $q \lor s$ is false, that is, with both q and s false.

p q r s	[(p → q) ∧ (r → s)]			→	[(p ∨ r) → (q ∨ s)]		
0 0 0 0	1	1	1	1	0	1	0
0 0 1 0	1	0	0	1	1	0	0
1 0 0 0	0	0	1	1	1	0	0
1 0 1 0	0	0	0	1	1	0	0
step 1 1 1 1	2	3	2	4	2	3	2

We are able to derive numerous logical equivalences and implications using the following.

Substitution Rules.

(a) If a compound proposition P is a tautology and if each occurrence of some variable of P, say p, is replaced by the same proposition E, then the resulting compound proposition P^* is also a tautology.

(b) If a compound proposition P contains a proposition Q and if Q is replaced by a logically equivalent proposition Q^*, then the resulting compound proposition P^* is logically equivalent to P.

To see why the substitution rules are true, one analyzes their effects on the corresponding truth tables. For example, in the case of rule (a), the truth table entries for P are all 1 regardless of the truth values for p. If we replaced all occurrences of p by a contradiction, for example, and considered a table for the resulting proposition, we would in effect be looking at just those rows in the table for P for which p is false, but they would still all have the value 1 for P. If we replace p by some other proposition E, then as soon as we determine the truth value of the proposition E we know which rows in the table for P to look at, but they all give the value 1 for P anyway, so who cares whether E is true or false?

For brevity, the equivalences and implications in Tables 1 and 2 will often be referred to as **rules.** Here are some illustrations of the use of these rules.

EXAMPLE 6   (a) According to the modus ponens rule 19,

$$P = \text{"}[p \land (p \to q)] \to q\text{"}$$

is a tautology. If we replace each occurrence of p by the proposition $E =$

"$q \rightarrow r$" we obtain the tautology

$$P^* = \text{``}[(q \rightarrow r) \wedge ((q \rightarrow r) \rightarrow q)] \rightarrow q.\text{''}$$

If instead we replace each occurrence of q by E we obtain the tautology

$$[p \wedge (p \rightarrow (q \rightarrow r))] \rightarrow (q \rightarrow r).$$

(b) Consider the proposition

$$P = \text{``}\neg[(p \rightarrow q) \wedge (p \rightarrow r)] \rightarrow [q \rightarrow (p \rightarrow r)]\text{''}$$

which is not a tautology. We obtain logically equivalent propositions if we replace $(p \rightarrow q)$ by the logically equivalent $(\neg p \vee q)$ or if we replace one or both occurrences of $(p \rightarrow r)$ by $(\neg p \vee r)$; see rule 10a. We could also replace $[(p \rightarrow q) \wedge (p \rightarrow r)]$ by $[p \rightarrow (q \wedge r)]$ thanks to rule 12b. Thus P is logically equivalent to the following propositions among others:

$$\neg[(\neg p \vee q) \wedge (p \rightarrow r)] \rightarrow [q \rightarrow (p \rightarrow r)],$$
$$\neg[(p \rightarrow q) \wedge (\neg p \vee r)] \rightarrow [q \rightarrow (p \rightarrow r)],$$
$$\neg[p \rightarrow (q \wedge r)] \rightarrow [q \rightarrow (\neg p \vee r)]. \quad \Box$$

EXAMPLE 7   (a) We illustrate substitution rules (a) and (b) by showing the nearly obvious equivalence

$$[(p \vee q) \vee (p \vee r)] \Leftrightarrow (p \vee q) \vee r$$

by successively substituting equivalent propositions.

Equivalent propositions	*Explanations*
$(p \vee q) \vee (p \vee r)$	given
$[(p \vee q) \vee p] \vee r$	associative law 3a with substitutions valid by substitution rule (a)
$[p \vee (q \vee p)] \vee r$	same
$[p \vee (p \vee q)] \vee r$	commutative law 2a
$[(p \vee p) \vee q] \vee r$	associative law 3a and substitution rule (a)
$[p \vee q] \vee r$	idempotent law 5a and substitution rule (b)

Here we carefully mentioned each application of substitution rules (a) and (b), but in practice one would explain the substitution involved at a given step only if it appeared that the reader might not see it without help.

(b) Now we derive the useful tautology

$$[(p \rightarrow q) \vee (p \rightarrow r)] \rightarrow [p \rightarrow (q \vee r)]$$

starting from a tautology based on the associative law:

$$[(p \vee q) \vee r] \rightarrow [p \vee (q \vee r)].$$

By part (a) and substitution rule (b),

$$[(p \lor q) \lor (p \lor r)] \to [p \lor (q \lor r)]$$

is also a tautology. Replacing each occurrence of p by $\neg p$, we get the tautology

$$[(\neg p \lor q) \lor (\neg p \lor r)] \to [\neg p \lor (q \lor r)].$$

Implication rule 10a and substitution rule (a) tell us

$$\neg p \lor q \Leftrightarrow p \to q, \qquad \neg p \lor r \Leftrightarrow p \to r, \qquad \neg p \lor (q \lor r) \Leftrightarrow p \to (q \lor r).$$

Applying substitution rule (b) three times, we conclude that

$$[(p \to q) \lor (p \to r)] \to [p \to (q \lor r)]$$

is a tautology. ▯

As illustrated in Example 7, we can use substitution to transform one compound proposition into a logically equivalent one. Normally one would use this procedure to obtain a more convenient proposition. What is "convenient" depends, of course, on what comes next. These rules can be considered analogous to the rules of ordinary algebra, with which we often rewrite expressions in forms more suited to whatever task we have at hand.

EXAMPLE 8   We find a proposition logically equivalent to $(p \land q) \to (\neg p \land q)$ that does not use the connective $\land$ by using the DeMorgan law 8d and substitution. Since $p \land q$ is equivalent to $\neg(\neg p \lor \neg q)$ and $\neg p \land q$ is equivalent to $\neg(\neg \neg p \lor \neg q)$, the given proposition is equivalent to

$$\neg(\neg p \lor \neg q) \to \neg(\neg \neg p \lor \neg q)$$

and so to

$$\neg(\neg p \lor \neg q) \to \neg(p \lor \neg q).$$

If desired, we could apply rule 10a to obtain the equivalent

$$\neg(p \to \neg q) \to \neg(q \to p),$$

which uses neither $\land$ nor $\lor$. On the other hand, we could avoid the use of the connective $\to$ by applying rule 10a. ▯

EXERCISES 2.2

1. Give the converse and contrapositive for each of the following propositions.
   (a) $p \to (q \land r)$.
   (b) If $x + y = 1$, then $x^2 + y^2 \geqq 1$.
   (c) If $2 + 2 = 4$, then $3 + 3 = 8$.
2. Consider the proposition "if $x > 0$, then $x^2 > 0$ for $x \in \mathbb{R}$."
   (a) Give the converse and contrapositive of the proposition.
   (b) Which of the following are true propositions: the original proposition, its converse, its contrapositive?

3. Consider the following propositions:

$$p \rightarrow q, \qquad \neg p \rightarrow \neg q, \qquad q \rightarrow p, \qquad \neg q \rightarrow \neg p,$$
$$q \wedge \neg p, \qquad \neg p \vee q, \qquad \neg q \vee p, \qquad p \wedge \neg q.$$

   (a) Which proposition is the converse of $p \rightarrow q$?
   (b) Which proposition is the contrapositive of $p \rightarrow q$?
   (c) Which propositions are logically equivalent to $p \rightarrow q$?

4. Verify the following logical equivalences using truth tables.
   (a) the distributive law, rule 4a
   (b) the identity laws 6a, 6b, 6c, 6d
   (c) the contrapositive, rule 9

5. Verify the following logical equivalences using truth tables.
   (a) rule 12a
   (b) the exportation law, rule 14
   (c) rule 15

6. Verify the following logical implications using truth tables.
   (a) modus tollens, rule 20
   (b) disjunctive syllogism, rule 21

7. Verify the following logical implications using truth tables and shortcuts as in Example 5.
   (a) rule 25b
   (b) rule 25c
   (c) rule 26b

8. Prove or disprove the following. Note that only *one* line of the truth table is needed to show that a proposition is *not* a tautology.
   (a) $(q \rightarrow p) \Leftrightarrow (p \wedge q)$
   (b) $(p \wedge \neg q) \Rightarrow (p \rightarrow q)$
   (c) $(p \wedge q) \Rightarrow (p \vee q)$

9. Show the following by the methods of Example 6.
   (a) $[(p \vee r) \wedge (q \rightarrow r)] \Leftrightarrow [(p \rightarrow q) \rightarrow r]$
   (b) $\neg q \Rightarrow [(p \vee q) \rightarrow p]$

10. Verify the following **absorption laws**.
   (a) $[p \vee (p \wedge q)] \Leftrightarrow p$
   (b) $[p \wedge (p \vee q)] \Leftrightarrow p$

11. Show that $(p \oplus q) \Leftrightarrow [(p \vee q) \wedge \neg(p \wedge q)]$, where $\oplus$ is the "exclusive or" introduced in Exercise 15 of § 2.1.

12. Prove or disprove:
   (a) $[p \rightarrow (q \rightarrow r)] \Leftrightarrow [(p \rightarrow q) \rightarrow (p \rightarrow r)]$
   (b) $[p \oplus (q \rightarrow r)] \Leftrightarrow [(p \oplus q) \rightarrow (p \oplus r)]$

13. Prove or disprove the "associative laws":
   (a) $[(p \rightarrow q) \rightarrow r] \Leftrightarrow [p \rightarrow (q \rightarrow r)]$
   (b) $[(p \leftrightarrow q) \leftrightarrow r] \Leftrightarrow [p \leftrightarrow (q \leftrightarrow r)]$
   (c) $(p \oplus q) \oplus r \Leftrightarrow p \oplus (q \oplus r)$

14. Every compound proposition can be written using only the connectives $\neg$ and $\vee$. This fact follows from the equivalences $(p \rightarrow q) \Leftrightarrow (\neg p \vee q)$, $(p \wedge q) \Leftrightarrow$

$\neg(\neg p \vee \neg q)$, and $(p \leftrightarrow q) \Leftrightarrow [(p \rightarrow q) \wedge (q \rightarrow p)]$. Find propositions logically equivalent to the following using only the connectives $\neg$ and $\vee$.

(a) $p \leftrightarrow q$ (b) $(p \wedge q) \rightarrow (\neg q \wedge r)$

(c) $(p \rightarrow q) \wedge (q \vee r)$ (d) $p \oplus q$

15. (a) Show that $p \vee q$ and $p \wedge q$ are logically equivalent to propositions using only the connectives $\neg$ and $\rightarrow$.

    (b) Show that $p \vee q$ and $p \rightarrow q$ are logically equivalent to propositions using only the connectives $\neg$ and $\wedge$.

    (c) Is $p \rightarrow q$ logically equivalent to a proposition using only the connectives $\wedge$ and $\vee$?

16. The **Sheffer stroke** is a connective $|$ defined by the truth table:

p	q	$p \vert q$
0	0	1
0	1	1
1	0	1
1	1	0

This connective is interesting because all compound propositions can be written using only this connective. This fact follows from the remarks in Exercise 14 and parts (a) and (b) below.

    (a) Show that $\neg p \Leftrightarrow p \vert p$.

    (b) Show that $p \vee q \Leftrightarrow (p \vert p) \vert (q \vert q)$.

    (c) Find a proposition equivalent to $p \wedge q$ using only the Sheffer stroke.

    (d) Do the same for $p \rightarrow q$.

    (e) Do the same for $p \oplus q$.

17. Consider the tautology $p \rightarrow [q \rightarrow (p \wedge q)]$. Show that if the first p is replaced by the proposition $p \vee q$, then the new proposition is not a tautology. This shows that substitution rule (a) must be applied with care.

18. Let P be the proposition $[p \wedge (q \vee r)] \vee \neg[p \vee (q \vee r)]$. Replacing all occurrences of $q \vee r$ by $q \wedge r$ yields

$$P^* = "[p \wedge (q \wedge r)] \vee \neg[p \vee (q \wedge r)]."$$

Since $q \wedge r \Rightarrow q \vee r$, one might suppose that $P \Rightarrow P^*$ or that $P^* \Rightarrow P$. Show that neither of these is the case.

§ 2.3 *Formal Proofs*

With the tautologies of § 2.2 we will be able to specify precisely what we mean by a valid proof in the propositional calculus. A **theorem** consists of some propositions $H_1, H_2, \ldots, H_n$, called its **hypotheses**, and a proposition C, called its **conclusion**. Here $H_1, H_2, \ldots, H_n$ and C represent propositions as discussed in § 2.1. A theorem with hypotheses $H_1, H_2, \ldots, H_n$ and conclusion C is **true** provided

$$H_1 \wedge H_2 \wedge \cdots \wedge H_n \Rightarrow C.$$

Thus the theorem is true if and only if $H_1 \wedge H_2 \wedge \cdots \wedge H_n \to C$ is a tautology.

A **formal proof** of a theorem consists of a sequence of propositions, ending with the conclusion C, that are regarded as valid for any of several reasons. To be **valid** a proposition may be one of the hypotheses, may be a known tautology, may be derived from propositions earlier in the sequence via the substitution rules in § 2.2, or may be inferred from earlier propositions according to certain **rules of inference**. A proposition Q can be inferred from propositions $P_1, P_2, \ldots, P_k$ provided $P_1 \wedge P_2 \wedge \cdots \wedge P_k \Rightarrow Q$. We symbolize such a **rule of inference** as

$$
\begin{array}{l}
P_1 \\
P_2 \\
\cdot \\
\cdot \\
\cdot \\
\underline{P_k} \\
\therefore\ Q
\end{array}
\quad [\therefore \text{ is read ``hence'' or ``therefore.''}]
$$

EXAMPLE 1 The logical implication modus ponens $[p \wedge (p \to q)] \Rightarrow q$ corresponds to the rule of inference

$$
\begin{array}{l}
P \\
\underline{P \to Q} \\
\therefore\ Q
\end{array}
$$

where P and Q represent compound propositions. In fact, every logical implication in Table 2 of § 2.2 corresponds to a rule of inference. We list some of them in Table 1. Note that rule 34 is based on the tautology $(p \wedge q) \to (p \wedge q)$. □

TABLE 1. Rules of Inference

28.	P		29.	$P \wedge Q$
	$\therefore\ P \vee Q$ addition			$\therefore\ P$ simplification
30.	P		31.	$P \to Q$
	$P \to Q$			$\neg Q$
	$\therefore\ Q$ modus ponens			$\therefore\ \neg P$ modus tollens
32.	$P \vee Q$		33.	$P \to Q$
	$\neg P$ disjunctive			$Q \to R$ hypothetical
	$\therefore\ Q$ syllogism			$\therefore\ P \to R$ syllogism
34.	P			
	Q			
	$\therefore\ P \wedge Q$ conjunction			

Note that if compound propositions P and Q are logically equivalent, then in particular $P \Rightarrow Q$, and so we have a corresponding rule of inference.

EXAMPLE 2   (a) From the logical equivalence 4a in Table 1 of § 2.2, we deduce $[(p \vee q) \wedge (p \vee r)] \Rightarrow [p \vee (q \wedge r)]$ and hence we have the rule of inference

$$P \vee Q$$
$$\underline{P \vee R}$$
$$\therefore \ P \vee (Q \wedge R).$$

(b) From the logical equivalence 12b in Table 1 of § 2.2 we obtain the rule of inference

$$P \rightarrow Q$$
$$\underline{P \rightarrow R}$$
$$\therefore \ P \rightarrow (Q \wedge R). \quad \square$$

A formal proof with a valid sequence of propositions is called a **valid proof** or **valid argument**. If one or more of the propositions is invalid then, regardless of what the conclusion is, the argument is called a **fallacy**. We give some examples that begin with propositions given in English.

EXAMPLE 3   We analyze the following argument. "If I study or if I am a genius, then I will pass the course. If I pass the course, then I will be allowed to take the next course. Therefore, if I am not allowed to take the next course, then I am not a genius." We let

$s = $ "I study,"
$g = $ "I am a genius,"
$p = $ "I will pass the course,"
$a = $ "I will be allowed to take the next course."

Then the theorem is: if $s \vee g \rightarrow p$ and $p \rightarrow a$, then $\neg a \rightarrow \neg g$. Here is a formal proof. In the explanations, the numbers prior to the semicolon refer to the earlier propositions from which the proposition is inferred.

Proof	*Explanations*
1. $s \vee g \rightarrow p$	hypothesis
2. $p \rightarrow a$	hypothesis

Our strategy is to use 1 to get $g \rightarrow p$, combine this with 2 to get $g \rightarrow a$, and then take the contrapositive.

3. $g \rightarrow g \vee s$	addition (rule 16)
4. $g \rightarrow s \vee g$	3; commutative law 2a
5. $g \rightarrow p$	4, 1; hypothetical syllogism (rule 33)
6. $g \rightarrow a$	5, 2; hypothetical syllogism (rule 33)
7. $\neg a \rightarrow \neg g$	6; contrapositive (rule 9)

We stress that this theorem can be proved in several ways. Thus there may be many valid proofs of a single theorem. □

EXAMPLE 4 "If I study or if I am a genius, then I will pass the course. I will not be allowed to take the next course. If I pass the course, then I will be allowed to take the next course. Therefore, I did not study." With the notation of Example 3, the theorem is: if $s \lor g \to p$, $\neg a$ and $p \to a$, then $\neg s$. We will combine the first and third hypotheses to get $s \to a$ and then we will apply modus tollens.

Proof	*Explanations*
1. $s \lor g \to p$	hypothesis
2. $\neg a$	hypothesis
3. $p \to a$	hypothesis
4. $s \to s \lor g$	addition (rule 16)
5. $s \to p$	4, 1; hypothetical syllogism (rule 33)
6. $s \to a$	5, 3; hypothetical syllogism (rule 33)
7. $\neg s$	6, 2; modus tollens (rule 31) □

In general, proving a theorem $H_1 \land H_2 \land \cdots \land H_n \Rightarrow C$ is equivalent to proving

$$H_1 \land H_2 \land \cdots \land H_n \land \neg C \Rightarrow \text{a contradiction}$$

in view of the logical equivalence reductio ad absurdum (rule 15). This approach to a proof is called a **proof by contradiction.**

EXAMPLE 5 We prove the assertion in Example 4 by contradiction.

Proof	*Explanations*
1. $s \lor g \to p$	hypothesis
2. $\neg a$	hypothesis
3. $p \to a$	hypothesis
4. $\neg(\neg s)$	negation of the conclusion
5. s	4; double negation (rule 1)
6. $s \to s \lor g$	addition (rule 16)
7. $s \to p$	6, 1; hypothetical syllogism (rule 33)
8. p	5, 7; modus ponens (rule 30)
9. a	8, 3; modus ponens (rule 30)
10. $a \land (\neg a)$	9, 2; conjunction (rule 34)
11. contradiction	10; rule 7b

Even though this proof is longer than the proof in Example 4, it may be conceptually more straightforward. In the real world, one resorts to proofs by contradiction when it is easier to use $\neg C$ *in conjunction with* the hypotheses than it is to derive *C from the hypotheses*. We will illustrate this in § 2.4. □

Here is another example.

EXAMPLE 6   "If I do not specify the initial conditions, then my program will not begin. If I program an infinite loop, then my program will not terminate. If the program does not begin or if it does not terminate, then the program will fail. Therefore, if the program does not fail, then I specified the initial conditions and I did not program an infinite loop." Let

$$i = \text{"I specified the initial conditions,"}$$
$$b = \text{"the program will begin,"}$$
$$l = \text{"I programmed an infinite loop,"}$$
$$t = \text{"the program will terminate,"}$$
$$f = \text{"the program fails."}$$

The theorem is: if $\neg i \to \neg b$, $l \to \neg t$ and $(\neg b \lor \neg t) \to f$, then $\neg f \to (i \land \neg l)$. We will first work for the contrapositive which, by a DeMorgan law, is equivalent to $\neg i \lor l \to f$. [Note that t does not stand for "tautology" here.]

Proof	*Explanations*
1. $\neg i \to \neg b$	hypothesis
2. $l \to \neg t$	hypothesis
3. $(\neg b \lor \neg t) \to f$	hypothesis
4. $(\neg i \lor l) \to (\neg b \lor \neg t)$	1, 2; the rule of inference based on the constructive dilemma 26a
5. $(\neg i \lor l) \to f$	4, 3; hypothetical syllogism (rule 33)
6. $\neg f \to \neg(\neg i \lor l)$	5; contrapositive (rule 9)
7. $\neg f \to (\neg \neg i \land \neg l)$	6; deMorgan law 8a
8. $\neg f \to (i \land \neg l)$	7; double negation (rule 1) □

EXAMPLE 7   "If the program does not fail, then the program will begin and terminate. The program begins and fails. Therefore the program did not terminate." With the notation of Example 6, the theorem is: if $\neg f \to b \land t$ and $b \land f$, then $\neg t$.

Proof?	*Explanations*
1. $\neg f \to b \land t$	hypothesis
2. $b \land f$	hypothesis
3. $b \land t \to t$	simplification (rule 17)
4. $\neg f \to t$	1, 3; hypothetical syllogism (rule 33)
5. f	2; simplification (rule 29)
6. $\neg t$	4, 5; see below

How would you infer proposition 6 from propositions 4 and 5? It appears that the best hope is modus tollens, but a closer look shows that modus tollens does not apply. What is needed is $P \to Q$, $\neg P$, $\therefore$ $\neg Q$ and this is *not* a valid rule of inference. The alleged proof above is invalid and is a fallacy. The proof is invalid, as just indicated, but this failure alone does not show that there is no correct proof; perhaps we simply went about the proof in the wrong way. In fact, no correct proof exists in this case because the theorem itself is not true. That is,

$$\{[\neg f \rightarrow (b \wedge t)] \wedge (b \wedge f)\} \rightarrow \neg t$$

is not a tautology. To see this, consider the logical possibility where b, f and t are all true. In other words, consider the last row of its truth table:

b	f	t	$\{[\neg f \rightarrow (b \wedge t)] \wedge (b \wedge f)\}$	$\rightarrow$	$\neg t$
1	1	1	0 1 1 1 1	0	0

In terms of the original hypotheses, the program might terminate and yet fail for some other reason.   ⬜

EXERCISES 2.3

1. Give the rules of inference corresponding to the logical implications 23, 26a and 27b.

2. Complete the following formal proofs by supplying explanations for each step.

(a) If $p \rightarrow (q \vee r)$, $q \rightarrow s$ and $r \rightarrow t$, then $p \rightarrow (s \vee t)$.

Proof

1. $p \rightarrow (q \vee r)$
2. $q \rightarrow s$
3. $r \rightarrow t$
4. $(q \vee r) \rightarrow (s \vee t)$ [See Exercise 1.]
5. $p \rightarrow (s \vee t)$

(b) If $p \rightarrow (q \wedge r)$, $(q \vee s) \rightarrow t$ and $p \vee s$, then t.

Proof

1. $p \rightarrow (q \wedge r)$
2. $(q \vee s) \rightarrow t$
3. $p \vee s$
4. $(q \wedge r) \rightarrow q$
5. $p \rightarrow q$
6. $(p \vee s) \rightarrow (q \vee s)$
7. $q \vee s$
8. t

(c) If $p \rightarrow (q \rightarrow r)$, $p \vee \neg s$ and q, then $s \rightarrow r$.

Proof

1. $p \rightarrow (q \rightarrow r)$
2. $p \vee \neg s$
3. q
4. $\neg s \vee p$

5. $s \to p$
6. $s \to (q \to r)$
7. $(s \wedge q) \to r$
8. $q \to [s \to (q \wedge s)]$
9. $s \to (q \wedge s)$
10. $s \to (s \wedge q)$
11. $s \to r$

3. Complete the following proof by contradiction, by supplying explanations for each step.

   If $p \to (q \wedge r)$, $(q \vee s) \to t$ and $p \vee s$, then t.

Proof
1. $p \to (q \wedge r)$
2. $(q \vee s) \to t$
3. $p \vee s$
4. $\neg t$
5. $\neg (q \vee s)$
6. $\neg q \wedge \neg s$
7. $\neg q$
8. $\neg s \wedge \neg q$
9. $\neg s$
10. $s \vee p$
11. p
12. $q \wedge r$
13. q
14. $q \wedge (\neg q)$
15. contradiction

4. Complete the following proof by contradiction.

   If $p \to (q \wedge r)$, $r \to s$ and $\neg (q \wedge s)$, then $\neg p$.

Proof
1. $p \to (q \wedge r)$
2. $r \to s$
3. $\neg (q \wedge s)$
4. $\neg (\neg p)$
5. p
6. $q \wedge r$
7. q
8. $r \wedge q$
9. r
10. s
11. $q \wedge s$
12. $(q \wedge s) \wedge \neg (q \wedge s)$
13. contradiction

5. Convert each of the following arguments into logical notation using the suggested variables. Then provide a formal proof.

(a) "If my computations are correct and I pay the electric bill, then I will run out of money. If I don't pay the electric bill, the power will be turned off. Therefore, if I don't run out of money and the power is still on, then my computations are incorrect." (*c, b, r, p*)

(b) "If the weather bureau predicts dry weather, then I will take a hike or go swimming. I will go swimming if and only if the weather bureau predicts warm weather. Therefore, if I don't go on a hike, then the weather bureau predicts wet or warm weather." (*d, h, s, w*)

(c) "If I get the job and work hard, then I will get promoted. If I get promoted, then I will be happy. I will not be happy. Therefore, either I will not get the job or I will not work hard." (*j, w, p, h*)

(d) "If I study law, then I will make a lot of money. If I study archeology, then I will travel a lot. If I make a lot of money or travel a lot, then I will not be disappointed. Therefore, if I am disappointed, then I did not study law and I did not study archeology." (*l, m, a, t, d*)

6. Construct formal proofs of the following theorems.
   (a) If $p \rightarrow (q \lor r)$ and $q \rightarrow s$, then $p \rightarrow (r \lor s)$.
   (b) If $p \rightarrow q$, $r \rightarrow s$ and $\neg(p \rightarrow s)$, then $q \land \neg r$.
   (c) If $p \rightarrow q$, $\neg r \rightarrow s$ and $\neg q \lor \neg s$, then $p \rightarrow r$.

7. Construct formal proofs by contradiction for the following theorems.
   (a) If $p \rightarrow q$, $r \rightarrow (p \land s)$, $(q \land s) \rightarrow (p \land t)$ and $\neg t$, then $p \rightarrow \neg r$.
   (b) If $p \lor (q \rightarrow r)$, $q \lor r$ and $r \rightarrow p$, then p.

8. For each of the following, give a formal proof of the theorem or show that it is false by exhibiting a suitable row of a truth table.
   (a) If $(q \land r) \rightarrow p$ and $q \rightarrow \neg r$, then p.
   (b) If $q \lor \neg r$ and $\neg(r \rightarrow q) \rightarrow \neg p$, then p.
   (c) If $p \rightarrow (q \lor r)$, $q \rightarrow s$ and $r \rightarrow \neg p$, then $p \rightarrow s$.

9. For the following sets of hypotheses, state a conclusion that can be inferred and specify the rules of inference used.
   (a) If the TV set is not broken, then I will not study. If I study, then I will pass the course. I will not pass the course.
   (b) If I passed the midterm and the final, then I passed the course. If I passed the course, then I passed the final. I failed the course.
   (c) If I pass the midterm or the final, then I will pass this course. I will take the next course only if I pass this course. I will not take the next course.

10. Consider the following hypotheses. If I take the bus or subway, then I will be late for my appointment. If I take a cab, then I will not be late for my appointment and I will be broke. I will be on time for my appointment.

    Which of the following conclusions *must* follow, i.e., can be inferred from the hypotheses? Justify your answers.
    (a) I will take a cab.
    (b) I will be broke.
    (c) I will not take the subway.
    (d) If I become broke, then I took a cab.
    (e) If I take the bus, then I won't be broke.

§ 2.4   *Methods of Proof*

The constant emphasis on logic and proofs is what sets mathematics apart from other pursuits. In § 2.3 we discussed proofs in the setting and symbolism of the propositional calculus. The proofs used in everyday working mathematics are based on the same logical framework as the propositional calculus but their structure is not usually displayed in the stylized format of § 2.3.

In this section we discuss some common methods of proof and the standard terminology that accompanies them. The most natural sort of proof is the **direct proof** in which the hypotheses $H_1, \ldots, H_n$ are shown to imply the conclusion C:

$$H_1 \wedge H_2 \wedge \cdots \wedge H_n \Rightarrow C.$$

The proofs in § 2.3, except for Example 5, are direct proofs in the propositional calculus.

One type of **indirect proof** is a proof of **the contrapositive** [compare rule 9, Table 1 of § 2.2]:

$$\neg C \Rightarrow \neg (H_1 \wedge H_2 \wedge \cdots \wedge H_n).$$

EXAMPLE 1   Let $m, n \in \mathbb{N}$. We wish to prove that if $m + n \geq 73$ then $m \geq 37$ or $n \geq 37$. To do this, we prove the contrapositive: not "$m \geq 37$ or $n \geq 37$" implies not "$m + n \geq 73$." By DeMorgan's law, the negation of "$m \geq 37$ or $n \geq 37$" is "not $m \geq 37$ and not $n \geq 37$," i.e., "$m \leq 36$ and $n \leq 36$." So the contrapositive proposition is: If $m \leq 36$ and $n \leq 36$, then $m + n \leq 72$. This proposition follows immediately from a general property about inequalities: $a \leq c$ and $b \leq d$ imply $a + b \leq c + d$ for real numbers a, b, c, d.   □

Another type of **indirect proof** is a **proof by contradiction**:

$$\neg C \wedge H_1 \wedge H_2 \wedge \cdots \wedge H_n \Rightarrow \text{a contradiction.}$$

[Compare rule 15, Table 1 of § 2.2.] Example 5 in § 2.3 contains a proof by contradiction in the propositional calculus.

EXAMPLE 2   We wish to prove that $\sqrt{2}$ is irrational. That is, if x is in $\mathbb{R}$ and $x^2 = 2$, then x is not a rational number. The property of irrationality is a negative sort of property and not easily verified directly. But we can show that x rational and $x^2 = 2$ together lead to a contradiction.

We prove that $\sqrt{2}$ is irrational by contradiction. So assume $x \in \mathbb{R}$, $x^2 = 2$ and x is rational. Then by the definition of a rational number, we have $x = p/q$ where $p, q \in \mathbb{Z}$ and $q \neq 0$. By reducing the fraction if necessary, we may assume that p and q have no common factors. In particular, p and q are not both even. Since $2 = x^2 = p^2/q^2$ we have $p^2 = 2q^2$ and so p^2 is even. This implies that p is even, as we will show in Example 4. Hence $p = 2k$

for some $k \in \mathbb{Z}$. Then $(2k)^2 = 2q^2$ and therefore $q^2 = 2k^2$. Thus q^2 and q are also even. But then p and q are both even, contradicting our earlier statement. Hence $\sqrt{2}$ is irrational. □

As already remarked, mathematical proofs could in principle be presented in the formal format of § 2.3 rather than in essay form. However, the proofs would quickly get long and cumbersome. For example, the proof of Example 2 could start out as follows.

Proof	*Explanation*
1. $x \in \mathbb{R}$	assumption
2. $x^2 = 2$	assumption
3. x is rational	negation of the conclusion
4. $x = p/q, q \neq 0$	definition of rational number
5. p, q have no common factors	fractions can be reduced
6. p and q not both even	5; otherwise 2 would be a common factor
7. $p^2 = 2q^2$	4, 2; algebra
Etc.	

EXAMPLE 3 We prove by contradiction that there are infinitely many primes. Thus assume that there are finitely many primes, say k of them. We write them as $p_1, p_2, \ldots, p_k$ so that $p_1 = 2$, $p_2 = 3$, etc. Consider $n = 1 + p_1 p_2 \cdots p_k$. Since $n > p_j$ for all $j = 1, 2, \ldots, k$, n itself is not prime. However, n is a product of primes [this believable fact is not trivial to prove and, in fact, we provide a proof later in Example 1 of § 6.3]. Therefore at least one of the p_j's must divide n. Since each p_j divides $n - 1$, at least one p_j divides both $n - 1$ and n, but this is impossible. Indeed, if p_j divides both $n - 1$ and n, then it divides their difference, 1, which is absurd. □

One should avoid artificial proofs by contradiction such as in the next example.

EXAMPLE 4 We prove by contradiction that the product of two odd integers is an odd integer. Assume $m, n \in \mathbb{N}$ are odd integers but mn is even. There exist k, l in $\mathbb{N}$ so that $m = 2k + 1$ and $n = 2l + 1$. Then

$$mn = 4kl + 2k + 2l + 1 = 2(2kl + k + l) + 1,$$

an odd number, contradicting the assumption that mn is even.

This proof by contradiction is artificial because we did not use the assumption "mn is even" until after we established that "mn is odd." The following direct proof is far preferable.

Consider odd integers m, n in $\mathbb{N}$. There exist $k, l \in \mathbb{N}$ so that $m = 2k + 1$ and $n = 2l + 1$. Then

$$mn = 4kl + 2k + 2l + 1 = 2(2kl + k + l) + 1,$$

which is odd.   ☐

Sometimes a result has the form

$$H_1 \vee H_2 \vee \cdots \vee H_n \Rightarrow C,$$

and sometimes it is convenient to convert a proposition into one of this form. Such a proposition is equivalent to

$$(H_1 \Rightarrow C) \wedge (H_2 \Rightarrow C) \wedge \cdots \wedge (H_n \Rightarrow C).$$

[For $n = 2$, compare rule 12a, Table 1 of §2.2.] Therefore a theorem like this can be proved by **cases**. The next example illustrates how boring and repetitive a proof by cases can be.

EXAMPLE 5   Recall that the **absolute value** $|x|$ of x in $\mathbb{R}$ is defined by the rule:

$$|x| = \begin{cases} x & \text{if } x \geq 0 \\ -x & \text{if } x < 0 \end{cases}.$$

Assuming the familiar order properties of $\leq$ on $\mathbb{R}$, we prove

$$|x + y| \leq |x| + |y| \quad \text{for} \quad x, y \in \mathbb{R}.$$

We consider four cases: (i) $x \geq 0$ and $y \geq 0$; (ii) $x \geq 0$ and $y < 0$; (iii) $x < 0$ and $y \geq 0$; (iv) $x < 0$ and $y < 0$.

Case (i). If $x \geq 0$ and $y \geq 0$, then $x + y \geq 0$ and so $|x + y| = x + y = |x| + |y|$.

Case (ii). If $x \geq 0$ and $y < 0$, then

$$x + y < x + 0 = |x| \leq |x| + |y|$$

and

$$-(x + y) = -x + (-y) \leq 0 + (-y) = |y| \leq |x| + |y|.$$

Either $|x + y| = x + y$ or $|x + y| = -(x + y)$; either way $|x + y| \leq |x| + |y|$ by the above inequalities.

Case (iii). The case $x < 0$ and $y \geq 0$ is similar to Case (ii).

Case (iv). If $x < 0$ and $y < 0$, then $x + y < 0$ and $|x + y| = -(x + y) = -x + (-y) = |x| + |y|$.
So in all four cases, $|x + y| \leq |x| + |y|$.   ☐

EXAMPLE 6   For every $n \in \mathbb{N}$, $n^3 + n$ is even. This fact can be easily proved by induction [see §2.5], but here we prove it by cases.

Case (*i*). Suppose n is even. Then $n = 2k$ for some $k \in \mathbb{N}$ and so

$$n^3 + n = 8k^3 + 2k = 2(4k^3 + k),$$

which is even.

Case (*ii*). Suppose n is odd; then $n = 2k + 1$ for some $k \in \mathbb{N}$ and so

$$n^3 + n = (8k^3 + 12k^2 + 6k + 1) + (2k + 1) = 2(4k^3 + 6k^2 + 4k + 1),$$

which is even.

Here is a more elegant proof by cases. Given n in $\mathbb{N}$, we have $n^3 + n$ $= n(n^2 + 1)$. If n is even, so is $n(n^2 + 1)$. If n is odd, then n^2 is odd, hence $n^2 + 1$ is even, and so $n(n^2 + 1)$ is even. ☐

An implication $p \rightarrow q$ is sometimes said to be **vacuously true** if p is false. This is because we have decreed $p \rightarrow q$ to be true whenever p is false and so, in this case, the truth of $p \rightarrow q$ tells us nothing about q. A **vacuous proof** is a proof of an implication $p \rightarrow q$ in which it is shown that p is false. Such implications rarely have intrinsic interest, but they arise as exceptional cases in proofs of general assertions.

EXAMPLE 7   (a) Consider finite sets A and B, and consider the assertion:

"if A has fewer elements than B, then there is a one-to-one mapping of A onto a proper subset of B."

This is vacuously true if B is the empty set because the hypothesis must be false. A vacuous proof consists of simply observing that in this case the hypothesis is impossible.

(b) Consider the assertion:

$$n \in \mathbb{N} \quad \text{and} \quad n \geq 4 \quad \text{implies} \quad n^2 \leq 2^n.$$

This is vacuously true for $n = 0, 1, 2, 3$. For these values of n, its truth does not depend on whether $n^2 \leq 2^n$ is true. For $n \geq 4$, an induction proof can be given [see § 2.5]. ☐

An implication $p \rightarrow q$ is sometimes said to be **trivially true** if q is true. This is because, in this case, the truth value of p is irrelevant. A **trivial proof** of $p \rightarrow q$ is one in which q is shown to be true without any reference to p.

EXAMPLE 8   If x and y are real numbers such that $xy = 0$, then $(x + y)^n = x^n + y^n$ for $n \geq 1$. This proposition is trivially true for $n = 1$; $(x + y)^1 = x^1 + y^1$ is obviously true and this fact does not depend on the hypothesis $xy = 0$. For $n \geq 2$, this hypothesis is needed. ☐

One encounters references to **constructive proofs** and **nonconstructive proofs** for the existence of mathematical objects satisfying certain properties.

A constructive proof either specifies the object [a number or a matrix, say] or indicates how it [or they] can be determined by some explicit procedure or algorithm. A nonconstructive proof establishes the existence of objects by some indirect means such as a proof by contradiction, without giving directions for how to find them.

EXAMPLE 9   In Example 3 we proved by contradiction that there are infinitely many primes. We did not construct an infinite list of primes. Our proof can be revised to give a constructive procedure for building an arbitrarily long list of distinct primes, provided we have some way of factoring integers. [This is Exercise 16.] ▯

In the next example we use the following axiom which will be discussed further in § 6.3:

Well-Ordering Principle   Every nonempty subset of $\mathbb{N}$ has a least element.

EXAMPLE 10   We prove that there is a least, i.e., smallest, natural number n such that

(*) $1^n + 2^n + 3^n + \cdots + (99)^n = \sum_{k=1}^{99} k^n < (100)^n.$

Since every nonempty subset of $\mathbb{N}$ has a least element, it suffices to show that the set

$$S = \{n \in \mathbb{N} : \sum_{k=1}^{99} k^n < (100)^n\}$$

is nonempty. We simplify the problem by noting that $k^n \leqq (99)^n$ for $k \leqq 99$ and so

$$\sum_{k=1}^{99} k^n \leqq \sum_{k=1}^{99} (99)^n = 99(99)^n.$$

Hence any n that satisfies $99(99)^n < (100)^n$ also satisfies (*) and belongs to S. Thus it suffices to show that some n satisfies the inequality $99(99)^n < (100)^n$ or $99 < (100/99)^n$. A direct calculation shows that this holds if n is sufficiently large. In fact, $n = 458$ works. Thus the set S is nonempty [it contains 458] and has a least element. What is its least element? The proof gives no clue, though we know it is no bigger than 458. The proof is nonconstructive because the well-ordering principle is nonconstructive; it doesn't specify how the least element might be found. ▯

EXAMPLE 11   Every positive integer n has the form $2^k m$ where $k \in \mathbb{N}$ and m is odd. This can be proved in several ways. They all suggest the following constructive procedure. If n is odd, let $k = 0$ and $m = n$. Otherwise, divide n by 2 and apply the procedure to $n/2$. Continue until an odd number is reached. Then k will equal the number of times division by 2 was necessary. Exercise 15 asks you to check out this procedure. ▯

We began this chapter with a painstaking development of a very limited system of logic, namely the propositional calculus. In this section, we relaxed the formality in order to discuss several methods of proof encountered in this book and elsewhere. We hope that you now have a better idea of what a mathematical proof is. In Chapter 6 we will study some more sophisticated aspects of logic.

Outside the realm of logic, and in particular in the remainder of this book, proofs are communications intended to convince the reader of the truths of assertions. Logic will serve as the foundation of the process and will recede into the background except where there is a communications gap. That is, usually it should not be necessary to consciously think of the logic presented in this chapter. But if a particular proof in this book or elsewhere is puzzling, then you may wish to analyze it more closely. What are the exact hypotheses? Is the author using hidden assumptions? Is the author giving an indirect proof?

Finally, there is always the possibility that the author has made an error or has not stated what was intended. Maybe you can show that the assertion is false. Or at least show that the reasoning is fallacious. Even some good mathematicians have made the mistake of trying to prove $P \Leftrightarrow Q$ by showing both $P \Rightarrow Q$ and $\neg Q \Rightarrow \neg P$, probably in some disguise.

EXERCISES 2.4

In all exercises with proofs, indicate the methods of proof used.

1. Prove that the product of two even integers is an even integer.
2. Prove that the product of an even and an odd integer is even.
3. Prove that $|xy| = |x| \cdot |y|$ for $x, y \in \mathbb{R}$.
4. Prove that $n^4 - n^2$ is divisible by 3 for all $n \in \mathbb{N}$.
5. Prove that $n^2 - 2$ is never divisible by 3 for $n \in \mathbb{N}$.
6. (a) Prove that $\sqrt{3}$ is irrational.
   (b) Prove that $\sqrt[3]{2}$ is irrational.
7. Prove or disprove:
   (a) The sum of two even integers is an even integer.
   (b) The sum of two odd integers is an odd integer.
   (c) The sum of two primes is never a prime.
   (d) The sum of three consecutive integers is divisible by 3.
   (e) The sum of four consecutive integers is divisible by 4.
   (f) The sum of five consecutive integers is divisible by 5.
8. (a) It is not known whether there are infinitely many **prime pairs**, i.e., odd primes whose difference is 2. Examples of prime pairs are $\langle 3, 5 \rangle$, $\langle 5, 7 \rangle$, $\langle 11, 13 \rangle$ and $\langle 71, 73 \rangle$. Give three more examples of prime pairs.
   (b) Prove that there are no "prime triples," i.e., odd primes $2k + 1$, $2k + 3$, $2k + 5$ where $k \in \mathbb{N}$. *Hint:* Show that one of these must be divisible by 3.

9. Prove the following assertions for a real number x and $n = 1$.
   (a) If $x \geq 0$, then $(1 + x)^n \geq 1 + nx$.
   (b) If $x^n = 0$, then $x = 0$.
   (c) If n is even, then $x^n \geq 0$.

10. Prove the result in Example 8. Use the fact that if $xy = 0$, then $x = 0$ or $y = 0$.

11. Prove that there is a smallest prime that is larger than 10^{21}. Is your proof constructive? If so, produce the prime.

12. Prove that there is a least positive integer n such that

$$\sum_{k=1}^{10} n^k < 2^n.$$

Is the proof constructive? *Hint:* $\sum_{k=1}^{10} n^k \leq \sum_{k=1}^{10} n^{10} = 10 \cdot n^{10}$. Compare $10 \cdot n^{10}$ and 2^n for $n = 70$.

13. (a) Prove that given n in $\mathbb{N}$, there exist n consecutive integers that are not prime, i.e., the set of prime integers has arbitrarily large gaps. *Hint:* Start with $(n + 1)! + 2$.
    (b) Is the proof constructive? If so, use it to give six consecutive nonprimes.
    (c) Give seven consecutive nonprimes.

14. Here is another proof that $\sqrt{2}$ is irrational. Show that if $\sqrt{2}$ is rational, then $\{n \in \mathbb{P} : \sqrt{2}\,n \in \mathbb{Z}\}$ is nonempty. Let m be the least element of the set. Obtain a contradiction by showing that $\sqrt{2}\,m - m$ is also in the set.

15. Use the procedure in Example 11 to write the following positive integers in the form $2^k m$ where $k \in \mathbb{N}$ and m is odd.
    (a) 14   (b) 73   (c) 96   (d) 1168

16. Suppose $p_1, p_2, \ldots, p_k$ is a given list of distinct primes. Explain how one could use an algorithm which factors integers into prime factors to construct a prime which is not in the list. *Suggestion:* Factor $1 + p_1 p_2 \cdots p_k$.

§ 2.5   *First Look at Induction*

Mathematical induction is a method of proof which we can often use when we want to establish the truth of an infinite list of propositions. The method is a natural one to use in a variety of situations in computer science. Some applications are quite mathematical in flavor, such as verifying that a certain formula holds for all positive integers. Another frequent use of the method is to show that a computer program with loops performs as expected.

We will eventually need fairly sophisticated versions of induction, but we feel that the student should first gain experience with the basic version. Accordingly, in this section we give a brief introduction to the subject, with examples and exercises, and a few remarks to indicate why it works. After we have studied some predicate calculus in Chapter 6, we will return to a more thorough and general treatment of induction. At that point it should become clear why we regard mathematical induction as a legitimate method of proof; for now we just see how to use it.

EXAMPLE 1   (a) Consider a video game which begins with a spaceship in the middle of the screen. In 5 seconds an alien appears. Five seconds later the alien splits into two aliens, which appear in two places on the screen. Five seconds later, each of these aliens splits into two, and so on. Every 5 seconds the number of aliens doubles. The player's task is to eliminate the aliens before they fill the screen.

Suppose the player is not very skillful and all the aliens survive. How many will there be 30 seconds after the game begins? By calculating the number of aliens at 5-second intervals we get the table

Time	5	10	15	20	25	30
Aliens	1	2	4	8	16	32

So the answer to our question is that there will be 32 aliens in 30 seconds.

Now suppose we want to find the number of aliens in 5 minutes. We could simply extend the table to the right, doubling the entries in the second row as we go along, but there's clearly an easier way. Let $A(n)$ be the number of aliens on the screen after n 5-second intervals. Then $A(1) = 1$, $A(2) = 2$, $A(3) = 4$, etc. We observe that $A(n) = 2^{n-1}$ for $n = 1, 2, 3, 4, 5, 6$, and it seems reasonable to guess that after 5 minutes, which is $5 \cdot 60$ seconds, the value of $A(60)$ will be 2^{59} [a *lot* of aliens]. How can we be sure this guess is correct without going through the calculations?

The method of mathematical induction applies to just such situations, ones in which

1. we know the answer in the beginning,
2. we know how to determine the answer at one stage from the answer at the previous stage, and
3. we have a guess at the general answer.

Of course, if our guess is wrong that's too bad; we won't be able to prove it's right with this method, or with any other. But if our guess is correct, then mathematical induction often gives us a framework for confirming the guess with a proof. We will return to this example shortly to see how the method applies.

(b) The following simple procedure starts with initial values of quantities called I and S. It calculates and prints successive values of S.

Step 1. Let $I = S = 1$.
Step 2. Print S.
Step 3. Replace S by $S + 2I + 1$.
Step 4. Replace I by $I + 1$ and go back to Step 2.

Figure 1(a) is a flowchart for this procedure.[1] Figure 1(b) lists the first few values of S which are printed. The steps of the program are completely dull; the only interesting feature is the loop caused by the return to Step 2.

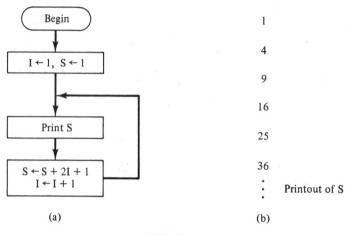

Begin	1
	4
$I \leftarrow 1, S \leftarrow 1$	9
	16
Print S	25
	36
$S \leftarrow S + 2I + 1$ $I \leftarrow I + 1$	⋮ Printout of S

(a)   (b)

FIGURE 1

A glance at the output shows that the procedure seems to be printing the squares of the positive integers in increasing order. How can we be sure? We check the operation of the loop. When we first come to Step 2, $I = 1$ and $S = 1 = I^2$. Now suppose that at some time when we come to Step 2 we find that I is a positive integer, say n, and $S = I^2$. We will print n^2, replace S by $n^2 + 2n + 1$, replace I by $n + 1$ and go back to Step 2. Since $n^2 + 2n + 1 = (n + 1)^2$, the new S is the square of the new I. We have observed:

$I = 1$ and $S = 1^2$ the first time we are at Step 2, and
If $I = n$ and $S = n^2$ when we are at Step 2, then $I = n + 1$ and $S = (n + 1)^2$ the next time we are at Step 2.

The obvious guess is that for each $n \in \mathbb{P}$ the value of S is n^2 the nth time we are at Step 2. The method of mathematical induction will confirm this guess [Example 2(b)]. ☐

Our first version of mathematical induction is concerned with propositions $p(n)$ that are indexed by $\mathbb{P}$. Section 1.3 contains some preparatory remarks and examples illustrating propositions indexed by $\mathbb{P}$.

---

[1]The reader who is not familiar with flowcharts can simply ignore this one and the few which appear later on. We have included them as possible aids to understanding, and not for their own interest. This particular flowchart gives a simple illustration of a loop in an algorithm. In the flowchart the loop is a chain of arrows that form a closed path.

Principle of Mathematical Induction

Consider a list $p(1)$, $p(2)$, $p(3)$, ... of propositions indexed by $\mathbb{P}$. All the propositions $p(n)$ are true provided

(B) $p(1)$ is true;

(I) $p(n+1)$ is true whenever $p(n)$ is true.

We will refer to (B), i.e., the fact that $p(1)$ is true, as the **basis for induction** and we will refer to (I) as the **inductive step**. In the notation of the propositional calculus, the inductive step is equivalent to:

the implication $p(n) \to p(n+1)$ is true for all $n \in \mathbb{P}$.

Notice that the Principle of Mathematical Induction is not itself a proof that $p(n)$ is true for all n, but it tells us that *if* we can somehow show (B) and (I) *then* all $p(n)$'s are true. There is no free lunch. The work goes into showing (B) and (I), which must be verified before the Principle of Mathematical Induction can be applied. In practice, (B) will usually be easy to check.

EXAMPLE 2

(a) In the video game of Example 1(a) we were given that $A(1) = 1$ and that $A(n+1) = 2 \cdot A(n)$ for $n \geqq 1$. We guessed that $A(n) = 2^{n-1}$ for every $n \in \mathbb{P}$, though actually we only cared about $n = 60$.

For each $n \in \mathbb{P}$ let the nth proposition $p(n)$ be "$A(n) = 2^{n-1}$." Then $p(1)$ is "$A(1) = 2^0$," which is true since $2^0 = 1$. Thus the basis (B) holds. We could also verify $p(2)$, i.e., $A(2) = 2^1$, as well as other particular cases, but there is no need to.

For the inductive step (I) we must simply check that for each n if $p(n)$ is true, i.e., if $A(n) = 2^{n-1}$, then $p(n+1)$ is true, i.e., $A(n+1) = 2^{(n+1)-1}$. Suppose $A(n) = 2^{n-1}$ for some $n \in \mathbb{P}$. Then

$$A(n+1) = 2 \cdot A(n) \quad \text{by the structure of the game}$$
$$= 2 \cdot 2^{n-1} \quad \text{by the supposition}$$
$$= 2^n = 2^{(n+1)-1},$$

as we wanted to check. Thus (I) holds. By the Principle of Mathematical Induction, all of the propositions $p(n)$ are true. In particular, we have $A(60) = 2^{59}$.

(b) For the looping procedure of Example 1(b) let $p(n)$ be:

"$S = n^2$ the nth time the procedure is at Step 2."

We already checked that $p(1)$ is true and that if $p(n)$ is true then $p(n+1)$ is true. It follows immediately from the Principle of Mathematical Induction that $p(n)$ is true for every $n \in \mathbb{P}$. Thus the procedure does indeed print the squares of the positive integers in increasing order. ⬚

EXAMPLE 3

(a) Here is an illustration of how mathematical induction is useful in mathematics. We calculate

$$2 = 1 \cdot 2, \quad 2 + 4 = 6 = 2 \cdot 3, \quad 2 + 4 + 6 = 12 = 3 \cdot 4,$$
$$2 + 4 + 6 + 8 = 20 = 4 \cdot 5,$$

and we begin to suspect that the sum of the first n even positive integers is always $n(n + 1)$. We could verify our guess for many more values of n. We might even call our guess a "conjecture," since that sounds more official. But how do we show our conjecture is true for all n? We use induction. Our nth proposition $p(n)$ is

$$\text{“} 2 + 4 + \cdots + (2n) = n(n + 1).\text{”}$$

Thus $p(1)$ asserts that "$2 = 1(1 + 1)$," $p(2)$ asserts that "$2 + 4 = 2(2 + 1)$," ..., $p(73)$ asserts that

$$\text{“} 2 + 4 + \cdots + 146 = 73(73 + 1) = 5402,\text{”}$$

etc. In particular, $p(1)$ is true by inspection and this establishes the basis for induction.

For the inductive step, suppose that $p(n)$ is true for some n. That is, suppose that

$$2 + 4 + \cdots + (2n) = n(n + 1)$$

is true. We wish to establish $p(n + 1)$:

$$2 + 4 + \cdots + (2n) + (2(n + 1)) = (n + 1)((n + 1) + 1),$$

i.e., we wish to establish

$$2 + 4 + \cdots + (2n) + (2n + 2) = (n + 1)(n + 2).$$

Since $p(n)$ is true by supposition, we have

$$\begin{aligned}
2 + 4 + \cdots + (2n) + (2n + 2) &= [2 + 4 + \cdots + (2n)] + (2n + 2) \\
&= n(n + 1) + (2n + 2) \\
&= n(n + 1) + 2(n + 1) \\
&= (n + 1)(n + 2).
\end{aligned}$$

Thus $p(n + 1)$ holds whenever $p(n)$ holds. By the Principle of Mathematical Induction, we conclude that $p(n)$ is true for all n.

(b) Dividing both sides of the identity proved in part (a) by 2 gives the familiar formula

$$1 + 2 + \cdots + n = \tfrac{1}{2}n(n + 1)$$

for the sum of the first n positive integers.   ☐

There are two basic ingredients for a valid induction proof: the basis and the inductive step. In addition, if there is any possible doubt, it should be made clear that one is giving a proof by induction.

It is worth emphasizing that, prior to the last sentence in the preceding proof, we did *not* prove "$p(n + 1)$ is true." We merely proved an implication: "if $p(n)$ is true, then $p(n + 1)$ is true." In a sense we proved an infinite number of assertions, namely: $p(1)$; if $p(1)$ is true then $p(2)$ is true; if $p(2)$ is true then

$p(3)$ is true; if $p(3)$ is true then $p(4)$ is true; etc. Then we applied mathematical induction to conclude: $p(1)$ is true; $p(2)$ is true; $p(3)$ is true; $p(4)$ is true; etc.

In Example 3, we could have written $2 + 4 + \cdots + (2n)$ as $\sum_{k=1}^{n} (2k)$ and used summation notation throughout the proof. We illustrate the use of summation notation in the next example.

EXAMPLE 4 We prove

$$\sum_{k=1}^{n} (3k - 2) = \tfrac{1}{2}(3n^2 - n) \quad \text{for all} \quad n \in \mathbb{P}.$$

Proof. Our nth proposition $p(n)$ is

$$\text{``} \sum_{k=1}^{n} (3k - 2) = \tfrac{1}{2}(3n^2 - n).\text{''}$$

Note that

$$p(1) = \text{``}1 = \tfrac{1}{2}(3 \cdot 1^2 - 1),\text{''}$$
$$p(2) = \text{``}1 + 4 = \tfrac{1}{2}(3 \cdot 2^2 - 2),\text{''}$$
$$p(3) = \text{``}1 + 4 + 7 = \tfrac{1}{2}(3 \cdot 3^2 - 3).\text{''}$$

In particular, $p(1)$ is true by inspection and this establishes the basis for induction. Suppose now that $p(n)$ is true for some n:

$$\sum_{k=1}^{n} (3k - 2) = \tfrac{1}{2}(3n^2 - n);$$

we need to show $p(n + 1)$:

$$\sum_{k=1}^{n+1} (3k - 2) = \tfrac{1}{2}[3(n + 1)^2 - (n + 1)].$$

Using $p(n)$, we obtain

$$\sum_{k=1}^{n+1} (3k - 2) = \sum_{k=1}^{n} (3k - 2) + [3(n + 1) - 2] = \tfrac{1}{2}(3n^2 - n) + (3n + 1).$$

To verify $p(n + 1)$, we need to verify that

$$\tfrac{1}{2}(3n^2 - n) + (3n + 1) = \tfrac{1}{2}[3(n + 1)^2 - (n + 1)].$$

This is a purely algebraic matter:

$$\tfrac{1}{2}(3n^2 - n) + (3n + 1) = \tfrac{1}{2}(3n^2 - n + 6n + 2) = \tfrac{1}{2}(3n^2 + 5n + 2)$$
$$= \tfrac{1}{2}(3n + 2)(n + 1) = \tfrac{1}{2}[3(n + 1) - 1](n + 1) = \tfrac{1}{2}[3(n + 1)^2 - (n + 1)].$$

We have shown that $p(n + 1)$ is true whenever $p(n)$ is true. Hence all the propositions $p(n)$ are true by the Principle of Mathematical Induction. We could also have derived this example from the previous one, since

$$\sum_{k=1}^{n} (3k - 2) = 3 \sum_{k=1}^{n} k - \sum_{k=1}^{n} 2 = 3[\tfrac{1}{2}n(n + 1)] - 2n = \tfrac{1}{2}(3n^2 - n). \quad \square$$

Not all induction proofs in mathematics involve sums.

EXAMPLE 5   All numbers of the form $7^n - 2^n$ are divisible by 5.

Proof. More precisely, we show that $7^n - 2^n$ is divisible by 5 for each $n \in \mathbb{P}$. Our nth proposition is

$$p(n) = \text{``}7^n - 2^n \text{ is divisible by } 5.\text{''}$$

The basis for induction $p(1)$ is clearly true, since $7^1 - 2^1 = 5$. For the inductive step, assume that $p(n)$ is true. Our task is to use this assumption somehow to establish $p(n + 1)$:

$$7^{n+1} - 2^{n+1} \text{ is divisible by } 5.$$

Thus we would like to write $7^{n+1} - 2^{n+1}$ somehow in terms of $7^n - 2^n$, in such a way that any remaining terms are easily seen to be divisible by 5. A little trick is to write this as $7(7^n - 2^n)$ plus appropriate terms to preserve the equality:

$$7^{n+1} - 2^{n+1} = 7(7^n - 2^n) + 7 \cdot 2^n - 2^{n+1}$$
$$= 7(7^n - 2^n) + 7 \cdot 2^n - 2 \cdot 2^n = 7(7^n - 2^n) + 5 \cdot 2^n.$$

Now $7^n - 2^n$ is divisible by 5 by assumption and $5 \cdot 2^n$ is obviously divisible by 5, so the same is true for $7^{n+1} - 2^{n+1}$. [In more detail: we can write $7^n - 2^n = 5m$ for some $m \in \mathbb{P}$ so that

$$7^{n+1} - 2^{n+1} = 7 \cdot 5m + 5 \cdot 2^n = 5(7m + 2^n).]$$

We have shown that the inductive step holds and so our proof is complete by the Principle of Mathematical Induction.   ☐

The Principle of Mathematical Induction is equally valid if the indexing begins with some integer m other than 1: *All the propositions $p(m)$, $p(m + 1)$, $p(m + 2)$, ... are true provided*

(B) *$p(m)$ is true;*
(I) *$p(n)$ implies $p(n + 1)$ for all $n \geqq m$.*

We will frequently use this with $m = 0$, i.e., when the propositions $p(n)$ are indexed by the set $\mathbb{N}$.

EXAMPLE 6   Let $\mathcal{P}(S)$ be the power set of some finite set S. If S has n elements, then $\mathcal{P}(S)$ has 2^n members. This was shown to be plausible in Example 2 of § 1.1. We prove it now.

Proof. This assertion was verified earlier for $n = 0, 1, 2$ and 3. In particular, the case $n = 0$ establishes the basis for induction. Before proving the inductive step, let's experiment a little and compare $\mathcal{P}(S)$ for $S = \{a, b\}$ and $S = \{a, b, c\}$. Note that

$$\mathcal{P}(\{a, b, c\}) = \{\varnothing, \{a\}, \{b\}, \{a, b\}, \{c\}, \{a, c\}, \{b, c\}, \{a, b, c\}\}.$$

The first four sets comprise $\mathcal{P}(\{a, b\})$; each of the remaining sets is a set in

$\mathcal{P}(\{a, b\})$ with c added to it. This is why $\mathcal{P}(\{a, b, c\})$ has twice as many sets as $\mathcal{P}(\{a, b\})$. This argument looks as if it generalizes: every time an element is added to S, the size of $\mathcal{P}(S)$ doubles.

To prove the inductive step, we assume the proposition is valid for n. We consider a set S with $n + 1$ elements; for convenience we use $S = \{1, 2, 3, \ldots, n, n + 1\}$. Let $T = \{1, 2, 3, \ldots, n\}$. The sets in $\mathcal{P}(T)$ are simply the subsets of S that do not contain $n + 1$. By the assumption for n, $\mathcal{P}(T)$ contains exactly 2^n sets. Each remaining subset of S contains $n + 1$, so it is the union of a set in $\mathcal{P}(T)$ with the one-element set $\{n + 1\}$. That is, $\mathcal{P}(S)$ has another 2^n sets that are not subsets of T. It follows that $\mathcal{P}(S)$ has $2^n + 2^n = 2^{n+1}$ members. This completes the inductive step, and hence the result holds for all n by mathematical induction. ☐

Notice that in Example 6 we experimented with a small value of n to get some idea how a general argument might go. Proofs by induction often arise in situations in which we have examined a few cases, think we see the pattern and want to show that our guess is right in general. Sometimes it helps to examine how one case follows from the one before, in order to help us construct an argument for the general inductive step. Such experimentation does not by itself prove anything general, but it can be enormously useful in pointing out what difficulties may arise in a full-dress argument.

EXAMPLE 7 Some experience with inequalities suggests that $n^2 \leq 2^n$ for sufficiently large n. Here is a careful verification of this fact. Some experimentation shows that this inequality holds for $n = 0, 1, 2$ and 4. It appears to hold for all $n \geq 4$. We prove this by induction by observing

(B) $4^2 \leq 2^4$,

and showing

(I) $n^2 \leq 2^n$ implies $(n + 1)^2 \leq 2^{n+1}$ for $n \geq 4$.

Thus we assume that $n^2 \leq 2^n$ for some fixed $n \geq 4$. Here is motivation and "scratch work" for the proof to follow in the next paragraph. We wish to infer $(n + 1)^2 \leq 2^{n+1}$ from $n^2 \leq 2^n$. Since $n^2 \leq 2^n$ implies $2^{n+1} = 2 \cdot 2^n \geq 2n^2$, it suffices to show $(n + 1)^2 \leq 2n^2$. This is equivalent to

$$\frac{(n + 1)^2}{n^2} \leq 2, \quad \text{i.e., to} \quad \frac{n + 1}{n} \leq \sqrt{2} \quad \text{and thus to} \quad 1 + \frac{1}{n} \leq \sqrt{2}.$$

For $n \geq 4$ we have $1 + 1/n \leq 1 + \frac{1}{4} < \sqrt{2}$, these inequalities hold, and we are in business.

Here is the formal proof of (I). Assume that $n^2 \leq 2^n$ and $n \geq 4$. Then $1 + 1/n < \sqrt{2}$, hence $n + 1 < \sqrt{2}\, n$ and so

$$(n + 1)^2 < 2n^2 \leq 2 \cdot 2^n = 2^{n+1},$$

as desired. We used the assumption $n^2 \leq 2^n$ at the last inequality. Since

(B) and (I) hold, the Principle of Mathematical Induction shows that $n^2 \leq 2^n$ for all $n \geq 4$.   ☐

EXAMPLE 8   Induction is useful in proving results about graphs and trees. As an example, if you did Exercise 9 of § 0.2 you probably conjectured:

$$p(n) = \text{"Every tree with } n \text{ vertices has exactly } n - 1 \text{ edges,"}$$

for $n \in \mathbb{P}$. For $n = 1$, this says that the trivial one-vertex tree has no edges at all, which is true. Note also that the only tree with 2 vertices has 1 edge. In § 6.4 we'll prove the inductive step, i.e., that $p(n)$ implies $p(n + 1)$ for all $n \in \mathbb{P}$. It will follow that all the propositions $p(n)$ are true.   ☐

We close the section with an indication of why induction works. Suppose that

(B) $p(1)$ is true;
(I) the truth of $p(n)$ implies the truth of $p(n + 1)$, for all $n \in \mathbb{P}$.

Imagine, if possible, that there are some values of n in $\mathbb{P}$ for which $p(n)$ is not true, and start looking for the first such bad n in the list $1, 2, 3, \ldots$. By (B) it's not 1. By (I), if we haven't yet found such a bad n, the next integer we look at won't be bad either. So we'll never find an n for which $p(n)$ is false. This argument will be made more precise in § 6.3.

EXERCISES 2.5

1. Prove
$$\sum_{k=1}^{n} k^2 = 1 + 4 + 9 + \cdots + n^2 = \frac{n(n + 1)(2n + 1)}{6} \quad \text{for} \quad n \in \mathbb{P}.$$

2. Prove
$$4 + 10 + 16 + \cdots + (6n - 2) = n(3n + 1) \quad \text{for all } n \in \mathbb{P}.$$

3. Prove
$$\sum_{k=0}^{n} a^k = \frac{a^{n+1} - 1}{a - 1} \quad \text{for} \quad a \in \mathbb{R}, a \neq 0, a \neq 1, \text{ and } n \in \mathbb{N}.$$

4. Prove
$$\frac{1}{1 \cdot 5} + \frac{1}{5 \cdot 9} + \frac{1}{9 \cdot 13} + \cdots + \frac{1}{(4n - 3)(4n + 1)} = \frac{n}{4n + 1} \quad \text{for} \quad n \in \mathbb{P}.$$

5. Modify the procedure of Example 1(b) by letting $I = 1$ and $S = 2$ in Step 1 but otherwise making no changes.
(a) List the first four printed values of S.
(b) Guess the value of S at the nth time the procedure is at Step 2 and prove your guess is correct for all $n \in \mathbb{P}$.

6. Consider the following procedure.
Step 1. Let $S = 1$.
Step 2. Print S.

Step 3. Replace S by $S + 2\sqrt{S} + 1$ and go back to Step 2.

(a) List the first four printed values of S.

(b) Use mathematical induction to show that the value of S is always an integer. [It is easier to prove the stronger statement that the value of S is always the square of an integer and in fact $S = n^2$ the nth time the procedure is at Step 2.]

7. Prove that $11^n - 4^n$ is divisible by 7 for all $n \in \mathbb{P}$.

8. Prove that $n^3 - 4n + 6$ is divisible by 3 for all $n \in \mathbb{N}$.

9. (a) Calculate $1 + 3 + \cdots + (2n - 1)$ for a few values of n, and then guess a general formula for this sum.

(b) Prove the formula obtained in part (a) by induction.

10. (a) Prove that $n^2 > n + 1$ for $n \geq 2$.

(b) Prove that $n! > n^2$ for $n \geq 4$. [$n!$ is defined in § 1.3.]

11. (a) Decide for which positive values of n the inequality $3n < n^2 - 1$ holds.

(b) Prove your claim in part (a).

12. Repeat Exercise 11 for $4n \leq n^2 - 7$.

13. Consider the proposition $p(n) = $ "$n^2 + 5n + 1$ is even."

(a) Prove that the truth of $p(n)$ implies the truth of $p(n + 1)$, for all $n \in \mathbb{P}$.

(b) For which values of n is $p(n)$ actually true? What is the moral of this exercise?

14. Prove $(2n + 1) + (2n + 3) + (2n + 5) + \cdots + (4n - 1) = 3n^2$ for $n \in \mathbb{P}$. The sum can also be written $\sum\limits_{k=n}^{2n-1} (2k + 1)$.

15. Prove that $5^n - 4n - 1$ is divisible by 16 for $n \in \mathbb{P}$.

16. Prove $1^3 + 2^3 + \cdots + n^3 = (1 + 2 + \cdots + n)^2$, i.e., $\sum\limits_{k=1}^{n} k^3 = (\sum\limits_{k=1}^{n} k)^2$ for $n \in \mathbb{P}$. *Hint:* Use the identity in Example 3(b).

17. This exercise requires a little knowledge of trigonometric identities. Prove that $|\sin nx| \leq n|\sin x|$ for all $x \in \mathbb{R}$ and all $n \in \mathbb{P}$.

18. Give examples of lists of propositions $p(1), p(2), p(3), \ldots$ for which:

(a) (B) holds but (I) fails.

(b) (I) holds but (B) fails.

Can you conclude that $p(n)$ is true for all n in either case?

CHAPTER HIGHLIGHTS

To check your understanding of the material in this chapter, we recommend that you consider each item listed below and:

(a) Satisfy yourself that you can define each concept and describe each method.

(b) Give at least one reason why the item was included in the chapter.

(c) Think of at least one example of each concept and at least one situation in which the fact or method would be useful.

Concepts

propositional calculus
  proposition
  logical connectives $\neg$, $\wedge$, $\vee$, $\rightarrow$, $\leftrightarrow$
  compound proposition
    truth table
    variable
  tautology, contradiction
  logical equivalence, implication, contrapositive
formal proof
  theorem, hypothesis, conclusion
  rule of inference
  valid, fallacy
methods of proof
  direct, indirect, by contradiction
  vacuous, trivial
  constructive, nonconstructive
induction
  basis, inductive step

Facts

Basic logical equivalences [Table 1 of § 2.2].
Basic logical implications [Table 2 of § 2.2].
Basic rules of inference [Table 1 of § 2.3].
Substitution rules [§ 2.2].
Well-ordering principle.
Principle of Mathematical Induction.

Methods

Use of truth tables.
Use of DeMorgan laws to eliminate $\wedge$ or $\vee$.
Use of rules of inference to construct proofs.
Use of mathematical induction to construct proofs.

3

FUNCTIONS AND SEQUENCES

||

This chapter begins with a study of functions, which leads naturally to the study of a special class of functions called sequences. This, in turn, leads to consideration of recursive definitions and algorithms.

§ 3.1 *Functions*

We begin with a working descriptive definition of "function." A **function** f assigns to each element x in some set S a unique element in a set T. We say such an f is **defined on** S with **values in** T. The set S is called the **domain of** f and is sometimes written $\text{Dom}(f)$. The element assigned to x is usually written $f(x)$. Care should be taken to avoid confusing a function f with its functional values $f(x)$, especially when people write, as we will later, "the function $f(x)$." A function f is completely specified by:

    (a) the set on which f is defined, namely $\text{Dom}(f)$;
    (b) the assignment, rule or formula giving the value $f(x)$ for each $x \in \text{Dom}(f)$.

For x in $\text{Dom}(f)$, $f(x)$ is called the **image of** x **under** f. The set of all images $f(x)$ is a subset of T called the **image of** f and written $\text{Im}(f)$. Thus we have

$$\text{Im}(f) = \{f(x) : x \in \text{Dom}(f)\}.$$

It is often convenient to specify a set T of allowable images, i.e., a set T containing $\text{Im}(f)$. Such a set is called a **codomain of** f. While a function f

has exactly one domain Dom(f) and exactly one image Im(f), any set containing Im(f) can serve as a codomain. Of course, when we specify a codomain we will try to choose one which is useful or informative in context. The notation $f: S \rightarrow T$ is shorthand for: "f is a function with domain S and codomain T." We sometimes refer to a function as a **map** or **mapping** and say that f **maps** S into T. When we feel the need of a picture we sometimes draw sketches such as those in Figure 1.

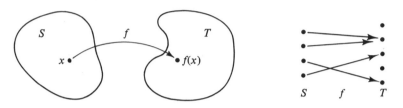

A function f mapping S into T

FIGURE 1

EXAMPLE 1   (a) Consider a function $f: \mathbb{R} \rightarrow \mathbb{R}$. This means that Dom($f$) = $\mathbb{R}$ and, for each $x \in \mathbb{R}$, $f(x)$ represents a unique number in $\mathbb{R}$. Thus $\mathbb{R}$ is a codomain for f but the image Im(f) may be a much smaller set. For example, if $f_1(x) = x^2$ for all $x \in \mathbb{R}$, then Im(f_1) = $[0, \infty)$ and we could write $f_1: \mathbb{R} \rightarrow [0, \infty)$. If f_2 is defined by

$$f_2(x) = \begin{cases} 1 & \text{if } x \geqq 0, \\ 0 & \text{if } x < 0, \end{cases}$$

then Im(f_2) = $\{0, 1\}$ and we could write $f_2: \mathbb{R} \rightarrow [0, \infty)$ or $f_2: \mathbb{R} \rightarrow \mathbb{N}$ or $f_2: \mathbb{R} \rightarrow \{0, 1\}$ among other choices.

(b) Consider the function $g: \mathbb{N} \rightarrow \mathbb{N}$ defined by $g(n) = n^2 - n$. Here it is useful to specify $\mathbb{N}$ as a codomain, since we might not be interested in the exact set Im(g). ☐

We will avoid the terminology "range of a function f" because many authors use "range" for what we call the image of f and many others use "range" for what we call a codomain.

There is a connection between functions and computer addresses, but they are not the same thing. Suppose that as part of a computer program we want to take whatever number is stored at address X, multiply it by itself and store the result at address SQ. We might write the program line

$$SQ \leftarrow X*X$$

or

$$SQ = X*X.$$

This line describes the squaring function f with rule $f(x) = x^2$ and domain the set of all numbers the computer can store at address X. To help us remember its rule, we might even want to call the function SQ, so that $SQ(x) = x^2$. So far as the computer is concerned, though, SQ is simply the name of a memory location, and we just happen to be storing a single value of the squaring function there.

In Chapter 0 we introduced two important concepts: graphs and trees. Unfortunately, the term "graph" has a somewhat different meaning in connection with functions. To be precise, we consider a function $f: S \rightarrow T$. The **graph of** f is the following subset of $S \times T$:

$$\text{Graph}(f) = \{\langle x, y \rangle \in S \times T : f(x) = y\}.$$

This definition is compatible with the use of the term in algebra and calculus. The graphs of the functions in Example 1 are sketched in Figure 2. Unlike

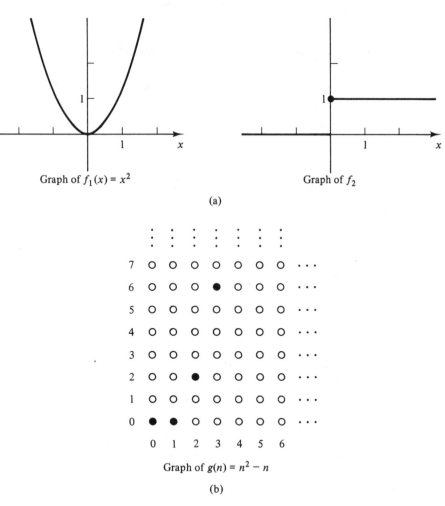

Graph of $f_1(x) = x^2$ Graph of f_2

(a)

Graph of $g(n) = n^2 - n$

(b)

FIGURE 2

the notation for matrices, the labels on the vertical axis of a graph decrease as one goes from top to bottom. This inconsistency is unfortunately completely standard.

Our working definition of "function" is incomplete; in particular, the term "assigns" is undefined. A very precise set-theoretical definition can be given. The key observation is this: Not only does a function determine its graph, but a function can be recovered from its graph. In fact, the graph of a function $f: S \to T$ is a subset G of $S \times T$ with the following property:

for each $x \in S$ there is exactly one $y \in T$ such that $\langle x, y \rangle \in G$.

Given G, we have $\text{Dom}(f) = S$ and, for each $x \in S$, $f(x)$ is the unique element in T such that $\langle x, f(x) \rangle \in G$. The point is that nothing is lost if we regard functions and their graphs as the same, and we gain some precision in the process.

Definition Let S and T be sets. A **function** with domain S and codomain T is a subset G of $S \times T$ satisfying:

for each $x \in S$ there is exactly one $y \in T$ such that $\langle x, y \rangle \in G$.

If S and T are subsets of $\mathbb{R}$ and if $S \times T$ is graphed so that S is part of the horizontal axis and T is part of the vertical axis, then a subset G of $S \times T$ is a function [or the graph of a function] if every vertical line through a point in S intersects G in exactly one point.

A function $f: S \to T$ is said to be **one-to-one** if distinct elements in S have distinct images in T under f:

$$x_1, x_2 \in S \quad \text{and} \quad x_1 \neq x_2 \quad \text{imply} \quad f(x_1) \neq f(x_2).$$

This is logically equivalent to the contrapositive:

$$x_1, x_2 \in S \quad \text{and} \quad f(x_1) = f(x_2) \quad \text{imply} \quad x_1 = x_2,$$

the form that is most useful in proofs. In terms of the graph G of f, f is one-to-one if:

for each $y \in T$ there is at most one $x \in S$ such that $\langle x, y \rangle \in G$.

If S and T are subsets of $\mathbb{R}$ and f is graphed as above, this condition states that horizontal lines intersect G at most once.

Given $f: S \to T$ we say that f maps **onto** a subset B of T provided $B = \text{Im}(f)$. In particular, we say f maps **onto** T provided $\text{Im}(f) = T$. In terms of the graph G of f, f maps S onto T if and only if:

for each $y \in T$ there is at least one $x \in S$ such that $\langle x, y \rangle \in G$.

A function $f: S \to T$ that is one-to-one and maps onto T is called a **one-to-one correspondence** between S and T. Thus f is a one-to-one correspondence if and only if:

for each $y \in T$ there is exactly one $x \in S$ such that $\langle x, y \rangle \in G$.

These three kinds of special functions are illustrated in Figure 3.

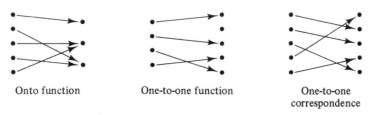

| Onto function | One-to-one function | One-to-one correspondence |

FIGURE 3

Before we turn to mathematical examples, we illustrate the ideas in a nonmathematical setting.

EXAMPLE 2 Suppose that each student in a class S is assigned a seat number from the set $T = \{1, 2, \ldots, 75\}$. This provides a function $f: S \to T$; thus for each student s, $f(s)$ represents his or her seat number. The function will be one-to-one provided no two students are assigned the same seat number. In this case, the class cannot have more than 75 students. The function will map S onto T provided every number in T has been assigned to at least one student. Note that for this to happen the class must have at least 75 students. The only way f could be a one-to-one correspondence of S onto T is if the class has exactly 75 students.

If we view the function f as a set of ordered pairs, then it will consist of pairs in $S \times T$ like $\langle$Les Moore, 73$\rangle$. □

EXAMPLE 3 (a) We define $f: \mathbb{N} \to \mathbb{N}$ by the rule $f(n) = 2n$. Then f is one-to-one since

$$f(n_1) = f(n_2) \quad \text{implies} \quad 2n_1 = 2n_2 \quad \text{implies} \quad n_1 = n_2.$$

However, f does not map $\mathbb{N}$ onto $\mathbb{N}$ since $\text{Im}(f)$ consists only of the even natural numbers.

(b) Let Σ be an alphabet. Then length$(w) \in \mathbb{N}$ for each word w in Σ^*; see § 1.1. Thus "length" is a function from Σ^* onto $\mathbb{N}$. [Note that functions can have fancier names than "f."] To see this, recall that Σ is nonempty and so Σ contains some letter, say a. Now $0 = \text{length}(\epsilon)$, $1 = \text{length}(a)$, $2 = \text{length}(aa)$, etc. The function length is not one-to-one unless Σ has only one element. □

EXAMPLE 4 We prove that $f: \mathbb{R} \to \mathbb{R}$ defined by $f(x) = 3x - 5$ is a one-to-one correspondence of $\mathbb{R}$ onto $\mathbb{R}$. To check that f is one-to-one we need to show

$$f(x) = f(x') \quad \text{implies} \quad x = x',$$

i.e.,

$$3x - 5 = 3x' - 5 \quad \text{implies} \quad x = x'.$$

But $3x - 5 = 3x' - 5$ implies $3x = 3x'$ [add 5 to both sides] and this implies that $x = x'$ [divide both sides by 3].

To show that f maps $\mathbb{R}$ onto $\mathbb{R}$ we consider an element y in $\mathbb{R}$. We need to find an x in $\mathbb{R}$ such that $f(x) = y$, i.e., $3x - 5 = y$. So we solve for x and obtain $x = (y + 5)/3$. Thus, given y in $\mathbb{R}$, $(y + 5)/3$ belongs to $\mathbb{R}$ and $f((y + 5)/3) = 3((y + 5)/3) - 5 = y$. This shows that every $y \in \mathbb{R}$ belongs to $\text{Im}(f)$ so that f maps $\mathbb{R}$ onto $\mathbb{R}$. $\square$

EXAMPLE 5 Consider the set $\mathfrak{M}_{m,n}$ of all $m \times n$ matrices. For $\mathbf{A} \in \mathfrak{M}_{m,n}$ let $\text{TRANS}(\mathbf{A}) = \mathbf{A}^T$, the transpose of $\mathbf{A}$. Then TRANS is a one-to-one correspondence between $\mathfrak{M}_{m,n}$ and $\mathfrak{M}_{n,m}$. To see this, first observe that

$$(\mathbf{A}^T)^T = \mathbf{A} \quad \text{for all} \quad \mathbf{A} \in \mathfrak{M}_{m,n}.$$

Suppose that $\mathbf{A}$ and $\mathbf{B}$ are in $\mathfrak{M}_{m,n}$ and that $\text{TRANS}(\mathbf{A}) = \text{TRANS}(\mathbf{B})$. Then $\mathbf{A}^T = \mathbf{B}^T$ and so $\mathbf{A} = (\mathbf{A}^T)^T = (\mathbf{B}^T)^T = \mathbf{B}$. Thus the function TRANS is one-to-one. To see that TRANS maps onto $\mathfrak{M}_{n,m}$, consider an arbitrary $\mathbf{C}$ in $\mathfrak{M}_{n,m}$. Then $\mathbf{C}^T$ belongs to $\mathfrak{M}_{m,n}$ and $\text{TRANS}(\mathbf{C}^T) = (\mathbf{C}^T)^T = \mathbf{C}$. Thus every member of $\mathfrak{M}_{n,m}$ is in $\text{Im}(\text{TRANS})$.

Notice how tempting it would have been to write $\text{TRANS}(\text{TRANS}(\mathbf{A}))$ instead of $(\mathbf{A}^T)^T$. Why didn't we? Because the function TRANS under discussion maps $\mathfrak{M}_{m,n}$ to $\mathfrak{M}_{n,m}$, but not the other way back unless $m = n$. There is another function, say SNART, from $\mathfrak{M}_{n,m}$ to $\mathfrak{M}_{m,n}$ defined by

$$\text{SNART}(\mathbf{A}) = \mathbf{A}^T.$$

The rules for defining SNART and TRANS look the same, but because they have different domains the two functions are different. $\square$

EXAMPLE 6 (a) We are now in a position to give a precise definition of a graph G. As noted in § 0.3, a graph consists of vertices and edges, and each edge connects certain vertices. Thus a graph G consists of a set $V(G)$, whose elements are called **vertices**, and a set $E(G)$, whose elements are called **edges**. In addition, there is a function γ [Greek lowercase gamma] mapping $E(G)$ into the family of two- and one-element subsets of $V(G)$. For each e in $E(G)$, if $\gamma(e) = \{u, v\}$ where $u \neq v$, then we say the edge e **joins** the vertices u and v. If $\gamma(e) = \{u\}$ then we call e a **loop** and say that e **joins** u to itself. The members of $\gamma(e)$ are called the **endpoints** of e. We say that edges e and f are **parallel** if $\gamma(e) = \gamma(f)$, i.e., if e and f have the same endpoints.

This precision is not only comforting, it also makes it clearer how a computer can view a graph as two sets plus a function γ that specifies the endpoints of the edges.

(b) If there are no parallel edges, then γ is one-to-one and the sets $\gamma(e)$ uniquely determine the edges e. That is, there is only one edge for each set $\gamma(e)$. In this case, we often dispense with the set $E(G)$ and the function γ and simply write the edges as sets, like $\{u, v\}$ or $\{u\}$, or as vertex sequences, like $u\,v$, $v\,u$ or $u\,u$. $\square$

EXAMPLE 7   In § 1.3 we indicated how various collections of objects can be indexed. For example, $\{A_k : k \in \mathbb{N}\}$ might represent a family of subsets of $\mathbb{R}$ indexed by $\mathbb{N}$, while $\{p(n) : n \in \mathbb{P}\}$ might represent a set of propositions indexed by $\mathbb{P}$. This indexing concept can be made more precise using functions, as we illustrate below.

The indexed family $\{A_k : k \in \mathbb{N}\}$ can be described by the function f with domain $\mathbb{N}$ such that $f(k) = A_k$ for all $k \in \mathbb{N}$. A codomain of f is the set $\mathcal{P}(\mathbb{R})$ of all subsets of $\mathbb{R}$. The function f will be one-to-one if and only if sets A_k and A_j with different subscripts are always different.

For the set $\{p(n) : n \in \mathbb{P}\}$, we can also view the symbol p as a function with domain $\mathbb{P}$, so that p is a proposition-valued function with domain $\mathbb{P}$. As before, this just means that for each $n \in \mathbb{P}$, $p(n)$ represents some proposition.

In general, an indexed family of objects $\{x_i : i \in I\}$ can be described with a function, say g, with domain I such that $g(i) = x_i$ for all $i \in I$. The indexing function g is one-to-one if and only if $x_i \ne x_j$ whenever $i \ne j$. ☐

Some special functions occur so often that they have special names. Let S be a nonempty set. The **identity function** 1_S on S is the function that maps each element of S to itself:

$$1_S(x) = x \quad \text{for all} \quad x \in S.$$

Thus the identity function is a one-to-one correspondence of S onto S.

A function $f: S \to T$ is called a **constant function** if there is some $y_0 \in T$ so that $f(x) = y_0$ for all $x \in S$. The value a constant function takes does not change or vary as x varies over S.

Consider a set S and a subset A of S. The function on S that takes the value 1 at members of A and the value 0 at the other members of S is called the **characteristic function of A** and is denoted χ_A [Greek lowercase chi, sub A]. Thus

$$\chi_A(x) = \begin{cases} 1 & \text{for} \quad x \in A, \\ 0 & \text{for} \quad x \in S \setminus A. \end{cases}$$

Note that $\chi_A : S \to \{0, 1\}$ is rarely one-to-one and is usually an onto map. In fact, χ_A maps S onto $\{0, 1\}$ unless $A = S$ or $A = \varnothing$. If either A or $S \setminus A$ has at least two members then χ_A is not one-to-one.

Now consider functions $f: S \to T$ and $g: T \to U$; see Figure 4. We define the **composition** $g \circ f: S \to U$ by the rule

$$g \circ f(x) = g(f(x)) \quad \text{for all} \quad x \in S.$$

One might read the left side "g circle f of x" or "g of f of x." Complicated operations that are performed in calculus or on a calculator can be viewed as the composition of simpler functions.

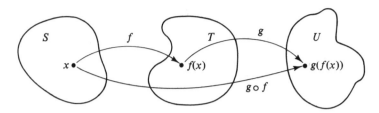

Composing functions

FIGURE 4

EXAMPLE 8   (a) Consider the function $h: \mathbb{R} \to \mathbb{R}$ given by

$$h(x) = (x^3 + 2x)^7.$$

The value $h(x)$ is obtained by first calculating $x^3 + 2x$ and then taking its seventh power. We write f for the first or inside function: $f(x) = x^3 + 2x$. We write g for the second or outside function: $g(x) = x^7$. The name of the variable x is irrelevant; we could just as well have written $g(y) = y^7$ for $y \in \mathbb{R}$. Either way, we see that

$$g(f(x)) = g(x^3 + 2x) = (x^3 + 2x)^7 = h(x) \quad \text{for} \quad x \in \mathbb{R}.$$

Thus $h = g \circ f$. The ability to view complicated functions as the composition of simpler functions is a critical skill in calculus. Note that the order of f and g is important. In fact,

$$f \circ g(x) = f(x^7) = (x^7)^3 + 2(x^7) = x^{21} + 2x^7 \quad \text{for} \quad x \in \mathbb{R}.$$

(b) Suppose that one wishes to calculate $h(x) = \sqrt{\log x}$ for certain positive values of x on a hand-held calculator. The calculator has the functions $\sqrt{x}$ and $\log x$, which stands for $\log_{10} x$. One works from the inside out. For example, if $x = 73$, one keys in this value, performs $\log x$ to obtain 1.8633, and then performs $\sqrt{x}$ to obtain 1.3650. Note that $h = g \circ f$ where $f(x) = \log x$ and $g(x) = \sqrt{x}$. As in part (a), order is important: $h \neq f \circ g$, i.e., $\sqrt{\log x}$ is not generally equal to $\log \sqrt{x}$. For example, if $x = 73$, then $\sqrt{x}$ is approximately 8.5440 and $\log \sqrt{x}$ is approximately .9317.

(c) Of course, some functions f and g do commute under composition, i.e., satisfy $f \circ g = g \circ f$. For example, if $f(x) = \sqrt{x}$ and $g(x) = 1/x$ for $x \in (0, \infty)$, then $f \circ g = g \circ f$ because

$$\sqrt{\frac{1}{x}} = \frac{1}{\sqrt{x}} \quad \text{for} \quad x \in (0, \infty).$$

For example, for $x = 9$ we have $\sqrt{1/9} = 1/3 = 1/\sqrt{9}$. ☐

We can compose more than two functions if we wish.

EXAMPLE 9 Consider the functions f, g and h that map $\mathbb{R}$ into $\mathbb{R}$ and are defined by

$$f(x) = x^4, \qquad g(y) = \sqrt{y^2 + 1}, \qquad h(z) = z^2 + 72.$$

We've used the different variable names x, y and z to help clarify our computations below. Let's calculate $h \circ (g \circ f)$ and $(h \circ g) \circ f$ and compare the answers. First, for $x \in \mathbb{R}$ we have

$$(h \circ (g \circ f))(x) = h(g \circ f(x)) \qquad \text{by definition of } h \circ (g \circ f)$$
$$= h(g(f(x))) \qquad \text{by definition of } g \circ f$$
$$= h(g(x^4)) \qquad \text{since } f(x) = x^4$$
$$= h(\sqrt{x^8 + 1}) \qquad y = x^4 \text{ in definition of } g$$
$$= (\sqrt{x^8 + 1})^2 + 72 \quad z = \sqrt{x^8 + 1} \text{ in definition of } h$$
$$= x^8 + 73 \qquad \text{algebra.}$$

On the other hand,

$$((h \circ g) \circ f)(x) = (h \circ g)(f(x)) \qquad \text{by definition of } (h \circ g) \circ f$$
$$= h(g(f(x))) \qquad \text{by definition of } h \circ g$$
$$= x^8 + 73 \qquad \text{exactly as above.}$$

We conclude that

$$(h \circ (g \circ f))(x) = ((h \circ g) \circ f)(x) = x^8 + 73 \quad \text{for all} \quad x \in \mathbb{R},$$

and so the functions $h \circ (g \circ f)$ and $(h \circ g) \circ f$ are exactly the same function. This is no accident, as we observe in the next general theorem. □

Associativity of Composition. Consider functions $f: S \to T$, $g: T \to U$ and $h: U \to V$. Then $h \circ (g \circ f) = (h \circ g) \circ f$.

The proof of this basic result amounts to checking that the functions $h \circ (g \circ f)$ and $(h \circ g) \circ f$ both map S into V and that, just as in Example 9, for each $x \in S$ the values $(h \circ (g \circ f))(x)$ and $((h \circ g) \circ f)(x)$ are both equal to $h(g(f(x)))$.

Since composition is associative, we can write $h \circ g \circ f$ unambiguously without any parentheses. We can also compose any finite number of functions without using parentheses.

EXAMPLE 10   (a) If $f(x) = x^4$ for $x \in [0, \infty)$, $g(x) = \sqrt{x + 2}$ for $x \in [0, \infty)$ and $h(x) = x^2 + 1$ for $x \in \mathbb{R}$, then

$$h \circ g \circ f(x) = h(g(x^4)) = h(\sqrt{x^4 + 2}) = (x^4 + 2) + 1$$
$$= x^4 + 3 \quad \text{for} \quad x \in \mathbb{R},$$
$$f \circ g \circ h(x) = f(g(x^2 + 1)) = f(\sqrt{x^2 + 1 + 2})$$
$$= (x^2 + 3)^2 \quad \text{for} \quad x \in \mathbb{R},$$
$$f \circ h \circ g(x) = f(h(\sqrt{x + 2})) = f(x + 2 + 1)$$
$$= (x + 3)^4 \quad \text{for} \quad x \in [0, \infty).$$

(b) The function F given by

$$F(x) = (\sqrt{x^2 + 1} + 3)^5 \quad \text{for} \quad x \in \mathbb{R}$$

can be written as $k \circ h \circ g \circ f$ where

$$f(x) = x^2 + 1 \quad \text{for} \quad x \in \mathbb{R},$$
$$g(x) = \sqrt{x} \quad\;\; \text{for} \quad x \in [0, \infty),$$
$$h(x) = x + 3 \quad \text{for} \quad x \in \mathbb{R},$$
$$k(x) = x^5 \quad\;\;\; \text{for} \quad x \in \mathbb{R}. \quad \square$$

EXERCISES 3.1

1. We define $f : \mathbb{R} \to \mathbb{R}$ as follows:

$$f(x) = \begin{cases} x^3 & \text{if } x \geqq 1, \\ x & \text{if } 0 \leqq x < 1, \\ -x^3 & \text{if } x < 0. \end{cases}$$

(a) Calculate $f(3)$, $f(\tfrac{1}{3})$, $f(-\tfrac{1}{3})$ and $f(-3)$.
(b) Sketch a graph of f.
(c) Find $\mathrm{Im}(f)$.

2. The functions sketched in Figure 5 have domain and codomain both equal to [0, 1].

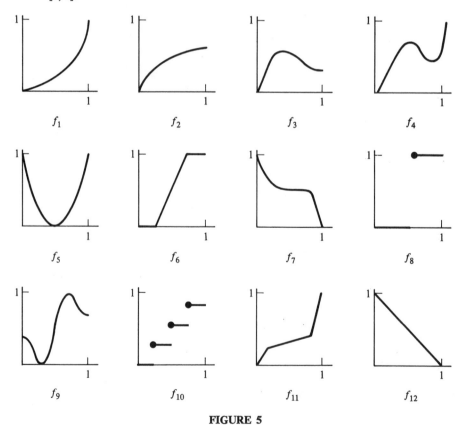

FIGURE 5

(a) Which of these functions are one-to-one?

(b) Which of these functions map [0, 1] onto [0, 1]?

(c) Which of these functions are one-to-one correspondences?

3. Let $S = \{1, 2, 3, 4, 5\}$ and $T = \{a, b, c, d\}$. For each question below: if the answer is YES give an example; if the answer is NO explain briefly.

(a) Are there any one-to-one functions from S into T?

(b) Are there any one-to-one functions from T into S?

(c) Are there any functions mapping S onto T?

(d) Are there any functions mapping T onto S?

(e) Are there any one-to-one correspondences between S and T?

4. Let $S = \{1, 2, 3, 4, 5\}$ and consider the following functions from S into S: $1_S(n) = n$, $f(n) = 6 - n$, $g(n) = \max\{3, n\}$, $h(n) = \max\{1, n - 1\}$.

(a) Write each of these functions as a set of ordered pairs, i.e., list the elements in their graphs.

(b) Sketch a graph of each of these functions.

(c) Which of these functions are one-to-one and onto?

5. Here is a one-to-one function from $\mathbb{N} \times \mathbb{N}$ into $\mathbb{N}$: $f(\langle m, n \rangle) = 2^m 3^n$.

(a) Calculate $f(\langle m, n \rangle)$ for five different elements $\langle m, n \rangle$ in $\mathbb{N} \times \mathbb{N}$.

(b) Explain why f is one-to-one.

(c) Does f map $\mathbb{N} \times \mathbb{N}$ onto $\mathbb{N}$? Explain.

(d) Show that $g(\langle m, n \rangle) = 2^m 4^n$ defines a function on $\mathbb{N} \times \mathbb{N}$ that is not one-to-one.

6. Consider the following functions from $\mathbb{N}$ into $\mathbb{N}$: $1_\mathbb{N}(n) = n$, $f(n) = 3n$, $g(n) = n + (-1)^n$, $h(n) = \min\{n, 100\}$, $k(n) = \max\{0, n - 5\}$.

(a) Which of these functions are one-to-one?

(b) Which of these functions map $\mathbb{N}$ onto $\mathbb{N}$?

7. Let A and B be nonempty sets. The projection map PROJ picks the first element from each pair in $A \times B$, i.e., PROJ: $A \times B \to A$ where PROJ$(\langle a, b \rangle) = a$.

(a) Does this function map $A \times B$ onto A? Justify.

(b) Is PROJ one-to-one? What if B has only one element?

8. Let $\mathfrak{M}_{n,n}$ be the set of $n \times n$ matrices. Here is an important function in linear algebra: trace(**A**) $= \sum_{i=1}^{n} a_{ii}$ where **A** $= [a_{ij}]$. Thus trace maps $\mathfrak{M}_{n,n}$ into $\mathbb{R}$. For this exercise, $n = 2$.

(a) Calculate trace(**A**) for the following matrices:

$$\begin{bmatrix} 2 & 3 \\ 4 & 5 \end{bmatrix}, \quad \begin{bmatrix} 1 & 0 \\ 0 & -1 \end{bmatrix}, \quad \begin{bmatrix} 1 & 1 \\ 1 & 1 \end{bmatrix}, \quad \begin{bmatrix} 0 & 17 \\ 8 & 73 \end{bmatrix}.$$

(b) Show that trace maps $\mathfrak{M}_{2,2}$ onto $\mathbb{R}$.

9. For $n \in \mathbb{Z}$, let $f(n) = \frac{1}{2}[(-1)^n + 1]$. The function f is the characteristic function for some subset of $\mathbb{Z}$. Which subset?

10. In Example 8(b), we compared the functions $\sqrt{\log x}$ and $\log \sqrt{x}$. Show that these functions take the same value for $x = 10{,}000$.

11. We define functions mapping $\mathbb{R}$ into $\mathbb{R}$ as follows: $f(x) = x^3 - 4x$, $g(x) = 1/(x^2 + 1)$, $h(x) = x^4$. Find

(a) $f \circ g \circ h$ (b) $f \circ h \circ g$ (c) $h \circ g \circ f$
(d) $f \circ f$ (e) $g \circ g$ (f) $h \circ g$
(g) $g \circ h$

12. Show that if $f: S \to T$ and $g: T \to U$ are one-to-one, then $g \circ f$ is one-to-one.

13. Prove that the composition of functions is associative.

14. Several important functions can be found on hand-held calculators. Why isn't the identity function, i.e., the function $1_\mathbb{R}$ where $1_\mathbb{R}(x) = x$ for all $x \in \mathbb{R}$, among them?

15. Consider the functions f and g mapping $\mathbb{Z}$ into $\mathbb{Z}$, where $f(n) = n - 1$ for $n \in \mathbb{Z}$ and g is the characteristic function χ_E of $E = \{n \in \mathbb{Z} : n \text{ is even}\}$.
    (a) Calculate $(g \circ f)(5)$, $(g \circ f)(4)$, $(f \circ g)(7)$ and $(f \circ g)(8)$.
    (b) Calculate $(f \circ f)(11)$, $(f \circ f)(12)$, $(g \circ g)(11)$ and $(g \circ g)(12)$.
    (c) Determine the functions $g \circ f$ and $f \circ f$.
    (d) Show that $g \circ g = g \circ f$ and that $f \circ g$ is the negative of $g \circ f$.

§ 3.2   Invertible Functions

Roughly speaking, if a function has an inverse, then the inverse function undoes the action of the function. See Figure 1. Thus if we compose a function and its inverse, we get a function that leaves values unchanged.

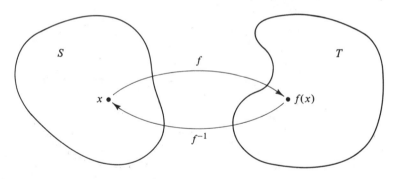

A function and its inverse

FIGURE 1

EXAMPLE 1   (a) The functions x^2 and $\sqrt{x}$ with domains $[0, \infty)$ are "inverses" to each other. If you apply these operations in either order to some value, the original value is obtained. Try it on a calculator! In other words,

$$\sqrt{x^2} = x \quad \text{and} \quad (\sqrt{x})^2 = x \quad \text{for} \quad x \in [0, \infty).$$

(b) The function $1/x$ is its own "inverse." If you apply the operation twice to some value, the original value is obtained. That is,

$$\frac{1}{1/x} = x \quad \text{for} \quad \text{all nonzero } x \text{ in } \mathbb{R}. \quad \square$$

To give a precise definition, we consider a function $f: S \to T$. A function $f^{-1}: T \to S$ is said to be the **inverse of** f if $f^{-1} \circ f = 1_S$ and $f \circ f^{-1} = 1_T$. In other words,

$$f^{-1}(f(x)) = x \quad \text{for all} \quad x \in S$$

and

$$f(f^{-1}(y)) = y \quad \text{for all} \quad y \in T.$$

A function f is said to be **invertible** if it has an inverse.

EXAMPLE 2   (a) Consider a positive real number b where $b \neq 1$. Important examples of b are 2, 10 and the number e that appears in calculus and is approximately 2.718. The function f_b given by $f_b(x) = b^x$ for $x \in \mathbb{R}$ has an inverse f_b^{-1} with domain $(0, \infty)$, which is called a **logarithm function**. We write $f_b^{-1}(y) = \log_b y$; by the definition of an inverse we have

$$\log_b b^x = x \quad \text{for} \quad x \in \mathbb{R}$$

and

$$b^{\log_b y} = y \quad \text{for} \quad y \in (0, \infty).$$

In particular, e^x and $\log_e x$ are inverse functions. The function $\log_e x$ is called the **natural logarithm** and is often denoted $\ln x$. The functions 10^x and $\log_{10} x$ are inverses, and so are 2^x and $\log_2 x$. The functions $\log_{10} x = \log$ and $\log_e x = \ln$ appear on many calculators; such calculators also allow one to compute their inverses 10^x and e^x.

(b) The functions TRANS: $\mathfrak{M}_{m,n} \to \mathfrak{M}_{n,m}$ and SNART: $\mathfrak{M}_{n,m} \to \mathfrak{M}_{m,n}$ in Example 5 of § 3.1 are inverses to each other, since

$$\text{SNART(TRANS(A))} = \mathbf{A} \quad \text{for all} \quad \mathbf{A} \in \mathfrak{M}_{m,n}$$

and

$$\text{TRANS(SNART(B))} = \mathbf{B} \quad \text{for all} \quad \mathbf{B} \in \mathfrak{M}_{n,m}. \quad \square$$

Not all functions have inverses. The next theorem tells us which ones do.

Theorem   Consider $f: S \to T$. The function f is invertible if and only if f is one-to-one and maps S onto T.

Proof. Suppose that f is invertible. Then there is a function $f^{-1}: T \to S$ such that $f^{-1} \circ f = 1_S$ and $f \circ f^{-1} = 1_T$. To see that f is one-to-one, we consider $x_1, x_2 \in S$ such that $f(x_1) = f(x_2)$. Then

$$x_1 = 1_S(x_1) = f^{-1}(f(x_1)) = f^{-1}(f(x_2)) = 1_S(x_2) = x_2.$$

Thus f is one-to-one. To see that f maps S onto T, we consider $y \in T$. Then $f^{-1}(y)$ belongs to S and

$$f(f^{-1}(y)) = f \circ f^{-1}(y) = 1_T(y) = y.$$

Thus $y \in \text{Im}(f)$. Since every y in T is in $\text{Im}(f)$, we conclude that $\text{Im}(f) = T$. That is, f maps S onto T.

Now suppose that f is one-to-one and maps S onto T. Then

for each $y \in T$ there is exactly one $x \in S$ such that $f(x) = y$.

This provides a ready-made formula for f^{-1}, namely: for $y \in T$, $f^{-1}(y) =$ that unique $x \in S$ such that $f(x) = y$. Consider x_0 in S. Then $f(x_0)$ is in T and so

$$f^{-1}(f(x_0)) = \text{that unique } x \in S \text{ such that } f(x) = f(x_0),$$

i.e., $f^{-1}(f(x_0)) = x_0$. This is true for all x_0 in S and so $f^{-1} \circ f = 1_S$. Now consider $y \in T$. Then $f^{-1}(y) = x$ where $f(x) = y$, and so $f(f^{-1}(y)) = f(x) = y$. Since this holds for all y in T, we have $f \circ f^{-1} = 1_T$. Thus f is invertible. $\quad\square$

EXAMPLE 3 Consider the function $f: \mathbb{R} \to \mathbb{R}$ given by $f(x) = x^3 + 1$. It is easy to check that f is one-to-one and maps $\mathbb{R}$ onto $\mathbb{R}$. Hence f is invertible by the theorem. We find its inverse f^{-1}. Note that $f^{-1}(y) = x$ if and only if $y = f(x) = x^3 + 1$. So we solve for x in the last equation:

$$x^3 + 1 = y \quad \text{or} \quad x^3 = y - 1 \quad \text{or} \quad x = \sqrt[3]{y - 1}.$$

Thus $f^{-1}(y) = \sqrt[3]{y - 1}$. This computation works for each y in $\mathbb{R}$ and so f^{-1} is completely determined. $\quad\square$

EXAMPLE 4 Consider the function $g: \mathbb{Z} \times \mathbb{Z} \to \mathbb{Z} \times \mathbb{Z}$ given by $g(\langle m, n \rangle) = \langle -n, -m \rangle$. We will check that g is one-to-one and onto, and then we'll find its inverse. To show that g is one-to-one we need to show that

$$g(\langle m, n \rangle) = g(\langle m', n' \rangle) \quad \text{implies} \quad \langle m, n \rangle = \langle m', n' \rangle.$$

First $g(\langle m, n \rangle) = g(\langle m', n' \rangle)$ implies $\langle -n, -m \rangle = \langle -n', -m' \rangle$. Since these ordered pairs are equal we must have $-n = -n'$ and $-m = -m'$. Hence $m = m'$ and $n = n'$ so that $\langle m, n \rangle = \langle m', n' \rangle$ as desired.

To show that g maps onto $\mathbb{Z} \times \mathbb{Z}$, we consider $\langle p, q \rangle$ in $\mathbb{Z} \times \mathbb{Z}$ and need to find $\langle m, n \rangle$ in $\mathbb{Z} \times \mathbb{Z}$ so that $g(\langle m, n \rangle) = \langle p, q \rangle$. Thus we need $\langle -n, -m \rangle = \langle p, q \rangle$, and this tells us that n should be $-p$ and m should be $-q$. In other words, given $\langle p, q \rangle$ in $\mathbb{Z} \times \mathbb{Z}$ we see that $\langle -q, -p \rangle$ is an element in $\mathbb{Z} \times \mathbb{Z}$ such that $g(\langle -q, -p \rangle) = \langle p, q \rangle$. That is, g maps $\mathbb{Z} \times \mathbb{Z}$ onto $\mathbb{Z} \times \mathbb{Z}$.

To find the inverse of g we need to consider $\langle p, q \rangle$ in $\mathbb{Z} \times \mathbb{Z}$ and find $g^{-1}(\langle p, q \rangle)$. But this is, by definition, exactly the element in $\mathbb{Z} \times \mathbb{Z}$ that g maps onto $\langle p, q \rangle$. So the work of the last paragraph must be relevant and, in fact, shows that g maps $\langle -q, -p \rangle$ onto $\langle p, q \rangle$. Hence $g^{-1}(\langle p, q \rangle) = \langle -q, -p \rangle$ for all $\langle p, q \rangle$ in $\mathbb{Z} \times \mathbb{Z}$.

It is interesting to note that $g = g^{-1}$ in this case. $\quad\square$

Inverses of functions are so useful that we sometimes restrict functions that are not one-to-one to smaller domains on which they are one-to-one. If we then arrange for the codomain to equal the image of the function, we obtain an invertible function.

EXAMPLE 5   (a) Consider $f: \mathbb{R} \to \mathbb{R}$ where $f(x) = x^2$. Then f is not one-to-one, but it is one-to-one if we restrict the domain to $[0, \infty)$. Thus we define a new function F by the same rule $F(x) = x^2$ but having $\text{Dom}(F) = [0, \infty)$. Then F is one-to-one. In fact, $F: [0, \infty) \to [0, \infty)$ is one-to-one and onto. It is this function that has $F^{-1}(x) = \sqrt{x}$ as its inverse; see Example 1(a).

The function F is called the **restriction** of f to $[0, \infty)$. This sort of restriction is clearly possible and desirable in many settings of interest.

(b) You should be able to follow this example even if you know no trigonometry. It turns out that none of the trigonometric functions are one-to-one. For example, consider the graph of $\sin x$ in Figure 2. But $\sin x$ is

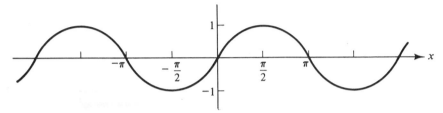

The function $\sin x$

FIGURE 2

one-to-one if its domain is restricted to, say, $[-\pi/2, \pi/2]$. See Figure 3(a) where we have denoted the restriction by $\text{Sin } x$. With codomain $[-1, 1]$, we obtain an invertible function; the inverse is given in Figure 3(b). This is the

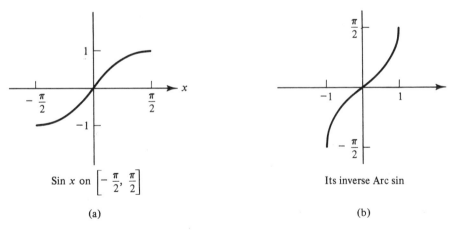

$\text{Sin } x$ on $\left[-\dfrac{\pi}{2}, \dfrac{\pi}{2}\right]$ Its inverse Arc sin

(a)   (b)

FIGURE 3

inverse sine or Arcsin encountered in trigonometry, calculus and many hand-held calculators. □

Consider a function $f: S \to T$. For a subset A of S, we define
$$f(A) = \{f(x) : x \in A\}.$$

Thus $f(A)$ is the set of images $f(x)$ as x varies over A. We call $f(A)$ the **image of the set A under f.**

If f is invertible and B is a subset of T, then clearly

$$f^{-1}(B) = \{f^{-1}(y) : y \in B\}.$$

Since $f^{-1}(y) = x$ if and only if $f(x) = y$, we have

$$f^{-1}(B) = \{x \in S : f(x) \in B\}.$$

The last set written makes sense even if f is not invertible. Because of this we use the useful, but misleading, notation $f^{-1}(B)$ for this last set *even when f^{-1} does not represent a function.* This standard notation will appear more natural in the context of relations later on. The reader needs to become comfortable with its usage now. We recapitulate: If $f: S \to T$ and $B \subseteq T$, then we define

$$f^{-1}(B) = \{x \in S : f(x) \in B\}.$$

The set $f^{-1}(B)$ is called the **pre-image of the set B under f.** This notation will be used whether f is invertible or not. If f is invertible, then the pre-image of the subset B of T under f equals the image of B under f^{-1}.

Finally, for $y \in T$ we write $f^{-1}(y)$ for the set $f^{-1}(\{y\})$. That is,

$$f^{-1}(y) = \{x \in S : f(x) = y\}.$$

This set is the **pre-image of the element y under f.** Note that solving the equation $f(x) = y$ for x is equivalent to finding the set $f^{-1}(y)$. That is, $f^{-1}(y)$ is the **solution set** for the equation $f(x) = y$. As with equations in algebra, the set $f^{-1}(y)$ might have one element, several elements or no elements at all.

EXAMPLE 6   (a) Consider $f: \mathbb{R} \to \mathbb{R}$ where $f(x) = x^2$. Then we have

$$f^{-1}(4) = \{x \in \mathbb{R} : x^2 = 4\} = \{-2, 2\},$$

the solution set of the equation $x^2 = 4$. The pre-image of the set $[1, 9]$ is

$$f^{-1}([1, 9]) = \{x \in \mathbb{R} : x^2 \in [1, 9]\} = \{x \in \mathbb{R} : 1 \leqq x^2 \leqq 9\}$$
$$= [-3, -1] \cup [1, 3].$$

Also we have $f^{-1}([-1, 0]) = \{0\}$ and $f^{-1}([-1, 1]) = [-1, 1]$.

(b) Consider the function $g: \mathbb{N} \times \mathbb{N} \to \mathbb{N}$ defined by $g(\langle m, n \rangle) = m^2 + n^2$. Then

$$g^{-1}(0) = \{\langle 0, 0 \rangle\}, \qquad g^{-1}(1) = \{\langle 0, 1 \rangle, \langle 1, 0 \rangle\},$$
$$g^{-1}(2) = \{\langle 1, 1 \rangle\}, \qquad g^{-1}(3) = \varnothing, \qquad g^{-1}(4) = \{\langle 0, 2 \rangle, \langle 2, 0 \rangle\},$$

etc. Note also that $g^{-1}(25) = \{\langle 0, 5 \rangle, \langle 3, 4 \rangle, \langle 4, 3 \rangle, \langle 5, 0 \rangle\}$.

(c) Let Σ be an alphabet and let L be the length function on Σ^*: $L(w) = \text{length}(w)$ for $w \in \Sigma^*$. Then $L: \Sigma^* \to \mathbb{N}$. For $k \in \mathbb{N}$, $L^{-1}(k) = \Sigma^k$ in the notation of Example 1(c), § 1.3. If $E = \{n \in \mathbb{N} : n \text{ is even}\}$, then

$$L^{-1}(E) = \{w \in \Sigma^* : \text{length}(w) \text{ is even}\} = \bigcup_{k=0}^{\infty} \Sigma^{2k}. \quad \square$$

A function defined on a set S can be used to cut S up into pieces. Consider a function f from S onto T. For each y in T, $f^{-1}(y)$ is a nonempty subset of S. Every x in S is in exactly one subset of the form $f^{-1}(y)$, namely the set $f^{-1}(f(x))$ which consists of all s in S with $f(s) = f(x)$. If $y \neq z$ then we have $f^{-1}(y) \cap f^{-1}(z) = \varnothing$. Thus the various sets $f^{-1}(y)$ are disjoint and their union $\bigcup_{y \in T} f^{-1}(y)$ is S. There is a technical term for such a family of sets.

Definition A **partition** of a nonempty set S is a collection of nonempty subsets which are disjoint and whose union is S.

If the partition is indexed by a set I, say $\{A_i : i \in I\}$, these requirements become

$A_i \neq \varnothing$ for each $i \in I$;

for each $i, j \in I$ either $A_i = A_j$ or $A_i \cap A_j = \varnothing$;

$\bigcup_{i \in I} A_i = S$.

EXAMPLE 7 (a) Let L be the length function on Σ^*, as in Example 6(c). The partition $\{L^{-1}(k) : k \in \mathbb{N}\}$ of Σ^* is exactly the partition $\{\Sigma^k : k \in \mathbb{N}\}$. The sets Σ^k are disjoint and their union $\bigcup_{k \in \mathbb{N}} \Sigma^k$ equals Σ^*.

(b) Consider the function $f \colon \mathbb{N} \times \mathbb{N} \to \mathbb{Z}$ defined by $f(\langle m, n \rangle) = m - n$. The partition $\{f^{-1}(k) : k \in \mathbb{Z}\}$ of $\mathbb{N} \times \mathbb{N}$ is sketched in Figure 4. For example,

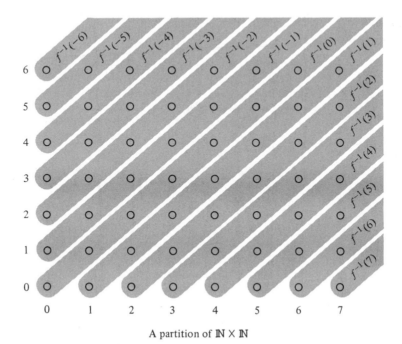

A partition of $\mathbb{N} \times \mathbb{N}$

FIGURE 4

the set $f^{-1}(2)$ consists of the pairs $\langle m, n \rangle$ with $m - n = 2$, i.e., $\langle 2, 0 \rangle$, $\langle 3, 1 \rangle$, $\langle 4, 2 \rangle$, etc. ▯

EXERCISES 3.2

1. Find the inverses of the following functions mapping $\mathbb{R}$ into $\mathbb{R}$.
   (a) $f(x) = 2x + 3$
   (b) $g(x) = x^3 - 2$
   (c) $h(x) = (x - 2)^3$
   (d) $k(x) = \sqrt[3]{x} + 7$

2. Many hand-held calculators have the functions $\log x$, x^2, $\sqrt{x}$ and $1/x$.
   (a) Specify the domains of these functions.
   (b) Which of these functions are inverses to each other?
   (c) Which of these functions commute with respect to composition?
   (d) Some hand-held calculators also have the functions $\sin x$, $\cos x$ and $\tan x$. If you know a little trigonometry, repeat parts (a), (b) and (c) for these functions.

3. Here are some functions from $\mathbb{N} \times \mathbb{N}$ to $\mathbb{N}$: $\text{SUM}(\langle m, n \rangle) = m + n$, $\text{PROD}(\langle m, n \rangle) = m * n$, $\text{MAX}(\langle m, n \rangle) = \max\{m, n\}$, $\text{MIN}(\langle m, n \rangle) = \min\{m, n\}$; $*$ denotes multiplication of integers.
   (a) Which of these functions map $\mathbb{N} \times \mathbb{N}$ onto $\mathbb{N}$?
   (b) Show that none of these functions is one-to-one.
   (c) For each of these functions F, how big is the set $F^{-1}(4)$?

4. Here are some functions mapping $\mathcal{P}(\mathbb{N}) \times \mathcal{P}(\mathbb{N})$ into $\mathcal{P}(\mathbb{N})$: $\text{UNION}(\langle A, B \rangle) = A \cup B$, $\text{INTER}(\langle A, B \rangle) = A \cap B$ and $\text{SYM}(\langle A, B \rangle) = A \oplus B$.
   (a) Show that each of these functions maps $\mathcal{P}(\mathbb{N}) \times \mathcal{P}(\mathbb{N})$ onto $\mathcal{P}(\mathbb{N})$.
   (b) Show that none of these functions are one-to-one.
   (c) For each of these functions F, how big is the set $F^{-1}(\varnothing)$? the set $F^{-1}(\{0\})$?

5. Here are two "shift functions" mapping $\mathbb{N}$ into $\mathbb{N}$: $f(n) = n + 1$ and $g(n) = \max\{0, n - 1\}$ for $n \in \mathbb{N}$.
   (a) Calculate $f(n)$ for $n = 0, 1, 2, 3, 4, 73$.
   (b) Calculate $g(n)$ for $n = 0, 1, 2, 3, 4, 73$.
   (c) Show that f is one-to-one but does not map $\mathbb{N}$ onto $\mathbb{N}$.
   (d) Show that g maps $\mathbb{N}$ onto $\mathbb{N}$ but is not one-to-one.
   (e) Show that $g \circ f = 1_{\mathbb{N}}$ but that $f \circ g \neq 1_{\mathbb{N}}$.

6. We define $f : \mathbb{N} \to \mathbb{N}$ and $g : \mathbb{N} \to \mathbb{N}$ as follows: $f(n) = 2n$ for all $n \in \mathbb{N}$, $g(n) = n/2$ if n is even and $g(n) = (n - 1)/2$ if n is odd.
   (a) Calculate $g(n)$ for $n = 0, 1, 2, 3, 4, 73$.
   (b) Show that $g \circ f = 1_{\mathbb{N}}$ but that $f \circ g \neq 1_{\mathbb{N}}$.

7. If $f : S \to S$ and $f \circ f = 1_S$, then f is its own inverse. Show that the following functions are their own inverses.
   (a) The function $f : (0, \infty) \to (0, \infty)$ where $f(x) = 1/x$.
   (b) Let S be a set and define $\phi : \mathcal{P}(S) \to \mathcal{P}(S)$ by $\phi(A) = A^c$.
   (c) Let $\mathfrak{M}_{n,n}$ be the set of $n \times n$ matrices and define $\text{TRANS}(A) = A^T$ for A in $\mathfrak{M}_{n,n}$.
   (d) Let C be a set and define $\text{REV}: C \times C \to C \times C$ by $\text{REV}(\langle x, y \rangle) = \langle y, x \rangle$.

8. Let A be a subset of some set S and consider the characteristic function χ_A of A. Find $\chi_A^{-1}(1)$ and $\chi_A^{-1}(0)$.

9. Let $f: S \to T$ and $g: T \to U$ be invertible functions. Show that $g \circ f$ is invertible and that $(g \circ f)^{-1} = f^{-1} \circ g^{-1}$.

10. Let $f: S \to T$ be an invertible function. Show that f^{-1} is invertible and that $(f^{-1})^{-1} = f$.

11. Consider functions $f: S \to T$ and $g: T \to S$ such that $g \circ f = 1_S$. Nontrivial examples of such pairs of functions appear in Exercises 5 and 6.
   (a) Prove that f is one-to-one.
   (b) Prove that g maps T onto S.

12. Consider the function $f: \mathbb{R} \times \mathbb{R} \to \mathbb{R} \times \mathbb{R}$ defined by
$$f(\langle x, y \rangle) = \langle x + y, x - y \rangle.$$
   (a) Prove that f is one-to-one on $\mathbb{R} \times \mathbb{R}$.
   (b) Prove that f maps $\mathbb{R} \times \mathbb{R}$ onto $\mathbb{R} \times \mathbb{R}$.
   (c) Find the inverse function f^{-1}.
   (d) Find the composite functions $f \circ f^{-1}$ and $f \circ f$.

13. Let $f: S \to T$.
   (a) Show that $f(f^{-1}(B)) \subseteq B$ for subsets B of T.
   (b) Show that $A \subseteq f^{-1}(f(A))$ for subsets A of S.
   (c) Show that $f^{-1}(B_1 \cap B_2) = f^{-1}(B_1) \cap f^{-1}(B_2)$ for subsets B_1 and B_2 of T.
   (d) Under what conditions on B does equality hold in part (a)?

14. Let $f: S \to T$. Prove or disprove. If false, a single example will suffice.
   (a) $f(A_1 \cap A_2) = f(A_1) \cap f(A_2)$ for subsets A_1 and A_2 of S.
   (b) $f(A_1 \setminus A_2) = f(A_1) \setminus f(A_2)$ for subsets A_1 and A_2 of S.
   (c) $f(A_1) = f(A_2)$ implies $A_1 = A_2$.

15. Consider the function $f: \mathbb{N} \times \mathbb{N} \to \mathbb{N}$ defined by $f(\langle m, n \rangle) = m + n$.
   (a) List the elements in each of the sets $f^{-1}(0)$, $f^{-1}(1)$, $f^{-1}(2)$ and $f^{-1}(3)$.
   (b) Sketch the partition $\{f^{-1}(k) : k \in \mathbb{N}\}$ of $\mathbb{N} \times \mathbb{N}$; compare Figure 4.

16. Consider the functions g and h mapping $\mathbb{Z}$ into $\mathbb{N}$ defined as follows: $g(n) = |n|$, $h(n) = 1 + (-1)^n$.
   (a) Describe the sets in the partition $\{g^{-1}(k) : k \in \mathbb{N}\}$ of $\mathbb{Z}$. How many sets are there?
   (b) Describe the sets in the partition $\{h^{-1}(k) : k \in \mathbb{N}\}$ of $\mathbb{Z}$. How many sets are there?

17. (a) One can show that if $f: T \to U$ is one-to-one and if $g: S \to T$ and $h: S \to T$ satisfy $f \circ g = f \circ h$, then $g = h$. Give examples of functions f, g and h for which $f \circ g = f \circ h$ but $g \neq h$.
   (b) Give examples of functions f, g and h for which $g \circ f = h \circ f$ but $g \neq h$.
   (c) Give a condition on f so that $g \circ f = h \circ f$ implies $g = h$.

§ 3.3 *Sequences*

An important family of functions consists of those whose domains are the set $\mathbb{N} = \{0, 1, 2, \ldots\}$ of natural numbers [or $\{m, m + 1, m + 2, \ldots\}$ for some integer m]. Such functions are called **sequences**. Thus a sequence on $\mathbb{N}$ is a function that has a specified value for each integer $n \in \mathbb{N}$. It has been

$$X+y-x-y+1 \qquad x-y-x+1+y$$

traditional in mathematics to denote a sequence by a letter such as s and to denote its value at n as s_n rather than $s(n)$. We frequently call s_n the nth **term** of the sequence. It is often convenient to denote the sequence itself by (s_n) or $(s_n)_{n \in \mathbb{N}}$ or $(s_0, s_1, s_2, \ldots)$.

EXAMPLE 1   (a) Consider the sequence $(s_n)_{n \in \mathbb{N}}$ where $s_n = n^2$. This is the sequence $(0, 1, 4, 9, 16, \ldots)$. Formally, of course, this is the function with domain $\mathbb{N}$ whose value at each n is n^2. The *set* of values is $\{0, 1, 4, 9, 16, \ldots\} = \{n^2 : n \in \mathbb{N}\}$.

(b) Consider the sequence given by $a_n = (-1)^n$ for $n \in \mathbb{N}$, i.e., $(a_n)_{n \in \mathbb{N}}$ where $a_n = (-1)^n$. This is the sequence $(1, -1, 1, -1, 1, -1, 1, \ldots)$. Formally, this is a function whose domain is $\mathbb{N}$ and whose *set* of values is $\{-1, 1\}$.   ▯

As the last example suggests, it is important to distinguish between a sequence and its set of values. We will always use parentheses $(\ )$ to signify a sequence and braces $\{\ \}$ to signify a set. The sequence given by $a_n = (-1)^n$ has an infinite number of terms even though their values are repeated over and over. On the other hand, the *set* $\{(-1)^n : n \in \mathbb{N}\}$ is exactly the set $\{-1, 1\}$ consisting of two numbers.

EXAMPLE 2   An important sequence is given by $s_n = n!$ for $n \geq 0$, where $n!$ represents "n factorial" introduced in § 1.3. As examples, $s_0 = s_1 = 1$, $s_5 = 120$ and $s_6 = 720$.   ▯

As we noted in § 1.4, in computer science it is desirable to communicate information in a linear fashion, without subscripts and other decorations. Accordingly, sequences are frequently written as functions with parentheses around the variable. Moreover, sequences and functions are frequently given suggestive abbreviated names, such as SEQ, FACT, SUM, etc.

EXAMPLE 3   (a) Let $\text{FACT}(n) = n!$ for $n \in \mathbb{N}$. This is exactly the same sequence as in Example 2; only its name [FACT, instead of s] has been changed. Note that $\text{FACT}(n + 1) = (n + 1)*\text{FACT}(n)$ for $n \in \mathbb{N}$, where $*$ denotes multiplication of integers.

(b) For $n \in \mathbb{N}$, let $\text{TWO}(n) = 2^n$. Then TWO is a sequence. Note that $\text{TWO}(n + 1) = 2*\text{TWO}(n)$ for $n \in \mathbb{N}$.   ▯

Our definition of sequence allows the domain to be any set of the form $\{m, m + 1, m + 2, \ldots\}$ where m is an integer.

EXAMPLE 4   Consider the sequence (b_n) given by $b_n = 1/n^2$ for $n \geq 1$. Clearly this sequence needs to have its domain avoid the value $n = 0$.   ▯

So far, all of our sequences have had real numbers as values. However, there is no such restriction in the definition and, in fact, we will be interested in sequences with values in other sets.

EXAMPLE 5 (a) For each $n \in \mathbb{P}$, we define the following subsets of $\mathbb{Z}$:

$$A_n = \{m \in \mathbb{Z} : m \text{ divides } n\}.$$

Thus $A_1 = \{1, -1\}$, $A_2 = \{1, -1, 2, -2\}, \ldots, A_6 = \{1, -1, 2, -2, 3, -3, 6, -6\}$, etc. These sets are the terms of a sequence $(A_n)_{n \in \mathbb{P}}$ of subsets of $\mathbb{Z}$.

(b) Another sequence $(D_n)_{n \in \mathbb{N}}$ of subsets of $\mathbb{Z}$ is defined by

$$D_n = \{m \in \mathbb{Z} : m \text{ is a multiple of } n\}$$
$$= \{0, \pm n, \pm 2n, \pm 3n, \ldots\}.$$

(c) Let Σ be an alphabet. For $k \in \mathbb{N}$ we define

$$\Sigma^k = \{w \in \Sigma^* : \text{length}(w) = k\}.$$

The sequence $(\Sigma^k)_{k \in \mathbb{N}}$ is a sequence of subsets of Σ^*.

(d) An example of a matrix-valued sequence $(\mathbf{M}_n)$ is given by

$$\mathbf{M}_n = \begin{bmatrix} n & (-1)^n \\ 1 & -n \end{bmatrix} \quad \text{for} \quad n \in \mathbb{N}.$$

The first few terms are:

$$\mathbf{M}_0 = \begin{bmatrix} 0 & 1 \\ 1 & 0 \end{bmatrix}, \quad \mathbf{M}_1 = \begin{bmatrix} 1 & -1 \\ 1 & -1 \end{bmatrix} \quad \text{and} \quad \mathbf{M}_2 = \begin{bmatrix} 2 & 1 \\ 1 & -2 \end{bmatrix}. \quad \square$$

Note that a sequence $(s_n)_{n \in \mathbb{N}}$ can always be viewed as a set indexed by $\mathbb{N}$ and that a set indexed by $\mathbb{N}$ can always be viewed as a sequence. See Example 5, parts (b) and (c).

We will also have occasion to use finite sequences. A **finite sequence** is a function whose domain is a finite subset of $\mathbb{Z}$ having the form $\{m, m + 1, \ldots, n\}$. Frequently m will be 0 or 1.

EXAMPLE 6 (a) Consider a finite set S with, say, n elements. The members of the set S can be listed as a sequence $s_1, s_2, \ldots, s_n$ in many ways, in fact in $n!$ ways. Often we choose a listing that will be useful for the problem at hand.

(b) If S is a finite set of real numbers, we might list S in increasing order, so that

$$s_1 < s_2 < s_3 < \cdots < s_{n-1} < s_n,$$

or in decreasing order, so that

$$s_1 > s_2 > s_3 > \cdots > s_{n-1} > s_n.$$

Sometimes we might know that the set S can be indexed by the set $\{1, 2, \ldots, n\}$ but not be sure that all the elements are distinct. In other words, S

has at most n elements and possibly fewer. If the set consists of real numbers, we might list it in nondecreasing order

$$s_1 \leq s_2 \leq s_3 \leq \cdots \leq s_{n-1} \leq s_n$$

or in nonincreasing order

$$s_1 \geq s_2 \geq s_3 \geq \cdots \geq s_{n-1} \geq s_n.$$

(c) The set of prime integers less than 65,536 can be listed as $p_1, p_2,$ $p_3, p_4, \ldots, p_m$ where $p_1 = 2, p_2 = 3, p_3 = 5$, etc. The exact value of m could be determined, but is probably not important.   ▯

EXAMPLE 7   (a) A path in a graph is a finite sequence $e_1, e_2, \ldots, e_n$ of edges that link up with each other. Such a path determines a sequence of vertices $v_1, v_2,$ $\ldots, v_n, v_{n+1}$. The last subscript is $n + 1$ because the number of vertices in a vertex sequence is always one larger than the number of edges.

(b) Computer programs often involve millions of repetitious calculations, but they do stop eventually. The successive values at some address will form a finite sequence. If, for example, the address contains the ith square $SQ(i) = i^2$ at the ith step and if the program terminates after n steps, then we obtain the finite sequence $(SQ(i))_{i=1}^n$, i.e., $1, 4, 9, 16, \ldots, n^2$.   ▯

The sequences in Example 3 have the property that the value of the sequence at $n + 1$ can be calculated in terms of the value at n. Indeed, $FACT(n + 1) = (n + 1) * FACT(n)$ and $TWO(n + 1) = 2 * TWO(n)$. In mathematics, and especially in computer science, it is frequently convenient to define sequences by such means, that is, it is convenient to define their values in terms of previous values. The next section deals with this method of defining sequences.

EXERCISES 3.3

1. Consider the sequence given by $a_n = \dfrac{n-1}{n+1}$ for $n \in \mathbb{P}$.

(a) List the first six terms of this sequence.

(b) Calculate $a_{n+1} - a_n$ for $n = 1, 2, 3$.

(c) Show that $a_{n+1} - a_n = \dfrac{2}{(n+1)(n+2)}$ for $n \in \mathbb{P}$.

2. Consider the sequence given by $b_n = [1 + (-1)^n]/2$ for $n \in \mathbb{N}$.

(a) List the first seven terms of this sequence.

(b) What is its set of values?

3. Consider the matrix-valued sequence (M_n) given by

$$\mathbf{M}_n = \begin{bmatrix} n & n-1 \\ n+1 & n \end{bmatrix}, \qquad n \in \mathbb{N}.$$

(a) Give the first four terms of this sequence.

(b) Calculate $\mathbf{M}_n + \mathbf{M}_n^T$ for $n = 0, 1$ and 2.

(c) Show that $\mathbf{M}_n + \mathbf{M}_n^T = \begin{bmatrix} 2n & 2n \\ 2n & 2n \end{bmatrix}$ for all n.

4. Calculate

(a) $\dfrac{5!}{2!\,3!}$ (b) $\dfrac{6!}{3!\,3!}$ (c) $\dfrac{4!}{0!\,4!}$

5. For $n \in \mathbb{N}$, let $\mathrm{SEQ}(n) = n^2 - n$.

(a) Calculate $\mathrm{SEQ}(n)$ for $n \leqq 6$.

(b) Show that $\mathrm{SEQ}(n+1) = \mathrm{SEQ}(n) + 2n$ for all $n \in \mathbb{N}$.

(c) Show that $\mathrm{SEQ}(n+1) = \dfrac{n+1}{n-1} * \mathrm{SEQ}(n)$ for $n \geqq 2$.

6. For $n = 1, 2, 3, \ldots$, let $\mathrm{SSQ}(n) = \sum\limits_{i=1}^{n} i^2$.

(a) Calculate $\mathrm{SSQ}(n)$ for $n = 1, 2, 3$ and 5.

(b) Observe that $\mathrm{SSQ}(n+1) = \mathrm{SSQ}(n) + (n+1)^2$ for $n \geqq 1$.

(c) It turns out that $\mathrm{SSQ}(73) = 132{,}349$. Use this to calculate $\mathrm{SSQ}(74)$ and $\mathrm{SSQ}(72)$.

7. For the following sequences, write the first several terms until the behavior of the sequence is clear.

(a) $a_n = [2n - 1 + (-1)^n]/4$ for $n \in \mathbb{N}$.

(b) (b_n) where $b_n = a_{n+1}$ for $n \in \mathbb{N}$ and a_n is as in part (a).

(c) $\mathrm{VEC}(n) = \langle a_n, b_n \rangle$ for $n \in \mathbb{N}$.

8. Each integer $n \geqq 2$ can be written uniquely as a product of primes:

$$n = \prod_{j=1}^{s} p_j^{k_j} = p_1^{k_1} p_2^{k_2} \cdots p_s^{k_s}$$

where $p_1 < p_2 < \cdots < p_s$ are primes and $k_1, k_2, \ldots, k_s$ are positive integers. For example, $504 = 2^3 \cdot 3^2 \cdot 7$, i.e., $s = 3$, $p_1 = 2$, $p_2 = 3$, $p_3 = 7$, $k_1 = 3$, $k_2 = 2$ and $k_3 = 1$. For each such n, let $\mathrm{PRIM}(n) = k_1 + k_2 + \cdots + k_s$. Thus $\mathrm{PRIM}(504) = 6$.

(a) Describe the set $\{n : \mathrm{PRIM}(n) = 1\}$.

(b) Calculate $\mathrm{PRIM}(n)$ for $n = 15, 16, 17, 18, 19$ and 20.

(c) Find the smallest n for which $\mathrm{PRIM}(n) = 7$.

(d) Show that $\mathrm{PRIM}(n * m) = \mathrm{PRIM}(n) + \mathrm{PRIM}(m)$ for $n, m \geqq 2$.

9. For each $n \in \mathbb{N}$, let B_n consist of the set of rational numbers that can be written as $k/2^n$ with $k \in \mathbb{Z}$. Then (B_n) is a sequence in $\mathcal{P}(\mathbb{Q})$, the set of subsets of the set $\mathbb{Q}$ of rational numbers.

(a) What is B_0?

(b) Give three numbers that are in $B_1 \backslash B_0$ and three that are in $B_2 \backslash B_1$.

(c) Give three rational numbers that do not belong to $\bigcup\limits_{n \in \mathbb{N}} B_n$.

(d) Show that $B_n \subseteq B_{n+1}$ for all $n \in \mathbb{N}$.

(e) Give an explicit one-to-one correspondence ϕ_n between the sets B_n and B_{n+1}.

(f) Give an explicit one-to-one correspondence between the sets B_0 and B_n.

10. Let (p_n) be the sequence of primes [starting with 2]. It is natural to list the primes in increasing order, so that $p_0 = 2, p_1 = 3, p_2 = 5$, etc. Show that $p_6 = p_0 + p_1 + p_2 + p_3$.

§ 3.4   Recursive Definitions

We say that a sequence is defined **recursively** provided:

(B) some finite set of values, usually the first one or first few, are specified,

(R) the remaining values of the sequence are defined in terms of previous values of the sequence. A formula which does this is called a **recursion formula** or **relation.**

The requirement (B) will provide the **basis** or starting point for the definition. The remainder of the sequence will be obtained by using the recursion relation (R) repeatedly. [The relation will occur again and again, i.e., it "recurs."]

EXAMPLE 1   (a) We define the sequence FACT via

(B) FACT(0) = 1,
(R) FACT($n + 1$) = $(n + 1)*$FACT(n) for $n \in \mathbb{N}$.

One can use (R) to calculate FACT(1), then FACT(2), then FACT(3), etc. and one quickly sees that FACT(n) = $n!$ for the first several values of n. This identity can be proved for all n by mathematical induction; a proof is requested in Exercise 17. Since we understand the sequence $n!$, the recursive definition above may seem silly, but we will try to convince you in part (b) that recursive definitions of even simple sequences are useful.

(b) Consider the sequence SUM(n) = $\sum_{i=0}^{n} 1/i!$. To write a computer program that calculates the values of SUM for large values of n, one would use the following recursive definition:

(B) SUM(0) = 1,
(R) SUM($n + 1$) = SUM(n) + $\dfrac{1}{(n + 1)!}$.

The added term in (R) is the reciprocal of $(n + 1)!$, so FACT($n + 1$) will be needed as the program progresses. At each n, one could instruct the program to calculate FACT($n + 1$) from scratch or one could store a large number of these values. Clearly, it would be more efficient to alternately calculate FACT($n + 1$) and SUM($n + 1$) using the recursive definition in part (a) for FACT and the recursive definition above for SUM.

(c) Define the sequence SEQ as follows:

(B) SEQ(0) = 1,

(R) SEQ($n + 1$) = ($n + 1$)/SEQ(n) for $n \in \mathbb{N}$.

With $n = 0$, we find SEQ(1) = 1/1 = 1. Then with $n = 1$, we find SEQ(2) = 2/1 = 2. Continuing in this fashion, we find that the first few terms are 1, 1, 2, 3/2, 8/3, 15/8, 16/5, 35/16. It is by no means apparent what a general formula for SEQ(n) might be. It is evident that SEQ(73) exists but it would take considerable calculation to find it. □

In Example 1, how did we *know* that SEQ(73) exists? Our certainty is based on the belief that recursive definitions do indeed define sequences on all of $\mathbb{N}$, unless some step leads to an illegal computation such as division by 0. We prove that the recursive definition in Example 1 defines a sequence by proving

$$p(n) = \text{"SEQ}(n) \text{ is defined and SEQ}(n) \neq 0\text{"}$$

for all $n \in \mathbb{N}$. We do so by induction. Since SEQ(0) = 1, $p(0)$ is clearly true. Assume that $p(n)$ is true. Then SEQ(n) $\neq 0$ and so ($n + 1$)/SEQ(n) is a well-defined real number. Thus SEQ($n + 1$) is defined by the recursive definition. Moreover, SEQ($n + 1$) $\neq 0$ since $n + 1 \neq 0$. That is, $p(n + 1)$ is true. Since $p(n)$ implies $p(n + 1)$ for all $n \in \mathbb{N}$, the Principle of Mathematical Induction shows that all $p(n)$'s are true.

The foregoing examples of recursive definitions were special in that the ($n + 1$)st value of the sequence depended only on the nth value of the sequence. Not all sequences have this property.

EXAMPLE 2

(a) The **Fibonacci sequence** is defined as follows:

(B) FIB(0) = FIB(1) = 1,

(R) FIB(n) = FIB($n - 1$) + FIB($n - 2$) for $n \geqq 2$.

Note that the recursion formula makes no sense for $n = 1$ and so FIB(1) had to be defined separately in the basis. The first few terms of this sequence are

$$1, 1, 2, 3, 5, 8, 13, 21, 34, 55, 89.$$

(b) Here is an easy way to define the sequence 0, 0, 1, 1, 2, 2, 3, 3, ...

(B) SEQ(0) = SEQ(1) = 0,

(R) SEQ(n) = 1 + SEQ($n - 2$) for $n \geqq 2$.

Compare Exercise 5 in § 3.3. □

EXAMPLE 3   In the video game of Example 1 of § 2.5, the number of aliens after 5n seconds was denoted by $A(n)$. If no aliens were eliminated, then $A(1) = 1$ and $A(n + 1) = 2 \cdot A(n)$ for $n \geqq 1$. This is a recursively defined sequence, actually a finite sequence in view of the limitations of a video screen. An easy induction argument in Example 2 of § 2.5 showed that $A(n) = 2^{n-1}$ for all possible *n*. ◻

EXAMPLE 4 Consider the graph in Figure 1. In § 0.3 we indicated that the matrix

$$\mathbf{M} = \begin{bmatrix} 1 & 1 \\ 1 & 0 \end{bmatrix}$$

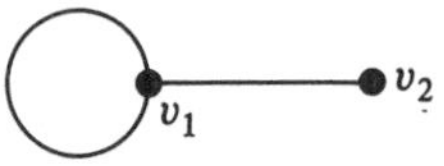

FIGURE 1

can be used to study this graph. In particular, the entries in the *n*th power $\mathbf{M}^n$ give the exact number of paths of length *n* that connect two vertices. Matrix multiplication is discussed in § 4.1, and Exercise 14 of that section asks for a proof that

$$\mathbf{M}^n = \begin{bmatrix} \text{FIB}(n) & \text{FIB}(n-1) \\ \text{FIB}(n-1) & \text{FIB}(n-2) \end{bmatrix} \quad \text{for} \quad n \geq 2.$$

Thus this simple graph leads to matrices whose entries are defined by the recursively defined Fibonacci sequence in Example 2. ◻

Of course we can give recursive definitions even if the sequence is not real-valued.

EXAMPLE 5 Let *S* be a set and let *f* be a function from *S* into *S*. We define

(B) $f^{(0)} = 1_S$ [the identity function on *S*],
(R) $f^{(n+1)} = f^{(n)} \circ f$.

Thus

(1) $f^{(1)} = f, \quad f^{(2)} = f \circ f, \quad f^{(3)} = f \circ f \circ f, \quad$ etc.

In other words,

(2) $f^{(n)} = f \circ f \circ \cdots \circ f \quad [n \text{ times}]$.

$f^{(n)}$ is simply the composite of the function *f*, *n* times. The recursive definition is more precise than the "etc." in (1) or the three dots in (2). ◻

As in Example 5, we will often use recursive definitions to give concise definitions for concepts that we already understand quite well.

EXAMPLE 6 Let *a* be a nonzero real number.

(B) $a^0 = 1$,
(R) $a^{n+1} = a^n \cdot a$ for $n \in \mathbb{N}$.

Equivalently,

(B) POW(0) = 1,

(R) POW($n + 1$) = POW(n)*a for $n \in \mathbb{N}$. □

EXAMPLE 7 Let $(a_j)_{j \in \mathbb{P}}$ be a sequence of real numbers. Then

(B) $\displaystyle\prod_{j=1}^{1} a_j = a_1,$

(R) $\displaystyle\prod_{j=1}^{n+1} a_j = a_{n+1} \cdot \prod_{j=1}^{n} a_j$ for $n \geq 1.$

Equivalently,

(B) PROD(1) = a_1,

(R) PROD($n + 1$) = a_{n+1}*PROD(n) for $n \geq 1$.

These recursive definitions start at $n = 1$. An alternative is to define the "empty product" to be 1, i.e.,

(B) $\displaystyle\prod_{j=1}^{0} a_j = 1$ [which looks peculiar],

or

(B) PROD(0) = 1.

Then the same recursive relation (R) as before serves to define the remaining terms of the sequence. □

EXERCISES 3.4

1. We recursively define $s_0 = 1$ and $s_{n+1} = 2/s_n$ for $n \in \mathbb{N}$.
   (a) List the first few terms of the sequence.
   (b) What is the set of values of s?

2. We recursively define SEQ(0) = 0 and SEQ($n + 1$) = $1/[1 + \text{SEQ}(n)]$ for $n \in \mathbb{N}$. Calculate SEQ(n) for $n = 1, 2, 3, 4$ and 6.

3. Consider the sequence $(1, 3, 9, 27, 81, \ldots)$.
   (a) Give a formula for the nth term SEQ(n) where SEQ(0) = 1.
   (b) Give a recursive definition for the sequence SEQ.

4. (a) Give a recursive definition for the sequence $(2, 2^2, (2^2)^2, ((2^2)^2)^2, \ldots)$, i.e., $(2, 4, 16, 256, \ldots)$.
   (b) Give a recursive definition for the sequence $(2, 2^2, 2^{(2^2)}, 2^{(2^{(2^2)})}, \ldots)$, i.e., $(2, 4, 16, 65536, \ldots)$.

5. Is the following a recursive definition for a sequence SEQ? Explain.

   (B) SEQ(0) = 1,
   (R) SEQ($n + 1$) = SEQ(n)$/[100 - n]$.

6. (a) Calculate SEQ(9) where SEQ is as in Example 1(c).
   (b) Calculate FIB(11) where FIB is as in Example 2(a).

7. We recursively define $a_0 = a_1 = 1$ and $a_n = a_{n-1} + 2a_{n-2}$ for $n \geq 2$.
   (a) Calculate a_n for $n \leq 6$.
   (b) Prove that all the terms a_n are odd integers.

8. Recursively define $b_0 = b_1 = 1$ and $b_n = 2b_{n-1} + b_{n-2}$ for $n \geq 2$.
   (a) Calculate b_n for $n \leq 5$.
   (b) Explain why all the terms b_n are odd integers.

9. Let $SEQ(0) = 1$ and $SEQ(n) = \sum_{i=0}^{n-1} SEQ(i)$ for $n \geq 1$. This is actually a simple, familiar sequence. What is it?

10. Consider the sequence defined by
    (B) $SEQ(0) = 1$, $SEQ(1) = 0$,
    (R) $SEQ(n) = SEQ(n-2)$ for $n \geq 2$.

    (a) List the first few terms of this sequence.
    (b) What is the set of values of this sequence?

11. Consider the sequence defined by
    (B) $SEQ(0) = 0$, $SEQ(1) = 1$,
    (R) $SEQ(n) = \dfrac{1}{n} * SEQ(n-1) + \dfrac{n-1}{n} * SEQ(n-2)$ for $n \geq 2$.

    (a) List the first few terms of this sequence.
    (b) Explain why $0 \leq SEQ(n) \leq 1$ for all n.

12. We recursively define $a_0 = 0$, $a_1 = 1$, $a_2 = 2$ and $a_n = a_{n-1} - a_{n-2} + a_{n-3}$ for $n \geq 3$.
    (a) List the first few terms of the sequence until the pattern is clear.
    (b) What is the set of values of the sequence?

13. Verify the equalities in formula (1) of Example 5.

14. Let $(a_1, a_2, \ldots)$ be a sequence of real numbers.
    (a) Give a recursive definition for $SUM(n) = \sum_{j=1}^{n} a_j$ for $n \geq 1$.
    (b) Revise your recursive definition for $SUM(n)$ by starting with $n = 0$. What is the "empty sum"?

15. Let $(A_1, A_2, \ldots)$ be a sequence of subsets of some set S.
    (a) Give a recursive definition for $\bigcup_{j=1}^{n} A_j$.
    (b) How would you define the "empty union"?
    (c) Give a recursive definition for $\bigcap_{j=1}^{n} A_j$.
    (d) How would you define the "empty intersection"?

16. Let $(A_1, A_2, \ldots)$ be a sequence of subsets of some set S. Define
    (B) $SYM(1) = A_1$,
    (R) $SYM(n+1) = A_{n+1} \oplus SYM(n)$ for $n \geq 1$.

    Recall that $\oplus$ denotes symmetric difference. It turns out that an element x in S belongs to $SYM(n)$ if and only if the set $\{k : x \in A_k \text{ and } k \leq n\}$ has an odd number of elements. Prove this by mathematical induction.

17. Prove that $\text{FACT}(n) = n!$ for $n \in \mathbb{N}$ where the sequence FACT is defined recursively in Example 1 and $n!$ is defined as in § 1.3.

§ 3.5   *General Recursive Definitions*

The recursive definitions in § 3.4 allowed us to define sequences, i.e., sets of objects that are conveniently indexed by $\mathbb{N}$. More generally, we say that a set of objects is defined **recursively** provided

(B) some members of the set are specified explicitly,

(R) the remaining members of the set are defined in terms of members already defined.

The specification in (B) is called the **basis** for the definition and the recipe in (R) the **recursive clause**.

We begin with an example that is familiar from algebra.

EXAMPLE 1   We recursively define the set POLY($\mathbb{R}$) of **polynomial functions** on $\mathbb{R}$.

(B) The constant functions and the function I, defined by $I(x) = x$ for all $x \in \mathbb{R}$, are polynomial functions.

(R) If f and g are polynomial functions, so are $f + g$ and fg.

We illustrate this definition by showing, step by step, that the function $f(x) = 5 + 2x^2$ is a polynomial function. Let $f_1(x) = 5$ and $f_2(x) = 2$ for all $x \in \mathbb{R}$. Then f_1 and f_2 are polynomial functions by (B). Since I is a polynomial function, so is its square I^2 and hence so is $f_3 = f_2 \cdot I^2$. Note that since $I^2(x) = I(x) \cdot I(x) = x^2$, we have $f_3(x) = 2x^2$ for all x. Finally, since $f = f_1 + f_3$, f is a polynomial function.   ☐

A third condition was implicit in the definition in Example 1, namely the so-called **extremal** condition:

(E) No object is a polynomial function unless it can be obtained from (B) and (R) in a finite number of steps.

We will usually omit the extremal condition, but it should be specified if there is any danger of confusion.

EXAMPLE 2   Let Σ be a finite alphabet. We define the set Σ^* as follows:

(B) The empty word ϵ is in Σ^*.

(R) If w is in Σ^* and x is in Σ, then wx is in Σ^*.

By wx we mean the word obtained by attaching x to the right of the word w.

To illustrate this definition, suppose that $\Sigma = \{a, b, c\}$. By (B), ϵ is in Σ^*. Since $c \in \Sigma$, (R) shows that $\epsilon c = c \in \Sigma^*$. Since $a \in \Sigma$, another application of (R) shows that $ca \in \Sigma^*$. Again, since $b \in \Sigma$, we conclude that $cab \in \Sigma^*$. Letters can be repeated, of course, so $cabb \in \Sigma^*$. In fact, any finite string of letters, using only a, b and c, will be in Σ^*. Note that, as in English, we have obtained the word "*cabb*" by building it from left to right.   ☐

EXAMPLE 3   (a) In reading about trees in Chapter 0, it may have occurred to you that they are built up from smaller trees. It seems as if one can just keep adding leaves, starting with the trivial tree, to get any tree. In fact, the following recursive definition provides an alternative way to describe the class of [finite] trees.

(B) A single vertex is a [trivial] tree.

(R) If T is a tree and v is some element that is not a vertex of T, then we obtain a new tree T' if we add v to the set of vertices of T and if we add a single edge connecting v to some vertex of T.

(b) To illustrate the recursive definition in part (a), we consider the tree T_1 in Figure 1 and pluck leaves, one by one, in any old way until a single vertex is left. We obtain T_2, T_3, T_4, T_5, T_6 in Figure 1. Now to obtain T_1

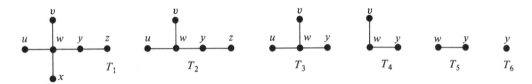

FIGURE 1

using the recursive definition we use Figure 1 *in reverse*. We begin with T_6, which is a tree by the basis (B). By (R), T_5 is a tree because it is obtained from T_6 by adding one vertex, namely w, and one edge, namely wy, connecting w to a vertex of T_6. By (R) again, T_4 is a tree because it is obtained from T_5 by adding v and the edge vw which connects v to a vertex of T_5. Three more such applications of (R) show that T_1 is a tree according to our recursive definition.   ☐

EXAMPLE 4   Sometimes subsets of sets can be defined recursively. For example, consider the following subset of $\mathbb{N} \times \mathbb{N}$:

$$S = \{\langle m, n \rangle : m \leqq 2n\}.$$

The set S is drawn in Figure 2. An examination of the picture suggests how membership in S can be based on membership of elements closer to $\langle 0, 0 \rangle$. If an ordered pair is in S, so are the ordered pairs immediately above it illustrated by the arrows in Figure 2. This observation can be converted into a

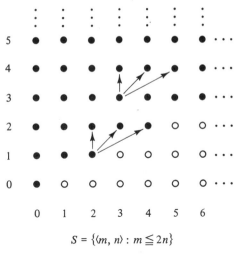

$$S = \{\langle m, n \rangle : m \leq 2n\}$$

FIGURE 2

recursive definition:

(B) $\langle 0, 0 \rangle \in S$.

(R) If $\langle m, n \rangle \in S$, then $\langle m, n + 1 \rangle$, $\langle m + 1, n + 1 \rangle$ and $\langle m + 2, n + 1 \rangle$ are in S.

We illustrate the above definition by showing that $\langle 5, 3 \rangle$ is in S. By the basis (B), $\langle 0, 0 \rangle \in S$. By (R), $\langle 1, 1 \rangle \in S$. Then by (R), $\langle 3, 2 \rangle \in S$ and again by (R) we have $\langle 5, 3 \rangle \in S$. There are other sequences of arguments that will show that $\langle 5, 3 \rangle \in S$. For example, we could apply (R) to conclude that $\langle 2, 1 \rangle$, then $\langle 4, 2 \rangle$, then $\langle 5, 3 \rangle$ are in S. ☐

To help motivate the next example, consider the following questions that probably did not arise in algebra: What is an acceptable formula? What is it that makes $(x + y)(x - y)$ look good and makes $(x + - (^4/y \text{ look worthless? An answer leads to the notion of a **well-formed formula** or **wff**.

EXAMPLE 5

(a) Here is a definition of wff's for algebra.

(B) Numerical constants and variables are wff's.

(R) If f and g are wff's, so are $(f + g)$, $(f - g)$, (fg), (f/g) and (f^g).

Being variables, x and y are wff's. Therefore both $(x + y)$ and $(x - y)$ are wff's. Finally, we conclude that $((x + y)(x - y))$ is a wff. The definition isn't entirely satisfactory, since the outside parentheses here seem extraneous. However, without them the square $(((x + y)(x - y))^2)$ would look like $((x + y)(x - y)^2)$ and these expressions have different meanings. The problem is that in algebra we traditionally allow the omission of parentheses in some circumstances. Taking all the exceptional cases into account, we would be led to a complicated definition. Note also that our definition does not exclude division by 0. Thus (0/0) is a wff even though we would not assign a numerical value to this expression.

(b) In computer science, the symbol ∗ is often used for multiplication and ↑ used for exponentiation [$a \uparrow b$ means a^b]. With this notation, the definition of wff's can be rewritten as:

(B) Numerical constants and variables are wff's.
(R) If f and g are wff's, so are $(f + g)$, $(f - g)$, $(f*g)$, (f/g) and $(f \uparrow g)$.

For example, $(((((X + Y) \uparrow 2) - (2*(X*Y))) - (X \uparrow 2)) - (Y \uparrow 2))$ is a wff.

(c) In § 9.4 we will discuss Polish notation, which is a parenthesis-free notation. The preceding examples and related exercises may help you appreciate its value.   ▢

EXAMPLE 6   (a) A recursive definition of wff's for the propositional calculus is as follows.

(B) Variables, such as p, q, r, are wff's.
(R) If P and Q are wff's, so are $(P \lor Q)$, $(P \land Q)$, $(P \to Q)$, $(P \leftrightarrow Q)$ and $\neg P$.

Note that we do not require parentheses when we negate a proposition. Consequently, the negation symbol $\neg$ always negates the shortest subexpression following it that is a wff. In practice, we tend to omit the outside parentheses and, for the sake of readability, we may use brackets [ ] or braces { } for parentheses.

(b) In the expression $\neg(p \lor q) \to r$, the negation sign negates $(p \lor q)$, i.e., the expression means $(\neg(p \lor q)) \to r$. To emphasize the difference between the expressions $\neg(p \lor q) \to r$ and $\neg((p \lor q) \to r)$ we describe the recursive procedures that lead to each of them. First, $\neg(p \lor q) \to r$ is a wff via the following recursive procedure: p, q, r are wff's; so $(p \lor q)$ is a wff; so $\neg(p \lor q)$ is a wff; finally $(\neg(p \lor q) \to r)$ is a wff. Compare this with the recursive procedure: p, q, r are wff's; so $(p \lor q)$ is a wff; so $((p \lor q) \to r)$ is a wff; and finally $\neg((p \lor q) \to r)$ is a wff.   ▢

Once a set S has been defined recursively, it is often possible and convenient to define a function f recursively on the set. The function definition can sort of ride along with the set definition in the following way:

(B) First define f for the members of the set specified in the basis for defining S.
(R) Whenever a member s of S is defined in terms of previously defined members according to the recursive clause for S, define $f(s)$ appropriately in terms of the values of f assigned to the previously defined members.

EXAMPLE 7   Let Σ^* be as defined in Example 2. Using that definition, we recursively define **length** for words in Σ^*.

(B) length(ϵ) $= 0$.
(R) If length(w) has been defined and $x \in \Sigma$, then length(wx) $= 1 + $ length(w).

For example, length(c) $=$ length(ϵc) $= 1 + $ length(ϵ) $= 1 + 0 = 1$, hence length(ca) $= 1 + $ length(c) $= 1 + 1 = 2$, and therefore length(cab) $= 1 + $ length(ca) $= 1 + 2 = 3$. ▯

One must be extremely careful with this sort of recursive definition. If members of the set can be recursively constructed in more than one way, then we must be certain that the function f is **well-defined**, that is, that the assigned value $f(s)$ does not depend on the way we think of s as constructed.

EXAMPLE 8   Consider the polynomial functions defined in Example 1. Note that if f and g are the polynomial functions defined by $f(x) = 2x^3 - x$ and $g(x) = x^7 + 4x^4 - 8$, then the degree of $f + g$ is 7 and the degree of fg is 10. Because of examples like this, it is tempting to recursively define the **degree** deg of polynomial functions as follows:

(B) deg(c) $= 0$ for constant functions c and deg(I) $= 1$.
(R) If deg(f) and deg(g) have been defined, then deg($f + g$) $=$ max $\{$deg(f), deg(g)$\}$ and deg(fg) $=$ deg(f) $+$ deg(g).

This fine-looking definition *does not work*. For example, let $f(x) = x + 3$, $g(x) = x^2 + x - 1$ and $h(x) = 4 - x^2$ for $x \in \mathbb{R}$. Using (B) and (R), one can show that deg(f) $= 1$ and deg(g) $=$ deg(h) $= 2$, as is reasonable. Then by (R), deg($g + h$) would equal 2, but $g + h$ is equal to the function f. The trouble is that f can be recursively constructed in more than one way and our definition of degree is ambiguous.

Incidentally, there seems to be no easy way to repair the unsuccessful definition above. One would have to prove that if f is a polynomial function there exists a *unique n* in $\mathbb{N}$ such that f can be written as

$$f(x) = \sum_{j=0}^{n} a_j x^j, \quad \text{i.e.,} \quad f = \sum_{j=0}^{n} a_j I^j,$$

where $a_0, a_1, \ldots, a_n$ are real numbers and $a_n \neq 0$. [Except for the uniqueness, this is done in Example 4 of § 6.4.] Then one can safely define deg(f) $= n$. ▯

EXERCISES 3.5

1. Use the definition in Example 1 to show that the following functions on $\mathbb{R}$ are polynomial functions.
   (a) $f(x) = 4 - 3x + 5x^3$
   (b) $g(x) = \pi$
   (c) $h(x) = (x + 1)^3$

2. Use the definition in Example 2 to show that the following objects are in Σ^*, where Σ is the usual English alphabet.
   (a) cat   (b) math
   (c) zzpq   (d) aint

3. Add enough parentheses to the following algebraic expressions so that they are wff's as defined in Example 5(a).
   (a) $x + y + z$ (b) $x + y/z$
   (c) xyz (d) $(x + y)^{x+y}$

4. Add enough parentheses to the following algebraic expressions so that they are wff's as defined in Example 5(b).
   (a) $X + Y + Z$ (b) $X*(Y + Z)$
   (c) $X \uparrow 2 + 2*X + 1$ (d) $X + Y/Z - Z*X$

5. Use the recursive definition of wff in Example 5 to show that the following are wff's.
   (a) $((x^2) + (y^2))$ (b) $(((X \uparrow 2) + (Y \uparrow 2)) \uparrow 2)$
   (c) $((X + Y)*(X - Y))$

6. Use the definition in Example 6 to show that the following are wff's in the propositional calculus.
   (a) $\neg(p \lor q)$ (b) $(\neg p \land \neg q)$
   (c) $((p \leftrightarrow q) \to ((r \to p) \lor q))$

7. Modify the definition in Example 6 so that the "exclusive or" connective $\oplus$ is allowable.

8. Show that if f and g are polynomial functions, so is $f - g$. See Example 1.

9. We recursively define **piecewise polynomial functions** in $\mathbb{R}$.

   (B) Polynomial functions are piecewise polynomial functions.
   (R) If f_1 and f_2 are piecewise polynomial functions and $a \in \mathbb{R}$, then so are f_3 and f_4 where

   $$f_3(x) = \begin{cases} f_1(x) & \text{for } x < a \\ f_2(x) & \text{for } x \geq a \end{cases}, \qquad f_4(x) = \begin{cases} f_1(x) & \text{for } x \leq a \\ f_2(x) & \text{for } x > a \end{cases}.$$

   Show that the following functions on $\mathbb{R}$ are piecewise polynomial functions.
   (a) The absolute value function $g_1(x) = |x|$.
   (b) The function $g_2(x) = |x|^3$.
   (c) The function f where

   $$f(x) = \begin{cases} 0 & \text{for } x < 0 \\ 1 & \text{for } x \geq 0 \end{cases}.$$

   (d) $h(x) = |x| + |x - 1|$.

10. Let $\Sigma = \{a, b\}$. We recursively define a subset S of Σ^* as follows:

    (B) $a \in S$ and $b \in S$,
    (R) if w is in S, then awb is in S.

    (a) List four different members of S.
    (b) Is $aaabb$ in S? Explain.
    (c) Is $aaabbb$ in S? Explain.

11. (a) Give a recursive definition for the following subset of $\mathbb{N} \times \mathbb{N}$:
$S = \{\langle m, n \rangle : n = 3m\}$.

(b) Use the recursive definition to show that $\langle 3, 9 \rangle \in S$.

12. (a) Give a recursive definition for the following subset of $\mathbb{N} \times \mathbb{N}$:
$T = \{\langle m, n \rangle : m \leq n\}$.

(b) Use the recursive definition to show that $\langle 3, 5 \rangle \in T$.

13. Let $\Sigma = \{a, b\}$ and let S be the set of words in Σ^* in which all the a's precede all the b's. For example, *aab*, *abbb*, *a*, *b* and even ϵ belong to S, but *bab* and *ba* do not.

(a) Give a recursive definition for the set S.

(b) Use the recursive definition to show that $abbb \in S$.

(c) Use the recursive definition to show that $aab \in S$.

14. Let $\Sigma = \{a, b\}$ and let T be the set of words in Σ^* which have exactly one a.

(a) Give a recursive definition for the set T.

(b) Use the recursive definition to show that $bbab \in T$.

15. We recursively define the **depth** of a wff as follows; see Example 5.

(B) Numerical constants and variables have depth 0.

(R) If depth(f) and depth(g) have been defined, then each of $(f + g)$, $(f - g)$, (fg), (f/g) and (f^g) has depth equal to $1 + \max\{\text{depth}(f), \text{depth}(g)\}$.

This turns out to be a well-defined definition; compare Example 8. Calculate the depth of the following algebraic expressions:

(a) $((x^2) + (y^2))$

(b) $(((X \uparrow 2) + (Y \uparrow 2)) \uparrow 2)$

(c) $((X + Y)*(X - Y))$

(d) $(((((X + Y) \uparrow 2) - (2*(X*Y))) - (X \uparrow 2)) - (Y \uparrow 2))$

(e) $(((x + (x + y)) + z) - y)$

(f) $(((X*Y)/X) - (Y \uparrow 4))$

16. Let Σ^* be as defined in Example 2. We define the **reversal** $\overleftarrow{w}$ of a word w in Σ^* recursively as follows:

(B) $\overleftarrow{\epsilon} = \epsilon$,

(R) if $\overleftarrow{w}$ has been defined and $x \in \Sigma$, then $\overleftarrow{wx} = x\overleftarrow{w}$.

This is another well-defined definition.

(a) Prove that $\overleftarrow{x} = x$ for all $x \in \Sigma$.

(b) Use this definition to find the reversal of *cab*.

(c) Use this definition to find the reversal of *abbaa*.

(d) If w_1 and w_2 are in Σ^*, what is $\overleftarrow{w_1 w_2}$ in terms of $\overleftarrow{w_1}$ and $\overleftarrow{w_2}$? What is $\overleftarrow{\overleftarrow{w_1}}$?

§ 3.6 *The Division Algorithm*

If we divide 25 by 7 we get 3, with a remainder of 4. That is,

$$25 = 3 \cdot 7 + 4.$$

This example is an instance of a general fact about integers.

Theorem 1
[The Division
Algorithm]

Let m be in $\mathbb{P}$. For each integer n there are unique integers q and r satisfying

$$n = qm + r \quad \text{and} \quad 0 \leq r < m.$$

The numbers q and r are called the **quotient** and **remainder**, respectively, when n is divided by m. In our illustration with $m = 7$ and $n = 25$ we have $q = 3$ and $r = 4$.

It may seem odd to call this theorem an algorithm, since the statement doesn't explain a procedure for finding either q or r. The name for the theorem is traditional, however, and in most applications the actual method of computation is unimportant.

Theorem 1 can be proved fairly quickly with a nonconstructive argument. We choose instead to develop a procedure which gives us values for q and r. First we consider how one might get these numbers by using a calculator. Notice first that we can rewrite the integer equation $n = qm + r$ as an equation in rational numbers:

$$\frac{n}{m} = q + \frac{r}{m}.$$

If $0 \leq r < m$, then $0 \leq r/m < 1$ and thus, by adding q to all terms, $q \leq n/m < q + 1$. That is, q is the largest integer less than or equal to n/m, and $r/m = n/m - q$. For n positive this means that q is the **integer part** of n/m and r/m is the **fractional part**, i.e., the number to the right of the decimal point in n/m.

EXAMPLE 1

(a) With $m = 7$ and $n = 25$ as above, we get

$$\frac{25}{7} = 3 + \frac{4}{7}$$

A pocket calculator gives[1]

$$25 \div 7 \approx 3.571428571,$$

so $4/7 \approx .571428571$ [actually this is a repeating decimal which repeats in blocks of length 6].

(b) To find q and r with $m = 2835$ and $n = 659{,}043$ we punch buttons on the calculator and get

$$659043 \div 2835 \approx 232.4666667.$$

Thus $q = 232$ and $r/2835 \approx .4666667$. Hence $r \approx 2835 \cdot .4666667 = 1323.000095$. That is, $r = 1323$, as we can check. Alternatively, since $q = 232$ we have $r = 659043 - 232 \cdot 2835 = 1323$.

(c) Now consider $m = 7$ and $n = -25$. Then $-25/7 = -3 - 4/7$ as

---

[1] The notation $\approx$ means "approximately equals."

in part (a) and our calculator gives

$$-25 \div 7 \approx -3.571428571.$$

Does this mean that $q = -3$ and $r = -4$? No, because r must be nonnegative. Recall that q is always the largest integer less than or equal to n/m. In our present case, $q = -4$ since $-4 < -3.571428571 < -3$. We have

$$-\frac{25}{7} = -3 - \frac{4}{7} = -4 + 1 - \frac{4}{7} = -4 + \frac{3}{7},$$

so $-25 = (-4)\cdot 7 + 3$ and the answer is $q = -4$ and $r = 3$. ☐

This example shows how to find q and r if we have n/m, but how do we get a value for n/m? At some point, we need a constructive procedure. Most pocket calculators and computers, which operate with a fixed number of decimal digits, perform division using a fairly sophisticated approximate method which is fast and is accurate to as many digits as the machine carries.

The method we are about to describe is much slower. It is exact rather than approximate, however, and its structure allows us to illustrate how some of the ideas we have been examining recently are used in program verification. Checking that the method works gives us a proof that q and r exist. If we then show they are unique we will have proved Theorem 1.

Consider first the case that n is positive. We want an integer q such that $0 \le n - qm < m$, so we simply test successive values $q = 0, 1, 2, \ldots$, producing numbers $n, n - m, n - 2m, \ldots$ of the form $n - qm$ as candidates for r until we hit the first one that's less than m. Then we stop. If we have $n - km < m \le n - (k - 1)m$ for some k, then subtracting m from all terms gives $n - (k + 1)m < 0 \le n - km$, so $0 \le n - km < m$. Thus $q = k$, $r = n - km$ and we are done. In this sense, division is repeated subtraction. Our procedure could be written as follows, starting with given values of $m \in \mathbb{P}$ and $n \in \mathbb{N}$.

DIVISION *Algorithm.*

Step 1. Let $q = 0$ and $r = n$. [These are guesses, and are probably not the final answers.]

Step 2. If $r \ge m$ then replace r by $r - m$, replace q by $q + 1$ and repeat Step 2.

Step 3. Stop. ☐

We can also describe this algorithm with a flowchart as in Figure 1(a) or in a program format as in Figure 1(b). The successive values of r and q produced by an initial choice of $m = 7$ and $n = 25$ are shown in Figure 1(c).

To verify that this algorithm computes q and r correctly, we must show that its execution stops sooner or later and that when it stops the values of

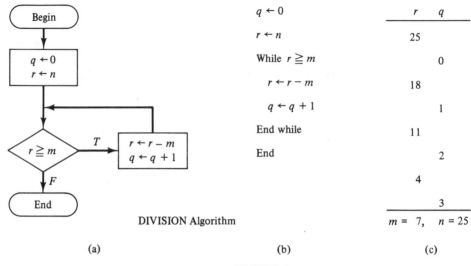

DIVISION Algorithm

(a)   (b)   (c)

FIGURE 1

q and r are the right ones. The stopping values of q and r are determined by the last execution of the loop in Step 2.

Denote by r_i and q_i the values of r and q when the algorithm begins Step 2 for the ith time. The instructions in Step 1 tell us that

$$r_1 = n, \qquad q_1 = 0$$

and Step 2 says that

$$\text{if} \quad r_i \geqq m \quad \text{then} \quad r_{i+1} = r_i - m \quad \text{and} \quad q_{i+1} = q_i + 1.$$

Thus the numbers $r_1, r_2, \ldots$ and $q_1, q_2, \ldots$ are defined recursively.

If k is such that $r_1 > r_2 > \cdots > r_{k-1} \geqq m > r_k$, then when the algorithm reaches Step 2 for the kth time it goes on to Step 3 and produces stopping values q_k and r_k. We want to show that there is such a k and that $n = q_k m + r_k$.

The standard method for proving facts about recursively defined sequences is mathematical induction. The trouble with using induction here is that if the procedure really does work, as we say it will, then the lists $r_1, r_2, \ldots$ and $q_1, q_2, \ldots$ are finite and so are not bona fide sequences. We can't logically say "Let's just ignore the terms that aren't there and use induction anyway," but in fact that is effectively what one does in situations like this. We give a careful, mathematically rigorous proof that the DIVISION algorithm works, as an elementary example of how to use induction to verify an algorithm which stops.

Proof That the DIVISION *Algorithm Works.* For $i \in \mathbb{P}$ let

$$p(i) = \text{``If } r_i \text{ is defined, then } r_i = n - q_i m \geqq 0$$
$$\text{and } q_i = i - 1.\text{''}$$

Then $p(1)$ is true since $q_1 = 0$, $r_1 = n = n - 0 \cdot m = n - q_1 m$ and $n \geqq 0$.

Assume inductively that $p(i)$ is true for some $i \in \mathbb{P}$, and consider $p(i + 1)$. If r_{i+1} is not defined then $p(i + 1)$ is *vacuously* true [at last a use for a vacuously true implication], so we may suppose that r_{i+1} is defined, i.e., that the algorithm gets to Step 2 at least $i + 1$ times. Then the instruction in Step 2 at the ith visit must have said to repeat Step 2. It follows that $r_i \geqq m$ and the recursion formulas $r_{i+1} = r_i - m$ and $q_{i+1} = q_i + 1$ are valid. Hence

$$r_{i+1} = r_i - m$$
$$= n - q_i m - m \qquad \text{by } p(i)$$
$$= n - (q_i + 1)m$$
$$= n - q_{i+1}m$$

and $r_{i+1} = r_i - m \geqq 0$. Since $q_i = i - 1$, we have

$$q_{i+1} = q_i + 1 = (i - 1) + 1 = (i + 1) - 1,$$

and so $p(i + 1)$ is true. By the Principle of Mathematical Induction $p(i)$ is true for every $i \in \mathbb{P}$.

If $j \geqq 2$ and r_j is defined then so is r_{j-1}, and by $p(j)$ and $p(j - 1)$ we have

$$r_j = n - q_j m = n - (j - 1)m = n - (j - 2)m - m$$
$$= n - q_{j-1}m - m = r_{j-1} - m < r_{j-1}.$$

Thus $r_1 > r_2 > \cdots > r_{j-1} > r_j > \cdots$ so long as the terms are defined. Since there are no infinite decreasing sequences in $\mathbb{N}$, there must be a k in $\mathbb{P}$ such that r_k is defined but r_{k+1} is not. That is, the algorithm must stop with some $r_k < m$, and then $r = r_k$ and $q = q_k$. By $p(k)$, $0 \leqq r_k = n - q_k m$, so $0 \leqq r < m$ and $n = qm + r$. $\quad\square$

In this proof we used two standard devices for adapting induction to verify an algorithm which stops at some undetermined time. We agreed in $p(i)$ to talk only about quantities r_i and q_i that made sense. We also called attention to a decreasing chain $r_1 > r_2 > \cdots$ in $\mathbb{N}$. No such chain can go on forever, since its terms form a subset of $\mathbb{N}$ which must have a smallest member. [In the proof above the last term is actually r_q.]

The DIVISION algorithm gives an explicit construction which proves the existence part, as contrasted with the uniqueness part, of Theorem 1 for $n \geqq 0$. Now suppose $n < 0$. One way to find q and r is to appeal to the algorithm for the positive case as follows.

NEGATIVE DIVISION *Algorithm.*

Step 1. Use the DIVISION algorithm to find q' and r with

$$-n = q'm + r \text{ and } 0 \leq r < m.$$

Step 2. Let $q = -q'$.

Step 3. If $r \neq 0$ replace q by $q - 1$ and r by $m - r$.

Step 4. Stop. ▯

This algorithm works, since if $-n = q'm + r$ then

$$n = (-q')m - r = \begin{cases} (-q')m + r & \text{if } r = 0 \\ (-q' - 1)m + (m - r) & \text{if } r \neq 0 \end{cases}$$

and $0 \leq m - r < m$ if $r \neq 0$.

EXAMPLE 2   Figure 2 lists the values of the variables in the execution of the NEGATIVE DIVISION algorithm with $m = 7$ and $n = -25$. ▯

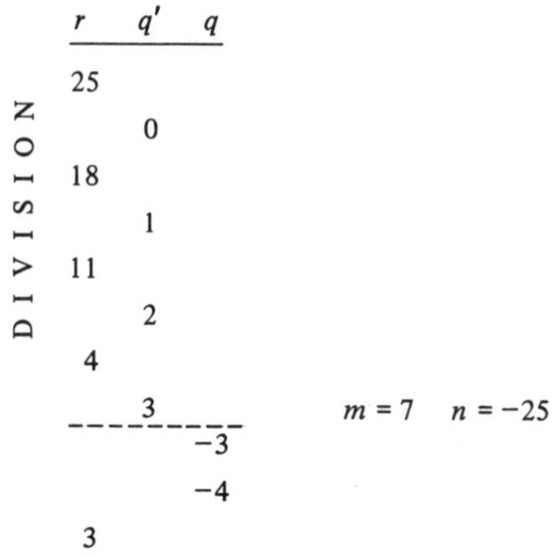

FIGURE 2

Another way to handle negative n would be to modify the DIVISION algorithm to add m's, and to look at $n, n + m, n + 2m, \ldots$ until we hit $n + q'm$ with $n + (q' - 1)m < 0 \leq n + q'm$. Let $r = n + q'm$ and $q = -q'$. Then $r - m < 0 \leq r$, so $0 \leq r < m$, and $n = -q'm + r = qm + r$.

We have seen how to find values of q and r for all integers n. To complete the proof of Theorem 1 we must show uniqueness, i.e., that these are the only possible values. Suppose that $n = q_1 m + r_1 = q_2 m + r_2$ with $0 \leq r_1 < m$ and $0 \leq r_2 < m$. We want to show that this forces $q_1 = q_2$ and $r_1 = r_2$. Now $r_1 = q_2 m + r_2 - q_1 m = (q_2 - q_1)m + r_2$. If $q_2 - q_1 > 0$, then $q_2 - q_1 \geq 1$, so $(q_2 - q_1)m \geq m$ and thus

$$r_1 = (q_2 - q_1)m + r_2 \geq m + r_2 \geq m + 0 = m,$$

contradicting $0 \leq r_1 < m$. Thus $q_2 - q_1 \leq 0$. Similarly, $q_1 - q_2 \leq 0$, so $q_1 = q_2$ and $r_1 = 0 \cdot m + r_2 = r_2$, as we wanted to prove.

The number of passes through the "while" loop in the DIVISION algorithm is q, which is about n/m. Since the other steps take a fixed amount of time, the total execution time for this algorithm is roughly proportional to n/m. The algorithm we learned as children is considerably faster. It's awkward to write out the details, but the next example reminds us of how it works.

EXAMPLE 3 Figure 3 shows the format with $n = 3369$ and $m = 13$.

$$
\begin{array}{r}
2\ 5\ 9 \\
13\ \overline{\rceil\ 3\ 3\ 6\ 9} \\
2\ 6 \\
\overline{7\ 6} \\
6\ 5 \\
\overline{1\ 1\ 9} \\
1\ 1\ 7 \\
\overline{2}
\end{array}
$$

FIGURE 3

For this example we:

1. Start at the left.
2. Divide 33 by 13, to get quotient 2 with remainder 7.
3. Slide over one digit to the right.
4. Divide 76 by 13, to get 5 with remainder 11.
5. Slide over one digit.
6. Divide 119 by 13, to get 9 with remainder 2.
7. Stop.

The answer is $q = 259$ and $r = 2$.

The three divide steps could each be done using the DIVISION algorithm, which would involve altogether $2 + 5 + 9 = 16$ loops subtracting 13 repeatedly. Even counting in the time for the start and slide steps this procedure is much faster than making 259 loops using the DIVISION algorithm alone. ☐

To estimate how long this childhood algorithm takes for a general m and n we count how many divide and slide steps there are and estimate how long each one takes. The number of divide steps depends on how many digits there are in the decimal expression for n. Call this number of digits DIGIT(n). Then there are DIGIT(n) − DIGIT(m) + 1 divide steps. Each divide step takes at most 9 subtraction loops, so for a fixed value of m the time to divide and slide is bounded by some constant, say B, which is determined by the time it takes to subtract m. Altogether there are at most DIGIT(n) steps, each of which takes time at most B, so the total time, disregarding starting and stopping, is at most $B \cdot$ DIGIT(n).

To divide n by m using the DIVISION algorithm takes about n/m subtraction loops. Suppose a subtraction loop takes time S. We know that B is roughly bounded by $9S$, so the childhood algorithm time is at most something like $9S \cdot$ DIGIT(n), compared with $(n/m)S$ for the DIVISION algorithm. The ratio is

$$\frac{(n/m)S}{9S \cdot \text{DIGIT}(n)} = \frac{n}{\text{DIGIT}(n)} \cdot \frac{1}{9m}.$$

For large values of n one can show that n is much, much greater than DIGIT(n), so the DIVISION algorithm takes much, much longer than the childhood method.

There is a notation, called the **"big-oh" notation**, which is commonly used to describe estimates of the sort we have just been making. Suppose f and g are functions with domain $\mathbb{N}$ and with nonnegative values. We say $f(n)$ is $O(g(n))$ [read "$f(n)$ is big oh of $g(n)$"] in case there is a constant C such that $f(n) \leqq Cg(n)$ for all large enough values of n.

EXAMPLE 4   (a) $f(n)$ is $O(1)$ if the values of $f(n)$ are bounded above by some constant for large n. Note that here 1 represents the function on $\mathbb{N}$ whose value is 1 at each $n \in \mathbb{N}$.

(b) $f(n)$ is $O(n)$ if $f(n)$ is bounded by some constant multiple of n for large n, that is, if $f(n) \leqq Cn$ for large n. For instance, using our notation from above, the time $T(n)$ to execute the DIVISION algorithm on n with a fixed divisor m is approximately $(n/m)S$ plus a start and stop time T_0. Since $T_0 \leqq n$ for all large enough n, $T(n) \leqq (S/m)n + n = (1 + S/m)n$ for large n. Thus $T(n)$ is $O(n)$.

(c) Let $f(n) = 3 - 4n^2 + 17n^3 + 2n^5$ for $n \in \mathbb{N}$. We claim that $f(n)$ is $O(n^5)$. We have $3 \leqq n^5$ for $n \geqq 2$, $-4n^2 \leqq 0$ for all $n \in \mathbb{N}$, and $17n^3 \leqq n^5$ for $n \geqq 5$. Thus

$$f(n) \leqq n^5 + 0 + n^5 + 2n^5 = 4n^5$$

for all large enough n.

(d) If $f(n)$ is $O(g(n))$ and $g(n)$ is $O(h(n))$ then $f(n)$ is $O(h(n))$ [Exercise 13(a)]. ⬚

EXAMPLE 5   The time $T_c(n)$ to execute the childhood algorithm on n with fixed m is bounded by $9S \cdot$ DIGIT(n), so $T_c(n)$ is $O(\text{DIGIT}(n))$.

The notation $O(\log n)$ is also used to describe $O(\text{DIGIT}(n))$. For readers familiar with logarithms we explain the connection. A moment's thought shows that

$$10^{\text{DIGIT}(n)-1} \leqq n < 10^{\text{DIGIT}(n)} \quad \text{for} \quad n \in \mathbb{P}.$$

This translates into the logarithmic statement

$$\text{DIGIT}(n) - 1 \leq \log n < \text{DIGIT}(n);$$

here log signifies $\log_{10}$. Since $\log n < \text{DIGIT}(n)$, $\log n$ is $O(\text{DIGIT}(n))$. If $f(n)$ is $O(\log n)$ then by Example 4(d) $f(n)$ is $O(\text{DIGIT}(n))$. On the other hand,

$$\text{DIGIT}(n) \leq 1 + \log n \leq \log n + \log n = 2 \log n$$

for $n \geq 10$, so $\text{DIGIT}(n)$ is $O(\log n)$. By Example 4(d) again, if $f(n)$ is $O(\text{DIGIT}(n))$ then $f(n)$ is $O(\log n)$. Thus $O(\text{DIGIT}(n))$ and $O(\log n)$ mean the same thing.

In computer science, logarithms are often to the base 2 rather than base 10, but since $\log_2 x = \log_2 10 \cdot \log_{10} x$ and $\log_2 10$ is a constant, $O(\log_2 n)$ and $O(\log_{10} n)$ mean the same thing. □

As a final note, we confess to having been sloppy in estimating time involved for various steps in our algorithm. How long it takes to start the algorithm up and how long the subtractions take may depend on n. The dependence is really on $\text{DIGIT}(n)$ rather than directly on n, however, so the effects we have ignored are secondary and do not change our general conclusions.

EXERCISES 3.6

1. Use any method to find q and r for the following values of n and m.
   (a) $n = 20, m = 3$ (b) $n = 20, m = 4$
   (c) $n = -20, m = 3$ (d) $n = -20, m = 4$
   (e) $n = 371{,}246, m = 65$ (f) $n = -371{,}246, m = 65$

2. Find an integer s and a rational number t such that $0 \leq t < 1$ and $s + t =:$
   (a) $20/3$ (b) $20/4$ (c) $-20/3$
   (d) $-20/4$ (e) $371{,}246/65$ (f) $-371{,}246/65$

3. List the successive values of r and q in the execution of the DIVISION algorithm for these starting values of n and m. [See Figure 1(c) for format.]
   (a) $n = 20, m = 7$ (b) $n = 20, m = 4$
   (c) $n = 200, m = 70$ (d) $n = 70, m = 200$

4. List the successive values of r, q' and q in the execution of the NEGATIVE DIVISION algorithm for these starting values of n and m. [See Figure 2 for format.]
   (a) $n = -20, m = 7$ (b) $n = -20, m = 4$
   (c) $n = -20, m = 40$

5. Give r_1, r_2, r_3, r_4 and the last value of r_i in the execution of the DIVISION algorithm for these starting values of n and m.
   (a) $n = 200, m = 13$ (b) $n = 201, m = 13$

6. Give q_1, q_2, q_3 and the last value of q_i in the execution of the DIVISION algorithm for these starting values of n and m.
   (a) $n = 200, m = 13$ (b) $n = 201, m = 13$

7. Write an algorithm to find q and r for negative n which performs the modification of the DIVISION algorithm described after Example 2.

8. Write an algorithm which finds q and r for all choices of n in $\mathbb{Z}$. *Hint:* Put together algorithms for $n \geq 0$ and $n < 0$.

9. How many subtractions of 17 are involved in dividing 14,095 by 17 using:
   (a) the childhood algorithm?
   (b) the DIVISION algorithm?

10. Assume the notation in the discussion of the DIVISION algorithm. For $i \in \mathbb{P}$ let

    $s(i) = $ "If r_i is defined, then $r_i = n - (i - 1)m$."

    Use mathematical induction to prove that $s(i)$ is true for every $i \in \mathbb{P}$.

11. Find $n/\mathrm{DIGIT}(n)$ in each case.
    (a) $n = 12$ (b) $n = 120$
    (c) $n = 1200$ (d) $n = 12{,}000$

12. Suppose $f(n)$ is $O(n^a)$ and $g(n)$ is $O(n^b)$. Prove
    (a) $f(n)g(n)$ is $O(n^{a+b})$.
    (b) $f(n) + g(n)$ is $O(n^{\max\{a,b\}})$.
    [In view of these facts we could write $O(n^a) \cdot O(n^b) = O(n^{a+b})$ and $O(n^a) + O(n^b) = O(n^{\max\{a,b\}})$.]

13. (a) Show that if $f(n)$ is $O(g(n))$ and $g(n)$ is $O(h(n))$ then $f(n)$ is $O(h(n))$. [Symbolically, $O(O(h(n))) = O(h(n))$.]
    (b) Give examples of $f(n)$, $g(n)$ and $h(n)$ such that $f(n)$ is $O(h(n))$ and $g(n)$ is $O(h(n))$ but $f(n)$ is not $O(g(n))$.

14. Show that if $f(n)$ is $O(g(n))$ and $g(n)$ is $O(f(n))$ then $O(f(n)) = O(g(n))$ in the sense that

    $$h(n) \text{ is } O(f(n)) \Leftrightarrow h(n) \text{ is } O(g(n)).$$

15. Show that
    (a) $(n + 1)^2$ is $O(n^2)$.
    (b) $O((n + 1)^2) = O(n^2)$ [see Exercise 14 for the meaning of this equation].
    (c) $O(500n) = O(n)$.

16. Show that n and n' give the same remainder value r on division by m if and only if $n - n'$ is a multiple of m.

CHAPTER HIGHLIGHTS

Satisfy yourself that you can define each concept and describe each method. Give at least one reason why the item was included in the chapter.
Think of at least one example of each concept and at least one situation in which the fact or method would be useful.

Concepts

function = map = mapping
  domain, codomain
  image of x, image of f = $\mathrm{Im}(f)$

graph of f
one-to-one, onto, one-to-one correspondence
well-defined
special functions
   identity function, constant function, characteristic function, logarithmic
     function, polynomial function
composition of functions
restriction, $f(A)$
pre-image, $f^{-1}(B), f^{-1}(y) = f^{-1}(\{y\})$
sequence, finite sequence
recursive definition [= basis + recursive clause]
     of a sequence, set, function
quotient, remainder [$n = qm + r$]
"big-oh" notation

Facts

Composition of functions is associative.
A function has an inverse if and only if it is one-to-one and onto.
Each function determines a partition of its domain.
The Division Algorithm: $n = qm + r$ with $0 \leq r < m$.

Methods

DIVISION, NEGATIVE DIVISION and childhood algorithm to find q and
   r in the Division algorithm.
Inductive verification of algorithm correctness.

4

MATRICES AND OTHER

SEMIGROUPS

The main aim of this chapter is to study situations in which the associative law holds. We begin by discussing addition and multiplication of matrices in § 4.1. Section 4.2 develops more matrix algebra. In § 4.3 we fit our earlier results into the more general context of semigroups and monoids.

§ 4.1 Matrices

We first encountered matrices in § 0.3, where we showed that they provide a useful way of studying graphs. In § 1.4 we discussed matrix notation and also considered the operations of transposition and matrix addition. We now want to focus attention on addition, and to do so we require that the matrices we are adding have the same shape and have entries we can add. Accordingly, we consider fixed positive integers m and n and look at members of $\mathfrak{M}_{m,\,n}$, the set of all $m \times n$ matrices with real entries.

Recall that if $\mathbf{A} = [a_{ij}]$ and $\mathbf{B} = [b_{ij}]$, then $\mathbf{A} + \mathbf{B}$ has (i, j) entry $a_{ij} + b_{ij}$ for each i and j; we simply add corresponding entries of $\mathbf{A}$ and $\mathbf{B}$ to get $\mathbf{A} + \mathbf{B}$. Before listing properties of addition we give a little more notation. Let $\mathbf{0}$ represent the $m \times n$ matrix all entries of which are 0. [Context will always make plain what size this matrix is.] For $\mathbf{A}$ in $\mathfrak{M}_{m,\,n}$ the matrix $-\mathbf{A}$, called the **negative of** $\mathbf{A}$, is obtained by negating each entry in $\mathbf{A}$. Thus if $\mathbf{A} = [a_{ij}]$, then $-\mathbf{A} = [-a_{ij}]$; equivalently $(-\mathbf{A})[i, j] = -\mathbf{A}[i, j]$.

148

Theorem   For all **A**, **B** and **C** in $\mathfrak{M}_{m,n}$

   (a) $\mathbf{A} + (\mathbf{B} + \mathbf{C}) = (\mathbf{A} + \mathbf{B}) + \mathbf{C}$ [associative law]
   (b) $\mathbf{A} + \mathbf{B} = \mathbf{B} + \mathbf{A}$ [commutative law]
   (c) $\mathbf{A} + \mathbf{0} = \mathbf{0} + \mathbf{A} = \mathbf{A}$ [additive identity]
   (d) $\mathbf{A} + (-\mathbf{A}) = (-\mathbf{A}) + \mathbf{A} = \mathbf{0}$ [additive inverses]

Proof. These properties of matrix addition are reflections of corresponding properties of addition of real numbers and are easy to check. We check (a) and leave the rest to Exercise 18.

Say $\mathbf{A} = [a_{ij}]$, $\mathbf{B} = [b_{ij}]$ and $\mathbf{C} = [c_{ij}]$. The (i, j) entry of $\mathbf{B} + \mathbf{C}$ is $b_{ij} + c_{ij}$, so the (i, j) entry of $\mathbf{A} + (\mathbf{B} + \mathbf{C})$ is $a_{ij} + (b_{ij} + c_{ij})$. Similarly, the (i, j) entry of $(\mathbf{A} + \mathbf{B}) + \mathbf{C}$ is $(a_{ij} + b_{ij}) + c_{ij}$. Since addition of real numbers is associative, corresponding entries of $\mathbf{A} + (\mathbf{B} + \mathbf{C})$ and $(\mathbf{A} + \mathbf{B}) + \mathbf{C}$ are equal, and so the matrices are equal.   ☐

Since addition of matrices is associative, we can write $\mathbf{A} + \mathbf{B} + \mathbf{C}$ without causing ambiguity.

Matrices can be multiplied by real numbers, which in this context are often called **scalars**. Given **A** in $\mathfrak{M}_{m,n}$ and c in $\mathbb{R}$, $c\mathbf{A}$ is the $m \times n$ matrix whose (i, j) entry is ca_{ij}; thus $(c\mathbf{A})[i, j] = c\mathbf{A}[i, j]$. This multiplication is called **scalar multiplication** and $c\mathbf{A}$ is called the **scalar product**.

EXAMPLE 1   (a) If

$$\mathbf{A} = \begin{bmatrix} 2 & 1 & -3 \\ -1 & 0 & 4 \end{bmatrix},$$

then

$$2\mathbf{A} = \begin{bmatrix} 4 & 2 & -6 \\ -2 & 0 & 8 \end{bmatrix} \quad \text{and} \quad -7\mathbf{A} = \begin{bmatrix} -14 & -7 & 21 \\ 7 & 0 & -28 \end{bmatrix}.$$

(b) In general, the scalar product $(-1)\mathbf{A}$ is the negative $-\mathbf{A}$ of **A**.   ☐

Addition and scalar multiplication of matrices are natural, but the definition of the product of matrices we are about to make may appear peculiar and unnatural. The standard linear algebra explanation for choosing this definition shows how matrices correspond to certain functions, called linear transformations; then multiplication of matrices corresponds to composition of the linear transformations. An explanation can also be given in terms of systems of linear equations. A treatment along these lines would take us too far into linear algebra, so we will present the rule for multiplying matrices without any algebraic justification.

Recall, however, that in § 0.3 we saw how the powers $\mathbf{M}^n$ of a matrix **M** of a graph contain useful information about the graph. Here's another example that involves two different graphs and matrices.

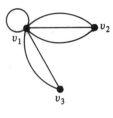

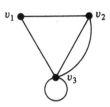

$$A = \begin{bmatrix} 1 & 3 & 2 \\ 3 & 0 & 0 \\ 2 & 0 & 0 \end{bmatrix}$$

$$B = \begin{bmatrix} 0 & 1 & 1 \\ 1 & 0 & 2 \\ 1 & 2 & 1 \end{bmatrix}$$

FIGURE 1

EXAMPLE 2 Consider the graphs and their matrices in Figure 1; note that they use the same set $\{v_1, v_2, v_3\}$ of vertices. Let **C** be the matrix whose (i,j) entry is the number of paths of length 2 from v_i to v_j whose first edge comes from the first graph and whose second edge comes from the second graph. As an example, let's calculate c_{13}, the number of paths like this from v_1 to v_3. The intermediate vertex can be v_1, v_2 or v_3:

Intermediate vertex v_l	Number of paths in first graph from v_1 to v_l	Number of paths in second graph from v_l to v_3	Total number of paths through v_l
v_1	$a_{11} = 1$	$b_{13} = 1$	$a_{11}b_{13} = 1$
v_2	$a_{12} = 3$	$b_{23} = 2$	$a_{12}b_{23} = 6$
v_3	$a_{13} = 2$	$b_{33} = 1$	$a_{13}b_{33} = \dfrac{2}{9}$

The answer 9 is exactly

$$c_{13} = a_{11}b_{13} + a_{12}b_{23} + a_{13}b_{33},$$

i.e.,

$$C[1, 3] = A[1, 1]B[1, 3] + A[1, 2]B[2, 3] + A[1, 3]B[3, 3].$$

Similar calculations yield the other entries of **C** and we find

$$C = \begin{bmatrix} 5 & 5 & 9 \\ 0 & 3 & 3 \\ 0 & 2 & 2 \end{bmatrix}.$$

This is the "product matrix" **AB** about to be defined. ☐

In general, matrices **A** and **B** can be multiplied to get **AB** provided the number of columns of **A** equals the number of rows of **B**. So consider an $m \times n$ matrix **A** and an $n \times p$ matrix **B**. Thus **A** is in $\mathfrak{M}_{m, n}$ and **B** is in $\mathfrak{M}_{n, p}$.

The **product AB** is the $m \times p$ matrix in $\mathfrak{M}_{m,p}$ defined by

$$c_{ik} = \sum_{j=1}^{n} a_{ij}b_{jk} \quad \text{for} \quad 1 \leqq i \leqq m \quad \text{and} \quad 1 \leqq k \leqq p.$$

In subscript-free notation

$$(\mathbf{AB})[i, k] = \sum_{j=1}^{n} \mathbf{A}[i, j]\mathbf{B}[j, k].$$

Schematically, the (i, k) entry of **AB** is obtained by multiplying terms of the ith row of **A** with corresponding terms of the kth column of **B** and summing. See Figure 2. One can calculate c_{ik} by mentally lifting the ith row of **A**, rotating it clockwise by 90°, placing it on top of the kth column of **B**, and then summing the products of the corresponding terms:

$$c_{ik} = a_{i1}b_{1k} + a_{i2}b_{2k} + \cdots + a_{in}b_{nk}.$$

For this calculation to make sense, the rows of **A** and the columns of **B** must have the same number of entries. If **A** is $m \times n$ and **B** is $r \times p$, the matrix product **AB** is only defined if $n = r$, in which case **AB** is an $m \times p$ matrix.

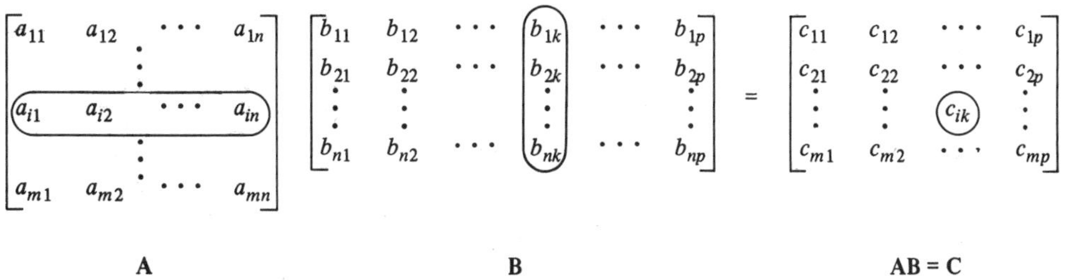

$$\mathbf{A} \qquad\qquad \mathbf{B} \qquad\qquad \mathbf{AB = C}$$

FIGURE 2

EXAMPLE 3   Consider matrices and vectors

$$\mathbf{A} = \begin{bmatrix} 3 & -1 \\ -2 & 4 \end{bmatrix}, \quad \mathbf{B} = \begin{bmatrix} -1 & 0 & 3 \\ 2 & 1 & -5 \end{bmatrix},$$

$$\mathbf{v}_1 = [2 \ \ -3 \ \ 4] \quad \text{and} \quad \mathbf{v}_2 = \begin{bmatrix} 1 \\ -3 \end{bmatrix}.$$

(a) To calculate **AB**, we begin by mentally placing the first row of **A** over the first, second and third columns of **B** in turn. These three computations give the first row of **AB**:

$$\mathbf{AB} = \begin{bmatrix} -3 - 2 & 0 - 1 & 9 + 5 \end{bmatrix} = \begin{bmatrix} -5 & -1 & 14 \end{bmatrix}.$$

Using the second row of **A** in the same way, we obtain the second row of **AB**:

$$\mathbf{AB} = \begin{bmatrix} -5 & -1 & 14 \\ 10 & 4 & -26 \end{bmatrix}.$$

(b) The product **BA** is not defined, since **B** is a 2×3 matrix, **A** is a 2×2 matrix and $3 \neq 2$. Furthermore, our schematic procedure breaks down, since the rows of **B** have three terms and the columns of **A** have two terms; so it is not clear how we would mentally place the rows of **B** on top of the columns of **A**.

(c) We have

$$\mathbf{A}^2 = \mathbf{AA} = \begin{bmatrix} 3 & -1 \\ -2 & 4 \end{bmatrix} \begin{bmatrix} 3 & -1 \\ -2 & 4 \end{bmatrix} = \begin{bmatrix} 11 & -7 \\ -14 & 18 \end{bmatrix}.$$

(d) We have

$$\mathbf{A}\mathbf{v}_2 = \begin{bmatrix} 3 & -1 \\ -2 & 4 \end{bmatrix} \begin{bmatrix} 1 \\ -3 \end{bmatrix} = \begin{bmatrix} 6 \\ -14 \end{bmatrix}.$$

(e) Neither $\mathbf{B}\mathbf{v}_1$ nor $\mathbf{v}_1\mathbf{B}$ is defined. But $\mathbf{v}_1\mathbf{B}^T$ and $\mathbf{B}\mathbf{v}_1^T$ are:

$$\mathbf{v}_1\mathbf{B}^T = \begin{bmatrix} 2 & -3 & 4 \end{bmatrix} \begin{bmatrix} -1 & 2 \\ 0 & 1 \\ 3 & -5 \end{bmatrix} = \begin{bmatrix} 10 & -19 \end{bmatrix}$$

and

$$\mathbf{B}\mathbf{v}_1^T = \begin{bmatrix} -1 & 0 & 3 \\ 2 & 1 & -5 \end{bmatrix} \begin{bmatrix} 2 \\ -3 \\ 4 \end{bmatrix} = \begin{bmatrix} 10 \\ -19 \end{bmatrix}.$$

The similarity of these two products is not an accident, as noted in Exercise 19.   ∎

EXAMPLE 4   Consider

$$\mathbf{A} = \begin{bmatrix} 3 & -1 \\ -2 & 4 \end{bmatrix}, \qquad \mathbf{B} = \begin{bmatrix} 1 & 2 \\ -3 & 1 \end{bmatrix}, \qquad \mathbf{C} = \begin{bmatrix} 1 & 0 \\ 2 & 3 \end{bmatrix}.$$

(a) We have

$$\mathbf{AB} = \begin{bmatrix} 3 & -1 \\ -2 & 4 \end{bmatrix} \begin{bmatrix} 1 & 2 \\ -3 & 1 \end{bmatrix} = \begin{bmatrix} 6 & 5 \\ -14 & 0 \end{bmatrix}$$

and

$$\mathbf{BA} = \begin{bmatrix} 1 & 2 \\ -3 & 1 \end{bmatrix} \begin{bmatrix} 3 & -1 \\ -2 & 4 \end{bmatrix} = \begin{bmatrix} -1 & 7 \\ -11 & 7 \end{bmatrix}.$$

This example shows that multiplication of matrices is not commutative! Even when both **AB** and **BA** are defined they may or may not be equal.

(b) Since

$$\mathbf{AB} = \begin{bmatrix} 6 & 5 \\ -14 & 0 \end{bmatrix},$$

we have

$$(\mathbf{AB})\mathbf{C} = \begin{bmatrix} 6 & 5 \\ -14 & 0 \end{bmatrix} \begin{bmatrix} 1 & 0 \\ 2 & 3 \end{bmatrix} = \begin{bmatrix} 16 & 15 \\ -14 & 0 \end{bmatrix}.$$

On the other hand,

$$\mathbf{BC} = \begin{bmatrix} 1 & 2 \\ -3 & 1 \end{bmatrix} \begin{bmatrix} 1 & 0 \\ 2 & 3 \end{bmatrix} = \begin{bmatrix} 5 & 6 \\ -1 & 3 \end{bmatrix}$$

and so

$$\mathbf{A(BC)} = \begin{bmatrix} 3 & -1 \\ -2 & 4 \end{bmatrix} \begin{bmatrix} 5 & 6 \\ -1 & 3 \end{bmatrix} = \begin{bmatrix} 16 & 15 \\ -14 & 0 \end{bmatrix}.$$

These rather different computations show that $(\mathbf{AB})\mathbf{C} = \mathbf{A(BC)}$ in this case. This is *not* an accident, as we will see later in this section. ☐

EXAMPLE 5   Consider the $n \times n$ matrix

$$\mathbf{I} = \begin{bmatrix} 1 & 0 & 0 & \cdots & 0 \\ 0 & 1 & 0 & \cdots & 0 \\ 0 & 0 & 1 & \cdots & 0 \\ \cdot & \cdot & \cdot & & \cdot \\ \cdot & \cdot & \cdot & & \cdot \\ \cdot & \cdot & \cdot & & \cdot \\ 0 & 0 & 0 & \cdots & 1 \end{bmatrix};$$

thus $\mathbf{I}[i, i] = 1$ for $i = 1, 2, \ldots, n$ and $\mathbf{I}[i, j] = 0$ for $i \neq j$. This special matrix is called the $n \times n$ **identity matrix**. Whenever we wish to specify its size explicitly we will denote it by $\mathbf{I}_n$. Thus for example

$$\mathbf{I}_2 = \begin{bmatrix} 1 & 0 \\ 0 & 1 \end{bmatrix} \quad \text{and} \quad \mathbf{I}_4 = \begin{bmatrix} 1 & 0 & 0 & 0 \\ 0 & 1 & 0 & 0 \\ 0 & 0 & 1 & 0 \\ 0 & 0 & 0 & 1 \end{bmatrix}.$$

Now consider any $m \times n$ matrix $\mathbf{A}$. Then the product $\mathbf{AI}_n$ is defined and

$$(\mathbf{AI}_n)[i, k] = \sum_{j=1}^{n} \mathbf{A}[i, j]\mathbf{I}_n[j, k]$$

for $1 \leq i \leq m$ and $1 \leq k \leq n$. For $j \neq k$, we have $\mathbf{I}_n[j, k] = 0$ and so this sum collapses to $\mathbf{A}[i, k]\mathbf{I}_n[k, k] = \mathbf{A}[i, k]$. This is true for all i and k, and hence

(1) $$\mathbf{AI}_n = \mathbf{A} \quad \text{for all} \quad \mathbf{A} \in \mathfrak{M}_{m, n}.$$

Next consider an $n \times p$ matrix $\mathbf{B}$. Then $\mathbf{I}_n\mathbf{B}$ is defined and

$$(\mathbf{I}_n\mathbf{B})[i, k] = \sum_{j=1}^{n} \mathbf{I}_n[i, j]\mathbf{B}[j, k] = \mathbf{B}[i, k].$$

Thus

(2) $$\mathbf{I}_n\mathbf{B} = \mathbf{B} \quad \text{for all} \quad \mathbf{B} \in \mathfrak{M}_{n, p}.$$

Assertions (1) and (2) both apply to square $n \times n$ matrices and so

(3) $$\mathbf{AI}_n = \mathbf{I}_n\mathbf{A} = \mathbf{A} \quad \text{for all} \quad \mathbf{A} \in \mathfrak{M}_{n, n}. \quad ☐$$

Consider a fixed n in $\mathbb{P}$. We claim that the set $\mathbb{R}^n$, the set $\mathfrak{M}_{n,1}$ of column vectors and the set $\mathfrak{M}_{1,n}$ of row vectors are in one-to-one correspondence with each other. In fact,

$$f(\langle x_1, x_2, \ldots, x_n \rangle) = [x_1 \quad x_2 \quad \cdots \quad x_n]$$

defines a one-to-one correspondence f between $\mathbb{R}^n$ and $\mathfrak{M}_{1,n}$, and TRANS(A) $= \mathbf{A}^T$ provides a one-to-one correspondence between $\mathfrak{M}_{1,n}$ and $\mathfrak{M}_{n,1}$. Composition of these correspondences provides a one-to-one correspondence between $\mathbb{R}^n$ and $\mathfrak{M}_{n,1}$.

Multiplication of matrices is associative [that is, $(\mathbf{AB})\mathbf{C} = \mathbf{A}(\mathbf{BC})$ whenever either side makes sense] as we illustrated in Example 4. At the computational level, this fact is rather mysterious; see Exercise 22. The mystery vanishes when we relate matrices to linear transformations, since the composition of functions is associative. However, we have not explained the connection between matrices and linear transformations, and so we state the general associative law without proof.

Associative Law   If $\mathbf{A}$ is an $m \times n$ matrix, $\mathbf{B}$ is an $n \times p$ matrix and $\mathbf{C}$ is a $p \times q$ matrix,
for Matrices   then $(\mathbf{AB})\mathbf{C} = \mathbf{A}(\mathbf{BC})$.

Since multiplication of matrices is associative, we can write $\mathbf{ABC}$ without ambiguity. Also, powers such as $\mathbf{A}^3 = \mathbf{AAA}$ are unambiguous.

To conclude this section we stress again that although *multiplication of matrices is associative* it is *not commutative*: $\mathbf{AB}$ need not equal $\mathbf{BA}$ even if both products are defined. Example 4(a) illustrates noncommutativity. Examples of other laws of arithmetic not satisfied by matrices appear in Exercises 17 and 20(b).

EXERCISES 4.1

1. Let

$$\mathbf{A} = \begin{bmatrix} 1 & 2 & 4 \\ 3 & 0 & 2 \end{bmatrix} \quad \text{and} \quad \mathbf{B} = \begin{bmatrix} 2 & 1 \\ -1 & 0 \\ -2 & 3 \end{bmatrix}.$$

Find the following when they exist.
(a) $\mathbf{AB}$ (b) $\mathbf{BA}$ (c) $\mathbf{ABA}$
(d) $\mathbf{A} + \mathbf{B}^T$ (e) $3\mathbf{A}^T - 2\mathbf{B}$ (f) $(\mathbf{AB})^2$

2. Let

$$\mathbf{C} = \begin{bmatrix} 1 \\ 0 \\ 1 \end{bmatrix}$$

and let $\mathbf{A}$ and $\mathbf{B}$ be as in Exercise 1. Find the following when they exist.
(a) $\mathbf{AC}$ (b) $\mathbf{BC}$ (c) $\mathbf{C}^2$
(d) $\mathbf{C}^T\mathbf{C}$ (e) $\mathbf{CC}^T$ (f) $73\mathbf{C}$

3. Let

$$A = \begin{bmatrix} 3 & -4 & 3 & 1 \\ 2 & 0 & 1 & -2 \\ -1 & 1 & 2 & 0 \end{bmatrix} \quad \text{and} \quad B = \begin{bmatrix} -1 & 1 & 0 \\ 1 & 2 & 1 \\ 0 & 1 & -1 \end{bmatrix}.$$

Find the following when they exist.

(a) A^2 (b) B^2 (c) AB
(d) BA (e) BA^T (f) A^TB

4. Let **A** and **B** be as in Exercise 3, and let $v = \begin{bmatrix} -2 & 1 & -1 \end{bmatrix}$. Find the following when they exist.

(a) vA (b) vB (c) Bv^T
(d) $(vB)^T$ (e) $5(vB)^T - 3Bv^T$

5. (a) Calculate both $(AB)C$ and $A(BC)$ for

$$A = \begin{bmatrix} -1 & 4 \\ 2 & 5 \end{bmatrix}, \quad B = \begin{bmatrix} 1 & 1 \\ 0 & 1 \end{bmatrix} \quad \text{and} \quad C = \begin{bmatrix} 2 & -1 \\ 1 & 3 \end{bmatrix}.$$

(b) Calculate both $B(AC)$ and $(BA)C$.

6. Let **A**, **B** and **C** be as in Exercise 5. Calculate
(a) both AB and BA
(b) both AC and CA
(c) A^2

7. Let

$$A = \begin{bmatrix} 3 & -1 \\ 2 & 1 \\ -2 & 4 \end{bmatrix}, \quad B = \begin{bmatrix} 1 & 2 \\ 0 & 1 \end{bmatrix} \quad \text{and} \quad C = \begin{bmatrix} -1 & 3 \\ 2 & 1 \end{bmatrix}.$$

(a) Calculate $A(BC)$ and $(AB)C$.
(b) Calculate $A(B^2)$ and $(AB)B$.

8. For **A** and **B** in $\mathfrak{M}_{m,n}$ let $A - B = A + (-B)$. Show that
(a) $(A - B) + B = A$
(b) $-(A - B) = B - A$
(c) $(A - B) - C \neq A - (B - C)$ in general

9. Consider **A**, **B** in $\mathfrak{M}_{m,n}$ and a, b, c in $\mathbb{R}$. Show
(a) $c(aA + bB) = (ca)A + (cb)B$
(b) $-aA = (-a)A = a(-A)$
(c) $(aA)^T = aA^T$
(d) $(aA)B = a(AB) = A(aB)$

10. Let **A** be a square matrix. Give a recursive definition for A^n.

11. Let

$$A = \begin{bmatrix} 1 & 0 \\ 0 & 0 \end{bmatrix}, \quad B = \begin{bmatrix} 0 & 1 \\ 0 & 0 \end{bmatrix} \quad \text{and} \quad C = \begin{bmatrix} 0 & 0 \\ 1 & 0 \end{bmatrix}.$$

Calculate

(a) AB (b) BA (c) AC
(d) CA (e) BC (f) CB

12. Let **A**, **B** and **C** be as in Exercise 11. Calculate
(a) A^n for all $n \in \mathbb{P}$,

(b) $\mathbf{B}^n$ for all $n \in \mathbb{P}$,

(c) $\mathbf{C}^n$ for all $n \in \mathbb{P}$.

13. Let

$$\mathbf{A} = \begin{bmatrix} 1 & 0 \\ 1 & 1 \end{bmatrix}.$$

(a) Calculate $\mathbf{A}^n$ for $n = 1, 2, 3, 4$.

(b) Guess a general formula for $\mathbf{A}^n$ and prove your guess is correct by induction.

14. Let

$$\mathbf{M} = \begin{bmatrix} 1 & 1 \\ 1 & 0 \end{bmatrix}$$

and let FIB be the Fibonacci sequence introduced in Example 2 of § 3.4. Prove that

$$\mathbf{M}^n = \begin{bmatrix} \text{FIB}(n) & \text{FIB}(n-1) \\ \text{FIB}(n-1) & \text{FIB}(n-2) \end{bmatrix} \quad \text{for} \quad n \geq 2.$$

15. (a) Let

$$\mathbf{A} = \begin{bmatrix} a & 0 \\ 0 & a \end{bmatrix}$$

for some fixed a in $\mathbb{R}$. Show that $\mathbf{AB} = \mathbf{BA}$ for all $\mathbf{B}$ in $\mathfrak{M}_{2,2}$.

(b) Consider a fixed matrix $\mathbf{A}$ in $\mathfrak{M}_{2,2}$ that satisfies $\mathbf{AB} = \mathbf{BA}$ for all $\mathbf{B} \in \mathfrak{M}_{2,2}$. Show that

$$\mathbf{A} = \begin{bmatrix} a & 0 \\ 0 & a \end{bmatrix} \quad \text{for some} \quad a \in \mathbb{R}.$$

Hint: Write

$$\mathbf{A} = \begin{bmatrix} a & b \\ c & d \end{bmatrix} \quad \text{and try} \quad \mathbf{B} = \begin{bmatrix} 1 & 0 \\ 0 & 0 \end{bmatrix} \quad \text{and} \quad \begin{bmatrix} 0 & 1 \\ 0 & 0 \end{bmatrix}.$$

16. Let

$$\mathbf{M} = \begin{bmatrix} 2 & 1 & 1 \\ 1 & 0 & 2 \\ 1 & 2 & 0 \end{bmatrix}.$$

(a) Draw a graph having $\mathbf{M}$ as its matrix, as in § 0.3.

(b) Calculate the matrix that counts the number of paths of length 2 between pairs of vertices.

17. Find 2×2 matrices that show that $(\mathbf{A} + \mathbf{B})(\mathbf{A} - \mathbf{B}) = \mathbf{A}^2 - \mathbf{B}^2$ does not generally hold.

18. Prove (b), (c) and (d) of the theorem.

19. Show that if $\mathbf{A}$ is an $m \times n$ matrix and $\mathbf{B}$ is an $n \times p$ matrix, then $(\mathbf{AB})^T = \mathbf{B}^T\mathbf{A}^T$. Note that both sides of the equality represent $p \times m$ matrices.

20. (a) Prove the cancellation law for $\mathfrak{M}_{m,n}$ under addition, i.e., prove that if $\mathbf{A}, \mathbf{B}, \mathbf{C}$ are in $\mathfrak{M}_{m,n}$ and $\mathbf{A} + \mathbf{C} = \mathbf{B} + \mathbf{C}$, then $\mathbf{A} = \mathbf{B}$.

(b) Show that the cancellation law for $\mathfrak{M}_{n,n}$ under multiplication fails, i.e., show that $\mathbf{AC} = \mathbf{BC}$ need not imply $\mathbf{A} = \mathbf{B}$.

21. (a) Let A and B be $m \times n$ matrices and let C be an $n \times p$ matrix. Show that the distributive law holds: $(\mathbf{A} + \mathbf{B})\mathbf{C} = \mathbf{AC} + \mathbf{BC}$.

(b) Verify the distributive law $A(B + C) = AB + AC$. First specify the sizes of the matrices for which this makes sense.

22. (a) Show directly that $A(BC) = (AB)C$ for matrices A, B and C in $\mathfrak{M}_{2,2}$.
(b) Did you enjoy part (a)? If yes, give a direct proof of the general associative law for matrices.

23. Let A and B be $n \times n$ matrices such that $AB = BA$.
(a) Prove that $BA^k = A^kB$ for all $k \in \mathbb{P}$.
(b) Prove that $(AB)^k = A^kB^k$ for all $k \in \mathbb{P}$.

24. Let A and B be $n \times n$ matrices such that $AB = BA = 0$. Prove that $(A + B)^k = A^k + B^k$ for all $k \in \mathbb{P}$.

§ *4.2   Inverses of Matrices*

Consider a square $n \times n$ matrix A. An $n \times n$ matrix B is said to be the inverse of A provided the products AB and BA are both equal to the identity $n \times n$ matrix I. A matrix A has at most one inverse, which we write as A^{-1}. So if A has an inverse, then

$$AA^{-1} = A^{-1}A = I,$$

A^{-1} is called the **inverse of** A and we say that A is **invertible**. Only square matrices can be invertible, so most of the matrices in this section will be square, i.e., $n \times n$ for some n. Since 1×1 matrices are trivial, we'll assume $n \geqq 2$. Even if A is a nonzero square matrix, A need not be invertible.

EXAMPLE 1   (a) We show that

$$A = \begin{bmatrix} 3 & -2 \\ -6 & 4 \end{bmatrix}$$

is not invertible. Assume A has an inverse, say

$$A^{-1} = \begin{bmatrix} a & b \\ c & d \end{bmatrix}.$$

Then we must have

$$\begin{bmatrix} 1 & 0 \\ 0 & 1 \end{bmatrix} = \begin{bmatrix} 3 & -2 \\ -6 & 4 \end{bmatrix}\begin{bmatrix} a & b \\ c & d \end{bmatrix} = \begin{bmatrix} 3a - 2c & 3b - 2d \\ -6a + 4c & -6b + 4d \end{bmatrix}.$$

Comparing the (1, 1) and (2, 1) entries, we find $3a - 2c = 1$ and $-6a + 4c = 0$. Thus

$$0 = -6a + 4c = -2(3a - 2c) = -2 \cdot 1 = -2,$$

a contradiction. So A is not invertible.

(b) Many square matrices are invertible. For example, we will verify in Example 2(c) that

$$\begin{bmatrix} 1 & 2 \\ 3 & 4 \end{bmatrix}$$

is invertible.

(c) For any n, the $n \times n$ identity matrix $\mathbf{I}$ is invertible and $\mathbf{I}^{-1} = \mathbf{I}$ since $\mathbf{II} = \mathbf{I}$. ☐

EXAMPLE 2   (a) Let

$$\mathbf{A} = \begin{bmatrix} 1 & 2 \\ 5 & 7 \end{bmatrix} \quad \text{and} \quad \mathbf{B} = \begin{bmatrix} 7 & -2 \\ -5 & 1 \end{bmatrix}.$$

Since

$$\begin{bmatrix} 1 & 2 \\ 5 & 7 \end{bmatrix}\begin{bmatrix} 7 & -2 \\ -5 & 1 \end{bmatrix} = \begin{bmatrix} -3 & 0 \\ 0 & -3 \end{bmatrix} = \begin{bmatrix} 7 & -2 \\ -5 & 1 \end{bmatrix}\begin{bmatrix} 1 & 2 \\ 5 & 7 \end{bmatrix},$$

$\mathbf{AB} = -3\mathbf{I} = \mathbf{BA}$. Hence we have $\mathbf{A}(-\frac{1}{3}\mathbf{B}) = -\frac{1}{3}\mathbf{AB} = -\frac{1}{3}(-3\mathbf{I}) = \mathbf{I}$ and likewise $(-\frac{1}{3}\mathbf{B})\mathbf{A} = \mathbf{I}$. Thus $\mathbf{A}^{-1} = -\frac{1}{3}\mathbf{B}$. That is,

$$\begin{bmatrix} 1 & 2 \\ 5 & 7 \end{bmatrix}^{-1} = -\frac{1}{3}\begin{bmatrix} 7 & -2 \\ -5 & 1 \end{bmatrix} = \begin{bmatrix} -\frac{7}{3} & \frac{2}{3} \\ \frac{5}{3} & -\frac{1}{3} \end{bmatrix},$$

as can be verified directly by multiplication.

(b) More generally, if

$$\mathbf{A} = \begin{bmatrix} a & b \\ c & d \end{bmatrix}$$

and if $ad - bc \neq 0$, then

$$\mathbf{A}^{-1} = \frac{1}{ad - bc}\begin{bmatrix} d & -b \\ -c & a \end{bmatrix},$$

since

$$\begin{bmatrix} a & b \\ c & d \end{bmatrix}\begin{bmatrix} d & -b \\ -c & a \end{bmatrix} = \begin{bmatrix} d & -b \\ -c & a \end{bmatrix}\begin{bmatrix} a & b \\ c & d \end{bmatrix} = \begin{bmatrix} ad - bc & 0 \\ 0 & ad - bc \end{bmatrix}.$$

If $ad - bc = 0$, it turns out that $\mathbf{A}$ is not invertible. So determining inverses of 2×2 matrices is easy.

(c) Let

$$\mathbf{C} = \begin{bmatrix} 1 & 2 \\ 3 & 4 \end{bmatrix}.$$

Part (b) applies with $a = 1$, $b = 2$, $c = 3$ and $d = 4$; hence

$$\mathbf{C}^{-1} = \frac{1}{-2}\begin{bmatrix} 4 & -2 \\ -3 & 1 \end{bmatrix} = \begin{bmatrix} -2 & 1 \\ \frac{3}{2} & -\frac{1}{2} \end{bmatrix}. \quad ☐$$

There are general techniques for finding inverses of arbitrary invertible matrices, but we will not need them in this book. We will, however, give a brief discussion of a way of telling whether or not a matrix in $\mathfrak{M}_{n,n}$ has an inverse without actually finding the inverse. Recall that in Example 2(b) we showed that a matrix $\mathbf{A}$ in $\mathfrak{M}_{2,2}$ is invertible if $ad - bc \neq 0$. The real number $ad - bc$ is determined by $\mathbf{A}$, and the correspondence $\mathbf{A} \to ad - bc$ defines a function from $\mathfrak{M}_{2,2}$ to $\mathbb{R}$. It turns out that for each n in $\mathbb{P}$ there is a function like this, called the **determinant function**, from $\mathfrak{M}_{n,n}$ to $\mathbb{R}$, which tests invertibility. Even though different n's give different functions, we will follow common practice and denote all of these functions by det. Thus det: $\mathfrak{M}_{n,n} \to \mathbb{R}$, and for **A** in $\mathfrak{M}_{n,n}$ we call det(**A**) the **determinant of A**. Since the value of the number det(**A**) is given by a rather complicated formula involving $n!$ terms, each a product of entries of **A**, and since the properties of the determinant function are more important to us than its definition, we simply state without proof two fundamental theorems on determinants. Consult any text on linear algebra or matrix theory for proofs of these facts.

Theorem 1   Each function det: $\mathfrak{M}_{n,n} \to \mathbb{R}$ has the following properties:

(a) det(**I**) $= 1$;
(b) det(**AB**) $=$ (det **A**)(det **B**) for **A**, **B** $\in \mathfrak{M}_{n,n}$.

Theorem 2   An $n \times n$ matrix **A** is invertible if and only if det(**A**) $\neq 0$.

For 2×2 matrices

$$\mathbf{A} = \begin{bmatrix} a & b \\ c & d \end{bmatrix},$$

det(**A**) $= ad - bc$ and Theorem 2 reminds us of what we already learned in Example 2(b): **A** is invertible if and only if $ad - bc \neq 0$. Many people calculate 2×2 determinants using the mental device in Figure 1. For 3×3 determinants, a similar mental device works; see Figure 2.

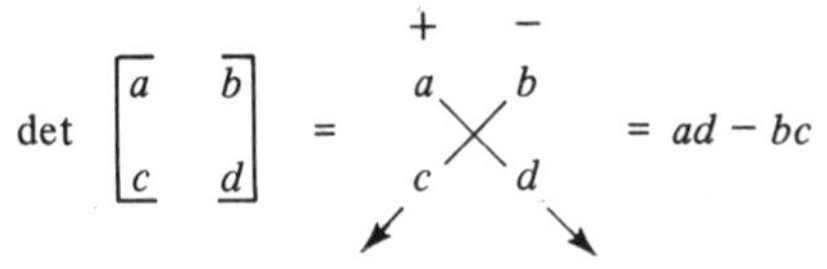

FIGURE 1

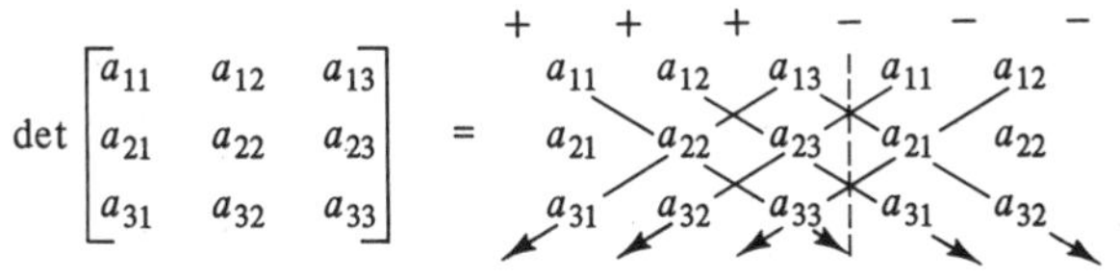

$$= a_{11}a_{22}a_{33} + a_{12}a_{23}a_{31} + a_{13}a_{21}a_{32} - a_{13}a_{22}a_{31} - a_{11}a_{23}a_{32} - a_{12}a_{21}a_{33}$$

FIGURE 2

EXAMPLE 3   We have

$$\det \begin{bmatrix} 2 & -1 & 1 \\ 3 & 4 & 2 \\ 1 & 0 & -3 \end{bmatrix} = 2(4)(-3) + (-1)(2)(1) + 1(3)(0)$$
$$- 1(4)(1) - 2(2)(0) - (-1)(3)(-3)$$
$$= -24 - 2 + 0 - 4 - 0 - 9 = -39. \quad \square$$

For $n \geq 4$, mental devices similar to the ones above do not work! They give the wrong answers. The determinant of a general $n \times n$ matrix is defined to be a certain sum and difference of $n!$ terms each of which is a product of n entries of the matrix, one from each column and one from each row. Again, see any linear algebra or matrix theory book for the full story on which terms to add and which to subtract. Computers generally don't calculate determinants from the definition, but use programs based on properties determinants enjoy; even computers can't handle $n!$ terms if n is very large.

At this point we have a test for whether or not a matrix has an inverse, but we have seen no reason to care what the answer is. Inverses play an important role in matrix theory and we give an example now of one way they can be useful.

Suppose first that we want to solve a matrix equation

$$\mathbf{AX} = \mathbf{C}$$

for $\mathbf{X}$, given the matrices $\mathbf{A}$ and $\mathbf{C}$. If $\mathbf{A}$, $\mathbf{X}$ and $\mathbf{C}$ were numbers a, x and c we would simply have $x = c/a$, unless $a = 0$. We cannot divide matrices, but multiplying by $\mathbf{A}^{-1}$ works as well, when we can do it. The answer is

$$\mathbf{X} = \mathbf{A}^{-1}\mathbf{C}$$

if $\mathbf{A}$ is invertible. To see this, suppose that $\det(\mathbf{A}) \neq 0$, so that $\mathbf{A}^{-1}$ exists. If $\mathbf{AX} = \mathbf{C}$, then $\mathbf{A}^{-1}\mathbf{AX} = \mathbf{A}^{-1}\mathbf{C}$. But $\mathbf{A}^{-1}\mathbf{AX} = \mathbf{IX} = \mathbf{X}$ by Example 5 of § 4.1, so $\mathbf{X} = \mathbf{A}^{-1}\mathbf{C}$. Conversely, if $\mathbf{X} = \mathbf{A}^{-1}\mathbf{C}$ then $\mathbf{AX} = \mathbf{AA}^{-1}\mathbf{C} = \mathbf{IC} = \mathbf{C}$. Notice here that the matrices $\mathbf{X}$ and $\mathbf{C}$ need not be square. If $\mathbf{A}$ is $n \times n$, then $\mathbf{X}$ and $\mathbf{C}$ can be $n \times m$ for any m. In particular, they can be $n \times 1$, as they naturally are when the matrix equation $\mathbf{AX} = \mathbf{C}$ comes from a system of linear equations.

EXAMPLE 4   (a) We solve

$$\begin{bmatrix} 2 & 3 \\ 4 & 5 \end{bmatrix} \mathbf{X} = \begin{bmatrix} -2 \\ 4 \end{bmatrix}.$$

In this case the determinant is $ad - bc = 2 \cdot 5 - 3 \cdot 4 = -2 \neq 0$. From Example 2(b) we have

$$\begin{bmatrix} 2 & 3 \\ 4 & 5 \end{bmatrix}^{-1} = \frac{1}{-2} \begin{bmatrix} 5 & -3 \\ -4 & 2 \end{bmatrix},$$

so

$$\mathbf{X} = \frac{-1}{2} \begin{bmatrix} 5 & -3 \\ -4 & 2 \end{bmatrix} \begin{bmatrix} -2 \\ 4 \end{bmatrix} = \frac{-1}{2} \begin{bmatrix} -22 \\ 16 \end{bmatrix} = \begin{bmatrix} 11 \\ -8 \end{bmatrix},$$

as one can check by multiplying

$$\begin{bmatrix} 2 & 3 \\ 4 & 5 \end{bmatrix} \begin{bmatrix} 11 \\ -8 \end{bmatrix} = \begin{bmatrix} -2 \\ 4 \end{bmatrix}.$$

(b) Consider the system of linear equations

$$2x_1 + 3x_2 = -2$$
$$4x_1 + 5x_2 = 4.$$

Since

$$\begin{bmatrix} 2 & 3 \\ 4 & 5 \end{bmatrix} \begin{bmatrix} x_1 \\ x_2 \end{bmatrix} = \begin{bmatrix} 2x_1 + 3x_2 \\ 4x_1 + 5x_2 \end{bmatrix},$$

this system can be written as a single matrix equation

$$\begin{bmatrix} 2 & 3 \\ 4 & 5 \end{bmatrix} \begin{bmatrix} x_1 \\ x_2 \end{bmatrix} = \begin{bmatrix} -2 \\ 4 \end{bmatrix}.$$

By part (a), $x_1 = 11$ and $x_2 = -8$.

(c) Now consider the system

$$2x_1 + 3x_2 = c_1$$
$$4x_1 + 5x_2 = c_2$$

where c_1 and c_2 are unspecified constants. Just as above, the solution is

$$\begin{bmatrix} x_1 \\ x_2 \end{bmatrix} = \mathbf{X} = -\frac{1}{2} \begin{bmatrix} 5 & -3 \\ -4 & 2 \end{bmatrix} \begin{bmatrix} c_1 \\ c_2 \end{bmatrix} = -\frac{1}{2} \begin{bmatrix} 5c_1 - 3c_2 \\ -4c_1 + 2c_2 \end{bmatrix},$$

so that $x_1 = -\frac{1}{2}(5c_1 - 3c_2)$ and $x_2 = -\frac{1}{2}(-4c_1 + 2c_2)$. □

In § 1.4 we suggested using matrices to describe systems of linear equations. This was illustrated in Example 4, though we admit that any solution method would work fine in that simple case. More generally, we can write a system

$$a_{11}x_1 + a_{12}x_2 + \cdots + a_{1n}x_n = c_1$$
$$a_{21}x_1 + a_{22}x_2 + \cdots + a_{2n}x_n = c_2$$
$$\vdots$$
$$a_{m1}x_1 + a_{m2}x_2 + \cdots + a_{mn}x_n = c_m$$

as a matrix equation

$$(*) \qquad \begin{bmatrix} a_{11} & a_{12} & \cdots & a_{1n} \\ a_{21} & a_{22} & \cdots & a_{2n} \\ \vdots & \vdots & & \vdots \\ a_{m1} & a_{m2} & \cdots & a_{mn} \end{bmatrix} \begin{bmatrix} x_1 \\ x_2 \\ \vdots \\ x_n \end{bmatrix} = \begin{bmatrix} c_1 \\ c_2 \\ \vdots \\ c_m \end{bmatrix} \qquad \text{or} \quad \mathbf{AX} = \mathbf{C}.$$

If $m = n$ and if the square matrix $\mathbf{A}$ has an inverse, then we can find $x_1, x_2,$ $\ldots, x_n$ by writing $\mathbf{X} = \mathbf{A}^{-1}\mathbf{C}$. If $\mathbf{A}$ is not square or if $\det(\mathbf{A}) = 0$ there may or may not be solutions. In such a case other methods will be necessary to solve the problem, and even in the invertible case other techniques are available which are faster for computations.

EXERCISES 4.2

1. Let

$$A = \begin{bmatrix} 2 & 5 \\ 1 & -3 \end{bmatrix} \quad \text{and} \quad B = \begin{bmatrix} 4 & 1 \\ -3 & -2 \end{bmatrix}.$$

Calculate
(a) det(**A**)   (b) det(**B**)   (c) det(**AB**)
(d) det(**BA**)   (e) det(**A**^{2})   (f) det(**B**$^{-1}$)

2. Let

$$A = \begin{bmatrix} 1 & 2 & 4 \\ 3 & 0 & 2 \end{bmatrix} \quad \text{and} \quad B = \begin{bmatrix} 2 & 1 \\ -1 & 0 \\ -2 & 3 \end{bmatrix}.$$

Find the following determinants when they exist.
(a) det(**A**)   (b) det(**B**)   (c) det(**AB**)
(d) det(**BA**)   (e) det(**B**^{T}**A**^{T})

3. Determine which of the following matrices are invertible. Find the inverses of the invertible matrices and check your answers.

(a) $I = \begin{bmatrix} 1 & 0 \\ 0 & 1 \end{bmatrix}$ (b) $A = \begin{bmatrix} 1 & 1 \\ 0 & 1 \end{bmatrix}$ (c) $B = \begin{bmatrix} 1 & 1 \\ 1 & 1 \end{bmatrix}$

(d) $C = \begin{bmatrix} 2 & -3 \\ 5 & 8 \end{bmatrix}$ (e) $D = \begin{bmatrix} 0 & 1 \\ 1 & 0 \end{bmatrix}$

4. Find the determinants of the following matrices and state whether the matrices are invertible.

(a) $\begin{bmatrix} 1 & 5 & 0 \\ -2 & 3 & 1 \\ 0 & 4 & 2 \end{bmatrix}$ (b) $\begin{bmatrix} 1 & 5 & 0 \\ 1 & 3 & 1 \\ 0 & 2 & -1 \end{bmatrix}$

(c) $\begin{bmatrix} 3 & 1 & -1 \\ 0 & 1 & 2 \\ -4 & 1 & -1 \end{bmatrix}$ (d) $\begin{bmatrix} 1 & 2 & 3 \\ 4 & 5 & 4 \\ 3 & 2 & 1 \end{bmatrix}$

5. Let

$$A = \begin{bmatrix} 3 & -1 \\ -1 & 1 \end{bmatrix}.$$

Find
(a) the transpose of **A**   (b) the determinant of **A**
(c) det(**A**^{10})   (d) the inverse of **A**
(e) **A**^{2} (f) det(**A** − λ**I**) for $\lambda \in \mathbb{R}$

6. Show that all matrices of the form

$$\begin{bmatrix} 1 & a & b \\ 0 & 1 & c \\ 0 & 0 & 1 \end{bmatrix}$$

are invertible.

7. For which values of x are the following invertible?

(a) $\begin{bmatrix} -1 & 2 & 1 \\ 1 & x & -2 \\ 0 & 2 & 3 \end{bmatrix}$
(b) $\begin{bmatrix} -1 & 3 & x \\ 1 & 2 & 0 \\ 2 & 4 & -1 \end{bmatrix}$

8. Show that the following matrices are inverses for each other.

$$\mathbf{A} = \begin{bmatrix} 2 & -1 & -4 \\ 3 & 8 & 2 \\ 2 & 5 & 1 \end{bmatrix}, \quad \mathbf{B} = \begin{bmatrix} 2 & 19 & -30 \\ -1 & -10 & 16 \\ 1 & 12 & -19 \end{bmatrix}.$$

9. Use Exercise 8 to solve the following systems of equations.

(a) $\begin{aligned} 2x - y - 4z &= 2 \\ 3x + 8y + 2z &= 1 \\ 2x + 5y + z &= 0 \end{aligned}$
(b) $\begin{aligned} 2x - y - 4z &= 1 \\ 3x + 8y + 2z &= 1 \\ 2x + 5y + z &= 0 \end{aligned}$

(c) $\begin{aligned} 2x + 19y - 30z &= 1 \\ -x - 10y + 16z &= 0 \\ x + 12y - 19z &= 1 \end{aligned}$
(d) $\begin{aligned} 2x + 19y - 30z &= 3 \\ -x - 10y + 16z &= 2 \\ x + 12y - 19z &= -1 \end{aligned}$

10. (a) Show that if $\mathbf{A}$ is an invertible matrix, then $\det(\mathbf{A}^{-1}) = 1/\det(\mathbf{A})$.
   (b) Use Theorem 1 to show that if $\det(\mathbf{A}) = 0$, then there is no matrix $\mathbf{B}$ such that $\mathbf{AB} = \mathbf{I}$.
   (c) Find $\det(\mathbf{A}^{-1})$ for

$$\mathbf{A} = \begin{bmatrix} 5 & 2 & 6 \\ 1 & -3 & -4 \\ 3 & 1 & -1 \end{bmatrix}.$$

   Parts (a) and (b) show that Theorem 2 is true given the truth of Theorem 1.

11. Let $\mathbf{A}$ and $\mathbf{B}$ be invertible $n \times n$ matrices.
   (a) Show that $\mathbf{AB}$ is invertible and that $(\mathbf{AB})^{-1} = \mathbf{B}^{-1}\mathbf{A}^{-1}$.
   (b) Prove or disprove: $\mathbf{A} + \mathbf{B}$ is invertible and $(\mathbf{A} + \mathbf{B})^{-1} = \mathbf{A}^{-1} + \mathbf{B}^{-1}$.
   (c) Prove or disprove: $\mathbf{A}^2$ is invertible.

12. (a) Find all real numbers λ for which the equation

$$\begin{bmatrix} 0 & 1 \\ -2 & 3 \end{bmatrix} \begin{bmatrix} x \\ y \end{bmatrix} = \lambda \begin{bmatrix} x \\ y \end{bmatrix}$$

   has nonzero solutions. *Hint:* Let

$$\mathbf{A} = \begin{bmatrix} 0 & 1 \\ -2 & 3 \end{bmatrix} \quad \text{and} \quad \mathbf{I} = \begin{bmatrix} 1 & 0 \\ 0 & 1 \end{bmatrix}.$$

   The above equation has nonzero solutions $\begin{bmatrix} x \\ y \end{bmatrix}$ only when $\mathbf{A} - \lambda\mathbf{I}$ is non-invertible. So by Theorem 2, it suffices to solve $\det(\mathbf{A} - \lambda\mathbf{I}) = 0$.
   (b) Do the same for

$$\begin{bmatrix} 2 & -1 \\ 1 & 0 \end{bmatrix} \begin{bmatrix} x \\ y \end{bmatrix} = \lambda \begin{bmatrix} x \\ y \end{bmatrix}.$$

13. Approximate entries or round-off errors can present serious problems in finding inverses or in solving matrix equations.

(a) Show that

$$A = \begin{bmatrix} 1 & \frac{1}{3} \\ 3 & 1 \end{bmatrix}$$

is not invertible.

(b) Show that

$$B = \begin{bmatrix} 1 & .3333 \\ 3 & 1 \end{bmatrix}$$

is invertible and find its inverse.

(c) How might a program for invertibility of matrices be designed to detect such anomalies?

§ 4.3   Semigroups

We have already seen several ways of combining mathematical objects, such as numbers and matrices, two at a time. In this section we look at associative operations for combining two elements of a set, and we consider what sorts of general statements are true in such a context. One merit of such a general abstract approach is that it allows one to focus on fundamental properties, without being distracted by the details of different settings. It also means that one can prove theorems once and for all, rather than again and again in various situations. Later on, in Chapter 11, we will give a much more complete treatment of associative operations.

Consider a nonempty set S. A function from $S \times S$ into S is sometimes called a **binary operation**. In this case, we usually have in mind some sort of addition or multiplication and we use notation such as $+$ or $*$ instead of functional notation. Moreover, we normally place the operation symbol between the variables. Thus we would write $s_1 + s_2$, not $+(\langle s_1, s_2 \rangle)$, for example.

EXAMPLE 1   (a) Addition on $\mathbb{R}$ is a binary operation. Formally, the operation is the function SUM: $\mathbb{R} \times \mathbb{R} \to \mathbb{R}$ defined by SUM$(\langle x, y \rangle) = x + y$. We will usually use the symbol $+$, not the formal functional notation SUM.

(b) The function SUM also gives a binary operation on $\mathbb{Z}, \mathbb{N}$ and $\mathbb{Q}$. All it takes for SUM to give a binary operation on a subset S of $\mathbb{R}$ is for it to map $S \times S$ into S, i.e.,

$$x + y \in S \quad \text{whenever} \quad x, y \in S.$$

It is common practice to say that S is **closed under** $+$, or under SUM, in this case. Note that $\mathbb{Z}, \mathbb{N}$ and $\mathbb{Q}$ are closed under $+$. The subset $\{1, 2, 3, 4, 5\}$ of $\mathbb{R}$ is not closed since, for example, $3 + 3 \notin \{1, 2, 3, 4, 5\}$; $+$ is not a binary operation on this subset.

(c) Multiplication $*$ on $\mathbb{R}$ is a binary operation. Formally, the operation is the function PROD: $\mathbb{R} \times \mathbb{R} \to \mathbb{R}$ defined by PROD$(\langle x, y \rangle) = x*y$. Multiplication is also a binary operation on $\mathbb{Z}, \mathbb{N}$ and $\mathbb{Q}$.

(d) Let $\mathfrak{M}_{m,n}$ be the set of all $m \times n$ matrices. Matrix addition $+$ is a binary operation on $\mathfrak{M}_{m,n}$ since

$$A, B \in \mathfrak{M}_{m,n} \quad \text{imply} \quad A + B \in \mathfrak{M}_{m,n}.$$

(e) Matrix multiplication is a binary operation on the set $\mathfrak{M}_{n,n}$ of $n \times n$ matrices.

(f) Let $\mathcal{P}(S)$ be the set of all subsets of some set S. Then union $\cup$ and intersection $\cap$ are binary operations on $\mathcal{P}(S)$. Formally, these are the functions UNION and INTER mapping $\mathcal{P}(S) \times \mathcal{P}(S)$ into $\mathcal{P}(S)$ and defined by

$$\text{UNION}(\langle A, B \rangle) = A \cup B \quad \text{and} \quad \text{INTER}(\langle A, B \rangle) = A \cap B. \quad \Box$$

We will sometimes use a little square $\square$ for a generic binary operation. This is a neutral symbol that does not suggest addition or multiplication or any other familiar operation like union or intersection. So consider a binary operation $\square$ on a nonempty set S. The operation $\square$ is said to be **associative** if

$$s_1 \square (s_2 \square s_3) = (s_1 \square s_2) \square s_3 \quad \text{for all} \quad s_1, s_2, s_3 \in S.$$

A set S with an associative binary operation $\square$ is said to be a **semigroup under** $\square$. To be brief, we will say that $(S, \square)$ is a **semigroup**. If the operation is understood, we may simply call S a **semigroup**. All the binary operations in Example 1 are associative and so all the sets in Example 1 are semigroups under the indicated binary operations. Of course not all useful binary operations are associative—subtraction and division are not, for example—but most of them are. By limiting our study to associative operations we will impose enough structure to be able to state some general facts without excluding the main examples. We will look at some operations in detail after a few basic definitions.

A semigroup $(S, \square)$ is **commutative** if

$$s_1 \square s_2 = s_2 \square s_1 \quad \text{for all} \quad s_1, s_2 \in S.$$

An element e in S will be called an **identity for S** provided

$$s \square e = e \square s = s \quad \text{for all} \quad s \in S.$$

A semigroup with an identity is called a **monoid**. A monoid can't have more than one identity, because if e and f are identities then $e = e \square f = f$. If S has an identity e, an element t such that $s \square t = e = t \square s$ is called an **inverse** of s, often written as s^{-1}. Inverses are unique, when they exist, because if r and t are inverses of s then $s \square t = e$ and $r \square s = e$ and so $r = r \square e = r \square (s \square t) = (r \square s) \square t = e \square t = t$. A monoid in which every element has an inverse is called a **group**. Thus a group is a semigroup with an identity and inverses.

In view of associativity, the expression $s_1 \square s_2 \square s_3$ is unambiguous in a semigroup.

EXAMPLE 2   (a) $(\mathbb{R}, +)$ is a commutative group. The identity is 0 since

$$x + 0 = 0 + x = x \quad \text{for all} \quad x \in \mathbb{R}.$$

For emphasis and clarity, 0 is often referred to as the **additive identity in** $\mathbb{R}$. Inverses with respect to the operation $+$ are called **additive inverses** and written $-x$ not x^{-1}, since the inverse law in this case says

for each $x \in \mathbb{R}$ there is an element $-x \in \mathbb{R}$ such that
$x + (-x) = (-x) + x = 0.$

(b) $(\mathbb{R}, *)$ is a commutative monoid. The identity [or **multiplicative identity**] is 1 since

$$x*1 = 1*x = x \quad \text{for all} \quad x \in \mathbb{R}.$$

Each nonzero x in $\mathbb{R}$ has an inverse [or **multiplicative inverse**], i.e., a number x^{-1} such that

$$x*x^{-1} = x^{-1}*x = 1.$$

Sometimes x^{-1} is written $1/x$ and is called the **reciprocal** of x. $(\mathbb{R}, *)$ is not quite a group because 0 has no multiplicative inverse: $0*x$ never equals 1.

(c) Since the product of nonzero real numbers is nonzero, $*$ is also a binary operation on $\mathbb{R}\backslash\{0\}$. Moreover, $(\mathbb{R}\backslash\{0\}, *)$ is a bona fide commutative group.   ☐

EXAMPLE 3   (a) $(\mathbb{Q}, +)$ and $(\mathbb{Q}\backslash\{0\}, *)$ are commutative groups. Note that $-x$ is in $\mathbb{Q}$ whenever x is in $\mathbb{Q}$ and that x^{-1} is in $\mathbb{Q}$ whenever x is a nonzero number in $\mathbb{Q}$.

(b) $(\mathbb{Z}, +)$ is a commutative group but $(\mathbb{Z}\backslash\{0\}, *)$ is not a group, since $n \in \mathbb{Z}\backslash\{0\}$ does not imply that $n^{-1} \in \mathbb{Z}\backslash\{0\}$. In fact, if n and n^{-1} are both in $\mathbb{Z}\backslash\{0\}$, then n must be 1 or -1. We can assert that $(\mathbb{Z}\backslash\{0\}, *)$ is a commutative monoid; its identity is 1.

(c) $(\mathbb{N}, +)$ is not a group, since $n \in \mathbb{N}$ does not imply that $-n \in \mathbb{N}$. $(\mathbb{N}, +)$ is a commutative monoid with additive identity 0.   ☐

EXAMPLE 4   (a) The set $\mathfrak{M}_{m,n}$ of all $m \times n$ matrices is a commutative group under addition. This fact is spelled out in the theorem in § 4.1.

(b) The set $\mathfrak{M}_{n,n}$ is a monoid under multiplication, with identity $\mathbf{I}_n$. The associative law is discussed at the end of § 4.1. Except for the trivial case $n = 1$, this monoid is not commutative: $\mathbf{AB}$ does not necessarily equal $\mathbf{BA}$. As pointed out in § 4.2, some, but not all, matrices in $\mathfrak{M}_{n,n}$ have inverses.

(c) The set of all invertible $n \times n$ matrices is a group under multiplication. This group is not commutative unless $n = 1$.   ☐

EXAMPLE 5   (a) Let $\mathcal{P}(S)$ be the set of all subsets of some set S. With the operation $\cup$, $\mathcal{P}(S)$ is a commutative semigroup with identity $\varnothing$; see laws 1a, 2a and 5a in Table 1 of § 1.2. Only the empty set itself has an inverse, since $A \cup B \neq \varnothing$ whenever $A \neq \varnothing$.

(b) $\mathcal{P}(S)$ is also a semigroup under the operations $\cap$ and $\oplus$; see Exercises 4 and 5. ☐

EXAMPLE 6 Consider a set $T = \{a, b, \ldots\}$ with at least two members. The set FUN(T, T) of all functions mapping T into T is a semigroup under composition; the associative law is discussed in § 3.1. The identity function 1_T on T is the identity for this semigroup, since

$$(1_T \circ f)(t) = 1_T(f(t)) = f(t) \quad \text{for all} \quad t \in T,$$

so that $1_T \circ f = f$ and similarly $f \circ 1_T = f$. This monoid is not commutative. For example, let f and g be the constant functions defined by $f(t) = a$ and $g(t) = b$ for all t in T. Then $(f \circ g)(t) = f(g(t)) = a$ for all t and $(g \circ f)(t) = b$ for all t. That is, $f \circ g = f \neq g = g \circ f$. ☐

EXAMPLE 7 (a) Let T be a nonempty set. The set FUN($T, \mathbb{N}$) of functions mapping T into $\mathbb{N}$ is a semigroup under the operation $\square$ defined by

$$(f \square g)(t) = f(t) + g(t) \quad \text{for all} \quad t \in T.$$

[Observe, for instance, that $(f \square g) \square h$ is defined by $((f \square g) \square h)(t) = (f \square g)(t) + h(t) = (f(t) + g(t)) + h(t)$ for all $t \in T$.] The identity element of FUN($T, \mathbb{N}$) is the constant function z defined by $z(t) = 0$ for all $t \in T$. An inverse for f would be a function g with $f(t) + g(t) = 0$ for all t, i.e., with $g(t) = -f(t)$ for all t. Since f and g have values in $\mathbb{N}$, no such g exists if $f(t) > 0$ for some t.

(b) Replace $\mathbb{N}$ by $\mathbb{Z}$ in (a). Now inverses exist; the inverse of f is the function $-f$ defined by $(-f)(t) = -f(t)$ for all $t \in T$. Thus FUN($T, \mathbb{Z}$) is a group under $\square$.

(c) The set FUN($\mathbb{R}, \mathbb{R}$) of real-valued functions on $\mathbb{R}$ is a group under the operation $+$ defined by $(f + g)(x) = f(x) + g(x)$ for all $x \in \mathbb{R}$. It is a monoid under the operation $\cdot$ defined by $(f \cdot g)(x) = f(x) * g(x)$ for all $x \in \mathbb{R}$. The identity now is the constant function c_1 where $c_1(x) = 1$ for all $x \in \mathbb{R}$. Both the additive group and the multiplicative monoid are commutative, since $\mathbb{R}$ itself has commutative addition and multiplication. ☐

The examples of semigroups we have looked at so far have almost all been infinite. They are familiar examples, but they are not the ones a computer works with. When we label a quantity as INTEGER or REAL in a computer program, we mean that it should be an integer or a real number within the capacity of the computer. Such notions as "infinite precision arithmetic" notwithstanding, too big is just too big. There is no way to deal with an enormously large integer or with π carried out to more digits than the number of bits of memory available.

The strategy that a typical arithmetic unit of a computer uses to add or multiply reasonable-sized numbers amounts to carrying out the operations in a very large finite semigroup rather than in $\mathbb{R}$ or $\mathbb{Z}$. If the numbers get too large, the computation produces an "overflow" message. To see one way to get finite semigroups we introduce the notion of **congruence**.

Let p be a fixed integer ≥ 2. Consider integers m and n. We say that m **is congruent to** n **modulo** p and we write $m \equiv n \pmod{p}$ provided $m - n$ is divisible by p. According to the Division Algorithm in § 3.6, m has the form $k_1 p + r_1$ and n has the form $k_2 p + r_2$ where $k_1, k_2 \in \mathbb{Z}$ and $r_1, r_2 \in \{0, 1, 2, \ldots, p - 1\}$. Then $m \equiv n \pmod{p}$ if and only if $r_1 = r_2$. If m and n are non-negative, then $m \equiv n \pmod{p}$ if and only if m and n leave the same remainders when divided by p.

EXAMPLE 8   (a) Two integers are congruent modulo 2 if they are both even or if they are both odd.

(b) The integers which are multiples of 5, namely

$$\ldots, -25, -20, -15, -10, -5, 0, 5, 10, 15, 20, 25, \ldots,$$

are all congruent to each other modulo 5 since the difference between any two numbers on this list is a multiple of 5.

If we add 1 to each member of this list we get a new list

$$\ldots, -24, -19, -14, -9, -4, 1, 6, 11, 16, 21, 26, \ldots.$$

The *differences* between numbers haven't changed, so the differences are still multiples of 5. For instance

$$16 - (-14) = (15 + 1) - (-15 + 1) = 15 + 1 - (-15) - 1$$
$$= 15 - (-15) = 30.$$

Thus the numbers on the new list are also congruent to each other modulo 5.

The integers

$$\ldots, -23, -18, -13, -8, -3, 2, 7, 12, 17, 22, 27, \ldots$$

are also congruent to each other modulo 5. So are the integers

$$\ldots, -22, -17, -12, -7, -2, 3, 8, 13, 18, 23, 28, \ldots,$$

and the integers

$$\ldots, -21, -16, -11, -6, -1, 4, 9, 14, 19, 24, 29, \ldots.$$

Each integer belongs to exactly one of these lists and each of these five lists contains exactly one of the numbers 0, 1, 2, 3, 4. That is, the lists form a partition of $\mathbb{Z}$. This shows that the next theorem holds with $p = 5$.   □

Theorem 1   Fix $p \geq 2$. For each $m \in \mathbb{Z}$ there is exactly one r in $\{0, 1, 2, \ldots, p - 1\}$ such that $m \equiv r \pmod{p}$.

Proof. By the Division Algorithm, m has the form $kp + r$ where $k \in \mathbb{Z}$ and $r \in \{0, 1, 2, \ldots, p - 1\}$. Then $m - r = kp$ and so $m \equiv r \pmod{p}$.

Now suppose r' in $\{0, 1, 2, \ldots, p - 1\}$ also satisfies $m \equiv r' \pmod{p}$. Then $m - r' = k'p$ for some $k' \in \mathbb{Z}$ and so $r - r' = (k' - k)p$. Hence $r - r'$

is a multiple of p. But we have $r - r' \leq p - 1$ and $r - r' \geq -(p - 1)$, and 0 is the only integer between $-(p - 1)$ and $p - 1$ that is a multiple of p. Consequently $r - r' = 0$ and $r = r'$. ☐

Congruences appear in real life.

EXAMPLE 9   An **odometer** is a device that measures the distance traveled by a vehicle. In most American automobiles, the odometer only goes up to 99,999 miles. In an old clunker an odometer reading of, say, 28,802 only tells us the true mileage modulo 100,000. That is, the clunker may have traveled 28,802 brutal miles, or 128,802 miles, or 228,802 miles, etc. ☐

The next theorem lists some basic properties of congruence. The labels R, S and T stand for reflexivity, symmetry and transitivity, notions that will be studied in Chapter 7.

Theorem 2   Fix $p \geq 2$.

(a) For integers a, b and c we have

(R) $a \equiv a \pmod p$;
(S) $a \equiv b \pmod p$ implies $b \equiv a \pmod p$;
(T) $a \equiv b \pmod p$ and $b \equiv c \pmod p$ imply $a \equiv c \pmod p$.

(b) If $a \equiv b \pmod p$ and $c \equiv d \pmod p$, then

$$a + c \equiv b + d \pmod p$$

and

$$ac \equiv bd \pmod p.$$

Proof. (a) Properties (R), (S) and (T) are immediate if we remember that "$a \equiv b \pmod p$" means "a and b have the same remainders on division by p."

(b) By assumption, $a - b = kp$ and $c - d = lp$ for some $k, l \in \mathbb{Z}$. Then

$$(a + c) - (b + d) = (a - b) + (c - d) = kp + lp = (k + l)p$$

and so $a + c \equiv b + d \pmod p$. To deal with the product, we resort to some algebraic chicanery:

$$ac - bd = ac - ad + ad - bd = a(c - d) + (a - b)d$$
$$= alp + kpd = (al + kd)p.$$

Since $al + kd$ is in $\mathbb{Z}$, $ac - bd$ is divisible by p and so $ac \equiv bd \pmod p$. ☐

We are now prepared to define the promised finite semigroups. For fixed $p \geq 2$, we write $\mathbb{Z}(p)$ for the set $\{0, 1, 2, \ldots, p - 1\}$. We are going to define an addition and multiplication for $\mathbb{Z}(p)$. It is traditional to use the symbols $+$ and $\cdot$ or $*$, but to avoid confusion with the ordinary operations on $\mathbb{Z}$ we will employ $+_p$ and $*_p$ in this section. For $m, n \in \mathbb{Z}(p)$, $m +_p n$ is defined to be the unique number in $\mathbb{Z}(p)$ satisfying

$$m +_p n \equiv m + n \pmod p.$$

Theorem 1 states that such a unique number exists; in fact, it is the remainder on dividing $m + n$ by p. Similarly, $m *_p n$ is the unique number in $\mathbb{Z}(p)$ satisfying

$$m *_p n \equiv mn \ (\text{mod } p).$$

To get $m *_p n$ multiply m by n, divide by p and take the remainder.

EXAMPLE 10   (a) For $\mathbb{Z}(5) = \{0, 1, 2, 3, 4\}$, we have $4 +_5 4 = 3$ since $4 + 4 \equiv 3$ (mod 5). Similarly, $4 *_5 4 = 1$ since $4 \cdot 4 \equiv 1$ (mod 5). The complete addition and multiplication tables for $\mathbb{Z}(5)$ are given in Figure 1.

$+_5$	0	1	2	3	4		$*_5$	0	1	2	3	4
0	0	1	2	3	4		0	0	0	0	0	0
1	1	2	3	4	0		1	0	1	2	3	4
2	2	3	4	0	1		2	0	2	4	1	3
3	3	4	0	1	2		3	0	3	1	4	2
4	4	0	1	2	3		4	0	4	3	2	1

$\mathbb{Z}(5)$

FIGURE 1

$+_2$	0	1		$*_2$	0	1
0	0	1		0	0	0
1	1	0		1	0	1

$\mathbb{Z}(2)$

FIGURE 2

(b) Very simple but very important semigroups are obtained using $\mathbb{Z}(2)$ as a starting point. The addition and multiplication tables for $\mathbb{Z}(2)$ are given in Figure 2. ☐

Theorem 3 The operations $+_p$ and $*_p$ are associative so that $\mathbb{Z}(p)$ is a semigroup under each of these binary operations.

Proof. Consider m, n and r in $\mathbb{Z}(p)$. By definition of $+_p$, we have

$$(m +_p n) +_p r \equiv (m +_p n) + r \ (\text{mod } p)$$

and

$$m +_p n \equiv m + n \ (\text{mod } p).$$

By Theorem 2(b) with $a = m +_p n$, $b = m + n$ and $c = d = r$, we see that

$$(m +_p n) +_p r \equiv (m + n) + r \ (\text{mod } p).$$

Similarly

$$m +_p (n +_p r) \equiv m + (n + r) \ (\text{mod } p).$$

Since addition in $\mathbb{Z}$ is associative, property (T) of Theorem 2 shows that

$$(m +_p n) +_p r \equiv m +_p (n +_p r) \pmod{p}.$$

Since both sides of this congruence are in $\mathbb{Z}(p)$, we conclude that

$$(m +_p n) +_p r = m +_p (n +_p r).$$

The associativity of $*_p$ is proved in exactly the same way. $\quad\Box$

In fact [Exercise 17] $(\mathbb{Z}(p), +_p)$ is a group; $(\mathbb{Z}(p), *_p)$ is not, though it does have an identity element.

Applications of congruence arithmetic to computing are outside the scope of this book, but a few comments may serve to give perspective. Computers commonly do arithmetic in $\mathbb{Z}(2)$ at the most primitive hardware level and in $\mathbb{Z}(L)$ where L is very large at the working register level. Really fast computers and really fast arithmetic programs have been designed to do arithmetic in several different $\mathbb{Z}(p)$'s, either all at once or in succession, and then fit the results together at the end. Many high-level programming languages have provisions, such as the MOD function in Pascal, for carrying out congruence arithmetic operations.

EXERCISES 4.3

1. $(\mathbb{N}, *)$ is a semigroup.
   (a) Is this semigroup commutative?
   (b) Is there an identity for this semigroup?
   (c) If yes, do inverses exist? If yes, specify them.
   (d) Is this a monoid? A group?

2. $(\mathbb{P}, +)$ is a semigroup. Repeat Exercise 1.

3. $(\mathbb{P}, *)$ is a semigroup. Repeat Exercise 1.

4. Let $\mathcal{P}(S)$ be the set of all subsets of a nonempty set S. $\mathcal{P}(S)$ is a semigroup with respect to $\cap$. Repeat Exercise 1 for this semigroup.

5. $\mathcal{P}(S)$ is a semigroup with respect to symmetric difference $\oplus$. Repeat Exercise 1 for this semigroup.

6. For a nonempty set S, let PERM(S) be the set of all permutations of S, i.e., all one-to-one functions from S onto S. PERM(S) is a semigroup under composition. Repeat Exercise 1.

7. Repeat Exercise 1 for the semigroup FUN($T, \mathbb{R}$) of real-valued functions on T under addition.

8. Repeat Exercise 1 for the semigroup FUN($T, \mathbb{R}$) under multiplication.

9. Consider the set SL_n of $n \times n$ matrices with determinant 1.
   (a) Show that SL_n is a semigroup with respect to matrix multiplication.
   (b) Is this semigroup commutative?
   (c) Is there an identity for this semigroup?
   (d) If yes, do inverses exist?
   (e) Is this semigroup a monoid? A group?

10. Show that $\mathbb{R}^+ = \{x \in \mathbb{R} : x > 0\}$ is not a semigroup with the binary operation $\langle x, y \rangle \to x/y$.

11. (a) Convince yourself that $\mathbb{N}$ is a semigroup under the binary operation $\langle m, n \rangle \to \min\{m, n\}$ and also under $\langle m, n \rangle \to \max\{m, n\}$.
    (b) Are the semigroups in part (a) monoids?

12. (a) Show that $\mathbb{P}$ is a semigroup with respect to $\langle m, n \rangle \to \gcd(m, n)$ where $\gcd(m, n)$ represents the greatest common divisor of m and n.
    (b) Show that $\mathbb{P}$ is a semigroup with respect to $\langle m, n \rangle \to \operatorname{lcm}(m, n)$ where $\operatorname{lcm}(m, n)$ represents the least common multiple of m and n.
    (c) Are the semigroups in parts (a) and (b) monoids?

13. Consider a binary operation on a nonempty set S and use functional notation f for the operation.
    (a) State the associative law for f.
    (b) State the commutative law for f.

14. List five integers that are congruent modulo 4 to each of the following:
    (a) 0   (b) 1   (c) 2
    (d) 3   (e) 4   (f) 73

15. (a) List the elements in the sets A_0, A_1 and A_2 where

$$A_k = \{m \in \mathbb{Z} : -10 \leq m \leq 10 \text{ and } m \equiv k \ (\text{mod } 3)\}.$$

    (b) What is A_3? A_4? A_{73}?

16. Give the complete addition and multiplication tables for $\mathbb{Z}(4)$. Compare the tables with those for $\mathbb{Z}(5)$ in Figure 1.

17. Prove that the semigroup $(\mathbb{Z}(p), +_p)$ is a commutative group.

18. Consider the semigroup $(\mathbb{Z}(p), *_p)$.
    (a) Show that this semigroup is a commutative monoid.
    (b) Use Figure 1 to show that $\mathbb{Z}(5) \setminus \{0\}$ is a group under multiplication $*_5$.
    (c) Use Exercise 16 to show that $\mathbb{Z}(4) \setminus \{0\}$ is not a group under $*_4$.

19. Prove that an element of a monoid cannot have two different inverses.

20. Fill in the details of the argument that $\operatorname{FUN}(\mathbb{R}, \mathbb{R})$ is a commutative group under addition; see Example 7(c).

21. Let A and B be subsets of $\mathbb{R}$.
    (a) Show that $\chi_{A \cap B} = \chi_A \cdot \chi_B$ where the right side of the equation is the ordinary product of functions as in Example 7(c).
    (b) Show that $\chi_{A \cup B} = \chi_A + \chi_B - \chi_{A \cap B}$.

22. Let $\mathbb{S}$ be a set of statements such that $p, q \in \mathbb{S}$ implies $p \wedge q$ and $p \oplus q$ are in $\mathbb{S}$; $p \oplus q$ is defined in Exercise 15 of § 2.1. Let $\phi(p) = 1$ if p is true and $\phi(p) = 0$ if p is false.
    (a) Show that $\phi(p \wedge q) = \phi(p)\phi(q)$ for all $p, q \in \mathbb{S}$.
    (b) Show that $\phi(p \oplus q) \equiv \phi(p) + \phi(q) \ (\text{mod } 2)$ for all $p, q \in \mathbb{S}$.

§ 4.4   *The Semigroups* Σ^* *and* $\mathcal{P}(\Sigma^*)$

After some preliminaries about general semigroups, we look in detail at two examples that are important in the study of formal languages and finite automata.

First consider an arbitrary semigroup $(S, \square)$. For $s \in S$ and $n \in \mathbb{P}$, we continue a familiar convention and write s^n for the $\square$-product of s with itself n times. A precise recursive definition for s^n is:

(B) $s^1 = s$,
(R) $s^{n+1} = s^n \square s$ for $n \in \mathbb{P}$.

If $(S, \square)$ is a monoid, i.e., if S has an identity e, then we also define $s^0 = e$. Alternatively, we could modify the recursive definition to read:

(B) $s^0 = e$,
(R) $s^{n+1} = s^n \square s$ for $n \in \mathbb{N}$.

With these definitions we can prove, once and for all, some familiar algebraic properties of exponents.

Theorem 1 Let $(S, \square)$ be a semigroup. For $s \in S$ and $m, n \in \mathbb{P}$, we have

(a) $s^m \square s^n = s^{m+n}$
(b) $(s^m)^n = s^{mn}$.

For a monoid, these formulas hold for $m, n \in \mathbb{N}$.

Proof. (a) We fix $m \in \mathbb{P}$ and prove

(1) $$s^m \square s^n = s^{m+n} \quad \text{for} \quad n \in \mathbb{P},$$

by induction on n. For $n = 1$, this follows from the recursive definition. Assume the equality is valid for some n. Then

$$\begin{aligned}
s^m \square s^{n+1} &= s^m \square (s^n \square s) && \text{definition of } s^{n+1} \\
&= (s^m \square s^n) \square s && \text{associativity} \\
&= s^{m+n} \square s && \text{inductive assumption} \\
&= s^{(m+n)+1} && \text{definition of } s^{(m+n)+1} \\
&= s^{m+(n+1)}.
\end{aligned}$$

The Principle of Mathematical Induction now shows that (1) holds for all n in $\mathbb{P}$.

(b) Again we fix m and prove

(2) $$(s^m)^n = s^{mn} \quad \text{for} \quad n \in \mathbb{P},$$

by induction on n. For $n = 1$, this is clear since $(s^m)^1 = s^m$ by the basis part of the recursive definition. If the equality holds for n, then

$$\begin{aligned}
(s^m)^{n+1} &= ((s^m)^n) \square s^m && \text{definition} \\
&= s^{mn} \square s^m && \text{inductive assumption} \\
&= s^{mn+m} && \text{part (a)} \\
&= s^{m(n+1)}.
\end{aligned}$$

Hence (2) holds for all n by induction.

If S is a monoid and m or n is 0, then (a) and (b) are simple to verify. ☐

We have treated the generic operation $\square$ the same way we would treat multiplication. Let's see how the foregoing would look when $\square$ is replaced by $+$. The general product s^n is replaced by the general sum ns and the first recursive definition becomes:

(B) $1s = s$,
(R) $(n + 1)s = ns + s$ for $n \in \mathbb{P}$.

Theorem 1 now says

(a) $ms + ns = (m + n)s$
(b) $n(ms) = (mn)s$

for $s \in S$ and $m, n \in \mathbb{P}$. It might be a useful exercise to rewrite the proof of Theorem 1 using this notation.

Now let Σ be an alphabet. The set Σ^* of all words is informally defined in § 1.1 and is recursively defined in Example 2 of § 3.5. Two words w_1 and w_2 in Σ^* are multiplied by **concatenation**; that is, $w_1 w_2$ is the word obtained by placing the string w_2 right after the string w_1. In other words, if $w_1 = a_1 a_2 \cdots a_m$ and $w_2 = b_1 b_2 \cdots b_n$ where the a_j's and b_k's are in Σ, then $w_1 w_2 = a_1 a_2 \cdots a_m b_1 b_2 \cdots b_n$. For example, if $w_1 = cat$ and $w_2 = nip$, then $w_1 w_2 = catnip$ and $w_2 w_1 = nipcat$. Multiplication by the empty word ϵ leaves the word unchanged:

$$w\epsilon = \epsilon w = w \quad \text{for all} \quad w \in \Sigma^*.$$

It is evident from the definition that concatenation is an associative binary operation. Since the empty word ϵ serves as an identity for Σ^*, Σ^* is a monoid.

Now consider the set $\mathcal{P}(\Sigma^*)$ of all subsets of Σ^*, i.e., all languages using letters from Σ. Of course, $\mathcal{P}(\Sigma^*)$ is a semigroup under binary operations such as $\cup$, $\cap$ and $\oplus$. But none of these operations reflects the special structure of Σ^*. When we speak of **the semigroup** $\mathcal{P}(\Sigma^*)$ we refer to the binary operation in the next definition.

Definition   For $A, B \in \mathcal{P}(\Sigma^*)$, the **set-product** AB is defined to be the set

$$AB = \{w_1 w_2 : w_1 \in A \quad \text{and} \quad w_2 \in B\}.$$

Thus AB is the set of all words obtained by concatenating a word in A with a word in B.

Using the associativity of concatenation in Σ^*, it is easy to see that set-product is associative:

$$(AB)C = A(BC) \quad \text{for all} \quad A, B, C \in \mathcal{P}(\Sigma^*).$$

Thus $\mathcal{P}(\Sigma^*)$ is a semigroup.

EXAMPLE 1   Here we compare and contrast the empty set $\varnothing$ and the set $\{\epsilon\}$ consisting of the empty word. These sets are different and they both belong to $\mathcal{P}(\Sigma^*)$. Since

$$A\{\epsilon\} = \{\epsilon\}A = A \quad \text{for all} \quad A \in \mathcal{P}(\Sigma^*),$$

$\{\epsilon\}$ is an identity for $\mathcal{P}(\Sigma^*)$. Thus $\mathcal{P}(\Sigma^*)$ is a monoid. For any set A,

$$A\varnothing = \{w_1 w_2 : w_1 \in A \quad \text{and} \quad w_2 \in \varnothing\};$$

since $w_2 \in \varnothing$ never occurs, this set is empty and so

$$A\varnothing = \varnothing A = \varnothing \quad \text{for all} \quad A \in \mathcal{P}(\Sigma^*). \quad \square$$

Powers A^n for $A \in \mathcal{P}(\Sigma^*)$ and $n \in \mathbb{N}$ are defined just as for general monoids. In particular, $A^0 = \{\epsilon\}$ for all $A \in \mathcal{P}(\Sigma^*)$. Note that for $k \in \mathbb{N}$, Σ^k consists of all words obtained by concatenating k letters from Σ, i.e.,

$$\Sigma^k = \{w \in \Sigma^* : \text{length}(w) = k\},$$

so that the new power notation is consistent with the definition in Example 1(c) of § 1.3.

EXAMPLE 2   Let $\Sigma = \{a, b, c\}$, $A = \{a, ab\}$, $B = \{\epsilon, b, bb\}$ and $C = \{w \in \Sigma^* : \text{length}(w)$ is even$\}$. Note that C contains the empty word ϵ. Then

$$AB = \{a, ab, abb, abbb\},$$
$$BA = \{a, ab, ba, bab, bba, bbab\},$$
$$A^2 = \{aa, aab, aba, abab\},$$
$$B^2 = \{\epsilon, b, bb, bbb, bbbb\},$$
$$A\Sigma = \{aa, ab, ac, aba, abb, abc\},$$
$$C\Sigma = \Sigma C = \{w \in \Sigma^* : \text{length}(w)$ is odd$\}.$$

Note that

$$C = \bigcup_{n=0}^{\infty} \Sigma^{2n}. \quad \square$$

For any language $A \subseteq \Sigma^*$, the set A^* defined by

$$A^* = \bigcup_{n=0}^{\infty} A^n$$

is called the **Kleene closure of** A. Note that A^* consists of all the possible words obtained by concatenating words from A, including the empty word ϵ since $A^0 = \{\epsilon\}$. For $A = \Sigma$ this notation is consistent with our earlier usage of Σ^* since $\Sigma^* = \bigcup_{n=0}^{\infty} \Sigma^n$. We also define the **positive closure** A^+ by

$$A^+ = \bigcup_{n=1}^{\infty} A^n.$$

In particular,

$$\Sigma^+ = \bigcup_{n=1}^{\infty} \Sigma^n = \{w \in \Sigma^* : \text{length}(w) > 0\} = \Sigma^* \setminus \{\epsilon\}.$$

Note that we always have $A^* = A^+ \cup \{\epsilon\}$ and that $A^* = A^+$ if and only if ϵ belongs to A [Exercise 12].

EXAMPLE 3   Let A, B and C be as in Example 2: $A = \{a, ab\}$, $B = \{\epsilon, b, bb\}$, $C = \{w \in \Sigma^* : \text{length}(w) \text{ is even}\}$. It is easy to verify that

$$C = \bigcup_{n=0}^{\infty} C^n = C^* = C^+$$

since $C^n \subseteq C$ for all $n \in \mathbb{N}$. It is also easy to show that

$$B^* = B^+ = \{w \in \Sigma^* : w \text{ uses only the letter } b\}$$

$$= \{\epsilon, b, bb, bbb, bbbb, \ldots\} = \{b^n : n \in \mathbb{N}\}.$$

The exact nature of the set A^* is less clear, though it is a subset of

$$D = \{w \in \Sigma^* : \text{the number of occurrences of } b \text{ is } \leq \text{ the}$$
$$\text{number of occurrences of } a\}.$$

This can be seen by proving that $A^n \subseteq D$ for all $n \in \mathbb{N}$ by induction. The inclusion $A^* \subseteq D$ is proper; for example, $aabb$ is not in A^*. Observe that $\epsilon \in A^*$ but $\epsilon \notin A^+$ so that $A^+ \neq A^*$.   ☐

Here are some other basic properties about the Kleene and positive closures.

Theorem 2   For a subset A of Σ^* we have

(a) $A^*A^* = A^*$,
(b) $(A^*)^* = A^*$,
(c) $A^+ = AA^* = A^*A = A^+A^* = A^*A^+$,
(d) $(A^+)^+ = A^+$,
(e) $(A^*)^+ = (A^+)^* = A^*$.

Proof.   We freely use the following obvious facts:

(1)   if $A \subseteq B$ and $C \subseteq D$, then $AC \subseteq BD$;

(2)   if $A \subseteq B$, then $A^n \subseteq B^n$ for all n, $A^+ \subseteq B^+$ and $A^* \subseteq B^*$;

(3) $A \subseteq A^+ \subseteq A^*$.

(a) Clearly $A^* = \{\epsilon\}A^* \subseteq A^*A^*$. For the other inclusion, consider $w \in A^*A^*$. Then $w = w_1w_2$ where $w_1 \in A^*$ and $w_2 \in A^*$. Hence for some $m, n \in \mathbb{N}$ we have $w_1 \in A^m$ and $w_2 \in A^n$. Consequently $w = w_1w_2 \in A^mA^n = A^{m+n} \subseteq A^*$. This shows that $A^*A^* \subseteq A^*$ and so (a) is established.

(b) Since $A \subseteq A^*$, we have $A^* \subseteq (A^*)^*$. To show

$$(A^*)^* = \bigcup_{n=0}^{\infty} (A^*)^n \subseteq A^*,$$

it suffices to prove

(4) $(A^*)^n \subseteq A^*$ for all $n \in \mathbb{N}$.

This is obvious for $n = 0$ and $n = 1$. With induction in mind, we assume the inclusion for some $n \geq 1$ and then obtain

$$(A^*)^{n+1} = (A^*)^n A^* \subseteq A^*A^* \quad \text{inductive assumption}$$
$$= A^* \qquad \text{by part (a)}.$$

By the Principle of Mathematical Induction, (4) holds.

(c) We will prove

(5) $$A^+ \subseteq AA^* \subseteq A^+A^* \subseteq A^+.$$

This will show that $A^+ = AA^* = A^+A^*$ and the other equalities in (c) have similar proofs. For each $n \geq 1$, we have $A^n = AA^{n-1} \subseteq AA^*$ and so $A^+ = \bigcup_{n=1}^{\infty} A^n \subseteq AA^*$. This establishes the first inclusion in (5) and the second inclusion is clear. If $w \in A^+A^*$, then $w = w_1 w_2$ with $w_1 \in A^+$ and $w_2 \in A^*$ so that $w_1 \in A^m$ and $w_2 \in A^n$ for some $m \in \mathbb{P}$ and $n \in \mathbb{N}$. Since $m + n$ is in $\mathbb{P}$, we see that $w = w_1 w_2 \in A^{m+n} \subseteq A^+$. This establishes the last inclusion in (5).

The proofs of parts (d) and (e) are left to Exercise 9.   □

Parts (a) and (c) can be given quick and intuitive proofs provided one is comfortable with manipulating infinite unions as in Exercise 10.

Loosely speaking, a closure operator is something which, if repeated, gives you nothing new. For example, A^* will usually be larger than A. But applying the star operator again, this time to A^*, gives nothing new since $(A^*)^* = A^*$. This is why * is called a closure operator. The $^+$ operator is another example of a closure operator.

The next theorem gives various representations of the Kleene closure of the union of two languages. The proof is made easy by applying Theorem 2; elementwise arguments can be avoided.

Theorem 3   For subsets A and B of Σ^* we have

$$(A \cup B)^* = (A^* \cup B^*)^* = (A^*B^*)^* = (B^*A^*)^*.$$

Proof. Since $A \cup B \subseteq A^* \cup B^* \subseteq A^*B^*$, we have

(1) $$(A \cup B)^* \subseteq (A^* \cup B^*)^* \subseteq (A^*B^*)^*.$$

Since $A \subseteq A \cup B$ and $B \subseteq A \cup B$, we have

$$A^*B^* \subseteq (A \cup B)^*(A \cup B)^* = (A \cup B)^*,$$

the equality following from Theorem 2(a). Hence

$$(A^*B^*)^* \subseteq ((A \cup B)^*)^* = (A \cup B)^*$$

where the equality follows from Theorem 2(b). This inclusion and (1) show that the first three sets of the theorem are equal. Now reversing the roles of A and B gives

$$(B^*A^*)^* = (B \cup A)^* = (A \cup B)^*.   \square$$

EXAMPLE 4   To remove some of the mystery from the equalities in Theorem 3, we illustrate the equality $(A \cup B)^* = (A^*B^*)^*$ for the sets $A = \{a, ad\}$ and $B = \{b, bdb\}$.

Each word in $(A \cup B)^*$ has the form $c_1 c_2 \ldots c_n$, where each c_i belongs to A or to B. For example,

$$w = aabdbadaababbdbada$$
$$= aa(bdb)(ad)aabab(bdb)(ad)a$$

is such a word. Neighboring elements in A can be grouped together to give a product in A^*. Similarly, adjacent elements of B give products in B^*. Thus one way to break up w is

$$w = \underbrace{aa}_{\in A^*} \quad \underbrace{(bdb)}_{\in B^*} \quad \underbrace{(ad)aa}_{\in A^*} \quad \underbrace{b}_{\in B^*} \quad \underbrace{a}_{\in A^*} \quad \underbrace{b(bdb)}_{\in B^*} \quad \underbrace{(ad)a.}_{\in A^*}$$

The empty word ϵ is in B^*. If we attach it to the end of w, we see that w belongs to $(A^*B^*)^4$ and hence to $(A^*B^*)^*$.

Now consider a typical word in $(A^*B^*)^*$, i.e., one of the form $w_1 w_2 \ldots w_m$ where each w_i is in A^*B^*. Each w_i is itself of the form $u_i v_i$ with $u_i \in A^*$ and $v_i \in B^*$. One example of such a word is $u_1 v_1 u_2 v_2 u_3 v_3$ with $u_1 = (ad)a(ad)$, $u_2 = aa$, $u_3 = (ad)(ad)a$ and $v_1 = bbbb$, $v_2 = \epsilon$, $v_3 = b(bdb)$. This is the word

$$adaadbbbbaaadadabbdb,$$

which is clearly in $(A \cup B)^*$.   ⬜

For any subset A of Σ^* the sets A^+ and A^* are closed under the concatenation operation on Σ^* by Theorem 2(a) and the obvious inclusion $A^+A^+ \subseteq A^+$. Hence each of these sets is a semigroup containing A; indeed A^* is a monoid, with identity ϵ.

In general, a **subsemigroup** of a semigroup $(S, \square)$ is a subset T of S which is closed under the operation $\square$, i.e., satisfies $t \square t' \in T$ for all $t, t' \in T$. A **submonoid** of a monoid $(M, \square)$ is a subsemigroup of M which contains the identity of M, and a **subgroup** of a group $(G, \square)$ is a submonoid of G which contains the inverses of all of its members. We will return to these ideas in Chapter 11.

In our present situation A^+ is a subsemigroup and A^* a submonoid of the monoid Σ^*. In fact, A^+ is the smallest subsemigroup of Σ^* containing A, and A^* is the smallest submonoid containing A. For surely any subsemigroup of Σ^* which contains A must contain A^n for $n = 1, 2, \ldots$ [an induction is hiding here] and so must contain A^+. Throw in ϵ to get the smallest submonoid.

EXERCISES 4.4

1. Let $(S, \square)$ be a group. How would you define s^n for s in S and negative integers n?

2. Let $\Sigma = \{a, b, c, d\}$ and consider the words: $w_1 = bad$, $w_2 = cab$ and $w_3 = abcd$.

(a) Determine $w_1 w_2$, $w_2 w_1$, $w_2 w_3 w_2 w_1$ and $w_3 w_2 w_3$.

(b) Determine w_1^2, w_2^3 and ϵ^4.

3. Let Σ be the usual English alphabet and consider the words: $w_1 = break$, $w_2 = fast$, $w_3 = lunch$ and $w_4 = food$.

   (a) Determine ϵw_1, $w_2 \epsilon$, $w_2 w_4$, $w_3 w_1$ and $w_4 \epsilon w_4$.

   (b) Compare $w_1 w_2$ and $w_2 w_1$.

   (c) Determine w_2^2, w_4^2, $w_2^2 w_4 w_1^2$ and ϵ^{73}.

4. Let $\Sigma = \{a, b, c\}$, $A = \{a, ab, aa\}$, $B = \{cab, bac, cc\}$ and $E = \{\epsilon\}$. Determine

   (a) AB (b) BA (c) AE

   (d) EA (e) $A\Sigma$ (f) ΣA

   (g) A^2 (h) B^2 (i) E^{73}

5. Let $\Sigma = \{a, b\}$, $A = \{ab, ba\}$ and $B = \{\epsilon, b^2\}$. Calculate

   (a) A^2 (b) AB (c) BA

   (d) B^2 (e) $A\Sigma$ (f) $\Sigma^2 \cap B$

6. Let Σ, A and B be as in Exercise 5.

   (a) Describe B^*.

   (b) Show that $A^* \subseteq \bigcup_{n=0}^{\infty} \Sigma^{2n}$.

   (c) Give an example of a word in $\Sigma^* \backslash A^*$ having even length.

   (d) Show that $A^* B \neq A B^*$.

7. (a) Explain why Σ^* is not a group. That is, exhibit a word having no inverse.

   (b) When is the monoid Σ^* commutative?

8. Let A and D be as in Example 3. Prove that $A^n \subseteq D$ for all $n \in \mathbb{N}$.

9. (a) Prove part (d) of Theorem 2.

   (b) Prove part (e) of Theorem 2.

10. (a) Let $\{C_i : i \in I\}$ be a family of subsets of Σ^* indexed by some set I. Prove that if B is also a subset of Σ^*, then $B(\bigcup_{i \in I} C_i) = \bigcup_{i \in I} BC_i$.

    (b) Use part (a) to prove parts (a) and (c) of Theorem 2.

11. Let A, B and C be languages over an alphabet Σ. Specify which statements below are true and which are false. For each false statement, provide an example that shows it is false.

    (a) $A \cap B \subseteq AB$. (b) $A^* = B^*$ implies $A = B$.

    (c) Σ^* is infinite. (d) ϵ is in A^*.

    (e) $AB = BA$. (f) $AB = A$ implies $B = \{\epsilon\}$.

    (g) $AB = AC$ implies $B = C$. (h) $A \subseteq A^2$.

    (i) $A \subseteq B$ implies $A^2 \subseteq B^2$. (j) $\epsilon \in AB$ implies $\epsilon \in A \cap B$.

    (k) $AA^* = A^*$. (l) $A^2 = B^2$ implies $A = B$.

    (m) $A^* = \Sigma^*$ implies $\Sigma \subseteq A$. (n) Every word in Σ has length 1.

12. For $A \subseteq \Sigma^*$, prove that $A^* = A^+$ if and only if ϵ is in A.

13. Let A be a nonempty language over an alphabet Σ such that $A^2 = A$. Prove that A contains the empty word ϵ. *Hint:* Consider a word in A having least length.

14. Consider languages A and B over an alphabet Σ.

    (a) Prove that $(BA)^{n+1} = B(AB)^n A$ for all $n \in \mathbb{N}$ by induction.

    (b) Prove that $(BA)^+ = B(AB)^* A$.

(c) Prove that if $AB = BA$, then $(BA)^n = B^n A^n$ for all $n \in \mathbb{N}$. *Hint:* Use induction and part (a).

15. Generalize parts (a) and (c) of Exercise 14 to an arbitrary monoid $(S, \square)$.

16. Let A and B be languages over an alphabet Σ.
    (a) Show that $(AB)^n \subseteq (A \cup B)^{2n}$ for $n = 0, 1$ and 2.
    (b) Prove, by induction, that $(AB)^n \subseteq (A \cup B)^{2n}$ for all $n \in \mathbb{N}$.
    (c) Show that $(AB)^* \subseteq (A \cup B)^*$.

17. Let A, B and C be languages over an alphabet Σ.
    (a) Prove $A(B \cup C) = AB \cup AC$.
    (b) Prove $A(B \cap C) \subseteq AB \cap AC$.
    (c) Show that the inclusion in part (b) can be proper.

18. (a) Show that the intersection of two subsemigroups of a semigroup S is a subsemigroup of S or the empty set.
    (b) How about the intersection of two submonoids of a monoid or two subgroups of a group?
    (c) How would the answers to parts (a) and (b) change if we intersected more than two sets?
    (d) Show that if S is a semigroup, if $A \subseteq S$ and $A \neq \varnothing$, then the intersection of all subsemigroups of S containing A is the smallest subsemigroup of S containing A.

19. Let $\Sigma = \{a, b\}$.
    (a) Find the smallest submonoid of Σ^* containing the set $\{a, ab\}$. That is, describe its members. Compare with the set A^* in Example 3.
    (b) Find the smallest submonoid of Σ^* containing $\{a, ba\}$.

CHAPTER HIGHLIGHTS

These lists of items should produce three kinds of responses. What three? [See the end of Chapter 0 for the answer.]

Concepts

matrix
    transpose, sum, product, scalar multiple
    identity, negative, inverse
    determinant
binary operation
    semigroup, subsemigroup
    monoid = semigroup with identity, submonoid
    group = monoid with inverses, subgroup
congruence modulo p, $\mathbb{Z}(p)$, $+_p$, $*_p$
Σ^* and $\mathcal{P}(\Sigma^*)$ as monoids
Kleene closure $= A^* = \bigcup\limits_{n=0}^{\infty} A^n$, A^+

Facts

Matrix multiplication is associative, but not commutative.

$\det(\mathbf{AB}) = (\det \mathbf{A})(\det \mathbf{B})$ and $\det(\mathbf{I}) = 1$.

A square matrix is invertible if and only if its determinant is non-0.

Properties of congruence [Theorem 2 of § 4.3].

$(\mathbb{Z}(p), +_p)$ and $(\mathbb{Z}(p), *_p)$ are semigroups.

The congruence classes mod p partition $\mathbb{Z}$.

In a semigroup $s^m \,\square\, s^n = s^{m+n}$ and $(s^m)^n = s^{mn}$.

Properties of A^* and A^+ [Theorems 2 and 3 of § 4.4].

Method

Use of inverses to solve matrix equations.

5

COUNTING

‖‖‖

The major goal of this chapter is to establish several techniques for counting large finite sets without actually listing their elements. Related techniques, such as the Pigeon-Hole Principle, will also be studied. The last section deals with infinite sets.

§ 5.1 Basic Counting Techniques

For any finite set S, we write $|S|$ for the number of elements in the set. Thus $|S| = |T|$ precisely when the finite sets S and T are of the same size. Observe that

$$|\varnothing| = 0 \quad \text{and} \quad |\{1, 2, \ldots, n\}| = n \quad \text{for} \quad n \in \mathbb{P}.$$

We begin with some counting rules with which you are probably more or less familiar.

Union Rules Let S and T be finite sets.

(a) If S and T are disjoint, i.e., if $S \cap T = \varnothing$, then $|S \cup T| = |S| + |T|$.

(b) In general, $|S \cup T| = |S| + |T| - |S \cap T|$.

The intuitive reason (b) holds is that, in calculating $|S| + |T|$, elements in $S \cap T$ are counted twice and so $|S \cap T|$ needs to be subtracted from the sum $|S| + |T|$ to obtain $|S \cup T|$. Assertion (b) can be obtained from (a) as follows. Applying (a) two times, we get

$$|S \cup T| = |S| + |T \backslash S| \quad \text{and} \quad |T| = |T \backslash S| + |S \cap T|.$$

Thus we have

$$|S \cup T| + |S \cap T| = |S| + |T \backslash S| + |S \cap T| = |S| + |T|$$

and this implies (b).

A general rule for counting unions of more than two sets, called the Inclusion-Exclusion Principle, appears in § 5.2.

EXAMPLE 1 How many integers in $S = \{1, 2, 3, \ldots, 1000\}$ are divisible by 3 or 5? We let

$$D_3 = \{n \in S : n \text{ is divisible by 3}\}$$

and

$$D_5 = \{n \in S : n \text{ is divisible by 5}\}.$$

We seek the number of elements in $D_3 \cup D_5$, which is not obvious. But $|D_3|$ is easily seen to be 333; just divide 1000 by 3 and round down. Doubters should note that

$$D_3 = \{3m : 1 \leq m \leq 333\}.$$

Likewise, $|D_5| = 200$. Since $D_3 \cap D_5 = \{n \in S : n \text{ is divisible by 15}\}$ and $1000/15$ is $66\ 2/3$, $|D_3 \cap D_5|$ equals 66. By the Union Rule (b),

$$|D_3 \cup D_5| = |D_3| + |D_5| - |D_3 \cap D_5| = 333 + 200 - 66 = 467. \quad \square$$

For finite sets S and T we have $|S \times T| = |S| \cdot |T|$, since

$$S \times T = \{\langle s, t \rangle : s \in S \quad \text{and} \quad t \in T\}$$

and for each of the $|S|$ choices of s in S there are $|T|$ choices of t in T to make up the ordered pair $\langle s, t \rangle$. The identity $|S \times T| = |S| \cdot |T|$ is illustrated in Figures 1 and 2 of § 1.4. A similar equality holds for the product of more than two sets.

Product Rules (a) For finite sets $S_1, S_2, \ldots, S_k$ we have

$$|S_1 \times S_2 \times \cdots \times S_k| = \prod_{j=1}^{k} |S_j|.$$

(b) More generally, suppose that a given set can be viewed as a set of ordered k-tuples $\langle s_1, s_2, \ldots, s_k \rangle$ with the following structure. There are n_1 possible choices of s_1. Given s_1 there are n_2 possible choices of s_2. Given s_1 and s_2 there are n_3 possible choices of s_3. In general, given $s_1, s_2, \ldots, s_{j-1}$ there are n_j choices of s_j. Then the set has $n_1 n_2 \cdots n_k$ elements.

often used
where order
matters .

In practice we will often use Product Rule (b), but almost never with the forbidding formalism suggested in its statement.

EXAMPLE 2 (a) We calculate the number of ways of selecting five cards with replacement from a deck of 52 cards. Thus we are counting ordered 5-tuples consisting of cards from the deck. **With replacement** means that each card is returned to the deck before the next card is drawn. The set of ways of selecting five cards with replacement is in one-to-one correspondence with $D \times D \times D \times D \times D = D^5$, where D is the 52-element set of cards. Thus by Product Rule (a), the set has 52^5 elements.

This problem can also be solved by Product Rule (b). There are 52 ways of selecting the first card. After selecting a few cards which have been returned to the deck, there are still 52 ways of selecting the next card. So there are $52 \cdot 52 \cdot 52 \cdot 52 \cdot 52$ ways of selecting five cards with replacement.

(b) Now we calculate the number of ways of selecting five cards without replacement from a deck of 52 cards. **Without replacement** means that, once a card is drawn, it is not returned to the deck. This time Product Rule (a) does *not* apply, since not all ordered 5-tuples in D^5 are allowed. Specifically, ordered 5-tuples with cards repeated are forbidden. But Product Rule (b) does apply. The first card can be selected in 52 ways. Once it is selected the second card can be selected in 51 ways. The third card can be selected in 50 ways, the fourth in 49 ways and the fifth in 48 ways. So five cards can be selected without replacement in $52 \cdot 51 \cdot 50 \cdot 49 \cdot 48$ ways.

So far we have only counted ordered 5-tuples of cards, not 5-card subsets. We will return to the subset question in Example 10.   ☐

EXAMPLE 3   (a) Let $\Sigma = \{a, b, c, d, e, f, g\}$. The number of words in Σ^* having length 5 is $7^5 = 16,807$, i.e., $|\Sigma^5| = 16,807$. This is seen by applying either Product Rule just as in Example 2(a). The number of words in Σ^5 that have no letters repeated is $7 \cdot 6 \cdot 5 \cdot 4 \cdot 3 = 2520$. This is because the first letter can be selected in 7 ways, then the second letter can be selected in 6 ways, etc.

(b) Let $\Sigma = \{a, b, c, d\}$. The number of words in Σ^2 without repetitions of letters is $4 \cdot 3 = 12$ by Product Rule (b). We can illustrate this by a picture called a tree; see Figure 1. Each path from the start corresponds to a word in

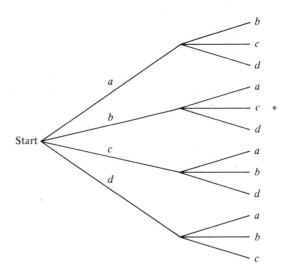

FIGURE 1

Σ^2 without repetitions. For example, the path ending at ∗ corresponds to the word *bc*. One can mentally imagine a similar but very large tree for the computation in part (a). ☐

EXAMPLE 4 In Exercise 6 of § 0.2 we asked you to count the number of spanning trees in two graphs, redrawn here in Figures 2(a) and 2(b). A direct count shows that the graph in Figure 2(a) has 8 spanning trees. Any spanning tree in Figure 2(b)

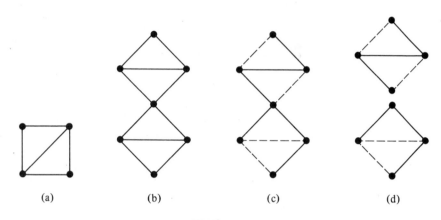

(a)	(b)	(c)	(d)

FIGURE 2

can be viewed as a pair of spanning trees, one for the upper half and one for the lower half of the graph. Each half of the spanning tree is a spanning tree for the graph in Figure 2(a). For example, the spanning tree in Figure 2(c) is built from the pair of spanning trees in Figure 2(d). By the Product Rule there are $8 \cdot 8 = 64$ such pairs, so the graph in Figure 2(b) has 64 spanning trees. ☐

EXAMPLE 5 (a) Let S and T be finite sets. We will count the number of functions $f: S \to T$. Here it is convenient to write

$$S = \{s_1, s_2, \ldots, s_m\} \quad \text{and} \quad T = \{t_1, t_2, \ldots, t_n\}$$

so that $|S| = m$ and $|T| = n$. A function $f: S \to T$ can be obtained by specifying $f(s_1)$ to be one of the n elements in T, then specifying $f(s_2)$ to be one of the n elements in T, etc. This process leads to $n^m = n \cdot n \cdots n$ [m times] different results, each of which specifies a different function. We conclude that there are n^m functions mapping S into T.

(b) In part (a) we determined $|\text{FUN}(S, T)|$ for the set $\text{FUN}(S, T)$ of all functions from S into T. Some people write T^S in place of $\text{FUN}(S, T)$. This is strange-looking notation, but it does allow one to write

$$|T^S| = |T|^{|S|},$$

giving a "power rule" analogous to our union rules and product rules. ☐

Consider a nonempty finite set S with n elements and consider a positive integer $r \leqq n$. An *r*-**permutation** of S is any ordered listing of r distinct elements of S. More precisely, an *r*-**permutation** is a one-to-one mapping σ [lowercase Greek sigma] of the set $\{1, 2, \ldots, r\}$ into S. An r-permutation σ is completely described by the ordered r-tuple $\langle \sigma(1), \sigma(2), \ldots, \sigma(r) \rangle$, and we will sometimes use the r-tuple as a notation for the r-permutation itself. An r-permutation can be obtained by assigning 1 to any of the n elements in S. Then 2 can be assigned to any of the $n - 1$ remaining elements, etc. Hence by Product Rule (b), the set S has $n(n - 1)(n - 2) \cdots$ r-permutations where the product consists of exactly r factors. The last factor turns out to be $n - r + 1$. We sometimes abbreviate the product as $P(n, r)$. Thus S has exactly

$$P(n, r) = n(n - 1)(n - 2) \cdots (n - r + 1) = \prod_{j=0}^{r-1} (n - j)$$

r-permutations. We call the n-permutations simply **permutations**. The set S has exactly $P(n, n) = n!$ permutations. Note that $P(n, r) \cdot (n - r)! = n!$ and so

$$P(n, r) = \frac{n!}{(n - r)!} \quad \text{for} \quad 1 \leqq r \leqq n.$$

It is also convenient to decree $P(n, 0) = 1$, the unique 0-permutation being the "empty permutation."

EXAMPLE 6   (a) The five cards drawn without replacement in Example 2(b) correspond exactly to 5-permutations of the 52-element set of cards. So the number of such drawings is exactly $P(52, 5) = 52 \cdot 51 \cdot 50 \cdot 49 \cdot 48$.

(b) Let Σ be the seven letter alphabet in Example 3(a). The words in Σ^5 that have no letters repeated are 5-permutations of Σ. There are $P(7, 5) = 7 \cdot 6 \cdot 5 \cdot 4 \cdot 3$ such 5-permutations. Note that the empty word ϵ is the empty permutation of Σ.

(c) The words in Σ^2 without repetitions in Example 3(b) are 2-permutations of the 4-element set Σ. There are $P(4, 2) = 4 \cdot 3 = 12$ of them.   ☐

EXAMPLE 7   In §0.2 we were interested in the spanning trees of a graph with 14 edges. We mentioned that there are 14! possible orderings of the edges. This is correct since these orderings are just the various permutations of the 14-element set of edges.   ☐

In counting problems where order matters, r-permutations are clearly relevant. Often order is irrelevant, in which case the ability to count sets becomes important. We already know that a set S with n elements has 2^n subsets altogether. For $0 \leqq r \leqq n$ let $\binom{n}{r}$ be the number of r-element subsets of S. The number $\binom{n}{r}$, called a **binomial coefficient**, is read "n choose r" and is sometimes called the number of **combinations** of n things taken r at a time.

Theorem 1   For $0 \leq r \leq n$ we have

$$\binom{n}{r} = \frac{n!}{(n-r)!\,r!}.$$

Proof. Let S be a set with n elements. For each r-element subset T of S, there are $r!$ permutations of S using the elements in T. Hence there are $\binom{n}{r} \cdot r!$ r-permutations of S in all, i.e.,

$$\binom{n}{r} \cdot r! = P(n, r) = \frac{n!}{(n-r)!}$$

and so

$$\binom{n}{r} = \frac{n!}{(n-r)!\,r!}. \quad \Box$$

EXAMPLE 8   We count the number of strings of 0's and 1's having length n that consist of exactly r 1's. This is equivalent to counting the number of functions from $\{1, 2, \ldots, n\}$ to $\{0, 1\}$ that take the value 1 exactly r times. In other words, we need to count the number of characteristic functions χ_A where $|A| = r$. This is exactly the number of r-element subsets of $\{1, 2, \ldots, n\}$, i.e., $\binom{n}{r}$. $\quad \Box$

EXAMPLE 9   Consider a graph with no loops that is **complete** in the sense that for each pair of distinct vertices there is exactly one edge connecting them. How many edges does the graph have if it has n vertices? Let's assume $n \geq 2$. Each edge determines a 2-element subset of the set V of vertices and, conversely, each 2-element subset of V determines an edge. In other words, the set of edges is in one-to-one correspondence with the set of 2-element subsets of V. Hence there are

$$\binom{n}{2} = \frac{n!}{(n-2)!\,2!} = \frac{n(n-1)}{2}$$

edges of the graph. $\quad \Box$

An excellent way to illustrate the techniques of this section is to calculate the numbers of various kinds of poker hands. A deck of cards consists of four suits called clubs, diamonds, hearts and spades. Each suit consists of thirteen cards with values A, 2, 3, 4, 5, 6, 7, 8, 9, 10, J, Q, K. Here A stands for ace, J for jack, Q for queen and K for king. There are four cards of each value, one from each suit. A **poker hand** is a set of 5 cards from a 52-card deck of cards. The order in which the cards are chosen is irrelevant. A straight consists of five cards whose values form a consecutive sequence such as 8, 9, 10, J, Q. The ace A can be at the bottom of a sequence A, 2, 3, 4, 5 or at the top of a sequence 10, J, Q, K, A. Poker hands are classified into disjoint sets as follows; they are listed in reverse order of their likelihood.

Royal flush: 10, J, Q, K, A all in the same suit.

Straight flush: a straight all in the same suit that is not a royal flush.

Four of a kind: four cards in the hand have the same value. For example, four 3's and a 9.

Full house: three cards of one value and two cards of another value. For example, three jacks and two 8's.

Flush: Five cards all in the same suit, but not a royal or straight flush.

Straight: A straight that is not a royal or straight flush.

Three of a kind: Three cards of one value, a fourth card of a second value and a fifth card of a third value.

Two pairs: Two cards of one value, two more cards of a second value and the remaining card a third value. For example, two queens, two 4's and a 7.

One pair: Two cards of one value but not classified above. For example, two kings, a jack, a 9 and a 6.

Nothing: None of the above.

EXAMPLE 10   (a) There are $\binom{52}{5}$ poker hands. Note that

$$\binom{52}{5} = \frac{52 \cdot 51 \cdot 50 \cdot 49 \cdot 48}{5 \cdot 4 \cdot 3 \cdot 2 \cdot 1} = 52 \cdot 17 \cdot 10 \cdot 49 \cdot 6 = 2,598,960.$$

(b) How many poker hands are full houses? Let's call a hand consisting of three jacks and two 8's a full house of type $\langle J, 8 \rangle$, with similar notation for other types of full houses. Order matters, since hands of type $\langle 8, J \rangle$ have three 8's and two jacks. Also, types like $\langle J, J \rangle$ and $\langle 8, 8 \rangle$ are impossible. So types of full houses correspond to 2-permutations of the set of possible values of cards; hence there are $13 \cdot 12$ different types of full houses.

Now we count the number of full houses of each type, say type $\langle J, 8 \rangle$. There are $\binom{4}{3} = 4$ ways to choose three jacks from four jacks, and there are then $\binom{4}{2} = 6$ ways to select two 8's from four 8's. Thus there are $4 \cdot 6 = 24$ hands of type $\langle J, 8 \rangle$. This argument works for all $13 \cdot 12$ types of hands and so there are $13 \cdot 12 \cdot 24 = 3744$ full houses.

(c) How many poker hands are two pairs? Let's say that a hand with two pairs is of type $\{Q, 4\}$ if it consists of two queens and two 4's. This time we have used set notation because order does not matter: hands of type $\{4, Q\}$ are hands of type $\{Q, 4\}$ and we don't want to count them twice. There are $\binom{13}{2}$ types of hands. For each type, say $\{Q, 4\}$, there are $\binom{4}{2}$ ways of choosing two queens, $\binom{4}{2}$ ways of choosing two 4's and $52 - 8 = 44$ ways of choosing the fifth card. Hence there are

$$\binom{13}{2}\binom{4}{2}\binom{4}{2} \cdot 44 = 123,552$$

poker hands consisting of two pairs.

(d) How many poker hands are straights? First we count all possible straights even if they are royal or straight flushes. Let's call a straight consisting of the values 8, 9, 10, J, Q a straight of type Q. In general, the type of a straight is the highest value in the straight. Since any of the values 5, 6, 7, 8, 9, 10, J, Q, K, A can be the highest value in a straight, there are 10 types of straights. Given a type of straight, there are 4 choices for each of the 5 values. So there are 4^5 straights of each type and $10 \cdot 4^5 = 10{,}240$ straights altogether. There are 4 royal flushes and 36 straight flushes and so there are 10,200 straights that are not of these exotic varieties.

(e) You are asked to count the remaining kinds of poker hands in Exercise 11, for which all answers are given. ☐

Binomial coefficients get their name from the next theorem.

Binomial Theorem For real numbers a and b and $n \in \mathbb{N}$, we have
$$(a + b)^n = \sum_{r=0}^{n} \binom{n}{r} a^r b^{n-r}.$$

This can be proved by induction using the following recursion relation:
$$\binom{n+1}{r} = \binom{n}{r-1} + \binom{n}{r} \qquad \text{for } 1 \leq r \leq n;$$

see Exercise 18. This relation, in turn, can be proved by algebraic manipulation, but let us give a set-theoretic explanation.

There are $\binom{n+1}{r}$ r-element subsets of $\{1, 2, \ldots, n, n+1\}$. We separate them into two classes. There are $\binom{n}{r}$ subsets which contain only members of $\{1, 2, \ldots, n\}$. There are also the remaining subsets, each of which consists of the number $n+1$ and some $r-1$ members of $\{1, 2, \ldots, n\}$. Since there are $\binom{n}{r-1}$ ways to choose the elements which aren't $n+1$, this second class of subsets consists of $\binom{n}{r-1}$ subsets. Hence there are exactly $\binom{n}{r} + \binom{n}{r-1}$ r-element subsets of $\{1, 2, \ldots, n, n+1\}$, so that $\binom{n}{r} + \binom{n}{r-1} = \binom{n+1}{r}$.

The recursion relation discussed above is the basis for the **Pascal triangle** in Figure 3, which is popular even though its usefulness is limited to small values of n. Each number in the $(n+1)$-st row of the triangle different from 1 has the form $\binom{n+1}{r}$ and the nearest numbers just above it are $\binom{n}{r-1}$ and $\binom{n}{r}$. The recursion relation just says that such an entry is the sum of the two nearest numbers just above it. For example, for $n=5$ and $r=2$ the recursion relation says
$$\binom{6}{2} = \binom{5}{1} + \binom{5}{2}, \quad \text{i.e.,} \quad 15 = 5 + 10.$$

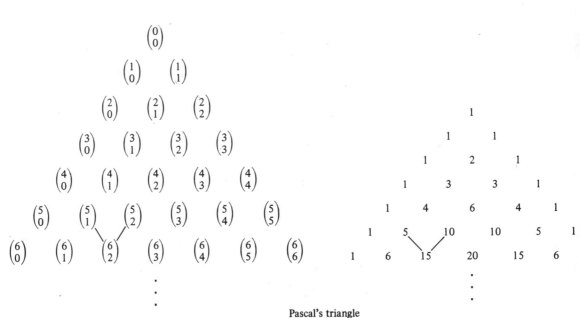

Pascal's triangle

FIGURE 3

EXERCISES 5.1

1. Calculate

(a) $\binom{8}{3}$ (b) $\binom{8}{0}$ (c) $\binom{8}{5}$

(d) $\binom{52}{50}$ (e) $\binom{52}{52}$ (f) $\binom{52}{1}$

2. Let $A = \{1, 2, 3, 4, 5, 6, 7, 8, 9, 10\}$ and $B = \{2, 3, 5, 7, 11, 13, 17, 19\}$.
   (a) Determine the sizes of the sets $A \cup B$, $A \cap B$ and $A \oplus B$.
   (b) How many subsets of A are there?
   (c) How many 4-element subsets of A are there?
   (d) How many 4-element subsets of A consist of 3 even and 1 odd number?

3. Among 150 people, 45 swim, 40 bike and 50 jog. Also, 32 people jog but don't bike, 27 people jog and swim, and 10 people do all three.
   (a) How many people jog but don't swim and don't bike?
   (b) If 21 people bike and swim, how many do none of the three activities?

4. A certain class consists of 12 men and 16 women. How many committees can be chosen from this class consisting of
   (a) seven people?
   (b) three men and four women?
   (c) seven women or seven men?

5. (a) How many committees consisting of 4 people can be chosen from 9 people?
   (b) Redo part (a) if there are two people, Ann and Bob, who will not serve on the same committee.

6. How many committees consisting of 4 men and 4 women can be chosen from a group of 8 men and 6 women?

7. Let $S = \{a, b, c, d\}$ and $T = \{1, 2, 3, 4, 5, 6, 7\}$.
   (a) How many one-to-one functions are there from T into S?
   (b) How many one-to-one functions are there from S into T?
   (c) How many functions are there from S into T?

8. Let $P = \{1, 2, 3, 4, 5, 6, 7, 8, 9\}$ and $Q = \{A, B, C, D, E\}$.
   (a) How many 4-element subsets of P are there?
   (b) How many permutations, i.e., 5-permutations, of Q are there?
   (c) How many license plates are there consisting of three letters from Q followed by two numbers from P? Repetition is allowed; for example, $DAD\ 88$ is allowed.

9. Cards are drawn from a deck of 52 cards with replacements.
   (a) In how many ways can ten cards be drawn so that the tenth card is not a repetition?
   (b) In how many ways can ten cards be drawn so that the tenth card is a repetition?

10. Let Σ be the alphabet $\{a, b, c, d, e\}$ and, as usual, let $\Sigma^k = \{w \in \Sigma^* : \text{length}(w) = k\}$. How many elements are there in each of the following sets?
    (a) Σ^k, for each $k \in \mathbb{N}$
    (b) $\{w \in \Sigma^3 : \text{no letter in } w \text{ is used more than once}\}$
    (c) $\{w \in \Sigma^4 : \text{the letter } c \text{ occurs in } w \text{ exactly once}\}$
    (d) $\{w \in \Sigma^4 : \text{the letter } c \text{ occurs in } w \text{ at least once}\}$

11. Count the number of poker hands of the following kinds:
    (a) four of a kind
    (b) flush [but not straight or royal flush]
    (c) three of a kind
    (d) one pair

12. (a) In how many ways can the letters a, b, c, d, e, f be arranged so that the letters a and b are adjacent?
    (b) In how many ways can the letters a, b, c, d, e, f be arranged so that the letters a and b are not adjacent?

13. Obtain the next two rows of the Pascal triangle in Figure 3.

14. Draw the 8 spanning trees of the graph in Figure 2(a).

15. (a) Give the matrix for a complete graph with n vertices; see Example 9.
    (b) Use the matrix in part (a) to count the number of edges of the graph. *Hint:* How many entries in the matrix are equal to 1?

16. Prove that $\sum_{r=0}^{n} (-1)^r \binom{n}{r} = 0$ for $n \in \mathbb{P}$. *Hint:* Use the binomial theorem.

17. (a) Show that $\binom{n}{r} = \binom{n}{n-r}$ for $0 \leqq r \leqq n$.
    (b) Give a set-theoretic interpretation of the identities in part (a).

18. (a) Prove the binomial theorem.

    (b) Prove $\binom{n+1}{r} = \binom{n}{r-1} + \binom{n}{r}$ for $1 \leq r \leq n$ algebraically.

19. Prove that $2^n = \sum_{r=0}^{n} \binom{n}{r}$

    (a) by setting $a = b = 1$ in the binomial theorem.

    (b) by counting subsets of an n-element set.

    (c) by induction using the recursion relation in Exercise 18(b).

§ 5.2   More Counting Techniques

In this section we introduce the general **Inclusion-Exclusion Principle**. We also discuss methods for counting partitions and solving related problems.

It is often easy to count elements in an intersection of sets, where the key connective is "and." On the other hand, it is often difficult to count directly the elements in a union of sets. The Inclusion-Exclusion Principle will tell us the size of a union in terms of the sizes of various intersections. Let $A_1, A_2, \ldots, A_n$ be finite sets. For $n = 2$, the Union Rule (b) asserts that

$$|A_1 \cup A_2| = |A_1| + |A_2| - |A_1 \cap A_2|.$$

For $n = 3$, the Inclusion-Exclusion Principle below asserts that

$$|A_1 \cup A_2 \cup A_3| = |A_1| + |A_2| + |A_3| - |A_1 \cap A_2| - |A_1 \cap A_3|$$
$$- |A_2 \cap A_3| + |A_1 \cap A_2 \cap A_3|$$

and for $n = 4$, it asserts that

$$|A_1 \cup A_2 \cup A_3 \cup A_4| = |A_1| + |A_2| + |A_3| + |A_4| - |A_1 \cap A_2|$$
$$- |A_1 \cap A_3| - |A_1 \cap A_4| - |A_2 \cap A_3|$$
$$- |A_2 \cap A_4| - |A_3 \cap A_4| + |A_1 \cap A_2 \cap A_3|$$
$$+ |A_1 \cap A_2 \cap A_4| + |A_1 \cap A_3 \cap A_4|$$
$$+ |A_2 \cap A_3 \cap A_4| - |A_1 \cap A_2 \cap A_3 \cap A_4|.$$

Inclusion-Exclusion Principle To calculate the size of $A_1 \cup A_2 \cup \cdots \cup A_n$, calculate the sizes of all possible intersections of sets from $\{A_1, A_2, \ldots, A_n\}$, add the results obtained by intersecting an odd number of the sets and subtract the results obtained by intersecting an even number of the sets.

In terms of the phrase "inclusion-exclusion," include or add the sizes of the sets, then exclude or subtract the sizes of all intersections of two sets, then include or add the sizes of all intersections of three sets, etc. A concise statement of the principle is offered in Exercise 16.

EXAMPLE 1   We count the number of integers in $S = \{1, 2, 3, \ldots, 2000\}$ that are divisible by 9, 11, 13 or 15. For each $k \in \mathbb{P}$, we let $D_k = \{n \in S : n \text{ is divisible by } k\}$ and we seek $|D_9 \cup D_{11} \cup D_{13} \cup D_{15}|$. Note that $|D_k|$ is the largest integer $\leq 2000/k$. Hence

$$|D_9| = 222, \qquad |D_{11}| = 181, \qquad |D_{13}| = 153, \qquad |D_{15}| = 133,$$

$$|D_9 \cap D_{11}| = |D_{99}| = 20, \qquad\qquad |D_9 \cap D_{13}| = |D_{117}| = 17,$$

$$|D_9 \cap D_{15}| = |D_{45}| = 44, \qquad\qquad |D_{11} \cap D_{13}| = |D_{143}| = 13,$$

$$|D_{11} \cap D_{15}| = |D_{165}| = 12, \qquad\qquad |D_{13} \cap D_{15}| = |D_{195}| = 10,$$

$$|D_9 \cap D_{11} \cap D_{13}| = |D_{1287}| = 1, \qquad |D_9 \cap D_{11} \cap D_{15}| = |D_{495}| = 4,$$

$$|D_9 \cap D_{13} \cap D_{15}| = |D_{585}| = 3, \qquad |D_{11} \cap D_{13} \cap D_{15}| = |D_{2145}| = 0,$$

$$|D_9 \cap D_{11} \cap D_{13} \cap D_{15}| = |D_{6435}| = 0.$$

Note that $D_9 \cap D_{15} = D_{45}$ [not D_{135}] since lcm$(9, 15) = 45$; similar care is needed in dealing with $D_9 \cap D_{11} \cap D_{15}$, $D_9 \cap D_{13} \cap D_{15}$, etc. Now by the Inclusion-Exclusion Principle, we have

$$\begin{aligned}
|D_9 \cup D_{11} \cup D_{13} \cup D_{15}| &= 222 + 181 + 153 + 133 \\
&\quad - (20 + 17 + 44 + 13 + 12 + 10) \\
&\quad + (1 + 4 + 3 + 0) - 0 = 581. \quad \square
\end{aligned}$$

EXAMPLE 2   We count the number of integers in $T = \{1000, 1001, \ldots, 9999\}$ with at least one digit that is 0, at least one that is 1 and at least one that is 2. For example, 1072 and 2101 are such numbers. It is easier to count numbers that exclude certain digits and so we deal with complements. That is, for $k = 0, 1$ and 2 we let

$$A_k = \{n \in T : n \text{ has no digit equal to } k\}.$$

Then each A_k^c consists of those n in T that have at least one digit equal to k and so $A_0^c \cap A_1^c \cap A_2^c$ consists of those n in T that have at least one 0, one 1 and one 2 among their digits. This is exactly the set whose size we are after. Since $A_0^c \cap A_1^c \cap A_2^c = (A_0 \cup A_1 \cup A_2)^c$ by DeMorgan's law, we will first calculate $|A_0 \cup A_1 \cup A_2|$ using the Inclusion-Exclusion Principle. By the Product Rule (a) we have $|A_1| = 8 \cdot 9 \cdot 9 \cdot 9$ since there are 8 choices for the first digit, which cannot be 0 or 1, and 9 choices for the other digits. Similar computations yield

$$|A_0| = 9 \cdot 9 \cdot 9 \cdot 9 = 6561, \qquad |A_1| = |A_2| = 8 \cdot 9 \cdot 9 \cdot 9 = 5832,$$

$$|A_0 \cap A_1| = |A_0 \cap A_2| = 8 \cdot 8 \cdot 8 \cdot 8 = 4096,$$

$$|A_1 \cap A_2| = 7 \cdot 8 \cdot 8 \cdot 8 = 3584,$$

$$|A_0 \cap A_1 \cap A_2| = 7 \cdot 7 \cdot 7 \cdot 7 = 2401.$$

By the Inclusion-Exclusion Principle,

$$|A_0 \cup A_1 \cup A_2| = 6561 + 5832 + 5832 - (4096 + 4096 + 3584)$$
$$+ 2401 = 8850$$

and so

$$|(A_0 \cup A_1 \cup A_2)^c| = |T| - |A_0 \cup A_1 \cup A_2| = 9000 - 8850 = 150.$$

There are 150 integers in T whose digits include at least one 0, 1 and 2.   ☐

An Explanation of the Inclusion-Exclusion Principle. The main barrier to proving the general principle is the notation [cf. Exercise 16]. The principle can be proved by induction on n. We show how the result for $n = 2$ leads to the result for $n = 3$. Using the $n = 2$ case we have

(1) $|A \cup B \cup C| = |A \cup B| + |C| - |(A \cup B) \cap C|$

and

(2) $|A \cup B| = |A| + |B| - |A \cap B|.$

Applying the distributive law for unions and intersections [rule 3b in Table 1 of § 1.2], we also obtain

(3) $|(A \cup B) \cap C| = |(A \cap C) \cup (B \cap C)|$
$$= |A \cap C| + |B \cap C| - |A \cap B \cap C|.$$

Substitution of (2) and (3) into (1) yields

(4) $|A \cup B \cup C| = |A| + |B| - |A \cap B| + |C| - |A \cap C|$
$$- |B \cap C| + |A \cap B \cap C|$$

and this is the principle for $n = 3$.   ☐

A much simpler counting principle which we will also find useful is just a formalization of common sense. If a box contains 30 marbles of different colors and if there are 6 marbles of each color, then there must be 5 colors of marbles. This is a special case of the next lemma if we let A be the set of marbles, B the set of colors, ϕ the function which maps each marble to its color, and note that $k = 6$.

Counting Lemma   If $\phi: A \to B$ maps the finite set A <u>onto</u> B and if the sets

$$\phi^{-1}(b) = \{a \in A : \phi(a) = b\}$$

have the same number of elements, say k, for all b in B then

$$|B| = |A|/k.$$

Proof. The set A is the union of the disjoint sets $\phi^{-1}(b)$ and so $|A|$
$= \sum_{b \in B} |\phi^{-1}(b)| = \sum_{b \in B} k = k \cdot |B|$. Therefore $|B| = |A|/k$.   ☐

We return to the problem of counting permutations of letters in a word. If all the letters are different, the problem is easy. For example, there are 9!

permutations of the letters in ALGORITHM. But how many permutations are there of the letters in CORRESPONDENCE? We solve this by first labeling the repeated letters: $C_1 O_1 R_1 R_2 E_1 S P O_2 N_1 D E_2 N_2 C_2 E_3$ so that all the letters are different. There are 14! permutations of these subscripted letters. For each such permutation σ, we let $\phi(\sigma)$ be the same word without the subscripts. Two permutations yield the same word w if only the two C's are permuted, the two N's are permuted, the two O's are permuted, the two R's are permuted and the three E's are permuted. Thus each $\phi^{-1}(w)$ contains 2! 2! 2! 2! 3! permutations. By the Counting Lemma, we conclude that there are

$$\frac{14!}{2!\,2!\,2!\,2!\,3!}$$

permutations of CORRESPONDENCE. Exactly this sort of argument can be used to prove the following principle.

Consider a set of n objects of k different types. If $n_1 + n_2 + \cdots + n_k = n$ where n_1 are alike, n_2 are alike, . . . , n_k are alike, then there are

$$\frac{n!}{n_1!\,n_2!\,\cdots\,n_k!}$$

distinguishable permutations of the n objects, where we distinguish between two permutations in case there is a position in which their entries are of different types.

EXAMPLE 3   Let $\Sigma = \{a, b, c\}$. The number of words in Σ^* having length 10 using 4 a's, 3 b's and 3 c's is

$$\frac{10!}{4!\,3!\,3!} = 4200.$$

The number of words using 5 a's, 3 b's and 2 c's is

$$\frac{10!}{5!\,3!\,2!} = 2520$$

and the number using 5 a's and 5 b's is

$$\frac{10!}{5!\,5!} = 252.$$

For comparison, note that Σ^{10} has $3^{10} = 59{,}049$ words. ☐

Recall that a partition of a set S is a collection of disjoint subsets whose union is the set S itself. An **ordered partition** is a partition in which the subsets are ordered; in this case, although the sets are ordered, the elements within the sets are not.

EXAMPLE 4   Let $S = \{1, 2, 3, 4, 5, 6, 7\}$.
      (a) Here are some ordered partitions of S:

$$\langle\{1, 3, 5\}, \{2, 4, 6, 7\}\rangle, \quad \langle\{2, 4, 6, 7\}, \{1, 3, 5\}\rangle, \quad \langle\{3, 6\}, \{2, 5\}, \{1, 4, 7\}\rangle,$$
$$\langle\{1\}, \{2, 4, 6\}, \{3, 5, 7\}\rangle \quad \text{and} \quad \langle\{1, 6\}, \{2, 5\}, \{3, 4\}, \{7\}\rangle.$$

(b) We count the number of ordered partitions of S of the form $\langle A, B, C \rangle$ where $|A| = 2, |B| = 3$ and $|C| = 2$. Given a permutation σ of S, we can form such a partition $\phi(\sigma)$ by letting A consist of the first two elements, B consist of the next three elements, and C the remaining two. There are 7! permutations of S. Given a permutation, say $\langle 3, 7, 4, 1, 6, 5, 2 \rangle$, if we permute the first two numbers, the second three and the last two, to obtain say $\langle 7, 3, 4, 6, 1, 5, 2 \rangle$, both permutations will be mapped by ϕ to the same ordered partition, namely $\langle \{3, 7\}, \{1, 4, 6\}, \{2, 5\} \rangle$. There are 2! 3! 2! such permutations that ϕ maps to the same ordered partition π. In other words, each $\phi^{-1}(\pi)$ has 2! 3! 2! elements. From the Counting Lemma we see that there are

$$\frac{7!}{2!\,3!\,2!} = 210$$

different ordered partitions of S where $|A| = |C| = 2$ and $|B| = 3$. □

The counting argument in Example 4(b) easily generalizes to establish the following.

Counting Ordered Partitions. If a set has n elements and if $n_1 + n_2 + \cdots + n_k = n$, then there are

$$\frac{n!}{n_1!\,n_2! \cdots n_k!}$$

ordered partitions $\langle A_1, A_2, \ldots, A_k \rangle$ of the set with $|A_j| = n_j$ for $j = 1, 2, \ldots, k$.

EXAMPLE 5   In how many ways can three disjoint committees be formed from twenty people if they must have 3, 5 and 7 people, respectively? This is equivalent to counting ordered partitions $\langle A, B, C, D \rangle$ of the set of twenty people where $|A| = 3, |B| = 5, |C| = 7$ and $|D| = 5$. The set D corresponds to the people with no committee assignment. There are

$$\frac{20!}{3!\,5!\,7!\,5!} \approx 5.587 \cdot 10^9$$

possible ways to form such committees. Note that although $|D| = |B|$, the committee B and the set D play different roles; the ordering of the partition is significant and we are not just interested in ways of breaking the big set up into a 3-element subset, a couple of 5-element subsets and a 7-element subset. □

EXAMPLE 6   (a) A **bridge deal** is an ordered partition of 52 cards involving four sets with 13 cards each. Thus there are

$$\frac{52!}{13!\,13!\,13!\,13!} = \frac{52!}{(13!)^4} \approx 5.3645 \cdot 10^{28}$$

bridge deals.

(b) We count the number of bridge deals in which each hand of 13 cards contains one ace. First we deal out the aces; this can be done in $4! = 24$ ways. Just as in part (a), the remaining cards can be partitioned in $48!/(12!)^4$ ways. So $24 \cdot 48!/(12!)^4$ of the bridge deals yield one ace in each hand. The fraction of such deals is

$$24 \frac{48!}{(12!)^4} \cdot \frac{(13!)^4}{52!} = \frac{(13)^3}{17 \cdot 25 \cdot 49} \approx .1055.$$

(c) A single **bridge hand** consists of 13 cards drawn from a 52-card deck. There are $\binom{52}{13} \approx 6.394 \cdot 10^{11}$ bridge hands. We say that a bridge hand has distribution n_1–n_2–n_3–n_4 where $n_1 \geq n_2 \geq n_3 \geq n_4$ and $n_1 + n_2 + n_3 + n_4 = 13$ if there are n_1 cards of some suit, n_2 cards of a second suit, n_3 cards of a third suit and n_4 cards of the remaining suit. To illustrate, we count the number of bridge hands having 4–3–3–3 distribution. There are $\binom{13}{4}\binom{13}{3}\binom{13}{3}\binom{13}{3}$ ways to choose 4 clubs and three of each of the other suits. We get the same result if we replace clubs by one of the other suits. So we conclude that there are

$$4\binom{13}{4}\binom{13}{3}^3 \approx 6.6906 \cdot 10^{10}$$

bridge hands having 4–3–3–3 distribution. Of all bridge hands, about $6.6906/63.94 \approx .1046$ proportion have 4–3–3–3 distribution. □

Sometimes problems reduce to counting unordered partitions. When this occurs, count ordered partitions first and then divide by suitable numbers to take into account the lack of order.

EXAMPLE 7 (a) In how many ways can twelve students be divided into three groups, with four students in each group, so that one group studies topic T_1, one studies topic T_2 and one studies topic T_3? Here order matters: if we permuted groups of students, the students would be studying different topics. So we count ordered partitions, of which there are

$$\frac{12!}{4! \, 4! \, 4!} = 34{,}650.$$

(b) In how many ways can twelve students be divided into three study groups, with four students in each group, so that each group will study the same topic? Now we wish to count unordered partitions, since we regard partitions like $\langle A, B, C \rangle$ and $\langle B, A, C \rangle$ as equivalent. They correspond to the same partitioning of the twelve students into three equal groups. From part (a), there are 34,650 ordered partitions. If we map each ordered partition $\langle A, B, C \rangle$ to the unordered partition $\phi(\langle A, B, C \rangle) = \{A, B, C\}$, we find that $\phi^{-1}(\{A, B, C\})$ has $3! = 6$ elements, namely $\langle A, B, C \rangle, \langle A, C, B \rangle, \langle B, A, C \rangle, \langle B, C, A \rangle, \langle C, A, B \rangle$ and $\langle C, B, A \rangle$. So by the Counting Lemma there are

34,650/6 = 5775 unordered partitions of the desired type. Hence the answer to our question is 5775.   ☐

EXAMPLE 8   (a) In how many ways can nineteen students be divided into five groups, two groups of five and three groups of three, so that each group studies a different topic? As in Example 7(a), we count ordered partitions, of which there are

$$\frac{19!}{5!\,5!\,3!\,3!\,3!} \approx 3.911 \cdot 10^{10}.$$

(b) In how many ways can the students in part (a) be divided if all five groups are to study the same topic? In part (a) we counted all ordered partitions $\langle A, B, C, D, E \rangle$ where $|A| = |B| = 5$ and $|C| = |D| = |E| = 3$. If A and B are permuted and C, D, E are permuted, we will get the same study groups, but we cannot permute groups of different sizes like A and D. To count unordered partitions we let $\phi(\langle A, B, C, D, E \rangle) = \langle \{A, B\}, \{C, D, E\} \rangle$. Each inverse image $\phi^{-1}(\langle \{A, B\}, \{C, D, E\} \rangle)$ has 2! 3! elements [such as $\langle B, A, C, E, D \rangle$] and so, by the Counting Lemma, there are

$$\frac{19!}{5!\,5!\,3!\,3!\,3!} \cdot \frac{1}{2!\,3!} \approx 3.26 \cdot 10^9$$

unordered partitions of students into study groups.   ☐

EXAMPLE 9   In how many ways can a set of 100 elements be partitioned into 50 sets with 2 elements each? More generally, we can ask in how many ways a set of $2n$ elements can be partitioned into n sets with 2 elements each. To answer the first question, replace each n by 50 in what follows. We are asking for unordered partitions. There are

$$\frac{(2n)!}{2 \cdot 2 \cdots 2} = \frac{(2n)!}{2^n}$$

ordered partitions $\langle A_1, A_2, \ldots, A_n \rangle$ where each set has 2 elements. Any permutation of the n sets gives the same unordered partition and so there are $(2n)!/2^n n!$ unordered partitions of $2n$ elements into n sets with 2 elements each. Note that

$$\frac{(2n)!}{2^n n!} = (2n - 1)(2n - 3)(2n - 5) \cdots 3 \cdot 1$$

since

$$\frac{(2n)!}{(2n - 1)(2n - 3) \cdots 3 \cdot 1} = (2n)(2n - 2)(2n - 4) \cdots 6 \cdot 4 \cdot 2$$

$$= 2 \cdot n \cdot 2(n - 1) \cdot 2(n - 2) \cdots 2 \cdot 3 \cdot 2 \cdot 2 \cdot 2 \cdot 1$$
$$\qquad \uparrow \quad\uparrow \qquad\quad\uparrow \qquad\qquad\quad\uparrow \quad\uparrow \quad\uparrow$$

$$= 2^n n!.$$

Here is another way to count the unordered partitions above. First list the elements of the set in some order. Pick the first element. There are $2n - 1$

possible elements that can join it to form a 2-element set. Now pick the next unused element. There are $2n - 3$ possible elements that can join it to form a second 2-element set. Continuing in this way, we find that there are $(2n - 1)(2n - 3) \cdots 3 \cdot 1$ ways to construct the desired unordered partitions.

$\square$

The last counting formula we consider arises in a variety of ways, but we offer it in a form that is easy to remember.

Placing Objects in Boxes. There are $\binom{n + k - 1}{k - 1}$ ways to place n indistinguishable objects into k distinguishable boxes.

Proof. The proof is both elegant and illuminating; we illustrate it for the case $n = 5$ and $k = 4$. We let five 0's represent the objects and then we add three 1's to serve as dividers among the four boxes. Thus we consider the set of all strings consisting of five 0's and three 1's and we claim there is a one-to-one correspondence between this set and the ways to place the five 0's into four boxes. Specifically, a string corresponds to the placement of the 0's before the first 1 into the first box, the 0's between the first and second 1 into the second box, the 0's between the second and third 1 into the third box, and the 0's after the third 1 into the fourth box. For example,

$$0\,0\,1\,1\,0\,0\,0\,1 \rightarrow 0\,0 \big| \big| 0\,0\,0 \big| \rightarrow$$

In this example, boxes 2 and 4 are empty because there are no 0's between the first and second dividers and there are no 0's after the last divider. More examples:

As noted in Example 8 of § 5.1, there are $\binom{8}{3}$ strings having five 0's and three 1's. This establishes the result for $n = 5$ and $k = 4$.

In the general case, we consider strings of n 0's and $k - 1$ 1's. The 0's correspond to objects and the 1's to dividers. There are $\binom{n + k - 1}{k - 1}$ such strings and, as above, there is a one-to-one correspondence between these strings and the placing of n 0's into k boxes. $\square$

EXAMPLE 10 (a) In how many ways can ten red marbles be placed into five distinguishable bags? Here $n = 10$, $k = 5$ and the answer is $\binom{10 + 5 - 1}{5 - 1} = \binom{14}{4} = 1001$.

(b) In how many ways can ten red marbles be placed into five indistinguishable bags? This is much harder. You should be aware that counting problems can get difficult quickly. Here one would like to apply part (a) and the Counting Lemma. The trouble is that if we let ϕ map distinguishable arrangements, like $\langle 1, 1, 3, 2, 3 \rangle$, to indistinguishable arrangements, like $\{1, 1, 2, 3, 3\}$, the inverse images would have *different* sizes. For example, $\phi^{-1}(\{2, 2, 2, 2, 2\})$ would have one element while $\phi^{-1}(\{0, 1, 2, 3, 4\})$ would have 120 elements. We abandon this problem. Any solution we are aware of involves the consideration of several cases. $\square$

Sometimes problems need to be manipulated before it is clear how to apply one of our principles.

EXAMPLE 11   How many numbers in $\{1, 2, 3, \ldots, 100000\}$ have the property that the sum of the digits is 7? We can ignore the very last number 100000 and we can assume that all the numbers have five digits by placing zeros in front if necessary. So, for example, we replace 1 by 00001 and 73 by 00073. Our question is now: How many strings of five digits have the property that the sum of the digits is 7? We can associate each such string with the placement of seven balls in five boxes; for example,

$$00142 \rightarrow \boxed{ \mid \mid 0 \mid \begin{matrix} 0\,0 \\ 0\,0 \end{matrix} \mid 0\,0} \;;$$

$$30121 \rightarrow \boxed{\begin{matrix} 0\,0 \\ 0 \end{matrix} \mid \mid 0 \mid 0\,0 \mid 0}\;.$$

There are $\binom{11}{4} = 330$ such placements and so there are 330 numbers with the desired property. $\square$

We now give a little different interpretation of the "Placing Objects in Boxes" principle. Consider the k boxes first and assume that each box contains an unlimited supply of objects labeled according to the boxes they are in. Applying the principle in reverse, we see that there are $\binom{n+k-1}{k-1}$ ways to remove n objects from the k boxes. In other words, *the number of ways of selecting n objects from k distinguishable objects, allowing repetitions, is* $\binom{n+k-1}{k-1}$.

EXAMPLE 12   In how many ways can ten coins be selected from an unlimited supply of pennies, nickels, dimes and quarters? This is tailor-made for the principle just stated. Let $n = 10$ [for the ten coins] and $k = 4$ [for the four types of coins]. Then the answer is $\binom{10 + 4 - 1}{4 - 1} = \binom{13}{3} = 286$.

The new interpretation can be avoided as follows. The problem is equivalent to counting ordered 4-tuples of nonnegative integers whose sum is 10. For example, $\langle 5, 3, 0, 2 \rangle$ corresponds to the selection of 5 pennies, 3 nickels and 2 quarters. Counting these ordered 4-tuples is equivalent to counting the ways of placing ten indistinguishable objects into 4 boxes and this can be done in $\binom{13}{3}$ ways.   □

The principles in this section may appear to be a bag of tricks needed to work the problems we set for ourselves. To some extent the subject of counting is like that, though we prefer to think of our techniques as tools rather than tricks. They *are* applicable in a variety of common situations, but won't handle every problem that comes up. The thought processes that we demonstrated in the proofs of the principles are as valuable as the principles themselves, since the same sort of analysis can often be used on problems where the ready-made tools don't apply.

EXERCISES 5.2

1. Among 200 people, 150 either swim or jog or both. If 85 swim and 60 swim and jog, how many jog?

2. Let $S = \{100, 101, 102, \ldots, 999\}$ so that $|S| = 900$.
   (a) How many numbers in S have at least one digit that is a 3 or a 7? Examples: 300, 707, 736, 103, 997.
   (b) How many numbers in S have at least one digit that is a 3 *and* at least one digit that is a 7? Examples: 736 and 377 but not 300, 707, 103, 997.

3. Find the number of integers in $\{1, 2, 3, \ldots, 1000\}$ that are divisible by 4, 5 or 6.

4. How many different mixes of candy are possible if a mix consists of 10 pieces of candy and if there are 4 different kinds of candy available in unlimited quantities?

5. From a total of 15 people, 3 committees consisting of 3, 4 and 5 people respectively are to be chosen.
   (a) How many such sets of committees are possible if no person may serve on more than one committee?
   (b) How many such sets of committees are possible if there is no restriction on the number of committees on which a person may serve?

6. An investor has 7 $1000 bills to distribute by mail among 3 mutual funds.
   (a) In how many ways can she invest her money?
   (b) In how many ways can she invest her money if each fund must get at least $1000?

7. Twelve identical letters are to be placed into four mailboxes.
   (a) In how many ways can this be done?
   (b) How many ways are possible if each mailbox must receive at least two letters?

8. Find the number of permutations that can be formed from all the letters of the following words.

(a) FLORIDA   (b) CALIFORNIA
(c) MISSISSIPPI   (d) OHIO

9. How many different signals can be created by lining up nine flags in a vertical column if 3 of them are white, 2 are red and 4 are blue?

10. Among the integers $\{1, 2, 3, \ldots, 1000\}$, how many of them are
   (a) divisible by 7?   (b) divisible by 11?
   (c) not divisible by 7 or 11?
   (d) divisible by 7 or 11 but *not* both?

11. (a) How many 4-digit numbers can be formed using only the digits 3, 4, 5, 6 and 7?
   (b) How many of the numbers in part (a) have some digit repeated?
   (c) How many of the numbers in part (a) are even?
   (d) How many of the numbers in part (b) are bigger than 5000?

12. Let $\Sigma = \{a, b, c\}$. If $n_1 \geqq n_2 \geqq n_3$ and $n_1 + n_2 + n_3 = 6$, we call a word in Σ^6 of type n_1–n_2–n_3 if one of the letters appears in the word n_1 times, another letter appears n_2 times and the other letter appears n_3 times. For example, *accabc* is of type 3–2–1 and *caccca* is of type 4–2–0. The number of words in Σ^6 of each type is:

type	6–0–0	5–1–0	4–2–0	4–1–1	3–3–0	3–2–1	2–2–2
number	3	36	90	90	60	360	90

Verify this assertion for three of the types.

13. In how many ways can $2n$ elements be partitioned into two sets with n elements each?

14. The English alphabet consists of 21 consonants and 5 vowels. The vowels are a, e, i, o, u.
   (a) Prove that no matter how the letters of the English alphabet are listed in order [e.g., zuvarqlgh$\cdots$] there must be 4 consecutive consonants.
   (b) Give a list to show that there need not be 5 consecutive consonants.
   (c) Suppose now that the letters of the English alphabet are put in a circular array; for example,

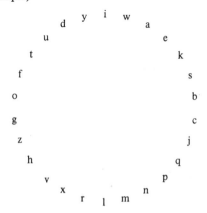

Prove that there must be 5 consecutive consonants in such an array.

15. (a) For how many integers between 1000 and 9999 is the sum of the digits exactly 9? Examples: 1431, 5121, 9000, 4320.

    (b) How many of the integers counted in part (a) have all nonzero digits?

16. Consider finite sets $\{A_1, A_2, \ldots, A_n\}$. Let $\mathcal{P}_+(n)$ be the set of nonempty subsets I of $\{1, 2, \ldots, n\}$. Show that the Inclusion-Exclusion Principle says that

$$\left| \bigcup_{i=1}^{n} A_i \right| = \sum_{I \in \mathcal{P}_+(n)} (-1)^{|I|+1} \cdot \left| \bigcap_{i \in I} A_i \right|.$$

17. Let S be the set of all sequences of 0's, 1's and 2's of length ten. For example, S contains 0211012201.

    (a) How many elements are in S?

    (b) How many sequences in S have exactly five 0's and five 1's?

    (c) How many sequences in S have exactly three 0's and seven 1's?

    (d) How many sequences in S have exactly three 0's?

    (e) How many sequences in S have exactly three 0's, four 1's and three 2's?

    (f) How many sequences in S have at least one 0, at least one 1 and at least one 2?

18. Consider finite sets satisfying $\chi_A + \chi_B = \chi_C + \chi_D$. Show that $|A| + |B| = |C| + |D|$.

19. In the proof of the "Placing Objects in Boxes" principle, we set up a one-to-one correspondence between strings of five 0's and three 1's and placements of five 0's in four boxes.

    (a) Give the placements that correspond to the following strings: 1 0 1 0 1 0 0 0, 0 1 0 0 1 0 0 1, 1 0 0 0 0 0 1 1, 1 1 1 0 0 0 0 0.

    (b) Give the strings that correspond to the following placements:

0	0	0	0 0

,

0 0		0	0 0

,

0 0 0			
0 0			

.

20. Use the Counting Lemma to give another proof of Theorem 1 in § 5.1.

§ 5.3 *Pigeon-Hole Principle*

The usual Pigeon-Hole Principle asserts that if m objects are placed in n boxes or pigeon-holes and if $m > n$, then some box will receive more than one object. Here is a slight generalization of this fact.

Pigeon-Hole Principle   If a finite set is partitioned into n sets, then at least one of the sets has $|S|/n$ or more elements.

Proof. Assume that the set S has a partition $\{A_i : i = 1, 2, \ldots, n\}$ satisfying $|A_i| < |S|/n$ for each i. Then S is the disjoint union of the sets A_i and so

$$|S| = \sum_{i=1}^{n} |A_i| < \sum_{i=1}^{n} \frac{|S|}{n} = |S|,$$

a contradiction. $\square$

We will often apply this principle when the partition is given by a function. The principle can then be stated as follows.

Pigeon-Hole   Consider a function $f: S \to T$ where S and T are finite sets with $|S| > k \cdot |T|$.
Principle   Then at least one of the sets $f^{-1}(t)$ has more than k elements.

Proof. The family $\{f^{-1}(t): t \in T\}$ partitions S into n sets with $n \leq |T|$. By the principle just proved, some set $f^{-1}(t)$ has at least $|S|/n$ members. Since $|S|/n \geq |S|/|T| > k$ by hypothesis, such a set $f^{-1}(t)$ has more than k elements.   ∏

When $k = 1$, this principle tells us that if $f: S \to T$ and $|S| > |T|$, then at least one of the sets $f^{-1}(t)$ has more than one element. It is remarkable how often this simple observation is helpful in problem-solving.

EXAMPLE 1   Given three integers, there must be two of them whose sum is even. This is because either two of the integers are even or else two are odd, and in either case their sum must be even. Here is a tighter argument. Let S be the set of three integers and for $m \in S$ let $f(m) = 0$ if m is even and $f(m) = 1$ if m is odd. Then $f: S \to \{0, 1\}$ and by the Pigeon-Hole Principle one of the sets $f^{-1}(0)$ or $f^{-1}(1)$ has more than one element. That is, either S contains two [or more] even integers or else S contains two [or more] odd integers.   ∏

EXAMPLE 2   We show that given p integers $a_1, a_2, \ldots, a_p$, not necessarily distinct, some of them add up to a number that is a multiple of p. By Theorem 1 in § 4.3, for each integer m there exists an integer $f(m)$ in $\mathbb{Z}(p)$ such that $m \equiv f(m)$ (mod p). We now consider this function restricted to the set

$$S = \{0, a_1, a_1 + a_2, a_1 + a_2 + a_3, \ldots, a_1 + a_2 + a_3 + \cdots + a_p\}.$$

Since $|S| = p + 1 > p = |\mathbb{Z}(p)|$, the Pigeon-Hole Principle shows that two distinct numbers m and n in S have the same image in $\mathbb{Z}(p)$. Since $m \equiv f(m)$ (mod p), $f(m) = f(n)$ and $f(n) \equiv n$ (mod p), we have $m \equiv n$ (mod p) by (T) of Theorem 2, § 4.3. Therefore the differences $n - m$ and $m - n$ are multiples of p. One of these differences has the form $a_k + a_{k+1} + \cdots + a_l$, i.e., it's a sum of integers from our list that is a multiple of p.

The result just proved is sharp, in the sense that we can give integers $a_1, a_2, \ldots, a_{p-1}$ for which no nonempty subset has sum that is a multiple of p. Simply let $a_j = 1$ for $j = 1, 2, \ldots, p - 1$.   ∏

EXAMPLE 3   Let A be some fixed 10-element subset of $\{1, 2, 3, \ldots, 50\}$. We show that A possesses two different 5-element subsets, the sums of whose elements are equal. Let $\mathcal{S}$ be the family of 5-element subsets B of A. For each B in $\mathcal{S}$, let $f(B)$ be the sum of the numbers in B. Note that we must have $f(B) \geq 1 + 2 + 3 + 4 + 5 = 15$ and $f(B) \leq 50 + 49 + 48 + 47 + 46 = 240$ so that $f: \mathcal{S} \to T$ where $T = \{15, 16, 17, \ldots, 240\}$. Since $|T| = 226$ and $|\mathcal{S}| = \binom{10}{5} = 252$, the Pigeon-Hole Principle shows that $\mathcal{S}$ contains different sets with the same image under f, i.e., different sets the sums of whose elements are equal. □

Some applications of the Pigeon-Hole Principle require considerable ingenuity.

EXAMPLE 4 Here we show that if $a_1, a_2, \ldots, a_{n^2+1}$ is a sequence of $n^2 + 1$ distinct real numbers, then there is a subsequence with $n + 1$ terms that is either increasing or decreasing. This means that there exist subscripts $k_1 < k_2 < \cdots < k_{n+1}$ so that either

$$a_{k_1} < a_{k_2} < \cdots < a_{k_{n+1}}$$

or

$$a_{k_1} > a_{k_2} > \cdots > a_{k_{n+1}}.$$

For each j in $\{1, 2, \ldots, n^2 + 1\}$, let $\text{INC}(j)$ be the length of the longest increasing subsequence stopping at a_j and $\text{DEC}(j)$ be the length of the longest decreasing sequence stopping at a_j. Then define $f(j) = \langle \text{INC}(j), \text{DEC}(j) \rangle$. For example, suppose that $n = 3$ and the original sequence is given by

a_1	a_2	a_3	a_4	a_5	a_6	a_7	a_8	a_9	a_{10}
11	3	15	8	6	12	17	2	7	1 .

Here $a_5 = 6$, $\text{INC}(5) = 2$ since a_2, a_5 is the longest increasing subsequence stopping at a_5 and $\text{DEC}(5) = 3$ since a_1, a_4, a_5 and a_3, a_4, a_5 are longest decreasing subsequences stopping at a_5. Similarly, $\text{INC}(6) = 3$ and $\text{DEC}(6) = 2$ and so $f(5) = \langle 2, 3 \rangle$ and $f(6) = \langle 3, 2 \rangle$. Indeed, in this example

$$f(1) = \langle 1, 1 \rangle \qquad f(2) = \langle 1, 2 \rangle \qquad f(3) = \langle 2, 1 \rangle$$
$$f(4) = \langle 2, 2 \rangle \qquad f(5) = \langle 2, 3 \rangle \qquad f(6) = \langle 3, 2 \rangle$$
$$f(7) = \langle 4, 1 \rangle \qquad f(8) = \langle 1, 4 \rangle \qquad f(9) = \langle 3, 3 \rangle$$
$$f(10) = \langle 1, 5 \rangle.$$

This particular example has increasing subsequences of length 4, such as a_2, a_5, a_6, a_7 since $\text{INC}(7) = 4$, and also decreasing subsequences of length 4, such as a_1, a_4, a_5, a_8 since $\text{DEC}(8) = 4$. Since $\text{DEC}(10) = 5$ it even has a decreasing subsequence of length 5. Note that f is one-to-one in this example so that f cannot map the 10-element set $\{1, 2, 3, \ldots, 10\}$ into the 9-element set $\{1, 2, 3\} \times \{1, 2, 3\}$. In other words, the one-to-oneness of f alone forces at least one $\text{INC}(j)$ or $\text{DEC}(j)$ to exceed 3 and this in turn forces our sequence to have an increasing or decreasing subsequence of length 4.

To prove the general result we first claim that f must be one-to-one, which we prove directly. Consider j, k in $\{1, 2, 3, \ldots, n^2 + 1\}$ with $j < k$. If $a_j < a_k$, then $\text{INC}(j) < \text{INC}(k)$ since a_k could be attached to the longest increasing sequence ending at a_j to get a longer increasing sequence ending at a_k. Similarly, if $a_j > a_k$, then $\text{DEC}(j) < \text{DEC}(k)$. In either case the *ordered pairs* $f(j)$ and $f(k)$ cannot be equal, i.e., $f(j) \neq f(k)$. Since f is one-to-one, f cannot map $\{1, 2, 3, \ldots, n^2 + 1\}$ into $\{1, 2, \ldots, n\} \times \{1, 2, \ldots, n\}$ by the

Pigeon-Hole Principle and so there is a j such that either $\text{INC}(j) \geqq n + 1$ or $\text{DEC}(j) \geqq n + 1$. Hence the original sequence has an increasing or decreasing subsequence with $n + 1$ terms. $\square$

EXAMPLE 5   You probably know that the decimal expansions of rational numbers repeat themselves, but you may never have seen a proof. For example,

$$\frac{29}{54} = .537037037037037 \cdots ;$$

check this *by long division* before proceeding further! The general fact can be seen as a consequence of the Pigeon-Hole Principle. We may assume that the given rational number has the form m/n where $0 < m < n$. We analyze the division algorithm. When we divide m by n we obtain $.d_1 d_2 d_3 \cdots$ where

$$10 \cdot m = n \cdot d_1 + r_1 \qquad 0 \leqq r_1 < n$$
$$10 \cdot r_1 = n \cdot d_2 + r_2 \qquad 0 \leqq r_2 < n$$
$$10 \cdot r_2 = n \cdot d_3 + r_3 \qquad 0 \leqq r_3 < n$$

etc. so that $10 \cdot r_j = n \cdot d_{j+1} + r_{j+1}$ where $0 \leqq r_{j+1} < n$. We illustrate this in Figure 1. The remainders r_j all take their values in $\{0, 1, 2, \ldots, n - 1\}$. By the Pigeon-Hole Principle, after a while the values must repeat. In fact, two of the numbers $r_1, r_2, \ldots, r_{n+1}$ must be equal. Hence there are k and m in $\{1, 2, \ldots, n + 1\}$ with $k < m$ and $r_k = r_m$. Let $l = m - k$ so that $r_k = r_{k+l}$.

$$.d_1 d_2 d_3 d_4 d_5 \cdots \quad = .53703 \cdots$$

54 ⟌ 290	$10 \cdot 29 = 10m$	
270	$54 \cdot 5 = nd_1$	
200	$10 \cdot 20 = 10 r_1$	$r_1 = 20$
162	$54 \cdot 3 = nd_2$	
380	$10 \cdot 38 = 10 r_2$	$r_2 = 38$
378	$54 \cdot 7 = nd_3$	
20	$10 \cdot 2 = 10 r_3$	$r_3 = 2$
0	$54 \cdot 0 = nd_4$	
200	$10 \cdot 20 = 10 r_4$	$r_4 = 20$
162	$54 \cdot 3 = nd_5$	
380	$10 \cdot 38 = 10 r_5$	$r_5 = 38$
378	etc.	

Long division

FIGURE 1

[In our carefully selected example, k can be 1 and l can be 3.] We will show that the sequences of r_i's and d_i's repeat every l terms beginning with $i = k + 1$. Since $10 r_k = 10 r_{k+l}$ we have $n d_{k+1} + r_{k+1} = n d_{k+l+1} + r_{k+l+1}$. Hence $r_{k+1} \equiv r_{k+l+1} \pmod{n}$; since both r_{k+1} and r_{k+l+1} are in $\mathbb{Z}(n)$, they must be equal. Thus $n d_{k+1} = n d_{k+l+1}$ and this implies that $d_{k+1} = d_{k+l+1}$. We have just checked the basis for an induction proof of

(*) $$d_j = d_{j+l} \quad \text{and} \quad r_j = r_{j+l}$$

for $j \geqq k + 1$. For once, the inductive step is no harder to prove. If fact, if (*) holds for j, then

$$nd_{j+1} + r_{j+1} = 10r_j = 10r_{j+l} = nd_{j+l+1} + r_{j+l+1}$$

so that $r_{j+1} \equiv r_{j+l+1} \pmod{n}$ and hence $r_{j+1} = r_{j+l+1}$. Consequently $nd_{j+1} = nd_{j+l+1}$ and $d_{j+1} = d_{j+l+1}$, which establishes (*) for $j + 1$. By mathematical induction, (*) holds for all $j \geqq k + 1$.

From (*) we have

$$d_{k+1} = d_{k+l+1}, \qquad d_{k+2} = d_{k+l+2}, \qquad \ldots, \qquad d_{k+l} = d_{k+2l}$$

so that

$$d_{k+1} d_{k+2} \cdots d_{k+l} = d_{k+l+1} d_{k+l+2} \cdots d_{k+2l}.$$

In fact, this whole block repeats indefinitely. In other words, the decimal expansion of m/n is a repeating expansion. □

The next example doesn't exactly apply the Pigeon-Hole Principle but it is a pigeon-hole problem in spirit.

EXAMPLE 6 Consider nine nonnegative real numbers $a_1, a_2, a_3, \ldots, a_9$ with sum 90.

(a) We show that there must be three of the numbers having sum at least 30. This is easy because

$$90 = (a_1 + a_2 + a_3) + (a_4 + a_5 + a_6) + (a_7 + a_8 + a_9)$$

and so at least one of the sums in parentheses must be at least 30.

(b) We show that there must be four of the numbers having sum at least 40. There are several ways to do this, but none of them is quite as simple as the method in part (a). Our first approach is to note that the sum of all the numbers in Figure 2 is 360 since each row sums to 90. Hence one of the nine columns must have sum at least $360/9 = 40$.

a_1	a_2	a_3	a_4	a_5	a_6	a_7	a_8	a_9
a_2	a_3	a_4	a_5	a_6	a_7	a_8	a_9	a_1
a_3	a_4	a_5	a_6	a_7	a_8	a_9	a_1	a_2
a_4	a_5	a_6	a_7	a_8	a_9	a_1	a_2	a_3

FIGURE 2

Our second approach is to use part (a) to select three of the numbers having sum $s \geqq 30$. One of the remaining six numbers must have value at least $\frac{1}{6}$ of their sum $90 - s$. Adding this to the selected three gives four numbers with sum at least

$$s + \tfrac{1}{6}(90 - s) = 15 + \tfrac{5}{6}s \geqq 15 + \tfrac{5}{6} \cdot 30 = 40.$$

Our third approach is to note that we may as well assume that $a_1 \geqq a_2 \geqq \cdots \geqq a_9$. Then it is clear that $a_1 + a_2 + a_3 + a_4$ is the largest sum using four of the numbers and our task is relatively concrete: to show $a_1 + a_2 + a_3 + a_4 \geqq 40$. Moreover, this suggests showing

$$(*) \qquad\qquad a_1 + a_2 + \cdots + a_n \geqq 10n$$

for $1 \leqq n \leqq 9$. We can do this by a finite induction, i.e., by noting that $(*)$ holds for $n = 1$ and showing that if $(*)$ holds for n, $1 \leqq n < 9$, then $(*)$ holds for $n + 1$. We will adapt the method of our second approach. Assume $(*)$ holds for n and let $s = a_1 + a_2 + \cdots + a_n$. Since a_{n+1} is the largest of the remaining $9 - n$ numbers, $a_{n+1} \geqq (90 - s)/(9 - n)$. Hence

$$a_1 + a_2 + \cdots + a_n + a_{n+1} = s + a_{n+1} \geqq s + \frac{90 - s}{9 - n}$$

$$= s + \frac{90}{9 - n} - \frac{s}{9 - n} = s\left(1 - \frac{1}{9 - n}\right) + \frac{90}{9 - n}$$

$$\geqq 10n\left(1 - \frac{1}{9 - n}\right) + \frac{90}{9 - n} \qquad \text{[inductive assumption]}$$

$$= 10n + \frac{90 - 10n}{9 - n} = 10n + 10 = 10(n + 1).$$

This finite induction argument shows that $(*)$ holds for $1 \leqq n \leqq 9$.

For this particular problem, the first and last approaches are far superior because they generalize in an obvious way without further tricks.   □

Most, but not all, of the following exercises involve the Pigeon-Hole Principle. They also provide more practice using the techniques from §§ 5.1 and 5.2. The exercises are not equally difficult and some may require extra ingenuity.

EXERCISES 5.3

1. (a) Given four integers, explain why two of them must be congruent modulo 3.
   (b) Prove that if $a_1, a_2, \ldots, a_{p+1}$ are integers, then two of them must be congruent modulo p.

2. (a) A sack contains 50 marbles of four different colors. Explain why there are at least 13 marbles of the same color.
   (b) If exactly 8 of the marbles are red, explain why there are at least 14 of the same color.

3. Let A be a 10-element subset of $\{1, 2, 3, \ldots, 50\}$. Show that A possesses two different 4-element subsets, the sums of whose elements are equal.

4. Let S be a 3-element set of integers. Show that S has two different nonempty subsets such that the sums of the numbers in each of the subsets are congruent modulo 6.

5. Let A be a subset of $\{1, 2, 3, \ldots, 149, 150\}$ consisting of 25 numbers. Show that there are two disjoint pairs of numbers from A having the same sum [for example, $\{3, 89\}$ and $\{41, 51\}$ have the same sum, namely 92].

6. For the following sequences, find an increasing or decreasing subsequence of length 5 if you can.
   (a) 4, 3, 2, 1, 8, 7, 6, 5, 12, 11, 10, 9, 16, 15, 14, 13
   (b) 17, 13, 14, 15, 16, 9, 10, 11, 12, 5, 6, 7, 8, 1, 2, 3, 4
   (c) 10, 6, 2, 14, 3, 17, 12, 8, 7, 16, 13, 11, 9, 15, 4, 1, 5

7. Find the decimal expansions for $1/7$, $2/7$, $3/7$, $4/7$, $5/7$ and $6/7$ and compare them.

8. (a) Show that if ten nonnegative integers have sum 101, there must be three with sum at least 31.
   (b) Prove a generalization of part (a): If $1 \leqq k \leqq n$ and if n nonnegative integers have sum m, there must be k with sum at least _____.

9. In this problem the twenty-four numbers $1, 2, 3, 4, \ldots, 24$ are permuted in some way, say $\langle n_1, n_2, n_3, n_4, \ldots, n_{24} \rangle$.
   (a) Show that there must be four consecutive numbers in the permutation that are less than 20, i.e., $\leqq 19$.
   (b) Show that $n_1 + n_2 + n_3 + \cdots + n_{24} = 300$.
   (c) Show that there must be three consecutive numbers in the permutation with sum $\geqq 38$.
   (d) Show that there must be five consecutive numbers in the permutation with sum $\geqq 61$.

10. A roulette wheel is divided into 36 sectors with numbers $1, 2, 3, \ldots, 36$. [We are omitting sectors with 0 and 00 that are included in Las Vegas and give the house the edge in gambling.]
    (a) Show that there are four consecutive sectors with sum greater than 74.
    (b) Show that there are five consecutive sectors with sum greater than 94.

11. Let n_1, n_2 and n_3 be distinct positive integers. Show that at least one of n_1, n_2, n_3, $n_1 + n_2$, $n_2 + n_3$ or $n_1 + n_2 + n_3$ is divisible by 3. *Hint:* Map $\{n_1, n_1 + n_2, n_1 + n_2 + n_3\}$ to $\mathbb{Z}(3)$ by f where $f(m) \equiv m$ (mod 3).

12. A club has six men and nine women members. How many ways can a committee of five be selected if
    (a) there are no restrictions on the committee make-up?
    (b) there must be two men and three women on the committee?
    (c) there must be at least one man and at least one woman on the committee?
    (d) the committee must consist of only men or else it must consist of only women.

13. Six-digit numbers are to be formed using the integers in the set $A = \{1, 2, 3, 4, 5, 6, 7, 8\}$.
    (a) How many such numbers can be formed if repetitions are allowed?
    (b) In part (a), how many of the numbers contain at least one 3 and at least one 5?
    (c) How many six-digit numbers can be formed if each digit in A can be used at most once?

(d) How many six-digit numbers can be formed that consist of one 2, two 4's and three 5's?

14. How many divisors are there of 6000? *Hint:* $6000 = 2^4 \cdot 3 \cdot 5^3$ and every divisor has the form $2^m 3^n 5^r$ where $m \leq 4$, $n \leq 1$ and $r \leq 3$.

15. Consider n in $\mathbb{P}$ and let S be a subset of $\{1, 2, \ldots, 2n\}$ consisting of $n + 1$ numbers.
    (a) Show that S contains two numbers that are relatively prime.
    (b) Show that S contains two numbers such that one of them divides the other.
    (c) Show that part (a) can fail if S has only n elements.
    (d) Show that part (b) can fail if S has only n elements.

16. (a) Consider a subset A of $\{0, 1, 2, \ldots, p\}$ such that $|A| > (p/2) + 1$. Show that A contains two different numbers whose sum is p.
    (b) For $p = 6$, find A with $|A| = (p/2) + 1$ not satisfying the conclusion in part (a).
    (c) For $p = 7$, find A with $|A| = [(p - 1)/2] + 1$ not satisfying the conclusion in part (a).

§ 5.4 Infinite Sets

Mathematicians have a way of classifying infinite sets according to their "size." First they generalize the concept "two sets are of the same size." The clue to the commonly accepted correct approach is the following elementary observation:

Two finite sets are of the same size if and only if there exists a one-to-one correspondence between them.

Accordingly, we regard two sets S and T, finite or infinite, to be of the **same size** if there is a one-to-one correspondence between them. In this book we will not study this classification scheme for sets in detail, but we will distinguish between two kinds of infinite sets.

Any set that is the same size as the set $\mathbb{P}$ of positive integers will be called **countably infinite**. Thus a set S is countably infinite if and only if there exists a one-to-one correspondence between $\mathbb{P}$ and S. A set is **countable** if it is finite or countably infinite. One is able to count or list such a nonempty set by matching it with $\{1, 2, \ldots, n\}$ for some $n \in \mathbb{P}$, or with $\mathbb{P}$. In the infinite case, the list will never end. As one would expect, a set is **uncountable** if it is not countable.

EXAMPLE 1   (a) The set $\mathbb{N}$ is countably infinite because $f(n) = n - 1$ defines a one-to-one function f mapping $\mathbb{P}$ onto $\mathbb{N}$. Its inverse f^{-1} is a one-to-one mapping of $\mathbb{N}$ onto $\mathbb{P}$; note $f^{-1}(n) = n + 1$ for $n \in \mathbb{N}$. Even though $\mathbb{P}$ is a proper subset of $\mathbb{N}$, by our definition $\mathbb{P}$ is the same size as $\mathbb{N}$. This may be surprising, since a similar situation does not occur for finite sets. Oh well, $\mathbb{N}$ has only one more element than $\mathbb{P}$.

(b) The set $\mathbb{Z}$ of *all* integers is also countably infinite. A one-to-one function f from $\mathbb{Z}$ onto $\mathbb{P}$ is indicated in Figure 1, where we have found it

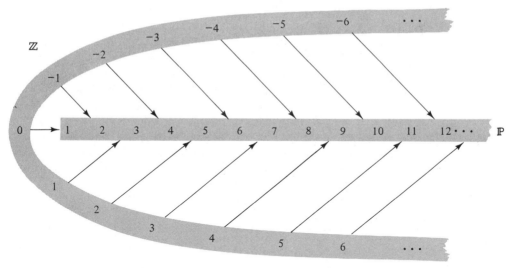

A one-to-one correspondence of $\mathbb{Z}$ onto $\mathbb{P}$

FIGURE 1

convenient to bend the picture of $\mathbb{Z}$. This function can be given by a formula, if desired:

$$f(n) = \begin{cases} 2n + 1 & \text{for } n \geqq 0, \\ -2n & \text{for } n < 0. \end{cases}$$

Even though $\mathbb{Z}$ looks about twice as big as $\mathbb{P}$, these sets are of the same size. Beware! For infinite sets, your intuition may be unreliable. Or, to take a more positive approach, you may need to refine your intuition when dealing with infinite sets.

(c) Even the set $\mathbb{Q}$ of all rational numbers is countably infinite. This is striking, because the set of rational numbers is distributed evenly throughout $\mathbb{R}$. To give a one-to-one correspondence between $\mathbb{P}$ and $\mathbb{Q}$, a picture is worth a thousand formulas. See Figure 2. The function f is obtained by following

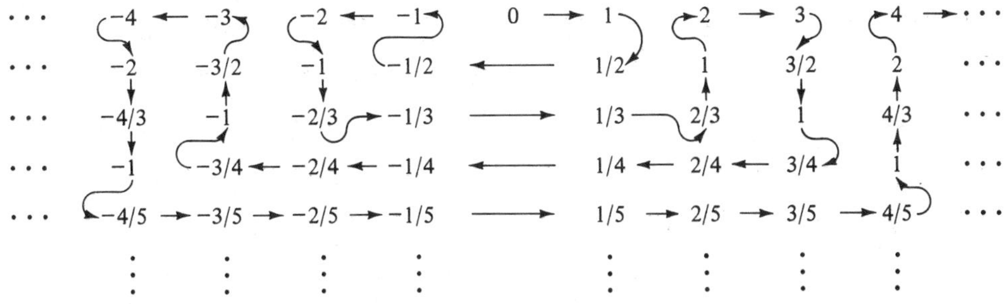

A listing of the rationals

FIGURE 2

the arrows and skipping over repetitions. Thus $f(1) = 0$, $f(2) = 1$, $f(3) = \frac{1}{2}$, $f(4) = -\frac{1}{2}$, $f(5) = -1$, $f(6) = -2$, $f(7) = -\frac{2}{3}$, etc. $\square$

EXAMPLE 2 So far, all of our examples of graphs and trees have had finitely many vertices and edges. However, there is no such restriction in the general definitions. Figure 3 contains partial pictures of some infinite graphs. The set of vertices in Figure 3(a) is $\mathbb{Z}$, and only consecutive integers are connected by an edge. Note that this is an infinite tree with *no* leaves; contrast this with the fact that every finite tree with more than one vertex has leaves. The set of vertices in Figure 3(b) is $\mathbb{Z} \times \{0, 1\}$; this tree has infinitely many leaves. The central vertex in the tree in Figure 3(c) has infinite degree; all its other vertices are leaves. There are only two vertices in the graph of Figure 3(d), but they are connected by infinitely many edges.

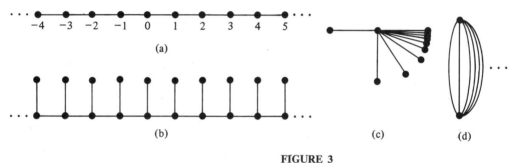

(a)

(b)   (c)   (d)

FIGURE 3

In all these examples, the sets of vertices and edges are countable. Graphs don't have to be countable, but it is hard to draw or visualize uncountable ones and we will have no need for them. $\square$

In the next example we illustrate a technique that goes back to Georg Cantor, the father of set theory. You may find the result in part (b) more interesting, but the details in part (a) are easier to follow.

EXAMPLE 3 (a) The set $\text{FUN}(\mathbb{P}, \{0, 1\})$ of all functions from $\mathbb{P}$ into $\{0, 1\}$ is uncountable. Equivalently, the set of all infinite strings of 0's and 1's is uncountable. Obviously $\text{FUN}(\mathbb{P}, \{0, 1\})$ is infinite, so if it were countable there would exist an infinite listing $\{f_1, f_2, \ldots\}$ of *all* the functions in this set. We define a function f^* on $\mathbb{P}$ as follows:

$$f^*(n) = \begin{cases} 0 & \text{if } f_n(n) = 1 \\ 1 & \text{if } f_n(n) = 0 \end{cases}.$$

For each n in $\mathbb{P}$, $f^*(n) \neq f_n(n)$ and so the functions f^* and f_n must be different. Thus $f^* \neq f_n$ for all $n \in \mathbb{P}$ and so $\{f_1, f_2, \ldots\}$ is not a listing of *all* functions in $\text{FUN}(\mathbb{P}, \{0, 1\})$. This contradiction shows that $\text{FUN}(\mathbb{P}, \{0, 1\})$ is uncountable.

(b) The interval $[0, 1)$ is uncountable. If it were countable, there would exist a one-to-one function f mapping $\mathbb{P}$ onto $[0, 1)$. We show that this is impossible. Each number in $[0, 1)$ has a decimal expansion $.d_1 d_2 d_3 \cdots$ where each d_j is a digit in $\{0, 1, 2, 3, 4, 5, 6, 7, 8, 9\}$. In particular, each number $f(k)$ has the form $.d_{1k} d_{2k} d_{3k} \cdots$; here d_{nk} represents the nth digit in $f(k)$. Consider Figure 4 and focus on the indicated "diagonal digits." We define d_n^* for $n \in \mathbb{P}$ as follows: if $d_{nn} \neq 1$, let $d_n^* = 1$ and if $d_{nn} = 1$, let $d_n^* = 2$. The point is that $d_n^* \neq d_{nn}$ for all $n \in \mathbb{P}$. Now $.d_1^* d_2^* d_3^* \cdots$ represents a number x in $[0, 1)$ which is different from $f(n)$ in the nth digit for each $n \in \mathbb{P}$. Thus x cannot be one of the numbers $f(n)$; i.e., $x \notin \text{Im}(f)$ and so f does not map $\mathbb{P}$ onto $[0, 1)$.

$$f(1) = .d_{11}\ d_{21}\ d_{31}\ d_{41}\ \cdots$$

$$f(2) = .d_{12}\ d_{22}\ d_{32}\ d_{42}\ \cdots$$

$$f(3) = .d_{13}\ d_{23}\ d_{33}\ d_{43}\ \cdots$$

$$f(4) = .d_{14}\ d_{24}\ d_{34}\ d_{44}\ \cdots$$

$$\vdots$$

Cantor's diagonal procedure

FIGURE 4

Note that we arranged for all of the digits of x to be 1's and 2's. This choice was quite arbitrary, except that we deliberately avoided 0's and 9's since there are some numbers whose expansions involve 0's and 9's that have two decimal expansions. For example, $.250000 \cdots$ and $.249999 \cdots$ represent the same number in $[0, 1)$. ☐

The proof in Example 3(b) can be modified to prove that $\mathbb{R}$ and $(0, 1)$ are uncountable; in fact, all intervals $[a, b]$, $[a, b)$, $(a, b]$ and (a, b) are uncountable for $a < b$. In view of Exercise 9, another way to show that these sets are uncountable is to show that they are in one-to-one correspondence with each other. In fact, they are also in one-to-one correspondence with unbounded intervals. Showing the existence of such one-to-one correspondences can be challenging. We provide a couple of the trickier arguments in the next example, and ask for some easier ones in Exercise 3.

EXAMPLE 4   (a) We show that $\mathbb{R}$ and $(0, 1)$ are in one-to-one correspondence, and hence are of the same size. Though trigonometric functions are not necessary here [Exercise 5], we will use a ready-made function from trigonometry, namely the tangent; see Figure 5(a). The function f given by $f(x) = \tan x$ is one-to-one on $(-\pi/2, \pi/2)$ and maps this interval onto $\mathbb{R}$. It is easy to find

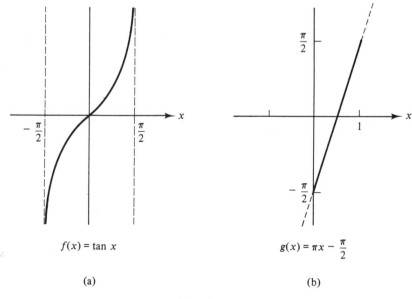

$$f(x) = \tan x$$

(a)

$$g(x) = \pi x - \frac{\pi}{2}$$

(b)

FIGURE 5

a linear function g mapping $(0, 1)$ onto $(-\pi/2, \pi/2)$, namely $g(x) = \pi x - \pi/2$; see Figure 5(b). The composite function $f \circ g$ is a one-to-one correspondence between $(0, 1)$ and $\mathbb{R}$.

(b) We show that $[0, 1)$ and $(0, 1)$ have the same size. No simple formula provides us with a one-to-one mapping between these sets. The trick is to isolate some infinite sequence in $(0, 1)$, say $\frac{1}{2}, \frac{1}{3}, \frac{1}{4}, \ldots$, and then map this sequence onto $0, \frac{1}{2}, \frac{1}{3}, \frac{1}{4}, \ldots$ while leaving the complement fixed. That is, let

$$C = (0, 1) \setminus \left\{ \frac{1}{n} : n = 2, 3, 4, \ldots \right\}$$

and define

$$f(x) = \begin{cases} 0 & \text{if } x = \frac{1}{2}, \\ \dfrac{1}{n-1} & \text{if } x = 1/n \text{ for some integer } n \geq 3, \\ x & \text{if } x \in C. \end{cases}$$

See Figure 6. □

$$(0, 1) = C \cup \{\tfrac{1}{2}, \tfrac{1}{3}, \tfrac{1}{4}, \tfrac{1}{5}, \ldots\}$$

$$\downarrow \qquad \downarrow \ \downarrow \ \downarrow \ \downarrow$$

$$[0, 1) = C \cup \{0, \tfrac{1}{2}, \tfrac{1}{3}, \tfrac{1}{4}, \ldots\}$$

$$f: (0, 1) \rightarrow [0, 1)$$

FIGURE 6

We next prove two basic facts about countable sets.

Theorem   (a) Subsets of countable sets are countable.

(b) The countable union of countable sets is countable.

Proof. (a) It is enough to show that subsets of $\mathbb{P}$ are countable. Consider a subset A of $\mathbb{P}$. Clearly A is countable if A is finite. Suppose that A is infinite. We define $f(1)$ to be the least element in A. Then we define $f(2)$ to be the least element in $A\backslash\{f(1)\}$; then $f(3)$ to be the least element in $A\backslash\{f(1), f(2)\}$, etc. This process continues, so that $f(n+1)$ is the least element in $A\backslash\{f(k) : 1 \leq k \leq n\}$ for each $n \in \mathbb{P}$. It is easy to verify that this recursive definition provides a one-to-one function f mapping $\mathbb{P}$ onto A [Exercise 10] and so A is countable.

(b) The statement in part (b) means that if I is a countable index set and if $\{A_i : i \in I\}$ is a family of countable sets, then the union $\bigcup_{i \in I} A_i$ is countable. We may assume that each A_i is nonempty and that $\bigcup_{i \in I} A_i$ is infinite, and we may assume that $I = \mathbb{P}$ or that I has the form $\{1, 2, \ldots, n\}$. If $I = \{1, 2, \ldots, n\}$ and we defined $A_i = A_n$ for $i > n$, we would obtain a family $\{A_i : i \in \mathbb{P}\}$ indexed by $\mathbb{P}$ with the same union. Thus we may assume that $I = \mathbb{P}$. Each set A_i is finite or countably infinite. By repeating elements if A_i is finite, we can list each A_i as follows:

$$A_i = \{a_{1i}, a_{2i}, a_{3i}, a_{4i}, \ldots\}.$$

The elements in $\bigcup_{i \in I} A_i$ can be listed in an array as in Figure 7. The arrows in the figure suggest a single listing for $\bigcup_{i \in I} A_i$:

(∗) $a_{11}, a_{12}, a_{21}, a_{31}, a_{22}, a_{13}, a_{14}, a_{23}, a_{32}, a_{41}, \ldots.$

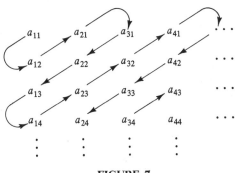

FIGURE 7

Some elements may be repeated, but the list includes infinitely many distinct elements since $\bigcup_{i \in I} A_i$ is infinite. Now a one-to-one mapping f of $\mathbb{P}$ onto $\bigcup_{i \in I} A_i$ is obtained as follows: $f(1) = a_{11}, f(2)$ is the next element listed in (∗) different from $f(1), f(3)$ is the next element listed in (∗) different from $f(1)$ and $f(2)$, etc. ☐

EXAMPLE 5 The argument in Example 1(c) that $\mathbb{Q}$ is countable is similar to the proof of part (b) of the theorem. In fact, we can use the theorem to give another proof that $\mathbb{Q}$ is countable. For each n in $\mathbb{P}$, let

$$A_n = \left\{ \frac{m}{n} : m \in \mathbb{Z} \right\}.$$

Thus A_n consists of all integer multiples of $1/n$. Each A_n is clearly in one-to-one correspondence with $\mathbb{Z}$ [map m to m/n] and so each A_n is countable. By part (b) of the theorem, the union

$$\bigcup_{n \in \mathbb{P}} A_n = \mathbb{Q}$$

is also countable. □

EXAMPLE 6   (a) If Σ is a finite alphabet, then the set Σ^* of all words using letters from Σ is countably infinite. Note that Σ is nonempty by definition. We already know that Σ^* is infinite. Recall that

$$\Sigma^* = \bigcup_{k=0}^{\infty} \Sigma^k$$

where each Σ^k is finite. Thus Σ^* is a countable union of countable sets, and hence Σ^* itself is countable by part (b) of the theorem.

(b) Imagine, if you can, a countably infinite alphabet Σ and let Σ^* consist of all words using letters of Σ, i.e., all finite strings of letters from Σ. For each $k \in \mathbb{P}$, the set Σ^k of all words of length k is in one-to-one correspondence with the product set $\Sigma^k = \Sigma \times \Sigma \times \cdots \times \Sigma$. In fact, the correspondence maps each word $a_1 a_2 \cdots a_k$ to the k-tuple $\langle a_1, a_2, \ldots, a_k \rangle$. So each set Σ^k is countable by Exercise 17. The 1-element set $\Sigma^0 = \{\epsilon\}$ is countable too. Hence $\Sigma^* = \bigcup_{k=0}^{\infty} \Sigma^k$ is countable by part (b) of the theorem.   □

EXAMPLE 7 Consider any graph and let V and E be the sets of vertices and edges. Even if V or E is infinite, each path has finite length by definition. Let Π [capital Greek pi] be the set of all paths of the graph.

(a) If E is nonempty, Π is infinite. For if e is any edge, then e, $e\,e$, $e\,e\,e$, etc. all describe paths in the graph.

(b) If E is finite, then Π is countable. For purposes of counting, let's view E as an alphabet. Since each path is a sequence of edges, it corresponds to a word in E^*. Of course, not all words in E^* correspond to paths, since endpoints of adjacent edges must match up. But the set Π is in one-to-one correspondence with some *subset* of E^*. The set E^* is countably infinite by Example 6(a) and so Π is countable by part (a) of the theorem.

(c) If E is countably infinite, then Π is still countable. Simply apply Example 6(b) instead of Example 6(a) in the discussion of part (b).   □

EXERCISES 5.4

1. Let A and B be finite sets with $|A| < |B|$. True or False.
   (a) There is a one-to-one map of A into B.
   (b) There is a one-to-one map of A onto B.
   (c) There is a one-to-one map of B into A.
   (d) There is a function mapping A onto B.
   (e) There is a function mapping B onto A.

2. True or false.
   (a) The set of positive rational numbers is countably infinite.
   (b) The set of all rational numbers is countably infinite.
   (c) The set of positive real numbers is countably infinite.
   (d) The intersection of two countably infinite sets is countably infinite.
   (e) There is a one-to-one correspondence between the set of all even integers and the set $\mathbb{N}$ of natural numbers.

3. Give one-to-one correspondences between the following pairs of sets.
   (a) $(0, 1)$ and $(-1, 1)$ (b) $[0, 1)$ and $(0, 1]$
   (c) $[0, 1]$ and $[-5, 8]$ (d) $(0, 1)$ and $(1, \infty)$
   (e) $(0, 1)$ and $(0, \infty)$ (f) $\mathbb{R}$ and $(0, \infty)$

4. Let $E = \{n \in \mathbb{N} : n \text{ is even}\}$. Show that E and $\mathbb{N} \backslash E$ are countable by exhibiting one-to-one functions $f \colon \mathbb{P} \to E$ and $g \colon \mathbb{P} \to \mathbb{N} \backslash E$.

5. Here is another one-to-one function f mapping $(0, 1)$ onto $\mathbb{R}$:
   $$f(x) = \frac{2x - 1}{x(1 - x)}.$$
   (a) Sketch the graph of f.
   (b) If you know some calculus, prove that f is one-to-one by showing that its derivative is positive on $(0, 1)$.

6. Which of the following sets are countable? countably infinite?
   (a) $\{0, 1, 2, 3, 4\}$ (b) $\{n \in \mathbb{N} : n \leq 73\}$
   (c) $\{n \in \mathbb{Z} : n \leq 73\}$ (d) $\{n \in \mathbb{Z} : |n| \leq 73\}$
   (e) $\{5, 10, 15, 20, 25, \ldots\}$ (f) $\mathbb{N} \times \mathbb{N}$
   (g) $[\frac{1}{4}, \frac{1}{3}]$

7. Let Σ be the alphabet $\{a, b, c\}$. Which of the following sets are countably infinite?
   (a) Σ^{73} (b) Σ^*
   (c) $\bigcup_{k=0}^{\infty} \Sigma^{2k} = \{w \in \Sigma^* : \text{length}(w) \text{ is even}\}$
   (d) $\bigcup_{k=0}^{3} \Sigma^k$ (e) $\bigcup_{k=1}^{3} \Sigma^{2k}$

8. A set A has m elements and a set B has n elements. How many functions from A into B are one-to-one? *Hint:* Consider the cases $m \leq n$ and $m > n$ separately.

9. Let S be an infinite set.
   (a) Show that if there is a one-to-one correspondence of S onto some countable set, then S itself is countable.
   (b) Show that if there is a one-to-one correspondence of S onto some uncountable set, then S is uncountable.

10. Complete the proof of part (a) of the theorem by showing that f is one-to-one and that f maps $\mathbb{P}$ onto A.

11. (a) Prove that if S and T are countable, then $S \times T$ is countable.
    (b) Prove that if f maps S onto T and S is countable, then T is countable.
    (c) Use parts (a) and (b) to give another proof that $\mathbb{Q}$ is countable. *Suggestion:* For $\langle m, n \rangle$ in $\mathbb{Z} \times \mathbb{P}$, define $f(\langle m, n \rangle) = m/n$.

12. Show that if S and T have the same size, so do $\mathcal{P}(S)$ and $\mathcal{P}(T)$.

13. (a) Show that $\mathrm{FUN}(\mathbb{P}, \{0, 1\})$ is in one-to-one correspondence with the set $\mathcal{P}(\mathbb{P})$ of all subsets of $\mathbb{P}$.
    (b) Show that $\mathcal{P}(\mathbb{P})$ is uncountable.

14. Show that any disjoint family of nonempty subsets of a countable set is countable.

15. Show that if S is countable, then $S^n = S \times S \times \cdots \times S$ [n times] is countable for each n. *Hint:* Use Exercise 11(a) and induction.

CHAPTER HIGHLIGHTS

See the end of Chapter 0 if you have forgotten how to use the following lists to review. Think always of examples.

Concepts

number of elements in $S = |S|$
selection with/without replacement
r-permutation, permutation
countable, countably infinite, uncountable

Facts

$|S \cup T| = |S| + |T| - |S \cap T|$ for finite sets.

$|S_1 \times \cdots \times S_k| = \prod_{j=1}^{k} |S_j|$.

$\binom{n}{r} = \dfrac{n!}{(n-r)!\, r!}$.

Binomial theorem: $(a + b)^n = \sum_{r=0}^{n} \binom{n}{r} a^r b^{n-r}$.

Counting Lemma.

Formula $\dfrac{n!}{n_1! \cdots n_k!}$ for counting ordered partitions.

Formula $\binom{n+k-1}{k-1}$ for ways to place n objects in k boxes.

Inclusion-Exclusion Principle.
Pigeon-Hole Principle.
Every rational number has a repeating decimal expansion.
Subsets and countable unions of countable sets are countable.

Methods

Cantor's diagonalization procedure.
Numerous clever ideas illustrated in examples.

6

MORE LOGIC AND

INDUCTION

After developing quantifiers in § 6.1, we give in § 6.2 a brief introduction to the predicate calculus. Sections 6.3 and 6.4 concern some sophisticated aspects of mathematical induction, and serve as an elaboration on the treatment given in § 2.5.

§ 6.1   Quantifiers

The propositional calculus is a nice, complete, self-contained theory of logic, but it is totally inadequate for most of mathematics. The problem is that the propositional calculus does not allow the use of an infinite number of propositions. In addition, the notation is awkward for handling a large finite number of propositions. For example, we frequently encounter an infinite sequence of propositions $p(n)$ indexed by $\mathbb{N}$. The informal statement "$p(n)$ is true for all n" means "$p(0)$ is true, $p(1)$ is true, $p(2)$ is true, etc." The only symbolism from the propositional calculus would be $p(0) \wedge p(1) \wedge p(2) \wedge \cdots$, but this is not acceptable in the propositional calculus. Similarly, the informal statement "$p(n)$ is true for some n" would correspond to the unacceptable $p(0) \vee p(1) \vee p(2) \vee \cdots$. To get around this sort of problem we just need some new symbols, a symbol that means "for all" and one that means "for some." Then we need to know the rules for using the new symbols and combining them with the old ones. The augmented system of symbols and rules is called the **predicate calculus**.

The new symbols we introduce are called **quantifiers**. Suppose that $\{p(x): x \in U\}$ is a family of propositions indexed by a set U that may be infinite; the set U is called the **universe of discourse** or **domain of discourse**. The **universal quantifier** $\forall$, an upside-down A as in "for *A*ll," is used to build compound propositions of the form

$$\forall x \, p(x)$$

which we read as "for all x, $p(x)$." Other translations of $\forall$ are "for each," "for every," "for any." The compound proposition $\forall x \, p(x)$ is assigned truth values as follows:

$\forall x \, p(x)$ is true if $p(x)$ is true for every x in U;
otherwise $\forall x \, p(x)$ is false.

The **existential quantifier** $\exists$, a backward E as in "there *E*xists," is used to form propositions like

$$\exists x \, p(x)$$

which we read as "there exists an x such that $p(x)$," "there is an x such that $p(x)$," or "for some x, $p(x)$." The compound proposition $\exists x \, p(x)$ has these truth values:

$\exists x \, p(x)$ is true if $p(x)$ is true for at least one x in U;
$\exists x \, p(x)$ is false if $p(x)$ is false for every x in U.

EXAMPLE 1   (a) Let $\mathbb{N}$ be the universe of discourse and for each n in $\mathbb{N}$ let $p(n)$ be the proposition "$n^2 = n$." Then $\forall n \, p(n)$ is false because, for example, $p(3)$, i.e., $3^2 = 3$, is false. On the other hand, $\exists n \, p(n)$ is true because at least one proposition $p(n)$ is true; in fact, exactly two of them are true, namely $p(0)$ and $p(1)$.

For the same universe of discourse, let $q(n)$ be the proposition "$(n + 1)^2 = n^2 + 2n + 1$." We can use $p(n)$, $q(n)$ and connectives from the propositional calculus to obtain other quantified propositions. For example, $\exists n[\neg q(n)]$ is false since every proposition $\neg q(n)$ is false. The proposition $\forall n[p(n) \lor q(n)]$ is true because each proposition $p(n) \lor q(n)$ is true. Of course, the weaker proposition $\exists n[p(n) \lor q(n)]$ is also true.

(b) Let $p(x)$ be "$x \leq 2x$" and $q(x)$ be "$x^2 \geq 0$," with universe of discourse $\mathbb{R}$. Since $\mathbb{R}$ cannot be listed as a sequence, it would really be impossible to symbolize $\exists x \, p(x)$ or $\forall x \, q(x)$ in the propositional calculus. Clearly $\exists x \, p(x)$ is true; $\forall x \, p(x)$ is false because $p(x)$ is false for negative x. Both $\forall x \, q(x)$ and $\exists x \, q(x)$ are true and $\exists x[\neg q(x)]$ is false.

(c) Quantifiers are useful in mathematics and computer science when the universe of discourse is finite, but large. Suppose, for example, that propositions $p(n)$ are indexed by the universe of discourse $\{n \in \mathbb{N} : 0 \leq n \leq$

65,535}. The notation $\forall n\, p(n)$ is clearly preferable to

$$p(0) \wedge p(1) \wedge p(2) \wedge p(3) \wedge \cdots \wedge p(65{,}535)$$

though we might invent the acceptable $\bigwedge\limits_{n=0}^{65{,}535} p(n)$. □

EXAMPLE 2   Occasionally we are confronted with a constant function in algebra, such as $f(x) = 2$ for $x \in \mathbb{R}$, so that the variable x does not appear in the right side of the definition of f. Although the value of $f(x)$ does not depend on the choice of x, we nevertheless regard f as a function of x. Similarly, in logic we occasionally encounter propositions $p(x)$ whose truth values do not depend on the choice of x in U. As artificial examples, consider $p(n) =$ "2 is prime" and $q(n) =$ "16 is prime," with universe of discourse $\mathbb{N}$. Since all propositions $p(n)$ are true, $\exists n\, p(n)$ and $\forall n\, p(n)$ are both true. Since all propositions $q(n)$ are false, $\exists n\, q(n)$ and $\forall n\, q(n)$ are both false. Propositions $p(x)$ whose truth values do not depend on x are essentially the ones we studied earlier in the propositional calculus. In a sense the propositional calculus fills the same place in the predicate calculus that the constant functions fill in the study of all functions. □

Let's analyze the proposition $\forall x\, p(x)$ more closely. The expression $p(x)$ is called a predicate. In ordinary grammatical usage a predicate is the part of a sentence which says something about the subject of the sentence. For example, "_____ went to the moon" and "_____ is bigger than a bread box" are predicates. To make a sentence, we supply the subject. For example, the predicate "_____ is bigger than a bread box" becomes the sentence "This book is bigger than a bread box" if we supply the subject "This book." If we call the predicate p, then the sentence could be denoted p(This book). Each subject yields a sentence.

In our symbolic logic setting a **predicate** is a function which produces a proposition whenever we feed it a member of the universe, that is, a proposition-valued function with domain U. We follow our usual practice and denote such a function by $p(x)$. The variable x in the expression $p(x)$ is called a **free variable** of the predicate. As x varies over U the truth value of $p(x)$ may vary. In contrast, the proposition $\forall x\, p(x)$ has a fixed meaning and truth value and does not vary with x. The variable x in $\forall x\, p(x)$ is called a **bound variable**; it is bound by the quantifier $\forall$. Since $\forall x\, p(x)$ has a fixed meaning and truth value, it would be pointless and unnatural to quantify it again. That is, it would be pointless to introduce $\forall x[\forall x\, p(x)]$ and $\exists x[\forall x\, p(x)]$ since their truth values are the same as that of $\forall x\, p(x)$.

We can also consider predicates which are functions of more than one variable, perhaps from more than one universe of discourse, and in such cases multiple use of quantifiers is natural.

EXAMPLE 3   (a) Let $\mathbb{N}$ be the universe of discourse and for each m and n in $\mathbb{N}$ let $p(m, n)$ be the proposition "$m < n$." We could think of these propositions as being indexed by $\mathbb{N} \times \mathbb{N}$ and think of $\mathbb{N} \times \mathbb{N}$ as the universe of discourse, but for the present we prefer to treat the variables m and n separately. Both variables m and n are free in the sense that the meanings and truth values of $p(m, n)$ vary with both m and n. In the expression $\exists m\, p(m, n)$, the variable m is bound but the variable n is free. The proposition $\exists m\, p(m, n)$ reads "there is an m in $\mathbb{N}$ with $m < n$," so $\exists m\, p(m, 0)$ is false, $\exists m\, p(m, 1)$ is true, $\exists m\, p(m, 2)$ is true, etc. For each choice of n the proposition $\exists m\, p(m, n)$ is either true or false; its truth value does not depend on m but depends on n alone. It is meaningful to quantify $\exists m\, p(m, n)$ with respect to the free variable n to obtain $\forall n[\exists m\, p(m, n)]$ and $\exists n[\exists m\, p(m, n)]$. The proposition $\forall n[\exists m\, p(m, n)]$ is false because $\exists m\, p(m, 0)$ is false and the proposition $\exists n[\exists m\, p(m, n)]$ is true because, for example, $\exists m\, p(m, 1)$ is true. Henceforth we will usually omit the brackets [   ] and write $\forall n\, \exists m\, p(m,n)$ and $\exists n\, \exists m\, p(m, n)$.

There are eight ways to apply the two quantifiers to the two variables: $\forall m\, \forall n$, $\forall n\, \forall m$, $\exists m\, \exists n$, $\exists n\, \exists m$, $\forall m\, \exists n$, $\exists n\, \forall m$, $\forall n\, \exists m$, $\exists m\, \forall n$. The first two turn out to be logically equivalent, since they have the same meaning as $\forall \langle m, n\rangle\, p(m, n)$ where $\langle m, n\rangle$ varies over the new universe of discourse $\mathbb{N} \times \mathbb{N}$. Similarly, $\exists m\, \exists n\, p(m, n)$ and $\exists n\, \exists m\, p(m, n)$ are logically equivalent. The remaining four must be approached carefully. For our example, we already observed that $\forall n\, \exists m\, p(m, n)$ is false. No matter what m is, $\forall n\, p(m, n)$ is false since $p(m, 0)$ is false. Therefore $\exists m\, \forall n\, p(m, n)$ is false. To analyze $\forall m\, \exists n\, p(m, n)$, note that for each m, $\exists n\, p(m, n)$ is true because $p(m, m + 1)$ is true. Therefore $\forall m\, \exists n\, p(m, n)$ is also true. To analyze $\exists n\, \forall m\, p(m, n)$, note that for each n, $\forall m\, p(m, n)$ is false because, for example, $p(n, n)$ is false. Therefore $\exists n\, \forall m\, p(m, n)$ is false. We repeat:

for this example,
$$\forall m\, \exists n\, p(m, n) \text{ is true, while } \exists n\, \forall m\, p(m, n) \text{ is false.}$$

The left proposition asserts, correctly, that for every m, there is a bigger n. The right proposition asserts, incorrectly, that there is an n bigger than all m.

(b) Here is a less mathematical example illustrating the importance of order when using both quantifiers $\forall$ and $\exists$. Let the universe of discourse consist of all people and consider

$$p(x, y) = \text{"}y \text{ is a mother of } x.\text{"}$$

Then $\forall x\, \exists y\, p(x, y)$ asserts that everyone has a mother, which is true. On the other hand, $\exists y\, \forall x\, p(x, y)$ asserts that someone is the mother of everyone else, which is false.

The proposition $\forall y\, \exists x\, p(x, y)$ asserts that everyone is a mother, and $\exists x\, \forall y\, p(x, y)$ asserts that someone has everyone for his or her mother. These are both clearly false statements.   ☐

With these examples in mind we turn now to a more formal account. Let $U_1, U_2, \ldots, U_n$ be nonempty sets. An *n*-**place predicate** over $U_1 \times U_2 \times \cdots \times U_n$ is a function $p(x_1, x_2, \ldots, x_n)$ with domain $U_1 \times U_2 \times \cdots \times U_n$ which has propositions as its function values. The variables $x_1, x_2, \ldots, x_n$ for $p(x_1, x_2, \ldots, x_n)$ are all **free variables** for the predicate, and each x_j varies over the corresponding universe of discourse U_j. The term "free" is short for "free for substitution," meaning that the variable x_j is available in case we wish to substitute a particular value from U_j for all occurrences of x_j.

If we substitute a value for x_j, say for definiteness we substitute a for x_1 in $p(x_1, x_2, \ldots, x_n)$, we get the predicate $p(a, x_2, \ldots, x_n)$ which is free on the $n - 1$ remaining variables $x_2, \ldots, x_n$ but no longer free on x_1. An application of a quantifier $\forall x_j$ or $\exists x_j$ to a predicate $p(x_1, x_2, \ldots, x_n)$ gives a predicate $\forall x_j \, p(x_1, x_2, \ldots, x_n)$ or $\exists x_j \, p(x_1, x_2, \ldots, x_n)$ whose value depends only on the values of the remaining $n - 1$ variables. We say the quantifier **binds** the variable x_j, making x_j a **bound variable** for the predicate. Application of n quantifiers, one for each variable, makes all variables bound and yields a proposition whose truth value can be determined by applying the rules for $\forall x$ and $\exists x$ specified prior to Example 1 to the universes $U_1, U_2, \ldots, U_n$.

EXAMPLE 4   (a) Consider the proposition

(1) $$\forall m \, \exists n [n > 2^m];$$

here $p(m, n) = $ "$n > 2^m$" is a 2-place predicate over $\mathbb{N} \times \mathbb{N}$. That is, m and n are both allowed to vary over $\mathbb{N}$. Recall our convention that (1) represents

$$\forall m [\exists n [n > 2^m]].$$

Both variables m and n are bound. To decide the truth value of (1), we consider the inside expression $\exists n [n > 2^m]$ in which n is a bound variable and m is a free variable. We mentally fix the free variable m and note that the proposition "$n > 2^m$" is true for some choices of n in $\mathbb{N}$, for example $n = 2^m + 1$. It follows that $\exists n [n > 2^m]$ is true. This thought process is valid for each m in $\mathbb{N}$, so we conclude that $\exists n [n > 2^m]$ is true for all m. That is, (1) is true.

If we reverse the quantifiers in (1), we obtain

(2) $$\exists n \, \forall m [n > 2^m].$$

This is false because $\forall m [n > 2^m]$ is false for each n, since "$n > 2^m$" is false for $m = n$.

(b) Consider the propositions

(3) $$\forall x \, \exists y [x + y = 0],$$

(4) $$\exists y \, \forall x [x + y = 0],$$

(5) $$\forall x \, \exists y [xy = 0],$$

(6) $$\exists y \, \forall x [xy = 0],$$

where each universe of discourse is $\mathbb{R}$.

To analyze (3) we consider a fixed x. Then $\exists y[x + y = 0]$ is true, because the choice $y = -x$ makes "$x + y = 0$" true. That is, $\exists y[x + y = 0]$ is true for all x and so (3) is true.

To analyze (4) we consider a fixed y. Then $\forall x[x + y = 0]$ is not true, because the choice $x = 1 - y$ makes "$x + y = 0$" false. That is, for each y, $\forall x[x + y = 0]$ is false and so (4) is false.

Proposition (5) is true, because $\exists y[xy = 0]$ is true for all x. In fact, the choice $y = 0$ makes "$xy = 0$" true.

To deal with (6) we analyze $\forall x[xy = 0]$ in two cases. If $y = 0$, this proposition is clearly true. But if $y \neq 0$ this proposition is false, since the choice $x = 1$ makes "$xy = 0$" false in this case. Thus $\forall x[xy = 0]$ is true if and only if $y = 0$. Since $\forall x[xy = 0]$ is true for some y, namely $y = 0$, the proposition (6) is true.

In the next section we will see that the truth of (6) implies the truth of (5) on purely logical grounds; that is,

$$\exists y \, \forall x \, p(x, y) \rightarrow \forall x \, \exists y \, p(x, y)$$

is always true. $\square$

We have already noted that an n-place predicate becomes an $(n - 1)$-place predicate when we bind one of the variables with a quantifier. Its truth value depends on the truth values of the remaining $n - 1$ free variables, and in particular doesn't depend on what name we choose to call the bound variable. Thus if $p(x)$ is a 1-place predicate with universe of discourse U, then $\forall x \, p(x)$, $\forall y \, p(y)$ and $\forall t \, p(t)$ all have the same truth value, namely true if $p(u)$ is true for every u in U and false otherwise. Similarly, if $q(x, y)$ is a 2-place predicate with universes U and V, then $\exists y \, q(x, y)$, $\exists t \, q(x, t)$ and $\exists s \, q(x, s)$ all describe the same 1-place predicate, namely the predicate which has truth value true for a given x in U if and only if $q(x, v)$ is true for some v in the universe V in which the second variable lies. On the other hand, the predicate $\exists x \, q(x, x)$ is *not* the same as these last three. The difference is that the quantifier in this instance binds both of the free variables.

EXAMPLE 5   Let U and V be $\mathbb{N}$ and let $q(x, y) =$ "$x > y$." Then $\exists x \, q(x, y)$ is the 1-place predicate "some member of $\mathbb{N}$ is greater than y," and so is $\exists t \, q(t, y)$. The predicate $\exists y \, q(x, y)$ is the 1-place predicate "there is a member of $\mathbb{N}$ less than x," which is the same predicate as $\exists s \, q(x, s)$ and has the value true for $x > 0$ and false for $x = 0$. But $\exists x \, q(x, x)$ is the proposition "$x > x$ for some x," which has the value false. $\square$

In practice, it is common to omit leading universal quantifiers.

EXAMPLE 6   The associative and cancellation laws for $\mathbb{R}$ are often written

(a) $$（x + y) + z = x + (y + z),$$

(b) $$xz = yz \quad \text{and} \quad z \neq 0 \quad \text{imply} \quad x = y.$$

The intended meanings are

$$\forall x \, \forall y \, \forall z[(x + y) + z = x + (y + z)],$$
$$\forall x \, \forall y \, \forall z[(xz = yz \land z \neq 0) \rightarrow x = y],$$

where the universe of discourse is $\mathbb{R}$. When writing informally, the universal quantifiers sometimes follow the predicate, so that (a) might be written as

$$(x + y) + z = x + (y + z) \quad \forall x \, \forall y \, \forall z,$$

or

$$(x + y) + z = x + (y + z) \quad \forall x, y, z \in \mathbb{R},$$

or

$$(x + y) + z = x + (y + z) \quad \text{for all} \quad x, y, z \in \mathbb{R}. \quad \square$$

Another common practice is to build in a description of the universe of discourse just after the variable being quantified. For example, instead of "Let $\mathbb{R}$ be the universe ... $\forall x \, p(x)$" one might write $\forall x \in \mathbb{R} \, p(x)$. Similarly, $\exists x \in \mathbb{R} \, \forall n \in \mathbb{P}[x^n > x]$ is read as "there is a real number x such that for every n in $\mathbb{P}$, $x^n > x$" or as "there is a real number x such that $x^n > x$ for every n in $\mathbb{P}$." Along the same lines, one might write $\forall \epsilon > 0 \, \exists \delta > 0$, rather than the cumbersome $\forall \epsilon \in (0, \infty) \, \exists \delta \in (0, \infty)$.

EXERCISES 6.1

1. Determine the truth values of the following, where the universe of discourse is $\mathbb{N}$.
   (a) $\forall m \, \exists n[2n = m]$ (b) $\exists n \, \forall m[2m = n]$
   (c) $\forall m \, \exists n[2m = n]$ (d) $\exists n \, \forall m[2n = m]$
   (e) $\forall m \, \forall n[\neg \{2n = m\}]$

2. Determine the truth values of the following, where the universe of discourse is $\mathbb{R}$.
   (a) $\forall x \, \exists y[xy = 1]$
   (b) $\exists y \, \forall x[xy = 1]$
   (c) $\exists x \, \exists y[xy = 1]$
   (d) $\forall x \, \forall y[(x + y)^2 = x^2 + y^2]$
   (e) $\forall x \, \exists y[(x + y)^2 = x^2 + y^2]$
   (f) $\exists y \, \forall x[(x + y)^2 = x^2 + y^2]$
   (g) $\exists x \, \exists y[(x + 2y = 4) \land (2x - y = 2)]$
   (h) $\exists x \, \exists y[x^2 + y^2 + 1 = 2xy]$

3. Write the following sentences in logical notation. Be sure to bind all variables. When using quantifiers, specify universes; use $\mathbb{R}$ if no universe is indicated.
   (a) If $x < y$ and $y < z$, then $x < z$.
   (b) For every $x > 0$, there exists an n in $\mathbb{N}$ such that $n > x$ and $x > 1/n$.
   (c) For every $m, n \in \mathbb{N}$ there exists $p \in \mathbb{N}$ such that $m < p$ and $p < n$.
   (d) There exists $u \in \mathbb{N}$ so that $un = n$ for all $n \in \mathbb{N}$.
   (e) For each $n \in \mathbb{N}$, there exists $m \in \mathbb{N}$ such that $m < n$.
   (f) For every $n \in \mathbb{N}$, there exists $m \in \mathbb{N}$ such that $2^m \leq n$ and $n < 2^{m+1}$.

4. Determine the truth values of the propositions in Exercise 3.

5. Write the following sentences in logical notation; the universe of discourse is the set Σ^* of words using letters from a finite alphabet Σ.
   (a) If $w_1 w_2 = w_1 w_3$, then $w_2 = w_3$.
   (b) If length$(w) = 1$, then $w \in \Sigma$.
   (c) $w_1 w_2 = w_2 w_1$ for all $w_1, w_2 \in \Sigma^*$.

6. Determine the truth values of the propositions in Exercise 5.

7. Specify the free and bound variables in the following expressions.
   (a) $\forall x \, \exists z [\sin(x + y) = \cos(z - y)]$
   (b) $\exists x [xy = xz \to y = z]$
   (c) $\exists x \, \exists z [x^2 + z^2 = y]$

8. Consider the expression $x + y = y + x$.
   (a) Specify the free and bound variables in the expression.
   (b) Apply universal quantifiers over the universe $\mathbb{R}$ to get a proposition. Is the proposition true?
   (c) Apply existential quantifiers over the universe $\mathbb{R}$ to get a proposition. Is the proposition true?

9. Repeat Exercise 8 for the expression $(x - y)^2 = x^2 - y^2$.

10. Consider the proposition $\forall m \, \exists n [m + n = 7]$.
    (a) Is the proposition true for the universes of discourse $\mathbb{N}$?
    (b) Is the proposition true for the universes of discourse $\mathbb{Z}$?

11. Repeat Exercise 10 for $\forall n \, \exists m [m + 1 = n]$.

12. Consider the proposition $\forall x \, \exists y [(x^2 + 1)y = 1]$.
    (a) Is the proposition true for the universes of discourse $\mathbb{N}$?
    (b) Is the proposition true for the universes of discourse $\mathbb{Q}$?
    (c) Is the proposition true for the universes of discourse $\mathbb{R}$?

13. Another useful quantifier is $\exists !$ where $\exists ! \, x \, p(x)$ is read "there exists a unique x such that $p(x)$." This compound proposition is assigned truth value true if $p(x)$ is true for exactly one value of x in the universe of discourse; otherwise it is false. Write the following sentences in logical notation.
    (a) There is a unique x in $\mathbb{R}$ such that $x + y = y$ for all $y \in \mathbb{R}$.
    (b) The equation $x^2 = x$ has a unique solution.
    (c) Exactly one set is a subset of all sets in $\mathcal{P}(\mathbb{N})$.
    (d) If $f : A \to B$, then for each $a \in A$ there is exactly one $b \in B$ such that $f(a) = b$.
    (e) If $f : A \to B$ is a one-to-one function, then for each $b \in B$ there is exactly one $a \in A$ such that $f(a) = b$.

14. Determine the truth values of the propositions in Exercise 13.

15. In this problem $A = \{0, 2, 4, 6, 8, 10\}$ and the universe of discourse is $\mathbb{N}$. True or False.
    (a) A is the set of even integers in $\mathbb{N}$ less than 12.
    (b) $A = \{0, 2, 4, 6, \ldots\}$
    (c) $A = \{n \in \mathbb{N} : 2n < 24\}$
    (d) $A = \{n \in \mathbb{N} : \forall m [2m = n \to m < 6]\}$
    (e) $A = \{n \in \mathbb{N} : \forall m [2m = n \wedge m < 6]\}$

(f) $A = \{n \in \mathbb{N} : \exists m[2m = n \rightarrow m < 6]\}$

(g) $A = \{n \in \mathbb{N} : \exists m[2m = n \wedge m < 6]\}$

(h) $A = \{n \in \mathbb{N} : \exists ! \, m[2m = n \wedge m < 6]\}$ [see Exercise 13]

(i) $A = \{n \in \mathbb{N} : n$ is even and $n^2 \leq 100\}$

(j) $\forall n[n \in A \rightarrow n \leq 10]$

(k) $3 \in A \rightarrow 3 < 10$

(l) $12 \in A \rightarrow 12 < 10$

(m) $8 \in A \rightarrow 8 < 10$

16. With universe of discourse $\mathbb{N}$, let $p(n) = $ "n is prime" and $e(n) = $ "n is even." Write the following in ordinary English.

(a) $\exists m \, \forall n[e(n) \wedge p(m + n)]$

(b) $\forall n \, \exists m[\neg e(n) \rightarrow e(m + n)]$

Translate the following into logical notation using p and e.

(c) There are two prime integers whose sum is even.

(d) If the sum of two primes is even, then neither of them equals 2.

(e) The sum of two prime integers is odd.

17. Determine the truth values of the propositions in Exercise 16.

§ 6.2 Predicate Calculus

The ideas of "proof" and "theorem" which we discussed in § 2.3 for the propositional calculus can be extended to the predicate calculus setting. Not surprisingly, with more possible expressions we also get more complications. A moderately thorough account of the subject would form a substantial part of another book. In this section we limit ourselves to discussing some of the most basic and useful connections between quantifiers and logical operators.

In Chapter 2 we used the term "compound proposition" in an informal way to describe propositions built up out of simpler ones. In § 3.5 we gave a recursive definition of wff's for the propositional calculus; these are the compound propositions of Chapter 2. In the same way, we will use a recursive definition in order to precisely define "compound propositions" for the predicate calculus. At the same time we want to look more closely at what we did in the propositional calculus.

We built up five propositions from symbols p, q, r, etc. which we considered to be names for other propositions. The symbols could be considered to be variables, and a compound proposition such as $p \wedge (\neg q)$ could be considered a function of the two variables p and q; its value is true or false, depending on the truth values of p and q and the form of the compound proposition. The truth table for the compound proposition is simply a list of the function values as the variables range independently over the set {true, false}. Variables of this sort which can take on just the two values true and false are called **logical variables**. For the propositional calculus they are all we need, but for the predicate calculus we must also consider variables associated with other universes of discourse, such as $\mathbb{R}$, $\mathbb{Z}$ and $\mathfrak{M}_{m,n}$.

Suppose now that we have available a collection of nonempty universes of discourse with which the free variables of all n-place predicates we consider are associated. We define the class of **compound predicates** as follows:

(B_1) Logical variables are compound predicates.

(B_2) n-place predicates are compound predicates for $n \geqq 1$.

(R_1) If $p(x)$ and $q(x)$ are compound predicates with free variable x, then so are

$$\neg p(x), \quad (p(x) \lor q(x)), \quad (p(x) \land q(x)),$$
$$(p(x) \to q(x)) \quad \text{and} \quad (p(x) \leftrightarrow q(x)).$$

(R_2) If $p(x)$ is a compound predicate with free variable x, then

$$(\forall x \, p(x)) \quad \text{and} \quad (\exists x \, p(x))$$

are compound predicates for which x is not a free variable.

(E) The only compound predicates are those required by (B_1), (B_2), (R_1) and (R_2).

When we write "$p(x)$" here we mean to indicate that the given compound predicate has x as one of its free variables. We admit the possibility that the truth value of $p(x)$ is actually independent of the choice of x. In particular, we can view a proposition as trivially having a free variable, so that $p(x)$ and $q(x)$ in (R_1) might just be propositions p and q. If we delete (B_2) and (R_2) and the reference to free variables in (R_1) we obtain the recursive description of wff's for the propositional calculus in Example 6 of § 3.5. In our present setting there are compound predicates which are propositions besides those made from (B_1) and (R_1). If all of the variables in a compound predicate are bound then the predicate is a proposition. We extend our definition and say that a **compound proposition** is a compound predicate with no free variables. For example,

$$((\exists x (\exists z \, p(x, z))) \to (\forall y (\neg r(y))))$$

is a compound proposition with no free variables. In contrast,

$$(p(x) \lor (\neg \forall y \, q(x, y)))$$

and

$$((\exists z \, p(x, z)) \to (\forall y (\neg r(y))))$$

are compound predicates with free variable x.

The number and the placement of parentheses in a compound predicate are explicitly prescribed by our recursive definition. In practice, for clarity, we may add or suppress some parentheses. For example, we may write $((\forall x \, p(x)) \to (\exists x \, p(x)))$ as $\forall x \, p(x) \to \exists x \, p(x)$ and we may write $(\exists x \, \neg p(x))$ as $\exists x (\neg p(x))$. We sometimes also use brackets or braces instead of parentheses.

The truth value of a compound proposition ordinarily depends on the choices of the universes of discourse that the bound variables are quantified over, but there are important instances in which the truth value not only does not depend on the universe choices but is in fact independent of the values of the logical variables as well. A compound proposition which has the value true for all universes of discourse and all values of its logical variables is called a **tautology**. This definition extends the usage in Chapter 2, where there were no universes to worry about.

EXAMPLE 1   (a) An important class of tautologies consists of the generalized DeMorgan laws; compare rules 8a–8d in Table 1 of § 2.2. These are

(1) $$\neg\forall x\, p(x) \leftrightarrow \exists x[\neg p(x)],$$

(2) $$\neg\exists x\, p(x) \leftrightarrow \forall x[\neg p(x)],$$

(3) $$\forall x\, p(x) \leftrightarrow \neg\exists x[\neg p(x)],$$

(4) $$\exists x\, p(x) \leftrightarrow \neg\forall x[\neg p(x)].$$

To see (1), note that $\neg\forall x\, p(x)$ has truth value true exactly when $\forall x\, p(x)$ has truth value false, and this occurs whenever there exists an x in the universe of discourse such that $p(x)$ is false, i.e., $\neg p(x)$ is true. Thus $\neg\forall x\, p(x)$ is true precisely when $\exists x[\neg p(x)]$ is true. This argument does not rely on the choice of universe, so (1) is a tautology. The DeMorgan law (2) can be analyzed in a similar way. Alternatively, we can derive (2) from (1) by applying (1) to the 1-place predicate $\neg p(x)$ to obtain

$$\neg\forall x[\neg p(x)] \leftrightarrow \exists x[\neg\,\neg p(x)].$$

The substitution rules in § 2.2 are still valid and so we may substitute $p(x)$ for $\neg\,\neg p(x)$ and obtain the equivalent expression

$$\neg\forall x[\neg p(x)] \leftrightarrow \exists x[p(x)].$$

This is DeMorgan's law (4) and, if we negate both sides, we obtain (2). An application of (2) to $\neg p(x)$ yields (3).

(b) The following holds for a 2-place predicate $p(x, y)$:

(5) $$\exists x\, \forall y\, p(x, y) \rightarrow \forall y\, \exists x\, p(x, y).$$

If the left side of (5) has truth value true, then there exists an x_0 in the universe of discourse such that $\forall y\, p(x_0, y)$ is true, and so $p(x_0, y)$ is true for all y. Thus for each y, $\exists x\, p(x, y)$ is true; in fact, the same x_0 works for each y. Since $\exists x\, p(x, y)$ is true for all y, the right side of (5) has truth value true. Therefore (5) is a tautology.

(c) The converse to (5), namely

$$\forall y\, \exists x\, p(x, y) \rightarrow \exists x\, \forall y\, p(x, y),$$

is not generally true as we noted in Example 3 of § 6.1. To emphasize the difference, we suppose that the x and y vary over a three-element universe U, say $U = \{a, b, c\}$. Then the 2-place predicate $p(x, y)$ takes nine possible values:

$$p(a, a) \qquad p(a, b) \qquad p(a, c)$$

$$p(b, a) \qquad p(b, b) \qquad p(b, c)$$
$$p(c, a) \qquad p(c, b) \qquad p(c, c).$$

As noted in the proof of (5), $\exists x\, \forall y\, p(x, y)$ is true if $\forall y\, p(x_0, y)$ is true for some x_0. Since x_0 must equal a, b or c, we see that $\exists x\, \forall y\, p(x, y)$ is true if and only if all the propositions in some row above are true. In contrast, $\forall y\, \exists x\, p(x, y)$ will be true provided at least one proposition in each column is true. For example, if we consider a predicate $p(x, y)$ with truth values

$$
\begin{array}{ccc}
T & F & F \\
F & F & T \\
F & T & T,
\end{array}
$$

then $\forall y\, \exists x\, p(x, y)$ will be true, while $\exists x\, \forall y\, p(x, y)$ will be false. For this choice of predicate $p(x, y)$, $\exists x\, p(x, y)$ is true for every y, but the suitable x depends on y; no single x works for all y.   □

As in the propositional calculus, we say that two compound propositions P and Q are **logically equivalent** if and only if $P \leftrightarrow Q$ is a tautology; and we write $P \Leftrightarrow Q$ in this case. Also, P **logically implies** Q provided $P \to Q$ is a tautology, in which case we write $P \Rightarrow Q$. In Table 1, we give some useful logical equivalences and implications. We begin numbering the rules with 35, since Chapter 2 contains rules 1 through 34.

***Table 1. Logical Relationships
in the Predicate Calculus***

35a. $\forall x\, \forall y\, p(x, y) \Leftrightarrow \forall y\, \forall x\, p(x, y)$

   b. $\exists x\, \exists y\, p(x, y) \Leftrightarrow \exists y\, \exists x\, p(x, y)$

36. $\exists x\, \forall y\, p(x, y) \Rightarrow \forall y\, \exists x\, p(x, y)$

37a. $\neg \forall x\, p(x) \Leftrightarrow \exists x[\neg p(x)]$

   b. $\neg \exists x\, p(x) \Leftrightarrow \forall x[\neg p(x)]$ ⎫

   c. $\forall x\, p(x) \Leftrightarrow \neg \exists x[\neg p(x)]$ ⎬ DeMorgan laws

   d. $\exists x\, p(x) \Leftrightarrow \neg \forall x[\neg p(x)]$ ⎭

In Example 1 we discussed the tautologies corresponding to rules 36 and 37. The remaining rules are easy to verify.

EXAMPLE 2   To verify rule 35b, that is, to verify that

$$\exists x\, \exists y\, p(x, y) \leftrightarrow \exists y\, \exists x\, p(x, y)$$

is a tautology, we must check that this proposition has the value true for all possible universes of discourse. By the definition of $\leftrightarrow$, we need only check that $\exists x\, \exists y\, p(x, y)$ has the value true for a given universe if and only if $\exists y\, \exists x\, p(x, y)$ has the value true for that universe. Suppose $\exists x\, \exists y\, p(x, y)$ is true. Then $\exists y\, p(x_0, y)$ is true for some x_0 in the universe, so $p(x_0, y_0)$

is true for some y_0 in the universe. Hence $\exists x\, p(x, y_0)$ is true and thus $\exists y\, \exists x\, p(x, y)$ is true. The implication in the other direction follows similarly. Moreover, both $\exists x\, \exists y\, p(x, y)$ and $\exists y\, \exists x\, p(x, y)$ are logically equivalent to the proposition $\exists \langle x, y \rangle\, p(x, y)$ where $\langle x, y \rangle$ varies over $U_1 \times U_2$, with U_1 and U_2 the universes of discourse for the variables x and y. ☐

The DeMorgan laws 37a–37d can be used repeatedly to negate any quantified proposition. For example,

$$\neg \exists w\, \forall x\, \exists y\, \exists z\, p(w, x, y, z)$$

is successively logically equivalent to

$$\forall w[\neg \forall x\, \exists y\, \exists z\, p(w, x, y, z)]$$

$$\forall w\, \exists x[\neg \exists y\, \exists z\, p(w, x, y, z)]$$

$$\forall w\, \exists x\, \forall y[\neg \exists z\, p(w, x, y, z)]$$

$$\forall w\, \exists x\, \forall y\, \forall z[\neg p(w, x, y, z)].$$

This illustrates the general rule: The negation of a quantified predicate is logically equivalent to the proposition obtained by replacing each $\forall$ by $\exists$, replacing each $\exists$ by $\forall$, and by replacing the predicate itself by its negation.

EXAMPLE 3   (a) The negation of

(1) $$\forall x\, \forall y\, \exists z[x < z < y]$$

is

$$\exists x\, \exists y\, \forall z\{\neg[x < z < y]\}.$$

Applying DeMorgan's law, we see that

$$\neg[x < z < y] \Leftrightarrow \neg[x < z \wedge z < y]$$

$$\Leftrightarrow \neg(x < z) \vee \neg(z < y) \Leftrightarrow (x \geq z) \vee (z \geq y).$$

Hence the negation of (1) is logically equivalent to

$$\exists x\, \exists y\, \forall z[(z \leq x) \vee (z \geq y)].$$

(b) Consider universes U_1, U_2 and U_3 made up of companies, components and computers, respectively. Let $p(x, y)$ be the predicate "x produces y" and $q(y, z)$ be "y is a component part of z." The predicate

$$p(x, y) \wedge q(y, z)$$

has the meaning "x produces y, which is a component of z." The proposition

$$\forall x\, \forall z\, \exists y[p(x, y) \wedge q(y, z)]$$

means that each company produces some component of each computer. Its negation is

$$\neg \forall x\, \forall z\, \exists y[p(x, y) \wedge q(y, z)]$$

which is logically equivalent, by the DeMorgan laws, to

$$\exists x \, \exists z \, \forall y [\neg p(x, y) \lor \neg q(y, z)].$$

This negation has the interpretation that there exist a company x_0 and a computer z_0 so that for each choice of a component either x_0 does not produce it or it's not a component of z_0. An equivalent form of the negation is

$$\exists x \, \exists z \, \neg \forall y [p(x, y) \land q(y, z)],$$

with the interpretation that there exist a company x_0 and a computer z_0 so that no component part is both produced by x_0 and a component of z_0.

Compare this example with part (a). In the case of part (a), the negation is also equivalent to

$$\exists x \, \exists y \, \neg \exists z [x < z < y],$$

i.e., there exist x_0 and y_0 with no z strictly between them.

(c) The negation of

(2) $$\forall x \, \forall y [x < y \rightarrow x^2 < y^2]$$

is

$$\exists x \, \exists y \{ \neg [x < y \rightarrow x^2 < y^2] \}.$$

By rule 10a in Table 1 of § 2.2, and DeMorgan's law, $\neg(p \rightarrow q) \Leftrightarrow \neg(\neg p \lor q) \Leftrightarrow p \land \neg q$. So $\neg [x < y \rightarrow x^2 < y^2] \Leftrightarrow (x < y) \land (x^2 \geq y^2)$. Therefore the negation of (2) is logically equivalent to

$$\exists x \, \exists y [(x < y) \land (x^2 \geq y^2)]. \quad \square$$

EXAMPLE 4   Let the universe of discourse U consist of a and b. The DeMorgan law 37a then becomes

$$\neg [p(a) \land p(b)] \Leftrightarrow [\neg p(a)] \lor [\neg p(b)].$$

Except for the names $p(a)$ and $p(b)$, in place of p and q, this is the DeMorgan law 8b in Table 1 of § 2.2. $\square$

A general proposition often has the form $\forall x \, p(x)$ where x ranges over some universe of discourse. This is false if and only if $\exists x [\neg p(x)]$ is true, by DeMorgan's law 37a. Thus $\forall x \, p(x)$ is false if some x_0 can be exhibited for which $p(x_0)$ is false. Such an x_0 is called a **counterexample** to the proposition $\forall x \, p(x)$. It provides an example that is counter to [or contrary to] the general assertion $\forall x \, p(x)$.

EXAMPLE 5   (a) The number 2 provides a counterexample to the assertion "All prime numbers are odd numbers" or, if you prefer,

$$\forall n \, [n \text{ is prime} \rightarrow n \text{ is odd}].$$

(b) The number 7 provides a counterexample to the statement "Every positive integer is the sum of three squares of integers." Incidentally, it can be proved that every positive integer is the sum of four squares of integers, e.g., $1 = 1^2 + 0^2 + 0^2 + 0^2$, $7 = 2^2 + 1^2 + 1^2 + 1^2$, $73 = 8^2 + 3^2 + 0^2 + 0^2$.

(c) The number 23 provides a counterexample to the assertion "Every positive integer is the sum of eight cubes." However, it can be proved that every positive integer is the sum of nine cubes, e.g., $73 = 4^3 + 2^3 + 1^3 +$ some 0's.

(d) The matrices

$$\begin{bmatrix} 1 & 0 \\ 0 & 0 \end{bmatrix}, \quad \begin{bmatrix} 0 & 0 \\ 1 & 1 \end{bmatrix}$$

provide a counterexample to the assertion "If 2×2 matrices **A** and **B** satisfy **AB** = **0**, then **A** = **0** or **B** = **0**." This general assertion could have been written

$$\forall \mathbf{A} \ \forall \mathbf{B}[\mathbf{AB} = \mathbf{0} \rightarrow (\mathbf{A} = \mathbf{0} \lor \mathbf{B} = \mathbf{0})].$$

(e) The proposition "Every connected graph has an Euler circuit" is quite false. In view of Euler's theorem in § 0.1, any connected graph having a vertex of odd degree will serve as a counterexample to this assertion. The simplest counterexample has two vertices and one edge connecting them.

(f) Gerald Ford is a counterexample to the assertion "All American presidents were right handed." □

One compound proposition which is *almost* a tautology is

$$\forall x \ p(x) \rightarrow \exists x \ p(x),$$

with the corresponding logical relationship

$$\forall x \ p(x) \Rightarrow \exists x \ p(x).$$

The proposition has the value true for every nonempty universe, since if $\forall x \ p(x)$ is true for a nonempty U then $p(x_0)$ is true for each member x_0 of U and so $\exists x \ p(x)$ is true. On the other hand, if the universe is empty, then $\forall x \ p(x)$ has the value true vacuously, whereas $\exists x \ p(x)$ is false. It is true that everyone with three heads is rich. [You disagree? Give a counterexample.] But it is not true that there is a rich person with three heads. Here the universe consists of all three-headed people and $p(x)$ denotes "x is rich."

We left this relationship off of the list in Table 1, even though it is an important relationship, because it is not *always* true. We can combine it with other relationships to get implications which hold for all nonempty universes. For instance

$$[\forall x \ p(x) \rightarrow \exists x \ p(x)] \Leftrightarrow (\neg[\exists x \ p(x)] \rightarrow \neg[\forall x \ p(x)])$$

by the contrapositive rule 9. For a nonempty universe the expression on the left is true, so

$$\neg[\exists x \ p(x)] \rightarrow \neg[\forall x \ p(x)]$$

is also true. Using the DeMorgan laws 37b and 37a we find that

$$\forall x[\neg p(x)] \rightarrow \exists x[\neg p(x)]$$

is true, as is

$$\forall x[\neg p(x)] \rightarrow \neg[\forall x\, p(x)].$$

Thus, *for a nonempty universe*

$$\forall x[\neg p(x)] \Rightarrow \exists x[\neg p(x)]$$
$$\Leftrightarrow \neg[\forall x\, p(x)].$$

But note that the fact that every three-headed person is not rich, which is true, does not imply that there is a three-headed person who is not rich.

EXERCISES 6.2

1. Consider a universe U_1 consisting of members of a club, and a universe U_2 of airlines. Let $p(x, y)$ be the predicate "x has been a passenger on y" or equivalently "y has had x as a passenger." Write out the meanings of the following.
   (a) rule 35a   (b) rule 35b   (c) rule 36

2. Consider the universe U of all university professors. Let $p(x)$ be the predicate "x likes punk rock."
   (a) Express the proposition "not all university professors like punk rock" in predicate calculus symbols.
   (b) Do the same for "every university professor does not like punk rock."
   (c) Does either of the propositions in part (a) or (b) imply the other? Explain.
   (d) Write out the meaning of rule 37b for this U and $p(x)$.
   (e) Do the same for rule 37d.

3. Show that the following rules in Table 1 collapse to rules from Table 1 of § 2.2 when the universe of discourse U has two elements, a and b.
   (a) rule 37d   (b) rule 37b

4. (a) Show that the logical implication

   $$[\exists x\, p(x)] \wedge [\exists x\, q(x)] \Rightarrow \exists x[p(x) \wedge q(x)]$$

   is false. You may do this either by defining predicates $p(x)$ and $q(x)$ where this implication fails, or by taking a small universe of discourse, say $U = \{a, b\}$, and assigning truth values to the four propositions $p(a), p(b), q(a), q(b)$.
   (b) Do the same for the logical implication

   $$\exists x\, \forall y\, p(x, y) \Rightarrow \forall x\, \exists y\, p(x, y).$$

   Compare this with the true implication of rule 36.

5. Write the negation of $\forall n[p(n) \rightarrow p(n + 1)]$ without using the quantifier $\forall$, where the universe of discourse is $\mathbb{N}$.

6. Write the negation of $\exists x\, \forall y\, \exists z[z > y \rightarrow z < x^2]$ without using the connective $\neg$.

7. (a) Write the negation of

$$P = \forall x \; \forall y [x < y \to \exists z \{x < z < y\}]$$

without using the connective $\neg$.

(b) Determine the truth value of P when the universe of discourse is $\mathbb{R}$ or $\mathbb{Q}$.

(c) Determine the truth value of P when the universe of discourse is $\mathbb{N}$ or $\mathbb{Z}$.

8. Give a counterexample for each of the following assertions.

(a) Every even integer is the product of two even integers.

(b) $|S \cup T| = |S| + |T|$ for any two finite sets S and T.

(c) Every positive integer of the form $6k - 1$ is a prime.

(d) If the matrix $\begin{bmatrix} a & b \\ c & d \end{bmatrix}$ is invertible, then a, b, c and d are all nonzero numbers.

(e) Every graph has an even number of edges.

(f) All mathematics courses are fun.

9. Our definition of compound predicate does not permit expressions such as $\exists x \, p(x, x)$ with $p(x, y)$ a 2-place predicate. Describe a predicate $q(x, y)$ such that

$$\exists x \; \exists y [p(x, y) \wedge q(x, y)]$$

is true if and only if $p(x, x)$ is true for some x.

10. In the case that the universe of discourse is empty, $\forall x \, p(x)$ vacuously has the value true regardless of $p(x)$, and $\exists x \, p(x)$ is false. Describe the situation for a universe with exactly one member.

§ 6.3 *Mathematical Induction*

The principle of mathematical induction studied in § 2.5 is often called the First Principle of Mathematical Induction. We restate it here in the form of a rule of inference.

First Principle of Mathematical Induction. Let m be an integer and let $p(n)$ be a 1-place predicate over the universe of discourse $\{n \in \mathbb{Z} : n \geq m\}$.

(B) $p(m)$

(I) $\forall_{n \geq m} [p(n) \to p(n + 1)]$

∴ $\forall_{n \geq m} \, p(n)$

In the inductive step (I), each proposition is true provided the proposition immediately preceding it is true. To use this principle as a framework for constructing a proof, we need to check that $p(m)$ is true and that each proposition is true *assuming that the proposition just before it is true*. It is this right to assume the immediately previous case that makes the method of proof by induction so powerful. It turns out that in fact we are permitted to assume *all* previous cases. This apparently stronger assertion is a consequence of the following principle, whose proof we discuss at the end of this section.

Second Principle of Mathematical Induction. Let m be an integer and let $p(n)$ be a 1-place predicate over the universe of discourse $\{n \in \mathbb{Z} : n \geq m\}$.

(B) $p(m)$

(I) $\forall_{n>m}[p(m) \land \cdots \land p(n-1) \to p(n)]$

∴ $\forall_{n \geq m} p(n)$

The first three implications in (I), corresponding to $n = m+1$, $m+2$ and $m+3$, are

$$p(m) \to p(m+1),$$

$$p(m) \land p(m+1) \to p(m+2),$$

$$p(m) \land p(m+1) \land p(m+2) \to p(m+3).$$

To verify (I) in general one considers an $n > m$, assumes that the propositions $p(k)$ are true for $m \leq k < n$ and shows that $p(n)$ is true. The Second Principle of Mathematical Induction is the appropriate version to use when the truths of the propositions follow from predecessors other than the immediate predecessors.

EXAMPLE 1   Every integer $n \geq 2$ can be written as a product of primes.

Proof. Note that if n is prime the "product of primes" is simply the number n by itself. For $n \geq 2$ let $p(n)$ be the proposition

"n can be written as a product of primes."

Observe that the First Principle of Mathematical Induction is really unsuitable here. The lone fact that 1,311,819, say, happens to be a product of primes is of no help in showing that 1,311,820 is also a product of primes. We apply the Second Principle. Clearly $p(2)$ is true, since 2 is a prime.

Consider $n > 2$ and assume that $p(k)$ is true for all k satisfying $2 \leq k < n$. We need to show that this implies $p(n)$ is true. If n is prime, then $p(n)$ is clearly true. Otherwise, n can be written as a product jk where j and k are integers greater than 1. Thus $2 \leq j < n$ and $2 \leq k < n$. Since both $p(j)$ and $p(k)$ are assumed to be true, we can write j and k as products of primes. Then $n = jk$ is also a product of primes. We have checked the basis and induction step for the Second Principle of Mathematical Induction, and so we infer that all the propositions $p(n)$ are true.   □

Often the general proof of the inductive step (I) does not work for the first few values of n. In this case, these first few values of n need to be checked separately, so they may serve as part of the basis. We restate the Second Principle of Mathematical Induction in a more general version which applies in such situations.

Second Principle of Mathematical Induction. Let m be an integer, let $p(n)$ be a 1-place predicate over $\{n \in \mathbb{Z} : n \geq m\}$ and let l be an integer ≥ 0.

(B) $p(m), \ldots, p(m + l)$
(I) $\forall_{n>m+l}[p(m) \wedge \cdots \wedge p(n - 1) \to p(n)]$
$\therefore \qquad \forall_{n \geq m} p(n)$

If $l = 0$ this is our original version of the Second Principle.

In § 3.4 we saw that many sequences are defined recursively using earlier terms other than the immediate predecessors. The Second Principle is the natural form of induction for proving results about such sequences.

EXAMPLE 2   (a) In Exercise 8 of § 3.4 we recursively defined $b_0 = b_1 = 1$ and $b_n = 2b_{n-1} + b_{n-2}$ for $n \geq 2$. In part (b), we asked for an explanation of why all b_n's are odd integers. We were hoping you would stumble upon the need for the Second Principle of Mathematical Induction. We now give a proof.

The nth proposition is $p(n) = $ "b_n is odd." In the inductive step we will use the relation $b_n = 2b_{n-1} + b_{n-2}$ and so we'll need $n \geq 2$. Hence we'll check the cases $n = 0$ and 1 separately. Thus we will use the Second Principle with $m = 0$ and $l = 1$.

(B)   The propositions $p(0)$ and $p(1)$ are obviously true, since $b_0 = b_1 = 1$.

(I)   Consider $n \geq 2$ and assume that b_k is odd for all k satisfying $0 \leq k < n$. In particular, b_{n-2} is odd. Clearly $2b_{n-1}$ is even, and so $b_n = 2b_{n-1} + b_{n-2}$ is the sum of an even and an odd integer. Thus b_n is odd. It follows from the Second Principle of Mathematical Induction that all b_n's are odd.

Note that in this proof the oddness of b_n followed from the oddness of b_{n-2}.

(b) For the sequence above, we prove that $b_n < 6b_{n-2}$ for $n \geq 4$. Direct computation shows that $b_2 = 3$, $b_3 = 7$, $b_4 = 17$ and $b_5 = 41$. For $n = 4$ the inequality says $b_4 < 6b_2$ or $17 < 6 \cdot 3$ and for $n = 5$ it says $b_5 < 6b_3$ or $41 < 6 \cdot 7$; these are true. We now consider $n \geq 6$ and assume that

$$b_k < 6b_{k-2} \qquad \text{for} \quad 4 \leq k < n.$$

Since $n - 1$ and $n - 2$ are both ≥ 4 we have $b_{n-1} < 6b_{n-3}$ and $b_{n-2} < 6b_{n-4}$ by assumption. Hence

$$\begin{aligned} b_n &= 2b_{n-1} + b_{n-2} && \text{definition of } b_n \\ &< 2(6b_{n-3}) + 6b_{n-4} && \text{inductive assumption} \\ &= 6[2b_{n-3} + b_{n-4}] && \text{algebra} \\ &= 6b_{n-2} && \text{definition of } b_{n-2}. \end{aligned}$$

Hence by the Second Principle of Mathematical Induction the inequality holds for all $n \geq 4$.

Note that we checked the assertion for $n = 4$ and $n = 5$ before going on to the inductive step. Thus we applied the Second Principle with $m = 4$ and $l = 1$. Why did we check the inequality for $n = 5$, as well as for $n = 4$, before proceeding with the inductive step? Before we wrote up the proof we had observed that in the inductive step we were going to need to use $b_k < 6b_{k-2}$ for $k = n - 2$ and so we would need $n - 2 \geq 4$ or $n \geq 6$. In other words, the inductive step wouldn't work for $n = 5$: $b_5 = 2b_4 + b_3$, but b_3 isn't less than $6b_1$. ☐

EXAMPLE 3   We recursively define $a_0 = a_1 = a_2 = 1$ and $a_n = a_{n-2} + a_{n-3}$ for $n \geq 3$. The first few terms of the sequence are 1, 1, 1, 2, 2, 3, 4, 5, 7, 9, 12, 16, 21, 28, 37, 49. We prove that $a_n \leq (\frac{4}{3})^n$ for all $n \in \mathbb{N}$. This inequality is clear for $n = 0, 1$ and 2. So we consider $n \geq 3$ and assume that $a_k < (\frac{4}{3})^k$ for $0 \leq k < n$. In particular, $a_{n-2} \leq (\frac{4}{3})^{n-2}$ and $a_{n-3} \leq (\frac{4}{3})^{n-3}$. Thus we have

$$a_n = a_{n-2} + a_{n-3} \leq \left(\frac{4}{3}\right)^{n-2} + \left(\frac{4}{3}\right)^{n-3} = \left(\frac{4}{3}\right)^{n-3}\left(\frac{4}{3} + 1\right).$$

Since we want to conclude that $a_n \leq (\frac{4}{3})^n$, we observe that if only $(\frac{4}{3} + 1) \leq (\frac{4}{3})^3$ held, then we could conclude

$$a_n \leq \left(\frac{4}{3}\right)^{n-3}\left(\frac{4}{3} + 1\right) \leq \left(\frac{4}{3}\right)^{n-3}\left(\frac{4}{3}\right)^3 = \left(\frac{4}{3}\right)^n,$$

as desired. Direct computation shows that $(\frac{4}{3} + 1) \leq (\frac{4}{3})^3$ [do it!] and so we conclude that $a_n \leq (\frac{4}{3})^n$. This establishes the inductive step. Hence we infer from the Second Principle of Mathematical Induction [with $m = 0$ and $l = 2$] that $a_n \leq (\frac{4}{3})^n$ for all $n \in \mathbb{N}$.

In this proof we were lucky that $(\frac{4}{3} + 1) \leq (\frac{4}{3})^3$ [close, wasn't it?]. If this inequality hadn't held, we would have had to find another proof, prove something else, or abandon the problem. Induction gives us a framework for proofs, but it doesn't provide the details, which are determined by the particular problem at hand. ☐

We have already applied the First Principle of Mathematical Induction to finite sequences, for instance in Example 6 in § 5.3. Both principles can be stated and used for finite sequences. The changes are simple. Suppose that the propositions $p(n)$ are defined for $m \leq n \leq m^*$. The First Principle then reads

(B) $p(m)$

(I) $\forall_{m \leq n < m^*}[p(n) \to p(n + 1)]$

∴ $\forall_{m \leq n \leq m^*} p(n)$

and the general Second Principle reads

(B) $p(m), \ldots, p(m + l)$
(I) $\forall_{m+l<n\leq m}\cdot[p(m) \wedge \cdots \wedge p(n-1) \rightarrow p(n)]$
$\therefore \quad \forall_{m\leq n\leq m}\cdot p(n).$

We return to the infinite principles of induction and end this section by discussing the logical relationship between the two principles and explaining why we regard both as valid rules of inference for constructing proofs.

It turns out that each of the two principles implies the other, in the sense that if we accept either as a valid rule of inference then the other is also valid. It is clear that the Second Principle implies the First principle since, if we are allowed to assume all previous cases, then we are surely allowed to assume the immediately preceding case. A rigorous proof can be given by showing that (B) and (I) of the Second Principle are consequences of (B) and (I) of the First Principle.

It is perhaps more surprising that the First Principle implies the Second. A proof can be given using the propositions

$$q(n) = p(m) \wedge \cdots \wedge p(n) \quad \text{for} \quad n \geq m$$

and showing that if the sequence $p(n)$ satisfies (B) and (I) of the Second Principle, then $q(m)$ and $\forall_{n\geq m}[q(n) \rightarrow q(n+1)]$ are true. Then every $q(n)$ will be true by the First Principle so that $p(n)$ will also be true for every n.

The equivalence of the two principles is of less concern to us than an assurance that they are valid rules. For this we rely on a fundamental property of $\mathbb{N}$:

Well-Ordering Principle Every nonempty subset of $\mathbb{N}$ has a smallest member.

This property is not a consequence of the rules for arithmetic in $\mathbb{N}$ and is an independent axiom. The Well-Ordering Principle implies that:

Given $m \in \mathbb{Z}$, every nonempty subset of $\{n \in \mathbb{Z} : n \geq m\}$ has a smallest member.

To see this, consider a nonempty subset S of $\{n \in \mathbb{Z} : n \geq m\}$. Then $\{n - m : n \in S\}$ is a nonempty subset of $\mathbb{N}$. If its smallest member is n_0, then $n_0 + m$ is the smallest member of S [Exercise 18].

Proof of the Second Principle. Assume

(B) $p(m), \ldots, p(m + l)$ are all true,
(I) $\forall_{n>m+l}[p(m) \wedge \cdots \wedge p(n-1) \rightarrow p(n)]$ is true,

but that $\forall_{n\geq m} p(n)$ is false. Then the set

$$S = \{n \in \mathbb{Z} : n \geq m \text{ and } p(n) \text{ is false}\}$$

is nonempty. By the Well-Ordering Principle, S has a smallest element n_0. In view of (B) we must have $n_0 > m + l$. Since $p(n)$ is true for $m \leq n < n_0$, the compound proposition $p(m) \wedge \cdots \wedge p(n_0 - 1)$ is true. By (I), so is the implication

$$p(m) \wedge \cdots \wedge p(n_0 - 1) \rightarrow p(n_0).$$

Hence $p(n_0)$ is also true [modus ponens, rule 19 in Table 2 of § 2.2], contradicting the fact that n_0 belongs to S. It follows that if (B) and (I) hold, then $\forall_{n \geq m} \, p(n)$ is true. ∎

A similar proof can be given for the First Principle but, since the principles are equivalent, it is not needed.

Some of the exercises for this section require only the First Principle of Mathematical Induction and are included to provide extra practice.

EXERCISES 6.3

1. Prove $3 + 11 + \cdots + (8n - 5) = 4n^2 - n$ for $n \in \mathbb{P}$.

2. For $n \in \mathbb{P}$, prove

    (a) $1 \cdot 2 + 2 \cdot 3 + \cdots + n(n + 1) = \frac{1}{3}n(n + 1)(n + 2)$

    (b) $\dfrac{1}{1 \cdot 2} + \dfrac{1}{2 \cdot 3} + \cdots + \dfrac{1}{n(n + 1)} = \dfrac{n}{n + 1}$

3. Prove that $n^5 - n$ is divisible by 10 for all $n \in \mathbb{P}$.

4. (a) Calculate b_6 for the sequence (b_n) in Example 2.

    (b) Use the recursive definition of (a_n) in Example 3 to calculate a_9.

5. Is the First Principle of Mathematical Induction adequate to prove the fact in Exercise 7(b) of § 3.4? Explain.

6. Recursively define $a_0 = a_1 = 1$ and $a_n = 3a_{n-1} - 2a_{n-2}$ for $n \geq 2$.

    (a) Calculate the first few terms of the sequence.

    (b) Using part (a), guess the general formula for a_n.

    (c) Prove the guess in part (b).

7. Recursively define $a_0 = 1$, $a_1 = 2$ and $a_n = 2a_{n-1} - a_{n-2}$ for $n \geq 2$. Repeat Exercise 6 for this sequence.

8. Recursively define $a_0 = 1$, $a_1 = 3$ and $a_n = 2a_{n-1} - a_{n-2}$ for $n \geq 2$. Repeat Exercise 6 for this sequence.

9. Recursively define $a_0 = 1$, $a_1 = 2$ and $a_n = a_{n-1} + 2a_{n-2}$ for $n \geq 2$. Repeat Exercise 6 for this sequence.

10. Recursively define $a_0 = 1$, $a_1 = 2$ and $a_n = 2a_{n-1} + a_{n-2}$ for $n \geq 2$.

    (a) Calculate a_n for $n = 2, 3, 4, 5, 6$.

    (b) Prove that $a_n \leq (\frac{5}{2})^n$ for all $n \in \mathbb{N}$.

11. Recursively define $a_0 = a_1 = a_2 = 1$ and $a_n = a_{n-1} + a_{n-2} + a_{n-3}$ for $n \geq 3$.

    (a) Calculate the first few terms of the sequence.

    (b) Prove that all the a_n's are odd.

    (c) Prove that $a_n \leq 2^{n-1}$ for all $n \geq 1$.

12. Recursively define $a_0 = a_1 = 1$ and $a_n = 2a_{n-1} + 3a_{n-2}$ for $n \geq 2$.

    (a) Calculate a_n for $n = 2, 3, 4, 5, 6$.

(b) Prove that $a_n > 3^{n-1}$ for $n \geqq 2$.

(c) Prove that $a_n < 2 \cdot 3^{n-1}$ for $n \geqq 2$.

13. Recursively define $b_0 = b_1 = b_2 = 1$ and $b_n = b_{n-1} + b_{n-3}$ for $n \geqq 3$.

(a) Calculate b_n for $n = 3, 4, 5, 6$.

(b) Show that $b_n \geqq 2b_{n-2}$ for $n \geqq 3$.

(c) Prove the inequality $b_n \geqq (\sqrt{2})^{n-2}$ for $n \geqq 2$.

14. As in Exercise 9 of § 3.4, let $\text{SEQ}(0) = 1$ and $\text{SEQ}(n) = \sum_{i=0}^{n-1} \text{SEQ}(i)$ for $n \geqq 1$.

Prove that $\text{SEQ}(n) = 2^{n-1}$ for $n \geqq 1$.

15. In Exercise 11 of § 3.4, we defined $\text{SEQ}(0) = 0$, $\text{SEQ}(1) = 1$ and

$$\text{SEQ}(n) = \frac{1}{n} * \text{SEQ}(n-1) + \frac{n-1}{n} * \text{SEQ}(n-2)$$

for $n \geqq 2$. Prove that $0 \leqq \text{SEQ}(n) \leqq 1$ for all $n \in \mathbb{N}$.

16. Recall the Fibonacci sequence in Example 2 of § 3.4:

(B) $\text{FIB}(0) = \text{FIB}(1) = 1$,

(R) $\text{FIB}(n) = \text{FIB}(n-1) + \text{FIB}(n-2)$ for $n \geqq 2$.

Prove that

$$\text{FIB}(n) = 1 + \sum_{k=0}^{n-2} \text{FIB}(k) \quad \text{for} \quad n \geqq 2.$$

17. The **Lucas sequence** is defined as follows:

(B) $\text{LUC}(1) = 1$ and $\text{LUC}(2) = 3$,

(R) $\text{LUC}(n) = \text{LUC}(n-1) + \text{LUC}(n-2)$ for $n \geqq 3$.

(a) List the first eight terms of the Lucas sequence.

(b) Prove that $\text{LUC}(n) = \text{FIB}(n) + \text{FIB}(n-2)$ for $n \geqq 2$, where FIB is the Fibonacci sequence defined in Exercise 16.

18. Let S be a nonempty subset of $\{n \in \mathbb{Z} : n \geqq m\}$. Show that n_0 is the smallest member of $S' = \{n - m : n \in S\}$ if and only if $n_0 + m$ is the smallest member of S. *Suggestion*: It might help to first check this out on an example, say with $m = 5$ and $S = \{9, 17, 73\}$.

§ *6.4 A Generalization of Induction*

Recall from § 3.5 that a set S of objects is defined recursively provided

(B) some members of the set are specified explicitly,

(R) the remaining members of the set are defined in terms of members already defined.

We showed in § 3.5 that once a set itself has been defined recursively, functions can be recursively defined on it. If the image of such a function consists of propositions, i.e., if the function is a predicate, then it may be possible to prove all the propositions in the image true by a generalized version of induction which we now describe.

Generalized Principle of Induction   Let p be a proposition-valued function on a recursively defined set S. Suppose that

(B) $p(s)$ is true for the members s in S specified in the basis;

(I) whenever a member s of S is defined in terms of a set of previously defined members, say $D_s = \{t_1, \ldots, t_k\}$, then $p(t_1) \wedge \cdots \wedge p(t_k) \rightarrow p(s)$ is true.

Then $p(s)$ is true for every $s \in S$.

To see why this principle is valid, let $T = \{s \in S : p(s)$ is true$\}$. Then condition (B) states that all the members of the basis for S are in T, and condition (I) says that every member of S which is defined in terms of members of T is itself in T. Together they say that every member of S which can be built up out of basis members—i.e., every member of S— is in T.

EXAMPLE 1   (a) For a finite alphabet Σ, Σ^* was defined recursively in § 3.5 as follows:

(B) the empty word ϵ is in Σ^*,

(R) if w is in Σ^* and x is in Σ, then wx is in Σ^*.

Each new word wx is defined in terms of a word w in Σ^* already defined and a letter x in Σ. Thus, in terms of the general scheme, we have $D_{wx} = \{w\}$. If p is a proposition-valued function on Σ^*, then $\forall w\, p(w)$ is true provided

(B) $p(\epsilon)$ is true;

(I) $p(w) \rightarrow p(wx)$ is true for all $w \in \Sigma^*$ and $x \in \Sigma$.

This is the principle of induction for Σ^*. We illustrate its use in the next two parts of this example.

(b) Consider any subset S of Σ^*. For $w \in \Sigma^*$ we define $wS = \{ww_1 : w_1 \in S\}$. We claim that if $xS \subseteq S$ for all $x \in \Sigma$, then $wS \subseteq S$ for all $w \in \Sigma^*$.

Proof. We prove the claim by the inductive procedure in part (a). To each w in Σ^* we associate the proposition

$$p(w) = \text{``}wS \subseteq S.\text{''}$$

$p(\epsilon)$ is clearly true since $\epsilon w_1 = w_1$ for all words w_1. This establishes the basis of induction. For the inductive step, consider w in Σ^* and x in Σ; we need to prove $p(w) \rightarrow p(wx)$ is true, i.e.,

$$wS \subseteq S \quad \text{implies} \quad wxS \subseteq S.$$

In fact, if $wS \subseteq S$ and $x \in \Sigma$, then

$$wxS \subseteq wS \quad \text{since} \quad xS \subseteq S \quad \text{for } x \in \Sigma,$$

$$\subseteq S \quad \text{since} \quad wS \subseteq S \quad \text{by assumption.}$$

Thus the inductive step (I) has been established, so $p(w)$ is true for all $w \in \Sigma^*$.

(c) For words w in Σ^*, length(w) was recursively defined in § 3.5 as follows:

(B) length(ϵ) = 0;
(R) if length(w) has been defined and $x \in \Sigma$, then

$$\text{length}(wx) = 1 + \text{length}(w).$$

We prove that

$$\text{length}(w_1 w_2) = \text{length}(w_1) + \text{length}(w_2)$$

for $w_1, w_2 \in \Sigma^*$.

Proof. We fix w_1 and we inductively prove all the propositions

$$p(w) = \text{``length}(w_1 w) = \text{length}(w_1) + \text{length}(w).\text{''}$$

Since $w_1\epsilon = w_1$ and length(ϵ) = 0, the proposition $p(\epsilon)$ is true. For the inductive step, consider w in Σ^* and x in Σ; we prove $p(w) \to p(wx)$. Thus we assume that

(1) $$\text{length}(w_1 w) = \text{length}(w_1) + \text{length}(w)$$

and we want to show

(2) $$\text{length}(w_1 wx) = \text{length}(w_1) + \text{length}(wx).$$

From (1) it is evident that

$$1 + \text{length}(w_1 w) = \text{length}(w_1) + 1 + \text{length}(w).$$

The recursive definition of length shows that

$$\text{length}(w_1 wx) = 1 + \text{length}(w_1 w) \quad \text{and} \quad \text{length}(wx) = 1 + \text{length}(w),$$

and so (2) holds. □

EXAMPLE 2   (a) Well-formed formulas [wff's] for algebra were defined recursively in § 3.5 as follows:

(B) Numerical constants and variables are wff's.
(R) If f and g are wff's, so are $(f + g)$, $(f - g)$, (fg), (f/g) and (f^g).

The new wff's are all defined in terms of f and g and so, in terms of the general scheme, $D_{(f+g)} = \{f, g\}$, etc. If p is a proposition-valued function on the set of wff's, then all the propositions $p(f)$ are true provided

(B) $p(f)$ is true for all numerical constants and variables f;
(I) $[p(f) \wedge p(g)] \to [p((f+g)) \wedge p((f-g)) \wedge p((fg)) \wedge p((f/g)) \wedge p((f^g))]$ is true for all wff's f and g.

(b) We use the principle of induction in part (a) to prove that the number $L(f)$ of left parentheses in a wff f is equal to the number $R(f)$ of right parentheses in f.

Proof. To each wff f we associate the proposition

$$p(f) = \text{``}L(f) = R(f).\text{''}$$

If f is a numerical constant or variable, then clearly $L(f) = 0$ and $R(f) = 0$, and so $p(f)$ is true. This takes care of the basis of induction. For the inductive step, we consider wff's f and g. We need to prove that if $L(f) = R(f)$ and $L(g) = R(g)$, then similar identities hold for $(f + g)$, $(f - g)$, (fg), (f/g) and (f^g). All five cases are similar, so we deal only with $(f + g)$. It is clear that

$$L((f + g)) = L(f) + L(g) + 1$$

and that

$$R((f + g)) = R(f) + R(g) + 1,$$

from which it follows that $L((f + g)) = R((f + g))$.   □

EXAMPLE 3   (a) Finite trees were recursively defined in § 3.5:

(B) A single vertex is a [trivial] tree.
(R) If T is a tree and v is not a vertex of T, then T' is a tree if we add v as a vertex and add a single edge connecting v to some vertex of T.

Let p be a proposition-valued function on the class of finite trees. All the propositions are true provided

(B) $p(T_0)$ is true for the trivial tree T_0;
(I)   if $p(T)$ is true and T' is obtained from T as in the recursive definition, then $p(T')$ is true.

(b) We use the generalized principle of induction in part (a) to prove that every nontrivial tree has at least two leaves, i.e., vertices of degree 1.

Proof. For each tree T the proposition is

$$p(T) = \text{``if } T \text{ is nontrivial, then } T \text{ has at least two leaves.''}$$

For the trivial tree this is vacuously true, and so the basis holds. To prove the inductive step, we consider T and T', and assume $p(T)$ is true. There are two cases: either T is trivial or T has at least two leaves.

If T is trivial, it consists of a single vertex v_0. Then T' has two vertices, v_0 and v, and one edge connecting them. Therefore both v_0 and v are leaves in this case, and so $p(T')$ is true.

If T is nontrivial, then T has at least two leaves by assumption; let v_1 and v_2 be two of them. The new vertex v is a leaf of T' and cannot be connected to both v_1 and v_2. Hence at least one of v_1 and v_2 is also a leaf of T', and so T' has at least two leaves.

This establishes the inductive step and the proof is completed by appealing to the generalized principle of induction in part (a).

(c) In this part and in part (d) we are going to give two proofs of the assertion: If a tree T has n vertices then it has $n - 1$ edges. The proofs will have different structures. One will use induction on n, using part (b) and the old familiar First Principle of Mathematical Induction. The other proof will be more direct and will use induction on T using the principle in part (a).

First we use induction on n. The nth proposition $p(n)$ is

"if a tree has n vertices, then it has $n - 1$ edges."

This is clear for $n = 1$. Assume that $p(n)$ is true for some $n \geq 1$ and consider a tree with $n + 1$ vertices. It cannot be trivial, so by part (b) it has leaves. If we remove one leaf and the edge connected to it, we will obtain another tree having only n vertices. By proposition $p(n)$, the new tree has $n - 1$ edges and so the original tree has $(n - 1) + 1 = n$ edges. That is, a tree with $n + 1$ vertices has $(n + 1) - 1$ edges. In other words, $p(n) \to p(n + 1)$ is true for all $n \geq 1$. The result follows from the First Principle of Mathematical Induction.

(d) This time we prove the propositions

$$q(T) = \text{"if the tree } T \text{ has } n \text{ vertices, then it has } n - 1 \text{ edges."}$$

This is clear for the trivial tree which has 1 vertex and 0 edges. Assume $q(T)$ is true and consider T' recursively defined from T as in part (a). Then T' has one more vertex and one more edge than T has. So $q(T')$ is true if $q(T)$ is. Consequently, all the assertions $q(T)$ hold by the generalized principle of induction in part (a). ☐

EXAMPLE 4   (a) Polynomial functions on $\mathbb{R}$ are defined recursively in Example 1 of § 3.5. Here is the generalized induction procedure for a proposition-valued function p defined on the set of polynomial functions on $\mathbb{R}$. All the propositions $p(f)$ are true provided

(B) $p(f)$ is true for constant functions f,
   and $p(I)$ is true, where $I(x) = x$ for all $x \in \mathbb{R}$;
(I) $p(f) \wedge p(g) \to p(f + g) \wedge p(fg)$ for all f, g.

(b) We prove that if f is a polynomial function on $\mathbb{R}$, then there exist $n \in \mathbb{N}$ and constants $a_0, a_1, \ldots, a_n$ such that

(1) $f(x) = a_n x^n + a_{n-1} x^{n-1} + \cdots + a_1 x + a_0 \quad \text{for all} \quad x \in \mathbb{R}.$

Proof. If c is a constant and $f(x) = c$ for all $x \in \mathbb{R}$, then (1) holds for f with $n = 0$ and $a_0 = c$. Also, (1) holds for the function I with $n = 1$, $a_1 = 1$ and $a_0 = 0$. These observations establish the basis for induction.

For the inductive step, suppose that f has the form (1) and that g is given by

(2) $g(x) = b_m x^m + b_{m-1} x^{m-1} + \cdots + b_1 x + b_0 \quad \text{for all} \quad x \in \mathbb{R}$

and some $m \in \mathbb{N}$. Then we have

$$(f + g)(x) = c_p x^p + c_{p-1} x^{p-1} + \cdots + c_1 x + c_0$$

where $p = \max\{m, n\}$ and $c_i = a_i + b_i$ for $0 \leq i \leq p$ where we agree that $c_i = a_i$ if $i > m$ and $c_i = b_i$ if $i > n$. Also

$$(fg)(x) = d_{m+n} x^{m+n} + d_{m+n-1} x^{m+n-1} + \cdots + d_1 x + d_0$$

where each d_i is the sum of all products $a_j b_k$ such that $j + k = i$. [This is seen by multiplying the polynomials f and g and collecting together all the x^i terms.] Thus $f + g$ and fg have the form (1) and so all polynomial functions have this form by the general induction procedure. ☐

As in § 6.3, some of the exercises below require only the First Principle of Mathematical Induction.

EXERCISES 6.4

1. Prove that

$$\frac{1}{n+1} + \frac{1}{n+2} + \cdots + \frac{1}{2n} = 1 - \frac{1}{2} + \frac{1}{3} - \frac{1}{4} + \cdots + \frac{1}{2n-1} - \frac{1}{2n}$$

for $n \in \mathbb{P}$. For $n = 1$ this says $\frac{1}{2} = 1 - \frac{1}{2}$ and for $n = 2$ this says $\frac{1}{3} + \frac{1}{4} = 1 - \frac{1}{2} + \frac{1}{3} - \frac{1}{4}$.

2. For $n \in \mathbb{P}$, prove

   (a) $\sum_{k=1}^{n} \frac{1}{\sqrt{k}} \geq \sqrt{n}$ (b) $\sum_{k=1}^{n} \frac{1}{\sqrt{k}} \leq 2\sqrt{n} - 1$

3. Prove that $5^{n+1} + 2 \cdot 3^n + 1$ is divisible by 8 for $n \in \mathbb{N}$.

4. Prove that $8^{n+2} + 9^{2n+1}$ is divisible by 73 for $n \in \mathbb{N}$.

5. Here is a recursive definition for a subset S of $\mathbb{N} \times \mathbb{N}$:

   (B) $\langle 0, 0 \rangle \in S$,
   (R) if $\langle m, n \rangle \in S$, then $\langle m + 2, n + 3 \rangle \in S$.

   (a) List four members of S.
   (b) Prove that if $\langle m, n \rangle \in S$, then 5 divides $m + n$.
   (c) Is the converse to the assertion in part (b) true?

6. Here is a recursive definition for another subset T of $\mathbb{N} \times \mathbb{N}$:

   (B) $\langle 0, 0 \rangle \in T$,
   (R) if $\langle m, n \rangle \in T$, then each of $\langle m + 1, n \rangle$, $\langle m + 1, n + 1 \rangle$ and $\langle m + 1, n + 2 \rangle$ is in T.

   (a) List six members of T.
   (b) Prove that $2m \geq n$ for all $\langle m, n \rangle \in T$.

7. Consider the following recursive definition for a subset A of $\mathbb{N} \times \mathbb{N}$:

   (B) $\langle 0, 0 \rangle \in A$,
   (R) if $\langle m, n \rangle \in A$, then $\langle m + 1, n \rangle$ and $\langle m, n + 1 \rangle$ are in A.

   (a) Show that $A = \mathbb{N} \times \mathbb{N}$.
   (b) Let $p(m, n)$ be a proposition-valued function on $\mathbb{N} \times \mathbb{N}$. Use part (a) to devise a general recursive procedure for proving $p(m, n)$ true for all m and n.

8. Let $\Sigma = \{a, b\}$ and let B be the subset of Σ^* defined recursively as follows:

   (B) a and b are in B,
   (R) if $w \in B$, then abw and baw are in B.

   (a) List six members of B.
   (b) Prove that if $w \in B$, then length(w) is odd.
   (c) Is the converse to the assertion in part (b) true?

9. Let Σ be a finite alphabet. For words w in Σ^*, the reversal $\overleftarrow{w}$ is defined in Exercise 16 of § 3.5.

   (a) Prove length($\overleftarrow{w}$) = length(w) for all $w \in \Sigma^*$.

(b) Prove $\overleftarrow{w_1 w_2} = \overleftarrow{w_2}\,\overleftarrow{w_1}$ for all $w_1, w_2 \in \Sigma^*$.

10. Well-formed formulas P for the propositional calculus are defined recursively in Example 6 of § 3.5.

    (a) Give a general recursive procedure for a proposition-valued function on the set of wff's for the propositional calculus.

    (b) Prove that the number $L(P)$ of left parentheses in P always equals the number $R(P)$ of right parentheses in P.

11. Throughout this exercise, let p, q be *fixed* propositions. We recursively define the family $\mathfrak{F}$ of compound propositions using only $p, q, \wedge$ and $\vee$ as follows:

    (B) $p, q \in \mathfrak{F}$;

    (R) if $P, Q \in \mathfrak{F}$, then $(P \wedge Q)$ and $(P \vee Q)$ are in $\mathfrak{F}$.

    (a) Use this definition to verify that $(p \wedge (p \vee q))$ is in $\mathfrak{F}$.

    (b) Prove that if p and q are false, then all the propositions in $\mathfrak{F}$ are false.

    (c) Show that $p \to q$ is not logically equivalent to any proposition in $\mathfrak{F}$.

CHAPTER HIGHLIGHTS

These lists should be used as always to check understanding. See the end of Chapter 0 for a reminder on how to review.

Concepts

predicate calculus
    quantifiers, $\forall, \exists$
    predicate = proposition-valued function
        compound predicate
            free/bound variable
            logical variable
    tautology [extended version for compound predicates]
    logical equivalence, implication
    counterexample

Facts

Basic logical relationships [Table 1 of § 6.2].
$\forall$ and $\exists$ do not commute with each other:

    $\exists x \,\forall y \, p(x, y) \to \forall y \,\exists x \, p(x, y)$ is a tautology,
    but $\forall y \,\exists x \, p(x, y) \to \exists x \,\forall y \, p(x, y)$ is not.

First, Second and Generalized Principles of Mathematical Induction.
    First Principle can be viewed as a special case of Second Principle.

Methods

Use of DeMorgan laws to negate quantified predicates.
Construction of proofs using mathematical induction:
    Second Principle [$n \geq m$ version] for recursively defined sequences.
    Generalized Principle for predicates on recursively defined sets.

7

RELATIONS

One frequently wants to compare or contrast various members of a set, perhaps to arrange them in some appropriate order or to group together those with similar properties. The mathematical framework to describe this kind of organization of sets is the theory of relations. This chapter begins with order relations, then treats equivalence relations [the ones which group related elements together] and finally examines more general types of relations.

§ 7.1 *Partially Ordered Sets*

Suppose that there is some natural way to compare the members of a set, so that whenever we are given two members of the set we know how they compare with each other.

EXAMPLE 1   (a) We are used to comparing real numbers. For example, 3 is less than 5, -1 is less than 4 and -1 is greater than -3. We compare two numbers by observing which is larger and which is smaller.

(b) If the set S is indexed by $\mathbb{P}$ or $\mathbb{N}$ so that different elements have different indexes, we can compare two members of S by observing which of them has the smaller index. Different ways of indexing S give different ways of ordering the members. The element which has the lowest subscript of all for one indexing might have many members precede it using another indexing. ☐

A set whose members can be compared in such a way is said to be **ordered**, and the specification of how its members compare with each other is called an **order relation** on the set. To say anything useful about ordered sets we need to make these definitions more precise. First note, however, that in many sets which arise naturally we know how to compare some elements with others but also have pairs which are not comparable.

EXAMPLE 2   (a) If we try to compare makes of automobiles we can perhaps agree that Make X is not as good as Make Y but may not be able to say that either of Make Z or Make W is better than the other.

(b) We can agree to compare two numbers in $\{1, 2, 3, \ldots, 73\}$ in case one is a factor of the other. Then 6 and 72 are comparable and so are 6 and 3, but 6 and 8 are not, since neither 6 nor 8 is a factor of the other.

(c) We can compare two subsets of a set S [i.e., members of $\mathcal{P}(S)$] if one is contained in the other. If S has more than one member it has some incomparable subsets. For example, if $s_1 \neq s_2$ and s_1 and s_2 belong to S, then the sets $\{s_1\}$ and $\{s_2\}$ are incomparable.   □

Sets with comparison relations which allow the possibility of incomparable elements such as those in Example 2 are said to be partially ordered. They form an important class, which we now define precisely.

Suppose we are given a relation on a set S, in the sense that for each pair $\langle x, y \rangle$ in $S \times S$ we know whether or not x is related to y. Write $x \leqq y$ if and only if x is related to y. The relation is called a **partial order** on S if it satisfies the following:

(R) $s \leqq s$ for every s in S;
(AS) $s \leqq t$ and $t \leqq s$ imply $s = t$;
(T) $s \leqq t$ and $t \leqq u$ imply $s \leqq u$.

The conditions (R), (AS) and (T) are the **reflexive, antisymmetric** and **transitive** laws, and $\leqq$ is called reflexive, antisymmetric or transitive if it satisfies them. If $\leqq$ is a partial order on S the pair $(S, \leqq)$ is called a **partially ordered set** or **poset** for short. We use the notation "$\leqq$" as a general-purpose name for a partial order. If there is already a notation, such as "$\leq$" or "$\subseteq$," for a particular partial order we will generally use it in preference to "$\leqq$."

In Example 2 the understood relations were "is not as good as," "is a factor of" and "is a subset of." We could just as well have considered the relations "is as good as," "is a multiple of" and "contains," since these relations convey the same comparative information as the chosen ones. Each partial order on a set determines an **inverse** relation in which x and y are related if and only if y and x are related in the original way. The inverse of a partial order $\leqq$ is usually denoted by $\geqq$. The inverse relation is also a partial order [Exercise 12(a)].

Given a partial order $\leqq$ on a set S we can define another relation $\prec$ on

S by

$$x \prec y \quad \text{if and only if} \quad x \leq y \quad \text{and} \quad x \neq y.$$

For example if $\leq$ is set inclusion $\subseteq$, then $A \prec B$ means A is a proper subset of B, i.e., $A \subset B$. The relation $\prec$ satisfies:

(AR) $s \prec s$ is false for all s in S;
(T) $s \prec t$ and $t \prec u$ imply $s \prec u$.

A relation satisfying (AR) is said to be **antireflexive**. We call a relation which satisfies (AR) and (T) a **quasi-order**. Each partial order on S yields a quasi-order, and conversely if $\prec$ is a quasi-order on S then the relation $\leq$ defined by

$$x \leq y \quad \text{if and only if} \quad x \prec y \quad \text{or} \quad x = y$$

is a partial order on S [Exercise 12(b)]. Whether one considers a partial order or its associated quasi-order to describe comparisons between members of a set depends on the particular problem at hand. We will generally use the partial order but switch back and forth as convenient.

It is possible, at least in principle, to draw a diagram which shows at a glance the order relation on a finite poset. Given a partial order $\leq$ on S, we say the element t **covers** the element s in case $s \prec t$ and there is no u in S with $s \prec u \prec t$. A **Hasse** [pronounced HAH-suh] **diagram** of the poset $(S, \leq)$ is a figure consisting of points [or small circles] labeled by the members of S, with a line segment directed generally upward from s to t whenever t covers s.

EXAMPLE 3   (a) Let $S = \{1, 2, 3, 4, 5, 6\}$. We write $m \,|\, n$ in case m divides n, i.e., n is an integer multiple of m. The diagram in Figure 1 is a Hasse diagram of the poset $(S, |)$. There is no segment between 1 and 6 because 6 does not cover 1.

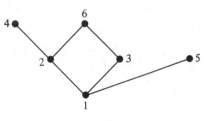

FIGURE 1

We can see from the diagram, though, that $1 \,|\, 6$ because the relation is transitive and there is a chain of segments corresponding to $1 \,|\, 2$ and $2 \,|\, 6$. Similarly, we can see that $1 \,|\, 4$ from the chain $1 \,|\, 2 \,|\, 4$. Note that, in general, transitive relations can be run together without causing confusion: $x \leq y \leq z$ means $x \leq y$, $y \leq z$ *and* $x \leq z$.

(b) Let S be the power set $\mathcal{P}(\{a, b, c\})$ with $\subseteq$ as partial order. Figure 2 shows a Hasse diagram of $(S, \subseteq)$. Note that the lines from $\{a\}$ to $\{a, c\}$ and from $\{b\}$ to $\{a, b\}$ happen to cross, but this crossing is simply a feature of the drawing and has no significance as far as the partial order is concerned. In particular, the intersection of the two lines does *not* represent an element of the poset.

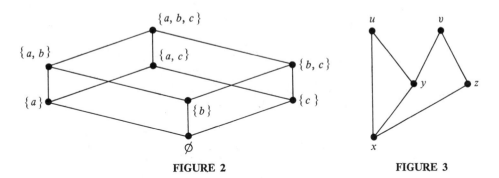

FIGURE 2   FIGURE 3

(c) The diagram in Figure 3 is not a Hasse diagram, because u cannot cover x if u also covers y and y covers x. If any of the line segments connecting u, x and y were removed, then the figure would be a Hasse diagram.

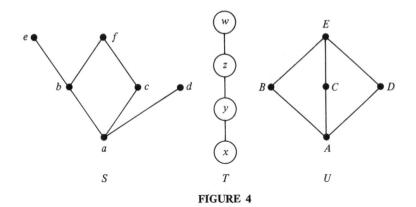

S   T   U

FIGURE 4

(d) The diagrams in Figure 4 are Hasse diagrams of posets, whose order relations can be read off directly from the diagrams. All elements are related to themselves. In addition:

For $S = \{a, b, c, d, e, f\}$ we have $a \leqq b, a \leqq c, a \leqq d, a \leqq e, a \leqq f$, $b \leqq e, b \leqq f$ and $c \leqq f$. We saw this picture before in part (a) of this example.

For $T = \{x, y, z, w\}$ we have $x \leqq y, x \leqq z, x \leqq w, y \leqq z, y \leqq w$ and $z \leqq w$. This is the picture we would get for divisors of 8 or of 27 or of 125 with order relation $|$.

For $U = \{A, B, C, D, E\}$ we have $A \leqq B, A \leqq C, A \leqq D, A \leqq E$, $B \leqq E, C \leqq E$ and $D \leqq E$. This picture is the Hasse diagram of the poset consisting of the sets $\{1\}, \{1, 2\}, \{1, 3\}, \{1, 4\}, \{1, 2, 3, 4\}$ with set inclusion as order relation. ⬚

In general, given a Hasse diagram for a poset, we see that $s \leq t$ in case either $s = t$ or there is an upward chain of edges from s to t. The reflexive and transitive laws are understood, and the covering information tells us the rest. The fact that every finite poset has a Hasse diagram is intuitively obvious and is an easy consequence of properties of directed graphs, as we will explain after Theorem 2 of § 8.1. Some infinite posets also have Hasse diagrams. A Hasse diagram of $\mathbb{Z}$ with the usual order $\leq$ is a vertical line with dots spaced along it. On the other hand, no real number covers any other in the usual $\leq$ order, so $(\mathbb{R}, \leq)$ has no Hasse diagram.

EXAMPLE 4   For an alphabet Σ, we make Σ^* into an infinite poset as follows. For words w_1, w_2 in Σ^* define $w_1 \leq w_2$ if w_1 is an **initial segment** of w_2, i.e., if there is a word w in Σ^* with $w_1 w = w_2$. For example, we have $ab \leq abbaa$. This conforms to our definition since, if $w_1 = ab$ and $w_2 = abbaa$, then $w_1 w = w_2$ for $w = baa$. Also, $\epsilon \leq w$ for all words because $w = \epsilon w$. Note that $abbaa$ does not cover ab since $u = abb$ and $u = abba$ both satisfy $ab \prec u \prec abbaa$. However, $abbaa$ covers $abba$, $abba$ covers abb, and abb covers ab. In general, if w_2 covers w_1 then $\text{length}(w_2) = 1 + \text{length}(w_1)$.

For $\Sigma = \{a, b\}$, part of the Hasse diagram for $(\Sigma^*, \leq)$ is drawn in Figure 5. This Hasse diagram is a tree. In § 9.2 we will view this as a "rooted tree," at which point tradition will force us to draw it upside down. ⬚

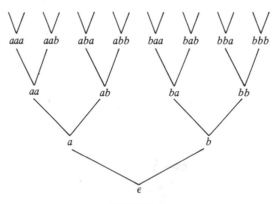

FIGURE 5

The elements corresponding to points near the top or bottom of a Hasse diagram often turn out to be important. If $(P, \leq)$ is a poset we call an element x of P **maximal** in case there is no y in P with $x \prec y$, and call x **minimal** if there is no y in P with $y \prec x$. In the posets with Hasse diagrams shown in

Figure 4 the elements d, e, f, w and E are maximal, while a, x and A are minimal. The infinite poset in Figure 5 has no maximal elements; the empty word ϵ is its only minimal element.

A subset S of a poset P inherits the partial order on P and is itself a poset, since the laws (R), (AS) and (T) apply to all members of P. We call S a **subposet** of P.

EXAMPLE 5   (a) The sets $\{2, 3, 4, 5, 6\}$ and $\{1, 2, 3, 6\}$ are subposets of the poset $\{1, 2, 3, 4, 5, 6\}$ given in Example 3(a), with Hasse diagrams shown in Figure 6. [Notice the placement of the primes in Figure 6(a).]

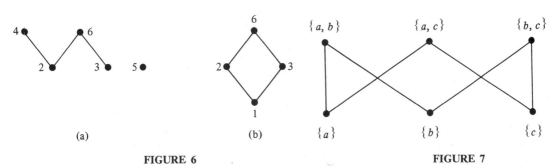

FIGURE 6   FIGURE 7

(b) The set of nonempty proper subsets of $\{a, b, c\}$ is a subposet of $\mathcal{P}(\{a, b, c\})$ with partial order $\subseteq$. Figure 7 shows a Hasse diagram for it. Compare with Figure 2.   ☐

If S is a subposet of a poset $(P, \leq)$, it may happen that S has a member M such that $s \leq M$ for every s in S. In Figure 6(b), $s \leq 6$ for every s, while no such element M exists in Figures 6(a) or 7. An element M with this property is called the **largest member** of S or the **maximum** of S and denoted max(S). [There is at most one such M; why?] This notation is consistent with our usage of max$\{m, n\}$ to denote the larger of the two numbers m and n. Similarly, if S has a member m such that $m \leq s$ for every s in S, then m is called the **smallest member** of S or the **minimum** of S and is denoted min(S).

EXAMPLE 6   Consider again the poset $(\{1, 2, 3, 4, 5, 6\}, |)$ illustrated in Figure 1. This poset has no largest member or maximum even though 4, 6 and 5 are all maximal elements. The element 1 is a minimum of the poset and is the only minimal element. The subset $\{2, 3\}$ has no largest member [3 is larger than 2 in the usual order, but not in the order under discussion].   ☐

Even if a subposet S of a poset $(P, \leq)$ has no largest member, it may happen that there is an element x in P with $s \leq x$ for every s in S. [For example, both elements in the set $\{2, 3\}$ of Example 6 divide 6.] Such an element is called an **upper bound** for S in P. If x is an upper bound for S in P such that $x \leq y$ for every upper bound y for S in P, x is called a **least upper bound** of S in P, and we write $x = \mathrm{lub}(S)$. Similarly, an element z in P such that $z \leq s$ for all s in S is a **lower bound** for S in P. A lower bound z such that $w \leq z$ for every lower bound w is called a **greatest lower bound** of S in P and denoted by $\mathrm{glb}(S)$. By the antisymmetric law (AS), a subset of P cannot have two different least upper bounds or two different greatest lower bounds.

EXAMPLE 7   (a) In the poset $(\{1, 2, 3, 4, 5, 6\}, |)$ the subset $\{2, 3\}$ has exactly one upper bound, namely 6, and so $\mathrm{lub}\{2, 3\} = 6$. Similarly, $\mathrm{glb}\{2, 3\} = 1$. The subset $\{4, 6\}$ has no upper bounds in the poset; 2 and 1 are both lower bounds and so $\mathrm{glb}\{4, 6\} = 2$. The subset $\{3, 6\}$ has 6 as an upper bound and 3 and 1 as lower bounds; hence $\mathrm{lub}\{3, 6\} = 6$ and $\mathrm{glb}\{3, 6\} = 3$. Thus least upper bounds and greatest lower bounds might or might not exist, and if they do they might or might not belong to the subset.

(b) In the poset P shown in Figure 8 the subset $\{b, c\}$ has d, e, g and h as upper bounds in P, and h is an upper bound for $\{d, f\}$. The set $\{b, c\}$ has no least upper bound in P [why?] but $h = \mathrm{lub}\{d, f\}$. The elements a and c are lower bounds for $\{d, e, f\}$, which has no greatest lower bound because a and c are not comparable. Element a is the greatest lower bound of $\{b, d, e, f\}$. ☐

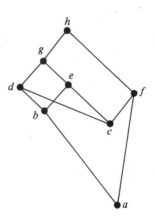

FIGURE 8

Many of the posets which come up in practice have the property that every 2-element subset has both a least upper bound and a greatest lower bound. Such a poset is called a lattice. Thus a poset $(P, \leq)$ is called a **lattice** if $\mathrm{lub}\{x, y\}$ and $\mathrm{glb}\{x, y\}$ exist for every x and y in P. If $(P, \leq)$ is a lattice, then we introduce the new notation $x \vee y = \mathrm{lub}\{x, y\}$ and $x \wedge y = \mathrm{glb}\{x, y\}$ for $x, y \in P$. We read $x \vee y$ as "x join y" and $x \wedge y$ as "x meet y" or, more informally, as "x bird y" and "x hat y."

Observe that $\vee$ and $\wedge$ are binary relations on P. Also, note that $x \wedge y = x$ if and only if $x \leq y$ if and only if $x \vee y = y$. In particular, we can recover the relation $\leq$ if we know either binary relation $\wedge$ or $\vee$; see Exercise 8. One can show by induction [Exercise 19(b)] that every finite subset of a lattice has both a least upper bound and a greatest lower bound.

EXAMPLE 8   (a) The poset $(\mathcal{P}(\{a, b, c\}), \subseteq)$ shown in Figure 2 is a lattice. For instance

$$\{a\} \vee \{c\} = \{a, c\}, \quad \{a, b\} \vee \{a, c\} = \{a, b, c\}, \quad \{a, b\} \wedge \{c\} = \varnothing$$

and

$$\{a, b\} \wedge \{b, c\} = \{b\}.$$

In general, for any set U, $(\mathcal{P}(U), \subseteq)$ is a lattice with $A \vee B = A \cup B$ and $A \wedge B = A \cap B$ so that

$$\text{lub}\{A, B, \ldots, Z\} = A \cup B \cup \cdots \cup Z$$

and

$$\text{glb}\{A, B, \ldots, Z\} = A \cap B \cap \cdots \cap Z.$$

The poset shown in Figure 7 is not a lattice; for example $\{a, b\}$ and $\{a, c\}$ have no least upper bound in the poset.

(b) Define the partial order $|$ on $\mathbb{P}$ by $m | n$ if and only if m divides n. The subposet $S = \{1, 2, 3, 4, 5, 6\}$ of $\mathbb{P}$, shown in Figure 1, is not a lattice since $\{3, 4\}$ has no upper bound in S. The full poset $(\mathbb{P}, |)$ is a lattice, however. For m and n in $\mathbb{P}$ an upper bound for $\{m, n\}$ is an integer k in $\mathbb{P}$ such that m divides k and n divides k, i.e., a common multiple of m and n. The least upper bound $m \vee n$ is the **least common multiple** of m and n. Similarly the greatest lower bound $m \wedge n$ is the **greatest common divisor** of m and n, the largest positive integer which divides both m and n. For instance, $12 \vee 10 = 60$ and $12 \wedge 10 = 2$. The numbers $m \vee n$ and $m \wedge n$ can be determined from the factorizations of m and n into products of primes. The primes themselves are the minimal members of the subposet obtained by deleting the element 1 from $\mathbb{P}$.

(c) Consider the set $\text{FUN}(\{a, b, c\}, \{0, 1\})$ of all functions from the 3-element set $\{a, b, c\}$ to $\{0, 1\}$. We obtain a partial order $\leq$ on this set by defining

$$f \leq g \quad \text{if and only if} \quad f(x) \leq g(x) \quad \text{for} \quad x = a, b, c.$$

It is convenient to label the eight functions in this poset with subscripts, like 101, that list the values the functions take at a, b and c, respectively. For example, f_{101} represents the function such that $f_{101}(a) = 1, f_{101}(b) = 0$ and $f_{101}(c) = 1$. The Hasse diagram for the poset $(\text{FUN}(\{a, b, c\}, \{0, 1\}), \leq)$ is given in Figure 9. $\square$

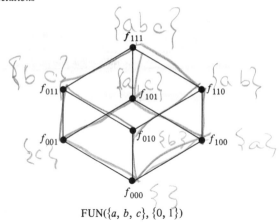

FUN($\{a, b, c\}, \{0, 1\}$)

FIGURE 9

EXAMPLE 9 Up to this section we have used the symbols $\lor$ and $\land$ as logical connectives. Our new usage is consistent with the previous notation. The poset $(\{0, 1\}, \leqq)$ with the usual order is a lattice in which

$$0 \lor 0 = 0 \land 0 = 0 \land 1 = 0 \quad \text{and} \quad 1 \land 1 = 1 \lor 1 = 1 \lor 0 = 1,$$

i.e., $x \lor y = \max\{x, y\}$ and $x \land y = \min\{x, y\}$. The table

p	q	$p \lor q$	$p \land q$
0	0	0	0
0	1	1	0
1	0	1	0
1	1	1	1

shows that the truth values of $p \lor q$ and $p \land q$ are the maximum and minimum values, respectively, of the truth values of p and q. In Chapter 10 we will discuss in detail how to make a set of propositions into a lattice, called a Boolean algebra.   ⬚

The definitions of $\lor$ and $\land$ imply that a lattice satisfies the following laws:

$x \lor x = x$	$x \land x = x$
$x \lor y = y \lor x$	$x \land y = y \land x$
$(x \lor y) \lor z = x \lor (y \lor z)$	$(x \land y) \land z = x \land (y \land z).$

A proof of the associativity of the join operation $\lor$ is outlined in Exercise 19. The laws in the left-hand column above match those on the right. The symmetry in the way $\lor$ and $\land$ are defined means that we can take the proof of a statement on one side, interchange $\lor$ and $\land$ and get a proof of the statement on the other side. This observation can be developed into a formal **principle**

of duality for lattices, which says that if we interchange $\vee$ and $\wedge$ in a true theorem about lattices we get another true theorem.

We began this section by considering sets in which we could compare any two members, but since then we have dealt almost exclusively with posets which have incomparable pairs of elements. In the next section we return to the special case in which each element is related to every other. We also discuss how to use orders on relatively simple sets to produce orders for more complicated ones.

EXERCISES 7.1

1. Draw Hasse diagrams for the following posets.
   (a) ($\{1, 2, 3, 4, 6, 8, 12, 24\}, |$) where $m|n$ means m is a factor of [i.e., divides] n.
   (b) The set of subsets of $\{3, 7\}$ with $\subseteq$ as partial order.

2. (a) Give examples of two posets which come from everyday life or from other courses.
   (b) Do your examples have maximal or minimal elements? If so, what are they?
   (c) What are the inverses of the partial orders in your examples?

3. Figure 10 shows the Hasse diagrams of three posets.

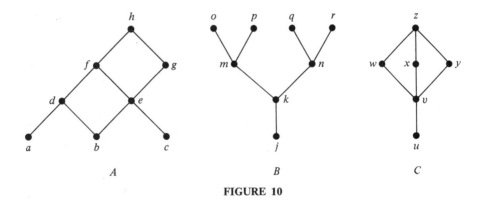

FIGURE 10

   (a) What are the maximal members of these posets?
   (b) Which of these posets have minimal elements?
   (c) Which of these posets have smallest members?
   (d) Which elements cover the element e?
   (e) Find each of the following if it exists.

$$\text{lub}\{d, c\}, \qquad \text{lub}\{w, y, v\}, \qquad \text{lub}\{p, m\}, \qquad \text{glb}\{a, g\}.$$

   (f) Which of these posets are lattices?

4. Find the maximal proper subsets of the 3-element set $\{a, b, c\}$. That is, find the maximal members of the subposet of $\mathcal{P}(\{a, b, c\})$ consisting of proper subsets of $\{a, b, c\}$.

5. Define the relations $<$, $\leqq$ and $\leqq$ on the plane $\mathbb{R} \times \mathbb{R}$ by

$$\langle x, y \rangle < \langle z, w \rangle \quad \text{if } x^2 + y^2 < z^2 + w^2,$$
$$\langle x, y \rangle \leqq \langle z, w \rangle \quad \text{if } \langle x, y \rangle < \langle z, w \rangle \text{ or } \langle x, y \rangle = \langle z, w \rangle,$$
$$\langle x, y \rangle \leqq \langle z, w \rangle \quad \text{if } x^2 + y^2 \leqq z^2 + w^2.$$

(a) Which of these relations are partial orders? Explain.

(b) Which are quasi-orders? Explain.

(c) Draw a sketch of $\{\langle x, y \rangle : \langle x, y \rangle \leqq \langle 3, 4 \rangle\}$.

(d) Draw a sketch of $\{\langle x, y \rangle : \langle x, y \rangle \leqq \langle 3, 4 \rangle\}$.

6. Let $\mathcal{E}(\mathbb{N})$ be the set of all finite subsets of $\mathbb{N}$ which have an even number of elements, with partial order $\subseteq$.

(a) Let $A = \{1, 2\}$ and $B = \{1, 3\}$. Find four upper bounds for $\{A, B\}$.

(b) Does $\{A, B\}$ have a least upper bound in $\mathcal{E}(\mathbb{N})$? Explain.

(c) Is $\mathcal{E}(\mathbb{N})$ a lattice?

7. Is every subposet of a lattice a lattice? Explain.

8. The table in Figure 11 has been partially filled in. It gives the value of $x \vee y$ for x and y in a certain lattice $(L, \leqq)$. For example $b \vee c = d$.

$\vee$	a	b	c	d	e	f
a	e	a	e	e		a
b		d	d	e		b
c			d	e		c
d				e		d
e						e
f						

FIGURE 11

(a) Fill in the rest of the table.

(b) Which are the largest and smallest elements of L?

(c) Show that $f \leqq c \leqq d \leqq e$.

(d) Draw a Hasse diagram for L.

9. Consider $\mathbb{R}$ with the usual order $\leqq$.

(a) Is $\mathbb{R}$ a lattice? If it is, what are the meanings of $a \vee b$ and $a \wedge b$ in $\mathbb{R}$?

(b) Give an example of a nonempty subset of $\mathbb{R}$ which has no least upper bound.

(c) Find $\text{lub}\{x \in \mathbb{R} : x < 73\}$.

(d) Find $\text{lub}\{x \in \mathbb{R} : x \leqq 73\}$.

(e) Find $\text{lub}\{x \in \mathbb{R} : x^2 < 73\}$.

(f) Find $\text{glb}\{x \in \mathbb{R} : x^2 < 73\}$.

10. (a) Show that every finite poset has a minimal element. *Hint:* Use induction.

(b) Give an example of a poset with a maximal element but no minimal element.

11. Consider the poset C whose Hasse diagram is shown in Figure 10. Show that $w \vee (x \wedge y) \neq (w \vee x) \wedge (w \vee y)$ and $w \wedge (x \vee y) \neq (w \wedge x) \vee (w \wedge y)$. This shows that lattices need not satisfy "distributive laws."

12. (a) Show that if $\leq$ is a partial order on a set S then so is its inverse relation $\geq$.

(b) Show that if $\prec$ is a quasi-order on a set S then the relation $\leq$ defined by

$$x \leq y \quad \text{if and only if} \quad x \prec y \quad \text{or} \quad x = y$$

is a partial order on S.

13. Let Σ be an alphabet. For $w_1, w_2 \in \Sigma^*$, let $w_1 \leq w_2$ mean length$(w_1) \leq$ length(w_2). Is $\leq$ a partial order on Σ^*? Explain.

14. Verify that the partial order $\leq$ on Σ^* in Example 4 is reflexive and transitive.

15. Let Σ be an alphabet.

(a) For $w_1, w_2 \in \Sigma^*$ define $w_1 \leq w_2$ if there are w and w' in Σ^* with $w_2 = ww_1w'$. Is $\leq$ a partial order on Σ^*? Explain.

(b) Answer part (a) if w and w' are restricted to belong to Σ.

16. Let S be a set of subroutines of a computer program. For A and B in S write $A \prec B$ if A must be completed before B can be completed. What sort of restriction must be placed on subroutine calls in the program to make $\prec$ a quasi-order on S?

17. Let $\mathcal{F}(\mathbb{N})$ be the collection of all *finite* subsets of $\mathbb{N}$. Then $(\mathcal{F}(\mathbb{N}), \subseteq)$ is a poset.

(a) Does $\mathcal{F}(\mathbb{N})$ have a maximal element? If yes, give one. If no, explain.

(b) Does $\mathcal{F}(\mathbb{N})$ have a minimal element? If yes, give one. If no, explain.

(c) Given A, B in $\mathcal{F}(\mathbb{N})$, does $\{A, B\}$ have a least upper bound in $\mathcal{F}(\mathbb{N})$? If yes, specify it. If no, provide a specific counterexample.

(d) Given A, B in $\mathcal{F}(\mathbb{N})$, does $\{A, B\}$ have a greatest lower bound in $\mathcal{F}(\mathbb{N})$? If yes, specify it. If no, provide a specific counterexample.

(e) Is $\mathcal{F}(\mathbb{N})$ a lattice? Explain.

18. Repeat Exercise 17 for the collection $\mathcal{I}(\mathbb{N})$ of all *infinite* subsets of $\mathbb{N}$.

19. (a) Consider elements x, y, z in a poset. Show that if lub$\{x, y\} = a$ and lub$\{a, z\} = b$, then lub$\{x, y, z\} = b$.

(b) Show that every finite subset of a lattice has a least upper bound.

(c) Show that if x, y and z are members of a lattice then $(x \vee y) \vee z = x \vee (y \vee z)$.

20. Let $\mathcal{S}$ be a set of compound propositions, and for P and Q in $\mathcal{S}$ define $P \leq Q$ if $P \Rightarrow Q$. Must $(\mathcal{S}, \leq)$ be a poset? Explain.

§ 7.2 *Special Orderings*

Partially ordered sets arise in a variety of ways, and in many cases the fact that there are pairs of elements which cannot be compared is an essential feature of the context. The important class of data structures called trees, which we will study in detail in Chapter 9, can be thought of as consisting of Hasse diagrams, such as those shown in Figure 1, in which lub$\{x, y\}$ exists for all x and y but glb$\{x, y\}$ exists only if $x \leq y$ or $y \leq x$. Trees are useful data structures, even though they have incomparable elements, because it is possible to start at the top and follow the tree to get to any element fairly quickly. Efficient algorithms are also known for examining all elements of a tree.

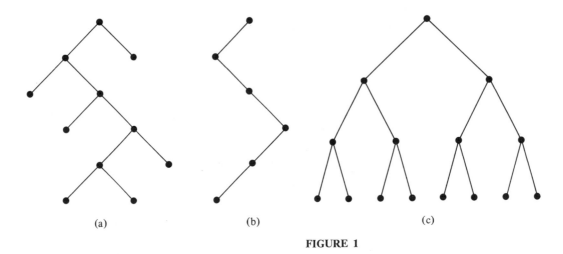

(a)   (b)   (c)

FIGURE 1

An even more common data structure consists of a list or sequence in which, no matter what two elements are chosen, one comes before the other. Such a structure is an example of a **chain** which we define to be a poset in which every two elements are comparable. A partial order is called a **total order** or **linear order** if for each choice of s and t in S either $s \leqq t$ or $t \leqq s$. Thus a chain is a poset with a total order. The terms "totally ordered set" and "linearly ordered set" are sometimes used as synonyms for "chain."

EXAMPLE 1   (a) The poset of Figure 1(b) is a chain, but the other posets in Figure 1 are not.

(b) The set $\mathbb{R}$ with the usual order $\leqq$ is a chain.

(c) The lists of names in a phone book or words in a dictionary are chains if we define $w_1 \leqq w_2$ to mean that $w_1 = w_2$ or w_1 comes before w_2. ∐

Every subposet of a chain is itself a chain. For example the posets $(\mathbb{Z}, \leqq)$ and $(\mathbb{Q}, \leqq)$ are subposets of $(\mathbb{R}, \leqq)$ and are linearly ordered by the orders they inherit from $\mathbb{R}$. The words in the dictionary between "start" and "stop" form a subchain of the chain of all words in Example 1(c).

A poset which is not itself a chain will have subposets which are. For a given poset, it is often useful to know something about the subposets which are chains.

EXAMPLE 2   (a) Let S be a set of people at a family reunion, and write $m \prec n$ in case m is a descendent of n. Then $\prec$ is a quasi-order which defines a partial order $\leqq$ by $m \leqq n$ if and only if $m \prec n$ or $m = n$. A chain in the poset $(S, \leqq)$ is a set of the form $\{m, n, p, \ldots, r\}$ in which m is a descendent of n, n a descendent of p, and so on. It would be unusual for such a chain to have more than 5 members, though the set S itself might be quite large.

(b) The Hasse diagram shown in Figure 2 describes a poset with a number of subchains [49 if we count the 1-element chains but not the empty chain]. ▯

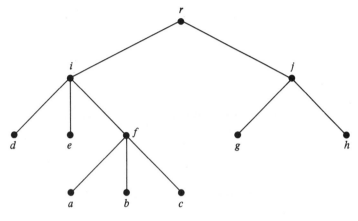

FIGURE 2

We are frequently interested in the maximal chains of a poset. To define these we first observe that if $(S, \leq)$ is a poset and if $\mathfrak{C}(S)$ is the set of chains in S then $(\mathfrak{C}(S), \subseteq)$ is also a poset. A **maximal chain** in S is defined to be a maximal member of $\mathfrak{C}(S)$, i.e., a chain which is not properly contained in another chain.

EXAMPLE 3   (a) In the poset of Figure 2 the maximal chains are $\{a, f, i, r\}$, $\{b, f, i, r\}$, $\{c, f, i, r\}$, $\{d, i, r\}$, $\{e, i, r\}$, $\{g, j, r\}$ and $\{h, j, r\}$. Notice that the maximal chains are not all the same size.

(b) In the poset shown in Figure 3 the two maximal chains $\{a, c, d, e\}$ and $\{a, b, e\}$ containing a and e have different numbers of elements. This poset has 4 maximal chains in all. ▯

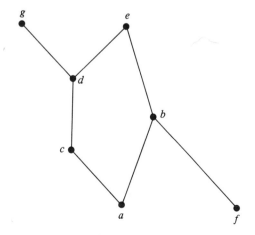

FIGURE 3

A finite chain must have a smallest member, and so must each of its nonempty subchains. Infinite chains, on the other hand, can exhibit a variety of behaviors. The infinite chains $(\mathbb{R}, \leqq)$ and $(\mathbb{Z}, \leqq)$ with their usual orders do not have smallest members. The chain $(\{x \in \mathbb{R} : 0 \leqq x\}, \leqq)$ has a smallest member, namely 0, but has subsets such as $\{x \in \mathbb{R} : 1 < x\}$ without smallest members. The infinite chain $(\mathbb{N}, \leqq)$ has a smallest member, and the well-ordering property of $\mathbb{N}$ stated in § 6.3 says that every nonempty subset does too.

We say that a chain C is **well-ordered** in case each nonempty subset of C has a smallest member. If C is well-ordered, and if for each c in C we have a statement $p(c)$, then we can hope to prove all statements $p(c)$ true by supposing the set $\{c \in C : p(c) \text{ is false}\}$ is nonempty, considering the smallest c for which $p(c)$ is false and deriving a contradiction. This was the idea behind our explanation of the validity of the principles of induction in § 6.3. Since every finite chain is well-ordered, the method applies to finite chains, and in particular to any set $\{n \in \mathbb{Z} : m \leqq n \leqq m^*\}$ with the usual order. Hence it can be used to justify the finite principles of induction stated after Example 3 of § 6.3.

In the rest of this section we study how to build new partial orders from known ones. Suppose first that $(S, \leqq)$ is a given poset and that T is a nonempty set. We can define a partial order, which we denote $\preceq$, on the set $\mathrm{FUN}(T, S)$ of functions from T to S by defining

$$f \preceq g \quad \text{if} \quad f(t) \leqq g(t) \quad \text{for all} \quad t \text{ in } T.$$

The verification that this new relation is a partial order is straightforward [Exercise 7(a)].

EXAMPLE 4   (a) If $S = T = \mathbb{R}$ with the usual order then $f \preceq g$ means that the graph of f lies on or below the graph of g, as in Figure 4.

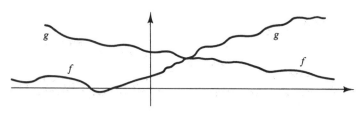

FIGURE 4

(b) Consider $S = \{0, 1\}$ with $0 < 1$. The functions in $\mathrm{FUN}(T, \{0, 1\})$ are the characteristic functions of subsets of T. Each subset A of T has a corresponding function χ_A in $\mathrm{FUN}(T, \{0, 1\})$ with $\chi_A(x) = 1$ if $x \in A$ and 0 if $x \notin A$. Then $\chi_A \preceq \chi_B$ if and only if $x \in B$ whenever $x \in A$, hence if and only if $A \subseteq B$. Thus the Hasse diagram for $(\mathrm{FUN}(T, \{0, 1\}), \preceq)$ is the same as the diagram for $(\mathscr{P}(T), \subseteq)$. See Figure 9 of § 7.1 for the diagram with $T = \{a, b, c\}$. □

Example 4(b) shows that (FUN(T, S), $\leq$) need not be a chain even if S is a chain. The poset (FUN(T, S), $\leq$) does inherit some properties from S, however. If S has largest or smallest elements so does FUN(T, S), and if S is a lattice so is FUN(T, S). For more in this vein see Exercise 7.

Another way to combine two sets into a new one is to form their product. Suppose that ($S, \leq_1$) and ($T, \leq_2$) are posets, where we use the subscripts to keep track of which partial order is which. There is more than one natural way to make $S \times T$ into a poset. Our preference will depend on the problem at hand.

The first partial order we describe for $S \times T$ is called the **product order**. For $s, s' \in S$ and $t, t' \in T$ define

$$\langle s, t \rangle \leq \langle s', t' \rangle \quad \text{if} \quad s \leq_1 s' \quad \text{and} \quad t \leq_2 t'.$$

EXAMPLE 5   Let $S = T = \mathbb{N}$ with the usual order $\leq$ in each case. Then $\langle 2, 5 \rangle \leq \langle 3, 7 \rangle$ since $2 \leq 3$ and $5 \leq 7$. Also $\langle 2, 5 \rangle \leq \langle 3, 5 \rangle$ since $2 \leq 3$ and $5 \leq 5$. But the pairs $\langle 2, 7 \rangle$ and $\langle 3, 5 \rangle$ are not comparable; $\langle 2, 7 \rangle \leq \langle 3, 5 \rangle$ would mean $2 \leq 3$ and $7 \leq 5$, while $\langle 3, 5 \rangle \leq \langle 2, 7 \rangle$ would mean $3 \leq 2$ and $5 \leq 7$. Figure 5 indicates the pairs $\langle m, n \rangle$ in $S \times T = \mathbb{N} \times \mathbb{N}$ with $\langle 2, 1 \rangle \leq \langle m, n \rangle \leq \langle 3, 4 \rangle$.   ▢

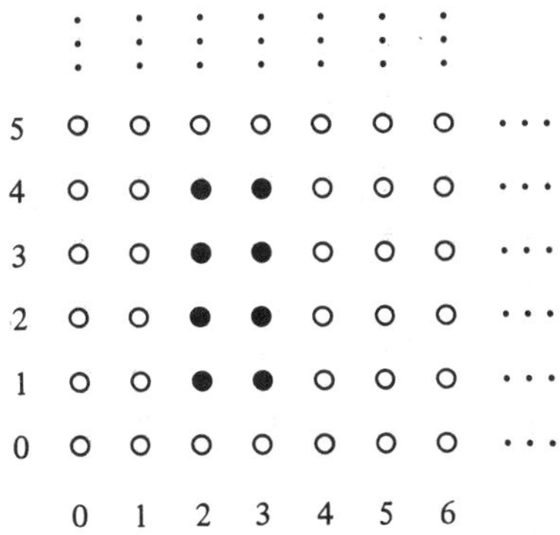

FIGURE 5

Consider, again, two posets ($S, \leq_1$) and ($T, \leq_2$). The fact that the product order $\leq$ is a partial order on $S \times T$ is almost immediate from the definition. For example, if $\langle s, t \rangle \leq \langle s', t' \rangle$ and $\langle s', t' \rangle \leq \langle s, t \rangle$, then $s \leq_1 s'$, $t \leq_2 t'$, $s' \leq_1 s$ and $t' \leq_2 t$. Since $\leq_1$ and $\leq_2$ are antisymmetric $s = s'$ and $t = t'$. So $\langle s, t \rangle = \langle s', t' \rangle$. Thus $\leq$ is antisymmetric.

There is no difficulty in extending this idea to define a partial order on the product $S_1 \times S_2 \times \cdots \times S_n$ of a number of posets. We define

$$\langle s_1, s_2, \ldots, s_n \rangle \leq \langle s'_1, s'_2, \ldots, s'_n \rangle \quad \text{if} \quad s_i \leq_i s'_i \quad \text{for all} \quad i.$$

In Example 5, $\mathbb{N}$ is a chain but $\mathbb{N} \times \mathbb{N}$ is not; for instance $\langle 2, 4 \rangle$ and $\langle 3, 1 \rangle$ are not related in the product order. In fact, the product order is almost never a total order [Exercise 12]. On the other hand, if $S_1, S_2, \ldots, S_n$ are chains, there is another natural order on $S_1 \times S_2 \times \cdots \times S_n$ which makes it a chain, which we now illustrate.

EXAMPLE 6 If $S = \{0, 1, 2, \ldots, 9\}$ with the usual order, the set $S \times S$ consists of pairs $\langle m, n \rangle$, which we can identify with the integers $00, 01, 02, \ldots, 98, 99$ from 0 to 99. To make $S \times S$ a chain we can simply define $\langle m, n \rangle \prec \langle m', n' \rangle$ if the corresponding integers are so related, i.e., if $m < m'$ or if $m = m'$ and $n < n'$. For example this order makes $\langle 5, 7 \rangle \prec \langle 6, 3 \rangle$ since $57 < 63$, and $\langle 3, 5 \rangle \prec \langle 3, 7 \rangle$ since $35 < 37$.

In a similar way we can identify the set $S \times S \times S$ with the set of integers from 0 to 999 and make $S \times S \times S$ into a chain by defining $\langle m, n, p \rangle \prec \langle m', n', p' \rangle$ if $m < m'$ or if $m = m'$ and $n < n'$ or if $m = m', n = n'$ and $p < p'$. □

The idea of this example works in general. If $(S_1, \leqq_1), \ldots, (S_n, \leqq_n)$ are posets we can define a relation $\prec$ on $S_1 \times \cdots \times S_n$ by

$$\langle s_1, s_2, \ldots, s_n \rangle \prec \langle t_1, t_2, \ldots, t_n \rangle \text{ if } s_1 \prec_1 t_1 \text{ or if there is an } r \text{ in } \{2, \ldots, n\}$$
$$\text{such that } s_1 = t_1, \ldots, s_{r-1} = t_{r-1} \text{ and } s_r \prec_r t_r.$$

Then $\prec$ is a quasi-order [Exercise 21] which induces a partial order $\leqq$ on $S_1 \times S_2 \times \cdots \times S_n$ called the **filing order**.

EXAMPLE 7 If $S = \{a, b, c, \ldots, z\}$ and $T = \{0, 1, \ldots, 9\}$ with the usual orders we can identify the members of $S \times T$ with 2-symbol strings such as $a5$ and $x3$. Imagine a device which has subassemblies, labeled by letters, each of which has at most 10 parts. It would be reasonable to label spare parts with letter-number combinations and to file them in bins arranged according to the filing order on $S \times T$. Then bin $a5$ would come before bin $x3$ because a precedes x, but $a5$ would come after $a3$ since $3 < 5$. □

The filing order is primarily useful if each S_i is a chain.

Theorem 1 Let $(S_1, \leqq_1), \ldots, (S_n, \leqq_n)$ be chains. Then, with the filing order $\leqq$, the product $S_1 \times \cdots \times S_n$ is a chain.

Proof. We already know that $\leqq$ is a partial order on $S_1 \times \cdots \times S_n$. Now let $\langle s_1, \ldots, s_n \rangle$ and $\langle t_1, \ldots, t_n \rangle$ be distinct elements in $S_1 \times \cdots \times S_n$. Since $s_r \neq t_r$ for some r, there is a first r for which $s_r \neq t_r$. Since $(S_r, \leqq_r)$ is a chain, either $s_r \prec_r t_r$ or $t_r \prec_r s_r$. In the first case $\langle s_1, \ldots, s_n \rangle \prec \langle t_1, \ldots, t_n \rangle$; in the second $\langle t_1, \ldots, t_n \rangle \prec \langle s_1, \ldots, s_n \rangle$. In either case, the two elements of $S_1 \times \cdots \times S_n$ are comparable. □

The special case in which all the posets $(S_i, \leqq_i)$ are the same is important enough to warrant a notation of its own. If $(S, \leqq)$ is a poset and $k \in \mathbb{P}$ we write $\leqq^k$ for the filing order on $S^k = S \times \cdots \times S$.

In the remainder of this section we are primarily interested in the case in which S is an alphabet. Accordingly, from now on we go Greek and write Σ instead of S. We also make the natural identification of k-tuples $\langle a_1, \ldots, a_k \rangle$ in the product Σ^k with words $a_1 \cdots a_k$ of length k in Σ^*. We still have in mind some given partial order $\leq$ on Σ. The set Σ^0 is $\{\epsilon\}$, and we define $\leq^0$ on Σ^0 in the only possible way: $\epsilon \leq^0 \epsilon$.

EXAMPLE 8 If $\Sigma = \{a, b, c, \ldots, z\}$ with the usual linear order on the English alphabet then Σ^k consists of all strings of letters of length k and $\leq^k$ is the usual alphabetical order on Σ^k. For example if $k = 3$, then

$$fed \leq^3 few \leq^3 one \leq^3 six \leq^3 ten \leq^3 two \leq^3 won. \quad \square$$

Since $\Sigma^* = \Sigma^0 \cup \Sigma^1 \cup \Sigma^2 \cup \cdots$ we can piece the partial orders $\leq^0$, $\leq^1, \leq^2, \ldots$ together to get an order $\leq^*$ for Σ^*, called the **standard order**, in which ϵ comes first, then all words of length 1, then all of length 2, and so on. More precisely

$$w_1 \leq^* w_2 \quad \text{if either } w_1 \in \Sigma^k \text{ and } w_2 \in \Sigma^r \text{ and } k < r$$
$$\text{or } w_1, w_2 \in \Sigma^k \text{ for the same } k \text{ and } w_1 \leq^k w_2.$$

If $(\Sigma, \leq)$ is a chain, as it was in Example 8, then $(\Sigma^*, \leq^*)$ is also a chain.

EXAMPLE 9 (a) Let Σ be the English alphabet in the usual order. The first few terms of Σ^* in the standard order are

$$\epsilon, a, b, \ldots, z, aa, ab, \ldots, az, ba, bb, \ldots, bz, ca, cb, \ldots, cz,$$
$$da, db, \ldots, dz, \ldots, za, zb, \ldots, zz, aaa, aab, aac, \ldots.$$

(b) Let $\Sigma = \{0, 1\}$ with $0 < 1$. The first few terms of Σ^* in the standard order are

$$\epsilon, 0, 1, 00, 01, 10, 11, 000, 001, 010, 011,$$
$$100, 101, 110, 111, 0000, 0001, 0010, \ldots. \quad \square$$

Note that if a dictionary were constructed using the standard order in Example 9(a) all the short words would be at the beginning of the dictionary, and to find a word it would be essential to know its exact length. [In fact, some dictionaries designed for crossword puzzle solvers are arranged this way.] To find words in a dictionary with the ordinary alphabetical order, one scans words from left to right looking for differences and ignoring the lengths of the words. Thus "aardvark" is listed before "axe" and "break" precedes "breakfast." Alphabetical order is based on the usual alphabet ordered in the usual way. The idea generalizes naturally to an arbitrary Σ with partial order $\leq$.

The **lexicographic** or **dictionary order** $\leq_L$ on Σ^* is defined as follows. For $a_1, \ldots, a_m$ and $b_1, \ldots, b_n$ in Σ let $k = \min\{m, n\}$. We define

$$a_1 \cdots a_m \prec_L b_1 \cdots b_n \quad \text{if} \quad a_1 \cdots a_k \prec^k b_1 \cdots b_k$$
$$\text{or if} \quad k = m < n \quad \text{and} \quad a_1 \cdots a_k = b_1 \cdots b_k.$$

Then $\prec_L$ is a quasi-order which defines the partial order $\leq_L$.

We can describe $\leq_L$ in another way. For words w and z in Σ^*, $w \leq_L z$ if and only if either

(a) w is an initial segment of z, i.e., $z = wu$ for some $u \in \Sigma^*$, or
(b) $w = xu$ and $z = xv$ for words u and v in Σ^* such that the first letter of u precedes the first letter of v in the ordering of Σ.

Note that in (b) x can be any word, possibly the empty word.

Lexicographic order, standard order and filing order all agree if we consider words in some fixed Σ^k, but lexicographic and standard orders differ in the treatment they give to words of different lengths.

EXAMPLE 10   Let $\Sigma = \{a, b\}$ with $a \prec b$. The first few terms of Σ^* in the lexicographic order are

$$\epsilon, a, aa, aaa, aaaa, aaaaa, \ldots.$$

Any word using the letter b is preceded by an *infinite* number of words, including all the words using only the letter a. Moreover, Σ^* contains infinite decreasing sequences of words; for example,

$$\ldots, aaaaab, \ldots, aaaab, \ldots, aaab, \ldots, aab, \ldots, ab, \ldots, b.$$

And there are infinitely many words between each of these; for example,

$$aaab, aaaba, aaabaa, aaabaaa, aaabaaaa, \ldots$$

all precede *aab*. Thus the lexicographic order on the infinite set Σ^* is very complicated and is difficult to visualize. Nevertheless, it defines a chain, as we show in the next theorem.   □

Theorem 2   If $(\Sigma, \leq)$ is a chain, then $(\Sigma^*, \leq^*)$ is well-ordered and $(\Sigma^*, \leq_L)$ is a chain.

Proof. We know from Theorem 1 that each $(\Sigma^k, \leq^k)$ is a chain. The standard order $\leq^*$ simply links these chains end to end for $k = 0, 1, 2, \ldots$, so $(\Sigma^*, \leq^*)$ is a chain. Now consider a nonempty subset A of Σ^*. Let k be the shortest length of a word in A. Since $A \cap \Sigma^k$ is nonempty and finite, $A \cap \Sigma^k$ possesses a smallest element w_0 in $(\Sigma^k, \leq^k)$. It follows that $w_0 \leq^* w$ for all w in A so that w_0 is the smallest member of A.

For the lexicographic order $\leq_L$, consider two elements $a_1 \cdots a_m$ and $b_1 \cdots b_n$ in Σ^* where $m \leq n$. If $a_1 \cdots a_m = b_1 \cdots b_m$, then $a_1 \cdots a_m \leq_L b_1 \cdots b_n$ by definition. Otherwise, since $(\Sigma^m, \leq^m)$ is a chain, one of $a_1 \cdots a_m$ and $b_1 \cdots b_m$ precedes the other in $(\Sigma^m, \leq^m)$ and so $a_1 \cdots a_m$ and $b_1 \cdots b_n$ are comparable in $(\Sigma^*, \leq_L)$. Thus every two members of Σ^* are comparable under $\leq_L$, and $\leq_L$ is a total order.   □

If Σ has more than one element, then $(\Sigma^*, \leq_L)$ is *not* well-ordered. For example, the set $\{b, ab, aab, aaab, aaaab, \ldots\}$ in Example 10 has no smallest member. Of course, every *finite* subset of Σ^* has a smallest member, since it is itself a finite chain.

EXERCISES 7.2

1. Let P be the set of all subsets of $\{1, 2, 3, 4, 5\}$.
   (a) Give two examples of maximal chains in $(P, \subseteq)$.
   (b) How many maximal chains are there in $(P, \subseteq)$?

2. Let $A = \{1, 2, 3, 4\}$ with the usual order and let $S = A \times A$ with the product order.
   (a) Find a chain in S with 7 members.
   (b) Can a chain in S have 8 members? Explain.

3. Let $(S, |)$ be the set $\{2, 3, 4, \ldots, 999, 1000\}$ with partial order "is a factor of."
   (a) There are exactly 500 maximal elements of $(S, |)$. What are they?
   (b) Give two examples of maximal chains in $(S, |)$.
   (c) Does every maximal chain contain a minimal element of S? Explain.

4. (a) Suppose that no chain in the poset $(S, \leq)$ has more than 73 members. Must a chain in S with 73 members be a maximal chain? Explain.
   (b) Give an example of a poset which has two maximal chains with four members and four maximal chains with two members.

5. Is every chain a lattice? Explain.

6. Let $(C_1, \leq_1), (C_2, \leq_2), \ldots, (C_n, \leq_n)$ be a set of disjoint chains. Describe a way to make $C_1 \cup C_2 \cup \cdots \cup C_n$ into a chain.

7. (a) Show that if $(S, \leq)$ is a poset and T is a set, then the relation $\leq$ on FUN(T, S) given by

$$f \leq g \quad \text{if} \quad f(t) \leq g(t) \quad \text{for all } t \text{ in } T$$

   is a partial order.
   (b) Show that if m is a maximal element in S then the function f_m defined by $f_m(t) = m$ for all $t \in T$ is a maximal element of FUN(T, S).
   (c) Show that if S is a lattice and if $f, g \in$ FUN(T, S), then the function h defined by $h(t) = f(t) \vee g(t)$ for $t \in T$ is the least upper bound of $\{f, g\}$.

8. Let $\mathbb{N} \times \mathbb{N}$ have the product order. Draw a sketch like the one in Figure 5 which shows $\{\langle m, n \rangle : \langle m, n \rangle \leq \langle 5, 2 \rangle\}$.

9. Let $S = \{0, 1, 2\}$ with the usual order and let $T = \{a, b\}$ with $a < b$.
   (a) Draw a Hasse diagram for the poset (FUN$(T, S), \leq$) with order $\leq$ described in Exercise 7. *Hint:* See Example 8(c) of § 7.1.
   (b) Draw a Hasse diagram for the poset $(S \times S, \leq)$ with the product order $\leq$.
   (c) Draw a Hasse diagram for $S \times T$ with the product order.

10. Suppose that $(S, \leq_1)$ and $(T, \leq_2)$ are posets and we define $\leq$ on $S \times T$ by

$$\langle s, t \rangle \leq \langle s', t' \rangle \quad \text{if} \quad s \leq_1 s' \quad \text{or} \quad t \leq_2 t'.$$

   Is $\leq$ a partial order? Explain.

11. Let $(S, \leq)$ be a poset and T a nonempty set. Define the partial order $\leq$ on FUN(T, S) as in Exercise 7. Under what conditions is (FUN$(T, S), \leq$) a chain? Explain.

12. Suppose that $(S, \leq_1)$ and $(T, \leq_2)$ are posets, each with more than one element. Show that $S \times T$ with the product order is not a chain.

13. Let $S = \{0, 1, 2\}$ and $T = \{3, 4\}$ with both sets given the usual order. List the members of the following sets in increasing filing order.
(a) $S \times S$ (b) $S \times T$ (c) $T \times S$

14. Let $(S, \leq_1)$ and $(T, \leq_2)$ be posets and give $S \times T$ the filing order.
(a) Show that if m_1 is maximal in S and m_2 is maximal in T, then $\langle m_1, m_2 \rangle$ is maximal in $S \times T$.
(b) Does $S \times T$ have other maximal elements besides the ones described in part (a)? Explain.
(c) Suppose $S \times T$ has a largest element. Must S or T have a largest element? Explain.

15. Define the order relation $\geq$ on $\mathbb{N}$ by letting $m \geq n$ if $n \leq m$. [Thus $\geq$ is the inverse of $\leq$.] Let $(S_1, \leq_1) = (\mathbb{N}, \leq)$ and $(S_2, \leq_2) = (\mathbb{N}, \geq)$ and let $S = S_1 \times S_2$ with the filing order. That is, $\langle m, n \rangle \leq \langle m', n' \rangle$ if $m < m'$ or if $m = m'$ and $n \geq n'$.
(a) Is $(S, \leq)$ a chain?
(b) Does S have a largest or a smallest element? Explain.
(c) Is $(S, \leq)$ well-ordered? Explain.

16. Show that in a finite poset $(S, \leq)$ every maximal chain contains a minimal element of S.

17. Let $\mathbb{B} = \{0, 1\}$ with the usual order. List the elements $101, 010, 11, 000, 10, 0010, 1000$ of $\mathbb{B}^*$ in increasing order
(a) for the lexicographic order,
(b) for the standard order.

18. Let $(\Sigma, \leq)$ be a nonempty chain.
(a) Does $(\Sigma^*, \leq^*)$ have a maximal member? Explain.
(b) Does $(\Sigma^*, \leq_L)$ have a maximal member? Explain.

19. Let Σ be the English alphabet with the usual order.
(a) List the words of this sentence in increasing standard order.
(b) List the words of this sentence in increasing lexicographic order.

20. Under what conditions on Σ are the lexicographic order and standard order on Σ^* the same?

21. Let $(S_1, \leq_1), \ldots, (S_n, \leq_n)$ be posets and define $\prec$ on $S_1 \times \cdots \times S_n$ by

$$\langle s_1, \ldots, s_n \rangle \prec \langle t_1, \ldots, t_n \rangle \quad \text{if } s_1 \prec_1 t_1 \text{ or if there is an } r \text{ in}$$
$$\{2, \ldots, n\} \text{ such that } s_1 = t_1, \ldots, s_{r-1} = t_{r-1} \text{ and } s_r \prec_r t_r.$$

Show that $\prec$ is a quasi-order.

22. Let $(S_1, \leq_1), \ldots, (S_n, \leq_n)$ be posets and let $S = S_1 \times \cdots \times S_n$ with the product order $\leq$.
(a) Show that if m_i is a maximal element of S_i for $i = 1, \ldots, n$, then $\langle m_1, \ldots, m_n \rangle$ is maximal in S.
(b) Show that if x_i and y_i are in S_i for $i = 1, \ldots, n$ and if $\text{lub}\{x_i, y_i\}$ exists for each i, then

$$\text{lub}\{\langle x_1, \ldots, x_n \rangle, \langle y_1, \ldots, y_n \rangle\} = \langle \text{lub}\{x_1, y_1\}, \ldots, \text{lub}\{x_n, y_n\}\rangle.$$

(c) Would parts (a) and (b) remain true if "maximal" were replaced by "minimal," "largest" or "smallest" or if "lub" were replaced by "glb?"
(d) Show that if each S_i is a lattice so is S.

§ 7.3   *Equivalence Relations*

In this section we study equivalence relations, which are relations that group together elements that have similar characteristics or share some property. These relations occur throughout mathematics and other fields, even though they are not always formally identified as such.

EXAMPLE 1   (a) Let S be a set of marbles. We might regard marbles s and t as equivalent if they have the same color, in which case we might write $s \sim t$. Note that the relation $\sim$ satisfies three properties:

(R) $s \sim s$ for all marbles s,
(S) if $s \sim t$ then $t \sim s$,
(T) if $s \sim t$ and $t \sim u$, then $s \sim u$.

These are nearly obvious; for example (T) asserts that if marbles s and t have the same color and t and u have the same color, then s and u have the same color. Note also that we can partition S into disjoint subsets so that elements belong to the same subset if and only if they are equivalent, i.e., if and only if they have the same color. If we let C be the set of possible colors and define the function $f: S \to C$ by $f(s) =$ "the color of s" for each s in S then the partition is $\{f^{-1}(c) : c \in C\}$, a partition of the sort studied in § 3.2.

(b) For the same set S of marbles, we might regard marbles s and t as equivalent if they are of the same size, and write $s \approx t$ in this case. All the comments in part (a) apply to $\approx$, with obvious changes.   ☐

Let S be any set and suppose that we have a relation $\sim$ on S, i.e., for each pair $\langle x, y \rangle$ in $S \times S$ we know whether $x \sim y$ or not. The relation $\sim$ is called an **equivalence relation** provided it satisfies:

(R) $s \sim s$ for every $s \in S$;
(S) if $s \sim t$ then $t \sim s$;
(T) if $s \sim t$ and $t \sim u$, then $s \sim u$.

The conditions (R), (S) and (T) are the **reflexive, symmetric** and **transitive** laws. If $s \sim t$ we say that s and t are **equivalent**; depending on the circumstances we might also say that s and t are **similar** or **congruent** or **isomorphic**. Other notations sometimes used for equivalence relations are $s \approx t, s \cong t$, $s \equiv t$ and $s \leftrightarrow t$. Unlike the notations for order, these notations all convey the idea that s and t have equal [or equivalent] status. This is reasonable, because of the symmetry law.

EXAMPLE 2   Triangles T_1 and T_2 in the plane are said to be **similar**, and we write $T_1 \approx T_2$, if their angles can be put in one-to-one correspondence so that corresponding angles are equal. If the corresponding sides are also equal, we say that the triangles are **congruent,** and we write $T_1 \cong T_2$. In Figure 1, $T_1 \cong T_2$, $T_1 \approx T_3$ and $T_2 \approx T_3$, but T_3 is not congruent to T_1 or T_2. Both $\approx$ and $\cong$ are equivalence relations on the set of all triangles in the plane. All the laws (R), (S) and (T) are evident for these relations.   ∎

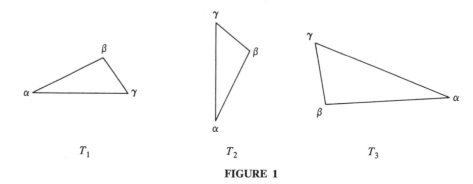

T_1 T_2 T_3

FIGURE 1

EXAMPLE 3   Consider a graph and let V be the set of its vertices. For vertices u and v we define $u \sim v$ provided $u = v$ or there is a path connecting u to v. Then $\sim$ is an equivalence relation on V. You may have verified symmetry and transitivity back at Exercise 8 of § 0.1.   ∎

EXAMPLE 4   (a) Consider a black box, perhaps an automaton, which accepts input strings in Σ^* for some alphabet Σ and generates output strings. We can define an equivalence relation $\sim$ on Σ^* by $w_1 \sim w_2$ if the box generates the same output string for either w_1 or w_2 as input.

(b) Consider a set S of black boxes which accept inputs in Σ^* and generate outputs. Define relations $\approx_1, \approx_2, \approx_3, \ldots$ on S by writing $B \approx_k C$ for boxes B and C in S if B and C produce the same output for every choice of input word of length k. Define $\approx$ on S by letting $B \approx C$ if $B \approx_k C$ for all $k \in \mathbb{P}$. Then all the relations $\approx_k$ and $\approx$ are equivalence relations on S, and two boxes are equivalent under $\approx$ if and only if they produce the same response to all input words with letters from Σ.   ∎

EXAMPLE 5   (a) Matrices **A** and **B** in the set $\mathfrak{M}_{n,n}$ of $n \times n$ matrices are **equivalent** if there are invertible matrices **P** and **Q** in $\mathfrak{M}_{n,n}$ such that **B** = **PAQ**. If we write **A** $\sim$ **B**, then we obtain an equivalence relation $\sim$ on $\mathfrak{M}_{n,n}$. The (R), (S) and (T) laws are not as obvious as in the previous examples and deserve verification.

(R) We always have **A** $\sim$ **A** because **A** = **IAI**, where **I** is the $n \times n$ identity matrix.

(S) Suppose **A** $\sim$ **B**; we need to show **B** $\sim$ **A**. Since **A** $\sim$ **B** we have **B** = **PAQ** for invertible matrices **P** and **Q**. Hence $\mathbf{P}^{-1}\mathbf{B}\mathbf{Q}^{-1} = \mathbf{P}^{-1}\mathbf{PAQQ}^{-1}$ = **IAI** = **A**. Since $\mathbf{P}^{-1}$ and $\mathbf{Q}^{-1}$ are also invertible, we conclude that **B** $\sim$ **A**.

(T) Suppose $\mathbf{A} \sim \mathbf{B}$ and $\mathbf{B} \sim \mathbf{C}$; we need to show $\mathbf{A} \sim \mathbf{C}$. Since $\mathbf{A} \sim \mathbf{B}$ and $\mathbf{B} \sim \mathbf{C}$, we have $\mathbf{B} = \mathbf{PAQ}$ and $\mathbf{C} = \mathbf{RBS}$, where $\mathbf{P}$, $\mathbf{Q}$, $\mathbf{R}$ and $\mathbf{S}$ are invertible. Then $\mathbf{C} = \mathbf{RBS} = \mathbf{RPAQS}$. Since $(\mathbf{RP})^{-1} = \mathbf{P}^{-1}\mathbf{R}^{-1}$ and $(\mathbf{QS})^{-1} = \mathbf{S}^{-1}\mathbf{Q}^{-1}$ [Exercise 11 of § 4.2], $\mathbf{RP}$ and $\mathbf{QS}$ are invertible and so $\mathbf{A} \sim \mathbf{C}$.

(b) It turns out that two matrices are equivalent provided one can be converted into the other via the elementary row and column operations that are encountered in solving systems of equations. In particular, all invertible $n \times n$ matrices are equivalent to each other. ◻

EXAMPLE 6   Consider the set $\mathcal{P}(S)$ of all subsets of some set S. For $A, B \in \mathcal{P}(S)$, we define $A \sim B$ if their symmetric difference $A \oplus B$ is a finite set. Then $\sim$ is an equivalence relation on $\mathcal{P}(S)$, as we now verify.

(R) Since $A \oplus A = \varnothing$ and $\varnothing$ is finite, we have $A \sim A$ for all $A \in \mathcal{P}(S)$.

(S) Symmetry is clear because $A \oplus B = B \oplus A$.

(T) Suppose $A \sim B$ and $B \sim C$ so that $A \oplus B$ and $B \oplus C$ are finite sets. We need to show that $A \sim C$, i.e., that $A \oplus C$ is finite. This is relatively easy *if* one remembers Exercise 8 of § 1.2; part (b) of that exercise asserts that $A \oplus B \subseteq (A \oplus C) \cup (B \oplus C)$. Interchanging B and C and using commutativity, we find

$$A \oplus C \subseteq (A \oplus B) \cup (B \oplus C).$$

Since the right-hand side is a finite set, $A \oplus C$ is also a finite set, and so $A \sim C$. ◻

EXAMPLE 7   (a) Let $\S$ be a set of compound propositions. Recall that $P \Leftrightarrow Q$ signifies that P and Q are logically equivalent, i.e., that P and Q have the same truth table columns. The relation $\Leftrightarrow$ on $\S$ is an equivalence relation:

(R) $P \Leftrightarrow P$ for all $P \in \S$;

(S) if $P \Leftrightarrow Q$, then $Q \Leftrightarrow P$;

(T) if $P \Leftrightarrow Q$ and $Q \Leftrightarrow R$, then $P \Leftrightarrow R$.

For instance, (T) is true because if P and Q have the same truth table columns and if Q and R do, too, then so do P and R.

(b) By the way, when we state a theorem in the form "The following are [logically] equivalent," we really have in mind the equivalence relation in part (a), where the compound propositions are probably propositions in the predicate calculus. The assertion means that for each choice of variables, all the propositions are true or else all the propositions are false. Thanks to the transitivity of $\Rightarrow$, if the propositions are named $P_1, P_2, \ldots, P_n$, it suffices to prove $P_1 \Rightarrow P_2 \Rightarrow \cdots \Rightarrow P_n \Rightarrow P_1$. See the lemma below for a typical illustration of this. ◻

Consider again an equivalence relation $\sim$ on a set S. For each $s \in S$ we define

$$[s] = \{t \in S : s \sim t\};$$

$[s]$ is called the **equivalence class** containing s. For us, "class" and "set" are synonymous, so that $[s]$ could have been called an "equivalence set," but it never is. The set of all equivalence classes of S is denoted by $[S]$, i.e., $[S] = \{[s] : s \in S\}$. We will sometimes attach subscripts to $[s]$ or $[S]$ to clarify exactly which of several possible equivalence relations is being used.

EXAMPLE 8   (a) In the marble setting of Example 1(a) the equivalence class $[s]$ of a given marble s is the set of all marbles that are the same color as s; this includes s itself. The equivalence classes are {blue marbles}, {red marbles}, {green marbles}, etc.

   (b) Consider the equivalence relation in Example 3 on the set V of vertices of a graph. Two vertices are equivalent precisely if they belong to the same connected part of the graph. For example, the equivalence classes for the graph in Figure 2 are $\{v_1, v_6, v_8\}$, $\{v_2, v_4, v_{10}\}$ and $\{v_3, v_5, v_7, v_9, v_{11}, v_{12}\}$. If a graph is connected, then the only equivalence class is the set V itself.   □

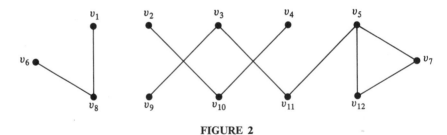

FIGURE 2

EXAMPLE 9   Let p be an integer ≥ 2. Recall from §4.3 that for $m, n \in \mathbb{Z}$ we defined $m \equiv n \pmod{p}$ provided $m - n$ is divisible by p. This definition gives an equivalence relation on $\mathbb{Z}$, called **congruence modulo** p, as we noted in Theorem 2(a) of §4.3.

   For the equivalence relation congruence modulo p we denote the equivalence class containing m by $[m]_p$. That is,

$$[m]_p = \{n \in \mathbb{Z} : m \equiv n \pmod{p}\}.$$

For $p = 5$, we have

$$[0]_5 = \{\ldots, -20, -15, -10, -5, 0, 5, 10, 15, 20, \ldots\},$$
$$[1]_5 = \{\ldots, -19, -14, -9, -4, 1, 6, 11, 16, 21, \ldots\},$$
$$[2]_5 = \{\ldots, -18, -13, -8, -3, 2, 7, 12, 17, 22, \ldots\},$$
$$[3]_5 = \{\ldots, -17, -12, -7, -2, 3, 8, 13, 18, 23, \ldots\},$$
$$[4]_5 = \{\ldots, -16, -11, -6, -1, 4, 9, 14, 19, 24, \ldots\}.$$

Moreover, every equivalence class $[m]_5$ is one of these five sets. For example, $[18]_5 = [3]_5$ and $[-73]_5 = [2]_5$. More generally, we have

$$[\mathbb{Z}]_p = \{[r]_p : r = 0, 1, 2, \ldots, p - 1\}$$

in view of Theorem 1 of § 4.3, since $[m]_p = [r]_p$ if and only if $m \equiv r \pmod{p}$.

□

In Examples 8 and 9 the equivalence classes form a partition of the underlying set. This reflects a general property of equivalence relations, which we give in Theorem 1. First we prove a lemma.

Lemma   Let $\sim$ be an equivalence relation on a set S. For s and t in S the following assertions are logically equivalent:

(i) $s \sim t$;
(ii) $[s] = [t]$;
(iii) $[s] \cap [t] \neq \varnothing$.

Proof. By "logically equivalent" we mean here, as in Example 7(b), that all three assertions are true or else all are false. We prove (i) $\Rightarrow$ (ii), (ii) $\Rightarrow$ (iii) and (iii) $\Rightarrow$ (i).

(i) $\Rightarrow$ (ii). Suppose $s \sim t$ and consider $s' \in [s]$. Then $s \sim s'$. By symmetry $t \sim s$. Since $t \sim s$ and $s \sim s'$, transitivity shows $t \sim s'$. Thus $s' \in [t]$. We've shown that every s' in $[s]$ belongs to $[t]$, and hence $[s] \subseteq [t]$. Similarly $[t] \subseteq [s]$.

(ii) $\Rightarrow$ (iii) is obvious.

(iii) $\Rightarrow$ (i). Select u in $[s] \cap [t]$. Then $s \sim u$ and $t \sim u$. By symmetry $u \sim t$. Since $s \sim u$ and $u \sim t$, we have $s \sim t$ by transitivity.   □

Theorem 1   (a) If $\sim$ is an equivalence relation on a nonempty set S, then $[S]$ is a partition of S.

(b) Conversely, if $\{A_i : i \in I\}$ is a partition of S, then the sets A_i are the equivalence classes corresponding to some equivalence relation on S.

Proof. (a) To show that $[S]$ partitions S, we need to show

(1) $\bigcup_{s \in S} [s] = S$;

(2)   for $s, t \in S$ either $[s] = [t]$ or $[s] \cap [t] = \varnothing$.

Clearly $[s] \subseteq S$ for each s in S, so that $\bigcup_{s \in S} [s] \subseteq S$. Given s_0 in S, we have $s_0 \sim s_0$ and so $s_0 \in [s_0]$; hence $S \subseteq \bigcup_{s \in S} [s]$. Therefore (1) holds.

Assertion (2) is logically equivalent to

(3) $[s] \cap [t] \neq \varnothing$ implies $[s] = [t]$

and this was proved in the lemma.

(b) Given a partition $\{A_i : i \in I\}$ of S, we define the relation $\sim$ on S by $s \sim t$ if s and t belong to the same set A_i. Properties (R), (S) and (T) are obvious, and so $\sim$ is an equivalence relation on S. Given a nonempty set A_i we have $A_i = [s]$ for all $s \in A_i$, and so the partition consists precisely of all equivalence classes $[s]$. $\square$

EXAMPLE 10   Let $\mathcal{S}$ be a family of sets, and for $S, T \in \mathcal{S}$ define $S \sim T$ if there exists a one-to-one function mapping S onto T. The relation $\sim$ is an equivalence relation on $\mathcal{S}$. Indeed:

(R) $S \sim S$ because the identity function $1_S \colon S \to S$ is a one-to-one mapping of S onto S.

(S) If $S \sim T$, then there is a one-to-one mapping f of S onto T. Its inverse f^{-1} is a one-to-one mapping of T onto S and so $T \sim S$.

(T) If $S \sim T$ and $T \sim U$, then there are one-to-one correspondences $f \colon S \to T$ and $g \colon T \to U$. It is easy to check that $g \circ f$ is a one-to-one correspondence of S onto U. This also follows from Exercise 9 of § 3.2 in conjunction with the theorem of that section. In any event, we conclude that $S \sim U$.

Observe that if S is finite, then $[S]$ consists of all sets in $\mathcal{S}$ that are the same size as S. If S is countably infinite, then $[S]$ consists of all countably infinite sets in $\mathcal{S}$. If S is uncountable, then $[S]$ will consist of some of the uncountable sets in $\mathcal{S}$ but probably not all of them, because not all uncountable sets are equivalent to each other. This last assertion is not obvious and is not justified in this book. $\square$

Sometimes an equivalence relation is defined in terms of a function on the underlying space. In a sense, which we will make precise in Theorem 2, every equivalence relation arises in this way.

EXAMPLE 11   (a) Consider $\mathbb{N} \times \mathbb{N}$ and define $\langle m, n \rangle \sim \langle j, k \rangle$ provided $m^2 + n^2 = j^2 + k^2$. It is easy to show directly that $\sim$ is an equivalence relation on $\mathbb{N} \times \mathbb{N}$. We take a slightly different approach. We define $f \colon \mathbb{N} \times \mathbb{N} \to \mathbb{N}$ by the rule

$$f(\langle m, n \rangle) = m^2 + n^2.$$

Then ordered pairs are equivalent exactly when they have equal images under f. The equivalence classes are simply the nonempty sets $f^{-1}(r)$, where $r \in \mathbb{N}$. Some of the sets $f^{-1}(r)$, like $f^{-1}(3)$, are empty, but this does no harm.

(b) Let Σ be an alphabet and let's regard two languages A and B in $\mathcal{P}(\Sigma^*)$ as equivalent if their Kleene closures A^* and B^* are equal. In symbols, $A \sim B$ if $A^* = B^*$. Again it is easy to check directly that $\sim$ is an equivalence relation. One way to see this is to consider the function ϕ where $\phi(A) = A^*$. The domain of ϕ is $\mathcal{P}(\Sigma^*)$ and its image is the set of all submonoids of Σ^*. Then $A \sim B$ if and only if $\phi(A) = \phi(B)$. The equivalence classes are the sets

$$\phi^{-1}(M) = \{A \in \mathcal{P}(\Sigma^*) \colon A^* = M\}$$

for submonoids M of Σ^*. $\square$

Theorem 2   (a) Let S be a nonempty set. Let f be a function with domain S, and define $s_1 \sim s_2$ if $f(s_1) = f(s_2)$. Then $\sim$ is an equivalence relation on S, and the equivalence classes are the nonempty sets $f^{-1}(t)$, where t is in the codomain T of S.

(b) Every equivalence relation $\sim$ on a set S is determined by a suitable function with domain S as in part (a).

Proof. We check that $\sim$ is an equivalence relation.

(R) $f(s) = f(s)$, so $s \sim s$ for all $s \in S$.

(S) If $f(s_1) = f(s_2)$, then $f(s_2) = f(s_1)$, so $s_1 \sim s_2$ implies $s_2 \sim s_1$.

(T) If $f(s_1) = f(s_2)$ and $f(s_2) = f(s_3)$, then $f(s_1) = f(s_3)$, and so $\sim$ is transitive.

The statement about equivalence classes is just the definition of $f^{-1}(t)$.

To prove (b), we define $\phi(s) = [s]$ for $s \in S$. The function ϕ maps S onto the set $[S]$ of equivalence classes and is called the **natural mapping** of S onto $[S]$. By the lemma before Theorem 1 we have $\phi(s) = \phi(t)$ if and only if $s \sim t$, and so $\sim$ is the equivalence relation determined by ϕ. Note that we have $\phi^{-1}([s]) = [s]$ for all $s \in S$. ☐

Normally we use notation like $\sim$ or $\equiv$ only when we have an equivalence relation. Of course the use of such notation does not automatically guarantee that we have an equivalence relation.

EXAMPLE 12   (a) Let $(P, \leq)$ be a finite poset and consider its Hasse diagram. Define $x \sim y$ if $x = y$ or if x and y are connected by a single line segment. The relation $\sim$ is certainly reflexive and symmetric. But it is probably not transitive: $x \sim y$ and $y \sim z$ need not imply $x \sim z$. The element y might be connected to both x and z by single line segments, and yet x and z might not be connected to each other. See Figure 4 of § 7.1. In the left-hand figure, $a \sim b$ and $b \sim f$ but $a \not\sim f$.

(b) For $m, n \in \mathbb{Z}$, define $m \sim n$ in case $m - n$ is odd. The relation is symmetric but is highly nonreflexive and nontransitive. In fact,

$$m \not\sim m \quad \text{for all} \quad m \in \mathbb{Z}$$

and

$$m \sim n \quad \text{and} \quad n \sim p \quad \text{always imply} \quad m \not\sim p.$$

(c) Consider the set $S = \text{FUN}([0, 1], \mathbb{R})$ of all functions mapping $[0, 1]$ into $\mathbb{R}$. Define $f \sim g$ provided $|f(x) - g(x)| < 1$ for all $x \in [0, 1]$. Then $\sim$ is reflexive and symmetric on S, but it fails to be transitive. For example, if $f(x) = 0$, $g(x) = x/2$ and $h(x) = x$ for $x \in [0, 1]$, then $f \sim g$ and $g \sim h$ but $f \not\sim h$. ☐

One of the most common sources of error in dealing with equivalence classes is attempting to define a function or relation on $[S]$ in terms of the members of the equivalence classes.

EXAMPLE 13   (a) Every member of $[\mathbb{Z}]_6$ is an equivalence class of the form $[m]_6$, with m in $\mathbb{Z}$, so let's define a function from $[\mathbb{Z}]_6$ to $\mathbb{Z}$ by the rule

$$f([m]_6) = m^2.$$

For example, $f([2]_6) = 2^2 = 4$. Of course $[2]_6 = [8]_6$ in $[\mathbb{Z}]_6$, so $f([2]_6) = f([8]_6) = 8^2 = 64 \neq 4$. Oops! We have a problem. Our intended function is *not well-defined*; that is, the definition given is ambiguous.

Where did we go wrong? The trouble is that $[2]_6$ contains many integers, including 2 and 8. We tried to base our definition of $f([2]_6)$ on the member of $[2]_6$ we chose, but different choices gave different answers.

(b) Now let's try to define a function g from $[\mathbb{Z}]_6$ to $[\mathbb{Z}]_{12}$ by letting $g([n]_6) = [n^2]_{12}$. This time we can do it. For suppose that $[n]_6 = [m]_6$. Then $n - m$ is a multiple of 6, say $n = m + 6k$; hence

$$n^2 = (m + 6k)^2 = m^2 + 12mk + 36k^2 \equiv m^2 \text{ (mod 12)}$$

and $[n^2]_{12} = [m^2]_{12}$. In this case we get the same answer regardless of the choice of representative of the equivalence class, so g is well-defined.   □

In the last illustrations we attempted to define a function value on an equivalence class in terms of the individual members of the class. We ran into trouble if different individuals in a class could give different results. To check that a function, relation or operation is well-defined on a set $[S]$ one must verify that using different members of a class does not change the proposed definition. Exercises 19 and 20 contain further illustrations.

EXAMPLE 14   Let $\mathbb{Q}$ be the set of rational numbers. Each number in $\mathbb{Q}$ has the form m/n with $m, n \in \mathbb{Z}$ and $n \neq 0$. Can we define a function f on $\mathbb{Q}$ by the rule $f(m/n) = m + n$? Since $\frac{2}{3} = \frac{4}{6}$ we would want $f(\frac{2}{3}) = 2 + 3 = 5$ and also $f(\frac{2}{3}) = f(\frac{4}{6}) = 10$. Trouble again, but where is the equivalence relation that causes it? The problem is that we can use different symbols m/n [such as $\frac{2}{3}$ and $\frac{4}{6}$] for the same number in $\mathbb{Q}$.

Let S be the set of all symbols m/n with $m, n \in \mathbb{Z}$ and $n \neq 0$. We define the relation $\approx$ on S by

$$m/n \approx p/q \quad \text{if} \quad mq = np.$$

One can check that $\approx$ is an equivalence relation, and that two symbols m/n and p/q are equivalent if and only if the numerical ratios of m to n and p to q are the same. [Check that $\frac{2}{3} \approx \frac{4}{6}$.] The equivalence classes in S are thus in one-to-one correspondence with the members of $\mathbb{Q}$, and we can [and probably should] think of $\mathbb{Q}$ as the set of equivalence classes. In our fancy notation, we'd write $[\frac{2}{3}] = [\frac{4}{6}]$ rather than $\frac{2}{3} = \frac{4}{6}$.

Now a function on $\mathbb{Q}$ will be well-defined provided the definition does not depend on which form the rationals take, i.e., provided it does not depend on which member of the equivalence class is used. Since $\frac{2}{3} \approx \frac{4}{6}$ and yet $2 + 3 \neq 4 + 6$, our definition $f(m/n) = m + n$ was not well-defined.   □

EXERCISES 7.3

1. Which of the following describe equivalence relations? For those which are not equivalence relations, specify which of (R), (S) and (T) fail, and illustrate the failures with examples.
   (a) $L_1 \parallel L_2$ for straight lines in the plane if L_1 and L_2 are the same or are parallel.
   (b) $L_1 \perp L_2$ for straight lines in the plane if L_1 and L_2 are perpendicular.
   (c) $p_1 \sim p_2$ for Americans if p_1 and p_2 live in the same state.
   (d) $p_1 \approx p_2$ for Americans if p_1 and p_2 live in the same state or in neighboring states.
   (e) $p_1 \approx p_2$ for people if p_1 and p_2 have a parent in common.
   (f) $p_1 \cong p_2$ for people if p_1 and p_2 have the same mother.

2. (a) List all equivalence classes of $\mathbb{Z}$ for the equivalence relation congruence modulo 4.
   (b) How many different equivalence classes of $\mathbb{Z}$ are there with respect to congruence modulo 73?

3. Let S be a set. Is equality $=$ an equivalence relation?

4. Matrices $\mathbf{A}$ and $\mathbf{B}$ in $\mathfrak{M}_{n,n}$ are **similar** if $\mathbf{B} = \mathbf{PAP}^{-1}$ for an invertible matrix $\mathbf{P}$, in which case we write $\mathbf{A} \approx \mathbf{B}$.
   (a) Prove that $\approx$ is an equivalence relation on $\mathfrak{M}_{n,n}$.
   (b) Show that if $\mathbf{A} \approx \mathbf{B}$, then $\det(\mathbf{A}) = \det(\mathbf{B})$.

5. Let $\mathcal{SEQ}$ be the set of all sequences (s_n) of real numbers and define $(s_n) \approx (t_n)$ if $\{n \in \mathbb{N} : s_n \neq t_n\}$ is finite. Show that $\approx$ is an equivalence relation on $\mathcal{SEQ}$.

6. Can you think of situations in the real world where you'd use the term "equivalent" and where a natural equivalence relation is involved?

7. Let S be a set and let G be a group of one-to-one functions f mapping S onto S. That is, G satisfies
   (i) the identity function 1_S is in G;
   (ii) if $f, g \in G$ then $f \circ g \in G$;
   (iii) if $f \in G$ then $f^{-1} \in G$.
   For $x, y \in S$ define $x \sim y$ if $f(x) = y$ for some $f \in G$. Show that $\sim$ is an equivalence relation on S.
   Note. Each of the equivalence relations for triangles in Example 2 is of this sort if G is selected suitably.

8. Verify the claims in Example 12(b).

9. Define the relation $\approx$ on $\mathbb{Z}$ by $m \approx n$ in case $m^2 = n^2$.
   (a) Show that $\approx$ is an equivalence relation on $\mathbb{Z}$.
   (b) Describe the equivalence classes for $\approx$. How many are there?

10. For m, n in $\mathbb{N}$ define $m \sim n$ if $m^2 - n^2$ is a multiple of 3.
    (a) Show that $\sim$ is an equivalence relation on $\mathbb{N}$.
    (b) List four elements in the equivalence class [0].
    (c) List four elements in the equivalence class [1].
    (d) Do you think there are any more equivalence classes?

11. Consider the equivalence relation $\sim$ on $\mathcal{P}(S)$ discussed in Example 6.
    (a) Describe the sets in the equivalence class containing the empty set $\varnothing$.
    (b) Describe the sets in the equivalence class containing S.

12. On the set $\mathbb{N} \times \mathbb{N}$ define $\langle m, n \rangle \sim \langle k, l \rangle$ if $m + l = n + k$.
   (a) Show that $\sim$ is an equivalence relation on $\mathbb{N} \times \mathbb{N}$.
   (b) Show that the set of equivalence classes is exactly the partition of $\mathbb{N} \times \mathbb{N}$ in Figure 4 of § 3.2.

13. The definition of $m \equiv n \pmod{p}$ makes sense even if $p = 1$ or $p = 0$.
   (a) Describe this equivalence relation for $p = 1$ and the corresponding equivalence classes in $\mathbb{Z}$.
   (b) Repeat part (a) for $p = 0$.

14. Let P be a set of computer programs and regard programs p_1 and p_2 as equivalent if they always produce the same outputs for given inputs. Is this an equivalence relation? Explain.

15. Let Σ be an alphabet, and for w_1 and w_2 in Σ^* define $w_1 \sim w_2$ if length(w_1) = length(w_2). Explain why $\sim$ is an equivalence relation, and describe the equivalence classes.

16. Consider $\mathbb{P} \times \mathbb{P}$ and define $\langle m, n \rangle \sim \langle p, q \rangle$ if $mq = np$.
   (a) Show that $\sim$ is an equivalence relation on $\mathbb{P} \times \mathbb{P}$.
   (b) Show that $\sim$ is the equivalence relation corresponding to the function $\mathbb{P} \times \mathbb{P} \to \mathbb{Q}$ given by $f(\langle m, n \rangle) = m/n$; see Theorem 2(a).

17. How many equivalence relations are there on $\{0, 1, 2, 3\}$? *Hint:* Count unordered partitions. Why does this solve the problem?

18. In the proof of Theorem 2(b), we obtained the equality $\phi^{-1}([s]) = [s]$. Does this mean that ϕ^{-1} is the identity function on $[S]$? Discuss.

19. As in Exercise 9, define $\approx$ on $\mathbb{Z}$ by $m \approx n$ in case $m^2 = n^2$.
   (a) What is wrong with the following "definition" of $\leqq$ on $[\mathbb{Z}]$? Let $[m] \leqq [n]$ if and only if $m \leqq n$.
   (b) What, if anything, is wrong with the following "definition" of a function $f : [\mathbb{Z}] \to \mathbb{Z}$? Let $f([m]) = m^2 + m + 1$.
   (c) Repeat part (b) with $g([m]) = m^4 + m^2 + 1$.
   (d) What, if anything, is wrong with the following "definition" of the operation $\oplus$ on $[\mathbb{Z}]$? Let $[m] \oplus [n] = [m + n]$.

20. Which of the following are well-defined definitions of functions on $\mathbb{Q}^+ = \{m/n : m, n \in \mathbb{P}\}$?
   (a) $f(m/n) = n/m$ (b) $g(m/n) = m^2 + n^2$
   (c) $h(m/n) = \dfrac{m^2 + n^2}{mn}$

§ 7.4   *General Relations*

When we introduced partial orders $\leqq$ and equivalence relations $\sim$ on a set S we indicated that for each pair $\langle x, y \rangle$ in $S \times S$ either the relation [$x \leqq y$ or $x \sim y$] held or it did not. Also we shrewdly left the term "relation" undefined. Knowing or specifying for which pairs a relationship holds on S is exactly the same as knowing or specifying a subset of $S \times S$. So we now formally define a **binary relation on S** as any subset R of $S \times S$.

By now we hope you have developed a feeling for partial orders and equivalence relations. They are quite different; partial orders sort of "flow" from small to large, while equivalence relations partition the set into unrelated blocks [called equivalence classes]. On the other hand, the notion of binary relation is so general and abstract that there really isn't anything to get a feeling for beyond the obvious fact that binary relations are subsets of $S \times S$. We study such general objects to help us see the common features of the more familiar orderings, equivalence relations and also functions. Viewing binary relations as subsets of $S \times S$ will make them easier to create and manipulate. Finally, machines can store useful information by storing ordered pairs, i.e., members of some relation. Manipulating information, then, corresponds to manipulating relations.

For a binary relation R on S we will often use the notation $x R y$ [read "x is R-related to y"] to signify $\langle x, y \rangle \in R$. In addition, $x \not R y$ means $\langle x, y \rangle \notin R$. This usage is compatible with our special notation $x \leq y$ and $x \sim y$. We now define, once and for all, what we mean by a relation R being **reflexive**, **antireflexive**, **symmetric**, **antisymmetric** or **transitive**:

(R) $x R x$ for all $x \in S$,
(AR) $x \not R x$ for all $x \in S$,
(S) $x R y$ implies $y R x$ for all $x, y \in S$,
(AS) $x R y$ and $y R x$ imply $x = y$,
(T) $x R y$ and $y R z$ imply $x R z$.

Each of these definitions can be written using ordered-pair notation. For example,

(S) $\langle x, y \rangle \in R$ implies $\langle y, x \rangle \in R$ for all $\langle x, y \rangle \in S \times S$.

From our present point of view, a **partial order on** S is a relation [i.e., subset of $S \times S$] satisfying (R), (AS) and (T). A **quasi-order on** S is a relation satisfying (AR) and (T) [so (AS) is vacuously true]. And an **equivalence relation on** S is a relation satisfying (R), (S) and (T).

It is often convenient to consider the **matrix A** of a relation R, when the set S is finite. The rows and columns of **A** are indexed by S, with entries $A[x, y] = 1$ if $x R y$ and $A[x, y] = 0$ if $x \not R y$.

EXAMPLE 1   We illustrate several relations on $S = \{1, 2, 3, 4\}$, whose matrices are given in Figure 1.

$$
\begin{array}{c|cccc}
 & 1 & 2 & 3 & 4 \\
\hline
1 & 0 & 1 & 1 & 1 \\
2 & 0 & 0 & 1 & 1 \\
3 & 0 & 0 & 0 & 1 \\
4 & 0 & 0 & 0 & 0
\end{array}
\qquad
\begin{bmatrix}
1 & 1 & 0 & 0 \\
1 & 1 & 1 & 0 \\
0 & 1 & 1 & 1 \\
0 & 0 & 1 & 1
\end{bmatrix}
\qquad
\begin{bmatrix}
1 & 0 & 0 & 1 \\
0 & 1 & 0 & 0 \\
0 & 0 & 1 & 0 \\
1 & 0 & 0 & 1
\end{bmatrix}
\qquad
\begin{bmatrix}
1 & 0 & 0 & 0 \\
0 & 1 & 0 & 0 \\
0 & 0 & 1 & 0 \\
0 & 0 & 0 & 1
\end{bmatrix}
$$

$\qquad\qquad R_1 \qquad\qquad\qquad\qquad R_2 \qquad\qquad\qquad\qquad R_3 \qquad\qquad\qquad\qquad E$

Matrices of relations

FIGURE 1

(a) Let R_1 be the relation defined by $m < n$. That is, $m\, R_1\, n$ if and only if $m < n$, and $R_1 = \{\langle m, n\rangle \in S \times S : m < n\}$. The relation R_1 is anti-reflexive and transitive, i.e., a quasi-order as expected. The relation R_1 is also antisymmetric vacuously:

$$m < n \quad \text{and} \quad n < m \quad \text{imply} \quad n = m$$

because the condition "$m < n$ and $n < m$" is always false. Indeed, the same argument shows that all quasi-orders are antisymmetric.

(b) Let R_2 be the relation defined by $m\, R_2\, n$ if $|m - n| \leq 1$. This relation is reflexive since $|m - m| \leq 1$ for $m \in S$, and it is symmetric since $|m - n| \leq 1$ implies $|n - m| \leq 1$. It is not transitive since, for instance, $2\, R_2\, 3$ and $3\, R_2\, 4$ but $2\, \not{R}_2\, 4$.

(c) Define R_3 by $m \equiv n$ (mod 3), so that $m\, R_3\, n$ if and only if $m \equiv n$ (mod 3). This relation is reflexive, symmetric and transitive [Theorem 2 of § 4.3] and so R_3 is an equivalence relation on S.

(d) Let E be the "equality relation" on S:

$$E = \{\langle m, n\rangle \in S \times S : m = n\} = \{\langle m, m\rangle : m \in S\}.$$

In other words, $m\, E\, n$ if and only if $m = n$. It is clear that E is an equivalence relation on S. Note that the matrix for the relation E is the 4×4 identity matrix. ☐

EXAMPLE 2   For $m, n \in \mathbb{Z}$, define $m\, R\, n$ if $m + n$ is a multiple of 3, i.e., $m + n \equiv 0$ (mod 3). This relation is not reflexive since $1\, \not{R}\, 1$ for example. It isn't anti-reflexive either since $3\, R\, 3$ for example. The relation R is symmetric since $m + n = n + m$ for $m, n \in \mathbb{Z}$. The relation R is not transitive; for instance $4\, R\, 2$ and $2\, R\, 1$ while $4\, \not{R}\, 1$. ☐

EXAMPLE 3   Consider a graph with no parallel edges or multiple loops. We define a relation R on the set V of vertices by $u\, R\, v$ whenever $\{u, v\}$ is an edge of the graph. The graph determines R, of course, and R also determines the graph since the graph has no parallel edges or multiple loops. More precisely, for every pair $\langle u, v\rangle$ of vertices, exactly one edge connects u to v if $u\, R\, v$, and no edges connect u to v otherwise. The matrix for the graph, as discussed in § 0.3, is exactly the matrix for the relation R.

Note that the relation R is symmetric. It will be reflexive if and only if there is a loop at every vertex. It need not be transitive, generally speaking, since $\{u, v\}$ and $\{v, w\}$ may be edges while $\{u, w\}$ is not. Every symmetric relation is the relation for some graph as described in the last paragraph. In Figure 2 we have drawn the graphs for the symmetric relations whose matrices are in Figure 1. When we study directed graphs in Chapter 8 we will see that every relation, symmetric or not, corresponds to some directed graph. ☐

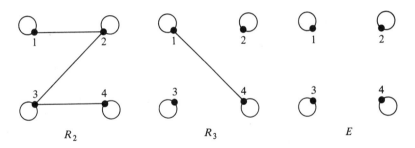

Graphs of symmetric relations

FIGURE 2

For any set S we will write E for the "equality relation": $E = \{\langle x, x \rangle : x \in S\}$. The next example includes some set-theoretic characterizations of properties (R) and (AR). Set-theoretic characterizations of (S), (AS) and (T) will be given later in this section and in the next section.

EXAMPLE 4 Let R be a binary relation on a set S.

(a) R is reflexive if and only if $E \subseteq R$. This is evident, since R is reflexive precisely in case

$$\langle x, x \rangle \in R \quad \text{for all} \quad x \in S,$$

i.e., in case every ordered pair in E belongs to R.

(b) R is antireflexive if and only if $E \cap R = \varnothing$. In fact, R is antireflexive provided

$$\langle x, x \rangle \notin R \quad \text{for all} \quad x \in S,$$

i.e., provided no ordered pair in E belongs to R.

(c) In § 7.1, prior to Example 3, we indicated how to get quasi-orders from partial orders and vice versa. In short, we observed that if R is a partial order then $R \backslash E$ is a quasi-order, and if R is a quasi-order then $R \cup E$ is a partial order. Exercise 15 contains a slightly more general result. ☐

We have introduced binary relations on a set; it is only the tiniest generalization to define them from one set to another. A **binary relation from a set S to a set T** is a subset of $S \times T$. Matrices for these relations are constructed just as before. The only difference is that the matrices won't be square matrices unless $|S| = |T|$.

EXAMPLE 5 Let $S = \{1, 2, 3, 4, 5\}$ and $T = \{a, b, c\}$, and let

$$R = \{\langle 1, a \rangle, \langle 2, a \rangle, \langle 2, c \rangle, \langle 3, a \rangle, \langle 3, b \rangle, \langle 4, a \rangle, \langle 4, b \rangle, \langle 4, c \rangle, \langle 5, b \rangle\}.$$

The matrix for R is given in Figure 3. ☐

$$
\begin{array}{c}
\quad a \quad b \quad c \\
\begin{array}{c}
1 \\
2 \\
3 \\
4 \\
5
\end{array}
\left[
\begin{array}{ccc}
1 & 0 & 0 \\
1 & 0 & 1 \\
1 & 1 & 0 \\
1 & 1 & 1 \\
0 & 1 & 0
\end{array}
\right]
\end{array}
$$

FIGURE 3

EXAMPLE 6 A mail-order record company has a list L of customers. Each customer indicates interest in certain categories of recordings: classical, easy-listening, Latin, religious, popular, rock, etc. Let C be the set of possible categories. The set of all ordered pairs $\langle$name, selected-category$\rangle$ is a relation R from L to C. This relation might contain such pairs as $\langle$K. A. Ross, classical$\rangle$, $\langle$C. R. B. Wright, classical$\rangle$ and $\langle$C. R. B. Wright, punk rock$\rangle$. ☐

EXAMPLE 7 A university would be interested in the relation given by all ordered pairs whose first entries are students and whose second entries are the courses the students are currently enrolled in. This is a relation R_1 from the set S of university students to the set C of courses offered. Note that if student s in S is fixed, then $\{c \in C : \langle s, c \rangle \in R_1\}$ is the set of courses taken by s. On the other hand, if course c in C is fixed, then $\{s \in S : \langle s, c \rangle \in R_1\}$ is the class list for the course.

Another relation R_2 consists of all ordered pairs whose first entries are courses and whose second entries are the departments for which the course is a major requirement. Thus R_2 is a relation from C to the set D of departments in the university. For fixed $c \in C, \{d \in D : \langle c, d \rangle \in R_2\}$ is the set of departments for which c is a major requirement. For fixed $d \in D, \{c \in C : \langle c, d \rangle \in R_2\}$ is the list of courses required for that department's majors. A computerized degree-checking program would need to use a data structure which contained enough information to determine the relations R_1 and R_2. ☐

EXAMPLE 8 (a) Consider a set P of programs written to be carried out on a computer and a catalog C of canned programs available for use. We get a relation from C to P if we say that a canned program c is related to a program p in P provided p calls c as a subroutine. A frequently used c might be related to a number of p's while a c which is never called is related to no p.

(b) A translator from decimal representations to binary representations can be viewed as the relation consisting of all ordered pairs whose first entries are allowable decimal representations and whose second entries are the corresponding binary representations. Actually this relation is a function. ☐

Recall that in § 3.1 we indicated how functions can be identified with their graphs and hence regarded as sets of ordered pairs. In fact, if $f: S \to T$ we identified f with the set

$$R_f = \{\langle x, y \rangle \in S \times T : y = f(x)\},$$

which is a relation from S to T. Of course, not all relations are functions. From this point of view a **function from S to T** is a relation R from S to T such that

for each $x \in S$ there is exactly one $y \in T$ such that $\langle x, y \rangle \in R$.

This is simply a restatement of the definition in § 3.1.

Consider again an arbitrary relation R from a set S to a set T, i.e., $R \subseteq S \times T$. The **inverse relation** R^{-1} is the relation from T to S defined by:

$$R^{-1} = \{\langle y, x \rangle \in T \times S : \langle x, y \rangle \in R\}.$$

Since every function $f: S \to T$ is a relation, f^{-1} always exists:

as a relation $f^{-1} = \{\langle y, x \rangle \in T \times S : y = f(x)\}.$

This relation is a function precisely when f is an invertible function as defined in § 3.2.

EXAMPLE 9   (a) Recall that if $f: S \to T$ is a function and $A \subseteq S$, then the image of A under f is

$$f(A) = \{f(x): x \in A\} = \{y \in T: y = f(x) \quad \text{for some} \quad x \in A\}.$$

If we view f as the relation R_f, then this set equals

$$\{y \in T: \langle x, y \rangle \in R_f \quad \text{for some} \quad x \in A\}.$$

Similarly, for any relation R from S to T we can define

$$R(A) = \{y \in T: \langle x, y \rangle \in R \quad \text{for some} \quad x \in A\}.$$

Since R^{-1} is a relation from T to S, for $B \subseteq T$ we also have

$$R^{-1}(B) = \{x \in S: \langle y, x \rangle \in R^{-1} \quad \text{for some} \quad y \in B\}$$
$$= \{x \in S: \langle x, y \rangle \in R \quad \text{for some} \quad y \in B\}.$$

If R is actually R_f for a function f from S to T this gives

$$R_f^{-1}(B) = \{x \in S: y = f(x) \quad \text{for some} \quad y \in B\} = \{x \in S: f(x) \in B\},$$

which is exactly the definition we gave for $f^{-1}(B)$ in § 3.2.

(b) For a concrete example of part (a), let S be a set of suppliers and T a set of products, and define $x \mathrel{R} y$ if supplier x sells product y. For a given set A of suppliers, the set $R(A)$ is the set of products sold by at least one member of A. For a given set B of products, $R^{-1}(B)$ is the set of suppliers who sell at least one product in B. The relation R is R_f for a function f from S to T if and only if each supplier sells exactly one product. □

Now consider a binary relation R on a single set S, i.e., $R \subseteq S \times S$. Then

$$R^{-1} = \{\langle y, x \rangle \in S \times S : \langle x, y \rangle \in R\}.$$

This definition of inverse is compatible with the definition of the inverse $\geq$ of a partial order $\leq$ given in § 7.1, since $y \geq x$ if and only if $x \leq y$. We did not introduce the inverse of an equivalence relation in § 7.3 because we would get nothing new. For in general, $R = R^{-1}$ if and only if R is symmetric; in Exercise 19 you are asked to show this and to show that R is antisymmetric if and only if $R \cap R^{-1} \subseteq E$.

EXERCISES 7.4

1. Give matrices for the following relations on $S = \{0, 1, 2, 3\}$ and specify which of the properties (R), (AR), (S), (AS) and (T) the relations satisfy.
   (a) $m\, R_1\, n$ if $m + n = 3$
   (b) $m\, R_2\, n$ if $m \equiv n \pmod 2$
   (c) $m\, R_3\, n$ if $m \leq n$
   (d) $m\, R_4\, n$ if $m + n \leq 4$
   (e) $m\, R_5\, n$ if $\max\{m, n\} = 3$

2. Draw graphs for the symmetric relations in Exercise 1.

3. (a) Which of the relations in Exercise 1 are partial orders?
   (b) Which of the relations in Exercise 1 are equivalence relations?

4. Let $A = \{0, 1, 2\}$. Each of the statements below defines a relation R on A by $m\, R\, n$ if the statement is true for m and n. Write each of the relations as a set of ordered pairs.
   (a) $m \leq n$ (b) $m < n$ (c) $m = n$
   (d) $mn = 0$ (e) $mn = m$ (f) $m + n \in A$
   (g) $m^2 + n^2 = 2$ (h) $m^2 + n^2 = 3$ (i) $m = \max\{n, 1\}$

5. Which of the relations in Exercise 4 are reflexive? symmetric?

6. Give a matrix for each of the relations in Exercise 4.

7. The following binary relations are defined on $\mathbb{N}$.
   (a) Write the binary relation R_1 defined by $m + n = 5$ as a set of ordered pairs.
   (b) Do the same for R_2 defined by $\max\{m, n\} = 2$.
   (c) The binary relation R_3 defined by $\min\{m, n\} = 2$ consists of infinitely many ordered pairs. List five of them.

8. For each of the relations in Exercise 7, specify which of the properties (R), (AR), (S), (AS) and (T) it satisfies.

9. Which of the following relations on $\mathbb{Z}$ are equivalence relations? For the equivalence relations, identify the equivalence classes. For the other relations, specify which of (R), (S) and (T) fail.
   (a) $n \equiv m \pmod 4$ (b) $nm = 0$
   (c) $nm > 0$ (d) $n \leq m$

10. Consider the relation R on $\mathbb{Z}$ defined by $m\, R\, n$ if and only if $m^3 - n^3 \equiv 0 \pmod 5$.

(a) Which of the properties (R), (AR), (S), (AS) and (T) are satisfied by R?

(b) Is R an equivalence relation? a partial order?

11. Let $\Sigma = \{a, b\}$ and define the binary relation $\leqq$ on $\mathcal{P}(\Sigma^*)$ by $A \leqq B$ if and only if $A^* \subseteq B^*$.

   (a) Which of the properties (R), (AR), (S), (AS) and (T) does the relation $\leqq$ satisfy? Verify your answers.

   (b) Is $\leqq$ a partial order? a quasi-order?

12. Let $\Sigma = \{a, b, c, d, e, f, g\}$. Give a matrix for the equivalence relation on Σ determined by the partition $\{\{a, d\}, \{c, e, f\}, \{b, g\}\}$.

13. (a) Consider the **empty relation** $\varnothing$ on a nonempty set S. Which of the properties (R), (AR), (S), (AS) and (T) does $\varnothing$ possess?

   (b) Repeat part (a) for the **universal relation** $U = S \times S$ on S.

14. Give an example of a relation that is:

   (a) antisymmetric and transitive but not reflexive,

   (b) symmetric but not reflexive or transitive.

15. Let R be an antisymmetric and transitive relation on a set S.

   (a) Prove that $R \cup E$ is a partial order on S.

   (b) Prove that $R \backslash E$ is a quasi-order on S.

16. Let R_1 and R_2 be binary relations on a set S.

   (a) Show that $R_1 \cap R_2$ is reflexive if R_1 and R_2 are.

   (b) Show that $R_1 \cap R_2$ is symmetric if R_1 and R_2 are.

   (c) Show that $R_1 \cap R_2$ is transitive if R_1 and R_2 are.

   (d) Observe that the intersection of equivalence relations is an equivalence relation.

17. Let R_1 and R_2 be binary relations on a set S.

   (a) Must $R_1 \cup R_2$ be reflexive if R_1 and R_2 are?

   (b) Must $R_1 \cup R_2$ be symmetric if R_1 and R_2 are?

   (c) Must $R_1 \cup R_2$ be transitive if R_1 and R_2 are?

   (d) Must $R_1 \cup R_2$ be an equivalence relation if R_1 and R_2 are?

18. If $\mathbf{A}$ is the matrix for a relation R from a set S to a set T, what is the matrix for the inverse relation R^{-1}?

19. Let R be a binary relation on a set S.

   (a) Prove that R is symmetric if and only if $R = R^{-1}$.

   (b) Prove that R is antisymmetric if and only if $R \cap R^{-1} \subseteq E$, where $E = \{\langle x, x \rangle : x \in S\}$.

20. Let R_1 and R_2 be binary relations from a set S to a set T.

   (a) Show that $(R_1 \cup R_2)^{-1} = R_1^{-1} \cup R_2^{-1}$.

   (b) Show that $(R_1 \cap R_2)^{-1} = R_1^{-1} \cap R_2^{-1}$.

   (c) Show that if $R_1 \subseteq R_2$ then $R_1^{-1} \subseteq R_2^{-1}$.

§ 7.5   *Composition of Relations*

In this section we generalize the familiar concept of composition of functions to relations. To help motivate this, we first consider functions $f: S \to T$ and $g: T \to U$, and recall that the composite function $g \circ f$ maps S into U and is defined by $g \circ f(x) = g(f(x))$ for all $x \in S$. As in § 7.4 we write R_f for the relation corresponding to f:

$$R_f = \{\langle x, y \rangle \in S \times T : y = f(x)\}.$$

Likewise R_g and $R_{g \circ f}$ represent the relations given by g and $g \circ f$. In particular,

$$R_{g \circ f} = \{\langle x, z \rangle \in S \times U : z = g(f(x))\}.$$

Now $z = g(f(x))$ means that $z = g(y)$ where $y = f(x)$, and so $\langle x, z \rangle$ belongs to $R_{g \circ f}$ if and only if there is some $y \in T$ such that $\langle y, z \rangle \in R_g$ and $\langle x, y \rangle \in R_f$. That is,

$$R_{g \circ f} = \{\langle x, z \rangle \in S \times U : \text{for some } y \in T, \quad \langle x, y \rangle \in R_f$$
$$\text{and} \quad \langle y, z \rangle \in R_g\}.$$

If we call this set $R_g \circ R_f$, then we can immediately generalize as follows. For a relation R_1 from S to T and a relation R_2 from T to U, we define $R_2 \circ R_1$ from S to U by

$$R_2 \circ R_1 = \{\langle x, z \rangle \in S \times U : \text{for some } y \in T, \quad \langle x, y \rangle \in R_1$$
$$\text{and} \quad \langle y, z \rangle \in R_2\}.$$

The relation $R_2 \circ R_1$ is called the **composite** of R_2 and R_1. Since we think of R_1 first and R_2 second, on esthetic grounds alone this general definition seems backwards. Moreover, it will turn out to be backwards when we observe the connection between composition of relations and products of their matrices. Accordingly, many people write "$R_1 \circ R_2$" in place of $R_2 \circ R_1$; since functions are relations, this usage is inconsistent and a source of confusion. To avoid this confusion, we will write $R_1 R_2$, rather than "$R_1 \circ R_2$," for $R_2 \circ R_1$. We summarize:

Definition   Given relations R_1 from S to T and R_2 from T to U, the **composite relation**

$$\{\langle x, z \rangle \in S \times U : \text{for some } y \in T, \quad \langle x, y \rangle \in R_1 \quad \text{and} \quad \langle y, z \rangle \in R_2\}$$

will be denoted by either $R_1 R_2$ or $R_2 \circ R_1$. Thus $x\, R_1 R_2\, z$ precisely if there exists $y \in T$ such that $x\, R_1\, y$ and $y\, R_2\, z$.

EXAMPLE 1   Read Example 7 of § 7.4, which concerns university students and courses, again. The relations are

$$R_1 = \{\langle s, c \rangle \in S \times C : s \text{ is enrolled in } c\}$$

and

$$R_2 = \{\langle c, d \rangle \in C \times D : c \text{ is required by } d\}.$$

Observe that

$$R_1 R_2 = \{\langle s, d \rangle \in S \times D : \text{for some } c \in C, \quad \langle s, c \rangle \in R_1$$
$$\text{and} \quad \langle c, d \rangle \in R_2\}.$$

Therefore $\langle s, d \rangle$ belongs to $R_1 R_2$ provided student s is taking some course that is required by department d.

Note that $R_2 R_1$ makes no sense, because the second entries of R_2 lie in the set D while the first entries of R_1 lie in S; it could not happen that $\langle c, t \rangle \in R_2$ and $\langle t, c' \rangle \in R_1$. Of course, $R_2 \circ R_1$ makes sense; this is just another name for $R_1 R_2$. $\square$

EXAMPLE 2 To illustrate working with general relations, we establish some elementary facts. Consider relations R_1 and R_2 from S to T and relations R_3 and R_4 from T to U.

(a) If $R_1 \subseteq R_2$ and $R_3 \subseteq R_4$, then $R_1 R_3 \subseteq R_2 R_4$. To see this, consider $\langle x, z \rangle \in R_1 R_3$. Then for some $y \in T$ we have $\langle x, y \rangle \in R_1$ and $\langle y, z \rangle \in R_3$. Since $R_1 \subseteq R_2$ and $R_3 \subseteq R_4$ we also have $\langle x, y \rangle \in R_2$ and $\langle y, z \rangle \in R_4$. So $\langle x, z \rangle \in R_2 R_4$. This shows that $R_1 R_3 \subseteq R_2 R_4$.

(b) We show

$$(R_1 \cup R_2)R_3 = R_1 R_3 \cup R_2 R_3.$$

Since $R_1 \subseteq R_1 \cup R_2$ we have $R_1 R_3 \subseteq (R_1 \cup R_2)R_3$ from part (a); likewise $R_2 R_3 \subseteq (R_1 \cup R_2)R_3$ and so

$$R_1 R_3 \cup R_2 R_3 \subseteq (R_1 \cup R_2)R_3.$$

To check the reverse inclusion, consider $\langle x, z \rangle \in (R_1 \cup R_2)R_3$. For some $y \in T$ we have $\langle x, y \rangle \in R_1 \cup R_2$ and $\langle y, z \rangle \in R_3$. Then either $\langle x, y \rangle \in R_1$ so that $\langle x, z \rangle \in R_1 R_3$ or else $\langle x, y \rangle \in R_2$ so that $\langle x, z \rangle \in R_2 R_3$. Either way, $\langle x, z \rangle \in R_1 R_3 \cup R_2 R_3$ and hence

$$(R_1 \cup R_2)R_3 \subseteq R_1 R_3 \cup R_2 R_3. \quad \square$$

In § 3.1 we observed that composition of functions is associative. So is composition of relations.

Associative Law for Relations If R_1 is a relation from S to T, R_2 is a relation from T to U and R_3 is a relation from U to V, then

$$(R_1 R_2)R_3 = R_1(R_2 R_3).$$

Proof. We show that an ordered pair $\langle x, v \rangle$ in $S \times V$ belongs to $(R_1 R_2)R_3$ if and only if

(1) there exist $y \in T$ and $z \in U$ so that

$$\langle x, y \rangle \in R_1, \ \langle y, z \rangle \in R_2 \text{ and } \langle z, v \rangle \in R_3.$$

A similar argument shows that $\langle x, v \rangle$ belongs to $R_1(R_2 R_3)$ if and only if (1) holds.

Consider $\langle x, v \rangle$ in $(R_1 R_2)R_3$. Since $R_1 R_2$ is a relation from S to U, this means that there exists $z \in U$ such that $\langle x, z \rangle \in R_1 R_2$ and $\langle z, v \rangle \in R_3$. Since $\langle x, z \rangle \in R_1 R_2$ there exists $y \in T$ such that $\langle x, y \rangle \in R_1$ and $\langle y, z \rangle \in R_2$. Thus (1) holds.

Now suppose that (1) holds for an element $\langle x, v \rangle$ in $S \times V$. Then $\langle x, y \rangle$

$\in R_1$ and $\langle y, z\rangle \in R_2$ so that $\langle x, z\rangle \in R_1R_2$. Since also $\langle z, v\rangle \in R_3$, we conclude that $\langle x, v\rangle \in (R_1R_2)R_3$. $\square$

In view of the associative law, we may write $R_1R_2R_3$ for either $(R_1R_2)R_3$ or $R_1(R_2R_3)$. As shown in the proof, $\langle x, v\rangle$ belongs to $R_1R_2R_3$ provided there exist $y \in T$ and $z \in U$ such that $\langle x, y\rangle \in R_1$, $\langle y, z\rangle \in R_2$ and $\langle z, v\rangle \in R_3$.

The sets and relations we have been considering could have been finite or infinite. We now consider relations R_1 from S to T and R_2 from T to U where S, T and U are finite. Let $\mathbf{A}_1$ and $\mathbf{A}_2$ be the matrices for the relations R_1 and R_2. What is the matrix for the composite relation R_1R_2?

EXAMPLE 3 Let $S = \{1, 2, 3, 4, 5\}$, $T = \{a, b, c\}$ and $U = \{e, f, g, h\}$. Consider the relations

$$R_1 = \{\langle 1, a\rangle, \langle 2, a\rangle, \langle 2, c\rangle, \langle 3, a\rangle, \langle 3, b\rangle, \langle 4, a\rangle, \langle 4, b\rangle, \langle 4, c\rangle, \langle 5, b\rangle\},$$

$$R_2 = \{\langle a, e\rangle, \langle a, g\rangle, \langle b, f\rangle, \langle b, g\rangle, \langle b, h\rangle, \langle c, e\rangle, \langle c, g\rangle, \langle c, h\rangle\},$$

so that

$$R_1R_2 = \{\langle 1, e\rangle, \langle 1, g\rangle, \langle 2, e\rangle, \langle 2, g\rangle, \langle 2, h\rangle, \langle 3, e\rangle, \langle 3, f\rangle, \langle 3, g\rangle, \langle 3, h\rangle, \langle 4, e\rangle, \langle 4, f\rangle, \langle 4, g\rangle, \langle 4, h\rangle, \langle 5, f\rangle, \langle 5, g\rangle, \langle 5, h\rangle\}.$$

$\mathbf{A}_1$

	a	b	c
1	1	0	0
2	1	0	1
3	1	1	0
4	1	1	1
5	0	1	0

$\mathbf{A}_2$

	e	f	g	h
a	1	0	1	0
b	0	1	1	1
c	1	0	1	1

$\mathbf{A}$

	e	f	g	h
1	1	0	1	0
2	1	0	1	1
3	1	1	1	1
4	1	1	1	1
5	0	1	1	1

$\mathbf{A}_1\mathbf{A}_2$

	e	f	g	h
1	1	0	1	0
2	2	0	2	1
3	1	1	2	1
4	2	1	3	2
5	0	1	1	1

FIGURE 1

The matrices $\mathbf{A}_1$, $\mathbf{A}_2$ and $\mathbf{A}$ for these relations are given in Figure 1. Compare the matrix $\mathbf{A}$ with the product $\mathbf{A}_1\mathbf{A}_2$. The 1's in the matrix $\mathbf{A}$ occur where the nonzero entries occur in $\mathbf{A}_1\mathbf{A}_2$. This is not an accident, as we now explain. Consider $x \in \{1, 2, 3, 4, 5\}$ and $z \in \{e, f, g, h\}$. The (x, z)-entry of $\mathbf{A}_1\mathbf{A}_2$ is

$$\sum_{y \in \{a,b,c\}} \mathbf{A}_1[x, y]\mathbf{A}_2[y, z].$$

The sum is positive if any product term is positive. A product $\mathbf{A}_1[x, y]\mathbf{A}_2[y, z]$ is 0 unless both $\mathbf{A}_1[x, y]$ and $\mathbf{A}_2[y, z]$ are 1, in which case we have $\langle x, y\rangle \in R_1$ and $\langle y, z\rangle \in R_2$. Thus the sum is 0 if $\langle x, z\rangle \notin R_1R_2$, and is greater than 0 if $\langle x, z\rangle \in R_1R_2$. More precisely, the sum is exactly the number

$$|\{y \in \{a, b, c\} : \langle x, y\rangle \in R_1 \quad \text{and} \quad \langle y, z\rangle \in R_2\}|.$$

For example, the $(2, e)$-entry is 2 because

$$\{y \in \{a, b, c\} : \langle 2, y \rangle \in R_1 \quad \text{and} \quad \langle y, e \rangle \in R_2\} = \{a, c\}.$$

The $(2, f)$-entry is 0 because

$$\{y \in \{a, b, c\} : \langle 2, y \rangle \in R_1 \quad \text{and} \quad \langle y, f \rangle \in R_2\} = \varnothing,$$

i.e., $\langle 2, f \rangle \notin R_1 R_2$. □

As Example 3 shows, the matrix for the relation $R_1 R_2$ need not be the product $\mathbf{A}_1 \mathbf{A}_2$ of the matrices for R_1 and R_2, but there is a connection: both have 0's in the same places. We could define a new product for matrices, letting $\mathbf{A}_1 * \mathbf{A}_2$ be the matrix obtained from $\mathbf{A}_1 \mathbf{A}_2$, by replacing each nonzero entry with 1. An equivalent and superior approach involves the use of slightly different operations on the entries which are in $\mathbb{Z}(2) = \{0, 1\}$. We use the **Boolean operations** $\vee$ and $\wedge$ on $\mathbb{Z}(2)$ defined by Table 1. These are the

TABLE 1

$\vee$	0	1
0	0	1
1	1	1

$\wedge$	0	1
0	0	0
1	0	1

familiar logical operations "or" and "and" on the set $\{0, 1\}$ of truth values. Note that for $m, n \in \mathbb{Z}(2)$ we have $m \vee n = \max\{m, n\}$ and $m \wedge n = \min\{m, n\}$. Consider **Boolean matrices** $\mathbf{A}_1$ and $\mathbf{A}_2$, i.e., matrices all of whose entries are 0's and 1's. If $\mathbf{A}_1$ is $m \times n$ and $\mathbf{A}_2$ is $n \times p$, we define the **Boolean product** $\mathbf{A}_1 * \mathbf{A}_2$ to be the usual product, but with the addition and multiplication operations replaced by $\vee$ and $\wedge$. That is, $\mathbf{A}_1 * \mathbf{A}_2$ is the $m \times p$ matrix whose (i, k)-entry is

$$\mathbf{A}_1 * \mathbf{A}_2[i, k] =$$

$$(\mathbf{A}_1[i, 1] \wedge \mathbf{A}_2[1, k]) \vee (\mathbf{A}_1[i, 2] \wedge \mathbf{A}_2[2, k]) \vee \cdots \vee (\mathbf{A}_1[i, n] \wedge \mathbf{A}_2[n, k]);$$

this may be written as

$$\bigvee_{j=1}^{n} (\mathbf{A}_1[i, j] \wedge \mathbf{A}_2[j, k]).$$

EXAMPLE 4 The Boolean product $\mathbf{A}_1 * \mathbf{A}_2$ of the matrices in Figure 1 is the matrix $\mathbf{A}$ in Figure 1. For example, the $(3, g)$-entry of $\mathbf{A}_1 * \mathbf{A}_2$ is $(1 \wedge 1) \vee (1 \wedge 1) \vee (0 \wedge 1) = 1 \vee 1 \vee 0 = 1$. The $(5, e)$-entry is $(0 \wedge 1) \vee (1 \wedge 0) \vee (0 \wedge 1) = 0 \vee 0 \vee 0 = 0$. □

The discussion in Example 3 can be modified to prove the following result.

Theorem 1   Consider relations R_1 from S to T and R_2 from T to U where S, T and U are finite. If $\mathbf{A}_1$ and $\mathbf{A}_2$ are the matrices for the relations R_1 and R_2, then the Boolean product $\mathbf{A}_1 * \mathbf{A}_2$ is the matrix for the composite relation $R_1 R_2$.

The Boolean product operation $*$ on Boolean matrices is associative. This can be shown directly or by applying the associativity of the corresponding relations, as advised in Exercise 17.

For the remainder of this section, except for Example 10, we consider relations on a single set S, i.e., subsets of $S \times S$.

Theorem 2   For a set S, let $\mathcal{P}(S \times S)$ denote the set of all relations on S. Under the composition operation, $\mathcal{P}(S \times S)$ is a monoid.

Proof. First note that if R_1 and R_2 are in $\mathcal{P}(S \times S)$, so is their composite $R_1 R_2$. Associativity of composition has already been verified. Thus $\mathcal{P}(S \times S)$ is a semigroup. The identity for this semigroup is the "equality relation" E:

$$E = \{\langle x, x \rangle \in S \times S : x \in S\}. \quad \square$$

The usual notational conventions apply to this monoid. Thus if R is a relation on S, then $R^0 = E$ and, for $n \in \mathbb{P}$, R^n is the composition of R with itself n times. Note that if $n > 1$, then $\langle x, z \rangle$ belongs to R^n provided there exist $y_1, y_2, \ldots, y_{n-1}$ in S such that $\langle x, y_1 \rangle, \langle y_1, y_2 \rangle, \ldots, \langle y_{n-1}, z \rangle$ are all in R. In other words, $x \, R^n \, z$ if x and z are R-related through a chain of length n.

EXAMPLE 5   (a) Consider a graph with no parallel edges or multiple loops and the relation R on its set V of vertices satisfying $u \, R \, v$ whenever $\{u, v\}$ is an edge. An example is illustrated in Figure 2. We have $u \, R^n \, w$ provided there exist vertices $v_1, \ldots, v_{n-1}$ so that $u \, R \, v_1, v_1 \, R \, v_2, \ldots, v_{n-1} \, R \, w$, i.e., provided there is a path of length n connecting u and w. If $\mathbf{A}$ is the Boolean matrix for R, the Boolean power

$$\mathbf{A} * \mathbf{A} * \cdots * \mathbf{A} \quad [n \text{ times}]$$

is the Boolean matrix for R^n and tells us exactly which pairs of vertices are connected by paths of length n. If we also wanted the number of such paths, we would calculate the ordinary matrix power $\mathbf{A}^n$, as discussed in §0.3.

$$\begin{bmatrix} 0 & 1 & 1 & 1 \\ 1 & 0 & 0 & 0 \\ 1 & 0 & 1 & 1 \\ 1 & 0 & 1 & 1 \end{bmatrix}$$

$\mathbf{A}$ = matrix for R Graph for R

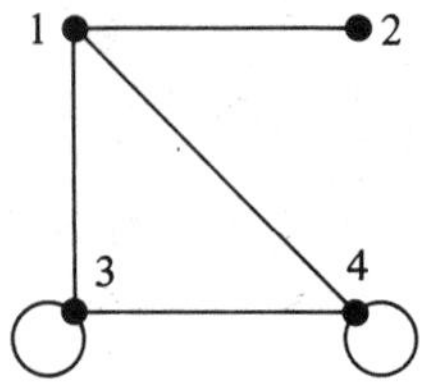

FIGURE 2

(b) If the relation R on $\{1, 2, 3, 4\}$ has the matrix and graph of Figure 2, then the relation R^2 has the matrix and graph of Figure 3. The (3, 4)-entry of **A∗A** tells us that there is at least one path in Figure 2 of length two from vertex 3 to vertex 4. That is why there is an edge from 3 to 4 in the graph of R^2. The (3, 4)-entry of $\mathbf{A}^2$ is 3 and so there are exactly 3 paths of length two in Figure 2 from vertex 3 to vertex 4. What are they? □

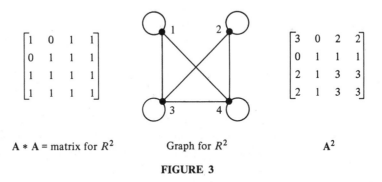

$$\mathbf{A} * \mathbf{A} = \text{matrix for } R^2 \qquad \text{Graph for } R^2 \qquad \mathbf{A}^2$$

FIGURE 3

EXAMPLE 6   Let R be the relation on $\{1, 2, 3\}$ with matrix

$$\mathbf{A} = \begin{bmatrix} 1 & 0 & 0 \\ 1 & 0 & 1 \\ 1 & 1 & 0 \end{bmatrix}.$$

The relation R^2 has matrix

$$\mathbf{A} * \mathbf{A} = \begin{bmatrix} 1 & 0 & 0 \\ 1 & 0 & 1 \\ 1 & 1 & 0 \end{bmatrix} * \begin{bmatrix} 1 & 0 & 0 \\ 1 & 0 & 1 \\ 1 & 1 & 0 \end{bmatrix} = \begin{bmatrix} 1 & 0 & 0 \\ 1 & 1 & 0 \\ 1 & 0 & 1 \end{bmatrix}.$$

The relation R^3 has matrix

$$\mathbf{A} * (\mathbf{A} * \mathbf{A}) = \begin{bmatrix} 1 & 0 & 0 \\ 1 & 0 & 1 \\ 1 & 1 & 0 \end{bmatrix} * \begin{bmatrix} 1 & 0 & 0 \\ 1 & 1 & 0 \\ 1 & 0 & 1 \end{bmatrix} = \begin{bmatrix} 1 & 0 & 0 \\ 1 & 0 & 1 \\ 1 & 1 & 0 \end{bmatrix}.$$

Note that $R = R^3$. In fact, we have $R^n = R^{n+2}$ for $n \geqq 1$, since

$$R^{n+2} = R^{(n-1)+3} = R^{n-1}R^3 = R^{n-1}R = R^n. \quad \square$$

It is sometimes helpful to visualize small relations R by representing the set by points and drawing an arrow from x to y whenever $\langle x, y \rangle \in R$. Figure 4 contains such a picture for the relations R and R^2 in Example 6. Note that R^2 is reflexive; there is an arrow from each point to itself. A relation is symmetric if for every arrow between points x and y there is also an arrow from y to x. Finally, note that R^2 can be drawn using the picture of R:

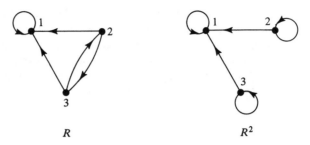

R   R²

FIGURE 4

draw an arrow from x to y if a chain of two arrows of R [one from x to some u and one from u to y] leads from x to y. Thus $1 \rightarrow 1$ in R^2 because $1 \rightarrow 1 \rightarrow 1$ in R, $2 \rightarrow 1$ in R^2 because $2 \rightarrow 1 \rightarrow 1$ in R [also $2 \rightarrow 3 \rightarrow 1$ in R], $2 \rightarrow 2$ in R^2 because $2 \rightarrow 3 \rightarrow 2$ in R, etc. Note also that $2 \rightarrow 3$ is not true in R^2, even though $2 \rightarrow 3$ in R, since there is no chain of length 2 in R from 2 to 3.

The monoid $\mathcal{P}(S \times S)$ is almost never commutative.

EXAMPLE 7   Let $S = \{1, 2\}$ and let R_1 and R_2 be the relations with matrices

$$\mathbf{A}_1 = \begin{bmatrix} 1 & 1 \\ 1 & 0 \end{bmatrix} \quad \text{and} \quad \mathbf{A}_2 = \begin{bmatrix} 1 & 1 \\ 0 & 1 \end{bmatrix}.$$

Then $R_1 R_2 \neq R_2 R_1$ since

$$\mathbf{A}_1 * \mathbf{A}_2 = \begin{bmatrix} 1 & 1 \\ 1 & 0 \end{bmatrix} * \begin{bmatrix} 1 & 1 \\ 0 & 1 \end{bmatrix} = \begin{bmatrix} 1 & 1 \\ 1 & 1 \end{bmatrix}$$

$$\neq \begin{bmatrix} 1 & 1 \\ 1 & 0 \end{bmatrix} = \begin{bmatrix} 1 & 1 \\ 0 & 1 \end{bmatrix} * \begin{bmatrix} 1 & 1 \\ 1 & 0 \end{bmatrix} = \mathbf{A}_2 * \mathbf{A}_1.$$

To be explicit, this nonequality shows that $\langle 2, 2 \rangle$ belongs to $R_1 R_2$ but not to $R_2 R_1$. □

The next theorem formalizes the fact that we can study finite relations by studying their matrices.

Theorem 3   Let S be a finite set with n elements. There is a one-to-one correspondence between the set $\mathcal{P}(S \times S)$ of relations on S and the set of $n \times n$ Boolean matrices. This correspondence preserves the semigroup operations: if R_1, R_2 and R are relations with Boolean matrices $\mathbf{A}_1$, $\mathbf{A}_2$ and $\mathbf{A}$, then

$$R_1 R_2 = R \quad \text{if and only if} \quad \mathbf{A}_1 * \mathbf{A}_2 = \mathbf{A}.$$

We have proved all of this theorem except the first assertion, which should be obvious upon a moment's reflection.

It should be evident from the definition that composition is somehow related to transitivity. The next theorem shows how simple the connection is.

Theorem 4   If R is a relation on a set S, then R is transitive if and only if $R^2 \subseteq R$.

Proof. Suppose first that R is transitive and consider $\langle x, z \rangle \in R^2$. By definition of R^2 there exists $y \in S$ such that $\langle x, y \rangle \in R$ and $\langle y, z \rangle \in R$. Since R is transitive, $\langle x, z \rangle$ is also in R. We've shown that every $\langle x, z \rangle$ in R^2 is in R, i.e., $R^2 \subseteq R$.

For the converse, suppose that $R^2 \subseteq R$. Consider $\langle x, y \rangle$ and $\langle y, z \rangle$ in R. Then $\langle x, z \rangle$ is in R^2 and hence in R. This proves that R is transitive.   ∎

For Boolean $m \times n$ matrices $\mathbf{A}_1$ and $\mathbf{A}_2$, let's write $\mathbf{A}_1 \leqq \mathbf{A}_2$ if every entry of $\mathbf{A}_1$ is less than or equal to the corresponding entry of $\mathbf{A}_2$, that is,

$$\mathbf{A}_1[i, j] \leqq \mathbf{A}_2[i, j] \quad \text{for} \quad 1 \leqq i \leqq m \quad \text{and} \quad 1 \leqq j \leqq n.$$

If R_1 and R_2 are relations from S to T, with matrices $\mathbf{A}_1$ and $\mathbf{A}_2$, then

$$R_1 \subseteq R_2 \quad \text{if and only if} \quad \mathbf{A}_1 \leqq \mathbf{A}_2;$$

think about where the 1's and 0's are in $\mathbf{A}_1$ and $\mathbf{A}_2$ [Exercise 16]. In particular, a relation R on a set S satisfies $R^2 \subseteq R$ if and only if its matrix satisfies $\mathbf{A}*\mathbf{A} \leqq \mathbf{A}$. So R is transitive if and only if $\mathbf{A}*\mathbf{A} \leqq \mathbf{A}$.

EXAMPLE 8   Consider the relation R on $\{1, 2, 3\}$ with matrix

$$\mathbf{A} = \begin{bmatrix} 1 & 0 & 0 \\ 1 & 0 & 0 \\ 1 & 1 & 0 \end{bmatrix}.$$

Since

$$\mathbf{A}*\mathbf{A} = \begin{bmatrix} 1 & 0 & 0 \\ 1 & 0 & 0 \\ 1 & 1 & 0 \end{bmatrix} * \begin{bmatrix} 1 & 0 & 0 \\ 1 & 0 & 0 \\ 1 & 1 & 0 \end{bmatrix} = \begin{bmatrix} 1 & 0 & 0 \\ 1 & 0 & 0 \\ 1 & 0 & 0 \end{bmatrix} \leqq \begin{bmatrix} 1 & 0 & 0 \\ 1 & 0 & 0 \\ 1 & 1 & 0 \end{bmatrix} = \mathbf{A},$$

R is transitive. The transitivity of R can also be seen from its picture in Figure 5. Whenever a chain of two arrows connects x to y, a single arrow also does. For example, $3 \rightarrow 2 \rightarrow 1$ and also $3 \rightarrow 1$. Similarly, $2 \rightarrow 1 \rightarrow 1$ and also $2 \rightarrow 1$.   ∎

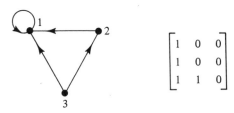

The relation R Its matrix $\mathbf{A}$

FIGURE 5

We next consider how inverses and compositions of relations interact. We begin with a

Warning. If R is a relation on a set S, then R^{-1} is also a relation on S. However, R^{-1} is not necessarily an inverse in the algebraic sense: RR^{-1} need not equal $R^{-1}R$ or E.

EXAMPLE 9   Let $S = \{1, 2\}$ and let R be the relation with matrix

$$\mathbf{A} = \begin{bmatrix} 1 & 1 \\ 0 & 0 \end{bmatrix}.$$

The matrix for R^{-1} is the transpose

$$\mathbf{A}^T = \begin{bmatrix} 1 & 0 \\ 1 & 0 \end{bmatrix}.$$

So the relations RR^{-1} and $R^{-1}R$ have matrices

$$\mathbf{A}*\mathbf{A}^T = \begin{bmatrix} 1 & 0 \\ 0 & 0 \end{bmatrix} \quad \text{and} \quad \mathbf{A}^T*\mathbf{A} = \begin{bmatrix} 1 & 1 \\ 1 & 1 \end{bmatrix}.$$

Thus $RR^{-1} \neq R^{-1}R$. Since E has matrix

$$\begin{bmatrix} 1 & 0 \\ 0 & 1 \end{bmatrix},$$

neither RR^{-1} nor $R^{-1}R$ equals E.   ☐

In spite of Example 9, the inverse relation satisfies some familiar properties.

EXAMPLE 10   Let R_1 be a relation from S to T and R_2 a relation from T to U. Then $(R_1R_2)^{-1}$ and $R_2^{-1}R_1^{-1}$ are relations from U to S. We show that they are equal:

$$(R_1R_2)^{-1} = R_2^{-1}R_1^{-1}.$$

Suppose that $\langle z, x \rangle \in (R_1R_2)^{-1}$. Then $\langle x, z \rangle \in R_1R_2$ and so there exists $y \in T$ such that $\langle x, y \rangle \in R_1$ and $\langle y, z \rangle \in R_2$. It follows that $\langle z, y \rangle \in R_2^{-1}$ and $\langle y, x \rangle \in R_1^{-1}$, and hence $\langle z, x \rangle \in R_2^{-1}R_1^{-1}$. Thus every $\langle z, x \rangle$ in $(R_1R_2)^{-1}$ is in $R_2^{-1}R_1^{-1}$, and so $(R_1R_2)^{-1} \subseteq R_2^{-1}R_1^{-1}$. The reverse inclusion is proved by reversing the steps of the proof above.   ☐

Throughout §§ 7.4 and 7.5 we have seen that Boolean matrices help us study finite relations. We will summarize the connections below. First we make two simple and sensible definitions. For Boolean $m \times n$ matrices $\mathbf{A}_1$ and $\mathbf{A}_2$ we define $\mathbf{A}_1 \vee \mathbf{A}_2$ by

$$(\mathbf{A}_1 \vee \mathbf{A}_2)[i, j] = \mathbf{A}_1[i, j] \vee \mathbf{A}_2[i, j] \quad \text{for} \quad 1 \leq i \leq m \quad \text{and} \quad 1 \leq j \leq n.$$

The matrix $\mathbf{A}_1 \wedge \mathbf{A}_2$ has a similar definition. For example, if

$$\mathbf{A}_1 = \begin{bmatrix} 1 & 0 & 1 & 1 \\ 0 & 1 & 1 & 0 \\ 1 & 1 & 0 & 1 \end{bmatrix} \text{ and } \mathbf{A}_2 = \begin{bmatrix} 1 & 1 & 1 & 0 \\ 0 & 1 & 1 & 1 \\ 1 & 0 & 1 & 0 \end{bmatrix},$$

then

$$\mathbf{A}_1 \vee \mathbf{A}_2 = \begin{bmatrix} 1 & 1 & 1 & 1 \\ 0 & 1 & 1 & 1 \\ 1 & 1 & 1 & 1 \end{bmatrix} \text{ and } \mathbf{A}_1 \wedge \mathbf{A}_2 = \begin{bmatrix} 1 & 0 & 1 & 0 \\ 0 & 1 & 1 & 0 \\ 1 & 0 & 0 & 0 \end{bmatrix}.$$

Summary. Let R be a relation on a finite set S with Boolean matrix $\mathbf{A}$. Then

(R)　R is reflexive if and only if all diagonal entries of $\mathbf{A}$ are 1;

(AR)　R is antireflexive if and only if all diagonal entries of $\mathbf{A}$ are 0;

(S)　R is symmetric if and only if $\mathbf{A} = \mathbf{A}^T$;

(AS)　R is antisymmetric if and only if $\mathbf{A} \wedge \mathbf{A}^T \leq \mathbf{I}$ where $\mathbf{I}$ is the identity matrix;

(T)　R is transitive if and only if $\mathbf{A} * \mathbf{A} \leqq \mathbf{A}$.

Let R_1 and R_2 be relations from a finite set S to a finite set T with Boolean matrices $\mathbf{A}_1$ and $\mathbf{A}_2$. Then

(a)　$R_1 \subseteq R_2$ if and only if $\mathbf{A}_1 \leqq \mathbf{A}_2$;

(b)　$R_1 \cup R_2$ has Boolean matrix $\mathbf{A}_1 \vee \mathbf{A}_2$;

(c)　$R_1 \cap R_2$ has Boolean matrix $\mathbf{A}_1 \wedge \mathbf{A}_2$.

Finally, composition of relations corresponds to the Boolean product of their matrices as explained in Theorems 1 and 3.

EXERCISES 7.5

1. For each of the following Boolean matrices, consider the corresponding relation R on $\{1, 2, 3\}$. Find the Boolean matrix for R^2 and determine whether R is transitive.

(a) $\begin{bmatrix} 1 & 1 & 0 \\ 0 & 1 & 1 \\ 1 & 0 & 1 \end{bmatrix}$ (b) $\begin{bmatrix} 1 & 0 & 1 \\ 0 & 1 & 0 \\ 1 & 0 & 1 \end{bmatrix}$ (c) $\begin{bmatrix} 0 & 0 & 1 \\ 0 & 1 & 0 \\ 1 & 0 & 0 \end{bmatrix}$

2. Draw pictures of the relations in Exercise 1.

3. Let $S = \{1, 2, 3\}$ and $T = \{a, b, c, d\}$. Let R_1 and R_2 be the relations from S to T with the Boolean matrices

$$\mathbf{A}_1 = \begin{bmatrix} 1 & 0 & 1 & 0 \\ 0 & 1 & 0 & 0 \\ 1 & 0 & 0 & 1 \end{bmatrix} \text{ and } \mathbf{A}_2 = \begin{bmatrix} 0 & 1 & 0 & 0 \\ 1 & 0 & 0 & 1 \\ 0 & 1 & 1 & 0 \end{bmatrix}.$$

(a) Find Boolean matrices for R_1^{-1} and R_2^{-1}.

(b) Find Boolean matrices for $(R_1 \cap R_2)R_1^{-1}$ and $R_1 R_1^{-1} \cap R_2 R_1^{-1}$.

(c) Find Boolean matrices for $R_2(R_1^{-1} \cup R_2^{-1})$ and $R_2 R_1^{-1} \cup R_2 R_2^{-1}$.

(d) Compare your answers to parts (b) and (c) with assertions in Exercise 11.

4. Let $S = \{1, 2, 3\}$ and $R = \{\langle 1, 1 \rangle, \langle 1, 2 \rangle, \langle 1, 3 \rangle, \langle 3, 2 \rangle\}$.

(a) Find the matrices for R, RR^{-1} and $R^{-1}R$.

(b) Draw pictures of the relations in part (a).

(c) Show that R is transitive, i.e., $R^2 \subseteq R$, but that $R^2 \neq R$.

(d) Is $R \cup R^{-1}$ transitive? Explain.

(e) Find R^n for all $n = 2, 3, \ldots$.

5. Let $S = \{1, 2, 3\}$ and $R = \{\langle 2, 1 \rangle, \langle 2, 3 \rangle, \langle 3, 2 \rangle\}$.

(a) Find the matrices for R, R^{-1} and R^2.

(b) Draw pictures of the relations in part (a).

(c) Is R transitive?

(d) Is R^2 transitive?

(e) Is $R \cup R^2$ transitive?

6. Let R be the relation on $\{1, 2, 3\}$ with Boolean matrix

$$\mathbf{A} = \begin{bmatrix} 0 & 1 & 0 \\ 1 & 1 & 1 \\ 0 & 1 & 0 \end{bmatrix}.$$

(a) Find the Boolean matrix for R^n for $n \in \mathbb{Z}$.

(b) Is R reflexive? symmetric? transitive?

7. Repeat Exercise 6 for

$$\mathbf{A} = \begin{bmatrix} 1 & 0 & 0 \\ 0 & 1 & 1 \\ 1 & 0 & 1 \end{bmatrix}.$$

8. Let P be the set of all people and consider the relation R where $p\,R\,q$ if p "likes" q.

(a) Describe in words the relations $R \cap R^{-1}$, $R \cup R^{-1}$ and R^2.

(b) Is R reflexive? symmetric? transitive? Discuss.

9. Consider the functions f and g from $\{1, 2, 3, 4\}$ to itself defined by $f(m) = \max\{2, 4 - m\}$ and $g(m) = 5 - m$.

(a) Find the Boolean matrices $\mathbf{A}_f$ and $\mathbf{A}_g$ for the relations R_f and R_g corresponding to f and g.

(b) Find the Boolean matrices for $R_f R_g$ and $R_{f \circ g}$ and compare.

(c) Find the Boolean matrices for R_f^{-1} and R_g^{-1}. Do these relations correspond to functions?

10. Let R be a relation on a finite set S and consider its picture. How do you modify the picture to get the picture of R^{-1}?

11. Consider relations R_1 and R_2 from S to T and relations R_3 and R_4 from T to U.

(a) Show that $R_1(R_3 \cup R_4) = R_1 R_3 \cup R_1 R_4$.

(b) Show that $(R_1 \cap R_2)R_3 \subseteq R_1 R_3 \cap R_2 R_3$ and that equality need not hold.

(c) How are the relations $R_1(R_3 \cap R_4)$ and $R_1 R_3 \cap R_1 R_4$ related?

12. Let R_1 and R_2 be relations on a set S. Prove or disprove:
    (a) If R_1 and R_2 are reflexive, so is $R_1 R_2$.
    (b) If R_1 and R_2 are symmetric, so is $R_1 R_2$.
    (c) If R_1 and R_2 are transitive, so is $R_1 R_2$.

13. Let R be the relation from $S = \{1, 2, 3, 4\}$ to $T = \{a, b, c\}$ with Boolean matrix

$$\mathbf{A} = \begin{bmatrix} 1 & 0 & 1 \\ 0 & 0 & 1 \\ 1 & 0 & 0 \\ 0 & 1 & 0 \end{bmatrix}.$$

    (a) Show that RR^{-1} is a symmetric relation on S.
    (b) Show that $R^{-1}R$ is a symmetric relation on T.
    (c) Are the relations RR^{-1} and $R^{-1}R$ equivalence relations?

14. Let R be a relation from a set S to a set T.
    (a) Prove that RR^{-1} is a symmetric relation on S. Don't use Boolean matrices, since S or T might be infinite.
    (b) Use part (a) to quickly infer that $R^{-1}R$ is a symmetric relation on T.
    (c) When will RR^{-1} be reflexive?

15. Verify Example 10 for the case that S, T and U are finite, using Boolean matrices.

16. Let R_1 and R_2 be relations from $S = \{1, 2, \ldots, m\}$ to $T = \{1, 2, \ldots, n\}$, with matrices $\mathbf{A}_1$ and $\mathbf{A}_2$. Show that $R_1 \subseteq R_2$ if and only if $\mathbf{A}_1 \leq \mathbf{A}_2$.

17. Use the associative law for relations to prove that the Boolean product is an associative operation.

18. Let S be a set. Is $\mathcal{P}(S \times S)$ a group with inverses R^{-1}? Explain.

§ 7.6 *Closures of Relations*

In this section we consider fairly abstract questions like the following. Let R be a relation on a set S, i.e., $R \subseteq S \times S$. What is the smallest transitive relation containing R? This is a loaded question, for how do we know there is such a relation? We will see in what follows that there is always a smallest transitive relation containing R, which we will denote by $t(R)$, and we will learn how to find it. There are also smallest relations containing R that are reflexive and symmetric; we'll denote them by $r(R)$ and $s(R)$. But there might not be a smallest antireflexive relation containing R.

Consider a property p that a relation on S might or might not satisfy. We will call the property **closable** if for each relation R on S there is a unique smallest relation, say $p(R)$, which contains R and has property p. In other words, for each R

(a) $R \subseteq p(R)$;
(b) $p(R)$ has property p;
(c) every relation containing R that has property p also contains $p(R)$.

As we remarked in the last paragraph, the properties r = reflexivity, s = symmetry and t = transitivity are closable. Before turning to a general treatment, let's look at an example.

EXAMPLE 1 Consider the relation R on $\{1, 2, 3, 4\}$ whose Boolean matrix is

$$\mathbf{A} = \begin{bmatrix} 0 & 0 & 1 & 1 \\ 0 & 1 & 0 & 0 \\ 0 & 0 & 1 & 0 \\ 1 & 0 & 0 & 0 \end{bmatrix}.$$

See Figure 1 for the picture of R.

(a) The relation R is not reflexive, since neither 1 nor 4 is related to itself. To obtain the reflexive relation $r(R)$, all we need to do is add the two ordered pairs $\langle 1, 1 \rangle$ and $\langle 4, 4 \rangle$. The Boolean matrix $\mathbf{r(A)}$ of $r(R)$ is simply the matrix $\mathbf{A}$ with all the diagonal entries equal to 1:

$$\mathbf{r(A)} = \begin{bmatrix} 1 & 0 & 1 & 1 \\ 0 & 1 & 0 & 0 \\ 0 & 0 & 1 & 0 \\ 1 & 0 & 0 & 1 \end{bmatrix}.$$

To get the picture for $r(R)$ in Figure 1, we simply added all the missing arrows from points to themselves.

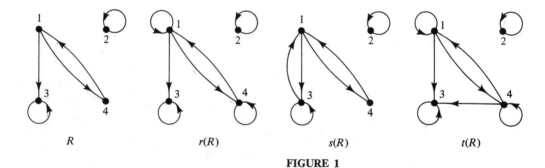

R   r(R)   s(R)   t(R)

FIGURE 1

(b) The relation R is not symmetric, since 1 R 3 but 3 $\not\!R$ 1. If we add the ordered pair $\langle 3, 1 \rangle$ to R we get the symmetric relation $s(R)$. Its Boolean matrix is

$$\mathbf{s(A)} = \begin{bmatrix} 0 & 0 & 1 & 1 \\ 0 & 1 & 0 & 0 \\ 1 & 0 & 1 & 0 \\ 1 & 0 & 0 & 0 \end{bmatrix}.$$

To get the picture of $s(R)$ from the picture of R, we simply add the missing reverses of all the arrows.

(c) The relation R isn't transitive either. For example, we have $4 \, R \, 1$ and $1 \, R \, 3$ but $4 \, \not R \, 3$. The scheme for finding $t(R)$ [or its Boolean matrix $\mathbf{t(A)}$] is not so simple as those for $r(R)$ and $s(R)$. Since $4 \, R \, 1$ and $1 \, R \, 3$, $t(R)$ will also contain $\langle 4, 1 \rangle$ and $\langle 1, 3 \rangle$. Since $t(R)$ must be transitive, $t(R)$ must contain $\langle 4, 3 \rangle$, so we must put $\langle 4, 3 \rangle$ in $t(R)$. In general, if there is a chain from x to y, i.e., if there are points $x_1, x_2, \ldots, x_{m-1}$ so that

$$ x \, R \, x_1, \, x_1 \, R \, x_2, \ldots, x_{m-1} \, R \, y, $$

then $\langle x, y \rangle$ must be in $t(R)$. If there is a chain from x to y and also one from y to z, then there is one from x to z. So the set of all pairs $\langle x, y \rangle$ connected by chains is a transitive relation and is the smallest transitive relation $t(R)$ containing R.

To get the picture of $t(R)$ in Figure 1 from the picture of R, we added an arrow connecting a point x to a point y whenever some sequence of arrows in R connected x to y and there wasn't an arrow from x to y already. For example, we added $4 \to 3$ because $4 \to 1 \to 3$ in R, and we added $1 \to 1$ because $1 \to 4 \to 1$ in R.

(d) The relation R is not antisymmetric, because $1 \, R \, 4$, $4 \, R \, 1$ and yet $1 \neq 4$. Any relation that contains R also contains $\langle 1, 4 \rangle$ and $\langle 4, 1 \rangle$, so it cannot possibly be antisymmetric. Thus surely there is no smallest antisymmetric relation containing R. This example shows that *antisymmetry is not a closable property*. □

The next proposition is nearly obvious. Think about why it's true before you read its proof.

Proposition If p is a closable property for relations, then

(a) $R = p(R)$ if and only if R has property p;
(b) $p(p(R)) = p(R)$.

Proof. (a) If $R = p(R)$ then R has property p, since $p(R)$ does. Conversely, if R has property p, then R is clearly the smallest such relation containing R, and so $R = p(R)$.

(b) Since $p(R)$ has property p, assertion (a) tells us that $p(R) = p(p(R))$. □

The function on $\mathcal{P}(S \times S)$ that maps R to $p(R)$ is called a **closure operator,** and we will call $p(R)$ the **p-closure** of R. Assertion (b) says that repeating the function gives nothing new; this was our loose definition of a closure operator in § 4.4.

The next theorem and its rather formal proof simply confirm that our intuitive discussions in Example 1 were valid.

Theorem 1   The properties r, s and t are closable. If R is a relation on a set S and if $E = \{\langle x, x \rangle : x \in S\}$, as usual, then

(r) $r(R) = R \cup E$;

(s) $s(R) = R \cup R^{-1}$;

(t) $t(R) = \bigcup\limits_{k=1}^{\infty} R^k$.

The sets $r(R), s(R)$ and $t(R)$ are called the **reflexive, symmetric** and **transitive closures** of R.

Proof. (r) As noted in Example 4 of § 7.4, a relation is reflexive if and only if it contains E. Hence $R \cup E$ is reflexive and every reflexive relation that contains R must contain $R \cup E$. So $R \cup E$ is the smallest reflexive relation containing R. This shows that r is a closable property and $r(R) = R \cup E$.

(s) Recall that a relation R_1 is symmetric if and only if $R_1^{-1} = R_1$ [Exercise 19 of § 7.4]. If $\langle x, y \rangle \in R \cup R^{-1}$, then $\langle y, x \rangle \in R^{-1} \cup R = R \cup R^{-1}$; thus $R \cup R^{-1}$ is symmetric. Consider any other symmetric relation R_1 that contains R. If $\langle x, y \rangle \in R^{-1}$ then $\langle y, x \rangle \in R \subseteq R_1$ and, since R_1 is symmetric, $\langle x, y \rangle \in R_1$. This shows that $R^{-1} \subseteq R_1$. Since $R \subseteq R_1$ we conclude that $R \cup R^{-1} \subseteq R_1$. This shows that $R \cup R^{-1}$ is the smallest symmetric relation containing R. Hence s is closable and $s(R) = R \cup R^{-1}$.

(t) First we show that the union $U = \bigcup\limits_{k=1}^{\infty} R^k$ is transitive. Consider x, y, z in S such that $\langle x, y \rangle \in U$ and $\langle y, z \rangle \in U$. Then we must have $\langle x, y \rangle \in R^k$ and $\langle y, z \rangle \in R^j$ for some k and j in $\mathbb{P}$. Then $\langle x, z \rangle$ belongs to $R^k R^j = R^{k+j}$, so that $\langle x, z \rangle \in U$. Thus U is a transitive relation containing R.

Now consider any transitive relation R_1 containing R. To show $U \subseteq R_1$, we prove $R^k \subseteq R_1$ by induction. This inclusion is obvious for $k = 1$. If the inclusion holds for k then

$$R^{k+1} = R^k R \subseteq R_1 R_1 \subseteq R_1;$$

the last inclusion is valid because R_1 is transitive [Theorem 4 of § 7.5]. The principle of induction shows that $R^k \subseteq R_1$ for all $k \in \mathbb{P}$, and so $U \subseteq R_1$. Thus U is the smallest transitive relation containing R, and

$$t(R) = U = \bigcup\limits_{k=1}^{\infty} R^k. \quad \square$$

EXAMPLE 2   (a) Suppose that R is a relation on a set S with n elements and that $\mathbf{A}$ is its Boolean matrix. In the next theorem we'll learn that

$$t(R) = \bigcup\limits_{k=1}^{n} R^k.$$

The results summarized in § 7.5 show that the Boolean matrices of $t(R)$, $s(R)$ and $r(R)$ are

$$\mathbf{t(A)} = \mathbf{A} \vee \mathbf{A^2} \vee \cdots \vee \mathbf{A}^n,$$

$$\mathbf{s(A)} = \mathbf{A} \vee \mathbf{A}^T$$

and

$$\mathbf{r(A)} = \mathbf{A} \vee \mathbf{I},$$

where $\mathbf{I}$ is the $n \times n$ identity matrix. Since $\mathbf{t(A)}$, $\mathbf{s(A)}$ and $\mathbf{r(A)}$ determine the relations $t(R)$, $s(R)$ and $r(R)$, these equations provide algorithms for determining transitive, symmetric and reflexive closures. In § 8.9 we will obtain more efficient algorithms for calculating transitive closures.

(b) For the relation R back in Example 1, it is easy to see that $\mathbf{s(A)} = \mathbf{A} \vee \mathbf{A}^T$ and $\mathbf{r(A)} = \mathbf{A} \vee \mathbf{I}$ where $\mathbf{I}$ is the 4×4 identity matrix. One can also verify that

$$\mathbf{t(A)} = \mathbf{A} \vee \mathbf{A}^2 \vee \mathbf{A}^3 \vee \mathbf{A}^4.$$

Of course, for such a simple relation it's easier to find $t(R)$ by using the picture of R. ▯

Theorem 2 If R is a relation on a set S with n elements, then

$$t(R) = \bigcup_{k=1}^{n} R^k.$$

Proof. For motivation we can think of the picture of R. The pair $\langle x, y \rangle$ is in $t(R)$ if and only if there is a path from x to y in the picture. If there is such a path, there's one which doesn't go through the same vertex twice. It can't involve more than n vertices, so it can't have length more than n.

Now let's write the argument using ordered pairs. Consider $\langle x, y \rangle$ in $t(R)$. If $\langle x, y \rangle \in R$ then clearly $\langle x, y \rangle$ is in $\bigcup_{k=1}^{n} R^k$. Otherwise, there is a chain $x_1, \ldots, x_{m-1}$, with $m \geq 2$, so that $x R x_1, x_1 R x_2, \ldots, x_{m-1} R y$. We can suppose that m is as small as possible for such a chain. Let $x_m = y$. If two of $x_1, \ldots, x_m$ are equal, say $x_i = x_j$ with $1 \leq i < j \leq m$, we can omit $x_i, \ldots, x_{j-1}$ and still get a chain from x to y, contrary to the minimal choice of m. Thus $x_1, \ldots, x_m$ are m different members of the n-element set S, so $m \leq n$. Thus $\langle x, y \rangle \in R^m \subseteq \bigcup_{k=1}^{n} R^k$. ▯

We may combine closure operators. For example, $sr(R)$ represents the symmetric closure of the reflexive closure of R.

EXAMPLE 3 For the relation R in Example 1 we obtained

$$\mathbf{r(A)} = \begin{bmatrix} 1 & 0 & 1 & 1 \\ 0 & 1 & 0 & 0 \\ 0 & 0 & 1 & 0 \\ 1 & 0 & 0 & 1 \end{bmatrix} \quad \text{and} \quad \mathbf{s(A)} = \begin{bmatrix} 0 & 0 & 1 & 1 \\ 0 & 1 & 0 & 0 \\ 1 & 0 & 1 & 0 \\ 1 & 0 & 0 & 0 \end{bmatrix}.$$

The Boolean matrix for $sr(R)$ is

$$\mathbf{sr(A)} = \begin{bmatrix} 1 & 0 & 1 & 1 \\ 0 & 1 & 0 & 0 \\ 1 & 0 & 1 & 0 \\ 1 & 0 & 0 & 1 \end{bmatrix}.$$

This is also the matrix $\mathbf{rs(A)}$ for $rs(R)$ and so $rs(R) = sr(R)$. This is not an accident [Exercise 11]. The transitive closure of $sr(R) = rs(R)$ turns out to have matrix

$$\mathbf{tsr(A)} = \mathbf{trs(A)} = \begin{bmatrix} 1 & 0 & 1 & 1 \\ 0 & 1 & 0 & 0 \\ 1 & 0 & 1 & 1 \\ 1 & 0 & 1 & 1 \end{bmatrix}.$$

This is the matrix of the equivalence relation on $\{1, 2, 3, 4\}$ whose equivalence classes are $\{2\}$ and $\{1, 3, 4\}$. Thus $tsr(R)$ is transitive, symmetric and reflexive. This is not obvious from the notation tsr, as you might think. It is conceivable, for example, that applying the t-closure to a symmetric relation might destroy its symmetry. Actually this does not happen, as we will explain in the lemma to Theorem 3, but applying the s-closure to a transitive relation can destroy its transitivity, as we show in the next example.   ☐

EXAMPLE 4   Let R be the relation on $\{1, 2, 3\}$ with Boolean matrix

$$\mathbf{A} = \begin{bmatrix} 1 & 1 & 1 \\ 0 & 0 & 0 \\ 0 & 0 & 1 \end{bmatrix}.$$

Since $\mathbf{A} * \mathbf{A} = \mathbf{A}$, R is transitive. The relation $s(R)$ has matrix

$$\mathbf{s(A)} = \begin{bmatrix} 1 & 1 & 1 \\ 1 & 0 & 0 \\ 1 & 0 & 1 \end{bmatrix}$$

and this relation is not transitive. For example, $\langle 2, 1 \rangle$ and $\langle 1, 3 \rangle$ are in $s(R)$ but $\langle 2, 3 \rangle$ is not.   ☐

In view of the next lemma, Example 4 illustrates the only way the closure operators r, s and t can destroy reflexivity, symmetry or transitivity; namely, the operator s can destroy transitivity.

Lemma   (a) If R is reflexive, so are $s(R)$ and $t(R)$.
(b) If R is symmetric, so are $r(R)$ and $t(R)$.
(c) If R is transitive, so is $r(R)$.

Proof. (a) This is obvious, because if $E \subseteq R$ then $E \subseteq s(R)$ and $E \subseteq t(R)$. Part (b) is left to Exercise 10.

(c) Suppose that R is transitive and consider $\langle x, y \rangle$ and $\langle y, z \rangle$ in $r(R)$ $= R \cup E$. If $\langle x, y \rangle \in E$ then $x = y$ and so $\langle x, z \rangle = \langle y, z \rangle$ is in $R \cup E$. If $\langle y, z \rangle \in E$ then $y = z$ and so $\langle x, z \rangle = \langle x, y \rangle$ is in $R \cup E$. If neither $\langle x, y \rangle$ nor $\langle y, z \rangle$ is in E, then they are both in R and so $\langle x, z \rangle \in R \subseteq R \cup E$ by the transitivity of R. Hence $\langle x, z \rangle \in R \cup E$ in all cases. $\square$

We next show that the property of being an equivalence relation is closable.

Theorem 3 For any relation R on a set S, $tsr(R)$ is the smallest equivalence relation containing R.

Proof. Since $r(R)$ is reflexive, two applications of (a) of the lemma show that $tsr(R)$ is reflexive. Since $sr(R)$ is automatically symmetric, one application of (b) of the lemma shows that $tsr(R)$ is symmetric. Finally, $tsr(R)$ is automatically transitive, and so $tsr(R)$ is an equivalence relation.

Consider any equivalence relation R_1 such that $R \subseteq R_1$. Then $r(R) \subseteq r(R_1) = R_1$, hence $sr(R) \subseteq s(R_1) = R_1$ and thus $tsr(R) \subseteq t(R_1) = R_1$. Therefore $tsr(R)$ is the smallest equivalence relation containing R. $\square$

EXAMPLE 5
(a) In Example 3, $tsr(R)$ was shown to be the equivalence relation with equivalence classes $\{2\}$ and $\{1, 3, 4\}$.

(b) Let R be the relation on $\{1, 2, 3\}$ in Example 4. Then

$$r(A) = \begin{bmatrix} 1 & 1 & 1 \\ 0 & 1 & 0 \\ 0 & 0 & 1 \end{bmatrix}, \qquad sr(A) = \begin{bmatrix} 1 & 1 & 1 \\ 1 & 1 & 0 \\ 1 & 0 & 1 \end{bmatrix}, \qquad tsr(A) = \begin{bmatrix} 1 & 1 & 1 \\ 1 & 1 & 1 \\ 1 & 1 & 1 \end{bmatrix}.$$

The smallest equivalence relation containing R is the universal relation $\{1, 2, 3\} \times \{1, 2, 3\}$. These computations can be double-checked by drawing pictures for the corresponding relations. $\square$

EXERCISES 7.6

1. Consider the relation R on $\{1, 2, 3\}$ with Boolean matrix $A = \begin{bmatrix} 0 & 1 & 0 \\ 0 & 0 & 0 \\ 0 & 0 & 1 \end{bmatrix}$.

   Find the Boolean matrices for
   (a) $r(R)$ (b) $s(R)$ (c) $rs(R)$
   (d) $sr(R)$ (e) $tsr(R)$

2. Repeat Exercise 1 with $A = \begin{bmatrix} 0 & 1 & 1 \\ 0 & 0 & 1 \\ 0 & 0 & 0 \end{bmatrix}$.

3. For Exercise 1, list the equivalence classes of $tsr(R)$.

4. For Exercise 2, list the equivalence classes of $tsr(R)$.

5. Repeat Exercise 1 for the relation R on $\{1, 2, 3, 4\}$ with Boolean matrix

$$\mathbf{A} = \begin{bmatrix} 0 & 1 & 0 & 1 \\ 1 & 0 & 1 & 0 \\ 0 & 1 & 1 & 0 \\ 1 & 0 & 1 & 0 \end{bmatrix}.$$

6. For Exercise 5, list the equivalence classes of $tsr(R)$.

7. Let R be the usual quasi-order relation on $\mathbb{P}$: $m\ R\ n$ in case $m < n$. Find or describe:

   (a) $r(R)$ (b) $sr(R)$ (c) $rs(R)$

   (d) $tsr(R)$ (e) $t(R)$ (f) $st(R)$

8. Repeat Exercise 7 where $m\ R\ n$ means that m divides n.

9. The Fraternal Order of Hostile Hermits is an interesting organization. Hermits know themselves. In addition, everyone knows the High Hermit but neither he nor any of the other members knows any other member. Define the relation R on the F.O.H.H. by $h_1\ R\ h_2$ if h_1 knows h_2. Determine $st(R)$ and $ts(R)$ and compare.

10. (a) Show that if $\{R_k\}$ is a sequence of symmetric relations on a set S, then the union $\bigcup\limits_{k=1}^{\infty} R_k$ is symmetric.

    (b) Let R be a symmetric relation on S. Show that R^n is symmetric for all $n \in \mathbb{P}$.

    (c) Show that if R is symmetric, so are $r(R)$ and $t(R)$.

11. Consider a relation R on a set S.

    (a) Show that $sr(R) = rs(R)$.

    (b) Show that $tr(R) = rt(R)$.

12. Show that $st(R) \neq ts(R)$ for the relation R in Example 4.

13. Show that there does not exist a smallest antireflexive relation containing the relation R on $\{1, 2\}$ whose Boolean matrix is $\begin{bmatrix} 1 & 0 \\ 1 & 0 \end{bmatrix}$. This shows that antireflexivity is not a closable property.

14. We say that a relation R on a set S is an **onto relation** if for every $y \in S$ there exists $x \in S$ such that $\langle x, y \rangle \in R$. Show that there does not exist a smallest onto relation containing the relation R on $\{1, 2\}$ specified in Exercise 13. Thus "onto relation" is not a closable property.

15. Suppose that a property p of relations on a nonempty set S satisfies:

    (i) the universal relation $S \times S$ has property p;

    (ii) p is **closed under intersections**, i.e., if $\{R_i : i \in I\}$ is a nonempty indexed family of relations on S possessing property p, then the intersection $\bigcap\limits_{i \in I} R_i$ also possesses property p.

    (a) Prove that p is closable.

    (b) Observe that properties r, s and t satisfy both (i) and (ii).

    (c) Which of (i) and (ii) does antireflexivity fail to satisfy?

    (d) Which of (i) and (ii) does the property "onto relation" fail to satisfy?

§ 7.7   *The Lattice of Partitions*

Consider the collection of all equivalence relations on a set S. This collection is partially ordered by inclusion. The minimal element is the equality relation E and the maximal element is the universal relation $U = S \times S$, since $E \subseteq R \subseteq U$ for all equivalence relations R on S. This collection is actually a lattice, as defined in § 7.1, if we define

$$R_1 \wedge R_2 = R_1 \cap R_2 \quad \text{and} \quad R_1 \vee R_2 = tsr(R_1 \cup R_2).$$

The definition of $R_1 \wedge R_2$ is straightforward, since the intersection of equivalence relations is again an equivalence relation [Exercise 16(d) of § 7.4] and so $R_1 \cap R_2$ is the largest equivalence relation contained in both R_1 and R_2. Similarly, $tsr(R_1 \cup R_2)$ is the smallest equivalence relation containing both R_1 and R_2. Note that $tsr(R_1 \cup R_2) = t(R_1 \cup R_2)$ since $R_1 \cup R_2$ is already reflexive and symmetric.

EXAMPLE 1   Consider again a sack S of marbles and the following two equivalence relations on S:

$\langle s, t \rangle \in R_1$ if s and t have the same color;
$\langle s, t \rangle \in R_2$ if s and t are of the same size.

Then $\langle s, t \rangle \in R_1 \wedge R_2$ if and only if s and t are of the same color *and* size. The pair $\langle s, t \rangle$ will be in $R_1 \vee R_2 = t(R_1 \cup R_2)$ if we can find a sequence of marbles $t_1, \ldots, t_{m-1}$ in S so that

$$\langle s, t_1 \rangle, \langle t_1, t_2 \rangle, \ldots, \langle t_{m-1}, t \rangle \quad \text{are all in} \quad R_1 \cup R_2.$$

For example, if the sack S includes the marbles pictured in Figure 1, then $\langle s, t \rangle$ is in $R_1 \vee R_2$. Actually, the consecutive pairs can alternate between R_1 and R_2, so that marble t_2 was not needed.   ⬜

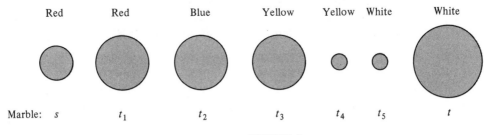

| Red | Red | Blue | Yellow | Yellow | White | White |

Marble: s t_1 t_2 t_3 t_4 t_5 t

FIGURE 1

EXAMPLE 2   For the set $\mathbb{P}$ of positive integers, consider the equivalence relations R_6 and R_8 where $\langle m, n \rangle \in R_6$ if $m \equiv n \pmod{6}$ and $\langle m, n \rangle \in R_8$ if $m \equiv n \pmod{8}$.
(a) If $\langle m, n \rangle \in R_6 \wedge R_8$, then $m - n$ must be divisible by both 6 and 8. This occurs precisely when $m - n$ is divisible by their least common multiple

24. So $\langle m, n \rangle \in R_6 \wedge R_8$ if and only if $m \equiv n \pmod{24}$. With obvious notation, $R_6 \wedge R_8 = R_{24}$.

(b) We will show that $R_6 \vee R_8 = R_2$, where $\langle m, n \rangle \in R_2$ if $m \equiv n \pmod{2}$. Note that 2 is the greatest common divisor of 6 and 8. Since $R_6 \cup R_8 \subseteq R_2$ and R_2 is an equivalence relation, we obviously have $R_6 \vee R_8 \subseteq R_2$. We show that

$$R_2 \subseteq R_6 \vee R_8 = t(R_6 \cup R_8).$$

First we note that

(*) $\langle k, k + 2 \rangle \in R_6 \vee R_8$ for all $k \in \mathbb{P}$,

since both $\langle k, k + 8 \rangle$ and $\langle k + 8, k + 2 \rangle$ are in $R_6 \cup R_8$. Now consider $\langle m, n \rangle \in R_2$ with, say, $m < n$. Then $n - m$ is even, so that $n = m + 2r$ for some $r \in \mathbb{P}$. Now by (*) all the pairs

$$\langle m, m + 2 \rangle, \langle m + 2, m + 4 \rangle, \ldots, \langle m + 2r - 2, m + 2r \rangle$$

are in $R_6 \vee R_8$. By transitivity, $\langle m, m + 2r \rangle = \langle m, n \rangle$ is also in $R_6 \vee R_8$. Every $\langle m, n \rangle$ in R_2 is in $R_6 \vee R_8$, and so $R_2 \subseteq R_6 \vee R_8$. ☐

Theorem 1 of § 7.3 described a one-to-one correspondence between the set of equivalence relations on a set S and the set $\Pi(S)$ of all partitions of S. Statements about equivalence relations on S correspond to statements about partitions of S and conversely we can translate partition statements into relation statements. We have just seen that the set of equivalence relations forms a lattice. There is a corresponding lattice structure on $\Pi(S)$, which we now describe.

Consider equivalence relations R_1 and R_2 with corresponding partitions π_1 and π_2. Then $R_1 \subseteq R_2$ if and only if every two R_1-related elements are also R_2-related, i.e., if and only if two members of the same R_1-class always belong to the same R_2-class. Thus $R_1 \subseteq R_2$ if and only if each set in π_1 is a subset of some set in π_2; we say π_1 **refines** π_2 and write $\pi_1 \lesssim \pi_2$ in this case. See Figure 2. The relation $\lesssim$ is a partial order on $\Pi(S)$ [Exercise 13] and $\Pi(S)$

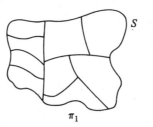

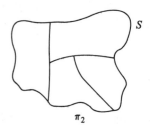

π_1 refines π_2

FIGURE 2

becomes a lattice with $\pi_1 \wedge \pi_2$ and $\pi_1 \vee \pi_2$ corresponding to $R_1 \cap R_2$ and $R_1 \vee R_2$ respectively. The partition $\pi_1 \wedge \pi_2$ is easy to find; it consists of all nonempty sets obtained by intersecting a set in π_1 with a set in π_2. Just as in the case of equivalence relations, it is usually less clear what the partition $\pi_1 \vee \pi_2$ corresponding to $R_1 \vee R_2$ is.

EXAMPLE 3 (a) For the sack of marbles in Example 1, each set in the partition $\pi_1 \wedge \pi_2$ consists of all marbles of a particular color and size. The nature of $\pi_1 \vee \pi_2$ depends on just what marbles are in S and how they are related. It might just consist of the set S by itself. Some possibilities are given in Exercises 1 to 4.

(b) The partition $\pi_6 \wedge \pi_8$ of $\mathbb{P}$ corresponding to $R_6 \wedge R_8 = R_{24}$ in Example 2 consists of the equivalence classes determined by the congruence $m \equiv n \pmod{24}$. There are 24 sets in the partition, one that contains 1, one that contains 2, etc. If this isn't obvious, reread Example 9 of § 7.3.

In this case, the partition $\pi_6 \vee \pi_8$ corresponding to $R_6 \vee R_8$ is also easy to describe, because we have already shown that $R_6 \vee R_8 = R_2$. The corresponding partition of $\mathbb{P}$ consists of two equivalence classes: the set of even numbers in $\mathbb{P}$ and the set of odd numbers in $\mathbb{P}$. □

We devote the rest of the section to presenting algorithms for finding $\pi_1 \wedge \pi_2$ and $\pi_1 \vee \pi_2$ when S is finite. For definiteness, consider a partition π of $S = \{1, 2, \ldots, n\}$. For each set A in π we select a fixed element m_A and define $\alpha(k) = m_A$ for $k \in A$; for example, m_A might be taken to be the smallest number in A. Each member of S belongs to some A in π so we obtain a function $\alpha: S \to S$ satisfying:

(1) $\alpha(j) = \alpha(k)$ if and only if j and k belong to the same set in π;

(2) $\alpha(\alpha(k)) = \alpha(k)$ for all k.

For each $k \in S$ the set in π which contains k is the set which contains $\alpha(k)$, so it is $\alpha^{-1}(\alpha(k))$. Thus π is determined by α. If R denotes the equivalence relation for which π is the set of equivalence classes, property (1) asserts:

(1') $\alpha(j) = \alpha(k)$ if and only if $j \, R \, k$.

Thus α is a function of the sort described in Theorem 2 of § 7.3.

EXAMPLE 4 Let R be an equivalence relation on $S = \{1, 2, 3, \ldots, 10\}$ whose partition π of equivalence classes is $\{\{1, 4, 6\}, \{2\}, \{3, 7, 10\}, \{5, 9\}, \{8\}\}$. The function α that selects the smallest number in each class is given by

k	1	2	3	4	5	6	7	8	9	10
$\alpha(k)$	1	2	3	1	5	1	3	8	5	3

Note that α satisfies (1) and (2). Another function α' that works is given by

k	1	2	3	4	5	6	7	8	9	10
$\alpha'(k)$	4	2	3	4	9	4	3	8	9	3

For partitions π_1 and π_2 of $S = \{1, 2, \ldots, n\}$, let α and β be corresponding functions satisfying (1) and (2). Note that π_1 refines π_2 provided

$$\alpha(i) = \alpha(j) \quad \text{implies} \quad \beta(i) = \beta(j) \quad \text{for all} \quad i, j \in S.$$

We seek the corresponding functions for $\pi_1 \wedge \pi_2$ and $\pi_1 \vee \pi_2$. The first algorithm provides the function γ for $\pi_1 \wedge \pi_2$.

Algorithm INTERSECT PARTITIONS.

Step 1. Set $\gamma(k) = 0$ for $k = 1, 2, \ldots, n$.
Step 2. Choose $k = 1$.
Step 3. If $\gamma(k) \neq 0$ go to Step 4. Otherwise, for each $j = k, k+1, \ldots,$ n satisfying $\alpha(j) = \alpha(k)$ and $\beta(j) = \beta(k)$ change $\gamma(j)$ to k.
Step 4. If $k = n$, stop. Otherwise replace k by $k + 1$ and go to Step 3.

After a little experimentation or thought, it is evident that this algorithm works, i.e., produces γ for $\pi_1 \wedge \pi_2$. However, writing out a careful justification is a bit tedious; see Exercise 15.

EXAMPLE 5 Let π_1 and π_2 be the partitions of $\{1, 2, 3, \ldots, 8\}$ with corresponding functions α and β as follows:

j	1	2	3	4	5	6	7	8
$\alpha(j)$	3	2	3	2	3	7	7	2
$\beta(j)$	5	4	4	4	5	5	5	4

Thus $\pi_1 = \{\{1, 3, 5\}, \{2, 4, 8\}, \{6, 7\}\}$; π_2 consists of two sets. In Table 1 we

TABLE 1

k	$\gamma(1)$	$\gamma(2)$	$\gamma(3)$	$\gamma(4)$	$\gamma(5)$	$\gamma(6)$	$\gamma(7)$	$\gamma(8)$
0	0	0	0	0	0	0	0	0
1	1	0	0	0	1	0	0	0
2	1	2	0	2	1	0	0	2
3	1	2	3	2	1	0	0	2
4	1	2	3	2	1	0	0	2
5	1	2	3	2	1	0	0	2
6	1	2	3	2	1	6	6	2
7	1	2	3	2	1	6	6	2
8	1	2	3	2	1	6	6	2

illustrate Algorithm INTERSECT PARTITIONS step by step. The partition $\pi_1 \wedge \pi_2$ can be read from the last line of Table 1; it consists of four sets. ☐

The next algorithm converts the function α for π_1 to the function α corresponding to $\pi_1 \vee \pi_2$.

Algorithm MERGE PARTITIONS.

Step 1. Choose $k = 1$.
Step 2. If $\alpha(\beta(k)) = \alpha(k)$ go to Step 3. Otherwise, for each $j = 1, 2, \ldots$, n satisfying $\alpha(j) = \alpha(k)$ change $\alpha(j)$ to $\alpha(\beta(k))$.
Step 3. If $k = n$, stop. Otherwise, replace k by $k + 1$ and go to Step 2.
☐

EXAMPLE 6 Let π_1 and π_2 be partitions with functions α and β as follows:

j	1	2	3	4	5	6	7	8
$\alpha(j)$	1	2	5	4	5	1	7	4
$\beta(j)$	3	4	3	4	5	6	6	8

So the partitions π_1 and π_2 each have five sets. We illustrate Algorithm MERGE PARTITIONS in Table 2. Since $\alpha(\beta(1)) = \alpha(3) = 5 \neq \alpha(1)$, each $\alpha(1) = 1$ is changed to $\alpha(\beta(1)) = 5$ in line $k = 1$. Using the new α from line

TABLE 2

k	$\alpha(1)$	$\alpha(2)$	$\alpha(3)$	$\alpha(4)$	$\alpha(5)$	$\alpha(6)$	$\alpha(7)$	$\alpha(8)$
given α	1	2	5	4	5	1	7	4
1	5	2	5	4	5	5	7	4
2	5	4	5	4	5	5	7	4
3	5	4	5	4	5	5	7	4
4	5	4	5	4	5	5	7	4
5	5	4	5	4	5	5	7	4
6	5	4	5	4	5	5	7	4
7	5	4	5	4	5	5	5	4
8	5	4	5	4	5	5	5	4

$k = 1$, we find $\alpha(\beta(2)) = \alpha(4) = 4 \neq \alpha(2)$ and so each $\alpha(2) = 2$ is changed to $\alpha(\beta(2)) = 4$ in line $k = 2$. Using the new α from line $k = 2$, we find $\alpha(\beta(3)) = \alpha(3)$, and so α is not changed in line $k = 3$. The algorithm continues in this way. The final α in line $k = 8$ corresponds to the partition $\pi_1 \vee \pi_2$, which has two sets. Figure 3 illustrates this example. In the figure the sets in

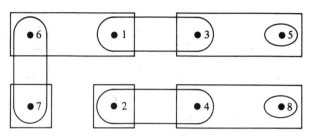

FIGURE 3

π_1 are indicated by rectangles and the ones in π_2 by ovals. The algorithm first links $\{1, 6\}$ to $\{3, 5\}$, then $\{2\}$ to $\{4, 8\}$ and later $\{7\}$ to $\{1, 3, 5, 6\}$.   □

Theorem   Algorithm MERGE PARTITIONS works.

    Proof. We restate the algorithm for ease of reference.

    Step 1. Choose $k = 1$.

    Step 2. If $\alpha(\beta(k)) = \alpha(k)$ go to Step 3. Otherwise, for each $j = 1, 2, \ldots,$ n satisfying $\alpha(j) = \alpha(k)$ change $\alpha(j)$ to $\alpha(\beta(k))$.

    Step 3. If $k = n$, stop. Otherwise, replace k by $k + 1$ and go to Step 2.

    For convenience denote the final function α by α^*. Notice first that the only place where $\alpha(j)$ can change during the execution of the algorithm is in Step 2. At that point, if $\alpha(i) = \alpha(j)$ then $\alpha(i)$ and $\alpha(j)$ both change to the same thing, namely $\alpha(\beta(k))$. Thus

(1)   if $\alpha(i)$ and $\alpha(j)$ are ever equal at some stage then they are equal from then on, so $\alpha^*(i) = \alpha^*(j)$.

We next observe that

(2) $\alpha^*(\beta(j)) = \alpha^*(j)$ for every j,

for if $\alpha(\beta(j)) = \alpha(j)$ when we reach Step 2 with $k = j$ then $\alpha^*(\beta(j)) = \alpha^*(j)$ by (1), while if $\alpha(\beta(j)) \neq \alpha(j)$ at that stage then Step 2 leaves $\alpha(\beta(j))$ unchanged and changes $\alpha(j)$ to $\alpha(\beta(j))$ on the spot.

    Now if $\alpha(i) = \alpha(j)$ for some i and j then $\alpha^*(i) = \alpha^*(j)$ by (1), and if $\beta(i) = \beta(j)$ then $\alpha^*(i) = \alpha^*(\beta(i)) = \alpha^*(\beta(j)) = \alpha^*(j)$ by (2). Thus

(3)   if $\alpha(i) = \alpha(j)$ *or* if $\beta(i) = \beta(j)$ then $\alpha^*(i) = \alpha^*(j)$,

which says that π_1 and π_2 both refine the partition π given by α^*. To show that $\pi = \pi_1 \vee \pi_2$ we only need to show that π refines $\pi_1 \vee \pi_2$, i.e., that

(4)   if $\alpha^*(i) = \alpha^*(j)$ then $\langle i, j \rangle \in R$

for the equivalence relation R corresponding to the partition $\pi_1 \vee \pi_2$.

    To show (4) it's enough to show

(5) $\langle j, \alpha^*(j) \rangle \in R$ for every j,

since if (5) holds and if $\alpha^*(i) = \alpha^*(j)$ then $\langle i, \alpha^*(i) \rangle \in R$ and $\langle \alpha^*(j), j \rangle \in R$ by symmetry of R, so $\langle i, j \rangle \in R$ by transitivity of R.

To show (5) finally, it's enough to show that $\langle j, \alpha(j) \rangle \in R$ for every j at every stage of the execution of the algorithm. This is clear at the beginning since α describes π_1 then. Suppose $\alpha(j)$ changes at some point, from $\alpha(k)$ to $\alpha(\beta(k))$. Assuming that $\langle j, \alpha(j) \rangle \in R$ before the change, we have $\langle j, \alpha(k) \rangle \in R$. Since R corresponds to the partition $\pi_1 \vee \pi_2$ we also have $\langle \alpha(k), k \rangle$, $\langle k, \beta(k) \rangle$ and $\langle \beta(k), \alpha(\beta(k)) \rangle$ in R. Transitivity of R gives $\langle j, \alpha(\beta(k)) \rangle \in R$, i.e., $\langle j, \alpha(j) \rangle \in R$ after the change. [An inductive argument is in the background here, of course.] □

EXERCISES 7.7

1. Suppose that the sack in Example 3 has ten marbles: 6 small green ones, 3 large red ones and 1 large green one. Describe $\pi_1 \wedge \pi_2$ and $\pi_1 \vee \pi_2$. How many sets are in each of these partitions?

2. How would your answers to Exercise 1 change if the single large green marble were lost?

3. Repeat Exercise 1 if the sack has ten marbles: 4 small yellow ones, 3 medium blue ones, 2 medium white ones and 1 large yellow one.

4. How would your answer to Exercise 3 change if 1 large blue marble were dropped into the sack?

5. Consider the equivalence relations R_3 and R_5 on $\mathbb{P}$ where $\langle m, n \rangle \in R_3$ if $m \equiv n \pmod 3$ and $\langle m, n \rangle \in R_5$ if $m \equiv n \pmod 5$, with corresponding partitions π_3 and π_5.
   (a) Describe the equivalence relation $R_3 \wedge R_5$.
   (b) Describe the partition $\pi_3 \wedge \pi_5$.
   (c) It turns out [Exercise 6] that $R_3 \vee R_5$ is the universal relation on $\mathbb{P}$, so all numbers in $\mathbb{P}$ are related to each other. Verify that $\langle 1, 2 \rangle, \langle 1, 3 \rangle, \langle 1, 73 \rangle$, $\langle 47, 73 \rangle$ and $\langle 72, 73 \rangle$ are in $R_3 \vee R_5$.
   (d) Describe the partition $\pi_3 \vee \pi_5$.

6. Prove that the relation $R_3 \vee R_5$ in Exercise 5 is the universal relation.

7. For each partition below of $\{1, 2, 3, 4, 5, 6\}$ give a function α satisfying conditions (1) and (2) stated prior to Example 4.
   (a) $\pi_1 = \{\{1, 3, 5\}, \{2, 6\}, \{4\}\}$
   (b) $\pi_2 = \{\{1, 2, 4\}, \{3, 6\}, \{5\}\}$
   (c) $\pi_3 = \{\{1\}, \{2\}, \{3\}, \{4\}, \{5\}, \{6\}\}$
   (d) $\pi_4 = \{\{1, 2, 3, 4, 5, 6\}\}$
   (e) What equivalence relation corresponds to π_3?
   (f) What equivalence relation corresponds to π_4?

8. Give the partitions $\pi_1, \pi_2, \pi_3, \pi_4$ of $\{1, 2, 3, \ldots, 8\}$ defined by the functions $\alpha_1, \alpha_2, \alpha_3$ and α_4 below:

k	1	2	3	4	5	6	7	8
$\alpha_1(k)$	1	1	3	1	5	6	3	5
$\alpha_2(k)$	2	2	6	8	5	6	7	8
$\alpha_3(k)$	4	4	3	4	5	3	3	4
$\alpha_4(k)$	3	2	3	8	2	3	7	8

9. Use the algorithms of this section to find functions corresponding to the partitions $\pi_1 \wedge \pi_2$ and $\pi_1 \vee \pi_2$ where π_1 and π_2 are as in Exercise 8.

10. Repeat Exercise 9 for π_3 and π_4.

11. Repeat Exercise 9 for π_2 and π_3.

12. Would Algorithm MERGE PARTITIONS work just as well if the roles of α and β were interchanged?

13. (a) Show that the relation $\leq$ defined on $\Pi(S)$ by $\pi_1 \leq \pi_2$ if and only if π_1 refines π_2 is a partial order on $\Pi(S)$.
    (b) Show that if π_1, π_2 and π_3 are in $\Pi(S)$ and if $\pi_3 \leq \pi_1$ and $\pi_3 \leq \pi_2$ then $\pi_3 \leq \pi_1 \wedge \pi_2$.

14. Analyze the algorithms INTERSECT PARTITIONS and MERGE PARTITIONS in case π_1 refines π_2 by considering the example where $S = \{1, 2, 3, 4, 5, 6, 7\}$ and

k	1	2	3	4	5	6	7
$\alpha(k)$	1	4	3	4	1	6	7
$\beta(k)$	5	4	5	4	5	4	7

15. Verify that Algorithm INTERSECT PARTITIONS works by showing the following.
    (a) The value of $\gamma(j)$ changes at least once for each j during execution of the algorithm.
    (b) If the value of $\gamma(j)$ changes when $k = k_0$ and if $k_0 \leq k'$ with $\alpha(k') = \alpha(j)$ and $\beta(k') = \beta(j)$ then $\gamma(k')$ changes to k_0.
    (c) The value of each $\gamma(j)$ changes exactly once during the execution.
    (d) If $0 \neq \gamma(i) = \gamma(j)$ then $\alpha(i) = \alpha(j)$ and $\beta(i) = \beta(j)$.
    (e) If $\alpha(i) = \alpha(j)$ and $\beta(i) = \beta(j)$, then $\gamma(i) = \gamma(j)$ at the conclusion of the algorithm.

CHAPTER HIGHLIGHTS

See the end of Chapter 0 for a reminder on how to use these lists to review. Think of examples.

Concepts

binary relation on S or from S to T
  reflexive, antireflexive, symmetric, antisymmetric, transitive [for relations on S]
  inverse relation R^{-1}
  composite $R_2 \circ R_1 = R_1 R_2$
  matrix of a relation

partial order, poset, subposet
  quasi-order
  Hasse diagram
  maximal, minimal, largest, smallest elements
  lattice
  chain = totally ordered set = linearly ordered set
  product order on $S_1 \times \cdots \times S_n$
  filing order on $S_1 \times \cdots \times S_n$
  standard order on Σ^*
  lexicographic = dictionary order on Σ^*
equivalence relation
  equivalence class $[s]$
  natural mapping $s \rightarrow [s]$
closure, closable
$R_1 \wedge R_2, R_1 \vee R_2$
refine [partitions]

Facts

Composition of relations is associative.
The matrix of a composite $R_1 R_2$ of relations is the Boolean product $\mathbf{A_1} * \mathbf{A_2}$
  of their matrices.
Matrix analogues of relation statements are given in the summary at the end
  of § 7.5.
Filing order on $S_1 \times \cdots \times S_n$ is linear if each S_i is a chain.
If Σ is a chain then standard order on Σ^* is a well-ordering and lexicographic
  order is linear but not a well-ordering.
A partition is essentially the same thing as the set of all equivalence classes
  for an equivalence relation.
Functions define equivalence relations on their domains.
$$r(R) = R \cup E, \ s(R) = R \cup R^{-1} \text{ and } t(R) = \bigcup_{k=1}^{\infty} R^k \ [= \bigcup_{k=1}^{n} R^k \text{ if } |S| = n].$$
The smallest equivalence relation containing R is $tsr(R)$.

Methods

INTERSECT PARTITIONS to give $\pi_1 \wedge \pi_2$.
MERGE PARTITIONS to give $\pi_1 \vee \pi_2$.

8

GRAPHS

Chapter 0 contained an informal introduction to graphs. We discussed and illustrated a number of ideas, but didn't prove theorems or justify algorithms. In this chapter we take another, closer look at the subject and fill in the arguments to support our conclusions. In Chapter 0 we avoided the graphs involving arrows, the so-called directed graphs. This time we begin by studying directed graphs—ones like flowcharts in which the connecting lines have directions associated with them. Then we give the connecting lines "weights," and also consider what happens if we leave off the directions. A road map with mileages as weights can be used to find the shortest highway distance between two points. In § 8.6 we discuss questions such as finding a shortest route for a traveling salesperson. Section 8.7 links graphs with relations and matrices, and §§ 8.8 and 8.9 describe some graph-theoretic algorithms.

This chapter is logically independent of Chapter 0, in the sense that we will develop everything anew. In particular, all the definitions will be repeated here at the appropriate places. We will now stress the theory, however, since motivation has been provided in Chapter 0.

§ 8.1   Directed Graphs

The essential features of a directed graph [digraph for short] are its objects and directed lines. Specifically, a **digraph** G consists of two sets, the nonempty set $V(G)$ of **vertices** of G and the set $E(G)$ of **edges** of G, together with a function γ [Greek lowercase gamma] from $E(G)$ to $V(G) \times V(G)$. If e is an edge of G and $\gamma(e) = \langle p, q \rangle$, then p is called the **initial vertex** of e and q the **terminal vertex** of e and we say e **goes from** p to q. This definition makes sense if $V(G)$ or $E(G)$ is infinite, but because our applications are to finite sets we will assume in this chapter that $V(G)$ and $E(G)$ are finite.

A **picture** of the digraph G is a diagram consisting of points corresponding to the members of $V(G)$ and arrows corresponding to the members of $E(G)$ such that if $\gamma(e) = \langle p, q \rangle$ then the arrow corresponding to e goes from the point labeled p to the point labeled q.

EXAMPLE 1   Consider the digraph G with $V(G) = \{w, x, y, z\}$, $E(G) = \{a, b, c, d, e, f, g, h\}$ and γ given by the table in Figure 1(a). The diagrams in Figures 1(b) and 1(c) are both pictures of G. In Figure 1(b) we labeled the arrows to make the correspondence to $E(G)$ plain. In Figure 1(c) we simply labeled the points and let the arrows take care of themselves. This causes no confusion because, in this case, there are no **parallel edges**, i.e., there is at most one edge with a given initial vertex and terminal vertex. In other words, the function γ is one-to-one. Note also that we omitted the arrow head on edge d since z is clearly both the initial and terminal vertex. □

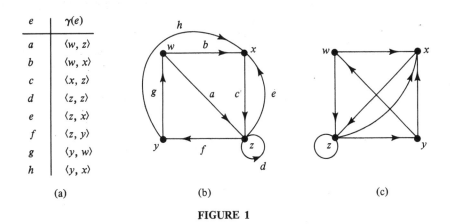

e	$\gamma(e)$
a	$\langle w, z \rangle$
b	$\langle w, x \rangle$
c	$\langle x, z \rangle$
d	$\langle z, z \rangle$
e	$\langle z, x \rangle$
f	$\langle z, y \rangle$
g	$\langle y, w \rangle$
h	$\langle y, x \rangle$

(a)   (b)   (c)

FIGURE 1

If $\gamma\colon E(G) \to V(G) \times V(G)$ is one-to-one, then we can identify the edges e with their images $\gamma(e)$ in $V(G) \times V(G)$ and consider $E(G)$ to *be* a subset of $V(G) \times V(G)$. In fact, some people define digraphs to have $E(G) \subseteq V(G) \times V(G)$ and call the more general digraphs we are considering "directed multigraphs."

Given a picture of G we can reconstruct G itself since the arrows tell us all about γ. We will commonly describe digraphs by giving pictures of them rather than tables of γ but the pictorial description is chosen just for human convenience. A computer stores a digraph by storing the function γ in one way or another.

Many of the important questions connected with digraphs can be stated in terms of sequences of edges leading from one vertex to another. A **path** in a digraph G is a sequence of edges such that the terminal vertex of one edge is the initial vertex of the next. Thus if $e_1, \ldots, e_n$ are in $E(G)$, then $e_1 e_2 \cdots e_n$ is a path provided there are vertices $x_1, x_2, \ldots, x_n, x_{n+1}$ so that $\gamma(e_i) = \langle x_i, x_{i+1} \rangle$ for $i = 1, 2, \ldots, n$. We say that $e_1 e_2 \cdots e_n$ is a path of **length** n **from** x_1 **to** x_{n+1}. The path is **closed** if $x_1 = x_{n+1}$.

EXAMPLE 2   In the digraph G in Figure 1 the sequence $f g a e$ is a path of length 4 from z to x. The sequences $c e c e c$ and $f g a f h c$ are also paths, but $f a$ is not a path since $\gamma(f) = \langle z, y \rangle$, $\gamma(a) = \langle w, z \rangle$ and $y \neq w$. The paths $f g a f h c, c e c e$ and d are closed; $f h c e$ and $d f$ are not.   ☐

A path $e_1 \cdots e_n$ with $\gamma(e_i) = \langle x_i, x_{i+1} \rangle$ has an associated sequence of vertices $x_1 x_2 \cdots x_n x_{n+1}$. If each e_i is the only edge from x_i to x_{i+1} then this sequence of vertices uniquely determines the path, and we could describe the path by listing the vertices in succession.

EXAMPLE 3   (a) In Figure 1 the path $f g a e$ has vertex sequence $z y w z x$. Observe that this vertex sequence alone determines the path. The path can be recovered from $z y w z x$ by looking at Figure 1(b) or 1(c) or using the table of γ in Figure 1(a). Since this digraph has no parallel edges, all its paths are determined by their vertex sequences.

(b) For the digraph pictured in Figure 2 the vertex sequence $y z z z$ corresponds only to the path $f g g$ but the sequence $y v w z$ belongs to both $c a e$ and $c b e$.   ☐

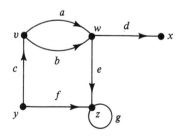

FIGURE 2

A closed path of length at least 1 with vertex sequence $x_1 x_2 \cdots x_n x_1$ is called a **cycle** if $x_1, \ldots, x_n$ are all different. The language of graph theory has not been standardized: various authors use "circuit" and "loop" for what we call a cycle, and "cycle" is sometimes used as a name for a closed path. A digraph with no cycles is called **acyclic**. A path is **acyclic** if the digraph consisting of the vertices and edges of the path is acyclic.

EXAMPLE 4   In Figure 1 the path $a f g$ is a cycle since its vertex sequence is $w z y w$. Likewise, the paths $c f h$ and $c f g b$, with vertex sequences $x z y x$ and $x z y w x$, are cycles. The short path $c e$ and the loop d are also cycles, since their vertex sequences are *x z x* and *z z* respectively. The path *c f g a e* is not a cycle, since its vertex sequence is *x z y w z x* and the vertex *z* is repeated. ☐

EXAMPLE 5 Hasse diagrams may be thought of as digraphs. Consider a poset $(P, \leqq)$ and let *H* be the digraph with $V(H) = P$ and with an edge from *x* to *y* whenever *y* covers *x*. Figure 3 shows two pictures of *H* for the poset $(\{1, 2, 3, 4, 5, 6\}, |)$. The picture on the left is correct but seems less helpful than the one on the right.

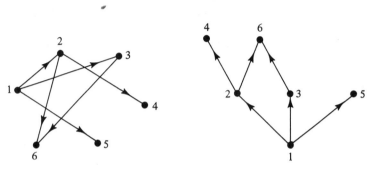

FIGURE 3

A path in *H* has a vertex sequence $x_1 x_2 \cdots x_{n+1}$ in which x_2 covers x_1, x_3 covers x_2, etc., and so $x_1 < x_2 < \cdots < x_{n+1}$. By transitivity and antisymmetry $x_1 < x_{n+1}$, so in particular $x_1 \neq x_{n+1}$ and the path is not closed. Hence *H* is acyclic. ☐

Theorem 1 If *u* and *v* are different vertices of a digraph *G*, and if there is a path in *G* from *u* to *v*, then there is an acyclic path from *u* to *v*.

Proof. Among all paths from *u* to *v* consider one of smallest length, say having vertex sequence $x_1 \cdots x_n x_{n+1}$ with $x_1 = u$ and $x_{n+1} = v$. Suppose that $x_i = x_j$ for some *i* and *j* with $1 \leqq i < j \leqq n + 1$. Then the path $x_i x_{i+1} \cdots x_j$ from x_i to x_j is closed [see Figure 4 for an illustration] and the path $x_1 \cdots x_i x_{j+1} \cdots x_{n+1}$ obtained by omitting this part still goes from *u* to *v*.

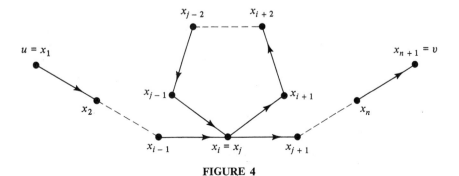

FIGURE 4

Since $x_1 \cdots x_n x_{n+1}$ had smallest length, this shorter path is impossible. We conclude that x_i and x_j must be different if $i \neq j$. Thus the path under consideration is acyclic. [This is essentially the argument that showed $t(R) \subseteq \bigcup_{k=1}^{n} R^k$ in the proof of Theorem 2 of § 7.6.]   ∎

Corollary 1   If there is a closed path from v to v then there is a cycle from v to v.

Proof. If there is an edge e of the graph from v to v, then the one-element sequence e is a cycle from v to v. Otherwise there is a closed path from v to v having the form $v\, x_2 \cdots x_n\, v$ where $x_n \neq v$. Then by Theorem 1 there is an acyclic path from v to x_n. Tacking on the last edge from x_n to v gives the desired cycle.   ∎

Corollary 2   A path is acyclic if and only if all its vertices are distinct.

Proof. If a path has no repeated vertex, then it is surely acyclic. If a path has a repeated vertex, then it contains a closed path, so by Corollary 1 it contains a cycle.   ∎

If G is an acyclic digraph we can define a natural quasi-order on $V(G)$ by defining $u \prec v$ if there is a path from u to v. This quasi-order gives us a way of comparing vertices of G. In fact, we can do a bit more. We can label the vertices with integers so that smaller vertices have smaller labels. Before we discuss such a labeling we need an observation. Call a vertex of a digraph a **sink** if it is not an initial vertex of any edge. Sinks correspond to points with no arrows leading away from them.

Lemma   Every finite acyclic digraph has at least one sink.

First proof. Since the digraph is acyclic, every path in it is acyclic. Since the digraph is finite, the path lengths are bounded and there must be a path of largest length, say $v_1 v_2 \cdots v_n$. Then v_n must be a sink. [Of course, if the digraph has no edges at all, every vertex is a sink.]   ∎

This proof is short and elegant, but it doesn't tell us how to find v_n or any other sink. Our next argument is constructive.

Second proof. Choose any vertex v_1. If v_1 is a sink, we are done. If not, there is an edge from v_1 to some v_2. If v_2 is a sink, we are done. If not, etc. We obtain in this way a sequence $v_1, v_2, v_3, \ldots$ such that $v_1 v_2 \cdots v_k$ is a path for each k. As in the first proof, such paths cannot be arbitrarily long, so at some stage we reach a sink.   ∎

Here is an algorithm based on the construction in the second proof, which returns a sink when it is applied to a finite acyclic digraph G. The algorithm uses **immediate successor** sets $\mathrm{SUCC}(v)$ defined by $\mathrm{SUCC}(v) =$

$\{u \in V(G)$: there is an edge from v to $u\}$. These data sets SUCC(v) would be supplied in the description of the digraph G when the algorithm is carried out.

Algorithm SINK.

Step 1. Choose v in $V(G)$.
Step 2. If SUCC(v) $= \varnothing$ go to Step 3. Otherwise choose u in SUCC(v),
    replace v by u and repeat Step 2.
Step 3. Let SINK(G) $= v$. Stop. ☐

EXAMPLE 6 Consider the acyclic digraph G shown in Figure 5. The immediate successor sets are SUCC(t) $= \{u, w, x\}$, SUCC(u) $= \{v\}$, SUCC(v) $= \varnothing$, SUCC(w) $= \{y\}$, SUCC(x) $= \{y\}$, SUCC(y) $= \varnothing$ and SUCC(z) $= \{w\}$. One possible sequence of choices using algorithm SINK on G is t, w, y. Others starting with t are t, x, y and t, u, v. A different first choice could lead to z, w, y. We could even get lucky and choose a sink first time. In any case the value SINK(G) returns is either v or y. ☐

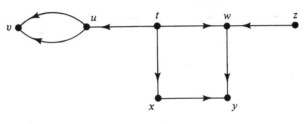

FIGURE 5

The following algorithm gives another way of finding sinks from immediate successor sets.

Algorithm THINK.

Step 1. Rummage through $V(G)$ until you find a v with SUCC(v) $= \varnothing$.
Step 2. Let THINK(G) $= v$. Stop. ☐

This algorithm depends for its effectiveness on having the members of $V(G)$ listed in some way so they can be examined one after the other without repeating. It may be faster or slower than algorithm SINK, depending on the characteristics of the digraph being examined.

Sinks correspond to points with no arrows leading away from them. Points with no arrows leading into them are also special. We call a vertex of a digraph a **source** if it is not a terminal vertex of any edge. Facts and algorithms about sinks have analogues for sources, obtained by reversing all the arrows. In particular, every finite acyclic digraph has at least one source [Exercise 17].

The proof of the next theorem gives one reason for considering sinks.

Theorem 2   An acyclic digraph with n vertices can have its vertices numbered from 1 to n in such a way that $i < j$ if there is a path from vertex i to vertex j.

Proof. We use induction on n, and note that the assertion is obvious for $n = 1$. Assume inductively that acyclic digraphs with fewer than n vertices can be labeled as described, and consider an acyclic digraph G with n vertices. By the last lemma G has a sink, say s. Give s the number n. Form a new graph H with $V(H) = V(G)\backslash\{s\}$ and with edges all those edges of G which do not have s as a vertex. Since G has no cycles, H has no cycles. Since H has only $n - 1$ vertices, by the inductive assumption we can number H with $\{1, 2, \ldots, n - 1\}$ in the way described in the theorem. The vertex s is numbered n, so every vertex in $V(G)$ has a number.

Now suppose there is a path in G from vertex i to vertex j. If the path lies entirely in H then $i < j$ since H is properly numbered. Otherwise, some vertex along the path is s, and since s is a sink it must be the last vertex, vertex j. But then $j = n$, so $i < j$ in this case too. Hence G, with n vertices, has its vertices labeled as in the statement of the theorem. The Principle of Mathematical Induction now shows that the theorem holds for all n. □

The idea of the proof of Theorem 2 can be developed into a constructive procedure for numbering a given graph.

Algorithm NUMBERING VERTICES.

Step 1. If $V(G) = \varnothing$ stop. If $V(G) \neq \varnothing$ find a sink of G and label it $|V(G)|$, the number of vertices in $V(G)$.

Step 2. Replace G by the digraph obtained by removing from G the sink and all attached edges. Go to step 1. □

This algorithm works with a set $V(G)$, which is the set of vertices of a digraph until it is empty, at which point the algorithm stops. In Step 1 we could use algorithm SINK to find the sink of G, in effect calling SINK as a subroutine. You may find it instructive to apply this algorithm to number the graph of Figure 5. Also see Exercise 18 for a procedure which begins numbering with 1.

The second proof of the lemma for Theorem 2 consisted of constructing a path from a given vertex v to a sink. We call a vertex u **reachable from** v in G if there is a path of length at least 1 in G from v to u, and we define

$$R(v) = \{u \in V(G) : u \text{ is reachable from } v\}.$$

Then $R(v) = \varnothing$ if and only if v is a sink, and the lemma's second proof showed in effect that in an acyclic digraph each nonempty set $R(v)$ contains at least one sink.

Even if G is not acyclic, the sets $R(v)$ may be important. As we shall see in § 8.7, determining all sets $R(v)$ amounts to finding the transitive closure of a certain relation. In § 8.9 we will study algorithms for finding the $R(v)$'s, as well as for answering other graph-theoretic questions.

One consequence of Theorem 2 is that every finite poset has a Hasse diagram. The discussion in Example 5 showed that if $(P, \leq)$ is a poset and H is the digraph with $V(H) = P$ and with an edge from x to y whenever y covers x then H is acyclic. We can use Theorem 2 to label H with $\{1, 2, \ldots, n\}$, and then draw a picture of H so that the height of the point corresponding to a vertex increases as its label increases. Since each edge points from a lower-numbered vertex to a higher-numbered one, any edge from an x to a y which covers x points upward. That is, the picture of H is a Hasse diagram for $(P, \leq)$.

Essentially the same reasoning shows that every acyclic digraph has a picture in which the arrows all go in more or less the same direction, for instance from left to right or from top to bottom. The digraph in Figure 6(b) is acyclic and all its arrows point generally from left to right.

EXAMPLE 7 According to Theorem 2 it is possible to number college courses so that all prerequisites for a course have lower numbers than the course itself. ◻

EXERCISES 8.1

1. Give a table of the function γ for each of the digraphs pictured in Figure 6.

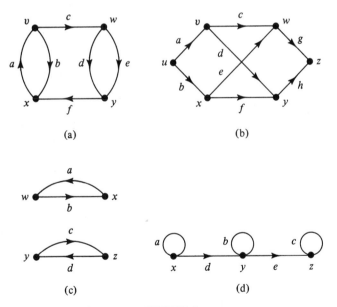

(a)   (b)

(c)   (d)

FIGURE 6

2. Draw a picture of the digraph G with $V(G) = \{w, x, y, z\}$, $E(G) = \{a, b, c, d, e, f, g\}$ and γ given by the following table.

e	a	b	c	d	e	f	g
$\gamma(e)$	$\langle x, w \rangle$	$\langle w, x \rangle$	$\langle x, x \rangle$	$\langle w, z \rangle$	$\langle w, y \rangle$	$\langle w, z \rangle$	$\langle z, y \rangle$

3. Which of the following vertex sequences describe paths in the digraph pictured in Figure 7(a)?

(a) *z y v w t*

(b) *x z w t*

(c) *v s t x*

(d) *z y s u*

(e) *x z y v s*

(f) *s u x t*

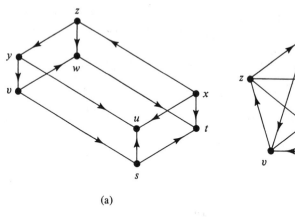

(a)   (b)

FIGURE 7

4. Find the length of a shortest path from *x* to *w* in the digraph shown in Figure 7(a).

5. Consider the digraph pictured in Figure 7(b). Describe an acyclic path

(a) from *x* to *y*

(b) from *y* to *z*

(c) from *v* to *w*

(d) from *x* to *z*

(e) from *z* to *v*

6. There are four basic blood types: A, B, AB and O. Type O can donate to any of the four types, A and B can donate to AB as well as to their own types but type AB can only donate to AB. Draw a digraph which presents this information. Is the digraph acyclic?

7. (a) Give the immediate successor sets SUCC(*v*) for all vertices in the digraph shown in Figure 8.

(b) What value for SINK(*G*) does an initial choice of vertex *w* give?

(c) What sinks of *G* are in *R*(*x*)?

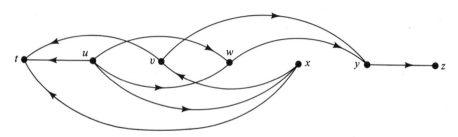

FIGURE 8

8. Give an example of a digraph with vertices x, y and z in which there is a cycle with x and y as vertices and another cycle with y and z, but there is no cycle with x and z as vertices.

9. Consider the digraph G pictured in Figure 9.
   (a) Find $R(v)$ for each vertex v in $V(G)$.
   (b) Find all sinks of G.
   (c) Is G acyclic?

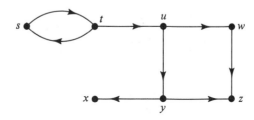

FIGURE 9

10. Does Algorithm SINK work on digraphs which have cycles? Explain.

11. Consider a digraph G with the following immediate successor sets: $\text{SUCC}(r) = \{s, u\}$, $\text{SUCC}(s) = \varnothing$, $\text{SUCC}(t) = \{r, w\}$, $\text{SUCC}(u) = \varnothing$, $\text{SUCC}(w) = \{r, t, x, y\}$, $\text{SUCC}(x) = \varnothing$, $\text{SUCC}(y) = \{w, z\}$ and $\text{SUCC}(z) = \varnothing$.
   (a) Draw a picture of such a digraph.
   (b) Do these sets $\text{SUCC}(v)$ determine $E(G)$ uniquely? Explain.
   (c) Find all sinks in G.
   (d) Find paths from the vertex w to three different sinks in the digraph.

12. A **tournament** is a digraph in which every two vertices have exactly one edge between them. [Think of $\langle x, y \rangle$ as an edge provided x defeats y.]
   (a) Give an example of a tournament with 4 vertices.
   (b) Show that a tournament cannot have two sinks.
   (c) Can a tournament with a cycle have a sink? Explain.
   (d) Would you like to be the sink of a tournament?

13. Let G be an acyclic digraph. Show that the relation $\prec$, defined by $u \prec v$ if there is a path from u to v, is a quasi-order on $V(G)$.

14. Let G be a digraph and define the relation $\sim$ on $V(G)$ by $x \sim y$ if $x = y$ or if x is reachable from y and y is reachable from x.
   (a) Show that $\sim$ is an equivalence relation.
   (b) Find the equivalence classes for the digraph pictured in Figure 9.
   (c) Describe the relation $\sim$ in the case that G is acyclic.

15. (a) Show that in Theorem 1 and Corollary 1 the path without repeated vertices can be constructed from edges of the given path. Thus every closed path contains at least one cycle.
   (b) Show that if u and v are vertices of a digraph and if there is a path from u to v, then there is a path from u to v in which no edge is repeated. [Consider the case $u = v$, as well as $u \neq v$.]

16. Let G be a digraph.
   (a) Show that if u is reachable from v then $R(u) \subseteq R(v)$.

(b) Give an alternate proof of the lemma for Theorem 2 by choosing v in $V(G)$ with $|R(v)|$ as small as possible.

(c) Does your proof in part (b) lead to a useful constructive procedure? Explain.

17. The **reverse** of a digraph G is the digraph $\hat{G}$ obtained by reversing all the arrows of G. That is, $V(\hat{G}) = V(G)$, $E(\hat{G}) = E(G)$ and if $\gamma(e) = \langle x, y \rangle$ then $\hat{\gamma}(e) = \langle y, x \rangle$.

(a) Use $\hat{G}$ and the lemma for Theorem 2 to show that if G is acyclic [and finite] then G has a source.

(b) Find all sources in the digraphs of Figures 5 through 9.

18. (a) Modify Algorithm NUMBERING VERTICES by using sources instead of sinks to produce an algorithm that numbers $V(G)$ in increasing order.

(b) Use your algorithm to number the digraph of Figure 5.

19. Let H be the Hasse diagram of a poset $(P, \leqq)$.

(a) Using the terminology of this section, describe the elements of H corresponding to the minimal elements of P.

(b) Answer part (a) with "maximal" instead of "minimal."

20. Modify algorithm THINK to obtain an algorithm which finds *all* sinks of G.

§ 8.2   *Isomorphisms and Invariants*

Digraphs are like grains of sand on the beach. A little experimentation shows that the number of different digraphs we can build with just a few vertices and edges is quite large, and in fact this number becomes astronomical in a hurry as we increase the numbers of vertices and edges allowed. If $|V(G)| = n$ and $|E(G)| = m$, then $|V(G) \times V(G)| = n^2$ and there are $(n^2)^m$ functions γ from $E(G)$ to $V(G) \times V(G)$, each of which determines a digraph. For $n = 4$ and $m = 5$ this number is already over a million.

On the other hand, several different functions may determine essentially the same digraph. If we had some way to sift through the million-odd digraphs we get from our $(4^2)^5$ functions and could eliminate essential duplicates, we might hope to get a more manageable list which would still have one sample of each of the kinds of digraphs with 4 vertices and 5 edges. As a practical matter this plan will fail, if not for 4 and 5 then for larger numbers, but it is still a helpful approach when we are looking for digraphs with special properties, as in Exercise 10.

EXAMPLE 1   Figure 1 shows pictures of two digraphs G_1 and G_2 with the same vertex set $\{w, x, y, z\}$ and the same edge set $\{d, f, g, h, i\}$, but described by different functions γ_1 and γ_2, defined as follows.

	d	f	g	h	i
γ_1	$\langle w, x \rangle$	$\langle w, x \rangle$	$\langle w, y \rangle$	$\langle y, y \rangle$	$\langle z, y \rangle$
γ_2	$\langle z, w \rangle$	$\langle z, x \rangle$	$\langle x, x \rangle$	$\langle y, x \rangle$	$\langle z, w \rangle$

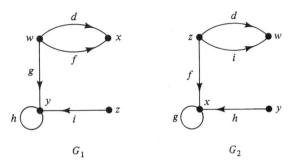

$$G_1 \qquad\qquad G_2$$

FIGURE 1

We can see from their pictures that the two digraphs are essentially the same, except that they have been labeled differently. It is clear from Figure 1 how to relabel G_1 to make it into G_2. We can describe the relabeling with the pair of functions $\alpha\colon \{w, x, y, z\} \to \{w, x, y, z\}$ and $\beta\colon \{d, f, g, h, i\} \to \{d, f, g, h, i\}$ given by the following tables.

v	w	x	y	z
$\alpha(v)$	z	w	x	y

e	d	f	g	h	i
$\beta(e)$	d	i	f	g	h

If we replace each vertex v in the table defining γ_1 by $\alpha(v)$ and each edge e by $\beta(e)$, then starting with

	d	f	g	h	i
γ_1	$\langle w, x \rangle$	$\langle w, x \rangle$	$\langle w, y \rangle$	$\langle y, y \rangle$	$\langle z, y \rangle$

we get the table

d	i	f	g	h
$\langle z, w \rangle$	$\langle z, w \rangle$	$\langle z, x \rangle$	$\langle x, x \rangle$	$\langle y, x \rangle$

which is in fact just the defining table for γ_2, with the entries in another order.   ☐

We say that two digraphs G and H are **isomorphic** [pronounced eye-so-MOR-fik] and we write $G \simeq H$ if there are one-to-one correspondences $\alpha\colon V(G) \to V(H)$ and $\beta\colon E(G) \to E(H)$ such that whenever an edge e of $E(G)$ joins vertices u and v of $V(G)$, the corresponding edge $\beta(e)$ joins the corresponding points $\alpha(u)$ and $\alpha(v)$ in $V(H)$. Figure 2 illustrates the concept. The left-hand arrow is part of the picture of G if and only if the corresponding right-hand arrow is in the picture of H. In symbols, if G and H are described by γ_1 and γ_2, respectively, and if $\gamma_1(e) = \langle u, v \rangle$, then $\gamma_2(\beta(e)) = \langle \alpha(u), \alpha(v) \rangle$.

FIGURE 2

Two isomorphic digraphs are essentially the same except for the labeling of their vertices and edges. Generally speaking, two sets with some mathematical structure are said to be **isomorphic** if there exist one-to-one correspondences between them which preserve [i.e., are compatible with] the structure. For example, two semigroups $(S, \square)$ and $(T, \triangle)$ are isomorphic if there is a one-to-one correspondence $\phi: S \to T$ such that $\phi(s_1 \square s_2) = \phi(s_1) \triangle \phi(s_2)$ for all s_1, s_2 in S; compare Exercise 22 of § 4.3.

It follows from the definition that $G \simeq G$ for every digraph G, and if $G \simeq H$ with correspondences α and β, then α^{-1} and β^{-1} are also one-to-one and so $H \simeq G$. If $G \simeq H$ and $H \simeq K$ then $G \simeq K$ [Exercise 14]. Thus if $\mathcal{S}$ is a set of digraphs, the relation $\simeq$ is an equivalence relation on $\mathcal{S}$. The equivalence classes are called **isomorphism classes**.

If G and H have no parallel edges, we've seen that we can consider $E(G)$ to be a subset of $V(G) \times V(G)$, and $E(H)$ a subset of $V(H) \times V(H)$. In this situation the isomorphism condition is particularly simple: G is isomorphic to H if there is a one-to-one correspondence $\alpha: V(G) \to V(H)$ such that $\langle u, v \rangle$ is in $E(G)$ if and only if $\langle \alpha(u), \alpha(v) \rangle$ is in $E(H)$. Such an α is called an **isomorphism** of G onto H.

EXAMPLE 2   Consider the digraphs G and H pictured in Figure 3, with

$$E(G) = \{\langle w, x \rangle, \langle w, z \rangle, \langle x, y \rangle, \langle x, z \rangle, \langle y, w \rangle, \langle z, x \rangle, \langle z, y \rangle\}$$

and

$$E(H) = \{\langle p, q \rangle, \langle p, r \rangle, \langle q, s \rangle, \langle r, p \rangle, \langle r, q \rangle, \langle s, p \rangle, \langle s, r \rangle\}.$$

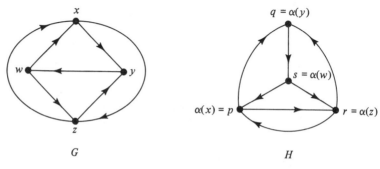

G H

FIGURE 3

It may not be obvious, but these digraphs are isomorphic. To see this, define α by $\alpha(w) = s$, $\alpha(x) = p$, $\alpha(y) = q$, $\alpha(z) = r$. The result of replacing each vertex in the description of $E(G)$ by its image under α is

$$\{\langle s, p \rangle, \langle s, r \rangle, \langle p, q \rangle, \langle p, r \rangle, \langle q, s \rangle, \langle r, p \rangle, \langle r, q \rangle\},$$

which is $E(H)$. Thus $G \simeq H$. The function α we used is not the only possible choice. $\square$

Given two digraphs, how do we determine whether they are isomorphic? In general we would probably look first for obvious differences or for the kind of obvious similarity we saw in Figure 1. The problem may not be easy to solve. In fact, one of the main messages of this section could be phrased "The graph isomorphism problem is hard."

Figure 4 shows pictures of four digraphs. The pictures all look quite different, so we might try to find ways in which the digraphs themselves are essentially different. A human being could attack the problem of the digraphs in Figure 4 in a variety of ways and could shift from one approach to another;

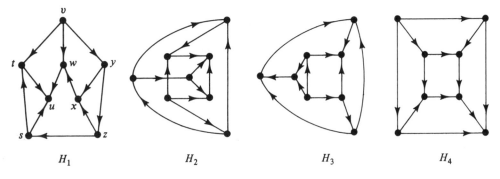

H_1 H_2 H_3 H_4

FIGURE 4

a computer program or algorithm must be spelled out in advance and might not be so flexible. One simpleminded algorithm we could write would simply label the vertices of the two candidate digraphs $v_1, v_2, \ldots, v_8$ and $w_1, w_2, \ldots, w_8$, label their edges $e_1, e_2, \ldots, e_{12}$ and $f_1, f_2, \ldots, f_{12}$, and examine each pair of functions

$$\alpha : \{v_1, \ldots, v_8\} \longrightarrow \{w_1, \ldots, w_8\} \quad \text{and} \quad \beta : \{e_1, \ldots, e_{12}\} \longrightarrow \{f_1, \ldots, f_{12}\}$$

to see if α and β meet the isomorphism conditions. This would involve $(8!)(12!) \approx 1.93 \cdot 10^{13}$ examinations. The computation could be speeded up considerably by taking one α at a time and rejecting whole bunches of β's as impossible for a given α. For example, if e_1 goes from v_1 to v_2 and if $\alpha(v_1) = w_3$ and $\alpha(v_2) = w_7$, we can reject β unless $\beta(e_1)$ goes from w_3 to w_7, without looking at what β does to the other edges. Even this quicker algorithm would have to go through all $8!$ possible α's before concluding that the two digraphs are not isomorphic. If they *were* isomorphic it might also take a while to find an isomorphism by this exhaustive process.

At the present time no isomorphism-detecting algorithm is known which is qualitatively much faster than the simpleminded scheme we just considered. To fully explain this last sentence would require the introduction of technical material which we have no other use for here, but the basic idea is this: The time it takes known algorithms to check for isomorphism of two given digraphs with n vertices can be comparable to $n!$ and in particular is not bounded by some polynomial in n. Polynomial-time algorithms are known to exist for some special classes of digraphs, however. Work in complexity theory has shown that the existence of a polynomial-time algorithm for digraph isomorphism is equivalent to the existence of polynomial-time algorithms to solve a number of other important types of problems, so the search for digraph isomorphism algorithms is an active one.

What the last paragraph means in our present context is that we should not be surprised if checking isomorphism or nonisomorphism turns out to be hard in specific cases.

One way we could hope to discover quickly that two digraphs are not isomorphic is to show that they differ in some aspect which would be the same for isomorphic graphs. For instance, if $G_1 \simeq G_2$ then obviously $|V(G_1)| = |V(G_2)|$ and $|E(G_1)| = |E(G_2)|$. Thus if our given digraphs have different numbers of vertices or edges, they are surely not isomorphic. A quantity, such as number of vertices or number of edges, is called an **isomorphism invariant** if its value is the same for any two isomorphic digraphs. Invariants are especially useful for showing that digraphs are *not* isomorphic. A set of invariants is **complete** if whenever two digraphs are not isomorphic there is at least one invariant in the set with different values for the two digraphs. A complete set of invariants would let us show that two digraphs *are* isomorphic by showing that each invariant is the same for both digraphs. Unfortunately, no complete set of invariants is known.

All of the digraphs in Figure 4 have 8 vertices and 12 edges, so the invariants $|V(G)|$ and $|E(G)|$ are no help in this case and we must look more closely. First, let's consider some easier examples.

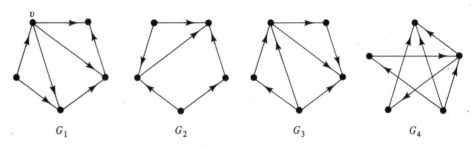

G_1 G_2 G_3 G_4

FIGURE 5

EXAMPLE 3   Figure 5 shows pictures of four digraphs. All have 5 vertices. By counting edges we see that G_2 with 6 edges is not isomorphic to any of the other three, which have 7. Digraphs G_1 and G_3 look somewhat alike though three arrows seem to have changed directions. As we saw in Example 2, it is possible for two digraphs with different-looking pictures to be isomorphic, so G_1 and G_3 could conceivably be isomorphic. They aren't. Digraph G_1 has a vertex v with one arrow coming in and three going out, while G_3 has no such vertex. If G_1 and G_3 were isomorphic, with mappings α and β as above, then β would have to take each of the three edges $\langle v, w \rangle$ with v as initial vertex to an edge $\langle \alpha(v), \alpha(w) \rangle$ with $\alpha(v)$ as initial vertex. No vertex in G_3 could serve as $\alpha(v)$. A similar argument could be based on terminal vertices. We will return to this example shortly and discuss G_4. ☐

The idea of counting arrows is a useful one. Let v be a vertex of a digraph G. The **indegree** of v is the number of edges of G with v as terminal vertex, and the **outdegree** of v is the number with v as initial vertex. The **degree** of v, $\deg(v)$, is the sum of the indegree and outdegree; in symbols

$$\deg(v) = \text{indeg}(v) + \text{outdeg}(v).$$

An edge from v to v gets counted twice here, once going out and once coming in.

As we noticed in Example 3, if α and β describe an isomorphism of G onto H and if $v \in V(G)$ then $\text{indeg}(v) = \text{indeg}(\alpha(v))$ and $\text{outdeg}(v) = \text{outdeg}(\alpha(v))$, so also $\deg(v) = \deg(\alpha(v))$. For each pair $\langle i, j \rangle$ of integers let

$$D_{i,j}(G) = \{v \in V(G) : \text{indeg}(v) = i \quad \text{and} \quad \text{outdeg}(v) = j\}.$$

Then the one-to-one correspondence α must map $D_{i,j}(G)$ onto $D_{i,j}(H)$; in particular $|D_{i,j}(G)|$ and $|D_{i,j}(H)|$ must be equal. That is, the numbers $|D_{i,j}(G)|$ are isomorphism invariants.

EXAMPLE 4   (a) For the digraphs of Figure 5 these invariants are as follows. [We omit the pairs $\langle i, j \rangle$ for which $D_{i,j}(G)$ is empty for all G's under consideration.]

$\langle i,j \rangle$	$\langle 0,2 \rangle$	$\langle 0,3 \rangle$	$\langle 1,1 \rangle$	$\langle 1,3 \rangle$	$\langle 2,0 \rangle$	$\langle 2,1 \rangle$	$\langle 2,2 \rangle$	$\langle 3,0 \rangle$
G_1	1	0	0	1	1	2	0	0
G_2	2	0	1	0	0	1	0	1
G_3	0	1	2	0	0	0	1	1
G_4	0	1	2	0	0	0	1	1

We can see at once that the only two of these digraphs which can possibly be isomorphic are G_3 and G_4. In fact, just checking one of $|D_{0,2}(G)|$, $|D_{1,1}(G)|$ or $|D_{2,1}(G)|$ would tell us that much. The table of values of $|D_{i,j}(G)|$ does not show that G_3 and G_4 *are* isomorphic. To show isomorphism, one would still need to give a function α. In Exercise 5 you are asked to show that G_3 and G_4 are, in fact, isomorphic.

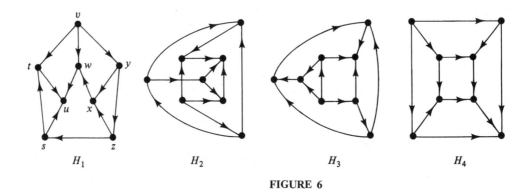

H_1 H_2 H_3 H_4

FIGURE 6

(b) Now let's go back to the digraphs of Figure 4, drawn again in Figure 6. Their invariants $|D_{i,j}(G)|$ are as follows.

$\langle i,j \rangle$	$\langle 0, 3 \rangle$	$\langle 1, 2 \rangle$	$\langle 2, 1 \rangle$	$\langle 3, 0 \rangle$
H_1	1	3	3	1
H_2	1	3	3	1
H_3	1	3	3	1
H_4	1	3	3	1

Not much help here. We must look still more closely. It turns out [Exercise 4] that H_1 and H_2 are, in fact, isomorphic. Exercise 6 suggests one way to show that H_1 and H_3 are not isomorphic by looking hard at these digraphs near their sources. The same idea will show that H_4 is not isomorphic to any of the others so, of the four, only H_1 and H_2 are isomorphic.

Another way to separate H_4 from the others is to observe that each of the other digraphs has three edges e, f, g so that the path $e\,f$ leads from the initial vertex of g to its terminal vertex. [For instance let $e = y\,z, f = z\,x$ and $g = y\,x$ in H_1.] Digraph H_4 has no such edges.

It turns out that H_1 and H_3 would be isomorphic if we reversed all arrows on one of them. Such digraphs are called **anti-isomorphic.** [See Exercise 6.]

                                                     ∎

The ideas we used in Example 4 can be extended to get other isomorphism invariants. We could count cycles of a given length, count sources, count triples of edges e, f, g with $e\,f$ a path from initial vertex of g to terminal vertex of g, count vertices with given in- and outdegrees, etc. Some of these invariants are related to others, as the following result illustrates.

Theorem   The sum of all the indegrees of a digraph equals the sum of all the outdegrees, which equals the number of edges of the digraph. In symbols,

$$\sum_{v \in V(G)} \text{indeg}\,(v) = \sum_{v \in V(G)} \text{outdeg}\,(v) = |E(G)|.$$

Hence

$$\sum_{v \in V(G)} \deg(v) = 2 \cdot |E(G)|, \text{ an even number.}$$

Proof. Each edge contributes 1 to the indegree of one vertex, so contributes 1 to the indegree sum. Thus the indegree sum is just the total number of edges. Similarly for the outdegrees. □

We can get the sum of all the indegrees by adding up all the indegrees which are 0, then all which are 1, then 2, and so on. For each $d \in \mathbb{N}$ let $V_d(G) = \{v \in V(G) : \text{indeg}(v) = d\}$. Then $\sum_{v \in V_d(D)} \text{indeg}(v)$ is a sum of $|V_d(G)|$ terms, each of which equals d, so $\sum_{v \in V_d(G)} \text{indeg}(v) = d \cdot |V_d(G)|$. Since $V(G) = \bigcup_{d=0}^{\infty} V_d(G)$, the theorem shows that

$$|E(G)| = \sum_{d \geq 0} (\sum_{v \in V_d(G)} \text{indeg}(v)) = \sum_{d \geq 0} d \cdot |V_d(G)|$$
$$= 0 \cdot |V_0(G)| + 1 \cdot |V_1(G)| + 2 \cdot |V_2(G)| + \cdots$$

This gives us a relationship among the invariants $|E(G)|, |V_1(G)|, |V_2(G)|, \ldots$.

EXAMPLE 5 The digraph G shown in Figure 7 has 7 edges and has indegrees and outdegrees as follows.

	w	x	y	z	sum
indeg	1	1	3	2	7
outdeg	0	3	1	3	7
deg	1	4	4	5	14

The nonempty sets $V_d(G)$ are: $V_1(G) = \{w, x\}$, $V_2(G) = \{z\}$, $V_3(G) = \{y\}$. Sure enough, $7 = 1 \cdot 2 + 2 \cdot 1 + 3 \cdot 1$. We could play the same game with outdegrees, letting $V_d^+ = \{v \in V(G) : \text{outdeg}(v) = d\}$. Then $V_0^+ = \{w\}$, $V_1^+ = \{y\}$, $V_2^+ = \varnothing$, $V_3^+ = \{x, z\}$ and $7 = 0 \cdot 1 + 1 \cdot 1 + 2 \cdot 0 + 3 \cdot 2$. □

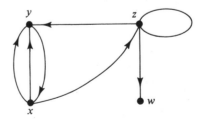

FIGURE 7

The idea of isomorphism is also useful as a means of describing the symmetry of a given digraph. The identity mappings $1_{V(G)}$ and $1_{E(G)}$ are defined by $1_{V(G)}(v) = v$ and $1_{E(G)}(e) = e$ for all v and e. The functions $\alpha = 1_{V(G)}$ and $\beta = 1_{E(G)}$ satisfy the conditions to give $G \simeq G$, but there may be other choices of α and β that work too. Roughly speaking, the more ways we can map G isomorphically back onto itself the more symmetry G has. We call an isomorphism of a digraph onto itself an **automorphism** of the digraph.

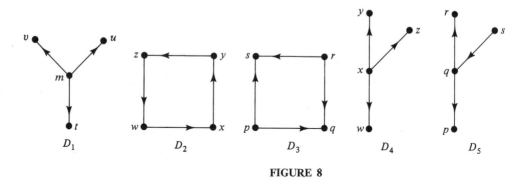

FIGURE 8

EXAMPLE 6   Figure 8 shows examples of digraphs with several different kinds of symmetry. These digraphs have no parallel edges, so we can describe their automorphisms by just giving the mappings α. Digraph D_1 has six different isomorphisms onto itself. Clearly $\alpha(m)$ must be m, but there are three choices for $\alpha(t)$ and then two remaining choices for $\alpha(u)$. The rows in Figure 9(a) list

m	t	u	v
m	t	u	v
m	t	v	u
m	u	t	v
m	u	v	t
m	v	t	u
m	v	u	t

w	x	y	z
w	x	y	z
x	y	z	w
y	z	w	x
z	w	x	y

Automorphisms of D_1 Automorphisms of D_2

(a)   (b)

FIGURE 9

the various possible assignments $\alpha(m)$, $\alpha(t)$, $\alpha(u)$, $\alpha(v)$. Digraph D_2 has four isomorphisms onto itself. There are four choices for $\alpha(w)$, but then $\alpha(x)$, $\alpha(y)$ and $\alpha(z)$ are completely determined; see Figure 9(b). Digraph D_3 also has four automorphisms [Exercise 7], but the digraph has a different kind of symmetry from that of D_2. We can rotate D_2 a quarter turn, while we can flip D_3 over along a diagonal. To describe the difference in terms of isomorphisms we need first to observe that the composition of two isomorphisms is again an isomorphism. Then we need to check how the various automorphisms for D_2 and D_3 compose with each other. We return to this question in Chapter 11 where we have the necessary terminology to describe the answer.

The kind of symmetry we are considering may not show up as symmetry of the picture of a digraph. Digraph D_4 doesn't look particularly symmetric as it's drawn, but in fact this digraph is isomorphic to D_1, so D_4 has six isomorphisms onto itself, just as D_1 does. Digraph D_5 also has an asymmetric picture but has two different isomorphisms onto itself [Exercise 7]. We could have drawn more symmetric pictures of these digraphs, of course, but for more complicated digraphs it may be impossible to construct a picture which displays the full symmetry involved, and the techniques of Chapter 11 become more appropriate. ◻

EXERCISES 8.2

1. (a) Assign directions to the edges in the picture in Figure 10(b) to get a digraph isomorphic to the one pictured in Figure 10(a).
   (b) In how many ways could part (a) be answered correctly? *Hint:* Think of sources and sinks.

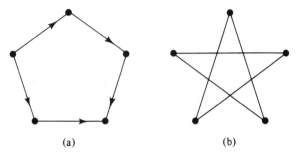

(a)   (b)

FIGURE 10

2. Draw pictures of all six digraphs with 2 vertices and 2 edges. "All" here means one example from each isomorphism class of such digraphs.

3. Consider the digraphs G_1 and G_2 pictured in Figure 11.
   (a) Find two different isomorphisms of G_1 onto G_2. You need only give the correspondences α.
   (b) Find an isomorphism of G_2 onto G_1.

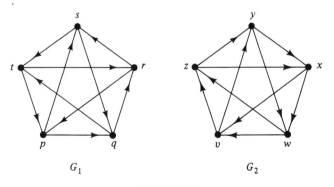

G_1 G_2

FIGURE 11

4. Label the vertices of digraph H_2 of Figure 6 and find an isomorphism α of H_1 onto H_2. *Hint:* Start with sources and sinks.

5. Label the vertices of digraphs G_3 and G_4 of Figure 5 and find a correspondence α to show that the two digraphs are isomorphic.

6. (a) Show that digraphs H_1 and H_3 of Figure 6 are not isomorphic. *Hint:* Consider edges from the sources of the two digraphs and look at the indegrees and outdegrees of their terminal vertices.

(b) Label the vertices of H_3 and find a correspondence α to show that H_1 and H_3 are anti-isomorphic. *Hint:* Start with sources and sinks.

(c) Are digraphs H_2 and H_3 of Figure 6 anti-isomorphic? Explain.

7. (a) Describe the two automorphisms of the digraph D_5 of Figure 8 onto itself.

(b) List all four automorphisms of the digraph D_3 of Figure 8 onto itself.

8. Consider the digraphs G and H of Example 2. Find an isomorphism of G onto H different from the one chosen in the example.

9. (a) List the nonempty sets $D_{i,j}(H_1)$ for the digraph H_1 in Figure 6.

(b) Repeat part (a) for the digraph G_1 in Figure 11.

10. A digraph is **regular** if there is some $k \in \mathbb{N}$ such that indeg(v) = outdeg(v) = k for all vertices v.

(a) Draw pictures of all five regular digraphs with 4 vertices and 4 edges. See Exercise 2 for the meaning of "all" in this context.

(b) How many nonisomorphic regular digraphs are there with 4 vertices and 6 edges? Explain.

11. A student was once given two digraphs G and H and asked if they were isomorphic. In an effort to get the question at least half right, he said that G was isomorphic but H was not. What do you think of this answer?

12. (a) Verify the equations of the theorem in this section for the digraph H_3 of Figure 6. If you haven't done Exercise 6(b), first label the vertices.

(b) Give the sets $V_d(G)$ for this digraph and verify that $|E(G)| = \sum_{d \geqq 0} d \cdot |V_d(G)|$.

13. Suppose that digraphs G and H are isomorphic, with α and β as in the text. If v is a sink of G, must $\alpha(v)$ be a sink of H? Explain.

14. Suppose that digraphs G and H are isomorphic, with correspondences α_1 and β_1 as in the text, and that H and K are isomorphic, with correspondences α_2 and β_2. Verify that G and K are isomorphic, with correspondences $\alpha_2 \circ \alpha_1$ and $\beta_2 \circ \beta_1$.

15. Show that a digraph must have an even number of vertices of odd degree.

16. Show that if G and H are isomorphic digraphs and if H is acyclic then G is acyclic.

17. (a) Show that the number of sources of a digraph is an isomorphism invariant.

(b) Is the number of vertices of indegree 3 an isomorphism invariant? Explain.

18. How many different isomorphisms are there of the digraph G_1 of Figure 11 onto the digraph G_2? Explain.

§ 8.3 Weighted Digraphs

In many applications of digraphs one wants to know if a given vertex v is reachable from another vertex u, that is, if it is possible to get to v from u by following arrows. For instance suppose each vertex represents a state a machine can be in such as FETCH, DEFER or EXECUTE, and there is an edge from s to t whenever the machine can change from state s to state t in response to some input. If the machine is in state u can it later be in state v? The answer is "yes" if and only if the digraph contains a path from u to v.

Now suppose there is a cost associated with each transition from one state to another, i.e., with each edge in the digraph. Such a cost might be monetary, might be a measure of the time involved to carry out the change, or might have some other meaning. We could now ask for a path from u to v with the smallest total associated cost, obtained by adding all the costs for the edges in the path.

If all edges cost the same amount then the cheapest path is simply the shortest. In general, however, edge costs might differ. A digraph with no parallel edges is called **weighted** if each edge has an associated number, called its **weight**. In a given application it might better be called "cost" or "length" or "capacity" or have some other interpretation. Weights are normally assumed to be nonnegative, but many of the results about weighted digraphs are true without such a limitation. We can describe the weighting of a digraph G with a function W from $E(G)$ to $\mathbb{R}$ where $W(e)$ is the weight of the edge e. The **weight** of a path $e_1 e_2 \cdots e_m$ in G is then the sum $\sum_{i=1}^{m} W(e_i)$. Since a weighted digraph has no parallel edges, we may suppose that $E(G) \subseteq V(G) \times V(G)$, and write $W(u, v)$ for the weight of an edge $\langle u, v \rangle$ from u to v.

EXAMPLE 1 (a) The digraph shown in Figure 1 is stolen from Figure 1 of § 0.1, where it described a rat and some cages. It could just as well describe a machine with states A, B, C and D, and the number next to an arrow [the weight of the edge] could be the number of microseconds necessary to get from its initial

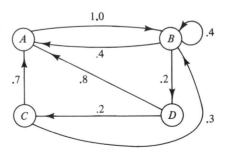

FIGURE 1

state to its terminal state. With that interpretation it takes .3 microsecond to go from state C to state B, .9 microsecond to go from D to A by way of C, .8 microsecond to go directly from D to A and .4 microsecond to stay in state B in response to an input. What is the shortest time to get from D to B?

(b) Figure 2 shows a more complicated example. In this case the shortest paths $s\, v\, x\, f$ and $s\, w\, x\, f$ from s to f have weights $6 + 7 + 4 = 17$ and $3 + 7 + 4 = 14$, respectively, but the longer path $s\, w\, v\, y\, x\, z\, f$ has weight $3 + 2 + 1 + 3 + 1 + 3 = 13$, which is less than either of these. Thus length is not directly related to weight. This example also shows a path $s\, w\, v$ from s to v which has smaller weight than the edge from s to v.

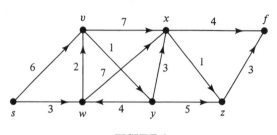

FIGURE 2

This digraph has a cycle $w\, v\, y\, w$. Clearly the whole cycle cannot be part of a path of minimum weight, but pieces of it can be. For instance $w\, v\, y$ is the path of smallest weight from w to y and the edge $y\, w$ is the path of smallest weight from y to w. □

If we wish, we can display the weight function W in a tabular form by indexing rows and columns of an array with the members of $V(G)$ and entering the value of $W(u, v)$ at the intersection of row u and column v.

EXAMPLE 2 The array for the digraph in Figure 2 is given in Figure 3(a). The numbers appear in locations corresponding to edges of the digraph. Later in this chapter we will consider how to make a useful matrix by filling in the blank spaces

W	s	v	w	x	y	z	f
s		6	3				
v				7	1		
w		2		7			
x					1	4	
y			4	3		5	
z							3
f							

(a)

W^*	s	v	w	x	y	z	f
s	0	5	3	9	6	10	13
v		0	5	4	1	5	8
w		2	0	6	3	7	10
x				0		1	4
y		6	4	3	0	4	7
z						0	3
f							0

(b)

FIGURE 3

appropriately. The table in Figure 3(a) contains enough information to let us reconstruct the weighted digraph, since from the table we know just where the edges go and what their weights are.

Figure 3(b) is a tabulation of the function W^* where $W^*(u, v)$ is the smallest weight of a path from u to v if such a path exists. The zero entries on the diagonal could be left out. They signify the obvious weights of the trivial paths of length 0. ⬚

For convenience we call the smallest weight of a path from u to v the **min-weight** from u to v; we will generally denote it by $W^*(u, v)$ as in Example 2. We also call a path from u to v having this weight a **min-path**. According to this definition a path of length 0 is a min-path. In Example 2 we simply announced the values of W^*, and the example is small enough that the values given can be easily verified. For more complicated digraphs the determination of W^* and of the min-paths can be nontrivial problems. In § 8.8 we will describe algorithms for finding W^*, but until then we will stare at the picture until the answer is clear. For small digraphs this method is as good as any.

Unlike the weight function W the min-weight function W^* does not completely determine the digraph.

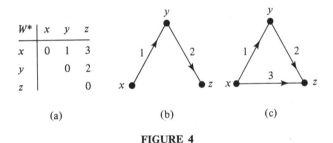

(a) (b) (c)

FIGURE 4

EXAMPLE 3 The table of W^* given in Figure 4(a) goes with each of the digraphs pictured in Figures 4(b) and 4(c), and with others as well. We cannot tell from the table whether there is an edge from x to z. We can see, though, that in any case there is a min-path from x to z through y, since going from x to y and then from y to z costs no more than any other way to get from x to z. ⬚

The function W^* does not give us the digraph but it does allow us to find min-paths.

EXAMPLE 4 Consider again the function W^* given in Figure 3(b). Let's try to find a min-path from v to f just by looking at the table of W^*. Since $W^*(v, f) = 8$, if we can find a vertex t different from v and f with $W^*(v, t) + W^*(t, f) = W^*(v, f) = 8$, then stringing together a min-path from v to t and one from

t to f will yield a min-path from v to f. From the table we see that

$$W^*(v, x) + W^*(x, f) = 4 + 4 = 8,$$
$$W^*(v, y) + W^*(y, f) = 1 + 7 = 8,$$
$$W^*(v, z) + W^*(z, f) = 5 + 3 = 8,$$

so we could let t be any one of x, y, z. Say we choose $t = x$.

Now we repeat the process with the pairs $\langle v, x \rangle$ and $\langle x, f \rangle$. We look for t different from v and x, with $W^*(v, t) + W^*(t, x) = W^*(v, x) = 4$. Only $t = y$ works. This means that there is a min-path from v to x through y, and since y is the only intermediate vertex on such a path, $v\, y\, x$ must *be* a min-path. This takes care of the pair $\langle v, x \rangle$ and leaves $\langle x, f \rangle$.

The table of W^* shows that z is the only t other than x and f with

$$W^*(x, t) + W^*(t, f) = W^*(x, f).$$

Hence there is a min-path from x to f through z, and it must be the path $x\, z\, f$. In fact, there is another min-path from x to f in the digraph of Figure 2 which gave us this table of W^*, but we cannot detect its existence from the table.

Piecing together the two min-paths $v\, y\, x$ and $x\, z\, f$ gives the min-path $v\, y\, x\, z\, f$ from v to f.   ☐

The ideas in this example lead to the following algorithm FILL-IN which uses a table of W^* to find a min-path between chosen vertices u and v. The algorithm is recursive; it keeps calling itself to attack simpler and simpler problems, until eventually it deals with edges.

Algorithm FILL-IN.

Step 1. If $W^*(u, v)$ is not given in the table or if $u = v$, stop.

Step 2. If there is a vertex t other than u and v with $W^*(u, t) + W^*(t, v) = W^*(u, v)$ choose such a t and go to Step 3. Otherwise let FILL-IN(u, v) be the edge from u to v.

Step 3. Apply Algorithm FILL-IN to the pairs $\langle u, t \rangle$ and $\langle t, v \rangle$ in place of $\langle u, v \rangle$ to obtain min-paths FILL-IN(u, t) from u to t and FILL-IN(t, v) from t to v. Let FILL-IN(u, v) be FILL-IN(u, t) followed by FILL-IN(t, v).   ☐

This algorithm produces a min-path from u to v, if there is one. Its success depends on the following fact.

Proposition   If $u \cdots t \cdots v$ is a min-path, then so are the first part $u \cdots t$ and the second part $t \cdots v$. Thus $W^*(u, v) = W^*(u, t) + W^*(t, v)$.

Proof. If $u \cdots t$ weren't a min-path already, we could replace it with one and get a path from u to t of smaller weight than the one we have. We could use it instead, and reduce the path weight from u to v. This is impossible, since the given path from u to v is a min-path. Thus $u \cdots t$ and, similarly, $t \cdots v$ are min-paths already. ☐

To carry out Algorithm FILL-IN on a computer, for example to analyze a complicated data structure, we would need to establish addresses FILL-IN(x, y) for paths which have not yet been determined. As the algorithm proceeds each of these addresses gets assigned a min-path, either determined by two previously computed min-paths or consisting of a single edge.

One way to store a path is to start with the initial vertex and associate with it a pointer to the next vertex, then a pointer from there to the next, and so on. To describe a path $x\, y\, z\, w$ we need pointers from x to y, from y to z and from z to w, which we could describe with a function p such that $p(x) = y$, $p(y) = z$ and $p(z) = w$. We could define $p(v)$ in some arbitrary way for other vertices v in $V(G)$ or simply define p just on $\{x, y, z\}$.

Suppose that the path $u \cdots v\, w\, x \cdots z$ is acyclic, and a pointer function p is already defined so that it describes $u \cdots v\, w$ and $w\, x \cdots z$. Then $p(v) = w$ and $p(w) = x$, so p already describes $u \cdots v\, w\, x \cdots z$ and the linking involves no extra work.

The simplicity of this linked-list point of view suggests that we might want to generate the vertices of a min-path successively from initial vertex to final vertex rather than jump in the middle. If all weights are positive, Algorithm FILL-IN can be modified to do this. In Step 2 among all possible vertices t with $W^*(u, t) + W^*(t, v) = W^*(u, v)$ choose one with $W^*(u, t)$ as small as possible. Then the min-path from u to t must be an edge [Exercise 13]. The added time it takes to compare values of $W^*(u, t)$ is a fairly small cost, but by deciding to take only the smallest one, we commit ourselves to examining the values of $W^*(u, t)$ for all t. In the original algorithm, we don't care about size, so we can take the first t we find with $W^*(u, t) + W^*(t, v) = W^*(u, v)$, and perhaps save time.

If we have stored a table of the weight function W as well as the min-weight function W^* we can avoid much of the search time by using the following algorithm. Again, we begin with the pair $\langle u, v \rangle$ of vertices we want to join.

Algorithm MIN-PATH.

Step 1. If $W^*(u, v)$ is not in the table or if $u = v$, stop.
Step 2. Choose a vertex t with $W(u, t) + W^*(t, v) = W^*(u, v)$.
Step 3. Let $p(u) = t$. Replace u by t and go to Step 1. ☐

If v is reachable from u, this algorithm yields a sequence $p(u)$, $p(p(u))$, $p(p(p(u)))$, ... of values of the pointer p, terminating in v and consisting of the successive vertices in a min-path from u to v. [If $v = u$ the procedure stops at once and yawns.] The algorithm works because every min-path of length at least 1 starts with an edge, and what remains after removing the edge is still a min-path.

EXAMPLE 5　We apply Algorithm MIN-PATH to the weighted digraph with picture and tables given in Figure 5.

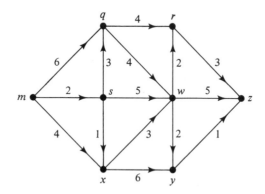

W	m	q	r	s	w	x	y	z
m		6		2		4		
q			4		4			
r								3
s		3			5	1		
w			2				2	5
x					3		6	
y								1
z								

W^*	m	q	r	s	w	x	y	z
m	0	5	8	2	6	3	8	9
q		0	4		4		6	7
r			0					3
s		3	6	0	4	1	6	7
w			2		0		2	3
x			5		3	0	5	6
y							0	1
z								0

FIGURE 5

First we determine a min-path from m to z. Set $u = m$, $v = z$. Then $W^*(u, v) = W^*(m, z) = 9$. Only $t = s$ works:

$$W(m, s) + W^*(s, z) = 2 + 7 = 9.$$

Let $p(m) = s$. Set $u = s$. Then $W^*(u, v) = W^*(s, z) = 7$. Only $t = x$ works:

$$W(s, x) + W^*(x, z) = 1 + 6 = 7.$$

Let $p(s) = x$. Set $u = x$. Then $W^*(u, v) = W^*(x, z) = 6$. Only $t = w$ works:

$$W(x, w) + W^*(w, z) = 3 + 3 = 6.$$

Let $p(x) = w$. Set $u = w$. Then $W^*(u, v) = W^*(w, z) = 3$. Only $t = y$ works:

$$W(w, y) + W^*(y, z) = 2 + 1 = 3.$$

Let $p(w) = y$. Set $u = y$. Then $W^*(u, v) = W^*(y, z) = 1$. Only $t = z$ works:

$$W(y, z) + W^*(z, z) = 1 + 0 = 1.$$

Let $p(y) = z$. Set $u = z$. Then $u = v$ so stop.

The resulting function p gives $p(m) = s$, $p(s) = x$, $p(x) = w$, $p(w) = y$, $p(y) = z$, corresponding to the min-path $m\ s\ x\ w\ y\ z$. In this case the answer is unique.

Applying the algorithm with the initial choices $u = q$, $v = z$ produces the values $p(q) = r$, $p(r) = z$ or the values $p(q) = w$, $p(w) = y$, $p(y) = z$, depending on how the first choice in Step 2 is made. Both $q\ r\ z$ and $q\ w\ y\ z$ are acceptable solutions to the min-path problem. ☐

Each time Algorithm MIN-PATH comes to Step 2 it makes a search for a new vertex t. Since the search only involves immediate successors of u, and since the other operations are quick to carry out, the algorithm is fairly fast.

In many situations described by weighted graphs the min-weights and min-paths are the important concerns. One class of problems of considerable importance in business and manufacturing, where weighted digraphs are useful, but where min-paths are irrelevant, is the scheduling of processes which involve a number of steps. The following example illustrates the sort of situation which arises.

EXAMPLE 6 Consider a cook preparing a simple meal of curry and rice. The curry recipe calls for the following steps.

(a) Cut up meat—about 10 minutes.
(b) Grate onion—about 2 minutes with a food processor.
(c) Peel and quarter potatoes—about 5 minutes.
(d) Marinate meat, onions and spices—about 30 minutes.
(e) Heat oil—4 minutes. Fry potatoes—15 minutes.
   Fry cumin seed—2 minutes.
(f) Fry marinated meat—4 minutes.
(g) Bake fried meat and potatoes—60 minutes.

In addition, there is

(h) Cook rice—20 minutes.

We have grouped three steps together in (e), since they must be done in sequence. Some of the other steps can be done simultaneously if enough help is available. We suppose our cook has all the help needed.

Figure (6a) gives a digraph which shows the sequence of steps and the possibilities for parallel processing. Cutting, grating, peeling and rice cooking can all go on at once. The dotted arrows after cutting and peeling indicate that frying and marinating cannot begin until cutting and peeling are completed. The other two dotted arrows have similar meanings. The picture has

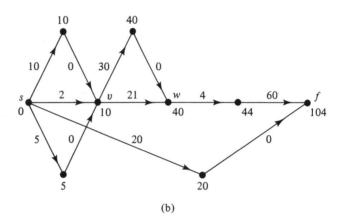

(a)

(b)

FIGURE 6

been redrawn in Figure 6(b) with weights on the edges to indicate time involved. [Ignore the numbers on the vertices for the moment.] The vertices denote stages of partial completion of the overall process, starting at the left and finishing at the right. In this case the min-path from left to right has weight 20, but there is much more total time required to prepare the meal than just the 20 minutes to cook the rice. The min-weight is no help. The important question here is: What is the smallest total time required to complete all steps in the process?

To answer the question we first examine vertices from left to right. Suppose we start at s at time 0. What is the earliest time we can have completed cutting, grating and peeling and arrive at vertex v? Clearly 10 minutes, since we must wait for the cutting no matter how soon we start grating or peeling. In fact, 10 is the *largest* weight of a path from s to v. Now what is the earliest time we can arrive at vertex w? The shortest time to get from v to w is 30 minutes [the largest weight of a path from v to w], so the shortest time to get from s to w is $10 + 30 = 40$ minutes. Similarly, the earliest we can complete the whole process and arrive at f is $40 + 4 + 60 = 104$ minutes after we start.

In each instance, the smallest time to arrive at a given vertex is the largest weight of a path from s to that vertex. The numbers beside the vertices in Figure 6(b) give these smallest times. □

An acyclic digraph with nonnegative weights and with unique source and sink, such as the digraphs in Figures 5 and 6, is called a **scheduling network**. For the rest of this section we suppose that we are dealing with a scheduling network G with source s [start] and sink f [finish]. For vertices u and v of G a **max-path** from u to v is a path of largest weight, and its weight is the **max-weight** from u to v, which we denote by $M(u, v)$. Max-weights and max-paths can be analyzed in much the same way as min-weights and min-paths. In § 8.8 we describe how to modify an algorithm for W^* to get one for M. For now we determine M by staring at the digraph.

A max-path from s to f is called a **critical path**, and an edge belonging to such a path is a **critical edge**. If $\langle u, v \rangle$ is an edge of G then

$$M(s, u) + W(u, v) + M(v, f) \leqq M(s, f)$$

since a path $s \cdots u\, v \cdots f$ certainly has no greater weight than a critical path from s to f, and equality holds if and only if $\langle u, v \rangle$ is part of a critical path. We define the **float time** $F(u, v)$ of the edge $\langle u, v \rangle$ by

$$F(u, v) = M(s, f) - M(s, u) - W(u, v) - M(v, f).$$

Then $F(u, v) \geqq 0$ for all edges $\langle u, v \rangle$, and $F(u, v) = 0$ if and only if $\langle u, v \rangle$ is a critical edge.

To get a meaningful interpretation of $F(u, v)$ we define two functions A and L on $V(G)$. If we start from s at time 0, the earliest time we can arrive at a vertex v having completed all tasks preceding v is $M(s, v)$. We denote this earliest arrival time by $A(v)$. In particular, $A(f) = M(s, f)$, the time in which the whole process can be completed. Let $L(v) = M(s, f) - M(v, f) = A(f) - M(v, f)$. Since $M(v, f)$ represents the shortest time required to complete all steps from v to f, $L(v)$ is the latest time we can leave v and still complete all remaining steps by time $A(f)$. To calculate $M(v, f)$ we work backwards from f.

EXAMPLE 7   The functions A and L for the scheduling network shown in Figure 7(a) are given in Figure 7(b). Since $A(x) = 5 = L(x)$ we must leave x as soon as we arrive to avoid delaying arrival at f. Similarly, we can't dawdle at u or y. Since $L(v) - A(v) = 9 - 7 = 2$ we may be able to delay departure from v by 2 time units without affecting the overall time from s to f. In this example the path $s\,u\,x\,y\,f$ is the unique critical path. □

To describe the float time $F(u, v)$ in terms of A, L and W observe that

$$F(u, v) = M(s, f) - M(v, f) - W(u, v) - M(s, u)$$
$$= L(v) - W(u, v) - A(u).$$

Thus $L(v) - A(u) = W(u, v) + F(u, v)$, i.e., the difference between the earliest we can arrive at u and the latest we can leave v is the time along the edge $\langle u, v \rangle$ plus the float time for that edge. An edge $\langle u, v \rangle$ is critical if and only if $L(v) - A(u) = W(u, v)$.

EXAMPLE 8   (a) For the example in Figure 7 the float time of the edge $\langle u, w \rangle$ is $L(w) - A(u) - W(u, w) = 7 - 2 - 2 = 3$. We could start along this edge as much as 3 time units after $A(u)$ and still arrive at w soon enough not to delay completion of the process. This edge $\langle u, w \rangle$ is not critical. On the other hand, we saw earlier that we must leave u on time in order to get to x on time. The edge $\langle u, x \rangle$ has float time $L(x) - A(u) - W(u, x) = 5 - 2 - 3 = 0$; it is critical.

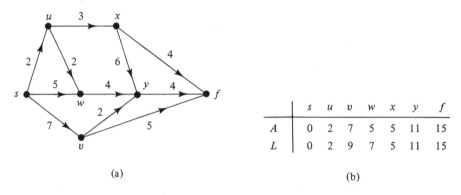

	s	u	v	w	x	y	f
A	0	2	7	5	5	11	15
L	0	2	9	7	5	11	15

(a)   (b)

FIGURE 7

(b) In the curry dinner problem of Example 6 the steps (a), (d), (f) and (g) are critical. The float time for cooking the rice is $104 - 0 - 20 = 84$ minutes [and in fact one would normally wait about 74 minutes before starting the rice to allow it to "rest" 10 minutes at the end]. The float time for heating the oil and frying potatoes and cumin seed is $40 - 10 - 21 = 9$ minutes. Speeding up these steps will have no effect on the total preparation time and there is no harm done if frying takes as many as 9 more minutes than expected.   ☐

As we just saw, shortening the time required for a noncritical edge does not decrease the total time $M(s, f)$ required for the process. Identification of critical edges focuses attention on those steps in a process where improvement may make a difference and where delays will surely be costly. Since its introduction in the 1950s the method of critical path analysis, sometimes called PERT for Program Evaluation and Review Technique, has been a popular way of dealing with industrial management scheduling problems.

EXERCISES 8.3

1. Give tables of W and W^* for the digraph of Figure 1 with the loop at B removed.

2. Give a table of W^* for the digraph of Figure 7(a).

3. Describe the possible weight functions W for an acyclic digraph with the min-weight function W^* given in Figure 4(a).

4. The path $s\,w\,v\,y\,x\,z\,f$ is a min-path from s to f in the digraph of Figure 2. Find another min-path from s to f in that digraph.

5. Figure 8 shows a weighted digraph. The directions and weights have been left off the edges, but the number at each vertex v is $W^*(s, v)$.
   (a) Give three different weight functions W which yield these values of $W^*(s, v)$. [An answer could consist of three pictures with appropriate numbers on the edges.]
   (b) Do the different weight assignments yield different min-paths between points? Explain.

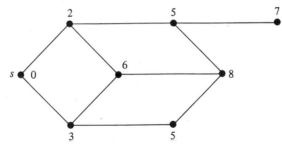

FIGURE 8

6. Apply Algorithm MIN-PATH to the digraph of Figure 5 using the format of Example 5 to find min-paths from
   (a) m to r (b) s to z (c) q to s

7. (a) Find a critical path for the digraph of Figure 2 with the edge from y to w removed.
   (b) Why does the critical path method apply only to acyclic digraphs?

8. How would you revise the digraph in Figure 5 if each vertex is also assigned a weight, say 2, that must be included in calculating the total weight of each path?

9. (a) Label the vertices in the digraph of Figure 9 and find all critical edges of the digraph.
   (b) How many critical paths does this digraph have?
   (c) What is the largest float time for an edge in this digraph?
   (d) Which edges have the largest float time?

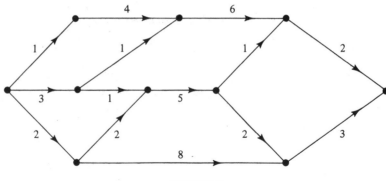

FIGURE 9

10. If the cook in Example 6 has no helpers, then steps (a), (b) and (c) must be done one after the other, but otherwise the situation is as in the example.
    (a) Draw a scheduling network for the no-helper process.
    (b) Find a critical path for this process.
    (c) Which steps in the process are not critical?

11. In Example 6 we used edges of weight 0 as a device to indicate that some steps could not start until others were finished.
    (a) Explain how to avoid such 0-edges if parallel edges are allowed.
    (b) Draw a digraph for the process of Example 6 to illustrate your answer.

12. Suppose that u, v and w are vertices of a weighted digraph with min-weight function W^* and that $W^*(u, v) + W^*(v, w) = W^*(u, w)$. Explain why there is a min-path from u to w through v.

13. Suppose all weights are positive. Show that if u and v are given, if t is chosen different from u such that $W^*(u, t) + W^*(t, v) = W^*(u, v)$ and if $W^*(u, t)$ is as small as possible with this property then there is an edge from u to t.

14. Write an algorithm based on solving the equation

$$W^*(u, t) + W(t, v) = W^*(u, v)$$

which finds min-paths from tables of W and W^* by working backwards from final vertex to starting vertex.

Note. The remaining exercises concern scheduling networks. The functions A, L and F are defined prior to Example 7.

15. (a) Show that $A(u) = \max\{A(w) + W(w, u) : \langle w, u \rangle \in E(G)\}$.
    (b) Show that $L(u) = \min\{L(v) - W(u, v) : \langle u, v \rangle \in E(G)\}$.

16. Define the **slack time** $S(v)$ of a vertex v in a scheduling network by $S(v) = L(v) - A(v)$.
    (a) Show that $S(v) \geq 0$ for all v.
    (b) Show that if $\langle u, v \rangle$ is a critical edge then $S(u) = S(v) = 0$. *Hint:* Use part (a) and Exercise 15.
    (c) If $\langle u, v \rangle$ is an edge with $S(u) = S(v) = 0$, must $\langle u, v \rangle$ be critical? Explain.

17. The float time $F(u, v)$ can be thought of as the amount of time we can delay starting along the edge $\langle u, v \rangle$ without delaying completion of the entire process.

Define the **free-float time** $FF(u, v)$ to be the amount of time we can delay starting along $\langle u, v \rangle$ without increasing $A(v)$.

(a) Find an expression for $FF(u, v)$ in terms of the functions A and W.

(b) Find $FF(u, v)$ for all edges of the digraph in Figure 7.

(c) What is the difference between $F(u, v)$ and $FF(u, v)$?

18. (a) Show that increasing the weight of a critical edge in a scheduling network increases the max-weight from the source to the sink.

(b) Is there any circumstance in which reducing the amount of time for a critical step in a process does not reduce the total time required for the process? Explain.

§ 8.4   *Undirected Graphs*

We now turn to the study of graphs where the edges have no directions associated with them. These are the sorts of graphs that were introduced in Chapter 0. Readers may wish to reread that chapter to reacquaint themselves with the kinds of problems that arise in this connection. However, the development here will be self-contained. This section is devoted to presenting basic definitions and properties of graphs of this type. Much of the material parallels the theory of digraphs we developed in the last three sections, but the questions we ask and the answers we get have a distinctly different character. The first few definitions were actually given in Example 6 of § 3.1.

Instead of being associated with an ordered pair of vertices, as edges in digraphs are, an undirected edge has an unordered set of vertices. Following the pattern we used for digraphs, we define an [undirected] **graph** G to consist of two sets, the set $V(G)$ of **vertices** of G and the set $E(G)$ of **edges** of G, together with a function γ from $E(G)$ to the set $\{\{u, v\} : u, v \in V(G)\}$ of all subsets of $V(G)$ with one or two members. For an edge e in $E(G)$ the members of $\gamma(e)$ are called the **vertices** of e or the **endpoints** of e; we say that e **joins** its endpoints. A **loop** is an edge with only one endpoint. Distinct edges e and f with $\gamma(e) = \gamma(f)$ are called **parallel** or **multiple** edges.

What we have just described is called a **multigraph** by some authors who reserve the term "graph" for those graphs with no loops or parallel edges. If a graph has no parallel edges we may identify an edge by listing its endpoints, in which case we will commonly write $e = \{u, v\}$ instead of $\gamma(e) = \{u, v\}$; we will also write $e = \{u, u\}$ instead of $e = \{u\}$ if e is a loop with vertex u.

A **picture** of a graph G is a diagram consisting of points corresponding to the vertices of G and arcs corresponding to edges, such that if $\gamma(e) = \{u, v\}$ then the arc for the edge e joins the points labeled u and v.

EXAMPLE 1   If we leave the direction arrows off of the edges in Figure 1 of § 8.1 we get the picture in Figure 1(a). A table of γ for this graph is given in Figure 1(b). This graph has parallel edges c and e joining x and z, and has a loop d with

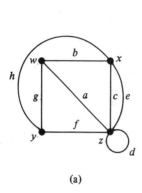

e	$\gamma(e)$
a	$\{w, z\}$
b	$\{w, x\}$
c	$\{x, z\}$
d	$\{z\}$ or $\{z, z\}$
e	$\{x, z\}$
f	$\{y, z\}$
g	$\{w, y\}$
h	$\{x, y\}$

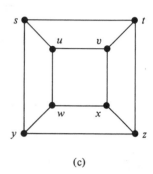

(a)   (b)   (c)

FIGURE 1

vertex z. The graph pictured in Figure 1(c) has no parallel edges, so for that graph a description such as "the edge $\{x, z\}$" is unambiguous. The same phrase could not be applied to the graph in Figure 1(a). □

A **path** of **length** n from the vertex u to the vertex v is a sequence $e_1 \cdots e_n$ of edges together with a sequence $x_1 \cdots x_{n+1}$ of vertices with $\gamma(e_i) = \{x_i, x_{i+1}\}$ for $i = 1, \ldots, n$ and $x_1 = u$, $x_{n+1} = v$. We will not have occasion to use paths of length 0; in what follows the length will always be a positive integer. If $e_1 e_2 \cdots e_n$ is a path from u to v with vertex sequence $x_1 x_2 \cdots x_{n+1}$, then $e_n \cdots e_2 e_1$ with vertex sequence $x_{n+1} x_n \cdots x_1$ is a path from v to u. We may speak of either of these paths as a **path between** u and v. If $u = v$ the path is **closed**.

The edge sequence of a path usually determines the vertex sequence, and we will sometimes use phrases such as "the path $e_1 e_2 \cdots e_n$" without mentioning vertices. Example 2 illustrates the possible fuzziness in such usage. If a graph has no parallel edges then the vertex sequence completely determines the edge sequence. In that setting, or if the actual choice of edges is unimportant, we will commonly use vertex sequences as descriptions for paths.

A path is called **simple** if all of its edges are different. Thus a simple path cannot use any edge twice, though it may go through the same vertex more than once. A closed simple path with vertex sequence $x_1 \cdots x_n x_1$ is called a **cycle** if the vertices $x_1, \ldots, x_n$ are distinct. A graph is **acyclic** if it contains no cycle. A path is **acyclic** if the "subgraph" consisting of the vertices and edges of the path is acyclic. In general a graph H is a **subgraph** of a graph G if $V(H) \subseteq V(G)$, $E(H) \subseteq E(G)$ and the function γ for G defined on $E(G)$ agrees with the γ for H on $E(H)$. If G has no parallel edges and if we think of $E(G)$ as a set of one- or two-element subsets of $V(G)$, the condition on γ follows from $E(H) \subseteq E(G)$.

EXAMPLE 2   (a) Consider the graph pictured in Figure 2(a). The path $e\,e$ with vertex sequence $x_1\,x_2\,x_1$ is a closed path, but it is not a cycle because it is not simple. Neither is the path $e\,e$ with vertex sequence $x_2\,x_1\,x_2$. This graph is acyclic.

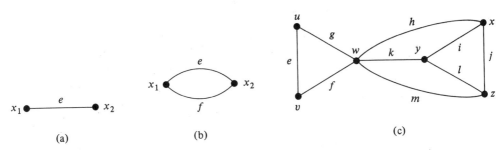

(a)   (b)   (c)

FIGURE 2

(b) The path $e\,f$ with vertex sequence $x_1\,x_2\,x_1$ in the graph of Figure 2(b) is a cycle. So is the path $e\,f$ with vertex sequence $x_2\,x_1\,x_2$.

(c) In the graph of Figure 2(c) the path $e\,f\,h\,i\,k\,g$ of length 6 with vertex sequence $u\,v\,w\,x\,y\,w\,u$ is closed and simple but is not a cycle because the first six vertices u, v, w, x, y and w are not all different. The path with vertex sequence $u\,w\,v\,w\,u\,v\,u$ also fails to be a cycle. The graph as a whole is not acyclic, and neither are these two paths, since $u\,v\,w\,u$ is a cycle in both of their subgraphs. □

A path $e_1\,\cdots\,e_n$ with all of $x_1,\ldots,x_{n+1}$ distinct must surely be simple since no two edges in it can have the same set of endpoints. Example 2(a) shows, however, that a closed path with $x_1,\ldots,x_n$ distinct need not be simple. That bad example is essentially the only one there is, as the following shows.

Proposition 1   Every closed path $e_1\,\cdots\,e_n$ of length at least 3 with $x_1,\ldots,x_n$ distinct is a cycle.

Proof. We only need to show that $e_1,\ldots,e_n$ are different. Since $x_1,\ldots,$ x_n are distinct, the path $e_1\,\cdots\,e_{n-1}$ is simple. That is, $e_1,\ldots,e_{n-1}$ are all different. But $\gamma(e_n)=\{x_n,x_1\}$ and $\gamma(e_i)=\{x_i,x_{i+1}\}$ for $i<n$. Since $n\geq 3$, $e_n\neq e_i$ for $i<n$ and so the path is simple. □

For paths which are not closed, distinctness of vertices can be characterized another way.

Proposition 2   A path has all vertices distinct if and only if it is simple and acyclic.

Proof. Consider first a path with distinct vertices. It must be simple, as we observed earlier. We prove it is acyclic by induction on its length. If the length is 1 the path is clearly acyclic. Suppose the path has length $n>1$

with vertex sequence $x_1 \cdots x_n x_{n+1}$. By the inductive assumption, the path $x_1 \cdots x_n$ is acyclic, so any cycle in our path must contain the edge joining x_n and x_{n+1}. But x_{n+1} is not a vertex of any other edge in the path, so it's not on any closed path made from edges in the path. Thus our path contains no cycle. The conclusion now follows by induction.

For the converse, suppose a simple path has vertex sequence $x_1 \cdots x_{n+1}$ with some repeated vertices. Consider two such vertices, say x_i and x_j with $i < j$ and with the difference $j - i$ as small as possible. Then $x_i, x_{i+1}, \ldots, x_{j-1}$ are all distinct, so the simple path $x_i x_{i+1} \cdots x_{j-1} x_j$ is a cycle [even if $j = i + 1$] and the original path contains a cycle.   ☐

It follows from Proposition 2 that every simple closed path contains a cycle, and in fact the proof shows that such a cycle can be built out of successive edges in the path.

The following result is analogous to Theorem 1 of § 8.1.

Theorem 1   If u and v are distinct vertices of a graph G and if there is a path in G from u to v, then there is a simple acyclic path from u to v.

Proof. Among all paths from u to v in G choose one of smallest length, say with vertex sequence $x_1 \cdots x_{n+1}$, $x_1 = u$ and $x_{n+1} = v$. Just as in the proof of Theorem 1 of § 8.1 the vertices $x_1, \ldots, x_{n+1}$ are distinct. By Proposition 2, the path is simple and acyclic.   ☐

Corollary   If there is a simple closed path in G with u as a vertex, then there is a cycle in G with u as a vertex.

Proof. If there is a loop with u as vertex we are done, so suppose there is no such loop. Then the given simple closed path $e_1 e_2 \cdots e_n$ has at least two edges. We may assume the vertex sequence is $x_1 \cdots x_n x_{n+1}$ with $x_1 = x_{n+1} = u$. Then $e_1 \cdots e_{n-1}$ is a simple path from u to x_n. Since $e_1, \ldots, e_n$ are distinct, the path $e_1 \cdots e_{n-1}$ lies in the graph $G \setminus \{e_n\}$ obtained from G by leaving out the edge e_n. Applying Theorem 1 to the graph $G \setminus \{e_n\}$ we get a simple acyclic path $f_1 \cdots f_m$ from u to x_n in $G \setminus \{e_n\}$. Then the path $f_1 \cdots f_m e_n$ is closed. Since $f_1 \cdots f_m$ is simple and acyclic, its vertices are distinct by Proposition 2. Thus only the first and last vertices of $f_1 \cdots f_m e_n$ are equal; i.e., $f_1 \cdots f_m e_n$ is a cycle through u.   ☐

We will have other occasions, especially in Chapter 9, to remove an edge e to get a new graph $G \setminus \{e\}$. The graph $G \setminus \{e\}$ is the subgraph of G with $V(G \setminus \{e\}) = V(G)$ and $E(G \setminus \{e\}) = E(G) \setminus \{e\}$.

The portion of § 8.1 after Theorem 1 and its corollary dealt with sinks in acyclic digraphs. For undirected graphs the corresponding ideas lead to the notion of connectedness, which we examine in the next two sections, and to the study of trees in Chapter 9, where we will need the following fact.

Theorem 2 If the graph G has two distinct vertices u and v and has two different simple paths from u to v then G contains a cycle.

We will most frequently use this theorem in its contrapositive form:

If G is acyclic and if u and v are distinct vertices of G then there is at most one simple path in G from u to v.

Proof of Theorem 2. If G has a loop or has parallel edges it clearly contains a cycle and we are done. Thus suppose G has no loops or parallel edges. Then each path is completely described by its vertex sequence. Suppose $x_0 \cdots x_n$ and $y_0 \cdots y_m$ are vertex sequences for two different simple paths with $x_0 = y_0 = u$ and $x_n = y_m = v$. If either path contains a cycle we are done, so suppose both paths are acyclic. The idea is to build a cycle out of parts of these paths. Since the paths are different, there is an index i such that $x_0 = y_0, \ldots, x_{i-1} = y_{i-1}$, but $x_i \neq y_i$. Let $w = x_{i-1} = y_{i-1}$. Since $x_n = y_m$ there is at least one pair of indices $\langle j, k \rangle$ such that $i \leqq j$, $i \leqq k$ and $x_j = y_k$. Consider such a pair with $j + k$ as small as possible, and let $z = x_j = y_k$.

Now form the path $w x_i \cdots x_{j-1} z y_{k-1} \cdots y_i w$, going out from w to z along the x-path and back from z to w along the y-path. Since $x_i \neq y_i$ this closed path has length at least 3. We claim it's a cycle. By Proposition 1 we only need to show that $w, x_i, \ldots, x_{j-1}, z, y_{k-1}, \ldots, y_i$ are distinct. Since the x-path and y-path are acyclic, the vertices going out are all different and the ones coming back are all different. By the choice of $\langle j, k \rangle$, none of $x_i, \ldots, x_{j-1}$ can be any of $y_i, \ldots, y_{k-1}$. Thus the path is a cycle. ☐

EXAMPLE 3 For the graph of Figure 2(c), $x\,z\,w\,u$ and $x\,z\,y\,w\,v\,u$ are simple paths from x to u. In the notation of the proof of Theorem 2, $x_0 = x$, $x_1 = z$, $x_2 = w$, $x_3 = u$ and $y_0 = x$, $y_1 = z$, $y_2 = y$, $y_3 = w$, $y_4 = v$, $y_5 = u$. Since $x_1 = y_1$ and $x_2 \neq y_2$, $i = 2$. Since $x_2 = y_3 = w$, $j = 2$ and $k = 3$. The path $x_1\,w\,y_2\,y_1$, i.e., $z\,w\,y\,z$, is the cycle constructed by the proof. The path $x_2\,x_3\,y_4\,y_3$, i.e., $w\,u\,v\,w$, is also a cycle made from parts of the x-path and the y-path. ☐

The ideas of isomorphism and invariant which we encountered in § 8.2 have natural counterparts for graphs which are not directed. If G and H are graphs without parallel edges and we consider edges to be one- or two-element sets of vertices, an **isomorphism** of G onto H is a one-to-one correspondence $\alpha: V(G) \to V(H)$ such that $\{u, v\}$ is in $E(G)$ if and only if $\{\alpha(u), \alpha(v)\}$ is in $E(H)$. Two graphs G and H are **isomorphic**, written $G \simeq H$, if there is an isomorphism α of one onto the other, in which case the inverse correspondence α^{-1} is also an isomorphism. For graphs with parallel edges the situation is slightly more complicated: we require two one-to-one correspondences $\alpha: V(G) \to V(H)$ and $\beta: E(G) \to E(H)$ such that an edge e of $E(G)$

joins vertices u and v in $V(G)$ if and only if the corresponding edge $\beta(e)$ joins $\alpha(u)$ and $\alpha(v)$.

EXAMPLE 4 The correspondence α with $\alpha(t) = t'$, $\alpha(u) = u', \ldots, \alpha(z) = z'$ is an isomorphism between the graphs pictured in Figures 3(a) and 3(b). The graphs shown in Figures 3(c) and 3(d) are also isomorphic to each other, but not to the graphs in parts (a) and (b). ▯

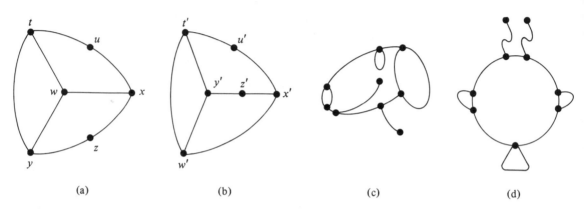

(a)   (b)   (c)   (d)

FIGURE 3

To tell the graphs of Figures 3(a) and 3(c) apart we can simply count vertices. Just as we observed when dealing with digraphs, isomorphic graphs have the same number of vertices and the same number of edges. These two numbers are examples of **isomorphism invariants** for graphs. Other examples include the number of loops and number of simple paths of a given length.

As in the case of digraphs we can count the number of edges attached to a particular vertex. To get the right count we need to treat loops differently from edges with two distinct vertices. We define $\deg(v)$, the **degree** of the vertex v, to be the number of 2-vertex edges with v as a vertex plus twice the number of loops with v as vertex. The number $D_k(G)$ of vertices of degree k in G is an isomorphism invariant, as is the **degree sequence** $(D_0(G), D_1(G), D_2(G), \ldots)$.

EXAMPLE 5   (a) The graphs shown in Figures 3(a) and 3(b) each have degree sequence $(0, 0, 2, 4, 0, 0, \ldots)$. Those in Figures 3(c) and 3(d) have degree sequence $(0, 2, 0, 6, 1, 0, 0, \ldots)$.

(b) Erasing the arrows from the digraphs of Figure 6 of § 8.2 gives the graphs pictured in Figure 4. All four graphs have eight vertices of degree 3 and no others. It turns out that $H_1 \simeq H_2 \simeq H_3$, but that none of these three is isomorphic to H_4. Having the same degree sequence does not guarantee isomorphism. ▯

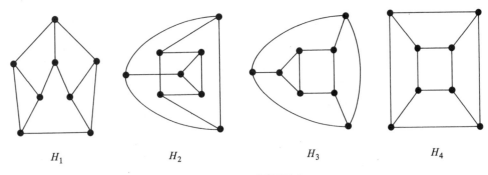

H_1 H_2 H_3 H_4

FIGURE 4

Graphs in which all vertices have the same degree, such as those in Figure 4, are called **regular** graphs. As the example shows, regular graphs with the same number of vertices need not be isomorphic. Graphs without loops or multiple edges and in which every vertex is joined to every other by an edge are called **complete** graphs. A complete graph with n vertices has vertices of degree $n - 1$, so such a graph is regular. All complete graphs with n vertices are isomorphic to each other and so we use the symbol K_n for any of them.

EXAMPLE 6   Figure 5(a) shows the first five complete graphs. The graph in Figure 5(b) has four vertices, each of degree 3, but is not complete. ☐

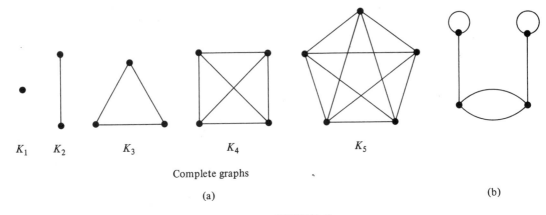

K_1 K_2 K_3 K_4 K_5

Complete graphs

(a)   (b)

FIGURE 5

A complete graph K_n contains subgraphs isomorphic to the graphs K_m for $m = 1, 2, \ldots, n$. Such a subgraph can be obtained by selecting any m of the n vertices and using all the edges in K_n joining them. Thus K_5 contains $\binom{5}{2} = 10$ subgraphs isomorphic to K_2, $\binom{5}{3} = 10$ subgraphs isomorphic to K_3 [i.e., triangles], and $\binom{5}{4} = 5$ subgraphs isomorphic to K_4. In fact, K_n contains subgraphs isomorphic to all of the graphs with n or fewer vertices and with no loops or parallel edges.

Complete graphs have a high degree of symmetry. Each permutation α of the vertices of a complete graph gives an isomorphism of the graph onto itself, since both $\{u, v\}$ and $\{\alpha(u), \alpha(v)\}$ are edges whenever $u \neq v$.

The next theorem is an analogue to the theorem of § 8.2. You may have anticipated part (a) if you worked Exercise 12 in § 0.1.

Theorem 3   (a) The sum of the degrees of the vertices of a graph is twice the number of edges. That is,

$$\sum_{v \in V(G)} \deg(v) = 2 \cdot |E(G)|.$$

(b) $D_1(G) + 2D_2(G) + 3D_3(G) + 4D_4(G) + \cdots = 2 \cdot |E(G)|.$

Proof. (a) Each edge, whether a loop or not, contributes 2 to the degree sum.

(b) The total degree sum contribution from the $D_k(G)$ vertices of degree k is $k \cdot D_k(G)$.   ☐

EXAMPLE 7   (a) The graph of Figure 1(a) has vertices w, x, y and z of degrees 3, 4, 3 and 6, and has eight edges. The degree sequence is $(0, 0, 0, 2, 1, 0, 1, 0, 0, \ldots)$. Sure enough,

$$3 + 4 + 3 + 6 = 2 \cdot 8 = 1 \cdot 0 + 2 \cdot 0 + 3 \cdot 2 + 4 \cdot 1 + 5 \cdot 0 + 6 \cdot 1.$$

(b) The complete graph K_n has n vertices, each of degree $n - 1$, and has $n(n - 1)/2$ edges.   ☐

Most of the remaining observations of § 8.2 are still true in the undirected context. In particular, the problem of determining when two graphs are isomorphic is still a difficult one.

EXERCISES 8.4

1. (a) Give a table of the function γ for the graph G pictured in Figure 6.
   (b) List the edges of this graph, considered as subsets of $V(G)$. For example, $a = \{w, x\}$.

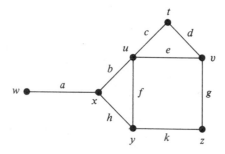

FIGURE 6

2. Draw a picture of the graph G with $V(G) = \{x, y, z, w\}$, $E(G) = \{a, b, c, d, f,$ $g, h\}$ and γ given by the table:

e	a	b	c	d	f	g	h
$\gamma(e)$	$\{x, y\}$	$\{x, y\}$	$\{w, x\}$	$\{w, y\}$	$\{y, z\}$	$\{y, z\}$	$\{w, z\}$

3. Consider the graph of Figure 6. Carry out the steps in the proof of Theorem 2 to construct cycles starting with the pairs of simple paths with the given vertex sequences.
   (a) $v\,u\,y\,x$ and $v\,z\,y\,u\,x$
   (b) $w\,x\,u\,v\,t\,u\,y$ and $w\,x\,y$
   (c) $w\,x\,u\,t\,v\,z\,y$ and $w\,x\,y$

4. (a) Draw pictures of all 14 graphs with three vertices and three edges. "All" here means one example from each isomorphism class.
   (b) Draw pictures of all graphs with four vertices and four edges which have no loops or parallel edges.
   (c) List the four graphs in parts (a) and (b) which are regular.

5. (a) Draw pictures of all five of the regular graphs with four vertices, each vertex of degree 2.
   (b) Draw pictures of all of the regular graphs with four vertices, each of degree 3, and with no loops or parallel edges.
   (c) Draw pictures of all of the regular graphs with five vertices, each of degree 3.

6. Suppose that a graph H is isomorphic to the graph G of Figure 6.
   (a) How many vertices of degree 1 does H have?
   (b) Give the degree sequence of H.
   (c) How many different isomorphisms are there of G onto G? Explain.
   (d) How many isomorphisms are there of G onto H?

7. Which, if any, of the pairs of graphs shown in Figure 7 are isomorphic? Justify your answer by describing an isomorphism or explaining why one does not exist.

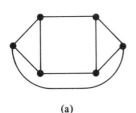

(a)

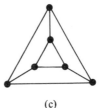

(b)   (c)

(d)

FIGURE 7

8. Describe an isomorphism between the graphs shown in Figure 8.

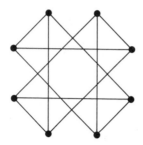   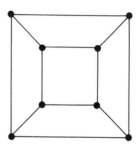

FIGURE 8

9. Consider the complete graph K_8 with vertices $v_1, v_2, \ldots, v_8$.
   (a) How many subgraphs of K_8 are isomorphic to K_5?
   (b) How many simple paths with 3 or fewer edges are there from v_1 to v_2?
   (c) How many simple paths with 3 or fewer edges are there altogether in K_8?

10. How many different isomorphisms are there of the graph K_n onto itself?

11. (a) A graph with 21 edges has 7 vertices of degree 1, 3 of degree 2, 7 of degree 3 and the rest of degree 4. How many vertices does it have?
   (b) How would your answer to part (a) change if the graph also had 6 vertices of degree 0?

12. Show that the number of vertices of odd degree is even.

13. Which of the following are degree sequences of graphs? In each case either draw a graph with the given degree sequence or explain why no such graph exists.
   (a) $(1, 1, 0, 3, 1, 0, 0, \ldots)$ (b) $(4, 1, 0, 3, 1, 0, 0, \ldots)$
   (c) $(0, 1, 0, 2, 1, 0, 0, \ldots)$ (d) $(0, 0, 2, 2, 1, 0, 0, \ldots)$
   (e) $(0, 0, 1, 2, 1, 0, 0, \ldots)$ (f) $(0, 1, 0, 2, 1, 0, 0, \ldots)$
   (g) $(0, 0, 0, 4, 0, 0, 0, \ldots)$ (h) $(0, 0, 0, 0, 5, 0, 0, \ldots)$

14. Show that a path in a graph G is a cycle if and only if it is possible to assign directions to the edges of G so that the path is a [directed] cycle in the resulting digraph.

15. Show that every finite graph in which each vertex has degree at least 2 contains a cycle.

16. Show that every graph with n vertices and at least n edges contains a cycle. *Hint:* Use induction on n and Exercise 15.

17. Show that
$$2|E(G)| - |V(G)| = -D_0(G) + D_2(G) + 2D_3(G) + \cdots + (k-1)D_k(G) + \cdots.$$

18. (a) Let S be a set of graphs. Show that isomorphism $\simeq$ is an equivalence relation on S.
   (b) How many equivalence classes are there if S consists of the four graphs in Figure 4?

§ 8.5   *Edge Traversal Problems*

Euler's solution to the Königsberg bridge problem is discussed in § 0.1; the Königsberg graph is shown in Figure 5 of that section. FLEURY'S algorithm, which provides a constructive solution to the problem, is discussed in § 0.2. In this section we prove Euler's theorem and some related results and justify FLEURY'S algorithm. A simple path which contains all edges of a graph G is called an **Euler path** of G, and a closed Euler path is called an **Euler circuit**. Euler's solution to the Königsberg bridge problem began with the following elementary observation, whose simple proof is given on page 6.

Theorem 1   A graph which has an Euler circuit must have all vertices of even degree.

Corollary   A graph which has an Euler path has either 2 vertices of odd degree or no vertices of odd degree.

Proof. Suppose G has an Euler path starting at u and ending at v. If $u = v$, the path is closed and Theorem 1 says all vertices have even degree. If $u \neq v$, create a new edge e joining u and v. The new graph $G \cup \{e\}$ has an Euler circuit consisting of the Euler path for G followed by e, so all vertices of $G \cup \{e\}$ have even degree. Remove e. Then u and v are the only vertices of $G = (G \cup (\{e\})\backslash\{e\}$ of odd degree.   □

EXAMPLE 1   The graph shown in Figure 1(a) has no Euler circuit, since u and v have odd degree, but the path $b\,a\,c\,d\,g\,f\,e$ is an Euler path. The graph in Figure 1(b) has all vertices of even degree and in fact has an Euler circuit. The graph in Figure 1(c) has all vertices of even degree but has no Euler circuit, for the obvious reason that the graph is disconnected into two subgraphs which are not connected to each other. Each of the subgraphs, however, has its own Euler circuit.   □

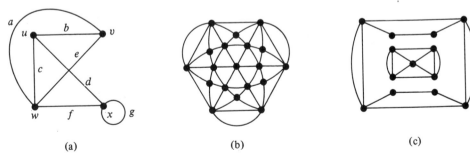

(a)   (b)   (c)

FIGURE 1

Theorem 1 shows that the even-degree condition is necessary for the existence of an Euler circuit. Euler's major contribution to the problem was his proof that, except for the sort of obvious trouble we ran into in Figure 1(c), the condition is also sufficient to guarantee an Euler path.

We need some terminology to describe the exceptional cases. A graph is called **connected** if each pair of distinct vertices is joined by a path in the graph. The graphs in Figures 1(a) and 1(b) are connected, but the one in Figure 1(c) is not. A connected subgraph of a graph G which is not contained properly in another connected subgraph of G is called a **component** of G. We will show in § 8.7 that the component containing a given vertex v consists of v and all vertices and edges on paths starting at v. For now, we will think of components as maximal connected subgraphs.

EXAMPLE 2   (a) The graphs of Figures 1(a) and 1(b) are connected. In these cases the graph has just one component, namely the graph itself.

(b) The graph of Figure 1(c) has two components, the one drawn on the outside and the one on the inside. Another picture of this graph is shown in Figure 2(a). In this picture there is no "inside" component, but of course there are still two components.

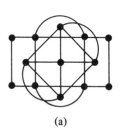   

(a)   (b)

FIGURE 2

(c) The graph of Figure 2(b) has seven components, two of which are isolated vertices.   □

We now restate Euler's theorem in § 0.1.

Theorem 2   A finite connected graph in which every vertex has even degree has an Euler circuit.

Before we prove this theorem we illustrate the idea of the proof in a concrete case.

EXAMPLE 3   Consider the graph shown in Figure 3(a). We want a closed simple path which includes all edges, and we observe that $a\,b\,c\,d\,e$ is at least closed and simple, even though it does not contain all edges. We remove the edges a, b, c, d, e. What's left is almost the graph of Figure 3(b). To get Figure 3(b) we also removed the vertex v which would otherwise have been isolated. Now

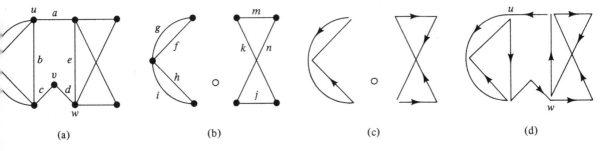

FIGURE 3

we can look at the two components of Figure 3(b) and see that they have their own Euler circuits $g\,i\,h\,f$ and $j\,k\,m\,n$, as illustrated in Figure 3(c). We can attach those circuits to the cycle $a\,b\,c\,d\,e$ at u and w to get the simple closed path $a\,g\,i\,h\,f\,b\,c\,d\,j\,k\,m\,n\,e$ of Figure 3(d), which is an Euler circuit for the original graph. □

Proof of Theorem 2. Suppose G is a finite connected graph with every vertex of even degree. If G has just one vertex the theorem is trivial, so assume $|V(G)| \geqq 2$. Since G is connected, each vertex has degree at least 1, and hence at least 2 since all degrees are even.

We first claim that G contains at least one cycle. Let $v_1\,v_2 \cdots v_n$ be the vertex sequence of a path of largest possible length with distinct vertices. Since $\deg(v_n) \geqq 2$ there is an edge at v_n different from the last edge in the path. It must join v_n and some v_i with $i \leqq n$, or else our chosen path would not be longest possible. Then the path $v_i\,v_{i+1} \cdots v_n\,v_i$ with the new edge at the end is a cycle.

Now choose a cycle C in G and remove from G all the edges in C and all the vertices of degree 2 on C, to obtain the subgraph $G \setminus C$. Since C is closed its removal decreases the degree of each vertex by an even number, so every vertex of $G \setminus C$ has even degree. If $G \setminus C$ is empty, then $G = C$ and we are done. Otherwise each of the components of $G \setminus C$ satisfies the hypotheses of the theorem.

It's time for induction. We could have supposed to begin with that the theorem is true for all graphs with fewer edges than G has. Then each component of $G \setminus C$ has its own Euler circuit. [To make a constructive algorithm out of this proof, call the algorithm itself recursively on the components.] The components were connected to all the vertices of C before we removed the edges of C, so each has at least one vertex on C. Choose such a vertex in each component. As in Example 3, proceed along C and at each of the chosen vertices attach the corresponding component Euler circuit. The resulting path is closed, simple and contains all the edges of G; it is an Euler circuit for G. □

Corollary   A finite connected graph which has exactly two vertices of odd degree has an Euler path.

> *Proof.* Say u and v have odd degree. Create a new edge e joining them. Then $G \cup \{e\}$ has all vertices of even degree and so has an Euler circuit by Theorem 2. Remove e again. What remains of the circuit is an Euler path for G. ⬜

The arguments used in the proofs of Theorems 1 and 2 can be easily modified to prove the following analogous result for digraphs.

Digraph   Suppose G is a digraph with more than one edge in which every vertex is
Version   reachable from every other vertex. There is a closed [directed] path in G which contains all edges of G if and only if indeg (v) = outdeg (v) for every vertex v.

We can make the proof of Theorem 2 into an algorithm for actually finding an Euler circuit. The following algorithm gives a different way of constructing Euler paths and circuits, one edge at a time. When the algorithm terminates, the sequence ES is the edge sequence of an Euler path or circuit and VS is its vertex sequence.

FLEURY'S *Algorithm.*

Step 1. Start at any vertex v of odd degree if there is one. Otherwise start at any vertex v. Let VS = v and let ES = ϵ [the empty sequence].

Step 2. If there is no edge remaining at v, stop.

Step 3. If there is exactly one edge remaining at v, say e from v to w, then remove e from $E(G)$ and v from $V(G)$ and go to Step 5.

Step 4. If there is more than one edge remaining at v, choose such an edge, say e from v to w, whose removal will not disconnect the graph; then remove e from $E(G)$.

Step 5. Add w to the end of VS, add e to the end of ES, replace v by w and go to Step 2. ⬜

This algorithm was illustrated at the beginning of § 0.2. Before discussing why it works, we give another example to illustrate its use.

EXAMPLE 4   Consider the graph of Figure 4(a). This graph does not have an Euler circuit, but it does have an Euler path joining the vertices z and y of odd degree. We start from z; i.e., let $v = z$ in Step 1. Thus VS = z and ES = ϵ. The only edge at z is i. So we go to Step 3, choose $e = i$ and $w = y$, remove i from $E(G)$, remove z from $V(G)$ and go to Step 5. Then VS = zy and ES = i. The new G with both i and z deleted is shown in Figure 4(b). Let $v = y$ and return to Step 2. There are three edges at v, so Step 4 applies.

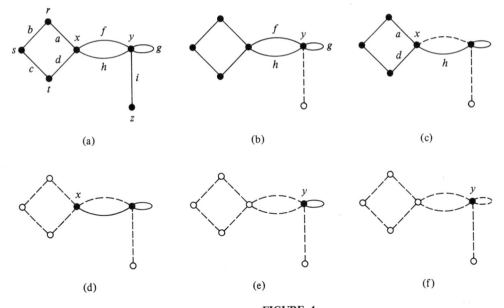

FIGURE 4

Now e can be f, g or h. Let's take $e = f$ in Step 4. Step 5 gives VS $= z\, y\, x$, ES $= i\, f$, $v = x$ and the new G shown in Figure 4(c). Return to Step 2. Again there are three edges at v and Step 4 applies.

Now e can be either a or d, but not h since removing h would disconnect the graph. Let's choose $e = a$; Step 5 gives VS $= z\, y\, x\, r$, ES $= i\, f\, a$ and $v = r$.

The next three moves are forced. Each leads to Step 3 and the removal of a vertex as well as an edge. We arrive at VS $= z\, y\, x\, r\, s\, t\, x$, ES $= i\, f\, a\, b\, c\, d$, $v = x$ and the graph shown in Figure 4(d).

The remaining two moves are also forced and lead to the graphs in Figures 4(e) and 4(f). The final vertex and edge sequences are VS $= z\, y\, x\, r\, s\, t\, x\, y\, y$ and ES $= i\, f\, a\, b\, c\, d\, h\, g$. $\square$

To prove that FLEURY'S algorithm works, we need the next theorem. It will also play a major role in our treatment of trees in Chapter 9.

Theorem 3   Let e be an edge of a connected graph G. The following are equivalent:

    (a) $G\backslash\{e\}$ is connected.
    (b) e is an edge of some cycle in G.
    (c) e is an edge of some simple closed path in G.

Proof. First note that if e is a loop, then $G \backslash \{e\}$ is connected, while e is a cycle all by itself. Since cycles are simple closed paths, the theorem holds in this case, and we may assume that e is not a loop. Thus e connects distinct vertices u and v. If f is another edge connecting u and v, then clearly $G \setminus \{e\}$ is connected and $e f$ is a cycle containing e. So the theorem also holds in this case. Hence we may assume that e is the unique edge connecting u and v.

(a) $\Rightarrow$ (b). Suppose that $G \setminus \{e\}$ is connected. By Theorem 1 of § 8.4 there is a simple acyclic path $x_1 x_2 \cdots x_m$ with $u = x_1$ and $x_m = v$. Since there is no edge from u to v in $G \setminus \{e\}$, we have $x_2 \neq v$ and so $m \geq 3$. As noted in Proposition 2 of § 8.4, the vertices $x_1, x_2, \ldots, x_m$ are distinct and so $x_1 x_2 \cdots x_m u$ is a cycle in G containing the edge e.

(b) $\Rightarrow$ (c). This is obvious since cycles are simple closed paths.

(c) $\Rightarrow$ (a). Now suppose that e is an edge of some simple closed path. Since e is not a loop or parallel edge, e belongs to a simple closed path $v_1 v_2 \cdots v_{n+1}$ where $v_1 = u$, $v_2 = v$, $v_{n+1} = u$ and $n \geq 3$. Consider any vertices x and y of G. Since G is connected, there is some path $w_1 w_2 \cdots w_r$ with $x = w_1$ and $w_r = y$. If u and v appear as consecutive w_i's, replace the edge $u v$ in the path from x to y by the path $v_{n+1} v_n \cdots v_3 v$. If v and u appear as consecutive w_i's, replace $v u$ by $v v_3 \cdots v_n v_{n+1}$. In this way we obtain a path from x to y that doesn't use e, i.e., a path in $G \setminus \{e\}$. Thus any two vertices of G are connected by a path in $G \setminus \{e\}$ and so $G \setminus \{e\}$ is connected. $\quad\square$

Proof That FLEURY'S Algorithm Works. We consider a finite connected graph all of whose vertices have even degree, and we show that FLEURY'S algorithm produces an Euler circuit. Modifications showing that we get an Euler path in the case of two vertices of odd degree are straightforward.

Each pass through the loop from Step 2 through Step 5 removes an edge from G and adds it to ES in such a way that the edges in ES form a path. Since G has only a finite number of edges to begin with, the algorithm must stop—or break down—sooner or later, and no edge can appear more than once in the path determined by ES. We need to show that the algorithm does not break down, and that when it stops ES contains every edge of G.

The only possible breakdown would occur in Step 4. Say G' is the current value of G and v' the current value of v. How do we know that if G' has more than one edge at v' then there is an edge at v' whose removal does not disconnect G'? Since the edges in ES form a path, either G' has two vertices of odd degree, one of which is v' and the other the vertex v_0 chosen in Step 1, or else $v' = v_0$ and G' has no vertices of odd degree. In the first case, G' has an Euler path from v' to v_0 by the corollary to Theorem 2, and in the second case G' has an Euler circuit by Theorem 2 itself. Either way, since v' has degree at least 2 and every edge of G' is involved in the Euler path or circuit of G', there is a simple closed path in G' which includes two edges at v'. Removing one of these edges cannot disconnect G', in view of Theorem 3. Thus the algorithm does not break down.

Why are there no edges left at the end? At the start the graph is connected, when we execute Step 4 the graph remains connected, and when we execute Step 3 the graph also remains connected, because after we remove the edge *e* we also remove the isolated vertex *v* which is left. So at all times the graph is connected. When we're forced to stop because there is no edge left at *v'* there must not be any other vertices left in *G'* either. Hence *G'* has no edges whatever and ES contains every edge of *G*.   ☐

EXERCISES 8.5

1. Consider the graph shown in Figure 5(a).
   (a) Describe an Euler path for this graph or explain why there isn't one.
   (b) Describe an Euler circuit for this graph or explain why there isn't one.

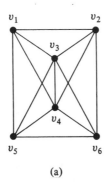
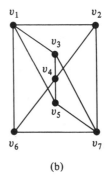

(a)   (b)

FIGURE 5

2. Repeat Exercise 1 for the graph of Figure 5(b).

3. Is it possible for an insect to crawl along the edges of a cube so as to travel along each edge exactly once? Explain.

4. Draw an Euler circuit in the style of Figure 3(d) for the graph of Figure 1(b).

5. Which complete graphs K_n have Euler circuits?

6. Apply FLEURY'S algorithm as in Example 4 to get an Euler path for the graph of Figure 1(a). Sketch the intermediate graphs obtained in the application of the algorithm, as was done in Figure 4.

7. Construct a graph with vertex set $\{0, 1\}^3$ and with an edge between vertices *v* and *w* if *v* and *w* differ in two coordinates.
   (a) How many components does the graph have?
   (b) How many vertices does the graph have of each degree?
   (c) Does the graph have an Euler circuit?

8. Answer the same questions as in Exercise 7 for the graph with vertex set $\{0, 1\}^3$ and with an edge between *v* and *w* if *v* and *w* differ in two or three coordinates.

9. (a) Show that if a connected graph *G* has exactly 2*k* vertices of odd degree then *E(G)* is the disjoint union of the edge sets of *k* simple paths. *Hint:* Add more edges, as in the proof of the corollary to Theorem 2.
   (b) Find two disjoint simple paths whose edge set union is *E(G)* for the Königsberg graph in Figure 5 on page 5.
   (c) Do the same for the graph in Figure 5(b) of Exercise 1.

10. (a) Use the proof of Theorem 2 to create an algorithm for finding Euler circuits.

(b) How would you modify the algorithm so that it would find Euler paths?

§ *8.6   Vertex Traversal Problems*

In § 0.2 we discussed Hamilton circuits and pointed out that characterizing them and finding techniques for discovering them in graphs are very difficult problems. Some facts can be proved, however, and this is our next task. We also discuss a couple of applications.

A path with vertex sequence $x_1 \, x_2 \cdots x_n$ is called a **Hamilton path** for the graph G if $x_1, x_2, \ldots, x_n$ are distinct and $\{x_1, x_2, \ldots, x_n\} = V(G)$. A closed path $x_1 \, x_2 \cdots x_n \, x_1$ is called a **Hamilton circuit** of G if $x_1 \, x_2 \cdots x_n$ is a Hamilton path, and a graph which has a Hamilton circuit is called a **Hamiltonian graph**. A Hamilton path must clearly be simple, and by Proposition 1 of § 8.4 if G has at least 3 vertices a Hamilton circuit of G must be a cycle.

EXAMPLE 1   (a) The graph shown in Figure 1(a) has Hamilton circuit $v \, w \, x \, y \, z \, v$.

(b) Adding more edges can't hurt, so the graph K_5 of Figure 1(b) is also Hamiltonian. In fact, every complete graph K_n for $n \geqq 3$ is Hamiltonian; we can go from vertex to vertex in any order we please.

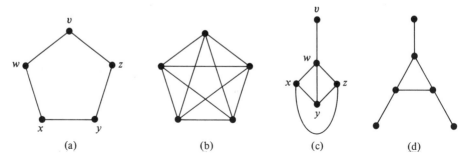

FIGURE 1

(c) The graph of Figure 1(c) has the Hamilton path $v \, w \, x \, y \, z$ but has no Hamilton circuit since no cycle goes through v.

(d) The graph of Figure 1(d) has no Hamilton path.   ☐

A Hamiltonian graph with n vertices must have at least n edges. This necessary condition may not be sufficient, as Figure 1(d) illustrates. Of course loops and parallel edges are of no use. The following gives a simple sufficient condition.

Theorem 1   If the graph G has no loops or parallel edges, if $|V(G)| = n \geqq 3$ and if $\deg(v) \geqq n/2$ for each vertex v of G, then G is Hamiltonian.

EXAMPLE 2   (a) The graph K_5 in Figure 1(b) has $\deg(v) = 4$ for each v and $|V(G)| = 5$, so it satisfies the condition of Theorem 1.

(b) Each of the graphs in Figure 2 has $|V(G)|/2 = 5/2$ and has a vertex of degree 2. They do not satisfy the hypotheses of Theorem 1, but are nevertheless Hamiltonian.   ∏

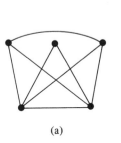
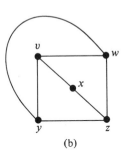

(a)   (b)

FIGURE 2

Theorem 1 imposes a uniform condition on all the vertices. Our next theorem requires only that there be enough edges somewhere in the graph. We will establish both of these sufficient conditions as consequences of Theorem 3, which gives a criterion in terms of degrees of pairs of vertices.

Theorem 2   A graph with n vertices and with no loops or parallel edges which has at least $\frac{1}{2}(n-1)(n-2) + 2$ edges is Hamiltonian.

EXAMPLE 3   (a) The Hamiltonian graph of Figure 2(a) has $n = 5$ so $\frac{1}{2}(n-1)(n-2) + 2 = 8$. It has 8 edges and so it satisfies the hypotheses and the conclusion of Theorem 2.

(b) The Hamiltonian graph of Figure 2(b) also has $n = 5$ and $\frac{1}{2}(n-1)(n-2) + 2 = 8$, but it has only 7 edges. It fails to satisfy the hypotheses of Theorem 2, as well as Theorem 1. If there were no vertex in the middle, we would have K_4 with $n = 4$ so $\frac{1}{2}(n-1)(n-2) + 2 = 5$, and the 6 edges would be more than enough. As it stands, the graph satisfies the hypotheses of the next theorem.   ∏

Theorem 3   Suppose the graph G has no loops or parallel edges and has $|V(G)| = n \geq 3$. If

$$\deg(v) + \deg(w) \geq n$$

for each two vertices v and w not connected by an edge, then G is Hamiltonian.

EXAMPLE 4   For the graph in Figure 2(b), $n = 5$. There are three pairs of distinct vertices that are not connected by an edge. We verify the hypotheses of Theorem 3 by examining them:

$$\text{for } \langle v, z \rangle, \qquad \deg(v) + \deg(z) = 3 + 3 = 6 \geqq 5;$$
$$\text{for } \langle w, x \rangle, \qquad \deg(w) + \deg(x) = 3 + 2 = 5 \geqq 5;$$
$$\text{for } \langle x, y \rangle, \qquad \deg(x) + \deg(y) = 2 + 3 = 5 \geqq 5. \quad \square$$

Proof of Theorem 3. Suppose the theorem is false for some n, and let G be a counterexample with $|E(G)|$ as large as possible. Now G is a subgraph of the Hamiltonian graph K_n. Adjoining to G an edge from K_n would give a graph which still satisfies the degree condition but has more than $|E(G)|$ edges. By the choice of G, any such graph would have a Hamilton circuit. This means that G must already have a Hamilton *path*, say with vertex sequence $v_1 v_2 \cdots v_n$. Since G has no Hamilton circuit, v_1 and v_n are not connected by an edge in G, and so $\deg(v_1) + \deg(v_n) \geqq n$.

Define subsets S_1 and S_n of $\{2, \ldots, n\}$ by

$$S_1 = \{i : \{v_1, v_i\} \in E(G)\} \quad \text{and} \quad S_n = \{i : \{v_{i-1}, v_n\} \in E(G)\}.$$

Then $|S_1| = \deg(v_1)$ and $|S_n| = \deg(v_n)$. Since $|S_1| + |S_n| \geqq n$ and $S_1 \cup S_n$ has at most $n - 1$ elements, $S_1 \cap S_n$ must be nonempty. Thus there is an i for which both $\{v_1, v_i\}$ and $\{v_{i-1}, v_n\}$ are edges of G. Then [see Figure 3] the path $v_1 \cdots v_{i-1} v_n \cdots v_i v_1$ is a Hamilton circuit in G, contradicting the choice of G as a counterexample. $\quad \square$

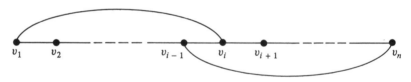

FIGURE 3

Our first two sufficient conditions follow easily from Theorem 3.

Proofs of Theorems 1 and 2. Suppose G has no loops or parallel edges and $|V(G)| = n \geqq 3$.

If $\deg(v) \geqq n/2$ for each v then $\deg(v) + \deg(w) \geqq n$ for any v and w whether joined by an edge or not, so the hypothesis of Theorem 3 is satisfied and G is Hamiltonian.

Suppose $|E(G)| \geqq \frac{1}{2}(n-1)(n-2) + 2 = \binom{n-1}{2} + 2$, and consider vertices u and v with $\{u, v\} \notin E(G)$. Remove from G the vertices u and v and all edges with u or v as a vertex. Since $\{u, v\} \notin E(G)$ we have removed $\deg(u) + \deg(v)$ edges and 2 vertices. The graph G' which is left is a subgraph of K_{n-2}, so

$$\binom{n-2}{2} = |E(K_{n-2})| \geqq |E(G')| \geqq \binom{n-1}{2} + 2 - \deg(u) - \deg(v).$$

Hence

$$\deg(u) + \deg(v) \geqq \binom{n-1}{2} - \binom{n-2}{2} + 2$$
$$= \tfrac{1}{2}(n-1)(n-2) - \tfrac{1}{2}(n-2)(n-3) + 2$$
$$= \tfrac{1}{2}(n-2)[(n-1) - (n-3)] + 2$$
$$= \tfrac{1}{2}(n-2)[2] + 2 = n.$$

Again, G satisfies the hypothesis of Theorem 3. □

Theorems 1, 2 and 3 are somewhat unsatisfactory in two ways. Not only are their sufficient conditions not necessary, the theorems give no guidance for finding a Hamilton circuit when one is guaranteed to exist. As we explained in § 0.2, the problem is related to the Traveling Salesperson Problem. As of this writing no efficient algorithm is known for solving it or for finding Hamilton paths or circuits. On the positive side, a Hamiltonian graph must certainly be connected, so all three theorems give sufficient conditions for a graph to be connected.

EXAMPLE 5   One way to convert the angular position of a rotating pointer into digital form is to divide the circle into 2^n equal segments, label the segments with the binary numbers from 0 to $2^n - 1$ and record the number of the segment the pointer points to. Figure 4 shows two possible ways of assigning labels for such a device with $n = 2$. To read the label electrically, we can provide n segmented

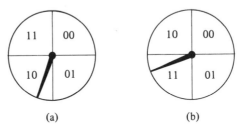

(a)   (b)

FIGURE 4

concentric rings so that the pointer makes contact with ring i if and only if the ith digit of the label is 1. Figure 5 shows the rings associated with the labelings of Figure 4. We have numbered the rings from the outside in, so that the outside rings correspond to the first digit and the inside rings correspond to the second digit.

If the pointer is near the boundary between 00 and 11 in Figure 5(a) a slight irregularity in contacts can cause a reading of 01 or 10. The arrangement of Figure 5(b) is better, because a contact error at a boundary can affect

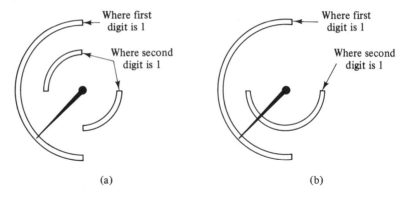

(a)   (b)

FIGURE 5

only one digit and in case of error the false label is just across the boundary from the true one.

A **Gray code** of length n is a labeling of the 2^n equal segments of a circle with binary strings of length n in such a way that the labels of adjacent segments differ in exactly one digit.

We can view the construction of a Gray code as a graph-theoretic problem. Let $V(G)$ be the set $\{0, 1\}^n$ of binary n-tuples, and join u and v by an edge if u and v differ in exactly one digit. A Gray code of length n is, in effect, a Hamilton circuit of the graph G. Figure 6(a) shows the graph G for $n = 2$.

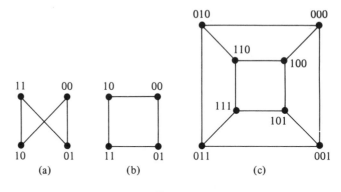

(a)   (b)   (c)

FIGURE 6

Figure 6(b) shows the same graph redrawn. Compare these pictures with the labels in Figure 4. This graph has two Hamilton circuits, one in each direction, which shows that there are two [essentially equivalent] Gray codes of length 2. Figure 6(c) shows the graph for $n = 3$. There are 12 Gray codes of length 3. Figure 7(a) shows the Hamilton path corresponding to one such code, and Figure 7(b) shows the associated segmented rings. Note that a contact error at any boundary would affect only one digit.   ☐

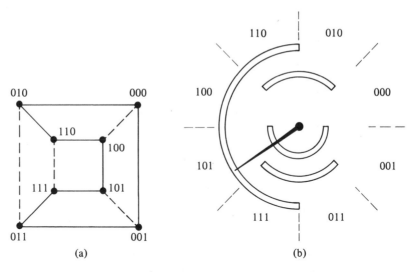

(a) (b)

FIGURE 7

The vertices in the graphs we constructed in Example 5 can be partitioned into two sets, those with an even number of 1's and those with an odd number, so that each edge joins a member of one set to a member of the other. We conclude this section with some observations about Hamilton circuits in graphs with this sort of partition.

A graph G is called **bipartite** if $V(G)$ is the union of two disjoint nonempty subsets V_1 and V_2 such that every edge of G joins a vertex of V_1 to a vertex of V_2. A graph is called a **complete bipartite** graph if, in addition, every vertex of V_1 is joined to every vertex of V_2 by a unique edge.

EXAMPLE 6 The graphs shown in Figure 8 are all bipartite. All but the one in Figure 8(b) are complete bipartite graphs. ☐

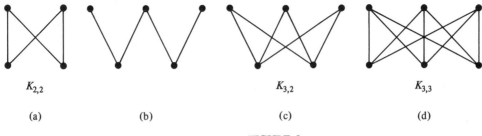

$K_{2,2}$ $K_{3,2}$ $K_{3,3}$

(a) (b) (c) (d)

FIGURE 8

Given m and n, the complete bipartite graphs with $|V_1| = m$ and $|V_2| = n$ are all isomorphic to each other; we denote them by $K_{m,n}$. Note that $K_{m,n}$ and $K_{n,m}$ are isomorphic.

Theorem 4 Let G be a bipartite graph with partition $V(G) = V_1 \cup V_2$. If G has a Hamilton circuit, then $|V_1| = |V_2|$. If G has a Hamilton path, then the numbers $|V_1|$ and $|V_2|$ differ by at most 1. For complete bipartite graphs with at least 3 vertices the converse statements are also true.

Proof. The vertices on a path in G alternately belong to V_1 and V_2. If $x_1 x_2 \cdots x_n x_1$ is a closed path that goes through each vertex once, then $x_1, x_3, x_5, \ldots$ must belong to one of the sets, say V_1. Since $\{x_n, x_1\}$ is an edge, n must be even and $x_2, x_4, \ldots, x_n$ all belong to V_2. So $|V_1| = |V_2|$. Similar remarks apply to a nonclosed path $x_1 x_2 \cdots x_n$, except that n might be odd, in which case one of V_1 and V_2 will have an extra vertex.

Now suppose $G = K_{m,n}$. If $m = n$ we can simply go back and forth from V_1 to V_2, since edges exist to take us wherever we want. If $m = n + 1$ we should start in V_1 to get a Hamilton path. $\quad\Box$

A respected computer scientist we know tells the story of how he once spent over two weeks on a computer searching for a Hamilton path in a bipartite graph with 42 vertices before he realized that the graph violated the condition of Theorem 4. The story has two messages: (1) people do have practical applications for bipartite graphs and Hamilton paths, and (2) *thought should precede computation.*

EXERCISES 8.6

1. Consider the graph shown in Figure 5(a) of § 8.5.
   (a) Is this a Hamiltonian graph?
   (b) Is this a complete graph?
   (c) Is this a bipartite graph?
   (d) Is this a complete bipartite graph?

2. Answer the same questions as in Exercise 1 for the graph in Figure 5(b) of § 8.5.

3. (a) How many Hamilton circuits does the graph $K_{n,n}$ have for $n \geq 2$? [Count circuits as different if they have different starting points or vertex sequences.]
   (b) How many Hamilton paths does $K_{n,n-1}$ have for $n \geq 2$?
   (c) Which complete bipartite graphs $K_{m,n}$ have Euler paths?

4. Redraw the graphs in Figure 6 and mark each of the subsets V_1 and V_2 of the bipartite partition of $V(G)$.

5. Arrange eight 0's and 1's in a circle so that each 3-digit binary number occurs as a string of 3 consecutive symbols somewhere in the circle. *Hint:* Find a Hamilton circuit in the graph with vertex set $\{0, 1\}^3$ and with an edge between vertices $\langle v_1, v_2, v_3 \rangle$ and $\langle w_1, w_2, w_3 \rangle$ whenever $\langle v_1, v_2 \rangle = \langle w_2, w_3 \rangle$ or $\langle v_2, v_3 \rangle = \langle w_1, w_2 \rangle$.

6. Give two other examples of Gray codes of length 3 besides the one in Example 5. For each code draw the associated segmented rings as in Figure 7(b).

7. Does the graph in Exercise 7 of § 8.5 have a Hamilton circuit? Does it have a Hamilton path?

8. Does the graph in Exercise 8 of § 8.5 have a Hamilton circuit? Does it have a Hamilton path?

9. For $n \geq 4$ build the graph K_n^+ from the complete graph K_{n-1} by adding one more vertex in the middle of an edge of K_{n-1}. [Figure 2(b) shows K_5^+.]
   (a) Show that K_n^+ does not satisfy the condition of Theorem 2.
   (b) Use Theorem 3 to show that K_n^+ is nevertheless Hamiltonian.

10. For $n \geq 4$ build the graph K_n^{++} from the complete graph K_{n-1} by adding one more vertex and an edge from the new vertex to a vertex of K_{n-1}. [Figure 1(c) shows K_5^{++}.] Show that K_n^{++} is not Hamiltonian. Observe that K_n^{++} has n vertices and $\frac{1}{2}(n-1)(n-2)+1$ edges. This example shows that the number of edges required in Theorem 2 cannot be decreased.

11. The **complement** of a graph G is the graph with vertex set $V(G)$ and with an edge between distinct vertices v and w if G does *not* have an edge joining v and w.
   (a) Draw the complement of the graph of Figure 2(b).
   (b) How many components does the complement in part (a) have?
   (c) Show that if G is not connected then its complement is connected.
   (d) Give an example of a graph which is isomorphic to its complement.
   (e) Is the converse to the statement in part (c) true?

12. Suppose that the graph G is regular of degree $k \geq 1$ [i.e., each vertex has degree k] and has at least $2k + 2$ vertices. Show that the complement of G is Hamiltonian. *Hint:* Use Theorem 1.

13. Show that Gray codes of length n always exist. *Hint:* Use induction on n and consider the graph G_n in which a Hamilton circuit corresponds to a Gray code of length n, as described in Example 5.

14. Explain why none of the theorems in this section can be used to solve Exercise 13.

§ 8.7 *Matrices, Relations and Graphs*

The pictures of relations in § 7.5 look just like pictures of digraphs in § 8.1. It is not surprising, then, that there is an intimate connection between relations and digraphs. In § 0.3 we briefly examined the connection between matrices and graphs, and in § 7.5 we saw that relations correspond to Boolean matrices. We now tie all these topics together. A relation on a set S determines a digraph G in a natural way: let $V(G) = S$ and put an edge from v to w whenever v is related to w. This was the procedure we used in § 8.1 to get the Hasse diagram of a poset from the covering relation on the poset. In the opposite direction, given a graph or digraph G we can define a relation on $V(G)$ by saying that v is related to w if there is an edge from v to w, or more generally if there is a path of some specified type from v to w.

To begin with, consider an undirected graph G. We call vertices v and w **adjacent** and write $v A w$ if there is an edge in $E(G)$ from v to w. Thus $v A w$ if there is a path of length 1 in G from v to w. Then A is a relation on $V(G)$, called the **adjacency relation**. Since G is undirected, the relation A is symmetric. A vertex v is A-related to itself if and only if G has a loop at v, so A is not reflexive in general. Nor is A usually transitive; we can have an edge from u to v and one from v to w without an edge from u to w.

To get a transitive relation from A we must consider chains of edges, from u_1 to u_2, u_2 to u_3, etc. As we saw in § 8.1 the appropriate notion is reachability. Define the **reachable relation** R on $V(G)$ by

$v \, R \, w$ if there is a path of length at least 1 in G from v to w.

Then R is transitive, and also symmetric since G is undirected. Since we require all paths to have length at least 1, R might not be reflexive. Let $\bar{R} = R \cup E$, the reflexive closure of R, so that $v \, \bar{R} \, w$ if $v = w$ or if $v \, R \, w$. Then $\bar{R}$ is an equivalence relation on $V(G)$. In fact, R is the transitive closure of A, and $\bar{R}$ is the smallest equivalence relation on $V(G)$ which contains A [see the lemma to Theorem 3 of § 7.6].

EXAMPLE 1   (a) Consider the graph G of Figure 1(a). The relation A is $\{\langle v, w \rangle,$ $\langle v, x \rangle, \langle v, y \rangle, \langle w, v \rangle, \langle x, v \rangle, \langle x, x \rangle, \langle x, y \rangle, \langle y, v \rangle, \langle y, x \rangle\}$. It is not reflexive or transitive. The relation R is $V(G) \times V(G)$ since each vertex is reachable from every other and from itself. [For instance, there is a path from w to v to w, so $w \, R \, w$.] Hence $\bar{R} = R$.

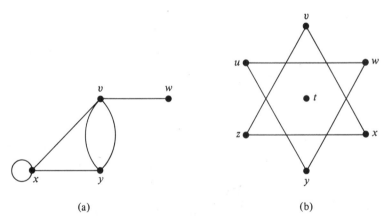

(a)   (b)

FIGURE 1

(b) The relation A for the graph of Figure 1(b) is $\{\langle u, w \rangle, \langle u, y \rangle, \langle v, x \rangle,$ $\langle v, z \rangle, \langle w, u \rangle, \langle w, y \rangle, \langle x, v \rangle, \langle x, z \rangle, \langle y, u \rangle, \langle y, w \rangle, \langle z, v \rangle, \langle z, x \rangle\}$. The relation R consists of the pairs in A together with the pairs $\langle u, u \rangle, \langle v, v \rangle, \langle w, w \rangle,$ $\langle x, x \rangle, \langle y, y \rangle$ and $\langle z, z \rangle$. The relation $\bar{R}$ is $R \cup \{\langle t, t \rangle\}$. In general, $R = \bar{R}$ if and only if G has no isolated vertices. The $\bar{R}$-equivalence classes of $V(G)$ are $\{u, w, y\}$, $\{v, x, z\}$ and $\{t\}$.   ☐

We have seen the $\bar{R}$-equivalence classes of $V(G)$ before; they are the vertex sets of the connected components of G. Recall that a graph is connected if each vertex is reachable from every other vertex, and a component of G is a connected subgraph H which is not contained in any other connected subgraph of G. The next theorem gives us a way of finding components. Simply choose a vertex v, find its $\bar{R}$-class, i.e., all vertices we can get to from v, and then take all edges joining the vertices found. In § 8.9 we will discuss algorithms for finding $\bar{R}$-classes, and hence components. At this point the statement of the theorem is more important to us than its proof.

Theorem 1   Let G be a graph. Let V be an $\bar{R}$-equivalence class of vertices of G and let H be the subgraph of G with $V(H) = V$ and $E(H) = \{e \in E(G) : e$ joins vertices in $V\}$. Then H is a component of G. Conversely, every component of G is determined by an $\bar{R}$-equivalence class in this way.

Proof. We show first that H is connected, i.e., that there is a path *in H* between any two different vertices in $V(H)$. Let u and v be distinct vertices in V. Since V is an $\bar{R}$-class of G, there is a path in G with vertex sequence $u = u_0 u_1 \cdots u_n = v$. All the vertices $u_1, u_2, \ldots$ on this path are reachable from u in G, so they are all $\bar{R}$-related to u. Thus each is in the $\bar{R}$-class V. Since H contains all edges in G that connect vertices in V, the path is a path in H, as we wished. Thus H is connected.

Now suppose H is contained in a connected subgraph K of G. Choose v in V and let w be any vertex in $V(K)$. Since K is connected and $V \subseteq V(K)$, v and w are joined by a path in K [or $v = w$] and so $w \bar{R} v$ in G. Thus w lies in the $\bar{R}$-class of v, i.e., in V. This shows that $V(K) \subseteq V$, so $V(K) = V$. Since $E(H)$ contains all edges of G between members of V, $E(H) = E(K)$ and thus $H = K$. We have shown that H is not contained in any other connected subgraph of G, so H is a component.

Now consider a component C of G and a vertex v in $V(C)$. Since C is connected, each vertex of C is in the $\bar{R}$-class of v. We just saw that the graph H with this $\bar{R}$-class as vertex set and with all possible edges is a component of G. Since C is contained in H and C is a component, $C = H$. ☐

As in § 7.5 we can use Boolean matrices to describe the relations A, R and $\bar{R}$ for finite graphs. We index the rows and columns of a matrix by the members of $V(G)$, and we put a 1 in the (u, v)-position if $\langle u, v \rangle$ is in the relation and put a 0 there otherwise.

EXAMPLE 2   (a) The relations A, R and $\bar{R}$ for the graph of Figure 1(a) give the following matrices.

$$
\mathbf{M}_A = \begin{array}{c} \\ v \\ w \\ x \\ y \end{array} \begin{array}{cccc} v & w & x & y \\ \left[\begin{array}{cccc} 0 & 1 & 1 & 1 \\ 1 & 0 & 0 & 0 \\ 1 & 0 & 1 & 1 \\ 1 & 0 & 1 & 0 \end{array}\right] \end{array}, \qquad \mathbf{M}_R = \mathbf{M}_{\bar{R}} = \begin{bmatrix} 1 & 1 & 1 & 1 \\ 1 & 1 & 1 & 1 \\ 1 & 1 & 1 & 1 \\ 1 & 1 & 1 & 1 \end{bmatrix}.
$$

Here we have shown the row and column headings on $\mathbf{M}_A$, but we will often omit them if the indexing is clear.

(b) The graph of Figure 1(b) gives the following.

$$
\mathbf{M}_A = \begin{array}{c} \\ u \\ v \\ w \\ x \\ y \\ z \\ t \end{array}
\begin{array}{ccccccc} u & v & w & x & y & z & t \\ \end{array}
\left[\begin{array}{ccccccc}
0 & 0 & 1 & 0 & 1 & 0 & 0 \\
0 & 0 & 0 & 1 & 0 & 1 & 0 \\
1 & 0 & 0 & 0 & 1 & 0 & 0 \\
0 & 1 & 0 & 0 & 0 & 1 & 0 \\
1 & 0 & 1 & 0 & 0 & 0 & 0 \\
0 & 1 & 0 & 1 & 0 & 0 & 0 \\
0 & 0 & 0 & 0 & 0 & 0 & 0
\end{array}\right],
\qquad
\mathbf{M}_{\bar{R}} = \left[\begin{array}{ccccccc}
1 & 0 & 1 & 0 & 1 & 0 & 0 \\
0 & 1 & 0 & 1 & 0 & 1 & 0 \\
1 & 0 & 1 & 0 & 1 & 0 & 0 \\
0 & 1 & 0 & 1 & 0 & 1 & 0 \\
1 & 0 & 1 & 0 & 1 & 0 & 0 \\
0 & 1 & 0 & 1 & 0 & 1 & 0 \\
0 & 0 & 0 & 0 & 0 & 0 & 1
\end{array}\right].
$$

With a different labeling we get a better idea of the structure.

$$
\mathbf{M}_A = \begin{array}{c} \\ u \\ w \\ y \\ v \\ x \\ z \\ t \end{array}
\begin{array}{ccccccc} u & w & y & v & x & z & t \\ \end{array}
\left[\begin{array}{ccccccc}
0 & 1 & 1 & 0 & 0 & 0 & 0 \\
1 & 0 & 1 & 0 & 0 & 0 & 0 \\
1 & 1 & 0 & 0 & 0 & 0 & 0 \\
0 & 0 & 0 & 0 & 1 & 1 & 0 \\
0 & 0 & 0 & 1 & 0 & 1 & 0 \\
0 & 0 & 0 & 1 & 1 & 0 & 0 \\
0 & 0 & 0 & 0 & 0 & 0 & 0
\end{array}\right],
\qquad
\mathbf{M}_{\bar{R}} = \left[\begin{array}{ccccccc}
1 & 1 & 1 & 0 & 0 & 0 & 0 \\
1 & 1 & 1 & 0 & 0 & 0 & 0 \\
1 & 1 & 1 & 0 & 0 & 0 & 0 \\
0 & 0 & 0 & 1 & 1 & 1 & 0 \\
0 & 0 & 0 & 1 & 1 & 1 & 0 \\
0 & 0 & 0 & 1 & 1 & 1 & 0 \\
0 & 0 & 0 & 0 & 0 & 0 & 1
\end{array}\right].
$$

The blocks of 1's in $\mathbf{M}_{\bar{R}}$ correspond to the components. ☐

Notice that since the relations are symmetric and we have always labeled rows and columns in the same order, the matrices we get are symmetric. Diagonal 1's in $\mathbf{M}_A$ correspond to loops. In $\mathbf{M}_{\bar{R}}$ all diagonal entries are 1.

The relation R is the transitive closure of A, so by Theorem 2 of § 7.6 we have

$$ R = \bigcup_{k=1}^{\infty} A^k. $$

Thus $\bar{R} = E \cup R = \bigcup_{k=0}^{\infty} A^k$. The relations $A^2, A^3, \ldots$ have their own graph-theoretic interpretations. By definition, $u\,A^2\,v$ means there is a vertex z with $u\,A\,z$ and $z\,A\,v$, i.e., there is a path in G of length 2 from u to z to v. Similarly, $u\,A^k\,v$ means there is a path of length k in G joining u and v [Exercise 14]. We saw in Theorem 1 of § 7.5 that if T and U are relations on a set S with matrices $\mathbf{M}_T$ and $\mathbf{M}_U$ then $\mathbf{M}_{TU}$ is the Boolean product $\mathbf{M}_T * \mathbf{M}_U$. Thus the matrix of A^k is the Boolean product $\mathbf{M}_A * \mathbf{M}_A * \cdots * \mathbf{M}_A$ with k factors.

EXAMPLE 3   (a) Consider the graph of Figure 1(a) and its matrix M_A given in Example 2(a). We compute.

$$M_{A^2} = M_A * M_A = \begin{bmatrix} 0 & 1 & 1 & 1 \\ 1 & 0 & 0 & 0 \\ 1 & 0 & 1 & 1 \\ 1 & 0 & 1 & 0 \end{bmatrix} * \begin{bmatrix} 0 & 1 & 1 & 1 \\ 1 & 0 & 0 & 0 \\ 1 & 0 & 1 & 1 \\ 1 & 0 & 1 & 0 \end{bmatrix} = \begin{bmatrix} 1 & 0 & 1 & 1 \\ 0 & 1 & 1 & 1 \\ 1 & 1 & 1 & 1 \\ 1 & 1 & 1 & 1 \end{bmatrix}.$$

The 0's in M_{A^2} reflect the fact that there is no path of length 2 between v and w. One can easily check that for this example $M_A \vee M_{A^2} = M_{\bar{R}}$.

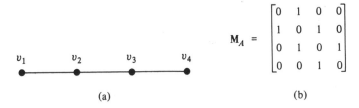

$$M_A = \begin{bmatrix} 0 & 1 & 0 & 0 \\ 1 & 0 & 1 & 0 \\ 0 & 1 & 0 & 1 \\ 0 & 0 & 1 & 0 \end{bmatrix}$$

(a)   (b)

FIGURE 2

(b) The graph of Figure 2(a) has the adjacency matrix given in Figure 2(b) with Boolean powers

$$M_{A^2} = \begin{bmatrix} 1 & 0 & 1 & 0 \\ 0 & 1 & 0 & 1 \\ 1 & 0 & 1 & 0 \\ 0 & 1 & 0 & 1 \end{bmatrix}, \qquad M_{A^3} = \begin{bmatrix} 0 & 1 & 0 & 1 \\ 1 & 0 & 1 & 0 \\ 0 & 1 & 0 & 1 \\ 1 & 0 & 1 & 0 \end{bmatrix},$$

$$M_{A^4} = \begin{bmatrix} 1 & 0 & 1 & 0 \\ 0 & 1 & 0 & 1 \\ 1 & 0 & 1 & 0 \\ 0 & 1 & 0 & 1 \end{bmatrix}.$$

Since $M_{A^2} \vee M_{A^3}$ has all entries equal to 1, the same is true for $M_R = M_{\bar{R}}$ and so R and R are the universal relation. Also $M_{A^2} = M_{A^4}$ and so $A^2 = A^4$. It follows that $A^3 = A^5$ and in general $A^{2k} = A^2$ and $A^{2k+1} = A^3$ for $k \geqq 2$. $\square$

Instead of forming the Boolean powers of M_A we could consider powers using ordinary matrix multiplication. The (u, w)-entry of $M_A M_A$ is the sum of all products $M_A[u, v] \cdot M_A[v, w]$ for v in $V(G)$. Such a product is 1 if there is a path from u to v to w and is 0 otherwise, since then at least one factor is 0. Thus the (u, w)-entry is the number of products which are 1, i.e., the number of v's in the middle of such paths. If G has no parallel edges this is simply the number of paths of length 2 from u to w.

EXAMPLE 4   (a) For the graph of Example 3(b) we have

$$\mathbf{M}_A \cdot \mathbf{M}_A = \begin{bmatrix} 1 & 0 & 1 & 0 \\ 0 & 2 & 0 & 1 \\ 1 & 0 & 2 & 0 \\ 0 & 1 & 0 & 1 \end{bmatrix} \quad \text{and} \quad \mathbf{M}_A \cdot \mathbf{M}_A \cdot \mathbf{M}_A = \begin{bmatrix} 0 & 2 & 0 & 1 \\ 2 & 0 & 3 & 0 \\ 0 & 3 & 0 & 2 \\ 1 & 0 & 2 & 0 \end{bmatrix}.$$

These matrices have non-0 entries just where $\mathbf{M}_{A^2}$ and $\mathbf{M}_{A^3}$ have them, but some of the entries are 2's and 3's. The diagonal 2's in $\mathbf{M}_A \cdot \mathbf{M}_A$ reflect the fact that there are two paths of length 2 from v_2 and v_3 back to themselves. Similarly, we observe that corresponding to the (4, 3)-entry 2 in $\mathbf{M}_A \cdot \mathbf{M}_A \cdot \mathbf{M}_A$ there are 2 paths of length 3 from v_4 to v_3. Their vertex sequences are $v_4\, v_3\, v_2\, v_3$ and $v_4\, v_3\, v_4\, v_3$.

(b) The graph of Figure 1(a) has parallel edges, so $\mathbf{M}_A$ doesn't give the correct number of paths of length 1 between vertices. The matrix

$$\mathbf{M}' = \begin{matrix} v \\ w \\ x \\ y \end{matrix} \begin{bmatrix} 0 & 1 & 1 & 2 \\ 1 & 0 & 0 & 0 \\ 1 & 0 & 1 & 1 \\ 2 & 0 & 1 & 0 \end{bmatrix}$$

does tell the number of edges between vertices of this graph, so its powers yield the number of paths of various lengths. For instance

$$(\mathbf{M}')^2 = \begin{bmatrix} 6 & 0 & 3 & 1 \\ 0 & 1 & 1 & 2 \\ 3 & 1 & 3 & 3 \\ 1 & 2 & 3 & 5 \end{bmatrix}$$

tells us that there are 6 paths of length 2 from v to itself, no paths of length 2 from v to w, 3 paths of length 2 from v to x, etc.   ☐

In § 0.3 an example similar to Example 4(b) was analyzed in some detail. There we used the notation $\mathbf{M}$ instead of $\mathbf{M}'$ since we were not also concerned with Boolean matrices. Both examples suggest one way to describe finite graphs with parallel edges using matrices. Choose a linear order for $V(G)$ and let $\mathbf{M}'$ be the matrix with rows and columns indexed by $V(G)$ and with (u, v)-entry the number of edges from u to v. Then $\mathbf{M}'$ completely determines G up to isomorphism and so contains enough information to let us draw a picture of G.

Since

$$\bar{R} = E \cup A \cup A^2 \cup A^3 \cup \cdots,$$

one way to get the relation $\bar{R}$ for a finite graph would be to compute the Boolean power matrices $\mathbf{M}_A, \mathbf{M}_{A^2}, \mathbf{M}_{A^3}, \ldots$ and form their least upper bound to get

$$\mathbf{M}_{\bar{R}} = \mathbf{M}_E \vee \mathbf{M}_A \vee \mathbf{M}_{A^2} \vee \mathbf{M}_{A^3} \vee \cdots.$$

There are only finitely many Boolean matrices of any given size, so only finitely many different matrices $\mathbf{M}_{A^k}$ can arise and this computation can actually be carried out. Indeed, Theorem 2 of § 7.6 points out that we don't need k's greater than $|V(G)|$. It turns out that this matrix procedure is very slow compared with other algorithms. We'll look at this question again in the next section and see some faster methods.

Many of the results we have developed in this section for undirected graphs have analogues for digraphs. Suppose for the rest of this section that G is a digraph. Again we define the **adjacency relation** A by $v\, A\, w$ if there is an edge in $E(G)$ from v to w. In the digraph setting A need not be symmetric. The transitive closure $R = t(A) = \bigcup_{k=1}^{\infty} A^k$ is the **reachable relation**, with $v\, R\, w$ if there is a path in G from v to w, i.e., if w is reachable from v. Even if R is reflexive it might not be an equivalence relation, since it might not be symmetric. The matrices $\mathbf{M}_A$ and $\mathbf{M}_R$ are defined just as in the undirected case. Here again

$$\mathbf{M}_R = \mathbf{M}_A \vee \mathbf{M}_{A^2} \vee \mathbf{M}_{A^3} \vee \cdots.$$

There is no natural analogue for digraphs of the notion of component. The concept of connectedness itself needs to be reexamined. What are we trying to call attention to when we say a digraph is connected? The following two definitions seem to be the most useful. We call a digraph **connected** if the graph we get from it by ignoring directions is connected as an undirected graph, and call a digraph **strongly connected** if $u\, R\, v$ for all vertices u and v. Every strongly connected digraph is connected, and a digraph is strongly connected if and only if the matrix of its reachability relation has all 1's as entries.

EXAMPLE 5   (a) The digraph of Figure 3(a) describes the operation of a **binary up-down counter**. The vertices stand for states of the machine, and the machine shifts from one state to another following arrows in response to inputs. An

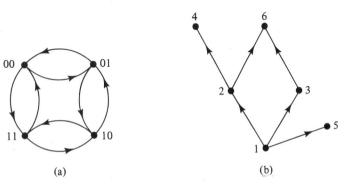

(a)   (b)

FIGURE 3

input 1 gives a clockwise shift, and 0 gives a counterclockwise shift. This digraph is strongly connected. Its associated matrices are

$$\mathbf{M}_A = \begin{matrix} 00 \\ 01 \\ 10 \\ 11 \end{matrix} \begin{bmatrix} 0 & 1 & 0 & 1 \\ 1 & 0 & 1 & 0 \\ 0 & 1 & 0 & 1 \\ 1 & 0 & 1 & 0 \end{bmatrix} \quad \text{and} \quad \mathbf{M}_R = \begin{bmatrix} 1 & 1 & 1 & 1 \\ 1 & 1 & 1 & 1 \\ 1 & 1 & 1 & 1 \\ 1 & 1 & 1 & 1 \end{bmatrix}.$$

(b) The Hasse diagram in Figure 3(b) has $v \, A \, w$ if w covers v, and has the adjacency and reachability matrices

$$\mathbf{M}_A = \begin{matrix} 1 \\ 2 \\ 3 \\ 4 \\ 5 \\ 6 \end{matrix} \begin{bmatrix} 0 & 1 & 1 & 0 & 1 & 0 \\ 0 & 0 & 0 & 1 & 0 & 1 \\ 0 & 0 & 0 & 0 & 0 & 1 \\ 0 & 0 & 0 & 0 & 0 & 0 \\ 0 & 0 & 0 & 0 & 0 & 0 \\ 0 & 0 & 0 & 0 & 0 & 0 \end{bmatrix} \quad \text{and} \quad \mathbf{M}_R = \begin{bmatrix} 0 & 1 & 1 & 1 & 1 & 1 \\ 0 & 0 & 0 & 1 & 0 & 1 \\ 0 & 0 & 0 & 0 & 0 & 1 \\ 0 & 0 & 0 & 0 & 0 & 0 \\ 0 & 0 & 0 & 0 & 0 & 0 \\ 0 & 0 & 0 & 0 & 0 & 0 \end{bmatrix}.$$

This digraph is connected, but not strongly connected. We can't tell that the digraph is connected just by looking at $\mathbf{M}_R$, though the matrix does contain enough information to answer the connectedness question. To check connectedness we could form $\mathbf{M}_A \vee \mathbf{M}_A^T$, the adjacency matrix for the associated undirected graph, and then take its Boolean powers as we did earlier. We could also do the same thing with the matrix $\mathbf{M}_R \vee \mathbf{M}_R^T$. In either case we would arrive at a matrix with all entries 1 and could conclude that the digraph is connected. Of course the easiest method for this example is to stare at the picture. ☐

EXERCISES 8.7

1. (a) Describe the adjacency relation A for an [undirected] graph G in terms of the function γ from $E(G)$ to $\{\{u, v\} : u, v \in V(G)\}$.
   (b) Give a description of A in terms of $\gamma : E(G) \to V(G) \times V(G)$ for a digraph G.

2. (a) Draw a picture of a graph with adjacency matrix

$$\begin{bmatrix} 0 & 0 & 1 & 1 & 0 & 1 \\ 0 & 0 & 0 & 0 & 1 & 0 \\ 1 & 0 & 1 & 0 & 0 & 0 \\ 1 & 0 & 0 & 0 & 0 & 1 \\ 0 & 1 & 0 & 0 & 0 & 0 \\ 1 & 0 & 0 & 1 & 0 & 0 \end{bmatrix}.$$

   (b) Find the components of the graph of part (a).

3. Find matrices $\mathbf{M}_A$, $\mathbf{M}_{A^2}$, $\mathbf{M}_{A^3}$, $\mathbf{M}_{A^4}$ and $\mathbf{M}_{\bar{R}}$ for the graph shown in Figure 4(a).

4. Find the matrices $\mathbf{M}_A$, $\mathbf{M}_{A^2}$, $\mathbf{M}_{A^4}$ and $\mathbf{M}_{A^{2001}}$ for the graph of Figure 4(b).

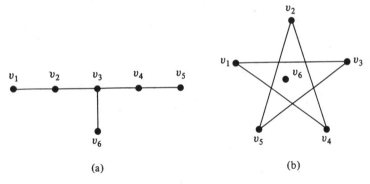

FIGURE 4

5. (a) Give the matrices $\mathbf{M}_A$ and $\mathbf{M}_R$ for the digraph of Figure 5(a).
  (b) Is the digraph connected? Strongly connected?

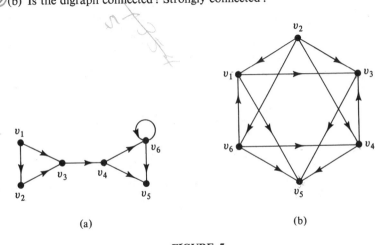

FIGURE 5

6. (a) Find the matrices $\mathbf{M}_A$, $\mathbf{M}_{A^2}$, $\mathbf{M}_{A^3}$, $\mathbf{M}_{A^4}$ and $\mathbf{M}_R$ for the digraph of Figure 5(b).
  (b) Is this digraph connected? Strongly connected?
  (c) Is this digraph acyclic? [Try to answer this part using your answer to part (a).]

7. (a) How many paths are there of length 3 from v_1 to v_3 in the graph of Figure 4(b). *Hint:* See Example 4.
  (b) How many paths are there of length 4 from v_1 to itself in this graph?
  (c) How many are there of length 4 from v_1 to v_2?

8. (a) Find $(\mathbf{M}_A)^2$ for the digraph of Figure 5(b).
  (b) How many paths are there of length 2 from v_2 to each of the other vertices in this digraph?
  (c) How many paths are there of length 4 from v_2 to other vertices?

9. Define the relation S on $V(G)$ by $v\,S\,w$ if $v = w$ or there is a path of even length from v to w.

(a) Find the relation S for the graph of Figure 4(a).

(b) Find S for the graph of Figure 4(b).

(c) Is S an equivalence relation in general? Explain.

(d) If G is a bipartite graph, what can you say about S?

10. (a) Describe the matrices $\mathbf{M}_A$ and $\mathbf{M}_{\bar{R}}$ for a complete graph K_n.

(b) Describe $\mathbf{M}_A$ and $\mathbf{M}_{\bar{R}}$ for a complete bipartite graph $K_{m,n}$. [Order the vertices in an intelligent way.]

11. (a) Say as much as you can about a connected graph whose reachability matrix has a 0 entry on the diagonal.

(b) Do the same for a connected digraph.

12. (a) Show that if all entries of one row of the reachability matrix for a graph are 1, then all entries of $\mathbf{M}_R$ are 1.

(b) Is a statement analogous to that in part (a) true for digraphs? Explain.

13. (a) Can two nonisomorphic graphs have the same adjacency matrix $\mathbf{M}_A$? Explain.

(b) Give a method for finding the degree of a vertex in a graph without parallel edges by looking at its adjacency matrix.

(c) Give a method for finding indegrees and outdegrees of a digraph without parallel edges by looking at its adjacency matrix.

(d) How would your answers to parts (b) and (c) change if parallel edges were allowed?

14. Show that if u and v are vertices of a graph with adjacency relation A and $k \in \mathbb{P}$, then u A^k v if and only if there is a path of length k from u to v. *Hint:* Use induction on k.

15. (a) Show that it is possible to order the vertices of a finite acyclic digraph so that the non-0 entries of $\mathbf{M}_A$ lie on or above the diagonal.

(b) Will the matrix $\mathbf{M}_R$ have the same property?

§ 8.8   *Graph Algorithms*

> algorithm *n*. Any peculiar method of computing.
> *The American College Dictionary*

Our study of digraphs and graphs has led us to a number of concrete questions. Given a digraph, what is the length of a shortest path from one vertex to another? If the digraph is weighted, what's the minimum or maximum weight of such a path? Is there any path at all? What are the components of a graph? Does removing an edge increase the number of components? Does a given edge belong to a cycle? Do any edges belong to cycles?

This section describes some algorithms for answering these questions and others, algorithms which can be implemented on computers as well as used to organize hand computations. The algorithms we have chosen are reasonably fast, and their workings are comparatively easy to follow. For a more complete discussion we refer the reader to books on the subject, such as *Design and Analysis of Computer Algorithms* by Aho, Hopcroft and Ullman.

We concentrate first on digraph problems, and deal later with modifications for the undirected case. As we noted in § 8.3, any min-weight algorithm can be used to get a shortest path-length algorithm simply by giving all edges weight 1. We can use such an algorithm to see if there is any path at all from u to v in G by creating fictitious edges of enormous weights between vertices which are not joined by edges in G. If the min-path from u to v in the enlarged graph has an enormous weight, it must be because no path exists made entirely from edges of G.

The min-weight problem is essentially a question about digraphs without loops or parallel edges, so we limit ourselves to that setting. Hence $E(G) \subseteq V(G) \times V(G)$, and we can describe the digraph with a table of the edge-weight function $W(u, v)$, as we did in § 8.3.

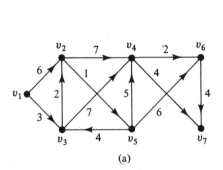

W	v_1	v_2	v_3	v_4	v_5	v_6	v_7
v_1		6	3				
v_2				7	1		
v_3	2			7			
v_4						2	4
v_5			4	5		6	
v_6							4
v_7							

(a)   (b)

FIGURE 1

EXAMPLE 1   Consider the weighted digraph G shown in Figure 1(a), which will be our running example through much of the following discussion. Figure 1(b) is the edge-weight table for G.   □

We will fill in the blanks of the table for the function W to get an $n \times n$ matrix which we will call **W**. For what follows next it will be appropriate to have diagonal matrix entries 0, corresponding to the paths of length 0 from vertices to themselves. If there is no edge from v_i to v_j for $i \neq j$ we use the fictitious edge idea and write ∞ in the (i, j)-position. In actual computations "∞" could be replaced by an enormous number or by a blank. The operating rules we'll need for ∞ are: $\infty + x = x + \infty = \infty$ for every x, and $\infty > a$ for every real number a.

EXAMPLE 2   Here is the matrix for the digraph of Example 1.

$$\mathbf{W} = \begin{bmatrix} 0 & 6 & 3 & \infty & \infty & \infty & \infty \\ \infty & 0 & \infty & 7 & 1 & \infty & \infty \\ \infty & 2 & 0 & 7 & \infty & \infty & \infty \\ \infty & \infty & \infty & 0 & \infty & 2 & 4 \\ \infty & \infty & 4 & 5 & 0 & 6 & \infty \\ \infty & \infty & \infty & \infty & \infty & 0 & 4 \\ \infty & \infty & \infty & \infty & \infty & \infty & 0 \end{bmatrix}. \quad \square$$

Our goal is to replace the entries in the initial matrix $\mathbf{W} = \mathbf{W}_0$ by the values of the min-weight function W^*.

Our first algorithm was described by T. C. Hu in 1967 in the *SIAM Journal of Applied Mathematics*. It proceeds through the matrix $\mathbf{W}$ row by row, from the top down, scanning each row from left to right and changing entries as it goes. At any given time, each entry $\mathbf{W}[i,j]$ is the smallest weight yet discovered for a path from v_i to v_j. When the algorithm reaches the (i,j)-position it compares the current value of $\mathbf{W}[i,j]$ with all sums $\mathbf{W}[i,k] + \mathbf{W}[k,j]$, i.e., with the minimum known weights of paths from v_i to v_j through v_k for all vertices v_k. If any of these path weights is smaller than $\mathbf{W}[i,j]$ the algorithm replaces $\mathbf{W}[i,j]$ by the smallest such sum.

HU'S *Algorithm.*

For $i = 1$ to n
  For $j = 1$ to n
    For $k = 1$ to n
      If $\mathbf{W}[i,j] > \mathbf{W}[i,k] + \mathbf{W}[k,j]$ then
        Replace $\mathbf{W}[i,j]$ by $\mathbf{W}[i,k] + \mathbf{W}[k,j]$
    End for
  End for
End for
End $\square$

We have written this algorithm in a style similar to a computer program, rather than in our usual "Step 1, Step 2, . . ." format, to make the looping clearer.

We can apply the algorithm to any $n \times n$ matrix $\mathbf{W}$ whose entries represent known weights of paths between vertices $v_1, \ldots, v_n$. To start with, we let $\mathbf{W}$ be the edge-weight matrix $\mathbf{W}_0$. HU'S algorithm yields a matrix $\mathbf{W}$ whose entries are no larger than the corresponding entries of $\mathbf{W}_0$ and are weights of paths. This matrix might or might not be the matrix $\mathbf{W}^*$ that we are after.

EXAMPLE 3   (a) We apply HU'S algorithm starting with the matrix $\mathbf{W}$ of Example 2. To illustrate the method we follow the computation of $\mathbf{W}[1,5]$. The values of $\mathbf{W}[1,1]$, $\mathbf{W}[1,2]$, $\mathbf{W}[1,3]$ and $\mathbf{W}[1,4]$ have already been computed. The value of $W[1, 2]$ has changed from 6 to 5 and $W[1, 4]$ has changed from ∞ to 10. The current matrix W is

$$\begin{bmatrix} 0 & 5 & 3 & 10 & \infty & \infty & \infty \\ \infty & 0 & \infty & 7 & 1 & \infty & \infty \\ \infty & 2 & 0 & 7 & \infty & \infty & \infty \\ \infty & \infty & \infty & 0 & \infty & 2 & 4 \\ \infty & \infty & 4 & 5 & 0 & 6 & \infty \\ \infty & \infty & \infty & \infty & \infty & 0 & 4 \\ \infty & \infty & \infty & \infty & \infty & \infty & 0 \end{bmatrix}$$

with $W[1, 5] = \infty$. The k-loop is

> For $k = 1$ to 7
>   If $W[1, 5] > W[1, k] + W[k, 5]$ then
>   Replace $W[1, 5]$ by $W[1, k] + W[k, 5]$
> End for.

The computation goes as follows.

$W[1, 1] + W[1, 5] = 0 + W[1, 5] = W[1, 5]$ no replacement

$W[1, 2] + W[2, 5] = 5 + 1 = 6$ replace ∞ by 6

$W[1, 3] + W[3, 5] = 3 + \infty = \infty$ no replacement

$W[1, 4] + W[4, 5] = 10 + \infty = \infty$ no replacement even though $W[1, 4]$ is updated from initial data

$W[1, 5] + W[5, 5] = 6 + 0 = 6$ using the current value of $W[1, 5]$ obtained 3 steps back; no replacement

$W[1, 6] + W[6, 5] = \infty + \infty = \infty$ no replacement

$W[1, 7] + W[7, 5] = \infty + \infty = \infty$ no replacement

The final value is $W[1, 5] = 6$. The corresponding path is $v_1\, v_3\, v_2\, v_5$.
  HU'S algorithm yields the final matrix

$$\begin{bmatrix} 0 & 5 & 3 & 10 & 6 & 12 & 14 \\ \infty & 0 & 5 & 6 & 1 & 7 & 10 \\ \infty & 2 & 0 & 7 & 3 & 9 & 11 \\ \infty & \infty & \infty & 0 & \infty & 2 & 4 \\ \infty & 6 & 4 & 5 & 0 & 6 & 9 \\ \infty & \infty & \infty & \infty & \infty & 0 & 4 \\ \infty & \infty & \infty & \infty & \infty & \infty & 0 \end{bmatrix}.$$

This turns out to be W^* for this example, as we'll see in Example 4.

The computation of $W[i, j]$ with HU'S algorithm is formally something like the calculation of the (i, j)-entry in the matrix product $W^2 = W \cdot W$. In HU'S algorithm the k-loop computes

$$\min_{k} \{W[i, k] + W[k, j]\} = \bigwedge_{k=1}^{n} (W[i, k] + W[k, j]),$$

while in the matrix product

$$W^2[i, j] = \sum_{k=1}^{n} (W[i, k] \cdot W[k, j]).$$

For hand calculations with HU'S algorithm we can run through the ith row and jth column of W in the way we would to compute $W^2[i, j]$. It is convenient to write W_0 in pencil, and write over the pencil entries in ink as the new values are computed.

(b) Consider the shortest path problem for the digraph in Figure 2(a).

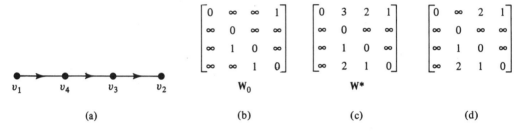

$$\begin{bmatrix} 0 & \infty & \infty & 1 \\ \infty & 0 & \infty & \infty \\ \infty & 1 & 0 & \infty \\ \infty & \infty & 1 & 0 \end{bmatrix} \quad \begin{bmatrix} 0 & 3 & 2 & 1 \\ \infty & 0 & \infty & \infty \\ \infty & 1 & 0 & \infty \\ \infty & 2 & 1 & 0 \end{bmatrix} \quad \begin{bmatrix} 0 & \infty & 2 & 1 \\ \infty & 0 & \infty & \infty \\ \infty & 1 & 0 & \infty \\ \infty & 2 & 1 & 0 \end{bmatrix}$$

W_0 W^*

(a)   (b)   (c)   (d)

FIGURE 2

The initial matrix W_0 is given in Figure 2(b), and the shortest path matrix W^* in Figure 2(c). HU'S algorithm yields the matrix in Figure 2(d), which indicates no known path from v_1 to v_2. The trouble is that when $W[1, 2]$ is being computed neither the path from v_1 to v_3 nor the path from v_4 to v_2 has yet been encountered. Here we could have avoided the trouble by relabeling vertices, but for larger values of n it might not be at all clear how to label the vertices to produce W^* with HU'S algorithm. ☐

We can apply HU'S algorithm repeatedly, starting each time with the matrix W produced from the previous application. Hu discovered the following striking facts.

1. Applying HU'S algorithm three times always gives W^*. [To see that three may be needed, see Exercise 4.]
2. So does applying HU'S algorithm once and then applying the same algorithm with i and j running backwards from n to 1.

Hu's proofs are elementary but too lengthy to include here. We will, however, show that in an important special case one application of HU'S algorithm is always enough.

Theorem 1   Suppose the finite digraph G is acyclic and is labeled so that $i < j$ if there is a path from v_i to v_j. Then HU'S algorithm produces the min-weight matrix for G.

Notice that Algorithm NUMBERING VERTICES following Theorem 2 in § 8.1 shows that every finite acyclic digraph has a labeling of the kind described in the theorem.

Proof of Theorem 1.   Given such a labeling, say with $\{1, 2, \ldots, n\}$, every path in G has its vertices numbered in increasing order. Suppose there is a path from i to j. We claim that HU'S algorithm computes $\mathbf{W}[i, j] = \mathbf{W}^*[i, j]$. Let $i_1 \, i_2 \cdots i_t$ be a min-path from i to j, with $i = i_1$ and $j = i_t$. Since the path is a min-path, each edge $\langle i_s, i_{s+1} \rangle$ is itself a min-path, so to begin with $\mathbf{W}[i_s, i_{s+1}] = \mathbf{W}^*[i_s, i_{s+1}]$, and this value of $\mathbf{W}[i_s, i_{s+1}]$ does not decrease as the algorithm proceeds.

Suppose the algorithm is computing $\mathbf{W}[i_1, i_r]$. Then it has already computed $\mathbf{W}[i_1, i_s]$ for $s = 2, \ldots, r - 1$. Assume inductively that for $s = 2, \ldots, r - 1$ the current value of $\mathbf{W}[i_1, i_s]$ is $\mathbf{W}^*[i_1, i_s]$. Then this will be the final value as well. When $k = r - 1$ in the replacement loop, $\mathbf{W}[i_1, i_{r-1}] + \mathbf{W}[i_{r-1}, i_r] = \mathbf{W}^*[i_1, i_{r-1}] + \mathbf{W}^*[i_{r-1}, i_r] = \mathbf{W}^*[i_1, i_r] \leqq \mathbf{W}[i_1, i_r]$. If $\mathbf{W}[i_1, i_r]$ is not already $\mathbf{W}^*[i_1, i_r]$, it will be after the replacement, and from then on. By induction each computed $\mathbf{W}[i_1, i_s]$ for $s = 2, \ldots, t$ is $\mathbf{W}^*[i_1, i_s]$. In particular, $\mathbf{W}[i, j] = \mathbf{W}[i_1, i_t] = \mathbf{W}^*[i, j]$, as we wanted to show.   ☐

Our next min-path algorithm is an adaptation of a procedure for finding shortest paths and the reachability relation. It looks superficially like HU'S algorithm but works quite differently. As for HU'S algorithm, we start with $\mathbf{W} = \mathbf{W}_0$, the edge-weight matrix.

WARSHALL'S *Algorithm.*

For $k = 1$ to n
  For $i = 1$ to n
    For $j = 1$ to n
      If $\mathbf{W}[i, j] > \mathbf{W}[i, k] + \mathbf{W}[k, j]$ then
        Replace $\mathbf{W}[i, j]$ by $\mathbf{W}[i, k] + \mathbf{W}[k, j]$
    End for
  End for
End for
End   ☐

Theorem 2   WARSHALL'S algorithm produces the min-weight matrix $\mathbf{W}^*$.

Proof.   We will prove the following assertion for each $k = 1, 2, \ldots, n$. At the conclusion of the execution of the loop for k, each $\mathbf{W}[i, j]$ is the smallest weight of any path from v_i to v_j whose intermediate vertices [if any] are all in $\{v_1, \ldots, v_k\}$. [The smallest weight is ∞ if there is no path of this kind.] It will follow that $\mathbf{W} = \mathbf{W}^*$ at the conclusion of the loop for $k = n$.

First consider the computation of the entry $W[i, j]$ in the loop for $k = 1$. The computed value of $W[i, j]$ is either the original value of $W[i, j]$ or is $W[i, 1] + W[1, j]$, so it is either ∞ or the weight of the edge $w_i\, w_j$ or the weight of the path $w_i\, w_1\, w_j$. It is the smallest of these, so the assertion for $k = 1$ in the last paragraph is true.

Now assume inductively that after execution of the loop for $k = m$ W is as described, and consider the computation of $W[i, j]$ in the loop for $k = m + 1$. Suppose first that among all paths from v_i to v_j with intermediate vertices in $\{v_1, \ldots, v_{m+1}\}$ there is one of smallest weight which does not go through v_{m+1}. By the inductive assumption its weight is the current value of $W[i, j]$. Since $W[i, m + 1] + W[m + 1, j]$ is the weight of a path from v_i to v_j through vertices in $\{v_1, \ldots, v_{m+1}\}$, we must have $W[i, j] \leq W[i, m + 1] + W[m + 1, j]$, and so no replacement occurs. The new value of $W[i, j]$ is the same as the old, and is the smallest weight for a path from v_i to v_j with intermediate vertices in $\{v_1, \ldots, v_{m+1}\}$.

Now suppose every path of smallest weight from v_i to v_j through $\{v_1, \ldots, v_{m+1}\}$ goes through v_{m+1}. Since such a path passes through each vertex at most once, the weight of such a path is $W[i, m + 1] + W[m + 1, j]$, where these entries still have the values they attained at the end of the loop for $k = m$. Since this sum is less than $W[i, j]$ at the end of the loop for $k = m$, the appropriate replacement is made. That is, after executing the loop for $k = m + 1$, W is as described in the first paragraph.

The claim for all $k = 1, 2, \ldots, n$ follows by finite induction. $\quad\square$

EXAMPLE 4 We apply WARSHALL'S algorithm to the digraph of Examples 1 and 2. Hand calculation with WARSHALL'S algorithm leads to n matrices, one for each value of k. For this example the matrices are the following.

$$
W_0 = W_1 = \begin{bmatrix}
0 & 6 & 3 & \infty & \infty & \infty & \infty \\
\infty & 0 & \infty & 7 & 1 & \infty & \infty \\
\infty & 2 & 0 & 7 & \infty & \infty & \infty \\
\infty & \infty & \infty & 0 & \infty & 2 & 4 \\
\infty & \infty & 4 & 5 & 0 & 6 & \infty \\
\infty & \infty & \infty & \infty & \infty & 0 & 4 \\
\infty & \infty & \infty & \infty & \infty & \infty & 0
\end{bmatrix},
$$

$$
W_2 = \begin{bmatrix}
0 & 6 & 3 & 13 & 7 & \infty & \infty \\
\infty & 0 & \infty & 7 & 1 & \infty & \infty \\
\infty & 2 & 0 & 7 & 3 & \infty & \infty \\
\infty & \infty & \infty & 0 & \infty & 2 & 4 \\
\infty & \infty & 4 & 5 & 0 & 6 & \infty \\
\infty & \infty & \infty & \infty & \infty & 0 & 4 \\
\infty & \infty & \infty & \infty & \infty & \infty & 0
\end{bmatrix},
$$

$$\mathbf{W}_3 = \begin{bmatrix} 0 & 5 & 3 & 10 & 6 & \infty & \infty \\ \infty & 0 & \infty & 7 & 1 & \infty & \infty \\ \infty & 2 & 0 & 7 & 3 & \infty & \infty \\ \infty & \infty & \infty & 0 & \infty & 2 & 4 \\ \infty & 6 & 4 & 5 & 0 & 6 & \infty \\ \infty & \infty & \infty & \infty & \infty & 0 & 4 \\ \infty & \infty & \infty & \infty & \infty & \infty & 0 \end{bmatrix},$$

$$\mathbf{W}_4 = \begin{bmatrix} 0 & 5 & 3 & 10 & 6 & 12 & 14 \\ \infty & 0 & \infty & 7 & 1 & 9 & 11 \\ \infty & 2 & 0 & 7 & 3 & 9 & 11 \\ \infty & \infty & \infty & 0 & \infty & 2 & 4 \\ \infty & 6 & 4 & 5 & 0 & 6 & 9 \\ \infty & \infty & \infty & \infty & \infty & 0 & 4 \\ \infty & \infty & \infty & \infty & \infty & \infty & 0 \end{bmatrix},$$

$$\mathbf{W}_5 = \mathbf{W}_6 = \mathbf{W}_7 = \mathbf{W}^* = \begin{bmatrix} 0 & 5 & 3 & 10 & 6 & 12 & 14 \\ \infty & 0 & 5 & 6 & 1 & 7 & 10 \\ \infty & 2 & 0 & 7 & 3 & 9 & 11 \\ \infty & \infty & \infty & 0 & \infty & 2 & 4 \\ \infty & 6 & 4 & 5 & 0 & 6 & 9 \\ \infty & \infty & \infty & \infty & \infty & 0 & 4 \\ \infty & \infty & \infty & \infty & \infty & \infty & 0 \end{bmatrix}.$$

We illustrate the computations by calculating $\mathbf{W}_3[5, 2]$. Here $k = 3$ and we look at $\mathbf{W}[5, 3] + \mathbf{W}[3, 2]$. The current value of $\mathbf{W}[5, 3]$ is $\mathbf{W}_2[5, 3] = 4$, and of $\mathbf{W}[3, 2]$ is $\mathbf{W}_3[3, 2] = 2$. Since $\mathbf{W}_2[5, 2] = \infty > 6 = \mathbf{W}_2[5, 3] + \mathbf{W}_3[3, 2]$, we replace ∞ by 6 and get $\mathbf{W}_3[5, 2] = 6$.

A given entry $\mathbf{W}[i, j]$ may change several times during the calculations of the outer loops [as k runs through its possible values]. In contrast, with HU'S algorithm all the changes occur during the calculation of the inner loop. $\square$

Either HU'S algorithm or WARSHALL'S algorithm can be modified to give a max-weight algorithm for acyclic digraphs with non-negative weights. Replace all the ∞'s by $-\infty$'s with $-\infty + x = -\infty = x + (-\infty)$ for all x and $-\infty < a$ for all real a. Change the inequality in the replacement loop to

$$\mathbf{W}[i, j] < \mathbf{W}[i, k] + \mathbf{W}[k, j].$$

Essentially the same arguments as in the proofs of Theorems 1 and 2 show that if an acyclic digraph is labeled as in the hypotheses of Theorem 1, the revised algorithms compute the function M of § 8.3. That is, the final $\mathbf{W}[i, j]$

is the max-weight from v_i to v_j if there is a path from v_i to v_j and is $-\infty$ otherwise.

If the goal is to find the max-weights from a source s to other vertices, then s can be labeled v_1 and only the first row of M is needed. For HU'S algorithm we can simply do the loop for $i = 1$. It can be shown that if the digraph is labeled as in Theorem 1 and the source is v_1, then WARSHALL'S algorithm also produces the correct first row if we fix $i = 1$.

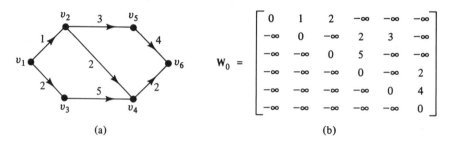

(a)   (b)

FIGURE 3

$$
\begin{bmatrix}
0 & 1 & 2 & 7 & 4 & 9 \\
-\infty & 0 & -\infty & 2 & 3 & 7 \\
-\infty & -\infty & 0 & 5 & -\infty & 7 \\
-\infty & -\infty & -\infty & 0 & -\infty & 2 \\
-\infty & -\infty & -\infty & -\infty & 0 & 4 \\
-\infty & -\infty & -\infty & -\infty & -\infty & 0
\end{bmatrix}
\qquad
\begin{bmatrix}
0 & 1 & 2 & 7 & 4 & -\infty \\
-\infty & 0 & -\infty & 2 & 3 & -\infty \\
-\infty & -\infty & 0 & 5 & -\infty & -\infty \\
-\infty & -\infty & -\infty & 0 & -\infty & 2 \\
-\infty & -\infty & -\infty & -\infty & 0 & 4 \\
-\infty & -\infty & -\infty & -\infty & -\infty & 0
\end{bmatrix}
$$

(a)   (b)

FIGURE 4

EXAMPLE 5   We find max-weights for the digraph of Figure 3(a) using the modified HU'S algorithm. The initial matrix $\mathbf{W_0}$ is given in Figure 3(b). The final matrix after one application of the algorithm is given in Figure 4(a). As a sample, we compute the $(1, 6)$-entry, with the other first-row entries all known and with $W[1, 6] = -\infty$ initially. Figure 4(b) gives the current matrix $\mathbf{W}$.

$$W[1, 1] + W[1, 6] = 0 - \infty = -\infty \qquad \text{no change}$$

$$W[1, 2] + W[2, 6] = 1 - \infty = -\infty \qquad \text{no change}$$

$$W[1, 3] + W[3, 6] = 2 - \infty = -\infty \qquad \text{no change}$$

$$W[1, 4] + W[4, 6] = 7 + 2 = 9 \qquad \text{change } W[1, 6] \text{ to } 9$$

$$W[1, 5] + W[5, 6] = 4 + 4 = 8 < 9 \qquad \text{no change}$$

$$W[1, 6] + W[6, 6] = 9 + 0 = 9 \qquad \text{no change}$$

This example is labeled so that $i < j$ if there is a path from v_i to v_j. Hence a single execution gives all max-weights.   □

In the next section we consider how to modify these algorithms to answer some of our basic questions about graphs.

E X E R C I S E S   8 . 8

1. (a) Find the min-weight matrix **W*** for the digraph shown in Figure 5.
   (b) Does one execution of HU'S algorithm produce **W***?

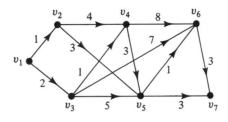

FIGURE 5

2. Find the max-weight matrix for the digraph of Figure 5.

3. Give the vertex sequence of all min-paths of weight at least 5 in the digraph in Figure 5.

4. Assign weight 1 to each edge in the digraph of Figure 6. Show that after two applications of HU'S algorithm the entry W[1, 2] is still ∞.

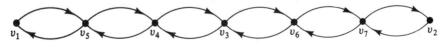

FIGURE 6

5. Use WARSHALL'S algorithm to find minimum path lengths in the digraph of Figure 6. Give the matrix **W** at the start of each k-loop.

6. (a) Use WARSHALL'S algorithm to find **W*** and min-paths for the digraph of Figure 3(a).
   (b) Find max-weights for the same digraph using the modified WARSHALL'S algorithm.

7. Give the final matrix **W** if WARSHALL'S algorithm is applied once to the matrix

$$\mathbf{W_0} = \begin{bmatrix} 0 & 11 & 9 & \infty & 2 \\ \infty & 0 & \infty & \infty & \infty \\ \infty & 1 & 0 & \infty & \infty \\ \infty & \infty & 2 & 0 & \infty \\ \infty & \infty & 6 & 3 & 0 \end{bmatrix}.$$

8. How could one test whether a digraph is acyclic using:
(a) HU'S algorithm?   (b) WARSHALL'S algorithm?

9. (a) Write a computer program to execute HU'S algorithm on digraphs with nonnegative weights using some negative number, such as -1, instead of ∞.

(b) Write a computer program to execute WARSHALL'S algorithm and test it on the graphs of Figures 1(a) and 5.

§ 8.9   *Modifications and Applications of the Algorithms*

We showed in § 8.3 how to use algorithms FILL-IN and MIN-PATH to construct min-paths once W^* is known. We can modify HU'S algorithm or WARSHALL'S algorithm to produce the min-paths directly. We create a "pointer" function P so that at any time either $\langle v_i, v_{P(i,j)} \rangle$ is the first edge on a path of smallest known weight from v_i to v_j, or $P(i,j) = i$ if no path is yet known from v_i to v_j. We consider P to be an $n \times n$ matrix with entries in $\{1, 2, \ldots, n\}$.

Initially, let $\mathbf{P}[i, j] = i$ if $\mathbf{W}[i, j] = \infty$ and $\mathbf{P}[i, j] = j$ otherwise. Change the replacement loop in either algorithm to read as follows.

> If $\mathbf{W}[i, j] > \mathbf{W}[i, k] + \mathbf{W}[k, j]$ then
>   Replace $\mathbf{W}[i, j]$ by $\mathbf{W}[i, k] + \mathbf{W}[k, j]$ and
>   Replace $\mathbf{P}[i, j]$ by $\mathbf{P}[i, k]$.

Then $\mathbf{P}[i, j]$ only changes when some path $v_i \cdots v_k \cdots v_j$ is discovered of smaller weight than the best known path from v_i to v_j. The first edge on the part from v_i to v_k is $\langle v_i, v_{\mathbf{P}[i,k]} \rangle$ and that becomes the first edge on the newly discovered best path from v_i to v_j.

The modified WARSHALL'S algorithm looks like this, starting with $\mathbf{W} = \mathbf{W}_0$ and with $\mathbf{P}[i, j] = j$ if there is an edge from i to j and $\mathbf{P}[i, j] = i$ if there is not.

> WARSHALL'S *Algorithm with a Pointer.*
>
> For $k = 1$ to n
>   For $i = 1$ to n
>   For $j = 1$ to n
>   If $\mathbf{W}[i, j] > \mathbf{W}[i, k] + \mathbf{W}[k, j]$ then
>   Replace $\mathbf{W}[i, j]$ by $\mathbf{W}[i, k] + \mathbf{W}[k, j]$ and
>   Replace $\mathbf{P}[i, j]$ by $\mathbf{P}[i, k]$
>   End for
>   End for
> End for
> End   ⬚

When the algorithm stops, $\mathbf{P}[i, j] = i$ if there is no min-path from v_i to v_j. Otherwise, the sequence

$$i, \quad \mathbf{P}[i, j], \quad \mathbf{P}[\mathbf{P}[i, j], j], \quad \mathbf{P}[\mathbf{P}[\mathbf{P}[i, j], j], j], \ldots$$

gives the indices of vertices on a min-path from v_i to v_j. Since each subscript l is followed by the subscript $\mathbf{P}[l, j]$, this is actually a simple recursively defined sequence.

We will illustrate the use of the "pointer" shortly in Example 1.

HU'S algorithm or WARSHALL'S algorithm can also be used to find the reachability relation R of a digraph. Simply change the initial diagonal entries to $\mathbf{W}[i, i] = \infty$ if there is no loop at i and $\mathbf{W}[i, i] = 1$ if there is a loop, and give all edges weight 1. The final value of $\mathbf{W}[i, j]$ is ∞ if there is no path from i to j and is a positive integer if there is a path. Modified with a pointer function, either algorithm gives shortest paths.

We saw in § 8.7 how to view transitive closure in terms of reachability. To use our algorithms to find $t(Q)$ for a relation Q on some finite set $\{s_1, \ldots, s_n\}$ let $\mathbf{W}[i, j] = 1$ if $s_i \ Q \ s_j$ and $\mathbf{W}[i, j] = \infty$ otherwise. In particular, this means that $\mathbf{W}[i, i] = \infty$ unless $s_i \ Q \ s_i$. When we set $\mathbf{W}[i, i] = 0$ in § 8.8, we observed that it was to account for the paths of length 0, with no edges. That choice of diagonal entries prevented us from arriving at false "min-paths" which included cycles. When we are considering the transitive closure of a relation Q which is not reflexive, we specifically want to know which x's are related to themselves in $t(Q)$. That is, we want to know for each x whether or not there is a path of length at least 1 from x to x in the associated digraph. The way to find out is to take $\mathbf{W}[i, i]$ to be ∞ initially if there is no loop at s_i. At the end of the execution, $\mathbf{W}[i, j] \neq \infty$ if and only if there is a path from s_i to s_j, i.e., $\langle s_i, s_j \rangle \in t(Q)$. In particular, $\mathbf{W}[i, i] \neq \infty$ if and only if s_i is related to itself in $t(Q)$. See Exercise 10 for a modification with 0 instead of ∞.

These algorithms can also be applied to undirected graphs, in effect by replacing each undirected edge $\{u, v\}$ with $u \neq v$ by two directed edges $\langle u, v \rangle$ and $\langle v, u \rangle$ and each loop $\{u, u\}$ by a loop $\langle u, u \rangle$. If the undirected edge has weight w, assign the directed edges the same weight w. If the graph is unweighted, assign weight 1 to all edges. The resulting matrix $\mathbf{W}[i, j]$ is symmetric.

EXAMPLE 1   (a) Consider the weighted undirected graph shown in Figure 1(a). We wish to find min-weights and min-paths between vertices, allowing travel in

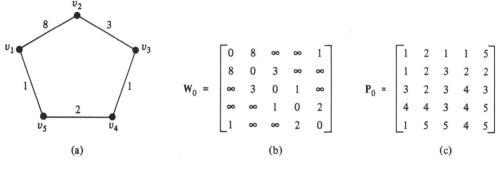

(a)   (b)   (c)

FIGURE 1

either direction along edges. The initial matrices $\mathbf{W}_0$ and $\mathbf{P}_0$ are given in Figures 1(b) and 1(c). After one execution of HU'S algorithm we arrive at

$$
\mathbf{W}_1 = \begin{bmatrix} 0 & 8 & 11 & 3 & 1 \\ 8 & 0 & 3 & 4 & 6 \\ 11 & 3 & 0 & 1 & 3 \\ 3 & 4 & 1 & 0 & 2 \\ 1 & 6 & 3 & 2 & 0 \end{bmatrix} \quad \text{and} \quad \mathbf{P}_1 = \begin{bmatrix} 1 & 2 & 2 & 5 & 5 \\ 1 & 2 & 3 & 3 & 3 \\ 2 & 2 & 3 & 4 & 4 \\ 5 & 3 & 3 & 4 & 5 \\ 1 & 4 & 4 & 4 & 5 \end{bmatrix}.
$$

The algorithm hasn't caught on to the fact that it is cheaper to get from v_1 to v_3 by way of v_5 and v_4. Note that in the computation of $\mathbf{P}[2, 5]$ the value of $\mathbf{P}[2, 4]$ has already changed to 3. The best known path from v_2 to v_5 goes through v_4 and starts out through v_3. Starting with $\mathbf{W}_1$ and $\mathbf{P}_1$ one more application of HU'S algorithm yields

$$
\mathbf{W}^* = \begin{bmatrix} 0 & 7 & 4 & 3 & 1 \\ 7 & 0 & 3 & 4 & 6 \\ 4 & 3 & 0 & 1 & 3 \\ 3 & 4 & 1 & 0 & 2 \\ 1 & 6 & 3 & 2 & 0 \end{bmatrix} \quad \text{and} \quad \mathbf{P}^* = \begin{bmatrix} 1 & 5 & 5 & 5 & 5 \\ 3 & 2 & 3 & 3 & 3 \\ 4 & 2 & 3 & 4 & 4 \\ 5 & 3 & 3 & 4 & 5 \\ 1 & 4 & 4 & 4 & 5 \end{bmatrix}
$$

which gives the final answer. Since

$$\mathbf{P}^*[1, 2] = 5, \quad \mathbf{P}^*[5, 2] = 4, \quad \mathbf{P}^*[4, 2] = 3 \quad \text{and} \quad \mathbf{P}^*[3, 2] = 2,$$

the path $v_1\, v_5\, v_4\, v_3\, v_2$ from v_1 to v_2 has minimum weight, namely 7. Machine calculation would be faster with WARSHALL'S algorithm for this example, but hand computation would be slow [Exercise 2].

(b) Consider the relation A with matrix

$$
\mathbf{M}_A = \begin{bmatrix} 0 & 0 & 0 & 0 & 0 & 1 \\ 0 & 1 & 0 & 0 & 1 & 0 \\ 0 & 0 & 0 & 0 & 0 & 1 \\ 0 & 0 & 0 & 0 & 0 & 0 \\ 0 & 1 & 0 & 0 & 0 & 0 \\ 1 & 0 & 1 & 0 & 0 & 0 \end{bmatrix}.
$$

The relation is symmetric and can be viewed as the adjacency relation of a graph with vertex set $\{1, 2, 3, 4, 5, 6\}$, which is why we labeled the matrix $\mathbf{M}_A$. We wish to find the transitive closure of A, i.e., the reachability relation R for the graph. The initial matrix $\mathbf{W}$ is

$$
\mathbf{W}_0 = \begin{bmatrix} \infty & \infty & \infty & \infty & \infty & 1 \\ \infty & 1 & \infty & \infty & 1 & \infty \\ \infty & \infty & \infty & \infty & \infty & 1 \\ \infty & \infty & \infty & \infty & \infty & \infty \\ \infty & 1 & \infty & \infty & \infty & \infty \\ 1 & \infty & 1 & \infty & \infty & \infty \end{bmatrix}.
$$

Notice the diagonal entries of $\mathbf{W_0}$. One application of HU'S algorithm turns out to be enough. It gives

$$
\mathbf{W^*} = \begin{bmatrix}
2 & \infty & 2 & \infty & \infty & 1 \\
\infty & 1 & \infty & \infty & 1 & \infty \\
2 & \infty & 2 & \infty & \infty & 1 \\
\infty & \infty & \infty & \infty & \infty & \infty \\
\infty & 1 & \infty & \infty & 2 & \infty \\
1 & \infty & 1 & \infty & \infty & 2
\end{bmatrix}, \quad \text{so} \quad \mathbf{M_R} = \begin{bmatrix}
1 & 0 & 1 & 0 & 0 & 1 \\
0 & 1 & 0 & 0 & 1 & 0 \\
1 & 0 & 1 & 0 & 0 & 1 \\
0 & 0 & 0 & 0 & 0 & 0 \\
0 & 1 & 0 & 0 & 1 & 0 \\
1 & 0 & 1 & 0 & 0 & 1
\end{bmatrix}.
$$

The picture of the graph in Figure 2 helps clarify the meaning of $\mathbf{M_R}$. The graph has three components. The components containing 1 and 2 can be read off from the first two rows of $\mathbf{M_R}$. The fourth row of $\mathbf{M_R}$ consists of 0's, but the fourth row of $\mathbf{M_{\bar{R}}}$ is 0 0 0 1 0 0, which gives the component {4}. ∎

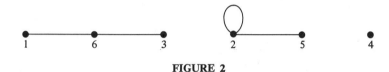

FIGURE 2

FLEURY'S algorithm in § 8.5 involves a check to see if removing a given edge e increases the number of components, i.e., if the endpoints of e are reachable from each other in the graph with e deleted. HU'S algorithm and WARSHALL'S algorithm can check reachability. Indeed, WARSHALL'S algorithm was originally designed for that purpose. We have discussed these algorithms just for graphs and digraphs with no parallel edges, but we can remove that restriction here. Let $\mathbf{W}[i, j]$ be the number of edges from v_i to v_j, if there are any, or ∞ if there are none. Suppose e goes from v_i to v_j. If $\mathbf{W}[i, j] \geq 2$, then e is one of several parallel edges, and so v_i and v_j are still adjacent if e is gone. If $\mathbf{W}[i, j] = 1$, replace $\mathbf{W}[i, j]$ by ∞ and use HU'S or WARSHALL'S algorithm to compute $\mathbf{W^*}[i, j]$. If $\mathbf{W^*}[i, j] = \infty$, v_j is not reachable from v_i in $G \backslash \{e\}$; otherwise it is.

A similar observation lets us use our algorithms to test whether an edge e belongs to a cycle. If e goes from v_i to v_j then e belongs to a cycle if and only if v_i is reachable from v_j in $G \backslash \{e\}$. By testing all edges of G we can determine whether G is acyclic.

We conclude this section by mentioning without proof another algorithm which can be used instead of HU'S or WARSHALL'S algorithms. The method is a modification of a reachability algorithm presented by Z. Bavel in his book *Math Companion for Computer Science*. Its form is somewhat different from the nested loop structures we have seen so far.

Initially, $\mathbf{W}$ is the edge-weight matrix $\mathbf{W_0}$ and, for $i = 1, \ldots, n$, $S(i)$ is the immediate successor list

$$S(i) = \text{SUCC}(i) = \{j : \text{there is an edge from } v_i \text{ to } v_j\}.$$

The algorithm keeps track of best known path weights, and also keeps lists of all vertices which are known to be reachable from each vertex. At the conclusion of the algorithm, $\mathbf{W} = \mathbf{W}^*$ and $S(i) = \{j : v_j \text{ is reachable from } v_i\}$. Two sets, P and M, are involved. Members of M can be thought of as marked with minus signs, which become plus signs when they move to P.

BAVEL'S *Algorithm.*

For $i = 1$ to n
  Let $P = \varnothing$ and $M = S(i)$
  While $M \neq \varnothing$
    Let $k = $ first member of M [in some ordering]
    Replace P by $P \cup \{k\}$
    Replace M by $M \cup S(k)$
    For j in M
      If $\mathbf{W}[i,j] > \mathbf{W}[i,k] + \mathbf{W}[k,j]$ then
        Replace $\mathbf{W}[i,j]$ by $\mathbf{W}[i,k] + \mathbf{W}[k,j]$
    End for
    Replace M by $M \setminus P$
  End while
  Let $S(i) = P$
End for
End   ☐

This algorithm, too, can be modified to give max-weights or can be given a pointer to produce paths.

BAVEL'S algorithm takes the following particularly simple form without the matrix $\mathbf{W}$ if all we want is the reachable sets.

For $i = 1$ to n
  Let $P = \varnothing$ and $M = S(i)$
  While $M \neq \varnothing$
    Let $k = $ first member of M
    Replace P by $P \cup \{k\}$
    Replace M by $(M \cup S(k)) \setminus P$
  End while
  Let $S(i) = P$
End for
End   ☐

If we just want $R(v)$ for a particular vertex $v = v_k$, we can simply execute the loop for $i = k$.

EXAMPLE 2   We calculate $R(v_1)$ for the digraph in Figure 3. For $i = 1$ we get the following successive values.

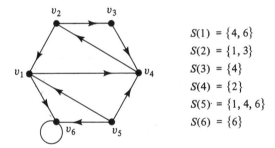

$$S(1) = \{4, 6\}$$
$$S(2) = \{1, 3\}$$
$$S(3) = \{4\}$$
$$S(4) = \{2\}$$
$$S(5) = \{1, 4, 6\}$$
$$S(6) = \{6\}$$

FIGURE 3

P	M	k	
∅	{4, 6}	4	
{4}	{$\not{4}$, 6, 2}	2	[we use the natural order on $\mathbb{P}$]
{4, 2}	{6, $\not{2}$, 1, 3}	1	
{4, 2, 1}	{6, $\not{1}$, 3, $\not{4}$, $\not{6}$}	3	
{4, 2, 1, 3}	{6, $\not{3}$, $\not{4}$}	6	
{4, 2, 1, 3, 6}	{$\not{6}$, $\not{6}$} = ∅		

So $S(1) = \{1, 2, 3, 4, 6\}$. Bavel's book contains worked examples illustrating the "plus-minus" format for hand computations. □

EXERCISES 8.9

1. (a) Give the initial and final min-path pointer matrices **P** for the digraph in Figure 4(a). [Compare with Exercise 3 of § 8.8.]

(b) Repeat part (a) for max-paths instead of min-paths.

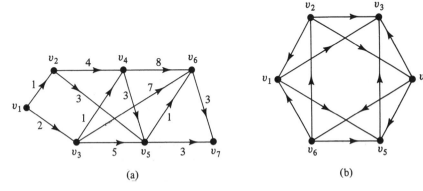

(a)   (b)

FIGURE 4

2. Use WARSHALL'S algorithm to find **W*** and min-paths for the graph of Figure 1(a).

3. (a) Give the initial matrix $\mathbf{W}_0$ to find the reachability relation for the digraph of Figure 4(b).

(b) Find the reachability matrix $\mathbf{M}_R$ for the digraph using HU'S algorithm.

(c) Is this digraph strongly connected?

4. Use BAVEL'S algorithm to find each of the following for the digraph of Figure 4(b).

(a) $R(v_1)$ (b) $R(v_4)$ (c) $R(v_5)$

5. Use BAVEL'S algorithm to find each of the following for the digraph of Figure 3.

(a) $R(v_3)$ (b) $R(v_5)$ (c) $R(v_6)$

6. Give the initial matrix $\mathbf{W}_0$ to find the transitive closure of each of the following relations.

(a) R on $\{1, 2, 3, 4, 5, 6\}$ where $i\,R\,j$ if $i = j - 1$,

(b) R on $\{1, 2, 3, 4, 5\}$ where $i\,R\,j$ if $|i - j| = 2$.

7. Find the transitive closures of the relations (a) and (b) in Exercise 6.

8. Give the final matrices $\mathbf{W}$ and $\mathbf{P}$ if HU'S algorithm is applied once to the matrix

$$\mathbf{W}_0 = \begin{bmatrix} 0 & 11 & 9 & \infty & 2 \\ \infty & 0 & \infty & \infty & \infty \\ \infty & 1 & 0 & \infty & \infty \\ \infty & \infty & 2 & 0 & \infty \\ \infty & \infty & 6 & 3 & 0 \end{bmatrix}.$$

Compare $\mathbf{W}$ with the answer to Exercise 7 of § 8.8.

9. (a) What happens if one applies HU'S algorithm once for max-weights to the digraph of Figure 5?

(b) Is the result meaningful?

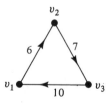

FIGURE 5

10. Modify HU'S and WARSHALL'S algorithms so that $\mathbf{W}[i, j] = 0$ if no path has been discovered from v_i to v_j and $\mathbf{W}[i, j] = 1$ if a path is known. *Hint:* Use $\mathbf{W}[i, k] \wedge \mathbf{W}[k, j]$.

11. (a) How could one use algorithms in this section and in § 8.8 to test whether a finite digraph is strongly connected?

(b) How could one use them to test whether a finite digraph is connected?

CHAPTER HIGHLIGHTS

For a reminder on how to use this material for review, see the end of Chapter 0.

Some of the material in this chapter was introduced long ago in Chapter 0. A good part of it is first discussed for digraphs and then modified for undirected graphs with similar definitions and no great surprises. Though there are lots of items on the lists below, there are not really as many new ideas to master as the lists would suggest. Have courage.

Concepts

digraph	**graph** [undirected]
vertex, edge	vertex, edge
initial/terminal vertex	endpoint
path	path
length	length
closed path, cycle	closed path, cycle
acyclic digraph, path	acyclic graph, path
isomorphism	isomorphism
class, invariant	class, invariant
degree, indegree, outdegree	degree
reachable	reachable
connected, strongly connected	connected
weight	component
min-weight, min-path	Euler path, circuit
scheduling network	Hamilton path, circuit
max-weight, max-path	Gray code
critical path, edge	adjacency relation
	reachable relation

Facts

A path in a digraph is acyclic if and only if its vertices are distinct.

There is at most one simple path between two vertices in an acyclic graph.

Graph and digraph isomorphism may be hard to check, but invariants can sometimes help.

Automorphisms help analyze digraph symmetry.

$\sum_v \text{indeg}(v) = \sum_v \text{outdeg}(v) = |E(G)|$ for digraphs.

$\sum_v \text{deg}(v) = 2|E(G)|$ for graphs and digraphs.

$L(v) - A(u) = W(u, v) + F(u, v)$ for scheduling networks.

Critical edge weights govern max-weight from source to sink in a scheduling network.

A graph has an Euler circuit if and only if it is connected and all vertices have even degree. An analogous statement holds for digraphs.

If e is an edge of a connected graph G then e belongs to some cycle if and only if $G \setminus \{e\}$ is connected. Thus a connectedness algorithm can test for cycles.

Components correspond to $\bar{R}$-classes. $\bar{R} = \bigcup_{k=0}^{\infty} A^k$.

The matrix of A^k is $\mathbf{M}_A * \cdots * \mathbf{M}_A$, with k factors.

If a graph G has no loops or parallel edges, and if $|V(G)| = n \geqq 3$, then G is Hamiltonian if any of the following are true:

(a) $\deg(v) \geqq n/2$ for each vertex v [high degrees].

(b) $|E(G)| \geqq \frac{1}{2}(n-1)(n-2) + 2$ [lots of edges].

(c) $\deg(v) + \deg(w) \geqq n$ whenever v and w are not connected by an edge.

Theorem 4 of § 8.6 gives information on Hamilton paths in bipartite graphs.

Methods

SINK and THINK to find a sink [or source] in a finite acyclic digraph.

NUMBERING VERTICES to assign numbers to vertices in a finite acyclic digraph so all paths lead from smaller to larger numbers.

FLEURY'S algorithm to find an Euler path of a graph.

FILL-IN to find a min-path between two vertices given W^*. It can be modified to produce the vertices in sequence.

MIN-PATH to find a min-path given W and W^*.

HU'S algorithm to find an approximation to W^* given W_0. Applied three times or forwards and backwards it gives W^*. It gives W^* at once if the digraph is acyclic and numbered properly.

WARSHALL'S and BAVEL'S algorithms to produce W^* given W_0.

For hand calculation HU'S algorithm involves less writing than WARSHALL'S. For machine computation there is no difference.

All three algorithms can be modified to find max-weights, min-paths or reachability [and hence transitive closure of a relation].

9

TREES

In this chapter we study a class of graphs, called trees, which arise frequently in computer science. Trees are especially suited to represent hierarchical structures and to represent addresses or labels in an organized manner. We give applications involving Polish notation, efficient codes and merging lists. We will also see how to use the structure of trees to process data they represent. This chapter begins with undirected trees and then deals with the most useful directed trees, the so-called "rooted trees," which arise naturally from undirected trees.

§ 9.1 Properties of Trees

A **tree** is a connected acyclic graph. In particular, a tree has no parallel edges and no loops.

EXAMPLE 1   The eleven trees with seven vertices are pictured in Figure 1. More precisely, there are eleven isomorphism classes of trees that have seven vertices, and we have drawn one from each class.   ☐

Consider any connected graph G. A subgraph T of G is called a **spanning tree** if T is a tree and if T includes every vertex of G, i.e., $V(T) = V(G)$. In other words, T is a tree obtained by removing some of the edges of G, perhaps, but keeping all of the vertices.

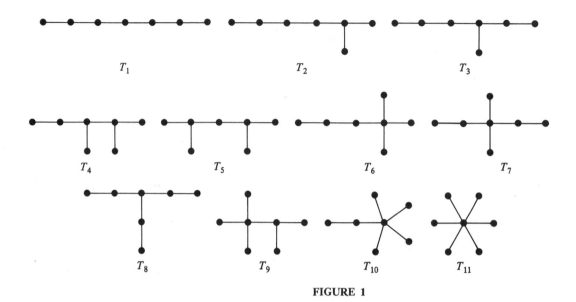

FIGURE 1

EXAMPLE 2   The graph H in Figure 2 has over 300 spanning trees, of which four have been sketched. They all have 6 edges.   ☐

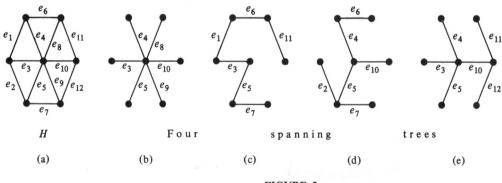

H	F o u r	s p a n n i n g	t r e e s	
(a)	(b)	(c)	(d)	(e)

FIGURE 2

The next theorem is a special case of Theorem 3 of § 8.5. Its corollary will show that all finite connected graphs have spanning trees.

Theorem 1   Let e be an edge of a connected graph G. Then $G \setminus \{e\}$ is connected if and only if e is in some cycle.

Corollary   Every finite connected graph G has a spanning tree.

Proof.   Consider a connected subgraph G' of G that uses all the vertices of G and has as few edges as possible. We claim that G' is acyclic, and hence is a spanning tree of G. Otherwise, G' has a cycle and the cycle involves some edge e of G'. By Theorem 1, $G' \setminus \{e\}$ would be a connected subgraph of G having fewer edges than G'. This contradiction shows that G' is acyclic. $\square$

EXAMPLE 3   (a) We illustrate Theorem 1 using the connected graph in Figure 3(a). Note that e_1 does not belong to a cycle and that $G \setminus \{e_1\}$ is disconnected: no path in $G \setminus \{e_1\}$ connects v to the other vertices. Likewise, e_5 belongs to no cycle and $G \setminus \{e_5\}$ is disconnected. The remaining edges belong to cycles. Removal of any *one* of them will not disconnect G.

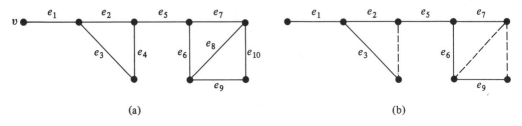

FIGURE 3

(b) To illustrate the corollary, note that $G \setminus \{e_{10}\}$ is still connected but has cycles. If we also remove e_8 the resulting graph still has a cycle, namely $e_2 \, e_3 \, e_4$. But if we then remove one of the edges in the cycle, say e_4, we obtain an acyclic connected subgraph, i.e., a spanning tree. See Figure 3(b). Clearly, several different spanning trees can be obtained in this way. $\square$

In characterizing trees we lose nothing by restricting our attention to graphs with no loops or parallel edges. Our first characterizations hold even if the graph is infinite.

Theorem 2   Let G be a graph with more than one vertex, no loops and no parallel edges. The following are equivalent:

(a) G is a tree.
(b) Each pair of distinct vertices is connected by exactly one simple path [and it is acyclic].
(c) G is connected, but will not be if any edge is removed.
(d) G is acyclic, but will not be if any edge is added.

Proof. This proof consists of four short proofs.

(a) $\Rightarrow$ (b). Suppose that G is a tree, so that G is connected and acyclic. By Theorem 1 of § 8.4, each pair of vertices is connected by at least one simple [acyclic] path. By the contrapositive version of Theorem 2 of § 8.4, there is just one simple path.

(b) $\Rightarrow$ (c). If (b) holds, G is clearly connected. Let $e = \{u, v\}$ be an edge of G and assume $G \setminus \{e\}$ is still connected. Note that $u \neq v$ since G has no loops. By Theorem 1 of § 8.4 there is a simple path in $G \setminus \{e\}$ from u to v.

Since this path and the one-edge path e are different simple paths in G from u to v, we contradict (b).

(c) $\Rightarrow$ (d). Suppose that (c) holds. If G had a cycle we could remove an edge from G and retain connectedness by Theorem 1. So G is acyclic. Now consider an edge e not in the graph G and let G' denote the graph G with this new edge adjoined. Since $G' \setminus \{e\} = G$ is connected, we apply Theorem 1 to G' to conclude that e belongs to some cycle of G'. In other words, adding e to G destroys acyclicity.

(d) $\Rightarrow$ (a). If (d) holds and G is not a tree, then G is not connected. Then there exist distinct vertices u and v that are not connected by any paths in G. Consider the new edge $e = \{u, v\}$. According to our assumption (d), $G \cup \{e\}$ has a cycle and e must be part of it. The rest of the cycle is a path in G that connects u and v. This contradicts our choice of u and v. Hence G is connected and G is a tree. ∎

In order to appreciate Theorem 2, draw a tree or look at a tree in one of the Figures 1 through 3 and observe that it possesses all the properties (a)–(d) in Theorem 2. Then draw or look at a nontree and observe that it possesses none of the properties (a)–(d).

We need two lemmas for our characterization of finite trees. For a tree, vertices of degree one are called **leaves** [the singular is **leaf**].

EXAMPLE 4   Of the trees in Figure 1: T_1 has two leaves; T_2, T_3 and T_8 have three leaves; T_4, T_5, T_6 and T_7 have four leaves; T_9 and T_{10} have five leaves; and T_{11} has six leaves. ∎

Lemma 1   A finite tree with at least one edge has at least two leaves.

Proof. Consider a longest simple acyclic path, say $v_1 v_2 \cdots v_n$. Then $v_1 \neq v_n$ and both v_1 and v_n are leaves. ∎

Lemma 2   A tree with n vertices has exactly $n - 1$ edges.

Proof. We apply induction. For $n = 2$ the lemma is clear. Assume the result is true for some n, and consider a tree T with $n + 1$ vertices. By Lemma 1, T has a leaf v_0. Let T_0 be the graph obtained by removing v_0 and the edge attached to v_0. Then T_0 is a tree, as is easily checked, and has n vertices. By the inductive assumption T_0 has $n - 1$ edges and so T has n edges. ∎

Lemma 2 holds, of course, for all the trees drawn in this section, and it will hold for any tree we can draw. Try drawing a tree and counting the number of edges as you add new vertices.

Theorem 3   Let G be a finite graph with n vertices, no loops and no parallel edges. The following are equivalent:

(a) G is a tree.

(b) G is acyclic and has $n - 1$ edges.

(c) G is connected and has $n - 1$ edges.

In other words, any two of the properties "connectedness," "acyclicity" and "having $n - 1$ edges" imply the third one.

Proof. The theorem is obvious for $n = 1$, so we assume $n \geqq 2$. Both (a) $\Rightarrow$ (b) and (a) $\Rightarrow$ (c) follow from Lemma 2.

(b) $\Rightarrow$ (a). Assume that (b) holds but that G is not a tree. Then (d) of Theorem 2 cannot hold. Since G is acyclic we can evidently add some edge and retain acyclicity. Now add as many edges as possible and still retain acyclicity. The graph G' so obtained will satisfy Theorem 2(d) and so G' will be a tree. Since G' has n vertices and at least n edges, this contradicts Lemma 2. Thus G is a tree.

(c) $\Rightarrow$ (a). Assume (c) holds but that G is not a tree. By the corollary to Theorem 1, G has a spanning tree T, which must have fewer than $n - 1$ edges. This contradicts Lemma 2 and so G is a tree. ☐

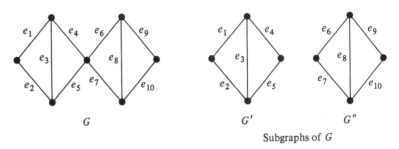

G $\qquad$ G' $\qquad$ G''

Subgraphs of G

FIGURE 4

EXAMPLE 5 (a) The graph G in Figure 4 has 64 spanning trees, as is explained in Example 4 of § 5.1. Each is obtained by taking the union of spanning trees of the subgraphs G' and G''.

(b) Some organized counting shows that the graph H in Figure 2 has 320 different spanning trees. You are asked to do some similar, but easier, counting in Exercises 5 and 7. ☐

The theorems characterizing trees suggest simple algorithms for finding spanning trees of a finite connected graph G. One algorithm starts out with all the edges and then removes edges without destroying connectedness, i.e., removes edges from existing cycles [Theorem 1]. Another algorithm starts out with no edges and then carefully adds edges without forming cycles. The problem becomes more interesting if the edges are **weighted**, i.e., if a non-negative number $W(e)$ is assigned to each edge e of G. The **weight** $W(G')$ of a subgraph G' of G is simply the sum of the weights of the edges of G', and the problem is to find a spanning tree of minimal weight. Thus we seek a spanning tree whose weight is less than or equal to that of any other spanning tree. Such spanning trees will be called **minimal spanning trees**. In the algorithms it will be assumed that the set $E(G)$ of edges $e_1, e_2, \ldots, e_m$ has been ordered with nondecreasing weights:

$$W(e_1) \leq W(e_2) \leq \cdots \leq W(e_m).$$

EXAMPLE 6   A weighted graph is given in Figure 5(a). The weights are indicated next to the edges. An ordering of the edges so that the weights are nondecreasing is indicated in Figure 5(b). □

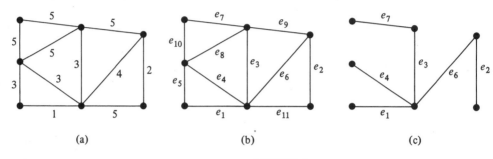

(a)   (b)   (c)

FIGURE 5

The first algorithm builds larger and larger acyclic subgraphs of G starting from the graph with vertex set $V(G)$ and with no edges, and adjoining edges one at a time. This is the algorithm that we illustrated in §0.2 in the discussion surrounding Figure 8. The notation $E \cup \{e_j\}$ in the statement of the algorithm stands for the subgraph whose edges are $E \cup \{e_j\}$.

Algorithm MIN-SPANNING TREE 1.

Step 1. Set $E = \emptyset$ and $j = 1$.
Step 2. If $E \cup \{e_j\}$ is acyclic, replace E by $E \cup \{e_j\}$ and go to Step 3. Otherwise go to Step 3.
Step 3. If $j < m$ replace j by $j + 1$ and go to Step 2. Otherwise stop. □

The second algorithm starts with all the edges, and removes edges with as large weights as possible without disconnecting the graph.

Algorithm MIN-SPANNING TREE 2.

Step 1. Set $E = E(G)$ and $j = m$.
Step 2. If e_j belongs to a cycle of E, replace E by $E \setminus \{e_j\}$ and go to Step 3. Otherwise go to Step 3.
Step 3. If $j > 1$ replace j by $j - 1$ and go to Step 2. Otherwise stop. □

As we will explain after Theorem 4, the two different algorithms always produce the same spanning tree.

EXAMPLE 7 If we apply the first algorithm to the weighted graph in Example 6 [and Figure 5] we obtain the spanning tree T with edges $e_1, e_2, e_3, e_4, e_6, e_7$ sketched in Figure 5(c). Edge e_5 was rejected because $e_1 e_4 e_5$ would form a cycle. Edges e_8 through e_{11} were rejected for similar reasons. The minimal spanning tree T has weight 18.

The second algorithm produces the same spanning tree. It successively removes edges e_{11}, e_{10}, e_9 and e_8, because each belongs to a cycle. At this point e_7 and e_6 do not belong to any cycles, so they are retained. Etc. ☐

If the graph G is not weighted we can assign each edge weight 1. Then the edges can be ordered in any way, and all spanning trees will be minimal since they all have weight $n - 1$, where n is the number of vertices of G.

EXAMPLE 8 If the first algorithm is applied to the graph in Figure 3(a) with the edges ordered $e_1, e_2, \ldots, e_{10}$, one obtains the spanning tree with edges $e_1, e_2, e_3, e_5, e_6, e_7, e_9$. This spanning tree is drawn in Figure 3(b). The second algorithm produces the same spanning tree and, in fact, the algorithm mimics the discussion in Example 3(b). ☐

Theorem 4 Both MIN-SPANNING TREE algorithms work.

Proof. These algorithms will work even if G has loops or parallel edges. The algorithms never choose loops, and they will select the first edge listed from a collection of parallel edges. Thus we may assume all loops and extra edges have been removed from $E(G)$. We begin by proving that each algorithm produces a tree.

Let E^* be the final set of edges produced by the first algorithm, and let T be the subgraph with $V(T) = V(G)$ and $E(T) = E^*$. Then T is acyclic since the graph is acyclic at each step in the algorithm. To see that T is connected, assume not. Then there are two vertices in $V(G)$ which are not joined by any path in E^*, and there is a path in G of shortest length joining these two vertices. Consider an edge e_j of this path. By our minimality condition, the edge e_j joins vertices not joined by any path in E^*. Thus $E^* \cup \{e_j\}$ is acyclic. But then at the jth step $E \cup \{e_j\}$ would be acyclic and e_j would have been added to E. That is, e_j would be in E^*, a contradiction.

At each step in the second algorithm, the graph is connected, by Theorem 1, since we only remove edges belonging to cycles. The final graph T is acyclic, because if it had a cycle the edge in the cycle with largest subscript would have been removed at the stage at which it was considered.

To prove that the algorithms produce minimal spanning trees, it is convenient to first consider the spanning tree T produced by *either* algorithm. Later in the proof we will consider the two algorithms separately. Among all *minimal* spanning trees of G consider an S that has as many edges as possible in common with T. It suffices to show $S = T$.

Suppose $S \neq T$ and let k be the smallest subscript of an edge in T but not in S. We add e_k to S to get $S^* = S \cup \{e_k\}$. In view of Theorem 2(d), S^* has a cycle C, which contains e_k since S is acyclic. Since T is acyclic there must be some other edge, call it e, in C which is not in T. Note that e is an edge of S. We now delete e from S^* to get $U = S^* \setminus \{e\} = (S \cup \{e_k\}) \setminus \{e\}$. Since U is connected [Theorem 1] and has the same number of edges as S, U is a spanning tree by Theorem 3. Moreover, U has one more edge, namely e_k, in common with T than S has. So by the choice of S, U is not a minimal spanning tree. Comparing the weights of S and U, we conclude that $W(e) < W(e_k)$, and so $e = e_i$ for some $i < k$.

Now suppose T is produced by the first algorithm. Since the edge e_i is rejected at the $j = i$ stage, at that stage $E \cup \{e_i\}$ contains a cycle C'. Since at that stage E consists of edges of T with subscripts less than i, and since $i < k$, we have $E \subseteq S$ by the choice of k. Since e_i is also in S, C' must be a cycle in S, which is a contradiction.

Finally, suppose T is produced by the second algorithm. The graph $T \cup \{e\}$ contains a cycle C'' which contains e. Since none of the other edges of C'' were rejected by the algorithm, they must all have subscripts less than i [otherwise the edge in C'' with largest subscript would have been rejected]. Again, by the choice of k, C'' must consist of edges in S, a contradiction.

These contradictions show that in both cases $T = S$ and so T is a minimal spanning tree.   ☐

A modification of the proof just given shows that if G is a finite connected weighted graph and if different edges have different weights, then G has a *unique* minimal spanning tree; Exercise 21 outlines a proof. Note that both algorithms depend only on the ordering of the edges and the structure of the graph G. That is, we chose the ordering of $E(G)$ to be consistent with the weighting, so that $W(e_i) \leq W(e_j)$ whenever $i \leq j$, but once this ordering is chosen the weights are never referred to again. We could reweight the graph so that $W'(e_j) = j$ for all j. The order would clearly be consistent with the new weight function W', and each algorithm would produce the same tree as before. By the result of Exercise 21 the two algorithms would then lead to the same tree, namely the unique minimal tree for the new weights, so they must have given the same tree in the first place.

In practice, the MIN-SPANNING TREE algorithms can be based on a connectivity algorithm for two points [see § 8.9]. At each stage of the first algorithm an edge $e = \{u, v\}$ is considered to see if it is part of a cycle. This is equivalent to determining whether the two vertices u and v are connected in $E \setminus \{e\}$, where E is built from the edges already considered. At each stage of the second algorithm E is connected, and so the connectedness of $E \setminus \{e\}$ can again be decided by checking whether u and v are connected in $E \setminus \{e\}$.

Of course either algorithm should be programmed to stop whenever the size of the set E of edges reaches $n - 1$.

EXERCISES 9.1

1. Find all trees with fewer than seven vertices.
2. The trees in Figure 6 have seven vertices. Specify which tree in Figure 1 each is isomorphic to.

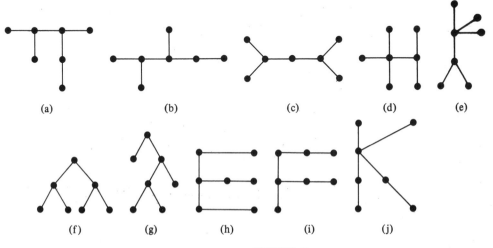

(a)   (b)   (c)   (d)   (e)

(f)   (g)   (h)   (i)   (j)

FIGURE 6

3. Draw the eight spanning trees of the graph G' in Figure 4.
4. Find the number of spanning trees of the graph in Figure 3(a).
5. Find the number of spanning trees of the graphs in Figure 7. *Hints for parts (a) and (d):* First classify the spanning trees by the number of "spokes" or "radii," i.e., by the degree of the vertex v. Then consider the various configurations formed by the spokes.

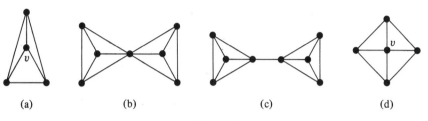

(a)   (b)   (c)   (d)

FIGURE 7

6. Find two nonisomorphic spanning trees of $K_{3,3}$.

7. Find the number of spanning trees of the graphs in Figure 8.

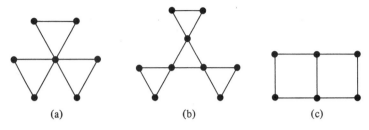

(a)   (b)   (c)

FIGURE 8

8. The **distance** between two vertices of a connected graph is defined to be the length of a shortest path joining them. The **diameter** of the graph is the maximum distance between two vertices if there is such a maximum and is ∞ otherwise.
   (a) Give the diameters of the graphs in Figure 7.
   (b) Give the diameters of the trees in Figure 1.
   (c) Sketch an infinite tree with diameter 2.
   (d) Sketch a tree that does not have finite diameter.

9. Sketch a tree with at least one edge and no leaves. *Hint:* See Lemma 1 to Theorem 3.

10. Does every edge of a finite connected graph with no loops belong to some spanning tree? Justify your answer.

11. Show that a connected graph with n vertices has at least $n - 1$ edges.

12. (a) Find all spanning trees of the graph in Figure 9.
    (b) Which edges belong to every spanning tree?
    (c) For a general finite connected graph, characterize the edges which belong to every spanning tree. Prove your assertion.

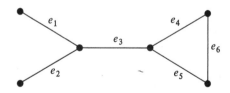

FIGURE 9

13. (a) Show that the sum of the degrees of the vertices of a tree with n vertices is $2n - 2$.
    (b) A tree has three vertices of degree 2, two of degree 3 and one of degree 4. If the remaining vertices have degree 1, how many vertices does the tree have?

14. (a) Show that there is a tree with six vertices of degree 1, one vertex of degree 2, one vertex of degree 3, one vertex of degree 5 and no others.
    (b) For $n \geq 2$, consider n positive integers $d_1, \ldots, d_n$ whose sum is $2n - 2$.

Show that there is a tree with n vertices whose vertices have degrees $d_1, \ldots, d_n$.

(c) Show that part (a) illustrates part (b) where $n = 9$.

15. (a) Reverse the order of the edges in the graph in Figure 3(a). That is, relabel e_1 by e_{10}, e_2 by e_9, etc.

    (b) Apply the two MIN-SPANNING TREE algorithms to the graph with these reordered edges.

16. Repeat Exercise 15 for the graph in Figure 5(b).

17. Find a minimal spanning tree of the weighted graph in Figure 10(a). What is its weight?

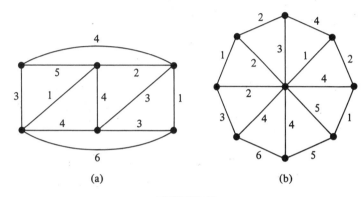

FIGURE 10

18. Repeat Exercise 17 for the graph in Figure 10(b).

19. An oil company wants to connect the cities in the mileage chart below by pipelines going directly between cities. What is the minimal number of miles of pipeline needed?

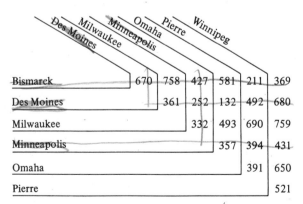

	Des Moines	Milwaukee	Minneapolis	Omaha	Pierre	Winnipeg
Bismarck	670	758	427	581	211	369
Des Moines		361	252	132	492	680
Milwaukee			332	493	690	759
Minneapolis				357	394	431
Omaha					391	650
Pierre						521

20. Let G be a finite connected weighted graph. Show that if e belongs to a cycle and has maximal weight among the edges in the cycle, then $G \backslash \{e\}$ contains a minimal spanning tree of G.

21. Let G be a finite connected weighted graph in which different edges have different weights. Show that G has exactly one minimal spanning tree. *Hint:* Assume G has more than one minimal spanning tree. Order the edges and consider the smallest subscript k of an edge that belongs to some but not all minimal spanning trees.

§ 9.2   *Rooted Trees*

In computer science trees often have distinguished vertices which can be used to give the trees directed structures. We can in general turn any undirected graph into a digraph by associating directions with its edges—putting arrows on them. If the original graph is a tree, the digraph we get is called a **directed tree**. If all of the arrows are directed away from a single vertex, the directed tree is called a rooted tree and that single vertex is its root. Rooted trees are often drawn as in Figure 1(a) so that the top vertex is the root and all the

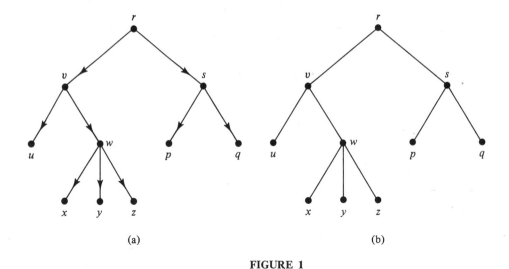

(a)   (b)

FIGURE 1

arrows point down and away from it. In this case, we may leave off the arrows, as in Figure 1(b). Thus the same picture will represent an ordinary tree or a rooted tree [or, later, an ordered rooted tree], depending on which we say it represents. We note in passing that our trees are upside-down from the ones in the woods.

EXAMPLE 1   (a) A binary search tree is a structure used to quickly determine the value or location of objects, such as numbers or alphabetized files, that are linearly ordered. The binary search tree in Figure 2 would be useful for searching for a number in $\{1, 2, 3, \ldots, 15\}$. The circled numbers represent keys. Given a

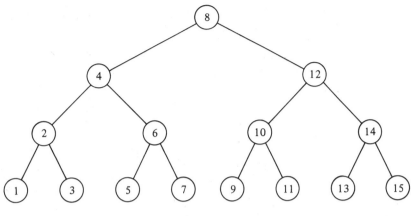

FIGURE 2

number in this set, it is first compared with 8: if it is less than 8, proceed to key 4; if it is bigger than 8, proceed to key 12; if it is equal to 8 the search is over. One proceeds down the tree in this manner until the number is found. Note that at most four keys will be needed.

(b) Data structures for diagnosis or identification can frequently be viewed as rooted trees. Figure 3 shows the idea. To use such a data structure we start at the top and proceed from vertex to vertex, taking an appropriate branch in each case to match the symptoms of the patient. The final leaf on

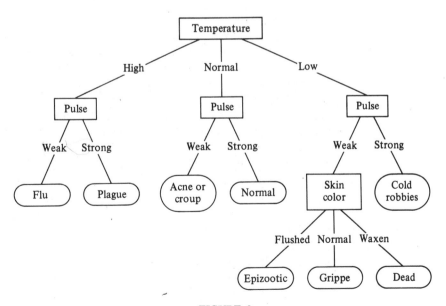

FIGURE 3

the path gives the name of the most likely condition or conditions for the given symptoms. The same sort of rooted tree structure is the basis for the key system used in field guides for identifying mushrooms, birds, wildflowers and the like.

(c) The chains of command of an organization can often be represented by a rooted tree. Part of the hierarchy of a university is indicated in Figure 4.

⬜

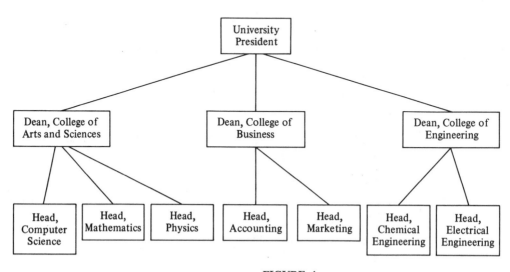

FIGURE 4

One natural way to get a rooted tree from an undirected tree is to choose a vertex, pick the tree up by that vertex and let gravity direct the edges, with arrows pointing down. We make this idea precise and use it to give the formal definition of a rooted tree. We begin with any [undirected] tree T, as in § 9.1, and select a vertex r which will be its **root.** Theorem 2 of § 9.1 shows that for each vertex $v \neq r$ there is a unique simple path connecting r and v. We direct the edges so that all these paths lead away from the root r. This directed tree is the **rooted tree** with root r made from the tree T; we denote it by T_r. Then an ordered pair $\langle v, w \rangle$ is a [directed] edge of the rooted tree T_r provided $\{v, w\}$ is an edge of the original tree T that is part of the unique simple path from r to the second entry w of the pair $\langle v, w \rangle$. Thus w will be farther from r than v.

EXAMPLE 2   Consider the [undirected] tree in Figure 5(a). If we select v, x and z to be the roots, we obtain the three rooted trees illustrated in Figures 5(b), 5(c) and 5(d). The exact placement of the vertices is unimportant; Figures 5(b) and 5(b′) represent the same rooted tree.

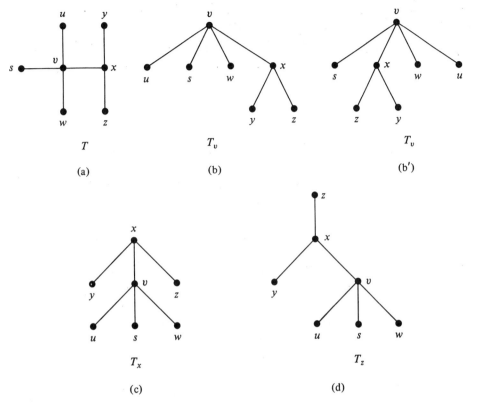

FIGURE 5

Note that $\langle v, w \rangle$ is an edge in Figure 5(d) because $\{v, w\}$ is an edge of the unique simple path in Figure 5(a) from z to w. On the other hand, $\langle w, v \rangle$ is not an edge of the rooted tree T_z; even though $\{w, v\}$ is an edge of the original tree, it is not an edge of the unique simple path from z to v. Similar remarks apply to all of the other edges.   ☐

The terms used to describe various parts of a tree are a curious mixture motivated both by the trees in the woods and by family trees. As before, the vertices of degree 1 are called **leaves**; there is one exception: occasionally [as in Figure 5(d)] the root will have degree 1 but we will not call it a leaf. Viewing a tree as a digraph, we see that its root is the sole source while the leaves are all sinks. The remaining vertices are sometimes called "branch nodes" or "interior nodes" and the leaves are sometimes called "terminal nodes." We adopt the convention that if $\langle v, w \rangle$ is an edge of a rooted tree, than v is the **parent** of w and w is a **child** of v. Every vertex except the root has exactly one parent. A parent may have several **children**. More generally, w is a **descendant** of v provided $w \neq v$ and v is a vertex of the unique simple path from r to *w*. Finally, for any vertex *v* the **subtree with root** *v* is precisely the tree consisting of *v*, all its descendants and all the directed edges connecting them. Whenever *v* is a leaf, the subtree with root *v* is a trivial one-vertex tree.

EXAMPLE 3   Consider the rooted tree in Figure 1 redrawn in Figure 6. There are six leaves. The parent *v* has two children, *u* and *w*, and five descendants: *u*, *w*, *x*, *y* and *z*. All the vertices except *r* itself are descendants of *r*. The whole tree itself is clearly a subtree rooted at *r*, and there are six trivial subtrees consisting of leaves. The interesting subtrees are given in Figure 6.   ☐

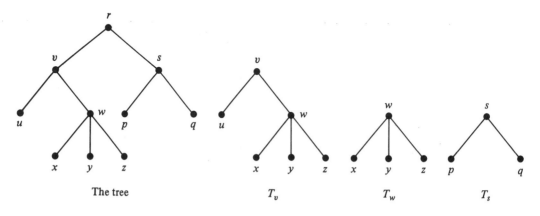

The tree   Subtrees of the tree

T_v T_w T_s

FIGURE 6

Our first theorem gives an intrinsic characterization of rooted trees. As we've seen, rooted trees are viewed both as directed trees and as ordinary undirected trees. Therefore, for clarity, we will sometimes refer to paths as **directed** or **undirected**.

Theorem 1   A directed tree is a rooted tree if and only if one vertex has indegree 0 and all others have indegree 1.

Proof. Suppose T_r is rooted with root *r*. If $\langle v, r \rangle$ were a directed edge, then $\{v, r\}$ would be an undirected edge on a simple path from *r* to *r*. But *T* is acyclic, so no such path exists. Thus indeg(r) = 0.

If *w* is a vertex other than *r*, there is a unique simple path from *r* to *w*, say with vertex sequence *r*, . . . , *u*, *w*. Then $\langle u, w \rangle$ is the unique directed edge with *w* as terminal vertex; thus indeg(w) = 1.

Now suppose *T* is a directed tree and has one vertex, call it *r*, of indegree 0 and the rest of indegree 1. Let *w* be a vertex different from *r*, and suppose the simple path from *r* to *w* has vertex sequence $r = u_0 u_1 u_2 \cdots u_{n-1} u_n = w$. Then $\{r, u_1\}$ is an undirected edge, so either $\langle r, u_1 \rangle$ or $\langle u_1, r \rangle$ is a directed edge. Since indeg(r) = 0, it must be $\langle r, u_1 \rangle$ which is the directed edge. Assume inductively that $\langle u_{k-1}, u_k \rangle$ is a directed edge for some $k < n$. Then $\langle u_{k+1}, u_k \rangle$ is not a directed edge, since indeg(u_k) = 1, so $\langle u_k, u_{k+1} \rangle$ must be a directed edge. By finite induction we conclude

$$\langle r, u_1 \rangle, \langle u_1, u_2 \rangle, \ldots, \langle u_{n-1}, u_n \rangle \text{ are directed edges.}$$

In particular, the unique directed edge of the form $\langle v, w \rangle$ is $\langle u_{n-1}, w \rangle$, and $\{u_{n-1}, w\}$ is the only undirected edge with vertex w on the simple path from r to w. We have shown that T is a rooted tree. ☐

Corollary 1 Every directed path in a rooted tree T is acyclic.

Proof. Consider a directed path $v_0\, v_1\, \cdots\, v_m$ in T. We may assume $v_0 = r$ since there is a directed path from r to v_0 which could be adjoined to the original path. Since v_0 has indegree 0, v_0 is not repeated in the sequence. Since no vertex has indegree $\geqq 2$, none of the other vertices is repeated either. Consequently the path is acyclic. ☐

Corollary 2 A rooted tree is an acyclic digraph.

A rooted tree is an **m-ary tree** if outdeg(v) $\leqq m$ for all vertices v. In other words, each parent has at most m children. The 2-ary trees are called **binary trees**. An m-ary tree [or binary tree] is a **regular m-ary tree** if outdeg(v) $= m$ for all vertices v that are not leaves.

The **level number** of a vertex v is the length of the unique simple path from the root to v. In particular, the root itself has level number 0. The **height** of a rooted tree is the largest level number of a vertex. Only leaves can have their level numbers equal to the height of the tree. A regular m-ary tree is said to be a **full m-ary tree** if all the leaves have the same level number, namely the height of the tree.

EXAMPLE 4 (a) The rooted tree in Figures 1 and 6 is a 3-ary tree and, in fact, is an m-ary tree for $m \geqq 3$. It is not a regular 3-ary tree since vertices v and s have outdegree 2. Vertices v and s have level number 1, vertices u, w, p and q have level number 2, and the leaves x, y and z have level number 3. The height of the tree is 3.

(b) The labeled tree in Figure 8(a) is a full regular binary tree of height 3. The labeled tree in Figure 8(b) is a regular 3-ary tree of height 3. It is not a full 3-ary tree since one leaf has level number 1 and five leaves have level number 2. ☐

EXAMPLE 5 Consider a full m-ary tree of height h. There are m vertices at level 1. Each parent at level 1 has m children, so there are m^2 vertices at level 2. A simple induction shows that the tree has m^l vertices at level l for each $l \leqq h$. Thus it has $1 + m + m^2 + \cdots + m^h$ vertices in all. Since

$$(m - 1)(1 + m + m^2 + \cdots + m^h) = m^{h+1} - 1,$$

as one can check by multiplying and canceling, we have

$$1 + m + m^2 + \cdots + m^h = \frac{m^{h+1} - 1}{m - 1}.$$

Note that the same tree has $p = (m^h - 1)/(m - 1)$ parents and $t = m^h$ leaves. ☐

An **ordered rooted tree** is simply a rooted tree such that the set of children of each parent is linearly ordered. When we draw such a tree, the children of each parent will be ordered from left to right.

EXAMPLE 6   (a) If we view Figure 5(b) as an ordered rooted tree, then the children of v are ordered: $u \prec s \prec w \prec x$. And the children of x are ordered: $y \prec z$. Figure 5(b′) is the picture of a different ordered rooted tree, since $s \prec x \prec w \prec u$ and $z \prec y$.

(b) As soon as we draw a rooted tree it looks like an ordered rooted tree, even if we do not care about the order structure. For example, the important structure in Figure 4 is the rooted tree structure. The ordering of the "children" is not important. The head of the computer science department precedes the head of the mathematics department simply because we chose to list the departments in alphabetical order.   ☐

Recall that in general two structures are isomorphic if there is a one-to-one correspondence between them that preserves the structure of concern. Two rooted trees T and T' are **isomorphic rooted trees** provided there exists a one-to-one correspondence α from $V(T)$ onto $V(T')$ so that

(i) if r is the root of T, then $\alpha(r)$ is the root of T';
(ii) if $\{w_1, \ldots, w_k\}$ is the set of children of a vertex v in T, then $\{\alpha(w_1), \ldots, \alpha(w_k)\}$ is the set of children of $\alpha(v)$.

Two ordered rooted trees T and T' are **isomorphic ordered rooted trees** if there is such an α satisfying (i) and

(ii′) if $\{w_1, \ldots, w_k\}$ is the set of children of a vertex v in T and if $w_1 \prec w_2 \prec \cdots \prec w_k$, then $\{\alpha(w_1), \ldots, \alpha(w_k)\}$ is the set of children of $\alpha(v)$ and $\alpha(w_1) \prec \alpha(w_2) \prec \cdots \prec \alpha(w_k)$.

Two ordinary trees are **isomorphic trees** if they are isomorphic as [undirected] graphs.

EXAMPLE 7   No two of the trees in Figures 5(b), 5(b′), 5(c) and 5(d) on page 413 are isomorphic as ordered rooted trees. To see this for the trees in Figures 5(b) and 5(b′), assume α is such an isomorphism from (b) to (b′). Then $\alpha(v) = v$ since α must map the root onto the root. Moreover, $\alpha(s) = x$ since α must map the second child of v onto the second child of $\alpha(v)$. But s is childless, while $\alpha(s) = x$ has two children.

As rooted trees, Figures 5(b) and 5(b') are isomorphic, but they are not isomorphic to the rooted trees in Figures 5(c) and 5(d). As ordinary trees, all five of the trees in Figure 5 are isomorphic. ☐

EXAMPLE 8   (a) Consider an alphabet Σ. We make Σ^* into a rooted tree as follows. The empty word ϵ will serve as the root. For any word w in Σ^*, its set of children is

$$\{wx : x \in \Sigma\}.$$

If Σ is ordered, then we order each set of children according to the lexicographic order to obtain an ordered rooted tree.

(b) Let $\Sigma = \{a, b\}$ where $a \prec b$. Each vertex has two children. For instance, the children of *abba* are *abbaa* and *abbab*. Part of the infinite ordered rooted tree Σ^* is drawn in Figure 7. ☐

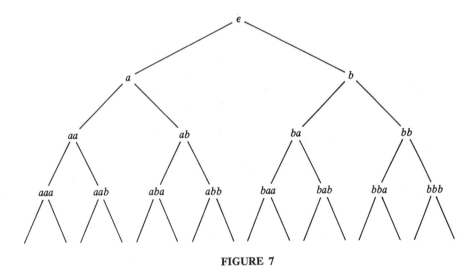

FIGURE 7

It is often convenient to label the vertices of an ordered rooted tree. This can be done in a variety of ways. One such scheme resembles Example 8: vertices of an *m*-ary tree can be labeled using words from Σ^* where $\Sigma = \mathbb{Z}(m) = \{0, 1, \ldots, m-1\}$. The ordered children of the root are labeled 0, 1, 2, etc. If a vertex is labeled by the word w, then its ordered children are labeled $w0$, $w1$, $w2$, etc. The label of a vertex tells us the exact location of the vertex in the tree. For example, a vertex labeled 1021 would be the second child of the vertex labeled 102 which, in turn, would be the third child of the vertex labeled 10, etc. The level of the vertex is the length of its label; a vertex labeled 1021 will be at level 4.

EXAMPLE 9   All of the vertices in Figure 8(a) except the root are labeled. In Figure 8(b) we have only labeled the leaves. The labels of the other vertices should be clear. ▯

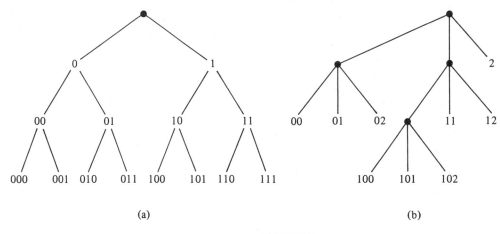

(a)   (b)

FIGURE 8

Labeled trees are useful for organizing or storing information. In fact, this scheme has been around a long time.

EXAMPLE 10   In old mathematics textbooks the paragraphs were frequently numbered using words in Σ^* where $\Sigma = \{1, 2, 3, \ldots\}$. Decimal points were used to set off the letters of the words in Σ^*, i.e., numbers. Thus 3.4.1.2 would refer to the second paragraph of the first subsection of the fourth section of Chapter 3, while 3.4.12 would refer to the twelfth subsection of the fourth section of Chapter 3. This scheme is not very pretty and so modern authors usually avoid it, but it has some real advantages which carry over to present-day uses of trees. One can always insert new paragraphs or sections without disrupting the numbering system. With a little care, paragraphs and sections can be deleted without causing trouble, especially if one doesn't mind gaps. Also the labels, such as 3.4.12, tell you exactly where the subsection or paragraph fits into the book. In contrast, one famous mathematics book has theorems numbered from 1 to 460. All the label "Theorem 303" tells us is that this theorem probably appears about two-thirds of the way through the book. ▯

Another advantage to labeled trees is that vertices can be reached via relatively short paths from the root. For example, a binary tree of height 12 can have up to $2^{12} = 4096$ leaves. Information stored at the leaves can be retrieved in 12 steps. A mindless linear search of the leaves might take thousands of steps.

EXERCISES 9.2

1. (a) For the tree in Figure 1, draw a rooted tree with new root v.
   (b) What is the level number of the vertex r?
   (c) What is the height of the tree?

2. Create a binary search tree for the usual English alphabet $\{a, b, \ldots, z\}$ with its usual order. Arrange it so that at most five keys will ever be needed.

3. (a) For each rooted tree in Figure 5, give the level numbers of the vertices and the height of the tree.
   (b) Which of the trees in Figure 5 are regular m-ary for some m?

4. Discuss why ordinary family trees are not rooted trees.

5. (a) Draw all binary trees of height 2. As usual "all" means up to isomorphism as rooted trees.
   (b) How many trees in part (a) are regular binary trees?
   (c) How many trees in part (a) are full binary trees?

6. Draw all regular binary trees of height 3.

7. (a) Draw full m-ary trees of height h for $m = 2$, $h = 2$; $m = 2$, $h = 3$; and $m = 3$, $h = 2$.
   (b) Which trees in part (a) have m^h leaves?

8. Consider a full binary tree T of height h.
   (a) How many leaves does T have?
   (b) How many vertices does T have?

9. Consider a full m-ary tree with p parents and t leaves. Show that $t = (m - 1)p + 1$ no matter what the height is.

10. Draw part of the rooted tree Σ^* where $\Sigma = \{a, b, c\}$ and $a \prec b \prec c$ as usual.

11. Let $\Sigma = \{a, b\}$ and consider the rooted tree Σ^*; see Example 8. Describe the set of vertices at level k. How big is this set?

12. Give some real-life examples of information storage that can be viewed as labeled trees. *Suggestions:* federal laws, handbooks of tables, parts catalogs.

13. (a) Show that the rooted trees in Figures 1 and 9 are isomorphic by giving an explicit isomorphism α.
    (b) How many such isomorphisms are there?

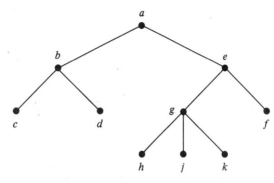

FIGURE 9

14. Show that the requirement (i) in the definition of isomorphic rooted trees is redundant. That is, show that (i) follows from (ii).

15. (a) Show that the rooted trees in Figures 5(b) and 5(c) are not isomorphic. (b) Do the same for Figures 5(c) and 5(d).

16. Consider an isomorphism α between rooted trees T and T'. Show that a vertex v in $V(T)$ is a leaf if and only if $\alpha(v)$ is a leaf.

17. Draw an ordered rooted tree that is not isomorphic to the tree in Figure 5(c) viewed as an ordered rooted tree but is isomorphic to that tree viewed simply as a rooted tree.

18. Repeat Exercise 17 for Figure 5(d).

§ 9.3   *More on Rooted Trees*

We have been thinking of our rooted trees as built from the root down. For finite trees we can also work from the leaves up, building larger and larger subtrees recursively. Such a construction makes rooted trees natural data structures to use for recursive computer programs. It also allows us to prove facts using our generalized principle of induction for recursively defined sets.

Definition 1   (B) A single vertex is a [trivial] rooted tree.

(R) If $T_1, \ldots, T_k$ are rooted trees with roots $r_1, \ldots, r_k$, if $V(T_1), \ldots, V(T_k)$ are disjoint and if r is an element not in $V(T_1) \cup \cdots \cup V(T_k)$, then T is a rooted tree where

$$V(T) = \{r\} \cup V(T_1) \cup \cdots \cup V(T_k),$$

r is a root with children $r_1, \ldots, r_k$ and all other vertices have the same children as before. Thus $T_1, \ldots, T_k$ are subtrees of T with corresponding roots $r_1, \ldots, r_k$.

EXAMPLE 1   Consider T in Figure 1. By (B), the vertices x, y and z each represent trivial trees. By (R), w is the root of a tree T_w with children x, y and z. Since these children were originally childless, they remain childless and are leaves of

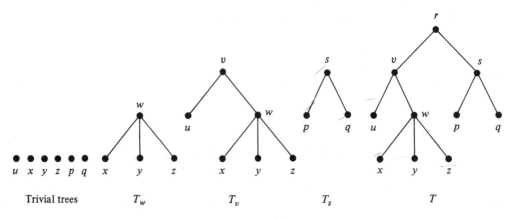

Trivial trees T_w T_v T_s T

FIGURE 1

T_w. By (B) again, the vertex u represents a trivial tree. By (R) again, v is the root of a tree T_v with children u and w. The vertex w still has three children. Similarly, s is the root of a tree T_s with leaves p and q. Finally, by (R) there is a tree with root r whose children v and s are roots of the subtrees T_v and T_s. The process is illustrated in Figure 1. $\square$

We can also recursively define the height function on the set of rooted trees.

Definition 2   (B) Trivial trees have height 0.
  (R) If T is defined as in Definition 1 and the subtrees $T_1, \ldots, T_k$ have heights $h_1, \ldots, h_k$, the height of T is $1 + \max\{h_1, \ldots, h_k\}$.

EXAMPLE 2   We use these recursive definitions to prove that an m-ary tree of height h has at most m^h leaves.

This is clear for the trivial trees since $m^0 = 1$. Consider an m-ary tree T, defined as in Definition 1, with the property that each subtree T_j has height h_j. Since T is an m-ary tree, each T_j is an m-ary tree and so it has at most m^{h_j} leaves. Let $h^* = \max\{h_1, \ldots, h_k\}$. Then the number of leaves of T is bounded by

$$m^{h_1} + \cdots + m^{h_k} \leqq m^{h^*} + \cdots + m^{h^*} = k \cdot m^{h^*}.$$

Since the root has at most m subtrees, $k \leqq m$ and so T has at most $m \cdot m^{h^*} = m^{h^*+1}$ leaves. Since $h^* + 1$ equals the height h of T, we are done. $\square$

A tree traversal algorithm is an algorithm for listing [or visiting or searching] all the vertices of a finite ordered rooted tree. The three most common such algorithms provide preorder traversal, inorder traversal [for binary trees *only*] and postorder traversal. All three are most easily described using the recursive definition of ordered rooted trees.

In the **preorder traversal**, the root is listed first and the subtrees are listed in order of their roots. Because of the way we draw ordered rooted trees, we will refer to the order as left to right. Here is the recursive algorithm.

Algorithm PREORDER.

Step 1. List the subtrees with the children of v as roots [using algorithm PREORDER].

Step 2. List T_v by stringing together v followed by the lists from Step 1 in order from left to right. $\square$

If v has no children, i.e., if v is a leaf, Step 1 is automatically vacuously completed, so the list of T_v is just v in that case.

In the **postorder traversal**, the subtrees are listed in order first, and then the root is listed at the end.

Algorithm POSTORDER.

Step 1. List the subtrees with the children of v as roots [using algorithm POSTORDER].

Step 2. List T_v by stringing together the lists from Step 1 in order from left to right *followed by v.*   ☐

EXAMPLE 3   (a) Consider the tree T in Figure 1. Each trivial tree is trivial to list. We now apply the preorder algorithm to the other trees in Figure 1, to obtain the following listings:

$$T_w: \quad w, x, y, z;$$
$$T_v: \quad v, u, T_w, \quad \text{i.e.,} \quad v, u, w, x, y, z;$$
$$T_s: \quad s, p, q;$$
$$T: \quad r, T_v, T_s, \quad \text{i.e.,} \quad r, v, u, w, x, y, z, s, p, q.$$

This listing can be obtained from the picture of T as illustrated in Figure 2(a). Just follow the dashed line, listing each vertex the first time it is reached.

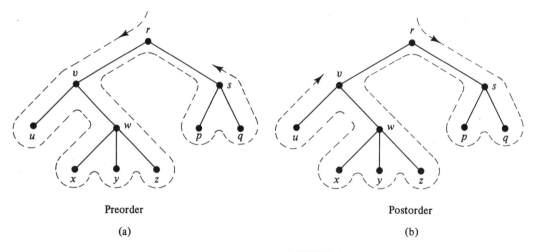

Preorder   Postorder

(a)   (b)

FIGURE 2

(b) Applying the postorder algorithm to the trees in Figure 1, we obtain:

$$T_w: \quad x, y, z, w;$$
$$T_v: \quad u, T_w, v, \quad \text{i.e.,} \quad u, x, y, z, w, v;$$
$$T_s: \quad p, q, s;$$
$$T: \quad T_v, T_s, r, \quad \text{i.e.,} \quad u, x, y, z, w, v, p, q, s, r.$$

This listing can be obtained from the picture of T in Figure 2(b), provided the vertices are written in reverse order, i.e., from right to left starting with r, then s, then q, etc.   ☐

For binary trees, the **inorder traversal** lists the root in between the left and right subtrees.

Algorithm INORDER.

Let T be a regular binary ordered rooted tree.
Step 1. List the left subtree.
Step 2. List the root of the tree.
Step 3. List the right subtree. ☐

If the tree T is not regular, then some vertices will have a single child. If each such single child is designated either a left child or a right child, then the algorithm above can be modified to list such trees; it simply skips Step 1 or Step 3 when a subtree is missing.

EXAMPLE 4 (a) Consider the recursively defined binary tree in Figure 3. Algorithm INORDER lists the subtrees as follows:

$$T_x: \quad y, x, z;$$
$$T_w: \quad v, w, T_x, \quad \text{i.e.,} \quad v, w, y, x, z;$$
$$T_s: \quad p, s, q;$$
$$T_u: \quad t, u, T_s, \quad \text{i.e.,} \quad t, u, p, s, q;$$
$$T: \quad T_w, r, T_u, \quad \text{i.e.,} \quad v, w, y, x, z, r, t, u, p, s, q.$$

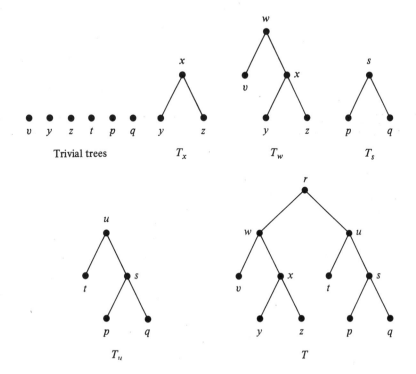

FIGURE 3

(b) Consider the labeled tree in Figure 8(a) of § 9.2. The inorder listing of the subtree with root 00 is 000, 00, 001; the other subtrees are also easy to list. The inorder listing of the entire tree is:

000, 00, 001, 0, 010, 01, 011, root, 100, 10, 101, 1, 110, 11, 111.   ⬜

It is of interest to know whether a particular listing determines the tree, that is, whether the tree can be recovered from the listing. It often cannot be, as we'll see in the next example.

EXAMPLE 5   Consider again the tree T in Figure 3. Figure 4 gives two more binary trees having the same inorder listing. The binary tree in Figure 5(a) has the same preorder listing as T and the tree in Figure 5(b) has the same postorder listing as T.   ⬜

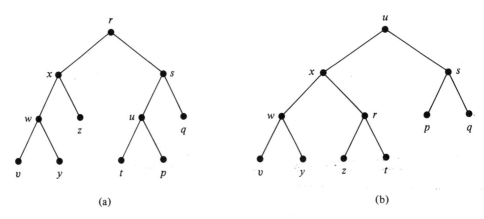

(a)   (b)

FIGURE 4

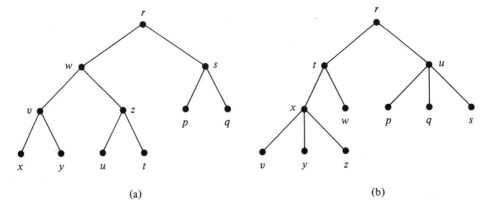

(a)   (b)

FIGURE 5

In spite of these examples, there are important situations under which trees can be recovered from their listings. Since our applications will be to Polish notation, and since the ideas are easier to grasp in that setting, we will return to this matter at the end of the next section.

EXERCISES 9.3

1. Use the schemes illustrated in Figure 2 to give the preorder and postorder listings of the vertices of the tree in Figure 4(a).

2. Repeat Exercise 1 for Figure 5(a).

3. Repeat Exercise 1 for Figure 5(b).

4. Give the inorder listing of the vertices of the labeled tree in Figure 6.

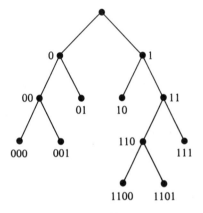

FIGURE 6

5. Use the PREORDER algorithm to list the vertices of the tree T in Figure 3.

6. Repeat Exercise 5 using the POSTORDER algorithm.

7. (a) Use the recursive definition of rooted tree in Definition 1 to show that Figure 4(b) represents a rooted tree.
   (b) Use the recursive definition of height in Definition 2 to calculate the height of the tree in part (a).

8. Use the recursive definition of height to calculate the height of the tree T in Figure 1.

9. Use the POSTORDER algorithm and the recursive definition in Exercise 7(a) to list the vertices in Figure 4(b).

10. Repeat Exercise 9 using the PREORDER algorithm.

11. Repeat Exercise 9 using the INORDER algorithm.

12. (a) Use the recursive definition of rooted tree to show that Figure 5(b) represents a rooted tree.
    (b) Calculate the height of the tree in part (a) using the recursive definition.

13. Use the POSTORDER algorithm and your answer to Exercise 12(a) to list the vertices of Figure 5(b).

14. Repeat Exercise 13 using the PREORDER algorithm.

15. (a) Give a recursive definition of m-ary trees.
    (b) Do the same for regular m-ary trees.
    (c) Do the same for full m-ary trees.

16. Show that a regular 3-ary tree has an odd number of leaves.

17. Consider an m-ary tree of height h and let t be the number of leaves. Observe that $t \leq m^h$ by Example 2. Show that $t \geq m + (m-1)(h-1)$ if the tree is regular.

18. Let T be a regular binary tree with t leaves $w_1, \ldots, w_t$. Show that if each leaf w_i is at level l_i then

$$\sum_{i=1}^{t} 2^{-l_i} = 1.$$

§ 9.4   *Polish Notation*

Preorder, postorder and inorder traversal give ways to list the vertices of an ordered rooted tree. If we label the vertices, we get a list of labels. If the labels are such things as numbers, addition signs, multiplication signs and the like our list may give a meaningful way to calculate a number; for instance, using ordinary algebraic notation, the list $4 * 3 \div 2$ determines the number 6. The list $4 + 3 * 2$ seems ambiguous; is it the number 14 or 10? Polish notation, which we describe below, is a method for defining algebraic expressions without parentheses, using lists obtained from trees. Of course it is important that the lists completely determine the corresponding labeled trees and their expressions. After we discuss Polish notation we prove that under even more general conditions the lists do determine the trees uniquely.

Polish notation can be used to write expressions which involve objects from some system [of numbers, or matrices, or propositions in the propositional calculus, etc.] and certain operations on the objects. The operations are usually, but not always, binary operations. The corresponding ordered rooted trees have leaves labeled with objects from the system [such as numbers] or by variables representing objects from the system [such as x]. The other vertices are labeled by the operations.

EXAMPLE 1   The algebraic expression

$$((x - 4) \uparrow 2) * ((y + 2)/3)$$

is represented by the tree in Figure 1(a). This expression uses several familiar binary operations on $\mathbb{R}$: $+, -, *, /, \uparrow$. Recall that $*$ represents multiplication and that $\uparrow$ represents exponentiation: $a \uparrow b$ means a^b. Thus our expression is equivalent to

$$(x - 4)^2 \left(\frac{y + 2}{3} \right).$$

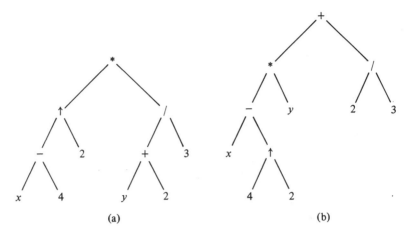

(a)   (b)

FIGURE 1

Note that this is an *ordered* tree; if x and 4 were interchanged, for example, the tree would represent a different algebraic expression.

It is clear that the ordered rooted tree determines the algebraic expression. Note that the inorder traversal of the vertices yields $x - 4 \uparrow 2 * y + 2 / 3$, and this is exactly the original expression *except for the parentheses.* Moreover, the parentheses are crucial since this expression determines neither the tree nor the original algebraic expression. This listing could just as well come from the algebraic expression

$$((x - (4 \uparrow 2)) * y) + (2/3)$$

whose tree is drawn in Figure 1(b). This algebraic expression is equivalent to $(x - 16)y + \frac{2}{3}$, a far cry from

$$(x - 4)^2 \left(\frac{y + 2}{3} \right).$$

Let us return to our original algebraic expression given by Figure 1(a). Preorder traversal yields

$$* \uparrow - x \, 4 \, 2 \, / + y \, 2 \, 3$$

and postorder traversal yields

$$x \, 4 - 2 \uparrow y \, 2 + 3 / *.$$

If turns out that each of these listings uniquely determines the tree, and hence the original algebraic expression. Thus these expressions are unambiguous *without parentheses.* This extremely useful observation was made by the Polish logician Łukasiewicz. The preorder listing is known now as **Polish notation** or **prefix notation**. The postorder listing is known as **reverse Polish notation** or **postfix notation**. Our usual algebraic notation, with the necessary parentheses, is known as **infix** notation. □

EXAMPLE 2   Consider the compound proposition $(p \to q) \lor (\neg p)$. We treat the binary operations $\to$ and $\lor$ as before. However, $\neg$ is a 1-ary or unary operation. We decree that its child is a right child since the operation precedes the proposition that it operates on. The corresponding ordered tree in Figure 2(a)

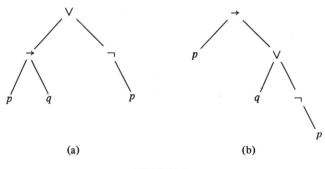

(a)   (b)

FIGURE 2

can be traversed in all three ways. The preorder is $\lor \to p\, q \, \neg\, p$ and the postorder is $p\, q \to p \, \neg\, \lor$. The inorder gives the original expression *without parentheses*. Another tree with the same inorder expression is drawn in Figure 2(b). As in Example 1, the preorder and postorder listings determine the tree and the original compound proposition. $\square$

As we illustrated in Example 5 of § 9.3, in general the preorder or post-order of vertices will not determine a tree, even a regular binary tree. More information is needed. It turns out that if we are provided with the level of each vertex, then the preorder or postorder list determines the tree. We will not pursue this. It also turns out that if we know how many children each vertex has, then the tree is determined by its preorder or postorder list.

EXAMPLE 3   We illustrate the last sentence by beginning with the expression

$$x\, 4 - 2 \uparrow y\, 2 + 3\, /\, *$$

in postfix notation. Each vertex $*$, $\uparrow$, $-$, $/$ and $+$ represents a binary operation and so has two children. The other vertices have no children, so we know exactly how many children each vertex has.

Let us recover the tree, but instead of drawing subtrees we'll determine their corresponding subexpressions. Starting at the left we find the first binary operation, $-$, which must apply to the two preceding subtrees, namely the leaves x and 4. Writing $(x - 4)$ for the corresponding subtree, we obtain the modified sequence $(x - 4)\, 2 \uparrow y\, 2 + 3\, /\, *$. Treating this expression in the same way, we obtain a subtree corresponding to $((x - 4) \uparrow 2)$ which leads us to $((x - 4) \uparrow 2)\, y\, 2 + 3\, /\, *$. Now the operation $+$ acts on the two preceding trees, namely the leaves y and 2. We get $((x - 4) \uparrow 2)(y + 2)\, 3\, /\, *$.

Now / acts on the preceding two trees, represented by $(y + 2)$ and 3. We obtain $((x - 4) \uparrow 2)((y + 2) / 3) *$. Now we have one operation, $*$, preceded by two expressions representing subtrees:

$$((x - 4) \uparrow 2) * ((y + 2)/3).$$

We've recovered the expression for the tree in Figure 1(a).

We briefly summarize the procedure of the last paragraph:

$$x\,4 - 2 \uparrow y\,2 + 3\,/\,*$$
$$(x - 4)\,2 \uparrow y\,2 + 3\,/\,*$$
$$((x - 4) \uparrow 2)\,y\,2 + 3\,/\,*$$
$$((x - 4) \uparrow 2)(y + 2)\,3\,/\,*$$
$$((x - 4) \uparrow 2)((y + 2)/3)\,*$$
$$((x - 4) \uparrow 2) * ((y + 2)/3).$$

There is another way to view this procedure, which will serve as a model for the proof of the theorem after Example 6. Working left to right, we can pick off the children of each vertex as follows: each binary operation gets the two nearest available children to its left. A child is "available" if it has not already been assigned to a parent. The other vertices get no children.

vertex	x	4	$-$	2	$\uparrow$	y	2	$+$	3	/	$*$
available children		x	$x, 4$	$-$	$-, 2$	$\uparrow$	$\uparrow, y$	$\uparrow, y, 2$	$\uparrow, +$	$\uparrow, +, 3$	$\uparrow, /$
assigned children			$x, 4$		$-, 2$			$y, 2$		$+, 3$	$\uparrow, /$

☐

EXAMPLE 4   The same method works for a compound proposition in reverse Polish notation, but when we meet the unary operation $\neg$, it acts on just the immediately preceding subexpression. For example,

$$p\,q \to p\,q \wedge \neg \vee$$
$$(p \to q)\,p\,q \wedge \neg \vee$$
$$(p \to q)(p \wedge q)\,\neg \vee \qquad \neg \text{ just acts on } (p \wedge q)$$
$$(p \to q)(\neg(p \wedge q)) \vee$$
$$(p \to q) \vee (\neg(p \wedge q)).$$

The reader can draw a tree representing this compound proposition. Alternatively, we can pick off the children working from left to right as in Example 3:

vertex	p	q	$\to$	p	q	$\land$	$\lnot$	$\lor$
available children	p	p,q	$\to$	$\to,p$	$\to,p,q$	$\to,\land$	$\to,\lnot$	
assigned children		p,q			p,q	$\land$	$\to,\lnot$	

Not all strings of operations and symbols lead to meaningful expressions.

EXAMPLE 5 Suppose it is alleged that

$$y + 2\,x * \uparrow 4 \quad \text{and} \quad q \lnot p\, q \lor \land \to$$

are in reverse Polish notation. The first one is hopeless right away, since $+$ is not preceded by two expressions. The second one breaks down when we attempt to decode it as in Example 4:

$$\underline{q \lnot}\, p\, q \lor \land \to$$
$$(\lnot q)\underline{p\, q \lor}\, \land \to$$
$$\underline{(\lnot q)(p \lor q)}\, \land \to$$
$$((\lnot q) \land (p \lor q)) \to .$$

Unfortunately, the operation $\to$ has only one subexpression preceding it. We conclude that neither of the strings of symbols given above represents a meaningful expression. □

Just as we did with ordinary algebraic expressions in § 3.5, we can recursively define what we mean by well-formed formulas [wff's] for Polish and reverse Polish notation. We give one example by defining **wff's for reverse Polish notation** of algebraic expressions:

(B) Numerical constants and variables are wff's.
(R) If f and g are wff's, so are $fg+$, $fg-$, $fg*$, $fg/$ and $fg\uparrow$.

EXAMPLE 6 We show that $x\, 2 \uparrow y - x\, y * /$ is a wff. All the variables and constants are wff's by (B). Then $x\, 2 \uparrow$ is a wff by (R). Hence $x\, 2 \uparrow y -$ is a wff where we use (R) with $f = x\, 2 \uparrow$ and $g = y$. Likewise, $x\, y *$ is a wff by (R). Finally, the entire expression is a wff by (R) since it has the form $fg/$ where $f = x\, 2 \uparrow y -$ and $g = x\, y *$. □

We end the section by proving the theorem that shows that expressions in Polish and reverse Polish notation uniquely determine the original expression. The proof is based on the second algorithm illustrated in Examples 3 and 4.

Theorem   Let T be a finite ordered rooted tree whose vertices have been listed by a preorder traversal or a postorder traversal. Suppose that the number of children is known for each vertex. Then the tree is determined, that is, the tree can be recovered from the listing.

Proof. We consider only the case of postorder traversal. For each vertex v of T let $S(v)$ be the set of children of v. We'll show that for $m = 1, 2, \ldots, n$ the set $S(v_m)$ and its order are uniquely determined by the postordered list $v_1\, v_2 \cdots v_n$ of T and the numbers $c_1, \ldots, c_n$ of children of $v_1, \ldots, v_n$.

Consider some vertex v_m. Then v_m is the root of the subtree T_m consisting of v_m and its descendants. When Algorithm POSTORDER lists v_m the subtrees of T_m have already been listed and their lists immediately precede v_m, in the order determined by the order of $S(v_m)$. Moreover, the algorithm does not insert entries later on into the list of T_m, so the list of T_m appears in the final list $v_1\, v_2 \cdots v_n$ of T as an unbroken string with v_m at the right end.

Since v_1 has no predecessors, v_1 is a leaf. Thus $S(v_1) = \varnothing$, and its order is vacuously determined. Assume inductively that for each k with $k < m$ the set $S(v_k)$ and its order are determined, and consider v_m. [We are using the second principle of induction here on the finite set $\{1, 2, \ldots, n\}$.] Then the set $U(m) = \{v_k : k < m\} \setminus \bigcup_{k<m} S(v_k)$ is determined. It consists of the vertices v_k to the left of v_m whose parents are not to the left of v_m. The children of v_m are the members of $U(m)$ which are in the tree T_m. Since the T_m list is immediately to the left of v_m, the children of v_m are the c_m members of $U(m)$ farthest to the right. Since $U(m)$ is determined and c_m is given, the set $S(m)$ of children of v_m is determined. Moreover, its order is the order of appearance in the list $v_1\, v_2 \cdots v_n$.

By induction, each ordered set $S(m)$ of children is determined by the postordered list and the sequence $c_1, c_2, \ldots, c_n$. The root of the tree is, of course, the last vertex v_n. Thus the complete structure of the ordered rooted tree is determined. □

EXAMPLE 7   The list $u\,x\,y\,z\,w\,v\,p\,q\,s\,r$ and sequence $0, 0, 0, 0, 3, 2, 0, 0, 2, 2$ give the following sets.

v_k	u	x	y	z	w	v	p	q	s	r
$U(v_k)$	$\varnothing$	$\{u\}$	$\{u, x\}$	$\{u, x, y\}$	$\{u, x, y, z\}$	$\{u, w\}$	$\{v\}$	$\{v, p\}$	$\{v, p, q\}$	$\{v, s\}$
$S(v_k)$	$\varnothing$	$\varnothing$	$\varnothing$	$\varnothing$	$\{x, y, z\}$	$\{u, w\}$	$\varnothing$	$\varnothing$	$\{p, q\}$	$\{v, s\}$

The ordered sets $S(v_k)$ can be assembled recursively into the tree T of Figure 1 of §9.3. □

EXERCISES 9.4

1. Write the algebraic expression given by Figure 1(b) in reverse Polish and in Polish notation.

2. For the ordered rooted tree in Figure 3(a), write the corresponding algebraic expression in reverse Polish notation and also in the usual infix algebraic notation.

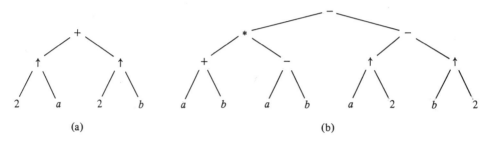

(a)   (b)

FIGURE 3

3. (a) For the ordered rooted tree in Figure 3(b), write the corresponding algebraic expression in Polish notation and also in the usual infix algebraic notation.
   (b) Simplify the algebraic expression obtained in part (a) and then draw the corresponding tree.

4. Calculate the following expressions given in reverse Polish notation.
   (a) $3\ 3\ 4\ 5\ 1\ -\ *\ +\ +$ (b) $3\ 3\ +\ 4\ +\ 5\ *\ 1\ -$
   (c) $3\ 3\ 4\ +\ 5\ *\ 1\ -\ +$

5. Calculate the following expressions given in reverse Polish notation.
   (a) $6\ 3\ /\ 3\ +\ 7\ 3\ -\ *$ (b) $3\ 2\uparrow 4\ 2\uparrow +\ 5\ /\ 2\ *$

6. Calculate the following expressions in Polish notation.
   (a) $-\ *\ 3\uparrow 5\ 2\ 2$ (b) $\uparrow *\ 3\ 5\ -\ 2\ 2$
   (c) $-\uparrow *\ 3\ 5\ 2\ 2$ (d) $/\ *\ 2\ +\ 2\ 5\uparrow +\ 3\ 4\ 2$
   (e) $*\ +\ /\ 6\ 3\ 3\ -\ 7\ 3$

7. Write the following algebraic expressions in reverse Polish notation.
   (a) $(3x - 4)^2$ (b) $(a + 2b)/(a - 2b)$
   (c) $x - x^2 + x^3 - x^4$

8. Write the algebraic expressions in Exercise 7 in Polish notation.

9. Write the following laws of algebra in reverse Polish notation.
   (a) $a + b = b + a$ (b) $a(bc) = (ab)c$
   (c) $a(b + c) = ab + ac$

10. Write the expression $x\ y\ +\ 2\uparrow x\ y\ -\ 2\uparrow -\ x\ y\ *\ /$ in the usual infix algebraic notation and simplify.

11. Consider the compound proposition represented by Figure 2(b).
    (a) Write the proposition in the usual infix notation [with parentheses].
    (b) Write the proposition in reverse Polish and in Polish notation.

12. The following compound propositions are given in Polish notation. Draw the corresponding rooted trees, and rewrite the expressions in the usual infix notation.

(a) $\leftrightarrow \neg \wedge \neg p \neg q \vee p q$ (b) $\leftrightarrow \wedge p q \neg \rightarrow p \neg q$

[These are laws from Table 1 of § 2.2.]

13. Repeat Exercise 12 for the following.

(a) $\rightarrow \wedge p \rightarrow p q q$

(b) $\rightarrow \wedge \wedge \rightarrow p q \rightarrow r s \vee p r \vee q s$

14. Write the following compound propositions in reverse Polish notation.

(a) $[(p \rightarrow q) \wedge (q \rightarrow r)] \rightarrow (p \rightarrow r)$ (b) $[(p \vee q) \wedge \neg p] \rightarrow q$

15. Illustrate the ambiguity of "parenthesis-free infix notation" by writing the following pairs of expressions in infix notation without parentheses.

(a) $(a/b) + c$ and $a/(b + c)$ (b) $a + (b^3 + c)$ and $(a + b)^3 + c$

16. Use the recursive definition for wff's for reverse Polish notation to show that the following are wff's.

(a) $3 \, x \, 2 \uparrow *$ (b) $x \, y + 1 \, x \, / \, 1 \, y \, / + *$

(c) $4 \, x \, 2 \uparrow y \, z + 2 \uparrow / -$

17. (a) Define wff's for Polish notation for algebraic expressions.

(b) Use the definition in part (a) to show that $\uparrow + x / 4 x 2$ is a wff.

18. Let $S_1 = x_1 \, 2 \uparrow$ and $S_{n+1} = S_n \, x_{n+1} \, 2 \uparrow +$ for $n \geq 1$. Here $x_1, x_2, \ldots$ represent variables.

(a) Show that each S_n is a wff for reverse Polish notation. *Hint:* Use induction on n.

(b) What does S_n look like in the usual infix notation?

19. (a) Define wff's for reverse Polish notation for the propositional calculus; see Example 6(a) of § 3.5.

(b) Use the definition in part (a) to show that $p q \neg \wedge \neg p q \neg \rightarrow \vee$ is a wff.

(c) Define wff's for Polish notation for the propositional calculus.

(d) Use the definition in part (c) to show that $\vee \neg \wedge p \neg q \rightarrow p \neg q$ is a wff.

20. (a) Draw the tree with postorder vertex sequence $t \, v \, y \, r \, z \, w \, u \, x \, q$ and number of children sequence 0, 0, 0, 2, 2, 0, 0, 0, 2, 3.

(b) Is there a tree with $s \, t \, v \, y \, r \, z \, w \, u \, x \, q$ as preorder vertex sequence and number of children sequence 0, 0, 0, 2, 2, 0, 0, 0, 2, 3? Explain.

§ 9.5   *Weighted Trees*

In this section we discuss general weighted trees and we give applications to prefix codes and sorted lists.

Consider a finite rooted tree T. We call T a **weighted tree** if a nonnegative real number is assigned to each leaf. This number is called the **weight** of the leaf. To establish some notation, we assume that T has t leaves whose weights are $w_1, w_2, \ldots, w_t$. We lose no generality if we also assume that $w_1 \leq w_2 \leq \cdots \leq w_t$. It will be convenient to label the leaves by their weights, and so we will often refer to the leaf by referring to its weight. Let $l_1, l_2, \ldots, l_t$ denote the corresponding levels of the leaves, so that l_i is the length of the path from the root to the leaf w_i. The **weight** of the tree T is the number

$$W(T) = \sum_{i=1}^{t} w_i l_i.$$

EXAMPLE 1   (a) Consider the weighted tree in Figure 1(a). The six leaves have weights 2, 4, 6, 7, 7 and 9. Thus $w_1 = 2$, $w_2 = 4$, $w_3 = 6$, $w_4 = 7$, $w_5 = 7$ and $w_6 = 9$. There are two leaves labeled 7, and it does not matter which we regard as w_4 and which we regard as w_5. For definiteness, we let w_4 represent the leaf labeled 7 at level 2. Then the level numbers are $l_1 = 3$, $l_2 = 1$, $l_3 = 3$, $l_4 = 2$, $l_5 = 1$ and $l_6 = 2$. Hence

$$W(T) = \sum_{i=1}^{6} w_i l_i = 2 \cdot 3 + 4 \cdot 1 + 6 \cdot 3 + 7 \cdot 2 + 7 \cdot 1 + 9 \cdot 2 = 67.$$

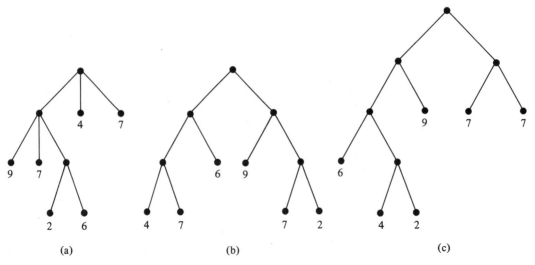

(a)   (b)   (c)

FIGURE 1

(b) The same six weights can be placed on a binary tree as in Figure 1(b), for instance. Now the level numbers are $l_1 = 3$, $l_2 = 3$, $l_3 = 2$, $l_4 = l_5 = 3$ and $l_6 = 2$ and so

$$W(T) = 2 \cdot 3 + 4 \cdot 3 + 6 \cdot 2 + 7 \cdot 3 + 7 \cdot 3 + 9 \cdot 2 = 90.$$

(c) Figure 1(c) shows another binary tree with these weights. Its weight is

$$W(T) = 2 \cdot 4 + 4 \cdot 4 + 6 \cdot 3 + 7 \cdot 2 + 7 \cdot 2 + 9 \cdot 2 = 88.$$

The total weight is less than in part (b), because the heavier leaves are near the root and the lighter ones are farther away. Later in this section we will discuss an algorithm for obtaining a binary tree with minimal weight for any specified sequence of weights $w_1, w_2, \ldots, w_t$. □

EXAMPLE 2 As we will explain later in this section, certain sets of binary numbers can serve as codes. An example of such a set is {00, 01, 100, 1010, 1011, 11}. These numbers are the labels of the leaves in the binary tree of Figure 2(a).

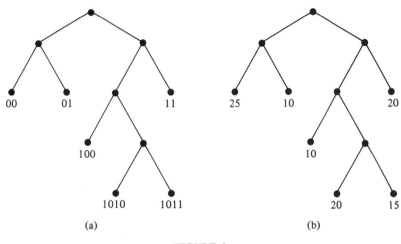

FIGURE 2

This set could serve as a code for the letters in an alphabet Σ which has six letters. Suppose that we also know how frequently each letter in Σ is used. In Figure 2(b) we have placed a weight at each leaf that signifies the percentage of code symbols using that leaf. For example, the letter coded 00 appears 25 percent of the time, the letter coded 1010 appears 20 percent of the time, etc. Since the length of each code symbol as a word in 0's and 1's is exactly its level in the binary tree, the average length of a code message using 100 letters from Σ will just be the weight of the weighted tree, in this case

$$25 \cdot 2 + 10 \cdot 2 + 10 \cdot 3 + 20 \cdot 4 + 15 \cdot 4 + 20 \cdot 2 = 280.$$

This weight measures the efficiency of the code. As we will see in Example 7, there are more efficient codes for this example, i.e., for the set of frequencies 10, 10, 15, 20, 20, 25. ☐

EXAMPLE 3 Consider some sorted lists, say $L_1, L_2, \ldots, L_n$, which could be alphabetically ordered files or some other subsets of a given poset, with each listed in increasing order. To illustrate the ideas involved, let's suppose each list is a set of real numbers. Suppose that we can merge lists two at a time to produce new lists. Our problem is to determine how to merge the lists most efficiently to produce a single sorted list.

Two lists are merged by comparing the largest numbers of each set and selecting the larger [either one if they are equal]. The selected number is removed and stored someplace, and the process is repeated for the remaining two lists. The process ends when one of the lists is empty. If the lists contain

j and k elements, respectively, this process must end after $j + k - 1$ or fewer comparisons. The goal is to merge $L_1, L_2, \ldots, L_n$ in pairs while minimizing the number of comparisons involved.

Let's consider a more concrete example. Suppose we have five lists L_1, L_2, L_3, L_4, L_5 with 15, 22, 31, 34, 42 items and suppose they are merged as indicated in Figure 3. There are 4 merges indicated by the circled numbers.

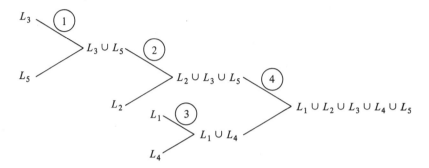

FIGURE 3

The first merge involves at most $|L_3| + |L_5| - 1 = 72$ comparisons. The second merge involves at most $|L_2| + |L_3| + |L_5| - 1 = 94$ comparisons. The third and fourth merges involve at most $|L_1| + |L_4| - 1 = 48$ and $|L_1| + |L_2| + |L_3| + |L_4| + |L_5| - 1 = 143$ comparisons. The entire process involves at most 357 comparisons. This number isn't very illuminating by itself, but note that

$$357 = 2 \cdot |L_1| + 2 \cdot |L_2| + 3 \cdot |L_3| + 2 \cdot |L_4| + 3 \cdot |L_5| - 4.$$

This is just 4 less than the weight of the tree in Figure 4. Note the intimate connection between Figures 3 and 4. No matter how we merge the five lists in pairs, there will be 4 merges. A computation like the one above shows that the merge will involve at most $W(T) - 4$ comparisons, where T is the tree corresponding to the merge. So finding a merge that minimizes the largest possible number of comparisons is equivalent to finding a binary tree with

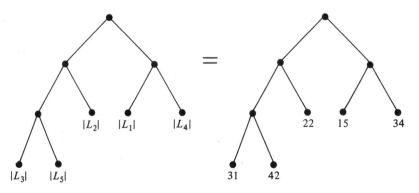

FIGURE 4

weights 15, 22, 31, 34, 42 having minimal weight. We return to this problem in Example 8.

The merging of n lists in pairs involves $n - 1$ merges. In general, a merge of n lists will involve at most $W(T) - (n - 1)$ comparisons, where T is the tree corresponding to the merge. □

Examples 2 and 3 suggest the following general problem. Consider t weights $w_1, w_2, \ldots, w_t$ where $0 \leq w_1 \leq w_2 \leq \cdots \leq w_t$. Find a binary weighted tree T with these weights so that $W(T)$ is as small as possible. We call such a T an **optimal binary tree** for the weights $w_1, w_2, \ldots, w_t$. We give a recursive algorithm for finding optimal binary trees. It reduces the problem to finding an optimal binary tree with one less leaf.

HUFFMAN'S *Algorithm.*

We are given weights $w_1, w_2, \ldots, w_t$ where $0 \leq w_1 \leq w_2 \leq \cdots \leq w_t$.

Step 1. Replace the weights by the weights $w_1 + w_2, w_3, \ldots, w_t$. Note that $w_1 + w_2$ might not be the smallest weight here, but the weights can be reordered so as to form a nondecreasing sequence.

Step 2. Obtain an optimal binary tree T' for the $t - 1$ weights $w_1 + w_2$, $w_3, \ldots, w_t$.

Step 3. Let T be the binary tree obtained from T' by replacing a leaf of weight $w_1 + w_2$ by a subtree with two leaves having weights w_1 and w_2. Then T is an optimal binary tree with weights w_1, $w_2, \ldots, w_t$. □

Ultimately HUFFMAN'S algorithm reduces to the problem of finding optimal binary trees with two leaves, and this problem is trivial.

EXAMPLE 4   Consider weights 9, 12, 14 so that $w_1 = 9$, $w_2 = 12$ and $w_3 = 14$. Clearly Figure 5(a) represents an optimal binary tree with weights $w_1 + w_2, w_3$, i.e., 21 and 14. If we replace the leaf of weight 21 by the subtree having weights 12 and 9, we obtain the tree in Figure 5(b). According to HUFFMAN'S algorithm this is an optimal binary tree with weights 9, 12, 14.

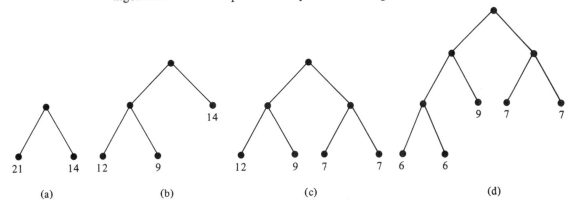

FIGURE 5

Now consider weights 7, 7, 9, 12 so that now $w_1 = w_2 = 7$, $w_3 = 9$ and $w_4 = 12$. Figure 5(b) is an optimal binary tree with weights $w_1 + w_2$, w_3, w_4, i.e., 14, 9, 12. We replace the leaf of weight 14 by the subtree having weights 7 at both leaves to obtain the optimal binary tree in Figure 5(c), with weights 7, 7, 9, 12.

Next consider weights 6, 6, 7, 7, 9. HUFFMAN'S algorithm requires an optimal binary tree with weights 12, 7, 7, 9 and such a tree is given in Figure 5(c). Hence Figure 5(d) shows an optimal binary tree with weights 6, 6, 7, 7, 9.

Finally, to obtain an optimal binary tree with weights 2, 4, 6, 7, 7, 9, we need an optimal binary tree with weights 6, 6, 7, 7, 9 such as that in Figure 5(d). Since HUFFMAN'S algorithm replaces a leaf of weight 6 by the subtree having weights 2 and 4, we conclude that the tree in Figure 1(c) is an optimal binary tree. As noted in Example 1(c), it has weight 88.   ☐

The only possible mystery in Example 4 is this: How did we know that we should consider the weights 9, 12, 14 and then the weights 7, 7, 9, 12, etc. in order to construct an optimal binary tree with weights 2, 4, 6, 7, 7, 9? Well, we started with the original weight sequence 2, 4, 6, 7, 7, 9 and combined the smallest two weights to obtain 6, 6, 7, 7, 9. We then repeated this process over and over, getting 7, 7, 9, 12, and then 9, 12, 14 and then 14, 21.

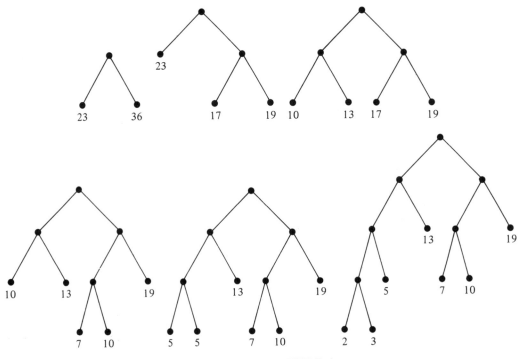

FIGURE 6

EXAMPLE 5 Let us find an optimal binary tree with weights 2, 3, 5, 7, 10, 13, 19. We repeatedly combine the smallest two weights to obtain the weight sequences

$$2, 3, 5, 7, 10, 13, 19 \rightarrow 5, 5, 7, 10, 13, 19$$

$$\rightarrow 7, 10, 10, 13, 19 \rightarrow 10, 13, 17, 19 \rightarrow 17, 19, 23$$

$$\rightarrow 23, 36.$$

Then we use HUFFMAN'S algorithm to build the optimal binary trees in Figure 6. After the fourth tree is obtained, either leaf of weight 10 could have been replaced by the subtree with weights 5 and 5. Thus the last two trees could have been as drawn in Figure 7. Either way, the final tree has weight 150 [Exercise 2]. Note that the optimal tree is by no means unique; the one in Figure 6 has height 4, while the one in Figure 7 has height 5. □

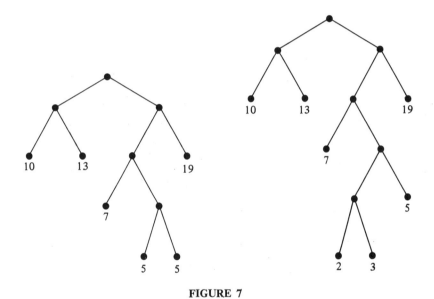

FIGURE 7

We now return to codes using binary numbers. Certain sets of binary numbers must be avoided; for example, a code should not use all three of 10, 01 and 0110, since strings like 100110 would be ambiguous. Actually, it is convenient to require that no code symbol consist of a string of digits which comprises the beginning digits of another code symbol. We can think of strings of 0's and 1's as vertices in a labeled binary tree, as in § 9.2. Reading the label of a vertex from left to right tells how to get to the vertex from the root: go left on 0, right on 1. Our restriction simply means that no vertex labeled with a code symbol lies below another in such a labeled binary tree, and means that there is a labeled binary tree whose leaves are exactly the code symbols. We also require that this binary tree be regular, so that every nonleaf has two children. Such a code is called a **prefix code**.

EXAMPLE 6 The set {00, 01, 100, 1010, 1011, 11} is a prefix code. It is the set of leaves for
the labeled binary tree in Figure 2(a), which we have redrawn in Figure 8(a)
with all vertices but the root labeled. Every string of 0's and 1's of length 4
begins with one of these code symbols, since every path of length 4 from the
root in the full binary tree in Figure 8(b) runs into one of the code vertices.

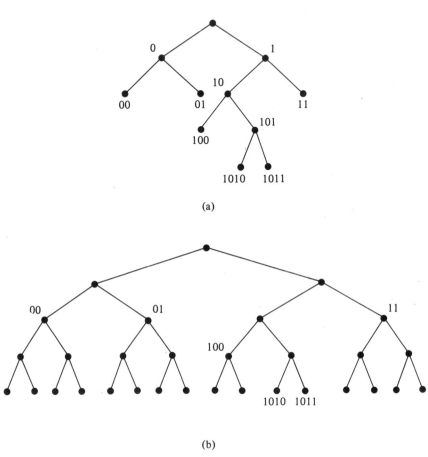

(a)

(b)

FIGURE 8

This means that we can attempt to decode any string of 0's and 1's by proceeding from left to right in the string, finding the first substring that is a code
symbol, then the next substring after that, and so on. This procedure either
uses up the whole string or it leaves at most three 0's and 1's undecoded at
the end.

For example, consider the string

1 1 1 0 1 0 1 1 0 1 1 0 0 0 1 0 0 1 1 1 1 1 0 0 1 0 .

We visit vertex 1, then vertex 11. Since vertex 11 is a leaf, we record 11 and return to the root. We next visit vertices 1, 10, 101 and 1010. Since 1010 is a leaf, we record 1010 and return again to the root. Proceeding in this way, we obtain the sequence of code symbols

$$11, 1010, 11, 01, 100, 01, 00, 11, 11, 100$$

and have 10 left over. This scheme for decoding arbitrary strings of 0's and 1's will work for any code with the property that every path from the root in a full binary tree runs into a unique code vertex. Prefix codes have this property by their definition.   ◻

EXAMPLE 7   We now solve the problem suggested by Example 2; that is, we find a prefix code for the set of frequencies 10, 10, 15, 20, 20, 25 that is as efficient as possible. Hence we want to minimize the average length of a code message using 100 letters from Σ. Thus all we need is an optimal binary tree for these weights. Using the procedure illustrated in Example 5, we obtain the weighted tree in Figure 9(a). We label this tree with binary digits in Figure 9(b). Then

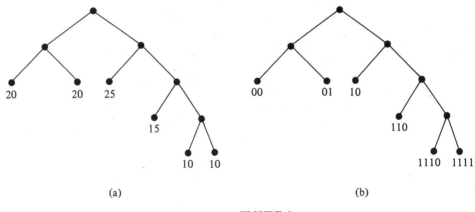

(a)   (b)

FIGURE 9

{00, 01, 10, 110, 1110, 1111} will be a most efficient code for Σ provided we match the letters of Σ to code symbols so that the frequencies of the letters are given by Figure 9(a). With this code, the average length of a code message using 100 letters from Σ is

$$20 \cdot 2 + 20 \cdot 2 + 25 \cdot 2 + 15 \cdot 3 + 10 \cdot 4 + 10 \cdot 4 = 255,$$

an improvement over the average length 280 obtained in Example 2.   ◻

EXAMPLE 8   We complete the discussion on sorted lists begun in Example 3. There we saw that we needed an optimal binary tree with weights 15, 22, 31, 34, 42. Using the procedure in Example 5, we obtain the tree in Figure 10. This tree

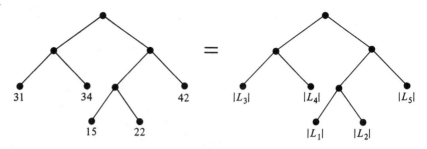

FIGURE 10

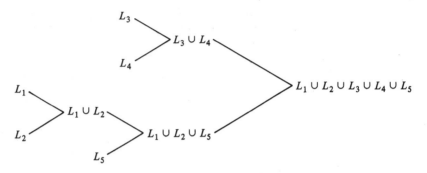

FIGURE 11

has weight 325. The corresponding merge in pairs given in Figure 11 will require at most $325 - 4 = 321$ comparisons. ☐

To show that HUFFMAN'S algorithm works, we first prove a lemma which tells us that in optimal binary trees the heavy leaves are near the root. The lemma and its corollary are quite straightforward if all the weights are distinct [Exercise 14]. However, we need the more general case. Even if we began with distinct weights, HUFFMAN'S algorithm might lead to the case where the weights are not all distinct, as occurred in Example 5.

Lemma   Let T be an optimal binary tree for weights $w_1, w_2, \ldots, w_t$. For $i = 1, 2, \ldots, t$, let l_i denote the level of w_i. If $w_j < w_k$ then $l_j \geqq l_k$.

Proof. Assume that $w_j < w_k$ and $l_j < l_k$ for some j and k. Let T' be the tree obtained by interchanging the weights w_j and w_k. In calculating $W(T)$ the leaves w_j and w_k contribute $w_j l_j + w_k l_k$, while in calculating $W(T')$ they contribute $w_j l_k + w_k l_j$. Since the other leaves contribute the same to both $W(T)$ and $W(T')$, we have

$$W(T) - W(T') = w_j l_j + w_k l_k - w_j l_k - w_k l_j$$
$$= (w_k - w_j)(l_k - l_j) > 0.$$

Hence $W(T') < W(T)$ and T is not an optimal binary tree, contrary to our hypothesis. □

Corollary There is an optimal binary tree T where the weights w_1 and w_2 are both at the lowest level l.

 Proof. There are at least two leaves at the lowest level, say w_j and w_k. If $w_1 < w_j$ then $l_1 \geq l_j = l$ by the lemma, and so $l_1 = l$ and w_1 is at level l. If $w_1 = w_j$ then conceivably $l_1 < l_j$, but we can interchange w_1 and w_j without changing the total weight of T. Similarly, by interchanging w_2 and w_k if necessary, we may suppose that w_2 is at level l. □

 The following result shows that HUFFMAN'S algorithm works.

Theorem Suppose that $0 \leq w_1 \leq w_2 \leq \cdots \leq w_t$. Let T' be an optimal binary tree with weights $w_1 + w_2, w_3, \ldots, w_t$ and let T be the weighted binary tree obtained from T' by replacing a leaf of weight $w_1 + w_2$ by a subtree with two leaves having weights w_1 and w_2. Then T is an optimal binary tree with weights $w_1, w_2, \ldots, w_t$.

 Proof. Since there are only finitely many binary trees with t leaves, there must be an optimal binary tree T_0 with weights $w_1, w_2, \ldots, w_t$. Our task is to show $W(T) = W(T_0)$. By the corollary of the lemma, we may suppose that the weights w_1 and w_2 for T_0 are at the same level. The total weight of T_0 won't change if weights at the same level are interchanged. Thus we may assume that w_1 and w_2 are children of the same parent p. These three vertices form a little subtree T_p.

 Now let T_0' be the tree with weights $w_1 + w_2, w_3, \ldots, w_t$ obtained from T_0 by replacing the subtree T_p by a leaf $\bar{p}$ of weight $w_1 + w_2$. Let l be the level of the vertex p and observe that in calculating $W(T_0)$ the subtree T_p contributes $w_1(l + 1) + w_2(l + 1)$, while in calculating $W(T_0')$, the vertex $\bar{p}$ with weight $w_1 + w_2$ contributes $(w_1 + w_2)l$. Thus

$$W(T_0) = W(T_0') + w_1 + w_2.$$

The same argument shows that

$$W(T) = W(T') + w_1 + w_2.$$

Since T' is optimal for the weights $w_1 + w_2, w_3, \ldots, w_t$, we have $W(T') \leq W(T_0')$ and so

$$W(T) = W(T') + w_1 + w_2 \leq W(T_0') + w_1 + w_2 = W(T_0).$$

Of course $W(T_0) \leq W(T)$, since T_0 is optimal for the weights $w_1, w_2, \ldots, w_t$, so $W(T) = W(T_0)$, as desired. That is, T is an optimal binary tree with weights $w_1, w_2, \ldots, w_t$. □

EXERCISES 9.5

1. (a) Calculate the weights of all the trees in Figure 5.
   (b) Calculate the weights of all the trees in Figure 6.

2. Calculate the weights of the two trees in Figures 6 and 7 with weights 2, 3, 5, 7, 10, 13, 19.

3. Construct an optimal binary tree for the following sets of weights and compute the weight of the optimal tree.

   (a) {1, 3, 4, 6, 9, 13}   (b) {1, 3, 5, 6, 10, 13, 16}
   (c) {2, 4, 5, 8, 13, 15, 18, 25}   (d) {1, 1, 2, 3, 5, 8, 13, 21, 34}

4. Find an optimal binary tree for the weights 10, 10, 15, 20, 20, 25 and compare your answer with Figure 9(a).

5. Which of the following sets of sequences are prefix codes? If the set is a prefix code, construct a binary tree whose leaves represent this binary code. Otherwise, explain why the set is not a prefix code.

   (a) {000, 001, 01, 10, 11}   (b) {00, 01, 110, 101, 0111}
   (c) {00, 0100, 0101, 011, 100, 101, 11}

6. Here is a prefix code: {00, 010, 0110, 0111, 10, 11}.
   (a) Construct a binary tree whose leaves represent this binary code.
   (b) Decode the string

   $$0\,0\,1\,0\,0\,0\,0\,1\,1\,0\,0\,1\,0\,0\,0\,1\,0\,0\,1\,1\,1\,1\,1\,0\,1\,1\,0$$

   if $00 = A$, $10 = D$, $11 = E$, $010 = H$, $0110 = M$ and 0111 represents the apostrophe '. You will obtain the very short poem titled "Fleas."
   (c) Decode

   $$0\,1\,0\,1\,1\,0\,1\,1\,0\,0\,0\,1\,0\,1\,1\,0\,1\,1\,0\,1\,1\,0\,1\,1\,0\,0\,0\,1\,0.$$

   (d) Decode the following soap opera. $1\,0\,0\,0\,1\,0\,0\,1\,0\,0\,0\,1\,0\,0\,1\,1\,0\,0\,0\,1\,0$
   $0\,0\,0\,1\,1\,0.\ \ 0\,1\,0\,1\,1\,0\,1\,1\,0\,0\,0\,1\,0\,1\,1\,0\,1\,1\,0\,0\,0\,0\,1\,1\,0\,0\,0\,1\,0.\ \ 0\,1\,1\,0\,0$
   $0\,0\,1\,1\,0\,0\,0\,1\,0\,1\,1\,1\,0\,0\,0\,1\,0\,1\,0\,1\,1\,0\,0\,1\,0.$

7. Suppose we are given a fictitious alphabet Σ of seven letters a, b, c, d, e, f and g with the following frequencies per 100 letters: $a - 11$, $b - 20$, $c - 4$, $d - 22$, $e - 14$, $f - 8$, $g - 21$.
   (a) Design an optimal binary prefix code for this alphabet.
   (b) What is the average length of a code message using 100 letters from Σ?

8. Repeat Exercise 7 for the frequencies: $a - 25$, $b - 2$, $c - 15$, $d - 10$, $e - 38$, $f - 4$, $g - 6$.

9. (a) Show that the code {000, 001, 10, 110, 111} satisfies all the requirements of a prefix code, except that the corresponding binary tree is not regular.
   (b) Show that some strings of binary digits are meaningless for this code.
   (c) Show that {00, 01, 10, 110, 111} is a prefix code, and compare its binary tree with that of part (a).

10. Repeat Exercise 7 for the frequencies: $a - 31$, $d - 31$, $e - 12$, $h - 6$, $m - 20$.

11. Let L_1, L_2, L_3, L_4 be sorted lists having 23, 31, 61 and 73 elements, respectively. How many comparisons at most are needed if the lists are merged as indicated?

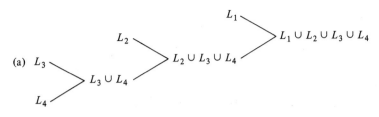

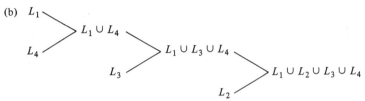

(a)

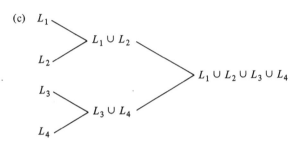

(c)

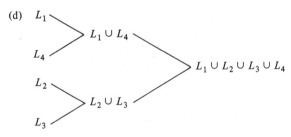

(e) How should the four lists be merged so that the total number of comparisons is a minimum? It is not sufficient to simply examine parts (a)–(d) since there are other ways to merge the lists.

12. Let $L_1, L_2, L_3, L_4, L_5, L_6$ be sorted lists having 5, 6, 9, 22, 29, 34 elements, respectively.
    (a) Show how the six lists should be merged so that the total number of comparisons can be kept to a minimum.
    (b) How many comparisons might be needed in your procedure?

13. Repeat Exercise 12 for seven lists having 2, 5, 8, 12, 16, 22, 24 elements, respectively.

14. Let T be an optimal binary tree whose weights satisfy $w_1 < w_2 < \cdots < w_t$. Show that the corresponding level numbers satisfy $l_1 \geqq l_2 \geqq l_3 \geqq \cdots \geqq l_t$.

15. Look at Exercise 1 again, and note that whenever a vertex of weight $w_1 + w_2$ in a tree T' is replaced by a subtree with weights w_1 and w_2, then the weight increases by $w_1 + w_2$. That is, the new tree T has weight $W(T') + w_1 + w_2$, just as in the proof of the theorem.

CHAPTER HIGHLIGHTS

As always, one of the best ways to use this material for review is to follow the suggestions at the end of Chapter 0. Ask yourself: What does it mean? Why is it here? How can I use it?

Concepts

tree, subtree
  leaf, parent, child, descendant
spanning tree, minimal spanning tree
directed tree
root, rooted tree, ordered rooted tree
binary/m-ary tree
  regular/full m-ary tree
preorder, postorder, inorder traversals
Polish, reverse Polish, infix notations
weighted tree, weight of a tree
optimal binary tree
  merge of lists, prefix code

Facts

The following statements about a graph with $n \geq 1$ vertices and no loops are equivalent:
  (a) G is a tree.
  (b) There is just one simple path between any two distinct vertices.
  (c) G is connected, but won't be if an edge is removed.
  (d) G is acyclic, but won't be if an edge is added.
  (e) G is acyclic and has $n - 1$ edges [as many as possible].
  (f) G is connected and has $n - 1$ edges [as few as possible].
Any vertex of a tree can be used as a root for a unique corresponding rooted tree.
Rooted trees and height can be defined recursively.
Rooted trees are natural data structures for random access to data and for branching and recursive programs.
An ordered rooted tree cannot always be recovered from its preorder, inorder or postorder listing.
It *can* be recovered from its preorder or postorder listing given knowledge of how many children each vertex has.

Methods

MIN-SPANNING TREE 1 and 2 to construct minimal spanning trees for weighted graphs.

PREORDER, POSTORDER and INORDER to list vertices of a finite ordered rooted tree.

Construction and deciphering of Polish and reverse Polish forms for algebraic expressions.

HUFFMAN'S recursive algorithm to find an optimal binary tree with given weights.

Use of binary weighted trees to determine efficient merging patterns and efficient prefix codes.

10

BOOLEAN ALGEBRA

The term "Boolean algebra" is used to describe a variety of related topics, ranging from symbolic logic and truth tables to the arithmetic performed by electrical relay networks or electronic computers. This chapter begins by developing abstract structures called Boolean algebras, starting from posets and lattices. The algebra involved is reminiscent of the truth tables of Chapter 2. The switching functions associated with electronic logic networks turn out to give important examples of Boolean algebras, and we are able to study the networks and their functions using the algebraic tools we develop. The chapter concludes with a brief discussion of Karnaugh maps, a tool somewhat like Venn diagrams, which can be useful in analyzing moderately complicated logical expressions.

§ 10.1 Lattices

Recall that in § 7.1 we called a poset $(P, \leq)$ a **lattice** provided every finite subset has both a least upper bound and a greatest lower bound. We also introduced two binary operations $\vee$ and $\wedge$ on P where

$$x \vee y = \text{lub}\{x, y\} \quad \text{and} \quad x \wedge y = \text{glb}\{x, y\}.$$

We will see in Theorem 1 that these binary operations satisfy the following properties:

1La. $x \vee y = y \vee x$ ⎫
   b. $x \wedge y = y \wedge x$ ⎬   commutative laws

2La. $(x \vee y) \vee z = x \vee (y \vee z)$ ⎫
   b. $(x \wedge y) \wedge z = x \wedge (y \wedge z)$ ⎬ associative laws

3La. $x \vee (x \wedge y) = x$ ⎫
   b. $x \wedge (x \vee y) = x$ ⎬   absorption laws

Theorem 2 will say that these six properties characterize lattices, in the sense that a set closed under two binary operations $\vee$ and $\wedge$ satisfying the properties can be given a natural partial ordering which makes it a lattice. Thus every general fact about lattices must somehow be a consequence of these six properties, and whenever we encounter a set with two binary operations satisfying these conditions we can view it as a lattice and immediately conclude that it has whatever general properties lattices have. One of our goals, then, will be to determine what can be proved just using the six listed properties. Let us call any set L with two binary operations $\vee$ and $\wedge$ that satisfy these six properties an **algebraic lattice**. We will sometimes write $(L, \vee, \wedge)$ to stress our interest in the operations $\vee$ and $\wedge$. As in § 7.1 we read $x \vee y$ as "x join y" and $x \wedge y$ as "x meet y."

Theorem 1   Consider a lattice $(P, \leq)$ and define $x \vee y = \mathrm{lub}\{x, y\}$ and $x \wedge y = \mathrm{glb}\{x, y\}$. Then $(P, \vee, \wedge)$ is an algebraic lattice.

    Proof. The commutative laws are clear. To check property 2La, consider $x, y, z \in P$ and let $u = (x \vee y) \vee z$ and $v = x \vee (y \vee z)$. Since $y \leq x \vee y \leq u$ and $z \leq u$, the element u is an upper bound for $\{y, z\}$. Since $y \vee z$ is the *least* upper bound, we have $y \vee z \leq u$. Also $x \leq x \vee y \leq u$, so u is an upper bound for $\{x, y \vee z\}$ and hence $x \vee (y \vee z) \leq u$. In other words, $v \leq u$. Similar reasoning shows that $u \leq v$ and therefore $u = v$.

    To check property 3La, consider $x, y \in P$. Since $x \leq x \vee w$ for any w, we have $x \leq x \vee (x \wedge y)$. Since $x \leq x$ and $x \wedge y \leq x$, the element x is an upper bound for $\{x, x \wedge y\}$ and so $x \vee (x \wedge y) \leq x$. Thus $x \vee (x \wedge y) = x$, as desired.

    Properties 2Lb and 3Lb have similar proofs.   ☐

    Before we prove results for algebraic lattices, we mention a **duality principle**. If we consider one of the six properties defining an algebraic lattice and we replace each $\vee$ by $\wedge$ and each $\wedge$ by $\vee$, then we obtain another one of the properties, which we might call the dual property. Thus 1La and 1Lb are duals for each other, etc. It follows that any theorem or identity that holds for an algebraic lattice will remain true if we dualize it, that is, if we replace each $\vee$ by $\wedge$ and each $\wedge$ by $\vee$.

Proposition Let $(L, \vee, \wedge)$ be an algebraic lattice.

(a) The operations $\vee$ and $\wedge$ satisfy the idempotent laws: $x \vee x = x$ and $x \wedge x = x$ for all $x \in L$.

(b) For $x, y \in L$ we have $x \vee y = y$ if and only if $x \wedge y = x$.

Proof. (a) With $y = x \vee x$, absorption law 3La gives the identity $x = x \vee [x \wedge (x \vee x)]$. But $[x \wedge (x \vee x)] = x$ by absorption law 3Lb, so $x = x \vee x$. The other idempotent law follows by duality.

(b) Suppose that $x \vee y = y$. Then

$$x = x \wedge (x \vee y) \quad \text{absorption law 3Lb}$$

$$= x \wedge y \qquad \text{since } x \vee y = y \text{ by supposition.}$$

The other implication follows by duality, interchanging the roles of x and y. $\square$

Theorem 1 shows that a lattice $(P, \leq)$ gives rise to an algebraic lattice. Theorem 2 provides a converse.

Theorem 2 Let $(L, \vee, \wedge)$ be an algebraic lattice. We define a relation $\leq$ on L as follows:

$$x \leq y \quad \text{if and only if} \quad x \vee y = y.$$

Then $\leq$ is a partial order, and $(L, \leq)$ is a lattice in which $\text{lub}\{x, y\} = x \vee y$ and $\text{glb}\{x, y\} = x \wedge y$ for all $x, y \in L$.

The proposition above shows that we could just as well define $x \leq y$ if and only if $x \wedge y = x$.

Proof. We check first that $\leq$ is a partial order.

(R)   Since $x \vee x = x$ by the idempotent laws, we have $x \leq x$.

(AS) Suppose $x \leq y$ and $y \leq x$, so that $x \vee y = y$ and $y \vee x = x$. Then $x = y \vee x = x \vee y = y$, using the commutative law.

(T)   Suppose that $x \leq y$ and $y \leq z$, so that $x \vee y = y$ and $y \vee z = z$. Then

$$x \vee z = x \vee (y \vee z) \quad \text{since } y \vee z = z$$

$$= (x \vee y) \vee z \quad \text{associative law}$$

$$= y \vee z \qquad \text{since } x \vee y = y$$

$$= z \qquad \text{since } y \vee z = z.$$

That is, $x \leq z$ as desired.

Next we verify $\text{lub}\{x, y\} = x \vee y$. Since $x \vee (x \vee y) = (x \vee x) \vee y = x \vee y$, the definition of $\leq$ shows that $x \leq x \vee y$. Similarly, $y \leq x \vee y$ and so $x \vee y$ is an upper bound for $\{x, y\}$. To show $x \vee y$ is the *least* upper bound, consider another upper bound u for $\{x, y\}$. Then $x \leq u$ and $y \leq u$, so that $x \vee u = u$ and $y \vee u = u$ and hence

$$(x \vee y) \vee u = x \vee (y \vee u) = x \vee u = u.$$

Therefore $x \vee y \leq u$. This shows that $x \vee y$ is the least upper bound for $\{x, y\}$, i.e., $x \vee y = \text{lub}\{x, y\}$. A similar [dual!] argument shows that $x \wedge y = \text{glb}\{x, y\}$. $\square$

Theorem 1 shows that if $(L, \preceq)$ is a lattice with $\vee$ and $\wedge$ defined by $x \vee y = \text{lub}\{x, y\}$ and $x \wedge y = \text{glb}\{x, y\}$ relative to the partial order $\preceq$, then $(L, \vee, \wedge)$ is an algebraic lattice. Theorem 2 shows that if we go on to define $\leq$ on L by $x \leq y$ if and only if $x \vee y = y$, then $(L, \leq)$ is a lattice. Is $(L, \leq)$ the lattice we started with? That is, is $\leq$ the same as $\preceq$? If $x \preceq y$ then $y = \text{lub}\{x, y\} = x \vee y$ and so $x \leq y$. Conversely, if $x \leq y$ then $y = x \vee y = \text{lub}\{x, y\}$, so $x \preceq y$. Thus $\leq$ is the partial order $\preceq$ we started with. A similar analysis shows that starting with an algebraic lattice, forming its poset and then forming its corresponding algebraic lattice gives us back our original algebraic lattice.

EXAMPLE 1 Consider any set S and let $\mathcal{P}(S)$ be the set of all subsets of S. With the operations $\cup$ and $\cap$, $\mathcal{P}(S)$ is an algebraic lattice. Motivated by Theorem 2, for A, B in $\mathcal{P}(S)$ we define

$$A \leq B \quad \text{if and only if} \quad A \cup B = B.$$

As noted back in Exercise 14 of § 1.2, $A \cup B = B$ if and only if $A \subseteq B$. So the relations $\leq$ and $\subseteq$ are the same. We have not defined a new relation, but we have given a slightly different and more algebraic definition of $\subseteq$ that is in terms of $\cup$ alone. $\square$

EXAMPLE 2 Let $\mathcal{S}$ be a set of compound propositions such that $P \wedge Q$ and $P \vee Q$ belong to $\mathcal{S}$ whenever P, Q belong to $\mathcal{S}$. [Here $\wedge$ and $\vee$ are the usual logical connectives.] We want to regard propositions in $\mathcal{S}$ as the same if they are logically equivalent, i.e., we want to view $\Leftrightarrow$ as an equivalence relation on $\mathcal{S}$ as in Example 7 of § 7.3.

Let $[\mathcal{S}]$ be the set of equivalence classes of $\mathcal{S}$. If P_1 and P_2 are logically equivalent and Q_1 and Q_2 are logically equivalent, then $P_1 \vee Q_1$ and $P_2 \vee Q_2$ are also logically equivalent. Consequently, the following definition on equivalence classes is unambiguous:

$$[P] \vee [Q] = [P \vee Q].$$

[See the end of § 7.3 for a discussion concerning this issue of unambiguous definitions on equivalence classes.] Similarly, the definition

$$[P] \wedge [Q] = [P \wedge Q]$$

is unambiguous. It is believable and easy to check that, with these operations $\vee$ and $\wedge$, $[\mathcal{S}]$ is an algebraic lattice. For example, we know $P \vee Q \Leftrightarrow Q \vee P$ from Table 1 of § 2.2, and so

$$[P] \vee [Q] = [P \vee Q] = [Q \vee P] = [Q] \vee [P].$$

Theorem 2 provides an order on [$\underline{S}$]:

$$[P] \leqq [Q] \quad \text{if and only if} \quad [P] \vee [Q] = [Q].$$

Now $[P] \vee [Q] = [Q]$ means $[P \vee Q] = [Q]$ so that $P \vee Q \Leftrightarrow Q$, which holds if and only if $P \Rightarrow Q$ since

$$[(P \vee Q) \leftrightarrow Q] \leftrightarrow [P \rightarrow Q]$$

is a tautology. We conclude that $[P] \leqq [Q]$ if and only if $P \Rightarrow Q$. □

In Examples 1 and 2, we began with an algebraic lattice and obtained a poset structure. Sometimes it is more natural to start with the poset.

EXAMPLE 3   Consider the set FUN($\mathbb{R}$, $\mathbb{R}$) of all functions from $\mathbb{R}$ to $\mathbb{R}$. As in Example 4 of § 7.2, we define $f \leq g$ provided $f(x) \leqq g(x)$ for all $x \in \mathbb{R}$. This poset is a lattice, so it is an algebraic lattice by Theorem 1. For f and g in FUN($\mathbb{R}$, $\mathbb{R}$), $f \vee g$ denotes the least upper bound for $\{f, g\}$, that is, the smallest function that is greater than or equal to both f and g. It is easy to show that

$$(f \vee g)(x) = \max\{f(x), g(x)\} \quad \text{for all} \quad x \in \mathbb{R}.$$

Likewise, the greatest lower bound $f \wedge g$ for $\{f, g\}$ is the function given by

$$(f \wedge g)(x) = \min\{f(x), g(x)\} \quad \text{for all} \quad x \in \mathbb{R}. \quad □$$

Consider again an algebraic lattice $(L, \vee, \wedge)$. An element in L that is greater than or equal to all other elements in L is called a **universal upper bound**. It is usually written 1; thus $x \leqq 1$, $x \vee 1 = 1$ and $x \wedge 1 = x$ for all $x \in L$. A **universal lower bound** is an element 0 such that $0 \leq x$ for all $x \in L$; note that $0 \vee x = x$ and $0 \wedge x = 0$. A lattice might or might not have universal upper and lower bounds.

Recall from § 7.1 that an element y **covers** an element x if $x \prec y$ and there is no u with $x \prec u \prec y$. If L has a universal lower bound 0 then the elements that cover 0 are called **atoms**.

EXAMPLE 4   (a) Consider the lattice $\mathcal{P}(S)$ of all subsets of S. The empty set $\varnothing$ is a universal lower bound, since $\varnothing \subseteq A$ for all $A \in \mathcal{P}(S)$. Likewise, S itself is a universal upper bound. The atoms are the one-element subsets of S.

(b) Consider the set FUN(S, $\mathbb{B}$) of functions from a set S to $\mathbb{B} = \{0, 1\}$, made into a lattice by $f \leq g$ provided $f(x) \leqq g(x)$ for all $x \in S$. As in Example 3, $(f \vee g)(x) = \max\{f(x), g(x)\}$, so

$$(f \vee g)(x) = \begin{cases} 1 & \text{if } f(x) = 1 \text{ or } g(x) = 1 \\ 0 & \text{otherwise} \end{cases}$$

and similarly,

$$(f \wedge g)(x) = \begin{cases} 1 & \text{if } f(x) = 1 \text{ and } g(x) = 1 \\ 0 & \text{otherwise.} \end{cases}$$

The atoms in $\text{FUN}(S, \mathbb{B})$ are the functions which have the value 1 at exactly one member of S and the value 0 at all other members, that is, the characteristic functions of the one-element subsets of S. □

An element x in an algebraic lattice is **join-irreducible** if $x = y \vee z$ implies $x = y$ or $x = z$, i.e., if x cannot be written as the join of two elements different from itself. We show that atoms are join-irreducible. Consider an atom a and assume $a = y \vee z$ where $a \neq y$ and $a \neq z$. Then $y \neq 0$ since otherwise a would equal z. Thus $0 \prec y$; and $y \prec a$ since $y \vee a = y \vee (y \vee z)$ $= (y \vee y) \vee z = y \vee z = a$. This shows that y is between 0 and a so that a cannot be an atom. An induction-like argument establishes the following theorem; see Exercise 17.

Theorem 3   In a finite algebraic lattice, every element can be written as the join of join-irreducible elements.

EXAMPLE 5   Consider $\mathcal{P}(S)$ where S is finite. If A is a subset of S, say $A = \{a_1, \ldots, a_m\}$, then

$$A = \{a_1\} \cup \{a_2\} \cup \cdots \cup \{a_m\}.$$

This shows that A is the join [union!] of atoms, which are join-irreducible. So Theorem 3 is nearly obvious in this case. □

Let $(L, \vee, \wedge)$ be an algebraic lattice. A subset M of L is a **sublattice** provided

$$x, y \in M \quad \text{imply} \quad x \vee y \in M \quad \text{and} \quad x \wedge y \in M,$$

i.e., provided M is closed under the operations $\vee$ and $\wedge$ of L.

EXAMPLE 6   Consider the lattice $(L, \leq)$ with Hasse diagram shown in Figure 1. The figure also shows Hasse diagrams of four subposets of $(L, \leq)$. The subset $M_1 = \{t, u, v, x\}$ is a sublattice of L, since the meet and join in L of any two members of M_1 belong to M_1. The subset $M_2 = \{t, u, v, w, x\}$ is not a sublattice of L

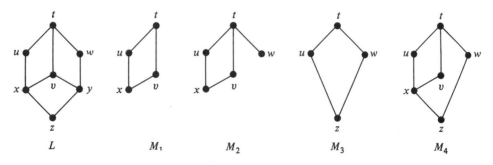

FIGURE 1

since, for example, $v \wedge w = y$ in L but $y \notin M_2$. In fact, $\{v, w\}$ has no lower bound in $(M_2, \leq)$ and so $(M_2, \leq)$ is not a lattice. The subset $M_3 = \{t, u, w, z\}$ is a sublattice of L since $u \vee w = t$ and $u \wedge w = z$ are in M_3. The subset $M_4 = \{t, u, v, w, x, z\}$ is not a sublattice of L. As was the case for M_2, M_4 does not contain $v \wedge w = y$. Notice, though, that the poset $(M_4, \leq)$ is a lattice in its own right, since z is the greatest lower bound of v and w in $(M_4, \leq)$. Thus *a subposet which is a lattice need not be a sublattice.* ☐

EXERCISES 10.1

1. Complete the proof of Theorem 1 by verifying properties 2Lb and 3Lb.

2. Verify the equalities in Example 3.

3. (a) Verify that [S] in Example 2 is a lattice.
  (b) If S contains a contradiction c, then $[c]$ is a universal lower bound. Why?
  (c) If S contains a tautology t, then $[t]$ is a universal upper bound. Why?

4. Write the duals of the following lattice equations [which are not always true].
  (a) $x \vee (y \wedge z) = (x \vee y) \wedge z$
  (b) $x \vee (y \wedge z) = (x \vee y) \wedge (x \vee z)$

5. Let L be an algebraic lattice with universal lower bound 0 and universal upper bound 1.
  (a) Is 0 join-irreducible? Explain.
  (b) Is 1 join-irreducible? Explain.

6. Consider a finite lattice $(P, \leq)$ and its Hasse diagram. Explain why an element is join-irreducible if and only if it covers at most one element.

7. Consider the lattice L in Figure 1.
  (a) List the atoms of the lattice.
  (b) List the join-irreducible elements of the lattice.
  (c) Write each element of the lattice as a join of join-irreducible elements.

8. Repeat Exercise 7 for Figure 2(a).

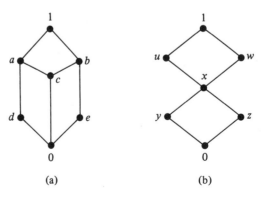

(a)   (b)

FIGURE 2

9. Consider the lattice $(\mathbb{P}, |)$; recall $m | n$ if m divides n.
   (a) What is the universal lower bound?
   (b) Does $\mathbb{P}$ have a universal upper bound?
   (c) Describe the atoms of $\mathbb{P}$.
   (d) Describe the join-irreducible elements of $\mathbb{P}$.

10. Repeat Exercise 7 for Figure 2(b).

11. Let D_{90} be the set of all divisors of 90, including 1 and 90. D_{90} is a lattice with the order $|$, where $m | n$ means m divides n.
    (a) Draw the Hasse diagram for this lattice.
    (b) Calculate $6 \vee 10$, $6 \wedge 10$, $9 \vee 30$ and $9 \wedge 30$.
    (c) List the atoms of D_{90}.
    (d) List the join-irreducible elements of D_{90}.
    (e) Write 90, 18 and 5 as joins of join-irreducible elements.

12. Find all sublattices of D_{90} that have four elements including 1 and 90.

13. Consider the lattices T and U in Figure 4 of § 7.1, page 251. Each has a universal lower bound.
    (a) List the atoms for each lattice.
    (b) Do either of these lattices have join-irreducible elements that are not atoms?
    (c) How many [nonempty] sublattices are there of T? of U?

14. For $x, y \in \mathbb{R}$ we define $x \vee y = \max\{x, y\}$ and $x \wedge y = \min\{x, y\}$.
    (a) Show that $(\mathbb{R}, \vee, \wedge)$ is an algebraic lattice.
    (b) What is the order on $\mathbb{R}$ given by Theorem 2?
    (c) Explain why all elements of $\mathbb{R}$ are join-irreducible.

15. Two algebraic lattices $(L_1, \vee, \wedge)$ and $(L_2, \cup, \cap)$ are **isomorphic** if there is a one-to-one correspondence $\phi : L_1 \to L_2$ such that

$$\phi(x \vee y) = \phi(x) \cup \phi(y) \quad \text{and} \quad \phi(x \wedge y) = \phi(x) \cap \phi(y)$$

   for all $x, y \in L_1$.
   (a) Show that in this case $\phi(x) \leq \phi(y)$ if and only if $x \leq y$.
   (b) Show that if $(L_1, \vee, \wedge)$ and $(L_2, \cup, \cap)$ are isomorphic, then x is an atom for L_1 if and only if $\phi(x)$ is an atom for L_2.
   (c) Show that the lattice L in Figure 1 is not isomorphic to the lattice in Figure 2(a).
   (d) Show that the lattice D_{30} of divisors of 30 is isomorphic to a lattice $\mathcal{P}(S)$ where $|S| = 3$. *Suggestion:* Use $S = \{2, 3, 5\}$.

16. Two algebraic lattices $(L_1, \vee, \wedge)$ and $(L_2, \cup, \cap)$ are **anti-isomorphic** if there is a one-to-one correspondence $\phi : L_1 \to L_2$ such that

$$\phi(x \vee y) = \phi(x) \cap \phi(y) \quad \text{and} \quad \phi(x \wedge y) = \phi(x) \cup \phi(y)$$

   for all $x, y \in L_1$. Show that the lattice L in Figure 1 is anti-isomorphic to the lattice in Figure 2(a). *Hint:* Turn one of their Hasse diagrams upside down.

17. Prove Theorem 3. *Hint:* If Theorem 3 fails for some finite algebraic lattice L, let B be the subset consisting of elements which aren't joins of join-irreducible

elements. Consider a minimal member m of the finite poset $(B, \leqq)$; see Exercise 10 of § 7.1.

18. Let $(P, \leqq)$ be a lattice. Show that if $x \leqq y$, then $x \vee (z \wedge y) \leqq (x \vee z) \wedge y$ for all $z \in P$.

§ 10.2   *Distributive and Boolean Lattices*

We are leading up to a discussion of Boolean algebras, which are probably the most important lattices in computer science. Their applications range from the analysis and design of electrical networks to abstract arguments in the theory of computational complexity. To begin the account we examine lattices which enjoy some, but perhaps not all, properties of Boolean algebras.

An algebraic lattice L is called a **distributive lattice** if the operations $\vee$ and $\wedge$ distribute over each other. That is, if

$$x \vee (y \wedge z) = (x \vee y) \wedge (x \vee z) \quad \text{and} \quad x \wedge (y \vee z) = (x \wedge y) \vee (x \wedge z)$$

for all $x, y, z \in L$.

EXAMPLE 1   (a) The lattice $\mathcal{P}(S)$ of subsets of a set S is a distributive lattice in view of the distributive laws in Table 1 of § 1.2.

(b) The lattice [§] of Example 2 of § 10.1 is a distributive lattice. This is a consequence of the distributive laws in Table 1 of § 2.2.

(c) Any chain, like $\mathbb{R}$ or $\mathbb{N}$ with the usual ordering, is a distributive lattice with $x \vee y = \max\{x, y\}$ and $x \wedge y = \min\{x, y\}$. One of the distributive laws says

$$\max\{x, \min\{y, z\}\} = \min\{\max\{x, y\}, \max\{x, z\}\}.$$

To verify this, we first suppose that $y \leqq z$. Then $\max\{x, y\} \leqq \max\{x, z\}$ and the asserted equality reduces to the identity

$$\max\{x, y\} = \max\{x, y\}.$$

The case $y \geqq z$ has a similar verification. The other distributive law has a similar proof.   ☐

EXAMPLE 2   (a) Consider the lattice $(\mathbb{P}, |)$ where $m | n$ means m divides n. This lattice is distributive. Here is the idea of the proof. If we write an integer k as a product of primes, each prime will occur a certain number of times, possibly 0. In particular, 2 will occur a certain number of times. Let's write $k = 2^u etc$ to signify that there are u factors of 2 in k. For examples,

$$12 = 2^2 \cdot 3 = 2^2 \ etc, \quad 62 = 2 \cdot 31 = 2^1 \ etc, \quad 64 = 2^6 \cdot 1 = 2^6 \ etc,$$

$$73 = 2^0 \ etc.$$

If $k = 2^u etc, m = 2^v etc$ and $n = 2^w etc$, then

$$k \vee m = \mathrm{lcm}\,(k, m) = 2^{\max\{u, v\}} \ etc$$

and

$$k \wedge m = \gcd(k, m) = 2^{\min\{u, v\}} \text{ etc.}$$

With this notation the distributive law $k \vee (m \wedge n) = (k \vee m) \wedge (k \vee n)$ becomes

$$2^{\max\{u, \min\{v, w\}\}} \text{ etc.} = 2^{\min\{\max\{u, v\}, \max\{u, w\}\}} \text{ etc.}$$

Example 1(c) shows that the exponents of 2 above are equal. Exactly the same argument works for counting the numbers of factors of the other primes. So when $k \vee (m \wedge n)$ and $(k \vee m) \wedge (k \vee n)$ are written as products of primes, they are identical. That is, $k \vee (m \wedge n) = (k \vee m) \wedge (k \vee n)$. The other distributive law has a similar proof.

(b) For an integer $m \geq 2$, consider the lattice $(D_m, |)$ where D_m is the set of all divisors of m. Since $(D_m, |)$ is a sublattice of $(\mathbb{P}, |)$ it is also a distributive lattice. The distributive lattice D_{12} is drawn in Figure 1(a). ▯

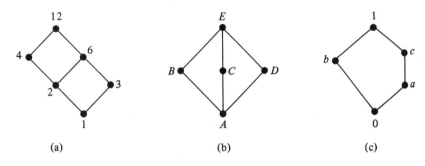

FIGURE 1

EXAMPLE 3   (a) The lattice in Figure 1(b) is not distributive. For example,

$$B \vee (C \wedge D) = B \vee A = B$$

while

$$(B \vee C) \wedge (B \vee D) = E \wedge E = E.$$

(b) The lattice in Figure 1(c) is not distributive either. For example,

$$a \vee (b \wedge c) = a \vee 0 = a$$

while

$$(a \vee b) \wedge (a \vee c) = 1 \wedge c = c. \quad ▯$$

It is interesting to note that it can be proved that a lattice is distributive if and only if it contains no sublattice that looks like either of the lattices in Figure 1(b) or 1(c). The next theorem shows that it is enough to check only one of the distributive laws, because then the other one holds automatically.

Theorem 1   For an algebraic lattice L the following properties imply each other:

(a) $x \vee (y \wedge z) = (x \vee y) \wedge (x \vee z)$ for all $x, y, z \in L$;

(b) $x \wedge (y \vee z) = (x \wedge y) \vee (x \wedge z)$ for all $x, y, z \in L$.

Proof. Suppose (a) holds. Then

$$
\begin{aligned}
(x \wedge y) \vee (x \wedge z) &= [(x \wedge y) \vee x] \wedge [(x \wedge y) \vee z] & \text{property (a)} \\
&= [x \vee (x \wedge y)] \wedge [z \vee (x \wedge y)] & \text{commutativity} \\
&= x \wedge [z \vee (x \wedge y)] & \text{absorption} \\
&= x \wedge [(z \vee x) \wedge (z \vee y)] & \text{property (a)} \\
&= [x \wedge (z \vee x)] \wedge (z \vee y) & \text{associativity} \\
&= [x \wedge (x \vee z)] \wedge (y \vee z) & \text{commutativity} \\
&= x \wedge (y \vee z) & \text{absorption.}
\end{aligned}
$$

So (a) implies (b); (b) implies (a) by the duality principle. □

For the remainder of this section we assume that L is an algebraic lattice with universal upper and lower bounds 1 and 0. Elements x and y in L are said to be **complements** if

$$x \vee y = 1 \quad \text{and} \quad x \wedge y = 0.$$

An element x in L might have no complements, might have a single unique complement or it might have more than one complement. It is easy to check that 0 and 1 are complements and that they are unique complements for each other. We call a lattice **complemented** if every element has at least one complement.

EXAMPLE 4   (a) The lattice in Figure 1(b) is complemented. The complements are not necessarily unique: both C and D are complements for B.

(b) The lattice in Figure 1(c) is also complemented. Again complements are not unique: both a and c are complements for b.

(c) The rather uninteresting lattice in Figure 2(a) illustrates a couple of important points. In the first place, it is not complemented. In fact, if we had

$$x \vee y = 1 \quad \text{and} \quad x \wedge y = 0,$$

then the first equality would force $y = 1$ while the second equality would force $y = 0$.

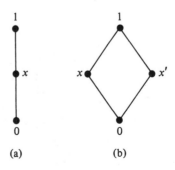

(a)   (b)

FIGURE 2

The second point is that this little lattice is distributive, as noted in Example 1(c). So distributive lattices with 1 and 0 need not be complemented. On the other hand, the next theorem shows that complements are unique in a complemented distributive lattice. ☐

Theorem 2 In a distributive lattice L with 1 and 0, if an element x has a complement then it is unique.

Proof. We assume that $x \vee y = 1, x \wedge y = 0, x \vee z = 1, x \wedge z = 0$, and will show $y = z$. Indeed

$$
\begin{aligned}
y &= y \vee 0 && \text{since } 0 \leq y \\
&= y \vee (x \wedge z) && \text{since } x \wedge z = 0 \\
&= (y \vee x) \wedge (y \vee z) && \text{distributive law} \\
&= 1 \wedge (y \vee z) && \text{since } y \vee x = x \vee y = 1 \\
&= (x \vee z) \wedge (y \vee z) && \text{since } x \vee z = 1 \\
&= (x \wedge y) \vee z && \text{distributive law} \\
&= 0 \vee z && \text{since } x \wedge y = 0 \\
&= z && \text{since } 0 \leq z. \quad ☐
\end{aligned}
$$

For a general lattice in which unique complements exist, we will often write x' for the complement of x. Then

$$x \vee x' = 1 \quad \text{and} \quad x \wedge x' = 0.$$

Note that in such a lattice, each x belongs to a sublattice that looks like Figure 2(b) where $(x')' = x$. It follows that the correspondence $x \to x'$ assigning each element to its complement is a one-to-one function from L onto itself.

A distributive lattice that is complemented is called a **Boolean lattice**. Such a lattice is a set with two binary operations, $\vee$ and $\wedge$, and a "unary operation," $x \to x'$, that satisfy a number of properties which we have already discussed. Boolean lattices are sometimes called Boolean algebras. They are usually called lattices when the emphasis is on the underlying partial order, while they are called algebras when the stress is on the algebraic operations $\vee$, $\wedge$ and $'$. In the next section we will define Boolean algebras in a purely algebraic way and we will show that the new definition and our present one coincide.

EXAMPLE 5 (a) Recall that $\mathcal{P}(S)$ is a distributive lattice with universal upper and lower bounds S and $\varnothing$. For any A in $\mathcal{P}(S)$,

$$A \cup A^c = S \quad \text{and} \quad A \cap A^c = \varnothing$$

and so $\mathcal{P}(S)$ is a complemented lattice with $A' = A^c$, and hence is a Boolean lattice. The complement of the element A in the lattice $\mathcal{P}(S)$ is the complement of the set A. This is clearly where complemented lattices got their name.

(b) The lattice [$\mathcal{S}$] of Example 2 of § 10.1 is a distributive lattice with universal upper and lower bounds $[t]$ and $[c]$, provided $\mathcal{S}$ contains a tautology t and a contradiction c. See Example 1(b) and also Exercise 3 of § 10.1. [$\mathcal{S}$] is a Boolean lattice if

$$P \in \mathcal{S} \quad \text{implies} \quad \neg P \in \mathcal{S}.$$

This is because

$$[P] \vee [\neg P] = [t] \quad \text{and} \quad [P] \wedge [\neg P] = [c]$$

which follow from rules 7 in Table 1 of § 2.2.

(c) Of course $(\mathbb{P}, |)$ is not a Boolean lattice; it doesn't have a universal upper bound. Some of its sublattices $(D_m, |)$ are Boolean and some aren't. For example, in the lattice D_{12} of Figure 1, the elements 2 and 6 have no complements. See Exercise 5 for more about this. □

We now have a general setting in which to prove the **DeMorgan laws**.

Theorem 3 If L is a Boolean lattice, then

$$(x \vee y)' = x' \wedge y' \quad \text{and} \quad (x \wedge y)' = x' \vee y'$$

for all $x, y \in L$.

Proof. We have

$$(x \vee y) \vee (x' \wedge y') = [(x \vee y) \vee x'] \wedge [(x \vee y) \vee y'] \quad \text{distributivity}$$

$$= [y \vee (x \vee x')] \wedge [x \vee (y \vee y')]$$

$$\text{associativity and commutativity}$$

$$= [y \vee 1] \wedge [x \vee 1] = 1 \wedge 1 = 1.$$

Similarly $(x \vee y) \wedge (x' \wedge y') = 0$, and so $(x \vee y)' = x' \wedge y'$.

The other DeMorgan law has an analogous proof. Since $(z')' = z$ for all z, we can also derive the other law from the one already proved:

$$x \wedge y = (x')' \wedge (y')' = (x' \vee y')'$$

and so

$$(x \wedge y)' = (x' \vee y')'' = x' \vee y'. \quad □$$

Suppose we interchange $\vee$ and $\wedge$ in some formula valid in a Boolean lattice L. Since 1 is defined by $x \vee 1 = 1$ for all x, and 0 by $x \wedge 0 = 0$ for all x, the elements 0 and 1 also switch roles. The conditions

$$x \vee x' = 1 \quad \text{and} \quad x \wedge x' = 0$$

become

$$x \wedge x' = 0 \quad \text{and} \quad x \vee x' = 1$$

and so the defining properties of x' are not changed by the switch. These remarks show that the following **duality principle** holds for Boolean lattices: if $\vee$ and $\wedge$ are interchanged and 0 and 1 are interchanged throughout a valid formula, another valid formula is obtained. In terms of the partial order $\leqq$

on L, the duality principle holds because the inverse partial order $\geqq$ also makes L a Boolean lattice.

EXERCISES 10.2

1. Consider the lattice L_1 with Hasse diagram in Figure 3(a).
   (a) List all the atoms of L_1.
   (b) List all join-irreducible elements of L_1.
   (c) Write 1 as the join of join-irreducible elements.
   (d) Give the complements, if they exist, for the following: $a, b, d, 0$.
   (e) Is L_1 a complemented lattice? Explain.
   (f) Is L_1 a distributive lattice? *Hint:* Use Theorem 2.

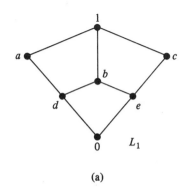 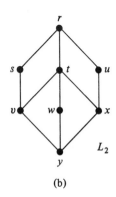

(a)   (b)

FIGURE 3

2. Consider the lattice L_2 with Hasse diagram in Figure 3(b).
   (a) Give the universal upper and lower bounds for L_2.
   (b) Find $v \vee x$, $s \vee v$ and $u \wedge v$.
   (c) Is L_2 a complemented lattice? Explain.
   (d) Find an element that has two complements.
   (e) Is L_2 a distributive lattice? Explain.

3. (a) Show that the elements 2 and 6 in the lattice D_{12} have no complements.
   (b) Consider any integer $m \geqq 2$. Prove that D_m is complemented if and only if m is a product of *distinct* primes, i.e., no prime appears more than once when m is written as a product of primes.

4. (a) Draw the Hasse diagram for the lattice $(D_{24}, |)$.
   (b) Give the complements, if they exist, for the following: 2, 3, 4, 6.
   (c) Is D_{24} a complemented lattice? Explain.
   (d) Is D_{24} a distributive lattice? Explain.
   (e) Is D_{24} a Boolean lattice? Explain.

5. (a) Show that Figure 4(a) is the Hasse diagram for the lattice $(D_{36}, |)$.
   (b) Is the lattice distributive?
   (c) Is it complemented?

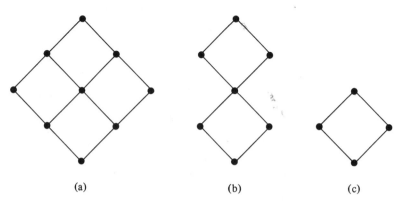

(a)   (b)   (c)

FIGURE 4

6. (a) Show that Figure 4(b) is the Hasse diagram for a distributive lattice.
   (b) Is it complemented? Explain.

7. Repeat Exercise 6 for Figure 4(c).

8. (a) Find the atoms for the lattice in Figure 1(a).
   (b) Find the join-irreducible elements.
   (c) Write the universal upper bound as the join of join-irreducible elements.

9. Repeat Exercise 8 for $(D_{36}, |)$ shown in Figure 4(a).

10. (a) Which chains have universal upper and lower bounds?
    (b) Which chains are distributive?
    (c) Which chains are complemented?

11. Let L be a distributive lattice. Prove that if x, y in L satisfy $x \vee a = y \vee a$ and $x \wedge a = y \wedge a$ for some $a \in L$, then $x = y$.

12. Use Theorem 2 to show that the lattices in Figures 1(b) and 1(c) are not distributive.

13. Let L be a lattice with 1 and 0. Show that 0 is the unique complement for 1 and vice versa.

14. Prove or disprove.
    (a) Every finite lattice is distributive.
    (b) Every finite lattice has a universal lower bound.

15. Let L be a Boolean lattice.
    (a) Prove that if $x \leqq y$ then $y' \leqq x'$.
    (b) Prove that if $y \wedge z = 0$ then $y \leqq z'$.
    (c) Prove that if $x \leqq y$ and $y \wedge z = 0$ then $z \leqq x'$.

§ 10.3 *Boolean Algebras*

Consider a Boolean lattice $(L, \leqq)$ with associated operations $\vee$, $\wedge$ and correspondence $x \to x'$. The lattice properties, the distributivity, and the existence of universal upper and lower bounds and complements translate into the following algebraic laws.

1Ba. $x \vee y = y \vee x$
  b. $x \wedge y = y \wedge x$ commutative laws

2Ba. $(x \vee y) \vee z = x \vee (y \vee z)$
  b. $(x \wedge y) \wedge z = x \wedge (y \wedge z)$ associative laws

3Ba. $x \vee (y \wedge z) = (x \vee y) \wedge (x \vee z)$
  b. $x \wedge (y \vee z) = (x \wedge y) \vee (x \wedge z)$ distributive laws

4Ba. $0 \vee x = x$
  b. $x \wedge 1 = x$ identity laws

5Ba. $x \vee x' = 1$
  b. $x \wedge x' = 0.$

We define a **Boolean algebra** to be a set with two binary operations $\vee$ and $\wedge$, a unary operation $'$ and distinct elements 0 and 1 satisfying these laws. Note that Boolean algebras satisfy the same principle of duality as stated for Boolean lattices at the end of § 10.2 [and for the same reasons].

Theorem 1 The following properties hold in a Boolean algebra:

6Ba. $x \vee x = x$
  b. $x \wedge x = x$ idempotent laws

7Ba. $x \vee 1 = 1$
  b. $x \wedge 0 = 0$ more identity laws

8Ba. $x \vee (x \wedge y) = x$
  b. $x \wedge (x \vee y) = x$ absorption laws

Proof. Here is 6Ba:

$$
\begin{aligned}
x \vee x &= (x \vee x) \wedge 1 & \text{identity law 4Bb}\\
&= (x \vee x) \wedge (x \vee x') & \text{5Ba}\\
&= x \vee (x \wedge x') & \text{distributive law 3Ba}\\
&= x \vee 0 & \text{5Bb}\\
&= 0 \vee x & \text{commutative law 1Ba}\\
&= x & \text{identity law 4Ba.}
\end{aligned}
$$

For 7Ba, observe

$$
\begin{aligned}
x \vee 1 &= x \vee (x \vee x') & \text{5Ba}\\
&= (x \vee x) \vee x' & \text{associative law 2Ba}\\
&= x \vee x' & \text{idempotent law 6Ba}\\
&= 1 & \text{5Ba.}
\end{aligned}
$$

And for 8Ba, we have

$$
\begin{aligned}
x \vee (x \wedge y) &= (x \wedge 1) \vee (x \wedge y) & \text{identity law 4Bb}\\
&= x \wedge (1 \vee y) & \text{distributive law 3Bb}\\
&= x \wedge (y \vee 1) & \text{commutative law 1Ba}\\
&= x \wedge 1 & \text{identity law 7Ba}\\
&= x & \text{identity law 4Bb.}
\end{aligned}
$$

Now 6Bb, 7Bb and 8Bb follow by duality. □

It turns out that the associative laws are redundant in the definition of a Boolean algebra. They are a consequence of the other defining laws for a Boolean algebra. In fact, Theorem 1 can be proved without using the associative laws. Proofs of these facts are tedious and not very informative, so we omit them.

Theorem 2   Boolean lattices are Boolean algebras and Boolean algebras are Boolean lattices.

Proof. We have already seen that Boolean lattices satisfy the laws 1Ba through 5Bb which define Boolean algebras. Now consider a Boolean algebra *A*. The absorption laws 8Ba and 8Bb proved in Theorem 1 together with 1Ba through 2Bb show that *A* is an algebraic lattice. Properties 3Ba through 5Bb show that *A* is distributive and complemented. Thus *A* is a Boolean lattice.   ☐

The theorem just proved shows that Boolean algebras satisfy any properties established for Boolean lattices. In particular, the DeMorgan laws hold by Theorem 3 of § 10.2:

9Ba. $(x \vee y)' = x' \wedge y'$
   b. $(x \wedge y)' = x' \vee y'$ }   DeMorgan laws.

EXAMPLE 1   (a) The Boolean lattices in Example 5 of § 10.2 are Boolean algebras. In particular, $\mathcal{P}(S)$ is a Boolean algebra with respect to the operations $\cup$, $\cap$ and complementation.

(b) We will see that every finite Boolean algebra, regardless of the setting in which it arises or the notation used, looks like [that is, is isomorphic to] $\mathcal{P}(S)$ for some finite set *S*. A very simple but important Boolean algebra is $\mathbb{B} = \{0, 1\}$ where $\vee$ and $\wedge$ are the usual Boolean operations "or" and "and" [Table 1 of § 7.5], $0' = 1$ and $1' = 0$.

(c) In Example 4(b) of § 10.1 we observed that the set $\mathrm{FUN}(S, \mathbb{B})$ of functions from *S* to $\mathbb{B} = \{0, 1\}$ is a lattice. Note that

$$(f \vee g)(x) = f(x) \vee g(x)$$

and

$$(f \wedge g)(x) = f(x) \wedge g(x)$$

for all $x \in S$; the operations $\vee$ and $\wedge$ on the right side are the operations in $\mathbb{B}$ mentioned in part (b). If we also define

$$(f')(x) = f(x)' \quad \text{for all} \quad x \in S,$$

then $\mathrm{FUN}(S, \mathbb{B})$ is a Boolean algebra. The universal lower bound is the constant function on *S* equal to 0 everywhere, and the universal upper bound is the constant function equal to 1 everywhere.

If $S = \{1, 2, \ldots, n\}$ we may write $\mathrm{FUN}(S, \mathbb{B})$ as $\mathbb{B}^n$ and view $\mathbb{B}^n$ as the set of all *n*-tuples of elements from $\mathbb{B} = \{0, 1\}$. The Boolean operations are then defined coordinatewise. For example [with $n = 3$], we have

$$\langle 1, 0, 1 \rangle \vee \langle 0, 1, 1 \rangle = \langle 1, 1, 1 \rangle,$$

$$\langle 1, 0, 1 \rangle \wedge \langle 0, 1, 1 \rangle = \langle 0, 0, 1 \rangle \quad \text{and} \quad \langle 1, 0, 1 \rangle' = \langle 0, 1, 0 \rangle.$$

The universal upper and lower bounds are $\langle 1, 1, 1 \rangle$ and $\langle 0, 0, 0 \rangle$. The atoms have exactly one entry equal to 1 and so the atoms are $\langle 1, 0, 0 \rangle, \langle 0, 1, 0 \rangle$ and $\langle 0, 0, 1 \rangle$. ▯

We next show that the atoms of a finite Boolean algebra are the building blocks for the algebra. Compare the result with Theorem 3 of § 10.1.

Theorem 3   Let A be a finite Boolean algebra with set of atoms $S = \{a_1, \ldots, a_n\}$. Each x in A can be written as a join of distinct atoms:

$$(1) \qquad\qquad\qquad x = a_{i_1} \vee \cdots \vee a_{i_k}.$$

Moreover, such an expression is unique, except for the order of the atoms. Indeed, the atoms $a_{i_1}, \ldots, a_{i_k}$ are precisely the atoms $\leq x$.

Proof. The proof that every element has the form (1) is a sort of induction. First we explain the idea. If $x = 0$ or x is an atom, we're done. Otherwise, there is a y in A such that $0 \prec y \prec x$. Then

$$x = x \vee y = (x \vee y) \wedge (y' \vee y) = (x \wedge y') \vee y.$$

Moreover, we have $x \wedge y' \prec x$ because otherwise $x \wedge y' = x, y \prec x = x \wedge y' \leq y'$ and $y \wedge y' = y$, which is impossible. So x is the join of the two smaller elements y and $x \wedge y'$. [Note that this shows that only atoms and 0 are join-irreducible.] If both y and $x \wedge y'$ are atoms, we're done. Otherwise we decompose them further into joins of smaller elements. Since A is finite, this process eventually stops and we've split x into a join of atoms. A recursive algorithm for finding an expression as a join of atoms can be based on this method.

A formal proof of (1) proceeds along the following lines. Assume some elements do not have the form (1) and let B be the nonempty subset of all such x. The poset $(B, \leq)$ has a smallest element. As in the last paragraph, the smallest element can be decomposed as the join of smaller elements. These smaller elements are not in B, so each is the join of atoms. Then the smallest element of B is also a join of atoms, a contradiction.

We next show that each x in A satisfies

$$(2) \qquad\qquad\qquad x = \vee\, \{a \in S : a \leq x\};$$

the notation on the right represents the join of all the elements in the set $\{a \in S : a \leq x\}$. We assume $x \neq 0$, since we view 0 as the join of the empty set of atoms. By (1), we know that 1 is the join of a set of atoms. It follows that

$$1 = \vee\, \{a \in S : a \leq 1\} = a_1 \vee \cdots \vee a_n,$$

since we could add the remaining atoms without destroying the identity. [Actually, in view of the theorem we are proving, there won't be any remaining atoms, but we don't know this yet.] Now

$$x = x \wedge 1 = x \wedge (a_1 \vee \cdots \vee a_n) = (x \wedge a_1) \vee \cdots \vee (x \wedge a_n).$$

Since $x \wedge a_i = a_i$ if $a_i \leq x$ and $x \wedge a_i = 0$ otherwise, this establishes the equality (2).

To check uniqueness, suppose $x = b_1 \vee \cdots \vee b_k$ is an expression for x as a join of atoms. Then $b_i \leq x$ for each i and so all the b_i's belong to $\{a \in S : a \leq x\}$. On the other hand, if $a \in S$ and $a \leq x$, then

$$0 \neq a = a \wedge x = a \wedge (b_1 \vee \cdots \vee b_k) = (a \wedge b_1) \vee \cdots \vee (a \wedge b_k).$$

Some $a \wedge b_i$ must be different from 0 and so $a \wedge b_i = a = b_i$ since a and b_i are atoms. Thus a is one of the b_i's. Consequently $\{b_1, \ldots, b_k\}$ is precisely the set of atoms $\leq x$. ☐

The next theorem tells us that a Boolean algebra is completely determined [up to isomorphism] by the number of atoms it has.

Theorem 4 If A is a finite Boolean algebra with set of atoms $S = \{a_1, \ldots, a_n\}$ and if B is a finite Boolean algebra with set of atoms $T = \{b_1, \ldots, b_n\}$, then there is a one-to-one correspondence ϕ of A onto B such that $\phi(a_i) = b_i$ for each i,

(1) $$\phi(x \vee y) = \phi(x) \vee \phi(y),$$

(2) $$\phi(x \wedge y) = \phi(x) \wedge \phi(y)$$

and

(3) $$\phi(x') = \phi(x)'$$

for all $x, y \in A$.

A one-to-one correspondence ϕ between Boolean algebras which satisfies properties (1), (2) and (3) is called a **Boolean algebra isomorphism**.

Proof. By Theorem 3, every x in A can be written uniquely in the form

$$x = a_{i_1} \vee \cdots \vee a_{i_k}.$$

We define

$$\phi(x) = b_{i_1} \vee \cdots \vee b_{i_k}.$$

In particular,

$$\phi(a_i) = b_i \quad \text{for} \quad i = 1, 2, \ldots, n.$$

By our definition and Theorem 3,

$$\phi(x) = \vee \{\phi(a) : a \in S \quad \text{and} \quad a \leq x\}$$

and also

$$\phi(x) = \vee \{b : b \in T \quad \text{and} \quad b \leq \phi(x)\}.$$

Since the expression for $\phi(x)$ is unique, we conclude that

(4) $a \leqq x$ if and only if $\phi(a) \leqq \phi(x)$

for $a \in S$. To verify (1), consider x, y in A and note that for $a \in S$:

$$\phi(a) \leqq \phi(x \vee y) \Leftrightarrow a \leqq (x \vee y) \Leftrightarrow a \leqq x \text{ or } a \leqq y \qquad [\text{see Exercise 9(a)}]$$
$$\Leftrightarrow \phi(a) \leqq \phi(x) \text{ or } \phi(a) \leqq \phi(y).$$

That is, for $b \in T$:

$$b \leqq \phi(x \vee y) \Leftrightarrow b \leqq \phi(x) \text{ or } b \leqq \phi(y) \Leftrightarrow b \leqq \phi(x) \vee \phi(y).$$

It follows from Theorem 3 applied to B that $\phi(x \vee y) = \phi(x) \vee \phi(y)$. Assertion (2) has a similar proof. Now

$$\phi(x) \vee \phi(x') = \phi(x \vee x') = \phi(1)$$

and

$$\phi(x) \wedge \phi(x') = \phi(x \wedge x') = \phi(0),$$

so $\phi(x') = \phi(x)'$.   ☐

If a set S has n elements, then the Boolean algebra $\mathcal{P}(S)$ [with operations $\cup, \cap$ and complementation] has exactly n atoms, namely the one-element subsets of S. So we have the following corollary.

Corollary   Every finite Boolean algebra with n atoms is isomorphic to the Boolean algebra $\mathcal{P}(S)$ of all subsets of an n-element set S, and hence has exactly 2^n elements.

As we have already indicated, finite Boolean algebras often arise in contexts different from $\mathcal{P}(S)$. Again let $\mathbb{B} = \{0, 1\}$ and for $n = 1, 2, \ldots$ let $\mathbb{B}^n$ be the Boolean algebra of Example 1. An **n-variable Boolean function** is a function

$$f : \mathbb{B}^n \to \mathbb{B}.$$

We write $\mathfrak{F}_n$ for the set of all n-variable Boolean functions, and if $f \in \mathfrak{F}_n$ and $\langle a_1, \ldots, a_n \rangle \in \mathbb{B}^n$ with each $a_i = 0$ or 1 we write $f(a_1, \ldots, a_n)$ for the value $f(\langle a_1, \ldots, a_n \rangle)$.

EXAMPLE 2   A 3-variable Boolean function is an f such that $f(a, b, c) = 0$ or 1 for each of the 2^3 choices of a, b and c. We could think of setting each of three switches to one of two positions. Then f behaves like a black box which produces an output of 0 or 1 depending on the settings of the switches and the internal structure of the box. Since there are 8 ways to set the switches and each setting can lead to either of 2 outputs, depending on the function, there are $2^8 = 256$ 3-variable Boolean functions. That is, $|\mathfrak{F}_3| = 256$.

A 3-variable Boolean function f can be viewed as a column in a truth table, for example:

a	b	c	f
0	0	0	1
0	0	1	1
0	1	0	0
0	1	1	1
1	0	0	0
1	0	1	0
1	1	0	0
1	1	1	1

This is just one of the 256 possible tables, since column f can be any arrangement of 0's and 1's. □

The counting argument in Example 2 works in general, so that $|\mathfrak{F}_n|$ $= 2^{(2^n)}$, a very big number unless n is very small. Just as in Example 1(c), $\mathfrak{F}_n$ is a Boolean algebra with the Boolean operations defined coordinatewise.

EXAMPLE 3   We illustrate the Boolean operations in $\mathfrak{F}_3$ in the following truth table for the indicated functions f and g:

a	b	c	f	g	$f \vee g$	$f \wedge g$	f'	$f' \wedge g$
0	0	0	1	0	1	0	0	0
0	0	1	1	1	1	1	0	0
0	1	0	0	0	0	0	1	0
0	1	1	1	0	1	0	0	0
1	0	0	0	1	1	0	1	1
1	0	1	0	0	0	0	1	0
1	1	0	0	1	1	0	1	1
1	1	1	1	0	1	0	0	0

Note that, since $f \wedge g$ takes the value 1 at exactly one point in $\mathbb{B}^3$, it is an atom of the Boolean algebra $\mathfrak{F}_3$. There are seven other atoms in $\mathfrak{F}_3$. As usual, it is of interest to write any member of a Boolean algebra, in this instance $\mathfrak{F}_3$, as a join of atoms. In the next section we will indicate how this is done using Boolean expressions. □

EXERCISES 10.3

1. (a) Verify that $\mathbb{B} = \{0, 1\}$ in Example 1(b) is a Boolean algebra by checking some of the laws 1Ba through 5Bb.
   (b) Do the same for FUN(S, $\mathbb{B}$) in Example 1(c).

2. (a) Let $S = \{a, b, c, d, e\}$ and write $\{a, c, d\}$ as a join of atoms in $\mathcal{P}(S)$.
   (b) Write $\langle 1, 0, 1, 1, 0 \rangle$ as a join of atoms in $\mathbb{B}^5$.
   (c) Let f be the function in FUN(S, $\mathbb{B}$) that maps a, c and d to 1 and b and e to 0. Write f as a join of atoms in FUN(S, $\mathbb{B}$).

3. The lattice $(D_{30}, |)$ is a Boolean lattice [Exercise 3 of § 10.2] and hence a Boolean algebra.
   (a) Draw a Hasse diagram for this poset.
   (b) List the atoms of D_{30}.
   (c) Find all Boolean subalgebras of D_{30}. Note that the subalgebras must contain 1 and 30.
   (d) Find a sublattice with four elements that is not a Boolean subalgebra.

4. The lattice $(D_{210}, |)$ is a Boolean algebra. Find a set S so that $\mathcal{P}(S)$ and D_{210} are isomorphic Boolean algebras and exhibit an isomorphism between them.

5. Find a set S so that $\mathcal{P}(S)$ and $\mathbb{B}^5$ are isomorphic Boolean algebras. Exhibit a Boolean algebra isomorphism from $\mathbb{B}^5$ to $\mathcal{P}(S)$.

6. Describe the atoms of $\text{FUN}(S, \mathbb{B})$ in Example 1(c). Is your description valid even if S is infinite?

7. (a) Is there a Boolean algebra with 6 elements? Explain.
   (b) Is every finite Boolean algebra isomorphic to a Boolean algebra $\mathcal{F}_n$ of Boolean functions? Explain.

8. (a) Describe the atoms of the lattice $\mathcal{P}(\mathbb{N})$.
   (b) Is every member of the lattice the join of atoms? Discuss.

9. Let x, y be elements of a Boolean algebra, and let a be an atom.
   (a) Show that $a \leq x \vee y$ if and only if $a \leq x$ or $a \leq y$.
   (b) Show that $a \leq x \wedge y$ if and only if $a \leq x$ and $a \leq y$.
   (c) Show that either $a \leq x$ or $a \leq x'$ and not both.

10. Let x and y be elements of a finite Boolean algebra, each written as a join of atoms:
$$x = a_1 \vee \cdots \vee a_n \quad \text{and} \quad y = b_1 \vee \cdots \vee b_m.$$
   (a) Explain how to write $x \vee y$ and $x \wedge y$ as joins of distinct atoms. Illustrate with examples.
   (b) How would you write x' as the join of distinct atoms?

11. Show that if ϕ is a Boolean algebra isomorphism between Boolean algebras A and B, then $x \leq y$ if and only if $\phi(x) \leq \phi(y)$.

12. Let $S = [0, 1)$ and let $\mathcal{C}$ consist of the empty set $\varnothing$ and all subsets of S that can be written as a finite union of intervals of the form $[a, b)$.
   (a) Show that each member of $\mathcal{C}$ can be written as a finite *disjoint* union of intervals of the form $[a, b)$.
   (b) Show that $\mathcal{C}$ is a Boolean algebra with respect to the operations $\cup$, $\cap$ and complementation.
   (c) Show that $\mathcal{C}$ has no atoms whatever.

§ 10.4 *Boolean Expressions*

The main purpose of this section is to introduce the mathematical terminology and ideas which are used in applying Boolean algebra methods to circuit design and logical analysis. The next section will discuss the applications themselves more fully.

A Boolean expression is a string of symbols involving 0 and 1, some variables and the Boolean operations. To be more precise, we define **Boolean expressions in n variables** $x_1, x_2, \ldots, x_n$ recursively by:

(B) The symbols 0 and 1 and $x_1, x_2, \ldots, x_n$ are Boolean expressions in $x_1, \ldots, x_n$.

(R) If E_1 and E_2 are Boolean expressions in $x_1, x_2, \ldots, x_n$ so are $(E_1 \vee E_2), (E_1 \wedge E_2)$ and E_1'.

As usual, in practice we will normally omit the outside parentheses and will freely use the associative laws.

EXAMPLE 1   (a) Here are four Boolean expressions in the three variables x, y, z:

$$(x \vee y) \wedge (x' \vee z) \wedge 1; \qquad (x' \wedge z) \vee (x' \wedge y) \vee z'; \qquad x \vee y; \qquad z.$$

The first two obviously involve all three variables. The last two don't. Whether we regard $x \vee y$ as an expression in two or three or more variables often doesn't matter. When it does matter and the context doesn't make the variables clear, we will be careful to say how we are viewing the expression.

The Boolean expressions 0 and 1 can be viewed as expressions in any number of variables, just as constant functions can be viewed as functions of one or of several variables.

(b) An example of a Boolean expression in n variables is

$$(x_1 \wedge x_2 \wedge \cdots \wedge x_n) \vee (x_1' \wedge x_2 \wedge \cdots \wedge x_n)$$
$$\vee (x_1 \wedge x_2' \wedge x_3 \wedge \cdots \wedge x_n). \quad \square$$

The usage of both symbols $\vee$ and $\wedge$ leads to bulky and awkward Boolean expressions, so we will usually replace the connective $\wedge$ by a dot or no symbol at all.

EXAMPLE 2   (a) With this new convention for $\wedge$, the first two Boolean expressions in Example 1(a) can be written as

$$(x \vee y) \cdot (x' \vee z) \cdot 1 \quad \text{and} \quad (x'z) \vee (x'y) \vee z'$$

or, more simply, as

$$(x \vee y)(x' \vee z)1 \quad \text{and} \quad x'z \vee x'y \vee z';$$

just as in ordinary algebra, the "product" $\wedge$ or $\cdot$ takes precedence over the "sum" $\vee$.

(b) The Boolean expression in Example 1(b) is

$$x_1 x_2 \cdots x_n \vee x_1' x_2 \cdots x_n \vee x_1 x_2' x_3 \cdots x_n.$$

(c) The expression $xyz \vee xy'z \vee x'z$ is shorthand for

$$(x \wedge y \wedge z) \vee (x \wedge y' \wedge z) \vee (x' \wedge z). \quad \square$$

If we substitute 0 or 1 for each occurrence of each variable in a Boolean expression, we get an expression involving $0, 1, \vee, \wedge$ and $'$ which has a meaning as a member of the Boolean algebra $\mathbb{B} = \{0, 1\}$. For example, replacing x by 0, y by 1 and z by 1 in the Boolean expression $x'z \vee x'y \vee z'$ gives

$$0'1 \vee 0'1 \vee 1' = (1 \wedge 1) \vee (1 \wedge 1) \vee 0 = 1 \vee 1 \vee 0 = 1.$$

In general, if E is a Boolean expression in the n variables $x_1, x_2, \ldots, x_n$, then E defines a **Boolean function** mapping $\mathbb{B}^n$ into $\mathbb{B}$ whose function value at $\langle a_1, a_2, \ldots, a_n \rangle$ is the element of $\mathbb{B}$ obtained by replacing x_1 by a_1, x_2 by a_2, $\ldots$, and x_n by a_n in E.

EXAMPLE 3   The Boolean function mapping $\mathbb{B}^3$ into $\mathbb{B}$ that corresponds to $x'z \vee x'y \vee z'$ is given in the following table where, just as with truth tables for propositions, we first calculate the Boolean functions for some of the subexpressions. The

x	y	z	$x'z$	$x'y$	z'	$x'z \vee x'y \vee z'$
0	0	0	0	0	1	1
0	0	1	1	0	0	1
0	1	0	0	1	1	1
0	1	1	1	1	0	1
1	0	0	0	0	1	1
1	0	1	0	0	0	0
1	1	0	0	0	1	1
1	1	1	0	0	0	0

fourth entry in the last column is the value we calculated a moment ago. Note that the Boolean expression z' corresponds to the function on $\mathbb{B}^3$ that maps each triple $\langle a, b, c \rangle$ to c' where $a, b, c \in \{0, 1\}$. Similarly, z corresponds to the function that maps each $\langle a, b, c \rangle$ to c.   □

We will regard two Boolean expressions as **equivalent** provided their corresponding Boolean functions are the same. For instance, $x(y \vee z)$ and $(xy) \vee (xz)$ are equivalent, since each corresponds to the function with value 1 at $\langle a, b, c \rangle = \langle 1, 1, 0 \rangle, \langle 1, 0, 1 \rangle$ or $\langle 1, 1, 1 \rangle$ and 0 otherwise. We will write $x(y \vee z) = (xy) \vee (xz)$, and in general we will write $E = F$ if the two Boolean expressions E and F are equivalent. The usage of "$=$" to denote this equivalence relation is customary and seems to cause no confusion.

The use of notation in this way is familiar from our experience with algebraic expressions and algebraic functions on $\mathbb{R}$. Technically, the algebraic expressions $(x + 1)(x - 1)$ and $x^2 - 1$ are different [because they *look* different] but the functions f and g defined by

$$f(x) = (x + 1)(x - 1) \quad \text{and} \quad g(x) = x^2 - 1$$

are equal. We regard the two expressions as equivalent and commonly use either $(x + 1)(x - 1)$ or $x^2 - 1$ as a name for the function they define. Similarly, we will often use Boolean expressions as names for the Boolean functions they define.

EXAMPLE 4   The function in $\mathfrak{F}_3$ named xy is defined by $xy(\langle a, b, c \rangle) = ab$ for all $\langle a, b, c \rangle$ in $\mathbb{B}^3$, so

$$xy(\langle a, b, c \rangle) = \begin{cases} 1 & \text{if } a = b = 1, \\ 0 & \text{otherwise.} \end{cases}$$

Similarly the functions named $x \vee z'$ and $xy'z$ satisfy

$$(x \vee z')(\langle a, b, c \rangle) = a \vee c' = \begin{cases} 1 & \text{if } a = 1 \quad \text{or} \quad c = 0, \\ 0 & \text{otherwise,} \end{cases}$$

and

$$xy'z(\langle a, b, c \rangle) = ab'c = \begin{cases} 1 & \text{if } a = 1, \ b = 0, \ c = 1, \\ 0 & \text{otherwise.} \end{cases}$$

Since $xy'z$ takes the value 1 at exactly one point in $\mathbb{B}^3$, it is an atom of the Boolean algebra $\mathfrak{F}_3$. The other seven atoms in $\mathfrak{F}_3$ are

$$xyz, \quad xyz', \quad xy'z', \quad x'yz, \quad x'yz', \quad x'y'z \quad \text{and} \quad x'y'z'. \quad \square$$

Suppose that E_1, E_2, E_3 are Boolean expressions in n variables. Since $\mathfrak{F}_n$ is a Boolean algebra, the Boolean expressions $E_1(E_2 \vee E_3)$ and $(E_1 E_2)$ $\vee (E_1 E_3)$ define the same function. Thus the two expressions are equivalent, and we can write the distributive law

$$E_1(E_2 \vee E_3) = (E_1 E_2) \vee (E_1 E_3).$$

In the same way, Boolean expressions satisfy all the other laws of a Boolean algebra as well, so long as we are willing to write equivalences as if they were equations.

Boolean expressions such as x or y' consisting of a single variable or its complement are called **literals**. The functions which correspond to them have the value 1 at half of the elements of $\mathbb{B}^n$. For example, the literal y' for $n = 3$ corresponds to the function with value 1 at all points $\langle a, 0, c \rangle$ in $\mathbb{B}^3$ and value 0 at all points $\langle a, 1, c \rangle$.

We saw in Example 4(b) of § 10.1 and Example 1(c) of § 10.3 that the atoms of $\mathfrak{F}_n$ are the functions which have the value 1 at exactly one member of $\mathbb{B}^n$. Each atom corresponds to a Boolean expression of a special form, called a minterm. A **minterm** in n variables is a meet [i.e., product] of n literals, each involving a different variable.

EXAMPLE 5   (a) The expressions $xy'z'$ and $x'yz'$ are minterms in the three variables x, y, z. The corresponding functions in $\mathfrak{F}_3$ have the value 1 only at $\langle 1, 0, 0 \rangle$ and $\langle 0, 1, 0 \rangle$, respectively.

(b) The expression xz' is a minterm in the two variables x, z. It is not a minterm in the three variables x, y, z; the corresponding function in $\mathfrak{F}_3$ has value 1 both at $\langle 1, 0, 0 \rangle$ and at $\langle 1, 1, 0 \rangle$.

(c) The expression $xyx'z$ is not a minterm since it involves the variable x in more than one literal. In fact, this expression is equivalent to 0. The expression $xy'zx$ is not a minterm either; it is equivalent to the minterm $xy'z$ in x, y, z, however.

(d) In the following table we list the eight elements of $\mathbb{B}^3$ and the corresponding minterms that take the value 1 at the indicated elements. Note that the literals corresponding to 0 entries are complemented while the other literals are not.

$\langle a, b, c \rangle$	Minterm with value 1 at $\langle a, b, c \rangle$
$\langle 0, 0, 0 \rangle$	$x'y'z'$
$\langle 0, 0, 1 \rangle$	$x'y'z$
$\langle 0, 1, 0 \rangle$	$x'yz'$
$\langle 0, 1, 1 \rangle$	$x'yz$
$\langle 1, 0, 0 \rangle$	$xy'z'$
$\langle 1, 0, 1 \rangle$	$xy'z$
$\langle 1, 1, 0 \rangle$	xyz'
$\langle 1, 1, 1 \rangle$	xyz

$\square$

According to Theorem 3 of § 10.3, every member of $\mathfrak{F}_n$ can be written as a join of atoms. Since atoms in $\mathfrak{F}_n$ correspond to minterms, every Boolean expression in n variables is equivalent to a join of distinct minterms. Moreover, such a representation as a join is unique, apart from the order in which the minterms are written. We call the join of minterms equivalent to a given Boolean expression E the **minterm canonical form** of E. [Another popular term, which we will not use, is **disjunctive normal form**, or DNF.] Parts (b) and (c) of the next example illustrate two different procedures for finding minterm canonical forms.

EXAMPLE 6 (a) The Boolean expression

$$x'yz \lor xy'z' \lor xy'z \lor xyz'$$

is a join of minterms in x, y, z as it stands, so this expression is its own minterm canonical form. The corresponding Boolean function has the values shown in the righthand column of the table. The 1's in the column tell which atoms in $\mathfrak{F}_3$ are involved, and hence determine the corresponding minterms. For instance, the 1 in the $\langle 1, 1, 0 \rangle$ row corresponds to xyz'.

x	y	z	$x'yz$	$xy'z'$	$xy'z$	xyz'	$x'yz \lor xy'z' \lor xy'z \lor xyz'$
0	0	0	0	0	0	0	0
0	0	1	0	0	0	0	0
0	1	0	0	0	0	0	0
0	1	1	1	0	0	0	1
1	0	0	0	1	0	0	1
1	0	1	0	0	1	0	1
1	1	0	0	0	0	1	1
1	1	1	0	0	0	0	0

(b) The Boolean expression $(x \lor yz')(yz)'$ is not written as a join of minterms. To get its minterm canonical form we can calculate the values of the corresponding Boolean function. For instance, $x = 0, y = 0, z = 0$ gives the value

$$(0 \lor 01)(00)' = (0 \lor 0)0' = 01 = 0$$

and $x = 1, y = 0, z = 1$ gives

$$(1 \lor 00)(01)' = (1 \lor 0)0' = 11 = 1.$$

When we calculate all eight values of the function we get the righthand column in the table in part (a). Thus $(x \lor yz')(yz)'$ is equivalent to the join of minterms in part (a), i.e., its minterm canonical form is $x'yz \lor xy'z' \lor xy'z \lor xyz'$.

(c) We can attack $(x \lor yz')(yz)'$ directly and try to convert it into a join of minterms using Boolean algebra laws. Recall that we write $E = F$ in case the Boolean expressions E and F are equivalent. By the Boolean algebra laws,

$$
\begin{aligned}
(x \lor yz')(yz)' &= (x \lor yz')(y' \lor z') && \text{DeMorgan law} \\
&= (x(y' \lor z')) \lor ((yz')(y' \lor z')) && \text{distributive law} \\
&= (xy' \lor xz') \lor (yz'y' \lor yz'z') && \text{distributive law twice} \\
&= (xy' \lor xz') \lor (0 \lor yz') && yy' = 0, \; z'z' = z' \\
&= xy' \lor xz' \lor yz' && \text{associative law and property of 0.}
\end{aligned}
$$

We first applied the DeMorgan laws to get all complementation down to the level of the literals. Then we distributed $\lor$ across meets as far as possible.

Now we have an expression as a join of meets of literals, but not as a join of minterms in x, y, z. Consider the subexpression xy' which is missing the variable z. Since $z \lor z' = 1$ we have $xy' = xy'1 = xy'(z \lor z') = xy'z \lor xy'z'$, which is a join of minterms. We can do the same sort of thing to the other two terms and get

$$xy' \lor xz' \lor yz' = (xy'z \lor xy'z') \lor (xyz' \lor xy'z') \lor (xyz' \lor x'yz')$$

which is a join of minterms. Deleting repetitions gives the minterm canonical form

$$xy'z \lor xy'z' \lor xyz' \lor x'yz'$$

for the expression $(x \lor yz')(yz)'$ we started with. This is of course the same as the answer obtained in part (b).   ☐

The methods illustrated in this example work in general. Given a Boolean expression, we can calculate the values of the Boolean function it defines—in effect, find its truth table. Then each value of 1 corresponds to a minterm in the canonical form of the expression. This is the method of Example 6(b). From this point of view the minterm canonical form is just another way of looking at the Boolean function.

Alternatively, we can obtain the minterm canonical form as in Example 6(c). First use the DeMorgan laws to move all complementation to the literals. Then distribute $\vee$ over products wherever possible. Then replace xx by x and xx' by 0 as necessary and insert missing variables using $x \vee x' = 1$. Finally, eliminate duplicates.

It is not always clear which technique is preferable for a given Boolean expression. One would not want to do a lot of calculations by hand using either method. Fortunately, the minterm canonical form is primarily useful as a theoretical tool, and when calculations do arise in practice they can be performed by machine using simple algorithms.

From a theoretical point of view, the minterm canonical form of a Boolean expression is very valuable, since it gives the expression in terms of its basic parts, namely minterms or atoms. As we will illustrate in § 10.5, Boolean expressions can be realized as electronic circuits and equivalent Boolean expressions correspond to electronic circuits that perform identically, i.e., give the same outputs for given inputs. Hence it is of interest to be able to "simplify" Boolean expressions, thereby obtaining "simplified" electronic circuits.

There are various ways to measure the simplification. It would be impossible to describe here all methods which have practical importance, but we can at least discuss one simple criterion. Let's say that a join of products [i.e., meets] of literals is **optimal** if there is no equivalent Boolean expression which is a join of fewer products and if among all equivalent joins of the same number of products there are none with fewer literals. Our task is to find an optimal join of products equivalent to a given Boolean expression. We can suppose that we have already found *one* equivalent join of products, namely the minterm canonical form.

EXAMPLE 7   (a) Consider the expression $(xy)'z$. The table shows the values of the Boolean function it defines. The minterm canonical form is thus $x'y'z \vee x'yz$

x	y	z	xy	$(xy)'$	$(xy)'z$
0	0	0	0	1	0
0	0	1	0	1	1
0	1	0	0	1	0
0	1	1	0	1	1
1	0	0	0	1	0
1	0	1	0	1	1
1	1	0	1	0	0
1	1	1	1	0	0

$\vee \; xy'z$. This expression is not optimal. By the Boolean algebra laws, $(xy)'z = (x' \vee y')z = x'z \vee y'z$, which is a join of only two terms with four literals. We will be able to show in § 10.6 that $x'z \vee y'z$ is optimal [or see Exercise 12].

This example illustrates a problem which can arise in practice. It seems plausible that a circuit to produce $x'z \vee y'z$ might be simpler than one to produce $x'y'z \vee x'yz \vee xy'z$, but perhaps a circuit to produce the original expression $(xy)'z$ would be simplest of all. We return to this point in § 10.6.

(b) Consider the join of products $E = x'z' \vee x'y \vee xy' \vee xz$. Is it optimal? We use Boolean algebra calculations, including the $x \vee x' = 1$ trick, to find its minterm canonical form:

$$E = x'yz' \vee x'y'z' \vee x'yz \vee x'yz' \vee xy'z \vee xy'z' \vee xyz \vee xy'z$$
$$= x'yz' \vee x'y'z' \vee x'yz \vee xy'z \vee xy'z' \vee xyz.$$

This has just made matters worse—more products and more literals. We want to repackage the expression in some clever way. Observe that we can group the six minterms together in pairs $x'yz'$ and $x'y'z'$, $x'yz$ and xyz, $xy'z$ and $xy'z'$, so that two minterms in the same pair differ in exactly one literal. Since

$$x'yz' \vee x'y'z' = x'(y \vee y')z' = x'z',$$
$$x'yz \vee xyz = yz \quad \text{and} \quad xy'z \vee xy'z' = xy',$$

$E = x'z' \vee yz \wedge xy'$. A different grouping gives

$$x'yz' \vee x'yz = x'y, \quad x'y'z' \vee xy'z' = y'z' \quad \text{and} \quad xy'z \vee xyz = xz,$$

so that $E = x'y \vee y'z' \vee xz$. Each of these product joins $x'z' \vee yz \vee xy'$ and $x'y \vee y'z' \vee xz$ will be shown to be optimal in Example 2(c) of § 10.6. That is, no join of products which is equivalent to E has fewer than three products, and no join with three products has fewer than six literals. Whether or not we believe this, each of these expressions looks simpler than the join of four products we started with. □

There is a method, called the **Quine-McCluskey procedure**, which builds optimal expressions by systematically grouping products together which differ in only one literal. The algorithm is tedious to use by hand but is readily programmed for computer calculation. Among other references, the textbooks *Applications-Oriented Algebra* by J. L. Fisher and *Modern Applied Algebra* by G. Birkhoff and T. C. Bartee contain readable accounts of the method.

Another procedure for finding optimal expressions, called the method of **Karnaugh maps**, has a resemblance to Venn diagrams. The methods works pretty well for Boolean expressions in three or four variables, where the problems are fairly simple anyway, but is less useful for more than four variables. The textbook *Computer Hardware and Organization* by M. E. Sloan devotes several sections to Karnaugh maps and discusses their advantages and disadvantages in applications. *Mathematical Structures for Computer Science* by J. L. Gersting contains a readable elementary account of the subject. We will illustrate the method in § 10.6, after we have described the elements of logical circuitry.

EXERCISES 10.4

1. Let $f: \mathbb{B}^3 \to \mathbb{B}$ be the Boolean function such that $f(0, 0, 0) = f(0, 0, 1) = f(1, 1, 0) = 1$ and $f(a, b, c) = 0$ for all other $\langle a, b, c \rangle \in \mathbb{B}^3$. Write the corresponding Boolean expression in minterm canonical form.

2. Give the Boolean function corresponding to the Boolean expression in Example 7(b).

3. For each of the following Boolean expressions in x, y, z describe the corresponding Boolean function and write the minterm canonical form.
   (a) xy (b) z' (c) $xy \lor z'$ (d) 1

4. Consider the Boolean expression $x \lor yz$ in x, y, z.
   (a) Determine the corresponding Boolean function $f: \mathbb{B}^3 \to \mathbb{B}$.
   (b) Write the expression in minterm canonical form.

5. Find the minterm canonical form for the four-variable Boolean expressions
   (a) $(x_1 x_2 x_3') \lor (x_1' x_2 x_3 x_4')$ (b) $(x_1 \lor x_2) x_3' x_4$

6. Use the method of Example 6(c) to find the minterm canonical form of the 3-variable Boolean expression $((x \lor y)' \lor z)'$.

7. (a) Find a join of products involving a total of three literals which is equivalent to the expression
   $$xz \lor [y' \lor y'z] \lor xy'z'.$$
   (b) Repeat part (a) for $[(xy \lor xyz) \lor xz] \lor z$.

8. The Boolean function $f: \mathbb{B}^3 \to \mathbb{B}$ is given by $f(a, b, c) = a +_2 b +_2 c$ for $\langle a, b, c \rangle \in \mathbb{B}^3$.
   (a) Determine a Boolean expression corresponding to f.
   (b) Write the expression in minterm canonical form with variables x, y, z.

9. Find an optimal expression equivalent to
   $$(x \lor y)' \lor z \lor x(yz \lor y'z').$$

10. Group the three minterms in $xyz \lor xyz' \lor xy'z$ in pairs to obtain an equivalent expression as a join of two products with two literals each.

11. There is a notion of maxterm dual to the notion of minterm. A **maxterm** in $x_1, \ldots, x_n$ is a join of n literals, each involving a different one of $x_1, \ldots, x_n$.
    (a) Use the DeMorgan laws to show that every Boolean expression in variables $x_1, \ldots, x_n$ is equivalent to a product of maxterms.
    (b) Write $xy' \lor x'y$ as a product of maxterms in x, y.

12. (a) Show that $x'z \lor y'z$ is not equivalent to a product of literals.
    (b) Show that $x'z \lor y'z$ is not equivalent to a join of products of literals in which one "product" is a single literal. [Parts (a) and (b) together show that $x'z \lor y'z$ is optimal.]

13. Prove that if E_1 and E_2 are Boolean expressions in $x_1, \ldots, x_n$ then $E_1 \lor E_2$ and $E_2 \lor E_1$ are equivalent.

§ 10.5   Logic Networks

Computer science at the hardware level involves designing devices to produce appropriate outputs from given inputs. For inputs and outputs which are 0's and 1's, this becomes a problem of designing circuitry to transform input data according to the rules for Boolean functions. In this section we will look briefly at ways in which Boolean algebra methods can be applied to logical design.

The basic building blocks of our logic networks are small units called **gates** which correspond to simple Boolean functions. Hardware versions of these units are available from manufacturers, packaged in a wide variety of configurations. Figure 1 shows the standard ANSI/IEEE symbols for the six

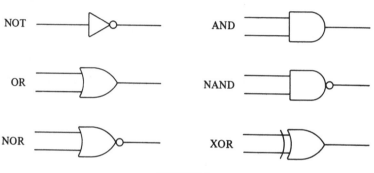

FIGURE 1

most elementary gates. We use the convention that the lines entering the symbol from the left are input lines, and the line on the right is the output line. Placing a small circle on an input or output line complements the signal on that line. The table shows the Boolean function values associated with

		x'	$x \vee y$	$(x \vee y)'$	xy	$(xy)'$	$x \oplus y$
x	y	NOT	OR	NOR	AND	NAND	XOR
0	0	1	0	1	0	1	0
0	1	1	1	0	0	1	1
1	0	0	1	0	0	1	1
1	1	0	1	0	1	0	0

these six gates and gives the corresponding Boolean function names for inputs x and y. AND, OR, NAND and NOR gates are also available with more than two input lines.

EXAMPLE 1   (a) The gate shown in Figure 2(a) corresponds to the Boolean function $(x \vee y')'$, or equivalently $x'y$.

(b) The 3-input AND gate in Figure 2(b) goes with the function $x'yz$.

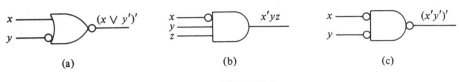

FIGURE 2

(c) The gate in Figure 2(c) gives $(x'y')'$ or $x \lor y$, so it acts like an OR gate. □

We consider the problem of designing a network of gates to produce a given complicated Boolean function of several variables. One major consideration is to keep the number of gates small. Another is to keep the length of the longest chain of gates small. Still other criteria arise in concrete practical applications.

EXAMPLE 2 Consider the foolishly designed network shown in Figure 3(a). [Dots indicate points where input lines divide.] There are four gates in the network. Reading from left to right there are two chains which are three gates long. We

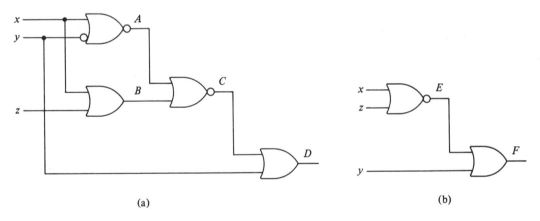

(a)   (b)

FIGURE 3

calculate the Boolean functions at A, B, C and D:

$$A = (x \lor y')'; \qquad B = x \lor z;$$
$$C = (A \lor B)' = ((x \lor y')' \lor (x \lor z))';$$
$$D = C \lor y = ((x \lor y')' \lor (x \lor z))' \lor y.$$

Boolean algebra laws give

$$D = ((x \lor y')(x \lor z)') \lor y = ((x \lor y') x'z') \lor y$$
$$= (xx'z' \lor y'x'z') \lor y = y'x'z' \lor y = (y' \lor y)(x'z' \lor y)$$
$$= x'z' \lor y.$$

The network shown in Figure 3(b) produces the same output, since

$$E = (x \vee z)' = x'z' \quad \text{and} \quad F = E \vee y = x'z' \vee y. \quad \square$$

This simple example shows how it is sometimes possible to redesign a complicated network into one using fewer gates. One reason for trying to reduce the lengths of chains of gates is that in many situations, including programmed simulations of hard-wired circuits, the operation of each gate takes a fixed basic unit of time, and the gates in a chain must operate one after the other. Long chains mean slow operation.

It happens that the expression $x'z' \vee y$ which we obtained for the complicated expression D in the last example is an optimal expression for D in the sense of § 10.4. Optimal expressions do not always give the simplest networks. For example, one can show [Exercise 7(a) of § 10.6] that $xz \vee yz$ is an optimal expression in x, y, z. Now $xz \vee yz = (x \vee y)z$, which can be implemented with an OR gate and an AND gate, whereas to implement $xz \vee yz$ directly would require two AND gates to form xz and yz and an OR gate to finish the job. What this means is that in practical situations our definition of "optimal" should change to match the hardware available.

In some settings it is desirable to have all gates of the same type or of at most two types. It turns out that we can do everything just with NAND or just with NOR. Which of these two types of gates is more convenient to use may depend on the particular transistor technology being employed. The table in Figure 4(a) shows how to write NOT, OR and AND in terms of NAND. Figure 4(b) shows the corresponding networks. This table also answers Exercise 16 of § 2.2, since NAND is another name for the Sheffer stroke referred to in that exercise. Exercise 2 asks for a corresponding table

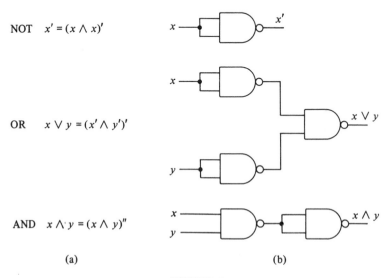

NOT $x' = (x \wedge x)'$

OR $x \vee y = (x' \wedge y')'$

AND $x \wedge y = (x \wedge y)''$

(a)   (b)

FIGURE 4

and figure for NOR. The network for OR in Figure 4 could also have been written as a single NAND gate with both inputs complemented. Complementing may or may not take separate gates in a particular application, depending on the technology involved and the source of the inputs. In most of our discussion we proceed as if complementation can be done at no cost.

Combinations of AND and OR such as those which arise in joins of products can easily be done entirely with NAND's.

EXAMPLE 3   Figure 5 shows a simple illustration. Just replace all AND's and OR's by NAND's in an AND-OR 2-stage network to get an equivalent network. An OR-AND 2-stage network can be replaced by a NOR network in a similar way [Exercise 4]. ☐

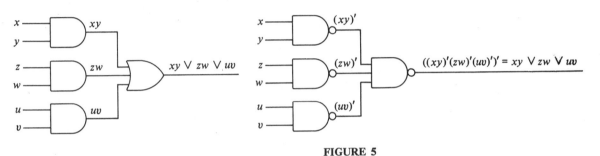

FIGURE 5

Logical networks can be viewed as acyclic digraphs with the sources labeled by variables $x_1, x_2, \ldots$, the other vertices labeled with $\vee$, $\wedge$ and $\oplus$, and some edges labeled $\neg$ for complementation. Each vertex then has an associated Boolean expression in the variables which label the sources.

EXAMPLE 4   The network of Figure 6(a) yields the digraph of Figure 6(b), with all edges directed from left to right. If we insert a 1-input $\wedge$-vertex in the middle of

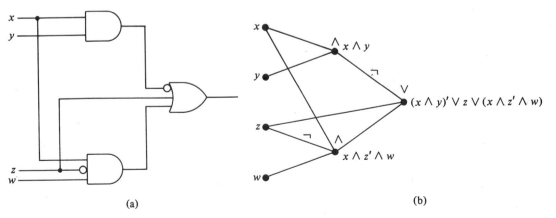

(a)   (b)

FIGURE 6

the edge from z to $(x \wedge y)' \vee z \vee (x \wedge z' \wedge w)$ we don't change the logic, and we get a digraph in which the vertices appear in columns—first a variable column, then an $\wedge$ column, then an $\vee$ column—and in which edges only go from one column to the next. ☐

The labeled digraph in Example 4 describes a computation of the Boolean function $(x \wedge y)' \vee z \vee (x \wedge z' \wedge w)$. In a similar way, any such labeled digraph describes computations for the Boolean functions which are associated with its sinks. Since every Boolean expression can be written as a join of products of literals, every Boolean function has a computation which can be described by a digraph like the one in Example 4, with a variable column, an $\wedge$ column and an $\vee$ column [consisting of a single vertex]. Indeed, as we saw in Example 3, all corresponding gates can be made NAND gates, so the $\vee$ vertex can be made an $\wedge$ vertex.

In a digraph of this sort no path has length greater than 2. The interpretation is that the associated computation takes just 2 units of time. The price we pay may be an enormous number of gates.

EXAMPLE 5   Consider the Boolean expression $E = x_1 \oplus x_2 \oplus \cdots \oplus x_n$. The corresponding Boolean function on $\mathbb{B}^n$ takes the value 1 at $\langle a_1, a_2, \ldots, a_n \rangle$ if and only if an odd number of the entries $a_1, a_2, \ldots, a_n$ are 1. The corresponding minterms are the ones with an odd number of uncomplemented literals. Hence the minimal canonical expression for E uses half of all the possible minterms and is a join of 2^{n-1} terms.

We claim that the minterm canonical expression for this E is optimal, i.e., whenever E is written as a join of products of literals, there will be at least 2^{n-1} terms. This is because such a join will have to include each of the minterms mentioned in the last paragraph. Otherwise some term would be a product of fewer than n literals; say x_1 and x_1' were both missing. Some choice of values of $a_1, a_2, \ldots, a_n$ will make this term have value 1. Note that an odd number of the entries $a_1, a_2, \ldots, a_n$ will be 1. If we change a_1 [from 0 to 1 or from 1 to 0], the term will still have value 1 but an even number of the entries $a_1, a_2, \ldots, a_n$ will be 1. No term of E can have this property, so each term for E must involve all n variables.

The observations of the last two paragraphs show that a length two digraph associated with $E = x_1 \oplus x_2 \oplus \cdots \oplus x_n$ must have at least $2^{n-1} + 1$ $\wedge$ and $\vee$ vertices, a number which grows exponentially with n. ☐

If we are willing to let the paths grow in length, we can divide and conquer to keep the total number of vertices manageable. Figure 7 shows the idea for $x_1 \oplus x_2 \oplus x_3 \oplus x_4$. This digraph has 9 $\wedge$ and $\vee$ vertices. So does the digraph associated with the join of products computation of $x_1 \oplus x_2 \oplus x_3 \oplus x_4$, since $2^3 + 1 = 9$; we have made no improvement. But how about

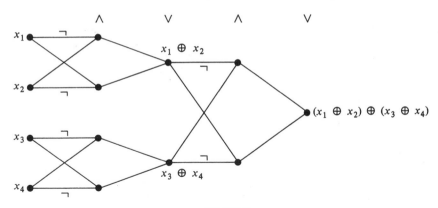

FIGURE 7

$x_1 \oplus x_2 \oplus \cdots \oplus x_8$? The join-of-product digraph has $2^7 + 1 = 129$ $\wedge$ and $\vee$ vertices, while the analogue of the Figure 7 digraph only has $9 + 9 + 2 + 1 = 21$ $\wedge$ and $\vee$ vertices [Exercise 11].

For $x_1 \oplus x_2 \oplus \cdots \oplus x_n$ in general, the comparison is $2^{n-1} + 1$ gates for the 2-stage computation versus only $3n - 1$ gates for the divide-and-conquer scheme, while the maximum path length increases from 2 to at most $2 \log n$ [Exercise 12]. Thus doubling the number of inputs increases path length by at most 2.

EXAMPLE 6   Circuits to perform operations in binary arithmetic are an important class of logical networks. Consider the problem of adding two binary integers. The example shown in Figure 8 illustrates the method, starting with the two integers 25 and 11 written in binary form and arranged one above the other with their digits in columns. Starting from the right we add the digits in a column. If the sum is 0 or 1 we write the sum in the answer line and carry a digit 0 one column to the left. If the sum is 2 or 3 [i.e., 10 or 11 in binary], we write 0 or 1, respectively, and go to the next column with a carry digit 1.

Carries $\longrightarrow$		1	1	0	1	1				
Numbers being $\Big\}\longrightarrow$		1	1	0	0	1	$25 =$	$16 + 8$		$+ 1$
added $\longrightarrow$	$+$		1	0	1	1	$+ 11 =$	8	$+ 2 + 1$	
Answer $\longrightarrow$	1	0	0	1	0	0	$36 = 32$	$+ 4$		

FIGURE 8

For the digit on the right which has no incoming carry digit, we could use the logical network called a **half-adder** shown in Figure 9. The value of S is the sum of x and y mod 2, and C gives the output carry digit. For the more general case with a carry input, C_I, as well as a carry output, C_o, we can combine two half-adders and an OR gate to get the network of Figure 10,

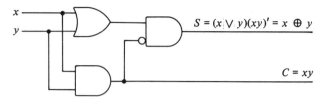

Half-adder

FIGURE 9

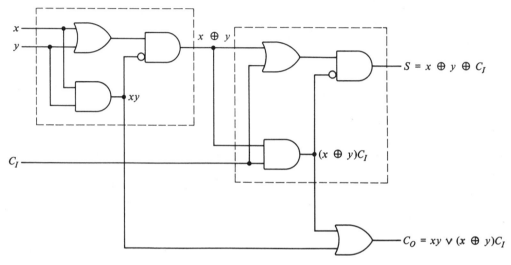

Full-adder

FIGURE 10

called a **full-adder**. Here C_O is 1 if and only if both x and y are 1 or exactly one of them is 1 and C_I is also 1, i.e., if and only if at least two of x, y and C_I are 1. Several full-adders can be combined into a network for adding n-digit binary numbers, or a single full-adder can be used repeatedly with suitable delay devices to feed the inputs in sequentially. In practice, each of these two schemes is slower than necessary. Fancy networks have been designed to add more rapidly and to perform other arithmetic operations. Our purpose in including this example was simply to illustrate the use of logical networks in hardware design.   ☐

The full-adder also shows how networks to implement two or more Boolean functions can be blended together. The minterm canonical form of $S = x \oplus y \oplus C_I$ is

$$xyC_I \vee xy'C_I' \vee x'yC_I' \vee x'y'C_I$$

which turns out to be optimal [Example 5, or Exercise 7(c) of § 10.6]. It can be implemented with a logic network using four AND gates and one OR gate if we allow four input lines. The optimal sum of products expression for C_O is $xy \vee xC_I \vee yC_I$, which can be produced with three AND gates and one OR gate. To produce S and C_O separately would appear to require $4 + 1 + 3 + 1 = 9$ gates, yet Figure 10 shows we can get by with 7 gates if we want both S and C_O at once. Moreover, each gate in Figure 10 has only two input lines. The message which we hope will be clear from this discussion is that the design of economical logic networks is not an easy problem.

EXERCISES 10.5

Note. In these exercises, inputs may be complemented unless otherwise specified.

1. (a) Describe the Boolean function which corresponds to the logical network shown in Figure 11.
   (b) Sketch an equivalent network consisting of two 2-input gates.

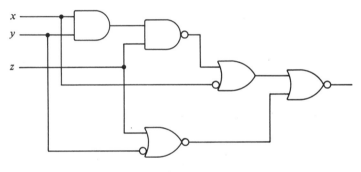

FIGURE 11

2. Write logical equations and sketch networks as in Figure 4 which show how to express NOT, OR and AND in terms of NOR without complementation of inputs.

3. Sketch logical networks equivalent to those in Figure 12, and composed entirely of NAND gates.

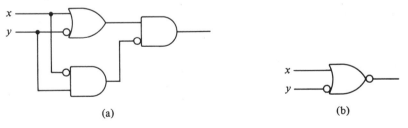

(a)   (b)

FIGURE 12

4. Sketch logical networks equivalent to those in Figure 13, and composed entirely of NOR gates.

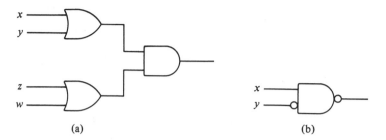

(a)   (b)

FIGURE 13

5. Sketch a logical network for the function XOR using:
   (a) two AND gates and one OR gate.
   (b) two OR gates and one AND gate.

6. Sketch a logical network which has output 1 if and only if:
   (a) exactly one of the inputs x, y, z has the value 1.
   (b) at least two of the inputs x, y, z, w have value 1.

7. Calculate the values of S and C_O for a full-adder with the given input values.
   (a) $x = 1, y = 0, C_I = 0$ (b) $x = 1, y = 1, C_I = 0$
   (c) $x = 0, y = 1, C_I = 1$ (d) $x = 1, y = 1, C_I = 1$

8. Find all values of x, y and C_I which produce the following outputs from a full-adder.
   (a) $S = 0, C_O = 0$ (b) $S = 0, C_O = 1$ (c) $S = 1, C_O = 1$

9. Consider the "triangle" and "circle" gates whose outputs are as shown in Figure 14. Show how to make a logic network from these two types of gates without complementation on input or output lines to produce the Boolean function:
   (a) x' (b) xy (c) $x \lor y$

FIGURE 14

10. AND-OR-INVERT gates are available commercially which produce the same effect as the logical network shown in Figure 15. What inputs should be used to make such a gate into an XOR gate?

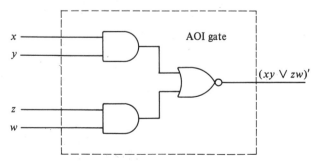

FIGURE 15

11. (a) Draw a digraph like the one in Figure 7 for a divide-and-conquer computation of $x_1 \oplus x_2 \oplus \cdots \oplus x_8$.
   (b) Draw the digraph for the 2-stage join-of-products computation of $x_1 \oplus x_2 \oplus x_3 \oplus x_4$.
   (c) How many $\wedge$ vertices are there in the digraph for the join-of-product computation of $x_1 \oplus x_2 \oplus \cdots \oplus x_8$?
   (d) Would you like to draw the digraph in part (c)?

12. Show by induction that for $n \geq 2$ there is a digraph for the computation of $x_1 \oplus x_2 \oplus \cdots \oplus x_n$ which has $3(n - 1)$ $\wedge$ and $\vee$ vertices and is such that if $2^m \geq n$ then every path has length at most $2m$. *Suggestion:* Consider k with $2^{k-1} < n \leq 2^k$ and combine digraphs for 2^{k-1} and $n - 2^{k-1}$ variables.

13. Draw a digraph for the computation of $x_1 \oplus x_2 \oplus \cdots \oplus x_6$ with 15 $\wedge$ and $\vee$ vertices and all paths of length at most 6. *Suggestion:* See Exercise 12.

§ 10.6   Karnaugh Maps

Instead of trying to find the most economical or "best" logic network possible, we may decide or be forced to settle for a solution which just seems reasonably good. Optimal solutions in the sense of §10.4 can be considered to be approximately best, so a technique for finding optimal solutions is worth having. The method of **Karnaugh maps**, which we now discuss briefly, is such a scheme.

We consider first the case of a three-variable Boolean function in x, y, z. The Karnaugh map of such a function is a 2×4 table, such as the ones in Figure 1. Each of the eight squares in the table corresponds to a minterm. The plus marks tell which minterms are involved in the function described by the table. The columns of a Karnaugh map are arranged so that neighboring

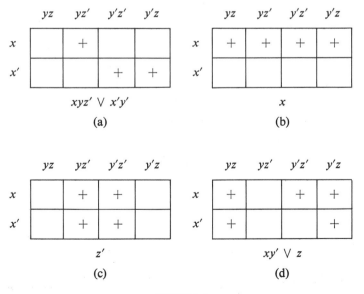

FIGURE 1

columns differ in just one literal. If we wrap the table around and sew the left edge to the right edge, then we get a cylinder whose columns still have this property.

EXAMPLE 1   (a) In Figure 1(a) the minterm canonical form is $xyz' \lor x'y'z' \lor x'y'z$. Since $x'y'z' \lor x'y'z = x'y'(z' \lor z) = x'y'$, the function can also be written as $xyz' \lor x'y'$.

(b) The Karnaugh maps for literals are particularly simple. The map for x in Figure 1(b) has the whole first row marked; x' has the whole second row marked. The map for y has the left 2×2 block marked and the one for y' has the right 2×2 block marked. The map for z' has just the entries in the middle 2×2 block marked; see Figure 1(c). If we sew the left edge to the right edge, the columns involving z also form a 2×2 block.

(c) The map in Figure 1(d) has all entries involving z marked, and also the minterm $xy'z'$. Since both xy' boxes are marked, the function can be written as $xy' \lor z$. ☐

We now have a cylindrical map on which the literals x and x' correspond to 1×4 blocks, the literals y, z, y' and z' correspond to 2×2 blocks, products of two literals correspond to 1×2 or 2×1 blocks and products of three literals correspond to 1×1 blocks.

To find an optimal expression for a given Boolean function in x, y, and z, we outline blocks corresponding to products by performing the following steps.

Step 1. Mark the squares on the Karnaugh map corresponding to the function.

Step 2. (a) Outline all marked blocks with 8 squares. [If all 8 boxes are marked, the function is 1. Yawn.]
(b) Outline all marked blocks with 4 squares which are not contained in other outlined blocks.
(c) Outline all marked blocks with 2 squares which are not contained in outlined blocks.
(d) Outline all marked squares which are not contained in outlined blocks.

Step 3. Select a set of outlined blocks which
(a) has every marked square in at least one selected block
(b) has as few blocks as possible and
(c) among all sets satisfying (b) gives an expression with as few literals as possible. ☐

We will need to say more about how to satisfy (b) and (c) in Step 3, but first we consider some examples.

EXAMPLE 2   (a) Consider the Boolean function with Karnaugh map in Figure 2(a). The "rounded rectangles" outline three blocks, one with four squares, corresponding to y, and two with two squares, corresponding to xz' and $x'z$. The

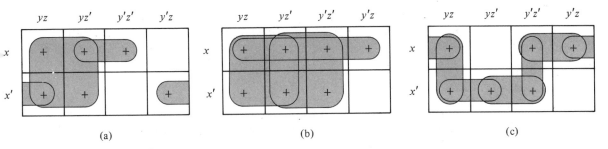

FIGURE 2

$x'z$ block is made from squares on the two sides of the seam where we sewed the left and right edges together. Since it takes all three outlined blocks to cover all marked squares, we must use all three blocks in Step 3. The resulting optimal expression is $y \lor xz' \lor x'z$.

(b) The Boolean function $(x'y'z)'$ is mapped in Figure 2(b). Here the outlined blocks go with x, y and z'. Again, it takes all three to cover the marked squares, so the optimal expression is $x \lor y \lor z'$.

(c) The Karnaugh map in Figure 2(c) has six outlined blocks, each with two squares. The marked squares can be covered with either of two sets of three blocks, corresponding to

$$x'y \lor xz \lor y'z' \quad \text{and} \quad x'z' \lor yz \lor xy'.$$

Since no fewer than three of the blocks can cover six squares, both of these expressions are optimal. We saw this Boolean function in Example 7(b) of § 10.4. ☐

Example 2(c) shows a situation in which more than one choice is possible. To illustrate the problems choices may cause in selecting the blocks in Step 3 we increase the number of variables to four, say w, x, y, z. Now the map is a 4×4 table, such as the ones in Figure 3, and we can think of sewing the top

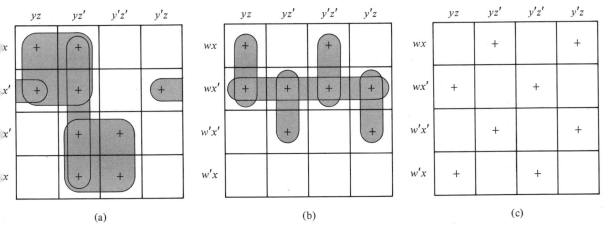

FIGURE 3

and bottom edges together to form a tube and then the left and right edges together to form a doughnut-shaped surface. The three-step procedure is the same as before, except that in Step 2 we start by looking for blocks with 16 squares.

EXAMPLE 3 (a) The map in Figure 3(a) has four outlined blocks, three with four squares corresponding to wy, yz' and $w'z'$, and one with two squares corresponding to $wx'z$. The two-square block is the only one containing the marked $wx'y'z$ square, and the blocks for wy and $w'z'$ are the only ones containing the squares for $wxyz$ and $w'x'y'z'$, respectively, so these three blocks must be used. Since they cover all the marked squares, they meet the conditions of Step 3. The optimal expression is $wx'z \lor wy \lor w'z'$.

(b) Bigger is not always better. The map in Figure 3(b) has five blocks. Each two-square block is essential, since each is the only block containing one of the marked squares. The big four-square wx' block is superfluous, since its squares are already covered by the other blocks. The optimal expression is $wyz \lor x'yz' \lor wy'z' \lor x'y'z$.

(c) The checkerboard pattern in Figure 3(c) describes the Boolean function $w \oplus x \oplus y \oplus z$ in w, x, y, z. In this case all eight blocks are 1×1 and the optimal expression is just the minterm canonical form. A similar conclusion holds for $x_1 \oplus x_2 \oplus \cdots \oplus x_n$ in general, as we saw in Example 5 of § 10.5. ☐

EXAMPLE 4 The maps in Example 3 offered no real choices; the essential blocks already covered all marked squares. The map of Figure 4(a) offers the opposite extreme. Every marked square is in at least two blocks. Clearly we must use at least one two-square block to cover $wx'yz'$. Suppose we choose the $wx'z'$ block. We can finish the job by choosing the four additional blocks shown in

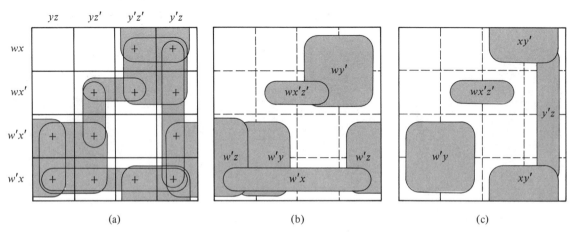

(a)   (b)   (c)

FIGURE 4

Figure 4(b). The resulting expression is

$$wx'z' \lor wy' \lor w'y \lor w'z \lor w'x.$$

Figure 4(c) shows another choice of blocks, this time with only four blocks altogether. The corresponding expression is

$$wx'z' \lor w'y \lor xy' \lor y'z.$$

This expression is better, but is it optimal? The only possible improvement would be to reduce to one two-square and two four-square blocks. Since there are twelve squares to cover, no such improvement is possible; the expression is optimal.   □

The rules for deciding which blocks to choose in situations like this are fairly complicated. It is not enough simply to choose the essential blocks because we are forced to, and then cover the remaining squares with the largest blocks possible. Such a procedure could lead to the nonoptimal solution of Figure 4(b).

For hand calculations, the tried-and-true method is to stare at the picture until the answer becomes clear. For machine calculations, which are necessary for more than five variables in any case, the Karnaugh map procedure is logically the same as the Quine-McCluskey method, for which software exists.

EXERCISES 10.6

For each of the Karnaugh maps in Exercises 1 through 4, give the corresponding minterm canonical form and an optimal expression.

1.

	yz	yz'	$y'z'$	$y'z$
x	+	+	+	+
x'	+			+

2.

	yz	yz'	$y'z'$	$y'z$
x	+	+		+
x'	+		+	+

3.

	yz	yz'	$y'z'$	$y'z$
x	+	+		+
x'			+	+

4.

	yz	yz'	$y'z'$	$y'z$
x	+			+
x'			+	

5. Draw the Karnaugh maps and outline the blocks for the given Boolean functions of x, y, z using the three-step procedure.
   (a) $x \lor x'yz$ (b) $(x \lor yz)'$
   (c) $y'z \lor xyz$ (d) $y \lor z$

6. Suppose the Boolean functions E and F each have Karnaugh maps consisting of a single block, and suppose the block for E contains the block for F.

(a) How are the optimal expressions for E and F related?

(b) Give examples of E and F related in this way.

7. Draw the Karnaugh map of each of the following Boolean expressions in x, y, z and show that the expression is optimal.

(a) $xz \lor yz$ (b) $xy \lor xz \lor yz$

(c) $xyz \lor xy'z' \lor x'yz' \lor x'y'z$

8. Repeat Exercise 7 for the following expressions in x, y, z, w.

(a) $x' \lor yzw$ (b) $x'z' \lor xy'z \lor w'xy$

(c) $wxz \lor wx'z' \lor w'x'z \lor w'xz'$

9. Find optimal expressions for the Boolean functions with these Karnaugh maps.

(a)

	yz	yz'	$y'z'$	$y'z$
wx	+	+	+	
wx'		+	+	+
$w'x'$	+	+	+	+
$w'x$	+	+	+	

(b)

	yz	yz'	$y'z'$	$y'z$
wx	+			
wx'				
$w'x'$	+	+	+	+
$w'x$		+	+	+

(c)

	yz	yz'	$y'z'$	$y'z$
wx	+	+	+	
wx'	+		+	+
$w'x'$		+	+	
$w'x$			+	+

(d)

	yz	yz'	$y'z'$	$y'z$
wx	+			+
wx'	+			+
$w'x'$		+	+	
$w'x$	+			+

CHAPTER HIGHLIGHTS

As usual: What does it mean? Why is it here? How can I use it? Think of examples.

Concepts

algebraic lattice
   sublattice
   join-irreducible, atom
   distributive lattice
   complement
   Boolean lattice, Boolean algebra
      duality principle

Boolean function, Boolean expression
  logical network, gate
  equivalent Boolean expressions, equivalent logical networks
    minterm canonical form
    optimal join of products
  labeled digraph
  Karnaugh map, block

Facts

Each lattice determines an algebraic lattice, and conversely. Boolean lattices
  correspond to Boolean algebras.
Every element of a finite algebraic lattice is a join of join-irreducible elements.
  This expression is essentially unique in a Boolean algebra.
Complements are unique in distributive lattices with 0 and 1.
The DeMorgan laws hold in Boolean algebras.
Any two Boolean algebras with n atoms are isomorphic.
Every logical network is equivalent to one using just NAND gates or just
  NOR gates.
Boolean expressions and logical networks correspond to labeled digraphs
  [§ 10.5].
Optimal Boolean expressions may not correspond to the simplest networks.
Choosing essential blocks first in a Karnaugh map and then greedily choosing
  the largest remaining blocks to cover may not give an optimal expression.

Methods

Use of the "truth table" of a Boolean expression to get its minterm canonical
  form.
Or use of the DeMorgan and distributive laws to get it.
Use of a Karnaugh map to find all optimal expressions equivalent to a given
  Boolean expression.

11

ALGEBRAIC SYSTEMS

A nonempty set which is closed under one or more binary operations is called an **algebra** or **algebraic system**. In Chapter 4 we considered semigroups, monoids and groups, which are algebras with one operation, and in Chapter 10 we studied lattices and Boolean algebras, which have more than one operation. In this chapter we will take a closer look at semigroups and groups. At the end, we will also briefly discuss rings and fields, algebras which can be thought of as generalizations of $\mathbb{Z}$ and $\mathbb{R}$ and of the set $\mathfrak{M}_{n,n}$ of $n \times n$ matrices.

Given an algebra, it turns out to be useful to look at its subalgebras and their relationship to each other and to the whole algebra. It also is helpful to consider the functions into other algebras from the given algebra which are compatible with the binary operations in a natural way. We first develop some of the basic facts about subgroups and about the appropriate functions for groups, and then show how to use the results to count the number of essentially different objects in collections with a high degree of symmetry.

§ 11.1 Generators

Chapter 4 contained an introduction to semigroups, using square matrices and the sets Σ^* and $\mathcal{P}(\Sigma^*)$ as examples. Since then we have seen many other examples, including Boolean algebras with $\vee$ or $\wedge$ as operations. Since most common binary operations are associative, we encounter semigroups virtually

494

every time we consider binary operations. In this section we consider how to build a semigroup or group out of a handful of its elements.

If a semigroup is at all large it may be impractical to keep a list of its elements, even in a computer, and of course there is no hope of listing all members of an infinite semigroup. Even if the elements *can* be stored, it may be impractical to examine them one at a time to test for a particular property. For a large semigroup S our goal is to find somehow a relatively small subset A of S such that all the elements of S can be built from members of A. In some sense the subset A will contain all the information about S.

The atoms of a Boolean algebra give an example of the sort of subset we want. By Theorem 3 of § 10.3, every element of a finite Boolean algebra is a join of atoms, i.e., every member of the algebra can be formed from atoms by joining elements repeatedly. If the algebra has 2^n members, we can build it out of its n atoms, and n is typically much smaller than 2^n.

Consider now a general semigroup $(S, \square)$ and a nonempty subset A of S. We define the set A^+ **generated by** A recursively as follows.

(B) $A \subseteq A^+$.
(R) If $x, y \in A^+$ then $x \square y \in A^+$.

These conditions imply, for example, that if $a_1, a_2, a_3, a_4 \in A$ then these four elements are in A^+, and so are $a_1 \square a_2$, $a_3 \square a_1 \square a_2$, $a_4 \square a_3 \square a_1 \square a_2$ and $a_1 \square a_2 \square a_3 \square a_1 \square a_2$. We call the members of A^+ the **products** formed from factors in A. Here "product" is a generic term for the result of combining elements of S using the operation $\square$. If the operation is $+$ or $\vee$ we will usually replace the word "product" by "sum" or "join," respectively. By (B) a product may have just one factor.

We say that A **generates** S if $A^+ = S$. Whether or not A generates S, A^+ is a subsemigroup of S by the following fact.

Theorem 1   Let A be a nonempty subset of the semigroup $(S, \square)$. Then A^+ is the unique smallest subsemigroup of S which contains A.

Proof. By (B), A^+ contains A. By (R), A^+ is closed under the operation $\square$, so by definition A^+ is a subsemigroup of S.

Now consider an arbitrary subsemigroup T of S which contains A. We'll show $A^+ \subseteq T$, from which it will follow that A^+ is the unique smallest subsemigroup containing A. We want to show that $x \in T$ for every x in A^+. Since A^+ is defined recursively, it's natural to use the Generalized Principle of Mathematical Induction introduced in § 6.4. Let $p(x)$ be the proposition "$x \in T$." To show that $p(x)$ is true for all x in A^+ we must establish that:

(B') $p(x)$ is true for the members of A^+ specified in the basis.
(I)   Whenever a member z of A^+ is specified by (R) in terms of previously defined members, say $z = x \square y$, then $p(x) \wedge p(y) \to p(z)$ is true.

Now (B′) is true since $A \subseteq T$ by the choice of T. Condition (I) just says "if $z = x \,\square\, y$ and if $x \in T$ and $y \in T$ then $z \in T$," which is true because T is a subsemigroup. The conditions for the Generalized Principle are met, so $x \in T$ for all x in A^+. ☐

Theorem 1 helps us describe the members of A^+ without recursion, as follows.

Theorem 2 Let A be a nonempty subset of the semigroup $(S, \square)$. Then A^+ consists of all elements of S of the form $a_1 \,\square\, \cdots \,\square\, a_n$ for $n \in \mathbb{P}$ and $a_1, \ldots, a_n \in A$.

Proof. Let X be the set of all products $a_1 \,\square\, \cdots \,\square\, a_n$. If $a_1, \ldots, a_n$, $b_1, \ldots, b_m$ are in A, then $a_1 \,\square\, \cdots \,\square\, a_n \,\square\, b_1 \,\square\, \cdots \,\square\, b_m$ is a product of this same form. Thus X is closed under $\square$, i.e., it's a subsemigroup of S. The case $n = 1$ gives $A \subseteq X$, so $A^+ \subseteq X$ by Theorem 1.

To show $X \subseteq A^+$, we use ordinary induction on n. Since $A \subseteq A^+$, $a_1 \in A^+$ whenever $a_1 \in A$. Assume inductively that $a_1 \,\square\, \cdots \,\square\, a_{n-1} \in A^+$ for some n and some $a_1, \ldots, a_{n-1}$ in A and let $a_n \in A$. Since $a_n \in A^+$, we have $a_1 \,\square\, \cdots \,\square\, a_{n-1} \,\square\, a_n \in A^+$ by (R) in the recursive definition of A^+. By induction, every member of X is in A^+. ☐

EXAMPLE 1 (a) Consider the semigroup $(\mathbb{Z}, +)$. The subsemigroup $\{2\}^+$ consists of all "products" of members of $\{2\}$. Since the operation here is $+$, $\{2\}^+$ consists of all sums $2 + 2 + \cdots + 2$, i.e., of all positive even integers. Thus $\{2\}^+ = 2\mathbb{P} = \{2n : n \in \mathbb{P}\}$.

(b) More generally, the subsemigroup of $(S, \square)$ generated by a single element x is the set

$$\{x\}^+ = \{x^n : n \in \mathbb{P}\}$$

[or $\{x\}^+ = \{nx : n \in \mathbb{P}\}$ if $\square$ is $+$]. Such a single-generator semigroup is called a **cyclic semigroup**.

(c) The subsemigroup $\{2\}^+$ of $(\mathbb{Z}, \cdot)$ is $\{2^n : n \in \mathbb{P}\} = \{2, 4, 8, 16, \ldots\}$. Notice that our notation is deficient; we can't tell from the expression $\{2\}^+$ alone whether we mean this subsemigroup or the one in part (a).

(d) The subsemigroup $\{2, 7\}^+$ of $(\mathbb{Z}, \cdot)$ generated by $\{2, 7\}$ is $\{2^m 7^n : m, n \in \mathbb{N}$ and $m + n \geq 1\}$.

(e) We show that the cyclic subsemigroup of $(\mathfrak{M}_{2,2}, \cdot)$ generated by the matrix

$$\mathbf{M} = \begin{bmatrix} 1 & 1 \\ 0 & 1 \end{bmatrix}$$

is

$$\{\mathbf{M}\}^+ = \left\{ \begin{bmatrix} 1 & n \\ 0 & 1 \end{bmatrix} : n \in \mathbb{P} \right\}.$$

By part (b) it will be enough to show that $\mathbf{M}^n = \begin{bmatrix} 1 & n \\ 0 & 1 \end{bmatrix}$ for $n \in \mathbb{P}$. This is clear for $n = 1$. Assume inductively that $\mathbf{M}^n = \begin{bmatrix} 1 & n \\ 0 & 1 \end{bmatrix}$ for some $n \in \mathbb{P}$. Then matrix multiplication gives

$$\mathbf{M}^{n+1} = \mathbf{M}^n \cdot \mathbf{M} = \begin{bmatrix} 1 & n \\ 0 & 1 \end{bmatrix} \begin{bmatrix} 1 & 1 \\ 0 & 1 \end{bmatrix} = \begin{bmatrix} 1 & 1+n \\ 0 & 1 \end{bmatrix}.$$

The result now follows by mathematical induction.

(f) Let Σ be an alphabet and let A be a language in $\mathcal{P}(\Sigma^*)$, i.e., a subset of Σ^*. In § 4.4 we defined the positive closure A^+ to be $\bigcup_{n=1}^{\infty} A^n$. In fact A^+ is the subsemigroup of Σ^* generated by A using the concatenation operation on Σ^*. ☐

Now consider a group $(G, \square)$, i.e., a semigroup with an identity, say e, in which inverses exist. If A is a nonempty subset of G we can still consider the subsemigroup A^+ of G generated by A, but it is often more natural to take advantage of the inverses and consider the **subgroup generated by** A, denoted by $\langle A \rangle$ and defined recursively as follows.

(B) $A \subseteq \langle A \rangle$.
(R$_1$)   If $x, y \in \langle A \rangle$ then $x \square y \in \langle A \rangle$.
(R$_2$)   If $x \in \langle A \rangle$ then $x^{-1} \in \langle A \rangle$.

Conditions (R$_1$) and (R$_2$) show that $\langle A \rangle$ is closed under the operations $\square$ and inversion. Consider an $a \in A$. Then $a \in \langle A \rangle$ by (B), so $a^{-1} \in \langle A \rangle$ by (R$_2$) and thus the identity $e = a \square a^{-1}$ also belongs to $\langle A \rangle$ by (R$_1$). Hence $\langle A \rangle$ is a subgroup of G. In fact, $\langle A \rangle$ is the unique smallest subgroup of G which contains A [Exercise 13].

EXAMPLE 2   (a) Consider the group $(\mathbb{Z}, +)$, in which the identity is 0 and the inverse of n is $-n$. The subgroup $\langle \{4\} \rangle$ must contain $4, 4 + 4, 4 + 4 + 4$, etc. by (R$_1$), so it must contain all positive multiples of 4. It also contains the inverses [i.e., negatives] of these elements by (R$_2$), so it must contain all integer multiples of 4. That is, $\langle \{4\} \rangle \supseteq 4\mathbb{Z}$. Since $4\mathbb{Z}$ is a subgroup containing 4, and since $\langle \{4\} \rangle$ is the smallest such subgroup, $\langle \{4\} \rangle = 4\mathbb{Z}$. Note that $\{4\}^+ = 4\mathbb{P}$, which is not the same as $\langle \{4\} \rangle$.

(b) Consider the subgroup $\langle \{4, -6\} \rangle$ of $(\mathbb{Z}, +)$. It contains $4 + (-6) = -2$ by (R$_1$), so contains $-(-2) = 2$ by (R$_2$). As in part (a), this means that $\langle \{4, -6\} \rangle \supseteq \langle \{2\} \rangle = 2\mathbb{Z}$. Now every number we can form from 4 and -6 by adding two numbers or taking negatives is still going to be even, so $\langle \{4, -6\} \rangle$ consists only of even numbers. Thus $\langle \{4, -6\} \rangle \subseteq 2\mathbb{Z}$ and so $\langle \{4, -6\} \rangle = 2\mathbb{Z}$. ☐

We say that a subset A of a group G **generates** G [as a group, now] or that A is a set of **generators** for G if $\langle A \rangle = G$. The subgroup $\langle A \rangle$ must contain elements such as $a_1 \,\square\, a_3 \,\square\, a_2$, $a_1 \,\square\, a_2^{-1}$ and $a_3^{-1} \,\square\, a_2 \,\square\, a_1^{-1} \,\square\, a_2$ for $a_1, a_2, a_3 \in A$. The next theorem says that products like this are all there are in $\langle A \rangle$.

Theorem 3   Let A be a nonempty subset of the group $(G, \square)$. Then $\langle A \rangle$ consists of all products formed from members of A and their inverses.

   Proof. For convenience, denote $\{a^{-1} : a \in A\}$ by A^{-1}. By Theorem 2, the set of products described in this theorem is the subsemigroup $(A \cup A^{-1})^+$. Thus we want to show that

$$\langle A \rangle = (A \cup A^{-1})^+.$$

By (B) and (R$_2$), $\langle A \rangle$ contains $A \cup A^{-1}$. Since $\langle A \rangle$ is closed under $\square$, and since $(A \cup A^{-1})^+$ is the smallest subsemigroup of G which contains $A \cup A^{-1}$, we have $\langle A \rangle \supseteq (A \cup A^{-1})^+$.

   To show the reverse inclusion, we use the Generalized Principle of Induction. Let $p(x)$ be the proposition "$x \in (A \cup A^{-1})^+$." We want to show that $p(x)$ is true for every x in $\langle A \rangle$.

   If $x \in A$ then $p(x)$ is true; thus $p(x)$ is true for the members x of $\langle A \rangle$ specified in (B).

   Now each member of $\langle A \rangle$ specified by (R$_1$) is of the form $x \,\square\, y$. We must check that

   (I$_1$) $p(x) \wedge p(y) \to p(x \,\square\, y)$ is true,

i.e., that if x and y are in $(A \cup A^{-1})^+$ then so is $x \,\square\, y$. Since $(A \cup A^{-1})^+$ is closed under $\square$, this condition is met.

   Finally, we must check

   (I$_2$) $p(x) \to p(x^{-1})$ is true.

Now if $p(x)$ is true, then $x \in (A \cup A^{-1})^+$, so by Theorem 2 $x = x_1 \,\square\, x_2 \,\square\, \cdots \,\square\, x_n$ for some $x_1, x_2, \ldots, x_n \in A \cup A^{-1}$. It is easy to check by multiplication by x that $x^{-1} = x_n^{-1} \,\square\, \cdots \,\square\, x_2^{-1} \,\square\, x_1^{-1}$. Since $(a^{-1})^{-1} = a$, the elements $x_1^{-1}, x_2^{-1}, \ldots, x_n^{-1}$ are also in $A \cup A^{-1}$, and so x^{-1} belongs to $(A \cup A^{-1})^+$ by Theorem 2. That is, $p(x^{-1})$ is true. $\square$

EXAMPLE 3   (a) If A has just one member, say $A = \{a\}$, we usually write $\langle a \rangle$ instead of $\langle \{a\} \rangle$. The subgroup $\langle a \rangle$ consists of all products of factors a and a^{-1}. We can cancel an a with an a^{-1}; for instance

$$a \,\square\, a \,\square\, a^{-1} \,\square\, a^{-1} \,\square\, a^{-1} \,\square\, a \,\square\, a^{-1} = a \,\square\, e \,\square\, a^{-1} \,\square\, e \,\square\, a^{-1}$$

$$= a \,\square\, a^{-1} \,\square\, a^{-1}$$

$$= e \,\square\, a^{-1} = a^{-1}.$$

So each such product is equal to a power of a or a power of a^{-1}. That is, $\langle a \rangle = \{a^k : k \in \mathbb{Z}\}$, where as always $a^0 = e$ and $a^{-k} = (a^{-1})^k$ for $k \in \mathbb{P}$. [If the operation is $+$, we have $\langle a \rangle = \{ka : k \in \mathbb{Z}\}$ with $0a = 0$ and $(-k)a = k(-a) = -(ka)$ for $k \in \mathbb{P}$.]

A group $\langle a \rangle$ generated by a single element is called a **cyclic group**. Such groups are always commutative.

(b) Consider the group $(\mathbb{Z}, +)$. For $n \in \mathbb{Z}$ we have $\langle n \rangle = n\mathbb{Z} = \{nk : k \in \mathbb{Z}\}$. In particular, $\langle 0 \rangle = \{0\}, \langle 1 \rangle = \mathbb{Z}$ and $\langle -1 \rangle = \mathbb{Z}$.

(c) The subgroup $\langle \{3, 5\} \rangle$ of $(\mathbb{Z}, +)$ is $\mathbb{Z}$ itself, since we know that $\langle \{3, 5\} \rangle$ contains $3 + 3 - 5 = 1$ so $\langle \{3, 5\} \rangle \supseteq \langle 1 \rangle = \mathbb{Z}$. Notice that neither 3 nor 5 by itself generates $\mathbb{Z}$. ∐

In fact, all subgroups of $(\mathbb{Z}, +)$ turn out to be cyclic, which is the simplest possible situation.

Theorem 4 Every subgroup of $(\mathbb{Z}, +)$ is of the form $n\mathbb{Z}$ for some $n \in \mathbb{N}$.

Proof. Consider a subgroup H of $(\mathbb{Z}, +)$. If $H = \{0\}$ then $H = 0\mathbb{Z}$, which is of the required form. Suppose $H \neq \{0\}$. If $0 \neq m \in H$ then also $-m \in H$. Thus $H \cap \mathbb{P}$ is nonempty, so it has a smallest element, say n. We show that $H = n\mathbb{Z}$. Since $n \in H$ and H is a subgroup, we have $n\mathbb{Z} \subseteq H$. Consider an element m of H. By the division algorithm $m = qn + r$ with $0 \leq r < n$. Since $n\mathbb{Z} \subseteq H, qn \in H$ and thus $r = m - qn \in H$. Since $r < n$ and n is the smallest positive member of H, we must have $r = 0$. That is, $m = qn \in n\mathbb{Z}$. Since m was arbitrary in $H, H \subseteq n\mathbb{Z}$ as claimed. ∐

In general we expect that a set A with more than one member will generate a subgroup which is not cyclic.

EXAMPLE 4 Consider the set G of all one-to-one functions of $\{1, 2, 3\}$ onto itself, i.e., all permutations of $\{1, 2, 3\}$. There are $3! = 6$ functions in G, and they form a group under composition, with identity e defined by $e(x) = x$ for $x = 1, 2, 3$. This group can be generated by two of its elements:

$$f \text{ defined by } f(1) = 2, \quad f(2) = 1, \quad f(3) = 3,$$

and

$$g \text{ defined by } g(1) = 2, \quad g(2) = 3, \quad g(3) = 1.$$

The following table gives the function values of six different products formed from f, g and g^{-1}.

	1	2	3
$f \circ f = e$	1	2	3
f	2	1	3
g	2	3	1
g^{-1}	3	1	2
$f \circ g$	1	3	2
$f \circ g^{-1}$	3	2	1

These must be the six different members of G, so $G = \langle \{f, g\} \rangle$. All products formed from f, g and g^{-1} must be somewhere in this list. For instance, one can check that $g \circ f = f \circ g^{-1}$, $g \circ f \circ g = f$ and $f \circ g \circ f \circ g = e$. Since $f \circ g \neq g \circ f$, G is not commutative, so it can't possibly be cyclic. ☐

One common use for generators is to show that all members of a group have a certain property by showing that the members of a generating set have the property.

EXAMPLE 5   (a) Consider a group G which consists of some permutations of $\{1, 2, 3, \ldots, 100\}$ onto itself, with composition as operation. In practice the members of G may not be known very well, but we may know a set A of generators of G. Suppose that we know that each a in A satisfies $a(1) = 1$, $a(2) = 3$ and $a(3) = 2$. We can conclude that:

$$g(1) = 1 \quad \text{for every} \quad g \in G,$$

and

$$\{g(2), g(3)\} = \{2, 3\} \quad \text{for every} \quad g \in G.$$

Here's how.

First look at $g(1)$. We claim that $\{g \in G : g(1) = 1\}$ is a subgroup of G, for if $g, h \in G$ with $g(1) = 1$ and $h(1) = 1$ then $(g \circ h)(1) = g(h(1)) = g(1) = 1$, and $g^{-1}(1) = g^{-1}(g(1)) = 1$. The subgroup contains A by assumption, so it contains $\langle A \rangle$. Since $\langle A \rangle = G$, we have $G = \{g \in G : g(1) = 1\}$, as claimed.

Similarly, one can check that $\{g \in G : \{g(2), g(3)\} = \{2, 3\}\}$ is a subgroup of G containing A, so it too must be G itself.

Note that we don't claim that $g(2) = 3$ for every $g \in G$, even though every generator in A has this property. The reason is that $\{g \in G : g(2) = 3\}$ is not a subgroup. In fact, it doesn't contain the identity.

(b) Consider a group G of isomorphisms of a graph onto itself, with composition as operation. If there is some vertex, edge or component which is sent into itself by all members of a generating set for G, then that vertex, edge or component is sent into itself by all members of G. The argument is essentially the argument in part (a). In general we say that the function f **fixes** the point x, the set S, the vertex $v, \ldots$ if $f(x) = x$, $f(S) = S$, $f(v) = v$, $\ldots$. If G is a group of permutations of some set S and $x \in S$ the set $\{g \in G : g(x) = x\}$ is always a subgroup of G, called the **subgroup fixing** x [Exercise 14]. If this subgroup contains a set of generators for G, it must be G itself. ☐

We saw in earlier examples that the subsemigroup $\{2\}^+ = 2\mathbb{P}$ and the subgroup $\langle 2 \rangle = 2\mathbb{Z}$ are different subsets of the infinite group $(\mathbb{Z}, +)$. For finite groups, only one subset arises.

Theorem 5   If $(G, \square)$ is a group, then every finite subsemigroup of G is a subgroup.

Proof. Consider a finite subsemigroup H of G. We just need to show that if $a \in H$ then $a^{-1} \in H$. Since H is finite, the function $n \to a^n$ mapping $\mathbb{P}$ to H cannot be one-to-one. Hence $a^n = a^m$ for some $n, m \in \mathbb{P}$ with $n < m$.

Then

$$e = a^n \,\square\, (a^{-1})^n = a^m \,\square\, (a^{-1})^n = a^{m-n}.$$

If $m - n = 1$, then $a = e$, so $a^{-1} = a \in H$. Otherwise $m - n \geq 2$ and so

$$a^{-1} = e \,\square\, a^{-1} = a^{m-n} \,\square\, a^{-1} = a^{m-n-1} \in H. \quad \square$$

This result is a time saver in practice. It means that to check to see if a finite subset of a known group is a subgroup it's only necessary to check closure under the operation of the group.

EXERCISES 11.1

1. Describe each of the following subsemigroups of $(\mathbb{Z}, +)$.
   (a) $\{1\}^+$ (b) $\{0\}^+$ (c) $\{-1, 2\}^+$
   (d) $\mathbb{P}^+$ (e) $\mathbb{Z}^+$ (f) $\{2, 3\}^+$
   (g) $\{6\}^+ \cap \{9\}^+$

2. Describe each of the following subsemigroups of $(\mathbb{Z}, \cdot)$.
   (a) $\{1\}^+$ (b) $\{0\}^+$ (c) $\{-1, 2\}^+$
   (d) $\mathbb{P}^+$ (e) $\mathbb{Z}^+$ (f) $\{2, 3\}^+$

3. Which of the semigroups in Exercise 1 are cyclic semigroups? Justify your answers.

4. Which of the semigroups in Exercise 2 are cyclic semigroups? Justify your answers.

5. Describe each of the following subgroups of $(\mathbb{Z}, +)$.
   (a) $\langle 1 \rangle$ (b) $\langle 0 \rangle$ (c) $\langle \{-1, 2\} \rangle$
   (d) $\langle \mathbb{Z} \rangle$ (e) $\langle \{2, 3\} \rangle$ (f) $\langle 6 \rangle \cap \langle 9 \rangle$

6. Which of the subgroups in Exercise 5 are cyclic groups? Justify your answers.

7. Recall that a monoid is a semigroup with an identity element. If A is a subset of a monoid $(M, \square)$ with identity e, the **submonoid generated by** A is defined to be $A^+ \cup \{e\}$. Find each of the following.
   (a) The submonoid of $(\mathbb{Z}, +)$ generated by $\{2\}$.
   (b) The submonoid of $(\mathbb{Z}, +)$ generated by $\{1, -1\}$.
   (c) The submonoid of $(\mathbb{Z}, +)$ generated by $\{0\}$.
   (d) The submonoid of $(\mathbb{Z}, \cdot)$ generated by $\{1\}$.
   (e) The submonoid of Σ^* generated by Σ, using concatenation on Σ^*.

8. (a) Give an example of a cyclic semigroup and a subsemigroup of it which is not cyclic.
   (b) Give an example of a cyclic group which is not a cyclic semigroup.
   (c) Give an example of a cyclic group which *is* a cyclic semigroup.

9. List the members of each of the following finite subsemigroups of $(\mathfrak{M}_{3,3}, \cdot)$.
   (a) $\left\{ \begin{bmatrix} 0 & 1 & 0 \\ 1 & 0 & 0 \\ 0 & 0 & 1 \end{bmatrix} \right\}^+$
   (b) $\left\{ \begin{bmatrix} 0 & 1 & 0 \\ 1 & 0 & 0 \\ 0 & 0 & 1 \end{bmatrix}, \begin{bmatrix} 0 & 0 & 1 \\ 1 & 0 & 0 \\ 0 & 1 & 0 \end{bmatrix} \right\}^+$

$$(c) \left\{ \begin{bmatrix} 0 & 2 & 3 \\ 0 & 0 & 4 \\ 0 & 0 & 0 \end{bmatrix}^+ \right\}$$

10. (a) Which of the subsemigroups in Exercise 9 are groups?
    (b) Which are commutative?
    (c) Which are cyclic?

11. The set S_4 of all one-to-one functions of $\{1, 2, 3, 4\}$ onto itself is a group under composition of functions. Which of the following are subgroups of $(S_4, \circ)$? Justify your answers.
    (a) $\{f \in S_4 : f(4) = 4\}$
    (b) $\{f \in S_4 : f(1) = 2\}$
    (c) $\{f \in S_4 : f(1) \in \{1, 2\}\}$
    (d) $\{f \in S_4 : f(1) \in \{1, 2\} \text{ and } f(2) \in \{1, 2\}\}$

12. (a) Find a 24-element subset of S_4 which generates the group $(S_4, \circ)$ in Exercise 11. [There are actually some 2-element generating sets for S_4, but they are harder to find.]
    (b) Is $(S_4, \circ)$ a cyclic group? Justify your answer.

13. Use the Generalized Principle of Mathematical Induction to show that $\langle A \rangle$ is the smallest subgroup of the group G containing A.

14. Consider a group G of permutations [i.e., one-to-one functions] of a set S onto itself, with composition of functions as operation. Show that $\{g \in G : g(x) = x\}$ is a subgroup of G for each x in S. *Suggestion:* See Example 5(a).

§ 11.2 Subsemigroups, Subgroups and Cosets

In § 11.1 we formed subsemigroups by building them up from the inside, using sets of elements to generate them. Once we have several subsemigroups on hand, we can form others by intersection.

Theorem 1 Let $(S, \square)$ be a semigroup. The intersection of any collection of subsemigroups of S is either empty or is itself a subsemigroup of S.

Proof. If s and t belong to the intersection, then they both belong to each subsemigroup in the collection, so their product $s \square t$ does too. That is, the intersection is closed under $\square$. ∎

Corollary 1 If S is a monoid, the intersection of any nonempty collection of submonoids of S is a submonoid of S.

Proof. A submonoid is a subsemigroup of S which contains the identity element e of S. If each member of the collection contains e, so does the intersection. ∎

Corollary 2 The intersection of any nonempty collection of subgroups of a group is a subgroup.

Proof. Every member of the intersection belongs to each subgroup, so its inverse does too. Thus its inverse also belongs to the intersection. Hence the intersection is a submonoid closed under taking inverses, i.e., a subgroup.

$\square$

EXAMPLE 1   (a) Both $2\mathbb{Z}$ and $3\mathbb{Z}$ are subsemigroups of $(\mathbb{Z}, \cdot)$. So is their intersection $6\mathbb{Z} = \{6k : k \in \mathbb{Z}\}$.

(b) The intersection $\mathbb{P} \cap 2\mathbb{Z} = \{2k : k \in \mathbb{P}\}$ is a subsemigroup of $(\mathbb{Z}, \cdot)$.

(c) Both $\mathbb{P}$ and $\{-k : k \in \mathbb{P}\}$ are subsemigroups of $(\mathbb{Z}, +)$. Their intersection is empty.

(d) Consider a group G of permutations of a set X, with composition as operation. For elements x and y in X the sets $\{g \in G : g(x) = x\}$ and $\{g \in G : g(y) = y\}$ are subgroups of G [Example 5(b) of § 11.1]. Their intersection $\{g \in G : g(x) = x \text{ and } g(y) = y\}$ is the subgroup of G fixing both x and y. More generally, if $Y \subseteq X$ the set $\{g \in G : g(x) = x \text{ for all } x \in Y\}$ is the intersection of the subgroups fixing the members of Y, so it is itself a subgroup of G. $\square$

EXAMPLE 2   (a) Consider a nonempty subset A of a semigroup S. By Theorem 1 the intersection of all of the subsemigroups which contain A [including S itself, naturally] is a subsemigroup which contains A. It must be the smallest subsemigroup containing A, namely A^+. This construction gives a way to define A^+ without describing its elements in terms of A.

(b) Consider a nonempty subset A of a group G. By Corollary 2, the intersection of all subgroups of G containing A is $\langle A \rangle$, the unique smallest subgroup of G containing A. $\square$

Semigroups are only required to be closed under an associative operation, so it is not particularly surprising that we can't say much of a general nature about the relationship between subsemigroups and the semigroup in which they are contained.

EXAMPLE 3   To see a sample of how wild things can get, consider an arbitrary nonempty set S, and define $\square$ on S by $x \square y = y$ for all $x, y \in S$; i.e., the product of two elements is always just the second element. Then $(x \square y) \square z = z = x \square z = x \square (y \square z)$, so $\square$ is associative and $(S, \square)$ is a semigroup. *Every* nonempty subset of S is a subsemigroup, since it's closed under $\square$. $\square$

Since, as this example shows, the subsemigroups of a semigroup may be pretty arbitrarily embedded in the whole semigroup, it is particularly striking that the subgroups of a group are quite strongly influenced by the structure of the group as a whole. Each subgroup defines a partition of the group in a natural way, which in the case of finite groups allows us to use arithmetic to draw significant group-theoretic conclusions. To state our main result we need to introduce some notation.

Consider a subgroup H of a group $(G, \square)$ with identity element e. A **coset** of H in G is a subset of the form

$$H \square x = \{h \square x : h \in H\}$$

for some x in G. The coset $H \square e$ is H itself, and indeed $H \square h = H$ for every h in H [Exercise 13(a)]. Since $e \in H$, the coset $H \square x$ contains $e \square x = x$. Thus every x in G belongs to at least one coset. In fact, x belongs to just one coset.

Theorem 2   The cosets of a subgroup of a group form a partition of the group.

Proof. Consider a group G with subgroup H. We just showed that G is the union of the various cosets $H \square x$, so we only need to show that any two distinct cosets are disjoint. Consider first an element $z \in H \square x$. Then $z = h \square x$ for some $h \in H$. For each $k \in H$, $k \square z = k \square (h \square x) = (k \square h) \square x \in H \square x$, because $k \square h$ is also in the subgroup H. Thus $H \square z \subseteq H \square x$. Moreover, $x = h^{-1} \square h \square x = h^{-1} \square z \in H \square z$, because h^{-1} is in the subgroup H, so the roles of x and z can be reversed and we conclude that $H \square x \subseteq H \square z$. [This is where the proof breaks down for semigroups.] We've shown that if $z \in H \square x$ then $H \square z = H \square x$.

Now suppose $z \in (H \square x) \cap (H \square y)$. Then by the argument above $H \square z = H \square x$ and $H \square z = H \square y$, so $H \square x = H \square y$. In other words, cosets which overlap are identical. ☐

EXAMPLE 4   Consider the subgroup $3\mathbb{Z}$ of the group $(\mathbb{Z}, +)$. The cosets are the sets of the form $3\mathbb{Z} + n = \{3k + n : k \in \mathbb{Z}\}$. There are just three of them, namely $3\mathbb{Z}$, $3\mathbb{Z} + 1$ and $3\mathbb{Z} + 2$, the congruence classes mod 3. Every n in $\mathbb{Z}$ can be written as $n = 3q + r$ with $r \in \{0, 1, 2\}$, so $\mathbb{Z}$ is the union of these three disjoint sets. Similarly, for every $m \in \mathbb{P}$ the cosets of $m\mathbb{Z}$ in $(\mathbb{Z}, +)$ are the congruence classes $[n]_m = m\mathbb{Z} + n$ mod m. ☐

Instead of the cosets $H \square x$ which we have been considering, we could just as easily have looked at **left cosets**, of the form $x \square H = \{x \square h : h \in H\}$. If G is commutative, then $H \square x = x \square H$, but in general the left coset $x \square H$ and right coset $H \square x$ are different subsets of G. The proof of Theorem 2 is still valid for left cosets, with the obvious right-left switches.

EXAMPLE 5   Consider the permutation group PERM(X) of all one-to-one functions of the nonempty set X onto itself, with composition as operation. Choose an element x_0 in X, and define the equivalence relation $\sim$ on PERM(X) by letting $f \sim g$ if and only if $f(x_0) = g(x_0)$. The function e defined by $e(x) = x$ for all x in X is the identity of PERM(X), and $f \sim e$ if and only if $f(x_0) = x_0$. We saw in Example 5(b) of § 11.1 that $\{f \in \text{PERM}(X) : f(x_0) = x_0\}$ is a subgroup of PERM(X); call this subgroup FIX. Then FIX is the equivalence class of e.

Now consider the equivalence class of some function g in $\mathrm{PERM}(X)$. We have $f \sim g$ if and only if $f(x_0) = g(x_0)$ if and only if $(g^{-1} \circ f)(x_0) = g^{-1}(f(x_0))$ $= g^{-1}(g(x_0)) = x_0$ if and only if $g^{-1} \circ f \in \mathrm{FIX}$. But $g^{-1} \circ f = h \in \mathrm{FIX}$ if and only if $f = g \circ g^{-1} \circ f = g \circ h \in g \circ \mathrm{FIX}$. That is, the left coset $g \circ \mathrm{FIX}$ is the equivalence class of g, consisting of all functions f in $\mathrm{PERM}(X)$ with $f(x_0) = g(x_0)$. In this case, the equivalence classes which partition $\mathrm{PERM}(X)$ are actually the left cosets of the subgroup FIX.

If $g \notin \mathrm{FIX}$ and X has at least three elements we can show that the right coset $\mathrm{FIX} \circ g$ is not the same as $g \circ \mathrm{FIX}$. Since $g \notin \mathrm{FIX}$, $g(x_0) \neq x_0$. Choose an f in $\mathrm{PERM}(X)$ with $f(x_0) = x_0$ but $f(g(x_0)) \neq g(x_0)$. Then $f \in \mathrm{FIX}$, so $f \circ g \in \mathrm{FIX} \circ g$, but $(f \circ g)(x_0) \neq g(x_0)$, so $f \circ g \notin g \circ \mathrm{FIX}$.

Exercise 9 deals with this example in detail for a three-element set X. ∎

Not only do the cosets of H in G partition G, they all have the same size, namely the size of H.

Theorem 3 Let H be a subgroup of the group $(G, \square)$ and let $x \in G$. The function ϕ given by $\phi(h) = h \square x$ is a one-to-one correspondence of H onto the coset $H \square x$.

Proof. The function ϕ certainly maps H into $H \square x$. The function ψ given by $\psi(k) = k \square x^{-1}$ is its inverse, since if $k = h \square x \in H \square x$ with $h \in H$ then $k \square x^{-1} = h \square x \square x^{-1} = h$. Since ϕ has an inverse on $H \square x$, it is a one-to-one correspondence of H onto $H \square x$. ∎

Our next result is one of the basic workhorses of finite group theory. To state it we need some notation. For H a subgroup of G, let G/H be the set of [right] cosets of H in G, and let $|H|, |G|$ and $|G/H|$ be the numbers of elements in H, G and G/H, respectively.

Corollary [Lagrange's Theorem] Let H be a subgroup of the finite group G. Then
$$|G| = |G/H| \cdot |H|.$$
In particular, $|H|$ and $|G/H|$ divide $|G|$.

Proof. There are $|G/H|$ cosets of H, each of which has $|H|$ members, by Theorem 3. They partition G by Theorem 2. ∎

One can show [Exercise 15] that G has the same number of left cosets of H as right cosets, so Lagrange's theorem is true whichever type of cosets we use.

EXAMPLE 6 (a) A group with 10 members can only have subgroups with 1, 2, 5 or 10 members. Contrast this with Example 3; a semigroup with 10 members can have subsemigroups with n members for $n = 1, 2, \ldots, 10$.

(b) A group with 81 members can only have subgroups with 1, 3, 9, 27 or 81 members.

(c) Suppose the set X has n elements. Then the group PERM(X) of Example 5 has $n!$ elements, and the subgroup FIX fixing x_0 has $(n-1)!$ elements. There are n left cosets $g \circ$ FIX, one for each possible value of $g(x_0)$. Lagrange's theorem in this case takes the form

$$n! = n \cdot (n-1)!.$$

(d) Let G be the group of isomorphisms of the graph in Figure 1 back onto itself, with composition as operation. One can use Lagrange's theorem to help check that G has 10 members. We see at once the five "rotations,"

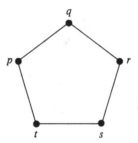

FIGURE 1

through angles of $0°$, $72°$, $144°$, $216°$ and $288°$, which form a subgroup, call it R. The correspondence g defined by $g(p) = p$, $g(q) = t$, $g(r) = s$, $g(s) = r$ and $g(t) = q$ is in G but not in R, so $|G| > |R| = 5$. By Lagrange's theorem $|G|$ is a multiple of 5, so it's at least 10. Now for an element f of G there are only five possible choices for $f(p)$, and then only two possible choices for $f(q)$ [one on each side of $f(p)$], after which the rest of the action of f is completely determined. So G has at most $5 \cdot 2 = 10$ members, and thus has exactly 10.

Half of the members of G are in R. The rest form the single coset $R \circ g$, where g is defined above. In this case $R \circ g = g \circ R$. [See also Exercise 14.]

The subgroup $\langle g \rangle$ consists just of e and g, since $g \circ g = e$, and so $|\langle g \rangle| = 2$. Since $10 = |G| = |G/\langle g \rangle| \cdot |\langle g \rangle|$, there are 5 cosets of $\langle g \rangle$ in G. In fact, $\langle g \rangle$ is the subgroup of G fixing the point p. As in part (c) above, the cosets of $\langle g \rangle$ are simply the five sets of isomorphisms in G taking p to each of its five possible images, namely $\{f \in G : f(p) = p\}$, $\{f \in G : f(p) = q\}$, $\{f \in G : f(p) = r\}$, etc.   □

The **order** of an element in a finite group is defined to be the number of elements in the cyclic subgroup it generates. By Lagrange's theorem, the order of every element of G divides $|G|$.

It is not hard to give examples of groups for which some divisors of $|G|$ are not orders of elements. Indeed, any noncyclic group is an example. An example of a group G which has no subgroup with n elements for some divisor n of $|G|$ is harder to describe, but in fact such groups are in a sense the most common.

EXERCISES 11.2

1. (a) Find the intersection of the subsemigroups $2\mathbb{P}$ and $3\mathbb{P}$ of the semigroup $(\mathbb{P}, +)$.
   (b) Is the intersection in part (a) cyclic? Explain.
   (c) Repeat part (b) with the semigroup $(\mathbb{P}, \cdot)$.

2. (a) Find the intersection of the subsemigroups of $(\mathbb{P}, \cdot)$ generated by 2 and 3, respectively.
   (b) Is the intersection in part (a) cyclic? Explain.

3. (a) Find the intersection of the three subsemigroups $4\mathbb{P}, 6\mathbb{P}, 10\mathbb{P}$ of the semigroup $(\mathbb{P}, \cdot)$.
   (b) Is the intersection in part (a) cyclic? Explain.
   (c) Repeat part (b) with the semigroup $(\mathbb{P}, +)$.

4. (a) Find the intersection of all the subgroups $n\mathbb{Z}$ of $(\mathbb{Z}, +)$, where $n \in \mathbb{P}$.
   (b) Is the intersection in part (a) cyclic? Explain.

5. (a) Give an example of a one-to-one correspondence between $4\mathbb{Z}$ and the coset $4\mathbb{Z} + 3$ in $(\mathbb{Z}, +)$.
   (b) Give another example.

6. Consider the group $(\mathbb{Z}, +)$. Write $\mathbb{Z}$ as a disjoint union of five cosets of a subgroup.

7. Give an example of a group G and subgroups H and K such that $H \cup K$ is not a subgroup of G.

8. (a) Show that the subgroup R in Example 6(d) is cyclic, and describe a generator for it.
   (b) Show that the group G in the example contains elements of orders 1, 2 and 5, but not 10.

9. Let $X = \{1, 2, 3\}$ and $x_0 = 1$ in Example 5.
   (a) Find $|\text{PERM}(X)|$.
   (b) Find $|\text{FIX}|$ and describe each of the functions in FIX.
   (c) The function g defined by $g(1) = 2$, $g(2) = 3$ and $g(3) = 1$ is not in FIX. Describe the members of the coset $\text{FIX} \circ g$.
   (d) Show that $\text{FIX} \circ g \neq g \circ \text{FIX}$.
   (e) Show that in fact $\text{FIX} \circ g$ is not a left coset at all.
   (f) How many cosets does FIX have in $\text{PERM}(X)$?

10. The table below describes a binary operation $\bullet$ on the set $G = \{a, b, c, d, e\}$ with e as identity element.

$\bullet$	e	a	b	c	d
e	e	a	b	c	d
a	a	e	c	d	b
b	b	d	a	e	c
c	c	b	d	a	e
d	d	c	e	b	a

(a) Show that the set $\{e, a\}$ is a group under $\bullet$ as operation.

(b) Without doing any calculations, use the result of part (a) and Lagrange's theorem to conclude that $(G, \bullet)$ is not a group.

11. The following table gives the binary operation for a group $(G, \bullet)$ with elements a, b, c, d, e, f.

$\bullet$	e	a	b	c	d	f
e	e	a	b	c	d	f
a	a	b	e	d	f	c
b	b	e	a	f	c	d
c	c	f	d	e	b	a
d	d	c	f	a	e	b
f	f	d	c	b	a	e

(a) List the members of the subgroup $\langle a \rangle$.

(b) Show that $\langle a \rangle \bullet c = c \bullet \langle a \rangle$.

(c) Find all the subgroups with two members.

(d) Find $|G/\langle d \rangle|$.

(e) Describe the right cosets of $\langle d \rangle$.

12. Repeat Exercise 11 for the group with the following table.

$\bullet$	e	a	b	c	d	f
e	e	a	b	c	d	f
a	a	b	e	d	f	c
b	b	e	a	f	c	d
c	c	d	f	a	b	e
d	d	f	c	b	e	a
f	f	c	d	e	a	b

13. (a) Show that if H is a subgroup of a group $(G, \square)$, and if $g \in G$, then $H \square g = H$ if and only if $g \in H$. Try to be clever and use Theorem 2.

(b) Show by example that the conclusion in part (a) can fail if G is just a semigroup and H a subsemigroup. *Suggestion:* Let $G = H = \mathbb{P}$.

14. Consider a finite group $(G, \square)$ with a subgroup H such that $|G| = 2|H|$. Show that $g \square H = H \square g$ for every g in G. *Suggestion:* Consider the two cases $g \in H$ and $g \notin H$ separately.

15. Let H be a subgroup of the group $(G, \square)$.

(a) Show that for each g in G the right coset $H \square g^{-1}$ consists of the inverses of the elements in the left coset $g \square H$.

(b) Describe a one-to-one correspondence between the set of left cosets of H in G and the set of right cosets.

16. Prove Theorem 3 without mentioning the inverse correspondence.

17. The set $\mathcal{L}(S)$ of all subsemigroups of a semigroup S is partially ordered by $\subseteq$.

(a) Show that the least upper bound $K \vee L$ of two members K, L of $\mathcal{L}(S)$ is $(K \cup L)^+$.

(b) Under what conditions on K and L does a greatest lower bound $K \wedge L$ exist? What is it when it exists?

(c) Show that if S is a finite group, then $(\mathfrak{L}(S), \subseteq)$ is a lattice. *Suggestion:* Appeal to Theorem 5 of § 11.1.

18. Show that if H is a subgroup of $(G, \bullet)$, then $x \bullet H \bullet x^{-1}$ is also a subgroup for each x in G.

§ 11.3   Homomorphisms

There is really only one natural way in which a function from one semigroup to another can take their algebraic structures into account: it must take products of elements to products of their images. In symbols, an "algebra-compatible" function h from a semigroup S with operation $\bullet$ to a semigroup T with operation $\square$ must satisfy

$$h(s_1 \bullet s_2) = h(s_1) \square h(s_2) \quad \text{for all} \quad s_1, s_2 \in S.$$

Such a function is called a **homomorphism**. If S and T are not just semigroups but are groups, we may emphasize the fact by calling h a **group homomorphism**.

EXAMPLE 1   (a) Let $(S, \bullet)$ and $(T, \square)$ both be $(\mathbb{Z}, +)$. The homomorphism condition is that

$$h(m + n) = h(m) + h(n) \quad \forall m, n \in \mathbb{Z}.$$

The function h defined by $h(n) = 5n$ for all n is an example of a homomorphism, since

$$h(m + n) = 5 \cdot (m + n) = 5m + 5n = h(m) + h(n).$$

There is nothing special about 5; any other integer would define a homomorphism in the same way.

(b) Let $(S, \bullet)$ be $(\mathbb{P}, +)$, let $(T, \square)$ be $(\mathbb{P}, \cdot)$, and let $h(m) = 2^m$ for m in $\mathbb{Z}$. Since

$$h(m + n) = 2^{m+n} = 2^m \cdot 2^n = h(m) \cdot h(n),$$

h is a homomorphism of $(\mathbb{P}, +)$ into $(\mathbb{P}, \cdot)$.

(c) The determinant of an $n \times n$ matrix is a real number. Theorem 1 of § 4.2 says that if $\mathbf{A}$ and $\mathbf{B}$ are $n \times n$ matrices, then

$$\det(\mathbf{A} \cdot \mathbf{B}) = \det(\mathbf{A}) \cdot \det(\mathbf{B}).$$

In other words, the mapping $\mathbf{A} \to \det(\mathbf{A})$ from $(\mathfrak{M}_{n,n}, \cdot)$ to $(\mathbb{R}, \cdot)$ is a homomorphism.

(d) Recall that $a = \log_2 b$ if and only if $b = 2^a$. The function h from $(\{x \in \mathbb{R} : x > 0\}, \cdot)$ to $(\mathbb{R}, +)$ given by $h(x) = \log_2 x$ is a homomorphism since $\log_2(xy) = \log_2(x) + \log_2(y)$.

(e) Consider a positive integer p. For $n \in \mathbb{Z}$, let $\text{Rem}_p(n)$ be the remainder when n is divided by p. Then Rem_p is a homomorphism of $(\mathbb{Z}, +)$ onto $(\mathbb{Z}(p), +_p)$, and also a homomorphism of $(\mathbb{Z}, \cdot)$ onto $(\mathbb{Z}(p), *_p)$. Theorems 1 and 2 of § 4.3 and the discussion after Theorem 2 give the details to verify that Rem_p is a homomorphism in each case. $\square$

If h is a homomorphism from $(S, \bullet)$ to $(T, \square)$, then the image $h(S)$ is a subsemigroup of T, since if $h(s_1)$ and $h(s_2)$ are members of $h(S)$ then $h(s_1)$ $\square\, h(s_2) = h(s_1 \bullet s_2) \in h(S)$, and so $h(S)$ is closed under $\square$. If $(S, \bullet)$ and $(T, \square)$ are groups, we can show that $h(S)$ is a subgroup of $(T, \square)$, as follows. Suppose e is the identity of S. Then $h(e) \square h(s) = h(e \bullet s) = h(s)$ for every s in S. So $h(e) = h(e) \square h(s) \square h(s)^{-1} = h(s) \square h(s)^{-1}$, which is the identity of T. That is, h sends the identity of S to the identity of T. Moreover, $h(e) = h(s^{-1} \bullet s) = h(s^{-1}) \square h(s)$, so

$$h(s)^{-1} = h(e) \square h(s)^{-1} = h(s^{-1}) \square h(s) \square h(s)^{-1} = h(s^{-1}).$$

Thus h takes inverses to inverses, and $h(S)$ contains the inverses of all of its elements. Since $h(S)$ is closed under products and taking inverses, it is a subgroup of T.

EXAMPLE 2 Let $(G, \square)$ be a group and let $g \in G$. Recall from Example 3(a) of § 11.1 that the cyclic group $\langle g \rangle$ generated by g is $\{g^n : n \in \mathbb{Z}\}$, where $g^{-k} = (g^{-1})^k$ for $k \in \mathbb{P}$. One can check by looking at cases that

$$g^{n+m} = g^n \square g^m \quad \forall n, m \in \mathbb{Z}.$$

That is, the function h from $(\mathbb{Z}, +)$ to $(G, \square)$ given by $h(n) = g^n$ is a homomorphism. Its image $h(\mathbb{Z})$ is $\langle g \rangle$. □

A homomorphism h from $(S, \bullet)$ to $(T, \square)$ defines a relation $\equiv$ on S by

$$s_1 \equiv s_2 \quad \text{if and only if} \quad h(s_1) = h(s_2).$$

We saw in Theorem 2 of § 7.3 that $\equiv$ is an equivalence relation. Denote the equivalence class of s by $[s]$. Then

$$h([s]) = \{h(s') : s' \in [s]\} = \{h(s') : h(s') = h(s)\} = \{h(s)\};$$

all members of $[s]$ have the same image under h, namely $h(s)$, and different classes have different images.

Since h is a special kind of function, $\equiv$ is a special kind of equivalence relation. Suppose $a \equiv b$ and $c \equiv d$. Then $h(a) = h(b)$ and $h(c) = h(d)$. Since h is a homomorphism,

$$h(a \bullet c) = h(a) \square h(c) = h(b) \square h(d) = h(b \bullet d),$$

and thus $a \bullet c \equiv b \bullet d$. That is,

(C) $$a \equiv b \text{ and } c \equiv d \Rightarrow a \bullet c \equiv b \bullet d.$$

An equivalence relation $\equiv$ which satisfies (C) is called a **congruence relation** on the semigroup $(S, \bullet)$, and its equivalence classes are called **congruence classes**. It turns out [Exercise 11(c)] that every congruence relation arises from a homomorphism in the same way that we have obtained $\equiv$ from h.

EXAMPLE 3   (a) Consider again the function $\text{Rem}_p : \mathbb{Z} \to \mathbb{Z}(p)$ in Example 1(e), which is a homomorphism of $(\mathbb{Z}, +)$ onto $(\mathbb{Z}(p), +_p)$ and also of $(\mathbb{Z}, \cdot)$ onto $(\mathbb{Z}(p), *_p)$. Since $\text{Rem}_p(m) = \text{Rem}_p(n)$ if and only if $m \equiv n \pmod{p}$, the congruence relation $\equiv$ defined by Rem_p is precisely the relation of congruence mod p defined on $\mathbb{Z}$ in § 4.3. Moreover, Theorem 2(b) of that section is just a statement of property (C), both for Rem_p as an additive homomorphism and as a multiplicative homomorphism.

(b) Define the relation $\equiv$ on $\mathbb{Z}$ by $m \equiv n$ if and only if m and n are both even or both odd. The corresponding congruence classes are $\text{EVEN} = \{n \in \mathbb{Z} : n \text{ is even}\}$ and $\text{ODD} = \{n \in \mathbb{Z} : n \text{ is odd}\}$. The relation $\equiv$ is a congruence relation on $(\mathbb{Z}, +)$. For instance, if a and b are both even and c and d are both odd, then $a + c$ and $b + d$ are both odd. The corresponding rule we learned as children is "EVEN plus ODD is ODD," and it doesn't matter which numbers are actually involved. This property reflects the fact that Rem_p in part (a) is an additive homomorphism for $p = 2$. $\square$

Condition (C) tells us that we get a representative of the congruence class $[b \bullet d]$ by using *any* representative a of the class $[b]$ and *any* representative c from $[d]$, and forming their product $a \bullet c$. Thus (C) says that

$$[a] = [b] \text{ and } [c] = [d] \Rightarrow [a \bullet c] = [b \bullet d].$$

Let $[S]$ denote the set of all congruence classes $[s]$. We define the binary operation $*$ on $[S]$ by

$$[s_1] * [s_2] = [s_1 \bullet s_2].$$

This product is well-defined because, as we just observed, we will get the same answer $[s_1 \bullet s_2]$ no matter which representatives of $[s_1]$ and $[s_2]$ we use. It is easy to check [Exercise 11(b)] that $([S], *)$ is a semigroup. If S has identity e then $[e]$ is the identity of $[S]$, and if $(S, \bullet)$ is a group then $[s^{-1}] = [s]^{-1}$, so $([S], *)$ is also a group [Exercise 11(d)].

The operation $*$ we have just defined is called the **natural operation** on the set $[S]$. It is understood to be the operation on $[S]$ if no other operation is specified. The semigroup $([S], *)$ may seem to be an unusual sort of object. Its members are themselves subsets of S, so we are combining subsets to get subsets. We have done this sort of thing before, though, using operations such as $\cup$, $\cap$ and $\oplus$, so only the definition of this particular operation $*$ is a new idea.

EXAMPLE 4   (a) Consider the relation $\equiv$ of congruence mod 2 on $\mathbb{Z}$ which we saw in Example 3(b). The congruence classes are $\text{EVEN} = [0]$ and $\text{ODD} = [1]$, and so $[\mathbb{Z}] = \{[0], [1]\}$. Let's look first at the additive group $(\mathbb{Z}, +)$. Then

$$\text{EVEN}*\text{EVEN} = [0]*[0] = [0 + 0] = [0] = \text{EVEN}$$

$$\text{EVEN}*\text{ODD} = [0]*[1] = [0 + 1] = [1] = \text{ODD}$$

$$\text{ODD}*\text{EVEN} = [1]*[0] = [1 + 0] = [1] = \text{ODD}$$

$$\text{ODD}*\text{ODD} = [1]*[1] = [1 + 1] = [2] = [0] = \text{EVEN}.$$

The symbol * here acts like "plus." We could summarize the results in a table.

*	[0]	[1]
[0]	[0]	[1]
[1]	[1]	[0]

The semigroup ([$\mathbb{Z}$], *) is a two-element group with identity [0], in which each element is its own inverse.

(b) Now consider the multiplicative semigroup ($\mathbb{Z}$, ·), with the same congruence relation as in part (a). We compute, and obtain a different table for the new product * on [$\mathbb{Z}$].

new *	[0]	[1]
[0]	[0]	[0]
[1]	[0]	[1]

For instance, [0]*[1] = [0·1] = [0], i.e., EVEN*ODD = EVEN. Now the symbol * acts like "times." The semigroup ([$\mathbb{Z}$], *) in this case has identity [1], but it is not a group.

We could just as well have used different names for the congruence classes. Since [16] = [0] and [73] = [1], the table

new *	[16]	[73]
[16]	[16]	[16]
[73]	[16]	[73]

is exactly the same as the last table except for the names.   □

The table in Example 4(a) looks just like the table for $+_2$ on $\mathbb{Z}(2)$ [Figure 2 of § 4.3], and the table in Example 4(b) looks like the table for $*_2$ on $\mathbb{Z}(2)$. This similarity follows from one of the most central facts about homomorphisms. To state the main theorem, we need to say what it means for two semigroups to look just alike. A semigroup homomorphism which is a one-to-one correspondence between two semigroups is called a **semigroup isomorphism**. We have seen isomorphisms before; graph isomorphisms were one-to-one correspondences preserving the graph structure, and Boolean algebra isomorphisms preserved the operations $\vee$, $\wedge$ and $'$. Semigroup isomorphisms preserve products. If h is a semigroup isomorphism of $(S, \bullet)$ onto $T, \square$) then

$$h(s_1 \bullet s_2) = h(s_1) \square h(s_2),$$

and since h is one-to-one

$$h(s_3) = h(s_1) \square h(s_2) \Leftrightarrow s_3 = s_1 \bullet s_2.$$

If there is a semigroup isomorphism of S onto T, we say S and T are **isomorphic** and write $S \simeq T$ [or $(S, \bullet) \simeq (T, \square)$ if the operations need to be mentioned].

Theorem [The fundamental theorem of homomorphisms] Let h be a homomorphism from the semigroup $(S, \bullet)$ to the semigroup $(T, \square)$. Define the congruence relation $\equiv$ on S by

$$s_1 \equiv s_2 \Leftrightarrow h(s_1) = h(s_2),$$

and let $[s]$ denote the congruence class of s. Then the mapping

$$[s] \to h(s)$$

is an isomorphism of $[S]$ onto $h(S)$.

Proof. When we defined $[s]$ earlier, we saw that all members of $[s]$ have the same image under h, so the mapping $[s] \to h(s)$ is well-defined and doesn't depend on which representative of $[s]$ we choose. Let's give this mapping a name, h^*; thus h^* from $[S]$ to $h(S)$ is defined by $h^*([s]) = h(s)$. We also saw earlier that if $[s] \neq [s']$ then $h(s) \neq h(s')$, so the mapping h^* is one-to-one. Its image is the set $h(S) = \{h(s) : s \in S\}$. We only need to check that h^* is a homomorphism. Since

$$
\begin{aligned}
h^*([s]*[s']) &= h^*([s \bullet s']) & &\text{definition of } * \\
&= h(s \bullet s') & &\text{definition of } h^* \\
&= h(s) \,\square\, h(s') & &h \text{ is a homomorphism} \\
&= h^*([s]) \,\square\, h^*([s']) & &\text{definition of } h^* \text{ again,}
\end{aligned}
$$

h^* is a homomorphism, and hence an isomorphism. □

This theorem says that the image semigroup $h(S)$ looks just like the semigroup $[S]$ made from the congruence classes. The isomorphism h^* is often called the **natural isomorphism** of $[S]$ onto $h(S)$. If S and T are groups, then $h(S)$ is a group, and so its isomorphic copy $[S]$ is also a group and h^* is a group isomorphism.

EXAMPLE 5 We saw in Example 1(e) that the mapping Rem_p from $(\mathbb{Z}, +)$ to $(\mathbb{Z}(p), +_p)$ is a homomorphism. The theorem says that $(\mathbb{Z}(p), +_p)$ is isomorphic to the semigroup $([\mathbb{Z}], *)$, with $[n] = \{m \in \mathbb{Z} : m \equiv n \,(\mathrm{mod}\ p)\}$ and $[n]*[n'] = [n + n']$. □

Consider again a homomorphism h from S to T. The mapping v [Greek lowercase nu] from S to $[S]$ given by $v(s) = [s]$ is also a homomorphism [Exercise 8(b)], called the **natural homomorphism**. For each $s \in S$ we have $h^*(v(s)) = h^*([s]) = h(s)$, so $h^* \circ v = h$. Figure 1 illustrates the relationship.

What if h is already one-to-one? Then h itself gives an isomorphism of S onto $h(S)$, and $[s] = \{s\}$ for all $s \in S$. In this case h^*, v and $[S]$ are not very

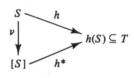

FIGURE 1

interesting. Since v is an isomorphism [Exercise 9], [S] looks just like S, and $h*$ is essentially h.

Isomorphisms get used in two different ways, as we saw when we looked at graph isomorphisms. Sometimes we want to call attention to the fact that two apparently different semigroups, such as [S] and $h(S)$, are actually identical in structure. At other times the identical structure is obvious, but we want to examine the various isomorphisms which are possible, for instance from S back onto itself, to see how much symmetry is present. We will explore symmetry more when we study groups in § 11.5.

Imagine now that we have a homomorphism h from a semigroup S to a semigroup T and that we know very little about S but all about T. If h is an isomorphism, then S is essentially identical with T and h tells us all about S. If h is one-to-one but not onto T, then at least we know that S looks just like the subsemigroup $h(S)$ of T. We can analyze S by looking at $h(S)$, which we know pretty well because it's inside the known semigroup T. Even if h is not one-to-one, we can still perhaps learn something about S by looking at $h(S)$. If S is complicated but $h(S)$ isn't, this may be a good way to begin to learn about the structure of S.

Such an approach works especially well if S is a group, as we will see in the next section.

EXERCISES 11.3

1. Which of the following functions h from ($\mathbb{Z}$, $+$) to ($\mathbb{Z}$, $+$) are homomorphisms?
   (a) $h(n) = 6n$ (b) $h(n) = n + 1$
   (c) $h(n) = -n$ (d) $h(n) = n^2$
   (e) $h(n) = (6n^2 + 3n)/(2n + 1)$

2. Which of the following functions h are homomorphisms from ($\mathbb{P}$, $+$) to ($\mathbb{P}$, $\cdot$)?
   (a) $h(n) = 6^n$ (b) $h(n) = n$
   (c) $h(n) = (-6)^n$ (d) $h(n) = n^2$
   (e) $h(n) = 2^{n+1}$

3. Which of the following relations are congruence relations on ($\mathbb{Z}$, $+$)?
   (a) $m \equiv n \Leftrightarrow m - n$ is even,
   (b) $m \equiv n \Leftrightarrow m - n$ is a multiple of 10,
   (c) $m \equiv n \Leftrightarrow m = n$,
   (d) $m \equiv n \Leftrightarrow m = 0$,
   (e) $m \equiv n \Leftrightarrow m^2 = n^2$.

4. (a) For each of the relations in Exercise 3 which is not a congruence relation explain how the relation fails to be a congruence relation.
   (b) For each of the relations in Exercise 3 which is a congruence relation describe the congruence class [15].

5. Let $F = \text{FUN}(\mathbb{R}, \mathbb{R})$, and define $+$ on F by
$$(f + g)(x) = f(x) + g(x) \quad \text{for all} \quad x \in \mathbb{R}.$$
   Define h from F to $\mathbb{R}$ by $h(f) = f(73)$.

(a) Show that h is a homomorphism of $(F, +)$ onto $(\mathbb{R}, +)$.

(b) Define $*$ on F by $(f * g)(x) = f(x) \cdot g(x)$ for all x. Show that h is a homomorphism of $(F, *)$ onto $(\mathbb{R}, \cdot)$.

6. Let X be a set. Define the function h from $\mathcal{P}(X)$ to $\mathcal{P}(X)$ by $h(A) = X \backslash A$ for $A \subseteq X$.

(a) Show that h is a homomorphism from $(\mathcal{P}(X), \cap)$ to $(\mathcal{P}(X), \cup)$.

(b) Show that h is also a homomorphism from $(\mathcal{P}(X), \cup)$ to $(\mathcal{P}(X), \cap)$.

(c) Show that h is an isomorphism in each case. [Thus $(\mathcal{P}(X), \cap) \simeq (\mathcal{P}(X), \cup)$.]

7. Let Σ be the English alphabet. Define h on Σ^* by $h(w) =$ length of w.

(a) Show that h is a homomorphism from Σ^* with its usual operation to $(\mathbb{N}, +)$.

(b) Describe an isomorphism between the semigroup $([\Sigma^*], *)$ and $(\mathbb{N}, +)$.

(c) Describe the members of the congruence class [*elephant*], and the image of this class under your isomorphism in part (b).

8. (a) Verify the assertions about Rem_p in Example 1(e).

(b) Verify that the mapping ν, defined after Example 5 by $\nu(s) = [s]$, is a homomorphism of $(S, \bullet)$ onto $([S], *)$.

9. Suppose the semigroup homomorphism h from $(S, \circ)$ to $(T, \square)$ is one-to-one.

(a) Describe the relation $\equiv$ determined by h.

(b) Describe the set $[S]$ and the operation $*$ on it.

(c) Describe the natural mapping ν from S to $[S]$ and show that it is an isomorphism.

10. Suppose that $(S, \bullet)$ is a monoid with identity e and that h is a semigroup homomorphism from $(S, \bullet)$ to $(T, \square)$.

(a) Show that $(h(S), \square)$ is a monoid with identity $h(e)$.

(b) Must $h(e)$ be an identity of $(T, \square)$? Justify your answer.

11. Let $\equiv$ be a congruence relation on the semigroup $(S, \bullet)$, and let $[S]$ be its set of congruence classes.

(a) Verify that the operation $*$ on $[S]$ given by $[s] * [t] = [s \bullet t]$ is well-defined, i.e., is independent of the representatives chosen from $[s]$ and $[t]$.

(b) Show that $([S], *)$ is a semigroup.

(c) Show that the mapping h, given by $h(s) = [s]$, is a homomorphism of $(S, \bullet)$ onto $([S], *)$, and that $h(s) = h(t) \Leftrightarrow s \equiv t$.

(d) Show that if $(S, \bullet)$ is a group, then $([S], *)$ is a group.

12. An element z of a semigroup $(S, \bullet)$ is called a **zero element** or **zero** of S in case

$$z \bullet s = s \bullet z = z \quad \text{for all } s \text{ in } S.$$

(a) Show that a semigroup cannot have more than one zero element.

(b) Give an example of an infinite semigroup which has a zero element.

(c) Give an example of a finite semigroup which has at least two members and which has a zero element.

13. Let z be a zero element of $(S, \bullet)$ and let h be a homomorphism from $(S, \bullet)$ to $(T, \square)$.

(a) Show that $h(z)$ is a zero element of $h(S)$.

(b) Must $h(z)$ be a zero element of $(T, \square)$? Justify your answer.

(c) Show that $[z]$ is a zero element of $([S], *)$.

14. (a) Show that if f is a homomorphism from $(S, \bullet)$ to $(T, \square)$, and if g is a homomorphism from $(T, \square)$ to $(U, \vartriangle)$, then $g \circ f$ is a homomorphism.

(b) Show that if h is an isomorphism of $(S, \bullet)$ onto $(T, \square)$, then h^{-1} is an isomorphism of $(T, \square)$ onto $(S, \bullet)$.

(c) Use the results of parts (a) and (b) to show that the relation $\simeq$ is reflexive, symmetric and transitive.

15. Let h be a semigroup homomorphism from $(S, \bullet)$ to $(T, \square)$, and define $[S]$ as in the theorem and its proof. Let U be a subsemigroup of S.

(a) Show that $h(U)$ is a subsemigroup of $h(S)$.

(b) Show that the set $\bar{U} = \{[u] : u \in U\}$ is a subsemigroup of $[S]$.

(c) Describe an isomorphism of $\bar{U}$ onto $h(U)$.

§ 11.4   Homomorphisms of Groups

In this section we will look at what happens when h is a homomorphism from a group $(G, \bullet)$ to a group $(H, \square)$. Let e be the identity element of G and let e' be the identity of H. Then, as we saw in § 11.3, $h(e) = e'$ and $h(x^{-1}) = h(x)^{-1}$ for each x in G. As before, h gives the congruence relation $\equiv$ on G, where $x \equiv y$ if and only if $h(x) = h(y)$. We can describe the congruence class $[x]$ as a coset of a certain subgroup K of G determined by h.

Theorem 1   With notation as above, let $K = \{x \in G : h(x) = e'\}$. Then

(a) K is a subgroup of G.

(b) $[x] = K \bullet x = x \bullet K$ for each x in G.

The subgroup K is called the **kernel** of the homomorphism h. Notice in particular, from (b), that $K = K \bullet e = [e]$, so K is a congruence class as well as a subgroup.

Proof. (a) If $x, y \in K$, then $h(x \bullet y) = h(x) \square h(y) = e' \square e' = e'$, so $x \bullet y \in K$. Moreover, $h(x^{-1}) = h(x)^{-1} = (e')^{-1} = e'$, so $x^{-1} \in K$. Since K is closed under products and inverses, it is a subgroup of G.

(b) If $k \in K$, then $h(k \bullet x) = h(k) \square h(x) = e' \square h(x) = h(x)$, so $k \bullet x \equiv x$. Similarly, $x \bullet k \equiv x$. Thus $K \bullet x = \{k \bullet x : k \in K\} \subseteq [x]$ and similarly $x \bullet K \subseteq [x]$. Now if $y \in [x]$ then $y \equiv x$, so $y \bullet x^{-1} \equiv x \bullet x^{-1} = e$, $h(y \bullet x^{-1}) = h(e) = e'$ and $y \bullet x^{-1} \in K$. Thus $y = (y \bullet x^{-1}) \bullet x \in K \bullet x$. Hence $[x] \subseteq K \bullet x$, and similarly $[x] \subseteq x \bullet K$.   ☐

The example in Exercise 9 shows that nothing like this theorem is true in general for semigroups; to get any good out of cosets we need a group structure. We saw in Theorem 3 of § 11.2 that all cosets $K \bullet x$ have the same number of elements, namely $|K|$, and this fact gives us a useful test for one-to-oneness of homomorphisms.

Corollary   A group homomorphism is one-to-one if and only if its kernel is just the identity element.

Proof. Since K is a subgroup, it contains the identity e for sure. Moreover, all cosets $K \bullet x$ have exactly one element if and only if K itself has just one element.   ☐

EXAMPLE 1   (a) Define the homomorphism h from $(\mathbb{Z}, +)$ to $(\mathbb{Z}, +)$ by $h(n) = 5n$. The kernel of h is $\{n \in \mathbb{Z} : 5n = 0\} = \{0\}$, and h is one-to-one. The congruence class $[n]$ is simply $\{0\} + n = \{n\}$.

(b) Consider Rem_6 from $(\mathbb{Z}, +)$ to $(\mathbb{Z}(6), +_6)$, where $\text{Rem}_6(n)$ is the remainder on dividing n by 6, as in Example 1(e) of § 11.3. Then $K = \{n \in \mathbb{Z} : n \text{ is a multiple of } 6\} = 6\mathbb{Z}$. The congruence classes are the cosets $6\mathbb{Z}$, $6\mathbb{Z} + 1, 6\mathbb{Z} + 2, 6\mathbb{Z} + 3, 6\mathbb{Z} + 4, 6\mathbb{Z} + 5$. ☐

It follows from Theorem 1 that the set $[G]$ of congruence classes is actually the set G/K of cosets of K in G that we considered in § 11.2. From (b) we see that it doesn't matter here whether we think of left or right cosets. Since $[x] = K \bullet x$, the natural operation $*$ on $[G]$ is the product

$$(K \bullet x)*(K \bullet y) = K \bullet (x \bullet y)$$

on G/K. We can restate our information about $[G]$ using the coset notation.

Theorem 2   Let h be a homomorphism from the group $(G, \bullet)$ to the group $(H, \square)$, with kernel K. Then

(a) G/K is a group, with product

$$(K \bullet x)*(K \bullet y) = K \bullet (x \bullet y).$$

(b) G/K is isomorphic to $h(G)$ under the isomorphism h^* defined by

$$h^*(K \bullet x) = h(x).$$

(c) The mapping $v: G \to G/K$ given by

$$v(x) = K \bullet x$$

is a homomorphism of G onto G/K. The kernel of v is K.

The only new fact here is the assertion that K is the kernel of v, which is true since $K = K \bullet e$ is the identity of G/K and $v(x) = K$ if and only if $x \in K$.

If G is finite, then Lagrange's theorem in § 11.2 says that $|G/K| = |G|/|K|$. Since $|h(G)| = |G/K|$ by Theorem 2(b), we have the following.

Corollary   Let h be a homomorphism defined on a finite group G, with kernel K. Then $|h(G)| = |G|/|K|$. In particular, $|h(G)|$ divides $|G|$.

EXAMPLE 2   (a) Consider the mapping $h: \mathbb{Z}(30) \to \mathbb{Z}(30)$ defined by $h(n) = 6 *_{30} n$. Then h is an additive homomorphism with image $h(\mathbb{Z}(30)) = 6 *_{30} \mathbb{Z}(30) = \{0, 6, 12, 18, 24\}$, which has 5 elements. The kernel $K = \{0, 5, 10, 15, 20, 25\}$ has 6 elements and

$$|h(\mathbb{Z}(30))| = 5 = 30/6 = |\mathbb{Z}(30)|/|K|.$$

(b) The mapping $h: \mathbb{Z}(6) \to \mathbb{Z}(15)$ defined by $h(n) = 5 *_{15} n$ is an additive homomorphism, with $h(0) = h(3) = 0$, $h(1) = h(4) = 5$, $h(2) = h(5) = 10$. The image is $\{0, 5, 10\} = 5 *_{15} \mathbb{Z}(15)$. The kernel is $\{0, 3\}$. Sure enough, we have $|5 *_{15} \mathbb{Z}(15)| = 3$ while also $|\mathbb{Z}(6)|/|\{0, 3\}| = 6/2 = 3$.

(c) The group PERM({1, 2, 3}), defined in Example 5 of § 11.2, has $3! = 6$ members. By the last corollary, its homomorphic images can only have 1, 2, 3 or 6 members. Actually, 3 is impossible, since no subgroup K of PERM({1, 2, 3}) with just two members satisfies $K \circ x = x \circ K$ for all x. This fact is essentially Exercise 9(d) of § 11.2. $\square$

A subgroup K with the property that $K \bullet x = x \bullet K$ for every x in G is called a **normal subgroup** of G. If G is commutative, every subgroup is normal, but in the general case there will be nonnormal subgroups. We've just seen that kernels of homomorphisms are normal. In fact, they are the *only* normal subgroups.

Theorem 3 Let K be a normal subgroup of the group $(G, \bullet)$. Then:
  (a) $(K \bullet x) \bullet (K \bullet y) = K \bullet (x \bullet y)$ for all $x, y \in G$.
  (b) The set G/K of cosets of K in G is a group under the operation $*$ defined by

$$(K \bullet x)*(K \bullet y) = K \bullet (x \bullet y).$$

  (c) The function $v: G \to G/K$ defined by $v(x) = K \bullet x$ is a homomorphism with kernel K.

This theorem looks a lot like Theorem 2. The difference here is that now we begin with a subgroup K and have to manufacture a homomorphism.

Proof of Theorem 3.   (a) By $(K \bullet x) \bullet (K \bullet y)$ we mean the set

$$K \bullet x \bullet K \bullet y = \{k_1 \bullet x \bullet k_2 \bullet y : k_1, k_2 \in K\}.$$

Since K is a subgroup of G, $K = K \bullet e \subseteq K \bullet K \subseteq K$, so $K = K \bullet K$. Since K is normal, we have $x \bullet K = K \bullet x$, and so

$$K \bullet x \bullet K \bullet y = K \bullet K \bullet x \bullet y = K \bullet (x \bullet y) \in G/K.$$

(b) According to (a), $(K \bullet x)*(K \bullet y)$ is $(K \bullet x) \bullet (K \bullet y)$ and thus $*$ is a well-defined binary operation on G/K. It is easy to check that it is associative, that K is the identity and that $K \bullet x^{-1} = (K \bullet x)^{-1}$.

(c) We have $v(x \bullet y) = K \bullet (x \bullet y) = (K \bullet x)*(K \bullet y) = v(x)*v(y)$ by definition of $*$, so v is a homomorphism. If $v(x) = v(e)$ then $x \in K \bullet x = K \bullet e = K$, and if $x \in K$ then $v(x) = K \bullet x = K = v(e)$. Thus K is the kernel of v. $\square$

The message of Theorem 2(b) is that to study homomorphic images of G, it is enough to look at the various groups G/K which can be made from cosets of certain subgroups K of G. The message of Theorem 3 is that we can identify the interesting subgroups; they are the ones satisfying the equations $K \bullet x = x \bullet K$ for all x.

Instead of comparing left and right cosets, we can test a subgroup for normality by looking at its **conjugates**, sets of the form $x \bullet K \bullet x^{-1}$. If K is a subgroup of G, then so is $x \bullet K \bullet x^{-1}$ for each x in G [Exercise 18 of § 11.2].

Moreover, $x \bullet K = K \bullet x$ if and only if $x \bullet K \bullet x^{-1} = K \bullet x \bullet x^{-1} = K$, so K is normal if and only if $K = x \bullet K \bullet x^{-1}$ for every x, i.e., if and only if all conjugates of K are equal to K. In fact, to show K normal it is enough to show $x \bullet K \bullet x^{-1} \subseteq K$ for all x in G, for in that case we have

$$K = x^{-1} \bullet (x \bullet K \bullet x^{-1}) \bullet x \subseteq x^{-1} \bullet K \bullet x \subseteq K$$

since x^{-1} is also in G.

EXERCISES 11.4

1. Find the kernel of each of the following homomorphisms h.
   (a) From $(\mathbb{Z}, +)$ to $(\mathbb{Z}, +)$, defined by $h(n) = 73n$.
   (b) From $(\mathbb{Z}, +)$ to $(\mathbb{Z}, +)$, defined by $h(n) = 0$ for all n.
   (c) From $(\mathbb{Z}, +)$ to $(\mathbb{Z}(5), +_5)$, defined by $h(n) =$ the remainder on division of n by 5.
   (d) From $(\mathbb{Z}, +)$ to $(\mathbb{Z}, +)$, defined by $h(n) = n$.

2. For each homomorphism in Exercise 1, describe the coset of the kernel which contains 73.

3. Suppose that h is a homomorphism defined on a group G and that $|G| = 12$ and $|h(G)| = 3$.
   (a) Find $|K|$ where K is the kernel of h.
   (b) How many members of G does h map onto each member of $h(G)$?
   (c) How many congruence classes does h determine in G?

4. Define $+$ on $\text{FUN}(\mathbb{P}, \mathbb{Z})$ by

$$(f + g)(n) = f(n) + g(n) \quad \text{for all } n \in \mathbb{P}.$$

   Define h from $\text{FUN}(\mathbb{P}, \mathbb{Z})$ to $\mathbb{Z}$ by $h(f) = f(73)$.
   (a) Verify that h is a homomorphism from $(\text{FUN}(\mathbb{P}, \mathbb{Z}), +)$ to $(\mathbb{Z}, +)$.
   (b) Find the kernel of h.

5. The **direct product** of two groups $(G, \bullet)$ and $(H, \square)$ is the group $(G \times H, \triangle)$ with operation $\triangle$ defined by

$$\langle g_1, h_1 \rangle \triangle \langle g_2, h_2 \rangle = \langle g_1 \bullet g_2, h_1 \square h_2 \rangle \ \forall g_1, g_2 \in G, \ \forall h_1, h_2 \in H.$$

   (a) Describe the identity element of $G \times H$ and the inverse of an element $\langle g, h \rangle$ in $G \times H$.
   (b) Verify that the mapping $f: G \times H \to G$ defined by $f(\langle g, h \rangle) = g$ is a homomorphism.
   (c) Find the kernel of the homomorphism f in part (b).
   (d) Find a normal subgroup of $G \times H$ which is isomorphic to H.

6. Define h from $(\mathbb{Z}, +)$ to $\mathbb{Z}(2) \times \mathbb{Z}(3)$ [see Exercise 5] by $h(n) = \langle n_2, n_3 \rangle$, where n_k is the remainder on division of n by k and the operation on $\mathbb{Z}(k)$ is $+_k$ for $k = 2, 3$.
   (a) Verify that h is a homomorphism.
   (b) Verify that $h(\mathbb{Z}) = \mathbb{Z}(2) \times \mathbb{Z}(3)$.
   (c) Find the kernel of h.
   (d) Show that $\mathbb{Z}(2) \times \mathbb{Z}(3) \simeq \mathbb{Z}(6)$.

7. Let G be the set of 2×2 matrices of the form $\begin{bmatrix} 1 & x \\ 0 & 1 \end{bmatrix}$, with matrix multiplication as operation.

(a) Verify that G is a group, with

$$\begin{bmatrix} 1 & x \\ 0 & 1 \end{bmatrix}^{-1} = \begin{bmatrix} 1 & -x \\ 0 & 1 \end{bmatrix}.$$

(b) Verify that

$$\begin{bmatrix} 0 & 1 \\ 1 & 0 \end{bmatrix} \cdot G \neq G \cdot \begin{bmatrix} 0 & 1 \\ 1 & 0 \end{bmatrix}.$$

This shows that G is not a normal subgroup of the multiplicative group of all invertible 2×2 matrices.

(c) Show that G is a normal subgroup of the group T of all 2×2 matrices of the form

$$\begin{bmatrix} y & z \\ 0 & 1/y \end{bmatrix}, \quad y \neq 0,$$

with multiplication as operation.

(d) The mapping h from T to $(\mathbb{R} \setminus \{0\}, \cdot)$ defined by

$$h\left(\begin{bmatrix} y & z \\ 0 & 1/y \end{bmatrix}\right) = y$$

is a homomorphism. Find its kernel.

(e) Show that T/G is isomorphic to the group of non-0 real numbers under multiplication.

8. An **antihomomorphism** from $(S, \bullet)$ to $(T, \square)$ is a function k such that

$$k(s_1 \bullet s_2) = k(s_2) \square k(s_1) \quad \text{for all} \quad s_1, s_2 \in S.$$

(a) Use the result of Exercise 19 of § 4.1 to show that the transpose mapping k given by $k(\mathbf{A}) = \mathbf{A}^T$ is an antihomomorphism from $\mathfrak{M}_{n,n}$ under multiplication into itself. [This k could be called an **anti-isomorphism** since it is one-to-one and onto.]

(b) Show that the mapping $x \to x^{-1}$ is always an antihomomorphism of a group onto itself.

(c) Show that if k_1 and k_2 are antihomomorphisms for which the composition $k_1 \circ k_2$ is defined, then $k_1 \circ k_2$ is a homomorphism.

(d) Give an example of an antihomomorphism which is also a homomorphism.

9. Let S and T be nonempty sets, and define $\bullet$ on S and $\square$ on T by

$$x \bullet y = y \quad \text{for all} \quad x, y \in S$$
$$a \square b = b \quad \text{for all} \quad a, b \in T.$$

Then $(S, \bullet)$ and $(T, \square)$ are semigroups [Example 3 of § 11.2].

(a) Show that every function h from S to T is a semigroup homomorphism.

(b) Assume S and T are finite. Partition S into $|T|$ or fewer sets, and assign a different member of T to each subset. Verify that the resulting mapping is a homomorphism, with the given subsets as congruence classes.

    (c) Can the congruence classes in part (b) be considered as cosets of a fixed subsemigroup of S? Justify your answer.

10. Show that if h is a homomorphism defined on the group G and if $h(g)$ has just one pre-image under h for some g in G, then h is one-to-one.

11. (a) Show that if S is a semigroup, if A generates S and if h is a homomorphism defined on S, then $h(A)$ generates $h(S)$.

    (b) Is the corresponding statement true for groups and group homomorphisms? Justify your answer.

12. Show that if H and K are normal subgroups of a group $(G, \bullet)$, then $H \cap K$ is a normal subgroup. *Suggestion:* Consider $x \bullet (H \cap K) \bullet x^{-1}$.

13. Let H be a subgroup of $(G, \bullet)$.

    (a) Show that $\{x \in G : x \bullet H \bullet x^{-1} = H\}$ is a subgroup of G.

    (b) Conclude that if G is generated by a subset A and if $x \bullet H \bullet x^{-1} = H$ for all $x \in A$, then H is a normal subgroup.

14. Consider a finite group G with a subgroup H such that $|G| = 2|H|$. Show that H must be a normal subgroup of G. *Suggestion:* See Exercise 14 of § 11.2.

§ *11.5* *Symmetry and Groups of Permutations*

Commutative groups frequently arise in settings in which the binary operation is addition. Noncommutative groups commonly occur where the operation is composition of functions. They are especially useful in describing the symmetry of other objects, such as graphs or digraphs.

EXAMPLE 1 Recall from § 8.2 that an automorphism of a digraph D is a graph isomorphism of D onto itself. One way to describe the symmetry of a digraph, such as the ones shown in Figure 1, is to list its automorphisms. We noted in § 8.2 that the composition of two digraph isomorphisms is also an isomorphism, and it's easy to check that the inverse of an isomorphism is also an isomorphism. This means that the set Aut(D) of automorphisms of a digraph D is a

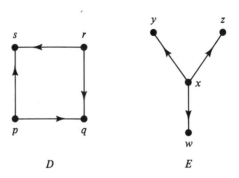

D E

FIGURE 1

group, with composition of functions as operation. In the case of the digraph *D* in Figure 1, which has two sources and two sinks, the automorphisms must send sources to sources and sinks to sinks. We can check that there are four different automorphisms, whose function values are given in Figure 2(a). The table in Figure 2(b) gives the products in the group (Aut(*D*), ∘). This group happens to be commutative.

	p	*q*	*r*	*s*			*e*	*f*	*g*	*h*
e	*p*	*q*	*r*	*s*		*e*	*e*	*f*	*g*	*h*
f	*p*	*s*	*r*	*q*		*f*	*f*	*e*	*h*	*g*
g	*r*	*q*	*p*	*s*		*g*	*g*	*h*	*e*	*f*
h	*r*	*s*	*p*	*q*		*h*	*h*	*g*	*f*	*e*

Aut(D)

(a)   (b)

FIGURE 2

This section contains several tables, such as the ones in Figure 2, which contain information about groups. It is a good idea on first reading to look quickly at the tables to see what kinds of information they contain, and perhaps to verify a few entries. Later on, especially when you are working the exercises, you can use the tables instead of making the calculations yourself.

The digraph *E* in Figure 1 has a different kind of symmetry and a different automorphism group. We see that every automorphism of *E* must send *x* to itself but otherwise can permute the remaining vertices in any way. Figure 3 gives the function values of the automorphisms of *E* and the table of (Aut(*E*), ∘). The group Aut(*E*) is essentially the same as—i.e., is isomorphic to—the noncommutative group PERM({*y*, *z*, *w*}), whose function values we get by suppressing the *x*-column in the table of values of Aut(*E*). We saw

	x	*y*	*z*	*w*		∘	*e*	*a*	*b*	*c*	*d*	*f*
e	*x*	*y*	*z*	*w*		*e*	*e*	*a*	*b*	*c*	*d*	*f*
a	*x*	*z*	*w*	*y*		*a*	*a*	*b*	*e*	*d*	*f*	*c*
b	*x*	*w*	*y*	*z*		*b*	*b*	*e*	*a*	*f*	*c*	*d*
c	*x*	*y*	*w*	*z*		*c*	*c*	*f*	*d*	*e*	*b*	*a*
d	*x*	*z*	*y*	*w*		*d*	*d*	*c*	*f*	*a*	*e*	*b*
f	*x*	*w*	*z*	*y*		*f*	*f*	*d*	*c*	*b*	*a*	*e*

Aut(E) ≃ PERM({y, z, w})

FIGURE 3

the table for $(\text{Aut}(E), \circ)$ before in Exercise 11 of § 11.2. Except for the names of the vertices, the group $\text{PERM}(\{y, z, w\})$ appears in Exercise 9 of § 11.2 and elsewhere. Every member of $\text{Aut}(E)$ fixes the vertex x. The subgroup of $\text{Aut}(E)$ fixing y is $\{e, c\}$. The subgroups $\{e, d\}$ and $\{e, f\}$ fix w and z, respectively. □

The groups which arise in analyzing symmetry are generally groups of permutations of sets. For instance, the automorphism group $\text{Aut}(D)$ in Example 1 consisted of certain permutations of the set $V(D)$ of vertices of D. The group $\text{PERM}(V(D))$ has $4! = 24$ members, but only four of them are in its subgroup $\text{Aut}(D)$.

Suppose that G is a group of permutations of the set S, i.e., a subgroup of $(\text{PERM}(S), \circ)$, and that T is a subset of S. Then the set $G_T = \{f \in G : f(T) = T\}$ is a subgroup of G, since if $f, g \in G$ then

$$(f \circ g)(T) = f(g(T)) = f(T) = T, \quad \text{and also} \quad f^{-1}(T) = f^{-1}(f(T)) = T$$

so that G is closed under composition and inverses. Since the intersection of subgroups is a subgroup, we can build subgroups of G such as $G_{\{x\}} \cap G_{\{y\}}$, $G_{\{x,y\}} \cap G_{\{x,z\}} \cap G_{\{z\}}$, etc. Complicated expressions can sometimes be simplified. For example,

$$G_{\{x,z\}} \cap G_{\{z\}} = G_{\{x\}} \cap G_{\{z\}},$$

because if

$$\{g(x), g(z)\} = g(\{x, z\}) = \{x, z\}$$

and if $g(z) = z$ then $g(x)$ must be x. Continuing this argument, we see that

$$G_{\{x,y\}} \cap G_{\{x,z\}} \cap G_{\{z\}} = G_{\{x,y\}} \cap G_{\{x\}} \cap G_{\{z\}} = G_{\{y\}} \cap G_{\{x\}} \cap G_{\{z\}}.$$

Automorphisms can also be used to look for isomorphisms between graphs. Consider two [undirected] connected graphs G and H, each with n vertices, and suppose $V(G) \cap V(H) = \varnothing$. We know that it is generally hard to tell if G and H are isomorphic. If they *are* isomorphic and we choose a vertex v of G, then there is a vertex w of H which corresponds to v under an isomorphism of G onto H. We can consider all n pairs $\langle v, w \rangle$ for w in H and look in each case to see if there is an isomorphism of G to H taking v to w.

Consider a particular pair $\langle v, w \rangle$ and build a new graph K by using all

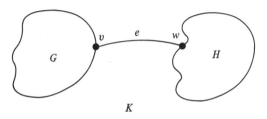

FIGURE 4

the vertices and edges of G and H and creating a new edge e joining v and w. Figure 4 illustrates the idea. If there is an isomorphism f from G onto H taking v to w, then f^{-1} is an isomorphism of H onto G taking w to v, and we can build an automorphism g of K onto itself by letting $g(x) = f(x)$ for x in G and $g(y) = f^{-1}(y)$ for y in H. The automorphism g takes the edge e to itself but interchanges its ends v and w. Conversely, if there is an automorphism of K turning e end for end, then its restriction to G is an isomorphism of G onto H. The problem of checking whether G and H are isomorphic has been turned into a question about automorphism groups of the n different graphs K which can be formed by choosing w in H.

The set

$$\text{Aut}(K)_e = \{f \in \text{Aut}(K) : f(e) = e\} = \text{Aut}(K)_{\{v, w\}}$$

is a subgroup of $\text{Aut}(K)$, and we have $\text{Aut}(K)_{\{v\}} \cap \text{Aut}(K)_{\{w\}} \subseteq \text{Aut}(K)_e$. The question now is whether the inclusion here is actually equality. If it is, no automorphism of K switches e end for end. Otherwise, one does. We have reduced the graph isomorphism problem to one of checking if two subgroups of $\text{Aut}(K)$ are equal. Unfortunately, this problem is hard too, but it can be attacked with group-theoretic machinery. The most successful work on graph isomorphisms has been based on this automorphism group approach.

Groups of permutations may appear to be rather special kinds of groups. Our first theorem says they are not; in a sense, every group is a permutation group.

Theorem 1 [Cayley] Let $(G, \square)$ be a group. Then G is isomorphic to a group of permutations of the set G itself.

Proof. We need to set up a one-to-one homomorphism λ of $(G, \square)$ into $(\text{PERM}(G), \circ)$. Then G will be isomorphic to the image $\lambda(G)$, which will be a subgroup of $\text{PERM}(G)$.

To each g in G we associate a function g^* from G to G defined by

$$g^*(x) = g \square x \quad \forall x \in G.$$

Since G is closed under $\square$, $g \square x$ is in G, so g^* does map G into G. Moreover

$$((g^{-1})^* \circ g^*)(x) = (g^{-1})^*(g^*(x)) = g^{-1} \square (g \square x) = x$$

for every x, and thus $(g^{-1})^* \circ g^*$ is the identity function on G. So is $g^* \circ (g^{-1})^*$ for a similar reason. Thus $(g^{-1})^*$ is the inverse of the function g^*. Since g^* has an inverse, it follows from the theorem of § 3.2 that g^* must be one-to-one and onto. Thus g^* belongs to $\text{PERM}(G)$.

We now define $\lambda: G \to \text{PERM}(G)$ by $\lambda(g) = g^*$ for all g in G. If g and h are in G, then $\lambda(g \square h) = (g \square h)^*$. But

$$(g \square h)^*(x) = (g \square h) \square x = g \square (h \square x) = g^*(h^*(x)) = (g^* \circ h^*)(x)$$

for every x in G, so $(g \,\square\, h)^* = g^* \circ h^*$. Thus

$$\lambda(g \,\square\, h) = g^* \circ h^* = \lambda(g) \circ \lambda(h),$$

and hence λ is a homomorphism from G into $\text{PERM}(G)$.

To check that λ is one-to-one, observe that if e is the identity element of G then

$$(\lambda(g))(e) = g^*(e) = g \,\square\, e = g,$$

so if $\lambda(g) = \lambda(h)$ then

$$g = (\lambda(g))(e) = (\lambda(h))(e) = h. \quad \square$$

Groups can be pretty complicated, and so Cayley's theorem can be viewed as saying that permutation groups must be pretty complicated. There is often some benefit to be gained, however, from taking a permutation group perspective.

Consider a group $(G, \square)$ with identity e and a homomorphism h of G into $(\text{PERM}(S), \circ)$ for some set S. In this case we say G **acts as** permutations on S, even if h is not one-to-one, and we call h a **permutation representation** of G on S. The group $h(G)$ and the homomorphism h may tell us something about G or about S. For g in G and s in S, it is common to write gs instead of $(h(g))(s)$.

For each s in S, the subset $\{gs : g \in G\}$ of S is called the **orbit** of s under G, and is denoted Gs. It consists of all the members of S that s can be taken to by the action of the various members of G. Since $h(e)$ is the identity of $\text{PERM}(S)$, $s = (h(e))(s) = es \in Gs$, and thus each s belongs to its orbit Gs. In particular, S is the union of all of the orbits under G.

EXAMPLE 2   (a) The group $\text{Aut}(E)$ of Example 1 acts on the set $\{x, y, z, w\}$ of vertices of E. Indeed, it *is* a subgroup of $\text{PERM}(\{x, y, z, w\})$. The orbit of y is

$$\text{Aut}(E)y = \{e(y), a(y), b(y), c(y), d(y), f(y)\}$$
$$= \{y, z, w, y, z, w\} = \{y, z, w\}.$$

Similarly $\text{Aut}(E)z = \text{Aut}(E)w = \{y, z, w\}$, and

$$\text{Aut}(E)x = \{e(x), a(x), b(x), c(x), d(x), f(x)\}$$
$$= \{x, x, x, x, x, x\} = \{x\}.$$

(b) The group $\text{Aut}(D)$ of Example 1 acts on the set $\{p, q, r, s\}$ with orbits

$$\text{Aut}(D)p = \text{Aut}(D)r = \{p, r\} = \{x : x \text{ is a source of } D\}$$
$$\text{Aut}(D)q = \text{Aut}(D)s = \{q, s\} = \{x : x \text{ is a sink of } D\}. \quad \square$$

Suppose now that G acts on S and that $s \in S$. It is easy to check that the set $G_s = \{g \in G : gs = s\}$ is a subgroup of G. It contains the kernel of the permutation representation h, since if $h(g)$ is the identity function on S then $gs = (h(g))(s) = s$ for every s. There is a link between the subgroup G_s of G and the orbit $Gs \subseteq S$.

Theorem 2   Suppose the group $(G, \square)$ acts as permutations on the finite set S. For each s in S we have

$$|Gs| = |G/G_s|.$$

Hence $|Gs|$ divides $|G|$.

Proof. Recall that $|G/G_s|$ is the number of cosets of the subgroup G_s in G. Consider first a chosen element x in G. For y in G we have $xs = ys \Leftrightarrow s = x^{-1}(xs) = x^{-1}(ys) = (x^{-1} \square y)s \Leftrightarrow x^{-1} \square y \in G_s \Leftrightarrow y = x \square x^{-1} \square y \in x \square G_s$. That is, y in G takes s to xs precisely if $y \in x \square G_s$. If we switch to a different coset $z \square G_s$, all of its members take s to zs, which must be an element of the orbit Gs different from xs. In this way, each coset $x \square G_s$ corresponds to a unique element xs of Gs, so Gs and G/G_s have the same number of elements. By Lagrange's theorem of §11.2, $|G/G_s|$ divides $|G|$.   □

Corollary   Suppose the group $(G, \square)$ acts on S as in Theorem 2. Choose $s_1, \ldots, s_m$ in S with exactly one s_i in each orbit Gs of G on S. Then

$$|S| = \sum_{i=1}^{m} |Gs_i| = \sum_{i=1}^{m} |G/G_{s_i}|.$$

Proof. The second equality follows from Theorem 2, so we just need to show that the orbits partition S. Suppose $Gs \cap Gt \neq \varnothing$ and let $u \in Gs \cap Gt$. Then $u = gs = ht$ for some $g, h \in G$, so $s = g^{-1}(ht) = (g^{-1} \square h)t \in Gt$ and thus $Gs \subseteq G(Gt) \subseteq (G \square G)t \subseteq Gt$. Similarly $Gt \subseteq Gs$. In other words, $Gs = Gt$ if $Gs \cap Gt \neq \varnothing$.   □

This corollary can be useful in the following sort of situation. Suppose that we know, for some reason, that every subgroup of G [except G itself] has an even number of cosets, and that $|S|$ is odd. The numbers $|G/G_{s_i}|$ cannot all be even, since by the corollary their sum is odd, so some G_{s_i} must be G itself. That is, there is an s_i in S such that $Gs_i = \{s_i\}$, which means that every g in G fixes s_i.

Here is another setting in which the corollary can be useful. Consider a group $(G, \square)$ acting as permutations on a finite set S. Then S breaks up into the disjoint union $S = Gs_1 \cup \cdots \cup Gs_m$ of orbits under G. We can view G as acting on each orbit separately, as follows. For g in G and $i = 1, 2, \ldots, m$, define the function g_i on Gs_i by $g_i(t) = gt$ for each t in Gs_i. Then $g_i(Gs_i) = gGs_i \subseteq Gs_i$, so g_i maps the orbit Gs_i back into itself; we call g_i the **restriction** of g to Gs_i. Since G acts as permutations on S, each g_i is one-to-one. Since Gs_i is finite, g_i must be onto Gs_i and hence $g_i \in$

PERM(Gs_i). Moreover, for $g, h \in G$ and $t \in Gs_i$ we have

$$(g \,\square\, h)_i(t) = (g \,\square\, h)(t) = g(ht) = g_i(h_i(t)) = (g_i \circ h_i)(t),$$

so $(g \,\square\, h)_i = g_i \circ h_i$. In other words, the mapping $\lambda_i: g \to g_i$ is a homomorphism of G into PERM(Gs_i), which is what it means to say that G acts on Gs_i.

Each orbit Gs_i gives us such a permutation representation λ_i of G on Gs_i. In a typical case, the sets Gs_i will be smaller than S, and we will be able to analyze the action of G on each orbit more easily than the action of G on S itself. Moreover, we will have lost nothing by breaking S up in this way, since the action of any member of G on S can be reconstructed from a knowledge of how the member acts on each orbit separately.

EXAMPLE 3 Consider the graph H in Figure 5. Let $G = \text{Aut}(H)$. Since graph automorphisms must preserve degrees of vertices, the orbit of w under G is contained in $\{u, w, x, y\}$. We can see by inspection that there actually are automorphisms of H taking w to any one of u, w, x, y, so the orbit is $Gw = \{u, w, x, y\}$. Similarly, we have $Gs = \{s, t\}$ and $Gr = \{r\}$.

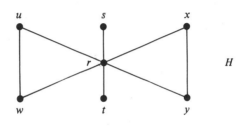

FIGURE 5

Consider an automorphism g of H. There are 4 choices for $g(w)$. Each such choice determines $g(u)$, but there are still two possibilities for $g(x)$. All told, there are 8 possible permutations g can produce on the orbit $\{u, w, x, y\}$. Moreover, for each of these 8 choices there are still two choices for $g(s)$. Thus $|G| = 16$. By Lagrange's theorem, the number of cosets of every subgroup of G divides 16, so all subgroups except G itself have an even number of cosets. The graph H has an odd number of vertices and sure enough, just as the corollary of Theorem 2 predicts, there is a vertex which is sent to itself by all members of $\text{Aut}(H)$.

The table in Figure 6(a) lists the sixteen members of G. The tables in Figures 6(b), 6(c) and 6(d) list their restrictions to the three orbits of G. Note the repetitions of blocks of rows in Figures 6(b), 6(c) and 6(d).

The first eight automorphisms in this table form the subgroup $G_s = G_t$. The first four listed form $G_s \cap G_{\{u,w\}}$. We see from Figures 6(c) and 6(d) that there are just two different possible restrictions of an element of $\text{Aut}(H)$ to $\{s, t\}$, and just eight to the set $\{u, w, x, y\}$.

r	s	t	u	w	x	y
r	s	t	u	w	x	y
r	s	t	w	u	x	y
r	s	t	u	w	y	x
r	s	t	w	u	y	x
r	s	t	x	y	u	w
r	s	t	x	y	w	u
r	s	t	y	x	u	w
r	s	t	y	x	w	u
r	t	s	u	w	x	y
r	t	s	w	u	x	y
r	t	s	u	w	y	x
r	t	s	w	u	y	x
r	t	s	x	y	u	w
r	t	s	x	y	w	u
r	t	s	y	x	u	w
r	t	s	y	x	w	u

G = Aut(H)

(a)

r	s	t	u	w	x	y
r	s	t	u	w	x	y
r	s	t	w	u	x	y
r	s	t	u	w	y	x
r	s	t	w	u	y	x
r	s	t	x	y	u	w
r	s	t	x	y	w	u
r	s	t	y	x	u	w
r	s	t	y	x	w	u
r	t	s	u	w	x	y
r	t	s	w	u	x	y
r	t	s	u	w	y	x
r	t	s	w	u	y	x
r	t	s	x	y	u	w
r	t	s	x	y	w	u
r	t	s	y	x	u	w
r	t	s	y	x	w	u

Restrictions to the orbits

(b)   (c)   (d)

FIGURE 6

Let λ_1, λ_2 and λ_3 be the homomorphisms of G into PERM($\{r\}$), PERM($\{s, t\}$) and PERM($\{u, w, x, y\}$) induced by restriction. Then λ_1 is boring: everything maps to the identity. The mapping λ_2 is less dull; its kernel is the normal subgroup $G_s \cap G_t = G_s$. The kernel of λ_3 is

$$G_u \cap G_w \cap G_x \cap G_y = G_u \cap G_x,$$

which has just two elements, shown in the first and ninth rows of Figure 6. Thus

$$|\lambda_1(G)| = 1, \quad |\lambda_2(G)| = \tfrac{16}{8} = 2 \quad \text{and} \quad |\lambda_3(G)| = \tfrac{16}{2} = 8.$$

An element g in G is completely determined by the triple $\langle \lambda_1(g), \lambda_2(g), \lambda_3(g) \rangle$ in

$$\text{PERM}(\{r\}) \times \text{PERM}(\{s, t\}) \times \text{PERM}(\{u, w, x, y\}).$$

There are $1 \cdot 2 \cdot 24 = 48$ such triples, but only 16 of them correspond to automorphisms of H.   □

Much more can be said about permutation groups, but to go farther we would need to introduce a good deal of specialized notation. This section

$$|F(\alpha_3)| = |\{u, v\}| = 2,$$
$$|F(\alpha_4)| = |F(\alpha_5)| = |F(\alpha_6)| = |F(\alpha_7)| = |\varnothing| = 0.$$

According to Theorem 1 the automorphism group has

$$\tfrac{1}{8}(6 + 4 + 4 + 2 + 0 + 0 + 0 + 0) = 2$$

orbits. In fact, we can see from the picture that there are exactly two orbits, namely $\{w, x, y, z\}$ and $\{u, v\}$, so Theorem 1 confirms our observation.

   (b) The group in part (a) has actions on other sets besides V. For example, it acts on the set T of all two-element subsets of V if we define $g(\{a, b\}) = \{g(a), g(b)\}$ for each graph automorphism g and for all vertices $a, b \in V$. This time $|F(e)| = |T| = \binom{6}{2} = 15$. Now α_1 sends each of the 2-element subsets of $\{u, v, y, z\}$ back to itself and also fixes $\{w, x\}$, since $\alpha_1(\{w, x\}) = \{\alpha_1(w), \alpha_1(x)\} = \{x, w\} = \{w, x\}$. Thus $|F(\alpha_1)| = \binom{4}{2} + 1 = 7$. Similarly, $|F(\alpha_2)| = 7$. Since α_3 only fixes $\{u, v\}$, $\{w, x\}$ and $\{y, z\}$, we have $|F(\alpha_3)| = 3$. In the same way, we find that $F(\alpha_4) = \{\{u, v\}, \{w, y\}, \{x, z\}\}$, $F(\alpha_5) = \{\{u, v\}\} = F(\alpha_6)$, and $F(\alpha_7) = \{\{u, v\}, \{w, z\}, \{x, y\}\}$.
   Theorem 1 then says that T consists of

$$\tfrac{1}{8}(15 + 7 + 7 + 3 + 3 + 1 + 1 + 3) = 5$$

orbits under G. This was not so obvious to begin with. Now we can observe that $\{w, u\}$, $\{w, v\}$, $\{w, x\}$, $\{w, y\}$ and $\{u, v\}$ belong to five different orbits. [Look at Figure 1(a) to see that none of these subsets can be mapped to another one by automorphisms of the graph.] If we had been asked originally to find a representative of each orbit, we would know we were done when we had exhibited these five subsets.   □

   Proof of Theorem 1. We have G acting on S, and we consider the set

$$W = \{\langle g, s \rangle \in G \times S : g(s) = s\},$$

which we count in two different ways.

   First, for each g in G we count pairs $\langle g, s \rangle$ with $g(s) = s$—there are $|F(g)|$ of them—and then add the answers. We get $|W| = \sum_{g \in G} |F(g)|$.

We can also count the members of W by counting for each $s \in S$ the set $\{g \in G : g(s) = s\}$, and then adding the answers for all values of s. For a single value of s the set $\{g \in G : g(s) = s\}$ is the subgroup G_s of G fixing s. By Theorem 2 of § 11.5, the size of the orbit Gs of s is given by $|Gs| = |G/G_s| = |G|/|G_s|$. Thus $|G_s| = |G|/|Gs|$, and so

$$|W| = \sum_{s \in S} \frac{|G|}{|Gs|} = |G| \cdot \sum_{s \in S} \frac{1}{|Gs|}.$$

Now we group together the terms in the sum which come from a given orbit Gs. Since $Gs = Gs'$ for each s' in Gs,

$$\sum_{s' \in Gs} \frac{1}{|Gs'|} = \sum_{s' \in Gs} \frac{1}{|Gs|} = |Gs| \cdot \frac{1}{|Gs|} = 1.$$

That is, the orbit contributes a total value of 1 to $\sum_{s \in S} \frac{1}{|Gs|}$. Thus if there are m orbits then

$$\sum_{s \in S} \frac{1}{|Gs|} = 1 + \cdots + 1 = m,$$

and we get $|W| = |G| \cdot m$.

It follows that $|G| \cdot m = |W| = \sum_{g \in G} |F(g)|$, so

$$m = \frac{1}{|G|} \sum_{g \in G} |F(g)|,$$

as claimed in the theorem.   □

Since there are $|G|$ terms in the sum $\sum_{g \in G} |F(g)|$, when we divide the sum by $|G|$ we obtain the average value of $|F(g)|$ over all members g of G. If some values are larger than average, then some must be smaller.

Corollary   If G acts transitively on S, i.e., if there is just one orbit of G on S, and if $|S| > 1$, then G contains an element g such that $g(s) \neq s$ for all $s \in S$.

Proof. By Theorem 1, the average value of $|F(g)|$ is 1, since there is just one orbit. Moreover, if e is the identity of G then $|F(e)| = |S| > 1$. Thus $|F(g)| < 1$ for at least one g, so $\{s \in S : g(s) = s\} = F(g) = \varnothing$.   □

Now let us go back to the question of coloring a cube with colors red, blue and green. A natural group to consider is the group G of all rotations of space which send the cube back onto itself, since this group describes the rotational symmetry of the cube. The group acts on the set of faces of the cube, and it also acts on a more complicated set which we now describe. Imagine the cube held in some position. A **coloring** of the cube is then simply a way of assigning a color to each of the six faces of the cube, i.e., a *function* f from the set F of faces to the set C of colors. We want to regard two colorings as essentially the same in case rotating the cube takes one into the other. To describe mathematically what we mean by this statement, consider a coloring $f : F \to C$ and a rotation g in G. Then $f \circ g : F \to C$ defined by $(f \circ g)(X) = f(g(X))$ for each face X is also a coloring of the cube [simply rotate by g and then color faces according to f]. We regard f and f' as equivalent in case $f' = f \circ g$ for some $g \in G$. We can view G as acting on the set $\text{FUN}(F, C)$ of all colorings by having g take f to $f \circ g^{-1}$. [The inverse is necessary here for technical reasons, to give $(g_1 \circ g_2)(f) = g_1(g_2(f))$, but is irrelevant to the main ideas.] Then the equivalence classes of colorings are just the orbits of $\text{FUN}(F, C)$ under G, and we can hope to count them using Theorem 1. To apply the theorem we need to count the colorings fixed by each member of G. The method we will use applies quite widely, so instead of answering the cube-coloring question just now, we first prove a general theorem and then apply it in Example 3 to the special case of the cube.

Theorem 2 Consider a finite group G acting on a set S. Then G also acts on FUN(S, C) for any set C if we define $g(f) = f \circ g^{-1}$ for $g \in G$ and $f: S \to C$. For each g in G, let $m(g)$ be the number of orbits of the cyclic group $\langle g \rangle$ on S. Then the number of orbits of G on FUN(S, C) is

$$\frac{1}{|G|} \sum_{g \in G} |C|^{m(g)}.$$

Proof. The action of G on FUN(S, C) is like the action of the rotation group on the set of face colorings of the cube which we just considered. According to Theorem 1, to show the formula is correct we just need to show that for each $g \in G$ we have

$$|\{f \in \text{FUN}(S, C) : g(f) = f\}| = |C|^{m(g)}.$$

Now $g(f) = f \circ g^{-1}$, so $g(f) = f$ if and only if $(f \circ g^{-1})(s) = f(s)$ for every $s \in S$, which is true if and only if $f(g^{-1}(s)) = f(s)$ for every s. Replacing $g^{-1}(s)$ by t gives $g(f) = f$ if and only if $f(t) = f(g(t))$ for every $t \in S$, i.e., if and only if for each t the values $f(t), f(g(t)), f(g^2(f)), f(g^3(t)), \ldots$ and $f(g^{-1}(t)), f(g^{-2}(t)), \ldots$ are all the same. That is, $g(f) = f$ if and only if the function f is constant on each orbit $\{g^n(t) : n \in \mathbb{Z}\}$ under $\langle g \rangle$. To describe such an f we simply give its value on each $\langle g \rangle$-orbit. There are $|C|$ possible function values and $m(g)$ orbits under $\langle g \rangle$, so there are $|C|^{m(g)}$ functions f which are constant on $\langle g \rangle$-orbits. The theorem follows. □

A coloring of a set S with colors from C is just a function from S to C, and we regard two colorings as equivalent under the action of G if they belong to the same G-orbit $\{f \circ g : g \in G\}$ in FUN(S, C). The G-orbits are the G-equivalence classes of colorings. With this terminology, Theorem 2 gives the following information.

Theorem 3 Consider a finite group G acting on a set S. For each positive integer k, let $C(k)$ be the number of [G-equivalence classes of] colorings of S using a set of k colors. Then

$$C(k) = \frac{1}{|G|} \sum_{g \in G} k^{m(g)}$$

where $m(g)$ is the number of orbits of $\langle g \rangle$ on S.

EXAMPLE 2 Before we get back to the cube, we color the vertices of a square with k colors, regarding two colorings as the same if we can turn one into the other by a suitable rotation of the square or by flipping it over. Figure 2(a) shows the square, and Figure 2(b) lists the relevant group of permutations of its vertex

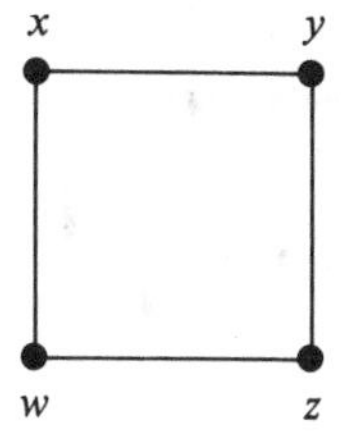

	x	y	z	w
e	x	y	z	w
r	y	z	w	x
r^2	z	w	x	y
r^3	w	x	y	z
h	w	z	y	x
v	y	x	w	z
d	x	w	z	y
f	z	y	x	w

(a)   (b)

FIGURE 2

$\langle e \rangle$	$\{x\}, \{y\}, \{z\}, \{w\}$	$m(e) = 4$
$\langle r \rangle$	$\{x, y, z, w\}$	$m(r) = 1$
$\langle r^2 \rangle$	$\{x, z\}, \{y, w\}$	$m(r^2) = 2$
$\langle r^3 \rangle$	$\{x, y, z, w\}$	$m(r^3) = 1$
$\langle h \rangle$	$\{x, w\}, \{y, z\}$	$m(h) = 2$
$\langle v \rangle$	$\{x, y\}, \{w, z\}$	$m(v) = 2$
$\langle d \rangle$	$\{x\}, \{z\}, \{y, w\}$	$m(d) = 3$
$\langle f \rangle$	$\{x, z\}, \{y\}, \{w\}$	$m(f) = 3$

FIGURE 3

set. One can check that $\langle e \rangle = \{e\}$, $\langle r \rangle = \langle r^3 \rangle = \{e, r, r^2, r^3\}$, $\langle r^2 \rangle = \{e, r^2\}$, $\langle h \rangle = \{e, h\}$, $\langle v \rangle = \{e, v\}$, $\langle d \rangle = \{e, d\}$ and $\langle f \rangle = \{e, f\}$. The table in Figure 3 lists the orbits of these cyclic subgroups. For example, since $\langle f \rangle = \{e, f\}$ the orbits of $\langle f \rangle$ are the sets $\{e(s), f(s)\}$ for s in $\{x, y, z, w\}$, so they are $\{e(x), f(x)\} = \{x, z\}$, $\{e(y), f(y)\} = \{y\}$, $\{e(z), f(z)\} = \{z, x\}$ and $\{e(w), f(w)\} = \{w\}$. There are just three different orbits; thus $m(f) = 3$.

According to Theorem 3 there are

$$C(k) = \tfrac{1}{8}(k^4 + k + k^2 + k + k^2 + k^2 + k^3 + k^3)$$
$$= \tfrac{1}{8}(k^4 + 2k^3 + 3k^2 + 2k)$$

different ways to color the vertices of the square with k colors. For $k = 1$, this number is of course 1. The table in Figure 4 gives the numbers of colorings possible for the first few values of k. Figure 4(b) indicates the six different possibilities for two colors, including both of the one-color colorings. ☐

k	Number of ways to color
1	1
2	6
3	21
4	55
5	120
6	231
7	406

(a)

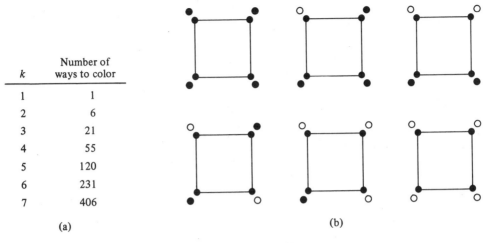

(b)

FIGURE 4

EXAMPLE 3   Now let us color the faces of the cube we started this section with. There are 24 rotations that send the cube back to itself. To list them all would take a fair amount of work, but in fact we only need to know their orbit sizes, and for that we can just count rotations of the five types illustrated in Figure 5(a).

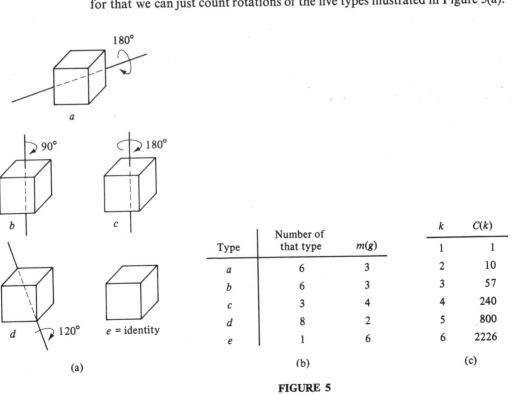

(a)

Type	Number of that type	$m(g)$
a	6	3
b	6	3
c	3	4
d	8	2
e	1	6

(b)

k	$C(k)$
1	1
2	10
3	57
4	240
5	800
6	2226

(c)

FIGURE 5

The table in Figure 5(b) tells how many there are of each type. It also gives the number $m(g)$ of orbits of their cyclic groups acting on the set of faces of the cube. For instance, consider the 90° rotation of type b. Each such rotation has an axis through the centers of two opposite faces. There are 6 faces, so there are 3 opposite pairs and hence 3 such axes. Figure 5(b) lists 6 rotations of type b: each axis gives two 90° rotations, one in each direction. A rotation g of type b has 3 $\langle g \rangle$-orbits: the faces the axes go through form orbits of size 1 and the other four faces form an orbit of size 4. Thus $m(g) = 3$. The remaining entries in Figure 5(b) have been determined by similar reasoning. Theorem 3 gives the formula

$$C(k) = \tfrac{1}{24}(6k^3 + 6k^3 + 3k^4 + 8k^2 + k^6)$$

for the number of colorings of the faces with k colors. Figure 5(c) lists the first few values of $C(k)$.   □

EXAMPLE 4 Consider now the problem of assigning different labels 1, 2, 3, 4, 5, 6 to the vertices of the graph in Figure 1 from Example 1(a), as illustrated in Figure 6. Two assignments are regarded as the same if there is a graph automorphism which takes one to the other. Thus the labelings shown in Figure 6 are all considered the same.

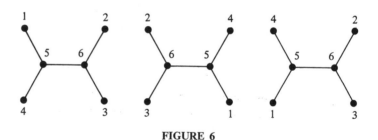

FIGURE 6

We can view this as a problem of coloring with exactly 6 colors. The formula from Theorem 3 gives us the number $C(k)$ of ways to color using at most k colors. Among the $C(6)$ colorings using at most 6 colors are some which use 5 or fewer colors, which we do not want to count. For $i = 1, 2, \ldots, 6$ let A_i be the set of colorings which do not use the ith color. Then $A_1 \cup A_2 \cup \cdots \cup A_6$ is the set of colorings using 5 or fewer of the colors, and the answer to our question is $C(6) - |A_1 \cup A_2 \cup \cdots \cup A_6|$. The Inclusion-Exclusion Principle of § 5.2 gives a formula for $|A_1 \cup A_2 \cup \cdots \cup A_6|$, namely

$$\sum_{i=1}^{6} |A_i| - \sum_{1 \le i < j \le 6} |A_i \cap A_j| + \sum_{1 \le i < j < k \le 6} |A_i \cap A_j \cap A_k| - \cdots,$$

where, for example, the third sum adds up the sizes of all the intersections of three *distinct* sets from among $A_1, \ldots, A_6$. Now

$$|A_i| = C(5) \quad \text{for each} \quad i,$$

$$|A_i \cap A_j| = |\{\text{colorings not using } i\text{th and } j\text{th colors}\}|$$
$$= C(4) \text{ for } i < j,$$
$$|A_i \cap A_j \cap A_k| = C(3) \quad \text{for} \quad i < j < k,$$

etc. Thus

$$|A_1 \cup A_2 \cup \cdots \cup A_6| = \tbinom{6}{1}C(5) - \tbinom{6}{2}C(4) + \tbinom{6}{3}C(3) - \tbinom{6}{4}C(2) + \tbinom{6}{5}C(1)$$

and so the number of colorings which use exactly 6 colors is

$$C(6) - \tbinom{6}{1}C(5) + \tbinom{6}{2}C(4) - \tbinom{6}{3}C(3) + \tbinom{6}{4}C(2) - \tbinom{6}{5}C(1).$$

The table in Figure 7(a) is based on the table of group elements in Figure 1(b). Theorem 3 gives the formula

$$C(k) = \tfrac{1}{8}(k^6 + k^5 + k^5 + k^4 + k^3 + k^2 + k^2 + k^3)$$
$$= \tfrac{1}{8}(k^6 + 2k^5 + k^4 + 2k^3 + 2k^2),$$

	Orbits		k	C(k)
$\langle e \rangle$	$\{u\},\{v\},\{w\},\{x\},\{y\},\{z\}$	$m(e) = 6$	1	1
$\langle \alpha_1 \rangle$	$\{u\},\{v\},\{w, x\},\{y\},\{z\}$	$m(\alpha_1) = 5$	2	21
$\langle \alpha_2 \rangle$	$\{u\},\{v\},\{w\},\{x\},\{y, z\}$	$m(\alpha_2) = 5$	3	171
$\langle \alpha_3 \rangle$	$\{u\},\{v\},\{w, x\},\{y, z\}$	$m(\alpha_3) = 4$	4	820
$\langle \alpha_4 \rangle$	$\{u, v\},\{w, y\},\{x, z\}$	$m(\alpha_4) = 3$	5	2850
$\langle \alpha_5 \rangle$	$\{u, v\},\{w, y, x, z\}$	$m(\alpha_5) = 2$	6	8001
$\langle \alpha_6 \rangle$	$\{u, v\},\{w, z, x, y\}$	$m(\alpha_6) = 2$	7	19306
$\langle \alpha_7 \rangle$	$\{u, v\},\{w, z\},\{x, y\}$	$m(\alpha_7) = 3$		

(a)   (b)

FIGURE 7

whose first seven values are shown in Figure 7(b). The number of colorings using exactly six colors is

$$8001 - 6 \cdot 2850 + 15 \cdot 820 - 20 \cdot 171 + 15 \cdot 21 - 6 \cdot 1 = 90.$$

Similarly, the number of colorings using exactly two colors is just $C(2) - \tbinom{2}{1}C(1) = 21 - 2 = 19$ and the number using exactly seven colors is

$$19306 - 7 \cdot 8001 + 21 \cdot 2850 - 35 \cdot 820 + 35 \cdot 171 - 21 \cdot 21 + 7 \cdot 1 = 0. \quad \square$$

Now let us return to the problem of building logical circuits, at first for just two inputs. There are $2^4 = 16$ Boolean functions of two variables, namely the members of $\text{FUN}(\mathbb{B} \times \mathbb{B}, \mathbb{B})$, where $\mathbb{B} = \{0, 1\}$. We may think of a circuit as a black box with two input leads, one for x_1 and one for x_2, and one output lead. Each element $\langle a_1, a_2 \rangle$ in $\mathbb{B} \times \mathbb{B}$ corresponds to a choice of values a_1 for x_1 and a_2 for x_2.

Interchanging the connections for x_1 and x_2 amounts to replacing $\langle a_1, a_2 \rangle$ by $\langle a_2, a_1 \rangle$, and corresponds to the permutation g of $\mathbb{B} \times \mathbb{B}$ that interchanges $\langle 0, 1 \rangle$ and $\langle 1, 0 \rangle$. We want to regard two black boxes as equivalent if one will produce the same results as the other, or will produce the same results if we interchange its input leads. That is, two boxes are equivalent if their Boolean functions f and f' are either the same or satisfy $f' = f \circ g$. Since $|\mathbb{B}| = 2$, the problem looks just like the 2-color question for a four-element set with two elements which are interchangeable. We apply Theorem 2 with $S = \mathbb{B} \times \mathbb{B}$, $C = \mathbb{B}$ and $G = \langle g \rangle = \{e, g\}$. The number of G-orbits is

$$\tfrac{1}{2}(2^4 + 2^3) = 12.$$

We can confirm this result using the table in Figure 8 which lists all sixteen Boolean functions from $\mathbb{B} \times \mathbb{B}$ to $\mathbb{B}$. Functions 2 and 4 can be performed with the same black box, as can functions 3 and 5, 10 and 12, and 11 and 13, so the number of orbits is $16 - 4 = 12$.

Function numbers

	0	1	2	3	4	5	6	7	8	9	10	11	12	13	14	15
$\langle 0, 0 \rangle$	0	1	0	1	0	1	0	1	0	1	0	1	0	1	0	1
$\langle 0, 1 \rangle$	0	0	1	1	0	0	1	1	0	0	1	1	0	0	1	1
$\langle 1, 0 \rangle$	0	0	0	0	1	1	1	1	0	0	0	0	1	1	1	1
$\langle 1, 1 \rangle$	0	0	0	0	0	0	0	0	1	1	1	1	1	1	1	1

FIGURE 8

Now suppose we also allow ourselves to complement inputs. Complementing the value on the first lead corresponds to interchanging $\langle 0, 0 \rangle$ with $\langle 1, 0 \rangle$, and $\langle 0, 1 \rangle$ with $\langle 1, 1 \rangle$. We denote this permutation of $\mathbb{B} \times \mathbb{B}$ by c_1 and the permutation corresponding to complementing the input on the second lead by c_2. Altogether the permutations g, c_1 and c_2 generate the group of permutations of $\mathbb{B} \times \mathbb{B}$ described in Figure 9(a). [This fact is not

	$\langle 0, 0 \rangle$	$\langle 0, 1 \rangle$	$\langle 1, 0 \rangle$	$\langle 1, 1 \rangle$
e	$\langle 0, 0 \rangle$	$\langle 0, 1 \rangle$	$\langle 1, 0 \rangle$	$\langle 1, 1 \rangle$
c_1	$\langle 1, 0 \rangle$	$\langle 1, 1 \rangle$	$\langle 0, 0 \rangle$	$\langle 0, 1 \rangle$
c_2	$\langle 0, 1 \rangle$	$\langle 0, 0 \rangle$	$\langle 1, 1 \rangle$	$\langle 1, 0 \rangle$
$c_1 \circ c_2$	$\langle 1, 1 \rangle$	$\langle 1, 0 \rangle$	$\langle 0, 1 \rangle$	$\langle 0, 0 \rangle$
g	$\langle 0, 0 \rangle$	$\langle 1, 0 \rangle$	$\langle 0, 1 \rangle$	$\langle 1, 1 \rangle$
$c_1 \circ g$	$\langle 1, 0 \rangle$	$\langle 0, 0 \rangle$	$\langle 1, 1 \rangle$	$\langle 0, 1 \rangle$
$c_2 \circ g$	$\langle 0, 1 \rangle$	$\langle 1, 1 \rangle$	$\langle 0, 0 \rangle$	$\langle 1, 0 \rangle$
$c_1 \circ c_2 \circ g$	$\langle 1, 1 \rangle$	$\langle 0, 1 \rangle$	$\langle 1, 0 \rangle$	$\langle 0, 0 \rangle$

	x	y	w	z
e	x	y	w	z
h	w	z	x	y
v	y	x	z	w
r^2	z	w	y	x
d	x	w	y	z
r^3	w	x	z	y
r	y	z	x	w
f	z	y	w	x

(a)   (b)

FIGURE 9

expected to be obvious; take our word for it.] This group also turns out to be isomorphic to the groups of Examples 1 and 2. It acts on the 4-element set $\mathbb{B} \times \mathbb{B}$ in the same way that the group in Example 2 acts on the vertices of the square, as we see by comparing Figure 9(a) with Figure 9(b), which is just Figure 2(b) rewritten with some rows and columns interchanged. The correspondence $\langle 0, 0 \rangle \to x, \langle 0, 1 \rangle \to y, \langle 1, 0 \rangle \to w, \langle 1, 1 \rangle \to z$ converts one table into the other. From Figure 4 we know that there are $C(2) = 6$ ways to 2-color the square, so there are six orbits of Boolean functions under the action of the group $\langle \{c_1, c_2, g\} \rangle$, i.e., six essentially different black boxes. Using the function numbers from Figure 8, the orbits in $\text{FUN}(\mathbb{B} \times \mathbb{B}, \mathbb{B})$ are

$$\{0\}, \quad \{1, 2, 4, 8\}, \quad \{3, 5, 10, 12\}, \quad \{6, 9\}, \quad \{7, 11, 13, 14\}, \quad \{15\}.$$

To build circuits, it would be enough to compute one function from each orbit, say the functions 0, 1, 3, 6, 7 and 15.

If we also allow ourselves to complement the output of a circuit, then a circuit which computes the function numbered n will also compute $15 - n$ and we need even fewer black boxes. A circuit for 0 will also compute 15, and one for 1 will compute 14 and hence also 7, 11 or 13. A circuit for 3 will also compute 12, which we already knew, and similarly a circuit for 6 will compute 9. The classes of functions are now

$$\{0, 15\}, \quad \{1, 2, 4, 8, 7, 11, 13, 14\}, \quad \{3, 5, 10, 12\} \quad \text{and} \quad \{6, 9\}.$$

It still requires four different circuits to compute all 2-variable Boolean functions, allowing complementation on both input and output leads.

Our methods generalize in theory to count the number of black boxes needed for n-input Boolean functions. In practice, the detailed determination of orbits for all elements of G gets exceedingly complicated. For 4-input functions the answer is that there are 222 different circuits required, even if we allow free complementation on input and output lines. This number is considerably smaller than $2^{16} = 65{,}536$.

Knowing how many different circuits there are does not help find representative circuits, though it does tell us when we have found enough. For 4-input functions, $\text{FUN}(\mathbb{B}^4, \mathbb{B})$ is small enough so that all 2^{16} of its members can be stored in a computer and one can find representatives in the following way using the algorithm MERGE PARTITIONS of § 7.7. As in the 2-input problem, the functions can be numbered $0, 1, \ldots, 2^{16} - 1$ so that n and $2^{16} - 1 - n$ are equivalent under complementation of outputs. It turns out that the group G which acts on $\mathbb{B}^4$ can be generated by three of its members. Each generator g partitions the set $\mathbb{B}^4$ into $\langle g \rangle$-orbits, and the join of these partitions with the $\{n, 2^{16} - 1 - n\}$ partition is the required 222-set partition. Exercises 15 and 16 illustrate the application of these ideas to 2-input functions.

Our methods have not taken systematic advantage of the symmetry of the group G itself. By using such symmetry one can obtain a formula for the number of G-orbits in $\text{FUN}(\mathbb{B}^n, \mathbb{B})$ whose members have exactly k of their values equal to 0 for $k = 1, 2, \ldots$. The textbook *Applied Modern Algebra* by Dornhoff and Hohn contains an account of such methods and the resulting formulas.

EXERCISES 11.6

1. The graph in Figure 10(a) has two automorphisms, which are described in Figure 10(b).
   (a) What is the average number of vertices fixed by the automorphisms of this graph?
   (b) Which of the automorphisms of this graph fix the average number of vertices?
   (c) Find the number of ways to color the vertices of this graph with k colors.

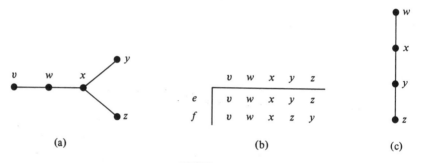

(a)   (b)   (c)

FIGURE 10

2. Verify Theorem 1 for:
   (a) The group of automorphisms of the graph in Figure 10(a) acting on the set of vertices of the graph.
   (b) The group in part (a) acting on the set of edges of the graph in Figure 10(a).
   (c) The group of rotations in Example 3 acting on the set of faces of the cube.

3. The graph in Figure 10(c) has two automorphisms.
   (a) How many ways are there to color the vertices of this graph with k colors?
   (b) How many ways are there to label the vertices of this graph with four different labels?

4. Show that the group $\langle \{g, c_1, c_2\} \rangle$ described in Figure 9(a) is also generated by $\{g, c_1\}$. *Suggestion:* Compute $g \circ c_1 \circ g$.

5. The graph in Figure 11(a) has six automorphisms, which are described in Figure 11(b).
   (a) Find the number of ways to color the vertices of this graph with k colors.
   (b) Find the number of ways to color the edges of this graph with k colors.

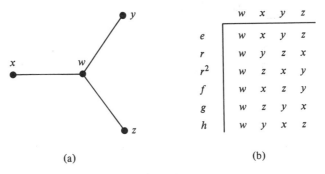

	w	x	y	z
e	w	x	y	z
r	w	y	z	x
r^2	w	z	x	y
f	w	x	z	y
g	w	z	y	x
h	w	y	x	z

(a)   (b)

FIGURE 11

6. (a) Use the Inclusion-Exclusion Principle and the answer to Exercise 5(a) to find the number of ways to color the vertices of the graph in Figure 11(a) with exactly 3 colors.
   (b) Describe all the different colorings in part (a), using the colors red, blue and green.
   (c) Find the number of ways to color the vertices of this graph with exactly 4 colors.

7. (a) How many ways are there to color the vertices of the square in Example 2 with exactly four colors?
   (b) List the different colorings which use all 4 of the colors red, blue, green, yellow.

8. How many different circular necklaces can be made from 5 beads of k different colors? Consider two necklaces to be the same if one looks just like the other when it is rotated or flipped over. *Hint:* The group here consists of e, four nontrivial rotations and five flips. See Example 2 for the 4-bead case.

9. Consider the group G of Example 1 acting on the set $S = \{u, v, w, x, y, z\}$.
   (a) How many pairs $\langle g, s \rangle$ in $G \times S$ are there with $g(s) = s$?
   (b) How many such pairs are there with $g = \alpha_3$?
   (c) How many such pairs are there with s in the G-orbit of x?
   (d) How many such pairs are there with s in the G-orbit of u?

10. Consider the problem of coloring the faces of a cube using crayons which are red, green and blue, as in Example 3.
    (a) How many colorings use exactly two of the three colors?
    (b) Use any method to find how many colorings have four red faces and two blue faces.
    (c) How many colorings have exactly four red faces?
    (d) Would you like to use the method of inspection to find all colorings with exactly two faces of each color?

11. (a) How many ways are there to color the vertices of a cube with k colors?
    (b) How many ways are there to color the edges of a cube with k colors?
       Two colorings in parts (a) and (b) are considered the same if one can be

turned into the other by a rotation of the cube. *Suggestion:* Use Figure 5(a) to create new tables like Figure 5(b) for the actions on vertices and edges.

12. Consider a group G acting on an n-element set S. Show that if $|F(g)| \geqq 1$ for each $g \in G$, then G has at least $1 + (n-1)/|G|$ orbits in S. For $n > 1$ this. implies the corollary to Theorem 1. *Hint:* Treat the element e of G separately from the others.

13. (a) How many different 2-input logical circuits are there if we only regard two circuits as the same if they have the same or complementary outputs?
    (b) How many are there if we also consider two circuits to be the same if they produce the same function when the input leads on one are interchanged?

14. Exhibit an isomorphism between the group described in Figure 1(b) and the group described in Figure 2(b). *Hint:* Neighboring leaves of the tree correspond to diagonally opposite corners of the square.

15. Let G_1 and G_2 be groups of permutations of a finite set S, and let G_0 be the group generated by $G_1 \cup G_2$. Let π_1 be the partition of S consisting of the G_1-orbits, with similar definitions for π_2 and π_0. Show that $\pi_0 = \pi_1 \vee \pi_2$. *Hint:* Let R_1 be the equivalence relation on S where $\langle s, t \rangle \in R_1$ if $g(s) = t$ for some $g \in G_1$, as in Exercise 15 of § 11.5. If R_2 and R_0 are defined analogously, then the equality $\pi_0 = \pi_1 \vee \pi_2$ is equivalent to $R_0 = R_1 \vee R_2$.

16. Let S be the set FUN($\mathbb{B} \times \mathbb{B}, \mathbb{B}$) which is illustrated in Figure 8 and used to count logical circuits. Let G_1 be the group $\langle \{c_1, c_2, g\} \rangle$, which corresponds to complementing or interchanging inputs, and let G_2 be the two-element group corresponding to complementation of the output. Let G_0, π_1, π_2 and π_0 be as in Exercise 15.
    (a) Convince yourself that
    $$\pi_1 = \{\{0\}, \{1, 2, 4, 8\}, \{3, 5, 10, 12\}, \{6, 9\}, \{7, 11, 13, 14\}, \{15\}\}$$
    and
    $$\pi_2 = \{\{0, 15\}, \{1, 14\}, \{2, 13\}, \{3, 12\}, \{4, 11\}, \{5, 10\}, \{6, 9\}, \{7, 8\}\}.$$
    (b) Explain why G_0 is the group that corresponds to complementation of inputs and outputs.
    (c) Determine π_0.

§ 11.7   Other Algebraic Systems

So far in this chapter we have been looking at sets with just one binary operation on them. A number of important and familiar algebraic structures have two binary operations, usually written $+$ and $\cdot$. The "additive" operation $+$ is typically very well-behaved, while the "multiplicative" operation $\cdot$ is generally less so, and there are usually distributive laws relating the two operations to each other. In this section we briefly introduce rings and fields, which are the two main kinds of algebraic structures with two operations, and we give some examples and discuss the basic facts about homomorphisms of such systems.

EXAMPLE 1   (a) The sets $\mathbb{Z}$, $\mathbb{Q}$ and $\mathbb{R}$ are each closed under ordinary addition and multiplication. Both $+$ and $\cdot$ are commutative and associative for each of these sets. Moreover, these operations satisfy the distributive laws:

$$a \cdot (b + c) = (a \cdot b) + (a \cdot c) \quad \text{and} \quad (a + b) \cdot c = (a \cdot c) + (b \cdot c).$$

(b) The set $\mathfrak{M}_{n,n}$ of $n \times n$ matrices with real entries is closed under matrix addition and also under matrix multiplication. Both operations are associative, and addition is commutative, but matrix multiplication is not commutative. For instance

$$\begin{bmatrix} 2 & 2 \\ 1 & 1 \end{bmatrix} \begin{bmatrix} 3 & -1 \\ -3 & 1 \end{bmatrix} = \begin{bmatrix} 0 & 0 \\ 0 & 0 \end{bmatrix} \neq \begin{bmatrix} 5 & 5 \\ -5 & -5 \end{bmatrix} = \begin{bmatrix} 3 & -1 \\ -3 & 1 \end{bmatrix} \begin{bmatrix} 2 & 2 \\ 1 & 1 \end{bmatrix}.$$

The distributive laws

$$\mathbf{A}(\mathbf{B} + \mathbf{C}) = (\mathbf{AB}) + (\mathbf{AC}) \text{ and } (\mathbf{A} + \mathbf{B})\mathbf{C} = (\mathbf{AC}) + (\mathbf{BC})$$

are valid.

(c) For $p \geqq 2$ the operations $+_p$ and $*_p$ on $\mathbb{Z}(p)$ are commutative and associative by Theorem 3 of § 4.3, and the distributive laws hold [Exercise 4].

(d) Consider any commutative group $(G, +)$ with identity 0, and define the operation $\cdot$ trivially on G by $a \cdot b = 0$ for all $a, b \in G$. It follows at once that $\cdot$ is commutative and associative, and that $(G, +, \cdot)$ satisfies the distributive laws. $\square$

Structures like the ones in Example 1 come up frequently enough to deserve a name. A **ring** is a set R closed under two binary operations, generally denoted $+$ and $\cdot$, such that

(a) $(R, +)$ is a commutative group,
(b) $(R, \cdot)$ is a semigroup,
(c) $a \cdot (b + c) = (a \cdot b) + (a \cdot c)$ and $(a + b) \cdot c = (a \cdot c) + (b \cdot c)$ for all $a, b, c \in R$.

If $(R, \cdot)$ is commutative, we say the ring $(R, +, \cdot)$ is **commutative.** The ring $(\mathfrak{M}_{n,n}, +, \cdot)$ in Example 1(b) is not commutative if $n > 1$. The other rings in Example 1 are commutative. A ring always has an additive identity element, denoted 0. If it has a multiplicative identity which is different from 0, we usually call the multiplicative identity 1 and we say the ring is a **ring with identity**. Each of the rings in Examples 1(a), (b) and (c) is a ring with identity. The **trivial ring** in Example 1(d) has no multiplicative identity unless G just consists of 0; since we require $1 \neq 0$, we do not consider $(\{0\}, +, \cdot)$ to be a ring with identity. The ring $(2\mathbb{Z}, +, \cdot)$ of even integers, with the usual sum and product, is another example of a commutative ring without identity.

The distributive laws make calculations in a ring behave very much like the arithmetic we are used to in $\mathbb{Z}$, allowing for the obvious fact that we need to watch out for noncommuting elements. For example, we have

$$(a + b)^2 = (a + b) \cdot (a + b) = [a \cdot (a + b)] + [b \cdot (a + b)]$$
$$= (a \cdot a) + (a \cdot b) + (b \cdot a) + (b \cdot b) = a^2 + a \cdot b + b \cdot a + b^2,$$

but this is not $a^2 + 2(a \cdot b) + b^2$ unless $a \cdot b = b \cdot a$. As another example, we get

$$(0 \cdot a) + (0 \cdot a) = (0 + 0) \cdot a = 0 \cdot a,$$

and so

$$0 \cdot a = (0 \cdot a) + (0 \cdot a) - (0 \cdot a) = (0 \cdot a) - (0 \cdot a) = 0.$$

Similarly $a \cdot 0 = 0$ for all a in a ring. One can also show that $(-a) \cdot b = -(a \cdot b) = a \cdot (-b)$ [Exercise 8].

We can never hope to divide by 0, but in the rings $(\mathbb{Q}, +, \cdot)$ and $(\mathbb{R}, +, \cdot)$ we can divide by every non-0 element. In $(\mathbb{Z}, +, \cdot)$ we can divide 6 by 3 successfully but cannot divide 6 by 5 to get an answer which is still in $\mathbb{Z}$. A **field** is a commutative ring $(R, +, \cdot)$ in which the non-0 elements form a group under multiplication. In a field the inverse of a non-0 a is usually written a^{-1} or $1/a$, and it has the property that $a^{-1} \cdot a = a \cdot a^{-1} = 1$. We also often write b/a for $b \cdot a^{-1}$, a notation which we justify by the fact that $(b/a) \cdot a = b \cdot a^{-1} \cdot a = b$.

If $a \cdot b = a \cdot c$ in a field and if $a \neq 0$, then $b = a^{-1} \cdot a \cdot b = a^{-1} \cdot a \cdot c = c$; i.e., a can be canceled in the equation $a \cdot b = a \cdot c$. Such cancellation is sometimes possible even if inverses do not exist—for example in $(\mathbb{Z}, +, \cdot)$. A commutative ring with identity in which each non-0 element is cancellable in this way is called an **integral domain**. These rings form an important class intermediate between fields and more general commutative rings. One can show [Exercise 14(c)] that every finite integral domain is a field.

EXAMPLE 2   (a) Groups are always nonempty, so the multiplicative identity in a field is always non-0. The smallest possible field is $(\mathbb{Z}(2), +_2, *_2)$ which has just two elements 0 and 1 and operations as shown in the tables.

$+_2$	0	1		$*_2$	0	1
0	0	1		0	0	0
1	1	0		1	0	1

(b) The set $\text{FUN}(\mathbb{R}, \mathbb{R})$ is a ring with $f + g$ and $f \cdot g$ defined by

$$(f + g)(x) = f(x) + g(x) \quad \text{and} \quad (f \cdot g)(x) = f(x) \cdot g(x)$$

for all $x \in \mathbb{R}$. The zero element is the constant function c_0 defined by $c_0(x) = 0$ for all x. This ring is commutative but is not an integral domain, even though it gets its multiplication from the field $\mathbb{R}$. For example, let $f(x) = 0$ for $x \leq 0$ and $f(x) = 1$ for $x > 0$, and let $g(x) = 1$ for $x \leq 0$ and $g(x) = 0$ for $x > 0$. Then $(f \cdot g)(x) = 0$ for every x, so $f \cdot g = 0 = f \cdot 0$ but $f \neq 0$ and $g \neq 0$. ∎

A **subring** of a ring R is simply a subset of R which is itself a ring under the two operations of R. A **subfield** of a field F is a subring of F which is itself a field; this means in particular that it contains the multiplicative identity 1 of F and is closed under taking inverses.

EXAMPLE 3   (a) The ring $(\mathbb{Z}, +, \cdot)$ has subrings $2\mathbb{Z}$, $73\mathbb{Z}$ and $\{0\}$ among others. In fact, one can show that the subrings of $\mathbb{Z}$ are precisely the rings $k\mathbb{Z}$ for k an integer. The ring $(\mathbb{Z}(p), +_p, *_p)$ is *not* a subring of $\mathbb{Z}$; in fact, the two rings have quite different structure. For example, for each a in $\mathbb{Z}(p)$ we have $a +_p a +_p \cdots +_p a = 0$ if there are p terms in the sum, whereas $a + a + \cdots + a = pa$ in $\mathbb{Z}$.

(b) Every subring R of a field F is an integral domain, because if $a, b, c \in R$ with $a \cdot b = a \cdot c$ and $a \neq 0$ then $b = c$ in F and hence also in R. In particular, the subring $(\mathbb{Z}, +, \cdot)$ of the field $(\mathbb{R}, +, \cdot)$ is an integral domain. It is not a field, since only 1 and -1 have multiplicative inverses in $\mathbb{Z}$. The field $(\mathbb{Q}, +, \cdot)$ is a subfield of $(\mathbb{R}, +, \cdot)$. □

The appropriate mappings to use in studying rings are the ones which are compatible with both the additive and multiplicative structure. A **ring homomorphism** from a ring $(R, +, \cdot)$ to a ring $(S, +, \cdot)$ is a function $h: R \to S$ such that

$$h(a + b) = h(a) + h(b) \quad \text{and} \quad h(a \cdot b) = h(a) \cdot h(b)$$

for all $a, b \in R$. The operations on the left sides of these equations are the operations in R; those on the right are in S. Thus a ring homomorphism is just a function which is both a group homomorphism from $(R, +)$ to $(S, +)$ and a semigroup homomorphism from $(R, \cdot)$ to $(S, \cdot)$.

EXAMPLE 4   (a) The function Rem_p from $\mathbb{Z}$ to $\mathbb{Z}(p)$, defined by $\text{Rem}_p(m) =$ the remainder when m is divided by p, is a ring homomorphism. This is because

$$m + n \equiv \text{Rem}_p(m) +_p \text{Rem}_p(n) \ (\text{mod } p)$$

and

$$m \cdot n \equiv \text{Rem}_p(m) *_p \text{Rem}_p(n) \ (\text{mod } p)$$

for all $m, n \in \mathbb{Z}$ by definition of $+_p$ and $*_p$.

(b) The determinant function from $\mathfrak{M}_{2,2}$ to $\mathbb{R}$ is not a ring homomorphism, even though $\det(\mathbf{AB}) = \det(\mathbf{A}) \cdot \det(\mathbf{B})$, because $\det(\mathbf{A} + \mathbf{B})$ is not generally $\det(\mathbf{A}) + \det(\mathbf{B})$.

(c) The function h from $\mathbb{Z}$ to $\mathbb{Z}$ defined by $h(m) = 3m$ is an additive group homomorphism but is not a ring homomorphism because $h(m \cdot n) = 3mn$, while $h(m) \cdot h(n) = 3m \cdot 3n = 9mn$.

(d) The mapping h of $\text{FUN}(\mathbb{R}, \mathbb{R})$ into $\mathbb{R}$ given by $h(f) = f(73)$ is a ring homomorphism, since

$$h(f + g) = (f + g)(73) = f(73) + g(73) = h(f) + h(g)$$

and

$$h(f \cdot g) = (f \cdot g)(73) = f(73) \cdot g(73) = h(f) \cdot h(g).$$

More generally, for any set S and ring R we can make FUN(S, R) into a ring just as we did for FUN$(\mathbb{R}, \mathbb{R})$, and each s in S gives rise to an evaluation homomorphism h from FUN(S, R) to R defined by $h(f) = f(s)$ for all f in FUN(S, R).

(e) The set POLY$(\mathbb{R})$ of all polynomials p, where $p(x) = a_0 + a_1 x + \cdots + a_n x^n$ with $n \in \mathbb{N}$ and with real coefficients $a_0, \ldots, a_n$, is a ring using $+$ and $\cdot$ defined in the usual way. We can think of POLY$(\mathbb{R})$ as a subring of FUN$(\mathbb{R}, \mathbb{R})$, since each polynomial defines a unique function and since one can show that two different polynomials must give different functions [i.e., have different graphs]. An evaluation homomorphism such as $f \to f(73)$ from FUN$(\mathbb{R}, \mathbb{R})$ to $\mathbb{R}$ yields a homomorphism from POLY$(\mathbb{R})$ to $\mathbb{R}$, defined in this instance by $p \to p(73)$. The evaluation homomorphism $p \to p(0)$ assigns to each polynomial p its constant coefficient a_0. □

Since ring homomorphisms are additive group homomorphisms, they have kernels. Suppose h is a homomorphism from $(R, +, \cdot)$ to $(S, +, \cdot)$. The kernel of h is the set $K = \{a \in R : h(a) = h(0)\}$, and for $a, b \in R$ we have

$$h(a) = h(b) \Leftrightarrow a - b \in K \Leftrightarrow a + K = b + K.$$

Everything is in additive dress here, so $a + K$ is the coset $\{a + k : k \in K\}$ of the subgroup K of $(R, +)$. As before, h is one-to-one if and only if $K = \{0\}$. The kernel of h is a special kind of subring of R. It is an additive subgroup of course, but it is also closed under multiplication not only by its own elements but even under multiplication by other elements in R, since if $h(a) = h(0)$ and if $r \in R$ then

$$h(a \cdot r) = h(a) \cdot h(r) = h(0) \cdot h(r) = h(0 \cdot r) = h(0)$$

and likewise $h(r \cdot a) = h(0)$.

An additive subgroup I of a ring $(R, +, \cdot)$ is called an **ideal** of R if $r \cdot a \in I$ and $a \cdot r \in I$ for all $a \in I$ and $r \in R$. Kernels of ring homomorphisms are ideals, as we noted in the last paragraph, and one can show [Exercise 10] that every ideal is the kernel of a homomorphism.

EXAMPLE 5   (a) The subgroup $\{0\}$ and the ring R itself are always ideals of R. These obvious ideals are the only ones there are in $\mathfrak{M}_{n,n}(\mathbb{R})$; a proof of this fact takes some work.

(b) If the ring R is commutative and if $a \in R$, then the set $R \cdot a = \{r \cdot a : r \in R\}$ is an ideal of R. To check this we observe that $r \cdot a + s \cdot a = (r + s) \cdot a \in R \cdot a$ and $-(r \cdot a) = (-r) \cdot a \in R \cdot a$ for every $r, s \in R$, so $R \cdot a$ is an additive subgroup of R. Since $s \cdot (r \cdot a) = (s \cdot r) \cdot a \in R \cdot a$ for every $r, s \in R$, $R \cdot a$ is closed under multiplication by elements of R. An ideal of the form $R \cdot a$ is called a **principal ideal**.

All of the subgroups of $(\mathbb{Z}, +)$ are of the form $n\mathbb{Z}$ by Theorem 4 of § 11.1, so every ideal of $(\mathbb{Z}, +, \cdot)$ is principal. So are the ideals of POLY($\mathbb{R}$), as it turns out, but such a situation is very special. For example, in the commutative ring POLY($\mathbb{Z}$) consisting of polynomials with integer coefficients, the set of all polynomials $a_0 + a_1 x + \cdots + a_n x^n$ in which a_0 is even is an ideal which is not principal [Exercise 17].

(c) Ideals of fields are boring. For suppose I is a non-0 ideal of a field F. Let $0 \neq a \in I$. For every $b \in F$ we have $b = (b \cdot a^{-1}) \cdot a \in F \cdot a \subseteq I$, so $I = F$. That is, F has only the obvious ideals $\{0\}$ and F. ⬚

If R is a ring with ideal I, then the group R/I consisting of additive cosets $r + I = \{r + i : i \in I\}$ can be made into a ring in a natural way. We define

$$(r + I) + (s + I) = (r + s) + I$$

and

$$(r + I) \cdot (s + I) = r \cdot s + I.$$

We've already seen in § 11.4 that the addition on R/I is well-defined; we check multiplication. If $r + I = r' + I$ and $s + I = s' + I$, then $r - r' \in I$ and $s - s' \in I$ and hence

$$r \cdot s - r' \cdot s' = r \cdot s - r \cdot s' + r \cdot s' - r' \cdot s'$$
$$= r \cdot (s - s') + (r - r') \cdot s' \in r \cdot I + I \cdot s' \subseteq I.$$

Thus $r \cdot s + I = r' \cdot s' + I$ and our definition of product is independent of the choice of representatives we take in the cosets $r + I$ and $s + I$. The rest of the properties of a ring are easy to check.

The fundamental homomorphism theorem for groups leads to a corresponding result for rings. Consider a ring homomorphism h from R to S with kernel I. Then h is an additive group homomorphism of $(R, +)$ into $(S, +)$, so we already know from Theorem 2 of § 11.4 that the mapping h^* from R/I to $h(R)$ defined by $h^*(r + I) = h(r)$ for $r \in R$ is a group isomorphism. Since

$$h^*((r + I) \cdot (r' + I)) = h^*((r \cdot r') + I) = h(r \cdot r')$$
$$= h(r) \cdot h(r') = h^*(r + I) \cdot h^*(r' + I),$$

h^* is in fact a ring homomophism. Therefore h^* is a **ring isomorphism** between R/I and $h(R)$, i.e., a ring homomorphism which is one-to-one and onto. We have shown the following.

Theorem 1 Let h be a homomorphism with kernel I from the ring R to the ring S. Then the mapping $r + I \rightarrow h(r)$ is an isomorphism of the ring R/I onto $h(R)$.

The ring R/I may have ideals of its own. They correspond to ideals of $h(R)$, by Theorem 1, but we can also associate them with ideals of R itself.

Theorem 2   Let h be a homomorphism from the ring R to the ring $h(R)$.
 (a) If I is an ideal of R, then $h(I)$ is an ideal of $h(R)$.
 (b) Every ideal of $h(R)$ is of the form $h(I)$ for some ideal I of R containing the kernel of h.

Proof. (a) Since I is a subgroup of $(R, +)$, $h(I)$ is a subgroup of $(h(R), +)$. If $h(r) \in h(R)$ and $h(a) \in h(I)$, then $h(a) \cdot h(r) = h(a \cdot r) \in h(I)$ since $a \cdot r$ is in the ideal I. Similarly, $h(r) \cdot h(a) \in h(I)$, so $h(I)$ is closed under multiplication by elements of $h(R)$.

(b) Suppose J is an ideal of $h(R)$. Let $I = h^{-1}(J) = \{a \in R : h(a) \in J\}$. If $a, b \in I$ then $h(a), h(b) \in J$, so $h(a + b) = h(a) + h(b)$ is in J and thus $a + b \in I$. Similarly, $-a \in I$ for $a \in I$, and both $a \cdot r$ and $r \cdot a$ are in I for all $a \in I$ and $r \in R$. Thus I is an ideal of R containing the kernel $\{a \in R : h(a) = 0\}$ of h. Clearly $h(I) = J$. ⬜

If K is an ideal of R, then the natural mapping $v : a \to a + K$ of R to R/K is a homomorphism with kernel K. Theorem 2, with v and R/K in place of h and $h(R)$, gives the following.

Corollary   Let K be an ideal of the ring R. The ideals of R/K are precisely the sets of the form I/K for I an ideal of R containing K. Moreover, for every ideal I of R the set $I + K = \{a + b : a \in I, b \in K\}$ is an ideal of R.

Proof. The second assertion is true because $v(I) = (I + K)/K$. ⬜

EXAMPLE 6   (a) The kernel of the ring homomorphism Rem_p from $\mathbb{Z}$ onto $\mathbb{Z}(p)$ defined in Example 4(a) is the ideal $p\mathbb{Z}$. The ideals in $\mathbb{Z}$ are of the form $k\mathbb{Z}$, and their images are of the form $\text{Rem}_p(k\mathbb{Z}) = \text{Rem}_p(k) *_p \text{Rem}_p(\mathbb{Z}) = \{\text{Rem}_p(k) *_p a : a \in \mathbb{Z}(p)\}$. For example, there are just four such ideals in $\mathbb{Z}(6)$, namely

$$\text{Rem}_6(\mathbb{Z}) = \mathbb{Z}(6) = \{0, 1, 2, 3, 4, 5\},$$
$$\text{Rem}_6(2\mathbb{Z}) = 2 *_6 \mathbb{Z}(6) = \{0, 2, 4\},$$
$$\text{Rem}_6(3\mathbb{Z}) = 3 *_6 \mathbb{Z}(6) = \{0, 3\},$$
$$\text{Rem}_6(6\mathbb{Z}) = 0 *_6 \mathbb{Z}(6) = \{0\}.$$

To see that these are all, we observe that an ideal $k\mathbb{Z}$ of $\mathbb{Z}$ contains another ideal $m\mathbb{Z}$ if and only if m is a multiple of k. According to Theorem 2(b), the ideals of $\mathbb{Z}(6)$ correspond to the ideals of $\mathbb{Z}$ which contain $6\mathbb{Z}$, namely $\mathbb{Z}, 2\mathbb{Z}, 3\mathbb{Z}$ and $6\mathbb{Z}$.

(b) We can make $\mathbb{Z}(2) \times \mathbb{Z}(3)$ into a ring by defining

$$\langle m, n \rangle + \langle j, k \rangle = \langle m +_2 j, n +_3 k \rangle$$

and

$$\langle m, n \rangle \cdot \langle j, k \rangle = \langle m *_2 j, n *_3 k \rangle.$$

The mapping $h: m \to \langle \text{Rem}_2(m), \text{Rem}_3(m) \rangle$ is a ring homomorphism from $\mathbb{Z}$ into $\mathbb{Z}(2) \times \mathbb{Z}(3)$. Its kernel is

$$\{m \in \mathbb{Z} : m \equiv 0 \ (\text{mod } 2) \text{ and } m \equiv 0 \ (\text{mod } 3)\}$$

$$= \{m \in \mathbb{Z} : m \equiv 0 \ (\text{mod } 6)\} = 6\mathbb{Z}.$$

Thus by Theorem 1 $h(\mathbb{Z})$ is isomorphic to $\mathbb{Z}/6\mathbb{Z}$, i.e., is isomorphic to $\mathbb{Z}(6)$. Since $|h(\mathbb{Z})| = |\mathbb{Z}(6)| = 6$ and $|\mathbb{Z}(2) \times \mathbb{Z}(3)| = 2 \cdot 3 = 6$, h must map $\mathbb{Z}$ onto $\mathbb{Z}(2) \times \mathbb{Z}(3)$. That is,

$$\mathbb{Z}(2) \times \mathbb{Z}(3) \quad \text{is ring-isomorphic to} \quad \mathbb{Z}(6).$$

One can check that the correspondence

$$\langle 0, 0 \rangle \to 0 \quad \langle 1, 1 \rangle \to 1 \quad \langle 0, 2 \rangle \to 2$$

$$\langle 1, 0 \rangle \to 3 \quad \langle 0, 1 \rangle \to 4 \quad \langle 1, 2 \rangle \to 5$$

is an isomorphism. The ideals of $\mathbb{Z}(2) \times \mathbb{Z}(3)$, which correspond to the ideals of $\mathbb{Z}(6)$ obtained in part (a), are the four subsets $\{\langle 0, 0 \rangle\}$, $\{\langle 0, 0 \rangle, \langle 0, 1 \rangle,$ $\langle 0, 2 \rangle\} = \{0\} \times \mathbb{Z}(3)$, $\{\langle 0, 0 \rangle, \langle 1, 0 \rangle\} = \mathbb{Z}(2) \times \{0\}$, and $\mathbb{Z}(2) \times \mathbb{Z}(3)$ itself. ☐

The ideas in Example 6(b) generalize. If $R_1, \ldots, R_n$ is a list of rings, not necessarily distinct, we make the product $R_1 \times \cdots \times R_n$ into a ring by defining

$$\langle r_1, \ldots, r_n \rangle + \langle s_1, \ldots, s_n \rangle = \langle r_1 + s_1, \ldots, r_n + s_n \rangle$$

and

$$\langle r_1, \ldots, r_n \rangle \cdot \langle s_1, \ldots, s_n \rangle = \langle r_1 \cdot s_1, \ldots, r_n \cdot s_n \rangle,$$

where the operations in each coordinate are the operations defined on the corresponding ring. If $h_1, \ldots, h_n$ are homomorphisms from some ring R to $R_1, \ldots, R_n$, respectively, then one can check [Exercise 12] that the mapping h from R to $R_1 \times \cdots \times R_n$ defined by $h(r) = \langle h_1(r), \ldots, h_n(r) \rangle$ is a homomorphism. Its kernel is $\{r \in R : h_i(r) = 0 \text{ for } i = 1, \ldots, n\}$, i.e., it is the intersection of the kernels of $h_1, \ldots, h_n$.

Suppose now that $I_1, \ldots, I_n$ are ideals of R, and that for $j = 1, \ldots, n$ each h_j is the natural homomorphism from R onto R/I_j given by $h_j(r) = r + I_j$. Then the homomorphism h described in the last paragraph is defined by $h(r) = \langle r + I_1, \ldots, r + I_n \rangle$ for $r \in R$. Since I_j is the kernel of h_j, we obtain the following.

Theorem 3   Let R be a ring with ideals $I_1, \ldots, I_n$. Then $I_1 \cap \cdots \cap I_n$ is an ideal of R and $R/(I_1 \cap \cdots \cap I_n)$ is isomorphic to a subring of $(R/I_1) \times \cdots \times (R/I_n)$.

In Example 6(b), with $I_1 = 2\mathbb{Z}$ and $I_2 = 3\mathbb{Z}$, the ring $\mathbb{Z}/(2\mathbb{Z} \cap 3\mathbb{Z})$ was isomorphic to the whole ring $(\mathbb{Z}/2\mathbb{Z}) \times (\mathbb{Z}/3\mathbb{Z})$, but in general $h(R)$ is only a subring of $R_1 \times \cdots \times R_n$. For example, in $\mathbb{Z}$ we have $6\mathbb{Z} \cap 10\mathbb{Z} \cap 15\mathbb{Z} = 60\mathbb{Z}$ [check this] and so $\mathbb{Z}/(6\mathbb{Z} \cap 10\mathbb{Z} \cap 15\mathbb{Z}) = \mathbb{Z}/60\mathbb{Z}$ has 60 members, while

$(\mathbb{Z}/6\mathbb{Z}) \times (\mathbb{Z}/10\mathbb{Z}) \times (\mathbb{Z}/15\mathbb{Z})$ has $6 \cdot 10 \cdot 15 = 900$ elements. Exercise 9 gives another example.

There is a great deal more which can be said about rings and fields. We have only introduced the most basic ideas and a few examples, but we hope to have given some feeling for the kinds of questions it might be reasonable to ask about these systems and the kinds of answers one might get. The study of groups, rings and fields makes up a large part of the area of mathematics called abstract algebra. At this point you are in a good position to read an introductory book in this area.

EXERCISES 11.7

In these exercises, the words "homomorphism" and "isomorphism" mean "ring homomorphism" and "ring isomorphism."

1. Which of the following sets are subrings of $(\mathbb{R}, +, \cdot)$?
   (a) $2\mathbb{Z}$ (b) $2\mathbb{R}$
   (c) $\mathbb{N}$ (d) $\{m + n\sqrt{2} : m, n \in \mathbb{Z}\}$
   (e) $\{m/2 : m \in \mathbb{Z}\}$ (f) $\{m/2^a : m \in \mathbb{Z}, a \in \mathbb{P}\}$

2. (a) For each subset in Exercise 1 which is a subring of $\mathbb{R}$ verify closure under addition and multiplication.
   (b) For each subset in Exercise 1 which is not a subring of $\mathbb{R}$ give a property of subrings which the subset does not satisfy.

3. Which of the following functions are ring homomorphisms? Justify your answer in each case.
   (a) $h : \text{FUN}(\mathbb{R}, \mathbb{R}) \to \mathbb{R}$ defined by $h(f) = f(0)$.
   (b) $h : \mathbb{R} \to \mathbb{R}$ defined by $h(r) = r^2$.
   (c) $h : \mathbb{R} \to \text{FUN}(\mathbb{R}, \mathbb{R})$ defined by $(h(r))(x) = r$. I.e., $h(r)$ is the constant function on $\mathbb{R}$ having value r at every x.
   (d) $h : \mathbb{Z} \to \mathbb{R}$ defined by $h(n) = n$.
   (e) $h : \mathbb{Z}/3\mathbb{Z} \to \mathbb{Z}/6\mathbb{Z}$ defined by $h(n + 3\mathbb{Z}) = 2n + 6\mathbb{Z}$.

4. Verify that the distributive laws hold in $(\mathbb{Z}(p), +_p, *_p)$.

5. Describe the ideals in the trivial ring G of Example 1(d).

6. Find the kernel of the homomorphism h from $\text{FUN}(\mathbb{R}, \mathbb{R})$ to $\mathbb{R}$ in Example 4(d).

7. Consider the ring $\mathbb{Z}$. Write each of the following in the form $n\mathbb{Z}$ with $n \in \mathbb{N}$.
   (a) $6\mathbb{Z} \cap 8\mathbb{Z}$ (b) $6\mathbb{Z} + 8\mathbb{Z}$
   (c) $3\mathbb{Z} + 2\mathbb{Z}$ (d) $6\mathbb{Z} + 10\mathbb{Z} + 15\mathbb{Z}$

8. Show that in a ring $(-a) \cdot b = -(a \cdot b) = a \cdot (-b)$ for every a and b.

9. (a) Verify that the mapping h from $\mathbb{Z}(12)$ to $\mathbb{Z}(4) \times \mathbb{Z}(6)$ given by $h(m) = \langle \text{Rem}_4(m), \text{Rem}_6(m) \rangle$ is a well-defined homomorphism.
   (b) Find the kernel of h.
   (c) Find an element of $\mathbb{Z}(4) \times \mathbb{Z}(6)$ which is not in the image of h.
   (d) Which elements in $\mathbb{Z}(12)$ are mapped to $\langle 1, 3 \rangle$ by h?

10. Let I be an ideal of a ring R.
    (a) Show that the mapping $r \rightarrow r + I$ is a ring homomorphism of R onto R/I.
    (b) Find the kernel of this homomorphism.

11. (a) Show that $(\mathbb{Z}(6), +_6, *_6)$ is not a field.
    (b) Show that $(\mathbb{Z}(5), +_5, *_5)$ is a field.
    (c) Show that if F and K are fields, then $F \times K$ is not a field.

12. If $R_1, \ldots, R_n$ are rings and if $h_1, \ldots, h_n$ are homomorphisms from a ring R into $R_1, \ldots, R_n$, respectively, then the mapping h defined by $h(r) = \langle h_1(r), \ldots, h_n(r) \rangle$ is a homomorphism of R into $R_1 \times \cdots \times R_n$. Verify this fact for $n = 2$.

13. (a) Show that if h is a ring homomorphism from a field F to a ring R, then either $h(a) = 0$ for all $a \in F$ or h is one-to-one.
    (b) Show that if I is an ideal of the ring R such that R/I is a field, then I and R are the only ideals of R which contain I.

14. Let R be a commutative ring with identity.
    (a) Show that R is an integral domain if and only if the mapping $a \rightarrow r \cdot a$ from R to R is one-to-one for each non-0 r in R.
    (b) Show that R is a field if and only if this mapping is a one-to-one correspondence of R onto itself for each non-0 r in R.
    (c) Show that every finite integral domain is a field.

15. (a) Find an ideal I of $\mathbb{Z}$ for which $\mathbb{Z}/I$ is isomorphic to $\mathbb{Z}(3) \times \mathbb{Z}(5)$.
    (b) Describe an isomorphism between $\mathbb{Z}(12)$ and $\mathbb{Z}(3) \times \mathbb{Z}(4)$.
    (c) Show that $\mathbb{Z}$ has no ideal I with $\mathbb{Z}/I$ isomorphic to $\mathbb{Z}(2) \times \mathbb{Z}(2)$.

16. (a) Draw a Hasse diagram for the set of ideals of $\mathbb{Z}(12)$, partially ordered by inclusion $\subseteq$.
    (b) Repeat part (a) for the ring $\mathbb{Z}(3) \times \mathbb{Z}(4)$.

17. Consider the ring $R = \text{POLY}(\mathbb{Z})$ of polynomials in x with integer coefficients.
    (a) Describe the members of the ideals $R \cdot 2$, $R \cdot x$ and $R \cdot 2 + R \cdot x$.
    (b) Show that there is no polynomial p in R for which $R \cdot p = R \cdot 2 + R \cdot x$.

18. The set $\mathbb{B} \times \mathbb{B}$ can be made into a ring in another way besides the one described in the text. Define $+$ and $\cdot$ by the tables:

$+$	$\langle 0, 0 \rangle$	$\langle 1, 0 \rangle$	$\langle 0, 1 \rangle$	$\langle 1, 1 \rangle$
$\langle 0, 0 \rangle$	$\langle 0, 0 \rangle$	$\langle 1, 0 \rangle$	$\langle 0, 1 \rangle$	$\langle 1, 1 \rangle$
$\langle 1, 0 \rangle$	$\langle 1, 0 \rangle$	$\langle 0, 0 \rangle$	$\langle 1, 1 \rangle$	$\langle 0, 1 \rangle$
$\langle 0, 1 \rangle$	$\langle 0, 1 \rangle$	$\langle 1, 1 \rangle$	$\langle 0, 0 \rangle$	$\langle 1, 0 \rangle$
$\langle 1, 1 \rangle$	$\langle 1, 1 \rangle$	$\langle 0, 1 \rangle$	$\langle 1, 0 \rangle$	$\langle 0, 0 \rangle$

$\cdot$	$\langle 0, 0 \rangle$	$\langle 1, 0 \rangle$	$\langle 0, 1 \rangle$	$\langle 1, 1 \rangle$
$\langle 0, 0 \rangle$	$\langle 0, 0 \rangle$	$\langle 0, 0 \rangle$	$\langle 0, 0 \rangle$	$\langle 0, 0 \rangle$
$\langle 1, 0 \rangle$	$\langle 0, 0 \rangle$	$\langle 1, 0 \rangle$	$\langle 0, 1 \rangle$	$\langle 1, 1 \rangle$
$\langle 0, 1 \rangle$	$\langle 0, 0 \rangle$	$\langle 0, 1 \rangle$	$\langle 1, 1 \rangle$	$\langle 1, 0 \rangle$
$\langle 1, 1 \rangle$	$\langle 0, 0 \rangle$	$\langle 1, 1 \rangle$	$\langle 1, 0 \rangle$	$\langle 0, 1 \rangle$

Verify that $\mathbb{B} \times \mathbb{B}$ is an additive group and that the non-0 elements form a group under multiplication. *Suggestion:* Save work by exhibiting known groups isomorphic to your alleged groups. [Finite fields such as this are important in algebraic coding to minimize the effects of noise on transmission channels.]

CHAPTER HIGHLIGHTS

Concepts

algebraic system
   semigroup, monoid, group
   ring, integral domain, field
     identity, zero
generate, set of generators
order of an element
coset, right coset
homomorphism
   isomorphism
   congruence relation
   kernel, normal subgroup, ideal
   natural operation on $[S]$
   natural isomorphism of $[S]$ onto $h(S)$
permutation action
   subgroup fixing something
   orbit
   coloring, G-equivalent colorings

Facts

Intersections of subsemigroups [subgroups, subrings, normal subgroups, ideals] are subsemigroups [subgroups, etc.].

The subsemigroup [subgroup] generated by A consists of all products of members of A [and their inverses].

The subgroups of $(\mathbb{Z}, +)$ are the sets $n\mathbb{Z}$, all of which are cyclic groups. They are the ideals of $(\mathbb{Z}, +, \cdot)$.

The cosets of a subgroup partition a group into subsets of equal size. Lagrange's theorem: $|G| = |G/H| \cdot |H|$.

The order of an element of G divides $|G|$.

Homomorphisms determine congruence relations.

Congruence classes [cosets of normal subgroups, of ideals] can be combined in a natural way to form a semigroup [group, ring].

Fundamental Theorem: If h is a homomorphism defined on S with set $[S]$ of congruence classes, then $[s] \rightarrow h(s)$ is an isomorphism of $[S]$ onto $h(S)$. If S is a group or ring and if h has kernel K, then $S/K \simeq h(S)$.

A group or ring homomorphism is one-to-one if and only if its kernel consists just of the identity element.

A homomorphism takes identities, inverses, subgroups, ideals to corresponding objects in the image.

Every subgroup [ideal] of the image of h is the image of a subgroup [ideal] which contains the kernel of h.

Cayley's theorem: Every group is isomorphic to a group of permutations.
The size of the G-orbit of s is the number of cosets of the subgroup fixing s,
   i.e., $|Gs| = |G/G_s|$.

$|S| = \sum_{i=1}^{m} |G/G_{s_i}|$ with one s_i from each orbit.

The number of orbits of G acting on S is the average number of elements of
   S fixed by members of G.

The number of orbits of G on FUN(S, C) is $\dfrac{1}{|G|} \sum_{g \in G} |C|^{m(g)}$.

$C(k) = \dfrac{1}{|G|} \sum_{g \in G} k^{m(g)}$.

If $I_1, \ldots, I_n$ are ideals of R, then $R/(I_1 \cap \cdots \cap I_n)$ is isomorphic to a
   subring of $(R/I_1) \times \cdots \times (R/I_n)$.

DICTIONARY

The words listed below are of three general sorts: English words with which the reader may not be completely familiar, common English words whose usage in mathematical writing is specialized, and technical mathematical terms which are assumed background for this book. For technical terms introduced in this book, see the index.

absurd. Clearly impossible, being contrary to some evident truth.

all. See *every*.

ambiguous. Capable of more than one interpretation or meaning.

anomaly. Something which is, or appears to be, inconsistent.

any. See *every*.

assume. "assume" and "suppose" mean the same thing and ask that we imagine a situation for the moment.

axiom. An assertion that is accepted and used without a proof. Obvious or self-evident axioms are preferred.

bona fide. Genuine or legitimate.

cf. Compare.

chicanery. Trickery.

class. See *set*.

collapse. To fall or come together.

collection. See *set*.

common factor. The integer m is a "common factor" or "common divisor" of two integers it divides them both. See *divisible by*.

comparable. Capable of being compared.

conjecture. A guess or opinion, preferably based on some experience or other source of wisdom.

corollary. See *theorem.*

define. Often this looks like an instruction [as in "Define $f(x) = x^2$"] when it is merely a [bad] mathematical way of saying "We define" or "Let".

disprove. The instruction "prove or disprove" means that the assertion should either be proved true or proved false. Which you do, of course, depends on whether the assertion is actually true or not.

distinct. Different.

distinguishable. A collection of objects is regarded as "distinguishable" if there is some property or characteristic that makes it possible to tell different objects apart. In contrast, we would regard ten red marbles of the same size as "indistinguishable."

divisible by. Consider integers m and n. We say that "n is divisible by m," that "m divides n," that "n is a multiple of m," or that "m is a factor of n" if $n = mk$ for some integer k. We write $m|n$ to signify any of these statements. For example, $3|6$, $4|20$ and $8|8$. Also $m|0$ for all m since $0 = mk$ for $k = 0$.

e.g. For example.

entries. The individual numbers or objects in ordered pairs, in matrices or in sequences.

even number. An integer that is exactly divisible by 2, i.e., any integer that can be written as $2k$ where $k \in \mathbb{Z}$. Note that 0 is an even number.

every. The expressions "for every," "for any" and "for all" mean the same thing. They all mean "for all choices of the variable in question," and so they correspond to the quantifier $\forall$ in § 6.1. The expression "for some" means "for at least one" and corresponds to the quantifier $\exists$ in § 6.1. It is generally good practice to avoid the use of "any," which is sometimes misunderstood. For example, "If $p(n)$ is true for any n" usually means "If $p(n)$ is true for some n," not "If $p(n)$ is true for every n."

factor. See *divisible by.*

family. See *set.*

fictitious. Imaginary, not actual.

gcd. If m and n are positive integers, then gcd(m, n) is the "greatest common divisor" of m and n, that is, the largest integer that divides both m and n. lcm(m, n) is their "least common multiple," i.e., the smallest integer that m and n both divide. For example gcd$(10, 25) = 5$ and lcm$(10,25) = 50$. gcd and lcm are often most easily calculated by writing m and n as products of primes. For example, for $m = 168$ and $n = 450$ we have $m = 2^3 \cdot 3 \cdot 7$ and $n = 2 \cdot 3^2 \cdot 5^2$, and so

$$\gcd(m, n) = 2 \cdot 3 = 6 \quad \text{and} \quad \text{lcm}(m, n) = 2^3 \cdot 3^2 \cdot 5^2 \cdot 7 = 12{,}600.$$

greatest common divisor. See *gcd.*

inclusion. We sometimes refer to the relation $A \subseteq B$ as an "inclusion" just as we may refer to $A = B$ as an "equality."

indices. Plural of index.

inspection. Something can be seen "by inspection" if it can be seen directly without calculation or modification.

irrational. An "irrational number" is a real number that is not rational, i.e., cannot be written as m/n for $m, n \in \mathbb{Z}, n \neq 0$. Examples include $\sqrt{2}$, $\sqrt{3}$, $\sqrt[3]{2}$, π and e.

lcm. See *gcd*.

least common multiple. See *gcd*.

lemma. See *theorem*.

loop. A part of a computer program that is used repeatedly.

matrices. Plural of matrix.

max. For two real numbers a and b, we write $\max\{a, b\}$ for the larger of the two. If $a = b$, then $\max\{a, b\} = a = b$.

min. For two real numbers a and b, we write $\min\{a, b\}$ for the smaller of the two. If $a = b$, then $\min\{a, b\} = a = b$.

multiple of. See *divisible by*.

necessary. We say a property p is "necessary" for a property q if p must hold whenever q holds, i.e., $q \Rightarrow p$. The property p is "sufficient" for q if p is enough to guarantee q, i.e., $p \Rightarrow q$. So p is necessary and sufficient for q provided $p \Leftrightarrow q$.

odd number. An integer that is not an even integer. An odd number can be written as $2k + 1$ for some $k \in \mathbb{Z}$.

permute. To change the order of a sequence of elements.

prime number. An integer ≥ 2 that cannot be written as the product of two integers that are both ≥ 2. The first few primes are 2, 3, 5, 7, 11, 13, 17, 19.

proposition. See *theorem*.

redundant. Unnecessary or excessive.

relatively prime. Two positive integers m and n are "relatively prime" if they have no common factors, i.e., if $\gcd(m, n) = 1$. See *gcd*.

sequence. A list of things following one another. A formal definition is given in § 3.3.

set. The terms "set," "collection," "class" and "family" are used interchangeably. We tend to refer to families of sets, for example, to avoid the expression "sets of sets."

some. See *every*.

sufficient. See *necessary*.

suppose. See *assume*.

synonym. A word having the same meaning as another word. Two words having the same meaning are *synonymous*.

theorem. A "theorem," "proposition," "lemma" or "corollary" is some assertion that has been or can be proved. The term "proposition" also has a special use in logic; see § 2.1. Theorems are usually the most important facts. Lemmas are usually not of primary interest and are used to prove later theorems or propositions. Corollaries are usually easy consequences of theorems or propositions just presented.

truncate. To shorten by cutting.

unambiguous. Not ambiguous. See *ambiguous.*

underlying set. The basic set on which the objects [like functions or operations] are defined.

vertices. Plural of vertex.

ANSWERS AND HINTS

Wise students will only look at these answers and hints after seriously working on the problems. When only hints are given, you should write out the details to check understanding as well as to get practice in communicating mathematical ideas.

Section 0.1, page 7

1. All but (b) and (d).

3. (c) is the only cycle listed.

5. (a) $s\,t\,v$ is one. (c) $u\,s\,t\,v\,w\,x\,z\,y$. There are no longest paths connecting vertices. For example, one can go from s to v as follows: $s\,u\,v\,u\,v\,u\,v\,\cdots\,u\,v$.

7. (a) is true and (b) is false. To see the failure of (b), consider the graph in Figure 9(a).

9. (a) and (b) are now both true.

11. Use a graph like Figure 3(b) of § 0.2.

13. If a cycle contains a loop at v, it must have vertex sequence $v\,v$, since otherwise v would be repeated in the middle of the cycle.

Section 0.2, page 14

1. Only Figure 9(b) has an Euler circuit. Only Figures 9(a) and 9(c) have Hamilton circuits.

3. It won't break down until the second visit to the other vertex of degree 3, namely t.

5. Figures 2(a) and 2(b) have Hamilton circuits.

560

7. Only the edges e_6 and e_7 are interchanged. Of course the new spanning tree has the same total weight, namely 1330, since they are both *minimal* spanning trees.

9. (b) A tree with n vertices has exactly $n - 1$ edges.

11. (b) For each pair of vertices in a tree, there is exactly one path connecting them that repeats no edges.

13. (a) $t\,u$, $t\,v$, $u\,v$, $u\,w$, $v\,w$, $x\,y$, $x\,z$ and $y\,z$. (b) $s\,t$ and $w\,x$.

15. (a) If the tree has n vertices, it must have $n - 7$ of degree 1. So we must have

$$5 + 5 + 3 + 3 + 3 + 2 + 2 + 1 \cdot (n - 7) = 2n - 2$$

by Exercise 14. Solve for n.

Section 0.3, page 22

1. Here are some answers for the trees labeled as indicated.

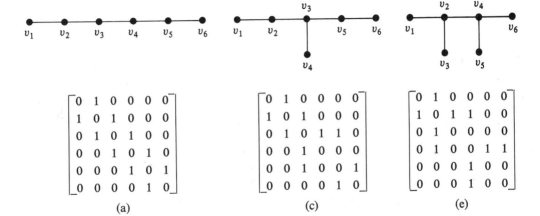

$$
\begin{bmatrix}
0 & 1 & 0 & 0 & 0 & 0 \\
1 & 0 & 1 & 0 & 0 & 0 \\
0 & 1 & 0 & 1 & 0 & 0 \\
0 & 0 & 1 & 0 & 1 & 0 \\
0 & 0 & 0 & 1 & 0 & 1 \\
0 & 0 & 0 & 0 & 1 & 0
\end{bmatrix}
\qquad
\begin{bmatrix}
0 & 1 & 0 & 0 & 0 & 0 \\
1 & 0 & 1 & 0 & 0 & 0 \\
0 & 1 & 0 & 1 & 1 & 0 \\
0 & 0 & 1 & 0 & 0 & 0 \\
0 & 0 & 1 & 0 & 0 & 1 \\
0 & 0 & 0 & 0 & 1 & 0
\end{bmatrix}
\qquad
\begin{bmatrix}
0 & 1 & 0 & 0 & 0 & 0 \\
1 & 0 & 1 & 1 & 0 & 0 \\
0 & 1 & 0 & 0 & 0 & 0 \\
0 & 1 & 0 & 0 & 1 & 1 \\
0 & 0 & 0 & 1 & 0 & 0 \\
0 & 0 & 0 & 1 & 0 & 0
\end{bmatrix}
$$

(a) \qquad\qquad\qquad (c) \qquad\qquad\qquad (e)

3. Yes. If Figure 6(c) is relabeled as indicated here, its matrix will be the same as for Figure 6(b).

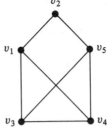

5. There are nine. "All" here means that every such graph is isomorphic to one of the nine, and no two of the nine are isomorphic to each other.

7. Consider loops to guess which two they are, and draw both. Then relabel the vertices on one of them.

9. (a) Either work it out pair by pair or multiply

$$\begin{bmatrix} 0 & 1 & 0 & 0 \\ 1 & 1 & 0 & 0 \\ 0 & 0 & 1 & 0 \\ 0 & 0 & 0 & 0 \end{bmatrix}$$

by itself and then draw the graph.

(b) No.   (c) $\begin{bmatrix} 1 & 1 & 0 & 0 \\ 1 & 2 & 0 & 0 \\ 0 & 0 & 1 & 0 \\ 0 & 0 & 0 & 0 \end{bmatrix}$.   (d) $\begin{bmatrix} 1 & 1 & 0 & 0 \\ 1 & 1 & 0 & 0 \\ 0 & 0 & 1 & 0 \\ 0 & 0 & 0 & 0 \end{bmatrix}$.

11. (b) No.   (c) $\begin{bmatrix} 1 & 0 & 1 & 0 & 0 & 0 \\ 0 & 2 & 0 & 1 & 1 & 0 \\ 1 & 0 & 3 & 0 & 0 & 1 \\ 0 & 1 & 0 & 1 & 1 & 0 \\ 0 & 1 & 0 & 1 & 2 & 0 \\ 0 & 0 & 1 & 0 & 0 & 1 \end{bmatrix}$ (d) $\begin{bmatrix} 1 & 1 & 1 & 1 & 1 & 1 \\ 1 & 1 & 1 & 1 & 1 & 1 \\ 1 & 1 & 1 & 1 & 1 & 1 \\ 1 & 1 & 1 & 1 & 1 & 1 \\ 1 & 1 & 1 & 1 & 1 & 1 \\ 1 & 1 & 1 & 1 & 1 & 1 \end{bmatrix}$.

13. The degree of vertex v_i is $2 \cdot \mathbf{M}[i, i]$ plus the sum of the other numbers in the ith row. If this doesn't look like a formula, how's this:

$$\text{degree}(v_i) = \mathbf{M}[i, i] + \mathbf{M}[i, 1] + \mathbf{M}[i, 2] + \cdots + \mathbf{M}[i, n]?$$

Section 1.1, page 32

1. (a) 0, 5, 10, 15, 20, say.   (c) $\varnothing$, {1}, {2, 3}, {3, 4}, {5}, say.   (e) 1, 1/2, 1/3, 1/4, 1/73, say.   (g) 1, 2, 4, 16, 18, say.

3. (a) ϵ, a, ab, cab, ba, say.   (c) $aaaa$, $aaab$, $aabb$, etc.

5. (a) 0.   (c) 138.   (e) 73.   (g) 0.   (i) ∞.   (k) ∞.   (m) ∞.   (o) ∞.

7. $A \subseteq A$, $B \subseteq B$, C is a subset of A and C, D is a subset of A, B and D.

9. (a) aba is in all three and has length 3 in each.   (c) cba is in Σ_1^* and length(cba) = 3.   (e) $caab$ is in Σ_1^* with length 4 and is in Σ_2^* with length 3.

11. (a) Yes.   (c) Delete first letters from the string until no longer possible. If ϵ is reached, the original string is in Σ^*. Otherwise, it isn't.

Section 1.2, page 40

1. (a) {1, 2, 3, 5, 7, 9, 11}.   (c) {1, 5, 7, 9, 11}.   (e) {3, 6, 12}.   (g) 16.

3. (a) [2, 3].   (c) [0, 2).   (e) $(-\infty, 0) \cup (3, \infty)$.

5. (a) $\varnothing$.   (c) $\varnothing$.   (e) {ϵ, ab, ba}.

7. $A \oplus A = \varnothing$ and $A \oplus \varnothing = A$.

9. $(A \cap B \cap C)^c = (A \cap B)^c \cup C^c$ and $(A \cap B)^c = A^c \cup B^c$ by DeMorgan law 9b. Now substitute.

11. Imitate one of the proofs in Example 4.

13. (a) Give elementwise argument or use Venn diagram. (b) This follows from part (a), since $A \cap (A \cup B) = (A \cap A) \cup (A \cap B) = A \cup (A \cap B)$. Supply reasons.

15. (a) False. Try $A = \varnothing$. (c) True. Show $x \in B$ implies $x \in C$ by considering two cases: $x \in A$ and $x \notin A$. Similarly, $x \in C$ implies $x \in B$. (e) The hint to part (c) also applies here.

17.

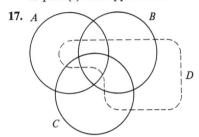

Section 1.3, page 48

1. (a) 42. (c) 1. (e) 154.

3. (a) 3, 12, 39 and 120. (c) 3, 9 and 45.

5. (a) $-2, 2, 0, 0$ and 0.

7. (a) D_{10}. (c) D_4. (e) $\{k \in \mathbb{Z} : k$ is divisible by 4 or 6 and not both$\} = \{0, \pm 4, \pm 6, \pm 8, \pm 16, \pm 18, \pm 20, \pm 28, \ldots\}$.

9. (a) $A_2 = \{2, 3, 4, \ldots\}$, $B_2 = \{0, 1, 2, 3, 4\}$,
   $A_4 = \{4, 5, 6, \ldots\}$, $B_4 = \{0, 1, 2, 3, 4, 5, 6, 7, 8\}$.
   (c) $A_1 \cap B_1 = \{1, 2\}$, $A_2 \cap B_2 = \{2, 3, 4\}$, $A_3 \cap B_3 = \{3, 4, 5, 6\}$, $A_7 \cap B_7 = \{7, 8, 9, \ldots, 14\}$, $A_1^c = \{0\}$, $A_2^c = \{0, 1\}$, $A_3^c = \{0, 1, 2\}$ and $A_7^c = \{0, 1, 2, 3, 4, 5, 6\}$.
   (e) $A_3, \mathbb{N}, B_3$ and $\varnothing$.

11. (a) $\{w \in \Sigma^* : \text{length}(w) \leq n\}$.

13. Imitate the proof in Example 3.

15. Divide $11^1 - 4^1 = 7$, $11^2 - 4^2 = 105$ and $11^3 - 4^3 = 1267$ by 7.

17. $p(n)$ is true for all $n \geq 4$.

Section 1.4, page 57

1. (a) $\langle a, a \rangle, \langle a, b \rangle, \langle a, c \rangle, \langle b, a \rangle$, etc. There are nine altogether.
   (c) $\langle a, a \rangle, \langle b, b \rangle$.

3. (a) $\langle 0, 0 \rangle, \langle 1, 1 \rangle, \langle 2, 2 \rangle, \ldots, \langle 6, 6 \rangle$, say.
   (c) $\langle 6, 1 \rangle, \langle 6, 2 \rangle, \langle 6, 3 \rangle, \ldots, \langle 6, 7 \rangle$, say.
   (e) The set has exactly five elements. List them.

5. (a)

7. (a) To find $A \cap B$, you need all $\langle x, y \rangle$ satisfying $2x - y = 4$ *and* $x + 3y = 9$. Solve this system of two equations in two unknowns. Answer: $A \cap B = \{\langle 3, 2 \rangle\}$.   (c) $\{\langle 9/7, 18/7 \rangle\}$.

9. (a) $\langle \epsilon, \epsilon \rangle$, $\langle a, a \rangle$, $\langle b, b \rangle$, $\langle a, b \rangle$, $\langle aa, bc \rangle$, etc.
   (b) There are eight, including $\langle a, b, a \rangle$ and $\langle b, a, a \rangle$.

11. (a) $\begin{bmatrix} -1 & 1 & 4 \\ 0 & 3 & 2 \\ 2 & -2 & 3 \end{bmatrix}$.   (c) $\begin{bmatrix} 5 & 8 & 7 \\ 5 & 1 & 5 \\ 7 & 3 & 5 \end{bmatrix}$.

   (e) $\begin{bmatrix} 5 & 5 & 7 \\ 8 & 1 & 3 \\ 7 & 5 & 5 \end{bmatrix}$.   (g) $\begin{bmatrix} 12 & 12 & 8 \\ 12 & -4 & 8 \\ 8 & 8 & 4 \end{bmatrix}$.   (i) $\begin{bmatrix} 4 & 8 & 9 \\ 6 & 4 & 3 \\ 11 & 5 & 8 \end{bmatrix}$.

13. (a) $\begin{bmatrix} 1 & -1 & 1 & -1 \\ -1 & 1 & -1 & 1 \\ 1 & -1 & 1 & -1 \end{bmatrix}$.   (c) Not defined.

   (e) $\begin{bmatrix} 3 & 2 & 5 & 4 \\ 2 & 5 & 4 & 7 \\ 5 & 4 & 7 & 6 \end{bmatrix}$.

15. (a) $\begin{bmatrix} 1 & 0 & 0 \\ 0 & 1 & 0 \\ 0 & 0 & 1 \end{bmatrix}$, $\begin{bmatrix} 1 & 0 & 0 \\ 0 & 0 & 1 \\ 0 & 1 & 0 \end{bmatrix}$, $\begin{bmatrix} 0 & 1 & 0 \\ 1 & 0 & 0 \\ 0 & 0 & 1 \end{bmatrix}$, $\begin{bmatrix} 0 & 1 & 0 \\ 0 & 0 & 1 \\ 1 & 0 & 0 \end{bmatrix}$, $\begin{bmatrix} 0 & 0 & 1 \\ 1 & 0 & 0 \\ 0 & 1 & 0 \end{bmatrix}$,
   $\begin{bmatrix} 0 & 0 & 1 \\ 0 & 1 & 0 \\ 1 & 0 & 0 \end{bmatrix}$.

   (b) Four of them equal their transposes.

17. (a) $\begin{bmatrix} 1 & 0 \\ n & 1 \end{bmatrix}$.   (c) $\{n \in \mathbb{N} : n \text{ is odd}\}$.

19. Clearly $s_1 = s_2$ and $t_1 = t_2$ imply $\langle s_1, t_1 \rangle = \langle s_2, t_2 \rangle$. If $\langle s_1, t_1 \rangle = \langle s_2, t_2 \rangle$, then

$$\{s_1\} = \{s_2\} \quad \text{and} \quad \{s_1, t_1\} = \{s_2, t_2\}.$$

Show that these equalities force $s_1 = s_2$ and $t_1 = t_2$.

Section 2.1, page 68

1. (a) $p \wedge q$.　(c) $\neg p \to (\neg q \wedge r)$.　(e) $\neg r \to q$.

3. (b) In Example 2, parts (b), (d) and (f) are true and parts (a) and (c) are false. The answer to part (e) depends on your interpretation.

5. The proposition is true for all $x, y \in [0, \infty)$, but is false when applied to all $x, y \in \mathbb{R}$.

7. (a) 0.　(c) 1.

Note. For truth tables, only the final columns are given.

9. (a)

p	q	$\neg(p \wedge q)$
0	0	1
0	1	1
1	0	1
1	1	0

(c)

p	q	$\neg p \wedge \neg q$
0	0	1
0	1	0
1	0	0
1	1	0

11.

p	q	r	final column
0	0	0	1
0	0	1	1
0	1	0	1
0	1	1	0
1	0	0	1
1	0	1	1
1	1	0	1
1	1	1	0

13.

p	q	r	part (a)	part (b)
0	0	0	0	0
0	0	1	1	0
0	1	0	1	1
0	1	1	1	0
1	0	0	1	1
1	0	1	1	0
1	1	0	1	1
1	1	1	1	0

15. (b)

p	$p \oplus p$
0	0
1	0

(d)

p	$(p \oplus p) \oplus p$
0	0
1	1

17. (a) $p \to q$.　(b) $p \to r$.　(c) $\neg r \to p$.　(d) $q \to p$.　(e) $r \to q$.
(f) $r \to (q \vee p)$ or $(r \to q) \vee p$.

19. Both possible truth values, true or false, lead to a contradiction. So this is not a proposition. It is an example of what is called a **paradox**.

Section 2.2, page 76

1. (a) Converse: $(q \wedge r) \to p$
Contrapositive: $\neg(q \wedge r) \to \neg p$.

(c) Converse: If $3 + 3 = 8$, then $2 + 2 = 4$.
Contrapositive: If $3 + 3 \neq 8$, then $2 + 2 \neq 4$.

3. (a) $q \to p$.   (c) $p \to q$, $\neg q \to \neg p$, $\neg p \lor q$.

7. (a) One need only consider rows in which $[(p \land r) \to (q \land r)]$ is false, i.e., $(p \land r)$ is true and $(q \land r)$ is false. This leaves one row to consider:

p	q	r
1	0	1

(c) One need only consider rows in which $[(p \land r) \to (q \land s)]$ is false, i.e., $(p \land r)$ is true and $(q \land s)$ is false. This leaves three rows to consider:

p	q	r	s
1	0	1	0
1	0	1	1
1	1	1	0

9. (a) We obtain successive equivalences using the indicated rules and suitable substitutions:

$[(p \lor r) \land (q \to r)]$	
$[(p \lor r) \land (\neg q \lor r)]$	rule 10a
$[(r \lor p) \land (r \lor \neg q)]$	rule 2a
$r \lor (p \land \neg q)$	rule 4a
$(p \land \neg q) \lor r$	rule 2a
$\neg(\neg p \lor \neg\neg q) \lor r$	rule 8d
$\neg(\neg p \lor q) \lor r$	rule 1
$\neg(p \to q) \lor r$	rule 10a
$(p \to q) \to r$	rule 10a

(b) $\neg q \Rightarrow \neg q \lor p$ by rule 16. So it suffices to show $(\neg q \lor p) \Leftrightarrow [(p \lor q) \to p]$. One proof of successive equivalences uses the rules in the following order: 10a, 8a, 2a, 4a, 7a, 6d, 2a.

11. Use truth tables.

13. (a) The propositions are not equivalent, as can be verified by comparing the first or third rows of their truth tables.   (b) and (c) are true. It is probably easiest to verify them using truth tables.

15. (a) See rules 11a and 11b.   (c) No. Any proposition involving only $p, q, \land$ and $\lor$ will have truth value 0 whenever p and q both have truth values 0. See Exercise 11 of § 6.4.

17. Consider the row of the truth table where p is false and q is true.

Section 2.3, page 83

1. For example, rule 23 corresponds to the rule of inference

$$\frac{\begin{array}{c} P \leftrightarrow Q \\ Q \leftrightarrow R \end{array}}{\therefore \ P \leftrightarrow R}$$

3. Lines 1, 2, 3 are hypotheses. Line 4 is the negation of the conclusion. Line 5 follows from lines 2 and 4 and the rule of inference 31 (modus tollens). Line 6 follows from line 5 and a DeMorgan law. Line 7 follows from line 6 and the rule of inference 29 (simplification). Etc.

5. (a) Let c = "my computations are correct," b = "I pay the electric bill," r = "I run out of money," and p = "the power stays on." Then the theorem is: if $(c \land b) \to r$ and $\neg b \to \neg p$, then $(\neg r \land p) \to \neg c$. Here is a formal proof; you should supply the missing explanations. Or give your own proof.

    1. $(c \land b) \to r$
    2. $\neg b \to \neg p$
    3. $\neg r \to \neg(c \land b)$
    4. $\neg r \to (\neg c \lor \neg b)$
    5. $p \to b$
    6. $(\neg r \land p) \to ((\neg c \lor \neg b) \land b)$ 4, 5; rule of inference corresponding to rule 26b
    7. $(\neg r \land p) \to (b \land (\neg c \lor \neg b))$
    8. $(\neg r \land p) \to ((b \land \neg c) \lor (b \land \neg b))$
    9. $(\neg r \land p) \to ((b \land \neg c) \lor$ contradiction$)$
    10. $(\neg r \land p) \to (b \land \neg c)$
    11. $(\neg r \land p) \to (\neg c \land b)$
    12. $(\neg c \land b) \to \neg c$ simplification [rule 17]
    13. $(\neg r \land p) \to \neg c$

(c) Let j = "I get the job," w = "I work hard," p = "I get promoted," and h = "I will be happy." Then the theorem is: if $(j \land w) \to p$, $p \to h$ and $\neg h$, then $\neg j \lor \neg w$. You should supply the formal proof.

7. (a) Here is a formal proof; you should supply all the explanations. Or give your own proof.

    1. $p \to q$ 9. $(p \land r) \to (q \land s)$
    2. $r \to (p \land s)$ 10. $q \land s$
    3. $(q \land s) \to (p \land t)$ 11. $p \land t$
    4. $\neg t$ 12. $t \land p$
    5. $\neg(p \to \neg r)$ 13. t
    6. $p \land r$ 14. $t \land \neg t$
    7. $(p \land s) \to s$ 15. contradiction
    8. $r \to s$

9. (a) With suggestive notation, the hypotheses are $\neg b \to \neg s$, $s \to p$ and $\neg p$. We can infer $\neg s$ using the contrapositive. We cannot infer either b or $\neg b$. Of course, we can infer more complex propositions, like $\neg p \lor s$ or $(s \land b) \to p$.
(c) The hypotheses are $(m \lor f) \to c$, $n \to c$ and $\neg n$. No interesting conclusions, such as m or $\neg c$, can be inferred.

Section 2.4, page 91

1. Give a direct proof using the following fact. If m and n are even integers, then there exist j and k in $\mathbb{Z}$ so that $m = 2j$ and $n = 2k$.

3. This can be done via four cases: see Example 5.

5. This can be done via three cases: (i) $n = 3k$ for some $k \in \mathbb{N}$; (ii) $n = 3k + 1$ for some $k \in \mathbb{N}$; (iii) $n = 3k + 2$ for some $k \in \mathbb{N}$.

7. (a) Give a direct proof, as in Exercise 1.   (c) False. Give an example.   (e) False. Finding an example will be easy; the sum of four consecutive integers is *never* divisible by 4.

9. (a) Trivially true.   (c) Vacuously true.

11. Since $\{n \in \mathbb{N} : n$ is prime and $n \leq 10^{21}\}$ is a finite set, Example 3 shows that $\{n \in \mathbb{N} : n$ is prime and $n > 10^{21}\}$ is nonempty. As in Example 10, this set has a least element. The proof relies on Example 3, which is nonconstructive.

13. (a) None of the numbers in the set

$$\{k \in \mathbb{N} : (n+1)! + 2 \leq k \leq (n+1)! + (n+1)\}$$

is prime, since if $2 \leq m \leq n+1$, then m divides $(n+1)!$ and so m also divides $(n+1)! + m$.

(b) Yes. Since $7! = 5040$, the proof shows that all the numbers from 5042 to 5047 are nonprime.

(c) Simply add 5048 to the list in part (b). Incidentally, a sequence of seven nonprimes starts with 90.

Section 2.5, page 100

Induction proofs should be written carefully and completely. These answers will serve only as guides, not as models.

1. Check the basis. For the inductive step, assume the equality holds for n. Then

$$\sum_{k=1}^{n+1} k^2 = \sum_{k=1}^{n} k^2 + (n+1)^2 = \frac{n(n+1)(2n+1)}{6} + (n+1)^2.$$

Some algebra shows that the right-hand side equals $\frac{(n+1)(n+2)(2n+3)}{6}$, and so the equality holds for $n+1$ whenever it holds for n.

3. The algebra for the inductive step is

$$\sum_{k=0}^{n+1} a^k = \sum_{k=0}^{n} a^k + a^{n+1} = \frac{a^{n+1}-1}{a-1} + a^{n+1} = \frac{a^{n+2}-1}{a-1}.$$

5. (a) $2, 5, 10, 17$.   (b) $S = n^2 + 1$.

7. Show that $11^{n+1} - 4^{n+1} = 11 \cdot (11^n - 4^n) + 7 \cdot 4^n$. Imitate Example 5.

11. (a) The inequality holds for all $n \geq 4$.

(b) Prove $3n < n^2 - 1$ for $n \geq 4$ by induction. For the inductive step, assume $3n < n^2 - 1$; you want $3(n+1) < (n+1)^2 - 1$, i.e., $3n + 3 < n^2 + 2n$. Since $3n + 3 < (n^2 - 1) + 3 = n^2 + 2$, it suffices to observe that $2 \leq 2n$.

13. (a) Assume $p(n)$ is true. Then $(n+1)^2 + 5(n+1) + 1 = (n^2 + 5n + 1) + (2n + 6)$. $n^2 + 5n + 1$ is even by assumption and $2n + 6$ is clearly even, so $p(n+1)$ is true.

(b) All propositions $p(n)$ are false. *Moral:* The basis of induction is crucial for mathematical induction.

15. *Hint:* $5^{n+1} - 4(n+1) - 1 = 5(5^n - 4n - 1) + 16n$.

17. Here $p(n)$ is the proposition "$|\sin nx| \leq n|\sin x|$ for all $x \in \mathbb{R}$." Clearly $p(1)$ holds. By algebra and trigonometry,

$$|\sin(n+1)x| = |\sin(nx+x)| = |\sin nx \cos x + \cos nx \sin x|$$
$$\leq |\sin nx| \cdot |\cos x| + |\cos nx| \cdot |\sin x| \leq |\sin nx| + |\sin x|.$$

Now assume $p(n)$ is true and show $p(n+1)$ is true.

Section 3.1, page 112

1. (a) $f(3) = 27, f(1/3) = 1/3, f(-1/3) = 1/27, f(-3) = 27$.
   (c) $\text{Im}(f) = [0, \infty)$.

3. (a) No; S is bigger than T. (c) Yes. For example, let $f(1) = a, f(2) = b$, $f(3) = c, f(4) = f(5) = d$. (e) No.

5. (a) $f(\langle 2, 1 \rangle) = 2^2 3^1 = 12, f(\langle 1, 2 \rangle) = 2^1 3^2 = 18$, etc.
   (b) If not, $2^m 3^n = 2^{m'} 3^{n'}$ for some $\langle m, n \rangle \neq \langle m', n' \rangle$. Then $m \neq m'$ [why?]. Say $m < m'$. Divide both sides by 2^m to get a number that is both odd and even, a contradiction. (c) Consider 5, for instance.

7. (a) Pick b_0 in B. For every $a \in A$, $\text{PROJ}(\langle a, b_0 \rangle) = a$ and so every a in A is in the image of PROJ. That is, PROJ maps $A \times B$ onto A.

9. $\{n \in \mathbb{Z} : n \text{ is even}\}$.

11. (a) $f \circ g \circ h(x) = (x^8 + 1)^{-3} - 4(x^8 + 1)^{-1}$.
    (c) $h \circ g \circ f(x) = [(x^3 - 4x)^2 + 1]^{-4}$.
    (e) $g \circ g(x) = (x^2 + 1)^2/[1 + (x^2 + 1)^2]$.
    (g) $g \circ h(x) = (x^8 + 1)^{-1}$.

13. Since $g \circ f : S \to U$ and $h : U \to V$, the composition $h \circ (g \circ f)$ is defined and maps S to V. A similar remark applies to $(h \circ g) \circ f$. Show that the functions' values agree at each $x \in S$.

15. (a) $1, 0, -1$ and 0.
    (c) $g \circ f$ is the characteristic function of $\mathbb{Z} \setminus E$. $f \circ f(n) = n - 2$ for all $n \in \mathbb{Z}$.

Section 3.2, page 120

1. (a) $f^{-1}(y) = (y - 3)/2$. (c) $h^{-1}(y) = 2 + \sqrt[3]{y}$.

3. (a) All of them; verify this.
   (c) $\text{SUM}^{-1}(4)$ has 5 elements, $\text{PROD}^{-1}(4)$ has 3 elements, $\text{MAX}^{-1}(4)$ has 9 elements, and $\text{MIN}^{-1}(4)$ is infinite.

5. (b) $g(0) = 0, g(1) = 0, g(2) = 1, g(3) = 2$, etc.
   (c) One-to-oneness is easy. Note that $0 \notin \text{Im}(f)$.
   (e) Evaluate $f \circ g$ at 0.

9. Since f and g are invertible, the functions $f^{-1} : T \to S$, $g^{-1} : U \to T$ and $f^{-1} \circ g^{-1} : U \to S$ exist. So it suffices to show $(g \circ f) \circ (f^{-1} \circ g^{-1}) = 1_U$ and $(f^{-1} \circ g^{-1}) \circ (g \circ f) = 1_S$.

11. (a) Prove the contrapositive: if $s_1, s_2 \in S$ and $f(s_1) = f(s_2)$, then $s_1 = s_2$. The proof will be very short.

13. (a) Suppose $t \in f(f^{-1}(B))$. Then $t = f(s)$ for some $s \in f^{-1}(B)$. $s \in f^{-1}(B)$ means that $f(s) \in B$. So $t \in B$. This works for any t, so $f(f^{-1}(B)) \subseteq B$.

15. (a) $f^{-1}(0) = \{\langle 0, 0 \rangle\}$, $f^{-1}(1) = \{\langle 0, 1 \rangle, \langle 1, 0 \rangle\}$, $f^{-1}(2) = \{\langle 0, 2 \rangle, \langle 1, 1 \rangle, \langle 2, 0 \rangle\}$, etc.

17. (a) The first sentence shows that the f in the example cannot be one-to-one. At the other extreme, if f is constant, $f \circ g = f \circ h$ for all g and h. Provide a specific example.

(c) f maps $\mathrm{Dom}(f)$ onto $\mathrm{Dom}(g) = \mathrm{Dom}(h)$.

Section 3.3, page 124

1. (a) $0, 1/3, 1/2, 3/5, 2/3, 5/7$.

(c) Note that $a_{n+1} = \dfrac{(n+1) - 1}{(n+1) + 1} = \dfrac{n}{n+2}$ for $n \in \mathbb{P}$.

3. (a) $\begin{bmatrix} 0 & -1 \\ 1 & 0 \end{bmatrix}, \begin{bmatrix} 1 & 0 \\ 2 & 1 \end{bmatrix}, \begin{bmatrix} 2 & 1 \\ 3 & 2 \end{bmatrix}, \begin{bmatrix} 3 & 2 \\ 4 & 3 \end{bmatrix}.$

5. (a) $0, 0, 2, 6, 12, 20, 30$.

(b) Just substitute the values into both sides. Induction is not needed.

(c) Same comment.

7. (a) $0, 0, 1, 1, 2, 2, 3, 3, \ldots$.

(c) $\langle 0, 0 \rangle, \langle 0, 1 \rangle, \langle 1, 1 \rangle, \langle 1, 2 \rangle, \langle 2, 2 \rangle, \langle 2, 3 \rangle, \langle 3, 3 \rangle, \ldots$.

9. (a) $\mathbb{Z}$.   (c) $1/3, 2/3, 1/73$.   (e) $\phi_n(x) = x/2$ for $x \in B_n$.

Section 3.4, page 129

1. (a) $1, 2, 1, 2, 1, 2, 1, 2, \ldots$.   (b) $\{1, 2\}$.

3. (a) $\mathrm{SEQ}(n) = 3^n$.

(b) (B) $\mathrm{SEQ}(0) = 1$,

(R) $\mathrm{SEQ}(n + 1) = 3*\mathrm{SEQ}(n)$ for $n \geqq 1$.

5. No. It's okay up to $\mathrm{SEQ}(100)$, but $\mathrm{SEQ}(101)$ is not defined, since we cannot divide by zero. If, in (R), we restricted n to be $\leqq 100$, we would obtain a recursively defined *finite* sequence.

7. (a) $1, 1, 3, 5, 11, 21, 43$.

(b) Since $2a_{n-2}$ is always even, the oddness of a_{n-1} implies the oddness of $a_{n-1} + 2a_{n-2} = a_n$. Give an induction proof.

9. $\mathrm{SEQ}(n) = 2^{n-1}$ for $n \geqq 1$.

11. (a) $0, 1, 1/2, 5/6, 7/12, 47/60, \ldots$.

(b) If $\mathrm{SEQ}(n - 2) \leqq 1$ and $\mathrm{SEQ}(n - 1) \leqq 1$, then $\mathrm{SEQ}(n) = \dfrac{1}{n}*\mathrm{SEQ}(n - 1)$

$+ \dfrac{n-1}{n}*\mathrm{SEQ}(n - 2) \leqq \dfrac{1}{n}*1 + \dfrac{n-1}{n}*1 = 1$. A similar argument shows $\mathrm{SEQ}(n) \geqq 0$.

13. $f^{(1)} = f^{(0)} \circ f$ by (R) with $n = 0$

$= 1_S \circ f$ by (B)

$= f$ by a property of 1_S.

Also [supply reasons]

$$f^{(2)} = f^{(1)} \circ f = f \circ f \quad \text{and} \quad f^{(3)} = f^{(2)} \circ f = (f \circ f) \circ f.$$

15. (a) (B) $\mathrm{UNION}(1) = A_1$,

(R) $\mathrm{UNION}(n) = A_n \cup \mathrm{UNION}(n - 1)$ for $n \geqq 2$.

(d) Empty intersection should be the universe, in this case S.

17. For the inductive step, assume FACT(n) = n! Then

$$
\begin{aligned}
\text{FACT}(n + 1) &= (n + 1)*\text{FACT}(n) && \text{definition of FACT} \\
&= (n + 1)*n! && \text{inductive assumption} \\
&= (n + 1)*1*2* \cdots *n && \text{definition of } n! \\
&= (n + 1)! && \begin{cases} \text{commutative law and} \\ \text{definition of } (n + 1)!. \end{cases}
\end{aligned}
$$

Section 3.5, page 135

1. (a) 4, -3 and 5 are polynomial functions by (B). $I(x) = x$ is a polynomial function by (B). So $-3x$ is a polynomial function by the (fg) part of (R). Also $I^2 = I \cdot I$ where $I^2(x) = x^2$ is a polynomial function by the (fg) part of (R). And so $I^2 \cdot I = I^3$ where $I^3(x) = x^3$ is a polynomial function by the (fg) part of (R).

Now $5x^3$ is a polynomial function by the (fg) part of (R). So $-3x + 5x^3$ is a polynomial function by the $(f + g)$ part of (R). Finally, $4 + (-3x + 5x^3)$ is a polynomial function by the $(f + g)$ part of (R). Tedious, isn't it?

3. (a) $((x + y) + z)$ or $(x + (y + z))$.
(c) $((xy)z)$ or $(x(yz))$.

5. (a) By (B), x, y and 2 are wff's. By the (f^g) part of (R), we conclude that (x^2) and (y^2) are wff's. So by the $(f + g)$ part of (R), $((x^2) + (y^2))$ is a wff.
(c) By (B), X and Y are wff's. By the $(f + g)$ part of (R), $(X + Y)$ is a wff. By the $(f - g)$ part of (R), $(X - Y)$ is a wff. Finally, by the $(f*g)$ part of (R), $((X + Y)*(X - Y))$ is a wff.

7. Simply add "$(P \oplus Q)$," to the recursive clause (R).

9. (a) First note that

$$
g_1(x) = \begin{cases} -x & \text{for} \quad x < 0 \\ x & \text{for} \quad x \geq 0 \end{cases}.
$$

Now x and $-x$ are piecewise polynomial functions (ppf's) by (B). So by (R) with $a = 0$, we see that g_1 is also a ppf.

11. (a) (B) $\langle 0, 0 \rangle \in S$,
(R) if $\langle m, n \rangle \in S$, then $\langle m + 1, n + 3 \rangle \in S$.
(b) By (B), $\langle 0, 0 \rangle \in S$. So by (R), $\langle 1, 3 \rangle \in S$. Again by (R), $\langle 2, 6 \rangle \in S$. And again by (R), $\langle 3, 9 \rangle \in S$.

13. (a) (B) ϵ is in S,
(R) if $w \in S$, then $aw \in S$ and $wb \in S$.
(b) $\epsilon \in S$ by (B). Now repeated use of (R) yields $a\epsilon \in S$, i.e., $a \in S$, so $ab \in S$, so $abb \in S$, so $abbb \in S$.

15. (a) 2. (c) 2. (e) 4.

Section 3.6, page 145

1. (a) $q = 6, r = 2$. (c) $q = -7, r = 1$. (e) $q = 5711, r = 31$.

3. (a)

r	q
20	
	0
13	
	1
6	
	2

$m = 7, \quad n = 20.$

(c)

r	q
200	
	0
130	
	1
60	
	2

$m = 70, \quad n = 200.$

5. (a) 200, 187, 174, 161, ..., 5.

7. Here is one version:

$$q \leftarrow 0$$
$$r \leftarrow n$$
While $r < 0$
$\quad r \leftarrow r + m$
$\quad q \leftarrow q - 1$
End while
End

9. (a) $8 + 2 + 9 = 19$.

11. (a) 6.   (c) 300.

13. (a) If $f(n) \leq C_1 g(n)$ and $g(n) \leq C_2 h(n)$ for constants C_1, C_2, then $f(n) \leq C_1 C_2 h(n)$.

15. (a) $(n + 1)^2 = n^2 + 2n + 1 = O(n^2) + O(n) + O(1) = O(n^2)$ by Exercise 12(b). Alternatively, observe that $n^2 + 2n + 1 \leq 2n^2$ for $n \geq 3$.
(c) Apply Exercise 14.

Section 4.1, page 154

1. (a) $\begin{bmatrix} -8 & 13 \\ 2 & 9 \end{bmatrix}$.   (c) $\begin{bmatrix} 31 & -16 & -6 \\ 29 & 4 & 26 \end{bmatrix}$.   (e) $\begin{bmatrix} -1 & 7 \\ 8 & 0 \\ 16 & 0 \end{bmatrix}$.

3. The products written in parts (a), (c) and (e) do not exist.

5. (a) $\begin{bmatrix} 1 & 10 \\ 11 & 19 \end{bmatrix}$.

7. (a) $\begin{bmatrix} 7 & 14 \\ 8 & 11 \\ 2 & -6 \end{bmatrix}$.

9. (a) The (i, j) entry of $a\mathbf{A}$ is $a\mathbf{A}[i, j]$. Similarly for $b\mathbf{B}$ and so the (i, j) entry of $a\mathbf{A} + b\mathbf{B}$ is $a\mathbf{A}[i, j] + b\mathbf{B}[i, j]$. So the (i, j) entry of $c(a\mathbf{A} + b\mathbf{B})$ is $ca\mathbf{A}[i, j] + cb\mathbf{B}[i, j]$. A similar discussion shows that this is the (i, j) entry of $(ca)\mathbf{A} + (cb)\mathbf{B}$. Since their entries are equal, the matrices $c(a\mathbf{A} + b\mathbf{B})$ and $(ca)\mathbf{A} + (cb)\mathbf{B}$ are equal.
(c) The (j, i) entries of both $(a\mathbf{A})^T$ and $a\mathbf{A}^T$ equal $a\mathbf{A}[i, j]$. Here $1 \leq i \leq m$ and $1 \leq j \leq n$. So the matrices are equal.

11. (a) $\mathbf{B}$.   (c) $\mathbf{0}$.   (e) $\mathbf{A}$.

15. (a) In fact, $\mathbf{AB} = \mathbf{BA} = a\mathbf{B}$ for all $\mathbf{B}$ in $\mathfrak{M}_{2,2}$.

(b) $\mathbf{AB} = \mathbf{BA}$ with $\mathbf{B} = \begin{bmatrix} 1 & 0 \\ 0 & 0 \end{bmatrix}$ forces $\begin{bmatrix} a & 0 \\ c & 0 \end{bmatrix} = \begin{bmatrix} a & b \\ 0 & 0 \end{bmatrix}$ and so $b = c = 0$.

So $\mathbf{A} = \begin{bmatrix} a & 0 \\ 0 & d \end{bmatrix}$. Now try $\mathbf{B} = \begin{bmatrix} 0 & 1 \\ 0 & 0 \end{bmatrix}$.

17. Since $(\mathbf{A} + \mathbf{B})(\mathbf{A} - \mathbf{B}) = \mathbf{A}^2 + \mathbf{BA} - \mathbf{AB} - \mathbf{B}^2$, it is enough to find $\mathbf{A}$ and $\mathbf{B}$ where $\mathbf{BA} \neq \mathbf{AB}$.

19. For $1 \leqq k \leqq p$ and $1 \leqq i \leqq m$,

$$(\mathbf{B}^T\mathbf{A}^T)[k, i] = \sum_{j=1}^{n} \mathbf{B}^T[k, j]\mathbf{A}^T[j, i] = \sum_{j=1}^{n} \mathbf{B}[j, k]\mathbf{A}[i, j].$$

Compare with the (k, i) entry of $(\mathbf{AB})^T$.

21. (a) Consider $1 \leqq i \leqq m$ and $1 \leqq k \leqq p$ and compare the (i, k) entries of $(\mathbf{A} + \mathbf{B})\mathbf{C}$ and $\mathbf{AC} + \mathbf{BC}$.

23. (a) This is an easy induction proof on k. At the inductive step, argue $\mathbf{BA}^{k+1} = \mathbf{BA}^k\mathbf{A} = \mathbf{A}^k\mathbf{BA} = \mathbf{A}^k\mathbf{AB} = \mathbf{A}^{k+1}\mathbf{B}$, with reasons, of course.
(b) Apply induction and part (a).

Section 4.2, page 162

1. (a) -11. (c) 55 [use parts (a) and (b); there is no need to calculate $\mathbf{AB}$].
(e) $(-11)^2 = 121$.

3. (a) $\mathbf{I}^{-1} = \mathbf{I}$. (c) Not invertible. (e) $\mathbf{D}^{-1} = \mathbf{D}$.

5. (a) $\mathbf{A}^T = \mathbf{A}$. (c) $2^{10} = 1024$. (e) $\begin{bmatrix} 10 & -4 \\ -4 & 2 \end{bmatrix}$.

7. (a) $x \neq -8/3$ since the matrix has determinant $-3x - 8$.

9. (a) The equation is $\mathbf{A}\begin{bmatrix} x \\ y \\ z \end{bmatrix} = \begin{bmatrix} 2 \\ 1 \\ 0 \end{bmatrix}$, so the solution is

$$\mathbf{A}^{-1}\begin{bmatrix} 2 \\ 1 \\ 0 \end{bmatrix} = \mathbf{B}\begin{bmatrix} 2 \\ 1 \\ 0 \end{bmatrix} = \begin{bmatrix} 23 \\ -12 \\ 14 \end{bmatrix}, \quad \text{i.e.,} \quad x = 23, y = -12, z = 14.$$

(c) $\mathbf{B}^{-1}\begin{bmatrix} 1 \\ 0 \\ 1 \end{bmatrix} = \mathbf{A}\begin{bmatrix} 1 \\ 0 \\ 1 \end{bmatrix} = \begin{bmatrix} -2 \\ 5 \\ 3 \end{bmatrix}$.

11. (a) It suffices to show $\mathbf{AB}(\mathbf{B}^{-1}\mathbf{A}^{-1}) = (\mathbf{B}^{-1}\mathbf{A}^{-1})\mathbf{AB} = \mathbf{I}$. (b) Suppose, for example, that $\mathbf{A} + \mathbf{B} = \mathbf{0}$.

13. (c) The program could indicate that any matrix $\mathbf{A}$ with small determinant, say $|\det(\mathbf{A})| < .001$, will be regarded as noninvertible. More sophisticated techniques are incorporated in most canned programs which involve matrix inversion or which are sensitive to small changes in matrix entries.

Section 4.3, page 171

1. (a) Yes. (b) Yes, 1. (c) No. Only 1 itself has an inverse. (d) It is a commutative monoid, but not a group.

3. Same answers as for Exercise 1.

5. (b) Yes, the empty set $\varnothing$, since $A \oplus \varnothing = A$ for all $A \in \mathcal{P}(S)$. (c) Yes, $A \oplus A = \varnothing$. Elements of $\mathcal{P}(S)$ are their own inverses with respect to this operation. (d) $(\mathcal{P}(S), \oplus)$ is a group.

7. See Example 7(b).

9. (a) $\mathfrak{M}_{n,n}$ is a semigroup with respect to matrix multiplication, so one only needs to check closure:

$$\mathbf{A}, \mathbf{B} \in SL_n \quad \text{implies} \quad \mathbf{AB} \in SL_n.$$

(c) Yes; the identity matrix $\mathbf{I}$ is in SL_n. (e) SL_n is a group.

11. (b) $(\mathbb{N}, \max)$ is a monoid because 0 is an identity. $(\mathbb{N}, \min)$ has no identity and so it is not a monoid. Check these claims.

13. (a) $f(\langle f(\langle s_1, s_2 \rangle), s_3 \rangle) = f(\langle s_1, f(\langle s_2, s_3 \rangle) \rangle)$ for all $s_1, s_2, s_3 \in S$.

15. (a) $A_0 = \{-9, -6, -3, 0, 3, 6, 9\}$, $A_1 = \{-8, -5, -2, 1, 4, 7, 10\}$ and $A_2 = \{-10, -7, -4, -1, 2, 5, 8\}$.

17. Commutativity is easy, since $m +_p n \equiv m + n \pmod{p} \equiv n + m \pmod{p} \equiv n +_p m \pmod{p}$. It is also easy to check that 0 is an additive identity. Additive inverses exist, because if $m \in \mathbb{Z}(p)$ and $m \neq 0$, then $p - m \in \mathbb{Z}(p)$ and $m +_p (p - m) = 0$.

19. Suppose that t and u are both inverses for s and consider tsu.

21. (a) For an element x, show $\chi_{A \cap B}(x) = \chi_A(x) \cdot \chi_B(x)$ by considering cases: $x \in A \cap B$; $x \notin A \cap B$.

Section 4.4, page 178

1. $s^n = (s^{-1})^{-n}$ for $n < 0$.

3. (a) *break, fast, fastfood, lunchbreak, foodfood.*

5. (a) $\{abab, abba, baab, baba\}$. (c) $\{ab, ba, bbab, bbba\}$.
(e) $\{aba, abb, baa, bab\}$.

7. (b) Σ^* is commutative if and only if Σ has exactly one element.

9. (b) Clearly $A^* \subseteq (A^+)^* \subseteq (A^*)^*$, and $(A^*)^* = A^*$ by Theorem 2(b). So all these sets are equal. A similar argument shows that $A^* = (A^*)^+$.

11. (a) False. (c) True. (e) False. (g) False. (i) True. (k) False.
(m) True. Don't forget to provide examples for the false statements.

15. (a) For $s, t \in S$, $(st)^{n+1} = s(ts)^n t$ for all $n \in \mathbb{N}$. As in Exercise 14, the proof is by induction.

17. (a) Clearly $AB \subseteq A(B \cup C)$ and $AC \subseteq A(B \cup C)$, so $AB \cup AC \subseteq A(B \cup C)$. For the reverse inclusion, consider w in $A(B \cup C)$ and show $w \in AB$ or $w \in AC$.

19. (a) The smallest monoid containing $\{a, ab\}$ consists of ϵ and all words that start with a and have no consecutive b's.

Section 5.1, page 190

1. (a) 56. (c) 56. (e) 1.

3. (a) Draw a Venn diagram and work from the inside out. The 10 is given as

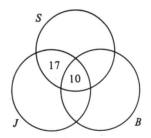

$|S \cap B \cap J|$. The 17 is calculated from $27 = |J \cap S|$. Etc. Answer $= 15$.
(b) 71.

5. (a) 126.   (b) 105.

7. (a) 0.   (b) 840.   (c) 2401.

9. (a) This is the same as the number of ways of drawing ten cards so that the *first* one is not a repetition. Hence $52(51)^9$.   (b) $52^{10} - 52(51)^9$.

11. (a) $13 \cdot \binom{4}{4} \cdot \binom{48}{1} = 624$.   (b) 5108.

  (c) $13 \cdot \binom{4}{3} \cdot \binom{12}{2} \cdot 4 \cdot 4 = 54{,}912$.   (d) 1,098,240.

15. (a) It is the $n \times n$ matrix with 0's on the diagonal and 1's elsewhere.

17. (b) Counting all the r-element subsets of an n-element set is the same as counting all their $(n-r)$-element complements.

19. (c) If true for n, then

$$\sum_{r=0}^{n+1} \binom{n+1}{r} = 1 + \sum_{r=1}^{n} \binom{n+1}{r} + 1 = 1 + \sum_{r=1}^{n} \binom{n}{r-1} + \sum_{r=1}^{n} \binom{n}{r} + 1$$
$$= \sum_{r=1}^{n+1} \binom{n}{r-1} + \sum_{r=0}^{n} \binom{n}{r} = 2 \sum_{r=0}^{n} \binom{n}{r} = 2 \cdot 2^n = 2^{n+1}.$$

Section 5.2, page 201

1. 125.

3. 466; remember $D_4 \cap D_6 = D_{12}$ not D_{24}.

5. (a) $\dfrac{15!}{3! \, 4! \, 5! \, 3!}$.   (b) $\binom{15}{3}\binom{15}{4}\binom{15}{5}$.

7. (a) $\binom{15}{3} = 455$.   (b) 35.

9. 1260.

11. (a) 625.   (b) 505.   (c) 250.   (d) 303.

13. There are $\dfrac{1}{2}\binom{2n}{n}$ unordered such partitions and $\binom{2n}{n}$ ordered partitions.

15. (a) 165.   (b) 56.

17. (a) 59,049.   (b) 252.   (c) 120.   (d) 15,360.   (e) 4200.   (f) 55,980.

19. (a)

		0
0	0	0 0

,

0	0 0	0 0	

, etc.

  (b) 01010100, etc.

Section 5.3, page 208

1. (a) Apply the Pigeon-Hole Principle to the partition $\{A_0, A_1, A_2\}$ of the set S of four integers where

$$A_i = \{n \in S : n \equiv i \,(\mathrm{mod}\ 3)\}.$$

Alternatively, apply the second version of the Pigeon-Hole Principle to the function $f: S \to \mathbb{Z}(3)$ defined so that $f(n) \equiv n \,(\mathrm{mod}\ 3)$ for each $n \in S$.
(b) Apply the Pigeon-Hole Principle to the function $f: \{1, 2, \ldots, p + 1\} \to \mathbb{Z}(p)$ defined so that $f(j) \equiv a_j \,(\mathrm{mod}\ p)$.

3. For each 4-element subset B of A, let $f(B)$ be the sum of the numbers in B. Explain why f maps the set of 4-element subsets of A into $\{10, 11, 12, \ldots, 194\}$. Note that A has $\binom{10}{4} = 210$ 4-element subsets. Apply the second version of the Pigeon-Hole Principle to f.

5. For each 2-element subset T of A, let $f(T)$ be the sum of the two elements. Then f maps the 300 2-element subsets of A into $\{3, 4, 5, \ldots, 299\}$.

7. The repeating blocks are various permutations of 142857.

9. (a) Look at the six blocks

$$\langle n_1, n_2, n_3, n_4 \rangle, \quad \langle n_5, n_6, n_7, n_8 \rangle, \quad \ldots, \quad \langle n_{21}, n_{22}, n_{23}, n_{24} \rangle.$$

(b) Use Example 3(b) of § 2.5.
(d) Look at the five blocks

$$\langle n_1, \ldots, n_5 \rangle, \quad \langle n_6, \ldots, n_{10} \rangle, \quad \langle n_{11}, \ldots, n_{15} \rangle,$$
$$\langle n_{16}, \ldots, n_{20} \rangle, \quad \langle n_{21}, \ldots, n_{24} \rangle.$$

11. If $0 \in \mathrm{Im}(f)$, then $n_1, n_1 + n_2$ or $n_1 + n_2 + n_3$ is divisible by 3. Otherwise f is not one-to-one and there are three cases:

$$n_1 \equiv n_1 + n_2 \,(\mathrm{mod}\ 3); \quad n_1 \equiv n_1 + n_2 + n_3 \,(\mathrm{mod}\ 3);$$
$$n_1 + n_2 \equiv n_1 + n_2 + n_3 \,(\mathrm{mod}\ 3).$$

13. (a) 262,144.   (b) 73,502.   (c) 20,160.   (d) 60.

15. (a) Show that S must contain both members of some pair $\langle 2k - 1, 2k \rangle$.
(b) For each $m \in S$, write $m = 2^k \cdot n$ where n is odd and let $f(m) = n$. Then $f: S \to \{1, 3, 5, \ldots, 2n - 1\}$.

Section 5.4, page 217

1. (a) True.   (c) False.   (e) True. Compare Exercise 3 of § 3.1.

3. (a) A function of the form $f(x) = ax + b$ will work if you choose a and b so that $f(0) = -1$ and $f(1) = 1$. Sketch your answer to see that it works.
(b) Use g where $g(x) = 1 - x$.
(c) Modify hint to part (a).
(d) $1/x$.
(e) Map $(1, \infty)$ onto $(0, \infty)$ using $h(x) = x - 1$ and compose with your answer in part (d).
(f) $f(x) = 2^x$, say. Sketch f to see that it works.

5. (a) Use the data

x	.1	.2	.3	.4	.5	.6	.7	.8	.9
$f(x)$	-8.89	-3.75	-1.90	$-.83$	0	.83	1.90	3.75	8.89

7. Only the sets in (b) and (c) are countably infinite.

9. (a) Let $f: S \to T$ be a one-to-one correspondence where T is a countable set. There is a one-to-one correspondence $g: T \to \mathbb{P}$ [why?]. Then $g \circ f$ is a one-to-one correspondence of S onto $\mathbb{P}$.

11. (a) Apply part (b) of the theorem to $S \times T = \bigcup_{t \in T} (S \times \{t\})$. Explain why each $S \times \{t\}$ is countable.
(b) For each $t \in T$, let $g(t)$ be an element in S such that $f(g(t)) = t$. Show that g is one-to-one and apply part (a) of the theorem.

13. (a) For each f in FUN($\mathbb{P}$, $\{0, 1\}$), define $\phi(f)$ to be the set $\{n \in \mathbb{P} : f(n) = 1\}$. Show ϕ is a one-to-one function from FUN($\mathbb{P}$, $\{0, 1\}$) onto $\mathcal{P}(\mathbb{P})$.
(b) Use Example 2(a) and Exercise 9.

15. For the inductive step, use the identity $S^n = S^{n-1} \times S$.

Section 6.1, page 225

1. (a) 0. (b) 0. (c) 1. (d) 0. (e) 0.

3. (a) $\forall x \, \forall y \, \forall z[((x < y) \land (y < z)) \to (x < z)]$; universes $\mathbb{R}$.
(c) $\forall m \, \forall n \, \exists p[(m < p) \land (p < n)]$; universes $\mathbb{N}$.
(e) $\forall n \, \exists m[m < n]$; universes $\mathbb{N}$.

5. (a) $\forall w_1 \, \forall w_1 \, \forall w_3[(w_1 w_2 = w_1 w_3) \to (w_2 = w_3)]$.
(c) $\forall w_1 \, \forall w_2[w_1 w_2 = w_2 w_1]$.

7. (a) x, z are bound; y is free. (c) Same answers as part (a).

9. (a) x, y are free; there are no bound variables.
(b) $\forall x \, \forall y[(x - y)^2 = x^2 - y^2]$ is false.
(c) $\exists x \, \exists y[(x - y)^2 = x^2 - y^2]$ is true.

11. (a) No. $\exists m[m + 1 = n]$ is false for $n = 0$. (b) Yes.

13. (a) $\exists! \, x \, \forall y[x + y = y]$. (c) $\exists! \, A \, \forall B[A \subseteq B]$. Here A, B vary over the universe of discourse $\mathcal{P}(\mathbb{N})$. Note that $\forall B[A \subseteq B]$ is true if and only if $A = \varnothing$.
(e) "$f: A \to B$ is a one-to-one function" $\to \forall b \, \exists! \, a[f(a) = b]$. Here a ranges over A and b ranges over B. One way to make this clear is to write
$\forall b \in B \, \exists! \, a \in A[f(a) = b]$.

15. (a) True. (c) False; e.g., 3 is in the right-hand set. (e) False; the right-hand set is empty. (g) True. (i) True. (k) True. (m) True.

17. (a) 0. (c) 1. (e) 0.

Section 6.2, page 234

1. (a) Every club member has been a passenger on every airline if and only if every airline has had every club member as a passenger. (c) If there is a club member who has been a passenger on every airline, then every airline has had a club member as a passenger.

3. (a) See rule 8c.

5. $\exists n[\neg\{p(n) \to p(n+1)\}]$ or $\exists n[p(n) \wedge \neg p(n+1)]$.

7. (a) $\exists x \, \exists y[(x < y) \wedge \forall z\{(z \leq x) \vee (y \leq z)\}]$.
   (c) 0; for example, $[x < y \to \exists z\{x < z < y\}]$ is false for $x = 3$ and $y = 4$.

9. One can let $q(x, y)$ be the predicate "$x = y$." Another way to handle $\exists x \, p(x, x)$ is to let $r(x)$ be the 1-place predicate $p(x, x)$. Then $\exists x \, r(x)$ is a compound predicate.

Section 6.3, page 240

3. Show that $n^5 - n$ is always even. Then use the identity $(n+1)^5 = n^5 + 5n^4 + 10n^3 + 10n^2 + 5n + 1$ [from the binomial theorem].

5. Yes. The oddness of a_n depends only on the oddness of a_{n-1}, since $2a_{n-2}$ is even whether a_{n-2} is odd or not.

7. (b) $a_n = n + 1$ for all $n \in \mathbb{N}$.
   (c) The basis needs to be checked for $n = 0$ and $n = 1$. For the inductive step, consider $n \geq 2$ and assume that $a_k = k + 1$ for $0 \leq k < n$. Then $a_n = 2a_{n-1} - a_{n-2} = 2n - (n-1) = n + 1$. This completes the inductive step, and so $a_n = n + 1$ for all $n \in \mathbb{N}$ by the Second Principle of Induction.

9. (b) $a_n = 2^n$ for all $n \in \mathbb{N}$.
   (c) The basis needs to be checked for $n = 0$ and $n = 1$. For the inductive step, consider $n \geq 2$ and assume that $a_k = 2^k$ for $0 \leq k < n$.

11. (b) The basis needs to be checked for $n = 0, 1$ and 2. For the inductive step, consider $n \geq 3$ and assume that a_k is odd for $0 \leq k < n$. Then $a_{n-1}, a_{n-2}, a_{n-3}$ are all odd. Since the sum of three odd integers is odd [if not obvious, prove it], a_n is also odd.
   (c) Since the inequality is claimed for $n \geq 1$ and since you will want to use the identity $a_n = a_{n-1} + a_{n-2} + a_{n-3}$ in the inductive step, you will need $n - 3 \geq 1$ in the inductive step. So check the basis for $n = 1, 2$ and 3. For the inductive step, consider $n \geq 4$ and assume that $a_k \leq 2^{k-1}$ for $1 \leq k < n$.

13. (a) 2, 3, 4, 6.
   (b) The inequality must be checked for $n = 3, 4$ and 5 before applying the Second Principle of Mathematical Induction to $b_n = b_{n-1} + b_{n-3}$.
   (c) The inequality must be checked for $n = 2, 3$ and 4. Then use the Second Principle of Mathematical Induction and part (b).

15. Check for $n = 0$ and 1 before applying induction. If may be simpler to prove "SEQ$(n) \leq 1$ for all n" separately from "SEQ$(n) \geq 0$ for all n."

17. (a) 1, 3, 4, 7, 11, 18, etc.
   (b) First check for $n = 2$ and 3. Then apply induction:

$$\text{LUC}(n) = \text{LUC}(n-1) + \text{LUC}(n-2)$$
$$= [\text{FIB}(n-1) + \text{FIB}(n-3)] + [\text{FIB}(n-2) + \text{FIB}(n-4)]$$
$$= [\text{FIB}(n-1) + \text{FIB}(n-2)] + [\text{FIB}(n-3) + \text{FIB}(n-4)]$$
$$= \text{FIB}(n) + \text{FIB}(n-2).$$

Be sure to supply explanations.

Section 6.4, page 246

1. *Hints:*

$$\frac{1}{n+2} + \cdots + \frac{1}{2n+2} = \left(\frac{1}{n+1} + \cdots + \frac{1}{2n}\right) + \left(\frac{1}{2n+1} + \frac{1}{2n+2} - \frac{1}{n+1}\right)$$

and

$$\frac{1}{2n+1} + \frac{1}{2n+2} - \frac{1}{n+1} = \frac{1}{2n+1} - \frac{1}{2n+2}.$$

Alternatively, to avoid induction, let $f(n) = \sum_{k=1}^{n} \frac{1}{k}$ and write both sides in terms of f.

3. *Hints:* $5^{n+2} + 2 \cdot 3^{n+1} + 1 = 5(5^{n+1} + 2 \cdot 3^n + 1) - 4(3^n + 1)$. Show that $3^n + 1$ is always even.

5. (a) $\langle 2, 3 \rangle$, $\langle 4, 6 \rangle$, etc.

   (b) (B) is clear since 5 divides $0 + 0$. For (R) you need to check

   "if 5 divides $m + n$, then 5 divides $(m + 2) + (n + 3)$."

   Alternatively, prove that every member of S is of the form $\langle 2k, 3k \rangle$ for $k \in \mathbb{N}$.

7. (a) Obviously $A \subseteq \mathbb{N} \times \mathbb{N}$. To show $\mathbb{N} \times \mathbb{N} \subseteq A$, apply the ordinary First Principle of Mathematical Induction to the propositions

   $$p(k) = \text{"if } \langle m, n \rangle \in \mathbb{N} \times \mathbb{N} \text{ and } m + n = k, \text{ then } \langle m, n \rangle \in A.\text{"}$$

9. (a) For w in Σ^*, let

   $$p(w) = \text{"length}(\overleftarrow{w}) = \text{length}(w).\text{"}$$

   Since $\overleftarrow{\epsilon} = \epsilon$, $p(\epsilon)$ is clearly true. You need to show $p(w) \to p(wx)$:

   $$\text{length}(\overleftarrow{w}) = \text{length}(w) \text{ implies } \text{length}(\overleftarrow{wx}) = \text{length}(wx).$$

   (b) Fix w_1, say, and work with $p(w) = \text{"}\overleftarrow{w_1 w} = \overleftarrow{w}\overleftarrow{w_1}.\text{"}$

11. (b) There are too many p's and P's around, so let's use $r(P)$ for the proposition-valued function on $\mathfrak{F}$, to which we wish to apply the general principle of induction. Then you need to prove all $r(P)$ are true where

    $$r(P) = \text{"if } p, q \text{ are false, then } P \text{ is false."}$$

Section 7.1, page 257

1. (a)

Supply labels

3. (a) h, o, p, q, r, z.   (c) B and C.   (e) f, z, p, does not exist.

5. (a) Only $\leqq$. $<$ is not reflexive and $\leqq$ is not antisymmetric.

(c)

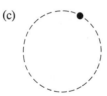

7. See Figures 2 and 6 or Exercise 6 for two different sorts of failure.

9. (a) $a \vee b = \max\{a, b\}$, $a \wedge b = \min\{a, b\}$.   (c) 73.   (e) $\sqrt{73}$.

13. Not if Σ has more than one element. Show that antisymmetry fails.

15. (a) Yes.   (b) The relation is not transitive.

17. (a) No. Every finite subset of $\mathbb{N}$ is a subset of a larger finite subset of $\mathbb{N}$.
   (c) $\mathrm{lub}\{A, B\} = A \cup B$. Note that $A \cup B \in \mathfrak{F}(\mathbb{N})$ for all $A, B \in \mathfrak{F}(\mathbb{N})$.
   (e) Yes; see parts (c) and (d).

19. (a) Show that b satisfies the definition of $\mathrm{lub}\{x, y, z\}$, i.e., $x \leqq b, y \leqq b$, $z \leqq b$ and if $x \leqq c, y \leqq c, z \leqq c$ then $b \leqq c$.
   (c) Use commutativity of $\vee$ and part (a).

Section 7.2, page 267

1. (a) $\{\varnothing, \{1\}, \{1, 4\}, \{1, 4, 3\}, \{1, 4, 3, 5\}, \{1, 4, 3, 5, 2\}\}$ is one.

3. (a) $501, 502, \ldots, 1000$.   (c) Yes. Think of primes or see Exercise 16.

5. Yes. If $a \leqq b$ then $a \vee b = b$ and $a \wedge b = a$.

7. (a) Transitivity, for example. If $f \leq g$ and $g \leq h$, then $f(t) \leqq g(t)$ and $g(t) \leqq h(t)$ in S, for all t in T. Since $\leqq$ is transitive on S, $f(t) \leqq h(t)$ for all t, so $f \leq h$ in $\mathrm{FUN}(T, S)$.
   (c) $f(t) \leqq f(t) \vee g(t) = h(t)$ for all t, so $f \leq h$. Similarly $g \leq h$, so h is an upper bound for $\{f, g\}$. Show that if $f \leq k$ and $g \leq k$ then $h \leq k$, so that h is the least upper bound for $\{f, g\}$.

9. Supply labels.   (a)

(c)

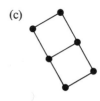

11. $|T| = 1$ and S is a chain, or $|S| = 1$. If S is not a chain, $\mathrm{FUN}(T, S)$ contains constant functions which are not comparable. If $|S| > 1$ and $|T| > 1$, select $s_1 \neq s_2$ and $t_1 \neq t_2$ and define f and g so that $f(t_1) = s_1, f(t_2) = s_2, g(t_1) = s_2, g(t_2) = s_1$.

13. (a) $\langle 0, 0 \rangle, \langle 0, 1 \rangle, \langle 0, 2 \rangle, \langle 1, 0 \rangle, \langle 1, 1 \rangle, \langle 1, 2 \rangle, \langle 2, 0 \rangle, \langle 2, 1 \rangle, \langle 2, 2 \rangle$.
   (c) $\langle 3, 0 \rangle, \langle 3, 1 \rangle, \langle 3, 2 \rangle, \langle 4, 0 \rangle, \langle 4, 1 \rangle, \langle 4, 2 \rangle$.

15. (a) Yes. Both $(\mathbb{N}, \leqq)$ and $(\mathbb{N}, \geqq)$ are chains. Apply Theorem 1.
(c) No. Consider $\{\langle 0, n \rangle : n \in \mathbb{N}\}$, for example. Note that $\langle 0, n + 1 \rangle \prec \langle 0, n \rangle$.

17. (a) $000, 0010, 010, 10, 1000, 101, 11$.

19. (a) in of the list this order words sentence standard increasing.

21. Antisymmetry is immediate. For transitivity consider cases. Suppose

$$\langle s_1, \ldots, s_n \rangle \prec \langle t_1, \ldots, t_n \rangle \text{ and } \langle t_1, \ldots, t_n \rangle \prec \langle u_1, \ldots, u_n \rangle.$$

If $s_1 \prec_1 t_1$ then $s_1 \prec_1 t_1 \leqq_1 u_1$, so $\langle s_1, \ldots, s_n \rangle \prec \langle u_1, \ldots, u_n \rangle$.
If $s_1 = t_1, \ldots, s_{r-1} = t_{r-1}, s_r \prec_r t_r$ and $t_1 = u_1, \ldots, t_{p-1} = u_{p-1}, t_p \prec_p u_p$
and $r < p$, then $s_1 = u_1, \ldots, s_{r-1} = u_{r-1}$ and $s_r \prec_r t_r = u_r$ and again
$\langle s_1, \ldots, s_n \rangle \prec \langle u_1, \ldots, u_n \rangle$. The remaining cases are similar.

Section 7.3, page 277

1. (a) is an equivalence relation. (c) is also an equivalence relation, unless one is concerned about those rare individuals who maintain residences in more than one state. (e) is not an equivalence relation. Why?

3. Very much so.

5. One needs to show:
(R) For each (s_n), the set $\{n \in \mathbb{N} : s_n \neq s_n\}$ is finite, i.e., $(s_n) \sim (s_n)$.
(S) If $\{n \in \mathbb{N} : s_n \neq t_n\}$ is finite, so is $\{n \in \mathbb{N} : t_n \neq s_n\}$, i.e., $(s_n) \sim (t_n)$ implies $(t_n) \sim (s_n)$.
(T) If $\{n \in \mathbb{N} : s_n \neq t_n\}$ and $\{n \in \mathbb{N} : t_n \neq u_n\}$ are finite, so is $\{n \in \mathbb{N} : s_n \neq u_n\}$, i.e., $(s_n) \sim (t_n)$ and $(t_n) \sim (u_n)$ imply $(s_n) \sim (u_n)$.

7. One needs to show:
(R) For each $x \in S$, $f(x) = x$ for some $f \in G$.
(S) If $f(x) = y$ for some $f \in G$, then $y = g(x)$ for some $g \in G$.
(T) If $f(x) = y$ for some $f \in G$ and $g(y) = z$ for some $g \in G$, then $h(x) = z$ for some $h \in G$.

9. (a) Verify directly, or apply Theorem 2(a) with $f(m) = m^2$ for $m \in \mathbb{Z}$.

11. (a) It consists of all finite subsets of S.

13. (a) $m \equiv n \pmod 1$ for all $m, n \in \mathbb{Z}$. There is only one equivalence class.

15. Apply Theorem 2, using the length function. The equivalence classes are the sets Σ^k, $k \in \mathbb{N}$.

17. Fifteen.

19. (a) Not well-defined: depends on the representative. For example $[3] = [-3]$ and $-3 \leqq 2$. If the definition made sense, we would have $[3] = [-3] \leqq [2]$ but not have $3 \leqq 2$.
(b) Trouble. For example, $[2] = [-2]$ but $(2)^2 + (2) + 1 \neq (-2)^2 + (-2) + 1$.
(c) Nothing wrong. If $[m] = [n]$ then $m^4 + m^2 + 1 = n^4 + n^2 + 1$.

Section 7.4, page 284

1. (a) R_1 satisfies (AR) and (S).
(c) R_3 satisfies (R), (AS) and (T).
(e) R_5 satisfies only (S).

3. R_3 is the only partial order, and R_2 is the only equivalence relation. Explain why each of the other relations isn't of one of these types.

5. Two of the relations are reflexive. Five of them are symmetric.

7. (a) $\{\langle 0, 5 \rangle, \langle 1, 4 \rangle, \langle 2, 3 \rangle, \langle 3, 2 \rangle, \langle 4, 1 \rangle, \langle 5, 0 \rangle\}$.

9. (a) This is an equivalence relation with 4 equivalence classes.
(c) This relation is not reflexive, since 0 is not related to 0. It is symmetric and transitive.

11. (a) The relation satisfies (R) and (T). Note that antisymmetry fails because $A^* = B^*$ need not imply $A = B$.

13. (a) The empty relation satisfies (AR), (S), (AS) and (T). The last three properties hold vacuously.

15. (a) To show that $R \cup E$ is a partial order, show
(R) $\langle x, x \rangle \in R \cup E$ for all $x \in S$,
(AS) $\langle x, y \rangle \in R \cup E$ and $\langle y, x \rangle \in R \cup E$ imply $x = y$,
(T) $\langle x, y \rangle \in R \cup E$ and $\langle y, z \rangle \in R \cup E$ imply $\langle x, z \rangle \in R \cup E$.
To verify (T), consider cases.

17. (a) Yes. This is clear: if $E \subseteq R_1$ and $E \subseteq R_2$ then $E \subseteq R_1 \cup R_2$.
(c) No. For a small example, let $S = \{a, b, c\}$, $R_1 = \{\langle a, b \rangle\}$ and $R_2 = \{\langle b, c \rangle\}$.

19. (a) Suppose R is symmetric. If $\langle x, y \rangle \in R$, then $\langle y, x \rangle \in R$ by symmetry and so $\langle x, y \rangle \in R^{-1}$. Similarly $\langle x, y \rangle \in R^{-1}$ implies $\langle x, y \rangle \in R$ [check] so that $R = R^{-1}$. For the converse, suppose that $R = R^{-1}$ and show R is symmetric.

Section 7.5, page 295

1. (a) $A*A = \begin{bmatrix} 1 & 1 & 1 \\ 1 & 1 & 1 \\ 1 & 1 & 1 \end{bmatrix}$. Since $A*A \leq A$ is not true, R is not transitive.
(c) Not transitive.

3. (b) Boolean matrices for $(R_1 \cap R_2)R_1^{-1}$ and $R_1 R_1^{-1} \cap R_2 R_1^{-1}$ are

$$[A_1 \wedge A_2]*A_1^T = \begin{bmatrix} 0 & 0 & 0 \\ 0 & 0 & 0 \\ 0 & 0 & 0 \end{bmatrix} \quad \text{and} \quad A_1*A_1^T \wedge A_2*A_1^T = \begin{bmatrix} 0 & 0 & 0 \\ 0 & 0 & 0 \\ 1 & 0 & 0 \end{bmatrix}.$$

(c) The Boolean matrices are $A_2*[A_1^T \vee A_2^T]$ and $(A_2*A_1^T) \vee (A_2*A_2^T)$. They are equal.

5. (a) The matrix for R is $A = \begin{bmatrix} 0 & 0 & 0 \\ 1 & 0 & 1 \\ 0 & 1 & 0 \end{bmatrix}$. Matrices for R^{-1} and R^2 are A^T and $A*A$.
(c) No; compare A and $A*A$ and note that $A*A \leq A$ fails.
(e) Yes.

7. (a) Matrix for R^0 is the identity matrix. Matrix for R^1 is A, of course. Matrix for R^n is $A*A$ for $n \geq 2$ as should be checked by induction. For $n < 0$, use transposes.
(b) R is reflexive, but not symmetric or transitive.

9. (a) $\mathbf{A}_f = \begin{bmatrix} 0 & 0 & 1 & 0 \\ 0 & 1 & 0 & 0 \\ 0 & 1 & 0 & 0 \\ 0 & 1 & 0 & 0 \end{bmatrix}$ and $\mathbf{A}_g = \begin{bmatrix} 0 & 0 & 0 & 1 \\ 0 & 0 & 1 & 0 \\ 0 & 1 & 0 & 0 \\ 1 & 0 & 0 & 0 \end{bmatrix}$.

(b) They will be different, since the Boolean matrix for $R_f R_g$ is $\mathbf{A}_f * \mathbf{A}_g$; this is the Boolean matrix for $R_{g \circ f}$ but not for $R_{f \circ g}$.

(c) One does and one doesn't.

11. Don't use Boolean matrices; the sets S, T, U might be infinite.

(a) $R_1 R_3 \cup R_1 R_4 \subseteq R_1(R_3 \cup R_4)$ by Example 2(a). For the reverse inclusion, consider $\langle x, z \rangle$ in $R_1(R_3 \cup R_4)$ and show $\langle x, z \rangle$ is in $R_1 R_3$ or $R_1 R_4$.

(c) $R_1(R_3 \cap R_4) \subseteq R_1 R_3 \cap R_1 R_4$. As in part (b), equality need not hold. For example, consider R_1, R_3, R_4 with Boolean matrices

$$\mathbf{A}_1 = \begin{bmatrix} 1 & 1 \\ 0 & 0 \end{bmatrix}, \qquad \mathbf{A}_3 = \begin{bmatrix} 0 & 0 \\ 0 & 1 \end{bmatrix}, \qquad \mathbf{A}_4 = \begin{bmatrix} 0 & 1 \\ 0 & 0 \end{bmatrix}.$$

13. (c) One is and one isn't.

15. Say S, T and U have m, n and p elements. The problem is equivalent to showing $(\mathbf{A} * \mathbf{B})^T = \mathbf{B}^T * \mathbf{A}^T$ where $\mathbf{A}$ and $\mathbf{B}$ are $m \times n$ and $n \times p$ Boolean matrices. Why? So compare (k, i)-entries of the two matrices where $1 \le i \le m$ and $1 \le k \le p$.

17. Given $m \times n$, $n \times p$ and $p \times q$ Boolean matrices $\mathbf{A}_1$, $\mathbf{A}_2$, $\mathbf{A}_3$, they correspond to relations R_1, R_2, R_3 where R_1 is a relation from $\{1, 2, \ldots, m\}$ to $\{1, 2, \ldots, n\}$, etc. The matrices for $(R_1 R_2)R_3$ and $R_1(R_2 R_3)$ are $(\mathbf{A}_1 * \mathbf{A}_2) * \mathbf{A}_3$ and $\mathbf{A}_1 * (\mathbf{A}_2 * \mathbf{A}_3)$ by four applications of Theorem 1.

Section 7.6, page 303

1. (a) $\begin{bmatrix} 1 & 1 & 0 \\ 0 & 1 & 0 \\ 0 & 0 & 1 \end{bmatrix}$.   **(c)** $\begin{bmatrix} 1 & 1 & 0 \\ 1 & 1 & 0 \\ 0 & 0 & 1 \end{bmatrix}$.   **(e)** $\begin{bmatrix} 1 & 1 & 0 \\ 1 & 1 & 0 \\ 0 & 0 & 1 \end{bmatrix}$.

3. $\{1, 2\}, \{3\}$.

5. (a) $\begin{bmatrix} 1 & 1 & 0 & 1 \\ 1 & 1 & 1 & 0 \\ 0 & 1 & 1 & 0 \\ 1 & 0 & 1 & 1 \end{bmatrix}$,   **(c)** $\begin{bmatrix} 1 & 1 & 0 & 1 \\ 1 & 1 & 1 & 0 \\ 0 & 1 & 1 & 1 \\ 1 & 0 & 1 & 1 \end{bmatrix}$.   **(e)** $\begin{bmatrix} 1 & 1 & 1 & 1 \\ 1 & 1 & 1 & 1 \\ 1 & 1 & 1 & 1 \\ 1 & 1 & 1 & 1 \end{bmatrix}$.

7. (a) $r(R)$ is the usual order $\le$.

(c) $rs(R)$ is the universal relation on $\mathbb{P}$.

(e) R is already transitive.

9. $\langle h_1, h_2 \rangle \in st(R)$ if $h_1 = h_2$ or if one of h_1, h_2 is the High Hermit. On the other hand, $ts(R)$ is the universal relation on F.O.H.H.

11. (a) Compare $(R \cup E) \cup (R \cup E)^{-1}$ and $(R \cup R^{-1}) \cup E$; see Exercise 20 of § 7.4.

13. Any relation that contains R will include the pair $\langle 1, 1 \rangle$. This violates anti-reflexivity.

15. (a) For any relation R, let $\{R_i : i \in I\}$ be the set of all relations containing R that have property p. Show that $\bigcap_{i \in I} R_i$ is the smallest such relation.

(c) $S \times S$ is not antireflexive.

(d) Intersect the onto relations on $\{1, 2\}$ having Boolean matrices $\begin{bmatrix} 1 & 1 \\ 1 & 0 \end{bmatrix}$ and $\begin{bmatrix} 1 & 0 \\ 1 & 1 \end{bmatrix}$. Is the intersection an onto relation?

Section 7.7, page 311

1. $\pi_1 \wedge \pi_2$ has 3 sets; $\pi_1 \vee \pi_2 = \{\{\text{all marbles}\}\}$.

3. $\pi_1 \vee \pi_2$ has 2 sets.

5. (b) $\pi_3 \wedge \pi_5$ has 15 sets.

(c) Since $\langle 1, 7 \rangle$ and $\langle 7, 2 \rangle$ are in $R_3 \cup R_5$, $\langle 1, 2 \rangle$ is in $R_3 \vee R_5$. To deal with $\langle 47, 73 \rangle$, note that $\langle 47, 2 \rangle$ is in $R_3 \cup R_5$ and you already know that $\langle 2, 1 \rangle$ and $\langle 1, 73 \rangle$ are in $R_3 \vee R_5$.

7. (a) For example, $\alpha(1) = \alpha(3) = \alpha(5) = 1$, $\alpha(2) = \alpha(6) = 2$, $\alpha(4) = 4$.

(c) $\alpha(n) = n$ for $n = 1, 2, 3, 4, 5, 6$.

(e) The "equality relation."

9. The γ for $\pi_1 \wedge \pi_2$ and the final α_1 for $\pi_1 \vee \pi_2$ should be

j	1	2	3	4	5	6	7	8
$\gamma(j)$	1	1	3	4	5	6	7	8
final $\alpha_1(j)$	5	5	6	5	5	6	6	5

11. The γ for $\pi_2 \wedge \pi_3$ and the final α_2 for $\pi_2 \vee \pi_3$ should be

j	1	2	3	4	5	6	7	8
$\gamma(j)$	1	1	3	4	5	3	7	4
final $\alpha_2(j)$	8	8	6	8	5	6	6	8

13. (a) Antisymmetry: If $\pi_1 \leq \pi_2$ and $\pi_2 \leq \pi_1$ and if A is a set in π_1 there are sets B in π_2 and C in π_1 with $A \subseteq B$ and $B \subseteq C$. The sets in π_1 are disjoint, so $A \subseteq C$ implies $A = C$. Thus $A = B \in \pi_2$. Similarly every set in π_2 is in π_1.

15. (a) $\gamma(j) = 0$ to start. If $\gamma(j)$ is still 0 when $k = j$, then $\gamma(j)$ changes to j at that point.

(c) The value changes at least once by part (a). If the first change occurs at $k = k_0$, then by part (b) the algorithm skips to Step 4 for later values $k = k'$.

(e) For any j, the final value of $\gamma(j)$ is the smallest k for which $\alpha(j) = \alpha(k)$ and $\beta(j) = \beta(k)$, by parts (b) and (c). If $\alpha(i) = \alpha(j)$ and $\beta(i) = \beta(j)$, then this value is the same for i and j.

Section 8.1, page 321

1. (a)

e	a	b	c	d	e	f
$\gamma(e)$	$\langle x, v \rangle$	$\langle v, x \rangle$	$\langle v, w \rangle$	$\langle w, y \rangle$	$\langle w, y \rangle$	$\langle y, x \rangle$

(c)

e	a	b	c	d
$\gamma(e)$	$\langle x, w \rangle$	$\langle w, x \rangle$	$\langle y, z \rangle$	$\langle z, y \rangle$

3. (a) Yes. (c) No. (e) Yes.

5. (a) $x\,w\,y$ is one. (c) $v\,x\,w$ is one. (e) $z\,y\,x\,w\,v$.

7. (a) $\text{SUCC}(t) = \varnothing$, $\text{SUCC}(u) = \{t, w, x\}$, $\text{SUCC}(v) = \{t, y\}$, $\text{SUCC}(w) = \{y\}$, etc. (c) t and z.

9. (a) $R(s) = \{s, t, u, w, x, y, z\} = R(t)$, $R(u) = \{w, x, y, z\}$, etc.

11. (a)

Supply labels.

(c) s, u, x, z.

13. Transitivity is a general property of reachability: string together a path from u to v and a path from v to w to get a path from u to w. Antisymmetry follows from acyclicity.

15. (a) In the proof of Theorem 1, choose a shortest path consisting of edges of the given path.

17. (a) Show that $\hat{G}$ is also acyclic. Apply the lemma to $\hat{G}$. A sink for $\hat{G}$ is a source for G.

19. (a) They are the sources of H.

Section 8.2, page 333

1. (a) Here is one way.

3. (a) One example is α where $\alpha(p) = v$, $\alpha(q) = y$, $\alpha(r) = w$, $\alpha(s) = z$, $\alpha(t) = x$.

5. The isomorphism is $\alpha(u) = u$ for all u if the digraphs are labeled as follows.

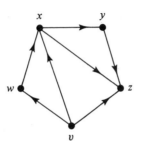

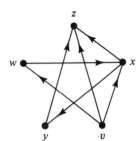

7. (a) One of them is the identity function and the other interchanges p and r. Define them explicitly.

9. (a) $D_{0,3} = \{v\}$, $D_{1,2} = \{s, y, z\}$, $D_{2,1} = \{t, w, x\}$, $D_{3,0} = \{u\}$.

11. It is terrible. Isomorphism is a binary relation; it makes no sense to say that "G is related." If you were asked "Are $1 + 1$ and 2 equal?" you wouldn't respond "$1 + 1$ is, but 2 isn't."

13. v is a sink if and only if $\operatorname{outdeg}(v) = 0$, and $\operatorname{outdeg}(v) = \operatorname{outdeg}(\alpha(v))$.

15. Use the second equation in the theorem.

17. (a) See the answer to Exercise 13. v is a source if and only if $\alpha(v)$ is a source.

Section 8.3, page 345

1.

W^*	A	B	C	D
A	0	1.0	1.4	1.2
B	.4	0	.4	.2
C	.7	.3	0	.5
D	.8	.5	.2	0

3.

W	x	y	z
x		1	*
y			2
z			

Here $* \geqq 3$ or else there is no entry there.

5. (a) Here is one example.

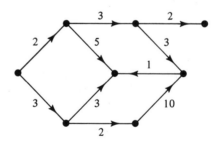

7. (a) $s\,v\,x\,f$ is one. There is another.

9. (a) Labeling as shown gives critical edges $\langle s, u \rangle$, $\langle u, w \rangle$, $\langle s, t \rangle$, $\langle t, w \rangle$, $\langle w, x \rangle$, $\langle x, y \rangle$ and $\langle y, f \rangle$.

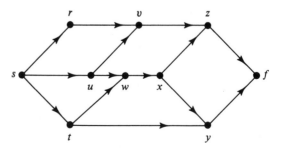

(c) 2.

11. (a) Shrink the 0-edges to make their two endpoints the same.

13. Consider a min-path $u\,w\,\cdots\,t$ from u to t and a min-path $t\,x\,\cdots\,v$ from t to v. Since

$$W^*(u, t) + W^*(t, v) = W^*(u, v),$$

$u\,w\,\cdots\,t\,x\,\cdots\,v$ is a min-path from u to v. So

$$W^*(u, t) = W^*(u, w) + W^*(w, t) \geqq W^*(u, w)$$

$$\text{and}\quad W^*(u, v) = W^*(u, w) + W^*(w, v) \quad \text{[why?]}.$$

But $W^*(u, t) \leqq W^*(u, w)$ so $W^*(w, t) = 0$. Since all weights are positive, $w = t$ and $u\,t$ is an edge.

15. (a) $A(u) = M(s, u) =$ weight of a max-path from s to u. If there is an edge $\langle w, u \rangle$, a max-path from s to w followed by that edge has total weight at most $M(s, u)$. That is, $A(w) + W(w, u) \leqq A(u)$. If $\langle w, u \rangle$ is an edge in a max-path from s to u, then $A(w) + W(w, u) = A(u)$.

17. (a) $FF(u, v) = A(v) - A(u) - W(u, v)$.   (c) The slack time at v.

Section 8.4, page 354

1. (a)

e	a	b	c	d	e	f	g	h	k
$\gamma(e)$	$\{w, x\}$	$\{x, u\}$	$\{t, u\}$	$\{t, v\}$	$\{u, v\}$	$\{u, y\}$	$\{v, z\}$	$\{x, y\}$	$\{y, z\}$

3. (a) In the notation of the proof $x_0 = y_0 = v, x_n = x_3 = x, y_m = y_4 = x$. Also $i = 1$ since $x_1 \neq y_1$. The pair $\langle j, k \rangle$ could be either $\langle 1, 3 \rangle$ [since $x_1 = y_3 = u$] or $\langle 2, 2 \rangle$ [since $x_2 = y_2 = y$]. The cycle is $v\,u\,y\,z\,v$ in either case.
   (c) The cycle is $x\,u\,t\,v\,z\,y\,x$.

5. (a)

   (c) See Exercise 12 or Theorem 3.

7. (a), (c) and (d) are regular, but (b) is not. Or count edges. (a) and (c) have cycles of length 3, but (d) does not. (a) and (c) are isomorphic; exhibit an isomorphism between them.

9. (a) $\binom{8}{5} = 56.$ (c) $8 \cdot 7 + 8 \cdot 7 \cdot 6 + 8 \cdot 7 \cdot 6 \cdot 6 = 2{,}408.$

11. (a) 19 [Use Theorem 3.]

13. (a) 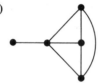 (e)

(c) See Exercise 12 or Theorem 3. (g) K_4.

15. Assume no loops or parallel edges. Consider a longest path $v_1 \cdots v_m$ with distinct vertices. There is another edge at v_m. Adjoin it to the path to get a closed path and use Proposition 1.

17. Use $|V(G)| = D_0(G) + D_1(G) + D_2(G) + \cdots$ and Theorem 3.

Section 8.5, page 363

1. (a) $v_3 \, v_1 \, v_2 \, v_3 \, v_6 \, v_2 \, v_4 \, v_6 \, v_5 \, v_1 \, v_4 \, v_5 \, v_3 \, v_4$ is one.

3. No. The edges and corners form a graph with 8 vertices, each of degree 3. It has no Euler path. See Figure 6(c) of § 8.6.

5. The ones with n odd.

7. $\{0, 1\}^3$ consists of 3-tuples of 0's and 1's, which we may view as binary strings of length 3. The graph is then

000   011   001   010

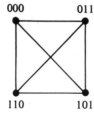 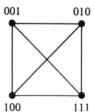

110   101   100   111

(a) 2. (c) No.

9. (a) Join the odd-degree vertices in pairs, with k new edges. The new graph has an Euler circuit, by Theorem 2. The new edges do not appear next to each other in the circuit and they partition the circuit into k simple paths of G.

(c) Imitate the proof. That is, add edges $\{v_2, v_3\}$ and $\{v_5, v_6\}$, say, create an Euler circuit, and then remove the two new edges.

Section 8.6, page 370

1. (a) Yes. Try $v_1 \, v_2 \, v_6 \, v_5 \, v_4 \, v_3 \, v_1$, for example.

(c) No. If v_1 is in V_1 then $\{v_2, v_3, v_4, v_5\} \subseteq V_2$, but v_2 and v_3 are joined by an edge.

3. (a) $2(n!)^2$. (c) m and n even, or m odd and $n = 2$, or $m = n = 1$.

5. One possible Hamilton circuit has vertex sequence 000, 001, 011, 111, 110, 101, 010, 100, 000 corresponding to the circular arrangement 0 0 0 1 1 1 0 1. Find another example.

7. No, for both questions. Why?

9. (a) K_n^+ has n vertices and just one more edge than K_{n-1} has, so it has exactly $\frac{1}{2}(n-1)(n-2)+1$ edges.

11. (a)

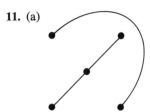

(c) Choose two vertices u and v in G. If they are *not* joined by an edge in G they are joined by an edge in the complement. If they *are* joined by an edge in G, they are in the same component of G. Choose w in some other component. Then $u\,w\,v$ is a path in the complement. In either case, u and v are joined by a path in the complement.

(e) No. Give an example.

13. Given G_{n+1}, consider the subgraph H_0 where $V(H_0)$ consists of all binary $(n+1)$-tuples with 0 in the $(n+1)$-*st* digit and $E(H_0)$ is the set of all edges of G_{n+1} connecting vertices in $V(H_0)$. Define H_1 similarly. Show H_0, H_1 are isomorphic to G_n, and so have Hamilton circuits. Use these to construct a Hamilton circuit for G_{n+1}. For $n=2$, see how this works in Figure 6.

Section 8.7, page 378

1. (a) $u\,A\,v$ if there is an edge e in $E(G)$ with $\gamma(e)=\{u,v\}$.

3. $\mathbf{M}_A = \begin{bmatrix} 0 & 1 & 0 & 0 & 0 & 0 \\ 1 & 0 & 1 & 0 & 0 & 0 \\ 0 & 1 & 0 & 1 & 0 & 1 \\ 0 & 0 & 1 & 0 & 1 & 0 \\ 0 & 0 & 0 & 1 & 0 & 0 \\ 0 & 0 & 1 & 0 & 0 & 0 \end{bmatrix}$, $\mathbf{M}_{A^t} = \begin{bmatrix} 1 & 0 & 1 & 0 & 1 & 0 \\ 0 & 1 & 0 & 1 & 0 & 1 \\ 1 & 0 & 1 & 0 & 1 & 0 \\ 0 & 1 & 0 & 1 & 0 & 1 \\ 1 & 0 & 1 & 0 & 1 & 0 \\ 0 & 1 & 0 & 1 & 0 & 1 \end{bmatrix}$, $\mathbf{M}_{\bar{R}}$ has all 1's.

5. (a) $\mathbf{M}_A = \begin{bmatrix} 0 & 1 & 1 & 0 & 0 & 0 \\ 0 & 0 & 1 & 0 & 0 & 0 \\ 0 & 0 & 0 & 1 & 0 & 0 \\ 0 & 0 & 0 & 0 & 1 & 1 \\ 0 & 0 & 0 & 0 & 0 & 0 \\ 0 & 0 & 0 & 0 & 1 & 1 \end{bmatrix}$ and $\mathbf{M}_R = \begin{bmatrix} 0 & 1 & 1 & 1 & 1 & 1 \\ 0 & 0 & 1 & 1 & 1 & 1 \\ 0 & 0 & 0 & 1 & 1 & 1 \\ 0 & 0 & 0 & 0 & 1 & 1 \\ 0 & 0 & 0 & 0 & 0 & 0 \\ 0 & 0 & 0 & 0 & 1 & 1 \end{bmatrix}$.

7. (a) 3. (c) 4.

9. (a) $S = \{\langle v_i, v_j \rangle : i - j \text{ is even}\}$.

(c) Yes. Check the reflexive, symmetric, transitive properties.

11. (a) It has 1 vertex and no edges.

13. (a) Yes, if we allow parallel edges. No, if we don't, since in that case M_A completely determines $E(G)$.

(c) The indegree of v is the sum of the entries in column v of M_A. Outdegrees are row sums.

15. (a) See Theorem 2 of § 8.1.

Section 8.8, page 389

1. (a)
$$\begin{bmatrix} 0 & 1 & 2 & 3 & 4 & 5 & 7 \\ \infty & 0 & \infty & 4 & 3' & 4 & 6 \\ \infty & \infty & 0 & 1 & 4 & 5 & 7 \\ \infty & \infty & \infty & 0 & 3 & 4 & 6 \\ \infty & \infty & \infty & \infty & 0 & 1 & 3 \\ \infty & \infty & \infty & \infty & \infty & 0 & 3 \\ \infty & \infty & \infty & \infty & \infty & \infty & 0 \end{bmatrix}.$$

3. The answer to Exercise 1(a) shows that there are at least two min-paths of weight 5, two of weight 6 and two of weight 7. It turns out that, for this example, there are exactly six min-paths of weight ≥ 5.

5. $\mathbf{W}_2 = \begin{bmatrix} 0 & \infty & \infty & \infty & 1 & \infty & \infty \\ \infty & 0 & \infty & \infty & \infty & \infty & 1 \\ \infty & \infty & 0 & 1 & \infty & 1 & \infty \\ \infty & \infty & 1 & 0 & 1 & \infty & \infty \\ 1 & \infty & \infty & 1 & 0 & \infty & \infty \\ \infty & \infty & 1 & \infty & \infty & 0 & 1 \\ \infty & 1 & \infty & \infty & \infty & 1 & 0 \end{bmatrix},$

$\mathbf{W}_4 = \begin{bmatrix} 0 & \infty & \infty & \infty & 1 & \infty & \infty \\ \infty & 0 & \infty & \infty & \infty & \infty & 1 \\ \infty & \infty & 0 & 1 & 2 & 1 & \infty \\ \infty & \infty & 1 & 0 & 1 & 2 & \infty \\ 1 & \infty & 2 & 1 & 0 & 3 & \infty \\ \infty & \infty & 1 & 2 & 3 & 0 & 1 \\ \infty & 1 & \infty & \infty & \infty & 1 & 0 \end{bmatrix},$ $\mathbf{W}_7 = \begin{bmatrix} 0 & 6 & 3 & 2 & 1 & 4 & 5 \\ 6 & 0 & 3 & 4 & 5 & 2 & 1 \\ 3 & 3 & 0 & 1 & 2 & 1 & 2 \\ 2 & 4 & 1 & 0 & 1 & 2 & 3 \\ 1 & 5 & 2 & 1 & 0 & 3 & 4 \\ 4 & 2 & 1 & 2 & 3 & 0 & 1 \\ 5 & 1 & 2 & 3 & 4 & 1 & 0 \end{bmatrix}.$

7. $\mathbf{W}^* = \begin{bmatrix} 0 & 8 & 7 & 5 & 2 \\ \infty & 0 & \infty & \infty & \infty \\ \infty & 1 & 0 & \infty & \infty \\ \infty & 3 & 2 & 0 & \infty \\ \infty & 6 & 5 & 3 & 0 \end{bmatrix}.$

9. (a) Replace the "If" line by:

If $\mathbf{W}[i, k] \geq 0$ and $\mathbf{W}[k, j] \geq 0$ and if
$\mathbf{W}[i, j] < 0$ or $\mathbf{W}[i, j] > \mathbf{W}[i, k] + \mathbf{W}[k, j]$ then

Section 8.9, page 395

1. (a)
$$\mathbf{P}_0 = \begin{bmatrix} 1 & 2 & 3 & 1 & 1 & 1 & 1 \\ 2 & 2 & 2 & 4 & 5 & 2 & 2 \\ 3 & 3 & 3 & 4 & 5 & 6 & 3 \\ 4 & 4 & 4 & 4 & 5 & 6 & 4 \\ 5 & 5 & 5 & 5 & 5 & 6 & 7 \\ 6 & 6 & 6 & 6 & 6 & 6 & 7 \\ 7 & 7 & 7 & 7 & 7 & 7 & 7 \end{bmatrix}, \quad \mathbf{P}_{\text{final}} = \begin{bmatrix} 1 & 2 & 3 & 3 & 2 & 2 & 2 \\ 2 & 2 & 2 & 4 & 5 & 5 & 5 \\ 3 & 3 & 3 & 4 & 4 & 4 & 4 \\ 4 & 4 & 4 & 4 & 5 & 5 & 5 \\ 5 & 5 & 5 & 5 & 5 & 6 & 7 \\ 6 & 6 & 6 & 6 & 6 & 6 & 7 \\ 7 & 7 & 7 & 7 & 7 & 7 & 7 \end{bmatrix}.$$

3. (a)
$$\mathbf{W}_0 = \begin{bmatrix} \infty & \infty & 1 & \infty & 1 & \infty \\ 1 & \infty & 1 & 1 & \infty & \infty \\ \infty & \infty & \infty & \infty & \infty & \infty \\ \infty & \infty & 1 & \infty & 1 & 1 \\ \infty & \infty & 1 & \infty & \infty & \infty \\ 1 & 1 & \infty & \infty & 1 & \infty \end{bmatrix}.$$
(c) No. Why?

5. (a) $\{v_1, v_2, v_3, v_4, v_6\}$.   (c) $\{v_6\}$.

7. (a) $i\,t(R)\,j$ if $i < j$.

9. (a) One gets $\begin{bmatrix} 0 & 6 & 13 \\ 17 & 23 & 30 \\ 10 & 16 & 46 \end{bmatrix}$.

11. (a) Use HU'S or WARSHALL'S algorithm to see if $\mathbf{W}^*$ has no ∞ entries. Or use BAVEL'S algorithm to see if $R(v) = V(G)$ for every v.

Section 9.1, page 407

1. There are fourteen, including the trivial tree with one vertex. Six of them are in Figure 3 of § 0.3.

5. (a) 16.   (c) 256.

7. (a) 27.   (c) 15.

9. Use $\mathbb{Z}$ for the set of vertices.

11. Use the corollary to Theorem 1.

13. (a) Apply Theorem 1 of § 8.4.

15. (b) You should obtain the tree whose edges have new labels $e_1, e_2, e_4, e_6, e_7, e_8, e_{10}$.

17. 10.

19. 1687 miles.

21. There exist minimal spanning trees S and T with $e_k \in T \setminus S$. Imitate the fifth paragraph of the proof of Theorem 4 to obtain $e_i \in S \setminus T$ where $i < k$. This will contradict your choice of k.

Section 9.2, page 419

1. (c) 3.
3. (a) Rooted trees in Figures 5(b) and 5(c) have height 2; the one in 5(d) has height 3.
   (b) Only the rooted tree in Figure 5(c) is a regular 3-ary tree.
5. (a) There are seven of them. (c) 1.
9. Use the formulas for p and t in Example 5.
11. There are 2^k words of length k.
13. (a) One such mapping is α where $\alpha(r) = a$, $\alpha(s) = b$, $\alpha(p) = d$, $\alpha(q) = c$, $\alpha(v) = e$, $\alpha(u) = f$, $\alpha(w) = g$, $\alpha(x) = j$, $\alpha(y) = k$, $\alpha(z) = h$.
15. (a) Suppose α were an isomorphism of the rooted tree in Figure 5(b) onto the rooted tree in Figure 5(c). Then $\alpha(v) = x$. Since α is one-to-one, v and x must have the same number of children. But v has four and x has three.

17. Say

Section 9.3, page 425

1. Postorder: $v, y, w, z, x, t, p, u, q, s, r$.
3. Preorder: $r, t, x, v, y, z, w, u, p, q, s$.
5. After the trivial trees are listed one obtains:
$$T_x: \quad x, y, z;$$
$$T_w: \quad w, v, T_x, \quad \text{i.e.,} \quad w, v, x, y, z;$$
$$T_s: \quad s, p, q;$$
$$T_u: \quad u, t, T_s, \quad \text{i.e.,} \quad u, t, s, p, q;$$
$$T: \quad r, T_w, T_u, \quad \text{i.e.,} \quad r, w, v, x, y, z, u, t, s, p, q.$$
7. (a) By (B), the leaves represent trivial trees. By (R), T_w, T_r and T_s are rooted trees. Use (R) with T_w and T_r to see that T_x is a rooted tree. Then use (R) with T_x and T_s to see that $T = T_u$ is a rooted tree. Draw the trees, as in Figure 1.
   (b) The trivial trees have height 0. So by (R),
$$\text{height}(T_w) = 1 + \max\{0, 0\} = 1.$$
   Similarly,
$$\text{height}(T_r) = \text{height}(T_s) = 1.$$
   Then
$$\text{height}(T_x) = 1 + \max\{1, 1\} = 2 \quad \text{and} \quad \text{height}(T) = 1 + \max\{2, 1\} = 3.$$
9. After the trivial trees are listed one obtains:
$$T_w: \quad v, y, w; \qquad T_r: \quad z, t, r; \qquad T_s: \quad p, q, s;$$
$$T_x: \quad T_w, T_r, x, \quad \text{i.e.,} \quad v, y, w, z, t, r, x; \qquad \text{etc.}$$
15. (a) (B) A single vertex is an m-ary tree.
    (R) If $T_1, \ldots, T_k$ are m-ary trees with roots $r_1, \ldots, r_k$, if $k \leq m$, if

$V(T_1), \ldots, V(T_k)$ are disjoint and if r is an element not in $V(T_1) \cup \cdots \cup V(T_k)$, then T is an m-ary tree where

$$V(T) = \{r\} \cup V(T_1) \cup \cdots \cup V(T_k), \quad \text{etc.}$$

(b) Require $k = m$ and all $T_1, \ldots, T_m$ to be regular m-ary trees.

(c) Require $k = m$ and all $T_1, \ldots, T_m$ to be full m-ary trees of the same height.

17. Use part (b) of Exercise 15 and generalized induction. At the recursive stage, one of the subtrees $T_1, \ldots, T_m$ has height $h - 1$ and so it must have at least $m + (m - 1)(h - 2)$ leaves. The other subtrees have at least one leaf each, so the tree T must have at least

$$m + (m - 1)(h - 2) + (m - 1) = m + (m - 1)(h - 1) \text{ leaves.}$$

Section 9.4, page 432

1. Reverse Polish: $x\, 4\, 2\uparrow - y * 2\, 3\, / \, +.$

3. (a) Polish: $- * + a\, b - a\, b - \uparrow a\, 2 \uparrow b\, 2;$
   infix: $(a + b)*(a - b) - ((a\uparrow 2) - (b\uparrow 2)).$

5. (a) 20. (b) 10.

7. (a) $3\, x * 4 - 2\uparrow.$
   (c) The answer depends on how the terms are associated. For $(x - x^2) + (x^3 - x^4)$, the answer is $x\, x\, 2\uparrow - x\, 3\uparrow x\, 4\uparrow - +.$

9. (a) $a\, b + = b\, a +.$ (c) $a\, b\, c + * = a\, b * a\, c * +.$

11. (b) Reverse Polish: $p\, q\, p \neg \lor \to$; Polish: $\to p \lor q \neg p.$

13. (a) Infix: $(p \land (p \to q)) \to q.$

15. (a) Both give $a\, / \, b + c.$

17. (a) (B) Numerical constants and variables are wff's.
   (R) If f and g are wff's, so are $+fg, -fg, *fg, /fg$ and $\uparrow fg.$

19. (a) (B) Variables, such as p, q, r, are wff's.
   (R) If P and Q are wff's, so are $P\,Q \lor, P\,Q \land, P\,Q \to, P\,Q \leftrightarrow$ and $P \neg.$
   (b) Argue, in turn, that $q \neg, p\, q \neg \land$ and $p\, q \neg \land \neg$ are wff's. Likewise, $p\, q \neg \to$ is a wff. Thus $p\, q \neg \land \neg p\, q \neg \to \lor$ is a wff.

Section 9.5, page 444

1. (a) 35, 56, 70, 82.

3. (a) Weight = 84. (c) Weight = 244.

5. All but (b) are prefix codes. In (b), 01 consists of the first two digits of 0111.

7. (b) 269.

9. (a) The vertex labeled 0 has only one child, 00. (b) Consider any string beginning with 01.

11. (a) 484. (c) 373. (e) It will involve at most 354 comparisons.

13. (b) 221.

Section 10.1, page 454

3. (a) The commutative and associative laws follow, as in Example 2, from the corresponding laws in Table 1 of §2.2. For the absorption laws, see Exercise 10 of §2.2.

(b) Because $c \Rightarrow P$ for all P. This can be verified by looking at the truth table of $c \to p$ or by applying rules 6c, 2b and 17 of § 2.2.

5. (a) Yes. (b) Maybe, maybe not. In Figure 4 of § 7.1, T and U are lattices. The universal upper bound for T is join-irreducible but the one for U is not.

7. (a) x, y. (b) u, w, x, y, z. (c) $t = u \lor w, v = x \lor y$ and the others are already join-irreducible.

9. (a) 1. (c) They are the primes. (d) They are the powers of primes, i.e., all integers of the form p^k where p is prime and $k \in \mathbb{P}$.

11. (a) Note $D_{90} = \{1, 2, 3, 5, 6, 9, 10, 15, 18, 30, 45, 90\}$. (c) 2, 3, 5.
(e) $90 = 2 \lor 9 \lor 5$; $18 = 2 \lor 9$; 5 is already join-irreducible.

13. (c) T has 15 and U has 19.

15. (a) $x \leqq y \Leftrightarrow x \lor y = y \Leftrightarrow \phi(x \lor y) = \phi(y) \Leftrightarrow \phi(x) \cup \phi(y) = \phi(y) \Leftrightarrow$
$\phi(x) \leqq \phi(y)$. Supply reasons.
(c) Use part (b).

17. Since m isn't itself join-irreducible, $m = x \lor y$ for some x and y different from m. Then $x \prec m$ and $y \prec m$. Hence x and y are not in B and so they are joins of join-irreducible elements. Use these facts to show that m is also a join of join-irreducible elements, a contradiction.

Section 10.2, page 461

1. (a) d, e. (c) $1 = a \lor c$. (e) No. b has no complement.

3. (b) It is straightforward to show D_m is complemented if m is a product of distinct primes; do it. Next assume m is not the product of distinct primes and show D_m is not complemented. To simplify notation, assume 2 is a prime that appears more than once so that $m = 2^u etc$ where $u \geqq 2$. Then 2 has no complement. In fact, if k were a complement for 2, we would have $\gcd(2, k) = 1$ and $\text{lcm}(2, k) = m$. Then k would be odd and so $\text{lcm}(2, k)$ would have only one factor of 2, a contradiction.

5. (b) See Example 2(b). (c) See Exercise 3(b).

7. The figure represents $(D_6, |)$.

9. (a) 2, 3. (b) 1, 2, 3, 4, 9.

11. Supply reasons:

$$x = x \land (x \lor a) = x \land (y \lor a)$$
$$= (x \land y) \lor (x \land a) = (x \land y) \lor (y \land a)$$
$$= (y \land x) \lor (y \land a) = y \land (x \lor a) = y \land (y \lor a) = y.$$

13. Assume $1 \lor x = 1$ and $1 \land x = 0$, and show $x = 0$. Then assume $0 \lor y = 1$ and $0 \land y = 0$, and show $y = 1$.

15. (a) Use $y' \lor x' = (y \land x)' = x'$.
(b) Show $y = y \land z'$, starting with $y = y \land 1 = y \land (z \lor z')$.
(c) Use parts (a) and (b).

Section 10.3, page 468

1. (a) Since the operations $\vee$ and $\wedge$ treat 0 and 1 just as if they represent truth values, checking the laws 1Ba through 5Bb for all cases amounts to checking corresponding truth tables. Do enough until the situation is clear to you.

3. (a) Note that $D_{30} = \{1, 2, 3, 5, 6, 10, 15, 30\}$.
    (c) $\{1, 30\}, \{1, 2, 15, 30\}, \{1, 3, 10, 30\}, \{1, 5, 6, 30\}, D_{30}$.

5. One solution is to set $S = \{1, 2, 3, 4, 5\}$ and define

$$\phi(\langle a_1, a_2, a_3, a_4, a_5\rangle) = \{i \in S : a_i = 1\}.$$

7. (a) No. A finite Boolean algebra has 2^n elements for some n.

9. (a) If $a \leq x$ or $a \leq y$, then surely $a \leq x \vee y$. Suppose $a \leq x \vee y$. Then $a = a \wedge (x \vee y) = (a \wedge x) \vee (a \wedge y)$. One of $a \wedge x$ and $a \wedge y$, say $a \wedge x$, must be different from 0. But $0 \prec a \wedge x \leq a$, so $a \wedge x = a$ and $a \leq x$.
    (c) $a \leq 1 = x \vee x'$, so $a \leq x$ or $a \leq x'$ by part (a). Both $a \leq x$ and $a \leq x'$ would imply $a \leq x \wedge x' = 0$ by part (b), a contradiction.

11. $x \leq y \Leftrightarrow x \vee y = y \Leftrightarrow \phi(x \vee y) = \phi(y) \Leftrightarrow \phi(x) \vee \phi(y) = \phi(y) \Leftrightarrow \phi(x) \leq \phi(y)$.

Section 10.4, page 477

1. $x'y'z' \vee x'y'z \vee xyz'$.

3. (c)

x	y	z	$xy \vee z'$	$x'y'z' \vee x'yz' \vee xy'z' \vee xyz' \vee xyz$.
0	0	0	1	
0	0	1	0	
0	1	0	1	
0	1	1	0	
1	0	0	1	
1	0	1	0	
1	1	0	1	
1	1	1	1	

5. (a) $x_1x_2x'_3x_4 \vee x_1x_2x'_3x'_4 \vee x'_1x_2x_3x'_4$.

7. (a) $xz \vee y'$.

9. $y' \vee z$.

11. (a) Find the minterm canonical form for E'. Then find $E = (E')'$ using De-Morgan's laws, first on joins and then on products.
    (b) $(x' \vee y')(x \vee y)$.

13. Show that the values of the corresponding Boolean functions are the same.

Section 10.5, page 485

1. (a) xyz.

3. (a)   (b)

5. (a)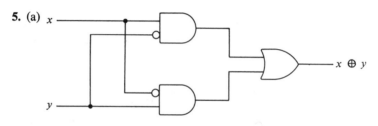

7. (a) $S = 1, C_O = 0.$ **(c)** $S = 0, C_O = 1.$

9. (a)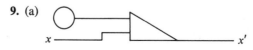

(c)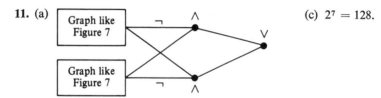

11. (a) 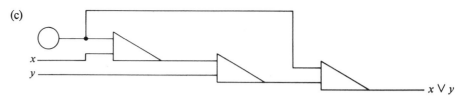   **(c)** $2^7 = 128.$

13.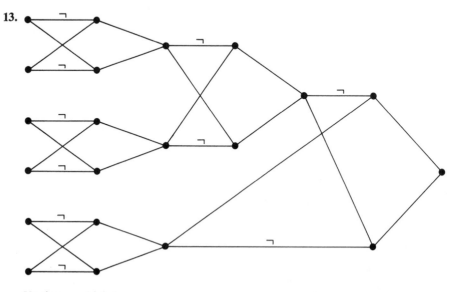

Vertices need labels.

Section 10.6, page 491

1. $xyz \lor xyz' \lor xy'z \lor xy'z \lor x'yz \lor x'y'z = x \lor z.$

3. $xyz \lor xyz' \lor xy'z \lor x'y'z' \lor x'y'z = xz \lor xy \lor x'y' = xy \lor y'z \lor x'y'.$

5. (a)   (c)

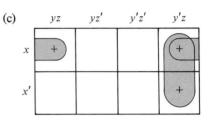

7. (a)

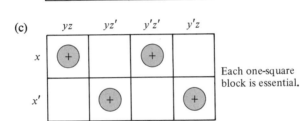

Each two-square block is essential.

(c)

Each one-square block is essential.

9. (a) $wxy \lor x'y' \lor w'y \lor z'.$
   (c) $w'x'z' \lor w'xy' \lor wxy \lor wx'z \lor y'z'$, not $w'x'z' \lor w'xy' \lor wx'y' \lor wyz \lor wxz'$, which also has five product terms but one more literal.

Section 11.1, page 501

1. (a) $\mathbb{P}$. (c) $\mathbb{Z}$. (e) $\mathbb{Z}$. (g) $18\mathbb{P} = \{18k : k \in \mathbb{P}\}.$

3. $\mathbb{P} = \{1\}^+, \{0\} = \{0\}^+, 18\mathbb{P} = \{18\}^+.$

5. (a) $\mathbb{Z}$. (c) $\mathbb{Z}$. (e) $\mathbb{Z}$.

7. (a) $2\mathbb{N} = \{2k : k \in \mathbb{N}\}.$ (c) $\{0\}$. (e) $\Sigma^*.$

9. (a) $\begin{bmatrix} 0 & 1 & 0 \\ 1 & 0 & 0 \\ 0 & 0 & 1 \end{bmatrix}$ and $\begin{bmatrix} 1 & 0 & 0 \\ 0 & 1 & 0 \\ 0 & 0 & 1 \end{bmatrix}.$

   (c) $\begin{bmatrix} 0 & 2 & 3 \\ 0 & 0 & 4 \\ 0 & 0 & 0 \end{bmatrix}, \begin{bmatrix} 0 & 0 & 8 \\ 0 & 0 & 0 \\ 0 & 0 & 0 \end{bmatrix}$ and $\begin{bmatrix} 0 & 0 & 0 \\ 0 & 0 & 0 \\ 0 & 0 & 0 \end{bmatrix}.$

11. (a) and (d). Check closure under $\circ$. For (b) and (c) give counterexamples.

13. Let H be a subgroup containing A. To show that $\langle A \rangle \subseteq H$, let $p(x)$ be
    "$x \in H$" and show that

    (B) $p(x) \, \forall x \in H$,

    (I_1) $p(x) \wedge p(y) \to p(x \square y)$,

    (I_2) $p(x) \to p(x^{-1})$

    are true.

Section 11.2, page 507

1. (a) $6\mathbb{P} = \{6k : k \in \mathbb{P}\}$.
   (c) No. For example, 6 and 12 are not both powers of the same member of $6\mathbb{P}$, so cannot both lie in the same cyclic subgroup.

3. (a) $60\mathbb{P}$.   (c) Yes. Give a generator.

5. (a) $f(n) = n + 3$ defines one.

7. Any example in which neither H nor K contains the other will work.

9. (a) $6 = 3!$.   (c) g and h, where $h(1) = 3$, $h(2) = 2$ and $h(3) = 1$.   (e) It contains g so could only be $g \circ$ FIX. Apply part (d).

11. (a) $\langle a \rangle = \{e, a, b\}$.   (c) $\langle c \rangle, \langle d \rangle, \langle f \rangle$.   (e) $\{e, d\}, \{a, c\}, \{b, f\}$.

13. (a) $H \square g$ contains $e \square g = g$. By Theorem 2, either $H \square g = H$ or else $H \square g$ and H are disjoint.

15. (a) For $h \in H$, $(g \square h)^{-1} = h^{-1} \square g^{-1} \in H \square g^{-1}$, so

    $$\{x^{-1} : x \in g \square H\} \subseteq H \square g^{-1}.$$

    Moreover, $h \square g^{-1} = (g \square h^{-1})^{-1}$ is in $\{x^{-1} : x \in g \square H\}$ for $h \in H$, so

    $$H \square g^{-1} \subseteq \{x^{-1} : x \in g \square H\}.$$

    (b) Use the result of part (a).

17. (a) See Example 2(a).   (c) By Theorem 5 of § 11.1, $\mathcal{L}(S)$ consists of 'subgroups of S. Any two subgroups intersect nontrivially by Corollary 2. Apply part (b).

Section 11.3, page 514

1. (a), (c), (e).

3. (a), (b), (c).

5. (a) $h(f + g) = (f + g)(73) = f(73) + g(73) = h(f) + h(g)$.

7. (a) See Example 1(c) of § 6.4.
   (c) $[elephant] = \{w : w$ is an eight-letter word$\}$. Its image is 8.

9. (a) $s_1 \equiv s_2 \Leftrightarrow s_1 = s_2$.   (c) $v(s) = \{s\}$.

11. (a) $[s_1] = [s_2]$ and $[t_1] = [t_2] \Rightarrow s_1 \equiv s_2$ and $t_1 \equiv t_2 \Rightarrow s_1 \bullet t_1 \equiv s_2 \bullet t_2$
    [why?] $\Rightarrow [s_1 \bullet t_1] = [s_2 \bullet t_2]$.
    (c) $h(s \bullet t) = [s \bullet t] = [s] * [t] = h(s) * h(t)$.
    (d) Show that $[s]^{-1} = [s^{-1}]$.

13. (a) Check that $h(z) \square h(s) = h(z \cdot s) = h(s) \square h(z)$ for every $s \in S$.
    (c) Check that $[z] * [s] = [s] = [s] * [z]$ for every $s \in S$, or use part (a) and the fundamental theorem.

15. (a) $h(u_1) \square h(u_2) = h(u_1 \bullet u_2) \in h(U)$ since $u_1 \bullet u_2 \in U$.

(c) $[u] \rightarrow h(u)$.

Section 11.4, page 519

1. (a) $\{0\}$. (c) $5\mathbb{Z} = \{5n : n \in \mathbb{Z}\}$.

3. (a) 4. (c) 3.

5. (a) The identity is $\langle e_G, e_H \rangle$, where e_G and e_H are the respective identities of G and H; $\langle g, h \rangle^{-1} = \langle g^{-1}, h^{-1} \rangle$.

(c) $\{\langle e_G, h \rangle : h \in H\}$.

7. (c) $\begin{bmatrix} y & z \\ 0 & 1/y \end{bmatrix} \begin{bmatrix} 1 & x \\ 0 & 1 \end{bmatrix} \begin{bmatrix} 1/y & -z \\ 0 & y \end{bmatrix} = \begin{bmatrix} 1 & xy^2 \\ 0 & 1 \end{bmatrix}$ is in G.

(e) Use the result of part (d) and Theorem 2(b).

9. (a) $h(x \bullet y) = h(y) = h(x) \square h(y)$.

(c) Not in general. If X is a subsemigroup, then $X \bullet s$ has one element and $s \bullet X$ has $|X|$ elements. By part (b), congruence classes can have lots of different sizes.

11. (a) More generally, if $A \subseteq S$ then

$$h(A^+) = h(\{x : x \text{ is a product } a_1 \cdots a_n \text{ of members of } A\})$$

$$= \{h(x) : x = a_1 \cdots a_n, \quad a_1, \ldots, a_n \in A\}$$

$$= \{y : y = h(a_1) \cdots h(a_n), \quad a_1, \ldots, a_n \in A\} = h(A)^+.$$

(b) Yes. Indeed, $h(\langle A \rangle) = \langle h(A) \rangle$.

13. (a) Use the identity

$$(x \bullet y) \bullet H \bullet (x \bullet y)^{-1} = x \bullet (y \bullet H \bullet y^{-1}) \bullet x^{-1}.$$

Also, if $H = x \bullet H \bullet x^{-1}$, then

$$x^{-1} \bullet H \bullet x = x^{-1} \bullet (x \bullet H \bullet x^{-1}) \bullet x = H.$$

Section 11.5, page 529

1. (a) 8. (c) Apply Lagrange's theorem.

3. (a) There would be a new column with all entries m. (c) There are 6 orbits.

5. (a) $\{e\}, \{e, f\}, \{e, g\}, \{e, h\}, \{e, f, g, h\}$.

(c) Kernel on $\{p, r\}$ is $\{e, f\}$, and kernel on $\{q, s\}$ is $\{e, g\}$.

7. (a) Rows of Figure 6(a) with u in the u-column. (c) w in each case.

9. They can only have 1, 3, 9 or 27 elements.

11. Imitate the proof of Cayley's theorem.

13. The functions a^*, b^*, c^* will be defined on $\{a, b, c, z\}$.

15. (b) The sets in π are the G-orbits in S.

Section 11.6, page 542

1. (a) 4. (c) $(k^5 + k^4)/2$.

3. (a) $C(k) = (k^4 + k^2)/2$.

5. (a) $C(k) = (k^4 + 2k^2 + 3k^3)/6$.

7. (a) 3.

9. (a) 16. [Count entries in Figure 1(b) which match their column headings.]
(c) 8.

11. (a) $C(k) = (k^8 + 17k^4 + 6k^2)/24$.

13. (a) 8.

15. As noted in § 7.7, $R_1 \vee R_2$ is the transitive closure of $R_1 \cup R_2$. We easily
have $R_1 \cup R_2 \subseteq R_0$, so $R_1 \vee R_2 \subseteq R_0$. If $\langle s, t \rangle \in R_0$, then $h(s) = t$ for some
$h \in \langle G_1 \cup G_2 \rangle$. Apply Theorem 3 of § 11.1 to conclude that

$$h = g_m \circ g_{m-1} \circ \cdots \circ g_2 \circ g_1$$

where each g_i is in $G_1 \cup G_2$. If $s_0 = s$ and $s_i = g_i(s_{i-1})$ for $i = 1, \ldots, m$, then
$s_m = t$ and each pair $\langle s_{i-1}, s_i \rangle$ belongs to $R_1 \cup R_2$. Hence $\langle s, t \rangle = \langle s_0, s_m \rangle$
is in $R_1 \vee R_2$ by Theorem 2 of § 7.6.

Section 11.7, page 552

1. (a), (b), (d), (f).

3. All but (b); (b) is not an additive homomorphism.

5. Every subgroup is an ideal.

7. (a) $24\mathbb{Z}$. (c) $\mathbb{Z} = 1\mathbb{Z}$, since $1 = 3 \cdot 1 + 2 \cdot (-1) \in 3\mathbb{Z} + 2\mathbb{Z}$.

9. (a) Verify well-definedness directly, or apply Theorem 1 to the homomorphism
$m \to \langle \text{Rem}_4(m), \text{Rem}_6(m) \rangle$ from $\mathbb{Z}$ to $\mathbb{Z}(4) \times \mathbb{Z}(6)$, as in Example 6(b).
(c) $\langle 1, 4 \rangle$ is one of the twelve; find another one.

11. (a) Since $2 *_6 3 = 0$, 2 has no inverse.
(b) Exhibit an inverse for each non-0 element. [In fact, $(\mathbb{Z}(p), +_p, *_p)$ is a field
if and only if p is prime. In case p is not prime, the idea in part (a) works. If p is
prime, the mapping $m \to k *_p m$ is a permutation of $\mathbb{Z}(p)$ for each non-0
$k \in \mathbb{Z}(p)$. The inverse permutation corresponds to the inverse of k.]
(c) Consider the inverse of $\langle 1, 0 \rangle$ for example.

13. (a) The kernel of h is either F or $\{0\}$ by Example 5(c).
(b) Part (a) and the corollary to Theorem 2 apply.

15. (a) $I = 15\mathbb{Z}$. (b) See Example 6(b).
(c) It would have to be $4\mathbb{Z}$ [why?], but $\mathbb{Z}/4\mathbb{Z}$ has an element a with $a + a \neq 0$.

17. (a) $R \cdot 2 = \{a_0 + a_1 x + \cdots + a_n x^n \in R : \text{every } a_i \text{ is even}\}$,
$R \cdot x = \{a_0 + a_1 x + \cdots + a_n x^n \in R : a_0 = 0\}$,
$R \cdot 2 + R \cdot x = \{a_0 + a_1 x + \cdots + a_n x^n \in R : a_0 \text{ is even}\}$.
(b) Suppose $R \cdot p = R \cdot 2 + R \cdot x$ for some $p \in R$. Since $2 \in R \cdot p$, p must be
constant, and since $x \in R \cdot p$, p is 1 or -1. But then $R \cdot p = R$, a contradiction.

INDEX

Note: Where page references for an entry are not in regular numerical sequence, the first reference listed is the *primary* reference.